Dewey Decimal Classification

Devised by Melvil Dewey

2023

Volume 4

Edited by

Alex Kyrios, Senior Editor

OCLC
OCLC, Inc.
Dublin, Ohio
2023

OCLC, Inc.
6565 Kilgour Place
Dublin, OH 43017-3395 USA
www.oclc.org/dewey

ISBN: (vol. 4) 978-1-55653-274-0

35mm cameras	771.32	'Abd al-Jabbār ibn Aḥmad	
100 Mile House (B.C.)	T2—711 75	al-Asadābādī	
401(k) plans	332.024 014 5	Koran commentary	297.122 74
		'Abd al-Razzāq ibn Hammām	
A		al-Ḥimyari	
		Hadith	297.125 56
A level examination	378.166 2	Abdel Aziz, Mohamed Ould	
Aachen (Germany)	T2—435 511	Mauritanian history	966.106 2
Aʻālī al-Nīl (South Sudan)	T2—629 3	Abdias (Biblical book)	224.91
Aar River (Switzerland)	T2—494 54	Abdo Benítez, Mario	
Aarau (Switzerland)	T2—494 562 84	Paraguayan history	989.207 48
Aarau (Switzerland :		Abdomen	573.997
Bezirk)	T2—494 562 8	biology	573.997
Aardvark	599.31	human anatomy	611.95
Aardwolf	599.743	human physiology	612.95
Aargau (Switzerland)	T2—494 56	injuries	617.550 44
Aarhus amt (Denmark)	T2—489 55	regional medicine	617.55
Abaca		surgery	617.550 59
botany	584.88	Abdominal muscles	
fiber crop	633.571	human anatomy	611.736
Abacus	513.028 4	Abdominal pregnancy	
Abalones	641.394	obstetrics	618.31
cooking	641.694	Abduction (Crime)	364.154
fishing and culture	639.483 2	law	345.025 4
food	641.394	prevention	364.4
zoology	594.32	self-defense	613.66
Abandoned children	305.230 869 45	social welfare	362.884
	T1—086 945	Abduction (Logic)	511.31
social group	305.230 869 45	'Abdu'l-Bahá	
social services	362.73	works by	297.938 24
Abattoirs	664.902 9	Abdul Rahman, Tunku, Putra	
Abaza language	499.962	Al-Haj	
	T6—999 62	Malaysian history	959.505 1
Abazin language	499.962	Abdul Razak bin Dato' Hussein,	
	T6—999 62	Tun Haji	
Abbeville County (S.C.)	T2—757 35	Malaysian history	959.505 2
Abbeys		Abdullah II, King of Jordan	
architecture	726.7	Jordanian history	956.950 45
church history	271	Abdullah bin Haji Ahmad	
religious significance of		Badawi, Datuk	
buildings	246.97	Malaysian history	959.506 1
Abbotsford (B.C.)	T2—711 37	Abel (Biblical person)	
Abbott, J. J. C. (John Joseph		Bible stories	222.110 950 5
Caldwell), Sir		Abel Tasman National Park	
Canadian history	971.055	(N.Z.)	T2—937 7
Abbott, Tony		Abelian categories	512.62
Australian history	994.072	Abelian groups	512.25
Abbreviated longhand	653.2	Abelian varieties	516.353
Abbreviation dictionaries	413.15	Aberconwy (Wales)	T2—429 27
specific languages	T4—315	Aberdare (Wales)	T2—429 78
specific subjects	T1—014 8	Aberdeen (Scotland)	T2—412 3
Abbreviations	411	Aberdeen (South Africa :	
specific languages	T4—11	District)	T2—687 53
specific subjects	T1—014 8	Aberdeen Angus cattle	636.223

1

Aberdeenshire (Scotland)	941.24	Abodah Zarah	296.123 4
	T2—412 4	Babylonian Talmud	296.125 4
Abergavenny (Wales)	T2—429 98	Mishnah	296.123 4
Abergele (Wales)	T2—429 27	Palestinian Talmud	296.124 4
Aberration		Abolition of slavery	326.8
astronomy	522.9	political science	326.8
Abertillery (Wales)	T2—429 95	sociology	306.362
'Abey 'Ahmed 'Ali		United States history	973.711 4
Ethiopian history	963.072 3	Abolitionists (Antislavery	
Abhidhammapiṭaka	294.382 4	activists)	326.809 2
Abhidharmapiṭaka	294.382 4	Abominable snowman	001.944
Abia State (Nigeria)	T2—669 45	Aboriginal Australian languages	499.15
Abidjan (Ivory Coast)	T2—666 8		T6—991 5
Ability	153.9	Aboriginal Australian literatures	899.15
Ability grouping in education	371.254	Aboriginal Australians	T5—991 5
Ability testing	153.93	religion	299.921 5
aptitudes	153.94	Aboriginal Malay languages	499.28
education	371.262		T6—992 8
intelligence	153.93	Aboriginal peoples	305.8
personnel selection	658.311 25	Australia	T5—991 5
Abitibi (Quebec : Regional		social group	305.8
County Municipality)	T2—714 134	Tasmania	T5—991 59
Abitibi, Lake (Ont. and		*see also* Indigenous peoples	
Quebec)	T2—713 142	Aboriginal Tasmanians	T5—991 59
Abitibi-Ouest (Quebec :		Aborigines	305.8
Regional County		*see also* Indigenous peoples	
Municipality)	T2—714 132	Abortifacient agents	
Abitibi-Témiscamingue		medicine	618.29
(Quebec : Administrative		pharmacokinetics	615.766
region)	T2—714 13	Abortifacients	
Abitibi-Témiscamingue		medicine	618.29
Region (Quebec)	T2—714 13	pharmacokinetics	615.766
Abkhaz language	499.962 3	Abortion	362.198 88
	T6—999 623	criminology	364.185
Abkhaz literature	899.962 3	law	345.028 5
Abkhazia (Georgia)	T2—475 8	demographic effect	304.667
Abkhazo-Adyghian languages	499.962	ethics	179.76
	T6—999 62	religion	205.697 6
Ablation of snow	551.578 464	Buddhism	294.356 976
Ablutions		Christianity	241.697 6
Islam	297.38	Hinduism	294.548 697 6
ABM (Missiles)	358.174 82	Islam	297.569 76
engineering	623.451 94	Judaism	296.369 76
military equipment	358.174 82	law	342.084
Abnaki Indians	974.004 973 4	legal right of fetuses	342.085
	T5—973 4	legal right of women	342.087 8
Abnaki language	497.34	medical law	344.041 92
	T6—973 4	medicine	618.88
Abnormal psychology	616.89	nonsurgical methods	
Abnormalities		medicine	618.29
human teratology	616.043	pharmacokinetics	615.766
physical anthropology	599.949	social problem	362.198 88
		law	344.054 6
		social services	362.198 88

Abused children (continued)	
social theology	201.762 76
Christianity	261.832 71
social welfare	362.76
see also Child abuse	
Abutments	721.3
architecture	721.3
construction	690.13
structural engineering	624.16
Abydos (Egypt : Extinct	
city)	T2—323
Abyssal zone	
biology	578.779
ecology	577.79
Abyssinia	T2—63
Abyssinian cat	636.826
Abyssinians	T5—928
Acacias	583.633
botany	583.633
forestry	634.973 633
ornamental arboriculture	635.977 363 3
Academic costume	378.28
Academic degrees	378.2
Academic dissertations	378.242
specific places	015
Academic freedom	371.104
higher education	378.121 3
law	344.078
Academic high schools	373.241
see also Secondary education	
Academic libraries	027.7
administration	025.197 7
collection development	025.218 77
use studies	025.587 7
Academic library buildings	
architecture	727.827
Academic placement	371.264
special education	371.904 3
see Manual at 371.262 vs.	
371.264	
Academic prognosis	371.264
special education	371.904 3
see Manual at 371.262 vs.	
371.264	
Academic status	371.104
higher education	378.121
Academic year	371.23
law	344.079 2
Academies (Organizations)	060
Academy schools	371.05
Acadia	971.501 7
	T2—715
Acadia National Park (Me.)	T2—741 45
Acadia Parish (La.)	T2—763 56

Acadians	T5—41
Acadians in Canada	T5—114
expulsion of	971.501 7
Acanthaceae	583.96
Acanthocephala	592.33
paleozoology	562.33
Acanthodii	567.2
Acanthopterygii	597.64
paleozoology	567.64
see also Fishes	
Acanthuses	635.933 96
botany	583.96
floriculture	635.933 96
Acari	595.42
Acarida	595.42
Acariformes	595.42
Acarina	595.42
Acarnania (Greece)	T2—495 18
ancient	T2—383
Acceleration	
biophysics	
humans	612.014 414
classical mechanics	531.112
extraterrestrial biophysics	
humans	612.014 534
Acceleration of particles	539.73
Acceleration principle	
(Macroeconomics)	339.41
Accelerator effect	
(Macroeconomics)	339.41
Accelerometers	
aircraft	629.135 2
Accent (Linguistics)	414.6
specific languages	T4—16
Accent (Poetry)	808.1
Acceptances (Commercial paper)	332.77
exchange medium	332.55
law	346.096
Access control (Computers)	005.83
management	658.478
Access points (Cataloging)	025.322
Access roads	388.13
see also Roads	
Access to airports	387.736 2
Accessioning	
archives	025.281 4
Accessories (Clothing)	391.44
care	646.6
commercial technology	687.19
customs	391.44
home economics	646.3
home sewing	646.48
see also Clothing	

Accident insurance	368.384	Accounting (continued)	
government-sponsored	368.42	literature	808.803 553
industrial casualty	368.7	history and criticism	809.933 553
law	346.086 384	specific literatures	T3B—080 355 3
see also Insurance		history and	
Accident investigation	363.106 5	criticism	T3B—093 553
technology	620.86	malpractice	346.063 1
Accidents	363.1	management policy	658.151 1
personal health	613.6	Accounts payable	657.74
psychology	155.936	accounting	657.74
social services	363.1	financial management	658.152 6
law	344.047	Accounts receivable	657.72
public administration	353.9	accounting	657.72
tort law	346.032 2	financial management	658.152 44
Accidents (Philosophy)	111.1	Accra (Ghana)	T2—667
Accipitridae	598.94	Accreditation	352.84
Acclimatization		education	379.158
animals	591.42	*see also* Licensing	
biology	578.42	Accreditation of prior learning	371.264
health	613.1	Acculturation	303.482
plants	581.42	Accumulators	
Accomack County (Va.)	T2—755 16	hydraulic	621.254
Accommodation (Optometry)	617.755	Accuracy drills and tests	
see also Eye diseases —		keyboarding	652.307
humans		shorthand	653.15
Accompaniment		Aceh (Indonesia)	959.811
musical technique	781.47		T2—598 11
see Manual at 781.47		Aceh (Indonesian people)	T5—992 242
Accomplices	364.3	Aceh language	499.224 2
see also Offenders			T6—992 242
Accordions	788.86	Aceh literature	899.224 2
instrument	788.861 9	Acetabularia	579.836
music	788.86	Acetals	668.423
see also Woodwind		Acetates	668.423
instruments		Acetobacter	579.33
Accountability		Acetylene	547.413
Christian doctrines	233.4	chemical engineering	661.814
ethics	170	gas technology	665.85
executive management	658.402	Achaea (Greece)	T2—495 27
military administration	355.685	ancient	T2—387
public administration	352.35	Achaia (Greece)	T2—495 27
public education	379.158	ancient	T2—387
teachers	371.144	Achariaceae	583.69
Accountancy	657	Achatocarpaceae	583.883
Accountants	657.092	Acheulian culture	930.124
Accounting	657	Achievement tests	371.262
arts	700.455 3	secondary education	373.126 2
	T3C—355 3	teacher-prepared tests	371.271
enterprises	338.761 657	Achinese	T5—992 242
law	346.063	Achinese language	499.224 2
corporation law	346.066 48		T6—992 242
public administration	343.034	Achinese literature	899.224 2
		Acholi (African people)	T5—965 584

Acholi language	496.558 4
	T6—965 584
Acid-base imbalances	
medicine	616.399 2
see also Digestive system	
diseases — humans	
Acid mine drainage	363.738 4
environmental protection	363.738 4
preventive technology	622.5
water pollution engineering	628.168 32
Acid pollution	
ecology	577.275 2
Acid precipitation	363.738 6
see also Acid rain	
Acid rain	363.738 6
law	344.046 336
meteorology	551.577 1
pollution technology	628.532
social welfare	363.738 6
weather forecasting	551.647 71
see also Pollution	
Acid rock	781.66
Acid-soil conditioners	631.821
chemical engineering	668.64
Acidification	
ecology	577.275 2
Acidosis	
medicine	616.399 2
see also Digestive system	
diseases — humans	
Acids	546.24
aromatic chemistry	547.637
chemical engineering	661.2
chemistry	546.24
human toxicology	615.921
organic chemistry	547.037
applied	661.86
see also Chemicals	
Acinonyx	599.759
Acipenseriformes	597.42
paleozoology	567.42
Acne	
medicine	616.53
see also Skin diseases —	
humans	
Acochlidacea	594.34
Acoela (Platyhelminthes)	592.42
Acoli (African people)	T5—965 584
Acoli language	496.558 4
	T6—965 584
Aconites	583.34
Acoraceae	584.42
Acorales	584.42

Acorns	
coffee substitute	
commercial processing	663.97
Acoustical communications	
engineering	621.382 8
Acoustical engineering	620.2
Acoustical engineers	620.209 2
Acoustical insulation	
buildings	693.834
Acoustical pattern recognition	006.45
engineering	621.399 4
Acoustical properties	
materials science	620.112 94
Acoustical prospecting	622.159 2
Acoustics	534
architectural design	729.29
engineering	620.2
see also Sound	
Acousto-optical communications	
engineering	621.382 8
Acquired immune deficiency	
syndrome	362.196 979 2
see also AIDS (Disease)	
Acquired immunity	571.96
humans	616.079
Acquisition of corporations	338.83
see also Mergers	
Acquisition of real property	333.33
economics	333.33
private ownership	333.33
public ownership	333.13
law	346.043 62
private ownership	346.043 62
public ownership	343.025 2
Acquisition of territory	325.32
law	342.041 2
law of nations	341.42
Acquisitions (Libraries)	025.2
Acquisitions (Museums)	069.51
Acrasia	579.52
Acre (Brazil)	T2—811 2
Acreage allotments	338.18
law	343.076 1
Acrididae	
agricultural pests	632.726
Acrobatic gymnastics	796.476
Acrobatics	796.476
biography	796.476 092
circuses	791.34
biography	791.340 92
sports	796.476
biography	796.476 092
see also Gymnastics	

Acrobats	796.476 092	Action	
circuses	791.340 92	philosophical anthropology	128.4
sports	796.476 092	psychology	150
Acrochordidae	597.967	Action games	
Acromegaly		indoor	793.4
medicine	616.47	Action Party (Italy : 1853–1867)	324.245 026
see also Endocrine		Action Party (Italy : 1942–1947)	324.245 06
diseases — humans		Action research	001.4
Acronym dictionaries	413.15		T1—072
specific languages	T4—315	Action toys	790.133
specific subjects	T1—014 8	manufacturing technology	688.728
Acronyms	411	*see also* Toys	
specific languages	T4—11	Actions (Law)	347.05
specific subjects	T1—014 8	Activated carbon	662.93
Acrostics	793.73	water treatment	628.166
Acrothoracica	595.35	Activated sludge process	628.354
Acrylic painting	751.426	Activewear	796
Acrylics	668.423 2	commercial technology	687.16
textiles	677.474 2	customs	391.48
see also Textiles		home economics	646.3
Acrylonitrile rubber	678.72	home sewing	646.47
Act		*see also* Athletic garments;	
philosophical anthropology	128.4	Sports clothes	
ACT (College testing program)	378.166 2	(Activewear); Sportswear	
Act of Union, 1840	971.039	(Activewear)	
ACTH (Hormone)		Activity-based costing	657.42
pharmacology	615.363	Activity therapy	
production		medicine	615.851 5
human physiology	612.492	Acton (Quebec : Regional	
Acting	792.028	County Municipality)	T2—714 525
motion pictures	791.430 28	Actors	792.028 092
radio	791.440 28	motion pictures	791.430 280 92
stage	792.028	collected biography	791.430 280 922
television	791.450 28	United States	791.430 280 922 73
variety shows		radio	791.440 280 92
Japan	792.702 809 52	stage	792.028 092
Actinide series	669.292	television	791.450 280 92
chemistry	546.42	*see Manual at* 780.92 and	
metallurgy	669.292	791.092	
see also Chemicals; Metals		Actresses	792.028 092
Actinium	669.292 1	*see also* Actors	
chemistry	546.421	Acts of the Apostles	226.6
metallurgy	669.292 1	pseudepigrapha	229.925
see also Chemicals; Metals		Actual grace	234.1
Actinomycetales	579.37	Actuarial science	368.01
Actinomycetes	579.37	Acuity (Visual perception)	
see Manual at 579.3		psychology	152.142 2
Actinopoda	579.45	Acupressure	
Actinopterygii	597	therapeutics	615.822 2
see also Fishes		Acupuncture	
Actinotherapy		therapeutics	615.892
medicine	615.831 5	Acylation	
		chemical engineering	660.284 4

Ad Dakhla (Western Sahara)	T2—648
Ad hoc networks (Computer networks)	004.685
Ada County (Idaho)	T2—796 28
Adages	398.9
Adair County (Iowa)	T2—777 73
Adair County (Ky.)	T2—769 675
Adair County (Mo.)	T2—778 264
Adair County (Okla.)	T2—766 89
Adam	
Bible stories	222.110 950 5
Islam	297.246
Adamawa-Eastern languages	496.361
	T6—963 61
Adamawa languages	496.361
	T6—963 61
Adamawa State (Nigeria)	T2—669 88
Adamawa-Ubangi languages	496.361
	T6—963 61
Adams, John	
United States history	973.44
Adams, John Quincy	
United States history	973.55
Adams County (Colo.)	T2—788 81
Adams County (Idaho)	T2—796 26
Adams County (Ill.)	T2—773 44
Adams County (Ind.)	T2—772 73
Adams County (Iowa)	T2—777 76
Adams County (Miss.)	T2—762 26
Adams County (N.D.)	T2—784 89
Adams County (Neb.)	T2—782 397
Adams County (Ohio)	T2—771 86
Adams County (Pa.)	T2—748 42
Adams County (Wash.)	T2—797 34
Adams County (Wis.)	T2—775 56
Adams Lake (B.C.)	T2—711 72
Adams River (B.C.)	T2—711 75
Adana İli (Turkey)	T2—564 7
ancient	T2—393 5
Adangme (African people)	T5—963 37
Adangme language	496.337
	T6—963 37
Adaptability	
psychology	155.24
children	155.418 24
late adulthood	155.672
situational influences	155.9
children	155.418 9
Adaptation (Biology)	578.4
animals	591.4
plants	581.4
Adaptive computing systems	004
Adaptive control systems	
automation engineering	629.836
'Ādāt law	
sources of fiqh	340.591 35
Addax	599.645
Added-value tax	336.271 4
Adders (Snakes)	597.963
Adder's-tongues (Ferns)	587.33
Addiction	362.29
customs	394.14
devotional literature	204.32
Christianity	242.4
medicine	616.86
pastoral theology	206.1
Christianity	259.429
personal health	613.8
religious guidance	204.42
Christianity	248.862 9
social theology	201.762 29
Christianity	261.832 29
social welfare	362.29
see also Substance abuse	
Addictive drugs	
pharmacokinetics	615.78
Addicts	T1—087 4
Addis Ababa (Ethiopia)	T2—633
Addison County (Vt.)	T2—743 5
Addison's disease	
medicine	616.45
see also Endocrine diseases — humans	
Addition (Chemical reaction)	541.39
organic chemistry	547.2
applied	660.284 4
Addition (Mathematics)	512.92
algebra	512.92
arithmetic	513.2
Additive manufacturing	621.988
Additive processes	
color photography	778.65
Addo Elephant National Park (South Africa)	T2—687 53
Addresses	080
Addresses to legislatures	352.238 4
United States	352.238 409 73
Adelaide (S. Aust.)	T2—942 31
Adelaide (South Africa : District)	T2—687 54
Aden	T2—533 5
Aden, Gulf of	551.461 532
	T2—165 32
Adenauer, Konrad	
German history	943.087 5

Adenomas	
incidence	614.599 9
medicine	616.993
Adenophorea	592.57
Adenosine triphosphate	572.475
Adenoviridae	579.244 3
Adephaga	595.762
Áder, János	
Hungarian history	943.905 45
Adhan	297.382 2
Adhesion	541.33
chemical engineering	660.293
Adhesiveness	
materials science	620.112 92
Adhesives	668.3
building materials	691.99
manufacturing technology	668.3
materials science	620.199
structural engineering	624.189 9
Adi Granth	294.682
Adige River (Italy)	T2—453
Adipocytes	
human cytology	611.018 276
Adipose tissues	571.57
human histology	611.018 27
Adirondack Mountains	
(N.Y.)	T2—747 5
Adıyaman İli (Turkey)	T2—565 2
ancient	T2—393 6
Adjectivals	415.5
specific languages	T4—55
Adjectives	415.5
specific languages	T4—55
Adjudication	347.07
competitions	T1—079
criminal law	345.07
law of nations	341.55
Adjustment (Insurance)	368.014
Adjustment (Psychology)	155.24
children	155.418 24
late adulthood	155.672
Adjustment disorders	
medicine	616.852
see also Mental disorders	
Adlerian psychology	150.195 3
Administration	658
	T1—068
public administration	351
see Manual at T1—068	
Administration of estates	346.056
Administration of justice	347
crimes against	364.134
law	345.023 4
criminal law	345.05

Administration régionale	
Kativik (Quebec)	T2—714 111
Administrative agencies	351
description and duties	351
government publications	
bibliographies	011.534
law	342.064
organization and structure	352.29
see Manual at 351 vs.	
352.29; *also at* 352–354	
see also Executive agencies;	
Government agencies;	
Governmental organizations	
see Manual at 352–354	
Administrative areas	
area planning	711.551
Administrative assistants	
office management	651.3
Administrative courts	342.066 4
Administrative discretion	342.066 4
Administrative law	342.06
Administrative personnel	
office management	651.3
Administrative procedure	
law	342.066
Administrative regulations	348.025
Administrative reports	T1—06
public administration	351.05
Administrative responsibility	658.402
military services	355.685
public administration	352.35
Administrative revenues	
public finance	336.16
Administrators (Public officials)	352.3
see also Public administrators	
Admirals	359.009 2
role and function	359.331
Admiralty courts	347.04
Admiralty Islands (Papua	
New Guinea)	T2—958 1
Admiralty law	343.096
see Manual at 341.45 vs.	
343.0962	
Admissibility of evidence	347.062
criminal law	345.062
Admission tests	371.262
higher education	378.166 2
Admission to the bar	344.017 613 4
Admissions	
schools	371.21
higher education	378.161
Adobe	
architectural construction	721.044 22
building construction	693.22

Adolescence	305.235	Adolescents (continued)	
arts	T3C—354	literature	808.803 523 5
literature	808.803 54	history and criticism	809.933 523 5
history and criticism	809.933 54	specific literatures	T3B—080 352 35
specific literatures	T3B—080 354	history and	
history and		criticism	T3B—093 523 5
criticism	T3B—093 54	physical fitness	613.704 3
psychology	155.5	physiology	612.661
social aspects	305.235	psychology	155.5
Adolescent boys	305.235 1	publications for	
	T1—083 51	bibliographies	011.625
see also Young men — under		reviews	028.162 5
twenty-one		reading	
Adolescent dentistry	617.600 835	library science	028.535
Adolescent development	305.235 5	religion	200.835
psychology	155.5	Christianity	270.083 5
sociology	305.235 5	devotional literature	242.63
Adolescent girls	305.235 2	guides to Christian life	248.83
	T1—083 52	pastoral care	259.23
see also Young women —		religious education	268.433
under twenty-one		guides to life	204.408 35
Adolescent gynecology	618.100 835	Judaism	296.083 5
Adolescent literature	808.899 283	guides to life	296.708 35
history and criticism	809.892 83	religious education	296.680 835
specific literatures	T3B—080 928 3	sex hygiene	613.951
history and criticism	T3B—099 283	social aspects	305.235
Adolescent medicine	616.008 35	social welfare	362.708 3
Adolescent obstetrics	618.200 835	law	344.032 708 3
Adolescent pharmacology	615.108 35	public administration	353.536 5
Adolescent psychiatry	616.890 083 5	Adolf Fredrik, King of Sweden	
Adolescent psychology	155.5	Swedish history	948.503 63
Adolescent surgery	617.008 35	Adopted children	306.874
Adolescent therapeutics	615.508 35		T1—085 4
Adolescent toxicology	615.900 835	family relationships	306.874
Adolescents	305.235	home care	649.145
	T1—083 5	psychology	155.445
arts	700.452 35	social welfare	362.829 8
	T3C—352 35	Adoption	362.734
civil and human rights	323.352	criminology	364.18
etiquette	395.123	law	345.028
government programs	353.536 5	law	346.017 8
health	613.043 3	religion	204.41
home care	649.125	social welfare	362.734
journalism for	070.483 3	Adoption leave	331.257 63
labor economics	331.347	government-sponsored	
law	344.013 47	insurance	368.454
legal status	346.013 083 5	labor economics	331.257 63
constitutional law	342.087 72	Adoptive parents	306.874
private law	346.013 083 5		T1—085
libraries for	027.626	Adoration of magi	232.923
		Adoration of shepherds	232.922
		ADP (Computing)	004
		Adrar (Algeria : Province)	T2—657

Adrenal gland diseases	
medicine	616.45
see also Endocrine	
diseases — humans	
pediatrics	618.924 5
Adrenal glands	573.46
biology	573.46
human anatomy	611.45
human physiology	612.45
medicine	616.45
surgery	617.461
see also Endocrine system	
Adrenal hormones	573.464
human physiology	612.45
pharmacology	615.364
see also Endocrine system	
Adrenocorticotrophic hormone	
pharmacology	615.363
production	
human physiology	612.492
Adrianople (Turkey)	T2—496 14
Adriatic Sea	551.461 385
	T2—163 85
Adsorbent carbons	662.93
Adsorbent charcoals	662.93
Adsorption	541.335
chemical engineering	660.284 235
chemistry	541.335
gaseous-state physics	530.435
semiconductors	537.622 6
Adult baptism	234.161 3
public worship	265.13
theology	234.161 3
Adult child abuse victims	
medicine	616.858 223 9
social theology	201.762 764
Christianity	261.832 73
social welfare	362.764
Adult child sexual abuse victims	
medicine	616.858 369
social theology	201.762 764
Christianity	261.832 73
social welfare	362.764
Adult children of alcoholics	
medicine	616.861 9
social welfare	362.292 4
Adult children of substance	
abusers	
medicine	616.869
social welfare	362.291 4
Adult easy literature	
rhetoric	808.067

Adult education	374
	T1—071 5
federal aid	379.121 5
law	344.074
public administrative support	353.84
public support	379.114
law	344.076 85
special education	371.904 75
university extension	378.175
Adultery	306.736
criminology	364.153
law	345.025 3
ethics	176.4
see also Sexual relations —	
ethics	
social theology	201.7
Christianity	261.835 736
sociology	306.736
Adulthood	305.24
psychology	155.6
social aspects	305.24
Adults	305.24
adult education	374.182
criminal offenders	364.3
development	
physiology	612.66
education	371.824
guides to religious life	204.4
health	613.043 4
higher education	378.198 2
journalism for	070.483 4
physical fitness	613.704 4
psychology	155.6
recreation	790.192
indoor	793.019 2
outdoor	796
religion	200
Christianity	230
devotional literature	242.64
guides to Christian life	248.84
religious education	268.434
secondary education	373.182 4
social aspects	305.24
Adur (England)	T2—422 69
Advaita (Philosophy)	181.482
Advanced placement (Education)	371.264
Advent	263.912
devotional literature	242.332
music	781.722
sermons	252.612
Advent Christian Church	286.73
see also Adventists	

Adventists	286.7	Advertising departments	659.112 2
biography	286.709 2	Advertising images	659.104 5
church government	262.067	Advertising lighting	621.322 9
local church	254.067	Advertising media planning	659.111
church law	262.986 7	Advertising themes	659.104 5
doctrines	230.67	Advice to readers	
catechisms and creeds	238.67	journalism	070.444
guides to Christian life	248.486 7	Advisory bodies	
missions	266.67	public administration	352.743
moral theology	241.046 7	Advisory opinions (Islamic law)	340.592 2
public worship	264.067	Advocacy	
religious associations	267.186 7	law	347.052
religious education	268.867	Advocates (Lawyers)	340.092
seminaries	230.073 67	Adygea (Russia)	T2—475 2
theology	230.67	Adyghe language	499.962 5
Adventure	904		T6—999 625
arts	700.458 2	Adyghe literature	899.962 5
	T3C—358 2	Aegadian Islands	T2—458 24
literature	808.803 582	Aegean (Greece :	
history and criticism	809.933 582	Decentralized	
specific literatures	T3B—080 358 2	administration)	T2—495 8
history and		Aegean architecture	722.61
criticism	T3B—093 582	Aegean Islands (Greece and	
specific places	930–990	Turkey)	949.58
Adventure fiction	808.838 7		T2—495 8
history and criticism	809.387	ancient	939.1
specific literatures	T3B—308 7		T2—391
individual authors	T3A—3	Aegean Sea	551.461 388
Adventure games	793.93		T2—163 88
computerized games	793.93	Aeolian instruments	786.69
Adventure racing	796.5	chamber music	785.669
see also Outdoor life		construction	786.691 923
Adverbials	415.76	by hand	786.691 923
specific languages	T4—576	by machine	681.866 9
Adverbs	415.76	Aeolian Islands (Italy)	T2—458 11
specific languages	T4—576	Aepyornithiformes	568.5
Adversary system	347	Aequian language	479.7
Adverse drug reactions			T6—797
pharmacokinetics	615.704	Aeration	
Advertisements	381.029	sewage treatment	628.35
	T1—029	water supply treatment	628.165
illustration	741.67	Aerial cinematography	777.6
Advertisers	659.109 2	Aerial microorganisms	579.175
Advertising	659.1	Aerial photography	778.35
design	744.66	military engineering	623.72
illustration	741.67	Aerial railways	385.6
law	343.082	engineering	625.5
managerial organization	659.112	transportation services	385.6
medical ethics	174.26	*see also* Railroads	
Advertising agencies	659.112 5	Aerial skiing	796.937
Advertising campaigns	659.113	*see also* Winter sports	
design	744.66	Aerial surveying	526.982
Advertising cards		Aerial videography	777.6
illustration	741.685		

12

Aerial warfare	358.4	Aextoxicaceae	583.82
see also Air warfare		Afan (Wales)	T2—429 85
Aerobatics	797.54	Afar (African people)	T5—935
Aerobic dancing	613.715	'Afãr kelel (Ethiopia)	T2—634
Aerobic exercise	613.71	Afar language	493.5
sports	796.44		T6—935
Aerobic gymnastics	796.44	AFDC (Social program)	362.713
Aerobic-microaerophilic		Affection	
gram-negative bacteria	579.323	psychology	152.41
Aerobic respiration	573.2	Affective disorders	362.25
Aerodynamic load	624.175	medicine	616.852 7
aeronautics	629.132 35	social welfare	362.25
Aerodynamics	533.62	*see also* Mental disorders	
aeronautics	629.132 3	Affects	
engineering	620.107 4	psychology	152.4
space flight	629.415 1	Affenpinscher	636.76
Aeroelasticity		Affine geometry	516.4
aeronautics	629.132 362	Affinity (Law)	346.015
Aeromechanics	533.6	Affirmative action	
aeronautics	629.132 3	education	379.26
engineering	620.107	employment	331.133
Aeronautical charts	629.132 54	*see also* Equal employment	
Aeronautical engineers	629.130 092	opportunity	
Aeronautics	629.13	government programs	353.53
law	343.097	law	342.087
Aerophones	788	constitutional law	342.087
see also Wind instruments		labor law	344.011 33
Aerosols	541.345 15	Affixes (Grammar)	415.92
chemical engineering	660.294 515	specific languages	T4—592
colloid chemistry	541.345 15	Affoltern (Switzerland :	
meteorology	551.511 3	Bezirk)	T2—494 572 1
Aerospace engineering	629.1	Afforestation	333.751 52
military	623.66	law	346.046 751 52
Aerospace engineers	629.109 2	resource economics	333.751 52
Aerospace medicine	616.980 21	silviculture	634.956
Aerospace photography	778.35	Afghan hound	636.753 3
Aerospace physiology		Afghan language	491.593
humans	612.014 4		T6—915 93
Aerostatics	533.61	Afghan literature	891.593
aeronautics	629.132 2	Afghan rugs	
engineering	620.107 3	arts	746.758 1
Aerotherapy		Afghan War, 2001–2021	958.104 7
medicine	615.836	Afghanistan	958.1
Aesthetics	111.85		T2—581
arts	701.17	ancient	939.6
literature	801.93		T2—396
music	781.17	Afghans	T5—915 93
philosophy	111.85	Afghans (Coverlets)	645.4
Aestivation	571.786	arts	746.430 437
Aeta (Philippine people)	T5—992 1	home sewing	646.21
Aetolia (Greece)	T2—383	household equipment	645.4
Aetolia and Acarnania		AFL (Labor)	331.883 209 73
(Greece)	T2—495 18	AFL-CIO	331.880 973
ancient	T2—383		

13

Aflatoxins	
human toxicology	615.952 956 57
Africa	960
	T2—6
geography	916
military operations	
World War I	940.416
World War II	940.542 3
travel	916.04
Africa, Black	T2—67
Africa, Central	967
	T2—67
Africa, East	967.6
	T2—676
Africa, North	961
	T2—61
ancient	939.7
	T2—397
see also North Africa	
Africa, Southern	968
	T2—68
Africa, Sub-Saharan	967
	T2—67
Africa, West	966
	T2—66
Africa proconsularis	T2—397 3
African American cooking	641.592 960 73
African American Methodist	
churches	287.8
see also Methodist Church	
African Americans	973.049 607 3
	T5—960 73
civil rights	323.119 607 3
civilization	973.049 607 3
education	371.829 960 73
military troops	
Civil War (United States)	973.741 5
World War II	940.540 3
social aspects	305.896 073
see Manual at T5—96073	
African bush pig	599.633
African clawed frog	597.865 4
African elephant	599.674
big game hunting	799.276 74
conservation technology	639.979 674
resource economics	333.959 674
African Hebrew Israelite Nation	
of Jerusalem	296.836
African independent churches	289.93
African languages	496
	T6—96
African lilies	584.78

African literature	808.899 6
history and criticism	809.896
in African languages	896
African Methodist Episcopal	
Church	287.83
see also Methodist Church	
African Methodist Episcopal	
Zion Church	287.83
see also Methodist Church	
African mole rat	599.359
African National Congress (South	
African political party)	324.268 083
African religions	299.6
African sleeping sickness	
incidence	614.533
medicine	616.936 3
see also Communicable	
diseases — humans	
African theater (World War II)	940.542 3
African violets	635.933 96
botany	583.96
floriculture	635.933 96
Africans	T5—96
Afrihili (Artificial language)	499.99
	T6—999 9
Afrikaans language	439.36
	T6—393 6
Afrikaans literature	839.36
Afrikaners	T5—393 6
Afro-Americans	973.049 607 3
	T5—960 73
see also African Americans	
Afro-Asian bloc	T2—171 65
Afro-Asiatic languages	492
	T6—92
non-Semitic	493
	T6—93
Afro-Asiatic literatures	892
non-Semitic	893
Afro-Asiatic peoples	T5—92
non-Semitic	T5—93
Afro-Cuban jazz	781.657 268 729 1
Afrohili (Artificial language)	499.99
	T6—999 9
After-dinner speeches	
literature	808.851
history and criticism	809.51
specific literatures	T3B—501
individual authors	T3A—5
rhetoric	808.512
Afterimages	
psychology	152.148

Agrammatism	
medicine	616.855 2
see also Communication	
disorders	
Agranulocytosis	
medicine	616.154
see also Cardiovascular	
diseases — humans	
Agraphia	
medicine	616.855 3
see also Communication	
disorders	
Agreement (Grammar)	415
specific languages	T4—5
Ağrı İli (Turkey)	T2—566 26
ancient	T2—395 5
Agricultural areas	T2—173 4
area planning	711.554
Agricultural assistance	
law	343.076
production economics	338.18
Agricultural banks	332.31
Agricultural chemicals	631.8
engineering	668.6
public safety	363.179 2
see also Hazardous materials	
use	631.8
Agricultural civilization	909
Agricultural commodities	338.17
see also Agricultural products	
Agricultural communities	307.72
Agricultural cooperative credit	
associations	334.2
Agricultural cooperatives	334.683
Agricultural credit	332.71
law	346.073
production economics	338.18
Agricultural ecology	577.55
Agricultural economics	338.1
Agricultural engineering	630
Agricultural enterprises	338.763
Agricultural equipment	631.3
manufacturing technology	681.763
Agricultural experiment stations	630.724
Agricultural extension	630.715
Agricultural genetics	631.523 3
Agricultural industries	338.1
accounting	657.863
economics	338.1
law	343.076
public administration	354.5

Agricultural insurance	368.096
crop	368.121
livestock liability	368.56
see also Insurance	
Agricultural laborers	
social class	305.563
Agricultural lands	333.76
biology	578.755
ecology	577.55
economics	333.76
sale and rental	333.335
Agricultural libraries	026.63
Agricultural life	
civilization	909
Agricultural lower classes	305.563
Agricultural machinery	631.3
manufacturing technology	681.763
shortages	
economics	338.14
Agricultural marketing	381.41
public administration	354.59
Agricultural meteorology	630.251 5
Agricultural occupations	
sociology	305.963
Agricultural pests	632.6
Agricultural pollution	363.738 498
effect on natural ecology	577.273
Agricultural price supports	
economics	338.18
public administration	354.528 5
Agricultural productivity	338.16
Agricultural products	338.17
commerce	381.41
economics	338.17
investment economics	332.644 1
military resources	355.245
public administration	354.59
see also Agricultural	
commodities; Farm	
produce; Produce	
(Agricultural products);	
Products — agricultural	
industries	
Agricultural runoff	363.738 498
Agricultural schools	630.71
Agricultural sociology	306.349
Agricultural structures	631.2
architecture	725.37
construction	690.537
domestic architecture	728.92
construction	690.892
use	631.2
Agricultural systems of labor	
sociology	306.364

Agricultural wastes	363.728 8	Ahimsa	294.548 697
animal feed	636.085 56	Buddhism	294.356 97
animal husbandry	636.083 8	Hinduism	294.548 697
sanitary engineering	628.74	Jainism	294.456 97
social services	363.728 8	Ahmadinejad, Mahmoud	
water pollution engineering	628.168 4	Iranian history	955.061
see also Waste control		Ahmadiyya movement	297.86
Agricultural workers	630.92	doctrines	297.204 6
labor economics	331.763	Ahom	T5—959 19
social group	305.963	Ahuachapán (El Salvador :	
Agricultural working class	305.563	Dept.)	T2—728 411
Agriculture	630	Ahvenanmaa (Finland)	T2—489 72
applied science	630	Ahvenanmaan lääni	
art representation	704.943	(Finland)	T2—489 72
arts	T3C—36	Aichi-ken (Japan)	T2—521 67
economics	338.1	Aid to families with dependent	
energy economics	333.796 6	children	362.713
enterprises	338.763	AIDS (Disease)	362.196 979 2
folklore	398.24	church work with patients	259.419 697 92
history and criticism	398.36	incidence	614.599 392
law	344.095 7	medicine	616.979 2
painting	758.5	law	344.043 697 92
public administration	354.5	nursing	616.979 202 31
Agriculture and state	338.18	pediatrics	618.929 792
Agriculturists	630.92	social services	362.196 979 2
	T1—088 63	social theology	201.762 196 979 2
Agrigento (Italy)	T2—458 221	Christianity	261.832 196 979 2
ancient	T2—378 221	*see also* Communicable	
Agrigento (Italy : Libero		diseases — humans	
consorzio comunale)	T2—458 22	Aigaio Nēsoi (Greece and	
ancient	T2—378 22	Turkey)	T2—495 8
Agrigentum (Italy)	T2—378 221	Aigaiou (Greece :	
Agroforestry	634.99	Decentralized	
Agromyzidae	595.774	administration)	T2—495 8
Agronomy	630	Aigle (Switzerland :	
Agrostis	633.23	District)	T2—494 524 9
botany	584.926	Aiken County (S.C.)	T2—757 75
forage crop	633.23	Aikido	796.815 4
Aguadilla (P.R. : District)	T2—729 54	physical fitness	613.714 815 4
Aguascalientes (Mexico :		*see also* Combat sports	
State)	T2—724 2	Ailanthuses	635.977 375
Agulhas National Park		botany	583.75
(South Africa)	T2—687 36	ornamental arboriculture	635.977 375
Agusan del Norte		Ailerons	629.134 33
(Philippines)	T2—599 726	Ailuropoda	599.789
Agusan del Sur		Ain (France)	T2—445 83
(Philippines)	T2—599 727	Aïn Chok-Hay Hassani	
Āḥād (Hadith)	297.125 24	(Morocco : Prefecture)	T2—643 8
Aḥādīth al-Qudsīyah	297.125 8	Aïn Defla (Algeria :	
Aharonim	296.180 92	Province)	T2—653
Ahidjo, Ahmadou		Aïn Sebaâ-Hay Mohamed	
Cameroonian history	967.110 41	(Morocco : Prefecture)	T2—643 8
Ahilot	296.123 6	Aïn Temouchent (Algeria :	
		Province)	T2—651

Ainu	T5—946	Air-cushion vehicles (continued)	
Ainu language	494.6	transportation services	388.35
	T6—946	inland water	386.22
Ainu literature	894.6	Air engines	621.42
Air		Air force personnel	358.400 92
gas technology	665.82	role and function	358.413 3
health	613.19	Air forces	358.4
Air artillery	358.43	Air freight	387.744
Air bags		airport services	387.736 4
automobile	629.276	law	343.097 8
Air bases	358.417	Air guns	
military engineering	623.66	art metalwork	739.73
World War I	940.443	manufacturing technology	683.4
World War II	940.544 3	Air holes	
see also Air warfare		aeronautics	629.132 327
Air circulation equipment		Air mail	383.144
buildings	697.932 5	*see also* Postal service	
Air compression engines		Air masses	551.551 2
automotive	629.250 7	Air mechanics	533.6
Air-compression-powered		aeronautics	629.132 3
automobiles		engineering	620.107
engineering	629.229 4	Air-mileage indicators	629.135 1
Air-compression-powered		Air motors	621.42
locomotives	385.365	Air national guards	358.413 7
engineering	625.265	Air operations (Military science)	358.414
transportation services	385.365	Air ordnance	358.418
see also Rolling stock		engineering	623.746 1
Air-compression-powered		military equipment	358.418
vehicles	388.349 4	Air pilots	629.130 92
transportation services	388.349 4	Air pockets	
Air compression technology	621.51	aeronautics	629.132 327
Air compressors	621.51	Air pollution	363.739 2
Air conditioning		crop damage	632.19
aircraft	629.134 42	ecology	577.276
automobile	629.277 2	law	344.046 342
buildings	697.93	public administration	354.373 5
health	613.5	social welfare	363.739 2
household management	644.5	technology	628.53
library buildings	697.978	toxicology	571.956
plant management	022.8	*see also* Pollution	
mining	622.42	Air pollution rights	363.739 26
museums	069.29	law	344.046 342
plant management	658.25	Air-position indicators	629.135 1
ships	623.853 7	Air pressure control	
vehicles	629.040 289	aircraft	629.134 42
Air conditioning engineers		spacecraft	629.477 5
building trades	697.930 92	Air propulsion	621.42
Air currents	551.517	Air pumps	621.69
aeronautics	629.132 4	Air raid shelters	363.35
Air-cushion vehicles	388.35	civil defense	363.35
engineering	629.3	law	344.053 5
land	388.35	military engineering	623.38
military engineering	623.748	public administration	353.95
ocean	387.2		

Air warfare (continued)	
Iraqi-Iranian Conflict	955.054 248
Korean War	951.904 248
Persian Gulf War, 1991	956.704 424 8
Vietnamese War	959.704 348
World War I	940.44
World War II	940.544
Airborne infantry	356.166
Airbrush drawing	741.29
Airbrush painting	751.494
Aircraft	387.73
engineering	629.133
law	343.097 5
military engineering	623.746
military equipment	358.418 3
piloting	629.132 52
psychological influence	155.965
sanitation services	363.729 3
see also Sanitation	
sports	797.5
see also Air sports	
theft of	364.162 862 913 3
law	345.026 286 291 33
transportation services	387.73
operation	387.740 44
see Manual at 629.046 vs. 388	
Aircraft accidents	363.124
see also Air safety	
Aircraft carriers	359.948 35
design	623.812 55
engineering	623.825 5
naval equipment	359.948 35
naval units	359.943 5
Aircraft detection	358.414
civil defense	363.35
Aircraft engineers	629.130 092
Aircraft failures	363.124 16
public safety	363.124 16
wreckage studies	629.132 55
see also Air safety	
Aircraft gunnery	623.555
Aircraft navigators	629.132 510 92
Aircraft noise	363.741
engineering	629.132 3
social welfare	363.741
see also Noise	
Aircraft operation	
transportation services	387.740 44
Aircraft racing	797.52
Airdrie (Scotland)	T2—414 52
Aire, River (England)	T2—428 15
Airflow	
aeronautics	629.132 32
Airfoils	629.134 32

Airframes	629.134 31
Airline cooking	641.575
Airline employees	387.709 2
Airlines	387.7
see also Air transportation	
Airplane accidents	363.124
see also Air safety	
Airplane-banner advertising	659.134 4
Airplane hijacking	364.155 2
law	345.025 52
Airplane racing	797.52
see also Air sports	
Airplanes	387.733 4
engineering	629.133 34
military engineering	623.746
piloting	629.132 52
transportation services	387.733 4
see also Aircraft	
Airport facilities	387.736 2
see also Airports	
Airport police	363.287 6
Airports	387.736
architecture	725.39
area planning	711.78
construction	690.539
engineering	629.136
institutional housekeeping	647.963 9
law	343.097 7
military engineering	623.66
public administration	354.79
transportation services	387.736
see also Aircraft	
Airships	387.732 4
engineering	629.133 24
military engineering	623.743
piloting	629.132 522
transportation services	387.732 4
see also Aircraft	
Airspace (Territorial right)	341.46
Airstrips	387.736
engineering	629.136 12
military engineering	623.661 2
transportation services	387.736
see also Airports	
Ais-Ais/Richtersveld	
Transfrontier Park	
(South Africa)	T2—687 17
Aisén (Chile : Province)	T2—836 22
Aisén del General Carlos	
Ibáñez del Campo	
(Chile : Region)	T2—836 2
Aisne (France)	T2—442 66
Aitkin County (Minn.)	T2—776 72

Alba (Romania : Judeţ)	T2—498 4
Albacete (Spain : Province)	T2—464 6
Albacore	597.783
Albanese, Anthony	
Australian history	994.072
Albania	949.65
	T2—496 5
ancient	939.865
	T2—398 65
Albania (Ancient kingdom)	939.534
	T2—395 34
Albanian language	491.991
	T6—919 91
Albanian literature	891.991
Albanians	T5—919 91
Albany (N.Y.)	T2—747 43
Albany (South Africa : District)	T2—687 53
Albany (W.A.)	T2—941 2
Albany County (N.Y.)	T2—747 42
Albany County (Wyo.)	T2—787 95
Albatrosses	598.42
Albay (Philippines)	T2—599 184
Albemarle County (Va.)	T2—755 482
Albemarle Sound (N.C.)	551.461 348
	T2—163 48
Alberni-Clayoquot (B.C.)	T2—711 2
Albert (N.B. : County)	T2—715 31
Albert (South Africa : District)	T2—687 57
Albert I, King of the Belgians	
Belgian history	949.304 1
Albert II, Holy Roman Emperor	
German history	943.028
Albert II, King of the Belgians	
Belgian history	949.304 4
Albert Falls Game Reserve (South Africa)	T2—684 7
Alberta	971.23
	T2—712 3
Albertine Statute	
Piedmontese history	945.108 3
Sardinian history	945.908 3
Alberton (South Africa : District)	T2—682 25
Albigensianism	273.6
denomination	284.4
persecution of	272.3
Albinism	
medicine	616.55
see also Skin diseases — humans	
Alborz (Iran)	T2—552 8
Albula (Switzerland)	T2—494 732 4

Albula (Switzerland : Region)	T2—494 732 4
Albumin glue	668.32
Albumins	572.66
see also Proteins	
Albuminuria	
medicine	616.63
see also Urologic diseases — humans	
Albuquerque (N.M.)	T2—789 61
Albury (N.S.W.)	T2—944 8
Alcedinidae	598.78
Alcelaphinae	599.645
Alces	599.657
Alchemy	540.112
Alcidae	598.33
Alcohol	547.031
see also Alcoholic beverages; Alcohols	
Alcohol abuse	362.292
see also Alcoholism	
Alcohol-related disorders	
perinatal medicine	618.326 861
Alcohol smuggling	364.133 61
law	345.023 361
Alcoholic beverages	641.21
commercial processing	663.1
cooking with	641.62
criminology	364.133 2
law	345.023 32
possession and use	364.173
law	345.027 3
customs	394.13
ethics	178.1
home preparation	641.874
product safety	363.192 9
see also Food — product safety	
public control	
criminology	364.173
law	344.054 1
public administration	353.37
smuggling	364.133 61
law	345.023 361
Alcoholics	T1—087 4
Alcoholics Anonymous	362.292 86
Alcoholism	362.292
law	344.044 61
medicine	616.861
pastoral theology	206.1
Christianity	259.429 2
personal health	613.81
pregnancy complications	
obstetrics	618.368 6

Alcoholism (continued)
  school problem   371.784
  social theology   201.762 292
    Christianity   261.832 292
  social welfare   362.292
  see also Substance abuse
Alcohols   547.031
  aromatic chemistry   547.631
  chemical engineering   661.82
  chemistry   547.031
  fuel   662.669 2
    cooking   641.585
  human toxicology   615.951 31
  pharmacokinetics   615.782 8
Alcona County (Mich.)   T2—774 79
Alcorn County (Miss.)   T2—762 993
Alcyonaria   593.6
Aldabra Island (Seychelles)   T2—696
Aldehydes   547.036
  aromatic chemistry   547.636
  chemical engineering   661.85
Alderflies   595.747
Alderney (Channel Islands)   T2—423 43
Alders   583.65
Aldosterone
  pharmacology   615.364
Ale   641.23
  commercial processing   663.42
  cooking with   641.623
  home preparation   641.873
Aleatory composition   781.32
Alekseĭ Mikhaĭlovich, Czar of
  Russia
  Russian history   947.048
Alemán, Arnoldo
  Nicaraguan history   972.850 542
Alemán, Miguel
  Mexican history   972.082 7
Alentejo (Portugal)   T2—469 5
Alentejo (Portugal : Region)   T2—469 5
Aleppo (Syria : Province)   T2—569 13
Alessandri, Jorge
  Chilean history   983.064 4
Alessandria (Italy :
  Province)   T2—451 4
  ancient   T2—371 8
Alethic logic   511.314
Aleut   979.800 497 19
     T5—971 9
Aleut language   497.19
     T6—971 9
Aleut literature   897.19
Aleutian Islands (Alaska)   T2—798 4

Aleutians East Borough
  (Alaska)   T2—798 4
Alevi-Bektashi   297.825 2
Alevis   297.825 2
Alexander I, Emperor of Russia
  Russian history   947.072
Alexander II, Emperor of Russia
  Russian history   947.081
Alexander III, Emperor of Russia
  Russian history   947.082
Alexander County (Ill.)   T2—773 999
Alexander County (N.C.)   T2—756 795
Alexander technique
  therapeutics   615.82
Alexandria (Egypt)
  ancient   T2—321
Alexandria (Egypt :
  Province)   T2—621
Alexandria (Scotland)   T2—414 32
Alexandria (South Africa :
  District)   T2—687 53
Alexandria (Va.)   T2—755 296
Alexandrian philosophy   186.4
Alexandrian school (Christian
  theology)   230.14
Alexis, Czar of Russia
  Russian history   947.048
Alfalfa   633.31
  botany   583.63
  forage crop   633.31
Alfalfa County (Okla.)   T2—766 22
Alfonsinos   597.64
Alfonso XII, King of Spain
  Spanish history   946.074
Alfonso XIII, King of Spain
  Spanish history   946.074
Alfred (South Africa :
  District)   T2—684 63
Alfred, King of England
  English history   942.016 4
Alfred Nzo District
  Municipality (South
  Africa)   T2—687 59
Alfred the Great, King of
  England
  English history   942.016 4
Algae   579.8
  paleontology   561.93
  physiology   571.298
  resource economics   333.953 8
Algarve (Portugal)   T2—469 6
Algarve (Portugal : Region)   T2—469 6

Algebra	512
numerical methods	518.42
primary education	372.71
Algebraic combinatorics	511.6
Algebraic curves	516.352
Algebraic function theory	512.74
Algebraic geometry	516.35
Algebraic groups	512.2
Algebraic K-theory	512.66
Algebraic logic	511.324
Algebraic number theory	512.74
Algebraic numbers	512.784
Algebraic operations	512.92
Algebraic progressions	515.24
Algebraic surfaces	516.352
Algebraic topology	514.2
Algebraic varieties	516.353
Alger County (Mich.)	T2—774 932
Algeria	965
	T2—65
ancient	T2—397 14
Algerians	T5—927 65
Algic languages	497.3
	T6—973
Algicides	632.95
agricultural use	632.95
chemical engineering	668.652
pest control technology	628.97
Algiers (Algeria : Province)	T2—653
Algiers, War with United States, 1815	973.53
Algologists	579.809 2
Algology	579.8
Algoma (Ont. : District)	T2—713 132
Algonkian era	551.715
geology	551.715
paleontology	560.171 5
Algonkian languages	497.3
	T6—973
Algonquian Indians	973.049 73
	T5—973
Algonquian languages	497.3
	T6—973
Algonquin Indians	971.300 497 33
	T5—973 3
Algonquin Provincial Park (Ont.)	T2—713 147
Algorithms	518.1
computer programming	005.13
Ali, Irfaan	
Guyanese history	988.103 36
Alicante (Spain : Province)	T2—467 65
Alice (South Africa : District)	T2—687 54

Alice Springs (N.T.)	T2—942 91
Alicyclic compounds	547.5
chemical engineering	661.8
Alien species	333.952 3
see also entries beginning with Nonnative	
Alienated classes	305.568
	T1—086 94
Alienation (Law)	346.043 6
Alienation (Social psychology)	302.544
arts	700.453
	T3C—353
literature	808.803 53
history and criticism	809.933 53
specific literatures	T3B—080 353
history and criticism	T3B—093 53
Aliens	305.906 91
	T1—086 91
see also Noncitizens	
Alimony	346.016 63
Aliphatic compounds	547.4
chemical engineering	661.8
Alismales	584.44
Alismataceae	584.44
Alismatales	584.44
Alismidae	584.44
Aliwal North (South Africa : District)	T2—687 57
Alizarines	667.256
Alkali heath	583.88
Alkali metals	669.725
chemistry	546.38
materials science	620.189 6
metallurgy	669.725
see also Chemicals; Metals	
Alkaline-earth metals	669.725
chemistry	546.39
materials science	620.189 6
metallurgy	669.725
see also Chemicals; Metals	
Alkaline-soil conditioners	631.825
chemical engineering	668.64
Alkalis	546.32
chemical engineering	661.3
human toxicology	615.922
Alkaloidal plants	581.63
agriculture	633.7
botany	581.63
Alkaloids	572.549
biochemistry	572.549
chemistry	547.7
pharmacognosy	615.321

Allocation (Rationing)	
public administration	352.86
Allocation of staff	658.312 8
public administration	352.66
Allodium	333.323 2
Alloecoela	592.42
Allopathy	610
therapeutic system	615.53
Allosaurus	567.912
Allotheria	569.29
Alloy binary systems	
metallurgy	669.94
Alloys	669
chemistry	546.3
materials science	620.16
metallography	669.95
metallurgy	669
ship design	623.818 2
shipbuilding	623.820 7
structural engineering	624.182
see Manual at 669	
Allspice	641.338 3
agriculture	633.83
botany	583.732
food	641.338 3
see also Spices	
Alluvial mining	622.292 7
Alluvium	551.354
Almanacs	030
astronomy	528
Almere (Netherlands)	T2—492 2
Almería (Spain : Province)	T2—468 1
Almonds	641.345 5
agriculture	634.55
botany	583.642
commercial processing	664.804 55
cooking	641.645 5
food	641.345 5
Almsgiving	204.46
Christianity	248.46
ethics	177.7
Islam	297.54
Almshouses	362.585
architecture	725.55
Alodium	333.323 2
Aloe barbadensis	
pharmacology	615.324 77
Aloe hemp	584.79
Aloe vera	
pharmacology	615.324 77
Aloes (Asparagaceae)	584.79
Aloes (Xanthorrhoeaceae)	584.77
botany	584.77
floriculture	635.934 77

Alopecia	
medicine	616.546
see also Skin diseases —	
humans	
Alopex	599.776 4
Alouatta	599.855
Alpaca wool textiles	677.32
see also Textiles	
Alpacas	636.296 6
Alpena County (Mich.)	T2—774 81
Alpenhorns	788.92
see also Brass instruments	
Alpes de Haute-Provence	
(France)	T2—449 5
Alpes-Maritimes (France)	T2—449 4
Alpha cellulose	676.4
Alpha decay	539.752 2
Alpha particles	539.723 2
Alphabetic subject catalog	017
Alphabets	411
applied linguistics	418
specific languages	T4—813
decorative arts	744.4
design	744.4
printing	686.21
specific languages	T4—11
Alphorns	788.92
see also Brass instruments	
Alpine biology	578.753 8
Alpine County (Calif.)	T2—794 43
Alpine ecology	577.538
Alpine gardens	635.952 8
Alpine plants	581.753 8
floriculture	635.952 8
Alpine skiing	796.935
see also Winter sports	
Alpine snowboarding	796.939
see also Winter sports	
Alps	949.47
	T2—494 7
Austria	T2—436 4
France	T2—445 8
Italy	T2—451
Switzerland	T2—494 7
Alpstein (Switzerland)	T2—494 71
Alsace (France)	T2—443 9
Alsatian (Dog)	636.737 6
Alsatian dialect	437.944 39
	T6—34
Alstroemeriaceae	584.6
Alta Verapaz (Guatemala)	T2—728 151
Altagracia (Dominican	
Republic : Province)	T2—729 385
Altaï (Russia : Republic)	T2—573

Aluminum (continued)
  shipbuilding — 623.820 7
  structural engineering — 624.182 6
  see also Chemicals; Metals
Aluminum lithography — 763.23
Aluminum soaps — 668.125
Alunite
  mineralogy — 549.755
Alur language — 496.558 4
        T6—965 584
Alvarado Quesada, Carlos
  Costa Rican history — 972.860 532
Alvarez, Luis Echeverría
  Mexican history — 972.083 2
Alveolar abscesses
  dentistry — 617.632
Alvra (Switzerland :
  Region) — T2—494 732 4
Älvsborgs län (Sweden) — T2—486 7
Alwa (Kingdom) — 962.620 22
Alyn and Deeside (Wales) — T2—429 33
Alyssums — 635.933 78
  botany — 583.78
  floriculture — 635.933 78
Alzheimer disease — 362.196 831 1
  diagnosis — 616.831 107 5
  drug therapy — 616.831 106 1
  etiology — 616.831 107 1
  genetics — 616.831 104 2
  geriatrics — 618.976 831 1
  medicine — 616.831 1
  pathology — 616.831 107
  social services — 362.196 831 1
  therapy — 616.831 106
  see also Nervous system
    diseases — humans
Alzheimer's disease — 362.196 831 1
  diagnosis — 616.831 107 5
  drug therapy — 616.831 106 1
  genetics — 616.831 104 2
  geriatrics — 618.976 831 1
  medicine — 616.831 1
  social services — 362.196 831 1
  therapy — 616.831 106
  see also Nervous system
    diseases — humans
AM radio stations — 384.545 3
  see also Radio stations
AM radio systems — 621.384 153
Amador County (Calif.) — T2—794 42
Amajuba District
  Municipality (South
  Africa) — T2—684 1

Amalgamations of corporations — 338.83
  see also Mergers
Amalgams
  dentistry — 617.675
Amambay (Paraguay) — T2—892 137
Amanzimtoti (South Africa) — T2—684 5
Amapá (Brazil : State) — T2—811 6
'Amāra kelel (Ethiopia) — T2—634
Amaranthaceae — 583.883
Amaranths — 583.883
  botany — 583.883
  cooking — 641.631
  field crop — 633.1
  floriculture — 635.933 883
  food — 641.331
  see also Grain amaranths
Amaryllidaceae — 584.78
Amaryllidoideae — 584.78
Amaryllises — 635.934 78
  botany — 584.78
  floriculture — 635.934 78
Amasya İli (Turkey) — T2—563 8
  ancient — T2—393 32
Amateur cinematography — 777
Amateur circuses — 791.3
Amateur motion pictures — 791.433
  see also Motion pictures
Amateur radio — 384.54
  communications services — 384.54
  engineering — 621.384 16
  law — 343.099 45
  public administration — 354.75
Amateur sports — 796.042
  see also Sports
  see Manual at 796.08 vs.
    796.04
Amateur theater — 792.022 2
Amateur video recording — 777
Amateur videography — 777
Amateur workshops — 684.08
Amathole District
  Municipality (South
  Africa) — T2—687 54
Amazon Region (Colombia) — T2—861 6
Amazon River — T2—811
  Brazil — T2—811
  Peru — T2—854 4
Amazonas (Brazil) — T2—811 3
Amazonas (Colombia :
  Dept.) — T2—861 7
Amazonas (Peru : Region)
  1989–2002 — T2—854 4
  2002– — T2—854 6
Amazonas (Venezuela) — T2—876 4

American literature	810
American loyalists	
Canadian history	971.024
United States history	973.314
American Lutheran Church	284.131
see also Lutheran church	
American-Mexican Border	
Region	T2—721
American Muslim Mission	297.87
American native languages	497
	T6—97
South America	498
	T6—98
American native literatures	897
South America	898
American native peoples	970.004 97
	T5—97
legal status	
United States	346.730 130 899 7
military troops	
American Revolution	973.343
War of 1812	973.524 2
World War II	940.540 3
religion	299.7
North America	299.7
South America	299.8
social aspects	305.897
South America	T5—98
tribal land	333.2
American Nazi Party	324.273 38
American opossums	599.276
American organs	786.55
instrument	786.551 9
music	786.55
see also Keyboard instruments	
American paint horse	636.13
American Party (U.S.)	324.273 2
American pocket billiards	794.733
American poetry	811
American Reformed Church	285.7
see also Reformed Church	
(American Reformed)	
American Revised version Bible	220.520 4
American Revolution, 1775–1783	973.3
societies	369.13
American saddlebred horse	636.13
American Samoa	996.13
	T2—961 3
American Sign Language	419.7
	T6—999 87
American Sign Language	
literature	899.987

American speeches	
African American authors	
collections	815.008 089 607 3
history and criticism	815.009 896 073
American Standard version Bible	220.520 4
American theater (World War II)	940.542 8
American Veterans of World War	
II, Korea, and Vietnam	369.186 2
Americans (U.S.)	T5—13
Americas	T2—7
Americium	546.441
see also Chemicals	
Amerind languages	497
	T6—97
South America	498
	T6—98
Amerind literatures	897
South America	898
Amerindians	T5—97
South America	T5—98
see also American native	
peoples	
Amersfoort (South Africa :	
District)	T2—682 78
Ameslan (Sign language)	419.7
	T6—999 87
Amethysts	553.87
see also Semiprecious stones	
Amhara (African people)	T5—928
Amharic language	492.87
	T6—928 7
Amharic literature	892.87
Amherst (N.S.)	T2—716 11
Amherst County (Va.)	T2—755 496
Amherst of Arracan, William Pitt	
Amherst, Earl	
Indian history	954.031 3
Ami (Taiwan people)	T5—992 5
Amiante (Quebec)	T2—714 712
Amicicide (Military science)	355.422
Amides	547.042
chemical engineering	661.894
Amiens (France)	T2—442 625
Amiiformes	597.41
Amin, Idi	
Ugandan history	967.610 42
Amination	547.27
chemical engineering	660.284 4
Amines	547.042
biochemistry	572.548
chemical engineering	661.894
Amino acid sequence	572.633

Amino acids	572.65	Amoebic dysentery	
applied nutrition	613.282	incidence	614.516
biochemistry	572.65	medicine	616.935 3
humans	612.015 756	*see also* Communicable	
see also Proteins		diseases — humans	
Aminoglycosides		Amoebida	579.432
pharmacology	615.329	Amoraim	296.120 092
Amish		Amorites	T5—921
biography	289.709 2	Amorphous computing	006.382
Amish churches	289.73	Amorphous solids	530.413
Amish cooking	641.566	Amos (Biblical book)	224.8
Amite County (Miss.)	T2—762 24	Ampere-hour meters	621.374 4
Amman (Jordan : Province)	T2—569 58	Amphetamine abuse	362.299 5
ancient	T2—335 8	medicine	616.864
Ammeters	621.374 4	personal health	613.84
Ammonia	546.711 2	social welfare	362.299 5
chemical engineering	661.34	*see also* Substance abuse	
Ammonite language	492.6	Amphibians	597.8
	T6—926	agriculture	639.378
Ammonium fertilizers	631.841	art representation	704.943 278
chemical engineering	668.624 1	arts	T3C—362 78
Ammonium hydroxide	546.711 2	commercial hunting	639.13
chemical engineering	661.34	conservation technology	639.977 8
Ammonium nitrate fertilizer	631.842	drawing	743.678
chemical engineering	668.624 2	food	641.396
Ammonium salts	546.711 24	cooking	641.696
chemical engineering	661.5	paleozoology	567.8
Ammonoidea	564.53	resource economics	333.957 8
Ammunition	355.825	zoology	597.8
military	355.825	Amphibious air-cushion vehicles	
engineering	623.45	engineering	629.325
use	355.825	military engineering	623.748 5
small arms engineering		Amphibious operations	355.46
military	623.451	marine forces	359.964 6
small arms manufacturing		Amphibious planes	387.733 48
technology	683.406	engineering	629.133 348
Amnesia		transportation services	387.733 48
medicine	616.852 32	*see also* Aircraft	
see also Mental disorders		Amphiboles	
Amnesty	364.65	mineralogy	549.66
law	345.077	Amphineura	594.27
penology	364.65	Amphipoda	595.378
Amniocentesis		Amphisbaenia	597.948
obstetrics	618.320 427 5	Amphisbaenidae	597.948
Amniotes	596	Amphissa (Greece)	T2—383
Amniotic fluid		Amphitheaters	796.068
human physiology	612.63	architecture	725.827
obstetrics	618.34	Amplifiers	621.381 535
Amoebas	579.432	electronic circuits	621.381 535
Amoebiasis		radio engineering	621.384 12
incidence	614.53	Amplitude-modulation radio	
medicine	616.936	systems	621.384 153
see also Communicable		Amplitude modulators	
diseases — humans		electronic circuits	621.381 536 2

Amputation of limbs	
surgery	617.580 59
Amsterdam (Netherlands)	T2—492 352
Amsterdam Island	969.9
	T2—699
Amto-Musan languages	T6—991 2
Amulets	133.44
Islamic popular practices	297.39
numismatics	737.23
religious significance	203.7
Amundsen Sea	551.461 74
	T2—167 4
Amur (Russia : Oblast)	T2—577
Amur River (China and	
Russia)	T2—577
Amurskaĩa oblast′ (Russia)	T2—577
Amusement parks	791.068
architecture	725.76
area planning	711.558
landscape architecture	712.5
recreation	791.068
Amusements	790
journalism	070.444
law	344.099
see also Recreation	
AMVETS (Veterans'	
organization)	369.186 2
Amyl nitrite abuse	362.299 3
medicine	616.86
personal health	613.8
social welfare	362.299 3
see also Substance abuse	
Amylases	572.756
see also Enzymes	
Amyloidosis	
medicine	616.399 5
see also Digestive system	
diseases — humans	
Amyotrophic lateral sclerosis	
medicine	616.839
see also Nervous system	
diseases — humans	
An Giang (Vietnam :	
Province)	T2—597 9
Anabaptists	284.3
Anabolism	572.45
see also Metabolism	
Anacampserotaceae	583.88
Anacardiaceae	583.75
botany	583.75
edible fruits	641.344 4
cooking	641.644 4
food	641.344 4
orchard crops	634.44

Anacondas	597.967
Anaerobic bacteria	579.314 9
Anaerobic digestion (Sewage	
treatment)	628.354
Anaerobic gram-negative rods	579.325
Anaerobic respiration	572.478
Anagrams	793.734
Anahim Lake (B.C.)	T2—711 75
Analgesic abuse	362.299
medicine	616.86
personal health	613.8
social welfare	362.299
see also Substance abuse	
Analgesics	
pharmacokinetics	615.783
Analog circuits	
electronics	621.381 5
Analog communications	621.382
Analog computers	004.19
communications	004.619
electronic	004.19
engineering	621.391 9
interfacing	004.619
nonelectronic	004.9
software development	005.29
Analog instruments	
technology	681.1
Analog-to-digital converters	
computer engineering	621.398 14
computer science	004.64
electronic engineering	621.381 59
Analogy	
logic	169
Analysis (Mathematics)	515
numerical methods	518.6
Analysis of covariance	519.538
Analysis of variance	519.538
Analysis situs	514
Analytic curves	516.362
Analytic functions	
spaces	515.73
Analytic geometry	516.3
Analytic number theory	512.73
Analytic spaces	515.942
Analytic surfaces	516.362
Analytic topology	514.7
Analytic trigonometry	516.34
Analytical bibliography	010.42
Analytical biochemistry	572.36
humans	612.015 85
Analytical chemistry	543
minerals	549.133
organic chemistry	543.17
Analytical guides (Music)	780.15

Analytical mechanics	531.015 15	Anchor ice	551.344
Analytical philosophy	146.4	Anchorages	387.1
Anambas Islands		engineering	627.22
(Indonesia)	T2—598 192	*see also* Ports	
Anambra State (Nigeria)	T2—669 48	Anchors	623.862
Ananda Mahidol, King of		Anchovies	641.392
Thailand		cooking	641.692
Thai history	959.304 3	food	641.392
Anaphora		zoology	597.45
linguistics	401.456	Ancienne-Lorette (Quebec)	T2—714 471
specific languages	T4—014 56	Ancient Arabic Order of the	
Anapsida	567.92	Nobles of the Mystic Shrine	
Anarchism	335.83	for North America	366.16
economics	335.83	biography	366.160 92
ideal state	321.07	Ancient architecture	722
political ideology	320.57	Ancient civilization	930
Anarchist communities	307.77	Ancient history	930
Anarchists	335.830 92		T1—090 1
Anarcho-syndicalism	335.82	Ancient law	340.53
economics	335.82	Ancient philosophy	180
political ideology	320.57	Ancient remedies	
Anarchy	335.83	therapeutics	615.880 901
see also Anarchism		Ancient sculpture	732
Anarthriaceae	584.9	Ancient world	930
Anas	598.413		T2—3
Anas platyrhynchos	598.413 4	geography	913
Anaspidea	594.37	*see Manual at* T2—3; *also at*	
Anatidae	598.41	T2—4–9 vs. T2—3	
Anatolia	T2—561	Ancistrocladaceae	583.887
Anatolian languages	491.998	Ancona (Italy : Province)	T2—456 71
	T6—919 98	ancient	T2—374 5
Anatolikē Attikē (Greece)	T2—495 12	Ancyclostomiasis	
Anatolikē Makedonia kai		incidence	614.555 4
Thrakē (Greece)	T2—495 7	medicine	616.965 4
Anatomic embryology		*see also* Communicable	
humans	611.013	diseases — humans	
Anatomy	571.3	Andalusia (Spain)	T2—468
domestic animals	636.089 1	Andalusite	
drawing		mineralogy	549.62
animals	743.6	Andaman and Nicobar	
humans	743.49	Islands	T2—548 8
humans	611	Andaman Sea	551.461 565
see Manual at 599.94 vs.			T2—165 65
611; *also at* 612 vs. 611		Andamanese	T5—959
microorganisms	571.633 29	Andamanese languages	495.9
plants	571.32		T6—959
Anatosaurus	567.914	Andean Region (Colombia)	T2—861 2
Anaxagorean philosophy	182.8	Andelfingen (Switzerland :	
Anbār (Iraq)	T2—567 4	Bezirk)	T2—494 574 9
Ancash (Peru)	T2—852 1	Anderson County (Kan.)	T2—781 672
Ancestors	T1—085 3	Anderson County (Ky.)	T2—769 463
family relationships	306.874	Anderson County (S.C.)	T2—757 25
objects of worship	202.13	Anderson County (Tenn.)	T2—768 73
Ancestry	929.1	Anderson County (Tex.)	T2—764 229

Andes	T2—8
Andes (Chile : Province)	T2—832 42
Andesite	552.23
Andhra language	494.827
	T6—948 27
Andhra literature	894.827
Andhra Pradesh (India)	T2—548 5
Andi languages	499.964
	T6—999 64
Andorra	946.79
	T2—467 9
Andreaeales	588.2
Andrew County (Mo.)	T2—778 126
Andrews County (Tex.)	T2—764 856
Androgens	
human physiology	612.61
Androgynous behavior	
psychology	155.33
Androgyny	
psychology	155.33
Andropogoneae	584.924
Andropov, ĨU. V. (ĨUriĩ	
Vladimirovich)	
Russian history	947.085 4
Andros (Greece : Regional	
unit)	T2—495 85
Andros Island (Bahamas)	T2—729 6
Andros Island (Greece)	T2—495 85
Androscoggin County (Me.)	T2—741 82
Androscoggin River (Me.)	T2—741 8
Anecdotes	
literature	808.882
history and criticism	809.982
specific literatures	T3B—802
individual authors	T3A—8
Anelytropsidae	597.952
Anemia	
medicine	616.152
see also Cardiovascular	
diseases — humans	
Anemones	583.34
botany	583.34
floriculture	635.933 34
Anesthesiologists	617.960 92
law	344.041 2
Anesthesiology	617.96
Anesthetics	
pharmacokinetics	615.781
Anesthetists	617.960 92
law	344.041 2
Aneuploidy	572.877

Aneurysms	
medicine	616.133
see also Cardiovascular	
diseases — humans	
Añez, Jeanine	
Bolivian history	984.054 3
Angas language	493.7
	T6—937
Angaston (S. Aust.)	T2—942 32
Angelfishes	597.72
Cichlidae	597.74
Pomacanthidae	597.72
Angelina County (Tex.)	T2—764 173
Angels	202.15
art representation	704.948 64
arts	T3C—382 021 5
Christianity	235.3
Islam	297.215
Judaism	296.315
literature	808.803 820 215
history and criticism	809.933 820 215
specific literatures	T3B—080 382 021 5
history and	
criticism	T3B—093 820 215
Anger	152.47
ethics	179.8
religion	205.698
psychology	152.47
see also Vices	
Ångermanland landskap	
(Sweden)	T2—488 5
Angers (France)	T2—441 84
Angina pectoris	
medicine	616.122
see also Cardiovascular	
diseases — humans	
Angiocardiography	
medicine	616.120 757 2
Angiology	616.13
Angioplasty	617.413
Angiosperms	583
paleobotany	561.3
Angle harps	787.94
see also Stringed instruments	
Angle trisection	516.204
Anglerfishes	597.62
Angles	516.152
Anglesey (Wales)	T2—429 21
Anglican cathedrals	
architecture	726.65
Anglican chant	782.322 3
Anglican Communion	283
church government	262.03
local church	254.03

Anglican Communion (continued)	
church law	262.983
doctrines	230.3
catechisms and creeds	238.3
general councils	262.53
guides to Christian life	248.483
liturgy	264.03
missions	266.3
moral theology	241.043
persecution by Queen Mary	272.6
public worship	264.03
religious associations	267.183
religious education	268.83
religious orders	255.83
church history	271.83
women	255.983
church history	271.983
seminaries	230.073 3
theology	230.3
Anglican sacred music	781.713
public worship	782.322 3
music	782.322 3
religion	264.030 2
Anglicans	
biography	283.092
Angling	799.12
Anglo-Boer War, 1880–1881	968.204 6
Anglo-Boer War, 1899–1902	968.048
Anglo-Dutch Wars, 1652–1653	949.204
Anglo-Egyptian Sudan	962.403
	T2—624
Anglo-Indians	T5—914 11
Anglo-Irish War, 1919–1921	941.508 21
Anglo-Saxon language	429
	T6—29
Anglo-Saxon law	349.420 902 1
Anglo-Saxon literature	829
Anglo-Saxons	T5—2
Anglo-Spanish War, 1739–1741	946.055
Angola	967.3
	T2—673
Angolans	T5—967 3
Angolese	T5—967 3
Angoni language	496.398
	T6—963 98
Angora cat	636.83
Angora goat	636.398 5
Angoulême, House of	944.028
Angoumois (France)	T2—446 5
Anguidae	597.959 2
Anguilla	972.973
	T2—729 73
Anguilla (Eels)	597.432
Anguillidae	597.432

Anguilliformes	597.43
Anguinomorphoidea	597.959
Angular momentum (Nuclear physics)	539.725
Angus (Scotland)	T2—412 6
Angus cattle	636.223
Anhalt (Germany)	T2—431 86
Anhimidae	598.41
Anhui Sheng (China)	T2—512 25
Anhwei Province (China)	T2—512 25
Anhydrite	
mineralogy	549.752
Anhydrous sulfates	
mineralogy	549.752
Aniliidae	597.967
Animal babies	591.392
domestic animals	636.07
mammals	599.139 2
Animal behavior	591.5
comparative psychology	156
Animal biography	590.929
	T1—092 9
Animal black	662.93
Animal body disposal	363.78
Animal breeding	636.082
Animal combat sports	791.8
Animal communication	591.59
physiology	573.92
Animal communities	591.782
Animal courtship	591.562
Animal defenses	591.47
Animal-derived drugs	
pharmacology	615.36
Animal-derived poisons	
human toxicology	615.94
Animal diseases	571.91
agricultural economics	338.14
veterinary medicine	636.089 6
Animal ecology	591.7
Animal experimentation	590.724
ethics	179.4
see also Animals — treatment of — ethics	
medicine	616.027
physiology	571.107 24
Animal fats	665.2
food	641.36
food technology	664.3
home cooking	641.66
industrial technology	665.2
Animal feeding	636.084
Animal feeds	636.085 5
see also Feeds	

Animal fibers	677.3
materials science	620.197
textiles	677.3
arts	746.043
economics	338.476 773
see also Textiles	
Animal flight	573.798
behavior	591.57
physiology	573.798
Animal food	636.085 5
see also Feeds	
Animal ghosts	133.14
Animal glue	668.32
Animal grooming	
agriculture	636.083 3
zoology	591.563
Animal heat	571.76
Animal hormones	573.44
Animal hospitals	636.083 21
Animal husbandry	636
agricultural economics	338.176
law	343.076 6
equipment manufacturing	
technology	681.763 6
public administration	354.56
Animal intelligence	591.513
comparative psychology	156.39
Animal language	591.59
Animal locomotion	573.79
Animal magnetism	154.72
parapsychology	133.89
Animal manures	
waste technology	628.76
Animal marking	590.723 2
Animal migration	591.568
Animal models	
human diseases	616.027
Animal navigation	591.568
Animal oils	665.2
food	641.36
food technology	664.3
home cooking	641.66
industrial technology	665.2
Animal performances	791.8
circuses	791.32
Animal pest control	363.78
see also Pest control	
Animal pests	591.65
Animal physiology	571.1
Animal-plant relationships	577.8
Animal populations	591.788
Animal psychology	591.5
comparative psychology	156

Animal racing	798
arts	700.457 9
	T3C—357 9
child care	649.57
ethics	175
journalism	070.449 798
law	344.099
literature	
history and criticism	809.933 579
specific literatures	T3B—080 357 9
history and	
criticism	T3B—093 579
motion pictures	791.436 579
public administrative support	353.78
safety	363.14
public administration	353.97
sociology	306.483
television programs	791.456 579
see also Sports	
Animal rescue	636.083 2
Animal resources	333.954
law	346.046 954
public administration	354.349
Animal rights	
ethics	179.3
see also Animals —	
treatment of — ethics	
Animal sacrifice	203.4
Animal shelters	636.083 2
Animal shows	791.8
animal husbandry	636.081 1
performing arts	791.8
Animal sounds	591.594
Animal swimming	591.57
Animal training	636.083 5
Animal viruses	579.2
Animal wastes	363.728 8
law	344.046 22
organic fertilizers	631.86
pollution	363.738
technology	628.76
water pollution engineering	628.168 46
Animal watching	590.723 4
Animal waxes	665.13
Animal weapons	591.47
Animal welfare	636.083 2
animal husbandry	636.083 2
law	344.049
Animals	590
agricultural pests	632.6
agriculture	636
agricultural economics	338.176
anatomy	571.31
art representation	704.943 2

Animals	590
arts	700.462
	T3C—362
bacterial diseases	571.993 11
Bible	220.859
cancer	571.978 1
care and maintenance	636.083
communicable diseases	571.981
conservation	333.954 16
see Manual at 333.955–.959	
vs. 639.97	
conservation technology	639.9
disease carriers	571.986
medicine	614.43
drawing	743.6
endoparasitic diseases	571.999 1
environmental diseases	571.951
folklore	398.245
history and criticism	398.369
food source	641.306
agriculture	636.088 3
growth	571.81
legendary	398.245 4
see also Legendary animals	
literature	808.803 62
history and criticism	809.933 62
specific literatures	T3B—080 362
history and	
criticism	T3B—093 62
mycoses	571.995 11
painting	758.3
parasitic diseases	571.999 1
physiology	571.1
protozoan infections	571.994 11
radiation injuries	571.934 51
regional anatomy	573.993 3
religious worship	202.12
resource economics	333.954
conservation	333.954 16
law	346.046 954 16
law	346.046 954
see Manual at 333.955–.959	
vs. 639.97	
rickettsial diseases	571.993 271 1
skin diseases	573.539
smuggling	364.133 67
law	345.023 367
theft of	364.162 859
therapeutic use	615.851 58
treatment of	
ethics	179.3
religion	205.693
Buddhism	294.356 93
Christianity	241.693

Animals	
treatment of	
ethics	
religion (continued)	
Hinduism	294.548 693
Judaism	296.369 3
use in mining	622.65
use in warfare	355.424
virus diseases	571.992 11
worm-caused diseases	571.999 1
zoology	590
see Manual at 800, T3C—362	
vs. 398.245, 590, 636	
Animals for specific purposes	636.088
see Manual at 636.1–.8 vs.	
636.088	
Animated cartoons	791.433 4
cinematography	777.7
drawing	741.58
motion pictures	791.433 4
Animated drawings	
drawing	741.58
Animated films	791.433 4
Animated graphics	
design	744.82
Animated television programs	791.453 4
Animation cels	741.58
Anime	791.433 4
drawing	741.58
motion pictures	791.433 4
Animism	
comparative religion	202.1
philosophy	147
Anis	598.74
Anise	641.338 2
botany	583.988 2
see also Flavorings	
Aniseikonia	
incidence	614.599 7
optometry	617.758
see also Eye diseases —	
humans	
Anisophylleaceae	583.66
Anjou (France)	T2—441 8
Anjou, House of	
Sicilian history	945.804
Southern Italian history	945.705
Ankara İli (Turkey)	T2—563 6
ancient	T2—393 2
Ankles	612.98
physiology	612.98
regional medicine	617.584
surgery	617.584
see also Lower extremities	

Anklets (Ornaments)	391.7	Annonaceae	584.286
customs	391.7	botany	584.286
making	739.278	edible fruits	641.344 1
costume jewelry	688.2	cooking	641.644 1
handicrafts	745.594 2	food	641.344 1
fine jewelry	739.278	orchard crops	634.41
Ankole (Kingdom)	967.610 1	Annotations to cases	348.047
	T2—676 1	Annotations to laws	348.027
Ankylosauria	567.915	Announcements	
Ankylosing spondylitis		design	744.75
medicine	616.73	etiquette	395.4
see also Musculoskeletal		Announcing	
diseases — humans		radio performances	791.443
Ann Arbor (Mich.)	T2—774 35	television performances	791.453
Anna, Empress of Russia		Annual leave	331.257 6
Russian history	947.061	personnel management	658.312 2
Annaba (Algeria : Province)	T2—655	Annual publications	050
Annam-Muong languages	495.92		T1—05
	T6—959 2	*see also* Annuals (Publications)	
Annam-Muong literatures	895.92	Annual reports	
Annam-Muong peoples	T5—959 2	design	744.552
Annamese	T5—959 22	Annual wage plan	331.236
Annamese language	495.922	Annual wages	331.216 2
	T6—959 22	personnel management	658.322 2
Annandale and Eskdale		Annuals (Plants)	582.12
(Scotland)	T2—414 7	floriculture	635.931 2
Annapolis (Md.)	T2—752 56	Annuals (Publications)	050
Annapolis (N.S. : County)	T2—716 33		T1—05
Annatto tree	583.77	almanacs	030
Anne (Mother of the Virgin		design	744.552
Mary), Saint	232.933	encyclopedia yearbooks	030
private prayers to	242.75	publishing	070.572
Anne, Queen of England		Annuities	
British history	941.069	insurance	368.37
English history	942.069	*see also* Insurance	
Scottish history	941.106 9	personal finance	332.024 014 5
Anne Arundel County (Md.)	T2—752 55	tax law	343.064
Annealing glass	666.129	Annulment	346.016 65
Annealing metals	671.36	Annunciation to Mary	232.912
Annelida	592.6	Anodynes	
paleozoology	562.6	pharmacokinetics	615.783
Annexation		Anointing of the sick	234.167
city government	320.859	public worship	265.7
law	342.041 3	theology	234.167
international politics	325.32	Anoka County (Minn.)	T2—776 65
law	342.041 2	Anoles	597.954 8
law of nations	341.42	Anolis	597.954 8
Anniellidae	597.959	Anomochloeae	584.92
Annihilation (Nuclear particles)	539.75	Anomura	595.387
Annihilationism	236.23	Anonymous works	
Anniversaries	394.2	bibliographies	014
see also Celebrations		Anoplura	595.756
Annobón (Equatorial			
Guinea)	T2—671 86		

Anorexia nervosa	362.25
medicine	616.852 62
social welfare	362.25
see also Mental illness	
Anostraca	595.32
Anoxygenic phototrophic	
bacteria	579.38
Anschluss	
Austrian history	943.605 22
Anser	598.417 3
Anseriformes	598.41
paleozoology	568.4
sports hunting	799.244
Anserini	598.417
Anson County (N.C.)	T2—756 753
Answers	
books of miscellaneous facts	030
study and teaching	T1—076
Ant algorithms	006.382 4
Ant bear	599.31
Ant lions	595.747
Antacids	
pharmacokinetics	615.73
Antakya (Turkey)	T2—564 8
ancient	T2—394 31
Antalya İli (Turkey)	T2—564 4
ancient	T2—392 8
eastern	T2—392 9
western	T2—392 8
Antananarivo (Madagascar :	
Province)	T2—691
Antarctic regions	T2—989
Antarctic waters	551.461 7
	T2—167
Antarctica	T2—989
Antártica Chilena (Chile :	
Province)	T2—836 48
Antbirds	598.822 6
Ante-Nicene church	270.1
Anteaters	599.314
Antelope County (Neb.)	T2—782 55
Antelopes	599.64
big game hunting	799.276 4
conservation technology	639.979 64
resource economics	333.959 64
Antenatal care	
obstetrics	618.24
Antennas	621.382 4
communications engineering	621.382 4
radar engineering	621.384 83
radio engineering	621.384 135
satellite communication	621.382 54
television engineering	621.388 35
Antenuptial contracts	346.016 62

Anterior chambers (Eyes)	
human physiology	612.841
Anthems	782.25
choral and mixed voices	782.525
single voices	783.092 5
Anthers	575.65
Anthocerotidae	588.3
Anthologies	080
literature	808.8
specific literatures	T3B—08
see Manual at T3B—08	
and T3B—09	
see Manual at 808.8	
see Manual at 080 vs. 800;	
also at 081–089	
Anthozoa	593.6
paleozoology	563.6
Anthracenes	547.616
chemical engineering	661.816
Anthracite coal	553.25
economic geology	553.25
mining	622.335
properties	662.622 5
Anthrax	
animals	
veterinary medicine	636.089 695 6
humans	
incidence	614.561
medicine	616.956
see also Communicable	
diseases — humans	
Anthribidae	595.768
Anthropogenesis	599.938
Anthropoidea	599.8
see also Primates	
Anthropological linguistics	306.44
Anthropologists	301.092
Anthropology	301
arts	700.455 2
	T3C—355 2
literature	808.803 552
history and criticism	809.933 552
specific literatures	T3B—080 355 2
history and	
criticism	T3B—093 552
philosophical anthropology	128
physical anthropology	599.9
theological anthropology	202.2
Anthropometric design	620.82
Anthropometry	599.94
see Manual at 599.94 vs. 611	
Anthropomorphism	
comparative religion	202.112
philosophy of religion	211

Anthroposophical therapy	
therapeutic system	615.53
Anthroposophy	299.935
biography	299.935 092
Anthuriums	635.934 442
botany	584.442
floriculture	635.934 442
Anti-allergic agents	
pharmacokinetics	615.796
Anti-anxiety drugs	
pharmacokinetics	615.788 2
Anti-arrhythmia agents	
pharmacokinetics	615.716
Anti-bacterial agents	
pharmacokinetics	615.792 2
Anti-federalist Party (U.S.)	324.273 26
Anti-HIV agents	
pharmacokinetics	615.792 4
Anti-infective agents	
pharmacokinetics	615.792
Anti-inflammatory agents	
pharmacokinetics	615.794
Anti-Lebanon	T2—569 14
Anti-Masonic Party (U.S.)	324.273 2
Anti-mission Baptists	286.4
see also Baptists	
Anti-retroviral agents	
pharmacokinetics	615.792 4
Anti-Semitism	305.892 4
political aspects	323.119 24
political ideology	320.569 924
social theology	
Christianity	261.26
Anti-Trinitarianism	289.1
Antiaircraft artillery	358.138 2
Antiaircraft artillery forces	358.13
Antiaircraft defenses	355.422
see also Air warfare	
Antiballistic missiles	358.174 82
engineering	623.451 94
military equipment	358.174 82
Antibiotics	615.329
chemistry	547.7
pharmacokinetics	615.792 2
pharmacology	615.329
Antibodies	571.967
human immunology	616.079 8
Antibody-dependent immune	
mechanisms	571.968
humans	616.079 9
Antichrist	236
Anticlines	551.86
Anticoagulants	
pharmacokinetics	615.718

Anticommunist international	
leagues	324.13
Anticonvulsants	
pharmacokinetics	615.784
Anticosti Island (Quebec)	T2—714 178 2
Anticyclones (Meteorology)	551.551 4
Antidepressants	
drug therapy	616.852 706 1
pharmacokinetics	615.78
Antidiuretics	
pharmacokinetics	615.761
Antidotes	
human toxicology	615.908
Antifreeze solutions	
automotive	629.256
Antifungal agents	
pharmacokinetics	615.792
Antigen-antibody reactions	571.967 7
human immunology	616.079 87
Antigen recognition	571.964 6
human immunology	616.079 5
Antigens	571.964 5
human immunology	616.079 2
Antigonish (N.S. : County)	T2—716 14
Antigua	T2—729 74
Antigua and Barbuda	972.974
	T2—729 74
Antiguans	T5—969 729 74
Antilipemic agents	
pharmacokinetics	615.739
Antillean Arawak Indians	972.900 497 92
	T5—979 2
Antilles	972.9
	T2—729
see also West Indies	
Antilles, Lesser	T2—729
Antilocapridae	599.639
Antilopinae	599.646
Antimacassars	645.4
arts	746.95
home sewing	646.21
household management	645.4
Antimasonic Party (U.S.)	324.273 2
Antimatter	530
Antimilitarism	355.021 3
military science	355.021 3
sociology	303.66
Antimissile defense forces	358.174
Antimissile missiles	358.174 82
engineering	623.451 94
military equipment	358.174 82
Antimission Baptists	286.4
see also Baptists	

Antimonides		Antisubmarine reconnaissance	
mineralogy	549.32	(Air warfare)	358.45
Antimony	669.75	Antisubmarine warfare	359.93
chemical engineering	661.071 6	World War I	940.451 6
chemistry	546.716	World War II	940.545 16
economic geology	553.47	Antitank artillery forces	358.12
materials science	620.189 5	Antitrust law	343.072 1
metallography	669.957 5	Antitrust policies	338.8
metallurgy	669.75	Antitrust violations	364.168
mining	622.347	law	345.026 8
physical metallurgy	669.967 5	public administration	353.43
see also Chemicals; Metals		Antiviral agents	
Antineoplastic agents		pharmacokinetics	615.792 4
pharmacokinetics	615.798	Antofagasta (Chile :	
Antinomianism	273.6	Province)	T2—831 38
Antioch (Turkey)	T2—564 8	Antofagasta (Chile : Region)	983.13
ancient	939.431		T2—831 3
	T2—394 31	Antoine-Labelle (Quebec)	T2—714 241
Antioquia (Colombia :		Antonines	255.18
Dept.)	T2—861 26	church history	271.18
Antioxidants		Antonym dictionaries	413.1
applied nutrition	613.286	specific languages	T4—312
Antiparasitic agents		specific subjects	T1—03
pharmacokinetics	615.792	Antrim (Northern Ireland :	
Antiparticles	539.72	Borough)	T2—416 12
Antipersonnel devices	623.451 4	Antrim (Northern Ireland :	
Antipodes Islands (N.Z.)	T2—939 9	County)	T2—416 1
Antiprotons	539.721 23	Antrim & Newtonabbey	
Antipsychotic drugs		(Northern Ireland)	T2—416 12
pharmacokinetics	615.788 2	Antrim County (Mich.)	T2—774 85
Antipyretics		Ants	595.796
pharmacokinetics	615.783	control technology	628.965 7
Antique (Philippines)	T2—599 532	culture	638.579 6
Antique furniture	749.1	Antsiranana (Madagascar :	
Antiques	745.1	Province)	T2—691
see Manual at 745.1		Antwerp (Belgium)	T2—493 222
Antiquities	930.1	Antwerp (Belgium :	
law	344.094	Province)	T2—493 22
Antiretroviral agents		Antwerpen (Belgium)	T2—493 222
pharmacokinetics	615.792 4	Antwerpen (Belgium :	
Antisepsis		Province)	T2—493 22
obstetrics	618.8	Anuak language	496.558 4
public health	614.48		T6—965 584
surgery	617.910 1	Anura	597.8
Antislavery movements	326.8	paleozoology	567.8
see also Abolition of slavery		Anus	
Antisocial people	305.906 92	human anatomy	611.35
	T1—086 92	human physiology	612.36
Antisocial personality disorders		medicine	616.35
medicine	616.858 2	surgery	617.555
see also Mental disorders		Anus diseases	
Antispasmodics		medicine	616.35
pharmacokinetics	615.784	*see also* Digestive system	
		diseases — humans	

Anvers (Belgium)	T2—493 222
Anvil Island (B.C. : Island)	T2—711 31
Anvils	682
blacksmithing	682
music	786.884 3
see also Percussion	
instruments	
Anwar Ibrahim	
Malaysian history	959.506 3
Anxiety	152.46
Anxiety disorders	
medicine	616.852 2
see also Mental disorders	
Anyi (African people)	T5—963 38
Anyi language	496.338
	T6—963 38
Anzoátegui (Venezuela :	
State)	T2—875 2
Aomori-ken (Japan)	T2—521 12
Aorta	573.185
human anatomy	611.13
human physiology	612.133
medicine	616.138
physiology	573.185
see also Cardiovascular system	
Aortic diseases	
medicine	616.138
see also Cardiovascular	
diseases — humans	
Aortic valve	573.185
human anatomy	611.12
human physiology	612.17
medicine	616.125
physiology	573.185
see also Cardiovascular system	
Aortic valve diseases	
medicine	616.125
see also Cardiovascular	
diseases — humans	
Aosta (Italy)	T2—451 11
ancient	T2—372 211
Aotearoa	T2—93
Aoudad	599.649
AP ammunition	623.451 8
Apache County (Ariz.)	T2—791 37
Apache Indians	979.004 972 5
	T5—972 5
Apachean Indians	T5—972 5
Apachean languages	497.25
	T6—972 5
Apalachicola River (Fla.)	T2—759 92
Apartheid	305.800 968 090 45
political ideology	320.569 090 68

Apartment buildings	647.92
architecture	728.314
construction	690.831 4
household management	647.92
see also Dwellings	
Apartment hotels	647.92
architecture	728.314
construction	690.831 4
household management	647.92
see also Dwellings	
Apartment-house districts	
area planning	711.58
Apartment houses	647.92
architecture	728.314
construction	690.831 4
household management	647.92
see also Dwellings	
Apartments	643.27
see also Apartment houses	
Apathy	
social psychology	302.17
Apatites	553.64
mineralogy	549.72
Apatosaurus	567.913 8
Apayao (Philippines)	T2—599 137
Apennines (Italy)	T2—45
Apes	599.88
animal husbandry	636.988
experimental animals	
medicine	616.027 38
Aphanite	552.2
Aphasia	
medicine	616.855 2
see also Communication	
disorders	
special education	371.914 2
Aphid flies	595.774
Aphids	595.752
agricultural pests	632.752
Aphorisms	398.9
Aphrodisiacs	
pharmacokinetics	615.766 9
Aphyllanthoideae	584.79
Aphyllophorales	579.597
Apiaceae	583.988 2
Apiales	583.988
Apical meristem	575.485
Apiculture	638.1
Apidae	595.799
APL (Educational credit)	371.264
Aplacophora	594.2

Aplastic anemia		Apparel	391
medicine	616.152	*see also* Clothing	
see also Cardiovascular		Apparel graphics	744.7
diseases — humans		Apparitions	133.1
Apnea		Apparitions of Mary	232.917
medicine	616.2	Appeal (Law)	347.08
see also Respiratory tract		Appeals of labor grievances	331.889 66
diseases — humans		*see also* Grievances (Labor)	
Apocalypse (Biblical book)	228	Appellate courts	347.03
Apocalypses (Biblical literature)	220.046	criminal law	345.014 4
New Testament		England	347.420 3
pseudepigrapha	229.94	Scotland	347.411 03
Old Testament pseudepigrapha	229.913	United States	347.732 4
Apocrita	595.79	Appellate procedure	347.08
Apocrypha (Bible)	229	Appendages	573.998
Apocryphal wisdom literature	229.3	Appendectomies	
Apocynaceae	583.956	surgery	617.554 5
Apoda (Amphibians)	597.82	Appendicitis	
Apodacea	593.96	medicine	616.34
Apodemus	599.358 5	*see also* Digestive system	
Apodi	598.762	diseases — humans	
Apodidae	598.762	surgery	617.554 5
Apodiformes	598.76	Appendix	
paleozoology	568.7	human anatomy	611.345
Apoidea	595.799	human physiology	612.33
Apollo project	629.454	medicine	616.34
Apologetics	202	surgery	617.554 5
Christianity	239	Appennino Tosco-Emiliano	
Islam	297.29	(Italy)	T2—454
Judaism	296.35	Appenzell (Switzerland)	T2—494 714 4
Aponogetonaceae	584.44	Appenzell (Switzerland :	
Apoplexy		Canton)	T2—494 71
medicine	616.81	Appenzell Ausser-Rhoden	
see also Nervous system		(Switzerland)	T2—494 712
diseases — humans		Appenzell Inner-Rhoden	
Apostates		(Switzerland)	T2—494 714
Christian polemics	239.7	Apperception	
Apostles	225.92	psychology	153.73
art representation	704.948 62	Appetite disorders	
Apostles' Creed	238.11	medicine	616.852 6
Apostleship (Spiritual gift)	234.13	*see also* Mental disorders	
Apostolic Church	270.1	Appetizers	641.812
Apostolic succession	262.11	Apples	641.341 1
Apostolicity	262.72	botany	583.642
Appalaches (Quebec)	T2—714 712	commercial processing	664.804 11
Appalachian dulcimers	787.75	cooking	641.641 1
see also Stringed instruments		food	641.341 1
Appalachian Mountains	T2—74	orchard crop	634.11
North Carolina	T2—756 8	Appaloosa	538.767 4
Appaloosa	636.13	Appleton layers	
Appanoose County (Iowa)	T2—777 89	Application development	
Apparatus	T1—028 4	environments	005.1
teaching aids	371.33	Application frameworks	005.1
	T1—078	Application generators	005.13

Application programming	005.13
see Manual at 005.1–.2 vs.	
005.42	
Application software	005.3
see Manual at 005.3, 005.5	
vs. 005.43–.45; *also at*	
005.3682 vs. 005.365,	
005.3684	
Application software	
development	005.1
see Manual at 005.1–.2 vs.	
005.42	
Applications for positions	650.142
job hunting	650.142
personnel selection	658.311 2
public administration	352.65
Applied chemistry	660
law	344.095 4
Applied ethics	170
Applied linguistics	418
specific languages	T4—8
Applied mathematics	519
Applied mechanics	620.1
Applied numerical analysis	518
Applied nutrition	363.8
see also Nutrition	
Applied optics	621.36
Applied physics	621
law	344.095 3
Applied psychology	158
children	155.419
Applied sciences	600
Applied sociology	360
Appling County (Ga.)	T2—758 784
Appliqué	
textile arts	746.445
Appointment power (Legislative	
bodies)	328.345 5
Appomattox County (Va.)	T2—755 625
Apportionment (Legislatures)	328.334 5
law	342.053
Appraisal	
archives	025.281 4
land economics	333.332
Appreciation	
arts	701.18
literature	801
music	781.17
Apprentices	
economics	331.55
Apprenticeship	331.259 22
	T1—071 55
economics	331.259 22
union control	331.889 6

Apprenticeship (continued)	
education	371.227
secondary level	373.27
personnel management	658.312 4
public administration	354.968
Approach piloting	623.892 9
Appropriate technology	338.927
Appropriation power (Legislative	
bodies)	328.341 2
Appropriations	352.49
enactment	328.37
law	343.034
see Manual at 300–330,	
355–390 vs. 342–347,	
352–354	
Approval plans	
library acquisitions	025.233
Approximation (Mathematics)	511.4
algebra	512.924
numerical methods	518.5
Approximation algorithms	
computer science	005.13
Apraxia of speech	
medicine	616.855 2
see also Communication	
disorders	
Apricots	641.342 1
botany	583.642
commercial processing	664.804 21
cooking	641.642 1
food	641.342 1
orchard crop	634.21
Aprons	391.44
commercial technology	687.19
leather	685.22
see also Accessories (Clothing)	
Apses	
Christian church architecture	726.593
Apterous insects	595.756
Apterygiformes	598.54
paleozoology	568.5
Apterygota	595.72
Apteryx	598.54
Aptitude tests	153.94
education	371.262
personnel selection	658.311 25
teacher-prepared tests	371.271
Aptitudes	153.9
Apulia (Italy)	T2—457 5
ancient	T2—377 5
Apure (Venezuela)	T2—874 2
Apurímac (Peru : Region)	T2—853 8
Aqaba, Gulf of	551.461 533
	T2—165 33

'Aqabah (Jordan : Province) T2—569 572
'Aqā'id (Islam)   297.2
Aquaculture   639.8
  economics   338.371 8
  green technology   639.802 86
Aquariums   597.073
  fish culture   639.34
Aquarius (Zodiac)   133.527 6
Aquaspirillum   579.323
Aquatic animals   591.76
  resource economics   333.954 8
Aquatic biological resources   333.952 8
  public administration   354.57
Aquatic biology   578.76
  see Manual at 578.76–.77 vs.
   551.46, 551.48
Aquatic birds   598.176
  resource economics   333.958 28
Aquatic ecology   577.6
  marine environments   577.7
Aquatic exercises   613.716
Aquatic gardens   635.967 4
  botany   581.760 73
  floriculture   635.967 4
Aquatic organisms   578.76
Aquatic plants   581.76
  floriculture   635.967 4
Aquatic resources   333.91
Aquatic sports   797
  arts   700.457 9
            T3C—357 9
  child care   649.57
  ethics   175
  human physiology   612.044
  journalism   070.449 797
  law   344.099
  literature
    history and criticism   809.933 579
    specific literatures T3B—080 357 9
     history and
      criticism   T3B—093 579
  motion pictures   791.436 579
  physical fitness   613.711
  public administrative support 353.78
  safety   363.14
   public administration   353.97
  sociology   306.483
  television programs   791.456 579
  see also Sports
Aquatinting   766.3
Aqueducts
  water supply engineering   628.15

Aqueous humors
  human anatomy   611.84
  human physiology   612.844
Aqueous solutions   541.342 2
  chemical engineering   660.294 22
Aquiculture   639.8
Aquifers   553.79
  see also Groundwater
Aquifoliaceae   583.982
Aquifoliales   583.982
Aquila (Italy : Province)   T2—457 11
  ancient   T2—377 34
Aquila chrysaetos   598.942 3
Aquileia (Italy)
  ancient   T2—373 81
Aquino, Benigno S., III
  Philippine history   959.905 2
Aquino, Corazon Cojuangco
  Philippine history   959.904 7
Aquitaine (France)   T2—447 1
Aquitania   T2—364 7
Aqvilgjuaq (Nunavut)   T2—719 55
Arab countries   909.097 492 7
            T2—174 927
Arab League   341.247 7
Arabesques (Music)   784.189 4
Arabia   953
            T2—53
  ancient   939.49
            T2—394 9
Arabia, Roman   T2—394 8
Arabia Deserta   939.49
            T2—394 9
  622–637   953.02
            T2—53
  Lower Mesopotamia   935.5
            T2—355
  Upper Mesopotamia   935.4
            T2—354
Arabia Felix   939.49
            T2—394 9
Arabia Petraea   939.48
            T2—394 8
Arabian Desert (Egypt)   T2—623
Arabian Peninsula   953
            T2—53
Arabian Sea   551.461 537
            T2—165 37
Arabic language   492.7
            T6—927
  Biblical texts   220.46
  Koran texts   297.122 4
  printing   686.219 27
Arabic literature   892.7

Arabic philosophy	181.92	Araucanía (Chile)	T2—834 6
Arabs	T5—927	Araucanian Indians	T5—987 2
Sicilian history	945.802	Araucanian languages	498.72
Araceae	584.442		T6—987 2
Arachnida	595.4	Araucariaceae	585.3
disease carriers	571.986	Arauco (Chile : Province)	T2—834 2
medicine	614.433	Arawak Indians	T5—983 9
paleozoology	565.4	South America	T5—983 9
Arad (Romania : Judeţ)	T2—498 4	West Indies	972.900 497 92
Araeoscelidia	567.93		T5—979 2
Arafura Sea	551.461 475	Arawakan languages	498.39
	T2—164 75		T6—983 9
Aragon (Kingdom)	946.03	Central America	497.92
Sardinian history	945.905		T6—979 2
Sicilian history	945.805	South America	498.39
Southern Italian history	945.706		T6—983 9
Spanish history	946.03	West Indies	497.92
Aragon (Spain)	946.55		T6—979 2
	T2—465 5	Arbitrage	332.645
Aragonite		Arbitration	
mineralogy	549.785	international relations	327.17
Aragua (Venezuela : State)	T2—873 4	labor economics	331.891 43
Arakhin	296.123 5	law	344.018 914 3
Babylonian Talmud	296.125 5	public administration	354.97
Mishnah	296.123 5	law	347.09
Aral Sea (Uzbekistan and		law of nations	341.522
Kazakhstan)	T2—587	personnel management	658.315 4
Arales	584.442	public administration	352.68
Araliaceae	583.988	Arbon (Switzerland :	
Aramaeans (Ancient)	T5—922	Bezirk)	T2—494 599
Aramaeans (Modern)	T5—923	Arborvitaes	585.4
Aramaic languages	492.2	Arboviruses	579.256 2
	T6—922	Arbuckle Mountains (Okla.)	T2—766 5
Biblical texts	220.42	Arc furnace practice	669.142 4
Midrashic texts	296.140 4	Arc length	
Talmudic texts	296.120 4	calculus	515.43
Aramaic literatures	892.2	integral geometry	516.362
Arameans (Ancient)	T5—922	Arc lighting	621.325
Arameans (Modern)	T5—923	*see also* Lighting	
Aran Islands (Ireland)	941.748	Arc welding	671.521 2
	T2—417 48	Arcade games	794.8
Araneae	595.44	Arcades	721.41
Araneida	595.44	architecture	721.41
Aransas County (Tex.)	T2—764 122	construction	690.141
Aranyakas	294.592 1	Arcadia (Greece)	T2—495 22
Arapaho Indians	978.004 973 54	ancient	T2—388
	T5—973 54	Arce Catacora, Luis	
Arapaho language	497.354	Bolivian history	984.054 3
	T6—973 54	Arcellinida	579.43
Arapahoe County (Colo.)	T2—788 82	Arch bridges	
Ararat (Vic.)	T2—945 7	construction	624.22
Arauan languages	498.9	Archaeobacteria	579.321
	T6—989	Archaeoceti	569.5
Arauca (Colombia : Dept.)	T2—861 98	Archaeocyatha	563.47

Archaeogastropoda	594.32	Architectural design	729
Archaeological thefts	364.162 89	*see Manual at* 729	
law	345.026 289	Architectural drawing	720.284
Archaeologists	930.109 2	Architectural drawings	720.222
Archaeology	930.1	Architectural orders	721.36
	T1—090 09	architecture	721.36
ancient places	931–939	construction	690.13
arts	T3C—358 301	Architectural schools and styles	720.9
Bible	220.93	ancient	722
law	344.094	construction details	721
literature	808.803 583 01	design and decoration	729
history and criticism	809.933 583 01	Architectural structure	720
modern places	940–990	Architecture	720
Archaeopteris	561.597	art representation	704.944
Archaeornithes	568.22	arts	T3C—357
Archaisms (Linguistics)	417.7	landscapes	712
specific languages	T4—7	literature	808.803 57
Archbishops	270.092	history and criticism	809.933 57
biography	270.092	specific literatures	T3B—080 357
specific denominations	280	history and	
see Manual at 230–280		criticism	T3B—093 57
ecclesiology	262.12	naval	623.81
Archean era	551.712	painting	758.7
geology	551.712	religious significance	203.7
paleontology	560.171 2	Christianity	246.9
Arched harps	787.94	*see also* Arts — religious	
see also Stringed instruments		significance	
Archeology	930.1	Spain	
see also Archaeology		medieval period	720.946 090 2
Archeozoic era	551.712	*see also* Arts	
geology	551.712	Archival materials	
paleontology	560.171 2	cataloging	025.341 4
Archer County (Tex.)	T2—764 543	library acquisitions	025.281 4
Archers	799.320 92	library treatment	025.171 4
Archery	799.32	records management	651.56
biography	799.320 92	Archival science	020
see also Target shooting		Archive buildings	
Arches (Structural elements)	721.41	architecture	725.15
architecture	721.41	Archives	027
construction	690.141	*see also* Libraries	
structural engineering	624.177 5	Archivists	020.92
concrete	624.183 45	Archosauria	567.9
Arches (Structures)	725.96	Archostemata	595.762
Arches National Park (Utah)	T2—792 58	Archuleta County (Colo.)	T2—788 32
Archetype (Psychology)		Arcs	516.152
Jungian system	150.195 4	Arctic animals	591.709 113
personality theory	155.264	Arctic Archipelago	
Archiannelida	592.62	(Nunavut and N.W.T.)	T2—719 52
Architarbi	565.4	Arctic Bay (Nunavut)	T2—719 52
Architects	720.92	Arctic biology	578.091 13
Architectural acoustics		Arctic climate	
construction	690.2	health	613.111
Architectural decoration	729	Arctic cod	597.632
see Manual at 729		Arctic cooking	641.591 1

Arctic ecology	577.091 13	Argentine literature	860
Arctic fox	599.776 4	Argentine Republic	T2—82
Arctic islands	T2—98	Argentineans	T5—688 2
Arctic Ocean	551.461 32	Argentines	T5—688 2
	T2—163 2	Argeş (Romania : Judeţ)	T2—498 2
see Manual at T2—163 and		Argolis (Greece)	T2—495 22
T2—164, T2—165		ancient	T2—388
Arctic plants	581.709 113	Argon	
floriculture	635.952	chemistry	546.753
Arctic regions	T2—113	gas technology	665.822
ecology	577.091 13	Argonne (France)	T2—443 81
Arctocephalinae	599.797 3	Argot	417.2
Arctocephalus	599.797 38	specific languages	T4—7
Ardabīl (Iran : Province)	T2—551 2	Arguloida	595.36
Ardahan İli (Turkey)	T2—566 22	Argument (Logic)	168
ancient	T2—393 37	Argyll and Bute (Scotland)	T2—414 2
Ardèche (France)	T2—445 89	Århus amt (Denmark)	T2—489 55
Ardeidae	598.34	Arhynchobdellida	592.66
Ardennes	T2—493 48	Ari liturgy	296.450 4
Ardennes (France)	T2—443 12	Ariana	T2—396
Ardennes, Battle of the,		Arianism	273.4
1944–1945	940.542 193 48	Arias Sánchez, Óscar	
Ards (Northern Ireland)	T2—416 54	Costa Rican history	972.860 521
Ards & North Down		1986–1990	972.860 521
(Northern Ireland)	T2—416 54	2006–2010	972.860 526
Area planning	307.12	Arica (Chile : Province)	T2—831 23
arts	711	Arid lands	551.415
community sociology	307.12		T2—154
Area studies	940–990	biology	578.754
collection development	025.29	ecology	577.54
Area treatment	T1—09	economics	333.736
Arecaceae	584.84	geography	910.915 4
Arecales	584.84	geomorphology	551.415
paleobotany	561.45	physical geography	910.021 54
Arecibo (P.R. : District)	T2—729 53	Ariège (France)	T2—447 35
Arecidae	584.84	Aries (Zodiac)	133.526 2
paleobotany	561.45	Arikara Indians	T5—979 32
Arena theater	792.022 8	Arikara language	497.932
Arenac County (Mich.)	T2—774 73		T6—979 32
Arenaviridae	579.256	Ariminum (Italy)	T2—372 686
Areolar tissues		Aristocracy	305.52
human histology	611.018 2		T1—086 21
Arequipa (Peru : Region)	985.32	political system	321.5
	T2—853 2	Aristolochiaceae	584.284
Arezzo (Italy)		Aristolochiales	584.284
ancient	T2—375 68	Aristotelian philosophy	185
Arezzo (Italy : Province)	T2—455 9	modern	149.91
ancient	T2—375 68	Arithmetic	513
Arfon (Wales)	T2—429 25	equipment	513.028 4
Argenteuil (Quebec :		numerical methods	518.45
Regional County		primary education	372.72
Municipality)	T2—714 23	Arithmetic progressions	515.24
Argentina	982	Arizona	979.1
	T2—82		T2—791

Arms (Body parts) (continued)	
surgery	617.574 059
see also Upper extremities	
Arms (Military)	355.82
art metalwork	739.7
customs	399
engineering	623.4
military equipment	355.82
procurement	355.621 2
see Manual at 355–359 vs. 623	
Arms (Small firearms)	
manufacturing technology	683.4
Arms control	327.174
international politics	327.174
law	341.733
military science	355.03
see also Arms race	
Arms race	327.174
ethics	172.422
social theology	201.727 5
Christianity	261.873 2
see also Arms control	
Armstrong (B.C.)	T2—711 5
Armstrong County (Pa.)	T2—748 88
Armstrong County (Tex.)	T2—764 833
Army artillery forces	358.12
Army engineer corps	358.22
Armyworms	595.78
agricultural pests	633.104 978
Arnhem (Netherlands)	T2—492 18
Arnhem Land (N.T.)	T2—942 95
Arno River (Italy)	T2—455
Arnold, Benedict	
treason	973.382
Arnsberg (Germany :	
Regierungsbezirk)	T2—435 63
Aromatherapy	615.321 9
Aromatic compounds	547.6
chemical engineering	661.8
Aromatic herbs	641.357
see also Herbs	
Aromatic hydrocarbons	
human toxicology	615.951 1
Aromatic teas	641.357
home preparation	641.877
see also Herb teas; Tea	
Aromatization	547.27
chemical engineering	660.284 4
Aroostook County (Me.)	T2—741 1
Árpád, House of	943.902
Arpeggiones	787.6
see also Stringed instruments	
Arpeggios	781.252
Arraignment	345.072

Arranged marriage	
law	346.016 2
Arrangement (Archives)	025.341 4
Arrangement (Music)	781.37
Arrangements (Music)	781.38
see Manual at 781.38	
Array processing	004.35
Array processors	004.35
Arrest	363.232
law	345.052 7
police services	363.232
Arretium (Italy)	T2—375 68
Arrhythmia	
medicine	616.128
see also Cardiovascular	
diseases — humans	
Arrondissements	320.83
see also Counties	
Arrow grasses	584.44
Arrow Lakes (B.C.)	T2—711 62
Arrowheads (Plants)	584.44
Arrowroot	641.336 8
botany	584.88
commercial processing	664.23
cooking	641.636 8
food	641.336 8
starch crop	633.68
Arrows	799.202 85
see also Bows and arrows	
Arrowworms	592.38
Arroyo, Gloria Macapagal-	
Philippine history	959.905 1
Ars antiqua	780.902
Ars nova	780.902
Arsenals	355.7
architecture	725.18
Arsenates	
mineralogy	549.72
Arsenic	669.75
chemical engineering	661.071 5
chemistry	546.715
economic geology	553.47
human toxicology	615.925 715
metallography	669.957 5
metallurgy	669.75
mining	622.347
organic chemistry	547.057 15
applied	661.895
physical metallurgy	669.967 5
see also Chemicals; Metals	
Arsenides	
mineralogy	549.32
Arson	364.164 2
law	345.026 42

Art	700
investment economics	332.63
sociology	306.47
theft of	364.162 87
law	345.026 287
therapeutics	615.851 56
see also Arts	
Art and religion	201.67
see also Arts and religion	
Art appreciation	701.18
Art brut	709.040 9
Art dealers	709.2
see Manual at 709.2 vs.	
381.457092	
Art deco	709.040 12
sculpture	735.230 412
Art galleries	708
architecture	727.7
law	344.093
Art libraries	026.7
Art metalwork	739
Art metalworkers	739.092
Art museums	708
architecture	727.7
institutional housekeeping	647.997
Art music	781.68
nonwestern	781.69
western	781.68
Art needlework	746.4
Art nouveau	709.034 9
19th century	709.034 9
20th century	709.040 14
architecture	724.6
decoration	744.090 34
Art paper	676.282 5
Art policy (Government policy)	700
Art posters	769.5
Art songs	782.421 68
Art therapy	
medicine	615.851 56
psychiatry	616.891 656
Arta (Greece : Regional	
unit)	T2—495 3
Artemisa (Cuba : Province)	T2—729 124
Arterial diseases	
medicine	616.13
see also Cardiovascular	
diseases — humans	
Arterial embolisms	
medicine	616.135
see also Cardiovascular	
diseases — humans	

Arterial occlusive diseases	
medicine	616.13
see also Cardiovascular	
diseases — humans	
Arterial thromboses	
medicine	616.135
see also Cardiovascular	
diseases — humans	
Arteries	573.185
animals	573.185
human anatomy	611.13
human physiology	612.133
medicine	616.13
physiology	573.185
surgery	617.413
see also Cardiovascular system	
Arteriosclerosis	
medicine	616.136
see also Cardiovascular	
diseases — humans	
Artesian wells	
engineering	628.114
hydrology	551.498
Arthabaska (Quebec :	
Regional County	
Municipality)	T2—714 565
Arthritis	
medicine	616.722
see also Musculoskeletal	
diseases — humans	
Arthrobacter	579.373
Arthrochirotida	563.96
Arthropoda	595
see also Arthropods	
Arthropods	595
agricultural pests	632.65
paleozoology	565
pesticides	
agricultural use	632.951 7
Arthur, Chester Alan	
United States history	973.84
Arthur, King	
English history	942.014
Arthur County (Neb.)	T2—782 785
Arthur's Pass National Park	
(N.Z.)	T2—938 1
Artibonite (Haiti : Dept.)	T2—729 446
Artichokes	641.353 2
botany	583.983
commercial processing	664.805 32
cooking	641.653 2
food	641.353 2
garden crop	635.32

Articles (Grammar)	415.5
specific languages	T4—55
Articles of Confederation, 1781	
United States history	973.318
Articulata	593.92
paleozoology	563.92
Articulatae	587.2
Articulated lorries	388.344
engineering	629.224
see also Trucks	
Articulation (Education)	371.21
Articulation disorders	
medicine	616.855
see also Communication disorders	
Articulations	
human anatomy	611.72
human physiology	612.752
Artificial arms	
medicine	617.574
Artificial environments	
health	613.5
Artificial eyes	
ophthalmology	617.79
Artificial feeding	
medicine	615.854 8
Artificial flies (Fishing)	
angling	799.124
making	688.791 24
Artificial flower arrangements	745.92
Artificial flowers	
handicrafts	745.594 3
Artificial gems	666.88
Artificial harbors	387.1
hydraulic engineering	627.2
military engineering	623.64
see also Ports	
Artificial heart	
surgery	617.412 059 2
Artificial immune systems	006.382 5
Artificial insemination	
animal husbandry	636.082 45
ethics	176.2
see also Reproduction — ethics	
family law	346.017
gynecology	618.178
health	613.94
Artificial intelligence	006.3
	T1—028 563
see Manual at 006.3 vs. 153	
Artificial islands	627.98
Artificial languages	499.99
	T6—999 9

Artificial legs	
medicine	617.58
Artificial life	006.382 6
Artificial-light gardening	635.048 3
floriculture	635.982 6
Artificial-light photography	778.72
Artificial limbs	
manufacturing technology	681.761
medicine	617.58
Artificial minerals	666.86
Artificial modification of weather	551.68
Artificial organs	
surgery	617.956
Artificial radioactivity	
physics	539.753
Artificial recharge (Groundwater)	627.56
Artificial respiration	
medicine	615.836 2
Artificial road surfaces	625.8
Artificial satellites	
engineering	629.46
flight	629.434
telecommunications	384.51
see also Satellite communication	
weather reporting	551.635 4
Artificial stone	666.89
architectural construction	721.044 4
building construction	693.4
building materials	691.3
materials science	620.139
Artificial sweeteners	
commercial processing	664.5
Artificial teeth	
dentistry	617.692
Artificial tissue	
surgery	617.956
Artigas (Uruguay : Dept.)	T2—895 36
Artillery	355.821
art metalwork	739.741
engineering	623.41
military equipment	355.821
Artillery ballistics	623.51
Artillery forces	358.12
Artillery installations	355.73
Artillery projectiles	623.451 3
Artiodactyla	599.63
paleozoology	569.63
Artisans	609.2
labor economics	331.794
Artistic études	784.189 49
Artistic gymnastics	796.442
Artistic lettering	744.42
Artistic principles	700.1

Artistic themes		Aruba	T2—729 86
arts	700.457	Arums	584.442
	T3C—357	Arun (England)	T2—422 67
folklore	398.277	Arunāchal Pradesh (India)	T2—541 63
history and criticism	398.357	Arundineae	584.92
literature	808.803 57	Arundinella	584.924
history and criticism	809.933 57	Arundinelleae	584.92
specific literatures	T3B—080 357	Arundinoideae	584.92
history and		Arusha Region (Tanzania)	T2—678 26
criticism	T3B—093 57	Arutani-Sape languages	498.9
Artists	700.92		T6—989
labor economics	331.761 7	Arvicola	599.354
see Manual at 700.92		Arya-Samaj	294.556 3
Artists' books	700	Aryan languages	
fine arts	709.040 82	(Indo-European)	410
20th century	709.040 82		T6—1
21st century	709.050 18	Aryan languages (Indo-Iranian)	491.1
techniques	702.81		T6—911
Artists' marks	702.78	Asanas	
	T1—027 8	health	613.704 6
Artists' sketches		therapeutics	615.824
criminal investigation	363.258	Asante (African people)	T5—963 385
Artois (France)	T2—442 72	Asante (Empire)	966.701 8
Arts	700	Asante (Kingdom)	T2—667
auction catalogs	700.29	Asbāb al-nuzūl	
awards	700.79	Koran	297.122 12
collections	700.74	Asbāb wurūd al-Ḥadīth	297.125 162
decorative	745	Asbestos	553.672
exhibitions	700.74	building material	691.95
auction catalogs	700.74	economic geology	553.672
festivals	700.74	human toxicology	615.925 392 24
influence on crime	364.254	materials science	620.195
law	344.097	mining	622.367 2
museums	700.74	pollution	363.738 494
primary education	372.5	law	344.046 335
public administrative support	353.77	*see also* Pollution	
religious significance	203.7	public safety	363.179 1
Buddhism	294.343 7	*see also* Hazardous materials	
Christianity	246	technology	666.72
Hinduism	294.537	textiles	677.51
Islam	297.3	*see also* Textiles	
Jainism	294.437	Asbestos (Quebec :	
Judaism	296.46	Regional County	
Native American religions	299.713 7	Municipality)	T2—714 573
sociology	306.47	Asbestos paper	676.289
Arts and crafts	745	Asbestosis	
sociology	306.47	medicine	616.244
Arts and religion	201.67	*see also* Respiratory tract	
Christianity	261.57	diseases — humans	
Islam	297.267	workers' compensation law	344.021 8
Judaism	296.377		
Arts policy (Government policy)	700		
Artvin İli (Turkey)	T2—566 22		
ancient	T2—393 37		

Ascariasis	
incidence	614.555 4
medicine	616.965 4
see also Communicable diseases — humans	
Ascension	997.34
	T2—973 4
Ascension Day	263.93
see also Ascensiontide	
Ascension Island (Atlantic Ocean)	997.34
	T2—973 4
Ascension of Jesus Christ	232.97
Ascension of Mary	232.914
Ascension Parish (La.)	T2—763 19
Ascensiontide	263.93
devotional literature	242.36
music	781.728
sermons	252.63
Ascent to Heaven of Muḥammad	297.633
Asceticism	204.47
Buddhism	294.344 47
Christianity	248.47
Hinduism	294.544 7
Islam	297.576
Sufi	297.446
Judaism	296.7
Aschaffenburg (Germany)	T2—433 31
Aschelminthes	592.5
paleozoology	562.5
Ascidiacea	596.2
Ascobolus	579.578
Ascoli Piceno (Italy : Province)	T2—456 75
ancient	T2—374 8
Ascomycetes	579.56
Ascomycotina	579.56
Ascophyllum	579.888
Ascothoracica	595.35
ASEAN	341.247 3
public administration	352.115 9
Asepsis	
obstetrics	618.8
public health	614.48
surgery	617.910 1
Asexual people	T1—086 6
psychology	155.34
social services	362.896
Asexual reproduction	571.89
microorganisms	571.842 9
plants	575.49
Asexual women	
social services	362.839 6
Asexual young people	
social services	362.786
Asexuality (Sexual orientation)	306.762
Asexuals	306.762
	T1—086 6
see also Asexual people	
Ash trays	
automobile	629.277
manufacturing	688.4
Ash Wednesday	263.925
devotional literature	242.35
sermons	252.625
Ashante language	496.338 5
	T6—963 385
Ashanti	966.701 8
Ashanti (African people)	T5—963 385
Ashanti (Kingdom)	T2—667
Ashburton District (N.Z.)	T2—938 6
Ashe County (N.C.)	T2—756 835
Ashes (Trees)	583.963
botany	583.963
forestry	634.973 963
Asheville (N.C.)	T2—756 88
Ashfield (England)	T2—425 25
Ashford (England : Borough)	T2—422 392
Ashkenazic liturgy	296.45
Ashland County (Ohio)	T2—771 29
Ashland County (Wis.)	T2—775 21
Ashley County (Ark.)	T2—767 83
Ashoka, King of Magadha	
Indian history	934.045
Ashtabula County (Ohio)	T2—771 34
Ashuapmushuam Wildlife Reserve (Quebec)	T2—714 142
Ashur (Extinct city)	T2—354
'Āshūrā'	297.36
Asia	950
	T2—5
geography	915
military operations	
World War I	940.415
travel	915.04
Asia (Roman diocese)	939.2
	T2—392
Asia (Roman province)	T2—392 3
Asia, Central	958
	T2—58
Asia, Southeastern	959
	T2—59
Asia Minor	956.1
	T2—561
ancient	939.2
	T2—392

54

Asian Americans	973.049 5	Asphalt (continued)	
	T5—950 73	mining	622.337
education	371.829 950 73	petroleum product	665.538 8
Asian Arctic seawaters	551.461 325	processing	665.4
	T2—163 25	Asphalt concrete	666.893
Asian flower arrangements	745.922 5	road engineering	625.85
Asian intergovernmental		Asphalt pavements	625.85
organizations	341.247	Asphodels	584.77
Asiana (Roman diocese)	939.2	Asphyxia	
	T2—392	medicine	617.18
Asians	T5—95	Asphyxiating gases	
Asiatic cholera		human toxicology	615.91
incidence	614.514	Aspidobothria	592.4
medicine	616.932	Aspidochirotacea	593.96
see also Communicable		Aspidocotylea	592.4
diseases — humans		Aspidogastrea	592.48
Asiatic elephant	599.676	Aspirin	615.313 7
Asilidae	595.773	Assa-Zag (Morocco)	T2—646 8
'Āṣim ibn Abī al-Nujūd		Assad, Bashar	
Koran readings	297.122 404 522	Syrian history	956.910 423
ASL (Sign language)	419.7	Assad, Hafez	
	T6—999 87	Syrian history	956.910 422
Asmā' al-Ruwāh	297.125 264	Assam (India)	T2—541 62
Asmara (Eritrea)	T2—635	Assamese	T5—914 51
Asoa language	496.56	Assamese language	491.451
	T6—965 6		T6—914 51
Asocial people	305.568	Assamese literature	891.451
	T1—086 92	Assassination	364.152 4
Aśoka, King of Magadha		law	345.025 24
Indian history	934.045	Assateague Island (Md. and	
Asotin County (Wash.)	T2—797 42	Va.)	T2—752 21
Asp (Viper)	597.963 6	Assault and battery	364.155 5
Asparagaceae	584.79	law	345.025 55
botany	584.79	criminal law	345.025 55
Asparagales	584.7	torts	346.033
Asparagus	641.353 1	social welfare	362.885 5
botany	584.79	Assaying	
commercial processing	664.805 31	metallurgy	669.92
cooking	641.653 1	Assemblage	
food	641.353 1	arts	702.814
garden crop	635.31	Assemblers (Computer software)	005.456
Aspect (Grammar)	415.63	Assemblies (Legislative bodies)	328
specific languages	T4—563	Assemblies of God	289.94
Aspect-oriented programming	005.117	Assembling machines	670.427
Aspects (Astrology)	133.530 44	Assembling products	670.42
Aspens	583.69	factory engineering	670.42
Asperger syndrome		production management	658.533
medicine	616.858 832	Assembly languages	005.136
pediatrics	618.928 588 32	Assembly-line methods	670.42
Aspergillus	579.565 7	production management	658.533
Asphalt	553.27	technology	670.42
building materials	691.96	Assertiveness training	
economic geology	553.27	applied psychology	158.2
materials science	620.196		

Asses	636.18
animal husbandry	636.18
zoology	599.665
Assessment tests	
education	371.262
Assimilation (Physiology)	
humans	612.39
Assimilation (Sociology)	303.482
Assiniboine Indians	T5—975 24
Assiniboine language	497.524
	T6—975 24
Assiniboine River (Sask.	
and Man.)	T2—712 73
Assistant teachers	371.141 24
Assisted living	362.61
Assisted suicide	
criminology	364.152 3
law	345.025 23
ethics	179.7
see also Right to die —	
ethics	
medical ethics	179.7
Associate-degree nurses	610.730 92
role and function	610.730 692
Association	302.3
Association analysis	519.537
Association football	796.334
electronic games	794.863 34
see also Ball games	
Association of ideas	
psychology	153.22
Association of South East Asian	
Nations	341.247 3
public administration	352.115 9
Associationism	
psychological system	150.194 4
Associations	060
fraternal organizations	369
Associations for religious work	206.5
Christianity	267
Judaism	296.67
Associative algebras	512.46
Associative learning	
psychology	153.152 6
Associative memory	004.5
Associative processing	004.35
Associative processors	004.35
engineering	621.391
Associative rings	512.46
Assomption (Quebec :	
Regional County	
Municipality)	T2—714 416
Assumption of Mary	232.914
Assumption Parish (La.)	T2—763 43

Assurance	368
see also Insurance	
Assyria	935.03
	T2—35
Mesopotamian history	935.03
Middle Eastern history	939.402
Palestinian history	933.03
Assyrian Church of the East	281.8
doctrines	230.18
catechisms and creeds	238.18
theology	230.18
see also Eastern churches	
Assyrian dialect	492.17
	T6—921
Assyrian literature	892.1
Assyrians (Ancient)	T5—921
Assyrians (Modern)	T5—923
Assyro-Babylonian language	492.1
	T6—921
Assyro-Babylonian literature	892.1
Astatine	546.735
Asteliaceae	584.7
Asteraceae	583.983
Asterales	583.983
Asteridae	583.9
Asterids	583.9
Asterinales	579.564
Asteroidea	593.93
Asteroids	523.44
	T2—992 4
astrology	133.539 8
Asteropeiaceae	583.88
Asterozoa	593.93
paleozoology	563.93
Asters	635.933 983
botany	583.983
floriculture	635.933 983
Asthma	
medicine	616.238
see also Respiratory tract	
diseases — humans	
pediatrics	618.922 38
Asti (Italy : Province)	T2—451 5
ancient	T2—371 7
Astigmatism	
optometry	617.755
see also Eye diseases —	
humans	
Astrakhan (Russia : Oblast)	T2—474 8
Astrakhanskaïa oblast′	
(Russia)	T2—474 8
Astral projection	133.95
Astrapotheria	569.62
Astrobiology	576.839

Astrolatry	202.12	Ataxia telangiectasia	
Astrologers	133.509 2	medicine	616.83
Astrology	133.5	*see also* Nervous system	
natural	520	diseases — humans	
Astrology and religion	201.613 35	Atayal (Taiwan people)	T5—992 5
Christianity	261.513	Atchison County (Kan.)	T2—781 36
Astromechanics		Atchison County (Mo.)	T2—778 113
engineering	629.411	Atelinae	599.858
Astrometry	522	Athabasca, Lake (Sask. and	
Astronautical engineering	629.47	Alta.)	T2—712 41
military	623.69	Athabascan languages	497.2
Astronautical engineers	629.409 2		T6—972
Astronautics	629.4	Athabaska River (Alta.)	T2—712 32
Astronauts	629.450 092	Athanasian Creed	238.144
selection and training	629.450 7	Athapascan-Eyak languages	497.2
Astronavigation	527		T6—972
Astronomers	520.92	Athapascan Indians	978.004 972
Astronomical almanacs	528		T5—972
Astronomical geography	525	Athapascan languages	497.2
Astronomical instruments	522.2		T6—972
Astronomical interpretation		Athapaskan languages	497.2
Bible	220.68		T6—972
Astronomical observatories	522.1	Atharvaveda	294.592 15
architecture	727.552	Atheism	211.8
Astronomy	520	Christian polemics	239.7
law	344.095 2	Christian view	261.21
see Manual at 520 vs. 523.1,		Jewish view	296.391
523.112, 523.8		religious freedom	
Astronomy and religion	201.652	law	342.085 222
Christianity	261.55	Atheistic religions	201.4
Islam	297.265 2	Atheists	211.809 2
philosophy of religion	215.2	Athelstan, King of England	
Astrophotography	522.63	English history	942.017 1
Astrophysics	523.01	Athenian supremacy	938.04
Asturias (Spain)	T2—461 9	Athens (Ga.)	T2—758 18
Asua language	496.56	Athens (Greece)	949.512
	T6—965 6		T2—495 12
Asunción (Paraguay)	T2—892 121	ancient	T2—385
Aswān (Egypt : Province)	T2—623	Athens County (Ohio)	T2—771 97
Asylum	323.631	Atheriniformes	597.66
law	342.083	paleozoology	567.66
Asymptotic curves	516.362	Atherosclerosis	
Asynchronous machinery	621.313 6	medicine	616.136
Asynchronous transfer mode		*see also* Cardiovascular	
communications engineering	621.382 16	diseases — humans	
computer communications	004.66	Atherospermataceae	584.288
engineering	621.398 1	Atherton (Qld.)	T2—943 6
Asyūṭ (Egypt : Province)	T2—622	Athletes	796.092
Atacama (Chile : Region)	T2—831 4	health	613.711
Atamasco lilies	584.78	occupational ethics	174.979 6
Atascosa County (Tex.)	T2—764 443	physical fitness	613.711
Atatürk, Kemal			
Turkish history	956.102 4		

Athlete's foot	
medicine	616.579
see also Skin diseases —	
humans	
Athletic club buildings	
architecture	725.85
Athletic fields	796.420 68
area planning	711.558
Athletic games	796
see also Sports	
Athletic garments	796
Athletic gloves and mitts	
manufacturing technology	688.7
Athletic injuries	
incidence	614.3
medicine	617.102 7
Athletic services	
armed forces	355.346
Athletic sports	796
see also Sports	
Athletics (Sports)	796
Athletics (Track and field)	796.42
Athos (Greece)	T2—495 65
Atjeh (Indonesia)	T2—598 11
Atkinson County (Ga.)	T2—758 822
Atlanta (Ga.)	T2—758 231
Atlanta Campaign, 1864	973.737 1
Atlantic City (N.J.)	T2—749 85
Atlantic Coast (Nicaragua)	T2—728 53
Atlantic Coastal Plain	T2—75
Maryland	T2—752 1
North Carolina	T2—756 1
South Carolina	T2—757 6
United States	T2—75
Virginia	T2—755 1
Atlantic cod	597.633
Atlantic County (N.J.)	T2—749 84
Atlantic intergovernmental	
organizations	341.243
Atlantic Islands	997
	T2—97
Atlantic languages (Africa)	496.32
	T6—963 2
Atlantic Ocean	551.461 3
	T2—163
World War II	940.542 93
see Manual at T2—163 and	
T2—164, T2—165	
Atlantic Provinces	971.5
	T2—715
Atlantic region	T2—182 1
Atlántico (Colombia :	
Dept.)	T2—861 15
Atlántida (Honduras)	T2—728 312

Atlantis	001.94
see also Legendary places	
Atlas Mountains	T2—64
Atlases	912
	T1—022 3
cataloging	025.346
geography	912
library treatment	025.176
pictorial works	T1—022 2
see Manual at T1—0222 vs.	
T1—0223	
Atmosphere	551.5
	T2—161
ecology	579.175
meteorology	551.5
public administration	354.37
Atmosphere-land interactions	551.523
Atmosphere-ocean interactions	551.524 6
Atmosphere-water interactions	551.524
Atmospheric disturbances	551.55
Atmospheric electricity	551.563
Atmospheric entry	
manned space flight	629.458 8
Atmospheric formations	551.551
Atmospheric ionization	538.767
Atmospheric nucleation	551.574 1
Atmospheric optics	551.565
Atmospheric pressure	551.54
Atmospheric radiation	
meteorology	551.527 3
Atmospheric thermodynamics	
space flight	629.415 2
Atoka County (Okla.)	T2—766 66
Atolls	551.424
	T2—142
geography	910.914 2
geomorphology	551.424
physical geography	910.021 42
Atomic bomb	355.825 119
see also Nuclear weapons	
Atomic emission spectroscopy	543.52
Atomic energy	333.792 4
economics	333.792 4
law	343.092 5
physics	539.7
Atomic mass	
chemistry	541.242
Atomic number	541.242
Atomic physics	539.7
astronomy	523.019 7
Atomic spectroscopy	543.5
Atomic structure	539.14
chemistry	541.24

Auckland (N.Z.)	T2—932 4
Auckland, George Eden, Earl of	
Indian history	954.031 4
Auckland City (N.Z.)	T2—932 4
Auckland Islands (N.Z.)	T2—939 9
Auckland Province (N.Z.)	T2—931 2
Auckland Region (N.Z.)	T2—932
Auction bridge	795.414
Auction catalogs	T1—029
bibliography	017.3
see also Catalogs	
commerce	381.170 29
Auctions	381.17
law	343.081 1
management	658.877
see also Commerce	
Aude (France)	T2—448 7
Audience participation programs	791.443
radio	791.443
television performances	791.453
Audiences	302.33
mass media	302.23
Audio books	
bibliographies	011.384
Audio input devices	
computer science	006.45
engineering	621.399 4
Audio-lingual language study	418
specific languages	T4—83
Audio output devices	
computer science	006.5
engineering	621.399
Audio publications	070.579
Audio systems	
automobile	629.277 4
Audio systems engineering	621.382 8
recording and reproduction	621.389 3
Audiobooks	
bibliographies	011.384
Audiologists	617.809 2
Audiology	617.8
pediatrics	618.920 978 9
Audiotex	384.646
see also Telephone	
Audiovisual engineering	621.389 7
Audiovisual equipment	
libraries	
management	022.9
museology	069.32
Audiovisual materials	
art appreciation use	701.1
bibliographies	011.37
cataloging	025.347
Christian religious education	268.635

Audiovisual materials (continued)	
design	744.82
instructional use	371.335
library treatment	025.177
primary education	372.133 5
reviews	028.137
Audiovisual media	302.234
sociology	302.234
wireless	
sociology	302.234 5
Audiovisual treatment	T1—020 8
Auditing	657.45
accounting	657.45
government accounts	657.835 045
Auditoriums	
architecture	725.83
Auditory canal diseases	
medicine	617.83
see also Ear diseases —	
humans	
Auditory canals	
human physiology	612.851
medicine	617.83
Auditory memory	153.133
Auditory perception	
psychology	152.15
Auditory tube diseases	
medicine	617.86
see also Ear diseases —	
humans	
Auditory tubes	
human physiology	612.854
medicine	617.86
Audits	657.45
accounting	657.45
government accounts	657.835 045
Audrain County (Mo.)	T2—778 332
Audubon County (Iowa)	T2—777 486
Auglaize County (Ohio)	T2—771 43
Augmented reality	006.8
Augrabies Falls National	
Park (South Africa)	T2—687 16
Augsburg (Germany)	T2—433 75
Augsburg, War of the League of,	
1688–1697	940.252 5
North American history	973.25
Augsburg Confession	238.41
Augusta (Ga.)	T2—758 64
Augusta (Me.)	T2—741 6
Augusta County (Va.)	T2—755 916
Augusta Praetoria (Italy)	T2—372 211
Augusta Taurinorum (Italy)	T2—372 221

Automatic data collection		Automobile driving	629.283
systems	006.2	law	343.094 6
engineering	621.399	recreation	796.7
Automatic data processing	004	Automobile engineers	629.222 092
	T1—028 5	Automobile insurance	368.092
Automatic firearms		inland marine	368.232
military engineering	623.442 4	law	346.086 092
military equipment	355.824 24	liability	368.572
Automatic identification and data		*see also* Insurance	
capture	006.24	Automobile noise	363.741
computer science	006.24	*see also* Noise	
engineering	621.384 192	Automobile parking	388.474
Automatic movements		*see also* Parking facilities	
psychology	152.32	Automobile racers	796.720 92
Automatic piloting		Automobile racing	796.72
aircraft	629.132 6	electronic games	794.867 2
Automatic pilots		*see also* Automotive	
aircraft	629.135 2	vehicles — sports	
Automatic pistols	683.432 5	Automobile rallies	796.73
see also Pistols		Automobile registration	354.765 284
Automatic rifles		law	343.094 4
military engineering	623.442 4	public administration	354.765 284
military equipment	355.824 24	Automobile safety	363.125
Automatic speech recognition	006.454	*see also* Highway safety	
Automatic sprinkler systems		Automobile theft	364.162 862 922 2
fire technology	628.925 2	law	345.026 286 292 22
Automatic text summarization		Automobile transportation	388.321
information science	025.410 285 635	engineering	629.222
Automatic theorem proving	511.360 285 63	law	343.094
Automatic train control		public administration	354.765
engineering	625.27	safety	363.125
Automatic transmissions		*see also* Highway safety	
automotive engineering	629.244 6	transportation services	388.321
Automatic writing (Spiritualism)	133.932	urban	388.413 21
Automation		Automobiles	388.342
agricultural economics	338.161	engineering	629.222
control engineering	629.8	economics	338.476 292 22
economics	338.064	law	343.078 629 222
manufacturing technology	670.427	law	343.094 4
mineral industries	338.26	licenses	354.765 284
production management	658.514	law	343.094 4
secondary industries	338.454	military engineering	623.747 2
social effects	303.483 4	repair	629.287 2
Automation engineers	629.809 2	sports	796.7
Automation training		*see also* Automotive	
personnel management	658.312 43	vehicles — sports	
Automatons	629.8	theft of	364.162 862 922 2
Automobile accidents	363.125	law	345.026 286 292 22
see also Highway safety		transportation services	388.342
Automobile bodies	629.26	travel	910
Automobile cars (Railroad)	385.34	*see Manual at* 629.046 vs. 388	
engineering	625.24	Automorphic functions	515.9
see also Rolling stock		calculus	515.9
		number theory	512.7

Automorphisms	511.326
geometry	516.1
topological algebras	512.55
Automotive electronics	629.272
Automotive engineering	629.2
economics	338.476 292
law	343.078 629 2
Automotive vehicles	388.34
engineering	629.2
law	343.094 4
military engineering	623.747
public administration	354.765
repair	629.287
safety	363.125
see also Highway safety	
safety engineering	629.204 2
sports	796.7
arts	700.457 9
	T3C—357 9
child care	649.57
ethics	175
journalism	070.449 796 7
law	344.099
literature	
history and criticism	809.933 579
specific literatures	T3B—080 357 9
history and criticism	T3B—093 579
motion pictures	791.436 579
public administrative support	353.78
safety	363.14
public administration	353.97
techniques	796.702 89
sociology	306.483
television programs	791.456 579
see also Sports	
transportation services	388.34
see Manual at 629.046 vs. 388	
Autonomic nervous system	
human anatomy	611.83
human physiology	612.89
medicine	616.856 9
Autonomic nervous system diseases	
medicine	616.856 9
see also Nervous system diseases — humans	
Autonomous agencies	
public administration	352.264
Autonomous Communities (Spain)	321.023
see also States (Members of federations)	

Autonomous motor land vehicles	629.204 6
engineering	629.204 6
Autonomous Republics (Soviet Union)	321.023
see also States (Members of federations)	
Autonomous vehicles	629.046
engineering	629.046
Autonomy in education	
higher education	378.1
public policy	379.15
Autonomy of states	320.15
Autopilots	
aircraft	629.135 2
Autopsy	
forensic medicine	614.1
medicine	616.075 9
Autoregression	519.536
Autumn	508.2
music	781.524 6
see also Seasons	
Autumn-flowering plants	581.43
floriculture	635.953
Auvergnat dialect (Occitan language)	T6—491
Auvergne (France)	T2—445 9
Auvergne-Rhône-Alpes (France)	T2—445 8
Auxiliaries (Foreign troops)	355.359
Auxiliary party organizations	324.3
Auxiliary power systems	
spacecraft	629.474 4
Auxiliary procedures	T1—028
Auxiliary routes	
marine	387.523
Auxiliary storage	
computer science	004.56
engineering	621.397 6
Auxiliary techniques	T1—028
Auyuittuq National Park (Nunavut)	T2—719 52
Available light photography	778.76
Avalanches	551.307
snow	551.578 48
Avant-garde arts	700.411
	T3C—11
literature	808.801 1
history and criticism	809.911
specific literatures	T3B—080 11
history and criticism	T3B—091 1
Avant-garde jazz	781.656

Avant-garde literary works	808.887	Avitaminosis	
history and criticism	809.987	medicine	616.39
specific literatures	T3B—807	*see also* Digestive system	
individual authors	T3A—8	diseases — humans	
Avant-garde music	780.904	Avocados	641.346 53
Avar language	499.964	agriculture	634.653
	T6—999 64	botany	584.288
Avaric language	499.964	commercial processing	664.804 653
	T6—999 64	cooking	641.646 53
Avarice	178	food	641.346 53
moral theology	205.68	Avodah Zarah	296.123 4
see also Vices		Babylonian Talmud	296.125 4
Avaro-Andi-Dido languages	499.964	Mishnah	296.123 4
	T6—999 64	Palestinian Talmud	296.124 4
Ave Maria	242.74	Avon (England)	T2—423 9
Aveiro (Portugal : District)	T2—469 34	Avon, River	
Avellino (Italy : Province)	T2—457 21	(Gloucestershire-Bristol,	
ancient	T2—377 31	England)	T2—423 9
Average costs	338.514 2	Avon, River	
management	658.155 3	(Leicestershire-Gloucestershire,	
Averaging	519.533	England)	T2—424 4
Aversion		Avon, River	
psychology	152.4	(Wiltshire-Dorset,	
Avery County (N.C.)	T2—756 862	England)	T2—423 1
Aves	598	Avot	296.123 47
Avesta	295.82	Avoyelles Parish (La.)	T2—763 71
Avestan language	491.52	Awadhi dialect	491.492
	T6—915 2		T6—914 92
Avestan literature	891.52	Awadhi literature	891.492
Aveyron (France)	T2—447 4	Awadhi-speaking people	T5—914 92
Aviaries	598.073	Awards	T1—079
animal husbandry	636.68	armed forces	355.134
architecture	728.927	biography	355.134 092
construction	690.892 7	*see also* Military	
Aviary birds	636.68	commemorations	
see also Birds		orders and decorations	929.81
Aviation	387.7	research	001.44
see also Air transportation		Awnings	645.3
Aviation fuel	665.538 25	household management	645.3
Aviation insurance	368.093	manufacturing technology	684
inland marine	368.24	Axes	621.93
liability	368.576	art metalwork	739.72
see also Insurance		military engineering	623.441 4
Aviation law	343.097	Axholme, Isle of (England)	T2—428 32
Aviation medicine	616.980 213	Axiology	121.8
Aviation meteorology	629.132 4	Axiom of choice	511.3
Aviation psychology	155.965	Axiomatic set theory	511.322
Avignon (France)	T2—449 22	Axioms	160
Avignon (Quebec)	T2—714 783	mathematical logic	511.3
Avila (Spain : Province)	T2—463 59	philosophical logic	160
Avila Camacho, Manuel		Axis Powers (World War II	
Mexican history	972.082 6	group)	940.533 4
Avionics	629.135		
military aircraft	623.746 049		

Axles	621.823	Azerbaijan	947.54
automotive engineering	629.245		T2—475 4
railroad engineering	625.21	ancient	939.534
Axolotl	597.858		T2—395 34
Axons		Azerbaijan (Iran)	T2—553
human cytology	612.810 46	Azerbaijan (Region)	T2—553
Ayacucho (Peru : Region)	T2—852 9	Azerbaijan	T2—475 4
Ayatollahs	297.092	Iran	T2—553
biography	297.092	Azerbaijani	T5—943 61
specific sects	297.8	Azerbaijani language	494.361
role and function	297.61		T6—943 61
see Manual at 297.092		Azerbaijani literature	894.361
Aydın İli (Turkey)	T2—562 6	Azeri	T5—943 61
ancient	T2—392 3	Azilal (Morocco : Province)	T2—644
Aye-ayes	599.83	Azimuth	526.63
conservation technology	639.979 83	'Azīz (Hadith)	297.125 24
resource economics	333.959 83	Azlon	
Ayers Rock (N.T.)	T2—942 91	textiles	677.472
Ayers Rock-Mount Olga		Azo compounds	547.043
National Park (N.T.)	T2—942 91	chemical engineering	661.894
Aylesbury Vale (England)	T2—425 93	Azo-oxy dyes	667.253
Aylwin Azócar, Patricio		Azo-tetrazo dyes	667.253
Chilean history	983.066 1	Azores	T2—469 9
Aymara Indians	T5—983 24	Azospirillum	579.323
Aymara language	498.324	Azov, Sea of (Ukraine and	
	T6—983 24	Russia)	551.461 389
Aymara literature	898.324		T2—163 89
Aymaran languages	498.324	Aztec calendar	529.329 784 52
	T6—983 24	Aztec language	497.452
Ayrshire (Scotland)	T2—414 6		T6—974 52
Ayrshire cattle	636.225	Aztec literature	897.452
Aysen (Chile : Province)	T2—836 22	Aztec period	972.018
Aythya	598.414	Aztecan languages	497.452
Ayub Khan, Mohammad			T6—974 52
Pakistani history	954.904 5	Aztecs	972
Ayurvedic cooking	641.563		T5—974 52
Ayurvedic medicine		Azua (Dominican Republic :	
therapeutic system	615.538	Province)	T2—729 372
India	615.538 095 4	Azuay (Ecuador)	T2—866 24
Ayutthaya (Kingdom)	959.302 3		
Az Zarqā' (Jordan :		**B**	
Province)	T2—569 593		
ancient	T2—335 93	B cells	571.967
Azad Kashmir	T2—549 138	human immunology	616.079 8
Azaleas	635.933 93	B-flat horns	788.974
botany	583.93	*see also* Brass instruments	
floriculture	635.933 93	B lymphocytes	571.967
Āzarbāyjān-i Bākhtarī (Iran)	T2—554	human immunology	616.079 8
Āzarbāyjān-i Khāvarī (Iran)	T2—553	Bà Rịa-Vũng Tàu (Vietnam)	T2—597 7
Azcona H., José		Baalbek (Lebanon)	
Honduran history	972.830 533	ancient	T2—394 4
		'Bab el Mandeb	551.461 532
			T2—165 32

Baba Batra	296.123 4	Babylonian dialect	492.17
Babylonian Talmud	296.125 4		T6—921
Mishnah	296.123 4	Babylonian Empire	935.502
Palestinian Talmud	296.124 4	Mesopotamian history	935.502
Baba Kamma	296.123 4	Middle Eastern history	939.402
Babylonian Talmud	296.125 4	Palestinian history	933.03
Mishnah	296.123 4	Babylonian literature	892.1
Palestinian Talmud	296.124 4	Babylonian Talmud	296.125
Baba Meẓia	296.123 4	Babylonians	T5—921
Babylonian Talmud	296.125 4	Babysitters' handbooks	649.102 48
Mishnah	296.123 4	Bắc Giang (Vietnam :	
Palestinian Talmud	296.124 4	Province)	T2—597 2
Babanango (South Africa :		Bắc Kạn (Vietnam :	
District)	T2—684 2	Province)	T2—597 1
Babangida, Ibrahim Badamosi		Bạc Liêu (Vietnam :	
Nigerian history	966.905 3	Province)	T2—597 9
Babblers	598.834	Bắc Ninh (Vietnam :	
Babenberg, House of	943.602 3	Province)	T2—597 2
Babergh (England)	T2—426 48	Baca County (Colo.)	T2—788 99
Babi Yar Massacre, 1941	940.531 844 5	Bacău (Romania : Judeţ)	T2—498 1
Babies	305.232	Baccarat	795.42
	T1—083 2	Bachelet, Michelle	
health	613.043 2	Chilean history	983.066 4
pediatrics	618.920 2	2006–2010	983.066 4
psychology	155.422	2014–2018	983.066 6
see also Infants		Bachelor parties	793.23
Bābil (Iraq : Province)	T2—567 5	Bachelorette parties	793.23
Babine language	497.2	Bachelors	306.815 2
Babirusa	599.633		T1—086 52
Babism	297.92	Bachelor's degree	378.2
Babists		Bacillaceae infections	
biography	297.920 92	incidence	614.512
Baboons	599.865	medicine	616.931
Babouvism (Socialist school)	335.2	*see also* Communicable	
Babur, Emperor of Hindustan		diseases — humans	
Indian history	954.025 2	Bacillariophyceae	579.85
Baby animals	591.392	Bacillary diseases	
domestic animals	636.07	incidence	614.512
mammals	599.139 2	medicine	616.931
Baby blue-eyes (Plant)	635.933 958	*see also* Communicable	
botany	583.958	diseases — humans	
floriculture	635.933 958	Bacillary dysentery	
Baby food	641.300 832	incidence	614.516
commercial preparation	664.62	medicine	616.935 5
cooking	641.562 22	*see also* Communicable	
feeding	649.3	diseases — humans	
food	641.300 832	Bacillus	579.362
Baby sign language		Back (Body part)	
for hearing people	419.108 32	human anatomy	611.9
Baby signing		human physiology	612.9
for hearing people	419.108 32	regional medicine	617.56
Babylon (Extinct city)	T2—355	surgery	617.560 59
Babylonia	935.5	Back muscles	
	T2—355	human anatomy	611.731

Back play	
American football	796.332 24
rugby	796.333 26
soccer	796.334 25
Backache	
medicine	617.564
Backgammon	795.15
Backhand	
tennis	796.342 23
Backpacking	796.51
equipment technology	688.765 1
Backyards	
biology	578.755 4
ecology	577.554
landscape architecture	712.6
Bacon	641.364
see also Pork	
Bacon County (Ga.)	T2—758 787
Bács-Kiskun Megye	
(Hungary)	T2—439 8
Bacteria	579.3
medical microbiology	616.920 1
paleontology	561.91
see Manual at 579.3	
Bacteria-enhanced oil recovery	622.338 27
Bacterial blood diseases	
incidence	614.577
medicine	616.94
see also Communicable	
diseases — humans	
Bacterial counts	
milk processing	637.127 7
Bacterial diseases	571.993
agriculture	632.32
animals	571.993 11
veterinary medicine	636.089 692
humans	362.196 92
incidence	614.57
medicine	616.92
social services	362.196 92
plants	571.993 12
agriculture	632.32
see also Communicable	
diseases	
Bacterial food poisons	
human toxicology	615.952 93
Bacterial pneumonia	
medicine	616.241 2
Bacterial viruses	579.26
Bactericides	668.653
agricultural use	632.953
chemical engineering	668.653
Bacteriological examination	
medicine	616.075 81

Bacteriologists	579.309 2
Bacteriology	579.3
medicine	616.920 1
see also Plants	
Bacteriophages	579.26
Bacteroides	579.325
Bactria	T2—396
Baculoviridae	579.243 6
Bad debts	
tax law	343.052 36
Bad Doberan (Germany :	
Landkreis)	T2—431 74
Badajoz (Spain : Province)	T2—462 7
Baden (Germany)	T2—434 64
Baden (Switzerland :	
Bezirk)	T2—494 566 3
Baden-Baden (Germany)	T2—434 643
Baden-Württemberg	
(Germany)	T2—434 6
Badenoch and Strathspey	
(Scotland)	T2—411 58
Badgers	599.767
Badges	
armed forces	355.134 2
Badlands National Park	
(S.D.)	T2—783 93
Badminton	796.345
biography	796.345 092
see also Ball games	
Badminton players	796.345 092
Badui language	499.223
	T6—992 23
Baetica	T2—366 8
Baffin (Nunavut)	971.952
	T2—719 52
Baffin Bay	551.461 327
	T2—163 27
Baffin Island (Nunavut)	T2—719 52
Bafia languages	496.396
	T6—963 96
Bafokeng (South Africa :	
District)	T2—682 41
Bag lunches	641.53
Bag papers	676.287
Bagasse	
fuel technology	662.88
plastic technology	668.411
Bagasse pulp	676.14
Bagaza, Jean-Baptiste	
Burundi history	967.572 041 5
Bagēmder (Ethiopia)	T2—634
Baggage cars	385.33
engineering	625.23
see also Rolling stock	

Baggage insurance	368.2	Bahrain	953.65
see also Insurance			T2—536 5
Baggage services	388.042	ancient	939.49
see also Passenger services			T2—394 9
Baghawī, al-Ḥusayn ibn Masʿūd		Bahraini	T5—927 536 5
Koran commentary	297.122 73	Baie-D'Urfé (Quebec)	T2—714 28
Baghdād (Iraq : Province)	T2—567 47	Baie-James (Quebec)	T2—714 115
Bagheli dialect	491.492	Baikal seal	599.792
	T6—914 92	Bail (Law)	345.056
Bagheli literature	891.492	Bailey County (Tex.)	T2—764 844
Bagheli-speaking people	T5—914 92	Bailments	346.025
Bagirmi language	496.566	Bairnsdale (Vic.)	T2—945 6
	T6—965 66	Bait-casting	799.126
Bagmati Pradesh (Nepal)	T2—549 63	Bait fishing	799.122
Bagpipes	788.49	Bait worm culture	639.75
instrument	788.491 9	Baixo Alentejo (Portugal)	T2—469 55
music	788.49	Baja California (Mexico :	
see also Woodwind		Peninsula)	T2—722
instruments		Baja California (Mexico :	
Bags	688.8	State)	T2—722 3
paper	676.33	Baja California Norte	
Baguios (Hurricanes)	551.552	(Mexico)	T2—722 3
see also Hurricanes		Baja California Sur	
Bahai Faith	297.93	(Mexico)	T2—722 4
Bahais		Baja Verapaz (Guatemala)	T2—728 152
biography	297.930 92	Baka (West African people)	T5—963 61
Bahama Islands	972.96	Baka language	T6—963 61
	T2—729 6	Baked goods	641.815
Bahamas	972.96	commercial processing	664.752
	T2—729 6	home preparation	641.815
Bahamians	T5—969 729 6	Baker County (Fla.)	T2—759 13
Bahasa Indonesia	499.221	Baker County (Ga.)	T2—758 967
	T6—992 21	Baker County (Or.)	T2—795 75
Bahasa Indonesia literature	899.221	Baker Lake (Nunavut)	T2—719 58
Bahasa Kebangsaan	499.28	Bakery goods	
	T6—992 8	commercial processing	664.752
Bahasa Malaysia	499.28	Baking	
	T6—992 8	commercial food preparation	664.02
Bahasa Melayu	499.28	home cooking	641.71
	T6—992 8	Baking powder	664.68
Baháʾuʾlláh		Baking soda	
works by	297.938 22	food technology	664.68
Bahāwalpur District		Bakongo (Kingdom)	967.320 1
(Pakistan)	T2—549 16		T2—673 2
Bahia (Brazil : State)	T2—814 2	Baʿlabakk (Lebanon)	
Bahía Blanca Estuary (Argentina)	551.461 368	ancient	T2—394 4
	T2—163 68	Balaena	599.527 6
Bahing-Vayu languages	495.49	Balaenidae	599.527
	T6—954 9	Balaenoptera	599.524
Bahoruco (Dominican		Balaenopteridae	599.524
Republic : Province)	T2—729 326	Balalaikas	787.875
Bahr al Ahmar (Egypt)	T2—623	instrument	787.875 19
Bahr al-Aḥmar (Sudan :		music	787.875
Province)	T2—625	see also Stringed instruments	

Balance beam (Gymnastic equipment)	796.442
Balance of payments	382.17
international banking	332.152
international commerce	382.17
Balance of power	327.112
Balance of trade	382.17
Balance sheets	657.3
accounting	657.3
financial management	658.151 2
investment analysis	332.632 042
Balancing machinery	621.816
Balanopaceae	583.69
Balanopales	583.69
Balanophoraceae	583.85
Balanopsidales	583.69
Balconies	721.84
architecture	721.84
construction	690.184
Balcony furniture	645.8
see also Outdoor furniture	
Balcony gardening	635.967 1
Bald cypresses	585.5
Bald eagle	598.943
conservation technology	639.978 943
resource economics	333.958 943
Baldachins	
church architecture	726.529 3
Baldness	
medicine	616.546
see also Skin diseases — humans	
Baldwin County (Ala.)	T2—761 21
Baldwin County (Ga.)	T2—758 573
Bâle-Ville (Switzerland)	T2—494 32
Baleares	T2—467 5
Balearic Islands	T2—467 5
Balearic Sea	551.461 382
	T2—163 82
Baleen whales	599.5
Balfour (South Africa : District)	T2—682 78
Bali language	499.223 8
	T6—992 238
Bali literature	899.223 8
Bali Sea (Indonesia)	551.461 474
	T2—164 74
Balıkesir İli (Turkey)	T2—562 3
ancient	T2—392 1
Balinese	T5—992 238
Balinese language	499.223 8
	T6—992 238
Balinese literature	899.223 8

Baling crops	631.56
equipment manufacturing technology	681.763 1
Balkan Mountains (Bulgaria)	T2—499
Balkan Peninsula	949.6
	T2—496
Balkan States	949.6
	T2—496
Balkan Wars	949.603 9
Balkar language	494.38
	T6—943 8
Ball bearings	621.822
Ball games	796.3
arts	700.457 9
	T3C—357 9
child care	649.57
equipment technology	688.763
ethics	175
human physiology	612.044
indoor	794.7
journalism	070.449 796 3
law	344.099
literature	
history and criticism	809.933 579
specific literatures	T3B—080 357 9
history and criticism	T3B—093 579
motion pictures	791.436 579
outdoor	796.3
physical fitness	613.711
public administrative support	353.78
safety	363.14
public administration	353.97
techniques	796.302 89
sociology	306.483
television programs	791.456 579
see also Sports	
Ball hockey	796.356 4
Ball lightning	551.563 4
Ballad operas	782.14
music	782.14
stage presentation	792.6
see also Theater	
Ballades (Music)	784.189 6
Ballads	
literature	808.814 4
history and criticism	809.144
specific literatures	T3B—104 4
individual authors	T3A—1
music	782.43
Ballarat (Vic.)	T2—945 7
Ballard County (Ky.)	T2—769 96
Ballast (Railroad)	625.141

Ballet	792.8	Baltic languages	491.9
see also Theater			T6—919
Ballet dancers	792.802 809 2	Baltic literatures	891.9
Ballet music	781.556	Baltic Sea	551.461 334
Balletts	782.43		T2—163 34
Ballina (N.S.W.)	T2—944 3	Baltic Sea Region	T2—485
Ballistic missile forces	358.17	Baltic States	947.9
Ballistic missiles	358.171 82		T2—479
engineering	623.451 95	Baltimore (Md.)	T2—752 6
military equipment	358.171 82	Baltimore County (Md.)	T2—752 71
Ballistics	531.55	Balto-Slavic languages	491.8
criminal investigation	363.256 2		T6—918
engineering	620.105	Balto-Slavic literatures	891.8
military engineering	623.51	Balts (Indo-European	
physics	531.55	people)	T5—919
Ballistocardiography		Baluchi	T5—915 98
medicine	616.120 754	Baluchi language	491.598
Balloons			T6—915 98
engineering	629.133 22	Baluchi literature	891.598
military engineering	623.742	Baluchistan	T2—549 15
piloting	629.132 522	Iran	T2—558 3
sports	797.51	Pakistan	T2—549 15
see also Outdoor life		Baluchistan (Pakistan)	T2—549 15
Ballots	324.65	Balustrades	721.8
Ballroom dancing	793.33	architecture	721.8
Balls (Dances)	793.38	artistic ironwork	739.48
Balls (Geometrical shapes)	516.156	construction	690.18
Balls (Gymnastic equipment)	796.443	Bamako (Mali)	T2—662 3
Balls (Recreational equipment)	796.3	Bamana language (Mandekan)	496.345 2
manufacturing technology	688.763		T6—963 452
Ballymena (Northern		Bambara (African people)	T5—963 452
Ireland : Borough)	T2—416 13	Bambara language	496.345 2
Ballymoney (Northern			T6—963 452
Ireland : District)	T2—416 14	Bambara literature	896.345 2
Balms	583.75	Bamberg (Germany)	T2—433 18
Balms (Burseraceae)	583.75	Bamberg County (S.C.)	T2—757 78
Balms (Lamiaceae)	583.96	Bamboo pulp	676.14
Balneotherapy		Bamboos	584.922
medicine	615.853	basketwork crop	633.58
Balochi	T5—915 98	botany	584.922
Balochi language	491.598	floriculture	635.934 922
	T6—915 98	handicrafts	745.51
Balochi literature	891.598	textiles	677.54
Balong language	496.396	*see also* Textiles	
	T6—963 96	Bambuseae	584.922
Balqā' (Jordan : Province)	T2—569 55	Bambusoideae	584.922
Balsa		Bambute (African people)	T5—963 94
botany	583.775	Bamileke (African people)	T5—963 6
forestry	634.973 775	Bamileke languages	496.36
Balsaminaceae	583.93		T6—963 6
Balsams (Plants)	583.93	Bamun language	496.36
Baltic-Finnic languages	494.54		T6—963 6
	T6—945 4	Bana (African people)	T5—963 6
Baltic-Finnic literatures	894.54		

Bana language	496.36	Bangkok (Thailand)	959.33
	T6—963 6		T2—593 3
Banach algebras	512.554	Bangladesh	954.92
Banach spaces	515.732		T2—549 2
Bananas	641.347 72	ancient	934.92
botany	584.88		T2—349 2
commercial processing	664.804 772	Bangladesh people	T5—914 126
cooking	641.647 72	Bangladeshis	T5—914 126
food	641.347 72	Bangor (Me.)	T2—741 3
horticulture	634.772	Bang's disease	636.208 969 57
Banat	949.84	Bangsamoro Autonomous	
	T2—498 4	Region in Muslim	
Yugoslavia	T2—497 1	Mindanao (Philippines)	T2—599 75
Banbridge (Northern		Bangui (Central African	
Ireland : District)	T2—416 57	Republic)	T2—674 1
Band leaders	784.092	Banī Suwayf (Egypt :	
Banda (African people)	T5—963 61	Province)	T2—622
Banda, H. Kamuzu (Hastings		Banjar	T5—992 256
Kamuzu)		Banjar language	499.225 6
Malawian history	968.970 41		T6—992 256
Banda, Joyce Hilda		Banjar literature	899.225 6
Malawian history	968.970 43	Banjar Malay language	499.225 6
Banda languages	496.361		T6—992 256
	T6—963 61	Banjar Malay literature	899.225 6
Banda Sea	551.461 474	Banjarese	T5—992 256
	T2—164 74	Banjarese language	499.225 6
Bandages	677.8		T6—992 256
manufacturing technology	677.8	Banjarese literature	899.225 6
surgical use	617.93	Banjoists	787.880 92
Bandera County (Tex.)	T2—764 885	Banjos	787.88
Bandi language	496.348	instrument	787.881 9
	T6—963 48	music	787.88
Bandicoots	599.26	*see also* Stringed instruments	
Bandjoun language	496.36	Banjul (Gambia)	T2—665 1
	T6—963 6	Bank accounts	332.175 2
Bandoneons	788.84	Bank deposit insurance	368.854
see also Woodwind		law	346.086 854
instruments		Bank examination	657.833 304 5
Bands	784	Bank failures	332.1
Bandundu (Congo :		Bank for International	
Province)	T2—675 116	Settlements	332.155
Bandy	796.963	Bank holding companies	332.16
Banff (Alta.)	T2—712 332	Bank mergers	332.16
Banff and Buchan		Bank notes	332.42
(Scotland)	T2—412 4	central banking	332.112
Banff National Park (Alta.)	T2—712 332	form of currency	332.404 4
Bangalore torpedoes	623.454 5	Bank reserves	332.1
Banghāzī (Libya)	T2—612	macroeconomic policy	339.53
Bangi-Ntomba languages	496.396 8	requirements	332.113
	T6—963 968	Bankers	332.109 2
Bangiophycideae	579.89	Banking	332.1
Bangka (Indonesia)	T2—598 196	*see also* Banks (Finance)	
Bangka Belitung		Banking cooperatives	334.2
(Indonesia)	T2—598 196	Banking services	332.17

Bankruptcy	332.75	Bantustans	968.29
accounting	657.47		T2—682 9
credit economics	332.75	Banyan	583.648
financial management	658.15	Banzer Suárez, Hugo	
law	346.078	Bolivian history	984.054 1
commercial law	346.078	Baobabs	583.775
public finance	343.037	Baoruco (Dominican	
public finance	336.368	Republic : Province)	T2—729 326
Banks (Finance)	332.1	Baoulé (African people)	T5—963 38
accounting	657.833 3	Baoulé language	496.338
architecture	725.24		T6—963 38
auditing	657.833 304 5	Baptism	234.161
credit regulation		customs	392.12
macroeconomic policy	339.53	etiquette	395.24
government guaranty of		music	781.582
deposits	368.854	public worship	265.1
law	346.082	theology	234.161
public administration	354.86	Baptism in the Holy Spirit	234.13
Banks County (Ga.)	T2—758 143	Baptism of Jesus Christ	232.95
Banks Island (N.W.T.)	T2—719 3	Baptismal fonts	247.1
Banks Peninsula (N.Z.)	T2—938 4	architecture	726.529 1
Banks Peninsula District		Baptismal names	929.44
(N.Z.)	T2—938 4	Baptismal records	
Banksias	583.38	genealogy	929.3
Bann River (Northern		Baptist General Conference of	
Ireland)	T2—416	America	286.5
Banned books	098.1	*see also* Baptists	
Banner County (Neb.)	T2—782 975	Baptist sacred music	781.716
Banners	929.92	public worship	782.322 6
armed forces	355.15	music	782.322 6
Bannock County (Idaho)	T2—796 47	religion	264.060 2
Bannock Indians	T5—974 577	Baptistries	
Bannock language	497.457 7	architecture	726.4
	T6—974 577	accessory building	726.4
Bannockburn, Battle of, 1314	941.102	part of church	726.596
Banquets	642.4	Baptists	286
Banská Bystrica (Slovakia :		biography	286.092
Province)	T2—437 34	church government	262.06
Banskobystrický kraj		local church	254.06
(Slovakia)	T2—437 34	church law	262.986
Bansuris	788.35	doctrines	230.6
see also Woodwind		catechisms and creeds	238.6
instruments		general councils	262.56
Bantams	636.587 1	guides to Christian life	248.486
Banten (Indonesia)	T2—598 23	missions	266.6
Banteng	599.642 2	moral theology	241.046
Bantoid languages	496.36	persecution of	272.8
	T6—963 6	public worship	264.06
Bantu languages	496.39	religious associations	267.186
	T6—963 9	religious education	268.86
see Manual at T6—9639		seminaries	230.073 6
Bantu literatures	896.39	theology	230.6
Bantu-speaking peoples	T5—963 9	Bar-code scanners	006.242
		computer engineering	621.399 4

Bar coding	006.242
computer science	006.242
materials management	658.780 285 624 2
Bar examination	340.076
Bar mitzvah	296.442 4
customs	392.14
etiquette	395.24
liturgy	296.454 24
music	781.583
Baraga County (Mich.)	T2—774 973
Barahona (Dominican Republic : Province)	T2—729 324
Barai language	499.12
	T6—991 2
Baraita	296.126 3
Baranya Megye (Hungary)	T2—439 7
Barbacoan languages	498.2
	T6—982
Barbadians	T5—969 729 81
Barbados	972.981
	T2—729 81
Barbary horse	636.11
Barbary States	T2—61
Barbecuing	641.76
indoor cooking	641.76
outdoor cooking	641.578 4
Barbels (Fishes)	597.482
sports fishing	799.174 82
Barber County (Kan.)	T2—781 82
Barbering	646.724
customs	391.5
Barberries	583.34
botany	583.34
cooking	641.647 4
floriculture	635.933 34
food	641.347 4
horticulture	634.74
Barbers	646.724 092
Barbershops	
sanitation services	363.729 9
see also Sanitation	
Barberton (South Africa : District)	T2—682 73
Barbets	598.72
Barbeuiaceae	583.883
Barbeyaceae	583.646
Barbeyales	583.646
Barbiturate abuse	362.299
medicine	616.86
personal health	613.8
social welfare	362.299
see also Substance abuse	
Barbiturates	
pharmacokinetics	615.782 1
Barbour County (Ala.)	T2—761 32
Barbour County (W. Va.)	T2—754 59
Barbs (Fishes)	597.482
Barbuda	T2—729 74
Barcaldine (Qld.)	T2—943 5
Barcelona (Spain : Province)	T2—467 2
Barents Sea	551.461 324
	T2—163 24
Barents Sea region	T2—48
Bargain theory of wages	331.210 1
Barge canals	386.48
engineering	627.138
transportation services	386.48
see also Canals	
Bargello	746.442
Barges	386.229
design	623.812 9
engineering	623.829
freight services	386.244
see also Ships	
Bari (Italy)	T2—457 511
ancient	T2—377 581
Bari (Italy : Città metropolitana)	T2—457 51
ancient	T2—377 58
Bari language	496.552
	T6—965 52
Bari languages	496.552
	T6—965 52
Baric languages	495.4
	T6—954
Barima-Waini Region (Guyana)	T2—881 1
Barinas (Venezuela : State)	T2—874 3
Baringo County (Kenya)	T2—676 274 8
Barisāl (Bangladesh : Division)	T2—549 26
Barite	553.662
mineralogy	549.752
Baritone voices	782.88
choral and mixed voices	782.88
single voices	783.88
Baritones (Horns)	
American	788.975
instrument	788.975 19
music	788.975
see also Brass instruments	
British	788.974
see also Brass instruments	
Barium	669.725
chemical engineering	661.039 5
chemistry	546.395
economic geology	553.499

Barium (continued)
  metallurgy 669.725
  physical metallurgy 669.967 25
  see also Chemicals
Barium (Italy) T2—377 581
Bark 581.47
  descriptive botany 581.47
  forest product 634.985
  physiology 575.452
Bark beetles 595.768
Barkerville (B.C.) T2—711 75
Barking and Dagenham
  (London, England) T2—421 75
Barkley, Lake (Ky. and
  Tenn.) T2—769 79
Barkly East (South Africa :
  District) T2—687 57
Barkly West (South Africa :
  District) T2—687 14
Barletta-Andria-Trani
  (Italy : Province) T2—457 59
  ancient T2—377 56
Barley 641.331 6
  botany 584.926
  cooking 641.631 6
  food 641.331 6
  food crop 633.16
  forage crop 633.256
Barley-free cooking 641.563 931 6
Barley-free diet
  health 613.268 316
Barley-free foods 641.309 316
Barlow, George Hilaro, Sir
  Indian history 954.031 2
Barmera (S. Aust.) T2—942 33
Barn owls 598.97
Barnabites 255.52
  church history 271.52
Barnacles 595.35
  paleozoology 565.35
Barnes County (N.D.) T2—784 32
Barnet (London, England) T2—421 87
Barnim (Germany :
  Landkreis) T2—431 53
Barnouic (Channel Islands) T2—423 49
Barns 631.22
  animal husbandry 636.083 1
  architecture 725.372
  construction 690.537 2
  domestic architecture 728.922
    construction 690.892 2
  use 631.22
Barnsley (England :
  Metropolitan Borough) T2—428 25

Barnstable County (Mass.) T2—744 92
Barnwell County (S.C.) T2—757 76
Barometric leveling 526.37
Barometric pressure 551.54
Baroque architecture 724.16
Baroque art 709.032
Baroque decoration 744.090 32
Baroque music 780.903 2
Baroque painting 759.046
Baroque sculpture 735.21
Barotse kingdoms (Zambian
  history) 968.940 1
Barracks 355.71
  architecture 725.18
  military housing 355.71
Barracudas 597.7
Barrage balloons
  military engineering 623.744
Barrages
  engineering 627.123
Barramunda 597.39
  culture 639.373 9
  fishing 639.273 9
Barrels 688.8
  wooden 674.82
Barren County (Ky.) T2—769 72
Barrhead (Scotland) T2—414 39
Barrier islands 551.423
  T2—142
  geography 910.914 2
  geomorphology 551.423
  physical geography 910.021 42
Barrios de Chamorro, Violeta
  Nicaraguan history 972.850 541
Barristers 340.092
Barron County (Wis.) T2—775 18
Barrow, Adama
  Gambian history 966.510 33
Barrow County (Ga.) T2—758 195
Barrow-in-Furness
  (England : Borough) T2—427 81
Barrow Island National Park
  (W.A.) T2—941 3
Barrow River (Ireland) T2—418
Barry (Wales) T2—429 89
Barry County (Mich.) T2—774 16
Barry County (Mo.) T2—778 76
Bars (Drinking places) 647.95
  see also Drinking places
Bars (Musical instruments) 786.82
  concussed 786.873
  friction 786.863
    set 786.863
  single 786.888

Bars (Musical instruments) (continued)
  percussed   786.843
    set   786.843
    single   786.884 3
  plucked   786.85
    set   786.85
    single   786.887
  see also Percussion instruments
Bars (Structural elements)   624.177 4
Bartending   641.874
Barter   332.54
Bartholomew County (Ind.) T2—772 24
Bartın İli (Turkey) T2—563 7
  ancient T2—393 17
Barton, Edmund, Sir
  Australian history   994.041
Barton County (Kan.) T2—781 52
Barton County (Mo.) T2—778 71
Bartow County (Ga.) T2—758 365
Baruch (Bible)   229.5
Baryons   539.721 64
Baryonyx   567.912
Barytons   787.6
  see also Stringed instruments
Bas-Congo (Congo) T2—675 114
Bas-Rhin (France) T2—443 95
Bas-Richelieu (Quebec) T2—714 39
Bas-Saint-Laurent (Quebec) T2—714 76
Bas-Saint-Laurent-Gaspésie
  Region (Quebec) T2—714 77
Basa (Cameroon people) T5—963 96
Basa (Liberian people) T5—963 3
Basaa language (Cameroon)   496.396
    T6—963 96
Basal angiosperms   584.2
  botany   584.2
  forestry   634.974
  paleobotany   561.4
Basal body   571.67
Basal ganglia
  human physiology   612.825
  medicine   616.83
Basal ganglia diseases
  medicine   616.83
    see also Nervous system
      diseases — humans
Basalt   552.26
Basari (Senegal-Guinea
  people) T5—963 2
Basari (Togo-Ghana people) T5—963 5
Base lines (Surveying)   526.33
Base running
  baseball   796.357 27

Base sequences (Nucleotides)   572.863 3
  humans   611.018 166 3
Baseball   796.357
  electronic games   794.863 57
  equipment manufacturing   688.763 57
  see also Ball games
Baseball cards   796.357 075
Baseball players   796.357 092
Baseband computer equipment   004.64
  engineering   621.398 1
Baseband local-area networks   004.68
  see also Computer
    communications
Basel (Switzerland) T2—494 32
Basel (Switzerland :
  Canton) T2—494 32
Basel-Landschaft
  (Switzerland : Canton) T2—494 33
Basel-Stadt (Switzerland) T2—494 32
Basellaceae   583.883
Baselland (Switzerland) T2—494 33
Basements
  home economics   643.5
Basenji   636.753 6
Bases (Chemicals)   546.32
  chemical engineering   661.3
  see also Chemicals
Bases (Military installations)   355.7
  law   343.015 7
Bashfulness   155.232
Bashir, Omar Hassan Ahmad al
  South Sudanese history   962.904 3
  Sudanese history   962.404 3
Bashkir language   494.38
    T6—943 8
Bashkiriĩa (Russia) T2—474 3
Bashkortostan T2—474 3
Basic Christian communities   250
  see Manual at 260 vs. 250
Basic education   370
  adults   374.012
  see also Education
Basic English   428
Basic skills education   370
  see also Education
Basic sulfates
  mineralogy   549.755
Basic training (Military)   355.54
  living conditions   355.129 2
Basidiomycete yeasts   579.59
Basidiomycetes   579.59
Basidiomycotina   579.59

Basil	641.357	Bass saxophones	788.75
botany	583.96	*see also* Woodwind	
see also Herbs		instruments	
Basil III, Czar of Russia		Bass Strait (Vic. and Tas.)	551.461 576
Russian history	947.042		T2—165 76
Basilan (Philippines :		Bass viols	787.65
Province)	T2—599 92	*see also* Stringed instruments	
Basilan Island (Philippines)	T2—599 92	Bass voices	782.89
Basildon (England :		choral and mixed voices	782.89
District)	T2—426 772	single voices	783.89
Basilians	255.17	Bassa (Cameroon people)	T5—963 96
church history	271.17	Bassa (Liberian people)	T5—963 3
Basilicata (Italy)	T2—457 7	Bassa language (Cameroon)	496.396
ancient	T2—377 7		T6—963 96
Basilisks (Mythical animal)	398.245 4	Bassa language (Liberia)	496.33
see also Legendary animals			T6—963 3
Basingstoke and Deane		Bassari (Senegal-Guinea	
(England)	T2—422 71	people)	T5—963 2
Basket stars	593.94	Bassari (Togo-Ghana	
Basketball	796.323	people)	T5—963 5
electronic games	794.863 23	Basse-Côte-Nord (Quebec :	
see also Ball games		Region)	T2—714 179
Basketball cards	796.323 075	Basse-Normandie (France)	T2—442 1
Basketball players	796.323 092	Basse-taille	
Basketry		ceramic arts	738.4
handicrafts	746.412	Basse Terre (Guadeloupe)	T2—729 76
Basketwork plants		Basses (Fishes)	597.73
agriculture	633.58	conservation technology	639.977 73
Basommatophora	594.38	cooking	641.692
Basotho	T5—968 85	culture	639.377 3
Basotho-Qwaqwa (South		food	641.392
Africa)	T2—685 1	resource economics	333.956 73
Basque (France)	T2—447 16	sports fishing	799.177 3
Basque language	499.92	zoology	597.73
	T6—999 2	Basses (Stringed instruments)	787.5
Basque literature	899.92	instrument	787.519
Basque nationalism	320.540 946 6	music	787.5
Basque Provinces (Spain)	T2—466	*see also* Stringed instruments	
Basques	T5—999 2	Basset horns	788.62
Basques (Quebec : Regional		Basset hound	636.753 6
County Municipality)	T2—714 766	Bassetlaw (England)	T2—425 21
Başrah (Iraq : Province)	T2—567 5	Basslets	597.73
Bass clarinets	788.65	Bassoon concertos	784.285 818 6
see also Woodwind		Bassoons	788.58
instruments		instrument	788.581 9
Bass drums	786.95	music	788.58
see also Percussion instruments		*see also* Woodwind	
Bass flutes	788.34	instruments	
see also Woodwind		Basswood	
instruments		botany	583.775
Bass recorders	788.367	forestry	634.972 77
see also Woodwind		lumber	674.142
instruments			

Bast fibers	
textiles	677.1
see also Textiles	
Bastille Day	394.263 5
Bastrop County (Tex.)	T2—764 32
Basutoland	968.850 2
	T2—688 5
Bat flies	595.774
Bat games	796.35
Bat mitzvah	296.443 4
customs	392.14
etiquette	395.24
liturgy	296.454 34
music	781.583
Bataan (Philippines :	
Province)	T2—599 153
Batak	T5—992 246
Batak Dairi language	499.224 66
	T6—992 246 6
Batak Dairi literature	899.224 66
Batak languages	499.224 6
	T6—992 246
Batak Toba language	499.224 62
	T6—992 246 2
Batak Toba literature	899.224 62
Batanes (Philippines)	T2—599 122
Batangas (Philippines :	
Province)	T2—599 177
Batavian Republic	949.205
Batch processing	004.3
see also Processing modes —	
computer science	
Batemans Bay (N.S.W.)	T2—944 7
Bates County (Mo.)	T2—778 43
Batfishes	597.62
Bath (England)	942.398
	T2—423 98
Bath and North East	
Somerset (England)	T2—423 98
Bath County (Ky.)	T2—769 555
Bath County (Va.)	T2—755 87
Bathhouses	
architecture	725.73
domestic	728.96
public	725.73
construction	690.573
domestic	690.896
public	690.573
Bathing	613.41
child training	649.63
customs	391.64
health	613.41
therapeutics	615.853

Bathing suits	
commercial technology	687.16
customs	391.48
home sewing	646.47
Bathrooms	643.52
construction	690.42
home economics	643.52
plumbing	696.182
residential interior decoration	747.78
Bathurst (N.B.)	T2—715 12
Bathurst (N.S.W.)	T2—944 5
Bathurst (South Africa :	
District)	T2—687 53
Bathurst Inlet (Nunavut)	T2—719 55
Bathyal zone	
biology	578.779
ecology	577.79
Bathyscaphes	387.27
design	623.812 7
engineering	623.827
transportation services	387.27
Bathyspheres	387.27
design	623.812 7
engineering	623.827
transportation services	387.27
Batik	746.662
Bating leather	675.22
Batlle Ibáñez, Jorge	
Uruguayan history	989.506 74
Batman İli (Turkey)	T2—566 78
ancient	T2—394 2
Batna (Algeria : Province)	T2—655
Batoidei	597.35
paleozoology	567.35
Baton Rouge (La.)	T2—763 18
Baton twirling	791.6
Batrachoidiformes	597.62
Bats (Animals)	599.4
conservation technology	639.979 4
paleozoology	569.4
resource economics	333.959 4
Bats (Sports equipment)	
baseball	796.357 26
manufacturing technology	688.763 57
cricket	796.358 26
manufacturing technology	688.763 58
Batswana (Ethnic group)	T5—963 977 5
Batswana (National group)	T5—968 83
Battalions (Military units)	355.31
Batten disease	
medicine	616.83
Battered wives	362.829 2
criminology	364.155 53
law	345.025 553

Battered wives (continued)		Bay laurel	641.357
social welfare	362.829 2	botany	584.288
see also Family violence		Bay of Bengal	551.461 564
Batteries (Artillery units)	358.123		T2—165 64
Batteries (Electric)	621.312 42	Bay of Biscay (France and Spain)	551.461 338
automotive	629.254 2		T2—163 38
Battery (Crime)	364.155 5	Bay of Fundy	551.461 345
law	345.025 55		T2—163 45
criminal law	345.025 55	Bay of Plenty Region (N.Z.)	T2—934 2
torts	346.033	Bay rum tree	583.732
social welfare	362.885 5	Bayadh (Algeria : Province)	T2—657
Batting (Sports)		Bayamón (P.R. : District)	T2—729 52
baseball	796.357 26	Bayberries (Myricaceae)	583.65
cricket	796.358 26	Bayberry wax	665.12
Battle-axes	623.441 4	Bayburt İli (Turkey)	T2—565 7
Battle games	793.92	ancient	T2—393 37
computerized games	793.92	Bayelsa State (Nigeria)	T2—669 41
Battle of the Atlantic, 1939–1945	940.542 93	Bayern (Germany)	T2—433
Battle tactics	355.42	Bayesian statistical decision	
Battleford (Sask.)	T2—712 42	theory	519.542
Battlefords (Sask.)	T2—712 42	Bayfield County (Wis.)	T2—775 13
Battles	355.4	Baylor County (Tex.)	T2—764 744
see also Land operations		Bayonet practice	355.547
see Manual at 930–990		Bayonets	623.441
Battleships	359.835 2	art metalwork	739.723
design	623.812 52	Bayono-Awbono languages	499.1
engineering	623.825 2		T6—991
naval equipment	359.835 2	Bayreuth (Germany)	T2—433 15
naval units	359.325 2	Bays	
Bauchi State (Nigeria)	T2—669 82	law of nations	341.448
Baudouin I, King of the Belgians		resource economics	333.916 4
Belgian history	949.304 3	Bayyūḍ, Ibrāhīm ibn 'Umar	
Bauxite	553.492 6	Koran commentary	297.122 77
economic geology	553.492 6	Bazaars	381.1
mineralogy	549.53	architecture	725.21
mining	622.349 26	management	658.87
Bava Batra	296.123 4	*see also* Commerce	
Babylonian Talmud	296.125 4	Bazookamen	356.162
Mishnah	296.123 4	Bazookas	356.162
Palestinian Talmud	296.124 4	engineering	623.442 6
Bava Kamma	296.123 4	ammunition	623.455
Babylonian Talmud	296.125 4	military equipment	356.162
Mishnah	296.123 4	Beach activities	
Palestinian Talmud	296.124 4	recreation	796.53
Bava Meẓia	296.123 4	Beach erosion	551.36
Babylonian Talmud	296.125 4	engineering	627.58
Mishnah	296.123 4	Beach flies	595.774
Palestinian Talmud	296.124 4	Beach volleyball	796.325 82
Bavaria (Germany)	943.3	Beaches	551.457
	T2—433		T2—146
Bavarian Alps (Germany)	T2—433 6	area planning	711.558
Baxter County (Ark.)	T2—767 21	geography	910.914 6
Bay County (Fla.)	T2—759 95	geomorphology	551.457
Bay County (Mich.)	T2—774 47	landscape architecture	714

Beaches (continued)
physical geography | 910.021 46
recreational resources | 333.784
resource economics | 333.917
sanitation services | 363.729 2
see also Sanitation
Beacons | 387.155
light
navigation aids | 623.894 4
transportation services | 387.155
Beaconsfield (Quebec) | T2—714 28
Beaconsfield (Tas.) | T2—946 5
Bead embroidery | 746.5
Beaded lizard | 597.959 5
Beadle County (S.D.) | T2—783 274
Beads | 391.7
customs | 391.7
handicrafts | 745.582
home sewing | 646.19
Beagle | 636.753 7
Beak | 591.44
descriptive zoology | 591.44
physiology | 573.355
Beak rushes | 584.94
Beaked reptiles | 597.945
Beaked whales | 599.545
Beam bridges
construction | 624.21
Beam warfare | 358.39
Beams (Light) | 535.5
Beams (Structural elements) | 624.177 23
naval architecture | 623.817 723
structural engineering | 624.177 23
concrete | 624.183 423
Beans | 641.356 5
botany | 583.63
commercial processing | 664.805 65
cooking | 641.656 5
field crop | 633.3
food | 641.356 5
garden crop | 635.65
Bear Lake County (Idaho) | T2—796 44
Beard | 646.724
care | 646.724
customs | 391.5
Beard fishes | 597.62
Bearded pig | 599.633 2
Bearded seal | 599.796
Beardworms | 592.3
Bearing walls | 721.2
architecture | 721.2
construction | 690.12
interior decoration | 747.3

Bearings | 621.822
clockwork | 681.112
machine engineering | 621.822
railroad engineering | 625.21
Béarn (France) | T2—447 16
Bears | 599.78
animal husbandry | 636.978
big game hunting | 799.277 8
conservation technology | 639.979 78
predator control technology | 636.083 9
conservation technology | 639.966
resource economics | 333.959 78
zoology | 599.78
Bearsden and Milngavie
(Scotland) | T2—414 36
Beasts of burden | 636.088 2
Beatification of saints | 235.24
Beating metals
decorative arts | 739.14
sculpture | 731.41
Beatitudes | 226.93
Christian moral theology | 241.53
Beatrix, Queen of the
Netherlands
Dutch history | 949.207 3
Beauce (Quebec) | T2—714 71
Beauce-Sartigan (Quebec) | T2—714 714
Beaufort County (N.C.) | T2—756 186
Beaufort County (S.C.) | T2—757 99
Beaufort Sea | 551.461 327
| T2—163 27
Beaufort West (South
Africa : District) | T2—687 39
Beauharnois-Salaberry
(Quebec) | T2—714 32
Beauregard Parish (La.) | T2—763 59
Beauticians | 646.720 92
Beauty | 111.85
personal
arts | 700.453
| T3C—353
literature | 808.803 53
history and criticism | 809.933 53
specific literatures | T3B—080 353
history and
criticism | T3B—093 53
philosophy | 111.85
Beauty contests | 791.66
Beauty pageants | 791.66
Beauty shops | 646.72
arts | T3C—356 4
literature | 808.803 564
history and criticism | 809.933 564
personal care | 646.72

Beauty shops (continued)		Bedsores	
sanitation services	363.729 9	medicine	616.545
see also Sanitation		*see also* Skin diseases —	
Beaver County (Okla.)	T2—766 14	humans	
Beaver County (Pa.)	T2—748 92	Bedspreads	645.4
Beaver County (Utah)	T2—792 46	arts	746.97
Beaverhead County (Mont.)	T2—786 69	home sewing	646.21
Beavers	599.37	household equipment	645.4
conservation technology	639.979 37	Bedwetting	
resource economics	333.959 37	medicine	616.849
trapping	639.113 7	*see also* Nervous system	
Beavers (Boy Scouts)	369.434	diseases — humans	
Bebop	781.655	pediatrics	618.928 49
Bécancour (Quebec :		Bee balms	583.96
Regional County		Bee County (Tex.)	T2—764 117
Municipality)	T2—714 55	Bee eaters	598.78
Béchar (Algeria : Province)	T2—657	Bee flies	595.773
Bechuanaland	968.830 2	Bee keeping	638.1
	T2—688 3	Bee lice	595.774
Becker County (Minn.)	T2—776 84	Bee products	638.16
Beckham County (Okla.)	T2—766 43	Bee venom	
Becoming		human toxicology	615.942
philosophy	116	Beeches	
Bed and breakfast		botany	583.65
accommodations	910.464	forestry	634.972 5
see also Lodging (Temporary		lumber	674.142
housing)		Beechworth (Vic.)	T2—945 5
Bedbugs	595.754	Beef	641.362
Bedclothes	645.4	commercial processing	
arts	746.97	economics	338.476 649 2
commercial technology	684.3	technology	664.92
home sewing	646.21	cooking	641.662
household equipment	645.4	food	641.362
Bedding (Bedclothes)	645.4	Beef cattle	
see also Bedclothes		agricultural economics	338.176 213
Bedford (England :		animal husbandry	636.213
Borough)	T2—425 61	Beefwoods	583.43
Bedford (South Africa :		Beefwoods (Casuarinaceae)	583.65
District)	T2—687 54	Beekeepers	638.109 2
Bedford (Va.)	T2—755 676	Beer	641.23
Bedford County (Pa.)	T2—748 71	commercial processing	663.42
Bedford County (Tenn.)	T2—768 583	cooking with	641.623
Bedford County (Va.)	T2—755 675	home preparation	641.873
Bedfordshire (England)	T2—425 6	Bees	595.799
Bédié, Henri Konan		agriculture	638.1
Ivorian history	966.680 52	Beeswax	
Bedouins	T5—927 2	apiculture processing	638.17
Bedrooms	643.53	Beet sugar	641.336 3
home economics	643.53	commercial processing	664.123
interior decoration	747.77	food	641.336 3
Beds (Furniture)	645.4	*see also* Sugar	
manufacturing technology	684.15		
see also Furniture			

Beet syrup	641.336 3
commercial processing	664.123
food	641.336 3
see also Sugar	
Beetles	595.76
agricultural pests	632.76
culture	638.576
paleozoology	565.76
Beetling textiles	677.028 25
Beets	641.351 1
botany	583.883
commercial processing	664.805 11
cooking	641.651 1
food	641.351 1
garden crop	635.11
sugar crop	633.63
Bega (N.S.W.)	T2—944 7
Beggar's lice	583.74
Beggar's lice (Fabaceae)	583.63
Begheli literature	891.492
Beginner cooking	641.512
Begoniaceae	583.66
Begoniales	583.66
Begonias	635.933 66
botany	583.66
floriculture	635.933 66
Behavior	
animals	591.5
comparative psychology	156
educational psychology	370.15
evolutionary psychology	155.7
general psychology	150
plants	575.9
social psychology	302
Behavior genetics	
psychology	155.7
Behavior modification	153.85
educational psychology	370.152 8
home child care	649.64
teaching methods	371.393
Behavior modification therapy	
psychiatry	616.891 42
Behavior therapy	
psychiatry	616.891 42
Behavioral adaptation	
animals	591.5
Behavioral pharmacology	615.78
Behavioral sciences	300
psychology	150
public administrative support	352.745
Behaviorism	150.194 3
Beijing (China)	T2—511 56
Beijing dialect	495.1
	T6—951 1

Being	111
Beira (Portugal : Province)	T2—469 3
Beira (Portugal : Region)	T2—469 3
Beira Alta (Portugal)	T2—469 31
Beira Baixa (Portugal)	T2—469 33
Beira Litoral (Portugal)	T2—469 35
Beirut (Lebanon)	T2—569 25
Beja (African people)	T5—935
Beja (Portugal : District)	T2—469 55
Beja language	493.5
	T6—935
Bejaïa (Algeria : Province)	T2—655
Békés Megye (Hungary)	T2—439 9
Bekhorot	296.123 5
Babylonian Talmud	296.125 5
Mishnah	296.123 5
Bekhterev, Vladimir	
Mikhailovich	
psychological system	150.194 4
Bektashi (Alevi-Bektashi sect)	297.825 2
Bektashi (Sufi order)	297.48
Bel and the Dragon (Bible)	229.6
Bela-Bela (South Africa :	
District)	T2—682 53
Belarus	947.8
	T2—478
Belarusian language	491.799
	T6—917 99
Belarusian literature	891.799
Belarusians	T5—917 99
Belau	996.6
	T2—966
Belfast (Northern Ireland)	941.67
	T2—416 7
Belfast (South Africa :	
District)	T2—682 76
Belfort (France : Territory)	T2—444 55
Belgian Congo	967.510 24
	T2—675 1
Belgian draft horse	636.15
Belgian hare	636.932 2
Belgian literature	
Flemish	839.31
French	840
Belgian malinois	636.737
Belgian tervuren	636.737
Belgians	T5—393 2
Belgica	T2—369 3
Belgium	949.3
	T2—493
ancient	936.93
	T2—369 3
Belgorod (Russia : Oblast)	T2—473 5

Belgorodskaĩa oblast′ (Russia)	T2—473 5
Belgrade (Serbia)	T2—497 1
Belief	
epistemology	121.6
Belief and doubt	
epistemology	121.6
Belief revision	
computer science	006.333
Belief systems	
social control	303.372
Belitung (Indonesia)	T2—598 196
Belize	972.82
	T2—728 2
Belize District (Belize)	T2—728 22
Belizeans	T5—969 728 2
Belknap County (N.H.)	T2—742 45
Bell County (Ky.)	T2—769 123
Bell County (Tex.)	T2—764 287
Bell-jar gardening	
floriculture	635.985
Bell magpies	598.8
Bell peppers	641.356 43
see also Sweet peppers	
Bell towers	
architecture	725.97
Bella Coola (B.C.)	T2—711 1
Bella Coola River (B.C.)	T2—711 1
Belladonna	
botany	583.959 3
human toxicology	615.952 395 93
pharmacology	615.323 959 3
Bellechasse (Quebec : Regional County Municipality)	T2—714 733
Bellenden Ker National Park (Qld.)	T2—943 6
Belles-lettres	800
history and criticism	809
specific literatures	T3B—09
see Manual at 800	
Bellflowers	635.933 983
botany	583.983
floriculture	635.933 983
Belligerency	341.62
Belligerent countries	T2—171 82
Bellingshausen Sea	551.461 74
	T2—167 4
Bellinzona (Switzerland)	T2—494 784 4
Bellinzona (Switzerland : Distretto)	T2—494 784

Bells	786.884 8
instrument	786.884 819
music	786.884 8
see also Percussion instruments	
Belluno (Italy : Province)	T2—453 7
ancient	T2—373 68
Bellville (South Africa : District)	T2—687 35
Belly dancing	793.3
Belmont County (Ohio)	T2—771 93
Beloit (Wis.)	T2—775 87
Belorussia	947.8
	T2—478
Belorussian language	491.799
	T6—917 99
Belorussian literature	891.799
Belorussians	T5—917 99
Belt buckles	391.7
customs	391.7
making	739.278
costume jewelry	688.2
handicrafts	745.594 2
fine jewelry	739.278
Belt conveyors	621.867 5
Beltrami County (Minn.)	T2—776 82
Belts (Clothing)	391.44
commercial technology	687.19
leather	685.22
see also Accessories (Clothing)	
Belts (Power transmission devices)	621.852
Beltways	388.122
see also Roads	
Beluga	599.542
Bemba (African people)	T5—963 915
Bemba kingdoms (Zambian history)	968.940 1
Bemba language	496.391 5
	T6—963 915
Bemba literature	896.391 5
Bembe language (Lake Tanganyika)	496.394
	T6—963 94
Ben Hill County (Ga.)	T2—758 852
Ben Lomond National Park (Tas.)	T2—946 4
Ben M'sik-Sidi Othmane (Morocco : Prefecture)	T2—643 8
Ben Slimane (Morocco : Province)	T2—643 9
Bến Tre (Vietnam : Province)	T2—597 8
Bena-Kinga languages	496.391
	T6—963 91

Benalla (Vic.)	T2—945 5	Benewah County (Idaho)	T2—796 93
Bench marks	526.32	Benga language	496.396
Bench-scale plants			T6—963 96
chemical engineering	660.280 71	Bengal (India)	T2—541 4
Bendel State (Nigeria)	T2—669 3	Bengal, Bay of	551.461 564
Bendel states (Nigeria)	T2—669 3		T2—165 64
Bendigo (Vic.)	T2—945 4	Bengal cat	636.822
Bending metals		Bengali	305.891 44
decorative arts	739.14		T5—914 4
sculpture	731.41	Bengali-Assamese languages	491.44
Bending tools	621.982		T6—914 4
Bendjedid, Chadli		Bengali language	491.44
Algerian history	965.053		T6—914 4
Bends		Bengali literature	891.44
medicine	616.989 4	Benghazi (Libya)	T2—612
see also Environmental		Bengkulu (Indonesia)	959.817
diseases — humans			T2—598 17
Benedictines	255.1	Bengo (Angola : Province)	T2—673 2
church history	271.1	Benguela (Angola :	
women	255.97	Province)	T2—673 4
church history	271.97	Benguet (Philippines :	
Benedictions	203.8	Province)	T2—599 132
Christianity	264.13	Beni (Bolivia)	T2—844 2
Judaism	296.45	Béni Mellal (Morocco :	
Benedictus	264.36	Province)	T2—644
music	782.323 2	Benign neoplasms	
Beneficial animals	591.63	incidence	614.599 9
Beneficial microorganisms	579.163	medicine	616.993
Beneficial organisms	578.63	Benign tumors	
Beneficial plants	581.63	incidence	614.599 9
Beneficiation (Ore dressing)	622.7	medicine	616.993
Benefit cost analysis	658.155 4	Benin	966.83
public administration	352.43		T2—668 3
Benefit societies	334.7	Benin (Kingdom)	966.930 1
economics	334.7		T2—669 3
insurance	368.3	Benin (Nigeria)	T2—669 3
see also Insurance		Benin City (Nigeria)	T2—669 32
Benefits (Insurance)	368.014	Beninese	T5—966 83
Benelux countries	949.2	Benishangul-Gumuz kelel	
	T2—492	(Ethiopia)	T2—633
Benesh choreology	792.82	Bennett, R. B. (Richard Bedford)	
Benevento (Italy)		Canadian history	971.062 3
ancient	T2—377 32	Bennett, Richard Bedford	
Benevento (Italy : Province)	T2—457 23	Bennett, 1st Viscount	
ancient	T2—377 32	Canadian history	971.062 3
Beneventum (Italy)	T2—377 32	Bennett County (S.D.)	T2—783 65
Benevolence		Bennettitales	561.592
ethics	177.7	Bennington County (Vt.)	T2—743 8
Benevolent and Protective Order		Benoni (South Africa :	
of Elks	366.5	District)	T2—682 25
Benevolent societies	334.7	Bensalah, Abdelkader	
economics	334.7	Algerian history	965.055
insurance	368.3	Benson County (N.D.)	T2—784 39
see also Insurance		Bent County (Colo.)	T2—788 97

Bermuda	972.99
	T2—729 9
Bermuda Islands	972.99
	T2—729 9
Bermuda Triangle	001.94
Bermudians	T5—969 729 9
Bern (Switzerland)	T2—494 542 4
Bern (Switzerland : Canton)	T2—494 54
Bernalillo County (N.M.)	T2—789 61
Berne (Switzerland)	T2—494 542 4
Berner Alpen (Switzerland)	T2—494 541
Berner Jura (Switzerland)	T2—494 547
Berner-Mitteland	
(Switzerland)	T2—494 542
Berner Oberland	
(Switzerland)	T2—494 541
Bernese Alps	T2—494 541
Bernese mountain dog	636.73
Bernier and Dorre Islands	
National Park (W.A.)	T2—941 3
Bernina (Switzerland)	T2—494 732 9
Berri (S. Aust.)	T2—942 33
Berrien County (Ga.)	T2—758 862
Berrien County (Mich.)	T2—774 11
Berries	581.464
commercial processing	664.804 7
cooking	641.647
descriptive botany	581.464
food	641.347
horticulture	634.7
physiology	575.67
Berry (France)	T2—445 5
Berry Islands (Bahamas)	T2—729 6
Berta language	496.57
	T6—965 7
Berthing structures	
engineering	627.32
Bertie County (N.C.)	T2—756 163
Berwickshire (Scotland)	T2—413 7
Beryciformes	597.64
Beryl	
mineralogy	549.64
Beryllium	669.724
chemical engineering	661.039 1
chemistry	546.391
economic geology	553.492 3
human toxicology	615.925 391
materials science	620.189 4
metallography	669.957 24
metallurgy	669.724
metalworking	673.724
mining	622.349 23
physical metallurgy	669.967 24
see also Chemicals; Metals	

Besançon (France)	T2—444 66
Bessarabia (Moldova and	
Ukraine)	T2—476
Bessel function	515.53
Bessemer steel	669.142 3
Best books	
bibliographies	011.73
Beta decay	539.752 3
Beta functions	515.52
Beta Israel	T5—924
Beta particles	539.721 12
Beta radiation	
biophysics	571.459
humans	612.014 486
Betatron-synchrotrons	539.735
Betatrons	539.734
Bété language	496.33
	T6—963 3
Bethal (South Africa :	
District)	T2—682 78
Bethlehem (South Africa :	
District)	T2—685 1
Bethulie (South Africa :	
District)	T2—685 7
Betrothal	392.4
see also Engagement	
(Betrothal)	
Betsimisaraka (Kingdom)	969.101
	T2—691
Betta (Fighting fish)	597.7
culture	639.377
Better business bureaus	381.347
Betting	306.482
see also Gambling	
Betting systems	795.01
Betulaceae	583.65
Betulales	583.65
Bevel gears	621.833 2
Beverage containers	
disposal	363.728 8
see also Waste control	
Beverage technologists	663.092
Beverage technology	663
equipment manufacturing	
technology	681.766 4
Beverages	641.2
commercial processing	663
cooking with	641.62
customs	394.12
health	613.2
home economics	641.2
home preparation	641.87

Bicol (Philippines : Region)	T2—599 18
Biculturalism	
sociolinguistics	306.446
sociology	305.8
Bicycle accidents	363.125 9
see also Highway safety	
Bicycle motocross	796.622
Bicycle paths	388.12
area planning	711.72
engineering	625.7
transportation services	388.12
urban	388.411
Bicycle racing	796.62
mountain	796.63
see also Cycling — sports	
Bicycle theft	364.162 862 922 72
law	345.026 286 292 272
Bicycle touring	910
Bicycle troops (Armed forces)	357.52
Bicycles	388.347 2
engineering	629.227 2
law	343.094 4
repair	629.287 72
riding	629.284 72
sports	796.6
theft of	364.162 862 922 72
law	345.026 286 292 272
transportation services	388.347 2
Bicycling	388.347 2
sports	796.6
see also Cycling — sports	
transportation services	388.347 2
Bidding	
games	
contract bridge	795.415 2
Biden, Joseph R., Jr.	973.934 092
United States history	973.934
Bié (Angola : Province)	T2—673 4
Biel (Switzerland :	
Verwaltungskreis)	T2—494 545 7
Bielefeld (Germany)	T2—435 655
Biella (Italy : Province)	T2—451 76
ancient	T2—372 236
Bielorussian language	491.799
	T6—917 99
Bielorussian literature	891.799
Bielsko (Poland :	
Voivodeship)	T2—438 58
Bienne (Switzerland :	
District)	T2—494 545 7
Biennials (Plants)	582.12
floriculture	635.931 4
Bienville Parish (La.)	T2—763 93
Bifidobacterium	579.373

Biflagellate molds	579.54
Bifurcation theory	515.392
Big air snowboarding	796.939
see also Winter sports	
Big bands	784.48
Big bang theory (Cosmogony)	523.18
Big Bend National Park	
(Tex.)	T2—764 932
Big Bend Region (Tex.)	T2—764 93
Big Black River (Miss.)	T2—762 4
Big brown bats	599.47
Big business	338.644
economics	338.644
management	658.023
personnel management	658.303
Big cats	599.755
Big Cypress Swamp (Fla.)	T2—759 44
Big game animals	599.6
conservation technology	639.979 6
resource economics	333.959 6
Big game fishes	597.7
Big game hunting	799.26
Big Horn County (Mont.)	T2—786 38
Big Horn County (Wyo.)	T2—787 33
Big Horn Mountains (Wyo.)	T2—787 3
Big Sandy River (Ky. and	
W. Va.)	T2—754 47
Kentucky	T2—769 2
West Virginia	T2—754 47
Big Sioux River (S.D. and	
Iowa)	T2—783 39
Iowa	T2—777 1
South Dakota	T2—783 39
Big Stone County (Minn.)	T2—776 432
Bigamy	364.183
law	345.028 3
Bigfoot	001.944
Bighead carp	597.482
Bighorn sheep	599.649 7
big game hunting	799.276 497
conservation technology	639.979 649 7
resource economics	333.959 649 7
Bignoniaceae	583.96
Bihar (India)	T2—541 23
Bihari	T5—914 54
Bihari language	491.454
	T6—914 54
Bihari literature	891.454
Bihor (Romania)	T2—498 4
Bikeways	388.12
see also Bicycle paths	
Bikini Atoll (Marshall	
Islands)	T2—968 3

Bình Dương (Vietnam :
  Province)   T2—597 7
Bình Phước (Vietnam :
  Province)   T2—597 7
Bình Thuận (Vietnam :
  Province)   T2—597 5
Bini (African people)   T5—963 3
Bini language   496.33
                     T6—963 3
Binocular-vision photography   778.4
Binoculars
  manufacturing technology   681.412 5
Binomial distribution   519.24
Binomial equations   512.942 2
  algebra   512.942 2
  calculus   515.252
Binuclear family   306.89
Bio, Julius Maada
  Sierra Leonean history   966.405 2
Bío Bío (Chile : Province)   T2—834 3
Bío Bío (Chile : Region)   T2—834 1
Bioactive proteins   572.69
Bioastronautics   571.499
  humans   612.014 5
Biobibliographies   012
  see Manual at 012 vs. 016,
    001–999
Biobío (Chile)   T2—834 1
Biochemical computing   006.384 2
Biochemical engineering   660.63
Biochemical evolution   572.38
Biochemical genetics   572.8
  humans   611.018 16
  see Manual at 576.5 vs. 572.8
Biochemical interactions   572.43
Biochemical reactions   572.43
Biochemicals   572
  organic chemistry   547
Biochemistry   572
  ecology   577.14
  humans   612.015
  origin of life   576.83
Bioclimatology   577.22
Biocomputing   006.384 2
Biodegradation
  materials science   620.112 23
Biodiesel fuel   665.37
  animal fats and oils   665.2
Biodiversity   333.95
  biology   578.7
  conservation   333.951 6
  ecology   577

Biodiversity (continued)
  resource economics   333.95
  see Manual at 333.7–.9 vs.
    363.1, 363.73, 577
Biodynamics   571.43
  humans   612.014 41
Bioelectricity   572.437
  electric organs   573.97
  humans   612.014 27
Bioelectrochemistry   572.437
Bioenergetics   572.43
  ecology   577.13
  humans   612.014 21
Bioethics   174.2
  religion   205.642
    Christianity   241.642
Biofeedback   152.188
  therapeutic use   615.851 4
Biofeedback therapy
  medicine   615.851 4
Biofeedback training
  therapeutic use   615.851 4
Biogas
  technology   665.776
Biogenesis   576.83
Biogeochemical cycles   577.14
Biogeochemical prospecting   622.12
Biogeochemistry   577.14
Biogeography   578.09
  animals   591.9
  plants   581.9
Biographers   920
Biographical dictionaries   T1—092 2
Biographical fiction   808.838 2
  history and criticism   809.382
  specific literatures   T3B—308 2
    individual authors   T3A—3
Biography   920
                     T1—092
  arts   700.45
                     T3C—35
  literary form   809.935 92
    specific literatures   T3B—094 92
  literature   808.803 5
    history and criticism   809.933 5
    specific literatures   T3B—080 35
      history and
        criticism   T3B—093 5
  see Manual at T1—092;
    also at 913–919; *also at*
    930–990
Bioinorganic chemistry   572.51
  humans   612.015 24
Bioko (Equatorial Guinea)   T2—671 86

Biosociology	304.5
biological ecology	577.8
sociology	304.5
see Manual at 302–307 vs. 156	
Biosolids	363.728 493
sanitary engineering	628.38
social services	363.728 493
use as fertilizer	631.869
Biospeleology	578.758 4
Biosphere	
resource economics	333.95
Biostatistics	570.151 95
Biosynthesis	572.45
humans	612.015 4
see also Metabolism	
Biotechnologists	660.609 2
Biotechnology	660.6
food technology	664.024
law	343.078 660 6
Bioterrorism	363.325 3
see also Terrorism	
Biotic communities	577.82
Bipolar disorder	
medicine	616.895
see also Mental disorders	
Bipolar memory	004.53
engineering	621.397 32
Bipolar transistors	621.381 528
Bira (African people)	T5—963 94
Bira-Huku languages	496.394
	T6—963 94
Biracial people	T5—05
Birational transformations	
algebraic geometry	516.35
Birches	583.65
botany	583.65
forestry	634.972 6
Bird attracting	639.978
zoology	598.072 34
Bird dogs	636.752
Bird hunting	799.24
Bird lice	595.757
Bird watching	598.072 34
Birdbanding	598.072 32
Birdhouses	636.508 31
animal husbandry	636.508 31
architecture	728.927
construction	690.892 7
Birds	598
agricultural pests	632.68
air transportation hazard	363.124 12
animal husbandry	636.5
art representation	704.943 28
arts	T3C—362 8

Birds (continued)	
commercial hunting	639.12
communicable diseases	571.981 8
conservation technology	639.978
control technology	628.968
agriculture	632.68
disease carriers	571.986
medicine	614.434
drawing	743.68
migration (Animals)	598.156 8
paleozoology	568
resource economics	333.958
sports hunting	799.24
see also Hunting — sports	
zoology	598
Bird's-eye fabrics	677.615
Bird's Head Peninsula	
(Indonesia)	T2—951 2
Bird's-nest fungi	579.599
Birds' nests	598.156 4
Birds of paradise	598.865
Birds of prey	598.9
conservation technology	639.978 9
resource economics	333.958 9
Biremes	387.21
design	623.812 1
engineering	623.821
handling	623.882 1
transportation services	387.21
see also Ships	
Birmingham (Ala.)	T2—761 781
Birmingham (England)	942.496
	T2—424 96
Birs River (Switzerland)	T2—494 3
Birth	573.67
mammals	573.67
reproductive behavior	599.156
see also Childbirth	
Birth certificates	
public administration	353.59
Birth control	363.96
demographic effect	304.666
ethics	176.3
religion	205.663
Buddhism	294.356 63
Christianity	241.663
Hinduism	294.548 663
Islam	297.566 3
Judaism	296.366 3
gynecology	618.18
health	613.94
law	344.048
medicine	618.18
public administration	353.59

Birth control (continued)		Bisexual people	T1—086 63
school programs	371.714	psychology	155.343
social services	363.96	social welfare	362.896 3
social theology	201.7	Bisexuality	306.765
Christianity	261.836	ethics	176.4
Judaism	296.38	*see also* Sexual relations —	
Birth defects		ethics	
medicine	616.043	psychology	155.343
Birth intervals		Bisexuals	306.765
demography	304.63		T1—086 63
Birth of Jesus Christ	232.92	*see also* Bisexual people	
Birth order	306.87	Bishops (Chessmen)	794.145
environmental psychology	155.924	Bishops (Clergy)	270.092
family relationships	306.87	biography	270.092
Birth rites		specific denominations	280
religion	203.81	*see Manual at* 230–280	
Birthday books		ecclesiology	262.12
astrology	133.540 42	Bishops' thrones	247.1
Birthday parties		architecture	726.529 3
cooking	641.568	Biskra (Algeria : Province)	T2—655
Birthdays		Bislama language	427.995 95
customs	394.2		T6—217
fortune-telling	133.335 4	Bismarck (N.D.)	T2—784 77
Birthmarks		Bismarck, Otto, Fürst von	
capillary hemangiomas		German history	943.083
medicine	616.993 15	Bismarck Archipelago (Papua	
medicine	616.55	New Guinea)	995.8
Births			T2—958
demography	304.63	Bismarck Range (Papua	
Birthwort	584.284	New Guinea)	T2—956
Bisa-Lamba languages	496.391	Bismarck Sea	551.461 476
	T6—963 91		T2—164 76
Bisayan Islands		Bismuth	669.75
(Philippines)	T2—599 5	chemical engineering	661.071 8
Biscay (Spain)	T2—466 3	chemistry	546.718
Biscay, Bay of (France and		economic geology	553.47
Spain)	551.461 338	materials science	620.189 5
	T2—163 38	metallography	669.957 5
Biscayne Bay (Fla.)	551.461 348	metallurgy	669.75
	T2—163 48	mining	622.347
Biscayne National Park		physical metallurgy	669.967 5
(Fla.)	T2—163 48	*see also* Chemicals; Metals	
Biscuit mixes	664.753	Bison	599.643
Biscuits (Breads)	641.815 7	animal husbandry	636.292
commercial processing	664.752 3	commercial hunting	639.116 43
home preparation	641.815 7	conservation technology	639.979 643
Biscuits (Cookies)	641.865 4	resource economics	333.959 643
commercial processing	664.752 5	subsistence hunting	639.116 43
home preparation	641.865 4	zoology	599.643
Biscuits (Crackers)	641.815	Bissau (Guinea-Bissau)	T2—665 7
commercial processing	664.752	Bistriţa-Năsăud (Romania)	T2—498 4
home preparation	641.815	Bithynia	T2—393 13
		Biting lice	595.757

Bitlis İli (Turkey)	T2—566 72
ancient	T2—394 2
Bitterns	598.34
Bitterroot Range (Idaho and	
Mont.)	T2—786 8
Idaho	T2—796 7
Montana	T2—786 8
Bittersweet (Celastraceae)	583.67
Bittersweet (Solanaceae)	583.959 3
Bitumens	553.27
see also Asphalt	
Bituminous coal	553.24
properties	662.622 4
see also Coal	
Bituminous materials	553.2
building materials	691.96
economic geology	553.2
materials science	620.196
structural engineering	624.189 6
Bituminous pavements	625.85
Bituminous sands	553.283
see also Tar sands	
Bituminous shale	553.283
see also Oil shale	
Bivalvia	594.4
fishing and culture	639.4
paleozoology	564.4
resource economics	333.955 4
Bivouac	355.412
military training	355.544
Biwas	787.85
see also Stringed instruments	
Bixaceae	583.77
Biya, Paul	
Cameroonian history	967.110 42
Bizana (South Africa :	
District)	T2—687 59
Bizerte (Tunisia)	T2—611
Blaby (England : District)	T2—425 41
Black Africa	T2—67
Black Americans	973.049 607 3
	T5—960 73
see also African Americans	
Black and tan coonhound	636.753 6
Black-and-white television	621.388 02
Black art (Witchcraft)	133.4
Black authors (African origin)	
literature	808.898 96
history and criticism	809.889 6
specific literatures	T3B—080 896
history and criticism	T3B—098 96
Black basses	597.738 8
sports fishing	799.177 388

Black bear	599.785
big game hunting	799.277 85
conservation technology	639.979 785
resource economics	333.959 785
Black Belt (Ala.)	T2—761 4
Black Canyon of the	
Gunnison National Park	
(Colo.)	T2—788 19
Black Carib Indians	T5—979 2
Black Carib language	497.92
	T6—979 2
Black Country (England)	T2—424 9
Black Death	
European history	940.192
incidence	614.573 2
Italian history	945.05
medicine	616.923 2
see also Communicable	
diseases — humans	
Tuscan history	945.505
Black Down Hills (England)	T2—423 57
Black duck	598.413
Black-eyed peas	641.356 592
botany	583.63
commercial processing	664.805 659 2
cooking	641.656 592
field crop	633.33
food	641.356 592
garden crop	635.659 2
Black-eyed Susans	583.99
Black-eyed Susans (Asteraceae)	583.983
Black feminism	305.420 899 6
Black-footed ferret	599.766 29
conservation technology	639.979 766 29
resource economics	333.959 766 29
Black Forest (Germany)	T2—434 6
Black grouse	598.634
Black Hawk County (Iowa)	T2—777 37
Black Hawk War, 1832	973.56
Black Hebrew Israelites	296.836
Black Hebrews	296.836
Black Hills (S.D. and Wyo.)	T2—783 9
Black holes (Astronomy)	523.887 5
Black lead	553.26
see also Graphite	
Black lung disease	362.196 244
medicine	616.244
social services	362.196 244
workers' compensation law	344.021 8
see also Respiratory tract	
diseases — humans	
Black magic	133.4
Black mangrove	583.96
Black mass	133.422

Blankets	645.4
arts	746.97
home sewing	646.21
household equipment	645.4
manufacturing technology	677.626
Blantyre (Malawi)	T2—689 7
Blasphemy	
criminology	364.188
ethics	179.5
religion	205.695
Christianity	241.695
law	345.028 8
Blast-furnace gas	665.772
Blast-furnace practice	669.141 3
Blast injuries	
medicine	617.19
Blast-resistant construction	624.176
buildings	693.854
Blasting	624.152 6
excavation	624.152 6
mining	622.23
underwater engineering	627.74
Blastozoa	563.92
Blastulas	571.865
Blattaria	595.728
Blazers	391.473
commercial technology	687.113
customs	391.473
home sewing	646.433
see also Clothing	
Blazonry	929.6
Bleaching	
clothes and related materials	667.14
home economics	648.1
oils and gases	665.028 3
Bleckley County (Ga.)	T2—758 525
Bledsoe County (Tenn.)	T2—768 76
Bleeding hearts (Papaveraceae)	635.933 35
botany	583.35
floriculture	635.933 35
Bleeding hearts (Plants)	635.933 35
botany	583.35
floriculture	635.933 35
Blekinge län (Sweden)	T2—486 2
Blekinge landskap (Sweden)	T2—486 2
Blended families	306.874 7
Blended waxes	665.19
Blenders	
use in cooking	641.589 3
Blending oils and gases	665.028 3
Blending petroleum distillates	665.534
Blenio (Switzerland :	
Distretto)	T2—494 782
Blennies	597.77

Blennioidei	597.77
Blessings	203.8
Christianity	264.13
Judaism	296.45
Blida (Algeria : Province)	T2—653
Blighted areas	
area planning	711.5
Blimps (Airships)	387.732 7
engineering	629.133 27
military engineering	623.743 7
transportation services	387.732 7
see also Aircraft	
Blind-deaf people	305.908 1
	T1—087 1
see also Blind people	
Blind people	305.908 1
	T1—087 1
education	371.911
library services	027.663
provision of necessities	362.418 3
social group	305.908 1
social welfare	362.41
Blind play (Chess)	794.17
Blind snakes	597.969
Blind workers	331.591
Blindman's buff	793.4
Blindness	
incidence	614.599 7
ophthalmology	617.712
see also Eye diseases —	
humans	
social welfare	362.41
Blinds	645.3
architecture	721.82
construction	690.182
household management	645.3
manufacturing technology	684
Blini	641.815 3
Bliss Bibliographic Classification	025.434
Blister beetles	595.769
Blitz tactics	355.422
Blizzards	551.555
social services	363.349 25
Bloc québécois (Canadian	
political party)	324.271 098 4
Block books	092
Block diagramming	
software design	005.120 28
Block Island (R.I.)	T2—745 8
Block printing	761
textile arts	746.62

Blockades	355.44	Blood coagulation	573.159
Civil War (United States)	973.75	human physiology	612.115
law of nations	341.584	physiology	573.159
law of war	341.63	*see also* Cardiovascular system	
military operations	355.44	Blood coagulation disorders	
World War I	940.452	medicine	616.157
World War II	940.545 2	*see also* Cardiovascular	
see also Naval operations		diseases — humans	
Blockbusters (Ammunition)	355.825 17	Blood diseases	573.153 9
engineering	623.451 7	humans	
military equipment	355.825 17	cancer	362.196 994 18
Blocking		incidence	614.599 941 8
American football	796.332 26	medicine	616.994 18
Blocks (Musical instruments)	786.82	social services	362.196 994 18
see also Bars (Musical		*see also* Cancer —	
instruments)		humans	
Bloemfontein (South		medicine	616.15
Africa)	T2—685 4	pharmacokinetics	615.718
Bloemfontein (South		*see also* Cardiovascular	
Africa : District)	T2—685 4	diseases	
Bloemhof (South Africa :		Blood-forming system	573.155
District)	T2—682 46	*see also* Hematopoietic system	
Blogs	006.752	Blood-forming system diseases	573.155 39
communications services	384.38	*see also* Hematopoietic system	
instructional use	371.334 675 2	diseases	
publishing	070.579 734	Blood groups	573.154
sociology	302.231 4	human physiology	612.118 25
Blood	573.15	physiology	573.154
animals	573.15	*see also* Cardiovascular system	
histology	573.153 5	Blood lipids	
human biophysics	612.118 1	human physiology	612.12
human histology	612.11	Blood plasma	573.156
human physiology	612.11	biology	573.156
biological markers	612.118 2	human histology	612.116
medicine	616.15	human physiology	612.116
physiology	573.15	pharmacology	615.39
see also Cardiovascular system		*see also* Cardiovascular system	
Blood analysis		Blood plasma banks	362.178 4
criminal investigation	363.256 2	*see also* Health services	
diagnosis		Blood plasma substitutes	615.399
general disease	616.075 61	Blood platelet disorders	
Blood banks	362.178 4	medicine	616.157
law	344.041 94	*see also* Cardiovascular	
see also Health services		diseases — humans	
Blood-brain barrier	573.862 1	Blood platelets	573.159
Blood cells	573.153 6	histology	573.159
human histology	612.11	human histology	612.117
see also Cardiovascular system		human physiology	612.117
Blood chemistry	573.154	medicine	616.157
human physiology	612.12	physiology	573.159
physiology	573.154	*see also* Cardiovascular system	
Blood cholesterol			
human physiology	612.12		

Blood pressure	573.134 3
human physiology	612.14
physiology	573.134 3
see also Cardiovascular system	
Blood River (South Africa)	T2—684 1
Blood River, Battle of, 1838	968.404 2
Blood substitutes	615.399
Blood sugar	
human physiology	612.12
Blood transfusion	362.178 4
law	344.041 94
pharmacology	615.39
social services	362.178 4
Blood types	573.154
human physiology	612.118 25
physiology	573.154
see also Cardiovascular system	
Blood vessel diseases	
medicine	616.13
see also Cardiovascular	
diseases — humans	
Blood vessels	573.18
animals	573.18
human anatomy	611.13
human physiology	612.13
medicine	616.13
physiology	573.18
pregnancy complications	
obstetrics	618.361 3
surgery	617.413
see also Cardiovascular system	
Bloodhound	636.753 6
Bloodroot	583.35
Bloodsucking animals	591.53
Bloodworts (Haemodoraceae)	584.86
Blotting paper	676.284 4
Blount County (Ala.)	T2—761 72
Blount County (Tenn.)	T2—768 885
Blouses	391.475
commercial technology	687.115
customs	391.475
home economics	646.3
home sewing	646.435
see also Clothing	
Blowers	621.61
Blowflies	595.774
Blowing glass	666.122
decorative arts	748.202 82
Blown tableware	
decorative arts	748.2
Blowpipes (Chemical apparatus)	542.4
Blowpipes (Weapons)	
sports	799.202 82
Blue and white transfer ware	738.27

Blue catfish	597.492
Blue collar workers	331.79
	T1—086 23
labor economics	331.79
labor force	331.119 042
labor market	331.129 042
labor unions	331.88
personnel management	658.304 4
training	658.312 45
public administration	354.93
social class	305.562
see also Working class	
Blue Earth County (Minn.)	T2—776 21
Blue goose	598.417 5
Blue-green algae	579.39
Blue monkeys	599.862
Blue Mountains (N.S.W.)	994.45
	T2—944 5
Blue Mountains (Or. and Wash.)	T2—795 7
Oregon	T2—795 7
Washington	T2—797 46
Blue Mountains National Park (N.S.W.)	T2—944 5
Blue Nile (Sudan)	T2—626 4
Blue Nile River (Ethiopia and Sudan)	T2—626 4
Blue Ridge Mountains	T2—755
Georgia	T2—758 2
North Carolina	T2—756 8
South Carolina	T2—757 2
Virginia	T2—755
Blue shark	597.34
Blue whale	599.524 8
Blue-winged teal	598.413
Bluebells (Asparagaceae)	635.934 79
botany	584.79
floriculture	635.934 79
Bluebells (Boraginaceae)	635.933 958
botany	583.958
floriculture	635.933 958
Bluebells (Campanulaceae)	635.933 983
botany	583.983
floriculture	635.933 983
Blueberries	641.347 37
botany	583.93
commercial processing	664.804 737
cooking	641.647 37
food	641.347 37
horticulture	634.737
Bluebirds	598.842
Bluebonnet	583.63
botany	583.63
floriculture	635.933 63

Body and soul	128.1
religion	202.2
Christianity	233.5
Judaism	296.32
philosophy of religion	218
Body art	709.040 752
Body contours	613.71
arts	T3C—356 1
customs	391.62
health	613.71
literature	808.803 561
history and criticism	809.933 561
specific literatures	T3B—080 356 1
history and criticism	T3B—093 561
sociology	306.461 3
Body covering (Animals)	573.5
descriptive zoology	591.47
physiology	573.5
Body fluid disorders	
medicine	616.399 2
see also Digestive system diseases — humans	
Body heat	
humans	612.014 26
Body image	306.461 3
Body language	302.222
psychology	153.69
social psychology	302.222
Body measurements	
humans	599.94
Body mechanics	
human physiology	612.76
Body piercing	
customs	391.7
Body shape	613.71
see also Body contours	
Body size	591.41
Body temperature	571.76
humans	612.014 26
Body weight	591.41
Bodybuilding	613.713
physical fitness	613.713
sports	796.41
Bodyguards	363.289
Bodywork	629.260 288
Boeotia (Greece)	T2—495 15
ancient	938.4
	T2—384
Boer War, 1880–1881	968.204 6
Boer War, 1899–1902	968.048
Bog mosses	588.29
Bog myrtle (Menyanthaceae)	583.983
Bog myrtle (Myricaceae)	583.65

Bog of Allen (Ireland)	T2—418 5
Bog turtle	597.925 7
Bogotá (Colombia)	T2—861 48
Bogs	
biology	578.768 7
ecology	577.687
Bogus wrapping paper	676.287
Bohemia (Czech Republic)	T2—437 1
Bohemia (Kingdom)	943.710 2
	T2—437 1
Bohemia and Moravia (Protectorate)	943.703 3
	T2—437
Bohemian Forest	T2—437 14
Czech Republic	T2—437 14
Germany	T2—433 5
Böhm-Bawerk, Eugen von	
economic school	330.157
Bohol (Philippines)	T2—599 556
Bohrium	
chemistry	546.54
Bohuslän landskap (Sweden)	T2—486 7
Boidae	597.967
Boiler and machinery insurance	368.7
see also Insurance	
Boiler-house practice	621.194
Boiler insurance	368.7
see also Insurance	
Boiler operations	621.194
Boilers	
heating buildings	697.07
steam	697.507
ship power plants	623.873
steam engineering	621.183
Boiling	
home cooking	641.73
Boiling points	536.44
Boils	
medicine	616.523
see also Skin diseases — humans	
Boina (Kingdom)	969.101
	T2—691
Boinae	597.967
Bois-Francs Region (Quebec)	T2—714 565
Boise (Idaho)	T2—796 28
Boise County (Idaho)	T2—796 74
Bojador (Morocco : Province)	T2—648
Bojanala Platinum District Municipality (South Africa)	T2—682 41

Bojutsu	796.855	Bolu İli (Turkey)	T2—563 4
Bok choy	641.353	ancient	T2—393 15
cooking	641.653	Boluarte, Dina	
food	641.353	Peruvian history	985.064 9
garden crop	635.3	Bolyai geometry	516.9
Bokkeveld Range (South		Bolzano (Italy : Province)	T2—453 83
Africa)	T2—687 17	ancient	T2—373 73
Bokmål language	439.82	Bomb disposal units	
	T6—398 2	armed forces	358.23
Bokmål literature	839.82	Bombacaceae	583.775
Boksburg (South Africa :		Bombacoideae	583.775
District)	T2—682 25	Bombala (N.S.W.)	T2—944 7
Boland (South Africa)	T2—687 33	Bombardment	
Bolaños Geyer, Enrique		military science	355.4
Nicaraguan history	972.850 543	particle physics	539.73
Bolas		solid-state physics	530.416
sports	799.202 82	Bombay (India)	T2—547 92
Boletaceae	579.6	Bombers	358.428 3
Boletes	579.6	engineering	623.746 3
Bolívar (Colombia : Dept.)	T2—861 14	military equipment	358.428 3
Bolívar (Ecuador :		Bombing (Terrorism)	363.325
Province)	T2—866 16	see also Terrorism	
Bolívar (Venezuela : State)	T2—876 3	Bombing forces	358.42
Bolívar, Simón		Bombs	355.825 1
South American history	980.02	military engineering	623.451
Bolivar County (Miss.)	T2—762 43	military equipment	355.825 1
Bolivia	984	Bombsights	623.46
	T2—84	Bombycillidae	598.852
Bolivia (Game)	795.418	Bombycoidea	595.78
Bolivian literature	860	Bombyliidae	595.773
Bolivians	T5—688 4	Bomet County (Kenya)	T2—676 274 2
Boll weevil		Bon (Tibetan religion)	299.54
agricultural pest	633.519 768	Bon Homme County (S.D.)	T2—783 395
Bollinger County (Mo.)	T2—778 94	Bonaire	T2—729 86
Bollworm		Bonaparte River (B.C.)	T2—711 72
agricultural pest	633.519 78	Bonasa	598.635
Bolobedu (South Africa :		Bonaventure (Quebec :	
District)	T2—682 59	Regional County	
Bologna (Italy)	T2—454 11	Municipality)	T2—714 785
ancient	T2—372 611	Bond (Law)	345.056
Bologna (Italy : Città		Bond County (Ill.)	T2—773 873
metropolitana)	T2—454 1	Bond insurance	368.853
Bolshevik International	324.175	Bond paper	676.282 3
Bolshevik parties	324.217 5	Bonded fabrics	677.69
Bolsonaro, Jair		see also Textiles	
Brazilian history	981.067	Bonding metals	671.58
Bolsover (England :		Bonding of employees	
District)	T2—425 15	insurance	368.83
Bolton (England :		law	346.086 83
Metropolitan Borough)	T2—427 37	Bonds (Chemical forces)	541.224
Bolts	621.882	biochemistry	572.33
Bolts (Locks)	683.31	Bonds (Securities)	332.632 3
Boltzmann statistics	530.132	accounting	657.75
		corporate law	346.066 6

Bonds (Securities) (continued)	
financial management	658.152 24
capital procurement	658.152 24
debt management	658.152 6
income tax	336.242 6
law	343.052 46
investment economics	332.632 3
law	346.092 2
see Manual at 332.632044 vs.	
332.6323; *also at* 332.6322	
vs. 332.6323	
Bône (Algeria : Dept.)	T2—655
Bone cancer	
incidence	614.599 947 1
medicine	616.994 71
see also Cancer — humans	
Bone carving	736.6
Bone char	662.93
Bone diseases	
medicine	616.71
see also Musculoskeletal	
diseases — humans	
pharmacokinetics	615.771
Bone marrow	573.155 6
biology	573.155 6
diseases	573.155 639
see also Hematopoietic	
system diseases	
human anatomy	611.41
human physiology	612.416
medicine	616.41
surgery	617.441
Bone marrow cancer	
incidence	614.599 944 1
medicine	616.994 41
see also Cancer — humans	
Bone marrow diseases	
medicine	616.41
see also Hematopoietic	
system diseases —	
humans	
Bone meal	
use as fertilizer	631.85
Bone tissues	
human histology	612.751 045
Bones	573.76
anthropometry	599.947
biology	573.76
drawing	
animals	743.6
humans	743.46
fractures	
medicine	617.15
human anatomy	611.71

Bones (continued)	
human physiology	612.751
medicine	616.71
pharmacokinetics	615.771
surgery	617.471
Bongo (Mammal)	599.642 3
Bongo, Ali Ben	
Gabonese history	967.210 43
Bongo, Omar	
Gabonese history	967.210 42
Bongo-Bagirmi languages	496.566
	T6—965 66
Bongo language	496.566
	T6—965 66
Bongos	786.95
see also Percussion instruments	
Bonin Islands (Japan)	T2—528
Bonito	641.392
cooking	641.692
food	641.392
zoology	597.783
Bonn (Germany)	T2—435 518
Bonner County (Idaho)	T2—796 96
Bonnetiaceae	583.69
Bonnets	391.43
see also Headwear	
Bonneville County (Idaho)	T2—796 53
Bono (Kingdom)	966.701 6
	T2—667
Bononia (Italy)	T2—372 611
Bonsai	635.977 2
Bontebok National Park	
(South Africa)	T2—687 36
Bonuses	331.216 4
labor economics	331.216 4
personnel management	658.322 5
Bony fishes	597
see also Fishes	
Bony ganoids	597.41
Boobies	598.43
resource economics	333.958 43
Booby traps	623.451 4
Booidea	597.967
Book arts	
design	744.52
technology	686
Book catalogs	025.313
bibliography	017
library science	025.313
Book clubs	070.5
Book collecting	002.075
Book editors	070.510 92
Book illumination	741.647
Book illustration	741.64

Bordeaux (France)	T2—447 144
Borden, Robert Laird, Sir	
Canadian history	971.061 2
Borden County (Tex.)	T2—764 853
Border Country (Scotland)	T2—413 7
Border defense	355.45
Border disputes	
law of nations	341.42
Border patrols	363.285
Borderline personality disorder	
medicine	616.858 52
see also Mental disorders	
Borders (Floriculture)	635.963
Borders (Geography)	320.12
see also Boundaries	
Borders Region (Scotland)	T2—413 7
Bordism theory	514.72
Bordj Bou Arréridj	
(Algeria : Province)	T2—655
Boreal forests	
biology	578.737
ecology	577.37
Borers (Insects)	
agricultural pests	634.049 7
Boric, Gabriel	
Chilean history	983.066 8
Boring	
mining	622.24
Boring tools	621.952
Boris Fyodorovich Godunov,	
Czar of Russia	
Russian history	947.044
Bornean languages	499.225
	T6—992 25
Borneo	T2—598 3
Indonesia	T2—598 3
Malaysia	T2—595 3
Borneo languages	499.225
	T6—992 25
Bornholm (Denmark)	T2—489 2
Bornholms amt (Denmark)	T2—489 2
Borno State (Nigeria)	T2—669 85
Bornu (Kingdom)	966.980 1
	T2—669 8
Boron	553.6
chemical engineering	661.067 1
chemistry	546.671
economic geology	553.6
organic chemistry	547.056 71
applied	661.895
see also Chemicals	
Boron fuels	662.86

Borrelia infections	
incidence	614.574
medicine	616.924
see also Communicable	
diseases — humans	
Borrowing	332.041 5
capital management	658.152 24
public finance	336.34
see also Public debt	
Borrowing power (Legislative	
bodies)	328.341 2
Borsod-Abaúj-Zemplén	
Megye (Hungary)	T2—439 9
Borstals	365.42
see also Penal institutions	
Boryaceae	584.7
Borzoi	636.753 5
Bos	599.642 2
Boshof (South Africa :	
District)	T2—685 3
Bosnia and Herzegovina	949.742
	T2—497 42
ancient	939.874 2
	T2—398 742
Bosniaks	T5—918 39
Bosnian language	491.839
	T6—918 39
Bosnian literature	891.839
Bosnian Muslims	T5—918 39
Bosnians	T5—918 39
Bosons	539.721
Bosporus (Turkey)	551.461 389
	T2—163 89
Bosque County (Tex.)	T2—764 518
Bossier Parish (La.)	T2—763 97
Boston (England : Borough)	T2—425 37
Boston (Mass.)	T2—744 61
Boston ivy	635.933 79
botany	583.79
floriculture	635.933 79
Boston Massacre, 1770	973.311 3
Boston Mountains (Ark. and	
Okla.)	T2—767 1
Arkansas	T2—767 1
Oklahoma	T2—766 8
Boston Port Bill, 1774	973.311 6
Boston Tea Party, 1773	973.311 5
Boston terrier	636.72
Bostonnais (Quebec)	T2—714 459
Bostrychoidea	595.763
Botanical drugs	
pharmacology	615.321

Bourgogne-Franche-Comté (France)	T2—444
Bourguiba, Habib	
Tunisian history	961.105 1
Bourke (N.S.W.)	T2—944 9
Bournemouth (England)	T2—423 38
Bouteflika, Abdelaziz	
Algerian history	965.054
Bouterse, Desire Delano	
Surinamese history	988.303 25
Boutonneuse fever	
incidence	614.526 3
medicine	616.922 3
see also Communicable diseases — humans	
Boutonnieres	745.923
Bouvet Island	T2—971 3
Bouvier des Flandres	636.737
Bovidae	599.64
animal husbandry	636.2
paleozoology	569.64
Bovinae	599.642
Bovine spongiform encephalopathy	
humans	
medicine	616.83
see also Nervous system diseases — humans	
Bovines	599.64
animal husbandry	636.2
Bow harps	787.94
see also Stringed instruments	
Bow River (Alta.)	T2—712 33
Bowed stringed instruments	787
see also Stringed instruments	
Bowell, Mackenzie, Sir	
Canadian history	971.055
Bowen (Qld.)	T2—943 6
Bowen Island (B.C. : Island)	T2—711 33
Bowfins	597.41
Bowhead whale	599.527 6
Bowie County (Tex.)	T2—764 197
Bowing techniques	784.193 69
Bowl games (Football)	796.332 63
Bowland, Forest of (England)	T2—427 685
Bowlers	794.609 2
Bowling	
biography	794.609 2
Bowling (Cricket)	796.358 22
Bowling (Game)	794.6
equipment technology	688.746
Bowling alleys	794.6
architecture	725.84
Bowman County (N.D.)	T2—784 92
Bowron Lake Provincial Park (B.C.)	T2—711 75
Bows and arrows	799.202 85
art metalwork	739.73
manufacturing technology	688.792 028 5
military engineering	623.441 6
shooting game	799.215
biography	799.215 092
sports	799.202 85
target shooting	799.32
Box (Plants)	583.395
botany	583.395
floriculture	635.933 395
Box Butte County (Neb.)	T2—782 94
Box Elder County (Utah)	T2—792 42
Box-girder bridges	
construction	624.215
Box lunches	641.53
Boxcars	385.34
engineering	625.24
see also Rolling stock	
Boxer (Dog)	636.73
Boxer Rebellion, 1899–1901	951.035
Boxers (Pugilists)	796.830 92
Boxes	688.8
paperboard	676.32
see also Containers	
Boxfishes	597.64
Boxing	796.83
law	344.099
see also Combat sports	
Boxwoods	583.395
botany	583.395
floriculture	635.933 395
Boy Scout camps	796.542 2
Boy Scouts	369.43
Boyacá (Colombia)	T2—861 44
Boycotts	
Holocaust, 1933–1945	940.531 813 2
international politics	327.117
law of nations	341.582
labor economics	331.893
law	344.018 93
restraint of trade	338.604 8
law	343.072 3
Boyd County (Ky.)	T2—769 27
Boyd County (Neb.)	T2—782 723
Boyle County (Ky.)	T2—769 523
Boyne River (Ireland)	T2—418 22
Boys	305.230 811
	T1—083
criminal offenders	364.36
education	371.821 1

Boys (continued)
  health 613.042 32
  home care 649.132
  journalism for 070.483 26
  psychology 155.432
  publications for
    bibliographies 011.624 1
  recreation 790.194
    indoor 793.019 4
    outdoor 796.083
  sex hygiene 613.953
  social aspects 305.230 811
Boys' clubs 369.42
Boys' scouting organizations 369.43
Boys' societies 369.42
Boysenberries 641.347 18
  commercial processing 664.804 718
  cooking 641.647 18
  food 641.347 18
  horticulture 634.718
Bozca Island (Turkey) T2—562 2
Bozcaada (Turkey) T2—562 2
Bozen (Italy : Province) T2—453 83
Bozizé, François
  Central African history 967.410 54
Brabant (Belgium) T2—493 3
Brabant Wallon (Belgium) T2—493 37
Bracelets 391.7
  customs 391.7
  making 739.278
    costume jewelry 688.2
    handicrafts 745.594 2
    fine jewelry 739.278
Brachiopoda 594.68
  paleozoology 564.68
Brachycera 595.773
Brachycera-Cyclorrhapha 595.774
Brachycera-Orthorrhapha 595.773
Brachyura 595.386
Bracing equipment
  aircraft 629.134 37
Bracken (Ferns) 587.3
Bracken County (Ky.) T2—769 325
Bracket fungi 579.597
Brackish water 553.72
  T2—169
  economic geology 553.72
  hydrology 551.48
Bracknell Forest (England) T2—422 98
Bradford County (Fla.) T2—759 15
Bradford County (Pa.) T2—748 57
Bradley County (Ark.) T2—767 63
Bradley County (Tenn.) T2—768 873
Bradoriida 565.3

Bradyodonti 567.3
Bradypodidae 599.313
Braga (Portugal : District) T2—469 12
Bragança (Portugal :
  District) T2—469 27
Braganza, House of 946.903
Brahma Samaj 294.556 2
Brahmanas 294.592 1
Brahmanism 294.5
Brahmans (Cattle) 636.291
Brahmans (People)
  biography 294.509 2
Brahmaputra River T2—549 2
  Bangladesh T2—549 2
  India T2—541 6
Brahui T5—948 3
Brahui language 494.83
  T6—948 3
Brahui literature 894.83
Braided rugs
  arts 746.73
Braiding hair 646.724 7
Braiding textiles 677.028 2
  arts 746.42
Braids (Hairstyling) 646.724 7
Braids (Mathematics) 514.224
Braids (Textile trim) 677.76
  arts 746.27
Brăila (Romania : Județ) T2—498 1
Braille 411
  printing 686.282
  specific languages T4—11
Braille publications
  bibliographies 011.63
  cataloging 025.349 2
  library treatment 025.179 2
  publishing 070.579 2
Brain 573.86
  biology 573.86
  human anatomy 611.81
  human biochemistry 612.822
  human biophysics 612.822
  human physiology 612.82
  medicine 616.8
  surgery 617.481
  see also Nervous system
Brain cancer
  incidence 614.599 948 1
  medicine 616.994 81
    see also Cancer — humans

Brain-damaged people	305.908 4	Brand preferences	
	T1—087 4	marketing research	658.834 3
education	371.91	Brandenburg (Germany)	T2—431 5
see also Mentally disabled		Brandenburg an der Havel	
people		(Germany)	T2—431 54
Brain diseases		Brandfort (South Africa :	
humans		District)	T2—685 3
cancer	362.196 994 81	Branding	744.6
incidence	614.599 948 1	design	744.6
medicine	616.994 81	Branding animals	636.081 2
social services	362.196 994 81	Brandon (Man.)	T2—712 73
see also Cancer —		Brands	
humans		sales promotion	658.827
incidence	614.598	Brandt, Willy	
medicine	616.8	German history	943.087 7
surgery	617.481	Brandy	641.253
Brain drain	331.127 91	commercial processing	663.53
Brain stem		Brant (Ont. : County)	T2—713 47
human anatomy	611.81	Branta	598.417 8
human physiology	612.826	Brantley County (Ga.)	T2—758 753
medicine	616.8	Bras d'Or Lake (N.S.)	T2—716 9
Braintree (England :		Brasília (Brazil)	T2—817 4
District)	T2—426 715	Braşov (Romania : Judeţ)	T2—498 4
Brainwashing	153.853	Brass	669.3
Braising		decorative arts	739.52
home cooking	641.73	materials science	620.182
Brakes (Devices)		metallography	669.953
automotive engineering	629.246	metallurgy	669.3
railroad engineering	625.25	metalworking	673.3
Brakes (Ferns)	587.3	physical metallurgy	669.963
Brakpan (South Africa :		Brass bands	784.9
District)	T2—682 25	Brass ensembles	785.9
Bran	641.331	Brass instruments	788.9
commercial processing	664.720 8	bands and orchestras	784
wheat	664.722 8	chamber ensembles	785
cooking	641.631	mixed	785.2–.5
food	641.331	single type	785.9
Branch banking	332.16	construction	788.919 23
Branch banks	332.16	by hand	788.919 23
Branch County (Mich.)	T2—774 21	by machine	681.889
Branch libraries		solo music	788.9
architecture	727.84	Brassicaceae	583.78
public librarianship	027.4	Brassicales	583.78
Branch stores	381.12	Bratislava (Slovakia)	T2—437 31
see also Commerce		Brauer groups	512.46
Branches of government	320.404	Braulidae	595.774
law	342.044	Braunschweig (Germany)	T2—435 976
Branching processes	519.234	Braunschweig (Germany :	
Branchiopoda	595.32	Regierungsbezirk)	T2—435 97
paleozoology	565.32	Braxton County (W. Va.)	T2—754 66
Branchiura	595.36	Brayer painting	751.49
Brand name products		Braziers	
sales promotion	658.827	ceramic arts	738.8
		heating buildings	697.1

Brest (France)	T2—441 12
Brèstskaĭa voblasts′ (Belarus)	T2—478 9
Bretagne (France)	T2—441
Breton language	491.68
	T6—916 8
Breton literature	891.68
Bretons	T5—916 8
Brevard County (Fla.)	T2—759 27
Breviaries	264.15
Roman Catholic	264.020 15
texts	264.024
Brewed alcoholic beverages	641.23
commercial processing	663.3
cooking with	641.62
home preparation	641.873
Brewed nonalcoholic beverages	641.877
commercial processing	663.9
home preparation	641.877
Brewster County (Tex.)	976.493 2
	T2—764 932
Brexias	583.67
Brezhnev, Leonid Il′ich	
Russian history	947.085 3
Brianskaĭa oblast′ (Russia)	T2—472 5
Briard (Dog)	636.737
Bribery of officials	364.132 3
law	345.023 23
public administration	353.46
Bribery of voters	364.132 4
law	345.023 24
Brick pavements	625.82
Bricklayers	693.210 92
Bricks	666.737
architectural construction	721.044 21
building construction	693.21
building materials	691.4
ceramic arts	738.6
materials science	620.142
structural engineering	624.183 6
Bride purchase	392.4
Bridge (Game)	795.415
Bridge circuits	621.374 2
electronics	621.381 548
Bridge engineers	624.209 2
Bridge harps	787.98
see also Stringed instruments	
Bridge River (B.C.)	T2—711 31
Bridge whist	795.413
Bridgend (Wales : County Borough)	T2—429 71
Bridges	388.132
architecture	725.98
construction	624.2
Bridges (continued)	
military engineering	623.67
public administration	354.76
transportation services	388.132
railroads	385.312
roads	388.132
Bridges (Dentistry)	617.692
Bridges (Electrical circuits)	621.374 2
Brie (Cheese)	641.373 53
cooking	641.673 53
food	641.373 53
processing	637.353
Brief psychotherapy	616.891 47
Briefcases	
manufacturing technology	685.51
Brig (Switzerland : Bezirk)	T2—494 794 3
Brigades (Military units)	355.31
Bright disease	
medicine	616.612
see also Urologic diseases — humans	
Brightness perception	
psychology	152.143
Brighton (England)	T2—422 56
Brighton and Hove (England)	T2—422 56
Brill's disease	
incidence	614.526 2
medicine	616.922 2
see also Communicable diseases — humans	
Brindisi (Italy)	T2—457 541
ancient	T2—377 631
Brindisi (Italy : Province)	T2—457 54
ancient	T2—377 63
Brine	553.72
Brine shrimps	595.32
Brined foods	
cooking	641.616 2
Brining foods	664.028 6
commercial preservation	664.028 6
home preservation	641.462
Briquettes	662.6
Brisbane (Qld.)	T2—943 1
Brisbane River (Qld.)	T2—943 2
Brisbane Water National Park (N.S.W.)	T2—944 2
Briscoe County (Tex.)	T2—764 839
Bristles	
animal husbandry	636.088 45
manufacturing technology	679.6
Bristletails	595.723

Bristling (Fish)	641.392	British New Guinea	995.402 1
cooking	641.692	British North America Act, 1867	971.049
food	641.392	British Open (Golf)	796.352 66
zoology	597.452	British pronunciation	421.55
Bristol (England)	942.393	British Sign Language	419.41
	T2—423 93		T6—999 841
Bristol (Va.)	T2—755 726	British Solomon Islands	T2—959 3
Bristol Avon River		British Somaliland	T2—677 3
(England)	T2—423 9	British spelling	421.55
Bristol Bay (Alaska)	551.461 434	British system (Measurement)	530.813
	T2—164 34	social aspects	389.15
Bristol Bay Borough		British Togoland	966.703
(Alaska)	T2—798 4		T2—667
Bristol board	676.288	British Virgin Islands	T2—729 725
Bristol County (Mass.)	T2—744 85	British western seawaters	551.461 337
Bristol County (R.I.)	T2—745 5		T2—163 37
Britain	941	Britons	T5—21
	T2—41	*see Manual at* T5—201–209	
ancient	936.1	vs. T5—2101–2109	
	T2—361	Brits (South Africa :	
see Manual at 941		District)	T2—682 41
Britain, Battle of, 1940	940.542 11	Britstown (South Africa :	
Britain, Northern	941.1	District)	T2—687 13
	T2—411	Brittania (Roman province)	T2—362
ancient	936.11	Brittany (Dog)	636.752
	T2—361 1	Brittany (France)	T2—441
Britain, Southern	942	Brittle stars	593.94
	T2—42	Brittleness	
ancient	936.2	materials science	620.112 6
	T2—362	Brixia (Italy)	T2—373 121
British Americans	T5—13	Brněnský kraj (Czech	
see Manual at T5—13 vs.		Republic)	T2—437 24
T5—2073, T5—21073		Broaching tools	621.954
British ancestry	T5—2	Broad beans	641.356 51
see Manual at T5—201–209		botany	583.63
vs. T5—2101–2109		cooking	641.656 51
British Antarctic Territory	T2—989	field crop	633.37
British Canadians	T5—112	food	641.356 51
see Manual at T5—112,		garden crop	635.651
T5—114 vs. T5—2,		Broad-gage railroads	385
T5—41		*see also* Railroads	
British Columbia	971.1	Broad jump	796.432
	T2—711	*see also* Track and field	
British Commonwealth of		Broad River (S.C.)	T2—757 4
Nations	T2—171 241	Broadband computer equipment	004.64
British Empire	T2—171 241	engineering	621.398 1
British Guiana	T2—881	Broadband local-area networks	004.68
British Honduras	T2—728 2	*see also* Computer	
British Isles	941	communications	
	T2—41	Broadbills	598.822
ancient	936.1	Broadcast advertising	659.14
	T2—361	Broadcast communications	004.693
see Manual at 941		communications services	384.36
British Kaffraria	T2—687 55	sociology	302.231 2

Broadcast media		Brokopondo (Suriname :	
journalism	070.19	District)	T2—883 92
Broadcast public speaking	808.51	Brome-Missisquoi (Quebec)	T2—714 62
Broadcast videotex	004.69	Bromegrasses	584.926
see also Computer		Bromeliaceae	584.98
communications		Bromeliads	584.98
Broadcasters	384.540 92	botany	584.98
Broadcasting	384.54	floriculture	635.934 98
law	343.099 4	Bromeliales	584.98
public administration	354.75	Bromes (Grasses)	584.926
see Manual at 384.54, 384.55,		Bromine	
384.8 vs. 791.4		chemical engineering	661.073 3
Broadcasting channels	384.545 2	chemistry	546.733
radio	384.545 2	economic geology	553.6
television	384.552 1	organic chemistry	547.02
Broadcasting networks	384.540 65	applied	661.891
see also Networks		Bromley (London, England)	T2—421 78
(Communications)		Bromoil process	773.8
Broadcasting stations	384.545 3	Bromsgrove (England :	
radio	384.545 3	District)	T2—424 42
see also Radio stations		Bromyard (England)	T2—424 2
television	384.552 2	Bronchi	
see also Television stations		human anatomy	611.23
Broadland (England)	T2—426 17	human physiology	612.234
Broads, The (England)	T2—426 17	medicine	616.23
Broadsides		surgery	617.544
cataloging	025.342	Bronchial asthma	
direct advertising	659.133	medicine	616.238
library treatment	025.172	*see also* Respiratory tract	
Broadwater County (Mont.)	T2—786 664	diseases — humans	
Broca aphasia		Bronchial diseases	
medicine	616.855 2	medicine	616.23
see also Communication		*see also* Respiratory tract	
disorders		diseases — humans	
Brocade	677.616	Bronchiectasis	
Brocatelle	677.616	medicine	616.23
Broccoli	641.353 5	*see also* Respiratory tract	
commercial processing	664.805 35	diseases — humans	
cooking	641.653 5	Bronchitis	
food	641.353 5	medicine	616.234
garden crop	635.35	*see also* Respiratory tract	
Brochures		diseases — humans	
design	744.57	Bronchodilator agents	
Brodiaeoideae	584.79	pharmacokinetics	615.72
Broiling	641.76	Bronchopneumonia	
Broken Hill (N.S.W.)	T2—944 9	medicine	616.241
Broken homes	362.829 4	Bronkhorstspruit (South	
social services	362.829 4	Africa : District)	T2—682 27
sociology	306.89	Brontosaurus	567.913 8
see also Families — social		Bronx (New York, N.Y.)	T2—747 275
welfare		Bronze	669.3
Brokers (Securities)	332.62	decorative arts	739.512
law	346.092 6	materials science	620.182
public administration	354.88	metallography	669.953

Bruises	
medicine	617.13
Brule County (S.D.)	T2—783 381
Brunches	642
cooking	641.52
customs	394.125 2
Brundusium (Italy)	T2—377 631
Brunei	959.55
	T2—595 5
Brunelliaceae	583.68
Bruniaceae	583.985
Bruniales	583.985
Brunswick County (N.C.)	T2—756 29
Brunswick County (Va.)	T2—755 575
Bruny Island (Tas.)	T2—946 2
Brush disposal	
forestry	634.955
Brush drawing	741.26
Brush-tailed possum	599.232
Brush turkeys	598.64
Brushes	679.6
Brushes (Generator parts)	621.316
Brussels (Belgium)	T2—493 32
Brussels-Capital Region	
(Belgium)	T2—493 32
Brussels griffon	636.76
Brussels sprouts	641.353 6
commercial processing	664.805 36
cooking	641.653 6
food	641.353 6
garden crop	635.36
Bruttium	T2—377 8
Bryales	588.2
Bryan County (Ga.)	T2—758 732
Bryan County (Okla.)	T2—766 62
Bryansk (Russia : Oblast)	T2—472 5
Bryce Canyon National Park	
(Utah)	T2—792 52
Bryde's whale	599.524
Bryophyta	588
paleobotany	561.8
pharmacology	615.322
Bryopodales	579.835
Bryopsida	588.2
Bryozoa	594.67
paleozoology	564.67
Brythonic languages	491.6
	T6—916
Brythonic literatures	891.6
Buamu language	496.35
	T6—963 5
Bubble memory	004.563

Bubbles	530.427 5
chemical engineering	660.293
chemistry	541.33
physics	530.427 5
Bube-Benga languages	496.396
	T6—963 96
Bubonic plague	
incidence	614.573 2
medicine	616.923 2
see also Communicable	
diseases — humans	
Bucconidae	598.72
Bucerotidae	598.78
Buchanan, James	
United States history	973.68
Buchanan County (Iowa)	T2—777 382
Buchanan County (Mo.)	T2—778 132
Buchanan County (Va.)	T2—755 752
Bucharest (Romania)	T2—498 2
Bucheggberg (Switzerland)	T2—494 359 5
Bücher, Karl	
economic school	330.154 2
Buckbeans	583.983
Buckeyes	583.75
Buckingham County (Va.)	T2—755 623
Buckinghamshire (England)	T2—425 9
Buckles	391.7
customs	391.7
making	739.278
costume jewelry	688.2
handicrafts	745.594 2
fine jewelry	739.278
Bucks County (Pa.)	T2—748 21
Buckthorns	583.646
Buckwheat	641.331 2
botany	583.888
commercial processing	664.72
cooking	641.631 2
food	641.331 2
food crop	633.12
București (Romania)	T2—498 2
Budapest (Hungary)	943.912
	T2—439 12
Buddha	294.363
art representation	704.948 943 63
arts	700.482 943 63
	T3C—382 943 63
Buddhism	294.3
art representation	704.948 943
arts	700.482 943
	T3C—382 943
Islamic polemics	297.294
religious freedom	
law	342.085 294 3

Buddhism and Islam	294.335 7
Buddhist view	294.335 7
Islamic view	297.284 3
Buddhism and Judaism	
Jewish view	296.399 43
Buddhist architecture	720.95
Buddhist calendar	529.324 3
religion	294.343 6
Buddhist education	294.375
Buddhist ethics	294.35
Buddhist holidays	294.343 6
customs	394.265 43
see also Holidays	
Buddhist monasteries	294.365 7
architecture	726.784 3
Buddhist philosophy	181.043
Buddhist sculpture	730.95
Buddhist temples and shrines	294.343 5
architecture	726.143
Buddhists	T1—088 294 3
biography	294.309 2
social group	305.694 3
Buddlejaceae	583.96
Budějovický kraj (Czech	
Republic)	T2—437 13
Budgerigars	636.686 4
animal husbandry	636.686 4
zoology	598.71
Budget deficits	352.48
macroeconomic policy	339.523
see also Budgets (Public)	
Budget in business	658.154
Budget messages	352.48
specific jurisdictions	352.493–.499
Budget surpluses	
macroeconomic policy	339.523
Budgeting	658.154
armed forces	355.622 8
public administration	352.48
see also Budgets (Public)	
Budgets (Business)	
management	658.154
Budgets (Public)	352.48
armed forces	355.622 8
specific jurisdictions	355.622 9
law	343.034
legislative enactment	328.378
specific international	
organizations	352.491
specific jurisdictions	352.493–.499
Buds	581.46
descriptive botany	581.46
physiology	575.486
plant propagation	631.533

Budworms	595.78
agricultural pests	632.78
Buena Vista (Va.)	T2—755 851
Buena Vista County (Iowa)	T2—777 18
Buenos Aires (Argentina)	T2—821 1
Buenos Aires (Argentina :	
Province)	T2—821 2
Buffalo	599.642
animal husbandry	636.293
Buffalo (Bison)	599.643
see also Bison	
Buffalo (N.Y.)	T2—747 97
Buffalo City Metropolitan	
Municipality (South	
Africa)	T2—687 55
Buffalo County (Neb.)	T2—782 45
Buffalo County (S.D.)	T2—783 31
Buffalo County (Wis.)	T2—775 48
Buffalo gnats	595.772
Buffers	
railroad engineering	625.25
Buffing metals	671.72
Buffing tools	621.922
Bufo	597.872
Bufonidae	597.87
Bufonoidea	597.87
Buganda	T2—676 1
Buganda (Kingdom)	967.610 1
Buginese	T5—992 262
Buginese language	499.226 2
	T6—992 262
Buginese literature	899.226 2
Bugis	T5—992 262
Bugis language	499.226 2
	T6—992 262
Bugis literature	899.226 2
Bugles	788.95
instrument	788.951 9
music	788.95
see also Brass instruments	
Bugs (Heteroptera)	595.754
Buhari, Muhammadu	
Nigerian history	966.905 7
Buḥayrah (Egypt)	T2—621
Buḥayrāt (South Sudan)	T2—629 4
Buhid	T5—992 1
Builders	690.092
Building	690
economics	338.476 9
enterprises	338.769
restrictive practices	338.826 9
government control	354.642 8
technology	690
see Manual at 624 vs. 690	

Building and loan associations	332.32	Bukovina	T2—498 1
law	346.082 32	Romania	T2—498 4
public administration	354.86	Ukraine	T2—477 9
Building codes	343.078 69	Bulacan (Philippines)	T2—599 158
criminology	364.142	Bülach (Switzerland :	
criminal law	345.024 2	Bezirk)	T2—494 572 4
enforcement	363.233	Bulawayo (Zimbabwe)	T2—689 1
Building construction services		Bulbs (Plants)	584.146
(Armed forces)	358.22	descriptive botany	584.146
Building cooperatives	334.1	nursery production	631.526
Building engineering services	696	ornamental plants	635.915 26
Building management	658.2	physiology	575.495
public administration	352.56	planting	631.532
Building materials	691	ornamental plants	635.915 32
architectural construction	721.04	Bulganin, Nikolay	
construction	691	Aleksandrovich	
synthetic	666.89	Russian history	947.085 2
Building paper	676.289	Bulgaria	949.9
Building remodeling	690.24		T2—499
home economics	643.7	ancient	939.89
see Manual at 690 vs. 643.7			T2—398 9
Building societies	332.32	Bulgarian Empire, 680–1014	949.901 3
Buildings	720	Bulgarian Empire, 1185–1396	949.901 4
architecture	720	Bulgarian language	491.81
area planning	711.6		T6—918 11
art representation	704.944	Bulgarian literature	891.81
capital procurement	658.152 42	Bulgarian Macedonia	T2—499 82
construction	690	Bulgarian Thrace	T2—499 5
enterprises	338.769	Bulgarians	T5—918 11
restrictive practices	338.826 9	Bulimia	
government control	354.642 8	medicine	616.852 63
see Manual at 624 vs. 690		*see also* Mental disorders	
economics	333.338	Bulk carriers (Ships)	387.245
energy economics	333.796 2	engineering	623.824 5
investment economics	332.632 43	*see also* Ships	
landscape architecture	717	Bulk mailings	383.124
management	658.2	*see also* Postal service	
public administration	352.56	Bulkley-Nechako (B.C.)	T2—711 82
planning		Bulkley River (B.C.)	T2—711 82
museums	069.22	Bull-roarers	788.29
Built-in furniture	645.4	*see also* Wind instruments	
decorative arts	749.4	Bull shark	597.34
manufacturing technology	684.16	Bull Shoals Lake (Ark. and	
see also Furniture		Mo.)	T2—767 193
Builth Wells (Wales)	T2—429 56	Bull terriers	636.755 9
Bujumbura (Burundi)	T2—675 72	Bulldog	636.72
Buka Island (Papua New		Bulldozers	624.152
Guinea)	T2—959 2	engineering	629.225
Bukele Ortez, Nayib Armando		repair	629.287 5
Salvadoran history	972.840 546	Buller District (N.Z.)	T2—937 3
Bukhārī, Muḥammad ibn Ismāʿīl		Bulletin boards	
Hadith	297.125 41	instructional use	371.335 6
Bukidnon (Philippines)	T2—599 772	management use	658.455

Bullets	
military engineering	623.455
Bullfighting	791.82
Bullfinches	598.885
Bullfrogs	597.892
Bullheads (Catfishes)	597.492
Bullitt County (Ky.)	T2—769 453
Bullmastiff	636.73
Bulloch County (Ga.)	T2—758 766
Bullock County (Ala.)	T2—761 483
Bullroarers	788.29
see also Wind instruments	
Bulls (Papal documents)	262.91
Bullying	302.343
education	371.58
social interaction	302.343
Bulrushes	584.94
Bulrushes (Cyperaceae)	584.94
Bulrushes (Sedges)	584.94
Bulrushes (Typhaceae)	584.99
Bultfontein (South Africa :	
District)	T2—685 3
Bulu language	496.396
	T6—963 96
Bumpers	
automobile	629.276
Bunbury (W.A.)	T2—941 2
Buncombe County (N.C.)	T2—756 88
Bundaberg (Qld.)	T2—943 2
Bundling (Customs)	392.4
Bündnis Zukunft Österreich	
(Political party)	324.243 603
Bungalows	
architecture	728.373
construction	690.837 3
Bungee jumping	797.5
see also Outdoor life	
Bungoma County (Kenya)	T2—676 286
Bunker Hill, Battle of, 1775	973.331 2
Bunker oils	665.538 8
Bunsen burners	542.4
Bunt (Fungi)	579.593
disease of wheat	633.119 493
Buntings	598.883
Bunun (Taiwan people)	T5—992 5
Bunya Mountains National	
Park (Qld.)	T2—943 2
Bunyoro (Kingdom)	967.610 1
	T2—676 1
Buoyancy	532.02
air mechanics	533.61
gas mechanics	533.12
liquid mechanics	532.25

Buoys	387.155
navigation aids	623.894 4
transportation services	387.155
Buprestoidea	595.763
Bur reeds	584.99
Būr Saʿīd (Egypt : Province)	T2—621 5
Burbots	597.632
Burdekin River (Qld.)	T2—943 6
Burdur İli (Turkey)	T2—562 7
ancient	T2—392 4
Bureau County (Ill.)	T2—773 372
Bureaucracy	302.35
public administration	352.63
sociology	302.35
Burgas (1987–1998)	
(Bulgaria : Oblast)	T2—499 5
Burgas (1999-) (Bulgaria :	
Oblast)	T2—499 52
Burgaska oblast	
(1987–1998) (Bulgaria)	T2—499 5
Burgaska oblast (1999-)	
(Bulgaria)	T2—499 52
Burgenland (Austria)	T2—436 15
Burglarproofing	
household security	643.16
Burglary	364.162 2
law	345.026 22
see also Theft	
Burglary insurance	368.82
see also Insurance	
Burgos (Spain : Province)	T2—463 53
Burgundian language	439.9
	T6—399
Burgundy (France)	T2—444 1
Burgundy-Franche-Comté	
(France)	T2—444
Burhou (Channel Islands)	T2—423 47
Burial insurance	368.366
see also Insurance	
Burial of dead	363.75
customs	393.1
see also Undertaking	
(Mortuary)	
Burial of Jesus Christ	232.964
Burial of waste	363.728 5
technology	628.445 64
see also Waste control	
Buriat	T5—942
Buriat language	494.2
	T6—942
Buriatiia (Russia)	T2—575
Burke County (Ga.)	T2—758 65
Burke County (N.C.)	T2—756 85
Burke County (N.D.)	T2—784 72

Burkina Faso	966.25	Bursae diseases	
	T2—662 5	medicine	616.76
Burkinabe	T5—966 25	*see also* Musculoskeletal	
Burkinans	T5—966 25	diseases — humans	
Burkitt lymphoma		Bursaries	T1—079
incidence	614.599 944 6	Burseraceae	583.75
medicine	616.994 46	Burt County (Neb.)	T2—782 243
see also Cancer — humans		Burundi	967.572
Burleigh County (N.D.)	T2—784 77		T2—675 72
Burleson County (Tex.)	T2—764 241	Burundi people	T5—967 572
Burlesque shows	792.7	Burundians	T5—967 572
see also Theater		Burushaski language	494.892
Burlington (Vt.)	T2—743 17		T6—948 92
Burlington County (N.J.)	T2—749 61	Burushaski literature	894.892
Burma	959.1	Burusho	T5—948 92
	T2—591	Bury (England :	
see also Myanmar		Metropolitan Borough)	T2—427 38
Burmanniaceae	584.52	Buryat	T5—942
Burmese	T5—958	Buryat language	494.2
Burmese cat	636.824		T6—942
Burmese language	495.8	Buryatia (Russia)	T2—575
	T6—958	Burying beetles	595.764 2
Burmese literature	895.8	Bus cooking	641.575
Burnaby (B.C.)	T2—711 33	Bus drivers	388.322 092
Burnet County (Tex.)	T2—764 63	Bus stops	388.33
Burnet-Llano region (Tex.)	T2—764 6	urban	388.473
Burnett County (Wis.)	T2—775 14	*see also* Bus transportation	
Burnie (Tas.)	T2—946 5	Bus terminals	388.33
Burnley (England :		architecture	725.38
Borough)	T2—427 642	urban	388.473
Burnout (Psychology)	158.723	*see also* Bus transportation	
Burns		Bus transportation	388.322
crop damage	632.18	law	343.094 82
medicine	617.11	public administration	354.765 3
Burramyidae	599.23	transportation services	388.322
Burreeds	584.99	urban	388.413 22
Burritos	641.84	law	343.098 2
Burros	636.182	public administration	354.769
animal husbandry	636.182	Buses	388.342 33
conservation technology	639.979 665	driving	629.283 33
resource economics	333.959 665	engineering	629.222 33
zoology	599.665	military engineering	623.747 23
Burrowing animals	591.564 8	operation	388.322 044
Burrowing toad	597.865	repair	629.287 233
Burrows	591.564 8	sanitation services	363.729 3
Bursa İli (Turkey)	T2—563 1	*see also* Sanitation	
ancient	T2—393 13	transportation services	388.342 33
Bursae		*see also* Automotive vehicles	
human anatomy	611.75	Bush, George	
human physiology	612.75	United States history	973.928
medicine	616.76	Bush, George W. (George	
surgery	617.475	Walker)	
		United States history	973.931
		Bush babies	599.83

118

Business presentations	
management use	658.452
Business records	
law	346.065
records management	651.5
Business relationships (Personal)	650.13
Business security	
management	658.47
Business success	650.1
Business tax	336.207
income tax	336.241 7
law	343.052 68
public administration	352.44
public finance	336.241 7
law	343.068
public administration	352.44
public finance	336.207
Business-to-business advertising	659.131 5
Business white pages	338.702 5
see Manual at T1—025 vs.	
T1—029	
Business writing	808.066 65
see Manual at 658.45 vs.	
651.7, 808.06665	
Businesses	338.7
Businessmen	338.092
see Manual at 338.092	
Businessowners insurance	368.094
see also Insurance	
Businesspeople	338.092
see Manual at 338.092	
Businesswomen	338.092
see Manual at 338.092	
Busing (School desegregation)	379.263
law	344.079 8
Buskerud fylke (Norway)	T2—482 6
Busoga (Kingdom)	967.610 1
	T2—676 1
Bustards	598.32
Busts (Sculpture)	731.74
Butadiene-styrene rubber	678.72
Butane	665.773
Butcher paper	676.287
Butene	665.773
Buṭlān (Islamic law)	340.591 2
Butler County (Ala.)	T2—761 37
Butler County (Iowa)	T2—777 29
Butler County (Kan.)	T2—781 88
Butler County (Ky.)	T2—769 755
Butler County (Mo.)	T2—778 93
Butler County (Neb.)	T2—782 322
Butler County (Ohio)	T2—771 75
Butler County (Pa.)	T2—748 91
Butomaceae	584.44

Butte (Mont.)	T2—786 68
Butte County (Calif.)	T2—794 32
Butte County (Idaho)	T2—796 59
Butte County (S.D.)	T2—783 43
Butter	641.372
cooking	641.672
food	641.372
processing	637.2
Butter prints and molds	
wood carving	736.4
Buttercups	583.34
Butterfat tests	
milk processing	637.127 6
Butterflies	595.789
conservation technology	639.975 789
culture	638.578 9
resource economics	333.955 7
Butterfly bushes	583.96
Butterfly farming	638.578 9
Butterfly fishes (Freshwater)	597.47
Butterfly fishes (Marine)	597.72
Butterfly flowers	
botany	583.952
Butterfly flowers (Solanaceae)	635.933 959 3
botany	583.959 3
floriculture	635.933 959 3
Butterfly gardening	638.578 9
Buttermilk	641.372 4
cooking	641.672 4
food	641.372 4
processing	637.24
Butternut tree	583.65
Butternuts	583.65
Butterworth (South Africa :	
District)	T2—687 54
Buttock muscles	
human anatomy	611.738
Button accordions	788.863
instrument	788.863 19
music	788.863
see also Woodwind	
instruments	
Button mangrove	583.73
Button quails	598.32
Buttonbushes	635.933 956
botany	583.956
floriculture	635.933 956
Buttons	391.45
commercial technology	687.8
customs	391.45
design	744.7
home sewing	646.19
numismatics	737.24
Butts County (Ga.)	T2—758 585

Butyrates	668.423	Byzantine Greek language	487.3
Buxaceae	583.395		T6—87
Buxales	583.395	Byzantine Greek literature	880
Buyers' guides	381.33	Byzantine law	340.54
	T1—029	Byzantine painting	759.021 4
see Manual at T1—025 vs.		Byzantine rite churches	281.5
T1—029		*see also* Eastern churches	
Buzău (Romania : Judeţ)	T2—498 2	Byzantine sculpture	734.224
Buzzards	598.94	Byzantium (City)	T2—398 618
Buzzards (Turkey vulture)	598.92	BZÖ (Austrian political party)	324.243 603
Buzzards Bay (Mass. : Bay)	551.461 346		
	T2—163 46		

C

Bwa (African people)	T5—963 5		
Bwamu language	496.35	C*-algebras	512.556
	T6—963 5	Cà Mau (Vietnam)	T2—597 9
Bwile language	496.393	Caaguazú (Paraguay :	
	T6—963 93	Dept.)	T2—892 134
By-products		Caazapá (Paraguay : Dept.)	T2—892 127
commercial food processing	664.08	Cabala	296.16
pulp	676.5	Jewish mysticism	
Byblidaceae	583.96	experience	296.712
Byblos (Lebanon)	T2—569 2	movement	296.833
ancient	T2—394 4	Jewish religious sources	296.16
Bydgoszcz (Poland :		occultism	135.47
Voivodeship)	T2—438 26	Cabañas (El Salvador)	T2—728 426
Byelarus	947.8	Cabaret shows	792.7
	T2—478	*see also* Theater	
Byelorussian language	491.799	Cabarrus County (N.C.)	T2—756 72
	T6—917 99	Cabbages	641.353 4
Byelorussian literature	891.799	botany	583.78
Byelorussians	T5—917 99	commercial processing	664.805 34
Bylot Island (Nunavut)	T2—719 52	cooking	641.653 4
Bypass surgery (Coronary)	617.412	food	641.353 4
Byrrhoidea	595.763	garden crop	635.34
Byssinosis		Cabell County (W. Va.)	T2—754 42
medicine	616.244	Cabin pressurization	
see also Respiratory tract		aircraft	629.134 42
diseases — humans		Cabinda (Angola : Province)	T2—673 1
Byzacium	T2—397 3	Cabinet government	321.804 3
Byzantine architecture	723.2	Cabinet-level committees	352.24
Byzantine art	709.021 4	Cabinet members	352.293
religious significance	246.1	Cabinet organs	786.55
Byzantine decoration	744.090 21	instrument	786.551 9
Byzantine Empire	949.502	music	786.55
	T2—495	*see also* Keyboard instruments	
Egyptian history	932.023	Cabinet secretariats	352.243
Libyan history	939.740 5	Cabinet secretaries	352.243 229 3
Moroccan history	939.712 06	Cabinetmakers	684.104 092
North African history	939.705	Cabinetmaking	684.104
Sardinian history	945.902	Cabinets (Furniture)	
Sicilian history	945.801	decorative arts	749.3
Southern Italian history	945.701	manufacturing technology	684.16
Tunisian history	939.730 5	Cabinets (Government councils)	321.804 3
		public administration	352.24

Cabins	643.1
architecture	728.73
home economics	643.1
see also Dwellings	
Cabins (Aircraft)	629.134 45
Cable communication systems	384.6
see also Telephone	
Cable railways	385.6
engineering	625.5
transportation services	385.6
see also Railroads	
Cable-stayed bridges	
construction	624.238
Cable television	384.555
engineering	621.388 57
law	343.099 46
see also Television	
Cables (Electrical conductors)	621.319 34
computer science	004.64
engineering	621.398 1
Cables (Ropes)	
knotting and splicing	623.888 2
metal	671.84
structural engineering	624.177 4
Cabo Delgado	
(Mozambique)	T2—679 8
Cabombaceae	584.23
Cabooses	385.32
engineering	625.22
transportation services	385.32
see also Rolling stock	
Cabs	388.342 32
see also Taxicabs	
Cacadu District	
Municipality (South	
Africa)	T2—687 53
Cacao	583.775
agriculture	633.74
botany	583.775
Cacao butter	665.354
see also Cocoa butter	
Cáceres (Spain : Province)	T2—462 8
Cachapoal (Chile :	
Province)	T2—833 2
Cache County (Utah)	T2—792 12
Cache Creek (B.C.)	T2—711 72
Cachets (Philately)	744.72
Cactaceae	583.885
Cactales	583.885

Cacti	583.885
botany	583.885
edible fruits	641.347 75
cooking	641.647 75
horticulture	634.775
floriculture	635.933 885
Cactuses	583.885
CAD (Computer-aided design)	620.004 202 85
CAD/CAM (Manufacturing)	670.285
Caddisflies	595.745
Caddo County (Okla.)	T2—766 41
Caddo Indians	T5—979 3
Caddo Lake (La. and Tex.)	T2—763 99
Caddo language	497.93
	T6—979 3
Caddo Parish (La.)	T2—763 99
Caddoan Indians	T5—979 3
Caddoan languages	497.93
	T6—979 3
Cadence (Music)	781.254
Cadenzas	784.186
Cadettes (Girl Scouts)	369.463 409 73
Cádiz (Spain : Province)	T2—468 8
Cadmium	669.56
chemical engineering	661.066 2
chemistry	546.662
human toxicology	615.925 662
materials science	620.184 6
metallography	669.955 6
metallurgy	669.56
metalworking	673.56
physical metallurgy	669.965 6
see also Chemicals	
Caecilians	597.82
Caedmon	829.2
Caen (France)	T2—442 24
Caenagnathiformes	568.5
Caenolestidae	599.27
Caere (Italy)	T2—375 9
Caerphilly (Wales : County	
Borough)	T2—429 76
Caesalpiniaceae	583.634
botany	583.634
Caesalpinioideae	583.634
Caesium	669.725
see also Cesium	
Café Filho, João	
Brazilian history	981.062
Cafeteria meal service	642.5
Cafeterias	647.95
see also Eating places	
Caffeine abuse	362.299
medicine	616.864
personal health	613.84

Calculus	515
numerical methods	518.6
Calculus of finite differences	515.62
Calculus of variations	515.64
Calcutta (India)	T2—541 47
Caldas (Colombia : Dept.)	T2—861 35
Calderdale (England)	T2—428 12
Calderón Fournier, Rafael Angel	
Costa Rican history	972.860 522
Calderón Hinojosa, Felipe	
Mexican history	972.084 2
Calderón Sol, Armando	
Salvadoran history	972.840 541
Caldwell County (Ky.)	T2—769 815
Caldwell County (Mo.)	T2—778 185
Caldwell County (N.C.)	T2—756 845
Caldwell County (Tex.)	T2—764 33
Caldwell Parish (La.)	T2—763 76
Caledon (South Africa :	
District)	T2—687 36
Caledon River (Lesotho and	
South Africa)	T2—685 7
Caledonia County (Vt.)	T2—743 34
Calendar reform	529.5
Calendars	529.3
chronology	529.3
design	744.76
illustration	741.682
liturgy	264
Anglican	264.031
Roman Catholic	264.021
religion	203.6
Christianity	263.9
Islam	297.36
Judaism	296.43
Calendering paper	676.234
Calendering rubber	678.27
Calendering textiles	677.028 25
Calgary (Alta.)	T2—712 338
Calhoun County (Ala.)	T2—761 63
Calhoun County (Ark.)	T2—767 64
Calhoun County (Fla.)	T2—759 943
Calhoun County (Ga.)	T2—758 956
Calhoun County (Ill.)	T2—773 853
Calhoun County (Iowa)	T2—777 43
Calhoun County (Mich.)	T2—774 22
Calhoun County (Miss.)	T2—762 81
Calhoun County (S.C.)	T2—757 72
Calhoun County (Tex.)	T2—764 121
Calhoun County (W. Va.)	T2—754 29
Calibration	530.8
electrical instruments	621.372
Calico bass	597.738

California	979.4
	T2—794
California, Gulf of (Mexico)	551.461 41
	T2—164 1
California, Southern	T2—794 9
California halibut	597.69
California laurel	584.288
California legless lizards	597.959
Californium	546.448
Caligoida	595.34
Caliphate	297.61
Caliphs	
companions of Muḥammad	297.648
religious biography	297.092
role and function	297.61
Calisthenics	613.714
child care	649.57
Calitzdorp (South Africa :	
District)	T2—687 37
Call to Islam	297.74
Calla lilies	635.934 442
botany	584.442
floriculture	635.934 442
Callahan County (Tex.)	T2—764 726
Callao (Peru : Province)	T2—852 6
Callao (Peru : Region)	T2—852 6
Callaway County (Mo.)	T2—778 335
Callejas Romero, Rafael	
Leonardo	
Honduran history	972.830 534
Caller ID telephone service	384.64
Calles, Plutarco Elías	
Mexican history	972.082 3
Calligraphy	744.42
Calliphoridae	595.774
Callipteris	561.597
Callithricidae	599.84
Callitrichidae	599.84
paleozoology	569.84
Callorhinus	599.797 3
Callosities	
medicine	616.544
see also Skin diseases —	
humans	
Calloway County (Ky.)	T2—769 92
Calls (Finance)	332.645 3
multiple forms of investment	332.645 3
stocks	332.632 283
Caloosahatchee River (Fla.)	T2—759 48
Caloric restriction	
health	613.25
Calorie counters	613.23
Calories	
applied nutrition	613.23

Campaign buttons	
numismatics	737.242
Campaign finance	324.78
law	342.078
Campaign finance offenses	364.132 4
law	345.023 24
Campaign literature	324.23
Campaign pins	
numismatics	737.242
Campaign strategy (Elections)	324.72
Campaigns (Military science)	355.4
see also Land operations	
Campaigns (Politics)	324.9
elections	324.9
law	342.078
nominations	324.5
specific countries	324.24–.29
techniques	324.7
see Manual at 909, 930–990	
vs. 320	
Campania (Italy)	T2—457 2
ancient	T2—377 2
Campanula	583.983
botany	583.983
floriculture	635.933 983
Campanulaceae	583.983
Campanulales	583.983
Campanulids	583.98
Campbell, Kim	
Canadian history	971.064 7
Campbell County (Ky.)	T2—769 34
Campbell County (S.D.)	T2—783 17
Campbell County (Tenn.)	T2—768 72
Campbell County (Va.)	T2—755 672
Campbell County (Wyo.)	T2—787 12
Campbell Island (N.Z.)	T2—939 9
Campbellites	286.6
Campbelltown (N.S.W.)	T2—944 6
Campbeltown (Scotland)	T2—414 2
Campeche (Mexico : State)	T2—726 4
Camperdown (South	
Africa : District)	T2—684 7
Campers (Vehicles)	388.346
cooking	641.575
engineering	629.226
see also Motor homes	
Campfires	796.545
Camphors	
chemistry	547.71
Campidano (Italy)	T2—459 8
Oristano	T2—459 4
South Sardinia	T2—459 8

Camping	796.54
biography	796.540 92
meal service	642.3
military operations	355.412
military training	355.544
Camping equipment	796.540 284
armed forces	355.81
manufacturing technology	685.53
Campo Formio, Treaty of, 1797	945.307
Campobasso (Italy :	
Province)	T2—457 192
ancient	T2—377 38
Campsites	910.468
household management	647.942
see also Lodging (Temporary	
housing)	
Campus Crusade for Christ	267.61
Campus ministry	259.24
Campus police	363.289
Campus unrest	371.81
Cams	621.838
Cần Thơ (Vietnam)	T2—597 9
Canaanite language	492.6
Canaanite languages	492.6
	T6—926
Canaanite literatures	892.6
Canaanites	T5—926
Canaanitic languages	492.6
	T6—926
Canaanitic literatures	892.6
Canada	971
	T2—71
2006–2015	971.073
2015–	971.074
English explorations	971.011 4
French explorations	971.011 3
Norse explorations	971.011 2
see Manual at T2—73 vs.	
T2—71	
Canada, Eastern	T2—713
Canada, Western	T2—712
Canada goose	598.417 8
Canadian Alliance (Political	
party)	324.271 04
Canadian Arctic	T2—719
Canadian Arctic	
Archipelago (Nunavut	
and N.W.T.)	T2—719 52
Canadian Cordillera	T2—711
Canadian County (Okla.)	T2—766 39
Canadian English dialects	T6—21
Canadian football	796.335
biography	796.335 092
see also Ball games	

Canadian football players	796.335 092	Canalboats (continued)	
Canadian French dialects	T6—41	towed	386.229
Canadian language		design	623.812 9
English	420.971	engineering	623.829
	T6—21	transportation services	386.229
French	440.971	Canalized rivers	386.3
	T6—41	engineering	627.13
Inuit	497.12	Canals	386.4
	T6—971 2	engineering	627.13
Canadian literature		law	343.096 4
English	810	law of nations	341.446
French	840	transportation services	386.4
Inuit	897.12	Canapés	641.812
Canadian Pacific seawaters	551.461 433	Cañar (Ecuador : Province)	T2—866 23
	T2—164 33	Canarese	T5—948 14
Canadian pronunciation		Canaries	636.686 25
English	421.52	animal husbandry	636.686 25
French	441.52	zoology	598.885
Canadian Reform Conservative		Canary grasses	584.926
Alliance (Political party)	324.271 04	Canary Islands	964.9
Canadian River (Okla.)	T2—766		T2—649
Canadian River, North		Canasta	795.418
(Okla.)	T2—766 1	Canberra (A.C.T.)	T2—947 1
Canadian Rockies (B.C. and		Cancellations (Philately)	744.72
Alta.)	T2—711	Cancer	571.978
Canadian Shield	T2—714	animals	571.978 1
Canada	T2—714	veterinary medicine	636.089 699 4
Manitoba	T2—712 72	humans	362.196 994
Ontario	T2—713 1	geriatrics	618.976 994
Canadian spelling		incidence	614.599 9
English	421.52	medicine	616.994
French	441.52	nursing	616.994 023 1
Canadians	T5—11	pediatrics	618.929 94
see Manual at T5—112,		social services	362.196 994
T5—114 vs. T5—2,		surgery	616.994 059
T5—41		Cancer (Zodiac)	133.526 5
Canaigre	633.87	Candelilla wax	665.12
agriculture	633.87	Candidiasis	
botany	583.888	incidence	614.559 3
Çanakkale İli (Turkey)	T2—562 2	medicine	616.969 3
ancient	T2—392 1	see also Communicable	
Asia	T2—562 2	diseases — humans	
Europe	T2—496 12	Candleberry	583.65
Canal Area (Panama)	T2—728 75	Candleberry wax	665.12
Canal transportation	386.4	Candler County (Ga.)	T2—758 773
see also Inland water		Candles	621.323
transportation		handicrafts	745.593 32
Canalboats		see also Lighting	
freight services	386.244	Candlesticks	621.323
power-driven	386.224 36	ceramic arts	738.8
design	623.812 436	handicrafts	745.593 3
engineering	623.824 36	see also Lighting	
transportation services	386.224 36	Candlewood	583.93
		Candomblé	299.673

Candy	641.853
commercial processing	664.153
home preparation	641.853
Candytufts (Plants)	583.78
Cane fruits	641.347 1
botany	583.642
cooking	641.647 1
food	641.347 1
horticulture	634.71
Cane rat	599.359
Cane sugar	641.336 1
commercial processing	664.122
food	641.336 1
see also Sugar	
Cane syrup	641.336 1
commercial processing	664.122
food	641.336 1
see also Sugar	
Cane textiles	677.54
see also Textiles	
Canea (Greece : Regional	
unit)	T2—495 9
Canella language	498.4
	T6—984
Canellaceae	584.282
Canellales	584.282
Canelones (Uruguay :	
Dept.)	T2—895 14
Canes (Sticks)	391.44
Caniapiscau (Quebec :	
Regional County	
Municipality)	T2—714 117
Canidae	599.77
paleozoology	569.77
Canindeyú (Paraguay)	T2—892 133
Canine police services	363.232
Canines	636.7
see also Dogs	
Canis	599.772
Çankırı İli (Turkey)	T2—563 7
ancient	T2—393 17
Canna (Scotland)	T2—411 54
Cannabaceae	583.648
Cannabis	
pharmacokinetics	615.782 7
Cannabis abuse	362.295
medicine	616.863 5
personal health	613.835
social welfare	362.295
see also Substance abuse	
Cannaceae	584.88
Cannas	635.934 88
botany	584.88
floriculture	635.934 88

Canned foods	
cooking	641.612
product safety	363.192 9
see also Food — product	
safety	
Cannel coal	553.23
economic geology	553.23
properties	662.622 3
Cannibalism	
customs	394.9
Cannibalism in animals	591.53
Canning, John Charles, Earl	
Indian history	954.031 7
Canning foods	664.028 2
commercial preservation	664.028 2
home preservation	641.42
Cannock Chase (England)	T2—424 67
Cannon County (Tenn.)	T2—768 535
Cannons	355.822
art metalwork	739.742
engineering	623.424
military equipment	355.822
Canoe racing	797.14
Canoeing	
sports	797.122
see also Aquatic sports	
Canoes	386.229
design	623.812 9
engineering	623.829
transportation services	386.229
Canoidea	599.76
paleozoology	569.76
Canon law	262.9
Canon of Bible	220.12
Canonization of saints	235.24
Canons (Music)	784.187 8
Canons regular	255.08
church history	271.08
women	255.908
church history	271.908
Canopies	
church architecture	726.529 3
Cant	417.2
specific languages	T4—7
Cantabria (Spain)	T2—463 51
Cantabrian Mountains	
(Spain)	T2—462
Cantal (France)	T2—445 92
Cantaloupes	641.356 117
cooking	641.656 117
food	641.356 117
garden crop	635.611 7

Cantatas	782.24
choral and mixed voices	782.524
single voices	783.092 4
Canteen cooking	641.577
Canteen meal service	642.5
Canteens	
armed forces	355.341
Canterbury Region (N.Z.)	T2—938
Cantharidae	595.764 4
Cantharoidea	595.764 4
Canticle of Canticles	223.9
Canticles	782.295
Cantilever bridges	
construction	624.219
Cantilever foundations	624.156
Canton (China)	T2—512 75
Cantonese dialects	495.179 512 7
	T6—951 7
Cantons	320.83
see also Counties	
Cantons-de-l'Est (Quebec)	T2—714 6
Cantors (Judaism)	296.462
biography	296.462 092
Cantus firmus	781.828
Canunda National Park (S.	
Aust.)	T2—942 34
Canute I, King of England	
English history	942.018 1
Canvas embroidery	746.442
Canvasback	598.414
Canyon County (Idaho)	T2—796 23
Canyoneering	796.524
Canyoning	796.524
see also Outdoor life	
Canyonlands National Park	
(Utah)	T2—792 59
Canyons	551.442
	T2—144
geography	910.914 4
geomorphology	551.442
physical geography	910.021 44
Canzonas	784.187 5
Cao Bằng (Vietnam :	
Province)	T2—597 1
Cap-de-la-Madeleine	
(Trois-Rivières, Quebec)	T2—714 451
Capacitance meters	621.374 2
Capacitors	
electrical engineering	621.315
radio engineering	621.384 133
Capacity (Law)	346.013
Cape (South Africa :	
District)	T2—687 35
Cape Baring (N.W.T.)	T2—719 3

Cape Breton (N.S. :	
Regional municipality)	T2—716 95
Cape Breton Highlands	
National Park (N.S.)	T2—716 91
Cape Breton Island (N.S.)	T2—716 9
Cape Cod (Mass.)	T2—744 92
Cape Cod Bay (Mass.)	551.461 345
	T2—163 45
Cape Dorset (Nunavut)	T2—719 52
Cape Fear River (N.C.)	T2—756 2
Cape Girardeau County	
(Mo.)	T2—778 96
Cape Hatteras (N.C.)	T2—756 175
Cape Le Grand National	
Park (W.A.)	T2—941 7
Cape May County (N.J.)	T2—749 98
Cape Metropolitan Area	
(South Africa)	T2—687 35
Cape of Good Hope (South	
Africa)	968.705
	T2—687
Cape of Good Hope (South	
Africa : Cape)	T2—687 356
Cape Peninsula (South	
Africa : Cape)	T2—687 356
Cape Peninsula National	
Park (South Africa)	T2—687 356
Cape Range National Park	
(W.A.)	T2—941 3
Cape Town (South Africa)	T2—687 355
Cape Verde	966.58
	T2—665 8
Cape Verde Islands	T2—665 8
Cape Verdeans	T5—966 58
Cape Winelands District	
Municipality (South	
Africa)	T2—687 33
Cape Wollaston (N.W.T.)	T2—719 3
Cape York Peninsula (Qld.)	T2—943 8
Capercaillies	598.634
Capers	641.338 2
botany	583.78
see also Flavorings	
Capes (Clothing)	391.46
see also Outerwear	
Capetian dynasty	944.021
genealogy	929.74
Capillaries	573.187
animals	573.187
human anatomy	611.15
human physiology	612.135
medicine	616.148
physiology	573.187

Capillaries (continued)	
surgery	617.415
see also Cardiovascular system	
Capillarity	530.427
chemical engineering	660.293
Capillary circulation	573.187
human physiology	612.135
see also Capillaries	
Capillary diseases	
medicine	616.148
see also Cardiovascular	
diseases — humans	
Capillary hemangiomas	
medicine	616.993 15
Capital	332.041
financial economics	332.041
income distribution	339.21
management	658.152
production economics	338.604 1
Capital (B.C.)	T2—711 28
Capital accounting	657.76
Capital budgets	658.154
Capital budgets (Public)	352.48
see also Budgets (Public)	
Capital cities	
area planning	711.45
Capital Federal (Argentina)	T2—821 1
Capital flight	332.042 4
Capital flows	332.042 4
Capital formation	332.041 5
agricultural industries	338.13
economics	332.041 5
financial management	658.152 2
macroeconomics	339.43
mineral industries	338.23
production economics	338.604 1
secondary industries	338.43
Capital gains tax	336.242 4
law	343.052 45
public administration	352.44
public finance	336.242 4
corporate income	336.243
individual income	336.242 4
Capital levy	336.22
law	343.054
Capital loss	
personal income tax deduction	336.242 4
Capital management	658.152
Capital markets	332.041 5
Capital movements	332.042 4

Capital punishment	364.66
ethics	179.7
religion	205.697
Buddhism	294.356 97
Christianity	241.697
Hinduism	294.548 697
Islam	297.569 7
Judaism	296.369 7
law	345.077 3
penology	364.66
social theology	201.764
Christianity	261.833 66
Capital Region (Denmark)	T2—489 13
Capital sources	332.041 5
financial management	658.152 2
Capital transactions (Balance of payments)	
international banking	332.152
international finance	332.042 4
Capitale-Nationale (Quebec)	T2—714 47
Capitalism	330.122
economics	330.122
social theology	201.73
Christianity	261.85
Judaism	296.383
sociology	306.342
Capitalization (Finance)	658.152
Capitalization (Writing)	411
specific languages	T4—11
Capitals (Architecture)	721.3
Capitán Prat (Chile : Province)	T2—836 28
Capitol Reef National Park (Utah)	T2—792 54
Capitols	
architecture	725.11
Capitonidae	598.72
Capiz (Philippines : Province)	T2—599 534
Cappadocia (Kingdom)	T2—393 4
Cappadocia (Turkey)	T2—564 1
Capparaceae	583.78
Capparales	583.78
Capparidales	583.78
Capra	599.648
Capreolus	599.659
Capri Island (Italy)	T2—457 3
Capricorn (Zodiac)	133.527 5
Capricorn District Municipality (South Africa)	T2—682 56
Caprifoliaceae	583.987
Caprimulgiformes	598.99
paleozoology	568.9

Carbonated beverages	641.26	Cardiac arrest	
commercial processing	663.62	medicine	616.123 025
home preparation	641.875	*see also* Cardiovascular	
Carbonated water		diseases — humans	
commercial processing	663.61	Cardiac asthma	
Carbonates		medicine	616.12
mineralogy	549.78	*see also* Cardiovascular	
Carbonia-Iglesia (Italy :		diseases — humans	
Province)	T2—459 8	Cardiac muscle tissues	
ancient	T2—379 8	human histology	612.740 45
Carboniferous period	551.75	Cardiff (Wales)	T2—429 87
geology	551.75	Cardigans	391.46
paleontology	560.175	commercial technology	687.14
Carboxylic acids	547.037	home sewing	646.45
chemical engineering	661.86	*see also* Outerwear	
Carbro process	773.1	Cardinal fishes	597.7
Carbuncles		Cardinal numbers	511.322
medicine	616.523	Cardinal sins	241.3
see also Skin diseases —		Cardinals (Birds)	598.883
humans		Cardinals (Clergy)	282.092
Carbureted-blue gas	665.772	biography	282.092
Carburetors	621.437	ecclesiology	262.135
automotive	629.253 3	Carding textiles	677.028 21
Carcharhinidae	597.34	arts	746.11
Carcharhiniformes	597.3	manufacturing technology	677.028 21
Carcharodon carcharias	597.33	Cardiology	616.12
Carchi (Ecuador)	T2—866 11	pediatrics	618.921 2
Carcinogenesis		Cardiopteridaceae	583.982
biology	571.978	Cardiopulmonary diseases	
medicine	616.994 071	medicine	616.1
Carcinoma	571.978	*see also* Cardiovascular	
incidence	614.599 9	diseases — humans	
medicine	616.994	Cardiopulmonary resuscitation	
see also Cancer		medicine	616.102 5
Card catalogs	025.313	Cardiotonic agents	
Card games	795.4	pharmacokinetics	615.711
biography	795.409 2	Cardiovascular agents	
Card players	795.409 2	pharmacokinetics	615.71
Card readers (Computers)	004.76	Cardiovascular diseases	573.139
engineering	621.398 6	animals	573.139
Card tricks	793.85	veterinary medicine	636.089 61
Card weaving		humans	362.196 1
arts	746.14	anesthesiology	617.967 41
Cardamom	641.338 32	cancer	362.196 994 1
agriculture	633.832	incidence	614.599 941
botany	584.88	medicine	616.994 1
food	641.338 32	social services	362.196 994 1
see also Spices		*see also* Cancer —	
Cardboard	676.288	humans	
Cárdenas, Lázaro		geriatrics	618.976 1
Mexican history	972.082 5	incidence	614.591
		medicine	616.1
		nursing	616.102 31
		pediatrics	618.921

Caries	
dentistry	617.67
incidence	614.599 6
Carillons	786.64
see also Mechanical musical	
instruments	
Caring	
ethics	177.7
religion	205.677
see also Love — ethics	
Carinthia (Austria)	T2—436 6
Carjacking	364.162 862 922 2
law	345.026 286 292 22
Carl XVI Gustaf, King of	
Sweden	
Swedish history	948.505 4
Carleton (N.B. : County)	T2—715 52
Carleton (Ont.)	T2—713 84
Carlisle (England : City)	T2—427 89
Carlisle County (Ky.)	T2—769 97
Carlow (Ireland : County)	T2—418 82
Carlsbad Caverns National	
Park (N.M.)	T2—789 42
Carlton County (Minn.)	T2—776 73
Carmarthen (Wales :	
District)	T2—429 65
Carmarthenshire (Wales)	T2—429 65
Carmelite Nuns	255.971
church history	271.971
Carmelites	255.73
church history	271.73
women	255.971
church history	271.971
Carnallite	553.636
mineralogy	549.4
Carnarvon (South Africa :	
District)	T2—687 13
Carnarvon National Park	
(Qld.)	T2—943 5
Carnations	635.933 883
botany	583.883
floriculture	635.933 883
Carnauba wax	665.12
Carnival	394.25
Carnivals	791.1
customs	394.26
Carnivora	599.7
conservation technology	639.979 7
paleozoology	569.7
resource economics	333.959 7
Carnivorous animals	591.53
Carnivorous dinosaurs	567.912

Carnivorous plants	583.887
botany	583.887
Byblidaceae	583.96
Cephalotaceae	583.68
floriculture	635.933 887
Lentibulariaceae	583.96
Nepenthales	583.887
physiology	575.99
Sarraceniaceae	583.93
Carnot cycle	536.71
Caro, Joseph	
Jewish legal codes	296.182
Carob	641.344 6
botany	583.63
cooking	641.644 6
food	641.344 6
orchard crop	634.46
Carolina (South Africa :	
District)	T2—682 78
Caroline County (Md.)	T2—752 31
Caroline County (Va.)	T2—755 362
Caroline Islands	T2—966
Carolingian dynasty	944.014
French history	944.014
German history	943.014
Italian history	945.02
Lombardian history	945.202
Piedmontese history	945.102
Tuscan history	945.502
Venetian history	945.302
Carols	782.28
choral and mixed voices	782.528
single voices	783.092 8
Carom billiards	794.72
Carotid body	
human anatomy	611.47
human physiology	612.49
medicine	616.4
Carp	641.392
cooking	641.692
culture	639.374 83
food	641.392
sports fishing	799.174 83
zoology	597.483
Carp family	597.482
Carpal tunnel syndrome	
medicine	616.856
see also Nervous system	
diseases — humans	
Carpals	
human anatomy	611.717
human physiology	612.751

Cartilage	573.763 56
human histology	612.751 7
human physiology	612.751 7
medicine	616.77
see also Musculoskeletal system	
Cartilage cells	
human cytology	612.751 76
Cartilage diseases	
medicine	616.77
see also Musculoskeletal diseases — humans	
Cartilaginous fishes	597.3
Cartilaginous ganoids	597.42
Cartographers	526.092
Cartographic materials	
cataloging	025.346
library treatment	025.176
Cartography	526
design	744.37
military engineering	623.71
military intelligence service	355.343 2
Cartomancy	133.324 2
Cartons	688.8
paperboard	676.32
Cartoon animation	741.58
Cartoon fiction	741.5
Cartoon films	791.433 4
cinematography	777.7
drawing	741.58
motion pictures	791.433 4
Cartoon television programs	791.453 4
cinematography	777.7
drawing	741.58
Cartooning	
techniques	741.51
Cartoonists	
biography	741.569 3–.569 9
see Manual at 741.593–.599 and 741.5693–.5699	
Cartoons	741.56
	T1—022 2
drawing	741.51
genres	
history, criticism, techniques	741.53
geographic treatment	741.569 3–.569 9
see Manual at 741.593–.599 and 741.5693–.5699	
humor	741.56
	T1—020 7

Cartoons (continued)	
journalism	
comic strips	070.444
editorial	070.442
see Manual at 741.5; *also at* 741.5 vs. 741.56	
Cartridge tapes (Computers)	004.563
engineering	621.397 63
Cartridges (Ammunition)	683.406
manufacturing technology	683.406
military engineering	623.455
Carts	388.341
manufacturing technology	688.6
Cārvāka	181.46
Carvalho, Evaristo	
Sao Tomean history	967.150 25
Carver County (Minn.)	T2—776 53
Carving	
artistic technique	730.28
architectural decoration	729.5
decorative arts	736
sculpture	731.46
table service	642.6
Caryocaraceae	583.69
Caryophyllaceae	583.883
Caryophyllales	583.88
Caryophyllidae	583.88
Casaba melon	641.356 117
cooking	641.656 117
food	641.356 117
garden crop	635.611 7
Casablanca (Morocco)	T2—643 8
Casablanca-Anfa (Morocco : Prefecture)	T2—643 8
Casanare (Colombia : Dept.)	T2—861 96
Cascade County (Mont.)	T2—786 611
Cascade Mountains (B.C.)	T2—711 5
Cascade Range	T2—795
British Columbia	T2—711 5
California	T2—794 2
Oregon	T2—795
Washington	T2—797 5
Cascades	
landscape architecture	714
Cascading style sheets	006.74
Case (Grammar)	415.5
specific languages	T4—55
Case-based reasoning	
computer science	006.333
Case grammar (Theory)	415.018 24
specific languages	T4—501 824
Case histories	
medicine	616.09

Casting metals	671.2	Casuistry	
arts	730.28	ethical systems	171.6
decorative arts	739.14	Caswell County (N.C.)	T2—756 575
sculpture	731.456	CAT (Air transportation hazard)	363.124 12
technology	671.2	Cat breeds	636.8
Casting plastics	668.412	*see Manual at* 636.82–.83	
Casting pottery	666.442	Cat briers	584.6
arts	738.142	Cat family (Felidae)	599.75
technology	666.442	CAT scan	
Castle Point (England)	T2—426 792	medicine	616.075 722
Castlegar (B.C.)	T2—711 62	Catabolism	572.48
Castlemaine (Vic.)	T2—945 3	*see also* Metabolism	
Castlereagh (Northern		Catahoula Parish (La.)	T2—763 74
Ireland : District)	T2—416 51	Catalan language	449.9
Castles			T6—499
architecture	728.81	Catalan literature	849.9
domestic	728.81	Catalans	T5—49
military	725.18	Catalases	572.791
Castles (Chessmen)	794.143	*see also* Enzymes	
Castor oil	665.353	Catalog marketing	381.142
Castor-oil plant	583.69	management	658.872
Castoridae	599.37	Catalog shopping	381.142
paleozoology	569.37	law	343.081 142 8
Castrato voices	782.86	Cataloging	
choral and mixed voices	782.86	library science	025.3
single voices	783.86	museology	069.52
Castro, Cipriano		Cataloging in publication	025.3
Venezuelan history	987.063 12	Catalogs	T1—021 6
Castro, Fidel		design	744.57
Cuban history	972.910 64	postal handling	383.124
Castro, Raúl		*see also* Postal service	
Cuban history	972.910 71	*see also* Auction catalogs	
Castro, Xiomara		Catalogs (Bibliographic catalogs)	\025.31
Honduran history	972.830 543	general catalogs	011
Castro County (Tex.)	T2—764 837	library science	025.31
Castroism	335.434 7	specific collections	017
economics	335.434 7	specific forms	011.3
political ideology	320.532 309 729 1	specific historical periods	011.09
Casual clothes	391	specific languages	011.2
see also Casual wear		specific places	015
Casual wear	391	specific subjects	016
commercial technology	687	*see Manual at* 011–017	
customs	391	Catalogs of exhibits	069.52
home economics	646.3		T1—074
home sewing	646.4	museology	069.52
see also Clothing		*see Manual at* T1—074 vs.	
Casual workers	331.544	T1—029	
Casualty insurance	368.5	Catalonia (Spain)	T2—467
law	346.086 5	Catalpas	635.977 396
see also Insurance		botany	583.96
Casuariiformes	598.53	ornamental arboriculture	635.977 396
paleozoology	568.5	Cataluña (Spain)	T2—467
Casuarinaceae	583.65		
Casuarinales	583.65		

Catalysis	541.395	Catechetics	268
chemical engineering	660.299 5	Catechisms	202
organic chemistry	547.215	Christianity	238
Catalytic cracking	665.533	Catechists	268
Catamarca (Argentina :		biography	268.092
Province)	T2—824 5	*see Manual at* 230–280	
Catamblyrhynchidae	598.88	role and function	268.3
Catana (Italy)	T2—378 131	Catechols	547.633
Catanduanes Island		Catechumenate	265.13
(Philippines)	T2—599 187	Categorial grammar	415.018 235
Catanduanes Province		specific languages	T4—501 823 5
(Philippines)	T2—599 187	Categories (Mathematics)	512.62
Catania (Italy)	T2—458 131	Category theory	512.62
ancient	T2—378 131	Catered meals	642.4
Catania (Italy : Città		Caterers	642.409 2
metropolitana)	T2—458 13	Catering	642.4
ancient	T2—378 13	Catering establishments	647.95
Catanzaro (Italy : Province)	T2—457 81	*see also* Eating places	
ancient	T2—377 81	Caterpillars	595.781 392
Catapults	355.822	culture	638.578 139 2
engineering	623.422	Catfishes	597.49
military equipment	355.822	Catfishes (Channel catfish)	641.392
Cataracts		conservation technology	639.977 492
ophthalmology	617.742	cooking	641.692
see also Eye diseases —		culture	639.374 92
humans		food	641.392
Catarrhini	599.86	resource economics	333.956 492
paleozoology	569.86	sports fishing	799.174 92
Catastrophes	904	zoology	597.492
see also Disasters		Catharine, the Great	
Catastrophes (Biological		Russian history	947.063
evolution)	576.84	Catharism	273.6
Catastrophes (Mathematics)	514.744	denomination	284.4
Catastrophic health insurance	368.382 8	persecution of	272.3
government-sponsored	368.42	Cathartics	
law	344.022	pharmacokinetics	615.732
law	346.086 382 8	Cathartidae	598.92
see also Insurance		Cathcart (South Africa :	
Catawba County (N.C.)	T2—756 785	District)	T2—687 54
Catawba Indians	T5—975 2	Cathedral systems	
Catawba language	497.52	Christian ecclesiology	262.3
	T6—975 2	Cathedrals	
Catawba River (N.C. and		architecture	726.6
S.C.)	T2—757 45	religious significance	246.96
Catbirds	598.844	Catherine I, Empress of Russia	
Catch-as-catch-can wrestling	796.812 3	Russian history	947.061
see also Combat sports		Catherine II, Empress of Russia	
Catch basins		Russian history	947.063
sewers	628.25	Catheterization	
Catchers' mitts		surgery	617.05
manufacturing technology	688.763 57	Cathode-ray tubes	621.381 542 2
Catching		television engineering	621.388 32
baseball	796.357 23	Catholic Church	282
Catchword indexing	025.486	Catholic epistles	227.9

Catholic regions	T2—176 12
Catholic schools	371.071 2
Catholicity	262.72
Catholics	282.092
Catnip	583.96
Catnip tea	641.357
see also Herb teas	
Catoosa County (Ga.)	T2—758 326
Catron County (N.M.)	T2—789 93
Cats	636.8
animal husbandry	636.8
arts	T3C—362 975 2
predator control technology	636.083 9
zoology	599.752
Cat's cradles	793.96
Catskill Mountains (N.Y.)	T2—747 38
Catsup	641.814
commercial processing	664.58
home preparation	641.814
Cattails (Plants)	584.99
Cattaraugus County (N.Y.)	T2—747 94
Cattle	636.2
agricultural economics	338.176 2
animal husbandry	636.2
theft of	364.162 863 62
law	345.026 286 362
zoology	599.642 2
Cattle cars	385.34
engineering	625.24
see also Rolling stock	
Cattle stealing	364.162 863 62
law	345.026 286 362
Cattlemen	636.213 092
CATV systems	384.554 6
see also Television	
Cauca (Colombia : Dept.)	T2—861 53
Caucasian Albania	T2—395 34
Caucasian languages	499.96
	T6—999 6
Caucasian literatures	899.96
Caucasian race	305.809
	T5—09
Caucasians (Peoples of the	
Caucasus)	T5—999 6
Caucasic languages	499.96
	T6—999 6
Caucasic literatures	899.96
Caucasoid race	T5—09
Caucasus	947.5
	T2—475
ancient	939.53
	T2—395 3
Russia	T2—475 2

Caucasus rugs	
arts	746.759
Cauchy integral	515.43
Cauchy problem	515.35
Caucus nomination	324.52
Caucuses (Legislative)	328.36
Caudal anesthesia	
surgery	617.964
Caudata	597.85
Caudofoveata	594.2
Caulerpales	579.835
Cauliflower	641.353 5
commercial processing	664.805 35
cooking	641.653 5
food	641.353 5
garden crop	635.35
Causation	
philosophy	122
Causative (Linguistics)	415.6
specific languages	T4—56
Cause	
philosophy	122
Causes of Holocaust	940.531 811
Causes of war	355.027
American Revolution	973.311
Civil War (United States)	973.711
Mexican War	973.621
South African War	968.048 1
Vietnamese War	959.704 31
World War I	940.311
World War II	940.531 1
Causeway Coast & Glens	
(Northern Ireland)	T2—416 14
Caustic potash	546.383 22
chemical engineering	661.332
Caustic soda	546.382 22
chemical engineering	661.322
Cautín (Chile)	T2—834 6
Cavalier County (N.D.)	T2—784 37
Cavalry (Horse mounted)	357.1
Cavalry (Mechanized)	357.5
Cavalry forces	357
Cavan (Ireland : County)	T2—416 98
Cave animals	591.758 4
Cave dwellers	569.9
Cave fishes	597.175 84
Cavefishes (Amblyopsidae)	597.62
Caves	551.447
	T2—144
biology	578.758 4
ecology	577.584
exploring	796.525
see also Outdoor life	
geography	910.914 4

Celebrations	394.2
armed forces	355.16
see also Military	
commemorations	
cooking	641.568
customs	394.2
public administrative support	353.77
Celeriac	641.351 28
cooking	641.651 28
food	641.351 28
garden crop	635.128
Celery	641.355 3
botany	583.988 2
commercial processing	664.805 53
cooking	641.655 3
food	641.355 3
garden crop	635.53
Celery root	641.351 28
see also Celeriac	
Celestas	786.83
instrument	786.831 9
music	786.83
see also Percussion instruments	
Celestial bodies	520
folklore	398.26
history and criticism	398.362
Celestial Church of Christ	289.93
see also Christian	
denominations	
Celestial mechanics	521
engineering	629.411
Celestial navigation	527
nautical	623.89
Celestial reference systems	522.7
Celestines	255.16
church history	271.16
Celestite	
mineralogy	549.752
Celiac disease	
medicine	616.399 12
see also Digestive system	
diseases — humans	
Celibacy	306.732
customs	392.6
ethics	176.4
religion	205.664
Buddhism	294.356 64
Christianity	241.664
Hinduism	294.548 664
psychology	155.3
religious practice	204.47
Buddhism	294.344 47
Christianity	248.47
clergy	262.140 865

Celibacy	
religious practice (continued)	
Hinduism	294.544 7
sociology	306.732
Cell biology	571.6
humans	611.018 1
Cell chemistry	572
Cell culture	571.638
experimental research	
medicine	616.027 7
Cell death	571.936
Cell determination	571.863 6
Cell differentiation	571.835
Cell digestion	572.4
Cell division	571.844
Cell lines	
experimental research	
medicine	616.027 7
Cell-mediated immunity	571.966
humans	616.079 7
Cell membrane receptors	572.696
Cell membranes	571.64
Cell metabolism	572.4
Cell movement	571.67
Cell physiology	571.6
humans	611.018 1
Cell receptors	572.696
Cell respiration	572.47
Cell walls	571.68
Cellists	787.409 2
Cello concertos	784.274 186
Cellos	787.4
instrument	787.419
music	787.4
see also Stringed instruments	
Cells (Biology)	571.6
anatomy	571.633
growth	571.84
humans	611.018 1
pathology	571.936
reproduction	571.84
Cells (Rooms)	
architecture	726.79
Cellular automata	511.35
computer science	006.382 2
mathematics	511.35
Cellular immunity	571.966
humans	616.079 7
Cellular pathology	571.936
humans	611.018 15
Cellular radio	384.535
engineering	621.384 56
Cellular slime molds	579.52

Central African Republic	
people	T5—967 41
Central Africans (National	
group)	T5—967 41
Central Algonquian languages	497.31
	T6—973 1
Central America	972.8
	T2—728
Central America (Federal	
Republic : 1823–1840)	972.804
	T2—728
Costa Rican history	972.860 42
Guatemalan history	972.810 42
Honduran history	972.830 4
Nicaraguan history	972.850 42
Salvadoran history	972.840 42
Central American native	
languages	497
	T6—97
Central American native	
literatures	897
Central American native	
peoples	T5—970 728
Central Americans	305.868 728
	T5—687 28
Central Asia	958
	T2—58
ancient	939.6
	T2—396
Central Athens (Greece)	T2—495 12
Central Australia	T2—942
Central banks	332.11
Central Bedfordshire	
(England)	T2—425 63
Central Black Earth Region	
(Russia)	T2—473 5
Central business district	
community redevelopment	307.342
Central Chernozem Region	
(Russia)	T2—473 5
Central Coast (B.C.)	T2—711 1
Central Denmark Region	
(Denmark)	T2—489 55
Central Dravidian languages	494.82
	T6—948 2
Central Dravidian literatures	894.82
Central Dravidians	T5—948 2
Central eastern Europe	943.7
	T2—437
Central Equatoria State	
(South Sudan)	T2—629 5
Central Europe	943
	T2—43
Central Finland (Finland)	T2—489 738

Central Fraser Valley (B.C.)	T2—711 37
Central Greece (Greece)	T2—495 15
Central Hawke's Bay	
District (N.Z.)	T2—934 69
Central heating	697.03
resource economics	333.793
Central Intelligence Agency	
(U.S.)	327.127 3
Central Italy	945.6
	T2—456
Central Java (Indonesia)	959.826
	T2—598 26
Central Kalimantan	
(Indonesia)	T2—598 34
Central Karoo District	
Municipality (South	
Africa)	T2—687 39
Central Kootenay (B.C.)	T2—711 62
Central Lowlands	
(Scotland)	T2—413
Central Luzon (Philippines :	
Region)	T2—599 15
Central Macedonia (Greece)	T2—495 65
Central Malayo-Polynesian	
languages	499.22
	T6—992 2
Central Mindanao	
(Philippines)	T2—599 74
Central nervous system	573.86
biology	573.86
human anatomy	611.81
human biochemistry	612.822
human biophysics	612.822
human physiology	612.82
medicine	616.8
see also Nervous system	
Central nervous system diseases	573.863 9
animals	573.863 9
humans	
medicine	616.8
see also Nervous system	
diseases	
Central Okanagan (B.C.)	T2—711 5
Central Ostrobothnia	
(Finland)	T2—489 735
Central Otago District	
(N.Z.)	T2—939 4
Central Pacific Basin	551.461 49
	T2—164 9
Central Pacific islands	T2—96
Central Powers (World War I)	940.334
Central processing units	004
engineering	621.39
Central Province (Kenya)	T2—676 26

Ceratophyllales	583.2	Cerebrovascular diseases	
paleobotany	561.3	medicine	616.81
Ceratopsia	567.915	*see also* Nervous system	
Cercidiphyllaceae	583.44	diseases — humans	
Cercidiphyllales	583.44	Cerebrum	
Cercopithecidae	599.86	human anatomy	611.81
paleozoology	569.86	human physiology	612.825
Cercopithecus	599.862	medicine	616.8
Cereal grains		Ceredigion (Wales)	T2—429 61
commercial processing	664.7	Ceremonial robes	391.48
Cereal grasses	584.926	commercial technology	687.15
botany	584.926	customs	391.48
forage crops	633.25	*see also* Clothing	
see Manual at 633–635		Ceremonials	264.022
Cereals	641.331	Ceremonies	394
agriculture	633.1	armed forces	355.17
animal feed	636.086	customs	394
botany	584.926	religion	203.8
commercial processing	664.7	*see also* Rites — religion	
ready-to-eat cereals	664.756	*see Manual at* 392, 393, 394	
cooking	641.631	vs. 793.2	
food	641.331	Ceres (Dwarf planet)	523.44
forage crops	633.25	Ceres (South Africa :	
see Manual at 633–635		District)	T2—687 33
Cerebellum		Cerigo Island (Greece)	T2—495 2
human anatomy	611.81	Cerium	
human physiology	612.827	chemistry	546.412
medicine	616.8	Cerium-group metals	
Cerebral commissures		economic geology	553.494 3
human physiology	612.826	Cerro Gordo County (Iowa)	T2—777 25
Cerebral hemispheres		Cerro Largo (Uruguay)	T2—895 23
human anatomy	611.81	Certainty	
human physiology	612.825	epistemology	121.63
medicine	616.8	Certhiidae	598.82
Cerebral infarction		Certificates (Awards)	T1—079
medicine	616.81	research	001.44
see also Nervous system		Certificates of deposit	332.175 2
diseases — humans		Certification	352.84
Cerebral ischemia		*see also* Licensing	
medicine	616.81	Certitude	
see also Nervous system		epistemology	121.63
diseases — humans		Cerveteri (Italy)	T2—456 3
Cerebral palsy		ancient	T2—375 9
medicine	616.836	Cervical caps	
see also Nervous system		health	613.943 5
diseases — humans		medicine	618.185
Cerebral peduncles		*see also* Birth control	
human physiology	612.826	Cervical vertebrae	
Cerebral sphingolipidosis		medicine	616.73
medicine	616.858 845	Cervicitis	
Cerebrospinal fluid		gynecology	618.142
human physiology	612.804 2	*see also* Female genital	
Cerebrovascular circulation		diseases — humans	
human physiology	612.824		

Chairs	645.4	Champagne	641.222 4
decorative arts	749.32	commercial processing	663.224
manufacturing technology	684.132	Champagne (France :	
outdoor furniture	645.8	Province)	T2—443 1
see also Outdoor furniture		Champagne-Ardenne	
see also Furniture		(France)	T2—443 1
Chaka, Zulu Chief		Champaign County (Ill.)	T2—773 66
KwaZulu-Natal history	968.403 9	Champaign County (Ohio)	T2—771 465
Chakwera, Lazarus McCarthy		Champlain (Quebec :	
Malawian history	968.970 45	County)	T2—714 455
Chalatenango (El Salvador :		Champlain (Quebec :	
Dept.)	T2—728 421	Regional County	
Chalcidice (Greece)	T2—495 65	Municipality)	T2—714 37
Chalcidoidea	595.79	Champlain, Lake	T2—747 54
Chalcids	595.79	New York	T2—747 54
Chalcis (Extinct city)	T2—384	Vermont	T2—743 1
Chalcocite		Champlevé	
mineralogy	549.32	ceramic arts	738.4
Chalcogens	546.72	Ch'an Buddhism	294.392 7
Chalcolithic Age	930.153	Chañaral (Chile : Province)	T2—831 42
Chaldean Empire	935.04	Chance	
	T2—35	philosophy	123.3
Chaldean Neo-Aramaic		probabilities	519.2
people	T5—923	Chance composition	781.32
Chaldeans (Religious order)	255.18	Chancel railings	247.1
church history	271.18	architecture	726.529 6
Chaldee (Aramaic) language	492.29	Chancellors (Prime ministers)	352.53
	T6—922 9	cabinet governments	321.804 3
Chalk	553.68	public administration	352.23
economic geology	553.68	Chancels	
petrology	552.58	architecture	726.593
Chalk drawing	741.23	Chancroid	
Chalkidikē (Greece)	T2—495 65	incidence	614.547
Challoner Bible	220.520 2	medicine	616.951 8
Chamaeidae	598.834	*see also* Communicable	
Chamaeleontidae	597.956	diseases — humans	
Chamaemyiidae	595.774	Chandeliers	
Chamber music	785	furniture arts	749.63
Chamber orchestras	784.3	Chandīgarh (India)	T2—545 52
Chambers County (Ala.)	T2—761 56	Chandra Shekhar	
Chambers County (Tex.)	T2—764 143	Indian history	954.052
Chambers of commerce	381.06	Changamire (Kingdom)	968.910 1
architecture	725.25		T2—689 1
Chambly (Quebec : County)	T2—714 365	Change	116
Chameleons	597.956	executive management	658.406
Chameleons (Anoles)	597.954 8	philosophy	116
Chamic languages	499.22	political science	320.011
	T6—992 2	sociology	303.4
Chamois	599.647	Changing voices	782.79
Chamomiles	583.983	choral and mixed voices	782.79
Chamorro	T5—995 2	single voices	783.79
Chamorro language	499.52	Chania (Greece : Regional	
	T6—995 2	unit)	T2—495 9
		Channel bass	597.725

Charitable donations		Charles VI, Holy Roman	
financial management	658.153	Emperor	
tax law	343.052 32	German history	943.052
Charitable trusts	361.763 2	Charles VI, King of France	
law	346.064 2	French history	944.026
income tax law	343.052 668	Charles VII, Holy Roman	
tax law	343.066 8	Emperor	
social welfare	361.763 2	German history	943.054
Charities	361.7	Charles VII, King of France	
see also Welfare services		French history	944.026
Chariton County (Mo.)	T2—778 25	Charles VIII, King of France	
Chariton River (Iowa and		French history	944.027
Mo.)	T2—778 2	Italian history	945.06
Charity		Tuscan history	945.506
ethics	177.7	Venetian history	945.306
religion	205.677	Charles IX, King of France	
Christianity	241.4	French history	944.029
see also Love — ethics		Charles IX, King of Sweden	
Charlemagne, Emperor		Swedish history	948.503 25
French history	944.014 2	Charles X, King of France	
German history	943.014	French history	944.062
Charles I, King of England		Charles X Gustav, King of	
British history	941.062	Sweden	
English history	942.062	Swedish history	948.503 43
Scottish history	941.106 2	Charles XI, King of Sweden	
Charles I, King of Spain		Swedish history	948.503 44
Spanish history	946.042	Charles XII, King of Sweden	
Charles II, King of England		Swedish history	948.503 45
British history	941.066	Charles XIII, King of Sweden	
English history	942.066	and Norway	
Scottish history	941.106 6	Swedish history	948.504 1
Charles II, King of Spain		Charles XIV John, King of	
Spanish history	946.053	Sweden and Norway	
Charles III, Duke of Savoy		Swedish history	948.504 1
Piedmontese history	945.106	Charles XV, King of Sweden and	
Charles III, King of Great Britain	941.086 209 2	Norway	
British history	941.086 2	Swedish history	948.504 1
English history	942.086 2	Charles City County (Va.)	T2—755 44
Scottish history	941.108 62	Charles County (Md.)	T2—752 47
Charles III, King of Spain		Charles Mix County (S.D.)	T2—783 382
Spanish history	946.057	Charles River (Mass.)	T2—744 4
Charles IV, Holy Roman		Charleston (S.C.)	T2—757 915
Emperor		Charleston (W. Va.)	T2—754 37
German history	943.027	Charleston County (S.C.)	T2—757 91
Charles IV, King of France		Charleville (Qld.)	T2—943 4
French history	944.024	Charlevoix (Quebec :	
Charles IV, King of Spain		Regional County	
Spanish history	946.058	Municipality)	T2—714 492
Charles V, Holy Roman Emperor		Charlevoix County (Mich.)	T2—774 86
German history	943.031	Charlevoix-Est (Quebec :	
Spanish history	946.042	Regional County	
Charles V, King of France		Municipality)	T2—714 494
French history	944.025	Charlotte (N.B.)	T2—715 33
		Charlotte (N.C.)	T2—756 76

Charlotte County (Fla.)	T2—759 49
Charlotte County (Va.)	T2—755 65
Charlottesville (Va.)	T2—755 481
Charlottetown (P.E.I.)	T2—717 5
Charlottetown Conference, 1864	971.049
Charlton County (Ga.)	T2—758 752
Charm	
life skills	646.76
Charms	203.32
Charms (Occultism)	133.44
Charnwood (England)	T2—425 47
Charophyceae	579.839
Chars	597.554
Charter of Fundamental Rights of	
the European Union, 2000	342.240 850 261
Charter schools	371.05
Charter services	388.042
air	387.742 8
bus	388.322 2
see also Passenger services	
Chartered banks	332.122
Chartered surveyors (United	
Kingdom)	
economics	333.08
Chartering	352.84
see also Licensing	
Charters	352.84
administrative law	342.066
constitutional law	342.02
private law	346.06
public administration	352.84
see also Licensing	
Charters Towers (Qld.)	T2—943 6
Chartreaux cat	636.82
Chartres (France)	T2—445 124
Charts	912
aeronautics	629.132 54
design	744.37
diagrammatic works	T1—022 3
geography	912
pictorial works	T1—022 2
see Manual at T1—0222 vs.	
T1—0223	
Chārvāka	181.46
Chase (B.C.)	T2—711 72
Chase County (Kan.)	T2—781 59
Chase County (Neb.)	T2—782 87
Chasing metals	
decorative arts	739.15
Chasms	551.442
	T2—144
geography	910.914 4
geomorphology	551.442
physical geography	910.021 44

Chassis	629.24
Chastity	
ethics	176.4
religion	205.664
Buddhism	294.356 64
Christianity	241.664
Hinduism	294.548 664
religious practice	204.47
Buddhism	294.344 47
Christianity	248.47
Hinduism	294.544 7
Chat groups	004.693
communications services	384.36
sociology	302.231 2
Chateau Clique	971.038
Châteauguay (Quebec :	
County)	T2—714 34
Chateaux	
architecture	728.8
Chatham County (Ga.)	T2—758 724
Chatham County (N.C.)	T2—756 59
Chatham Islands (N.Z.)	T2—939 9
Chatham-Kent (Ont.)	T2—713 33
Chatsworth (South Africa :	
District)	T2—684 5
Chattahoochee County (Ga.)	T2—758 476
Chattahoochee River	T2—758
Chattanooga (Tenn.)	T2—768 82
Chattanooga campaign, 1863	973.735 9
Chattel mortgages	
law	346.074
Chattisgarhi dialect	491.492
	T6—914 92
Chattisgarhi literature	891.492
Chattooga County (Ga.)	T2—758 344
Chaudière-Appalaches	
(Quebec)	T2—714 71
Chaudière River (Quebec)	T2—714 71
Chaunceys Line Reserve	
National Park (S. Aust.)	T2—942 32
Chausey Islands (France)	T2—423 48
Chautauqua County (Kan.)	T2—781 918
Chautauqua County (N.Y.)	T2—747 95
Chaves, Rodrigo	
Costa Rican history	972.860 533
Châvez Frias, Hugo	
Venezuelan history	987.064 2
Cheat River (W. Va. and	
Pa.)	T2—754 8
Cheatham County (Tenn.)	T2—768 462
Cheating	179.8
see also Vices	
Cheboygan County (Mich.)	T2—774 87
Chebyshev polynomials	515.55

Chechen	T5—999 641
Chechen language	499.964 1
	T6—999 641
Checheno-Ingushetia	
(Russia)	T2—475 2
Chechnia (Russia)	T2—475 2
Chechnya (Russia)	T2—475 2
Checkered beetles	595.763
Checkers	794.2
Checking accounts	332.175 22
Checklists	T1—021 6
Checkoff (Union dues)	331.889 6
Checks	332.76
law	346.096
Checks and balances	320.404
public administration	352.88
Cheddar cheese	641.373 54
cooking	641.673 54
food	641.373 54
processing	637.354
Cheeks	591.44
descriptive zoology	591.44
human anatomy	611.318
human physiology	612.31
medicine	616.31
physiology	573.355
see also Digestive system	
Cheerfulness	179.9
see also Virtues	
Cheerleading	791.64
Cheese	641.373
cooking	641.673
food	641.373
processing	637.3
side dishes	641.811 73
Cheese foods	641.373 58
cooking	641.673 58
food	641.373 58
processing	637.358
Cheese pies	641.824
commercial processing	664.65
cooking	641.824
home preparation	641.824
Cheese varieties	637.35
Cheesemaking	637.3
Cheetah	599.759
animal husbandry	636.89
Chefchaouen (Morocco :	
Province)	T2—642
Cheilostomata	594.676
Chekiang Province (China)	T2—512 42
Chelan County (Wash.)	T2—797 59
Chelates	547.590 442 42

Cheliabinskaia oblast'	
(Russia)	T2—474 3
Chelicerata	595.4
paleozoology	565.4
Cheliff (Algeria : Province)	T2—653
Chełm (Poland :	
Voivodeship)	T2—438 43
Chelmsford (England :	
Borough)	T2—426 752
Chelmsford, Frederic John	
Napier Thesiger, Viscount	
Indian history	954.035 7
Chelonia (Genus)	597.928
Chelonia (Order)	597.92
paleozoology	567.92
Cheloniidae	597.928
Chelonioidea	597.928
Cheltenham (England)	T2—424 16
Chelyabinsk (Russia :	
Oblast)	T2—474 3
Chelydridae	597.922
Chelyidae	597.929
Chemehuevi Indians	T5—974 576
Chemehuevi language	497.457 6
	T6—974 576
Chemical analysis	543
minerals	549.133
organic chemistry	543.17
Chemical arms control	
law	341.735
Chemical bonds	541.224
Chemical communication	573.929
Chemical compounds	546
engineering	660
Chemical contraceptives	
health	613.943 2
medicine	618.182
see also Birth control	
pharmacokinetics	615.766
Chemical crystallography	548.3
Chemical diagnosis	
medicine	616.075 6
Chemical engineering	660
economics	338.476 6
law	344.095 4
Chemical engineers	660.092
Chemical equilibrium	541.392
organic chemistry	547.212
Chemical fire extinction	628.925 4
Chemical forces (Armed	
services)	358.34
Chemical instruments	542
manufacturing technology	681.754
Chemical laboratories	542.1

Cherokee County (Okla.)	T2—766 88
Cherokee County (S.C.)	T2—757 42
Cherokee County (Tex.)	T2—764 183
Cherokee Indians	975.004 975 57
	T5—975 57
Cherokee language	497.557
	T6—975 57
Cherokee literature	897.557
Cherries	641.342 3
botany	583.642
commercial processing	664.804 23
cooking	641.642 3
food	641.342 3
orchard crop	634.23
ornamental arboriculture	635.977 364 2
Cherry County (Neb.)	T2—782 732
Cherry pickers (Machines)	621.873
Cherubim and Seraphim Church	289.93
see also Christian	
denominations	
Cherwell (England)	T2—425 73
Chesapeake (Va.)	T2—755 523
Chesapeake Bay (Md. and Va.)	551.461 347
	T2—163 47
Chesapeake Bay Region	
(Md. and Va.)	T2—755 18
Cheshire (England)	T2—427 1
Cheshire County (N.H.)	T2—742 9
Cheshire East (England)	T2—427 12
Cheshire swine	636.484
Cheshire West and Chester	
(England)	T2—427 14
Chess	794.1
equipment technology	688.741
Chess players	794.109 2
Chessmen	794.1
manufacturing technology	688.741
Chest	
human anatomy	611.94
human physiology	612.94
regional medicine	617.54
surgery	617.540 59
Chest bones	
human anatomy	611.712
human physiology	612.751
Chest muscles	
human anatomy	611.735
Chester (England : City)	T2—427 14
Chester County (Pa.)	T2—748 13
Chester County (S.C.)	T2—757 47
Chester County (Tenn.)	T2—768 265
Chester River (Md.)	T2—752 34
Chester White swine	636.484

Chesterfield (England :	
Borough)	T2—425 12
Chesterfield County (S.C.)	T2—757 63
Chesterfield County (Va.)	T2—755 594
Chesterfield Inlet (Nunavut)	T2—719 58
Chestnut bean	641.356 57
see also Chick-peas	
Chestnuts	583.65
botany	583.65
cooking	641.645 3
food	641.345 3
forestry	634.972 4
lumber	674.142
nut crop	634.53
Chests (Furniture)	645.4
manufacturing technology	684.16
see also Furniture	
Cheviot Hills (England)	T2—428 8
Chevrotains	599.63
Chewa (African people)	T5—963 918
Chewa language	496.391 8
	T6—963 918
Chewa literature	896.391 8
Chewing	
animal physiology	573.35
descriptive zoology	591.53
human physiology	612.311
Chewing gum	641.338
commercial processing	664.6
food	641.338
Chewing lice	595.757
Cheyenne (Wyo.)	T2—787 19
Cheyenne County (Colo.)	T2—788 92
Cheyenne County (Kan.)	T2—781 112
Cheyenne County (Neb.)	T2—782 96
Cheyenne Indians	978.004 973 53
	T5—973 53
Cheyenne language	497.353
	T6—973 53
Chhattīsgarh (India)	T2—541 37
Chhattisgarhi dialect	491.492
	T6—914 92
Chhattisgarhi literature	891.492
Chi-square test	519.56
Chiang, Ching-kuo	
Taiwanese history	951.249 058
Chiang, Kai-shek	
history	951.249 05
Chinese history	951.042
Taiwanese history	951.249 05
Chiaroscuro	701.8
Chiasmodontidae	597.7
Chiba-ken (Japan)	T2—521 37
Chibcha Indians	T5—982

Child custody	346.017 3
Child development	305.231
physiology	612.65
psychology	155.4
sociology	305.231
Child labor	331.31
law	344.013 1
Child molesting	364.153 6
law	345.025 36
medicine	616.858 36
Child neglect	362.76
see also Child abuse	
Child-parent relations	306.874
see also Parent-child relations	
Child prostitution	306.745
see also Prostitution	
Child protection	362.76
see also Child abuse	
Child psychology	155.4
Child rearing	649.1
customs	392.13
personal religion	204.41
Buddhism	294.344 41
Christianity	248.845
Hinduism	294.544 1
Islam	297.577
Judaism	296.74
Child study	305.23
physiology	612.65
psychology	155.4
sociology	305.23
Child support	346.017 2
Child training	649.6
Child war victims	305.230 869 48
Childbed fever	
obstetrics	618.74
Childbirth	618.4
arts	T3C—354
customs	392.12
etiquette	395.24
folklore	398.274
history and criticism	398.354
human physiology	612.63
literature	808.803 54
history and criticism	809.933 54
specific literatures	T3B—080 354
history and criticism	T3B—093 54
music	781.582
obstetrics	618.4
preparation	
obstetrics	618.24
psychology	155.646 3
social services	362.198 4

Childhood	305.23
psychology	155.4
sociology	305.23
Childhood disintegrative disorder	
medicine	616.858 83
pediatrics	618.928 588 3
Childhood of Jesus Christ	232.927
Childlessness	306.87
Children	305.23
	T1—083
art representation	704.942 5
arts	700.452 3
	T3C—352 3
civil and human rights	323.352
law	342.087 72
law of nations	341.485 72
cooking for	641.562 2
development	
human physiology	612.65
drawing	743.45
etiquette	395.122
government programs	353.536
grooming	646.704 6
health	613.043 2
home care	649.4
institutional buildings	
architecture	725.57
journalism for	070.483 2
labor economics	331.31
law	344.013 1
legal status	346.013 083
constitutional law	342.087 72
private law	346.013 083
literature	808.803 523
history and criticism	809.933 523
specific literatures	T3B—080 352 3
history and criticism	T3B—093 523
painting	757.5
physical fitness	613.704 2
psychology	155.4
publications for	
bibliographies	011.62
reviews	028.162
reading	
library science	028.53
recreation	790.192 2
indoor	793.019 22
outdoor	796.083
relations with government	323.352
religion	200.83
Christianity	270.083
devotional literature	242.62
guides to Christian life	248.82

Children		
religion		
Christianity (continued)		
pastoral care	259.22	
prayer books	242.82	
religious education	268.432	
guides to life	204.408 3	
Judaism	296.083	
guides to life	296.708 3	
religious education	296.680 83	
sex hygiene	613.951	
social aspects	305.23	
social welfare	362.7	
international organizations		
public administration	353.536 211	
public administration	353.536	
socialization	303.32	
treatment of		
ethics	179.2	
World War I	940.316 1	
World War II	940.531 61	
Children (Progeny)	306.874	
	T1—085 4	
Children of alcoholics		
pediatrics	618.928 619	
social welfare	362.292 3	
Children of minorities		
home care	649.157	
psychology	155.457	
Children of minorities (ethnic and national)		
home care	649.157	
Children of prisoners	362.829 5	
Children of substance abusers		
pediatrics	618.928 69	
social welfare	362.291 3	
Children of unmarried parents	306.874	
	T1—086 945	
legal status	346.017	
social welfare	362.787 4	
Children with communication disorders		
home care	649.151 4	
Children with developmental disabilities	305.908 508 3	
	T1—087 5	
home care	649.152	
Children with disabilities	305.908 083	
	T1—087	
home care	649.15	
	649.151	
psychology	155.45	

Children with emotional disturbances		
home care	649.154	
Children with hearing impairments	305.908 208 3	
	T1—087 2	
home care	649.151 2	
see also People with hearing impairments		
Children with learning disabilities		
home care	649.15	
Children with linguistic disorders		
home care	649.151 4	
Children with mental disabilities	305.908 408 3	
	T1—087 4	
education	371.92	
home care	649.152	
Children with mental illness		
home care	649.154	
Children with mobility impairments	305.908 308 3	
home care	649.151 6	
see also People with mobility impairments		
Children with moderate mental disabilities		
home care	649.152 6	
Children with physical disabilities		
home care	649.151	
Children with reading disorders		
home care	649.151 44	
Children with severe mental disabilities		
home care	649.152 8	
Children with speaking disorders		
home care	649.151 42	
Children with visual impairments		
home care	649.151 1	
Children's books		
bibliographies	011.62	
design	744.52	
illustration	741.642	
literature	808.899 282	
see also Children's literature		
publishing	070.508 3	
Children's church	264.008 3	
Children's clothing	391.3	
commercial technology	687.083	
customs	391.3	
home economics	646.36	
home sewing	646.406	
see also Clothing		
Children's cooking	641.512 3	

Children's Crusade, 1212	944.023	Chimaerae	597.38
Children's diseases	362.198 92	Chimaeriformes	597.38
medicine	618.92	Chimakuan languages	497.9
social welfare	362.198 92		T6—979
Children's homes	362.732	Chimaltenango	
Children's hospitals	362.198 92	(Guatemala : Dept.)	T2—728 161
see also Health care facilities		Chimborazo (Ecuador)	T2—866 17
Children's libraries	027.625	Chimbu Province (Papua	
administration	025.197 625	New Guinea)	T2—956 7
collection development	025.218 762 5	Chimeras (Fishes)	597.38
Children's literature	808.899 282	Chimes	786.848
history and criticism	809.892 82	*see also* Percussion instruments	
rhetoric	808.068	Chimneys	721.5
specific literatures	T3B—080 928 2	architecture	721.5
history and criticism	T3B—099 282	buildings	697.8
Children's parties	793.21	steam furnaces	621.183
Children's rights	323.352	Chimpanzees	599.885
law	342.087 72	Chin dynasty	931.04
law of nations	341.485 72	Ch'in dynasty	931.04
Children's sermons		China	951
Christianity	252.53		T2—51
Children's songs	782.420 83	ancient	931
Children's theater	792.022 6		T2—31
Children's voices	782.7	China (Porcelain)	666.5
choral and mixed voices	782.7	arts	738.2
single voices	783.7	China (Republic : 1949–)	951.249 05
Childress County (Tex.)	T2—764 754		T2—512 49
Chile	983	China cabinets	645.4
	T2—83	manufacturing technology	684.16
2022–	983.066 8	*see also* Furniture	
Chile saltpeter	553.64	China fir	585.5
economic geology	553.64	China grass plant	583.648
mineralogy	549.732	Chinaberry tree	635.977 375
Chilean cedar	585.4	botany	583.75
Chilean literature	860	ornamental arboriculture	635.977 375
Chileans	T5—688 3	Chinandega (Nicaragua :	
Chili	641.823 6	Dept.)	T2—728 511
commercial processing	664.65	Chinch bugs	
home preparation	641.823 6	agricultural pests	633.104 975 4
Chili peppers	641.338 4	zoology	595.754
agriculture	633.84	Chinchilla, Laura	
food	641.338 4	Costa Rican history	972.860 527
Chilko River (B.C.)	T2—711 75	Chinchillas	636.935 93
Chilled dishes		animal husbandry	636.935 93
cooking	641.79	zoology	599.359 3
Chilliwack (B.C.)	T2—711 37	Chinchillidae	599.359 3
Chiloé (Chile)	T2—835 6	Chincoteague pony	636.16
Chilopoda	595.62	Chinese	305.895 1
Chiltern (England)	T2—425 97		T5—951
Chiltern Hills (England)	T2—425	Chinese artichoke	641.352
Chilterns (England)	T2—425	agriculture	635.2
Chilton County (Ala.)	T2—761 81	botany	583.96
Chiluba, Frederick		cooking	641.652
Zambian history	968.940 42	food	641.352

Chivalry	394.7	Choapa (Chile : Province)	T2—832 38
arts	T3C—353	Chocó (Colombia)	T2—861 51
folklore	398.273	Choco languages	498.9
history and criticism	398.353		T6—989
literature	808.803 53	Central America	497.9
history and criticism	809.933 53		T6—979
specific literatures	T3B—080 353	Chocolate	641.337 4
history and		beverage	641.337 4
criticism	T3B—093 53	commercial processing	663.92
Chives	641.352 6	home preparation	641.877
botany	584.78	commercial processing	664.5
cooking	641.652 6	cooking with	641.637 4
food	641.352 6	food	641.337 4
garden crop	635.26	Choctaw County (Ala.)	T2—761 395
Chkalov (Russia : Oblast)	T2—474 3	Choctaw County (Miss.)	T2—762 694
Chlamydia infections		Choctaw County (Okla.)	T2—766 63
incidence	614.573 5	Choctaw Indians	976.004 973 87
medicine	616.923 5		T5—973 87
see also Communicable		Choctaw language	497.387
diseases — humans			T6—973 87
Chlamydias	579.327	Choice	
Chlamydomonadaceae	579.832	mathematics	511.65
Chlef (Algeria : Province)	T2—653	psychology	153.83
Chloranthaceae	584.26	Choice axiom	511.3
Chloranthales	584.26	Choice of entry (Cataloging)	025.322
paleobotany	561.4	Choice of vocation	331.702
Chlordane			T1—023
human toxicology	615.951 2	*see also* Vocational guidance	
Chlorideae	584.92	Choir lofts	
Chloridoideae	584.92	architecture	726.593
Chlorination		Choir stalls	247.1
water supply treatment	628.166 2	architecture	726.529 3
Chlorine	553.95	Choirs	782.5
chemical engineering	661.073 2	Choirs (Structural parts)	
chemistry	546.732	architecture	726.593
economic geology	553.95	Chokeberries	583.642
human toxicology	615.91	Chokwe (African people)	T5—963 99
organic chemistry	547.02	Chokwe-Luchazi languages	496.399
applied	661.891		T6—963 99
see also Chemicals		Chol language	497.428
Chlorite			T6—974 28
mineralogy	549.67	Cholan-Tzeltalan languages	497.428
Chlorococcales	579.833		T6—974 28
Chloromonadophyta	579.82	Cholera	
Chlorophyceae	579.83	incidence	614.514
Chlorophylls	572.46	medicine	616.932
chemical engineering	661.894	*see also* Communicable	
organic chemistry	547.593	diseases — humans	
Chlorophyta	579.83	Cholesterol	572.579 5
Chloroplastic DNA	572.869	applied nutrition	613.284
Chloroplasts	571.659 2	biochemistry	572.579 5
Chloroprene rubber	678.72	Choluteca (Honduras :	
Chlorpromazine		Dept.)	T2—728 351
pharmacokinetics	615.788 2		

Chon languages	498.7	Choroid diseases	
	T6—987	ophthalmology	617.72
Chondrichthyes	597.3	*see also* Eye diseases —	
paleozoology	567.3	humans	
Chondrocytes		Choroids	
human cytology	612.751 76	human physiology	612.842
Chondrophora	593.55	ophthalmology	617.72
Chondrostei	597.42	Chosen people (Judaism)	296.311 72
paleozoology	567.42	Chou dynasty	931.03
Chongqing (China)	T2—513 9	Chouteau County (Mont.)	T2—786 293
Chontales (Nicaragua)	T2—728 527	Chow chow	636.72
Chopi (African people)	T5—963 97	Chowan County (N.C.)	T2—756 147
Chopi languages	496.397	Chowan River (N.C.)	T2—756 15
	T6—963 97	Chrétien, Jean	
Choptank River (Del. and		Canadian history	971.064 8
Md.)	T2—752 31	Chris Hani District	
Choral music	782.5	Municipality (South	
Choral recitations		Africa)	T2—687 56
literature	808.855	Chrismation	
history and criticism	809.55	Christianity	234.162
specific literatures	T3B—505	public worship	265.2
individual authors	T3A—5	theology	234.162
Choral speaking	808.55	Christadelphians	289.9
literature	808.855	Christchurch (England :	
history and criticism	809.55	Borough)	T2—423 39
music	782.96	Christchurch (N.Z.)	T2—938 3
primary education	372.676	Christchurch City (N.Z.)	T2—938 3
rhetoric	808.55	Christening	265.1
Chorale preludes	784.189 92	customs	392.12
Chorales	782.27	etiquette	395.24
instrumental form	784.189 925	music	781.582
Chordata	596	Christian and Missionary	
Chordophones	787	Alliance	289.9
see also Stringed instruments		Christian art	704.948 2
Chords (Music)	781.252	religious significance	246
Chorea		Christian Brothers	255.78
medicine	616.83	church history	271.78
see also Nervous system		Christian calendars	529.4
diseases — humans		religion	263.9
Choreatic disorders		Christian church	260
medicine	616.83	history	270
see also Nervous system		local	250
diseases — humans		specific denominations	280
Choreographers	792.820 92	*see Manual at* 260 vs. 250	
Choreography	792.82	Christian Church (Disciples of	
ballet	792.82	Christ)	286.63
musical plays	792.62	Christian Churches and Churches	
Choreology	792.82	of Christ	286.63
Chorionic villi sampling		Christian County (Ill.)	T2—773 81
obstetrics	618.320 427 5	Christian County (Ky.)	T2—769 78
Chorley (England :		Christian County (Mo.)	T2—778 792
Borough)	T2—427 615	Christian Democracy (Italian	
		political party)	324.245 082 2

Christian Democratic Center		Christian Reformed Church	285.731
(Italian political party)	324.245 082	*see also* Reformed Church	
Christian democratic parties	324.218 2	(American Reformed)	
international organizations	324.182	Christian regions	T2—176 1
Christian Democratic People's		Christian sacred music	781.71
Party of Switzerland	324.249 404	public worship	782.32
Christian Democratic Union of		music	782.32
Germany (Political party)	324.243 04	choral and mixed voices	782.532
Christian denominations	280	single voices	783.093 2
	T1—088 28	religion	264.2
church government	262.01–.09	religious symbolism	246.75
local church	254.01–.09	Christian schools (General	
church law	262.98	education)	371.071
doctrines	230.1–.9	Christian Science	289.5
catechisms and creeds	238.1–.9	Christian Scientists	
general councils	262.5	biography	289.509 2
guides to Christian life	248.48	Christian Social Party (Austria)	324.243 602 4
missions	266.1–.9	Christian Social Party	
moral theology	241.04	(Switzerland)	324.249 407
pastoral theology	253.3	Christian Social Union (German	
public worship	264.01–.09	political party)	324.243 04
religious associations	267.18	Christian socialism	335.7
religious education	268.8	economics	335.7
religious orders	255	political ideology	320.531 2
church history	271	Christiana (South Africa :	
women's	255.9	District)	T2—682 46
seminaries	230.073	Christianity	230
theology	230.1–.9	art representation	704.948 2
see Manual at T1—0882 and		religious significance	246
200; *also at* 283–289		arts	700.482 3
Christian doctrine	230		T3C—382 3
Christian education	268	religious significance	246
see Manual at 207.5, 268 vs.		conversion to	248.246
200.71, 230.071, 292–299		from Judaism	248.246 6
Christian ethics	241	Islamic polemics	297.293
see Manual at 241 vs. 261.8		literature	808.803 823
Christian holidays	263.9	history and criticism	809.933 823
customs	394.266	specific literatures	T3B—080 382 3
devotional literature	242.3	history and	
sermons	252.6	criticism	T3B—093 823
see also Holidays		religious freedom	
Christian initiation	265.1	law	342.085 23
Christian Israelite Church	289.9	Christianity and anti-Semitism	261.26
Christian leadership	262.1	Christianity and atheism	261.21
local church	253	Christianity and culture	261
Christian life	248.4	Christianity and Islam	261.27
Christian-Marxist dialogue		Christian view	261.27
Christian theology	261.21	Islamic view	297.283
Christian Methodist Episcopal		Christianity and Judaism	261.26
Church	287.83	Christian view	261.26
see also Methodist Church		Jewish view	296.396
Christian names	929.44	Christianity and occultism	261.513
Christian philosophy	190	Christianity and other religions	261.2
		Christianity and politics	261.7

Chronic renal failure
  medicine 616.614
    see also Urologic diseases —
      humans
Chronicles 900
  see also History
Chronicles (Biblical books) 222.6
Chronobiology 571.77
Chronographs
  astronomy 522.5
  technology 681.118
Chronologies 902.02
  T1—020 2
Chronologists 529.092
Chronology 529
Chronometers
  astronomy 522.5
  technology 681.118
Chronoscopes
  technology 681.118
Chroococcales 579.39
Chrysanthemums 635.933 983
  botany 583.983
  floriculture 635.933 983
Chrysemys 597.925 92
Chrysobalanaceae 583.69
Chrysocloridae 599.335
Chrysocolla
  mineralogy 549.64
Chrysomelidae 595.764 8
Chrysomeloidea 595.764 8
Chrysophyceae 579.86
Chrysophyta 579.86
Chtouka-Aït Baha
  (Morocco) T2—646 6
Chubs 597.482
  sports fishing 799.174 82
Chūbu Region (Japan) T2—521 6
Chubut (Argentina) T2—827 4
Chuckchee Sea 551.461 325
  T2—163 25
Chucks 621.992
Chūgoku Region (Japan) T2—521 9
Chukchi (Russia : Okrug) T2—577
Chukchi-Kamchatkan languages 494.6
  T6—946
Chukchi Sea 551.461 325
  T2—163 25
Chukotko-Kamchatkan
  languages T6—946
Chukotskiĭ avtonomnyĭ
  okrug (Russia) T2—577
Chulalongkorn, King of Siam
  Thai history 959.303 5

Chulupí language 498.7
  T6—987
Chumash Indians 979.400 497 58
  T5—975 8
Chumash language 497.58
  T6—975 8
Chumash languages 497.58
  T6—975 8
Ch'ung-ch'ing shih (China) T2—513 9
Chungking (China) T2—513 9
Chuquisaca (Bolivia) T2—842 4
Chur (Switzerland) T2—494 732 24
Church 260
  ecclesiology 262
  history 270
    specific denominations 280
  local 250
Church and state 322.1
  social theology 201.72
    Christianity 261.7
  see also Politics and religion
  see Manual at 322.1 vs.
    201.72, 261.7, 292–299
Church authority 262.8
Church buildings
  architecture 726.5
  institutional housekeeping 647.985
  landscape architecture 712.7
  management 254.7
  religious significance 246.9
Church calendar 263.9
  chronology 529.44
Church camps 796.542 2
Church controversies 262.8
  local church 250
  specific denominations 280
Church etiquette 395.53
Church fathers 270
  biography 270.092
Church finance 262.006 81
  local church 254.8
Church furniture 247.1
Church government 262
  local church 254
  see Manual at 260 vs. 250
Church group work 253.7
Church growth
  local church 254.5
  missionary work 266
Church history 270
  specific denominations 280
Church holidays 263.9
  customs 394.266
  devotional literature 242.3

Churchill (Man.)	T2—712 71	Ciliatea	579.49
Churchill County (Nev.)	T2—793 52	Ciliates	579.49
Churchill River (Sask. and		Cilicia	939.35
Man.)	T2—712 71		T2—393 5
Chūsei period	952.02	Ciliophora	579.49
Chutes-de-la-Chaudière		CIM (Manufacturing)	670.285
(Quebec)	T2—714 59	Cimarron County (Okla.)	T2—766 132
Chutney	641.814	Cimbaloms	787.74
commercial processing	664.58	*see also* Stringed instruments	
home preparation	641.814	Cinchonas	583.956
Chuukese language	499.52	botany	583.956
	T6—995 2	medicinal crops	633.883 956
Chuvash language	494.315	Cincinnati (Ohio)	T2—771 78
	T6—943 15	Cinclidae	598.832
Chuvash literature	894.315	Cinder blocks	666.894
Chuvashes	T5—945 6	building construction	693.4
Chuvashia (Russia)	T2—474 6	building materials	691.3
Chuvashiĩa (Russia)	T2—474 6	manufacturing technology	666.894
Chyromyiidae	595.774	materials science	620.139
Chytridiomycetes	579.53	structural engineering	624.183 2
CIA (Intelligence agency)	327.127 3	Cinema	791.43
Cibola County (N.M.)	T2—789 91	*see also* Motion pictures	
Cicadas	595.752	Cinemas	
Ciceŵa language	496.391 8	architecture	725.823
	T6—963 918	Cinematography	777
Ciceŵa literature	896.391 8	*see Manual at* 791.43, 791.45	
Cichlidae	597.74	vs. 777	
culture	639.377 4	Cinnabar	
Cicindelidae	595.762	mineralogy	549.32
Ciconiidae	598.34	Cinnamon	641.338 34
Ciconiiformes	598.34	agriculture	633.834
paleozoology	568.3	botany	584.288
Cider	641.341 1	food	641.338 34
commercial processing	663.63	*see also* Spices	
cooking with	641.641 1	Cinque Ports (England)	T2—422 352
fermented	641.229	Cinquefoils	583.642
commercial processing	663.29	CIO (Labor)	331.883 309 73
food	641.341 1	CIP (Cataloging)	025.3
Ciechanów (Poland :		Ciphers (Cryptography)	652.8
Voivodeship)	T2—438 41	computer science	005.824
Ciego de Ávila (Cuba :		Circadian rhythms	571.77
Province)	T2—729 153	human physiology	612.022
Cienfuegos (Cuba :		Circassian languages	499.962 4
Province)	T2—729 143		T6—999 624
Cigar flower	583.73	Circassians	T5—999 624
Cigarette holders	688.4	Circle geometry	516.18
Cigarettes	679.73	Circle-squaring	516.204
smuggling	364.133 6	Circles	516.152
law	345.023 36	Circuit breakers	621.317
Cigars	679.72	Circuit courts	347.02
Cilia	571.67	Circuit switching	621.381 537
Ciliary bodies		communications engineering	621.382 16
human physiology	612.842	computer communications	004.66
ophthalmology	617.72	engineering	621.398 1

Circuits	621.319 2
computer engineering	621.395
electronics	621.381 5
microwave electronics	621.381 32
radio engineering	621.384 12
Circular buildings	720.48
architecture	720.48
construction	690.38
Circular dichroism	541.7
Circular manic-depressive psychoses	
medicine	616.895
see also Mental disorders	
Circulars	
direct advertising	659.133
postal handling	383.124
see also Postal service	
Circulation (Biology)	573.1
biology	573.1
brain	573.862 1
human physiology	612.824
see also Nervous system	
human physiology	612.1
plants	575.7
see also Cardiovascular system	
Circulation (Meteorology)	551.517
Circulation services	
library science	025.6
museology	069.13
Circulation theory (Economics)	332.401
Circulatory fluids	573.15
biology	573.15
plants	575.75
see also Cardiovascular system	
Circulatory organs	573.1
see also Cardiovascular system	
Circulatory system	573.1
biology	573.1
plants	575.7
see also Cardiovascular system	
Circumcision	392.1
customs	392.1
female	
surgery	618.160 59
Jewish rites	296.442 2
liturgy	296.454 22
male	
surgery	617.463
music	781.582
Circumcision of Jesus Christ	232.92
Circumstances of revelation of Koran	297.122 12

Circumstantial evidence	347.064
criminal investigation	363.25
criminal law	345.064
law	347.064
Circumterrestrial flights	
manned	629.454
unmanned	629.435 2
Circus animals	791.32
animal husbandry	636.088 8
Circus performers	791.309 2
Circuses	791.3
Cire perdue casting	
metals	671.255
Cirques (Geologic landforms)	551.315
Cirrhosis	
medicine	616.362 4
see also Digestive system diseases — humans	
Cirripedia	595.35
paleozoology	565.35
Cisalpine Gaul	T2—372
Cisalpine Republic	945.208 2
CISC (Computer science)	004.3
see also Processing modes — computer science	
Ciskei (South Africa)	T2—687 54
Cispadane Gaul	T2—372 6
Cistaceae	583.77
Cistercians	255.12
church history	271.12
women	255.97
church history	271.97
Citation analysis	
information science	020.727
Citation indexing	025.47
Citations	
armed forces	355.134
see also Military commemorations	
Citators to cases	348.047
United States	348.734 7
Citators to laws	348.027
United States	348.732 7
Citharinidae	597.48
Cities	307.76
	T2—173 2
arts	T3C—358 209 732
government	320.85
influence on precipitation	551.577 5
literature	808.803 582 097 32
history and criticism	809.933 582 097 32
specific literatures	T3B—080 358 209 732
history and criticism	T3B—093 582 097 32

Cities (continued)	
psychological influence	155.942
public administration	352.16
control by higher jurisdictions	353.336
see Manual at 351.3–.9 vs. 352.13–.19	
public administrative support	352.793
social services to residents	361.917 32
public administration	353.533 3
sociology	307.76
see Manual at T2—4–9; *also at* T2—41 *and* T2—42; *also at* T2—713 *and* T2—714; *also at* T2—93	
Citizen participation	323.042
crime prevention	364.43
election campaigns	324.72
social welfare	361.25
Citizens advice bureaus	361.06
Citizens and state	323
Citizens band radio	384.53
communications services	384.53
engineering	621.384 54
Citizenship	323.6
ethics	172.1
see also Political ethics	
law	342.083
political science	323.6
primary education	372.83
public administration	353.48
social theology	201.723
Christianity	261.7
Judaism	296.382
Citric acid cycle	572.475
Citronella	584.924
Citronella grass	584.924
Citrons	641.343 31
cooking	641.643 31
food	641.343 31
orchard crop	634.331
Citrus County (Fla.)	T2—759 72
Citrus fruits	641.343 04
botany	583.75
commercial processing	664.804 304
cooking	641.643 04
food	641.343 04
orchard crop	634.304
Citterns	787.85
see also Stringed instruments	
City churches	250.917 32
administration	254.22
pastoral theology	253.091 732

City colleges	378.052
see also Higher education	
City core	
community redevelopment	307.342
City directories	910.25
see Manual at T1—025 vs. T1—029	
City gas	665.772
City government	320.85
City government buildings	
architecture	725.13
City halls	
architecture	725.13
City manager government	320.854
City managers	
public administration	352.232 16
City noise	363.741
technology	620.23
see also Noise	
City of Cape Town Metropolitan Municipality (South Africa)	T2—687 35
City of Johannesburg Metropolitan Municipality (South Africa)	T2—682 21
City of Tshwane Metropolitan Municipality (South Africa)	T2—682 27
City planners	711.409 2
City planning	307.121 6
civic art	711.4
law	346.045
public administration	354.353
City schools	371.009 173 2
City-states	321.06
City traffic	388.41
law	343.098 2
City warfare	355.426
Cityscapes	
drawing	743.84
fine arts	704.944
painting	758.7
Ciudad da La Habana (Cuba)	T2—729 123
Ciudad Real (Spain : Province)	T2—464 5
Civets	599.742
Civic action of armed forces	355.34
Civic art	711

Civilian workers	331.79
armed forces	355.23
management	355.619
labor economics	331.79
labor force	331.119 042
labor market	331.129 042
Civilization	909
arts	700.458
	T3C—358
Bible	220.95
history	909
ancient	930
specific places	930–990
see also History	
literature	808.803 58
history and criticism	809.933 58
specific literatures	T3B—080 358
history and	
criticism	T3B—093 58
painting	758.99
primary education	372.89
sociology	306
see Manual at 306 vs. 305,	
909, 930–990; *also at* 909,	
930–990 vs. 910	
CJD (Disease)	
medicine	616.83
see also Nervous system	
diseases — humans	
Clackamas County (Or.)	T2—795 41
Clackmannan (Scotland :	
District)	T2—413 15
Clackmannanshire	
(Scotland)	T2—413 15
Cladding	
buildings	698
nuclear engineering	621.483 35
Cladding metals	671.73
Cladistic analysis	578.012
Cladocera	595.32
Cladocopa	595.33
paleozoology	565.33
Cladoselachii	567.3
Claiborne County (Miss.)	T2—762 285
Claiborne County (Tenn.)	T2—768 944
Claiborne Parish (La.)	T2—763 94
Claiming	
library acquisitions	025.236
Claims (Customer relations)	
marketing management	658.812
Claims (Insurance)	368.014
Claims adjustment	
insurance	368.014

Claims against government	
public administration	352.885
Claims courts	347.04
Clairaudience	133.85
Clairvoyance	133.84
Clairvoyants	133.840 92
Clallam County (Wash.)	T2—797 99
Clam shrimps	595.32
Clamming	639.44
sports	799.254 4
Clamps	621.992
Clams	594.4
conservation technology	639.974 4
cooking	641.694
fishing	639.44
food	641.394
commercial processing	664.94
paleozoology	564.4
resource economics	333.955 44
sports clamming	799.254 4
zoology	594.4
Clandestine publications	
bibliographies	011.56
Clanwilliam (South Africa :	
District)	T2—687 32
Clare (Ireland)	T2—419 3
Clare (S. Aust.)	T2—942 32
Clare County (Mich.)	T2—774 71
Clarendon County (S.C.)	T2—757 81
Clarinet concertos	784.286 218 6
Clarinetists	788.620 92
Clarinets	788.62
instrument	788.621 9
music	788.62
see also Woodwind	
instruments	
Clarion County (Pa.)	T2—748 69
Clark, Charles Joseph	
Canadian history	971.064 5
Clark, Joe	
Canadian history	971.064 5
Clark County (Ark.)	T2—767 49
Clark County (Idaho)	T2—796 57
Clark County (Ill.)	T2—773 71
Clark County (Ind.)	T2—772 185
Clark County (Kan.)	T2—781 77
Clark County (Ky.)	T2—769 54
Clark County (Mo.)	T2—778 343
Clark County (Nev.)	T2—793 13
Clark County (Ohio)	T2—771 49
Clark County (S.D.)	T2—783 22
Clark County (Wash.)	T2—797 86
Clark County (Wis.)	T2—775 28
Clarke County (Ala.)	T2—761 245

Clay County (Ala.)	T2—761 58
Clay County (Ark.)	T2—767 995
Clay County (Fla.)	T2—759 16
Clay County (Ga.)	T2—758 927
Clay County (Ill.)	T2—773 795
Clay County (Ind.)	T2—772 44
Clay County (Iowa)	T2—777 153
Clay County (Kan.)	T2—781 275
Clay County (Ky.)	T2—769 145
Clay County (Minn.)	T2—776 92
Clay County (Miss.)	T2—762 945
Clay County (Mo.)	T2—778 16
Clay County (N.C.)	T2—756 985
Clay County (Neb.)	T2—782 357
Clay County (S.D.)	T2—783 393
Clay County (Tenn.)	T2—768 49
Clay County (Tex.)	T2—764 542
Clay County (W. Va.)	T2—754 67
Clay pigeons	799.313 2
Clay pots	
use in cooking	641.589
Clayton County (Ga.)	T2—758 432
Clayton County (Iowa)	T2—777 36
Clean rooms	
safety engineering	620.86
Cleaning	
pneumatic engineering	621.54
technology	667.1
Cleaning crops	631.56
Cleaning house	648.5
Cleaning metals	671.7
Cleanliness	613.4
personal customs	391.64
personal health	613.4
Cleansing tissues	676.284 2
Clear-air turbulence	
transportation hazard	363.124 12
Clear Creek County (Colo.)	T2—788 61
Clearance (Banking)	332.178
central banking	332.113
commercial banking service	332.178
Clearfield County (Pa.)	T2—748 61
Clearing banks	332.12
Clearing houses (Banking)	332.12
Clearing of land	631.61
Clearwater County (Idaho)	T2—796 88
Clearwater County (Minn.)	T2—776 83
Clearwater River (B.C.)	T2—711 72
Clearwater River (Idaho)	T2—796 85
Cleavage	
geology	551.84
mineralogy	549.121
Cleburne County (Ala.)	T2—761 64
Cleburne County (Ark.)	T2—767 285

Cleethorpes (England : Borough)	T2—428 34
Cleft lip	
surgery	617.522
Cleft palate	
surgery	617.522 5
Clematises	635.933 34
botany	583.34
floriculture	635.933 34
Clemency	364.65
law	345.077
penology	364.65
Clemmys	597.925 7
Cleomaceae	583.78
Cleopatra, Queen of Egypt	
Egyptian history	932.021
Clerestories	
Christian church architecture	726.594
Clergy	200.92
biography	200.92
Christian	270.092
biography	270.092
specific denominations	280
see Manual at 230–280	
ecclesiology	262.1
see Manual at 260 vs. 250	
occupational ethics	241.641
pastoral theology	253
see Manual at 260 vs. 250	
personal religion	248.892
training	230.071 1
see also Ministers (Christian clergy); Pastors	
occupational ethics	174.1
religion	205.641
role and function	206.1
see also Rabbis; Religious leaders	
see Manual at 200.92 and 201–209, 292–299	
Clergymen's wives	
Christianity	253.22
see also Spouses of clergy — Christianity	
Clerical celibacy	
Catholic Church	262.142 086 5
Christianity	262.140 865
Clerical services	651.37
Clerihews	808.817
history and criticism	809.17
specific literatures	T3B—107
individual authors	T3A—1

Clerks	651.370 92	Climate (continued)	
office services	651.37	influence on crime	364.22
social group	305.965 137	psychological influence	155.915
Clerks regular	255.5	social effects	304.25
church history	271.5	*see Manual at* 551.5 vs. 551.6	
Clerks Regular of Somaschi	255.54	Climate control	551.68
church history	271.54	Climate-induced illnesses	
Clerks Regular of the Mother of		medicine	616.988
God	255.57	*see also* Environmental	
church history	271.57	diseases — humans	
Clermont (Qld.)	T2—943 5	Climate types	551.62
Clermont County (Ohio)	T2—771 794	Climatic changes	
Clermont-Ferrand (France)	T2—445 914	crop damage	632.1
Cleroidea	595.763	effect on natural ecology	577.22
Clethraceae	583.93	Climatological diseases	
Cleveland (England)	T2—428 5	medicine	616.988
Cleveland (Ohio)	T2—771 32	*see also* Environmental	
Cleveland, Grover		diseases — humans	
United States history	973.85	Climatologists	551.609 2
1885–1889	973.85	Climatology	551.6
1893–1897	973.87	Climatotherapy	
Cleveland bay horse	636.14	medicine	615.834
Cleveland County (Ark.)	T2—767 69	Climbing plants	582.18
Cleveland County (N.C.)	T2—756 775	floriculture	635.974
Cleveland County (Okla.)	T2—766 37	Clinch County (Ga.)	T2—758 812
Cleveland Hills (England)	T2—428 49	Clinch River (Va. and	
Clichés	418	Tenn.)	T2—768 73
dictionaries	413.1	Clingfishes	597.62
specific languages	T4—31	Clinical chemistry	616.075 6
rhetoric	808	Clinical drug trials	615.580 724
specific languages	T4—8	Clinical enzymology	616.075 6
Click beetles	595.765	Clinical immunology	616.079
Client-server computing	004.36	Clinical medicine	616
software development	005.276	diagnosis	616.075
Client-server processing	004.36	*see Manual at* 616 vs. 616.075	
Client-server software	005.376	Clinical neuropsychology	616.8
Cliff ecology	577.58	Clinical psychology	616.89
Clifford algebras	512.57	Clinical trials	615.507 24
Clifton Forge (Va.)	T2—755 816	Clinics	362.12
Climacteric		*see also* Health care facilities	
human physiology	612.665	Clinton (B.C.)	T2—711 72
Climacteric disorders		Clinton, Bill	
gynecology	618.175	United States history	973.929
see also Female genital		Clinton County (Ill.)	T2—773 875
diseases — humans		Clinton County (Ind.)	T2—772 553
male		Clinton County (Iowa)	T2—777 67
medicine	616.693	Clinton County (Ky.)	T2—769 653
see also Male genital		Clinton County (Mich.)	T2—774 24
diseases — humans		Clinton County (Mo.)	T2—778 155
medicine	618.175	Clinton County (N.Y.)	T2—747 54
Climate	551.6	Clinton County (Ohio)	T2—771 765
biophysics	571.49	Clinton County (Pa.)	T2—748 54
ecology	577.22	Clip spot embroidery	677.77
health	613.11		

Clipper ships	387.224	Cloning (continued)	
design	623.812 24	immunology	571.964 6
engineering	623.822 4	plants	575.49
handling	623.882 24	Clonmel (Ireland)	T2—419 25
transportation services	387.224	Clontarf, Battle of, 1014	941.501
see also Ships		Close air support (Tactics)	358.414 2
Clippings		Close corporations	338.74
cataloging	025.342	law	346.066 8
library treatment	025.172	management	658.045
Clitics	415.92	*see also* Corporations	
specific languages	T4—592	Close support aircraft	358.428 3
Clive, Robert Clive, Baron		engineering	623.746 3
Indian history	954.029 6	military equipment	358.428 3
Cloaks	391.46	Close-up cinematography	777.6
commercial technology	687.14	Close-up photography	778.324
home sewing	646.45	Close-up videography	777.6
see also Outerwear		Closed-circuit television	384.556
Clock towers		*see also* Television	
architecture	725.97	Closed-end mutual funds	332.632 7
Clockcases		Closed-loop systems	
art	739.3	automation engineering	629.83
decorative arts	749.3	Closed shop	331.889 2
Clockmakers	681.113 092	Closed stacks	025.81
Clocks	681.113	Closet drama	808.82
art metalwork	739.3	history and criticism	809.2
technology	681.113	specific literatures	T3B—2
Clockworks	681.112	individual authors	T3A—2
Clocolan (South Africa :		Closets	643.5
District)	T2—685 1	Closing (Real estate)	346.043 73
Clog dancing	793.32	Clostridium	579.364
Clogs	391.413	Clostridium infections	
commercial technology	685.32	incidence	614.512
customs	391.413	medicine	616.931
see also Clothing		*see also* Communicable	
Cloisonné		diseases — humans	
ceramic arts	738.42	Cloth	
Cloisters		ship design	623.818 97
cathedral		shipbuilding	623.820 7
architecture	726.69	Cloth covers	
monastic		bookbinding	686.343
architecture	726.79	Clothes dryers	
Clonal selection	571.964 6	home economics	648.1
human immunology	616.079 5	manufacturing technology	683.88
Cloning	571.89	Clothing	391
biotechnology	660.65	armed forces	355.81
human immunology	616.079 5	costume	355.14
human reproduction		arts	746.92
ethics	176.22	commercial manufacturing	687
religion	205.662 2	economics	338.476 87
see also		fur	685.24
Reproduction —		instruments	681.767 7
ethics — religion		leather	685.22
see also Reproduction —		customs	391
ethics		health	613.482

Coaching horses		Coast guard ships	363.286
recreation	798.6	design	623.812 63
Coagulants		engineering	623.826 3
pharmacokinetics	615.718	military service	359.978 3
Coagulation		police services	363.286
blood	573.159	Coast Mountains (B.C.)	T2—711 1
human physiology	612.115	Coast Province (Kenya)	T2—676 23
physiology	573.159	Coast Ranges	T2—795 1
see also Cardiovascular		California	T2—794 1
system		Oregon	T2—795 1
water supply treatment	628.162 2	Washington	T2—797 9
Coahoma County (Miss.)	T2—762 44	Coast Region (Tanzania)	T2—678 23
Coahuila (Mexico : State)	T2—721 4	Coastal defense	355.45
Coahuiltecan Indians	T5—979	Coastal engineering	627.58
Coahuiltecan languages	497.9	Coastal lands	551.457
	T6—979		T2—146
Coal	553.24	*see also* Coasts	
chemical engineering	662.62	Coastal pools	551.461 8
economic geology	553.24		T2—168
extractive economics	338.272 4	Coastal regions	551.457
heating buildings	697.042		T2—146
mining	622.334	*see also* Coasts	
law	343.077 52	Coastal wetlands	
pipeline transportation	388.57	biology	578.769
law	343.093 97	ecology	577.69
prospecting	622.182 4	Coastal zones	551.457
public administration	354.44		T2—146
public utilities	363.6	*see also* Coasts	
law	343.092 7	Coasting	
resource economics	333.822	snow sports	796.95
law	346.046 822	Coasts	551.457
Coal County (Okla.)	T2—766 67		T2—146
Coal gasification	665.772	biology	578.751
Coal mining	622.334	ecology	577.51
extractive economics	338.272 4	geography	910.914 6
law	343.077 52	geomorphology	551.457
Coal oil	665.538 3	law	346.046 917
Coal slurry	662.623	physical geography	910.021 46
pipeline transportation	388.57	recreational resources	333.784
law	343.093 97	resource economics	333.917
technology	662.624	law	346.046 917
technology	662.623	Coastwise routes	387.524
Coal tar	547.82	Coatbridge (Scotland)	T2—414 52
Coal tar chemicals	661.803	Coated paper	676.283
Coalition military forces	355.356	Coaticook (Quebec :	
Coalition War, 1690–1697	949.204	Regional County	
Coarse fishing (Sports)	799.11	Municipality)	T2—714 67
Coast artillery	358.168 2	Coating	667.9
engineering	623.417	latex	678.527
military equipment	358.168 2	metals	671.73
Coast artillery forces	358.16	paper	676.235
Coast guard	363.286	Coatings	667.9
military service	359.97	Coatis	599.763
police services	363.286		

Coats	391.46	Cochlear diseases	
commercial technology	687.14	medicine	617.882 2
indoor garments	687.113	*see also* Ear diseases —	
outdoor garments	687.14	humans	
customs	391.46	Cochleas	
indoor garments	391.473	human anatomy	611.85
outdoor garments	391.46	human physiology	612.858
home economics	646.3	medicine	617.882 2
home sewing	646.45	Cochran County (Tex.)	T2—764 845
indoor garments	646.433	Cochrane (Ont. : District)	T2—713 142
outdoor garments	646.45	Cockatiels	636.686 56
see also Clothing		animal husbandry	636.686 56
Coats Island (Nunavut)	T2—719 58	zoology	598.71
Coats of arms	929.6	Cockatoos	598.71
Cob (Building material)	693.22	animal husbandry	636.686 5
Cobalt	669.733	Cocke County (Tenn.)	T2—768 895
chemical engineering	661.062 3	Cockfighting	791.8
chemistry	546.623	Cockney dialect	427.942 1
economic geology	553.483		T6—21
materials science	620.189 33	Cockroaches	595.728
metallography	669.957 33	control technology	628.965 7
metallurgy	669.733	Cocks (Mechanisms)	621.84
metalworking	673.733	Cocksfoot (Grass)	633.22
mining	622.348 3	botany	584.926
organic chemistry	547.056 23	Cocktails	641.874
applied	661.895	commercial processing	663.1
physical metallurgy	669.967 33	Coclé (Panama : Province)	T2—728 721
see also Chemicals; Metals		Cocoa	641.337 4
Cobalt soaps	668.125	beverage	641.337 4
Cobar (N.S.W.)	T2—944 9	commercial processing	663.92
Cobb County (Ga.)	T2—758 245	home preparation	641.877
Cobbling	685.31	cooking with	641.637 4
Cobordism theory	514.72	food	641.337 4
Cobourg Peninsula National		*see also* Cacao	
Park (N.T.)	T2—942 95	Cocoa butter	665.354
Cobras	597.964 2	chemical technology	665.354
Coburg (Germany)	T2—433 11	cooking with	641.637 4
Cocaine abuse	362.298	food	641.337 4
medicine	616.864 7	food technology	664.3
personal health	613.84	Coconino County (Ariz.)	T2—791 33
social welfare	362.298	Coconucos Range	
see also Substance abuse		(Colombia)	T2—861 53
Cocas (Plants)	583.69	Coconut milk	
Coccidiosis		commercial processing	663.64
incidence	614.53	Coconut oil	665.355
medicine	616.936	Coconuts	641.346 1
see also Communicable		botany	584.84
diseases — humans		commercial processing	664.804 61
Coccinellidae	595.769	cooking	641.646 1
Cochabamba (Bolivia :		food	641.346 1
Dept.)	T2—842 3	food crop	634.61
Cochineal dyes	667.26	textiles	677.18
		see also Textiles	
		Cocoons	595.714 6

Cocoparra National Park (N.S.W.)	T2—944 8
Cocos (Keeling) Islands	969.9
	T2—699
Cocuy National Park (Colombia)	T2—861 44
Cocuy Range (Colombia)	T2—861 44
Cod-liver oil	
pharmacology	615.34
COD mail	383.184
see also Postal service	
CODASYL databases	
computer science	005.754
Code generators	
computer science	005.45
Code of Manu	294.592 6
Code telegraphy	384.14
wireless	384.524
see also Telegraphy	
Codependency	362.291 3
alcoholism	362.292 3
medicine	616.861 9
social welfare	362.292 3
devotional literature	204.32
Christianity	242.4
medicine	616.869
pastoral theology	206.1
Christianity	259.429
religious guidance	204.42
Christianity	248.862 9
social theology	201.762 29
Christianity	261.832 29
social welfare	362.291 3
Codes (Law)	348.023
United States	348.732 3
Codes of conduct	
moral theology	205
Christianity	241.5
Judaism	296.36
Codex iuris canonici (1917)	262.93
Codex iuris canonici (1983)	262.94
Codiaeum	583.69
Codiales	579.835
Codification	348.004
law of nations	341.026 7
United States	348.730 4
Coding data	005.72
Coding of programs	005.13
Coding of software	005.13
Coding theory	003.54
	T1—011 54
Codington County (S.D.)	T2—783 23
Codling moth	
agricultural pests	634.049 78
Codons	572.86
Cods	641.392
conservation technology	639.977 633
cooking	641.692
food	641.392
resource economics	333.956 633
zoology	597.633
Coeducation	371.821
Coefficient of expansion	536.41
Coefficient of restitution	531.382
Coelacanths	597.39
Coelenterata	593.5
paleozoology	563.5
Coelesyria (Lebanon)	T2—394 4
Coelomycetes	579.55
Coelophysis	567.912
Coenopteridales	561.73
Coenzymes	572.7
see also Enzymes	
Coercion	
social control	303.36
Coeur d'Alene language	497.943
	T6—979 43
Coeur d'Alene Mountains (Idaho and Mont.)	T2—796 91
Coevolution	576.87
Cofactors	572.7
Coffee	641.337 3
agricultural economics	338.173 73
agriculture	633.73
botany	583.956
commercial processing	
economics	338.476 639 3
technology	663.93
cooking with	641.637 3
food	641.337 3
home preparation	641.877
Coffee cakes	641.865 9
commercial processing	664.752 5
home preparation	641.865 9
Coffee County (Ala.)	T2—761 34
Coffee County (Ga.)	T2—758 823
Coffee County (Tenn.)	T2—768 64
Coffee grounds	
divination	133.324 4
Coffee substitutes	641.877
commercial processing	663.97
home preparation	641.877
Coffeehouses	647.95
see also Eating places	
Cofferdams	624.157
Coffey County (Kan.)	T2—781 645
Coffin flies	595.774
Coffs Harbour (N.S.W.)	T2—944 3

Cold sores	
medicine	616.522
see also Skin diseases —	
humans	
Cold-storing foods	664.028 52
commercial preservation	664.028 52
home preservation	641.452
Cold weather	
health	613.111
Cold-weather cooking	641.591 1
Cold-weather diseases	
medicine	616.988 1
see also Environmental	
diseases — humans	
Cold-weather photography	778.75
Cold-working operations	
metals	671.3
Coldwater River (B.C.)	T2—711 72
Cole County (Mo.)	T2—778 55
Coleman County (Tex.)	T2—764 725
Colemanite	
mineralogy	549.735
Coleoidea	594.5
Coleoptera	595.76
paleozoology	565.76
Coleraine (Northern	
Ireland : Borough)	T2—416 14
Coles County (Ill.)	T2—773 72
Colesberg (South Africa :	
District)	T2—687 13
Colfax County (N.M.)	T2—789 22
Colfax County (Neb.)	T2—782 532
Colic	
abdominal disorders	617.55
pediatrics	618.920 975 5
Coligny (South Africa :	
District)	T2—682 47
Coliiformes	598.75
paleozoology	568.7
Colima (Mexico : State)	T2—723 6
Colinus	598.627 3
Colitis	
medicine	616.344 7
see also Digestive system	
diseases — humans	
Collaboration	
musical technique	781.47
see Manual at 781.47	
Collaborative indexing	025.487
Collaborative tagging	025.487
Collage	702.812
Collage painting	751.493

Collagen	572.67
biochemistry	572.67
human histology	611.018 2
medicine	616.77
see also Musculoskeletal	
system; Proteins	
Collagen diseases	
medicine	616.77
see also Musculoskeletal	
diseases — humans	
Collards	641.353 47
cooking	641.653 47
food	641.353 47
garden crop	635.347
Collateral (Design)	744.65
Collateral kinsmen	306.87
	T1—085
Collect-on-delivery mail	383.184
see also Postal service	
Collected biography	920
	T1—092 2
see Manual at T1—0922;	
also at T1—0922 vs.	
T1—093–099; *also at*	
920.008 vs. 305–306, 362;	
also at 920.009, 920.03–.09	
vs. 909.09, 909.1–.8,	
930–990	
Collectibles	790.132
	T1—075
see Manual at 745.1	
Collecting	069.4
	T1—075
museology	069.4
recreation	790.132
Collecting of accounts	
law	346.077
management	658.88
Collection analysis	
library science	025.21
Collection development	
library science	025.21
Collection maintenance	
library operations	025.8
library science	025.21
Collection management	
library science	025.21
Collections	069.5
description	T1—074
fine arts	708
temporary	707.4
see Manual at 704.9 and	
753–758	

Collections (continued)
  literature   808.8
    specific literatures   T3B—08
     see Manual at T3B—08
      and T3B—09
    see Manual at 808.8
  museology   069.5
  of abstracts   080
    brief abstracts   011
  of texts   080
    see Manual at 080 vs. 800;
     also at 081–089
  preparation   T1—075
Collective bargaining   331.89
  economics   331.89
  law   344.018 9
  personnel management   658.315 4
     T1—068 3
    public administration   352.68
  public administration   354.97
  women workers   331.479
Collective security   327.116
Collective settlements   307.77
Collectivism   335
  economics   335
  political ideology   320.53
  see Manual at 335 vs. 306.345,
    320.53
College administration   378.101
College administrators
  biography   378.009 2
  role and function   378.111
College admissions   378.161
College applications   378.161 6
College basketball   796.323 63
College buildings   378.196
  architecture   727.3
  construction   690.73
  education   378.196
  institutional housekeeping   647.993
  interior decoration   747.873
College Canadian football   796.335 63
College costs   378.38
College dropouts   378.169 13
College education   378
  see also Higher education
College enrollment   378.161 9
College entrance examinations   378.166 2
College entrance requirements   378.161 7
College extension   378.175
College graduates
  choice of vocation   331.702 35
  labor force   331.114 45

College graduates (continued)
  social group   305.55
  unemployment   331.137 804
College-level accounting   657.044
College-level examinations   378.166 2
College libraries   027.7
  see also Academic libraries
College majors   378.241
College presidents
  biography   378.009 2
  role and function   378.111
College presses
  bibliographies of publications   011.54
  publishing   070.594
College readers (Reading
  comprehension textbooks)
  applied linguistics   418
  specific languages   T4—86
College readers (Rhetoric
  textbooks)   808
  specific languages   808.04
College sports   796.043
  see also Sports
  see Manual at 796.08 vs.
    796.04
College students
  guides to religious life
    Christianity   248.834
  pastoral care
    Christianity   259.24
College teachers   378.12
College teaching   378.125
College trustees   378.101 1
College volleyball   796.325 63
Colleges   378.154 2
   T1—071 1
  area planning   711.57
  liability   344.075
  see also Higher education
Colleges without walls   378.03
  see also Higher education
Collembola   595.725
Colleton County (S.C.)   T2—757 95
Collie (W.A.)   T2—941 2
Collier County (Fla.)   T2—759 44
Collies   636.737 4
Colligative properties
  chemical engineering   660.294 15
  chemistry   541.341 5
Collin County (Tex.)   T2—764 556
Collines-de-l'Outaouais
  (Quebec)   T2—714 223
Collingsworth County
  (Tex.)   T2—764 831

Collision prevention	
seamanship	623.888 4
Collisions (Physics)	
nuclear particles	539.757
solid-state physics	530.416
Colloid chemistry	541.345
applied	660.294 5
specific elements and	
compounds	546
Colloidal fuels	662.82
Colloids	541.345
specific elements and	
compounds	546
Colloquial language	418
specific languages	T4—8
Collor de Mello, Fernando	
Affonso	
Brazilian history	981.064
Collotype printing	686.232 5
Collusion	364.134
law	345.023 4
Cologne (Germany)	T2—435 514
Cologne (Germany :	
Regierungsbezirk)	T2—435 51
Colom Caballeros, Álvaro	
Guatemalan history	972.810 534
Colombia	986.1
	T2—861
Panamanian history	972.870 3
Colombian literature	860
Colombians	T5—688 61
Colombo (Sri Lanka)	T2—549 3
Colon	573.379
biology	573.379
human anatomy	611.347
human physiology	612.36
medicine	616.34
surgery	617.554 7
see also Digestive system	
Colón (Honduras : Dept.)	T2—728 313
Colón (Panama : Province)	T2—728 732
Colón, Archipiélago de	T2—866 5
Colon cancer	
incidence	614.599 943 47
medicine	616.994 347
see also Cancer — humans	
Colon Classification	025.435
Colonia (Uruguay)	T2—895 11
Colonial architecture	724.1
Colonial Heights (Va.)	T2—755 595
Colonial military forces	355.352
Colonial Phoenician architecture	722.32
Colonialism	325.3

Colonic diseases	
medicine	616.34
see also Digestive system	
diseases — humans	
Colonies (Territories)	321.08
see also Non-self-governing	
territories	
Colonization	325.3
Colonnades	721.2
architecture	721.2
construction	690.12
Colonnettes	721.3
architecture	721.3
construction	690.13
Color	535.6
animal physiology	573.5
animals	591.472
arts	701.85
biological adaptation	578.47
drawing	741.018
interior decoration	747.94
mineralogy	549.125
painting	752
physics	535.6
plants	581.47
religious significance	203.7
Christianity	246.6
see also Symbolism —	
religious significance	
technology	667
therapeutics	615.831 2
Color (Sound)	781.234
Color blindness	
incidence	614.599 7
ophthalmology	617.759
see also Eye diseases —	
humans	
Color materials	
pottery	666.42
arts	738.12
technology	666.42
Color perception	
psychology	152.145
Color photography	778.6
Color plants	
floriculture	635.968
Color printing	686.230 42
Color television	621.388 04
Color therapy	615.831 2
Color vision defects	
ophthalmology	617.759
see also Eye diseases —	
humans	

Combat sports	
arts (continued)	
child care	649.57
ethics	175
human physiology	612.044
journalism	070.449 796 8
law	344.099
literature	
history and criticism	809.933 579
specific literatures	T3B—080 357 9
history and criticism	T3B—093 579
motion pictures	791.436 579
physical fitness	613.711
public administrative support	353.78
safety	363.14
public administration	353.97
techniques	796.802 89
sociology	306.483
television programs	791.456 579
Combat squadrons (Air force)	358.413 1
Combat units	355.31
Combat vehicles	355.83
engineering	623.74
military equipment	355.83
Combat zones	
living conditions	355.129 4
Combatants	
law	343.01
law of war	341.67
Combination of grades	371.25
Combinations (Enterprises)	338.8
accounting	657.96
economics	338.8
law	346.065
management	658.046
initiation	658.114 6
see also International enterprises	
see Manual at 658.04 vs. 658.114, 658.402	
Combinations (Mathematics)	511.64
Combinatorial analysis	511.6
Combinatorial geometry	516.13
Combinatorial optimization	519.64
Combinatorial probabilities	519.2
Combinatorial set theory	511.322
Combinatorial topology	514.22
Combinatorics	511.6
Combinatory logic	511.3
Combined operations (Armed forces)	355.46
marine forces	359.964 6

Combined sewers	363.728 493
social services	363.728 493
technology	628.214
see also Sewage treatment	
Combines (Machines)	633.104 5
manufacturing technology	681.763 1
Combing textiles	677.028 21
arts	746.11
manufacturing technology	677.028 21
Combretaceae	583.73
Combs	646.724
customs	391.44
see also Accessories (Clothing)	
manufacturing technology	688.5
personal appearance	646.724
Combustion	541.361
chemical engineering	660.296 1
chemistry	541.361
diesel engines	621.436 1
heat engineering	621.402 3
Combustion gases	
ecology	577.276
human toxicology	615.91
pollution	363.738 7
pollution technology	628.532
toxicology	571.956
COMECON (Economic organization)	341.242 7
international commerce	382.914 7
international economics	337.147
law of nations	341.242 7
Comedians	792.702 809 2
Comedies (Drama)	792.23
literature	808.825 23
history and criticism	809.252 3
specific literatures	T3B—205 23
individual authors	T3A—2
motion pictures	791.436 17
radio programs	791.446 17
stage presentation	792.23
see also Theater	
television programs	791.456 17
Comedy	
arts	T3C—17
literature	808.801 7
history and criticism	809.917
specific literatures	T3B—080 17
history and criticism	T3B—091 7
Comets	523.6
	T2—993

Comfort equipment	
aircraft	629.134 42
automobile	629.277
vehicles	629.040 289
Comfort stations	363.729 4
technology	628.45
see also Sanitation	
Comfreys	583.958
botany	583.958
floriculture	635.933 958
Comic books	741.5
drawing	741.51
genres	
history, criticism, techniques	741.53
geographic treatment	741.593–.599
see Manual at 741.593–.599	
and 741.5693–.5699	
see Manual at 741.5; *also at*	
741.5 vs. 741.56	
Comic strips	741.56
drawing	741.51
genres	
history, criticism, techniques	741.53
geographic treatment	741.569 3–.569 9
see Manual at 741.593–.599	
and 741.5693–.5699	
journalism	070.444
see Manual at 741.5; *also at*	
741.5 vs. 741.56	
Comic style	
arts	T3C—17
literature	808.801 7
history and criticism	809.917
specific literatures	T3B—080 17
history and	
criticism	T3B—091 7
Comics (Comic books)	741.5
Comics (Comic strips)	741.56
see also Comic strips	
Cominform	324.175
Coming-of-age customs	392.15
etiquette	395.24
Commagene	T2—393 6
Command and control systems	
(Military)	355.330 41
Command economies	330.124
Command functions (Armed	
forces)	355.330 41
Commandeering military	
resources	355.28
Commander Islands	
(Russia)	T2—577

Commandments	
Jewish law	296.18
moral theology	205
Christianity	241.5
Judaism	296.36
Commando raids	355.422
Commandos (Armed forces)	356.167
Commelinaceae	584.86
Commelinales	584.86
Commelinidae	584.8
Commelinids	584.8
Commemorations	394.2
Holocaust, 1933–1945	940.531 862
see also Celebrations	
Commemorative medals	
numismatics	737.222
Commemorative stamps	744.72
Commencements	371.291 2
customs	394.2
Commensalism	577.852
Commentaries	
journalism	070.442
Commerce	381
accounting	657.839
agent of social change	303.482
arts	700.455 3
	T3C—355 3
energy economics	333.796 89
ethics	174.4
law	343.08
see Manual at 343.078 vs.	
343.08	
literature	808.803 553
history and criticism	809.933 553
specific literatures	T3B—080 355 3
history and	
criticism	T3B—093 553
public administration	354.73
sociology	306.34
see Manual at 380	
Commercial air conditioning	697.931 6
Commercial airplanes	387.733 404 23
engineering	629.133 340 423
piloting	629.132 521 6
transportation services	387.733 404 23
see also Aircraft	
Commercial areas	307.333
area planning	711.552 2
community sociology	307.333
land economics	333.77
Commercial aviation	387.7
see also Air transportation	

Commercial banks	332.12
international operations	332.15
law	346.082 12
services	332.17
see also Banks (Finance)	
Commercial bookbinding	686.3
Commercial buildings	
architecture	725.2
construction	690.52
institutional housekeeping	647.962
sale and rental	333.338 7
theft from	364.162 3
law	345.026 23
Commercial catalogs	381.029
T1—029	
see Manual at T1—025 vs.	
T1—029; *also at* T1—074	
vs. T1—029	
Commercial circulars	381.029
T1—029	
Commercial credit	332.742
Commercial crimes	364.168
law	345.026 8
Commercial fishing	338.372 7
economics	338.372 7
technology	639.2
see also Fisheries	
Commercial gardening	
economics	338.175
technology	635
Commercial general liability	
insurance	368.56
see also Insurance	
Commercial insurance	368.094
see also Insurance	
Commercial land use	333.77
community sociology	307.333
economics	333.77
Commercial languages	401.3
Commercial law	346.07
Commercial leases	
accounting	657.75
buildings	333.338 75
industrial lands	333.336 5
law	346.043 462
real property and equipment	
financial management	658.152 42
Commercial liability insurance	368.56
see also Insurance	
Commercial miscellany	381.029
T1—029	
Commercial multi-peril insurance	368.094
see also Insurance	
Commercial paper	332.77
exchange medium	332.55
Commercial policy	381.3
American Revolution cause	973.311 2
international commerce	382.3
Commercial property	333.77
taxation	336.225
Commercial property insurance	368.12
see also Insurance	
Commercial publishers	070.592
Commercial revenues	
public finance	336.1
Commercial vehicles	
(Automotive)	388.34
engineering	629.22
transportation services	388.34
see also Automotive vehicles	
Commercials	659.14
broadcast advertising	659.14
radio performances	791.443
television performances	791.453
Commewijne (Suriname :	
District)	T2—883 7
Commission government	
cities	320.854
Commissioned officers	355.009 2
role and function	355.332
Commissioning	
military personnel	355.223 6
Commissions (Governing boards)	352.25
libraries	021.82
Committees	302.34
legislative bodies	328.365
social psychology	302.34
Commodities	338.02
investment economics	332.632 8
law	346.092 2
production	338.02
speculation	332.632 8
Commodity brokers	332.62
public administration	354.88
Commodity exchanges	332.644
architecture	725.25
law	343.08
public administration	354.88
Commodity futures	332.632 8
Commodity futures markets	332.644
Commodity options	332.632 8
Commodity options markets	332.644
Commodity standards (Money)	332.42
Commodores	359.009 2
role and function	359.331
Common adder	597.963 6

Common beans	
commercial processing	664.805 652
field crop	633.372
garden crop	635.652
Common carp	641.392
see also Carp	
Common carriers	388.041
law	343.093
sanitation services	363.729 3
public administration	353.94
see also Sanitation	
truck	388.324 3
see also Freight services;	
Passenger services	
Common cold	
medicine	616.205
see also Respiratory tract	
diseases — humans	
Common dolphin	599.532
Common herring	597.452
Common lands	333.2
landscape architecture	712.5
Common law	340.57
see Manual at 340, 342–347	
vs. 340.57	
Common-law marriage	306.841
	T1—086 56
law	346.016 71
see also Marriage	
Common lectionary	264.34
preaching	251.6
Common Market	341.242 2
see also European Union	
Common mice	599.353
Common of the mass	264.36
music	782.323 2
choral and mixed voices	782.532 32
single voices	783.093 232
Common partridge	598.623 2
Common people	
customs	390.24
dress	391.024
Common quail	598.627 2
Common rats	599.352
Common Slavic language	491.8
	T6—918
Common stocks	332.632 2
speculation	332.632 28
Common Worship	264.03
Commons	
land economics	333.2
landscape architecture	712.5
Commonsense reasoning	
computer science	006.333

Commonwealth and Protectorate	
(Great Britain)	941.063
Commonwealth of Independent	
States	947.086
	T2—47
Commonwealth of Nations	909.097 124 1
	T2—171 241
Commonwealth of the	
Northern Mariana	
Islands	T2—967
Communal land	333.2
Communal living	307.774
Communalism	302.14
Communauté régionale de	
l'Outaouais (Quebec)	T2—714 221
Communes	307.774
production economics	338.7
Communicable diseases	571.98
agriculture	632.3
animals	571.981
veterinary medicine	636.089 69
biology	571.98
humans	362.196 9
geriatrics	618.976 9
incidence	614.5
medicine	616.9
law	344.043 69
nursing	616.904 231
pediatrics	618.929
pregnancy complications	
obstetrics	618.36
social services	362.196 9
public administration	353.63
plants	571.982
agriculture	632.3
Communication	302.2
	T1—014
animals	591.59
physiology	573.92
ethics	175
religion	205.65
Christianity	241.65
management	658.45
military administration	355.688 4
public administration	352.384
see also Communication in	
management	
see Manual at 658.45 vs.	
651.7, 808.06665	
office services	651.7
see Manual at 658.45 vs.	
651.7, 808.06665	
psychology	153.6
sociology	302.2

Communication design	744
see Manual at 744 vs. 741.6	
Communication disorders	362.196 855
geriatrics	618.976 855
incidence	614.598 55
medicine	616.855
pediatrics	618.928 55
social services	362.196 855
special education	371.914
Communication in management	658.45
see also Communication —	
management	
Communication in marketing	
management	658.802
Communication in teaching	371.102 2
Communication skills	
primary education	372.6
Communications	384
arts	T3C—355 8
computer science	004.6
see also Computer	
communications	
engineering	621.382
see also Communications	
engineering	
law	343.099
literature	808.803 558
history and criticism	809.933 558
military science	358.24
air forces	358.46
land forces	358.24
naval forces	359.983
police services	363.24
public administration	354.75
social effects	303.483 3
see Manual at 380	
Communications engineering	621.382
arts	T3C—356
manned space flight	629.457
military	623.73
ships	623.856
space flight	629.457
spacecraft	629.474 3
unmanned space flight	629.437
unmanned spacecraft	629.464 3
Communications engineers	621.382 092
Communications equipment	
computer science	004.64
engineering	621.398 1
military equipment	355.85
Communications facilities	384.042
architecture	725.23
area planning	711.8
construction	690.523

Communications facilities (continued)	
military resources	355.27
misuse	364.147
railroads	385.316
Communications media	302.23
see also Mass media	
Communications network	
architecture	
communications engineering	621.382 15
computer science	004.65
engineering	621.398 1
Communications networks	
computer science	004.6
technology	621.382 1
Communications protocols	
communications engineering	621.382 12
computer science	004.62
Communications satellites	384.51
see also Satellite	
communication	
Communications services	384.043
air forces	358.46
armed forces	358.24
naval forces	359.983
police services	363.24
Communications workers	384.092
Communicative disorders	362.196 855
see also Communication	
disorders	
Communion (Part of service)	264.36
music	782.323 5
Communion of saints	262.73
Communion service	264.36
music	782.323
Communism	335.4
economics	335.4
political ideology	320.532
Communism and Christianity	261.21
Communism and Islam	297.273 54
Communist bloc	T2—171 7
Communist ethics	171.7
Communist front organizations	
political science	324.3
Communist government	321.92
Communist Information Bureau	324.175
Communist International	324.175
Communist manifesto	335.422
Communist parties	324.217 5
Australia	324.294 097 5
France	324.244 075
international organizations	324.175
Communist Party of Australia	324.294 097 5
Communist Party of Austria	324.243 607 5
Communist Party of China	324.251 075

Communist Party of Germany	324.243 075	Community-school partnerships	371.19
Communist Party of the Soviet		primary education	372.119
Union	324.247 075	reading	372.425
Communist Party of the United		Community-school relations	306.432
States of America	324.273 75	education	371.19
Communist Party of the United		higher education	378.103
States of America (New York)	324.274 707 5	sociology	306.432
Communist Refoundation Party		Community schools	371.03
(Italy)	324.245 075	Community service	
Communists	335.409 2	education	371.19
Marxist-Leninist	335.430 92	higher education	378.103
Communities	307	secondary education	373.119
psychological influence	155.94	penology	364.68
see Manual at 307		Community suppers	642.4
Community action (Social		Commutation of sentence	364.65
welfare)	361.8	law	345.077
public administration	353.527 93	penology	364.65
Community antenna television		Commutative algebras	512.44
systems	384.554 6	Commutative groups	512.25
see also Television		Commutative rings	512.44
Community banks	332.1	Commutators (Generator parts)	621.316
see also Banks (Finance)		Commuter services	388.042
Community-based corrections	365.6	railroad	
Community centers		engineering	625.4
adult education	374.8	urban	388.4
architecture	727.9	*see also* Urban transportation	
area planning	711.55	*see also* Passenger services	
recreation centers	790.068	Como (Italy)	T2—452 31
Community chests	361.8	ancient	T2—372 264 1
Community colleges (Two-year		Como (Italy : Province)	T2—452 3
colleges)	378.154 3	ancient	T2—372 264
Community development	307.14	Comorans	T5—969 694
law	346.045	Comoro Islands	969.4
public administration	354.279 3		T2—694
Community ecology	577.82	Comoros	969.41
animals	591.782		T2—694 1
plants	581.782	Comox-Strathcona (B.C.)	T2—711 2
Community health services	362.12	Compact disc read-only memory	004.565
see also Health services		*see also* CDs (Compact	
Community information services		discs) — computer storage	
libraries	021.28	Compact discs	
Community mental health		computer storage	004.565
services	362.22	music	780
see also Mental health services		recordings	384
Community nursing	610.734 3	*see also* Sound recordings	
Community of Christ	289.333	Compact groups	512.55
seminaries	230.073 933 3	Compact spaces	514.32
Community planning	307.12	Companies	338.7
community sociology	307.12	law	346.066
public administration	352.793	*see also* Business enterprises	
Community property	346.042	Companies (Military units)	355.31
divorce law	346.016 64	Companions of Muḥammad	297.648
		Company law	346.066

Company meetings	
law	346.066 45
Company of New France	
Canadian history	971.016 2
Company records	
law	346.066 4
records management	651.5
Company towns	307.767
Company unions	331.883 4
see also Labor unions	
Compaoré, Blaise	
Burkinan history	966.250 53
Comparable worth	331.215 3
law	344.012 153
Comparative advantage	
economics	338.604 6
international commerce	382.104 2
Comparative anatomy	571.3
Comparative education	370.9
Comparative government	320.3
Comparative grammar	415
Comparative law	340.2
Comparative librarianship	020.9
Comparative linguistics	410
see Manual at 410	
Comparative literature	809
Comparative physiology	571.1
Comparative psychology	156
Comparative religion	200
see Manual at 201–209 and	
292–299	
Comparison shopping	381.33
consumer products	640.73
Comparisons of products	
and services	T1—029
Compass	912.028 4
manufacturing technology	681.753
Compatibility	
computer science	004
hardware	004
engineering	621.39
software	005.132 4
Compensation	331.21
economics	331.21
income distribution	339.21
law	344.012 1
personnel management	
armed forces	355.64
executives	658.407 2
public administration	352.67
public administration	354.98
Compensation (Legal remedy)	347.077
victims of crimes	
social welfare	362.881 87
Compensation differentials	331.22
Compensation plans	331.216
personnel management	658.322
Compensation scales	331.216
personnel management	658.322 2
Compensatory education	370.111
Competition	338.604 8
communications industry	384.041
economics	338.604 8
law	343.072 1
price determination	338.522
transportation services	388.049
Competition (Biology)	577.83
Competition (Social)	302.14
Competition law	343.072 1
Competitions	T1—079
recreation	790.134
research	001.44
use in advertising	659.17
Compilers (Computer software)	005.453
Complaints (Civil procedure)	347.053
Complaints (Customer relations)	
marketing management	658.812
Complement (Immunology)	571.968 8
humans	616.079 97
Complement fixation	
human immunology	616.079 97
Complete fertilizers	631.813
chemical engineering	668.62
Completeness theorem	511.3
Complex analysis	515.9
Complex functions	515.9
Complex groups (Sociology)	302.35
Complex instruction set	
computing	004.3
see also Processing modes —	
computer science	
Complex multiplication	516.35
Complex numbers	512.788
Complex salts	
chemical engineering	661.4
Complex-valued functions	515.7
Complex-variable functions	515.9
Complexes (Topology)	514.223
Compline	264.15
music	782.324
see also Liturgy of the hours	
Composers	780.92
see Manual at 780.92	
Composing machines	686.225 4
manufacturing technology	681.61
use	686.225 4
Compositae	583.983
Composite current transmission	621.319 15

Composite materials	
furniture	645.4
manufacturing technology	684.106
see also Furniture	
handicrafts	745.59
materials science	620.118
Composite media	709.040 7
20th century	709.040 7
21st century	709.050 1
painting	759.067
sculpture	735.230 47
Composite photography	778.8
Composite woods	674.83
Composites (Art)	
techniques	702.81
two-dimensional	740
Composition (Arts)	701.8
architectural design	729.11
design	744.32
drawing	741.018
painting	750.18
Composition (Law)	346.077
Composition (Music)	781.3
computers	781.34
primary education	372.874
Composition (Printing)	686.225
Composition (Writing)	808
applied linguistics	418
specific languages	T4—8
primary education	372.623
rhetoric	808
Composition of atmosphere	551.511
Composition of ocean floor	551.468 6
Compost	631.875
Compound bridges	
construction	624.2
Compound engines	
aircraft	629.134 352
Compound liquors	641.255
commercial processing	663.55
Compound microscopes	502.823
biology	570.282 3
Compound musical bows	787.93
instrument	787.931 9
music	787.93
see also Stringed instruments	
Compound words	
formation	415.92
specific languages	T4—592
usage (Applied linguistics)	
specific languages	T4—81
Compounds (Chemicals)	546
chemical engineering	661
chemistry	546

Comprehensive high schools	373.25
see also Secondary education	
Compressed air	621.51
Compressed-air transmission	621.53
Compressed gas vehicles	
engineering	629.229 73
Compressed workweek	331.257 22
economics	331.257 22
personnel management	658.312 1
Compressibility	
fluid mechanics	532.053 5
gas mechanics	533.28
liquid mechanics	532.58
Compressible flow	
aeronautics	629.132 323
Compression (Stress)	
materials science	620.112 42
Compromise of 1850	973.64
Civil War (United States) cause	973.711 3
Compulsive behavior	
medicine	616.858 4
see also Mental disorders	
Compulsive eating	
medicine	616.852 6
see also Mental disorders	
Compulsive gambling	362.27
medicine	616.858 41
social welfare	362.27
Compulsive personality disorder	
medicine	616.858 1
see also Mental disorders	
Compulsive shopping	
medicine	616.858 4
see also Mental disorders	
Compulsory education	379.23
law	344.079
Compulsory labor	331.117 3
Compulsory military service	355.223 63
law	343.012 2
Compulsory welfare services	361.614
Computability	511.352
Computable functions	511.352
Computational complexity	511.352
Computational intelligence	006.3
Computational learning theory	006.310 1
Computational linguistics	006.35
specific languages	T4—028 563 5
see Manual at 006.35 vs.	
410.285	
Computed tomography	
medicine	616.075 722
Computer access control	005.83
management	658.478
Computer-aided design	620.004 202 85

Computer-aided design/	
computer-aided manufacture	670.285
Computer-aided manufacture	670.427
Computer-aided software	
engineering	005.102 85
Computer algorithms	005.13
Computer animated films	791.433 4
Computer animation	006.696
computer art	776.6
Computer applications	T1—028 5
see Manual at T1—0285	
Computer architecture	004.22
engineering	621.392
see Manual at 004.21 vs.	
004.22, 621.392	
Computer art	776
see Manual at 776 vs. 006.5–.7	
Computer-assisted instruction	371.334
	T1—078 5
adult level	374.264
Computer-assisted printing	686.225 44
Computer communications	004.6
	T1—028 546
communications services	384.3
engineering	621.398 1
law	343.099 44
multimedia systems	384.38
public administration	354.75
sociology	302.231
software	005.713
software development	005.711
symbols	004.601 48
see Manual at 004.6 vs.	
005.71; *also at* 004.6 vs.	
384.3	
Computer composition (Music)	781.34
Computer composition (Printing)	686.225 44
Computer control	629.89
Computer crimes	364.168
law	345.026 8
Computer data security	
management	658.478
Computer engineering	621.39
arts	T3C—356
see Manual at 004–006 vs.	
621.39	
Computer engineers	621.390 92
Computer file sharing	
criminology	364.166 2
law	346.048 2
Computer fonts	744.45

Computer games	794.8
mobile computing devices	
software	794.815 35
software development	794.815 25
Computer graphics	006.6
	T1—028 566
engineering	621.399 6
instructional use	371.334 66
	T1—078 566
Computer graphics software	006.68
Computer hardware	004
engineering	621.39
see Manual at 004 vs. 005	
Computer-human interaction	004.019
engineering	621.398 4
Computer input devices	004.76
engineering	621.398 6
Computer input-output devices	004.75
engineering	621.398 5
Computer integrated	
manufacturing systems	670.285
Computer interfacing	004.6
software	005.713
software development	005.711
see Manual at 004.6 vs. 005.71	
Computer interfacing equipment	004.64
engineering	621.398 1
Computer languages	005.13
microprogramming	005.18
Computer literacy	004
primary education	372.34
Computer mathematics	004.015 1
see Manual at 004.0151 vs.	
511.1, 511.35	
Computer mice	004.76
engineering	621.398 6
Computer modeling	003.3
	T1—011 3
instructional use	371.397
Computer music	786.76
Computer network resources	025.042
Computer network security	005.8
certification	005.807 6
see also Computer security	
Computer networks	004.6
certification	004.607 6
communications services	384.3
processing modes	004.3
see also Processing	
modes — computer	
science	
security measures	005.8
see also Computer	
communications	

Computerized process control	629.895
chemical engineering	660.281 5
engineering	629.895
manufacturing technology	670.427 5
Computerized typesetting	686.225 44
Computers	004
access control	005.83
management	658.478
economics	338.470 04
engineering	621.39
instructional use	371.334
primary education	372.133 4
law	343.099 9
maintenance	004.028 8
music	780.285
musical instrument	786.76
see also Electrophones	
repair	004.028 8
social effects	303.483 4
theft of	364.162 800 4
law	345.026 280 04
see Manual at 004.1; *also at*	
004.1 vs. 004.3	
Comtism	146.4
Comum (Italy)	T2—372 264 1
Comunisti italiani (Political	
party)	324.245 075
Conakry (Guinea)	T2—665 2
Concealed weapons	364.143
law	345.024 3
Concealment	
military engineering	623.77
Concentration	
psychology of learning	153.153 2
Concentration camp inmates	362.88
	T1—086 949
Concentration camps	365.45
Holocaust, 1933–1945	940.531 85
penology	365.45
World War II	940.531 7
see also Internment camps;	
Penal institutions	
Concentricycloidea	593.93
Concepción (Chile :	
Province)	T2—833 9
Concepción (Paraguay)	T2—892 138
Concept-based retrieval	
information science	025.04
Concepts	
epistemology	121.4
psychology	153.23

Conceptual art	700
fine arts	709.040 75
20th century	709.040 75
21st century	709.050 15
painting	759.067 5
sculpture	735.230 475
see also Arts	
Conceptualism	
philosophy	149.1
Concert halls	
architecture	725.81
music	781.539
Concert zithers	787.75
see also Stringed instruments	
Concertantes	784.186
Concerti grossi	784.24
Concertinas	788.84
instrument	788.841 9
music	788.84
see also Woodwind	
instruments	
Concertinos	784.186 2
Concertos	784.23
musical form	784.186
Concerts	780.78
Concho County (Tex.)	T2—764 71
Conchostraca	595.32
Conciliation	
international politics	327.17
labor economics	331.891 4
law	347.09
Concord (N.H.)	T2—742 72
Concord, Battle of, 1775	973.331 1
Concordances	T1—03
Concordia Parish (La.)	T2—763 73
Concrete	666.893
architectural construction	721.044 5
building construction	693.5
building materials	691.3
foundation materials	624.153 36
materials science	620.136
ship design	623.818 34
ship hulls	623.845 4
shipbuilding	623.820 7
structural engineering	624.183 4
Concrete art	709.040 56
Concrete blocks	666.894
architectural construction	721.044 4
building construction	693.4
building materials	691.3
manufacturing technology	666.894
materials science	620.139
structural engineering	624.183 2
Concrete music	786.75

Conejos County (Colo.)	T2—788 33	Conflict (continued)	
Cones	516.154	social groups	305
Confections	641.86	sociology	303.6
Confederal Democratic Union		Conflict management	303.69
(Swiss political party)	324.249 408 2	business relationships	650.13
Confederate States of America	973.713	executive management	658.405 3
	T2—75	interpersonal relations	
Confederate sympathizers		personnel management	658.314 5
United States history	973.718	labor relations	
Confederated Benedictines	255.11	personnel management	658.315
church history	271.11	Conflict of interest	
Confederation of Arab		law	342.068 4
Republics	T2—62	occupational ethics	174
Confederation of the Rhine	943.06	political ethics	172
Confederations	321.02	public administration	353.46
law	342.042	Conflict of laws	340.9
public administration	351	domestic	342.042
Conference calls	384.64	*see Manual at* 340.9	
see also Telephone		Conflict resolution	303.69
Conference committees		international relations	327.17
legislative bodies	328.365 7	public safety	363.321 5
Conference on Data Systems		sociology	303.69
Languages databases		Conformal mapping	516.36
computer science	005.754	calculus	515.9
Conferences	060	differential geometry	516.36
Confession (Christian rite)	234.166	Conformal projections	526.82
public worship	265.62	Conformal transformations	516.35
theology	234.166	Conformation (Biochemical	
Confession (Law)	345.06	structure)	572.33
Confessionals	247.1	Conformity	303.32
architecture	726.529 1	psychology	153.854
Confessions of faith	202	Confraternities	267
Christianity	238	Confraternity Bible	220.520 5
Confidence regions	519.54	Confucianism	181.112
Confidential communications	323.448	art representation	704.948 995 12
civil right	323.448	arts	700.482 995 12
law	342.085 8		T3C—382 995 12
Confidentiality		philosophy	181.112
office services	651	religion	299.512
Confinement (Childbirth)	392.12	Confucianist holidays	
music	781.582	customs	394.265 951 2
Confirmation (Religious rite)	203.8	Confucianists	
Christianity	234.162	biography	181.112
public worship	265.2	religion	299.512 092
theology	234.162	Congenital adrenal hyperplasia	
etiquette	395.24	medicine	616.45
Judaism	296.442 4	Congenital diseases	
liturgy	296.454 24	humans	
women's	296.443 4	medicine	616.043
liturgy	296.454 34	pediatrics	618.920 043
music	781.583	Congenital heart defects	
Conflict	303.6	medicine	616.120 43
international politics	327.16	*see also* Cardiovascular	
law	341.5	diseases — humans	

Conjunctival diseases	
ophthalmology	617.77
see also Eye diseases —	
humans	
Conjunctivas	
human anatomy	611.84
human physiology	612.841
ophthalmology	617.77
Conjunctivitis	
incidence	614.599 7
ophthalmology	617.773
see also Eye diseases —	
humans	
Conjuring	
magic	133.43
recreation	793.8
Connacht (Ireland)	T2—417 1
Connaraceae	583.68
Connarales	583.68
Connecticut	974.6
	T2—746
Connecticut River	T2—74
Connecticut	T2—746
Massachusetts	T2—744 2
New Hampshire	T2—742
Vermont	T2—743
Connecting rods	621.827
internal-combustion engines	621.437
machine engineering	621.827
Connectionism	
artificial intelligence	006.32
Connections (Mathematics)	516.35
Connective tissue cells	
human cytology	611.018 26
Connective tissue diseases	
medicine	616.77
see also Musculoskeletal	
diseases — humans	
Connective tissues	571.56
biology	571.56
human anatomy	611.74
human histology	611.018 2
medicine	616.77
musculoskeletal system	573.735 6
human histology	612.757
human physiology	612.757
see also Musculoskeletal	
system	
Connochaetes	599.645 9
Conodonts	562.2
Conrad I, Holy Roman Emperor	
German history	943.022

Conscience	170
civil rights issues	323.442
ethical systems	171.6
religion	205
Buddhism	294.35
Christianity	241.1
Hinduism	294.548
Islam	297.5
Judaism	296.36
Conscientious objection	355.224
ethics	172.42
see also War — ethics	
law	343.012 6
social theology	201.727 3
see also War — social	
theology	
Conscientious objectors	355.224
see also Conscientious	
objection	
Conscious mental processes	153
children	155.413
comparative psychology	156.3
educational psychology	370.152
human physiology	612.823 3
late adulthood	155.671 3
men	155.332 3
women	155.333 3
Consciousness	153
philosophy	128.2
Consciousness-raising groups	305
Conscription (Draft)	355.223 63
law	343.012 2
Consecrations (Christian rites)	265.92
Consensus (Islamic law)	
sources of fiqh	340.591 33
Consent to marriage	
law	346.016 2
Consequential loss	
insurance	368.08
Consequentialism	
ethics	171.5
CONSER Project	025.343 2
Conservation (Maintenance	
and repair)	T1—028 8
arts	069.53
bibliographic materials	025.84
museology	702.88
Conservation of biodiversity	333.951 6
Conservation of energy (Physics)	531.62
Conservation of mass-energy	530.11
Conservation of natural resources	333.72
economics	333.72
law	346.044
public administration	354.334

Construction noise	363.741
see also Noise	
Construction services (Military)	358.22
land	358.22
naval	359.982
Construction specifications	692.3
Construction toys	790.133
manufacturing technology	688.725
see also Toys	
Construction workers	624.092
building trades	690.092
civil engineering	624.092
labor economics	331.762 4
public administration	354.942 4
Constructions (Grammar)	415
specific languages	T4—5
Constructive accounting	657.1
Constructive mathematics	511.36
Constructivism	
fine arts	709.040 57
painting	759.065 7
sculpture	735.230 457
Constructivism (Philosophy)	149
Consular law	342.041 2
law of nations	341.35
Consular service	327.2
public administration	353.132 63
Consulate (France)	944.046
Consulate buildings	
architecture	725.17
Consultants	001
management	658.46
public administration	352.373
marketing management	658.83
physicians	362.172
Consultative bodies	
public administration	352.743
Consumer attitudes	
marketing research	658.834 3
Consumer behavior	
marketing research	658.834 2
Consumer complaints	
marketing management	658.812
Consumer cooperatives	334.5
management	658.87
Consumer credit	332.743
law	346.073
marketing management	658.883
Consumer education	381.33
home economics	640.73
Consumer finance institutions	332.35
Consumer food prices	338.19
Consumer income	
macroeconomics	339.22

Consumer information	381.33
home economics	640.73
public administration	352.746
Consumer information labeling	381.33
Consumer movements	381.32
Consumer preferences	
marketing research	658.834 3
Consumer price indexes	338.528
Consumer protection	381.34
commerce	381.34
law	343.071
public administration	352.746
Consumer psychology	
marketing research	658.834 2
Consumer reports	381.33
	T1—029
see Manual at T1—025 vs.	
T1—029	
Consumer research	
marketing management	658.834
Consumer satisfaction	
customer relations	
marketing management	658.812
marketing research	658.834 3
Consumerism	381.3
Consumption	339.47
ethics	178
religion	205.68
Buddhism	294.356 8
Christianity	241.68
Hinduism	294.548 68
Islam	297.568
Judaism	296.368
macroeconomics	339.47
natural resources	333.713
sociology	306.3
Consumption-savings	
relationship	339.43
Contact allergies	
incidence	614.599 33
medicine	616.973
Contact dermatitis	
medicine	616.51
see also Skin diseases —	
humans	
Contact lenses	
manufacturing technology	681.41
optometry	617.752 3
Contact printing (Photography)	771.44
Contactors (Generator parts)	621.316
Contagious diseases	571.98
see also Communicable	
diseases	

Continuum hypothesis	511.322
Continuum physics	530
theory	530.14
Contortion	
sports	796.47
Contour farming	631.455
Contour surveying	526.981
Contra Costa County	
(Calif.)	T2—794 63
Contrabassoons	788.59
instrument	788.591 9
music	788.59
see also Woodwind	
instruments	
Contraception	363.96
ethics	176.3
see also Birth control	
Contraceptive drug implants	
health	613.943 2
medicine	618.182
see also Birth control	
Contraceptive drugs	
health	613.943 2
medicine	618.182
see also Birth control	
Contract bridge	795.415
Contract carriers	388.041
truck	388.324 3
see also Freight services	
Contract labor	331.542
economics	331.542
penology	365.65
sociology	306.363
Contracting	346.022
see also Contracts	
Contracting out	658.405 8
	T1—068 4
armed forces	355.621 2
management	658.405 8
public administration	352.538
Contraction (Effect of heat)	536.41
Contractions	
heart	573.17
human physiology	612.171
physiology	573.17
see also Cardiovascular	
system	
muscles	573.75
human physiology	612.741
see also Musculoskeletal	
system	
skin	573.5
human physiology	612.791
see also Skin	

Contractions (Linguistics)	411
specific languages	T4—11
specific subjects	T1—014 8
Contractors (Builders)	690.092
Contracts	346.022
air forces	358.416 212
armed forces	355.621 2
civil rights issues	323.46
collective bargaining	331.891
personnel management	658.315 4
public administration	352.68
construction	692.8
materials management	658.723
	T1—068 7
naval forces	359.621 2
public administration	352.53
Contractual liability insurance	368.56
see also Insurance	
Contradiction (Principle of)	111
Contradictions	
logic	165
Contralto voices	782.68
children's	782.78
choral and mixed voices	782.78
single voices	783.78
general works	782.68
choral and mixed voices	782.68
single voices	783.68
women's	782.68
choral and mixed voices	782.68
single voices	783.68
Contrapuntal forms	784.187
Contrastive linguistics	410
applied linguistics	418
see Manual at 410	
Contraventions (Criminal law)	345.02
Contributory negligence	346.032
Contrition (Christian rite)	234.166
public worship	265.61
theology	234.166
Control	
executive management	658.401 3
military services	355.685
public administration	352.35
export trade	382.64
see also Export trade	
public administration	352.8
external control	352.8
internal control	352.35
social process	303.33
Control circuits	621.381 537
Control devices	
electrical engineering	621.317
heating buildings	697.07

Converter substations		Cook Inlet (Alaska)	551.461 434
electrical engineering	621.312 6		T2—164 34
Converters		Cook Islands	T2—962 3
electrical engineering	621.313	Cook Strait (N.Z.)	551.461 478
electronic circuits	621.381 532 2		T2—164 78
Convertible tops	629.26	Cookbooks	641.5
Convertiplanes		Cooke County (Tex.)	T2—764 533
engineering	629.133 35	Cookery	641.5
military engineering	623.746 047 6	*see also* Cooking	
Converts	204.24	Cookies	641.865 4
Judaism	296.714	commercial processing	664.752 5
outreach activity for	296.69	home preparation	641.865 4
missions for	207.2	Cooking	641.5
Convex analysis	515.882	customs	392.37
Convex functions	515.882	primary education	372.373
Convex geometry	516.08	Cooking for one	641.561 1
Convex programming	519.76	Cooking for two	641.561 2
Convex sets		Cooking greens	641.354
geometry	516.08	commercial processing	664.805 4
Convex surfaces	516.362	cooking	641.654
Conveyancing	346.043 8	food	641.354
Conveying equipment	621.867	garden crop	635.4
mining	622.66	Cooking oils	641.338 5
pneumatic engineering	621.54	cooking	641.638 5
Conveyor belts	621.867 5	food	641.338 5
manufacturing technology	678.36	food technology	664.36
materials handling	621.867 5	Cooking utensils	643.3
Convict labor	365.65	manufacturing technology	683.82
economics	331.51	Cookout cooking	641.578
law	344.035 65	Cooks	641.509 2
penology	365.65	Cookstown (Northern	
Convicts	365.6	Ireland : District)	T2—416 4
	T1—086 927	Cool jazz	781.655
Convolutions		Coolants	621.564
cerebrum		nuclear engineering	621.483 36
human physiology	612.825	refrigeration engineering	621.564
Convolutions (Functions)	515.43	Coolgardie (W.A.)	T2—941 6
Convolvulaceae	583.959	Coolidge, Calvin	
Convulsions		United States history	973.915
medicine	616.845	Cooling coils	621.56
see also Nervous system		buildings	697.932 2
diseases — humans		Cooling systems	
Convulsive therapy		automotive	629.256
psychiatry	616.891 2	buildings	697.93
Conway County (Ark.)	T2—767 31	ships	623.853 5
Conway Range National		Cooling towers	621.197
Park (Qld.)	T2—943 6	Cooloola National Park	
Conwy (Wales: County		(Qld.)	T2—943 2
Borough)	T2—429 27	Coon cat	636.83
Cook, Joseph, Sir		Coonabarabran (N.S.W.)	T2—944 4
Australian history	994.041	Cooper County (Mo.)	T2—778 51
Cook County (Ga.)	T2—758 876	Cooperage	674.82
Cook County (Minn.)	T2—776 75	Cooperation	158
		social psychology	302.14

Coptic language	493.2	Coral Sea	551.461 476
	T6—932		T2—164 76
Biblical texts	220.49	Coral Sea Islands	T2—948
Coptic literature	893.2	Coral snakes	597.964 4
Coptic people	T5—932	Coralberry	583.675
Coptic period	932.023	Coralberry (Primulaceae)	583.93
Copts	T5—932	Corals	593.6
Copulation		paleozoology	563.6
sociology	306.77	Corby (England : Borough)	T2—425 51
Copying		Cordage	
office use	652.4	ship gear	623.862
Copying machines	686.4	textiles	677.71
see also Photocopying		Cordaitales	561.59
Copyright	346.048 2	Cordials	641.255
law	346.048 2	commercial processing	663.55
library operations	025.12	Cordierite	
public administration	352.749	mineralogy	549.64
Copyright deposits		Cordillera (Paraguay)	T2—892 135
library acquisitions	025.26	Cordillera Administrative	
Copyright infringement	346.048 2	Region (Philippines)	T2—599 13
criminal law	345.026 62	Cordillera Occidental	
criminology	364.166 2	(Colombia)	T2—861 5
law	346.048 2	Cordite	662.26
Copyright piracy	346.048 2	military engineering	623.452 6
criminal law	345.026 62	Córdoba (Argentina :	
criminology	364.166 2	Province)	T2—825 4
law	346.048 2	Córdoba (Colombia : Dept.)	T2—861 12
Coquihalla River (B.C.)	T2—711 37	Córdoba (Spain : Province)	T2—468 4
Coquimbo (Chile : Region)	T2—832 3	Cordoba caliphate	946.02
Coquitlam (B.C.)	T2—711 33	Cords (Textiles)	677.76
Cor pulmonale		textile arts	746.27
medicine	616.12	Corduroy	677.617
see also Cardiovascular		Cordylidae	597.958
diseases — humans		Core curriculum	375.002
Cora Indians	T5—974 54	Core eudicots	583
Cora language	497.454	paleobotany	561.3
	T6—974 54	Core memory	004.53
Coraciiformes	598.78	engineering	621.397 3
paleozoology	568.7	Core of earth	551.112
Coracles	386.229	Corfu (Greece : Regional	
design	623.812 9	unit)	T2—495 5
engineering	623.829	Coriariaceae	583.66
transportation services	386.229	Corinth (Greece : Regional	
Coral fungi	579.597	unit)	T2—495 22
Coral Harbour (Nunavut)	T2—719 58	ancient	T2—387
Coral reefs	578.778 9	Corinth, Isthmus of	
	T2—142	(Greece)	T2—495 22
biology	578.778 9	Corinthia (Greece)	T2—495 22
conservation technology	639.973 6	ancient	T2—387
ecology	577.789	Corinthians (Biblical books)	227.2
geography	910.914 2	Corito (Italy)	T2—375 68
physical geography	910.021 42	Cork	674.9
resource economics	333.955 3	forestry	634.985

Coronie (Suriname :	
District)	T2—883 2
Corowa (N.S.W.)	T2—944 8
Corozal District (Belize)	T2—728 21
Corpora (Linguistics)	410.188
specific languages	T4—018 8
Corpora quadrigemina	
human physiology	612.826 4
medicine	616.8
Corporal punishment	364.67
education	371.542
law	345.077 3
penology	364.67
Corporate bonds	332.632 34
Corporate crime	364.168
law	345.026 8
Corporate divestiture	
management	658.164
Corporate finance	338.604 1
management	658.15
Corporate governance	658.4
Corporate income tax	336.243
law	343.052 67
public administration	352.44
public finance	336.243
Corporate law	346.066
Corporate mergers	338.83
see also Mergers	
Corporate organization	338.74
economics	338.74
law	346.066 2
management	
initiation	658.114 5
internal organization	658.402
Corporate ownership	
land economics	333.324
Corporate planning	658.401 2
Corporate profits	
income distribution	339.21
Corporate reorganization	338.74
credit economics	332.75
law	346.066 26
management	658.16
production economics	338.74
Corporate retail chains	381.12
management	658.870 2
see also Commerce	
Corporate social responsibility	174.4
Corporate state (Government)	321.94
Corporate turnarounds	
executive management	658.406 3
Corporation meetings	
law	346.066 45
management use	658.456

Corporation records	
law	346.066 4
records management	651.5
Corporation tax	336.207
law	343.067
Corporations	338.74
accounting	657.95
law	346.066 48
economics	338.74
income tax	336.243
law	343.052 67
law	346.066
tort law	346.031
management	658.045
initiation	658.114 5
law	346.066 4
see Manual at 658.04 vs.	
658.114, 658.402	
taxes	336.207
law	343.067
Corps (Military units)	355.31
Corps of engineers	358.22
Corpus Christi (Tex.)	T2—764 113
Corpus iuris canonici	262.923
Corpus linguistics	410.188
specific languages	T4—018 8
Corpus striatum	
human physiology	612.825
medicine	616.8
Corpuscular theory of light	535.12
Correctional institutions	365
see also Penal institutions	
Corrections (Astronomy)	522.9
Corrections (Penology)	364.6
public administration	353.39
Correlation analysis	519.537
Correspondence (Letters)	383.122
see also Letters	
(Correspondence)	
Correspondence analysis	519.537
Correspondence art	709.040 84
Correspondence courses	371.356
adult education	374.4
	T1—071 5
higher education	378.175 6
Correspondence schools	374.4
	T1—071 5
Corrèze (France : Dept.)	T2—446 7
Corrientes (Argentina :	
Province)	T2—822 2
Corrodentia	595.732
Corrosion	620.112 23
Corrosion control	
chemical process equipment	660.283 04

Cost-benefit analysis	658.155 4
public administration	352.43
Cost control	658.155 2
public administration	352.85
Cost effectiveness	
financial management	658.155 4
Cost of living	339.42
Cost-output ratio	338.06
agricultural industries	338.16
economics	338.06
mineral industries	338.26
secondary industries	338.45
Cost reduction	658.155 2
Cost-volume-profit analysis	658.155 4
Costa, Manuel Pinto da	
Sao Tomean history	967.150 21
1975–1991	967.150 21
2011–	967.150 24
2011–2016	967.150 24
Costa e Silva, Arthur da	
Brazilian history	981.063
Costa Region (Ecuador)	T2—866 3
Costa Rica	972.86
	T2—728 6
Costa Rican literature	860
Costa Ricans	T5—687 286
Costaceae	584.88
Costanoan Indians	T5—974 13
Costanoan language	497.413
	T6—974 13
Costilla County (Colo.)	T2—788 35
Costs	338.51
accounting	657.42
agricultural industries	338.13
economics	338.51
financial management	658.155 2
macroeconomics	339.42
mineral industries	338.23
secondary industries	338.43
transportation services	388.049
Costume	391
arts	700.456 4
	T3C—356 4
literature	808.803 564
history and criticism	809.933 564
specific literatures	T3B—080 356 4
history and	
criticism	T3B—093 564
textile arts	746.92
see Manual at 391 vs. 646.3,	
746.92	

Costume jewelry	391.7
customs	391.7
handicrafts	745.594 2
making	688.2
Costume jewelry makers	688.209 2
Costumes	792.026
commercial technology	687.16
customs	391.48
dramatic performances	792.026
motion pictures	791.430 26
stage	792.026
television	791.450 26
home sewing	646.478
see also Clothing	
see Manual at 391 vs. 646.3,	
746.92	
Cot death	
pediatrics	618.920 26
Cotabato (Philippines :	
Province)	T2—599 748
Côte d'Azur (France)	T2—449 4
Côte-de-Beaupré (Quebec)	T2—714 48
Côte-de-Gaspé (Quebec)	T2—714 793
Côte d'Ivoire	966.68
	T2—666 8
Côte-d'Or (France)	T2—444 2
Côte-Nord (Quebec)	T2—714 17
Côte-Nord (Quebec :	
Administrative region)	T2—714 17
Côte-Saint-Luc (Quebec)	T2—714 28
Côtes-d'Armor (France)	T2—441 2
Cotillions	793.35
Cotingas	598.822
Cotingidae	598.822
Cotonou (Benin)	T2—668 3
Cotopaxi (Ecuador)	T2—866 14
Cotswold (England)	T2—424 17
Cotswold Hills (England)	T2—424 17
Cotswolds (England)	T2—424 17
Cottage cheese	641.373 56
cooking	641.673 56
food	641.373 56
processing	637.356
Cottage industries	338.634
labor economics	331.256 7
Cottages	
architecture	728.37
construction	690.837
Cottbus (Germany)	T2—431 51
Cottbus (Germany : Bezirk)	T2—431 51
Cotters	621.883
Cottle County (Tex.)	T2—764 751

Counties	320.83	Court costs	
government	320.83	judgments	
public administration	352.15	law	347.077
support and control	353.335	law	347.057
see Manual at 351.3–.9 vs.		Court decisions	
352.13–.19		law of nations	341.026 8
Counting	513.211	texts	348.044
Counting circuits	621.381 534	United States	348.734 4
Counting machines		Court handball	796.312
manufacturing technology	681.14	*see also* Ball games	
Counting-out rhymes	398.84	Court management	347.013
Counting rhymes	398.84	criminal law	345.012 3
Country and western music	781.642	Court of First Instance of the	
see also Country music		European Communities	341.242 228 2
Country clubs		Court of Justice of the European	
landscape architecture	712.7	Communities	341.242 228 4
Country music	781.642	Court records	347.013
songs	782.421 642	criminal law	345.012 3
Country musicians		genealogy	929.3
singers	782.421 642 092	Court reporters	347.016
Country Party (Australia)	324.294 04	criminal law	345.012 6
Country singers	782.421 642 092	Court reporting	
County charters	342.02	shorthand	653.18
County courts	347.02	Court rules	347.051
County executives	352.232 15	criminal law	345.05
County government buildings		Court settings	
architecture	725.13	music	781.536
County planning		Court tennis	796.34
civic art	711.3	Courtesy	
economics	338.9	ethics	177.1
Couples therapy		etiquette	395
psychiatry	616.891 562	Courthouses	
Coupling (Nuclear particles)	539.75	architecture	725.15
Couplings	621.825	Courtroom procedure	347.075
railroad engineering	625.25	criminal law	345.075
Coupons		Courts (Law)	347.01
sales promotion	658.82	England	347.420 1
Coups d'état	321.09	European Union	341.242 228
see Manual at 909, 930–990		law of nations	341.55
vs. 320.4, 321, 321.09		Scotland	347.411 01
Courage		United States	347.731
ethics	179.6	Courts-martial	343.014 3
Courland (Duchy)	T2—479 6	Courts of appeal	347.03
Cournot, A. A. (Antoine		England	347.420 3
Augustin)		Scotland	347.411 03
economic school	330.154 3	United States	347.732 4
Course in Miracles	299.93	Courts of first appeal	347.033
Courses of study	T1—071	criminal law	345.014 42
Court calendars	347.013	Courts of first instance	347.02
criminal law	345.012 3	criminal law	345.014 2
Court clerks	347.016	Courts of last appeal	347.035
criminal law	345.012 6	criminal law	345.014 44
		Courts of last resort	347.035
		criminal law	345.014 44

Cracking processes
petroleum 665.533
Cradle Mountain (Tas.) T2—946 3
Cradle Mountain-Lake
Saint Clair National Park
(Tas.) T2—946 3
Cradle of Humankind World
Heritage Site (South
Africa) T2—682 22
Cradock (South Africa :
District) T2—687 56
Craft (Ships) 387.2
see also Ships
Craft unions 331.883 2
United States 331.883 209 73
see also Labor unions
Crafts 680
arts 745
public administrative support 353.77
sociology 306.47
see Manual at 680 vs. 745.5
Craftsmen's marks T1—027 8
Craig County (Okla.) T2—766 98
Craig County (Va.) T2—755 795
Craigavon (Northern
Ireland : District) T2—416 6
Craighead County (Ark.) T2—767 98
Cranberries 641.347 6
botany 583.93
commercial processing 664.804 76
cooking 641.647 6
food 641.347 6
horticulture 634.76
Cranbrook (B.C.) T2—711 65
Crane County (Tex.) T2—764 915
Crane flies 595.772
Cranes (Birds) 598.32
conservation technology 639.978 32
resource economics 333.958 32
Cranes (Hoisting machinery) 621.873
Cranial nerve diseases
medicine 616.856
see also Nervous system
diseases — humans
Cranial nerves 573.85
human physiology 612.819
medicine 616.856
see also Nervous system
Craniata 596
Craniology 599.948
Craniotomy
obstetrical surgery 618.88
Cranks (Mechanisms) 621.827

Crape myrtle 635.977 373
botany 583.73
ornamental arboriculture 635.977 373
Crappies 597.738
sports fishing 799.177 38
Craps 795.12
Crash injuries
incidence 614.3
medicine 617.102 8
Crassulaceae 583.44
Crater Lake National Park
(Or.) T2—795 915
Craters (Depressions) 551.21
T2—144
geography 910.914 4
geology 551.21
physical geography 910.021 44
Craters of the Moon
National Monument
(Idaho) T2—796 59
Crates
wooden 674.82
Craven (England) T2—428 41
Craven County (N.C.) T2—756 192
Crawfishes 595.384
see also Crayfishes
Crawford County (Ark.) T2—767 35
Crawford County (Ga.) T2—758 562
Crawford County (Ill.) T2—773 75
Crawford County (Ind.) T2—772 28
Crawford County (Iowa) T2—777 45
Crawford County (Kan.) T2—781 98
Crawford County (Mich.) T2—774 77
Crawford County (Mo.) T2—778 62
Crawford County (Ohio) T2—771 27
Crawford County (Pa.) T2—748 97
Crawford County (Wis.) T2—775 74
Crawley (England) T2—422 61
Crawling
physiology 573.79
Crayfish culture 639.64
Crayfishes 595.384
cooking 641.695
culture 639.64
fishing 639.54
food 641.395
sports fishing 799.255 384
zoology 595.384
Crayfishing 639.54
sports 799.255 384
Crayon drawing 741.23

Cremation	363.75
customs	393.2
social services	363.75
see also Undertaking	
(Mortuary)	
Crematoriums	363.75
architecture	725.597
Cremona (Italy)	T2—452 71
Cremona (Italy : Province)	T2—452 7
ancient	T2—373 15
Crenshaw County (Ala.)	T2—761 36
Creodonta	569.7
Creole cooking	641.597 63
Creoles	
linguistics	417.22
specific languages	T4—7
see Manual at T4—7	
Creosote bush	583.62
Crepe myrtle	635.977 373
botany	583.73
ornamental arboriculture	635.977 373
Crepes	641.815 3
Creping paper	676.234
Creping textiles	677.028 25
Cresses	641.355 6
botany	583.78
cooking	641.655 6
food	641.355 6
garden crop	635.56
Creston (B.C.)	T2—711 62
Crests	929.6
Creswick (Vic.)	T2—945 3
Cretaceous period	551.77
geology	551.77
paleontology	560.177
Crete (Greece)	949.59
	T2—495 9
ancient	939.18
	T2—391 8
Crete (Greece :	
Decentralized	
administration)	T2—495 9
Crete (Greece : Island)	T2—495 9
ancient	T2—391 8
Crete, Sea of (Greece)	551.461 388
	T2—163 88
Creuse (France)	T2—446 8
Creutzfeldt-Jakob disease	
medicine	616.83
see also Nervous system	
diseases — humans	
Crewe and Nantwich	
(England)	T2—427 12
Crewelwork	746.446
Crib death	
pediatrics	618.920 26
Cribbage	795.411
Criblé engraving	765.6
Cricetidae	599.35
Cricetus	599.356
Cricket	
biography	796.358 092
Cricket (Game)	796.358
see also Ball games	
Cricket players	796.358 092
Crickets	595.726
culture	638.572 6
Cries (Rhymes)	398.87
Crime	364
arts	700.455 6
	T3C—355 6
correction	364.6
folklore	398.275 6
history and criticism	398.355 6
law	345
literature	808.803 556
history and criticism	809.933 556
specific literatures	T3B—080 355 6
history and	
criticism	T3B—093 556
social theology	201.764
Christianity	261.833
social welfare	362.88
Crime insurance	368.82
government-sponsored	
violent crimes	368.48
Crime prevention	364.4
criminology	364.4
public administration	353.39
management	658.473
penology	364.601
personal health	613.6
police services	363.23
public administration	353.36
school programs	371.782
Crime victims	362.88
	T1—086 949
Crimea (Ukraine : Oblast)	T2—477 1
Crimean Tatar language	494.388
	T6—943 88
Crimean Tatar literature	894.388
Crimean Tatars	T5—943 88
Crimean War, 1853–1856	947.073 8
Crimes	364.1
see also Criminal offenses	
Crimes against humanity	364.135
law	345.023 5

Croatian language	491.83	Crop-dusting	632.94
	T6—918 3	Crop-hail insurance	368.121
Croatian literature	891.83	see also Insurance	
Croatians	T5—918 3	Crop insurance	368.121
Croats	T5—918 3	see also Insurance	
Crocheted fabrics	677.662	Crop rotation	
arts	746.434	cultivation technique	631.582
manufacturing technology	677.662	economics	338.162
see also Textiles		soil conservation	631.452
Crocheted laces	677.662	Crop yields	338.1
arts	746.22	agricultural technology	631.558
manufacturing technology	677.662	economics	338.1
Crocheted rugs		see Manual at 338.1 vs.	
arts	746.73	631.558	
Crocheting	677.028 2	Crops	630
arts	746.434	economics	338.1
manufacturing technology	677.028 2	pathology	632
Crock-pot cooking	641.588 4	plant physiology	571.2
Crockett County (Tenn.)	T2—768 225	public administration	354.54
Crockett County (Tex.)	T2—764 875	Croquet	796.354
Crocodile River (Limpopo,		biography	796.354 092
South Africa)	T2—682 53	see also Ball games	
Crocodile River		Croquet players	796.354 092
(Mpumalanga, South		Crosby County (Tex.)	T2—764 848
Africa)	T2—682 73	Crosier Fathers	255.19
Crocodiles	597.982	church history	271.19
big game hunting	799.279 82	Cross-country races	
conservation technology	639.977 982	humans	796.428
paleozoology	567.98	Cross-country skiing	796.932
resource economics	333.957 982	see also Winter sports	
zoology	597.982	Cross County (Ark.)	T2—767 93
Crocodilians	597.98	Cross-cultural communication	303.482
Crocodilidae	597.982	Cross-cultural psychology	155.8
Crocodylus	597.982	Cross dressing	
Crocuses	635.934 75	sexual practices	306.778
botany	584.75	Cross-examination	347.075
floriculture	635.934 75	criminal law	345.075
Crohn disease		Cross-platform software	
medicine	616.344	development	005.132 42
see also Digestive system		Cross River languages	496.364
diseases — humans			T6—963 64
Cromwell, Oliver		Cross River State (Nigeria)	T2—669 44
British history	941.064	Cross-stitch	746.443
English history	942.064	Crossbills	598.885
Scottish history	941.106 4	Crossbows	623.441 6
Cromwell, Richard		Crossbreeding	
British history	941.065	agriculture	631.523
English history	942.065	animal husbandry	636.082
Scottish history	941.106 5	plant cultivation	631.523
Crook County (Or.)	T2—795 83	Crossdressing	
Crook County (Wyo.)	T2—787 13	sexual practices	306.778
Crop diversification		Crosses	
agriculture	631.58	religious significance	246.558
economics	338.162	Crossing over (Genetics)	572.877

Crutches	
manufacturing technology	681.761
Cryobiology	571.464 5
humans	612.014 467
Cryogenic engineering	621.59
Cryogenic engineers	621.590 92
Cryogenics	536.56
biophysics	571.464 5
humans	612.014 467
engineering	621.59
materials science	620.112 16
Cryolite	
mineralogy	549.4
synthetic	666.86
Cryometry	536.54
Cryosurgery	617.05
Cryotherapy	
medicine	615.832 9
Cryptanalysis	652.8
armed forces	355.343 2
Cryptococcales	579.55
Cryptogamia	586
paleobotany	561.6
Cryptography	652.8
armed forces	358.24
computer science	005.824
recreation	793.73
Cryptophyta	579.82
Cryptozoic eon	551.71
geology	551.71
paleontology	560.171
Crystal conduction counters	
nuclear physics	539.776
Crystal devices	
electronics	621.381 52
Crystal gazing	133.322
Crystal growth	548.5
Crystal lattices	548.81
Crystalline lens	
human anatomy	611.84
human physiology	612.844
ophthalmology	617.742
Crystalline solids	530.413
Crystallization	548.5
chemical engineering	660.284 298
sugar production	664.115
Crystallograms	548.83
Crystallographers	548.092
Crystallographic mineralogy	549.18
Crystallographic properties	
materials science	620.112 99
Crystallography	548
see Manual at 548 vs. 530.41;	
also at 549 vs. 548	

Crystals	548
occultism	133.254 8
divination	133.322
Csongrád Megye (Hungary)	T2—439 8
CSP (Austrian political party)	324.243 602 4
CSP (Swiss political party)	324.249 407
CSU (German political party)	324.243 04
CT (Tomography)	
medicine	616.075 722
Ctenophora	593.8
paleozoology	563.8
Ctenostomata	594.676
Ctenothrissiformes	567.5
Cuaiquer Indians	T5—982
Cuando Cubango (Angola)	T2—673 5
Cuanza Norte (Angola)	T2—673 2
Cuanza Sul (Angola :	
Province)	T2—673 2
Cub Scouts	369.434
Cuba	972.91
	T2—729 1
Cuban campaign, 1898	973.893 3
Cuban communism	335.434 7
economics	335.434 7
political ideology	320.532 309 729 1
Cuban literature	860
Cubans	T5—687 291
Cubas Grau, Raúl	
Paraguayan history	989.207 43
Cubature	515.43
Cube-doubling	516.204
Cube root	513.23
Cubes	516.156
Cubic equations	512.942 2
algebra	512.942 2
calculus	515.252
Cubism	709.040 32
painting	759.063 2
sculpture	735.230 432
Cubomedusae	593.53
Cuckoo shrikes	598.8
Cuckoos	598.74
Cucujoidea	595.769
Cuculiformes	598.74
paleozoology	568.7
Cucumber tree	583.22
Cucumber tree (Magnoliaceae)	584.286
Cucumbers	641.356 3
botany	583.66
commercial processing	664.805 63
cooking	641.656 3
food	641.356 3
garden crop	635.63
Cucurbitaceae	583.66

Cucurbitales	583.66
Cued speech	
applied linguistics	418
specific languages	T4—895 5
Cuenca (Spain : Province)	T2—464 7
Cuffs	
commercial technology	687.19
Cuitlateco language	497.9
	T6—979
Culberson County (Tex.)	T2—764 94
Culicidae	595.772
Cullinan (South Africa :	
District)	T2—682 27
Cullman County (Ala.)	T2—761 73
Culpeper County (Va.)	T2—755 392
Cultivated silk textiles	677.391
see also Textiles	
Cultivation	631.5
Cultivators	631.51
manufacturing technology	681.763 1
Cults	209
see Manual at 201–209 and	
292–299; *also at* 299.93	
Cultural anthropologists	306.092
Cultural anthropology	306
Cultural centers	
architecture	725.804 2
area planning	711.57
Cultural contact	303.482
Cultural ethnology	305.8
Cultural exchanges	303.482
law	344.08
public administration	353.7
sociology	303.482
Cultural heritage institutions	027
see also Libraries	
Cultural influence	
psychology	155.92
Cultural institutions	306
Cultural levels (Social	
classes)	T1—086 2
Cultural pluralism	305.8
education	370.117
political science	323.1
sociology	305.8
Cultural programs	
libraries	021.26
Cultural property	
historic preservation	363.69
law	344.094
Cultural relations	303.482
law	344.09
Cultural Revolution	951.056

Cultural symbols	
design	744.2
Culturally disadvantaged children	305.230 869 4
home care	649.156 7
psychology	155.456 7
social group	305.230 869 4
Culturally disadvantaged people	305.56
	T1—086 94
Culture	306
law	344.09
public administrative support	353.7
sociology	306
see Manual at 306 vs. 305,	
909, 930–990	
Cultured cells	
experimental research	
medicine	616.027 7
Cultured skim milk	641.371 476
cooking	641.671 476
food	641.371 476
processing	637.147 6
Cultured whole milk	641.371 46
cooking	641.671 46
food	641.371 46
processing	637.146
Culverts (Drainage)	625.734 2
Cumacea	595.376
Cumae (Extinct city)	T2—377 252
Cumberland (N.S. : County)	T2—716 11
Cumberland, Lake (Ky.)	T2—769 63
Cumberland County (Ill.)	T2—773 73
Cumberland County (Ky.)	T2—769 683
Cumberland County (Me.)	T2—741 91
Cumberland County (N.C.)	T2—756 373
Cumberland County (N.J.)	T2—749 94
Cumberland County (Pa.)	T2—748 43
Cumberland County (Tenn.)	T2—768 75
Cumberland County (Va.)	T2—755 615
Cumberland Mountains	T2—769 1
Kentucky	T2—769 1
Tennessee	T2—768 944
Cumberland Plateau	T2—768 7
Kentucky	T2—769 1
Tennessee	T2—768 7
Cumberland Presbyterian Church	285.135
see also Presbyterian Church	
Cumberland River (Ky. and	
Tenn.)	T2—768 5
Cumbernauld and Kilsyth	
(Scotland)	T2—414 52
Cumbria (England)	942.78
	T2—427 8
Cumbrian Mountains	
(England)	T2—427 8

Cuming County (Neb.)	T2—782 232	Currants (Grossulariaceae)	
Cumnock and Doon Valley		botany	583.44
(Scotland)	T2—414 67	Currency	332.4
Cumulative trauma disorders		*see also* Money	
medicine	617.172	Currency convertibility	332.456
Cuna Indians (Panama)	T5—978 3	Currency movements	332.042 4
Cuna language (Panama)	497.83	Currency paper	676.282 6
	T6—978 3	Currency power (Legislative	
Cuna literature (Panama)	897.83	bodies)	328.341 2
Cundinamarca (Colombia)	T2—861 46	Currency question	332.46
Cunene Province (Angola)	T2—673 5	Current accounts (Checking	
Cuneo (Italy : Province)	T2—451 3	accounts)	332.175 22
ancient	T2—371 6	Current assets	
Cunninghame (Scotland)	T2—414 61	accounting	657.72
Cunoniaceae	583.68	Current awareness services	
Cup fungi	579.57	information science	025.525
Cup games		Current liabilities	
soccer	796.334 64	accounting	657.74
Cupedidae	595.762	Current transactions	
Cupolas	721.5	balance of payments	
architecture	721.5	international commerce	382.17
construction	690.15	Curricula	375
Cupping			T1—071
therapeutics	615.89	adult education	374.01
Cuprammonium rayon	677.462	higher education	378.199
see also Textiles		law	344.077
Cupressaceae	585.4	primary education	372.19
paleobotany	561.54	public control	379.155
Cuprite		secondary education	373.19
mineralogy	549.522	special education	371.904 4
Cups		Curriculum change	375.006
paper	676.34	Curriculum development	375.001
Curaçao	T2—729 86	Curriculum evaluation	375.006
Curassows	598.64	Curriculum libraries	027.7
Curbs	625.888	Curriculum planning	375.001
Curculionidae	595.768	Curriculum vitae	650.142
Curculionoidea	595.768	Curriculums	375
agricultural pests	632.768	*see also* Curricula	
Curfew		Currituck County (N.C.)	T2—756 132
crime prevention	364.4	Curry County (N.M.)	T2—789 27
Curia Romana	262.136	Curry County (Or.)	T2—795 21
Curicó (Chile : Province)	T2—833 4	Curry powder	641.338 4
Curium	546.442	Curses	203.32
see also Chemicals		folklore	398.41
Curling		Curses (Occultism)	133.44
biography	796.964 092	Curtains	645.32
Curling (Sport)	796.964	arts	746.94
see also Winter sports		commercial technology	684.3
Currants	641.347 21	home sewing	646.21
botany	583.72	household management	645.32
cooking	641.647 21	Curtin, John	
food	641.347 21	Australian history	994.042
horticulture	634.721	Curvature (Mathematics)	516.362
		Curve fitting	511.42

Cutwork	
arts	746.44
Cutworms	595.78
agricultural pests	632.78
Cuyahoga County (Ohio)	T2—771 31
Cuyahoga River (Ohio)	T2—771 31
Cuyuni-Mazaruni Region (Guyana)	T2—881 9
Cuzco (Peru : Region)	985.37
	T2—853 7
CVP (Swiss political party)	324.249 404
Cyanamide fertilizers	631.841
chemical engineering	668.624 1
Cyanastraceae	584.7
Cyanite	
mineralogy	549.62
Cyanobacteria	579.39
Cyanophyta	579.39
Cybercrime	364.168
Cyberinfrastructure	004
Cybermetrics	025.042 072 7
Cybernetics	003.5
	T1—011 5
Cyberterrorism	363.325
criminology	364.168
see also Terrorism	
Cycadales	585.9
paleobotany	561.591
Cycadeoidales	561.592
Cycadofilicales	561.595
Cycads	585.9
paleobotany	561.591
Cyclades (Greece)	T2—495 85
ancient	T2—391 5
Cyclamens	635.933 93
botany	583.93
floriculture	635.933 93
Cyclanthaceae	584.55
Cyclanthales	584.55
Cyclarhidae	598.878
Cycles (Periodicity)	
philosophy	116
Cycles (Vehicles)	388.347
engineering	629.227
repair	629.287 7
riding	629.284 7
sports	796.6
transportation services	388.347
Cyclic compounds	547.5
chemical engineering	661.8
Cyclic groups	512.25
Cyclical unemployment	331.137 047
Cycling	
biography	796.609 2
sports	796.6
arts	700.457 9
	T3C—357 9
child care	649.57
ethics	175
human physiology	612.044
journalism	070.449 796 6
law	344.099
literature	
history and criticism	809.933 579
specific literatures	T3B—080 357 9
history and criticism	T3B—093 579
motion pictures	791.436 579
physical fitness	613.711
public administrative support	353.78
safety	363.14
public administration	353.97
sociology	306.483
television programs	791.456 579
see also Sports	
Cycling paths	388.12
see also Bicycle paths	
Cyclists	796.609 2
Cyclo-cross	796.624
Cyclo rubber	678.68
Cycloacetylenes	547.513
chemical engineering	661.815
Cyclones (Low-pressure systems)	551.551 3
Cyclones (Tornadoes)	551.553
see also Tornadoes	
Cycloolefins	547.512
chemical engineering	661.815
Cycloparaffins	547.511
chemical engineering	661.815
Cyclopedias	030
Cyclopoida	595.34
Cyclops (Animals)	595.34
Cycloramas	745.8
decorative arts	745.8
painting	751.74
Cyclorrhapha	595.774
Cyclosilicates	
mineralogy	549.64
Cyclostomata (Jawless fishes)	597.2
paleozoology	567.2
Cyclotomy (Number theory)	512.72
Cyclotrons	539.733
Cygninae	598.418
Cygnus	598.418
Cylinder recordings	
sound reproduction	621.389 32

Cylinders (Engine parts) 621.437
Cylinders (Shape) 516.154
Cylinders (Structural elements) 624.177 2
   concrete 624.183 42
Cylindrical bark beetles 595.769
Cymbals 786.873
   see also Percussion instruments
Cymodoceaceae 584.44
Cymraeg literature 891.66
Cymric language 491.66
       T6—916 6
Cymric literature 891.66
Cymry T5—916 6
Cynewulf 829.4
Cynic philosophy 183.4
Cynocephalidae 599.33
Cynocrambales 583.956
Cynocrambe 583.956
Cynomoriaceae 583.47
Cynomys 599.367
Cynon Valley (Wales) T2—429 78
Cyperaceae 584.94
Cyperales 584.94
Cypress Hills (Alta. and
   Sask.) T2—712 43
Cypress pine 585.4
Cypresses 585.4
   forestry 634.975 5
   lumber 674.144
Cyprinidae 597.482
Cypriniformes 597.48
   paleozoology 567.48
Cyprinodontidae 597.665
Cyprinodontoidei 597.66
Cyprinus 597.483
Cypriot architecture
   Phoenician 722.32
Cypriots T5—895
Cyprus 956.93
       T2—569 3
   ancient 939.37
       T2—393 7
   travel 915.693 04
Cyrenaic philosophy 183.5
Cyrenaica T2—397 5
   ancient 939.75
Cyrillic alphabet 491.8
   printing 686.219 18
Cyrrhestica T2—393 6
   southern T2—394 32
Cystic fibrosis
   medicine 616.372
     see also Digestive system
       diseases — humans

Cystitis
   medicine 616.623
     see also Urologic diseases —
       humans
Cystoidea 563.95
Cythera Island (Greece) T2—495 2
Cytinaceae 583.77
Cytochemistry 572
Cytodiagnosis
   medicine 616.075 82
Cytogenetics 572.8
   humans 611.018 16
Cytokines
   human immunology 616.079
Cytological examination
   medicine 616.075 82
Cytology 571.6
   humans 611.018 1
Cytometry
   diagnosis
     medicine 616.075 82
Cytopathology 571.936
   humans 611.018 15
Cytoplasm 571.65
Cytoplasmic inheritance 572.869
Cytoplasmic membranes 571.64
Cytoskeleton 571.654
Cytotaxonomy 578.012
Cytotoxic T cells 571.966
   human immunology 616.079 7
Cyzicus (Extinct city) T2—392 1
Czech language 491.86
       T6—918 6
Czech literature 891.86
Czech Republic 943.71
       T2—437 1
Czechia 943.71
       T2—437 1
Czechoslovak Republic 943.703 2
       T2—437
Czechoslovakia 943.703
       T2—437
Czechoslovaks T5—918 6
Czechs T5—918 6
Częstochowa (Poland :
   Voivodeship) T2—438 58

D

D region (Ionosphere) 538.767 2
Da capo form 781.822 5
   instrumental 784.182 2
Đà Nẵng (Vietnam) T2—597 5

Da Silva, Lula	
Brazilian history	981.065
2003–2011	981.065
2023–	981.068
Daba language	493.7
	T6—937
Đắc Lắc (Vietnam)	T2—597 6
Đắc Nông (Vietnam)	T2—597 6
Dacca (Bangladesh :	
Division)	T2—549 22
Daces	597.482
sports fishing	799.174 82
Dachau (Extermination camp)	940.531 853 36
Dachshund	636.753 8
Dacia	939.88
	T2—398 8
Dacorum (England)	T2—425 84
Dactylopteriformes	597.64
Dadaism	
fine arts	709.040 62
literature	808.801 162
history and criticism	809.911 62
specific literatures	T3B—080 116 2
history and	
criticism	T3B—091 162
painting	759.066 2
sculpture	735.230 462
Daddy longlegs	595.43
Dade County (Fla.)	T2—759 38
Dade County (Ga.)	T2—758 342
Dade County (Mo.)	T2—778 745
Dādra and Nagar Haveli and	
Daman and Diu (India)	T2—547 6
Daendels, Herman Willem	
Indonesian history	959.802 22
Daerah Khusus Ibukota	
Jakarta (Indonesia)	T2—598 22
Daffodils	635.934 78
botany	584.78
floriculture	635.934 78
Dagari (African people)	T5—963 5
Dagari language	496.35
	T6—963 5
Dagbani (African people)	T5—963 5
Dagbani language	496.35
	T6—963 5
Dagestan (Russia)	T2—475 2
Dagestan languages	499.964
	T6—999 64
Daggers	623.441 2
art metalwork	739.72
military engineering	623.441 2
Daggett County (Utah)	T2—792 15

Daghestan languages	499.964
	T6—999 64
Dagomba (African people)	T5—963 5
Dagomba language	496.35
	T6—963 5
Daguerreotype process	772.12
Dagur language	T6—942
Dahlias	635.933 983
botany	583.983
floriculture	635.933 983
Dahme-Spreewald	
(Germany : Landkreis)	T2—431 51
Dahomeans	T5—966 83
Dahomey	966.83
	T2—668 3
Dahomey (African people)	T5—963 37
Dahomey (Kingdom)	966.830 18
	T2—668 3
Dahūk (Iraq : Province)	T2—567 2
Dai language (Chad)	493.7
	T6—937
Daic languages	495.9
	T6—959
Daic literatures	895.9
Daic peoples	T5—959
Daʻīf (Hadith)	297.125 22
Daily devotions	204.46
Christianity	242.2
Judaism	296.45
Dairi Batak	T5—992 246 6
Dairi language	499.224 66
	T6—992 246 6
Dairi literature	899.224 66
Dairy cattle	
animal husbandry	636.214 2
Dairy cooperatives	334.683 7
Dairy farmers	636.214 209 2
Dairy farming	636.214 2
Dairy-free cooking	641.563 97
Dairy-free diet	
health	613.268 7
Dairy-free foods	641.309 7
Dairy industry	338.176 214 2
economics	338.176 214 2
law	343.076 621 42
products	338.476 37
economics	338.476 37
law	343.078 637
public administration	354.66
public administration	354.56
Dairy products	641.37
cooking	641.67
diet	613.277
food	641.37

Dances of the suite	793.3
music	784.188 3
Dancing	792.8
arts	700.457 9
	T3C—357 9
customs	394.3
ethics	175
etiquette	395.3
literature	808.803 579
history and criticism	809.933 579
specific literatures	T3B—080 357 9
history and	
criticism	T3B—093 579
musical plays	792.62
religious significance	203.7
Christianity	246.7
see also Arts — religious	
significance	
sociology	306.484 6
Dancing games	796.13
Dancing injuries	
medicine	617.102 75
Dandelions	583.983
botany	583.983
cooking	641.655 1
food	641.355 1
garden crop	635.51
Dandruff	
medicine	616.546
Dane County (Wis.)	T2—775 83
Danes	T5—398 1
Dangaleat language	493.7
	T6—937
Dangerous animals	591.65
Dangerous goods	363.17
see also Hazardous materials	
Dani	T5—991 2
Daniel (Biblical book)	224.5
Daniels County (Mont.)	T2—786 213
Danios	597.482
Danish language	439.81
	T6—398 1
Danish literature	839.81
Danish pastry	641.865 9
commercial processing	664.752 5
home preparation	641.865 9
Danish people	T5—398 1
Dannhauser (South Africa :	
District)	T2—684 1
Dano-Norwegian language	439.82
	T6—398 2
Dano-Norwegian literature	839.82

Danube River	T2—496
Austria	T2—436 12
Germany	T2—433
Danville (Va.)	T2—755 666
Danzig (Germany)	T2—438 22
Daphnes	583.77
Daqahlīyah (Egypt)	T2—621
DAR (Patriotic society)	369.135
biography	369.135 092
Dar es Salaam (Tanzania :	
Region)	T2—678 232
Darʻā (Syria : Province)	T2—569 14
Dard (Indic people)	T5—914 99
Dard languages	491.499
	T6—914 99
Dard literatures	891.499
Dardanelles Strait (Turkey)	551.461 389
	T2—163 89
Dardic languages	491.499
	T6—914 99
Dardic literatures	891.499
Dardic peoples	T5—914 99
Dare County (N.C.)	975.617 5
	T2—756 175
Darfur (Sudan)	T2—627
Dargi language	499.964
	T6—999 64
Dargwa language	499.964
	T6—999 64
Dari language	491.56
	T6—915 6
Dari literature	891.56
Darién (Panama : Province)	T2—728 778
Darien, Gulf of (Colombia)	551.461 365
	T2—163 65
Dārimī, ʻAbd Allāh ibn ʻAbd	
al-Raḥmān	
Hadith	297.125 54
Dark Ages	940.12
European history	940.12
see also Early Middle Ages	
see also Early Middle Ages	
Dark matter (Astronomy)	523.112 6
Darke County (Ohio)	T2—771 47
Darkling beetles	595.769
Darkroom practice	771.44
cinematography	777.55
negatives	771.43
photography	771.44
positives (photographs)	771.44
Darkrooms (Photography)	771.1
Darling Downs (Qld.)	T2—943 3
Darling Range (W.A.)	T2—941 2

Dates (Chronology)	902.02
Dates (Fruit)	641.346 2
agriculture	634.62
botany	584.84
commercial processing	664.804 62
cooking	641.646 2
food	641.346 2
Dating (Archaeological	
technique)	930.102 85
Dating (Social practice)	306.73
customs	392.6
life skills	646.77
sociology	306.73
Datiscaceae	583.66
Daturas	583.959 3
Daughters	306.874
	T1—085 4
Daughters of the American	
Revolution	369.135
biography	369.135 092
Dauphin (Man.)	T2—712 72
Dauphin County (Pa.)	T2—748 18
Dauphiné (France)	T2—445 86
Daur language	T6—942
D'Autray (Quebec)	T2—714 43
DAV (Veterans' organization)	369.186 3
Davao de Oro (Philippines)	T2—599 734
Davao del Norte	
(Philippines)	T2—599 735
Davao del Sur (Philippines)	T2—599 737
Davao Occidental	
(Philippines)	T2—599 738
Davao Oriental	
(Philippines)	T2—599 732
Davao Region (Philippines)	T2—599 73
Davenport (Iowa)	T2—777 69
Davenport Range (N.T.)	T2—942 91
Davenports	645.4
see also Furniture	
Daventry (England :	
District)	T2—425 56
David, King of Israel	
Biblical leader	222.409 2
Palestinian history	933.02
David and Goliath story	222.430 950 5
Davidson County (N.C.)	T2—756 68
Davidson County (Tenn.)	T2—768 55
Davie County (N.C.)	T2—756 69
Daviess County (Ind.)	T2—772 385
Daviess County (Ky.)	T2—769 864
Daviess County (Mo.)	T2—778 183
Davis County (Iowa)	T2—777 97
Davis County (Utah)	T2—792 27

Davis Strait	551.461 342
	T2—163 42
Davison County (S.D.)	T2—783 374
Da'wah	297.74
Dawes County (Neb.)	T2—782 93
Dawn	525.7
arts	T3C—33
literature	808.803 3
history and criticism	809.933 3
specific literatures	T3B—080 33
history and	
criticism	T3B—093 3
Dawson (Yukon)	T2—719 1
Dawson County (Ga.)	T2—758 263
Dawson County (Mont.)	T2—786 24
Dawson County (Neb.)	T2—782 46
Dawson County (Tex.)	T2—764 854
Dawson Creek (B.C.)	T2—711 87
Day camps	796.542 3
Day care	362.712
law	344.032 712
preschool education	372.21
social welfare	362.712
Day County (S.D.)	T2—783 142
Day language (Chad)	493.7
	T6—937
Day lilies	635.934 77
botany	584.77
floriculture	635.934 77
Day of the Lord	
Christianity	236.9
Daydreams	154.3
Daylesford (Vic.)	T2—945 3
Daylight saving time	389.17
law	343.07
Daylighting	729.28
Daylilies	635.934 77
floriculture	635.934 77
Daymarks	387.155
navigation aids	623.894 4
transportation services	387.155
Dayr al-Zawr (Syria :	
Province)	T2—569 12
Days	529.1
arts	T3C—33
chronology	529.1
folklore	398.236
history and criticism	398.33
literature	808.803 3
history and criticism	809.933 3
specific literatures	T3B—080 33
history and	
criticism	T3B—093 3
music	781.522

Death (continued)
customs 393
see Manual at 392, 393, 394
vs. 793.2
cytology 571.936
demography 304.64
ethics 179.7
religion 205.697
Buddhism 294.356 97
Christianity 241.697
Hinduism 294.548 697
Judaism 296.369 7
folklore 398.274 8
history and criticism 398.354 8
literature 808.803 548
history and criticism 809.933 548
specific literatures T3B—080 354 8
history and
criticism T3B—093 548
medical ethics 179.7
religion 205.697
medicine 616.078
music 781.588
philosophy 113.8
humans 128.5
psychology 155.937
religion 202.3
Christianity 236.1
Islam 297.23
Judaism 296.33
philosophy of religion 218
religious rites 203.88
Christianity 265.85
Islam 297.385
Judaism 296.445
liturgy 296.454 5
see also Rites — religion
social services 363.75
see also Undertaking
(Mortuary)
sociology 306.9
Death adders 597.964
Death certificates
public administration 353.59
Death of Jesus Christ 232.963
Death penalty 364.66
law 345.077 3
Death tax 336.276
law 343.053
public administration 352.44
Death Valley National Park
(Calif. and Nev.) T2—794 87
Death watch beetles 595.763
Debarkation 355.422

Debaters 809.53
Debates
literature 808.853
history and criticism 809.53
specific literatures T3B—503
individual authors T3A—5
rhetoric 808.53
Debating 808.53
Debit cards 332.76
banking services 332.178
credit economics 332.76
Debt collection
law 346.077
management 658.88
Debt limits
public finance 336.346
Debt management (Business) 658.152 6
Debt management (Personal) 332.024 02
Debt management (Public) 336.36
macroeconomic policy 339.523
public administration 352.45
public finance 336.36
Debtors
law 346.077
Debtors' prisons 365.4
see also Penal institutions
Debugging (Computer science) 004.24
engineering 621.392
software 005.14
Deburring metals 671.7
Debuts
customs 392.15
etiquette 395.24
music 781.584
Déby Itno, Idriss
Chadian history 967.430 44
Decalcomania 745.74
Decalogue 222.16
moral theology
Christianity 241.52
Judaism 296.36
Decapoda (Crustaceans) 595.38
conservation technology 639.975 38
resource economics 333.955 5
Decapoda (Mollusks) 594.58
paleozoology 564.58
Decathlon 796.42
Decatur County (Ga.) T2—758 993
Decatur County (Ind.) T2—772 16
Decatur County (Iowa) T2—777 875
Decatur County (Kan.) T2—781 143
Decatur County (Tenn.) T2—768 32
Decay
materials science 620.112 2

Decay (Sound)		Decompression sickness	
musical element	781.235	medicine	616.989 4
Decay schemes (Radioactivity)	539.752	*see also* Environmental	
Deccan (India)	T2—548	diseases — humans	
Deceleration		Deconstruction	
biophysics		philosophy	149.97
humans	612.014 414	Decoration	744
extraterrestrial biophysics		19th century	744.090 34
humans	612.014 534	architecture	729
Decentralization		arts	744
executive management	658.402	automobile	629.262
public administration	352.283	Decorations (Awards)	929.81
Deception	001.95	armed forces	355.134 2
military operations	355.41	*see also* Military	
Decidability	511.3	commemorations	
Decimal fractions	513.265	numismatics	737.223
Decimal numbers	513.55	Decorative arts	745
Decimal system	513.55	Decorative coloring	745.7
Decision analysis		Decorative lettering	744.42
management use	658.403 54	Decorative sculpture	731.72
Decision making		Decorative treatment	
executive management	658.403	glass	748.6
	T1—068 4	metals	739.15
military administration	355.683	pottery	666.45
production management	658.503 6	arts	738.15
psychology	153.83	technology	666.45
public administration	352.33	sculpture	731.4
social psychology	302.3	Decorative values	701.8
Decision tables		drawing	741.018
software design	005.120 28	painting	750.18
Decision theory	003.56	Decoupage	745.546
	T1—011 56	Decoys	
Decision theory (Mathematics)	519.542	handicrafts	745.593 6
Decks (Buildings)	721.84	Decubitus ulcers	
architecture	721.84	medicine	616.545
construction	690.184	*see also* Skin diseases —	
domestic	728.93	humans	
architecture	728.93	Dedications (Christian rites)	265.92
construction	690.893	Deduction (Logic)	162
Declaration of Independence,		psychology	153.433
1776	973.313	Deductive databases	
Declaration of intention	346.021	computer science	005.740 151 13
Declarative languages	005.115	Deductive reasoning	162
Declarative programming	005.115	computer science	006.333
Declaratory judgments	347.077	logic	162
Declension (Grammar)	415.5	psychology	153.433
specific languages	T4—55	Dee, River (Aberdeenshire,	
Decoding skills (Reading)		Scotland)	T2—412 4
primary education	372.46	Deeds	346.043 8
Decolonization	325.3	Deep-freezing foods	664.028 53
Decolorizing carbons	662.93	commercial preservation	664.028 53
Decomposition		home preservation	641.453
materials science	620.112 2	Deep sea biology	578.779
Decomposition method	518	Deep sea cods	597.63

Deep-sea diving	627.72
Deep sea ecology	577.79
Deep-sea fishing	639.22
commercial	639.22
sports	799.16
Deep-sea hydrothermal vents	
biology	578.779 9
ecology	577.799
Deer	599.65
agricultural pests	632.696 5
animal husbandry	636.294
big game hunting	799.276 5
commercial hunting	639.116 5
conservation technology	639.979 65
resource economics	333.959 65
zoology	599.65
Deer Lodge County (Mont.)	T2—786 87
Deer mice	599.355
Deerflies	595.773
Defamation	364.156
ethics	177.3
law	345.025 6
criminal law	345.025 6
torts	346.034
Default	332.75
Default logic	511.31
Defeasible logic	511.31
Defecation	
human physiology	612.36
Defendants	347.052
criminal law	345.05
Defense (Legal)	347.05
criminal law	345.050 44
Defense (Military operation)	355.4
engineering	623.3
Defense (National security)	355.03
law	343.01
Defense administration	355.6
Defense budgets	355.622 8
specific jurisdictions	355.622 9
Defense contracts	355.621 2
law	346.023
Defense departments	355.6
Defense mechanisms	
(Psychology)	155.2
Defense of home territory	355.45
Defense operations	355.4
Defenseless Mennonites	289.73
biography	289.709 2
Defiance County (Ohio)	T2—771 14
Defibrillation (Electric)	
medicine	616.128 064 5
Deficiency budgets (Public)	352.48
see also Budgets (Public)	

Deficiency diseases	
medicine	616.39
see also Digestive system	
diseases — humans	
Definite integrals	515.43
Definitive Treaty of Peace	
Between Great Britain and the	
United States	
United States history	973.317
Definitive Treaty of Peace with	
Spain, 1783	
United States history	973.317
Defla (Algeria : Province)	T2—653
Deflagrating explosives	662.26
Deflation (Economics)	332.41
Deflections	
structural analysis	624.171 4
Defluoridation	
water supply engineering	628.166 3
Defoid languages	496.33
	T6—963 3
Deformation	531.38
crystals	548.842
geology	551.8
materials science	620.112 3
naval architecture	623.817 6
physics	531.38
structural analysis	624.176
Deformities	
biology	571.976
human teratology	616.043
psychological influence	155.916
Degeneration (Pathology)	571.935
cytology	571.936
humans	616.07
Deglutition disorders	
medicine	616.323
see also Digestive system	
diseases — humans	
Dehumidification	
chemical engineering	660.284 29
Dehumidifiers	
air conditioning	
buildings	697.932 3
Dehydrated foods	
cooking	641.614
Dehydrating foods	664.028 4
commercial preservation	664.028 4
home preservation	641.44
Dehydrogenases	572.791
see also Enzymes	
Dehydrogenation	
chemical engineering	660.284 43
Deinonychus	567.912

Demand (continued)
natural resources 333.712
transportation services 388.049
Demand deposits 332.175 22
Dematerialization (Spiritualism) 133.92
Dementia 362.196 831
diagnosis 616.831 075
drug therapy 616.831 061
etiology 616.831 071
genetics 616.831 042
geriatrics 618.976 831
medicine 616.831
see also Nervous system
diseases — humans
pathology 616.831 07
social services 362.196 831
therapy 616.831 06
Demerara-Mahaica Region
(Guyana) T2—881 5
Demineralization
sewage treatment 628.358
water supply treatment 628.166 6
Demmin (Germany :
Landkreis) T2—431 72
Demobilization (Military science) 355.29
Democracy 321.8
educational objective 370.115
Democracy is Freedom-Daisy
(Italian political party) 324.245 05
Democratic centralism 335.43
economics 335.43
political ideology 320.532 2
Democratic government 321.8
Democratic Labor Party
(Australia) 324.294 06
Democratic Party (Italy) 324.245 06
Democratic Party (U.S.) 324.273 6
Democratic Party of the Left
(Italy) 324.245 07
Democratic Republic of East
Timor 959.870 4
Democratic Republic of the
Congo 967.51
T2—675 1
Democratic-Republican Party
(U.S.) 324.273 6
Democratic socialism 335.5
economics 335.5
political ideology 320.531 5
Democratici di sinistra (Italian
political party) 324.245 07
Democrats of the Left (Italian
political party) 324.245 07

Democrazia cristiana (Italian
political party) 324.245 082 2
Democrazia è libertà-La
Margherita (Italian political
party) 324.245 05
Democritean philosophy 182.7
Demodulation
electronics 621.381 536
Demodulators
electronic circuits 621.381 536
Demographic anthropology 304.6
Demography 304.6
Demolition (Military) 623.27
Demolition charges
military engineering 623.454 5
Demolition operations (Military) 358.23
underwater 359.984
Demoniac possession 133.426
occultism 133.426
religion 204.2
Demonology 133.42
religion 202.16
Demons 133.42
religion 202.16
Christianity 235.4
Demonstrations (Political
protests)
public safety 363.323
Demonstrative evidence 347.064
Demospongiae 593.46
paleozoology 563.4
Demotic language (Egyptian) 493.1
T6—931
Demotic language (Modern
Greek) 489.3
T6—89
Demotic literature (Modern
Greek) 889
Demotion
armed forces 355.112
personnel management 658.314 4
public administration 352.66
Demythologizing (Bible) 220.68
Denali Borough (Alaska) T2—798 6
Denali National Park and
Preserve (Alaska) T2—798 3
Denationalization 338.925
Denbigh (Wales) T2—429 37
Denbighshire (Wales) T2—429 37
Dendritic cells
human immunology 616.079
Dendrobatidae 597.877

Dendrobiums	584.72	Density pumps	621.699
botany	584.72	Dent County (Mo.)	T2—778 86
floriculture	635.934 72	Dental assistants	
Dendrochirotacea	593.96	law	344.041 3
Dendrocolaptidae	598.822	role and function	617.602 33
Dendrologists	582.160 92	Dental care	
Dendrology	582.16	dentistry	617.6
Dengue		social services	362.197 6
incidence	614.588 52	Dental diseases	573.356 39
medicine	616.918 52	*see also* Tooth diseases	
see also Communicable		Dental enamel	
diseases — humans		dentistry	617.634
Dengue fever		Dental hygiene	617.601
medicine	616.918 52	Dental implantation	
see also Communicable		dentistry	617.693
diseases — humans		Dental implants	
Dengue hemorrhagic fever		dentistry	617.693
incidence	614.588 52	Dental insurance	368.382 3
medicine	616.918 52	*see also* Insurance	
see also Communicable		Dental pulp	
diseases — humans		dentistry	617.634 2
Denial		Dental pulp diseases	
epistemology	121.5	dentistry	617.634 2
Denial of justice	364.134	Dental restoration	617.69
law	345.023 4	Dental surgery	617.605
Denial of rights	364.132 2	Dental technicians	
law	345.023 22	law	344.041 3
government liability	342.088	role and function	617.602 33
public administration	353.46	Dentin	
Denial of service attacks		dentistry	617.634
computer science	005.87	Dentinal material products	679.4
Denis-Riverin (Quebec)	T2—714 791	Dentistry	617.6
Denizli İli (Turkey)	T2—562 7	anesthesiology	617.967 6
ancient	T2—392 4	law	344.041 3
Denjoy integrals	515.43	pediatrics	617.645
Denman Island (B.C. :		Dentists	617.609 2
Island)	T2—711 2	law	344.041 3
Denmark	948.9	role and function	617.602 32
	T2—489	Dentition disorders	
ancient	936.89	dentistry	617.643
	T2—368 9	incidence	614.599 6
Denmark Strait	551.461 324	Denton County (Tex.)	T2—764 555
	T2—163 24	D'Entrecasteaux Islands	
Denominations	209	(Papua New Guinea)	T2—954 1
Christianity	280	Dentures	
Judaism	296.8	dentistry	617.692
see Manual at 201–209 and		Denver (Colo.)	T2—788 83
292–299		Denver County (Colo.)	T2—788 83
Dens		Deodorants	
home economics	643.58	pharmacokinetics	615.778
Density	531.14	Deodorization	
gas mechanics	533.15	sewers	628.23
liquid mechanics	532.4	Deontic logic	511.314
solid mechanics	531.54		

Deontology	
ethical systems	171.2
Deoxyribonucleic acid	572.86
humans	611.018 166
Department heads	
executive management	658.43
public administration	352.293
see Manual at 352–354	
Department stores	381.141
management	658.871
see also Commerce	
Departments (Organizational units)	
management	658.402
public administration	351
Departments (Territorial units)	320.83
see also Counties	
Departments of agriculture	354.5
Departments of commerce	354.73
Departments of defense	355.6
Departments of education	353.8
Departments of energy	354.4
Departments of foreign affairs	353.13
Departments of health	353.6
Departments of housing	353.55
Departments of interior	353.3
Departments of justice	353.4
Departments of labor	354.9
Departments of natural resources	354.3
Departments of state	351
Departments of transportation	354.76
Departments of treasury	352.4
Dependence	
personality trait	155.232
Dependency grammar	415.018 4
specific languages	T4—501 84
Dependency linguistics	410.184
specific languages	T4—018 4
Dependent children	
social welfare	362.713
Dependent personality disorder	
medicine	616.858 1
see also Mental disorders	
Dependent states	321.08
see also Semisovereign states	
Depletion allowance	336.243 16
tax law	343.052 34
Deportation	364.68
law	342.082
penology	364.68
Deposit insurance	368.854
Deposition (Geology)	551.303

Depository libraries	
acquisitions	025.26
government relations	021.8
Deposits (Bank)	332.175 2
government guaranty	368.854
public revenues	336.15
Depreciation	
accounting	657.73
tax law	343.052 34
Depressant abuse	362.299
medicine	616.86
personal health	613.8
social welfare	362.299
see also Substance abuse	
Depression (Mental state)	362.25
medicine	616.852 7
social welfare	362.25
see also Mental disorders	
Depressions (Economics)	
economic cycles	338.542
Depressions (Physiography)	551.44
	T2—144
geography	910.914 4
geomorphology	551.44
physical geography	910.021 44
Depressive disorder	
medicine	616.852 7
see also Mental disorders	
Depressive psychoses	362.26
medicine	616.895
see also Mental disorders	
Deputy chief executives	
executive management	658.42
law	342.062
public administration	352.239
Deputy heads of departments	
executive management	658.43
public administration	352.293
Dera Ismāīl Khān	
(Pakistan : District)	T2—549 124
Derby (England)	T2—425 17
Derbyshire (England)	942.51
	T2—425 1
Derbyshire Dales (England)	T2—425 13
Derivation (Morphology)	415.92
specific languages	T4—592
Derivational morphology	415.92
specific languages	T4—592
Derivatives (Speculation)	332.645 7
multiple forms of investment	332.645 7
securities	332.632
Derived spaces	514.32
Dermaptera	595.739
Dermatemydidae	597.926

Dermatitis		Descriptive bibliography	010.42
medicine	616.51	Descriptive biology	578
see also Skin diseases —		animals	590
humans		microorganisms	579
Dermatoglyphics	599.945	plants	580
Dermatology	616.5	*see Manual at* 578 vs. 304.2,	
Dermatomycoses		508, 910	
humans		Descriptive cataloging	025.32
incidence	614.595 79	Descriptive geometry	516.6
medicine	616.579	applied	604.201 516 6
see also Skin diseases —		Descriptive government	320.4
humans		Descriptive linguistics	410
Dermestoidea	595.763	*see Manual at* 410	
Dermochelyidae	597.928 9	Descriptive metadata	
Dermoptera	599.33	information science	025.3
paleozoology	569.33	Descriptive research	001.433
Derricks	621.873	T1—072 3	
Derry (Northern Ireland)	T2—416 21	public administrative support	352.75
Derry (Northern Ireland :		*see Manual at*	
County)	T2—416 2	T1—07201–07209 vs.	
Derry & Strabane (Northern		T1—0721	
Ireland)	T2—416 2	Descriptive statistics	519.53
Derwent, River (Derbyshire,		Descriptors (Terms)	025.47
England)	T2—425 1	Desegregation in education	379.263
Derwent, River (Yorkshire,		Desert biology	578.754
England)	T2—428 4	Desert ecology	577.54
Des Moines (Iowa)	T2—777 58	Desert plants	581.754
Des Moines County (Iowa)	T2—777 96	floriculture	635.952 5
Des Moines River (Minn.		Desert Storm, Operation, 1991	956.704 424
and Iowa)	T2—777	Desert tactics	355.423
Des Plaines River (Wis. and		Deserters	355.133 4
Ill.)	T2—773 2	Algerian Revolution	965.046 8
Desai, Morarji Ranchodji		American Revolution	973.38
Indian history	954.052	Chaco War	989.207 168
Desalinization	628.167	Civil War (England)	942.062 8
Descant recorders	788.364	Civil War (Spain)	946.081 8
see also Woodwind		Civil War (United States)	973.78
instruments		Crimean War	947.073 88
Descant viols	787.62	Falkland Islands War	997.110 248
see also Stringed instruments		Franco-German War	943.082 8
Descendants	T1—085 4	Hundred Years' War	944.025 8
family relationships	306.874	Indo-Pakistan War, 1971	954.920 518
Descent into hell of Jesus Christ	232.967	Indochinese War	959.704 18
Deschutes County (Or.)	T2—795 87	Iraq War, 2003–2011	956.704 438
Deschutes River (Or.)	T2—795 62	Iraqi-Iranian Conflict	955.054 28
Description		Korean War	951.904 28
literature	808.802 2	Mexican War	973.628
history and criticism	809.922	Napoleonic Wars	940.278
specific literatures	T3B—080 22	Persian Gulf War, 1991	956.704 428
history and		South African War	968.048 8
criticism	T3B—092 2	Spanish-American War	973.898
Description (Archives)	025.341 4	Thirty Years' War	940.248
Description logics		Vietnamese War	959.704 38
computer science	006.332	War of the Pacific	983.061 68

239

Deserters (continued)

World War I	940.48
World War II	940.548
Desertification	333.736
geomorphology	551.415
Desertion (Domestic relations)	306.88
law	346.016 6
Desertion (Military)	355.133 4
law	343.014
see also Deserters	
Deserts	551.415
	T2—154
biology	578.754
ecology	577.54
see also Arid lands	
Desha County (Ark.)	T2—767 85
Design	744
arts	744
automotive	629.231
engineering	620.004 2
Great Britain	
1940–1949	744.094 109 044
philosophy	124
primary education	372.52
road engineering	625.725
structural engineering	624.177 1
Design anthropometry	620.82
Design protection	346.048 4
Designer drugs	362.299
medicine	616.86
personal health	613.8
social welfare	362.299
see also Substance abuse	
Designs	
diagrammatic works	T1—022 3
pictorial works	T1—022 2
textiles	677.022
Désirade (Guadeloupe)	T2—729 76
Desjardins (Quebec)	T2—714 59
Desks	
decorative arts	749.3
household management	645.4
manufacturing technology	684.14
Desktop computers	004.16
see also Personal computers	
Desktop publishing	
composition	686.225 444 16
computer software	005.52
Desktop typesetting	686.225 444 16
Desmidiaceae	579.837
Desmids	579.837
Desmophyceae	579.87
Desmostylia	569.5

Desolation Sound Provincial	
Marine Park (B.C.)	T2—711 31
Despotism	321.9
Dessau (Germany :	
Regierungsbezirk)	T2—431 86
Desserts	641.86
Destiny	
philosophy	123
religion	202.2
Christianity	234.9
Destitute people	305.569
	T1—086 942
see also Poor people	
Destroyer escorts	359.835 4
design	623.812 54
engineering	623.825 4
naval equipment	359.835 4
naval units	359.325 4
Destroyers	359.835 4
design	623.812 54
engineering	623.825 4
naval equipment	359.835 4
naval units	359.325 4
Destruction of universe	523.19
Destructors	
military engineering	623.454 5
Desulfurization	
coal technology	662.623
Detail drawings	
construction	692.2
Detail finishing	
buildings	698
Detailing automobiles	629.287
Detection	
electronics	621.381 536
Detection of crime	363.25
see also Criminal investigation	
Detection of particles	539.77
Detection of radioactivity	539.77
Detective films	791.436 556
Detective plays	
literature	808.825 27
history and criticism	809.252 7
specific literatures	T3B—205 27
individual authors	T3A—2
Detective programs	791.446 556
radio	791.446 556
television	791.456 556
Detective stories	808.838 72
history and criticism	809.387 2
specific literatures	T3B—308 72
individual authors	T3A—3
Detectives	363.250 92
Detectors (Demodulators)	621.381 536

Detectors (Sensors)		Developed regions	909.097 22
manufacturing technology	681.2		T2—172 2
Detention	365	Developing (Photography)	771.44
Detention homes	365.34	negatives	771.43
see also Penal institutions		positives (photographs)	771.44
Detergents	668.14	Developing apparatus	
Deterioration		photography	771.44
materials science	620.112 2	Developing regions	909.097 24
Determinants	512.943 2		T2—172 4
Determinative mineralogy	549.1	Developing solutions	
Determinism	123	photography	771.54
literature	808.801 2	Development	
history and criticism	809.912	biology	571.8
specific literatures	T3B—080 12	*see also* Developmental	
history and		biology	
criticism	T3B—091 2	economics	338.9
Deterministic systems	003.7	natural resources	333.715
Deterrence (Nuclear strategy)	355.021 7	sociology	303.44
Detmold (Germany :		Development banks	332.153
Regierungsbezirk)	T2—435 65	domestic	332.28
Detonators	662.4	international	332.153
military engineering	623.454 2	Developmental abnormalities	571.938
Detroit (Mich.)	T2—774 34	Developmental biology	571.8
Detroit River (Mich. and		humans	612.6
Ont.)	T2—774 33	microorganisms	571.842 9
Deuel County (Neb.)	T2—782 913	Developmental disabilities	571.938
Deuel County (S.D.)	T2—783 25	medicine	616.858 8
Deuterium	546.212	nursing	616.858 802 31
see also Chemicals		pediatrics	618.928 588
Deuterium oxide		Developmental disorders	571.938
chemical engineering	661.08	*see also* Developmental	
chemistry	546.22	disabilities	
Deuteromycetes	579.55	Developmental genetics	571.85
Deuteromycotina	579.55	Developmental immunology	571.963 8
Deuteronomy (Bible)	222.15	Developmental linguistics	401.93
Deuterons	539.723 2		T4—019
Deutsche Kommunistische Partei	324.243 075	Developmental psychology	155
Deutsche Nationalsozialistische		comparative psychology	156.5
Arbeiterpartei (Austria)	324.243 602 38	*see Manual at* 155	
Deutsche Volksunion (Political		Developmental reading	418.4
party)	324.243 03	specific languages	T4—843
Deutsche Zentrumspartei	324.243 025	Developmentally disabled people	305.908 5
Deutscher Bund	943.07		T1—087 5
Deutzias	635.933 92	education	371.92
botany	583.92	social group	305.908 5
floriculture	635.933 92	social services	362.196 8
Deux-Montagnes (Quebec :		physical illness	362.196 8
Regional County		Developmentally disabled	
Municipality)	T2—714 252	workers	331.595
Deux-Sèvres (France)	T2—446 2	Deveron, River (Scotland)	T2—412 4
Devaluation of currency	332.414 2	Deviation (Social)	302.542
Devanagari alphabet	491.1	Device drivers	005.71
Developable surfaces	516.362	software	005.713
		software development	005.711

Devil	202.16	Dextrans	572.566
art representation	704.948 7	*see also* Carbohydrates	
arts	700.482 021 6	Dextrose	572.565
	T3C—382 021 6	*see also* Carbohydrates	
Christianity	235.4	Dhaka (Bangladesh :	
Islam	297.216	Division)	T2—549 22
Judaism	296.316	Dhammapada	294.382 322
literature	808.803 820 216	Dharma	
history and criticism	809.933 820 216	Hinduism	294.548
specific literatures	T3B—080 382 021 6	Dharmasastras	294.592 6
history and		Dhegiha languages	497.525
criticism	T3B—093 820 216		T6—975 25
occultism	133.422	Dhī Qār (Iraq : Province)	T2—567 5
Devil worship	202.16	Dhole	599.77
occultism	133.422	Dholuo language	496.558 42
Devolution, War of, 1667–1668	944.033		T6—965 584 2
Devon (England)	942.35	Dholuo literature	896.558 42
	T2—423 5	Diabetes	362.196 462
Devon cattle	636.226	medicine	616.462
Devonian period	551.74	pregnancy complications	
geology	551.74	obstetrics	618.364 6
paleontology	560.174	social services	362.196 462
Devonport (Tas.)	T2—946 5	*see also* Endocrine diseases —	
Devotional calendars	242.2	humans	
Devotional literature	204.32	Diabetes insipidus	
Buddhism	294.344 32	medicine	616.47
Christianity	242	*see also* Endocrine	
Hinduism	294.543 2	diseases — humans	
Islam	297.382	Diabetes mellitus	362.196 462
Sufi	297.438 2	cooking for	641.563 14
Judaism	296.72	medicine	616.462
Devotional theology	204	pediatrics	618.924 62
Buddhism	294.344	pregnancy complications	
Christianity	240	obstetrics	618.364 6
Hinduism	294.54	social services	362.196 462
Islam	297.57	*see also* Endocrine diseases —	
Sufi	297.4	humans	
Judaism	296.7	Diabetes mellitus (Type 1)	362.196 462 2
Dew	551.574 4	medicine	616.462 2
Dew points	536.44	pregnancy complications	
Dewberries	641.347 17	obstetrics	618.364 6
botany	583.642	social services	362.196 462 2
cooking	641.647 17	*see also* Endocrine diseases —	
food	641.347 17	humans	
horticulture	634.717	Diabetes mellitus (Type 2)	362.196 462 4
Dewdney-Alouette (B.C)	T2—711 37	medicine	616.462 4
Dewetsdorp (South Africa :		pregnancy complications	
District)	T2—685 7	obstetrics	618.364 6
Dewey County (Okla.)	T2—766 18	social services	362.196 462 4
Dewey County (S.D.)	T2—783 54	*see also* Endocrine diseases —	
Dewey Decimal Classification	025.431	humans	
Dewey shorthand system			
1936	653.428		
Dexter cattle	636.225		

Diaspore clay	553.61	Dictionaries	413
see also Clay		specific languages	T4—3
Diastrophism	551.8	*see Manual at* T4—3 vs.	
Diatessaron	226.1	T4—81	
Diathermy		specific subjects	T1—03
therapeutics	615.832 3	Dictionary catalogs	025.315
Diatomaceous earth	553.6	bibliography	017
economic geology	553.6	library science	025.315
mining	622.36	Dictyoptera	595.728
petrology	552.5	Didactic poetry	808.815
Diatoms	579.85	history and criticism	809.15
Diatonicism	781.262	specific literatures	T3B—105
Diatrymiformes	568.3	individual authors	T3A—1
Díaz, Porfirio		Didelphidae	599.276
Mexican history	972.081 4	Didiereaceae	583.883
Díaz-Canel, Miguel		Didjeridu	783.99
Cuban history	972.910 72	Dido language	499.964
Díaz Ordaz, Gustavo			T6—999 64
Mexican history	972.083 1	Didymelaceae	583.395
Diazepam		Didymelales	583.395
pharmacokinetics	615.788 2	Die casting	671.253
Diazines	547.593	Diefenbaker, John G.	
chemical engineering	661.894	Canadian history	971.064 2
Diazotization	547.27	Diefenbaker, Lake (Sask.)	T2—712 42
chemical engineering	660.284 4	Dieffenbachias	635.934 442
Diazotype processes	773.7	botany	584.442
Dibamidae	597.952	floriculture	635.934 442
Dice games	795.1	Diegueño Indians	T5—975 72
Dichapetalaceae	583.69	Dielectric materials	
Dichondras	583.959	materials science	620.195
Dickens County (Tex.)	T2—764 741	Dielectrics	537.24
Dickenson County (Va.)	T2—755 745	crystals	548.85
Dickey County (N.D.)	T2—784 54	Dielsdorf (Switzerland :	
Dickinson County (Iowa)	T2—777 123	Bezirk)	T2—494 572 3
Dickinson County (Kan.)	T2—781 56	Điện Biên (Vietnam :	
Dickinson County (Mich.)	T2—774 955	Province)	T2—597 1
Dickson County (Tenn.)	T2—768 44	Diencephalon	
Dicotyledons	583	human anatomy	611.81
botany	583	human physiology	612.826 2
forestry	634.972	medicine	616.8
paleobotany	561.3	Dies (Tools)	621.984
see Manual at 583–584		Diesel-electric locomotives	385.366 2
Dictation (Office practice)	651.74	engineering	625.266 2
shorthand	653.14	transportation services	385.366 2
Dictators	321.9	*see also* Rolling stock	
public administration	352.23	Diesel engines	621.436
Dictatorship	321.9	automotive	629.250 6
Diction	418	ships	623.872 36
applied linguistics	418	Diesel fuel	665.538 4
specific languages	T4—81	Diesel-hydraulic locomotives	385.366 4
rhetoric	808	engineering	625.266 4
		transportation services	385.366 4
		see also Rolling stock	

Digestive system diseases
humans (continued)
  anesthesiology — 617.967 43
   specific organs — 617.967 55
  cancer — 362.196 994 3
   incidence — 614.599 943
   medicine — 616.994 3
   social services — 362.196 994 3
   see also Cancer —
    humans
  geriatrics — 618.976 3
  incidence — 614.593
  medicine — 616.3
  pediatrics — 618.923
  pharmacokinetics — 615.73
  social services — 362.196 3
  surgery — 617.43
Digests — T1—020 2
Digests of cases — 348.046
 United States — 348.734 6
Digests of laws — 348.026
 United States — 348.732 6
Digital archives — 027
 see also Archives
Digital art — 776
 see Manual at 776 vs. 006.5–.7
Digital audio broadcasting
 communications — 384.54
 engineering — 621.384
Digital audio technology
 computer science — 006.5
 radiobroadcasting
  communications — 384.54
 sociology — 302.231
 sound reproduction — 621.389 3
Digital cameras — 771.3
Digital cinematography — 777
Digital circuits — 621.381 5
 computer engineering — 621.395
Digital codes (Computers) — 005.72
Digital communications — 384
 communications services — 384
 computer science — 004.6
 engineering — 621.382
 see Manual at 004.6 vs.
  621.382, 621.3981
Digital computers — 004
 see also Computers
Digital content management — 006.7
Digital ephemera
 design — 744.7
Digital images — 740
 photography — 779

Digital instruments
 technology — 681.1
Digital libraries — 027
Digital literacy
 primary education — 372.34
Digital media — 302.231
 advertising — 659.144
 sociology — 302.231
Digital photography — 770
Digital preservation — 025.84
 office records — 651.59
Digital publications — 070.579 7
 bibliographies — 011.39
Digital rights management
 computer science — 005.82
Digital signatures
 computer science — 005.824
Digital subscriber lines — 621.387 8
Digital television — 621.388 07
 sociology — 302.234 5
Digital-to-analog converters
 computer engineering — 621.398 14
 computer science — 004.64
 electronic engineering — 621.381 59
Digital video effects — 777.9
Digital video technology
 computer science — 006.696
  standards — 006.696 021 8
 instructional use — 371.334 669 6
 sociology — 302.231
Digital videography — 777
Digitalis
 pharmacokinetics — 615.711
Digitization
 office records — 651.59
Digitizer tablets — 006.62
 computer engineering — 621.399 6
Dignity of labor — 331.013
Digraphs — 511.54
Dihydroxy aromatics — 547.633
Dijon (France) — T2—444 26
Dik-diks — 599.646
Dika — 583.69
Dikes (Geology) — 551.88
Dikes (Levees) — 627.42
 reclamation from sea — 627.549
 road engineering — 625.734
Dilation
 heart
  human physiology — 612.171
Dilation and curettage
 surgery — 618.145 8

Diphtheria		Diplomatic service	327.2
incidence	614.512 3	public administration	353.132 63
medicine	616.931 3	Diplomats	327.209 2
see also Communicable		Diplopia	
diseases — humans		ophthalmology	617.762
Diphthongs (Phonology)	414.6	*see also* Eye diseases —	
specific languages	T4—16	humans	
Diplodocus	567.913	Diplopoda	595.66
Diplomacy	327.2	Diplura	595.724
customs	399	Dipnoi	597.39
law of nations	341.33	paleozoology	567.39
Diplomas	371.291 2	Dipodomys	599.359 87
prints	769.5	Dipole moments	537.243
Diplomatic causes of war	355.027 2	Dipped latex	678.533
World War I	940.311 2	Dipped rubber	678.36
World War II	940.531 12	Dippers (Birds)	598.832
Diplomatic customs	399	Dipperu National Park	
Diplomatic history	327.09	(Qld.)	T2—943 5
Algerian Revolution	965.046 2	Dipping animals	636.083 3
American Revolution	973.32	Dipping latex	678.527
Chaco War	989.207 162	Diprotodontia	599.2
Civil War (England)	942.062 2	Dips (Appetizers)	641.812
Civil War (Spain)	946.081 2	Dips (Geology)	551.85
Civil War (United States)	973.72	Dipsacales	583.987
Confederate States of		Diptera	595.77
America	973.721	Dipterocarpaceae	583.77
United States	973.722	Dīr District (Pakistan)	T2—549 122
Crimean War	947.073 82	Dirachmaceae	583.646
Falkland Islands War	997.110 242	Dirāyah	297.125 2
Franco-German War	943.082 2	Dirē Dawa (Ethiopia :	
Hundred Years' War	944.025 2	Administrative region)	T2—632
Indo-Pakistan War, 1971	954.920 512	Dirē Dawa na Īsa na	
Indochinese War	959.704 12	Gurgura Āwraja	
Iraq War, 2003–2011	956.704 432	(Ethiopia)	T2—632
Iraqi-Iranian Conflict	955.054 22	Direct advertising	659.133
Korean War	951.904 22	Direct broadcast satellite systems	384.552
Mexican War	973.622	Direct-current machinery	621.313 2
Napoleonic Wars	940.272	Direct-current transmission	621.319 12
Persian Gulf War, 1991	956.704 422	Direct distance dialing	384.64
South African War	968.048 2	communications services	384.64
Spanish-American War	973.892	engineering	621.385 7
Thirty Years' War	940.242	Direct-driven hoists	
Vietnamese War	959.704 32	mining	622.67
War of 1812	973.522	Direct energy conversion	
War of the Pacific	983.061 62	electrical engineering	621.312 4
World War I	940.32	Direct-fluid-pressure	
World War II	940.532	displacement pumps	621.699
Diplomatic immunities	327.2	Direct-mail advertising	659.133
law of nations	341.33	design	744.66
Diplomatic languages	401.3	Direct-mail marketing	381.142
Diplomatic law	342.041 2	design	744.66
law of nations	341.33	management	658.872
Diplomatic privileges	327.2	Direct marketing	381.1
law of nations	341.33	management	658.872

Disabled people (continued)
  footwear for
    manufacturing technology 685.38
  government programs 353.539
  Holocaust, 1933–1945 940.531 808 7
  home care 649.8
  institutional buildings
    architecture 725.54
  legal status 346.013 087
    private law 346.013 087
    United States 346.730 130 87
  libraries for 027.663
    administration 025.197 663
    collection development 025.218 766 3
  museum services 069.17
  pastoral care
    Christianity 259.44
  publications for
    bibliographies 011.63
    reviews 028.163
  recreation 790.196
    indoor 793.019 6
    outdoor 796.087
  social group 305.908
  social welfare 362.4
    biography 362.409 2
    public administration
      health services 353.66
  sports 796.087
  see Manual at 796.08 vs.
    796.04
  see Manual at 362.1–.4 vs. 610
Disabled veterans 362.408 697
  legal status 343.011 6
  social welfare 362.408 697
Disabled workers 331.59
  economics 331.59
  government programs 354.908 7
  law 344.015 9
  personnel management 658.300 87
Disarmament 327.174
  ethics 172.4
    religion 205.624
      Christianity 241.624
    see also Political ethics
  international politics 327.174
  law 341.733
  social theology 201.727 3
    Christianity 261.87
    Judaism 296.382 7
Disassembling tools 621.93
Disaster insurance 368.122
  see also Insurance
Disaster nursing 610.734 9

Disaster preparedness
  library operations 025.82
Disaster relief 363.348
  law 344.053 48
  public administration 353.95
Disaster technology 628.92
Disasters 904
  law 344.053 4
  management of enterprises 658.477
  personal safety 613.69
  psychology 155.935
  social effects 303.485
  social services 363.34
    public administration 353.95
  sociology 303.485
  see Manual at 900
Discarding
  library collections 025.216
  museology 069.51
Discharge (Military personnel) 355.114
Discharged offenders 364.8
  labor economics 331.51
Disciples of Christ 286.63
Discipline
  armed forces 355.13
    law 343.014
  education 371.5
  home child care 649.64
  labor economics 331.259 8
  labor unions 331.873
  legislators 328.366
  personnel management 658.314
    public administration 352.66
      law 342.068 4
  prisons 365.643
Disco dancing 793.33
Discoglossoidea 597.86
Discographies 011.38
  music 016.780 266
Discomycetes 579.57
Discount 332.84
Discount brokers 332.62
Discount clubs 381.149
  management 658.879
Discount rates 332.84
  economics 332.84
    central banking 332.113
    macroeconomic policy 339.53
Discount stores 381.149
  management 658.879
Discounts
  sales promotion 658.82

Diseases
- humans (continued)
  - medicine 616
    - *see Manual at* 610 vs. 616;
      - *also at* 616 vs. 612;
      - *also at* 616 vs. 617.4;
      - *also at* 616 vs. 618.92
    - pastoral theology 206.1
      - Christianity 259.41
    - pediatrics 618.92
    - prevalence 614.42
    - psychological influence 155.916
    - religious rites 203.8
      - Christianity 265.82
    - social services 362.1
    - social theology 201.762 1
      - Christianity 261.832 1
    - sociology 306.461
    - surgery 617
      - *see Manual at* 617
    - *see Manual at* 362.1–.4 and 614.4–.5
  - plants 571.92
    - agriculture 632.3
    - *see Manual at* 571–575 vs. 630

Diseconomies of scale 338.514 4

Disfigurement
- psychological influence 155.916

Dishes 642.7
- *see also* Tableware

Dishwashers
- installation 696.184
- manufacturing technology 683.88

Disinfection
- public health 614.48
- sewage treatment 628.32
- water supply treatment 628.166 2

Disinformation activities
- international politics 327.14

Disk drives 004.563
- engineering 621.397 63

Disks (Computers) 004.563
- engineering 621.397 63

Disks (Geometrical shapes) 516.154

Disks (Recording devices) 621.382 34

Dislocation (Aftermath of war) 355.028

Dislocation (Crystallography) 548.842

Dislocations (Geology) 551.872

Dislocations (Injuries)
- medicine 617.16

Dismal Swamp (N.C. and Va.) T2—755 523
- North Carolina T2—756 135
- Virginia T2—755 523

Dismissal of employees
- economics 331.259 6
  - unemployment 331.137
  - worker security 331.259 6
- law 344.012 596
- personnel management 658.313
  - public administration 352.69

Disordered solids 530.413

Disorderly conduct 364.143
- law 345.024 3

Disorders of sex development
- medicine 616.694

Dispatching 388.041
- production management 658.53
- *see also* Scheduling — transportation

Dispensaries 362.12
- armed forces 355.72
- *see also* Health care facilities

Dispensationalist theology 230.046 3

Dispensatories 615.13

Dispersion of light 535.4

Displaced persons 305.906 914
- T1—086 914
- law 342.083
- political science 325.21
- social welfare 362.87
- women
  - social welfare 362.839 814
- young people
  - social welfare 362.779 14
- *see also* Refugees

Display advertising 659.15
- design 744.68

Display lighting 621.322 9
- *see also* Lighting

Display of merchandise
- advertising 659.15

Display screens (Computers) 004.77
- engineering 621.398 7

Disposable personal income 339.32

Disposal of dead 363.75
- *see also* Undertaking (Mortuary)

Disposal of government property 352.54

Disposal of military supplies 355.621 37

Disposal of public lands 333.16
- economics 333.16
- public administration 352.574

Districting (Legislatures)	328.334 5
law	342.053
Districts (Local government	
units)	320.83
see also Counties	
Distrito Especial de Bogotá	
(Colombia)	T2—861 48
Distrito Federal (Brazil)	T2—817 4
Distrito Federal (Mexico)	972.53
	T2—725 3
Distrito Federal (Venezuela)	T2—877
Distrito Nacional	
(Dominican Republic)	T2—729 375
Ditches	
agriculture	631.62
road engineering	625.734
Ditsobotla (South Africa)	T2—682 47
Diuretics	
pharmacokinetics	615.761
Diurnal variations	
geomagnetism	538.742
Divehi language	491.489
	T6—914 89
Divehi literature	891.489
Divers	627.720 92
springboard sports	797.240 92
underwater sports	797.230 92
underwater technologists	627.720 92
Diversification	
production economics	338.6
production management	658.503 8
Diversity in the workplace	331.133
personnel management	658.300 8
Divertimentos	784.185 2
Divestment	
management	658.164
Divide County (N.D.)	T2—784 71
Divided catalogs	025.315
Dividends	332.632 21
accounting	657.76
financial management	658.155
income tax	336.242 6
law	343.052 46
law	346.092 2
Dividers	
road engineering	625.795
Divination	133.3
religion	203.2
African religions	299.613 2
Divinatory graphology	137
Divinatory signs	133.334
Divine law	
Christianity	241.2
Divine Light Mission	294

Divine office (Religion)	264.15
Anglican	264.030 15
music	782.324
choral and mixed voices	782.532 4
single voices	783.093 24
Roman Catholic	264.020 15
texts	264.024
Divine right of kings	321.6
Diving	627.72
engineering	627.72
sports	797.2
see also Aquatic sports	
Diving medicine	616.980 22
Diving petrels	598.42
Divining rods	133.323
Divinity of Jesus Christ	232.8
Divinity schools	230.071 1
Divisibility	512.72
Division	512.92
algebra	512.92
arithmetic	513.214
Division algebras	512.4
Division of labor	
production economics	338.6
sociology	306.368
Divisionism	709.034 5
painting	759.055
Divisions (Army units)	355.31
Divisions (Naval units)	359.31
Divorce	306.89
ethics	173
religion	205.63
Buddhism	294.356 3
Christianity	241.63
Hinduism	294.548 63
Islam	297.563
Judaism	296.363
Judaism	296.444 4
law	346.016 6
psychology	155.93
religion	204.41
social theology	201.7
Christianity	261.835 89
social welfare	362.829 4
see also Families — social	
welfare	
sociology	306.89
Divorced families	306.89
social welfare	362.829 4
Divorced men	306.892
guides to Christian life	248.842 3
psychology	155.643 2

Divorced people	306.89
	T1—086 53
Christian devotional literature	242.646
family relationships	306.89
guides to religious life	
Christianity	248.846
law	346.016 6
psychology	155.643
social group	306.89
social welfare	362.829 4
Divorced women	306.893
guides to Christian life	248.843 3
psychology	155.643 3
social welfare	362.839 59
Dixie County (Fla.)	T2—759 812
Dixiecrat Party (U.S.)	324.273 3
Dixieland jazz	781.653
Dixon County (Neb.)	T2—782 223
Dixon Entrance (B.C. and	
Alaska)	551.461 433
	T2—164 33
Diyālá (Iraq)	T2—567 4
Diyarbakır İli (Turkey)	T2—566 77
ancient	T2—394 2
Dizziness	
medicine	616.841
see also Nervous system	
diseases — humans	
Djakarta (Indonesia)	T2—598 22
Djamena (Chad)	T2—674 3
Djelfa (Algeria : Province)	T2—653
Djibouti	967.71
	T2—677 1
Djiboutians	T5—967 71
Djirbal language	499.15
	T6—991 5
Djotodia, Michel Am-Nondokro	
Central African history	967.410 55
DNA (Genetics)	572.86
humans	611.018 166
see Manual at 576.5 vs. 572.8	
DNA computing	006.384 2
DNA fingerprinting	572.863 3
biometric identification	
computer science	006.248 2
DNA topology	
humans	611.018 166 3
DNA virus infections	
incidence	614.581
medicine	616.911
see also Communicable	
diseases — humans	
DNA viruses	579.24

Dnepropetrovsk (Ukraine :	
Oblast)	T2—477 4
Dnestr River (Ukraine and	
Moldova)	T2—477 9
Dnieper River	T2—477
Dniester River (Ukraine and	
Moldova)	T2—477 9
Dnipropetrovs´ka oblast´	
(Ukraine)	T2—477 4
DNSAP (Austrian political party)	324.243 602 38
Do-it-yourself work	643.7
Dobby-weave fabrics	677.615
see also Textiles	
Doberai Peninsula	
(Indonesia)	T2—951 2
Doberman pinscher	636.736
Dobrich (Bulgaria : Oblast)	T2—499 42
Dobruja (Romania and	
Bulgaria)	T2—498 3
Bulgaria	T2—499 42
Romania	T2—498 3
Dobsonflies	595.747
Dock (Plant)	583.888
Docks (Port facilities)	387.15
engineering	627.31
see also Port facilities	
Doctors	610.92
see also Physicians	
Doctor's degree	378.2
Doctrinal controversies	
Christian church history	273
Doctrinal theology	202
Buddhism	294.342
Christianity	230
Hinduism	294.52
Islam	297.2
Sufi	297.41
Judaism	296.3
philosophy of religion	210
Tibetan Buddhism	294.342 042 3
Doctrine and Covenants (Latter	
Day Saint movement sacred	
book)	289.323
Document delivery services	025.6
Document markup languages	006.74
Documentary evidence	347.064
criminal investigation	363.256 5
law	347.064
Documentary films	
journalism	070.18
Documentary hypothesis	
(Pentateuchal criticism)	222.106 6
Documentary media	
journalism	070.1

Documentation	025
specific subjects	025.06
Dodders	583.959
Doddridge County (W. Va.)	T2—754 56
Dodecanese (Greece)	T2—495 87
ancient	T2—391 6
Dodecaphony	781.268
Dōdekanēsos (Greece)	T2—495 87
ancient	T2—391 6
Dodge County (Ga.)	T2—758 532
Dodge County (Minn.)	T2—776 153
Dodge County (Neb.)	T2—782 235
Dodge County (Wis.)	T2—775 82
Dodoma Region (Tanzania)	T2—678 26
Dodos	598.65
Doe, Samuel K. (Samuel Kanyon)	
Liberian history	966.620 32
Dog breeds	636.71
see Manual at 636.72–.75	
Dog family	599.77
Dog pounds	363.78
see also Pest control	
Dog racing	798.8
see also Animal racing	
Dog sled racing	798.83
see also Animal racing	
Dogbanes	583.956
Dogfishes	597.36
Dogmatism	
philosophy	148
Dogon (African people)	T5—963
Dogon language	496.3
	T6—963
Dogs	636.7
animal husbandry	636.7
arts	T3C—362 977 2
predator control technology	636.083 9
zoology	599.772
Dogwoods	635.977 392
botany	583.92
ornamental arboriculture	635.977 392
Doilies	642.7
arts	746.96
home sewing	646.21
table setting	642.7
Dolerite	552.3
Dolgan language	494.33
	T6—943 3
Dolichopodidae	595.773
Dolj (Romania)	T2—498 4

Doll clothing	688.722 1
handicrafts	745.592 21
manufacturing technology	688.722 1
see also Toys	
Doll furniture	688.723
handicrafts	745.592 3
manufacturing technology	688.723
see also Toys	
Dollard-des-Ormeaux (Quebec)	T2—714 28
Dollhouses	688.723
handicrafts	745.592 3
manufacturing technology	688.723
see also Toys	
Dolls	688.722 1
ceramic arts	738.83
handicrafts	745.592 21
manufacturing technology	688.722 1
see also Toys	
Dolly Varden trout	597.554
Dolnośląskie Voivodeship (Poland)	T2—438 52
Dolomite	553.516
economic geology	553.516
mineralogy	549.782
petrology	552.58
Dolores County (Colo.)	T2—788 26
Dolphinfishes	597.72
Dolphins	599.53
animal husbandry	636.953
conservation technology	639.979 53
resource economics	333.959 53
Domaine-du-Roy (Quebec)	T2—714 142
Domes	721.46
architecture	721.46
construction	690.146
structural engineering	624.177 5
concrete	624.183 45
Domestic animals	636
Domestic architecture	728
Domestic arts	640
Domestic cats	636.8
Domestic commerce	381
law	343.08
public administration	354.73
Domestic councils	
public administration	352.246
Domestic customs	392.3
Domestic employees	640.46
Domestic fowl	636.5
agricultural economics	338.176 5
zoology	598.625
Domestic industries	338.634
Domestic investment	332.6

Doppelgänger			Double houses	
literature	808.802 7		architecture	728.312
history and criticism	809.927		Double jeopardy	345.04
specific literatures	T3B—080 27		Double mini-trampoline	796.474
history and			Double-reed bagpipes	788.49
criticism	T3B—092 7		*see also* Woodwind	
Doppler effect	534.3		instruments	
Dorchester County (Md.)	T2—752 27		Double-reed instruments	788.5
Dorchester County (S.C.)	T2—757 94		*see also* Woodwind	
Dordogne (France)	T2—447 2		instruments	
Doris (Greece)	T2—383		Double salts	
Dormancy (Biology)	571.78		chemical engineering	661.4
Dormers	721.5		Double stars	523.841
architecture	721.5		Double sulfides	
construction	690.15		mineralogy	549.35
Dormice	599.359 6		Double taxation	336.294
Dormitories	371.871		law	343.052 6
architecture	727.38		public finance	336.294
Dorneck (Switzerland)	T2—494 355 7		Doubles (Literature)	808.802 7
Dorneck-Thierstein			history and criticism	809.927
(Switzerland)	T2—494 355		specific literatures	T3B—080 27
Dornoch Firth (Scotland)	T2—163 36		history and criticism	T3B—092 7
Dorsal muscles			Doubles (Tennis)	796.342 28
human anatomy	611.731		Doubling the cube	516.204
Dorset (England)	942.33		Doubs (France : Dept.)	T2—444 6
	T2—423 3		Doubs River (France and	
Dortmund (Germany)	T2—435 633		Switzerland)	T2—444 6
Dorval (Quebec)	T2—714 28		France	T2—444 6
Doryanthaceae	584.7		Switzerland	T2—494 36
Dosage determination			Doubt	
pharmacology	615.14		epistemology	121.5
Dosage forms			Dougherty County (Ga.)	T2—758 953
pharmaceutical chemistry	615.19		Douglas (South Africa)	T2—687 13
Dosimetry			Douglas County (Colo.)	T2—788 86
biophysics			Douglas County (Ga.)	T2—758 243
humans	612.014 480 287		Douglas County (Ill.)	T2—773 68
radiotherapy	615.842		Douglas County (Kan.)	T2—781 65
Dothideales	579.564		Douglas County (Minn.)	T2—776 45
Dotted swiss embroidery	677.77		Douglas County (Mo.)	T2—778 832
Douala (Cameroon)	T2—671 1		Douglas County (Neb.)	T2—782 254
Douay Bible	220.520 2		Douglas County (Nev.)	T2—793 59
Double basses	787.5		Douglas County (Or.)	T2—795 29
instrument	787.519		Douglas County (S.D.)	T2—783 383
music	787.5		Douglas County (Wash.)	T2—797 31
see also Stringed instruments			Douglas County (Wis.)	T2—775 11
Double-bassists	787.509 2		Douglas squirrel	599.363
Double bassoons	788.59		Doukkala-Abda (Morocco)	T2—646 2
instrument	788.591 9		Douro (Portugal : Region)	T2—469 15
music	788.59		Douro Litoral (Portugal)	T2—469 15
see also Woodwind			Dove, River (Derbyshire	
instruments			and Staffordshire,	
Double cropping	631.58		England)	T2—425 13
Double helix	572.863 3			

Dramatic monologues (Poetry)	808.812
history and criticism	809.12
specific literatures	T3B—102
individual authors	T3A—1
see Manual at T3A—2,	
T3B—2 vs. T3A—1,	
T3B—102	
Dramatic music	781.552
Dramatic poetry	808.812
history and criticism	809.12
specific literatures	T3B—102
individual authors	T3A—1
see Manual at T3A—2,	
T3B—2 vs. T3A—1,	
T3B—102	
Dramatic vocal forms	782.1
music	782.1
stage presentation	792.5
see Manual at 782.1 vs. 792.5,	
792.6	
Dramatists	809.2
collected biography	809.2
specific literatures	T3B—200 9
individual biography	T3A—2
Draped figures	704.942
drawing	743.4
painting	757
Draperies	645.32
arts	746.94
commercial technology	684.3
drawing	743.5
home sewing	646.21
household management	645.32
interior decoration	747.5
Draughts	794.2
Dravida languages	494.81
	T6—948 1
Dravida literatures	894.81
Dravidian languages	494.8
	T6—948
Dravidian literatures	894.8
Dravidians	T5—948
Drawbacks	
international commerce	382.7
Drawbridges	
construction	624.24
Drawers (Artists)	741.092
Drawing (Delineating)	741
arts	741
primary education	372.52
sociology	302.226
techniques	741.2
technology	604.2
Drawing glass	666.124

Drawing metals	671.34
decorative arts	739.14
sculpture	731.41
Drawing paper	676.282 5
Drawing rooms	643.54
home economics	643.54
interior decoration	747.75
Drawings	T1—022 2
arts	741
Drawn work	
arts	746.44
Dream books	135.3
Dream interpretation	154.63
Dreams	154.63
arts	T3C—353
human physiology	612.821
literature	808.803 53
history and criticism	809.933 53
specific literatures	T3B—080 353
history and	
criticism	T3B—093 53
parapsychology	135.3
psychology	154.63
Dred Scott decision, 1857	
Civil War (United States) cause	973.711 5
Dredgers (Ships)	
design	623.812 8
engineering	623.828
Dredging	627.73
Dredging services	
ports	387.168
Dredging spoil	363.728 4
engineering	627.73
social services	363.728 4
see also Waste control	
Drenthe (Netherlands)	T2—492 15
Dresden (Germany)	T2—432 142
Dresden (Germany :	
Direktionsbezirk)	T2—432 14
Dresden (Germany :	
Regierungsbezirk)	T2—432 14
Dress accessories	391.44
see also Accessories (Clothing)	
Dressage	798.23
Dressers	645.4
manufacturing technology	684.16
see also Furniture	
Dresses	391.472
commercial technology	687.112
customs	391.472
home economics	646.34
home sewing	646.432
see also Clothing	

Drought-resistant plants	581.754
floriculture	635.952 5
Droughts	
agricultural economics	338.14
crop damage	632.12
effect on natural ecology	577.22
meteorology	551.577 3
social services	363.349 29
agricultural industries	338.18
Drowning	
medicine	617.18
Drug abuse	362.29
see also Drugs (Narcotics);	
Marijuana abuse; Narcotics;	
Narcotics abuse; Stimulant	
abuse; Substance abuse;	
Tobacco abuse	
Drug administration routes	615.6
Drug adulteration	363.194
criminology	364.142
criminal law	345.024 2
see also Drugs	
(Pharmaceuticals) —	
product safety	
Drug allergies	
incidence	614.599 358
medicine	616.975 8
Drug compounding	615.19
Drug culture	306.1
Drug dependence	362.29
medicine	616.86
perinatal medicine	618.326 86
personal health	613.8
pregnancy complications	
obstetrics	618.368 6
social welfare	362.29
see also Substance abuse	
Drug design	615.19
Drug development	615.19
Drug enforcement agents	363.284
Drug-herb interactions	615.704 5
Drug incompatibilities	
pharmacokinetics	615.704 5
pharmacology	615.14
Drug interactions	
pharmacokinetics	615.704 5
Drug metabolism	
pharmacokinetics	615.7
Drug-nutrient interactions	615.704 52
Drug possession	364.177
law	345.027 7
see also Drug traffic	
Drug resistance	
microorganisms	616.904 1

Drug shock therapy	
psychiatry	616.891 2
Drug side effects	
pharmacokinetics	615.704 2
Drug smuggling	364.133 65
law	345.023 365
Drug testing	
personnel management	658.382 2
personnel selection	658.311 2
Drug therapy	
medicine	615.58
psychiatry	616.891 8
Drug toxicity	
pharmacokinetics	615.704
Drug traffic	364.133 65
criminology	364.177
law	345.027 7
see also Crime	
public administration	353.37
school problem	371.784
social problem	364.133 65
law	344.054 5
see also Drug possession; Drug	
use; Drugs (Narcotics);	
Narcotics; Narcotics traffic	
Drug use	362.29
see also Drug traffic;	
Substance abuse	
Drugged driving	364.147
causes of accidents	363.125 14
law	345.024 7
Drugs (Narcotics)	
customs	394.14
ethics	178.8
pharmacokinetics	615.782 2
smuggling	364.133 65
law	345.023 365
Drugs (Pharmaceuticals)	615.1
chemical analysis	615.190 1
economics	338.476 151
insurance	368.382 4
see also Insurance	
manufacturing technology	615.19
pharmacology	615.1
preservation	615.18
product safety	363.194
criminology	364.142
criminal law	345.024 2
law	344.042 33
public administration	353.998
see also Product safety	
see Manual at 615.1 vs.	
615.2–.3; *also at* 615.2–.3	
vs. 615.7	

262

Ducks	598.41
animal husbandry	636.597
conservation technology	639.978 41
resource economics	333.958 41
sports hunting	799.244
Duckweeds	584.442
Duct flutes	788.35
see also Woodwind	
instruments	
Ductility	
materials science	620.112 5
Duda, Andrzej	
Polish history	943.805 75
Dude farming	796.56
Dude ranching	796.56
Dudley (England :	
Metropolitan Borough)	T2—424 93
Due process of law	347.05
Dueling	394.8
customs	394.8
ethics	179.7
Duets	
chamber music	785.12
vocal music	783.12
Dufferin (Ont. : County)	T2—713 41
Dufferin and Ava, Frederick	
Temple Blackwood, Marquis	
of	
Indian history	954.035 4
Dugong	599.559
Dugongidae	599.559
Duhalde, Eduardo Alberto	
Argentine history	982.071
Duikers	599.64
Duisburg (Germany)	T2—435 536
Dukes County (Mass.)	T2—744 94
Dukhobors	289.9
Dulcimers	787.74
see also Stringed instruments	
Duluth (Minn.)	T2—776 771
Dumbarton (Scotland)	T2—414 32
Dumbarton (Scotland :	
District)	T2—414 32
Dumfries and Galloway	
(Scotland)	T2—414 7
Dumping (Trade)	
law	343.087
Dumps (Solid waste)	363.728 5
technology	628.445 62
see also Waste control	
Dumyāṭ (Egypt : Province)	T2—621
Dún Laoghaire (Ireland)	T2—418 38
Dunaliellaceae	579.832
Dundee (Scotland)	T2—412 7

Dundee (South Africa :	
District)	T2—684 8
Dundy County (Neb.)	T2—782 86
Dune buggies	
engineering	629.228 8
Dune stabilization	631.64
shore protection	627.58
Dunedin (N.Z.)	T2—939 2
Dunedin City (N.Z.)	T2—939 2
Dunes	551.375
see also Sand dunes	
Dunfermline (Scotland :	
District)	T2—412 9
Dung beetles	595.764 9
Dung flies	595.774
Dungannon (Northern	
Ireland : District)	T2—416 4
Dunkerque, Battle of, 1940	940.542 142 8
Dunkers	286.5
see also Baptists	
Dunkirk, Battle of, 1940	940.542 142 8
Dunklin County (Mo.)	T2—778 993
Dunn County (N.D.)	T2—784 82
Dunn County (Wis.)	T2—775 43
Dunoon (Scotland)	T2—414 2
Duodecimal system	513.5
Duodenal diseases	
medicine	616.34
see also Digestive system	
diseases — humans	
Duodenal ulcers	
medicine	616.343 3
see also Digestive system	
diseases — humans	
Duodenitis	
medicine	616.344
see also Digestive system	
diseases — humans	
Duodenum	573.378
biology	573.378
human anatomy	611.341
human physiology	612.33
medicine	616.34
surgery	617.554 1
see also Digestive system	
DuPage County (Ill.)	T2—773 24
Duplessis, Maurice	
Quebec history	971.404 1
Duplex houses	
architecture	728.312
Duplex-process steel	669.142 3

Dwellings	643.1
architecture	728
arts	700.456 4
	T3C—356 4
construction	690.8
customs	392.36
folklore	398.276 4
history and criticism	398.356 4
health	613.5
home economics	643.1
interior decoration	747
lighting	621.322 8
literature	808.803 564
history and criticism	809.933 564
specific literatures	T3B—080 356 4
history and criticism	T3B—093 564
theft from	364.162 2
law	345.026 22
see also Housing	
see Manual at 363.5 vs. 643.1	
Dwyfor (Wales)	T2—429 25
Dye lasers	621.366 4
Dye-producing plants	
agriculture	633.86
economic botany	581.636
Dyeing	667.3
home economics	648.1
textile arts	746.6
Dyeing leather	675.25
Dyeing yarns	
arts	746.13
Dyer County (Tenn.)	T2—768 15
Dyerma (African people)	T5—965 8
Dyerma language	496.58
	T6—965 8
Dyes	667.2
chemistry	547.86
technology	667.2
Dyfed (Wales)	T2—429 6
Dying	306.9
music	781.588
psychology	155.937
social aspects	306.9
Dying languages	306.44
Dying patients	362.175
pastoral theology	206.1
Christianity	259.417 5
social theology	201.762 175
Christianity	261.832 175
see Manual at 362.1–.4 vs. 610	
Dynamic logic	511.314
Dynamic oceanography	551.462
Dynamic programming	519.703

Dynamic psychology	150.193
Dynamic systems	003.85
Dynamical systems	
(Mathematics)	515.39
Dynamics	531.11
air	533.62
engineering	620.107 4
atmosphere	551.515
engineering	620.104
fluids	532.05
engineering	620.106 4
gases	533.2
engineering	620.107 4
liquids	532.5
engineering	620.106 4
particles	531.163
engineering	620.43
physics	531.11
solids	531.3
engineering	620.105 4
Dynamism	146
Dynamite	662.27
military engineering	623.452 7
Dynamos	621.313 2
Dysarthria	
medicine	616.855 2
see also Communication	
disorders	
Dysentery	
incidence	614.516
medicine	616.935
see also Communicable	
diseases — humans	
Dysfunctional families	
pastoral theology	206.1
Christianity	259.1
social relationships	306.87
social theology	201.7
Christianity	261.835 85
Dyslexia	
medicine	616.855 3
see also Communication	
disorders	
pediatrics	618.928 553
special education	371.914 4
Dysmenorrhea	
gynecology	618.172
see also Female genital	
diseases — humans	
Dyspepsia	
medicine	616.332
see also Digestive system	
diseases — humans	

Eastern Canadian Inuit language	497.124	Eastern Highlands Province	
	T6—971 24	(Papua New Guinea)	T2—956 9
Eastern Canadian Inuktitut	T5—971 24	Eastern Himalayan languages	495.49
Eastern Canadian Inuktitut			T6—954 9
language	497.124	Eastern Himalayan literatures	895.49
	T6—971 24	Eastern Himalayan peoples	T5—954 9
Eastern Canadian Inuktitut		Eastern Hindi languages	491.492
literature	897.124		T6—914 92
Eastern Cape (South Africa)	968.75	Eastern Hindi literatures	891.492
	T2—687 5	Eastern languages	
Eastern Catholic churches	281.52	(Adamawa-Eastern phylum)	496.361
doctrines	230.152		T6—963 61
catechisms and creeds	238.152	Eastern Macedonia and	
theology	230.152	Thrace (Greece)	T2—495 7
see also Eastern churches		Eastern Malayo-Polynesian	
Eastern churches	281.5	languages	499.5
church government	262.015		T6—995
local church	254.015	Eastern Malaysia	T2—595 3
church law	262.981 5	Eastern Mediterranean	
doctrines	230.15	region	T2—182 24
catechisms and creeds	238.15	ancient	938
general councils	262.515		T2—38
guides to Christian life	248.481 5	Eastern Mediterranean Sea	551.461 384
liturgy	264.015		T2—163 84
missions	266.15	Eastern Nilotic languages	496.552
monasticism	255.81		T6—965 52
church history	271.81	Eastern Ontario	T2—713 7
women	255.981	Eastern Oregon	T2—795 5
church history	271.981	Eastern Orthodox Church	281.9
moral theology	241.041 5	*see Manual at* 270, 230.11–.14	
public worship	264.015	vs. 230.15–.2, 281.5–.9,	
religious associations	267.181 5	282	
religious education	268.815	Eastern Panhandle (W. Va.)	T2—754 9
seminaries	230.073 15	Eastern Panjabi language	491.42
theology	230.15		T6—914 2
see Manual at 270, 230.11–.14		Eastern philosophy	181
vs. 230.15–.2, 281.5–.9, 282		Eastern Province (Kenya)	T2—676 24
Eastern Desert (Egypt)	T2—623	Eastern Province (Zambia)	T2—689 4
Eastern Empire	949.501 3	Eastern Region (China)	T2—512
Eastern England	942.6	Eastern Region (Ecuador)	T2—866 4
	T2—426	Eastern rite Catholics	281.52
Eastern Equatoria State		*see also* Eastern churches	
(South Sudan)	T2—629 5	Eastern rite churches	281.5
Eastern Europe	947	*see also* Eastern churches	
	T2—47	Eastern Roman Empire	949.501 3
Eastern Fijian languages	499.59	Eastern Saami languages	T6—945 76
	T6—995 9	Eastern Samar (Philippines)	T2—599 583
Eastern Finland (Finland)	T2—489 75	Eastern Sámi languages	T6—945 76
Eastern flying squirrel	599.369	Eastern Shore (Md. and Va.)	T2—752 1
Eastern France	T2—444	Eastern Siberia (Russia)	T2—575
Eastern front		Eastern Sudanic languages	496.54
World War I	940.414 7		T6—965 4
Eastern Hemisphere	T2—181 1	Eastern Townships	
		(Quebec)	T2—714 6

Ecological chemistry	577.14	Economic concentration	338.8
Ecological communities	577.82	Economic conditions	330.9
Ecological genetics	576.58	urban areas	330.917 32
Ecological heterogeneity	577	Economic cooperation	
Ecological niches	577.82	international economics	337.1
Ecological pyramids	577.16	*see Manual at* 337.3–.9 vs.	
Ecological succession	577.18	337.1	
Ecological toxicology	571.95	Economic development	338.9
Ecologism	320.58	banking	332.153
Ecology	577	domestic	332.28
animals	591.7	international	332.153
ethics	179.1	law	343.074
religion	205.691	natural resources	333.715
Buddhism	294.356 91	*see Manual at* 333.7–.9 vs.	
Christianity	241.691	363.1, 363.73, 577	
Hinduism	294.548 691	production economics	338.9
Judaism	296.369 1	public administration	354.27
microorganisms	579.17	*see Manual at* 300, 320.6 vs.	
physical anthropology	599.95	352–354	
plants	581.7	sociology	306.3
primary education	372.357	Economic ethics	174.4
social theology	201.77	Economic fluctuations	338.54
Christianity	261.88	Economic geography	330.9
Judaism	296.38	Economic geology	553
sociology	304.2	Economic growth	338.9
specific environments	577	macroeconomic policy	339.5
see Manual at 577.3–.7 vs.		production economics	338.9
578.73–.77		Economic history	330.9
see Manual at 333.7–.9 vs.		Economic integration	
363.1, 363.73, 577; *also at*		international economics	337.1
577.3–.7 vs. 579–590		Economic microbiology	579.16
Econometrics	330.015 195	Economic planning	338.9
management decision making	658.403 3	Economic policy	338.9
Economic aid		Economic power (Legislative	
international economics	338.91	bodies)	328.341 3
Economic anthropology	306.3	Economic rent	333.012
Economic assistance		Economic resources	
international economics	338.91	conservation	339.49
international politics	327.111	Economic rights	330
law	343.074	Economic services for workers	331.255
public administration	352.73	personnel management	658.383
foreign aid	353.132 73	Economic situation	330.9
Economic biology	578.6	Economic sociology	306.3
Economic botany	581.6	Economic stabilization	339.5
Economic causes of war	355.027 3	law	343.034
American Revolution	973.311	macroeconomic policy	339.5
World War I	940.311 3	Economic systems	330.12
World War II	940.531 13	Economic zoology	591.6
Economic classes	305.5	Economics	330
	T1—086 2	arts	700.455 3
civil rights	323.322		T3C—355 3
customs	390.1	forecasting	330.011 2
dress	391.01	information systems	025.063 3
relations with government	323.322	international politics	327.111

Edinburgh (Scotland)	941.34
	T2—413 4
Edirne (Turkey)	T2—496 14
Edirne İli (Turkey)	T2—496 14
Edisto River (S.C.)	T2—757 9
Editing	808.027
cinematography	777.55
journalism	070.41
videography	777.55
Editing music	780.149
Edition bookbinding	686.303 4
Editorial cartoons	070.442
Editorial design	744.55
Editorial policy	070.41
Editorial techniques	808.027
Editorials	070.442
Editors	
publishing	070.510 92
Edmonson County (Ky.)	T2—769 752
Edmonton (Alta.)	T2—712 334
Edmund I, King of England	
English history	942.017 2
Edmund II, King of England	
English history	942.017 4
Edmunds County (S.D.)	T2—783 15
Edo (African people)	T5—963 3
Edo language	496.33
	T6—963 3
Edo period (Japan)	952.025
Edo State (Nigeria)	T2—669 32
Edoid languages	496.33
	T6—963 3
Edom	939.464
	T2—394 64
EDP (Computing)	004
Edred, King of England	
English history	942.017 2
EDU (Swiss political party)	324.249 408 2
Education	370
	T1—071
arts	700.455 7
	T3C—355 7
federal aid	379.121
federal control	379.151
intergovernmental	
organizations	
aid	379.128
control	379.154
international aid	379.129
law	344.07
library role	021.24

Education (continued)		
literature		808.803 557
history and criticism		809.933 557
specific literatures	T3B—080 355 7	
history and		
criticism	T3B—093 557	
local control		379.153
local support		379.123
prisoner services		365.666
psychological influence		370.158
psychology		370.15
public administrative support		353.8
see Manual at 371 vs. 353.8,		
371.2, 379		
public policy		379
public support		379.11
sociology		306.43
state aid		379.122
state control		379.152
value		370.13
see also Public education		
see Manual at 371.01–.8 vs.		
372–374, 378		
Education and state		379
Education of employees		370.113
see also Vocational education		
Educational acceleration		371.28
Educational aid		379.11
financial management		371.206
Educational anthropology		306.43
Educational areas		
area planning		711.57
Educational buildings		371.6
architecture		727
construction		690.7
higher education		378.196
institutional housekeeping		647.99
interior decoration		747.87
special education		371.904 5
Educational consortia		
higher education		378.104
Educational counseling		371.422
Educational equalization		379.26
Educational exchanges		370.116
law		344.08
Educational exemptions		
customs duties		382.78
Educational facilities		371.6
see also Educational buildings		
Educational films		
instructional use		371.335 23
journalism		070.18

Educational games	790.1	Edward, the Elder, King of	
instructional use	371.337	England	
recreation	790.1	English history	942.016 5
Educational guidance	371.422	Edward, the Martyr, King of	
Educational institutions	371	England	
accounting	657.832 7	English history	942.017 3
Educational law	344.07	Edward I, King of England	
Educational leave	331.257 64	English history	942.035
labor economics	331.257 64	Edward II, King of England	
personnel management	658.312 2	English history	942.036
Educational media	371.33	Edward III, King of England	
journalism	070.1	English history	942.037
Educational planning	371.207	Edward IV, King of England	
Educational policy	379	English history	942.044
see Manual at 371 vs. 353.8,		Edward V, King of England	
371.2, 379		English history	942.045
Educational psychology	370.15	Edward VI, King of England	
Educational research	370.72	English history	942.053
Educational sociology	306.43	Edward VII, King of Great	
Educational technology	371.33	Britain	
Educational tests	371.26	British history	941.082 3
	T1—076	English history	942.082 3
see Manual at 371.262 vs.		Scottish history	941.108 23
371.264		Edward VIII, King of Great	
Educational therapy		Britain	
medicine	615.851 6	British history	941.084
Educational toys	790.133	English history	942.084
instructional use	371.337	Scottish history	941.108 4
manufacturing technology	688.725	Edwards County (Ill.)	T2—773 791
recreation	790.133	Edwards County (Kan.)	T2—781 782
see also Toys		Edwards County (Tex.)	T2—764 882
Educational vouchers	379.111	Edwards Plateau (Tex.)	T2—764 87
private schools	379.32	Edwy, King of England	
Educationally disadvantaged		English history	942.017 2
students	371.826 94	EEC (Economic organization)	341.242 2
Educators		*see also* European Union	
biography	370.92	Eelgrass	584.74
law	344.078	Eelgrass (Zosteraceae)	584.44
Eduyyot	296.123 4	Eelpouts	597.63
Babylonian Talmud	296.125 4	Eels	597.43
Mishnah	296.123 4	Eels (Freshwater)	597.432
Palestinian Talmud	296.124 4	commercial fishing	639.274 32
Edward, King of England, ca.		cooking	641.692
963–978		culture	639.374 32
English history	942.017 3	food	641.392
Edward, King of England, ca.		sports fishing	799.174 32
1003–1066		Eelworms	592.57
English history	942.019	agricultural pests	632.625 7
Edward, King of England, d. 924		Eerstehoek (South Africa :	
English history	942.016 5	District)	T2—682 78
Edward, the Confessor, King of		Efes (Extinct city)	T2—392 3
England		Effect	
English history	942.019	philosophy	122

Efficiency
agricultural industries	338.16
communications industry	384.041
economics	338.06
military administration	355.687 5
mineral industries	338.26
promotion of	
personnel management	658.314
production management	658.515
public administration	352.375
secondary industries	338.45
transportation services	388.049
Effigial slabs	736.5
Effingham County (Ga.)	T2—758 722
Effingham County (Ill.)	T2—773 796
Efik (African people)	T5—963 642
Efik language	496.364 2
	T6—963 642
Efik literature	896.364 2
EFP (Videography)	777.5
EFTA (Economic organization)	341.242
international commerce	382.914 3
international economics	337.143
law of nations	341.242
Egadi Islands	T2—458 24
Egba (African people)	T5—963 33
Egba language	496.333
	T6—963 33

Egbert, King of England
English history	942.016 1
Egg cells	571.845
Egg decorating	745.594 4
Egg-eating snakes	597.962
Egg-free cooking	641.563 975
Egg-free diet	
health	613.268 75
Egg-free foods	641.309 75
Egg production	636.088 42
Eggplants	641.356 46
botany	583.959 3
commercial processing	664.805 646
cooking	641.656 46
food	641.356 46
garden crop	635.646
Eggs	591.468
animal husbandry	636.088 42
poultry	636.514 2

see Manual at 636.1–.8 vs.
636.088
cooking	641.675
descriptive zoology	591.468
food	641.375
physiology	573.68
processing	637.5

Eglise de Jésus-Christ sur la
terre par le prophète Simon
Kimbangu	289.93

see also Christian
denominations
Egmont National Park	
(N.Z.)	T2—934 82
Ego (Psychology)	155.2
subconscious	154.2
Egoism	
ethical systems	171.9
Egrets	598.34
Egypt	962
	T2—62
ancient	932
	T2—32
Egyptian language	493.1
	T6—931
Egyptian literature	
Arabic	892.7
Egyptian	893.1
Egyptians (Ancient)	T5—931
Egyptians (Modern)	T5—927 62
Ehime-ken (Japan)	T2—523 2
Ehlanzeni District	
Municipality (South	
Africa)	T2—682 73
Ehlers-Danlos syndrome	
medicine	616.77

see also Musculoskeletal
diseases — humans
Eichsfeld (Germany :	
Landkreis)	T2—432 24
Eid al-Adha	297.36
Eid al-Fitr	297.36
Eiders	598.415
Eidetic imagery (Psychology)	153.32
Eidgenössisch-Demokratische	
Union (Swiss political party)	324.249 408 2
Eigenvalues	512.943 6
Eigenvectors	512.943 6
Eigg (Scotland)	T2—411 54
Eighteenth century	909.7
	T1—090 33
Eighth century	909.1
	T1—090 21
Eilean Siar (Scotland)	T2—411 4
Eindhoven (Netherlands)	T2—492 45
Einsiedeln (Switzerland :	
Bezirk)	T2—494 752 4
Einstein geometry	516.374
Einsteinium	546.449
Eire	941.7
	T2—417

Elderly people	305.26
	T1—084 6
see also Older people	
Elders (Plants)	583.987
Eleatic philosophy	182.3
Election (Christian doctrine)	234
Election campaigns	324.9
see also Campaigns (Politics)	
Election districts	328.334 5
Election fraud	324.66
criminology	364.132 4
law	345.023 24
Election law	342.07
Election monitoring	324.65
Election offenses	364.132 4
law	345.023 24
Election officials	324.65
Election procedures	324.6
law	342.07
Election returns	324.9
Election sermons	
Christianity	252.68
Election systems	324.6
Electioneering	324.7
law	342.078
Elections	324
labor unions	331.874
Elective courses	375.004
higher education	378.24
Electoral colleges	324.63
Electoral districts	328.334 5
Electoral law	342.07
Electoral power (Legislative bodies)	328.345 4
Electoral systems	324.63
Electorates (Election districts)	328.334 5
Electrets	537.24
Electric arcs	537.52
Electric automobiles	388.349 3
engineering	629.229 3
transportation services	388.349 3
Electric charge	537.21
Electric circuits	621.319 2
Electric clocks	
technology	681.116
Electric conductivity	537.62
Electric conductors	537.62
Electric control	629.804 3
Electric cooking	641.586
Electric countershock	
medicine	616.128 064 5
Electric currents	
measurement	621.374 4
physics	537.6

Electric defibrillation	
medicine	616.128 064 5
Electric eels	597.48
Electric energy	333.793 2
see also Electric power	
Electric eyes	621.381 542
Electric furnace practice	669.142 4
Electric generators	621.313
Electric heating	621.402 8
buildings	697.045
Electric injuries	
medicine	617.12
Electric lighting	621.32
mining	622.474
ships	623.852
see also Lighting	
Electric locomotives	385.363
engineering	625.263
transportation services	385.363
see also Rolling stock	
Electric meters	621.373
watt-hour usage	621.374 5
Electric motors	621.46
ships	623.872 6
Electric organs (Body parts)	573.97
Electric potential	537.21
measurement	621.374 3
Electric power	333.793 2
area planning	711.8
economics	333.793 2
engineering	621.31
law	343.092 9
measurement	621.374 5
mining	622.48
public administration	354.49
Electric power generation	621.312 1
nuclear steam generation	621.483
Electric power measurement	621.374 6
Electric power systems	
spacecraft	629.474 45
Electric-powered vehicles	388.349 3
engineering	629.229 3
transportation services	388.349 3
Electric propulsion	621.46
automotive	629.250 2
spacecraft	629.475 5
Electric railroads	385
electrification	621.33
see also Railroads	
Electric resistance	537.62
Electric shavers	
manufacturing technology	688.5
Electric shock therapy	
psychiatry	616.891 22

Electrolytic balance	571.75
humans	612.015 22
Electrolytic dissociation	541.372 2
chemical engineering	660.297 22
Electrolytic solutions	541.372
chemical engineering	660.297 2
Electromagnetic engineering	621.3
Electromagnetic engineers	621.309 2
Electromagnetic fields	530.141
effects in semiconductors	537.622 6
Electromagnetic induction	621.34
Electromagnetic interaction	539.754 6
Electromagnetic radiation	539.2
Electromagnetic spectrum	539.2
Electromagnetic theory	530.141
Electromagnetic theory of light	535.14
Electromagnetic wave theory of matter	530.141
Electromagnetic waves	539.2
Electromagnetism	537
astrophysics	523.018
biophysics	571.47
humans	612.014 42
engineering	621.3
Electromagnets	621.34
generator parts	621.316
Electrometallurgy	669.028 4
Electrometers	621.374 3
Electromyography	616.740 754 7
Electron arrangement	
crystallography	548.81
solid-state physics	530.411
Electron beam welding	671.521 4
Electron metallography	669.950 282
Electron microscopes	502.825
biology	570.282 5
manufacturing technology	681.413
Electron microscopy	502.825
biology	570.282 5
Electron-nuclear double resonance	538.362
Electron optics	
physics	537.56
Electron paramagnetic resonance	538.364
Electron paramagnetic resonance spectroscopy	543.67
Electron spectroscopy	543.62
Electron spin resonance	538.364
Electron spin resonance spectroscopy	543.67
Electronic aids	
marine navigation	623.893
Electronic bands	784.6

Electronic books	
bibliographies	011.39
publishing	070.573
Electronic bugging devices	621.389 28
Electronic bulletin boards	004.693
communications services	384.36
sociology	302.231 2
see also Computer communications	
Electronic circuits	621.381 5
Electronic commerce	381.142
law	343.081 142
marketing management	658.872
Electronic communications	
engineering	621.382
Electronic components	621.381 5
Electronic computers	004
see also Computers	
Electronic control	629.89
Electronic data processing	004
	T1—028 5
Electronic digital computers	004
see also Computers	
Electronic distance education	371.358
adult level	374.26
higher education	378.175 8
Electronic eavesdropping devices	621.389 28
Electronic engineering	621.381
Electronic engineers	621.381 092
Electronic field production (Videography)	777.5
Electronic flash photography	778.72
Electronic fuel injection systems	
automobiles	629.253
Electronic funds transfers	332.178
law	346.082 178
Electronic games	794.8
biography	794.809 2
equipment	794.802 84
Electronic interference	621.382 24
Electronic journals	T1—05
see also Serials	
Electronic mail	004.692
communications services	384.34
internal office communications	651.79
sociology	302.231 1
see also Computer communications	
Electronic mail lists	004.693
communications services	384.36
sociology	302.231 2
Electronic media	302.23
advertising	659.14
sociology	302.23

Elements (Chemicals)	546
chemistry	546
mineralogy	549.2
Elephant Butte Reservoir	
(N.M.)	T2—789 62
Elephant fishes	597.47
Elephant seals	599.794
Elephant shrews	599.337
Elephantiasis (Filarial)	
incidence	614.555 2
medicine	616.965 2
see also Communicable	
diseases — humans	
Elephants	599.67
animal husbandry	636.967
big game hunting	799.276 7
conservation technology	639.979 67
resource economics	333.959 67
Elephant's ears (Plants)	584.442
Elephas	599.676
Eleuthera Island (Bahamas)	T2—729 6
Eleutherodactylus	597.875 4
Elevated monorail systems	
engineering	625.44
Elevated rail transit systems	388.42
engineering	625.44
transportation services	388.42
see also Local rail transit	
systems	
Elevations (Architectural design)	729.1
Elevations (Physiography)	551.43
	T2—143
see also Mountains	
Elevator liability insurance	368.56
see also Insurance	
Elevators (Aircraft)	629.134 33
Elevators (Lifts)	
buildings	721.833
architecture	721.833
construction	690.183 3
mining	622.68
Elevenses	642
cooking	641.53
light meals	641.53
main meals	641.54
customs	394.125 3
light meals	394.125 3
main meals	394.125 4
Eleventh century	909.1
	T1—090 21
Elgeyo Marakwet County	
(Kenya)	T2—676 278 7
Elgin (Ont. : County)	T2—713 34

Elgin, James Bruce, Earl	
Indian history	954.035 1
Elgin, Victor Alexander Bruce,	
Earl of	
Indian history	954.035 5
Elian philosophy	183.7
Elis (Greece)	T2—495 27
ancient	T2—388
Elísa Piña (Dominican	
Republic : Province)	T2—729 343
Elites	305.52
	T1—086 21
Elitist systems of government	321.5
Elizabeth, Empress of Russia	
Russian history	947.062
Elizabeth I, Queen of England	
English history	942.055
Elizabeth II, Queen of Great	
Britain	
British history	941.085
English history	942.085
Scottish history	941.108 5
Elizabeth Islands (Mass.)	T2—744 94
Elk (Moose)	599.657
big game hunting	799.276 57
conservation technology	639.979 657
Elk (Wapiti)	599.654 2
animal husbandry	636.294 42
big game hunting	799.276 542
conservation technology	639.979 654 2
Elk County (Kan.)	T2—781 915
Elk County (Pa.)	T2—748 65
Elk Island National Park	
(Alta.)	T2—712 33
Elkhart County (Ind.)	T2—772 81
Elko County (Nev.)	T2—793 16
Elks (Fraternal order)	366.5
biography	366.509 2
Ellenborough, Edward Law, Earl	
of	
Indian history	954.031 5
Ellesmere Island (Nunavut)	T2—719 52
Ellesmere Port and Neston	
(England)	T2—427 14
Ellice Islands	T2—968 2
Elliot (South Africa :	
District)	T2—687 57
Elliotdale (South Africa :	
District)	T2—687 54
Elliott County (Ky.)	T2—769 255
Ellipses	516.152
Elliptic curves	516.352
Elliptic equations	515.353 3
Elliptic functions	515.983

Elliptic geometry	516.9	Emberizidae	598.883
Elliptic operators	515.724 2	Emberizinae	598.883
Ellis County (Kan.)	T2—781 19	Embezzlement	364.162 4
Ellis County (Okla.)	T2—766 155	law	345.026 24
Ellis County (Tex.)	T2—764 281 5	Embioptera	595.737
Ellisras (South Africa :		Embolisms	
District)	T2—682 53	arteries	
Ellsworth County (Kan.)	T2—781 535	medicine	616.135
Ellsworth Land (Antarctic		*see also* Cardiovascular	
regions)	T2—989	diseases — humans	
Elmbridge (England)	T2—422 145	lungs	
Elminidae	595.764 5	medicine	616.249
Elmore County (Ala.)	T2—761 52	*see also* Respiratory tract	
Elmore County (Idaho)	T2—796 29	diseases — humans	
Elms	635.977 364 8	medicine	616.135
botany	583.648	*see also* Cardiovascular	
forestry	634.972 8	diseases — humans	
lumber	674.142	veins	
ornamental arboriculture	635.977 364 8	medicine	616.145
Elocution	808.5	*see also* Cardiovascular	
Elopiformes	597.43	diseases — humans	
Elopomorpha	597.43	Embossing leather	675.25
paleozoology	567.43	Embouchure	784.193 4
Elqui (Chile : Province)	T2—832 32	Embrithopoda	569.62
Elves	398.21	Embroidered rugs	
see also Legendary beings		arts	746.74
Ely (England)	T2—426 56	Embroidery	
Ely, Isle of (England)	T2—426 53	arts	746.44
Emaciation		Embryo	571.86
medicine	616.396	human physiology	612.646
see also Digestive system		Embryo transfer	
diseases — humans		ethics	176.2
Emancipation of slaves	326.8	*see also* Reproduction —	
see also Abolition of slavery		ethics	
Emancipation Proclamation, 1863	973.714	surgery	618.178 059 9
Emanuel County (Ga.)	T2—758 684	Embryology	571.86
Ēmathia (Greece)	T2—495 65	human physiology	612.64
Embalming		Embryophyta	580
customs	393.3	*see also* Plants	
Embankments		Embryotomy	
flood-control engineering	627.42	obstetrical surgery	618.88
road engineering	625.733	Embu County (Kenya)	T2—676 248
structural engineering	624.162	Embumbulu (South Africa :	
Embargoes		District)	T2—684 63
international commerce	382.53	Emden (Lower Saxony,	
see also Import trade		Germany)	T2—435 917
law of nations	341.582	Emeralds	553.86
Embarrassment	152.4	economic geology	553.86
Embassies	327.2	jewelry	739.27
architecture	725.17	mining	622.386
public administration	353.13	Emergency care nursing	616.025
Embedded computer systems	006.22	Emergency legislation	343.01
Embellishments (Music)	781.247	Emergency management	
Emberá (Panama)	T2—728 776	management of enterprises	658.477

Emergency medical services	362.18
law	344.032 18
mental illness	362.204 251
Emergency medicine	616.025
injuries	617.102 6
Emergency planning	363.345 25
public administration	353.95
see also Disasters	
Emergency surgery	617.026
anesthesiology	617.960 42
Emergency telephone services	384.64
see also Telephone	
Emery County (Utah)	T2—792 57
Emery wheels	621.923
Emigrant remittances	332.042 46
Emigration	304.82
Jews	
Holocaust, 1933–1945	940.531 814 2
law	342.082
political science	325.2
social theology	
Christianity	261.838
sociology	304.82
Emigration from Mecca	297.634
Emilia-Romagna (Italy)	T2—454
ancient	T2—372 6
Eminent domain	343.025 2
land economics	333.13
Emission (Physics)	
solid-state physics	530.416
Emission control devices	
automotive	629.252 8
Emission of light	535.3
Emmanuel Philibert, Duke of	
Savoy	
Piedmontese history	945.107
Emmendingen (Germany :	
Landkreis)	T2—434 626
Emmental (Switzerland)	T2—494 549 7
Emmental-Oberaargau	
(Switzerland)	T2—494 549
Emmet County (Iowa)	T2—777 125
Emmet County (Mich.)	T2—774 88
Emmons County (N.D.)	T2—784 78
Emoticons	302.222 3
design	744.2
Emotional illness	362.2
social welfare	362.2
Emotional intelligence	152.4
Emotionally disturbed children	305.908 408 3
	T1—087 4
home care	649.154
see also People with mental	
illness	

Emotionally disturbed people	305.908 4
	T1—087 4
see also Mentally ill people	
Emotions	152.4
adolescents	155.512 4
arts	T3C—353
children	155.412 4
educational psychology	370.153 4
human physiology	612.823 2
literature	808.803 53
history and criticism	809.933 53
specific literatures	T3B—080 353
history and	
criticism	T3B—093 53
philosophy	128.37
Empangeni (South Africa)	T2—684 43
Empathy	
psychology	152.41
Empedoclean philosophy	182.5
Emphysema	
medicine	616.248
see also Respiratory tract	
diseases — humans	
Empididae	595.773
Empires	321.03
	T2—171 2
Empirical remedies	
therapeutics	615.88
Empiricism	146.44
ethics	171.2
Employee absenteeism	331.259 88
labor economics	331.259 88
personnel management	658.314
Employee assistance programs	
(Health and safety)	331.255
personnel management	658.382
see also Employee benefits	
Employee banks	332.37
credit unions	334.22
Employee benefits	331.255
economics	331.255
law	
public employees	342.068 6
personnel management	658.325
	T1—068 3
executives	658.407 25
public administration	352.67
public administration	354.98
Employee development	370.113
see also Vocational education	
Employee discounts	331.255
economics	331.255
personnel management	658.383

Employee dismissal	
economics	331.259 6
employment security	331.259 6
unemployment	331.137
law	344.012 596
personnel management	658.313
public administration	352.69
Employee evaluation	
military personnel	355.330 41
personnel management	658.312 5
executives	658.407 125
libraries	023.9
public administration	352.66
Employee fringe benefits	331.255
see also Employee benefits	
Employee housing	331.255
personnel management	658.383
see also Employee benefits	
Employee malfeasance	
personnel management	658.314
Employee management	658.3
	T1—068 3
see also Personnel management	
Employee morale	
personnel management	658.314
Employee motivation	
personnel management	658.314
executives	658.407 14
Employee organizations	331.88
economics	331.88
personnel management	658.315 3
military personnel	355.33
public administration	352.68
women workers	331.478
Employee orientation	
personnel management	658.312 42
Employee ownership	338.69
labor economics	331.216 49
personnel management	658.322 59
Employee participation in management	331.011 2
personnel management	658.315 2
public administration	352.68
Employee qualifications	331.114
see also Qualifications of employees	
Employee recognition	
personnel management	658.314 2
Employee representation in management	331.011 2
personnel management	658.315 2
Employee retention	
personnel management	658.314

Employee rights	331.011
law	344.010 1
Employee screening	
personnel management	658.311 2
Employee selection	
personnel management	658.311 2
	T1—068 3
libraries	023.9
public administration	352.65
Employee separation	
economics	331.259 6
employment security	331.259 6
unemployment	331.137
law	344.012 596
personnel management	658.313
public administration	352.69
Employee share ownership plans	
personnel management	658.322 59
Employee stock options	331.216 49
labor economics	331.216 49
personnel management	658.322 59
executives	658.407 225 9
Employee stock ownership plans	331.216 49
labor economics	331.216 49
personnel management	658.322 59
Employee theft	364.162 3
law	345.026 23
prevention	
management	658.473
Employee training personnel	
personnel management	658.312 404
Employee turnover	331.126
economics	331.126
personnel management	658.314
Employee utilization	
personnel management	658.312 8
public administration	352.66
Employees	331.11
bonding	
insurance	368.83
economics	331.11
household	640.46
journalism for	070.486
public administration	354.9
social class	305.562
Employer-employee relationships	
personnel management	658.315
libraries	023.9
public administration	352.68
public administration	354.97
Employer-supported services for workers	331.255
armed forces	355.34
economics	331.255

Employer-supported services for workers (continued)	
personnel management	658.38
	T1—068 3
executives	658.407 8
public administration	352.67
Employers' liability	346.031
Employers' liability insurance	368.56
see also Insurance	
Employment	331.125
Employment agencies	331.128
see also Employment services	
Employment conditions	331.2
see also Conditions of employment	
Employment interviewing	650.144
job hunting	650.144
personnel selection	658.311 24
Employment law	344.01
Employment rights	331.011
Employment security	331.259 6
law	344.012 596
public employees	342.068 6
public administration	354.98
Employment services	331.128
economics	331.128
public administration	354.96
social services	362.042 5
disabled people	362.404 84
law	344.032 042 5
mentally disabled people	362.384
people with disabilities	362.404 84
sick people	362.178 6
see also Sheltered employment; Vocational rehabilitation	
Employment subsidies	331.120 424
Employment tests	
personnel selection	658.311 25
Emporia (Va.)	T2—755 573
Emu	598.53
Emulsins	572.756
see also Enzymes	
Emulsions	541.345 14
chemical engineering	660.294 514
pharmaceutical chemistry	615.19
Emydidae	597.925
Ena language	496.394
	T6—963 94
Enactment of legislation	328.37
budgets	352.48
law	342.057
political science	328.37

Enamel (Dental)	
dentistry	617.634
Enameling	
ceramic arts	738.4
glass arts	748.6
Enamels	666.2
architectural decoration	729.6
ceramic arts	738.4
materials science	620.146
technology	666.2
Encampment	
military operations	355.412
military training	355.544
Encaustic painting	751.46
Encephalitis	
medicine	616.832
see also Nervous system diseases — humans	
Enclosures	
land economics	333.2
Encoding	
computer science	005.72
Encounter groups	
social psychology	302.14
social work	361.06
Encryption	652.8
computer science	005.824
Encyclicals	262.91
Encyclopedia yearbooks	030
	T1—03
Encyclopedias	030
	T1—03
Encyclopedists	
biography	030.92
End-blown flutes	788.35
see also Woodwind instruments	
End games (Chess)	794.124
End of the world	
controversial knowledge	001.9
religion	202.3
Christianity	236.9
End of universe	523.19
Endangered languages	306.44
Endangered species	333.952 2
Enderby (B.C.)	T2—711 5
Enderby Land (Antarctic regions)	T2—989
Endive	641.355 5
botany	583.983
food	641.355 5
garden crop	635.55

Energy (continued)	
law	346.046 79
philosophy	118
physics	530
plant management	658.26
public administration	354.4
quantum mechanics	530.12
resource economics	333.79
see Manual at 333.7–.9 vs. 363.6	
Energy budget (Nature)	
ecology	577.13
meteorology	551.525
Energy conservation	333.791 6
architectural consideration	720.472
economics	333.791 6
home economics	644
housing program	363.583
law	346.046 791 6
management of enterprises	658.26
public administration	354.43
see also Energy	
Energy development	333.791 5
law	346.046 791 5
public administration	354.427
see also Energy	
Energy engineering	621.042
buildings	696
Energy flow (Nature)	
ecology	577.13
meteorology	551.525
Energy levels (Nuclear physics)	539.725
Energy management	333.79
business	658.26
	T1—068 2
see also Energy	
Energy metabolism	572.43
human physiology	612.39
see also Digestive system	
Energy phenomena	
solid-state physics	530.416
Energy policy	333.79
see also Energy	
Energy production	333.79
Energy resources	333.79
economic geology	553.2
economics	333.79
extraction	622.33
economics	338.2
law	346.046 79
public administration	354.4
see also Energy	

Energy supply	333.791 1
law	343.092
see also Energy	
Enets language	494.4
	T6—944
Enewetak Atoll (Marshall Islands)	T2—968 3
Enfield (London, England)	T2—421 89
Enga language	499.12
	T6—991 2
Enga Province (Papua New Guinea)	T2—956 3
Engaged people	306.734
	T1—086 523
Engagement (Betrothal)	392.4
customs	392.4
etiquette	395.22
law	346.016 2
music	781.586
social aspects	306.734
Engcobo (South Africa : District)	T2—687 56
Engiadina Bassa/Val Müstair (Switzerland)	T2—494 732 7
Engineering	620
accounting	657.834
effect on natural ecology	577.272
law	343.078 62
primary education	372.358
Engineering analysis	
structures	624.17
Engineering design	620.004 2
Engineering drawing	604.2
Engineering geology	624.151
dams	627.81
railroads	625.122
roads	625.732
Engineering graphics	604.2
Engineering installations (Armed forces)	355.74
Engineering materials	620.11
Engineering mechanics	620.1
Engineering optics	621.36
Engineering services (Armed forces)	358.22
air force	358.47
navy	359.982
Engineering systems	
ships	623.85
Engineers	620.009 2
Engines	621.4
air-cushion vehicles	629.314
aircraft	629.134 35
automotive	629.25

Enteritis	
medicine	616.344
see also Digestive system	
diseases — humans	
Enterobacteriaceae	579.34
Enterobiasis	
incidence	614.555 4
medicine	616.965 4
see also Communicable	
diseases — humans	
Enteropneusta	593.99
paleozoology	563.99
Enterprise information	
integration	005.74
Entertainers	791.092
see Manual at 780.92 and	
791.092	
Entertaining	793.2
etiquette	395.3
indoor amusements	793.2
meal service	642.4
Entertainment advertising	659.131
Entertainment equipment	
automobile	629.277 4
Entertainment films	
performing arts	791.43
Entertainment law	344.099
Entertainment media	
accounting	657.84
Entertainment programs	
radiobroadcasting	
performing arts	791.44
television broadcasting	
performing arts	791.45
Entertainments (Parties)	793.2
cooking	641.568
etiquette	395.3
indoor amusements	793.2
interior decoration	747.93
meal service	642.4
see Manual at 392, 393, 394	
vs. 793.2	
Entertainments (Performances)	790.2
music	781.55
Enthusiasm	
psychology of learning	153.153 3
Entire functions	515.98
Entitlement spending	336.39
Entlebuch (Switzerland :	
Amt)	T2—494 551
Entombment	363.75
customs	393.1
see also Undertaking	
(Mortuary)	

Entomologists	595.709 2
Entomology	595.7
agriculture	632.7
medicine	616.968
Entoprocta	594.66
paleozoology	564.6
Entotrophi	595.724
Entrance examinations (Schools)	371.262
Entrance requirements (Schools)	371.217
Entre Douro e Minho	
(Portugal)	T2—469 1
Entre Ríos (Argentina)	T2—822 1
Entrées (Main dishes)	641.82
Entrées (Side dishes)	641.81
Entremont (Switzerland)	T2—494 796 6
Entrepreneurial management	658.421
Entrepreneurs	338.040 92
	T1—086 22
executive management	658.421
social class	305.554
see Manual at 300 vs. 600;	
also at 338.092	
Entrepreneurship	338.04
income distribution	339.21
management	658.421
production economics	338.04
Entropy	536.73
Enugu State (Nigeria)	T2—669 49
Enumeration (Combinatorial	
analysis)	511.62
Enumerative geometry	516.35
Enuresis	
medicine	616.849
see also Nervous system	
diseases — humans	
pediatrics	618.928 49
Environment	333.7
architectural consideration	720.47
arts	700.455 3
	T3C—355 3
economics	333.7
ethics	179.1
religion	205.691
Buddhism	294.356 91
Christianity	241.691
Hinduism	294.548 691
Judaism	296.369 1
literature	808.803 553
history and criticism	809.933 553
specific literatures	T3B—080 355 3
history and	
criticism	T3B—093 553
primary education	372.357
public administration	354.3

Equestrian sports (continued)
  literature
    history and criticism 809.933 579
    specific literatures T3B—080 357 9
      history and
        criticism T3B—093 579
    motion pictures 791.436 579
    physical fitness 613.711
    public administrative support 353.78
    safety 363.14
      public administration 353.97
      techniques 798.028 9
    sociology 306.483
    television programs 791.456 579
    see also Sports
Equestrians 798.092
Equidae 599.665
  animal husbandry 636.1
Equilibrium
  astronomy 521
  chemical engineering 660.299 2
  macroeconomic policy 339.5
Equipment T1—028 4
  educational use T1—078
  local Christian churches 254.7
  management 658.27
    T1—068 2
    public administration 352.55
  office services 651.2
  procurement 658.72
  teaching aids 371.33
    T1—078
Equipment research
  production management 658.577
Equipment sheds
  agricultural use 631.25
Equisetales 587.2
  paleobotany 561.72
Equisetum 587.2
Equitable remedies 347.077
Equity 346.004
Equivalent projections
  maps 526.85
Equus 599.665
Érable (Quebec) T2—714 575
Eragrosteae 584.92
Erath County (Tex.) T2—764 551
Erbium
  chemistry 546.418
Eremitical religious orders 255.02
  church history 271.02
  women 255.902
    church history 271.902
Erethizontidae 599.359 74

Eretrian philosophy (Ancient) 183.7
Erewash (England) T2—425 18
Erfurt (Germany) T2—432 248
Erfurt (Germany : Bezirk) T2—432 24
Ergative constructions 415
  specific languages T4—5
Ergodic theory 515.48
Ergonomics 620.82
  computers 004.019
  engineering 621.398 4
Erhard, Ludwig
  German history 943.087 6
Ericaceae 583.93
  botany 583.93
Ericales 583.93
Erie, Lake T2—771 2
  Ohio T2—771 2
  Ontario T2—713 3
Erie County (N.Y.) T2—747 96
Erie County (Ohio) T2—771 22
Erie County (Pa.) T2—748 99
Erik XIV, King of Sweden
  Swedish history 948.503 22
Erinaceidae 599.332
Erinaceus 599.332 2
Eriocaulaceae 584.96
Eriocaulales 584.96
Eritrea 963.5
  T2—635
Eritrean Orthodox Church 281.6
  see also Eastern churches
Eritreans T5—928 9
Erlangen (Germany) T2—433 22
Ermelo (South Africa :
  District) T2—682 78
Ermine 599.766 2
Erodiums 635.933 72
  botany 583.72
  floriculture 635.933 72
Erogeneity 155.31
Erosion 551.302
  agriculture 631.45
  by glaciers 551.313
  by water 551.352
  by wind 551.372
  engineering 627.5
  geology 551.302
  see Manual at 551.302–.307
    vs. 551.35
Erotetic logic 160.119
Erotic literature 808.803 538
  history and criticism 809.933 538
  specific literatures T3B—080 353 8
    history and criticism T3B—093 538

Erotic painting	757.8
Erotica	
arts	700.453 8
	T3C—353 8
literature	808.803 538
history and criticism	809.933 538
specific literatures	T3B—080 353 8
history and criticism	T3B—093 538
Errachidia (Morocco : Province)	T2—645
Error analysis (Mathematics)	511.43
Error-correcting codes	005.717
Error correctors	
automation engineering	629.831 5
Error detectors	
automation engineering	629.831 5
Errors	001.96
logic	165
psychology of perception	153.74
Errors and omissions insurance	368.564
see also Insurance	
Erudition	001.2
Eruptive variables	523.844 6
Eruvin	296.123 2
Babylonian Talmud	296.125 2
Mishnah	296.123 2
Palestinian Talmud	296.124 2
Erwinia	579.34
Erysipelas	
incidence	614.595 23
medicine	616.523
see also Skin diseases — humans	
Erysiphales	579.567
Erythroblastosis fetalis	
pediatrics	618.921 5
perinatal medicine	618.326 1
see also Cardiovascular diseases — humans	
Erythrocyte count	
human physiology	612.111 2
Erythrocyte disorders	
medicine	616.151
see also Cardiovascular diseases — humans	
Erythrocytes	573.153 6
human histology	612.111
human physiology	612.111
medicine	616.151
Erythroxylaceae	583.69

Erzgebirge (Czech Republic and Germany)	T2—437 15
Czech Republic	T2—437 15
Germany	T2—432 16
Erzincan İli (Turkey)	T2—566 74
ancient	T2—394 2
Erzurum İli (Turkey)	T2—566 24
ancient	T2—395 5
Es Semara (Morocco : Province)	T2—648
Esaki diodes	621.381 522
Escalators	621.867 6
architecture	721.832
building construction	690.183 2
Escalloniaceae	583.984
Escalloniales	583.984
Escallonias	583.984
Escambia County (Ala.)	T2—761 265
Escambia County (Fla.)	T2—759 99
Escape equipment	
aircraft	629.134 386
military aircraft	623.746 049
Escapements	
clockwork	681.112
Escapes	365.641
Eschatology	202.3
Buddhism	294.342 3
Christianity	236
Hinduism	294.523
Islam	297.23
Judaism	296.33
philosophy of religion	218
Escherichia	579.342
Escherichia coli infections	
incidence	614.57
medicine	616.926
see also Communicable diseases — humans	
Eschrichtidae	599.522
Escrows	346.043 73
Escuintla (Guatemala : Dept.)	T2—728 163
Esdras (Deuterocanonical book)	229.1
Eşfahān (Iran : Province)	T2—559 5
Eshowe (South Africa : District)	T2—684 43
Eskimo	305.897 1
	979.800 497 1
	T5—971
Eskimo-Aleut languages	497.1
	T6—971
Eskimo dogs	636.73
Eskimo languages	497.1
	T6—971

Eskimo literature	897.1
Eskişehir İli (Turkey)	T2—563 5
ancient	T2—392 6
Esmeralda County (Nev.)	T2—793 35
Esmeraldas (Ecuador :	
Province)	T2—866 35
Esocidae	597.59
Esophageal diseases	
medicine	616.32
see also Digestive system	
diseases — humans	
Esophagus	573.359
biology	573.359
human anatomy	611.32
human physiology	612.315
medicine	616.32
surgery	617.548
see also Digestive system	
Esoteric societies	366
Esox	597.59
ESP (Extrasensory perception)	133.8
Espaillat (Dominican	
Republic : Province)	T2—729 362
Espartos	584.926
botany	584.926
Esperance (W.A.)	T2—941 7
Esperance National Park	
(W.A.)	T2—941 7
Esperanto language	499.992
	T6—999 92
Esperanto literature	899.992
Espionage	327.12
armed forces	355.343 2
criminology	364.131
criminal law	345.023 1
ethics	172.4
see also Political ethics	
industrial management	658.472
international politics	327.12
labor economics	331.894
law of war	341.63
public administration	353.17
social theology	201.727
Christianity	261.87
see also International	
relations — social	
theology	
United States	327.127 3
history	327.127 300 9
Espírito Santo (Brazil :	
State)	T2—815 2
Esquimalt (B.C.)	T2—711 28
ESR (Magnetic resonance)	538.364

Essaouira (Morocco :	
Province)	T2—646 4
Essayists (Literature)	809.4
collected biography	809.4
specific literatures	T3B—400 9
individual biography	T3A—4
Essays	080
see Manual at 080 vs. 800;	
also at 081–089	
Essays (Literature)	808.84
criticism	809.4
theory	808.4
history and criticism	809.4
rhetoric	808.4
specific literatures	T3B—4
individual authors	T3A—4
Essen (Germany)	T2—435 538
Essence (Philosophy)	111.1
Essences (Flavorings)	641.338 2
see also Flavorings	
Essenes	296.814
Essential hypertension	
medicine	616.132
see also Cardiovascular	
diseases — humans	
Essential oils	
chemical engineering	661.806
chemistry	547.71
Essequibo Islands-West	
Demerara Region	
(Guyana)	T2—881 3
Essex (England)	T2—426 7
Essex (Ont. : County)	T2—713 31
Essex County (N.J.)	T2—749 31
Essex County (N.Y.)	T2—747 53
Essex County (Va.)	T2—755 34
Essex County (Vt.)	T2—743 25
Essonne (France)	T2—443 65
Estado Novo (Portugal)	946.904 2
Estate planning	332.024 016
law	346.052
tax law	343.053
Estate sales	381.19
Estate tax	336.276
law	343.053
Estate wines	641.22
commercial processing	663.2
Estates (Grounds)	
landscape architecture	712.6
Estates (Inheritance)	
accounting	657.47
administration	346.056
Estcourt (South Africa :	
District)	T2—684 9

Ethiopian Church	281.75	Ethnic groups (continued)	
see also Eastern churches		military troops	
Ethiopian languages	492.8	World War I	940.403
	T6—928	World War II	940.540 4
Ethiopian literatures	892.8	physical ethnology	599.97
Ethiopian Orthodox Tewahedo		psychology	155.82
Church	281.75	*see Manual at* 155.89 vs.	
see also Eastern churches		155.84	
Ethiopian War, 1895–1896	963.043	relations with government	323.11
Ethiopians	T5—928	religion	200.89
Ethiopic language	492.81	Christianity	270.089
	T6—928 1	social welfare	362.84
Biblical texts	220.46	public administration	353.533 9
Ethiopic literature	892.81	specific groups	353.534
Ethnic cleansing		*see Manual at* T5—0	
sociology	304.663	Ethnic minorities	305.8
Ethnic clubs	369.3	*see also* Ethnic groups	
Ethnic cooking	641.592	Ethnic nationalism	320.54
Ethnic differences		Ethnic relations	305.8
psychology	155.82	Ethnobotany	581.63
Ethnic groups	305.8	Ethnographers	305.800 92
	T1—089	Ethnography	305.8
arts	T3C—352 9	Ethnolinguistics	306.44
civil and human rights	323.11	Ethnological jurisprudence	340.52
law	342.087 3	Ethnologists	305.800 92
law of nations	341.485 3	Ethnology	305.8
collected biography	T1—092 3	physical anthropology	599.97
criminology	364.34	Ethnomusicology	780.89
education	371.829	Ethnopsychology	155.82
geographic treatment	T1—089 009	adolescents	155.508 9
see Manual at T1—09 vs.		children	155.457
T1—089		late adulthood	155.670 89
government programs	353.533 9	Ethology (Animal behavior)	591.5
specific groups	353.534	Etiology	
history	909.04	medicine	616.071
specific places	930–990	*see Manual at* 616.1–.9	
journalism for	070.484	Etiquette	395
labor	331.6	armed forces	355.133 6
economics	331.6	arts	700.455 9
law	344.016		T3C—355 9
personnel management	658.300 89	Etna, Mount (Italy)	T2—458 13
legal status	346.013 089	Etobicoke (Toronto, Ont.)	T2—713 541
constitutional law	342.087 3	Etorofu Island	T2—524
private law	346.013 089	Etowah County (Ala.)	T2—761 67
United States	346.730 130 89	Etruria	937.5
legal systems	340.52		T2—375
see Manual at 340.52		Etruria (Kingdom)	945.508 2
literature	808.898	Etruscan architecture	722.62
history and criticism	809.8	Etruscan language	499.94
specific literatures	T3B—080 8		T6—999 4
history and		Etruscan sculpture	733.4
criticism	T3B—098	Etruscans	937.501
see Manual at T3C—93–99,			T5—999 4
T3C—9174 vs. T3C—8			

Europe, Southeastern	949.6	Eustachian tube diseases	617.86
	T2—496	*see also* Ear diseases —	
ancient	939.8	humans	
	T2—398	Eustachian tubes	
Europe, Southern	940	human anatomy	611.85
	T2—4	human physiology	612.854
ancient	938	medicine	617.86
	T2—38	Euthanasia	
Europe, Western	940	ethics	179.7
	T2—4	religion	205.697
ancient	936	*see also* Death — ethics	
	T2—36	law	344.041 97
European Arctic seawaters	551.461 324	Eutheria	599
	T2—163 24	Eutrophication	577.631 58
European bison	599.643	Euvoia (Greece)	T2—495 15
European Commission	341.242 226	Evaluation of employee training	
European Common Market	341.242 2	personnel management	658.312 404
see also European Union		Evaluation research	001.4
European Community	341.242 2		T1—072
see also European Union		Evaluations of products and	
European Convention on Human		services	T1—029
Rights, 1950	342.240 850 261	Evangelical and Reformed	
European Court of Human Rights	342.240 850 269	Church	285.734
European Economic Community	341.242 2	*see also* Reformed Church	
see also European Union		(American Reformed)	
European federation	321.040 94	Evangelical churches	289.95
European Free Trade Association	341.242	Evangelical Congregational	
international commerce	382.914 3	Church	289.9
international economics	337.143	Evangelical Free Church of	
law of nations	341.242	America	289.95
European hedgehog	599.332 2	*see also* Christian	
European Investment Bank	332.153 4	denominations	
European literature	808.899 4	Evangelical Lutheran Church	284.131 2
European Parliament	341.242 224	*see also* Lutheran church	
European philosophy	190	Evangelical Lutheran Church in	
European polecat	599.766 28	America	284.135
European theater (World War II)	940.542 1	*see also* Lutheran church	
European Union	341.242 2	Evangelical Lutheran Synodical	
commerce	382.914 2	Conference of North America	284.132
economics	337.142	*see also* Lutheran church	
law of nations	341.242 2	Evangelical theology	230.046 24
public administration	352.114	Evangelical United Brethren	
European wildcat	599.752 6	Church	289.9
Europeans	T5—09	Evangelicalism	270.82
Europium		independent denominations	289.95
chemistry	546.415	Protestantism	280.4
Eurosids I	583.6	Evangeline Parish (La.)	T2—763 57
Eurosids II	583.7	Evangelische Kirche in	
Eurotiales	579.565	Deutschland	284.094 3
Euryapsida	567.93	*see also* Lutheran church	
Eurylaimidae	598.822	Evangelische Volkspartei der	
Eurypterida	565.493	Schweiz	324.249 408 2
Eurytania (Greece)	T2—495 15	Evangelism	269.2
ancient	T2—383	Evangelistic sermons	252.3

Evil spirits	133.423
arts	700.482 021 6
religion	202.16
see also Legendary beings	
Evolutes	516.362
Evolution	576.8
animals	591.38
biochemistry	572.38
biology	576.8
ethical systems	171.7
humans	599.938
microorganisms	579.138
molecular biology	572.838
philosophy	116
plants	581.38
see Manual at 576.8 vs. 560	
Evolution (Mathematics)	512.923
Evolution (Social change)	303.4
Evolution of stars	523.88
Evolution versus creation	202.4
Christianity	231.765 2
see Manual at 231.7652 vs.	
213, 500, 576.8	
Judaism	296.34
philosophy of religion	213
Evolutionary computation	006.382 3
Evolutionary cycles	576.84
Evolutionary genetics	572.838
Evolutionary programming	
computer science	006.382 3
Evolutionary psychology	155.7
Evolutionism	
philosophy	146.7
Evora (Portugal : District)	T2—469 52
EVP (Swiss political party)	324.249 408 2
Evreĭskaia avtonomnaia	
oblast´ (Russia)	T2—577
Evritania (Greece)	T2—495 15
Evros (Greece)	T2—495 7
Ewe (African people)	T5—963 374
Ewe language	496.337 4
	T6—963 374
Ewe literature	896.337 4
Ewenki (Asian people)	T5—941
Ewondo language	496.396
	T6—963 96
Ex-convicts	364.8
labor economics	331.51
Examination of witnesses	347.075
criminal investigation	363.254
criminal law	345.075

Examinations (Educational tests)	371.26
	T1—076
teacher-prepared tests	371.271
see Manual at 371.262 vs.	
371.264	
Excavating machinery	621.865
Excavation	624.152
archaeological technique	930.102 83
mining	622.2
road engineering	625.733
Excelsior	674.84
Excelsior (South Africa :	
District)	T2—685 1
Exceptional children	
education	371.9
home care	649.15
psychology	155.45
Exceptional students	371.9
Excess liability insurance	368.5
see also Insurance	
Excess profits tax	336.243 2
law	343.052 44
Exchange buildings	
architecture	725.25
Exchange rates	
foreign exchange	332.456
Exchanges	
library acquisitions	025.26
library-government relations	021.8
Excise tax	336.271
law	343.055 3
public administration	352.44
public finance	336.271
Excitation	
solid-state physics	530.416
Excited states	
solid-state physics	530.416
Excitons	
solid-state physics	530.416
Excluded classes	305.568
	T1—086 94
Exclusionary rule	347.062
Excommunication	
Judaism	296.67
Excretion	573.49
animals	573.49
biology	573.49
human physiology	612.46
plants	575.79
see also Urinary system	
Excretory organs	573.49
see also Urinary system	
Excretory system	573.49
see also Urinary system	

Exile
  arts (continued)
    literature   808.803 552
      history and criticism   809.933 552
      specific literatures   T3B—080 355 2
      history and
        criticism   T3B—093 552
Exiles   305.906 914
           T1—086 914
  social welfare   362.87
  women
    social welfare   362.839 814
  young people
    social welfare   362.779 14
  see also Refugees
Existence   111.1
Existence of God   212.1
  Christianity   231
  comparative religion   202.11
  Judaism   296.311
  philosophy of religion   212.1
Existential psychology   150.192
Existentialism   142.78
  arts   T3C—384
  ethics   171.2
  literature   808.803 84
    history and criticism   809.933 84
    specific literatures   T3B—080 384
    history and
      criticism   T3B—093 84
Existentialist theology   230.046
Exmoor (England)   T2—423 85
Exobasidiales   579.59
Exocoetidae   597.66
Exocrine glands   571.79
  human physiology   612.4
Exocrine secretions
  human physiology   612.4
Exodontics   617.66
Exodus (Bible)   222.12
Exogamy   306.82
Exogenous processes (Geology) 551.3
Exopterygota   595.73
Exorcism
  occultism   133.427
  religious rite   203.8
    Christianity   265.94
Exorcists   200.92
  biography   200.92
  religious role and function   206.1
  see Manual at 200.92 and
    201–209, 292–299

Exoskeleton   591.477
  descriptive zoology   591.477
  physiology   573.77
Exothermic reactions   541.362
  chemical engineering   660.296 2
Exotic species   333.952 3
Expanding universe theories 523.18
Expanding vaults   721.45
  architecture   721.45
  construction   690.145
Expansion (Effect of heat) 536.41
Expansion of enterprises
  executive management   658.406
Expansions (Mathematics) 511.4
Expatriates   305.906 91
          T1—086 91
  social welfare   362.899 1
  women
    social welfare   362.839 81
  young people
    social welfare   362.779 1
Expatriation   323.64
Expectant mothers
  employment economics   331.44
Expectant parents' handbooks 649.102 42
  medicine   618.24
Expectation
  probabilities   519.287
  statistical mathematics   519.54
Expectorants
  pharmacokinetics   615.72
Expeditionary forces   355.352
Expense statements
  financial management   658.151 2
Expenses
  financial management   658.155
Experience
  philosophical anthropology 128.4
  religion   204.2
    see also Religious
      experience
Experiential design   744.85
Experiment in International
  Living   373.011 62
Experimental animals   616.027
  care and maintenance   636.088 5
  medicine   616.027
Experimental arts   700.411
          T3C—11
Experimental biology   570.724
Experimental biomedical
  research   610.724
Experimental design
  (Mathematics)   519.57

Experimental literary works	808.887
history and criticism	809.987
specific literatures	T3B—807
individual authors	T3A—8
Experimental medicine	616.027
ethics	174.28
see also Medical ethics	
Experimental research	001.434
	T1—072 4
public administrative support	352.745
see Manual at	
T1—07201–07209 vs.	
T1—0721	
Experimental schools	371.04
higher education	378.03
Experimentation on animals	
ethics	179.4
see also Animals —	
treatment of — ethics	
medicine	616.027
Expert system shells	006.33
Expert systems	006.33
Expert testimony	347.067
criminal law	345.067
Expert witnesses	347.067
criminal law	345.067
Expertizing	
antiques	745.102 88
arts	702.88
ceramic arts	738.18
paintings	751.62
Experts	001
management use	658.46
Exploding wire phenomena	537.5
Explorations	910.9
geography	910.9
recreation	796.52
science	508
see Manual at 629.43, 629.45	
vs. 559.9, 919.904,	
910.919; *also at* 913–919	
Explorers	910.92
Explorers (Boy Scouts)	369.435
Explosion	541.361
chemical engineering	660.296 1
chemistry	541.361
Explosion insurance	368.12
see also Insurance	
Explosions	
mine safety engineering	622.82
social services	363.179 8
Explosive technologists	662.209 2

Explosives	662.2
control	
public administration	353.36
law	344.047 2
military engineering	623.452
public safety	363.179 8
see also Hazardous materials	
Exponents	512.922
algebra	512.922
arithmetic	513.22
Export controls	382.64
law	343.087 8
Export credit	332.742
law	346.073
Export-Import Bank of the	
United States	332.154 097 3
Export licensing	382.64
law	343.087 8
Export marketing	382.6
commerce	382.6
management	658.84
Export policy	382.63
Export restrictions	382.64
Export subsidies	382.63
Export tax	382.7
public finance	336.263
see also Customs (Tariff)	
Export trade	382.6
commerce	382.6
law	343.087 8
management	658.84
promotion	382.63
public administration	354.74
Exposition (Rhetoric)	808.066
speaking	808.5
writing	808.066
Expositions	907.4
see also Exhibitions	
Expository writing	808.066
Exposure meters	771.37
Exposure of the dead	
customs	393.4
Express freight services	388.044
air	387.744
bus	388.322 2
canal	386.404 24
ferry	386.6
inland waterway	386.244
lake	386.544
marine	387.544
railroad	385.23
special purpose	385.5
river	386.354
truck	388.324

Eyeglasses	
customs	391.44
manufacturing technology	681.411
optometry	617.752 2
Eyelid diseases	
ophthalmology	617.771
see also Eye diseases —	
humans	
Eyelids	
human physiology	612.847
ophthalmology	617.771
Eyes	573.88
anesthesiology	617.967 7
animal physiology	573.88
descriptive zoology	591.44
mammals	599.144
diseases	573.883 9
see also Eye diseases	
human anatomy	611.84
human physiology	612.84
injuries	617.713
ophthalmology	617.7
personal care	646.726
surgery	617.71
Eyre, Lake (S. Aust.)	T2—942 38
Eyre Peninsula (S. Aust.)	T2—942 38
Ezekiel (Biblical book)	224.4
Ezra (Biblical book)	222.7

F

F region (Ionosphere)	538.767 4
Fabaceae	583.63
Fabales	583.63
Fabian socialism	335.14
political ideology	320.531 2
Fabids	583.6
Fables	
folklore	398.24
Fabliaux	808.813
history and criticism	809.13
specific literatures	T3B—103
individual authors	T3A—1
Faboideae	583.63
Fabric furnishings	645.046
commercial technology	684.3
see also Furnishings	
Fabricating equipment	621.9
Fabrics	677.028 64
home economics	646.11
home furnishings	645.046
home sewing	646.11
textile technology	677.028 64
see also Textiles	

Facades	
architectural design	729.1
Face	
anthropometry	599.948
human anatomy	611.92
human physiology	612.92
personal care	646.726
regional medicine	617.52
surgery	617.520 59
Face perception	153.758
Facelift	617.520 592
Facial bones	
fractures	
medicine	617.156
human anatomy	611.716
human physiology	612.751
medicine	616.71
surgery	617.471
Facial recognition	
biometric identification	
computer science	006.248 399 5
Facility management	658.2
see also Plant management	
Facsimile transmission	384.14
engineering	621.382 35
postal service	383.141
see also Postal service	
wireless	384.524
see also Telegraphy	
Facsimiles	
bibliographies	011.47
Fact books	030
Fact finding	001.4
	T1—072
legislative activity	328.345 2
public administration	352.743
maladministration	353.46
public safety	363.106 5
Factitious disorders	
medicine	616.858 6
see also Mental disorders	
Factor algebras	512.57
Factor analysis	519.535 4
Factor proportions	
economics	338.512
Factorial experiment designs	519.57
Factorial series	515.243
Factories	
architecture	725.4
economics	338.476 7
institutional housekeeping	647.964
landscape architecture	712.7
manufacturing technology	670
organization of production	338.65

Falangism	335.6
economics	335.6
political ideology	320.533
Falasha	T5—924
Falcón (Venezuela)	T2—872 4
Falconidae	598.96
Falconiformes	598.9
paleozoology	568.9
Falconry	799.232
Falcons	598.96
animal husbandry	636.686 9
conservation technology	639.978 96
resource economics	333.958 96
Faliscan languages	479.4
	T6—794
Falkirk (Scotland)	T2—413 18
Falkland Islands	997.11
	T2—971 1
Falkland Islands War	997.110 24
Fall	508.2
music	781.524 6
see also Seasons	
Fall of humankind	233.14
Fall River County (S.D.)	T2—783 97
Fallacies	001.96
logic	165
Falling bodies	531.14
solid mechanics	531.5
Fallon County (Mont.)	T2—786 35
Fallopian tube diseases	
gynecology	618.12
see also Female genital	
diseases — humans	
Fallopian tubes	
gynecology	618.12
human anatomy	611.65
human physiology	612.625
Fallow deer	599.655
animal husbandry	636.294 5
Fallowing	631.581 2
Falls Church (Va.)	T2—755 293
Falls County (Tex.)	T2—764 286
False arrest	346.033 4
False chameleons	597.954 8
False coral snake (Aniliidae)	597.967
False coral snakes (Colubridae)	597.962
False Dmitri I	
Russian history	947.045
False Dmitri II	
Russian history	947.045
False impersonation	364.163 3
law	345.026 33
False imprisonment	346.033 4
False killer whales	599.53

False memory syndrome	
adult child abuse victims	
psychotherapy	616.858 223 906 51
adult child sexual abuse	
victims	
psychotherapy	616.858 369 065 1
False scorpions	595.47
Falsetto voices	782.86
choral and mixed voices	782.86
single voices	783.86
Falster (Denmark)	T2—489 3
Families	306.85
applied psychology	158.24
government programs	353.533 1
histories	929.2
see Manual at 929.2	
influence on crime	364.253
law	346.015
psychological influence	155.924
recreation	790.191
indoor	793.019 1
outdoor	796
religion	
guides to life	204.41
Christianity	248.4
see also Family life —	
religion	
pastoral theology	206.1
Christianity	259.1
social theology	201.7
Christianity	261.835 85
worship	204.3
Christianity	249
Judaism	296.45
social welfare	362.82
law	344.032 82
public administration	353.533 1
sociology	306.85
Families of clergy	
Christianity	
pastoral theology	253.22
Families of victims of terrorism	
social welfare	362.889 317 3
Family	306.85
system of government	321.1
see also Families	
Family abuse	362.829 2
sociology	306.87
see also Family violence	
Family behavior (Animals)	591.563
Family budgets	
macroeconomics	339.41

Fantasy fiction	808.838 766
history and criticism	809.387 66
specific literatures	T3B—308 766
individual authors	T3A—3
Fantasy games	793.93
computerized games	793.93
Fantasy sports	794.9
Fante (African people)	T5—963 385
Fante language	496.338 5
	T6—963 385
Fante literature	896.338 5
Fanti (African people)	T5—963 385
Fanti language	496.338 5
	T6—963 385
Fanti literature	896.338 5
Far East	950
	T2—5
Far East international	
organizations	341.247 3
Far North District (N.Z.)	T2—931 3
Far West Rand (South	
Africa)	T2—682 22
Farallones de Cali National	
Park (Colombia)	T2—861 52
Farces	792.23
literature	808.825 232
history and criticism	809.252 32
specific literatures	T3B—205 232
individual authors	T3A—2
stage presentation	792.23
Fareham (England :	
Borough)	T2—422 775
Fares	
transportation services	388.049
Fargo (N.D.)	T2—784 13
Faribault County (Minn.)	T2—776 22
Farm accounting	657.863
Farm buildings	631.2
architecture	725.37
construction	690.537
use	631.2
Farm costs	338.13
Farm cottages	
architecture	728.6
Farm forestry	634.99
Farm income	338.13
Farm investment	338.13
Farm law	343.076
Farm loans	332.71
law	346.073
Farm manure	631.861
Farm-owner insurance	368.096
see also Insurance	
Farm pests	632.6

Farm prices	338.13
Farm produce	338.17
see also Agricultural products	
Farm production quotas	
law	343.076 1
Farm profits	338.13
Farm property	333.76
resource economics	333.76
taxation	336.225
Farm roads	
use	631.28
Farm tenancy	333.335 53
economics	333.335 53
law	346.043 48
Farm tractors	629.225 2
see also Tractors	
Farm valuation	
tax economics	336.225
Farmers	630.92
	T1—088 63
social group	305.963
Farmers' markets	381.41
Farmers parties	324.218
Farmhouses	
agriculture	631.21
architecture	728.6
construction	690.86
Farming	630
Farmowner-ranchowner	
insurance	368.096
see also Insurance	
Farms	630
animal husbandry	636.01
Faro (Game)	795.42
Faro (Portugal : District)	T2—469 6
Faroe Islands	949.15
	T2—491 5
Faroese language	439.699
	T6—396 99
Faroese literature	839.699
Faroese people	T5—396 9
Farquhar Islands	
(Seychelles)	T2—696
Fārs (Iran)	T2—557 2
Farsi language	491.55
	T6—915 5
Farsi literature	891.55
Faruk I, King of Egypt	
Egyptian history	962.052
Fasād (Islamic law)	340.591 2
Fasciae	
human anatomy	611.74
human physiology	612.75
medicine	616.75

Fatty tissues	571.57	Fear of flying	
human histology	611.018 27	medicine	616.852 25
Fatwas	340.592 2	Feast days	
specific jurisdictions	348.3–.9	Christianity	263.9
Faucets	621.84	cooking	641.566
Faulk County (S.D.)	T2—783 213	devotional literature	242.3
Faulkner County (Ark.)	T2—767 74	sermons	252.6
Fault-tolerant computing	004.2	cooking	641.567
engineering	621.392	customs	394.2
firmware	005.18	religion	203.6
programming	005.13	*see also* Holy days	
Faults (Geology)	551.872	Feather products	
Fauna	590	manufacturing technology	679.47
see also Animals		Featherbedding	331.889 6
Fauquier County (Va.)	T2—755 275	Feathers	598.147
Fauresmith (South Africa :		animal husbandry	636.088 45
District)	T2—685 7	nonpoultry	636.61
Fauvism	709.040 43	poultry	636.514 5
painting	759.064 3	descriptive zoology	598.147
sculpture	735.230 443	physiology	573.597
Fava beans	641.356 51	Features	
see also Broad beans		journalism	070.44
Fax (Transmission)	384.14	Fecal incontinence	
see also Facsimile transmission		medicine	616.35
Fax directories	910.25	*see also* Digestive system	
see Manual at T1—025 vs.		diseases — humans	
T1—029		Feces	
Fayette County (Ala.)	T2—761 87	human physiology	612.36
Fayette County (Ga.)	T2—758 426	Federal administration	351
Fayette County (Ill.)	T2—773 797	Federal aid	
Fayette County (Ind.)	T2—772 623	education	379.121
Fayette County (Iowa)	T2—777 35	higher education	379.121 4
Fayette County (Ky.)	T2—769 47	law	344.076 84
Fayette County (Ohio)	T2—771 813	private schools	379.32
Fayette County (Pa.)	T2—748 84	Federal aid to preschool	
Fayette County (Tenn.)	T2—768 21	education	379.121 22
Fayette County (Tex.)	T2—764 251	Federal aid to primary education	379.121 2
Fayette County (W. Va.)	T2—754 71	Federal Capital Territory	
Faysal I, King of Iraq		(Nigeria)	T2—669 68
Iraqi history	956.704 1	Federal cases	
Faysal II, King of Iraq		United States	348.734
Iraqi history	956.704 2	Federal courts (United States)	347.732
Fayyūm (Egypt : Province)	T2—622	reports	348.734 1
FDP.The Liberals (Swiss political		Federal District (Brazil)	T2—817 4
party)	324.249 406	Federal District (Mexico)	T2—725 3
Fear	152.46	Federal government	321.02
arts	T3C—353	law	342.042
literature	808.803 53	public administration	351
history and criticism	809.933 53	Federal law (Treatises)	340
specific literatures	T3B—080 353	United States	349.73
history and		Federal laws	348.02
criticism	T3B—093 53	United States	348.732
social psychology	302.17	Federal Party (U.S.)	324.273 22
		Federal-provincial relations	321.023

Female genital diseases	
humans (continued)	
incidence	614.599 21
medicine	618.1
nursing	618.102 31
pediatrics	618.920 98
social services	362.198 1
surgery	618.105 9
Female genital organs	573.66
Female genital system	573.66
anesthesiology	617.968 1
biology	573.66
gynecology	618.1
human anatomy	611.65
human physiology	612.62
surgery	618.105 9
Female goddesses	202.114
see also Gods and goddesses	
Female prostitution	306.742
Female reproductive system	573.66
animals	573.66
plants	575.66
see also Female genital system	
Female sexual disorders	
gynecology	618.17
see also Female genital	
diseases — humans	
Female spouses	
social welfare	362.839 52
Female-to-male transgender	
people	306.768
	T1—086 7
social services	362.897
Female-to-male transgender	
young people	
social services	362.785
Females (Human)	305.4
	T1—082
health	613.042 4
see also Women	
Femininity	155.333
Femininity of God	202.114
Christianity	231.4
Judaism	296.311 2
Feminism	305.42
political ideology	320.562 2
religion	200.82
Christianity	270.082
Judaism	296.082
social aspects	305.42
Feminist theology	202.082
Christianity	230.082
Judaism	296.308 2
Feminist views	T1—082

Feminists	305.42
Femurs	
human anatomy	611.718
Fencers	796.862 092
Fences	631.27
agricultural use	631.27
landscape architecture	717
Fencing (Offense)	364.162 7
law	345.026 27
Fencing (Swordplay)	796.862
Fenders	
automobile	629.26
Feng shui	133.333 7
Fenians	941.708 1
Canadian history	971.048
Irish history	941.708 1
Fenland (England)	T2—426 53
Fennec fox	599.776
Fens, The (England)	942.6
	T2—426
Fentress County (Tenn.)	T2—768 69
Feral children	
psychology	155.456 7
Feral livestock	
agricultural pests	632.696
conservation technology	639.966
Ferdinand I, Holy Roman	
Emperor	
German history	943.032
Ferdinand II, Holy Roman	
Emperor	
German history	943.042
Ferdinand III, Holy Roman	
Emperor	
German history	943.043
Ferdinand V, King of Spain	
Spanish history	946.03
Ferdinand VI, King of Spain	
Spanish history	946.056
Ferdinand VII, King of Spain	
Spanish history	946.072
Fergus County (Mont.)	T2—786 292
Fermanagh (Northern	
Ireland)	T2—416 3
Fermanagh & Omagh	
(Northern Ireland)	T2—416 3
Fermat's last theorem	512.74
Fermentation	547.29
alcoholic beverages	663.13
biochemistry	572.49
chemical engineering	660.284 49
food technology	664.024
Fermented cider	
commercial processing	663.29

Fetal erythroblastosis	
pediatrics	618.921 5
perinatal medicine	618.326 1
see also Cardiovascular	
diseases — humans	
Fetal tissue	
experimental research	
medicine	616.027
Fetal tissue transplantation	
surgery	617.954
Fetal version	
obstetrics	618.82
Fetishism	
religion	202.1
sexual practices	306.777
Fetus	
human physiology	612.647
law	342.085
Feudal Age	
European history	940.14
Japanese history	952.02
Feudal law	340.55
Feudal tenure	321.3
land economics	333.322
political science	321.3
Feudalism	321.3
land economics	333.322
political science	321.3
Feuds	
influence on crime	364.256
Fever	
result of injury	
medicine	617.22
symptom	616.047
Fever blisters	
medicine	616.522
see also Skin diseases —	
humans	
Few-bodies problem	530.14
Fez-Boulemane (Morocco)	T2—643 4
Fez-Jdid Dar-Dbibegh	
(Morocco)	T2—643 4
Fez-Medina (Morocco)	T2—643 4
Fezile Dabi District	
Municipality (South	
Africa)	T2—685 2
Fianarantsoa (Madagascar :	
Province)	T2—691
Fiat money	332.42
Fiber (Diet)	
health	613.263
Fiber bundles	514.224
Fiber crops	633.5

Fiber glass	666.157
materials science	620.144
sculpture material	731.2
ship design	623.818 38
ship hulls	623.845 8
shipbuilding	623.820 7
textiles	677.52
arts	746.045 2
see also Textiles	
Fiber-glass-reinforced plastic	668.494 2
Fiber optic sensors	
manufacturing technology	681.25
Fiber optics	621.369 2
Fiber spaces	514.224
Fiberboards	676.183
Fiberglass	666.157
see also Fiber glass	
Fiberglass-reinforced plastic	668.494 2
Fibers (Histology)	
humans	611.018 2
Fibers (Materials)	
materials science	620.197
textile materials	677.028 32
Fibonacci numbers	512.72
Fibrin	
human physiology	612.115
Fibrinolytic agents	
pharmacokinetics	615.718
Fibrinoplastin	
human physiology	612.115
Fibrocartilage	
human histology	612.751 7
Fibromyalgia	
medicine	616.742
see also Musculoskeletal	
diseases — humans	
Fibrous cartilage	
human histology	612.751 7
Fibrous tunics	
human physiology	612.841
Fibulas	
human anatomy	611.718
Ficksburg (South Africa :	
District)	T2—685 1
Fiction	808.83
criticism	809.3
theory	808.3
folklore	398.2
history and criticism	809.3
rhetoric	808.3
specific literatures	T3B—3
individual authors	T3A—3
see Manual at T3B—3	

Figure skating	796.912
see also Winter sports	
Figured bass	781.47
Figured madras fabrics	677.615
see also Textiles	
Figures of speech	
literature	808.801
history and criticism	809.91
rhetoric	808.032
Figurines	666.68
ceramic arts	738.82
ceramic technology	666.68
earthenware	666.68
porcelain	666.58
glyptics	736.224
Figworts	583.96
Fiji	996.11
	T2—961 1
Fiji Sea	551.461 477
	T2—164 77
Fijian language	499.59
	T6—995 9
Fijian literature	899.59
Fijians	T5—995 9
Filamentous fungi	579.5
Filarial diseases	
incidence	614.555 2
medicine	616.965 2
see also Communicable	
diseases — humans	
Filariasis	
incidence	614.555 2
medicine	616.965 2
see also Communicable	
diseases — humans	
Filberts	641.345 4
agriculture	634.54
botany	583.65
cooking	641.645 4
food	641.345 4
File access methods	
computer science	005.741
File cabinets	651.54
manufacturing technology	684.16
use in records management	651.54
File clerks	
office services	651.374 3
File compression	005.746
File formats	
computer science	005.72

File management systems	
computer science	005.4
data file programs	005.74
data file software	005.74
see Manual at 005.74 vs.	
005.436	
File managers	
computer science	
data file programs	005.74
data file software	005.74
systems software	005.436
File organization	
computer science	005.4
data files	005.741
systems software	005.436
see Manual at 005.74 vs.	
005.436	
File processing	
databases	005.74
File structure	
computer science	
data files	005.741
File system management	
computer science	
systems software	005.436
Filefishes	597.64
Filers (Clerks)	651.374 3
Files (Data)	
computer science	005.74
Files (Tools)	621.924
Filicales	587.3
paleobotany	561.73
Filicopsida	587.3
paleobotany	561.73
Filing	
library operations	025.317 7
records management	651.53
Filing rules	
library science	025.317 7
Filipino language	499.211
	T6—992 11
Filipino literature	899.211
Filipinos	T5—992 1
Fillers	
plastic technology	668.411
Filling stations	
architecture	725.38
automotive engineering	629.286
Fillings	
dentistry	617.675
Fillmore, Millard	
United States history	973.64
Fillmore County (Minn.)	T2—776 16
Fillmore County (Neb.)	T2—782 342

Fires	363.37
crop damage	632.18
see also Fire safety	
Firewalls (Computer security)	005.83
Fireweeds (Asteraceae)	583.983
Fireweeds (Onagraceae)	583.73
Fireworks	662.1
Firing artillery	623.558
Firing clays	
arts	730.28
pottery	666.443
arts	738.143
technology	666.443
sculpture	731.47
Firing glass	666.126
Firing metallurgical furnaces	669.83
Firing of employees	
economics	331.259 6
employment security	331.259 6
unemployment	331.137
law	344.012 596
personnel management	658.313
public administration	352.69
Firmware	
hardware	004
engineering	621.395
microprograms	005.18
Firmware development	005.18
Firs	585.2
forestry	634.975 4
lumber	674.144
First aid	362.18
health services	362.18
injuries	
medicine	617.102 62
medicine	616.025 2
First aid stations	362.18
armed forces	355.72
First-class mail	383.122
see also Postal service	
First Crusade, 1096–1099	956.014
First editions	094.4
First Empire (France)	944.05
First International	324.17
First names	929.44
First Nations peoples	T5—97
see also American native peoples	
First-order logic	511.3
mathematical logic	511.3
philosophical logic	160
First Republic (Austria)	943.605 1
First Republic (France)	944.042
First Republic (Spain)	946.073

Firth of Clyde (Scotland)	551.461 337
	T2—163 37
Firth of Forth (Scotland)	551.461 336
	T2—163 36
Fiscal conservatism	
political ideology	320.512
Fiscal policy	336.3
law	343.034
macroeconomics	339.52
public finance	336.3
Fiscal tariffs	382.72
see also Customs (Tariff)	
Fischer-Tropsch processes	662.662 3
Fish	597
Fish culture	639.3
enterprises	338.763 93
Fish farmers	639.309 2
Fish farming	639.3
freshwater	639.31
Fish hatcheries	639.311
Fish lice	595.36
Fish-liver oils	
pharmacology	615.34
Fish oil	665.2
Fish ponds	639.31
ecology	577.636
Fisher (Mammal)	599.766 5
Fisher, Andrew	
Australian history	994.041
Fisher County (Tex.)	T2—764 732
Fisheries	338.372 7
economics	338.372 7
enterprises	338.763 92
law	343.076 92
products	338.372 7
commerce	381.437
public administration	354.57
technology	639.2
Fishermen	639.209 2
commercial	639.209 2
sports	799.109 2
Fishery law	343.076 92
Fishery technology	639.2
Fishes	597
art representation	704.943 27
arts	T3C—362 7
commercial fishing	
economics	338.372 7
conservation technology	639.977
cooking	641.692
culture	639.3
economics	338.371 3
drawing	743.67

Flags	929.92	Flatfishes	597.69
armed forces	355.15	sports fishing	799.176 9
law	344.09	Flathead County (Mont.)	T2—786 82
Flagstaff (South Africa :		Flathead Lake (Mont.)	T2—786 832
District)	T2—687 58	Flats	643.27
Flagstones	553.53	*see also* Apartment houses	
economic geology	553.53	Flattery	
quarrying	622.353	ethics	177.3
road engineering	625.81	Flatware	642.7
Flame	541.361	*see also* Tableware	
Flame emission spectroscopy	543.52	Flatworms	592.4
Flame-resistant fabrics	677.689	Flavivirus infections	
see also Textiles		humans	
Flame throwers	623.445	incidence	614.588 5
Flamenco	781.626 104 68	medicine	616.918 5
dance	793.319 468	Flavorings	641.338 2
music	781.626 104 68	agriculture	633.82
dance	784.188 2	commercial processing	664.5
songs	782.421 626 104 68	cooking with	641.638 2
Flameproof fabrics	677.689	economic botany	581.632
see also Textiles		food	641.338 2
Flamingos	598.35	Flax	
Flammability testing	628.922 2	botany	583.69
Flammable materials	363.179 8	fiber crop	633.52
fire safety technology	628.922 2	textiles	677.11
public safety	363.179 8	arts	746.041 1
technology	604.7	*see also* Textiles	
see also Hazardous materials		Flaxseed oil	665.352
Flanders	T2—493 1	Flea beetles	595.764 8
Flanders (Belgium)	T2—493 1	agricultural pests	632.764 8
Flanders (France)	T2—442 8	Flea-borne typhus	
Flannel	677.624	incidence	614.526 2
see also Textiles		medicine	616.922 2
Flap-footed lizards	597.952	*see also* Communicable	
Flaps (Aircraft)	629.134 33	diseases — humans	
Flare stars	523.844 6	Flea markets	381.192
Flares		management	658.87
nautical equipment	623.86	*see also* Commerce	
Flash drives	004.568	Fleabanes	583.983
engineering	621.397 68	Fleas	595.775
Flash welding	671.521 3	disease carriers	
Flashbulb photography	778.72	medicine	614.432 4
Flashcards		Fleets (Naval units)	359.31
cataloging	025.349 6	Fleming County (Ky.)	T2—769 56
library treatment	025.179 6	Flemings	T5—393 2
Flat-backed lutes	787.85	Flemish	T5—393 2
see also Stringed instruments		Flemish Brabant (Belgium)	T2—493 31
Flat-file databases		Flemish dialect	439.31
computer science	005.75		T6—393 1
Flat racing		Flemish literature	839.31
horses	798.4	Flesh flies	595.774
Flatcars	385.34	Fleshing leather	675.22
engineering	625.24	Fleshy-finned fishes	597.39
see also Rolling stock		Flevoland (Netherlands)	T2—492 2

Floors (continued)	
construction	690.16
housecleaning	648.5
interior decoration	747.4
Floppy disks	004.563
engineering	621.397 63
Floral arts	745.92
Floral oils	668.542
customs	391.63
Floral waters	668.542
customs	391.63
Florence (City-state)	945.5
Florence (Italy)	T2—455 11
ancient	T2—375 11
Florence (Italy :	
Metropolitan city)	T2—455 1
ancient	T2—375 1
Florence (Republic)	945.506
Florence County (S.C.)	T2—757 84
Florence County (Wis.)	T2—775 32
Florentia (Italy)	T2—375 11
Flores (Uruguay)	T2—895 26
Flores Facussé, Carlos	
Honduran history	972.830 536
Flores Island (Indonesia)	T2—598 68
Flores Pérez, Francisco	
Salvadoran history	972.840 542
Flores Sea (Indonesia)	551.461 474
	T2—164 74
Floriculture	635.9
Florida	975.9
	T2—759
Florida (Uruguay : Dept.)	T2—895 25
Florida, Straits of	551.461 363
	T2—163 63
Florida Keys (Fla.)	T2—759 41
Florida Panhandle	T2—759 9
Florideophycideae	579.89
Flórina (Greece : Regional	
unit)	T2—495 62
Flotation	
ores	622.752
Flotillas (Naval units)	359.31
Flounders	597.69
cooking	641.692
food	641.392
sports fishing	799.176 9
Flour	641.331
commercial processing	664.720 7
wheat	664.722 72
cooking	641.631
food	641.331
Flour beetles	595.769

Flow	
air mechanics	533.62
engineering	620.106 4
fluid mechanics	532.051
gas mechanics	533.21
liquid mechanics	532.51
Flow-charting	
computer software	
development	005.120 28
Flow meters	
manufacturing technology	681.28
Flow-of-funds accounts	
macroeconomics	339.26
Flowcharting	
computer software	
development	005.120 28
Flower arrangements	745.92
Flower beds	635.962
Flower flies	595.774
Flower gardening	635.9
Flower language	302.222
Flowering plants	583
landscape architecture	716
paleobotany	561.3
see Manual at 583 vs. 582.13;	
also at 583–584	
Flowering trees	635.977 13
botany	582.16
ornamental arboriculture	635.977 13
Flowers	582.13
art representation	704.943 43
arts	700.464 213
	T3C—364 213
cooking	641.659
descriptive botany	582.13
drawing	743.73
dress customs	391.44
floral arts	745.92
food	641.359
gardening	635.9
literature	808.803 642 13
history and criticism	809.933 642 13
specific literatures	T3B—080 364 213
history and	
criticism	T3B—093 642 13
painting	758.42
physiology	575.6
see Manual at 583 vs. 582.13;	
also at 635.9 vs. 582.1	
Flowmeters	
manufacturing technology	681.28
Floyd County (Ga.)	T2—758 35
Floyd County (Ind.)	T2—772 19
Floyd County (Iowa)	T2—777 26

FM radio stations	384.545 3
see also Radio stations	
FM radio systems	621.384 152
Foam glass	666.157
Foam latex	678.532
Foamed plastics	668.493
Foams	541.345 14
chemical engineering	660.294 514
Foard County (Tex.)	T2—764 748
Foccacia	641.815
Focusing apparatus	771.37
Foehns (Winds)	551.518 5
Fog	541.345 15
colloid chemistry	541.345 15
applied	660.294 515
meteorology	551.575
Fog signals	387.155
navigation aids	623.894
Foggia (Italy : Province)	T2—457 57
ancient	T2—377 53
Foils	
use in cooking	641.589
Foix (France : County)	T2—447 35
Fokís (Greece)	T2—495 15
Folding boxes	676.32
Folds (Geology)	551.875
Foliage plants	635.975
Foliations	514.72
Folk arts	745
Folk beliefs	
folklore	398.41
Folk dancers	793.319 2
Folk dancing	793.31
Folk drama	808.82
literature	
specific literatures	T3B—2
Folk high schools	374.83
Folk literature	398.2
see Manual at 398.2; *also at* 398.2 vs. 201.3, 230, 270, 292–299; *also at* 398.2 vs. 398.3–.4; *also at* 800 vs. 398.2	
Folk medicine	610
folklore	398.276 1
history and criticism	398.356 1
Folk music	781.62
modes	781.263
songs	782.421 62
see Manual at 781.62 vs. 780.89; *also at* 781.62 vs. 781.63–.66	
Folk musicians	781.620 092
singers	782.421 620 092
Folk poetry	808.81
specific literatures	T3B—1
Folk remedies	
therapeutics	615.88
Folk rock	781.661 72
Folk singers	782.421 620 092
Folk songs	782.421 62
Folklore	398
arts	700.455 9
	T3C—355 9
history and criticism	398.09
Folklorists	398.092
Folksonomies	025.487
Folkways	306
sociology	390
Follicles	
hair	
human anatomy	611.78
medicine	616.546
Fon (African people)	T5—963 37
Fon language	496.337
	T6—963 37
Fond du Lac County (Wis.)	T2—775 68
Fondues	
side dishes	641.811 73
Fonseca, Jorge Carlos de Almeida	
Cape Verdean history	966.580 34
Fonts (Typography)	744.452
Food	641.3
armed forces supplies	355.81
arts	700.456 4
	T3C—356 4
commercial processing	
economics	338.476 64
technology	664
cooking	641.5
customs	394.12
folklore	398.276 4
history and criticism	398.356 4
health	613.2
home economics	641.3
home preservation	641.4
literature	808.803 564
history and criticism	809.933 564
specific literatures	T3B—080 356 4
history and criticism	T3B—093 564
nutritional content	613.2
public administration	353.997
preservation techniques	664.028
commercial	664.028
home	641.4
primary education	372.373

Foot washing	
Christian rite	265.9
Football	796.33
electronic games	794.863 3
equipment technology	688.763 3
see also Ball games	
Football cards	796.332 075
Football players	796.330 92
American football	796.332 092
Australian football	796.336 092
Canadian football	796.335 092
rugby	796.333 092
soccer	796.334 092
Football rattles	786.886
see also Percussion instruments	
Footings	
walls	721.2
construction	690.12
Footpaths	388.12
see also Pedestrian paths	
Footwear	391.413
commercial technology	685.3
customs	391.413
see also Clothing	
For-hire carriers	388.041
truck	388.324 3
see also Freight services;	
Passenger services	
Forage crops	633.2
feeds	636.086
see Manual at 583–585 vs. 600	
Forage grasses	633.2
agriculture	633.2
botany	584.92
Forage legumes	633.3
botany	583.63
feeds	636.086
Foraminifera	579.44
paleontology	561.994
Forbes (N.S.W.)	T2—944 5
Forbs	582.12
Force (Energy)	
philosophy	118
Force (International politics)	327.117
Force and energy	531.6
Forced labor	
Holocaust, 1933–1945	940.531 813 4
World War II	940.540 5
Forced loans	336.344
Forces (Mechanics)	531.113
Forcing (Plants)	631.583
floriculture	635.982
gardening	635.048 3

Forcipulata	593.93
paleozoology	563.93
Ford, Gerald R.	
United States history	973.925
Ford County (Ill.)	T2—773 62
Ford County (Kan.)	T2—781 76
Forde, Francis Michael	
Australian history	994.042
Forearm techniques	
music	784.193 62
Forebrain	
human physiology	612.825
medicine	616.8
Forecasting	003.2
	T1—011 2
business	338.544
investments	332.678
management decision making	658.403 55
marketing management	658.818
occultism	133.3
social change	303.49
weather	551.63
Forecasting methods	
economics	338.544 2
Forecasts	003.2
	T1—011 2
business	338.544 3
social change	303.49
Foreclosure	346.043 64
Forehand	
tennis	796.342 22
Foreign affairs	327
Foreign affairs departments	353.13
Foreign aid	338.91
economics	338.91
law	343.074 8
international relations	327.111
law	342.041 2
military science	355.032
public administration	353.132 73
social welfare	361.26
governmental	361.6
private	361.77
Foreign assistance	338.91
Foreign direct investment	332.673
Foreign economic assistance	338.91
Foreign economic policies	337
Foreign economic relations	337
Foreign enterprises	338.88
Foreign exchange	332.45
law	343.032 5
Foreign income	
tax economics	336.24
tax law	343.052 48

Forest saltwater wetlands	
biology	578.769 7
ecology	577.697
Forest thinning	634.953
Forest wetlands	
biology	578.768 3
ecology	577.683
Forestation	333.751 52
Foresters	634.909 2
Forestry	634.9
agricultural economics	338.174 9
law	343.076 49
law	343.076 49
public administration	354.55
resource economics	333.75
law	346.046 75
Forests	333.75
	T2—152
see also Forest lands	
Forfeit games	793.5
Forge welding	671.529
Forgeries	
arts	702.874
books	098.3
financial instruments	332.9
museology	069.54
paintings	751.58
Forgery	364.163 5
law	345.026 35
Forget-me-nots	635.933 958
botany	583.958
floriculture	635.933 958
Forgetting	153.125
Forging	671.332
blacksmithing	682
decorative arts	739.14
sculpture	731.41
Forgiveness	
psychology	155.92
applied psychology	158.2
religious doctrine	202.2
Christianity	234.5
Forillon National Park	
(Quebec)	T2—714 793
Fork lifts	621.863
Forlì (Italy : Province)	T2—454 8
ancient	T2—372 68
Forlì-Cesena (Italy :	
Province)	T2—454 8
ancient	T2—372 68
Form (Concept)	
arts	701.8
drawing	741.018

Form (Concept) (continued)	
painting	750.18
philosophy	117
Form books	
law	347.055
Form criticism	
sacred books	208.2
Bible	220.663
Talmud	296.120 663
Form letters	
office use	651.752
Form of juristic acts	346.021
Form perception	
visual	
psychology	152.142 3
Formal analysis	
music	781.8
Formal dress	391.486
commercial technology	687.16
customs	391.486
home sewing	646.476
see also Clothing	
Formal grammars	511.3
programming languages	005.131
Formal groups	512.2
Formal languages	511.3
programming languages	005.131
Formal linguistics	410.182
grammar	415.018 2
specific languages	T4—501 82
phonology	414.018 2
specific languages	T4—150 182
semantics	401.430 182
specific languages	T4—014 301 82
specific languages	T4—018 2
Formal logic	511.3
mathematical logic	511.3
philosophical logic	160
Formal usage (Language)	418
specific languages	T4—8
Formaldehyde	
human toxicology	615.951 36
Format publishing	686
Formations	
sports	
American football	796.332 22
soccer	796.334 22
Formentera (Spain)	T2—467 56
Former communist bloc	909.097 17
	T2—171 7
Formicariidae	598.822 6
Formicidae	595.796
Formosa	951.249
	T2—512 49

Frankfurt an der Oder		Fraternal benefit societies	334.7
(Germany : Bezirk)	T2—431 53	economics	334.7
Frankia	579.37	insurance	368.3
Franking privileges	383.120 2	*see also* Insurance	
see also Postal service		Fraternal insurance	368.363
Franklin (Nunavut and		*see also* Insurance	
N.W.T.)	T2—719 52	Fraternal organizations	369
Franklin (State)	976.803	Fraternities	
	T2—768	education	371.855
Franklin (Va.)	T2—755 553	Fraud	364.163
Franklin County (Ala.)	T2—761 913	criminology	364.163
Franklin County (Ark.)	T2—767 34	law	345.026 3
Franklin County (Fla.)	T2—759 91	occultism	130
Franklin County (Ga.)	T2—758 135	prevention	
Franklin County (Idaho)	T2—796 42	management	658.473
Franklin County (Ill.)	T2—773 94	social welfare	362.889 63
Franklin County (Ind.)	T2—772 15	Fraud victims	362.889 63
Franklin County (Iowa)	T2—777 28	*see also* Victims of crime	
Franklin County (Kan.)	T2—781 66	Fraudulent claims	364.163
Franklin County (Ky.)	T2—769 432	criminology	364.163
Franklin County (Mass.)	T2—744 22	insurance	368.014
Franklin County (Me.)	T2—741 72	law	345.026 3
Franklin County (Miss.)	T2—762 27	Fraudulent elections	324.66
Franklin County (Mo.)	T2—778 63	criminology	364.132 4
Franklin County (N.C.)	T2—756 54	law	345.023 24
Franklin County (N.Y.)	T2—747 55	Frauenfeld (Switzerland)	T2—494 591 8
Franklin County (Neb.)	T2—782 377	Frauenfeld (Switzerland :	
Franklin County (Ohio)	T2—771 56	Bezirk)	T2—494 591
Franklin County (Pa.)	T2—748 44	Frazil ice	551.344
Franklin County (Tenn.)	T2—768 63	Freaks (Circuses)	791.35
Franklin County (Tex.)	T2—764 213	Fréchet algebras	512.55
Franklin County (Va.)	T2—755 68	Frederick, the Great	
Franklin County (Vt.)	T2—743 13	German history	943.053
Franklin County (Wash.)	T2—797 33	Frederick I, Holy Roman	
Franklin D. Roosevelt Lake		Emperor	
(Wash.)	T2—797 23	German history	943.024
Franklin District (N.Z.)	T2—933 1	Frederick II, Holy Roman	
Auckland Region	T2—932 7	Emperor	
Waikato Region	T2—933 1	German history	943.025
Franklin Parish (La.)	T2—763 77	Frederick II, King of Prussia	
Franz Josef Land (Russia)	T2—985	German history	943.053
Fraser, Malcolm		Frederick III, Emperor of	
Australian history	994.063	Germany	
Fraser Canyon (B.C.)	T2—711 37	German history	943.028
Fraser-Cheam (B.C.)	T2—711 37	Frederick III, German Emperor	
Fraser-Fort George (B.C.)	T2—711 82	German history	943.084
Fraser Island (Qld.)	T2—943 2	Frederick Barbarossa, Holy	
Fraser Plateau (B.C.)	T2—711 75	Roman Emperor	
Fraser River (B.C.)	T2—711 3	German history	943.024
Fraser Valley (B.C.)	T2—711 37	Frederick County (Md.)	T2—752 87
Fraserburg (South Africa :		Frederick County (Va.)	T2—755 992
District)	T2—687 17	Fredericksburg (Va.)	T2—755 366
		Fredericton (N.B.)	T2—715 515
		Frederiksberg (Denmark)	T2—489 13

Freeze-dried foods	
cooking	641.614
Freeze-drying foods	664.028 45
commercial preservation	664.028 45
home preservation	641.44
Freezers	621.57
kitchen appliances	641.453 028 4
low-temperature engineering	621.57
Freezing	536.42
Freezing foods	664.028 53
commercial preservation	664.028 53
home preservation	641.453
Fregatidae	598.43
Frei Montalva, Eduardo	
Chilean history	983.064 5
Frei Ruiz-Tagle, Eduardo	
Chilean history	983.066 2
Freiberge (Switzerland)	T2—494 368
Freiburg (Germany :	
Regierungsbezirk)	T2—434 62
Freiburg (Switzerland)	T2—494 535 4
Freiburg (Switzerland :	
Canton)	T2—494 53
Freiburg im Breisgau	
(Germany)	T2—434 626 2
Freie Demokratische Partei	
(Germany)	324.243 06
Freight and freightage	388.044
see also Freight services	
Freight cars	385.34
engineering	625.24
see also Rolling stock	
Freight insurance	368.2
see also Insurance	
Freight services	388.044
air	387.744
airport services	387.736 4
law	343.097 8
automobile	388.321
bus	388.322 2
law	343.094 82
terminal services	388.33
canal	386.404 24
ferries	386.6
ground	388.044
law	343.093 2
inland waterway	386.244
law	343.096 8
port services	386.864
lake	386.544
law	343.093 2
marine	387.544
law	343.096 8
port services	387.164

Freight services (continued)	
port services	387.164
engineering	623.888 1
public administration	354.764
railroad	385.24
law	343.095 8
public administration	354.767 4
special purpose	385.5
terminal services	385.264
river	386.354
truck	388.324
law	343.094 83
terminal services	388.33
urban	388.413 24
terminal services	388.473
Freight terminals	388.044
architecture	725.3
area planning	711.7
construction	690.53
inland waterway	386.853
ports	387.153
Freighters (Ships)	387.245
engineering	623.824 5
see also Ships	
Freiheitliche Partei Österreichs	324.243 603
Freiheits-Partei der Schweiz	324.249 403
Freisinnig-Demokratische Partei	
der Schweiz	324.249 406
Fremantle (W.A.)	T2—941 1
Fremont County (Colo.)	T2—788 53
Fremont County (Idaho)	T2—796 56
Fremont County (Iowa)	T2—777 77
Fremont County (Wyo.)	T2—787 63
French	T5—41
French and Indian War,	
1756–1763	940.253 4
North American history	973.26
French Broad River (N.C.	
and Tenn.)	T2—768 895
French bulldog	636.72
French Cameroons	T2—671 1
French-Canadian literature	840
French Canadians	T5—114
see Manual at T5—112,	
T5—114 vs. T5—2,	
T5—41	
French Communist Party	324.244 075
French Community	T2—171 244
French Congo (Brazzaville)	T2—672 4
French creole languages	447.9
	T6—417
French drama	842

Friaries
  architecture — 726.7
  church history — 271
  religious significance of
    buildings — 246.97
Fribourg (Switzerland) — T2—494 535 4
Friction — 531.113 4
  fluid mechanics — 532.053 3
  gas mechanics — 533.28
  liquid mechanics — 532.58
  machine engineering — 621.89
  solid mechanics — 531.4
Friction drums — 786.98
  see also Percussion instruments
Friction idiophones — 786.86
  set — 786.86
  single — 786.888
  see also Percussion instruments
Friction resistance
  materials science — 620.112 92
Frictional unemployment — 331.137 045
Friday
  Islamic observance — 297.36
Friedel-Crafts reaction
  chemical engineering — 660.284 4
Friedreich ataxia
  medicine — 616.83
  see also Nervous system
    diseases — humans
Friendly fire casualties (Military
  science) — 355.422
Friendly Islands — 996.12
   — T2—961 2
Friendly occupation
  law of nations — 341.722
Friendly societies — 334.7
  economics — 334.7
  insurance — 368.3
  see also Insurance
Friends (Religious society) — 289.6
  biography — 289.609 2
Friends of the library
  organizations — 021.7
Friendship — 177.62
  applied psychology — 158.25
  arts — T3C—353
  ethics — 177.62
    religion — 205.676 2
  folklore — 398.273
    history and criticism — 398.353

Friendship (continued)
  literature — 808.803 53
    history and criticism — 809.933 53
    specific literatures — T3B—080 353
    history and
      criticism — T3B—093 53
  psychological influence — 155.925
  social psychology — 302.34
Friesian language — 439.2
   — T6—392
Friesians — T5—392
Friesland (Germany) — T2—435 917
Friesland (Netherlands) — T2—492 13
Frieze (Fabric) — 677.617
  see also Textiles
Frigate birds — 598.43
Frigid zones — T2—11
  biology — 578.091 1
  diseases
    medicine — 616.988 1
    see also Environmental
      diseases — humans
  ecology — 577.091 1
  health — 613.111
Frigidity
  medicine — 616.858 32
Fringe benefits — 331.255
  see also Employee benefits
Fringes
  arts — 746.27
Fringes (Judaism) — 296.461
Fringillidae — 598.883
Frio County (Tex.) — T2—764 442
Frisian language — 439.2
   — T6—392
Frisian literature — 839.2
Friuli Venezia Giulia (Italy) — 945.39
Friuli-Venezia Giulia (Italy) — 945.39
Friuli Venezia Giulia (Italy) — T2—453 9
  ancient — T2—373 8
Friulian language — 459.92
   — T6—599 2
Friulian literature — 859.92
Friulians — T5—599 2
Frobisher Bay (Nunavut) — T2—719 52
Frogbits — 584.445
Frogfishes — 597.62
Frogmen (Navy) — 359.984
Frogmouths — 598.99

Fuchsias	635.933 73	Fujayrah (United Arab	
botany	583.73	Emirates : Emirate)	T2—535 7
floriculture	635.933 73	Fuji, Mount (Japan)	T2—521 66
Fucus	579.888	Fuji-san (Japan)	T2—521 66
Fuel alcohols	662.669 2	Fujian Sheng (China)	T2—512 45
Fuel cell vehicles	388.349 74	Fujimori, Alberto	
engineering	629.229 74	Peruvian history	985.064 3
transportation services	388.349 74	Fujiyama (Japan)	T2—521 66
Fuel cells	621.312 429	Fukien Province (China)	T2—512 45
Fuel element materials		Fukui-ken (Japan)	T2—521 55
nuclear reactors	621.483 35	Fukuoka-ken (Japan)	T2—522 2
Fuel engineers	662.609 2	Fukushima-ken (Japan)	T2—521 17
Fuel oils	665.538 4	Fula language	496.322
Fuel resources	333.82		T6—963 22
economics	333.82	Fula literature	896.322
extraction		Fulah (African people)	T5—963 22
economics	338.2	Fulah language	496.322
law	346.046 82		T6—963 22
public administration	354.4	Fulah literature	896.322
Fuel systems		Fulani (African people)	T5—963 22
automotive	629.253	Fulani Empire	966.950 1
Fueling	388.041		T2—669 5
aircraft	387.736 4	Fulani language	496.322
boats	387.168		T6—963 22
buses	388.33	Fulani literature	896.322
urban	388.473	Fulfulde language	496.322
ships	387.168		T6—963 22
trains	385.26	Fulfulde literature	896.322
trucks	388.33	Full-employment policy	331.120 424
urban	388.473	macroeconomics	339.5
Fuels	662.6	*see Manual at* 331.120424 vs.	
aircraft	629.134 351	331.1377	
automotive	629.253 8	Full orchestras	784.2
chemical engineering	662.6	Full-scale plants	
economic geology	553.2	chemical engineering	660.280 73
economics	338.476 626	Full scores	780
heat engineering	621.402 3	treatises	780.264
heating buildings	697.04	Full-text databases	025.04
marine engines	623.874	computer science	005.759
metallurgical furnaces	669.81	information science	025.04
military supplies	355.83	Full-text indexing	025.486
nuclear reactors	621.483 35	Full-year school	371.236
public administration	354.4	Fuller's earth	553.61
resource economics	333.82	economic geology	553.61
spacecraft	629.475	mining	622.361
steam engineering	621.182	Fulmars	598.42
unmanned spacecraft	629.465	Fulton County (Ark.)	T2—767 22
Fuelwood	333.953 97	Fulton County (Ga.)	T2—758 23
Fugitive slaves		Fulton County (Ill.)	T2—773 48
Civil War (United States) cause	973.711 5	Fulton County (Ind.)	T2—772 87
Fugues	784.187 2	Fulton County (Ky.)	T2—769 99
Fujairah (United Arab		Fulton County (N.Y.)	T2—747 47
Emirates : Emirate)	T2—535 7	Fulton County (Ohio)	T2—771 115
		Fulton County (Pa.)	T2—748 72

344

Fungal skin diseases	
humans	
incidence	614.595 79
medicine	616.579
Fungal viruses	579.27
Fungi	579.5
medical microbiology	616.969 01
paleontology	561.92
physiology	571.295
Fungi Imperfecti	579.55
Fungicides	632.952
agricultural use	632.952
chemical engineering	668.652
Fungus diseases	571.995
see also Mycoses	
Fungus weevils	595.768
Funicular railroads	385.6
engineering	625.32
transportation services	385.6
see also Railroads	
Funj Sultanate	962.402 3
	T2—624
Funnies	741.56
see also Comic strips	
Fur	599.714 7
descriptive zoology	599.714 7
physiology	573.58
Fur-bearing animals	599.7
animal husbandry	636.97
conservation technology	639.979 7
resource economics	333.959 7
small game hunting	799.259 7
trapping	639.117
zoology	599.7
Fur clothing	391
commercial technology	685.24
customs	391
home sewing	646.4
see also Clothing	
Fur farming	636.97
Fur goods	
commercial technology	685
Fur languages	496.57
	T6—965 7
Fur processing	675.3
economics	338.476 753
Fur seals	599.797 3
conservation technology	639.979 797 3
resource economics	333.959 797 3
Fur trapping	639.117
economics	338.372 97
Furans	547.592
chemical engineering	661.8

Furloughs	
armed forces	355.113
penology	365.643
Furnaces	
heat engineering	621.402 5
heating buildings	697.07
steam	697.507
steam engineering	621.183
Furnariidae	598.822 5
Furnas County (Neb.)	T2—782 384
Furneaux Islands (Tas.)	T2—946 7
Furnishings	645
commercial technology	684
customs	392.36
home cleaning	648.5
household management	645
interior decoration	747
libraries	
management	022.9
schools	371.63
Furniture	645.4
cleaning	648.5
customs	392.36
decorative arts	749
household management	645.4
libraries	
management	022.9
manufacturing technology	684.1
office services	651.23
ships	623.866
Furniture arrangement	645.4
Furniture covers	645.4
home sewing	646.21
household management	645.4
textile arts	746.95
Furniture designers	749.092
Furniture makers	684.100 92
Furriers	675.309 2
Furs	
handicrafts	745.537
home sewing materials	646.1
processing	675.3
products	
commercial technology	685
Further education	374
	T1—071 5
see also Adult education	
Furū' al-fiqh (Islamic law)	340.592
Furuncles	
medicine	616.523
see also Skin diseases —	
humans	

Furunculosis	
medicine	616.523
see also Skin diseases —	
humans	
Fusarium	579.567 7
Fused aromatic compounds	547.615
chemical engineering	661.816
Fused heterocyclic compounds	547.596
Fuselages	
aircraft	629.134 34
Fuses (Detonators)	662.4
military engineering	623.454 2
Fuses (Electrical)	621.317
Fusibility	
crystals	548.86
Fusion (Melting)	536.42
Fusion (Thermonuclear)	539.764
Fusion power plants	621.484
Fusion reactors	621.484
Future interests (Law)	346.042
Future life	
occultism	133.901 3
philosophy	129
religion	202.3
Buddhism	294.342 3
Christianity	236.2
Hinduism	294.523
Islam	297.23
Judaism	296.33
Future punishment	202.3
Futures	332.645 2
Futurism	
fine arts	709.040 33
literature	808.801 14
history and criticism	809.911 4
specific literatures	T3B—080 114
history and	
criticism	T3B—091 14
painting	759.063 3
sculpture	735.230 433
Futurology	003.2
occultism	133.3
social change	303.49
Fuzzy logic	511.313
Fuzzy mathematics	511.313
Fuzzy sets	511.322 3
Fuzzy systems	511.313
Fylde (England)	T2—427 662
Fylde (England : Borough)	T2—427 662
Fyn (Denmark)	T2—489 4
Fyns amt (Denmark)	T2—489 4
Fyodor I, Czar of Russia	
Russian history	947.044

Fyodor III, Czar of Russia	
Russian history	947.049

G

Gã (African people)	T5—963 378
Gã language	496.337 8
	T6—963 378
Gã literature	896.337 8
Gabbro	552.3
Gables	721.5
architecture	721.5
construction	690.15
Gabon	967.21
	T2—672 1
Gabonese	T5—967 21
Gaborone (Botswana)	T2—688 3
Gabrovo (Bulgaria : Oblast)	T2—499 26
Gadaba (Dravidian people)	T5—948 2
Gadaba (Munda people)	T5—959 5
Gadaba language (Dravidian)	494.82
	T6—948 2
Gadaba language (Munda)	495.95
	T6—959 5
Gadba (Dravidian people)	T5—948 2
Gadba (Munda people)	T5—959 5
Gadba language (Dravidian)	494.82
	T6—948 2
Gadba language (Munda)	495.95
	T6—959 5
Gadidae	597.632
Gadiformes	597.63
paleozoology	567.63
Gadolinium	
chemistry	546.416
Gadsden County (Fla.)	T2—759 925
Gadus	597.633
Gaelic languages	491.6
	T6—916
Irish	491.62
	T6—916 2
Scottish	491.63
	T6—916 3
Gaelic literatures	891.6
Irish	891.62
Scottish	891.63
Gaels	T5—916
Gaetulia	939.77
	T2—397 7
Gagauz language	494.36
	T6—943 6
Gage County (Neb.)	T2—782 286
Gagnon (Quebec)	T2—714 117

Gain sharing	331.216 47	Gallatin County (Ky.)	T2—769 365
labor economics	331.216 47	Gallatin County (Mont.)	T2—786 662
personnel management	658.322 5	Gallbladder	573.38
Gaines County (Tex.)	T2—764 855	biology	573.38
Gaining weight diet		human anatomy	611.36
health	613.24	human physiology	612.35
Gairdner, Lake (S. Aust.)	T2—942 38	medicine	616.365
Gait analysis		surgery	617.556 5
biometric identification		*see also* Digestive system	
computer science	006.248 379	Gallbladder diseases	
Gaitas	788.49	medicine	616.365
see also Woodwind		*see also* Digestive system	
instruments		diseases — humans	
Galagos	599.83	Gallegan language	469.9
Galapagos Islands	986.65		T6—699
	T2—866 5	Gallegan literature	869.9
travel	918.665 04	Galleons	387.22
Galapagos tortoise	597.924 6	design	623.812 2
Galați (Romania : Județ)	T2—498 1	engineering	623.822
Galatia	T2—393 2	transportation services	387.22
Galatia Salutaris	T2—393 2	*see also* Ships	
Galatians (Biblical book)	227.4	Galleries (Museums)	069
Galax	583.93		T1—074
Galax (Va.)	T2—755 715	Galleys (Ships)	387.21
Galaxies	523.112	design	623.812 1
see Manual at 520 vs. 523.1,		engineering	623.821
523.112, 523.8		handling	623.882 1
Galbulidae	598.72	transportation services	387.21
Galcha language	491.57	*see also* Ships	
	T6—915 7	Galli	598.6
Galcha literature	891.57	Gallia Cisalpina	T2—372
Galchah language	491.57	Gallia Cispadana	T2—372 6
	T6—915 7	Gallia County (Ohio)	T2—771 89
Galchah literature	891.57	Gallia Transalpina	T2—364
Galena		Gallia Transpadana	T2—372 2
mineralogy	549.32	Galliards	793.3
Galerkin method	518.63	music	784.188 2
Galibi language	498.422	Gallican schismatic churches	284.8
	T6—984 22	*see also* Old Catholic churches	
Galicia (Poland and		Galliformes	598.6
Ukraine)	T2—438 6	paleozoology	568.6
Poland	T2—438 6	sports hunting	799.246
Ukraine	T2—477 9	Gallinules	598.32
Galicia (Spain : Region)	T2—461	Gallipoli Campaign, 1915	940.426
Galician language	469.9	Gallipoli peninsula (Turkey)	T2—496 12
	T6—699	Gallium	669.79
Galician literature	869.9	chemical engineering	661.067 5
Galicians	T5—699	chemistry	546.675
Galilee (Israel)	956.945	metallurgy	669.79
	T2—569 45	*see also* Chemicals	
ancient	T2—334 5	Gallo-Roman period	936.402
Gall bladder	573.38	Galloway cattle	636.223
see also Gallbladder		Galls	
Gallatin County (Ill.)	T2—773 97	agriculture	632.2

Gametogenesis	571.845
Gaming	306.482
see also Gambling	
Gamka River (South Africa)	T2—687 37
Gamma decay	539.752 4
Gamma functions	515.52
Gamma particles	539.722 2
biophysics	571.459
humans	612.014 486
physics	539.722 2
Gamma-ray astronomy	522.686 2
Gamma-ray electronics	537.535
Gamma-ray photography	
engineering	621.367 3
Gamma-ray spectroscopes	
manufacturing technology	681.414 8
Gamma-ray spectroscopy	543.6
analytical chemistry	543.6
engineering	621.361
physics	537.535 2
Gamma rays	539.722 2
biophysics	571.459
humans	612.014 486
physics	539.722 2
Gan dialects (China)	495.179 512 22
	T6—951 7
Ganapataism	294.551 5
Ganda (African people)	T5—963 957
Ganda language	496.395 7
	T6—963 957
Ganda literature	896.395 7
Gandaki Pradesh (Nepal)	T2—549 64
Gandhi, Indira	
Indian history	954.045
1966–1971	954.045
1971–1977	954.051
1980–1984	954.052
Gandhi, Rajiv	
Indian history	954.052
Ganges River (India and	
Bangladesh)	T2—541
Ganglia	
basal	
medicine	616.83
human anatomy	611.83
human physiology	612.81
non-basal	
medicine	616.856
Gangrene	
medicine	616.047
Gangs	
criminology	364.106 6
social psychology	302.34
Gangsterism	364.106 6

Ganoidei	597.42
Gansu Sheng (China)	T2—514 5
Ganyesa (South Africa :	
District)	T2—682 46
Gaols	365.34
see also Penal institutions	
Gaonim	296.120 092
GAR (Organization)	369.15
Garage sales	381.195
management	658.87
see also Commerce	
Garages	
architecture	725.38
automotive engineering	629.286
construction	690.538
domestic	
architecture	728.98
construction	690.898
theft from	364.162 2
law	345.026 22
Garavance	641.356 57
see also Chick-peas	
Garbage collection	363.728 8
technology	628.442
Garbage disposal	363.728 8
technology	628.445
use as fertilizer	631.875
see also Waste control	
Garbage-disposal units	
installation	696.184
manufacturing technology	683.88
Garbanzo	641.356 57
see also Chick-peas	
García, Alan	
Peruvian history	985.064 5
Garcia, Carlos	
Philippine history	959.904 4
Garcinias	583.69
Gard (France)	T2—448 3
Garda, Lake (Italy)	T2—452 6
Garden County (Neb.)	T2—782 915
Garden crops	635
see Manual at 633–635	
Garden eggs	641.356 46
see also Eggplants	
Garden furniture	645.8
see also Outdoor furniture	
Garden legumes	641.356 5
horticulture	635.65
Garden lighting	621.322 9
see also Lighting	
Garden peas	641.356 56
see also Peas (Pisum sativum)	

Gas supply facilities	
area planning	711.8
Gas tubes	
electronics	621.381 513
Gas-turbine engines	621.433
aircraft	629.134 353
automotive	629.250 3
ships	623.872 33
Gas-turbine locomotives	385.362
engineering	625.262
transportation services	385.362
see also Rolling stock	
Gas welding	671.522
Gascogne (France)	T2—447 3
Gascon dialect (Occitan	
language)	T6—491
Gasconade County (Mo.)	T2—778 61
Gascony (France)	T2—447 3
Gascoyne River (W.A.)	T2—941 3
Gaseous-state chemistry	541.042 3
Gaseous-state lasers	621.366 3
Gaseous-state physics	530.43
Gaseous wastes	363.728
social services	363.728
technology	628.53
see also Waste control	
Gases	
chemical engineering	660.043
expansion and contraction	536.412
heat transfer	536.25
pneumatics	533
sound transmission	534.24
specific heat	536.65
state of matter	530.43
Gases (Fuels)	665.7
cooking	641.584
dowsing	133.323 7
mine safety engineering	622.82
natural	553.285
see also Natural gas	
plant management	658.26
public administration	354.46
public safety	363.179 8
public utilities	363.63
see also Hazardous materials	
Gases (Noxious)	
human toxicology	615.91
mine safety engineering	622.82
pollution	363.738 7
see also Pollution	
Gases in atmosphere	551.511 2
Gasohol	662.669 2

Gasoline	665.538 27
public safety	363.179 8
see also Hazardous materials	
Gasoline engines	621.434
Gašparovič, Ivan	
Slovak history	943.730 513
Gaspé Peninsula (Quebec)	T2—714 77
Gaspée (Ship), Burning of, 1772	973.311 2
Gaspésie (Quebec)	T2—714 77
Gaspésie-Îles-de-la-Madeleine	
(Quebec)	T2—714 77
Gaspésie National Park	
(Quebec)	T2—714 791
Gasteromycetes	579.599
Gasteropelecidae	597.48
Gasterosteidae	597.672
Gasterosteiformes	597.67
paleozoology	567.67
Gaston County (N.C.)	T2—756 773
Gastric analysis	
diagnosis	
general disease	616.075 63
Gastric secretions	573.363 79
human physiology	612.32
medicine	616.332
see also Digestive system	
Gastric ulcers	
medicine	616.334
see also Digestive system	
diseases — humans	
Gästrikland landskap	
(Sweden)	T2—488 1
Gastritis	
medicine	616.333
see also Digestive system	
diseases — humans	
Gastroenteritis	
medicine	616.33
see also Digestive system	
diseases — humans	
Gastroenterology	616.33
Gastroesophageal reflux	
medicine	616.324
see also Digestive system	
diseases — humans	
Gastrointestinal agents	
pharmacokinetics	615.73
Gastrointestinal diseases	
medicine	616.33
see also Digestive system	
diseases — humans	
Gastrointestinal microbiome	
human physiology	612.360 157 9

Gays	306.766	Ge'ez language	492.81
	T1—086 64		T6—928 1
see also Gay people		Biblical texts	220.46
Gaza (Mozambique :		Ge'ez literature	892.81
Province)	T2—679 2	Gegenschein	523.59
Gaza Strip	956.943	Geiger-Müller counters	
	T2—569 43	nuclear physics	539.774
ancient	933.3	Geingob, Hage Gottfried	
	T2—333	Namibian history	968.810 43
Gazankulu (South Africa)	T2—682 59	Geisel, Ernesto	
Gazehounds	636.753 2	Brazilian history	981.063
Gazella	599.646 9	Geishas	792.702 809 52
Gazelles	599.646 9	Gekkonidae	597.952
Gazetteers	910.3	Gekkonidea	597.952
Gazettes (Official publications)	351.05	Gela (Italy)	
Gaziantep İli (Turkey)	T2—564 9	ancient	T2—378 21
ancient	T2—393 6	Gelatin	
GB (Swiss political party)	324.249 408 7	commercial processing	664.26
Gbagbo, Laurent		Gelatin desserts	641.864 2
Ivorian history	966.680 53	Gelatin process	
Gbandi (Liberian people)	T5—963 48	printing	686.232 5
Gbandi language	496.348	Gelderland (Netherlands)	T2—492 18
	T6—963 48	Gelibolu (Turkey)	T2—496 12
Gbaya (African people)	T5—963 61	Gels	541.345 13
Gbaya language	496.361	chemical engineering	660.294 513
	T6—963 61	Gelsenkirchen (Germany)	T2—435 618
Gbe languages	496.337	Gem County (Idaho)	T2—796 27
	T6—963 37	Gemini (Zodiac)	133.526 4
GCSE (Educational tests)	373.126 2	Gemini project	629.454
Gdańsk (Poland :		Gempylidae	597.78
Voivodeship)	T2—438 22	Gems	553.8
GDP (Macroeconomics)	339.31	carving	736.2
GDVP (Austrian political party)	324.243 602 3	economic geology	553.8
Gê Indians	T5—984	jewelry	739.27
Gê language	498.4	materials science	620.198
	T6—984	mining	622.38
Gear-cutting tools	621.944	occultism	133.255 38
Gear-driven hoists		divination	133.322
mining	622.67	prospecting	622.188
Gears	621.833	synthetic	666.88
clockwork	681.112	Gen-Gbe language	496.337
Geary County (Kan.)	T2—781 29		T6—963 37
Geauga County (Ohio)	T2—771 336	Gen language	496.337
Geckos	597.952		T6—963 37
GED tests	373.126 2	Gender (Grammar)	415.5
Gedling (England)	T2—425 28	Gender identity	305.3
Geelong (Vic.)	T2—945 2		T1—081
Geelvink Bay languages	T6—991 2	arts	700.452 1
Geese	598.417		T3C—352 1
animal husbandry	636.598	labor economics	331.56
conservation technology	639.978 417	legal status	346.013 081
resource economics	333.958 417	private law	346.013 081
sports hunting	799.244 7		

Gender identity (continued)
  literature
    specific literatures   T3B—080 352 1
    history and
      criticism   T3B—093 521
  North American native peoples 305.308 997
  psychology   155.33
    adolescents   155.53
    children   155.43
Gender identity disorders
  medicine   616.858 3
Gender minorities   306.768
Gender non-conforming people   306.768
    T1—086 7
Gender nonconforming people   306.768
    T1—086 7
Gender nonconformity   306.768
Gender role   305.3
    T1—081
  arts   700.452 1
    T3C—352 1
  labor economics   331.56
  literature
    specific literatures   T3B—080 352 1
    history and
      criticism   T3B—093 521
Gene activation   572.865
Gene expression   572.865
Gene mapping   572.863 3
  humans   611.018 166 3
Gene pools   576.58
Gene silencing   572.865
Gene splicing
  biotechnology   660.65
Gene therapy
  law   344.041 96
  therapeutics   615.895
Genealogical registers   929.3
Genealogists   929.109 2
Genealogy   929.1
General accounting offices   352.43
  audit reports   352.439
General Agreement on Tariffs
  and Trade (1947)   382.92
  law   343.087 026 1
General anesthesia
  surgery   617.962
General assemblies
  presbyterian polity   262.42
General Carrera (Chile :
  Province)   T2—836 25
General catalogs   025.31
  bibliography   011
  library science   025.31

General certificate of education
  examination (United
  Kingdom)   371.262
  A level   378.166 2
  GCSE   373.126 2
General Conference Mennonite
  Church   289.73
General educational development
  tests   373.126 2
General services agencies   352.5
General Society of Colonial Wars
  (U.S.)   369.12
General Society of Mayflower
  Descendants   369.12
General staffs   355.330 42
General stores   381.14
  see also Commerce
General strikes   322.2
  economics   331.892 5
    see also Strikes (Work
      stoppages)
General topology   514.322
Generalized functions   515.782
Generalized system of preference 382.753
  see also Customs (Tariff)
Generals   355.009 2
  role and function   355.331
Generating electricity   621.312 1
Generating functions   515.55
Generating machinery
  electrical engineering   621.313
Generating steam   621.18
Generation gap   305.2
  family relationships   306.874
Generation of sound
  physics   534.1
Generative grammar   415.018 22
  specific languages   T4—501 822
Generative linguistics   410.182 2
  specific languages   T4—018 22
Generative organs   573.6
  see also Genital system
Generative phonology   414.018 2
  specific languages   T4—150 182
Generative semantics   401.430 182
  specific languages   T4—014 301 82
Genes   572.86
  humans   611.018 166
Genesee County (Mich.)   T2—774 37
Genesee County (N.Y.)   T2—747 92
Genesee River (Pa. and
  N.Y.)   T2—747 88
Genesis (Bible)   222.11

Genetic algorithms	
computer science	006.382 3
mathematics	519.625
Genetic code	572.863 3
humans	611.018 166 3
Genetic disorders	571.948
animals	571.948 1
humans	362.196 042
medicine	616.042
social services	362.196 042
Genetic engineering	660.65
agriculture	631.523 3
pest resistance	632.9
animal husbandry	636.082 1
cells	
research	
medicine	616.027 7
ethics	174.2
law	344.095 7
medical	344.041 96
tissue	
research	
medicine	616.027
Genetic evolution	572.838
Genetic factors	
influence on crime	364.24
physical ethnology	599.972
Genetic makeup	576.53
Genetic programming	
computer science	006.382 3
Genetic recombination	572.877
Genetic regulation	572.865
Genetic replication	572.864 5
Genetic resources	333.953 4
animals	333.954
economics	333.953 4
plants	333.953 4
Genetic screening	362.196 042 07
crime prevention	364.41
Genetic transcription	572.884 5
Genetic transduction	571.964 8
Genetic transformation	571.964 8
Genetic translation	572.645
Geneticists	576.509 2
Genetics	576.5
animal husbandry	636.082 1
animals	591.35
humans	599.935
sociology	304.5
microorganisms	579.135
plants	581.35
sociology	304.5
see Manual at 576.5 vs. 572.8	
Genets	599.742

Geneva (Switzerland :	
Canton)	T2—494 51
Geneva, Lake (Switzerland	
and France)	T2—494 52
France	T2—445 84
Switzerland	T2—494 52
Geneva Conventions	341.65
Geneva County (Ala.)	T2—761 292
Genève (Switzerland)	T2—494 516
Genève (Switzerland :	
Canton)	T2—494 51
Genf (Switzerland)	T2—494 516
Genf (Switzerland : Canton)	T2—494 51
Genghis Khan	
Asian history	950.21
Geniculate bodies	
human physiology	612.826 2
Genital diseases	573.639
animals	573.639
veterinary medicine	636.089 665
humans	362.196 65
anesthesiology	617.967 46
cancer	362.196 994 6
incidence	614.599 946
medicine	616.994 6
social services	362.196 994 6
see also Cancer —	
humans	
geriatrics	618.976 65
incidence	614.596 5
medicine	616.65
pediatrics	618.926 5
pharmacokinetics	615.766
social services	362.196 65
surgery	617.46
see also Urogenital diseases	
Genital herpes	
incidence	614.547
medicine	616.951 8
see also Communicable	
diseases — humans	
Genital organs	573.6
see also Genital system	
Genital system	573.6
anesthesiology	617.967 46
animals	573.6
diseases	573.639
see also Genital diseases	
human anatomy	611.6
human histology	612.604 5
human physiology	612.6
medicine	616.65

Geomancy	133.333	George V, King of Great Britain	
Geometric abstractionism	709.040 52	British history	941.083
painting	759.065 2	English history	942.083
sculpture	735.230 452	Scottish history	941.108 3
Geometric design	709.040 3	George VI, King of Great Britain	
painting	759.063	British history	941.084
sculpture	735.230 43	English history	942.084
Geometric number theory	512.75	Scottish history	941.108 4
Geometric probability	519.2	George County (Miss.)	T2—762 165
Geometric progressions	515.24	Georgetown (Guyana)	T2—881 5
Geometric shapes	516.15	Georgetown County (S.C.)	T2—757 89
Geometrical crystallography	548.81	Georgia	975.8
Geometrical optics	535.32		T2—758
Geometries over algebras	516.18	Georgia (Republic)	947.58
Geometries over rings	516.18		T2—475 8
Geometroidea	595.78	ancient	939.536
Geometry	516		T2—395 36
famous problems	516.204	Georgia, Strait of (B.C.)	551.461 433
primary education	372.76		T2—164 33
Geometry of numbers	512.75	Georgian architecture	724.19
Geomorphologists	551.410 92	Georgian Bay (Ont. : Bay)	T2—713 15
Geomorphology	551.41	Georgian language	499.969
Geomyidae	599.359 9		T6—999 69
Geonavigation		Georgian literature	899.969
nautical	623.892	Georgians	
Geonavigation aids		(Transcaucasians)	T5—999 69
marine navigation	623.893	Geotectonics	551.8
Geonim	296.120 092	Geothermal energy	333.88
Geophysical prospecting	622.15	economics	333.88
Geophysics	550	public administration	354.48
see Manual at 550 vs. 910		Geothermal engineering	621.44
Geopolitics	320.12	Geothermal prospecting	622.159
international relations	327.101	Gera (Germany)	T2—432 22
George (South Africa :		Gera (Germany : Bezirk)	T2—432 22
District)	T2—687 37	Geraldton (W.A.)	T2—941 2
George, Henry		Geraniaceae	583.72
economic school	330.155	Geraniales	583.72
George, Lake (N.Y.)	T2—747 51	Geraniums (Pelargoniums)	635.933 72
George I, King of Great Britain		botany	583.72
British history	941.071	floriculture	635.933 72
English history	942.071	Gerberas	583.983
Scottish history	941.107 1	botany	583.983
George II, King of Great Britain		floriculture	635.933 983
British history	941.072	Gerbils	636.935 83
English history	942.072	animal husbandry	636.935 83
Scottish history	941.107 2	zoology	599.358 3
George III, King of Great Britain		GERD (Disease)	
British history	941.073	medicine	616.324
English history	942.073	*see also* Digestive system	
Scottish history	941.107 3	diseases — humans	
George IV, King of Great Britain		Geriatric cardiology	618.976 12
British history	941.074		
English history	942.074		
Scottish history	941.107 4		

Gers (France)	T2—447 7
Gersau (Switzerland :	
Bezirk)	T2—494 752 8
Gert Sibande District	
Municipality (South	
Africa)	T2—682 78
Gerunds	415.54
specific languages	T4—554
Gesneriaceae	583.96
Gestalt psychology	150.198 2
Gestalt therapy	
psychiatry	616.891 43
Gestational diabetes	
pregnancy complications	
obstetrics	618.364 6
Gestures	302.222
drama	792.028
motion pictures	791.430 28
stage	792.028
television	791.450 28
preaching	251.03
psychology	153.69
expressive movements	152.384
nonverbal communication	153.69
rhetoric of speech	808.5
social psychology	302.222
Gettysburg, Battle of, 1863	973.734 9
Geysers	551.23
Gezira (Sudan : State)	T2—626 4
Ghana	966.7
	T2—667
Ghana Empire	966.101 6
	T2—661
Ghanaians	T5—966 7
Gharb al-Istiwā'īyah (South	
Sudan)	T2—629 5
Gharb Baḥr al Ghazāl	
(South Sudan)	T2—629 4
Gharb-Chrarda-Béni Hsen	
(Morocco)	T2—643 5
Gharb Dārfūr (Sudan :	
State)	T2—627
Gharb Kurdufān (Sudan)	T2—628
Gharbīyah (Egypt)	T2—621
Ghardaia (Algeria :	
Province)	T2—657
Gharīb	
Hadith	297.125 24
Ghazi I, King of Iraq	
Iraqi history	956.704 2
Ghazni dynasty	954.022 3
Ghazouani, Mohamed Ould	
Mauritanian history	966.106 3
Ghent (Belgium)	T2—493 142

Ghettos	307.336 6
Holocaust, 1933–1945	940.531 85
Ghor dynasty	954.022 5
Ghost pipefishes	597.67
Ghost sharks	597.38
Ghosts	133.1
arts	700.475
	T3C—375
fiction	808.838 733
history and criticism	809.387 33
specific literatures	T3B—308 733
individual authors	T3A—3
folklore	398.25
history and criticism	398.47
literature	808.803 75
history and criticism	809.933 75
specific literatures	T3B—080 375
history and	
criticism	T3B—093 75
occultism	133.1
Ghusl	297.38
Gia Lai (Vietnam)	T2—597 6
Giammattei, Alejandro	
Guatemalan history	972.810 537
Giant ferns	587.33
Giant forest hog	599.633
Giant otter	599.769
Giant panda	599.789
conservation technology	639.979 789
resource economics	333.959 789
Giant perches	597.72
Giant schnauzer	636.73
Giant slalom skiing	796.935
see also Winter sports	
Giant stars	523.88
Giants	
physical anthropology	599.949
Giant's Castle Game	
Reserve (South Africa)	T2—684 9
Giardiasis	
medicine	616.34
see also Digestive system	
diseases — humans	
Gibbons	599.882
Gibbs' phase rule	
thermochemistry	541.363
Gibraltar	946.89
	T2—468 9
Gibraltar, Strait of	551.461 381
	T2—163 81
Gibraltar Range National	
Park (N.S.W.)	T2—944 3
Gibson County (Ind.)	T2—772 35
Gibson County (Tenn.)	T2—768 23

Girl Scout camps	796.542 2
Girl Scouts	369.463
Girls	305.230 82
	T1—083
criminal offenders	364.36
education	371.822
health	613.042 42
home care	649.133
journalism for	070.483 27
psychology	155.433
publications for	
bibliographies	011.624 2
recreation	790.194
indoor	793.019 4
outdoor	796.083
sex hygiene	613.955
social aspects	305.230 82
Girls' clubs	369.46
Girls' scouting organizations	369.463
Girls' societies	369.46
Gironde (France)	T2—447 14
GIS (Geographic information	
systems)	910.285
	T1—028 5
mathematical geography	526.028 5
Gisborne District (N.Z.)	T2—934 4
Gisborne Region (N.Z.)	T2—934 4
Gisu (African people)	T5—963 95
Gisu language	496.395
	T6—963 95
Gittin	296.123 3
Babylonian Talmud	296.125 3
Mishnah	296.123 3
Palestinian Talmud	296.124 3
Giudicati	945.903
Giurgiu (Romania : Judeţ)	T2—498 2
Given names	929.44
Giyani (South Africa :	
District)	T2—682 59
Giza (Egypt)	T2—622
ancient	T2—322
Gjoa Haven (Nunavut)	T2—719 55
Glacial action	551.313
Glacial drift (Geologic	
landforms)	551.315
Glacial drift (Geologic material)	551.314
Glacier Bay National Park	
and Preserve (Alaska)	T2—798 2
Glacier County (Mont.)	T2—786 52
Glacier National Park (B.C.)	T2—711 68
Glacier National Park	
(Mont.)	T2—786 52

Glaciers	551.312
biology	578.758 6
ecology	577.586
Glaciology	551.31
Glades County (Fla.)	T2—759 51
Gladiolus	635.934 75
botany	584.75
floriculture	635.934 75
Gladstone (Qld.)	T2—943 5
Gladwin County (Mich.)	T2—774 72
Glamorgan, Vale of (Wales)	T2—429 89
Gland diseases	
medicine	616.4
see also Endocrine	
diseases — humans	
Glanders	
incidence	614.564
medicine	616.954
see also Communicable	
diseases — humans	
Glands	571.79
biology	571.79
endocrine system	573.4
human anatomy	611.4
human physiology	612.4
medicine	616.4
see also Endocrine system	
Glâne (Switzerland)	T2—494 532
Glanford (England)	T2—428 32
Glaris (Switzerland :	
Canton)	T2—494 74
Glarner Alps (Switzerland)	T2—494 74
Glarus (Switzerland)	T2—494 744
Glarus (Switzerland :	
Canton)	T2—494 74
Glascock County (Ga.)	T2—758 666
Glasgow (Scotland)	941.44
	T2—414 4
Glass	666.1
architectural construction	721.044 96
building construction	693.96
building materials	691.6
decorative arts	748
materials science	620.144
optical components	
manufacturing technology	681.42
sculpture material	731.2
ship design	623.818 38
ship hulls	623.845 8
shipbuilding	623.820 7
structural engineering	624.183 8
technology	666.1
Glass artists	748.092
Glass beads	748.85

Gloucestershire (England)	942.41	Gneiss	552.4
	T2—424 1	Gnetales	585.8
Glove compartments		Gneticae	585.8
automobile	629.277	paleobotany	561.58
Glove makers	685.409 2	Gnetum	585.8
Gloves	391.412	Gnosticism	299.932
commercial technology	685.4	Christian heresy	273.1
customs	391.412	GNP (Macroeconomics)	339.31
home economics	646.3	Gnus	599.645 9
home sewing	646.48	Go (Game)	794.4
see also Clothing		Goa (India : State)	T2—547 8
Glowworms	595.764 4	Goa, Daman and Diu (India)	T2—547 8
Gloxinias	635.933 96	Goajiro Indians	T5—983 9
botany	583.96	Goalkeeping	
floriculture	635.933 96	ice hockey	796.962 27
Glucose	572.565	soccer	796.334 26
see also Carbohydrates		Goat (Meat)	641.363 9
Glue	668.3	commercial processing	664.92
see also Adhesives		cooking	641.663 9
Glue abuse	362.299 3	food	641.363 9
medicine	616.86	Goat hair textiles	677.33
personal health	613.8	*see also* Textiles	
social welfare	362.299 3	Goatfishes	597.7
see also Substance abuse		Goats	636.39
Gluing		animal husbandry	636.39
bookbinding	686.35	zoology	599.648
Gluten-free cooking	641.563 931 1	Goat's milk	641.371 7
Gluten-free diet		cooking	641.671 7
health	613.268 311	food	641.371 7
Gluten-free foods	641.309 311	processing	637.17
Gluten intolerance		Goatsuckers	598.99
medicine	616.399 12	Gobi Desert (Mongolia and	
Gluttony	178	China)	T2—517 3
see also Consumption — ethics		Gobies	597.7
Glycemic index		Gobiesociformes	597.62
applied nutrition	613.283	God	211
human physiology	612.396	art representation	704.948
Glycerin	668.2	arts	700.482 11
Glycogen	572.566		T3C—382 11
see also Carbohydrates		Buddhism	294.342 11
Glycoproteins	572.68	Christianity	231
see also Proteins		comparative religion	202.11
Glycosides	572.567	Hinduism	294.521 1
see also Carbohydrates		Islam	297.211
Glyndŵr (Wales)	T2—429 37	Judaism	296.311
Glynn County (Ga.)	T2—758 742	literature	808.803 821 1
Glyptics	736.2	history and criticism	809.933 821 1
Glyptographers	736.209 2	specific literatures	T3B—080 382 11
Gmelina	583.96	history and	
botany	583.96	criticism	T3B—093 821 1
forestry	634.973 96	philosophy of religion	211
Gnassingbé, Faure		Goddess religions	201.43
Togolese history	966.810 43		
Gnats	595.772		

Goddesses	202.114	Goiás (Brazil : State)	T2—817 3
arts	700.482 021 14	Goidelic languages	491.6
	T3C—382 021 14		T6—916
literature	808.803 820 211 4	Goidelic literatures	891.6
history and criticism	809.933 820 211 4	Going public (Securities)	658.152 24
specific literatures	T3B—080 382 021 14	corporate law	346.066 2
history and		financial management	658.152 24
criticism	T3B—093 820 211 4	investment economics	332.632 2
see also Gods and goddesses		Goiter	
Gödel's theorem	511.3	medicine	616.442
Gods	202.11	*see also* Endocrine	
male	202.113	diseases — humans	
see also Male gods		surgery	617.539
see also Gods and goddesses		Gökçeada (Turkey)	T2—562 2
Gods and goddesses	202.11	Gold	669.22
African	299.612 11	chemical engineering	661.065 6
art representation	704.948	chemistry	546.656
arts	700.482 021 1	economic geology	553.41
	T3C—382 021 1	extractive economics	338.274 1
Australian	299.921 5	materials science	620.189 22
Buddhist	294.342 11	metallography	669.952 2
Celtic	299.161 211	metallurgy	669.22
Chinese	299.511 211	metalworking	673.22
classical	292.211	mining	622.342 2
folklore	398.21	monetary law	343.032
history and criticism	398.45	physical metallurgy	669.962 2
Germanic	293.211	prospecting	622.184 1
Greek	292.211	*see also* Chemicals; Metals	
Hawaiian	299.924 202 11	Gold Coast	966.703
Hindu	294.521 1		T2—667
literature	808.803 820 211	Gold coins	332.404 2
history and criticism	809.933 820 211	investment economics	332.63
specific literatures	T3B—080 382 021 1	monetary economics	332.404 2
history and		numismatics	737.43
criticism	T3B—093 820 211	Gold standard	332.422 2
Native American	299.712 11	foreign exchange	332.452
North American	299.712 11	Golden (B.C.)	T2—711 68
South American	299.812 11	Golden algae	579.86
Norse	293.211	Golden eagle	598.942 3
Polynesian	299.924 021 1	Golden Ears Provincial Park	
Roman	292.211	(B.C.)	T2—711 37
Scandinavian	293.211	Golden Gate Highlands	
Semitic	299.2	National Park (South	
Shinto	299.561 211	Africa)	T2—685 1
Goedelic languages	491.6	Golden hamsters	599.356
	T6—916	Golden Rule	
Goedelic literatures	891.6	Christianity	241.54
Goethite		Judaism	296.36
mineralogy	549.525	Golden Valley County	
Gogebic County (Mich.)	T2—774 983	(Mont.)	T2—786 311
Gogo languages	496.391	Golden Valley County	
	T6—963 91	(N.D.)	T2—784 95
Goh, Chok Tong		Goldeneyes	598.415
Singaporean history	959.570 52	Goldenrods	583.983

Goldfinches	598.885
Goldfish	639.374 84
culture	639.374 84
zoology	597.484
Goldi	T5—941
Goldi language	494.1
	T6—941
Golds	T5—941
Goldsmithing	739.22
Goldsmiths	739.220 92
Golestān (Iran : Province)	T2—552 2
Golf	796.352
equipment technology	688.763 52
see also Ball games	
Golf courses	796.352 068
Golfe-du-Saint-Laurent	
(Quebec)	T2—714 179
Golfers	796.352 092
Golgi apparatus	571.656
Goliad County (Tex.)	T2—764 123
Gombe State (Nigeria)	T2—669 84
Gomel′ (Belarus : Oblast)	T2—478 1
Gómez, Juan Vicente	
Venezuelan history	987.063 13
Goms (Switzerland)	T2—494 794 1
Göncz, Árpád	
Hungarian history	943.905 41
Gond (Dravidian people)	T5—948 23
Gondi language	494.823
	T6—948 23
Gondi literature	894.823
Gondola cars	385.34
engineering	625.24
see also Rolling stock	
Gonga (African people)	T5—935 9
Gongola State (Nigeria)	T2—669 88
Gongs	786.884 3
see also Percussion instruments	
Gonorhynchiformes	597.5
Gonorrhea	
incidence	614.547 8
medicine	616.951 5
see also Communicable	
diseases — humans	
Gonystylus	583.77
botany	583.77
forestry	634.973 77
Gonzales County (Tex.)	T2—764 257
González Macchi, Luis Angel	
Paraguayan history	989.207 44
Goochland County (Va.)	T2—755 455

Good and evil	111.84
ethics	170
religion	205
Christianity	241
Islam	297.5
Judaism	296.36
religion	202.118
Christianity	231.8
freedom of choice	233.7
comparative religion	202.118
Islam	297.2
freedom of choice	297.227
theodicy	297.211 8
Judaism	296.311 8
freedom of choice	296.32
philosophy of religion	214
Good Friday	263.925
devotional literature	242.35
music	781.726
sermons	252.625
Good Hope, Cape of (South	
Africa : Cape)	T2—687 356
Good luck charms	203.323
occultism	133.443
Good News Bible	220.520 82
Good spirits	202.15
Goodeniaceae	583.983
Goodhue County (Minn.)	T2—776 14
Gooding County (Idaho)	T2—796 36
Goodness-of-fit tests	519.56
Goodness of God	214
Christianity	231.8
comparative religion	202.112
Islam	297.211 2
Judaism	296.311 2
philosophy of religion	214
Goodwood (South Africa :	
District)	T2—687 35
Goole (England)	T2—428 39
Goose hunting	
sports	799.244 7
Gooseberries	641.347 25
botany	583.44
cooking	641.647 25
food	641.347 25
horticulture	634.725
Goosefishes	597.62
Goosefoots (Plants)	583.883
Gophers (Ground squirrels)	599.365
Gophers (Pocket gophers)	599.359 9
Gorbachev, Mikhail Sergeevich	
Russian history	947.085 4
Gordioida	592.59
Gordon (Scotland : District)	T2—412 4

Governing boards (continued)
libraries · 021.82
public administration · 352.25
Government · 320
ethics · 172.2
religion · 205.622
Buddhism · 294.356 22
Hinduism · 294.548 622
Islam · 297.562 2
Judaism · 296.362 2
see also Political ethics
see Manual at 320.9, 320.4 vs.
351
Government accounting · 657.835
law · 343.034
Government advisory boards · 352.743
Government agencies · 351
see also Administrative
agencies
Government and binding theory
(Linguistics) · 415.018 22
specific languages · T4—501 822
Government audit procedures · 657.835 045
Government bills · 332.632 32
see also Government securities
Government bonds · 332.632 32
see also Government securities
Government buildings
architecture · 725.1
area planning · 711.551
Government business enterprises · 338.749
see also Government
corporations
Government certificates · 332.632 32
see also Government securities
Government cities
area planning · 711.45
Government contracts · 352.53
armed forces · 355.621 2
law · 346.023
Government corporations · 338.749
law · 346.067
production economics · 338.749
public administration · 352.266
public revenue source · 336.19
see also Corporations;
Government business
enterprises; Public
enterprises
Government employees · 352.63
see also Government workers
Government expenditures · 336.39
see also Public expenditures
Government farm policies · 338.18

Government gazettes · 351.05
Government grants
production economics · 338.922
Government information services
international relations · 327.11
libraries · 027.5
public administration · 353.132 74
Government institutions
sociology · 306.2
Government investment · 332.672 52
international · 332.673 12
Government liability
law · 342.088
public administration · 352.885
Government libraries · 027.5
Government loans
credit economics · 332.7
economic development · 338.922
law · 343.074 2
public revenues · 336.15
Government notes · 332.632 32
see also Government securities
Government of Ireland Act, 1920 · 941.608 21
Government ownership
land economics · 333.1
Government policy · 320.6
Government procurement · 352.53
armed forces · 355.621 2
Government property
land economics · 333.1
law · 343.02
management · 352.5
Government publications
bibliographies · 011.53
cataloging · 025.343 4
library treatment · 025.173 4
Government publishers · 070.595
Government savings banks · 332.21
Government securities · 332.632 32
flotation · 336.344
income tax · 336.242 6
law · 343.052 46
investment economics · 332.632 32
law · 346.092 2
public administration · 352.45
public finance · 336.31
purchase
central banking · 332.114
see Manual at 332.632044 vs.
332.6323
Government service · 352.63
Government spending · 336.39
see also Public expenditures

Graphite	553.26	Graves County (Ky.)	T2—769 93
chemical engineering	662.92	Graves' disease	
economic geology	553.26	medicine	616.443
materials science	620.198	*see also* Endocrine	
mineralogy	549.27	diseases — humans	
mining	622.336	Graves registration service	
synthetic	666.86	(Armed forces)	355.699
Graphitic anthracite coal		Gravesham (England)	T2—422 315
properties	662.622 5	Gravestone inscriptions	
Graphology	155.282	genealogy	929.5
criminal investigation	363.256 5	Gravimetric analysis	543.2
divination	137	Gravitation	531.14
personnel selection	658.311 2	*see also* Gravity	
Graphs	511.5	Gravitational interaction	539.754
	T1—022	Gravitational prospecting	622.152
Graptemys	597.925 9	Gravitational waves	539.754
Graptolitoidea	563.55	Gravity	531.14
Grass carp	597.482	astromechanics	629.411 1
Grass owls	598.97	biophysics	571.435
Grass skiing	796.2	humans	612.014 412
see also Sports		celestial mechanics	521.1
Grass wax	665.12	extraterrestrial biophysics	
Grass wetlands		humans	612.014 532
biology	578.768 4	mechanics	531.14
ecology	577.684	solid mechanics	531.5
Grasses	584.92	Gravity concentration of ores	622.751
botany	584.92	Gravity determinations	
cereal crops	633.1	geodesy	526.7
floriculture	635.964	Gravity planes	
forage crops	633.2	mining	622.66
ornamental gardening	635.934 92	Gravity waves	551.515
paleobotany	561.49	Gray County (Kan.)	T2—781 74
Grasshoppers	595.726	Gray County (Tex.)	T2—764 827
agricultural pests	632.726	Gray fox	599.776
culture	638.572 6	Gray kangaroos	599.222
Grasslands	333.74	Gray partridge	598.623 2
	T2—153	Gray seal	599.793
animal husbandry	636.084 5	Gray squirrel	599.362
biology	578.74	Gray whale	599.522
ecology	577.4	conservation technology	639.979 522
economics	333.74	resource economics	333.959 522
geography	910.915 3	Gray wolf	599.773
geomorphology	551.453	Graylings	597.559
physical geography	910.021 53	Grays Harbor County	
Gratiot County (Mich.)	T2—774 49	(Wash.)	T2—797 95
Gratitude	179.9	Graysby	597.736
see also Virtues		Grayson County (Ky.)	T2—769 842
Graubünden (Switzerland)	T2—494 73	Grayson County (Tex.)	T2—764 557
Graupel	551.578 7	Grayson County (Va.)	T2—755 717
Gravel	553.626	Graywater	363.728 494
economic geology	553.626	Graz (Austria)	T2—436 55
materials science	620.191	Grazing	591.54
quarrying	622.362 6	animal husbandry	636.084 5
Gravel pavements	625.82	descriptive zoology	591.54

Great Valley (Calif.)	T2—794 5	Greeley County (Kan.)	T2—781 413
Great Victoria Desert		Greeley County (Neb.)	T2—782 49
(W.A.)	T2—941 5	Green algae	579.83
Great War, 1914–1918	940.3	Green Alliance (Swiss political	
Great whales	599.5	party)	324.249 408 7
Great White Brotherhood	299.93	Green bacteria	579.38
Great white shark	597.33	Green Bay (Wis.)	T2—775 61
Great Yarmouth (England :		Green Bay (Wis. and Mich.)	T2—775 63
Borough)	T2—426 18	Green County (Ky.)	T2—769 695
Greater Anchorage Area		Green County (Wis.)	T2—775 86
Borough (Alaska)	T2—798 35	Green fodder	
Greater Antilles	T2—729	forage crop	633.2
Greater Manchester		Green integral	515.43
(England)	T2—427 3	Green Lake County (Wis.)	T2—775 59
Greater Paris (France)	T2—443 6	Green living	
Greater Saint Lucia Wetland		household management	640.286
Park (South Africa)	T2—684 3	Green manures	631.874
Greater Sudbury (Ont.)	T2—713 133	Green marketing	
Greater Vancouver (B.C.)	T2—711 33	management	658.802
Grebes	598.443	Green monkeys	599.862
Grebo language	496.33	Green Mountains (Vt.)	T2—743
	T6—963 3	Green movement	320.58
Greco-Roman wrestling	796.812 2	Green parties	324.218 7
see also Combat sports		Green Party (Germany)	324.243 087
Greco-Turkish War, 1896–1897	949.507 2	Green Party of Switzerland	324.249 408 7
Greece	949.5	Green peppers	641.356 43
	T2—495	*see also* Sweet peppers	
ancient	938	Green politics	320.58
	T2—38	Green River (Ky. : River)	T2—769 8
Greed	178	Green River (Wyo.-Utah)	T2—792 5
moral theology	205.68	Utah	T2—792 5
see also Vices		Wyoming	T2—787 85
Greek architecture	722.8	Green seaweeds	579.83
Greek language	480	Green technology	628
	T6—8		T1—028 6
Biblical texts	220.48	agriculture	630.208 6
printing	686.218	aquaculture	639.802 86
Greek language (Modern)	489.3	architecture	720.47
	T6—89	chemical engineering	660.028 6
Greek law		construction	690.028 6
ancient	340.538	engineering	628
Greek-letter societies	371.85	forestry	634.902 86
	T1—06	horticulture	635.028 6
Greek literature	880	household management	640.286
Greek literature (Modern)	889	Green turtle	597.928
Greek philosophy	180	Greenbrier County (W. Va.)	T2—754 88
modern	199.495	Greenbrier River (W. Va.)	T2—754 88
Greek religion	292.08	Greenbriers	584.6
Greek revival architecture	724.23	Greene County (Ala.)	T2—761 42
Greek sculpture	733.3	Greene County (Ark.)	T2—767 993
Greeks (Ethnic group)	T5—8	Greene County (Ga.)	T2—758 612
ancient	T5—81	Greene County (Ill.)	T2—773 84
modern	T5—89	Greene County (Ind.)	T2—772 42
Greeks (National group)	T5—893	Greene County (Iowa)	T2—777 466

Grievances (Labor)	331.889 66
economics	331.889 66
law	344.018 896 6
personnel management	658.315 5
public administration	352.68
Grievances against government	
public administration	352.885
Griffith (N.S.W.)	T2—944 8
Griggs County (N.D.)	T2—784 34
Grilling (Cooking)	641.76
Grills (Cooking equipment)	
outdoor cooking	641.578 4
Grills (Screens)	
ironwork	
arts	739.48
Grimes County (Tex.)	T2—764 243
Grimoire	133.43
Grimsby (England)	T2—428 34
Grinding	
chemical engineering	660.284 22
coal	662.623
metals	671.35
ores	622.73
Grinding tools	621.92
Grindstones	621.923
Griqualand East (South Africa)	T2—684 67
Grise Fiord (Nunavut)	T2—719 52
Grisons (Animals)	599.766
Grisons (Switzerland)	T2—494 73
Grizzly bear	599.784
conservation technology	639.979 784
resource economics	333.959 784
Groblersdal (South Africa : District)	T2—682 55
Grocery trade	381.456 413
Grodno (Belarus : Oblast)	T2—478 8
Groined arches	721.44
architecture	721.44
construction	690.144
Groined vaults	721.44
architecture	721.44
construction	690.144
Groningen (Netherlands : Province)	T2—492 12
Grooming	646.7
child training	649.63
Grooming behavior (Animals)	591.563
Grooming of animals	636.083 3
Groote Eylandt (N.T.)	T2—942 95
Gros-de-Vaud (Switzerland)	T2—494 522 7
Gros Ventre language	497.354
	T6—973 54
Grosbeaks	598.883

Gross domestic product	339.31
Gross national product	339.31
Grossdeutsche Volkspartei (Austria)	324.243 602 3
Grosse Île (Montmagny, Quebec)	T2—714 735
Grosseto (Italy : Province)	T2—455 7
ancient	T2—375 64
Grossulariaceae	583.44
Grotesque	
arts	T3C—15
literature	808.801 5
history and criticism	809.915
specific literatures	T3B—080 15
history and criticism	T3B—091 5
Grottoes	551.447
	T2—144
see also Caves	
Ground bass	781.827
instrumental	784.182 7
Ground beetles	595.762
Ground cover	635.964
floriculture	635.964
landscape architecture	716
Ground-effect machines	
engineering	629.3
Ground forces (Military science)	355
Ground inspections	
aircraft	629.134 52
Ground ivy	583.96
Ground operations (Armed forces)	355.4
see also Land operations	
Ground photogrammetry	526.982 5
Ground squirrels	599.365
Ground substances (Histology)	
humans	611.018 2
Ground surveying	526.9
Ground testing facilities	
spacecraft	629.478
Ground tests	
aircraft	629.134 52
Ground transportation	388
engineering	629.049
law	343.093
military engineering	623.61
public administration	354.76
safety	363.12
see also Transportation safety	

Groupware	005.376
Grouse	598.63
conservation technology	639.978 63
resource economics	333.958 63
sports hunting	799.246 3
Growing layers (Plants)	575.48
Growing points (Plants)	575.48
Growlers (Ice formations)	551.342
Growth	571.8
animals	571.81
cells	571.849
developmental biology	571.8
human physiology	612.6
microorganisms	571.849 29
plants	571.82
Growth (Social development)	303.44
Growth hormones	571.837 4
Growth regulators	
agriculture	631.89
chemical engineering	668.6
Grues, Île aux (Quebec)	T2—714 735
Grues Island (Quebec)	T2—714 735
Gruidae	598.32
Gruiformes	598.32
paleozoology	568.3
Grundy County (Ill.)	T2—773 265
Grundy County (Iowa)	T2—777 537
Grundy County (Mo.)	T2—778 215
Grundy County (Tenn.)	T2—768 78
Grünen (German political party)	324.243 087
Grünen (Swiss political party)	324.249 408 7
Grünen - Die Grüne Alternative	
(Austrian political party)	324.243 608 7
Grünes Bündnis (Swiss political	
party)	324.249 408 7
Grunts (Fishes)	597.7
Gruyère (Switzerland :	
District)	T2—494 533
Grylloblattodea	595.726
GSP (Tariff)	382.753
see also Customs (Tariff)	
Guadalajara (Spain :	
Province)	T2—464 9
Guadalcanal (Solomon	
Islands)	T2—959 33
Guadalcanal, Battle of,	
1942–1943	940.542 659 33
Guadalquivir River (Spain)	T2—468
Guadalupe County (N.M.)	T2—789 25
Guadalupe County (Tex.)	T2—764 34
Guadalupe Mountains	
National Park (Tex.)	T2—764 94
Guadalupe River (Tex.)	T2—764 12

Guadeloupe	972.976
	T2—729 76
Guahiban languages	498.9
	T6—989
Guaicuru languages	498.7
	T6—987
Guainía (Colombia)	T2—861 67
Guairá (Paraguay)	T2—892 128
Guajira (Colombia : Dept.)	T2—861 17
Guam	T2—967
Guanacaste (Costa Rica :	
Province)	T2—728 66
Guanaco	599.636 7
animal husbandry	636.296 6
Guanaco wool textiles	677.32
see also Textiles	
Guanajuato (Mexico : State)	T2—724 1
Guanche language	493.3
	T6—933
Guangdong Sheng (China)	T2—512 7
Guangxi Zhuangzu Zizhiqu	
(China)	T2—512 8
Guangzhou (China)	T2—512 75
Guano	
agricultural use	631.866
Guans	598.64
Guantánamo (Cuba :	
Province)	T2—729 167
Guaraní Indians	T5—983 822
Guaraní language	498.382 2
	T6—983 822
Guaranteed annual wage	331.236
Guaranteed minimum income	362.582
law	344.032 582
public administration	353.54
Guaranteed wages	331.23
Guarantees (Insurance)	368.85
Guarantees (Law)	343.08
Guaranty (Suretyship)	346.074
Guard animals	636.088 6
Guard dogs	636.73
Guarda (Portugal : District)	T2—469 32
Guardian and ward	346.018
Guards (Safety equipment)	621.992
Guárico (Venezuela : State)	T2—874 7
Guatemala	972.81
	T2—728 1
Guatemala (Guatemala :	
Dept.)	T2—728 11
Guatemalan literature	860
Guatemalans	T5—687 281
Guavas	641.344 21
botany	583.732
commercial processing	664.804 421

Guavas (continued)
 cooking 641.644 21
 food 641.344 21
 orchard crop 634.421
Guaviare (Colombia) T2—861 66
Guayama (P.R. : District) T2—729 58
Guayaquil, Gulf of 551.461 41
  T2—164 1
Guayas (Ecuador :
 Province) T2—866 32
Guayule 583.983
Guebuza, Armando Emílio
 Mozambican history 967.905 3
Guelleh, Ismail Omar
 Djiboutian history 967.710 42
Guelma (Algeria : Province) T2—655
Guelmim (Morocco :
 Province) T2—646 8
Guelmim-Es Semara
 (Morocco) T2—646 8
Guelph (Ont.) T2—713 43
Guenons 599.862
Guernsey (Channel Islands) T2—423 42
Guernsey cattle 636.224
Guernsey County (Ohio) T2—771 92
Guernsey lily 635.934 78
Guerrilla tactics 355.425
Guerrilla troops 356.15
Guerrilla warfare 355.021 8
Guerrillas 322.42
Guests
 seating at table 642.6
Guevara, Ernesto
 Cuban communism 335.434 7
GUI (User interface)
 systems software 005.437
Guiana 988
  T2—88
Guidance
 crime prevention 364.48
 education 371.4
 manned space flight 629.453
 social welfare 361.06
  older people 362.66
 space flight 629.41
 unmanned space flight 629.433
Guidance systems
 spacecraft 629.474 2
 unmanned spacecraft 629.464 2
Guidebooks 910.202
 see Manual at 913–919; *also at*
  913–919 vs. 796.51
Guidebooks of exhibits T1—074

Guided aircraft
 control systems 629.132 6
 military engineering 623.746 9
Guided-light communication 621.382 75
Guided missile forces 358.17
 in space 358.8
 navy 359.981 7
Guided missiles 358.171 82
 engineering 623.451 9
 military equipment 358.171 82
Guided missiles in space 358.882
 engineering 623.451 98
 military equipment 358.882
Guided-way systems 388.42
 engineering 625.4
 see also Local rail transit
  systems
Guides to religious life 204.4
 Buddhism 294.344 4
 Christianity 248.4
 Hinduism 294.544
 Islam 297.57
  Sufi 297.44
 Judaism 296.7
Guiding equipment (Tools) 621.992
Guild socialism 335.15
Guild system 338.632
Guildford (England :
 Borough) T2—422 162
Guilford County (N.C.) T2—756 62
Guillain-Barré syndrome
 medicine 616.856
 see also Nervous system
  diseases — humans
Guilt
 psychology 152.44
 religion 202.2
  Christianity 233.4
  Judaism 296.32
Guilt (Law) 345.04
Guimaras (Philippines) T2—599 536
Guinea 966.52
  T2—665 2
Guinea, Gulf of 551.461 373
  T2—163 73
Guinea-Bissau 966.57
  T2—665 7
Guinea-Bissauans T5—966 57
Guinea fowl 636.593
 animal husbandry 636.593
 zoology 598.64

Guinea pigs	636.935 92
animal husbandry	636.935 92
experimental animals	
medicine	616.027 33
zoology	599.359 2
Guineans	T5—966 52
Guipúzcoa (Spain)	T2—466 1
Guiros	786.886
see also Percussion instruments	
Guitar concertos	784.278 718 6
Guitarfishes	597.35
Guitarists	787.870 92
Guitars	787.87
instrument	787.871 9
music	787.87
see also Stringed instruments	
Guizhou Sheng (China)	T2—513 4
Gujar	T5—914 79
Gujarat (India)	T2—547 5
Gujarati	T5—914 71
Gujarati language	491.47
	T6—914 71
Gujarati literature	891.47
Gulches	551.442
	T2—144
geography	910.914 4
geomorphology	551.442
physical geography	910.021 44
Gulf Coast (U.S.)	976
	T2—76
Gulf County (Fla.)	T2—759 947
Gulf Islands (B.C.)	T2—711 28
Gulf languages (North American	
native languages)	497.9
	T6—979
Gulf of Aden	551.461 532
	T2—165 32
Gulf of Alaska (Alaska)	551.461 434
	T2—164 34
Gulf of Aqaba	551.461 533
	T2—165 33
Gulf of Bothnia	551.461 334
	T2—163 34
Gulf of California (Mexico)	551.461 41
	T2—164 1
Gulf of Darien (Colombia)	551.461 365
	T2—163 65
Gulf of Finland	551.461 334
	T2—163 34
Gulf of Guayaquil	551.461 41
	T2—164 1
Gulf of Guinea	551.461 373
	T2—163 73

Gulf of Honduras	551.461 365
	T2—163 65
Gulf of Lions (France)	551.461 382
	T2—163 82
Gulf of Martaban (Burma)	551.461 565
	T2—165 65
Gulf of Mexico	551.461 364
	T2—163 64
Gulf of Oman	551.461 536
	T2—165 36
Gulf of Panama (Panama)	551.461 41
	T2—164 1
Gulf of Paria (Venezuela and	
Trinidad and Tobago)	551.461 366
	T2—163 66
Gulf of Riga (Latvia and Estonia)	551.461 334
	T2—163 34
Gulf of Saint Lawrence	551.461 344
	T2—163 44
Gulf of Siam	551.461 472
	T2—164 72
Gulf of Suez	551.461 533
	T2—165 33
Gulf of Taranto (Italy)	551.461 386
	T2—163 86
Gulf of Tehuantepec (Mexico)	551.461 41
	T2—164 1
Gulf of Thailand	551.461 472
	T2—164 72
Gulf of Urabá (Colombia)	551.461 365
	T2—163 65
Gulf of Venice (Italy)	551.461 385
	T2—163 85
Gulf Province (Papua New	
Guinea)	T2—954 7
Gulf Stream	551.462 131
Gulf War, 1980–1988	955.054 2
Gulf War, 1991	956.704 42
Gulfs	
resource economics	333.916 4
Gulistān (Iran : Province)	T2—552 2
Gullah dialect	427.975 799
	T6—217
Gulls	598.338
Gum-bichromate processes	773.5
Gum diseases	
dentistry	617.632
incidence	614.599 6
Gum trees (Eucalypti)	583.733
Gumatj language	499.15
	T6—991 5
Gumma-ken (Japan)	T2—521 33

Gustatory organs	573.878
see also Taste (Sense)	
Gustatory perception	
psychology	152.167
Gustav I Vasa, King of Sweden	
Swedish history	948.503 21
Gustav II Adolf, King of Sweden	
Swedish history	948.503 41
Gustav III, King of Sweden	
Swedish history	948.503 81
Gustav IV Adolf, King of	
Sweden	
Swedish history	948.503 82
Gustav V, King of Sweden	
Swedish history	948.505 1
Gustav VI Adolf, King of	
Sweden	
Swedish history	948.505 3
Gustavian period	948.503 8
Finnish history	948.970 138
Swedish history	948.503 8
Güstrow (Germany :	
Landkreis)	T2—431 74
Guthrie, Edwin R. (Edwin Ray)	
psychological system	150.194 34
Guthrie County (Iowa)	T2—777 49
Gutters	
road engineering	625.734
Guttiferae	583.69
Guyana	988.1
	T2—881
Guyandotte River (W. Va.)	T2—754 4
Guyane	988.2
	T2—882
Guyanese	T5—914 1
Guyenne (France)	T2—447
Guysborough (N.S. :	
County)	T2—716 21
Guzmán Blanco, Antonio	
Venezuelan history	987.062 8
Gwaun-cae-Gurwen (Wales)	T2—429 85
Gwent (Wales)	T2—429 9
Gwich'in Indians	T5—972
Gwinnett County (Ga.)	T2—758 223
Gwydir River (N.S.W.)	T2—944 4
Gwynedd (Wales)	T2—429 25
Gwynedd (Wales : County)	T2—429 2
Gymnascales	579.565
Gymnasiums (Secondary	
schools)	373.241
see also Secondary education	
Gymnasiums (Sports)	796.406 8
architecture	725.85
sports	796.406 8

Gymnastic exercises	613.714
Gymnastics	796.44
arts	700.457 9
	T3C—357 9
child care	649.57
ethics	175
human physiology	612.044
journalism	070.449 796 44
law	344.099
literature	
history and criticism	809.933 579
specific literatures	T3B—080 357 9
history and	
criticism	T3B—093 579
motion pictures	791.436 579
physical fitness	613.714
public administrative support	353.78
safety	363.14
public administration	353.97
techniques	796.440 289
sociology	306.483
television programs	791.456 579
see also Sports	
Gymnasts	796.440 92
Gymnolaemata	594.676
Gymnophiona	597.82
paleozoology	567.8
Gymnosomata	594.34
Gymnosperms	585
forestry	634.975
paleobotany	561.5
see also Plants	
Gymnotidae	597.48
Gympie (Qld.)	T2—943 2
Gynecologic cancer	
incidence	614.599 946 5
medicine	616.994 65
see also Cancer — humans	
Gynecologic disorders	362.198 1
see also Female genital	
diseases — humans	
Gynecologic nursing	618.102 31
Gynecologic surgery	618.105 9
Gynecologists	618.100 92
law	344.041 2
role and function	618.102 32
Gynecology	618.1
anesthesiology	617.968 1
geriatrics	618.978
pediatrics	618.920 98
surgery	618.105 9
Gynoplasty	618.105 92
Győr-Moson-Sopron Megye	
(Hungary)	T2—439 7

H

Hahnium	
chemistry	546.52
Hải Dương (Vietnam :	
Province)	T2—597 3
Haida Gwaii (B.C.)	971.112
	T2—711 12
Haida Indians	971.100 497 28
	T5—972 8
Haida language	497.28
	T6—972 8
Haida literature	897.28
Haidallah, Khouna Ould	
Mauritanian history	966.105 2
Haifa (Israel : District)	T2—569 46
Haiku	808.814 1
history and criticism	809.141
specific literatures	T3B—104 1
individual authors	T3A—1
Hail	551.578 7
crop damage	632.14
weather forecasting	551.647 87
Hail insurance	368.122
crops	368.121
see also Insurance	
Hail Mary	242.74
Haile Selassie I, Emperor of	
Ethiopia	
Ethiopian history	963.055
as emperor	963.055
as regent and king	963.054
Hailemariam Desalegn	
Ethiopian history	963.072 2
Hailstones	551.578 7
Hailstorms	551.554
social services	363.349 24
see also Disasters	
Hainan Sheng (China)	T2—512 9
Hainaut (Belgium)	T2—493 42
Haines (Alaska : Borough)	T2—798 2
Haiphong (Vietnam)	T2—597 3
Hair	599.147
animal husbandry	636.088 45
animal physiology	573.58
descriptive zoology	599.147
dramatic performances	792.027
motion pictures	791.430 27
stage	792.027
television	791.450 27
human anatomy	611.78
human physiology	612.799
medicine	616.546
personal care	646.724
surgery	617.477 9

Hair analysis	
criminal investigation	363.256 2
Hair diseases	
humans	
geriatrics	618.976 546
incidence	614.595 46
medicine	616.546
see also Skin diseases —	
humans	
pediatrics	618.925 46
pharmacokinetics	615.779
Hair dyeing	
personal care	646.724
Hair follicle diseases	
medicine	616.546
see also Skin diseases —	
humans	
Hair follicles	
medicine	616.546
Hair removal	
surgery	617.477 9
Hair seals	599.79
Hair transplantation	617.477 905 92
Haircutting	646.724
Hairdressers	646.724 092
Hairdressing	646.724
customs	391.5
Hairstyles	646.724
customs	391.5
Hairstyling	646.724
Hairweaving	646.724
Hairworms	592.59
Haiti	972.94
	T2—729 4
Haitian Creole	447.972 94
	T6—417
Haitian literature	840
Haitians	T5—969 729 4
Hajdú-Bihar Megye	
(Hungary)	T2—439 9
Hajeb (Morocco : Province)	T2—645
Ḥajj	297.352 4
Hakeas	583.38
Hakes	641.392
cooking	641.692
food	641.392
zoology	597.632
Hakka (Chinese people)	305.895 17
	T5—951 7
Hakka dialects	495.179 512
	T6—951 7
Hakkâri İli (Turkey)	T2—566 28
ancient	T2—395 5
Hala	584.55

Halogenation	547.27	Hamitic literatures	893
chemical engineering	660.284 4	Hamitic peoples	T5—93
Halogens		Hamito-Semitic languages	492
biochemistry	572.556		T6—92
chemical engineering	661.073	Hamito-Semitic literatures	892
chemistry	546.73	Hamlin County (S.D.)	T2—783 26
organic chemistry	547.02	Hammering metals	
alicyclic	547.52	sculpture	731.41
aliphatic	547.42	Hammers	621.973
applied	661.891	Hammersmith and Fulham	
Halophilic bacteria	579.321	(London, England)	T2—421 33
Haloragales	583.44	Hammurabi, King of Babylonia	
Hälsingland landskap		Mesopotamian history	935.502
(Sweden)	T2—488 1	Hampden County (Mass.)	T2—744 26
Halton (Cheshire, England)	T2—427 18	Hampshire (England)	T2—422 7
Halton (Ont.)	T2—713 533	Hampshire County (Mass.)	T2—744 23
Ham	641.364	Hampshire County (W. Va.)	T2—754 95
see also Pork		Hampshire swine	636.484
Ham radio		Hampstead (Quebec)	T2—714 28
engineering	621.384 16	Hampton (Va.)	T2—755 412
Hamadān (Iran : Province)	T2—555 2	Hampton County (S.C.)	T2—757 97
ancient	T2—357 52	Hampton Roads, Battle of, 1862	973.752
Ḥamāh (Syria : Province)	T2—569 13	Hamsters	636.935 6
Hamamelidaceae	583.44	animal husbandry	636.935 6
Hamamelidales	583.44	experimental animals	
Hamamelididae	583.44	medicine	616.027 33
Hamber Provincial Park		zoology	599.356
(B.C.)	T2—711 68	Han Chinese	T5—951
Hamblen County (Tenn.)	T2—768 923	Han dynasty	931.04
Hambleton (England)	T2—428 49	Ḥanafī school (Islamic law)	340.590 181 1
Hamburg (Germany)	T2—435 15	religious law	297.140 181 1
Häme (Finland : Lääni)	T2—489 73	Hanafites	
Hämeen lääni (Finland)	T2—489 73	religious law	297.140 181 1
Hamilton (N.Z.)	T2—933 4	Ḥanafīyah	
Hamilton (Ont.)	971.352	religious law	297.140 181 1
	T2—713 52	Ḥanbalī school (Islamic law)	340.590 181 4
Hamilton (Scotland :		religious law	297.140 181 4
District)	T2—414 57	Hanbalites	
Hamilton (Vic.)	T2—945 7	religious law	297.140 181 4
Hamilton City (N.Z.)	T2—933 4	Ḥanbalīyah	
Hamilton County (Fla.)	T2—759 84	religious law	297.140 181 4
Hamilton County (Ill.)	T2—773 95	Hancock County (Ga.)	T2—758 623
Hamilton County (Ind.)	T2—772 56	Hancock County (Ill.)	T2—773 43
Hamilton County (Iowa)	T2—777 52	Hancock County (Ind.)	T2—772 58
Hamilton County (Kan.)	T2—781 415	Hancock County (Iowa)	T2—777 24
Hamilton County (N.Y.)	T2—747 52	Hancock County (Ky.)	T2—769 862
Hamilton County (Neb.)	T2—782 354	Hancock County (Me.)	T2—741 45
Hamilton County (Ohio)	T2—771 77	Hancock County (Miss.)	T2—762 14
Hamilton County (Tenn.)	T2—768 82	Hancock County (Ohio)	T2—771 19
Hamilton County (Tex.)	T2—764 549	Hancock County (Tenn.)	T2—768 946
Hamilton-Wentworth (Ont.)	T2—713 52	Hancock County (W. Va.)	T2—754 12
Hamiltonian systems	515.39		
Hamitic languages	493		
	T6—93		

Hannover (Germany :
  Region)   T2—435 954
Hanoi (Vietnam)   T2—597 3
Hanover (South Africa :
  District)   T2—687 13
Hanover, House of   941.07
  British history   941.07
  English history   942.07
  genealogy   929.72
  Scottish history   941.107
Hanover County (Va.) T2—755 462
Hansen's disease
  incidence   614.546
  medicine   616.998
  see also Communicable
    diseases — humans
Hansford County (Tex.) T2—764 814
Hanson County (S.D.) T2—783 373
Hantavirus infections
  incidence   614.588
  medicine   616.918
  see also Communicable
    diseases — humans
Hants (England)   T2—422 7
Hants (N.S.)   T2—716 35
Hanukkah   296.435
  customs   394.267
  liturgy   296.453 5
Haouz (Morocco : Province) T2—646 4
Haploid cells   571.845
Haplosclerida   593.46
Haplotaxida   592.64
Happenings (Art style) 709.040 74
  20th century   709.040 74
  21st century   709.050 14
Happiness   152.42
  applied psychology 158
    children   155.419
  arts   T3C—353
  hedonism   171.4
  literature   808.803 53
    history and criticism 809.933 53
    specific literatures T3B—080 353
    history and
      criticism   T3B—093 53
  parapsychology   131
  psychology of emotions 152.42
  virtue ethics   171.3
Hapsburg, House of   943.603
  see also Habsburg, House of
Haptic devices   004.77
Haptophyceae   579.86
Harakmbet language   498.9
                       T6—989

Haralson County (Ga.) T2—758 38
Harare (Zimbabwe)   T2—689 1
Harari (African people) T5—928
Harari language   492.8
                       T6—928
Harari literature   892.8
Harassment   364.15
  social welfare   362.88
Harbor patrols   363.286
Harbor piloting   623.892 9
Harbor police   363.286
Harbor porpoises   599.539
Harbor seal   599.792 3
Harborough (England) T2—425 44
Harbors   387.1
  engineering   627.2
  see also Ports
Hard bop   781.655
Hard cheeses
  processing   637.354
Hard disk management 004.563
  systems software   005.436
Hard disks (Computers) 004.563
  engineering   621.397 63
Hard fiber crops   633.57
Hard rock   781.66
Hardanger
  arts   746.44
Hardanger fiddles   787.6
  see also Stringed instruments
Hardball hockey   796.356 64
Hardecanute, King of England
  English history   942.018 3
Hardee County (Fla.)   T2—759 57
Hardeman County (Tenn.) T2—768 28
Hardeman County (Tex.) T2—764 747
Hardening metals   671.36
Hardin County (Ill.)   T2—773 98
Hardin County (Iowa) T2—777 535
Hardin County (Ky.)   T2—769 845
Hardin County (Ohio)   T2—771 44
Hardin County (Tenn.) T2—768 31
Hardin County (Tex.)   T2—764 157
Harding, Warren G. (Warren
  Gamaliel)
  United States history 973.914
Harding County (N.M.) T2—789 24
Harding County (S.D.) T2—783 42
Hardinge, Henry Hardinge,
  Viscount
  Indian history   954.031 5
Hardinge of Penshurst, Charles
  Hardinge, Baron
  Indian history   954.035 6

Harrison County (Ky.)	T2—769 413
Harrison County (Miss.)	T2—762 13
Harrison County (Mo.)	T2—778 17
Harrison County (Ohio)	T2—771 68
Harrison County (Tex.)	T2—764 192
Harrison County (W. Va.)	T2—754 57
Harrison Lake (Fraser-Cheam, B.C.)	T2—711 37
Harrisonburg (Va.)	T2—755 921
Harrogate (England : Borough)	T2—428 42
Harrow (London, England)	T2—421 86
Harrows manufacturing technology	681.763 1
Harry Gwala District Municipality (South Africa)	T2—684 67
Harsha Indian history	934.07
Hart (England)	T2—422 723
Hart County (Ga.)	T2—758 155
Hart County (Ky.)	T2—769 715
Hartebeests	599.645
Hartford (Conn.)	T2—746 3
Hartford County (Conn.)	T2—746 2
Hartlepool (England : Borough)	T2—428 57
Hartley County (Tex.)	T2—764 823
Harts River (South Africa)	T2—687 14
Hartswater (South Africa : District)	T2—687 14
Hartz Mountains National Park (Tas.)	T2—946 2
Harvest mice	599.35
Harvest music	781.524 6
Harvesting	631.55
equipment manufacturing technology	681.763 1
production efficiency	338.163
Harvestmen (Arachnids)	595.43
Harvey County (Kan.)	T2—781 85
Haryana (India)	T2—545 58
Harz Mountains (Germany)	T2—431 82
Ḥasakah (Syria : Province)	T2—569 12
Hasan (Hadith)	297.125 21
Hashing (Computer science)	005.741
Hashish agriculture	633.79
Hashish abuse	362.295
medicine	616.863 5
personal health	613.835
social welfare	362.295
see also Substance abuse	
Hasidism	296.833 2
liturgy	296.450 44
Haskell County (Kan.)	T2—781 732
Haskell County (Okla.)	T2—766 77
Haskell County (Tex.)	T2—764 736
Haskovo (Bulgaria : Oblast)	T2—499 65
Hasmonean period	933.04
Hassan II, King of Morocco Moroccan history	964.052
Hassium chemistry	546.62
Hastings (England)	T2—422 59
Hastings (Ont. : County)	T2—713 585
Hastings, Battle of, 1066	942.021
Hastings, Francis Rawdon-Hastings, Marquess of Indian history	954.031 3
Hastings, Warren Indian history	954.029 8
Hastings District (N.Z.)	T2—934 65
Hatay İli (Turkey)	T2—564 8
ancient	939.431
	T2—394 31
Hatcheries fish culture	639.311
Hatchetfishes (Freshwater)	597.48
Hatchetfishes (Marine)	597.5
Hate	179.8
psychology	152.4
see also Vices	
Hate crimes	364.15
law	345.025
social welfare	362.88
Hatha yoga health	613.704 6
see Manual at 613.7046 vs. 615.824, 615.851, 615.852, 616–618	
therapeutics	615.824
see Manual at 613.7046 vs. 615.824, 615.851, 615.852, 616–618	
Hato Mayor (Dominican Republic : Province)	T2—729 381
Hatred	179.8
psychology	152.4
see also Vices	
Hats	391.43
see also Headwear	
Hattah Lakes National Park (Vic.)	T2—945 9
Hatteras, Cape (N.C.)	T2—756 175
Hatters	646.502 092

Hazardous materials (continued)
  public safety — 363.17
    law — 344.047 2
    technology — 604.7
    see Manual at 604.7 vs.
      660.2804
  transportation — 388.044
    law — 343.093 22
    technology — 604.7
    transportation services — 388.044
Hazardous wastes — 363.728 7
  law — 344.046 22
  public administration — 353.994
  social services — 363.728 7
  technology — 628.42
  see also Waste control
Hazelnuts — 641.345 4
  botany — 583.65
  see also Filberts
Hazelton (B.C.) — T2—711 85
Hazelton Mountains (B.C.) — T2—711 85
Hazing
  education — 371.58
HDTV (High-definition
  television) — 621.388 06
Head — 591.44
  animal physiology — 573.995
  anthropometry — 599.948
  descriptive zoology — 591.44
  human anatomy — 611.91
  human physiology — 612.91
  regional medicine — 617.51
  surgery — 617.510 59
Head lice
  medicine — 616.572
    see also Skin diseases —
      humans
Head muscles
  human anatomy — 611.732
Head scarves — 391.43
  see also Headwear
Head start (Education) — 372.21
Head teachers — 371.1
  biography — 371.100 92
  public control — 379.157
Headaches
  medicine — 616.849 1
    see also Nervous system
      diseases — humans
Headgear — 391.43
  see also Headwear
Headings (Cataloging) — 025.322

Headmasters
  biography — 371.200 92
  public control — 379.157
  role and function — 371.201 2
Heads of government — 352.23
Heads of state — 352.23
Headscarves — 391.43
  see also Headwear
Headstanders — 597.48
Headwear — 391.43
  commercial technology — 687.4
  customs — 391.43
  home economics — 646.3
  home sewing — 646.5
  see also Clothing
Healesville (Vic.) — T2—945 2
Healing
  religion — 203.1
    see Manual at 615.852 vs.
      203.1, 234.131, 292–299
  therapeutics — 615.5
Healing touch
  medicine — 615.852
Health — 613
  arts — T3C—356 1
  child care — 649.4
  literature — 808.803 561
    history and criticism — 809.933 561
    specific literatures — T3B—080 356 1
      history and
        criticism — T3B—093 561
  medicine — 613
  primary education — 372.37
  social theology — 201.762 1
    Christianity — 261.832 1
    Judaism — 296.38
  sociology — 306.461
  see Manual at 613 vs. 612,
    615.8
Health care — 362.1
  arts — T3C—356 1
  literature — 808.803 561
    history and criticism — 809.933 561
    specific literatures — T3B—080 356 1
      history and
        criticism — T3B—093 561
  see also Health services
Health care facilities — 362.1
  accounting — 657.832 2
  architecture — 725.51
  cooking — 641.579
  law — 344.032 1
  meal service — 642.56
  public administration — 353.68

Health care facilities (continued)	
safety	363.15
sanitation services	363.729 7
public administration	353.94
see also Sanitation	
social welfare	362.1
Health centers	362.12
see also Health care facilities	
Health cooking	641.563
Health ethics	174.2
Health foods	641.302
cooking	641.563 7
food	641.302
Health insurance	368.382
government-sponsored	368.42
law	344.022
United States	344.730 22
labor economics	331.255 4
law	346.086 382
public administration	353.69
Australia	353.690 994
United States	353.690 973
see also Insurance	
Health maintenance organizations	362.104 258 4
insurance	368.382
see also Insurance	
law	344.032 104 258 4
Health promotion	
medicine	613
public administration	353.627 4
Health protection service	
public administration	353.628
Health resorts	
personal health	613.122
Health services	362.1
Algerian Revolution	965.046 7
American Revolution	973.375
armed forces	355.345
Chaco War	989.207 167
Civil War (England)	942.062 7
Civil War (Spain)	946.081 7
Civil War (United States)	973.775
Crimean War	947.073 87
economics	338.473 621
employee programs	
personnel management	658.382
public administration	352.67
Falkland Islands War	997.110 247
Franco-German War	943.082 7
Hundred Years' War	944.025 7
Indo-Pakistan War, 1971	954.920 517
Indochinese War	959.704 17
Iraq War, 2003–2011	956.704 437
Iraqi-Iranian Conflict	955.054 27

Health services (continued)	
Korean War	951.904 27
labor economics	331.255 4
law	344.032 1
Napoleonic Wars	940.277
pastoral theology	206.1
Christianity	259.41
Persian Gulf War, 1991	956.704 427
prisoner services	365.667
public administration	353.6
United States	353.609 73
social theology	201.762 1
Christianity	261.832 1
social welfare	362.1
South African War	968.048 7
student welfare	371.71
Thirty Years' War	940.247
Vietnamese War	959.704 37
War of the Pacific	983.061 67
World War I	940.475
World War II	940.547 5
see Manual at 362.1–.4 vs. 610; *also at* 362.1–.4 and 614.4–.5	
Health surveys	614.42
Health visitors	610.734 3
medicine	610.734 3
social welfare	362.14
see also Nursing	
Heard County (Ga.)	T2—758 422
Hearing	573.89
human physiology	612.85
psychology	152.15
see also Ears	
Hearing aids	
audiology	617.89
Hearing devices	
audiology	617.89
Hearing disorders	
medicine	617.8
see also Ear diseases — humans	
Hearing examiners (Law)	342.066 4
Hearing-impaired children	305.908 208 3
	T1—087 2
home care	649.151 2
see also People with hearing impairments	
Hearing-impaired people	305.908 2
	T1—087 2
education	371.912
library services	027.663
social group	305.908 2
social welfare	362.42

Hearing impairment
  medicine   617.8
    see also Ear diseases —
      humans
Hearing people
  sign languages   419.1
      T6—999 8
Hearings
  legislative   328.345
Hearsay evidence   347.064
Heart   573.17
  animals   573.17
  human anatomy   611.12
  human biochemistry   612.173
  human biophysics   612.171
  human metabolism   612.173
  human physiology   612.17
  medicine   616.12
  physiology   573.17
  surgery   617.412
  see also Cardiovascular system
Heart attacks
  medicine   616.123 025
    myocardial infarction   616.123 7
    see also Cardiovascular
      diseases — humans
Heart depressants
  pharmacokinetics   615.716
Heart diseases
  cooking for   641.563 11
  medicine   616.12
    see also Cardiovascular
      diseases — humans
  pediatrics   618.921 2
  surgery   617.412
Heart failure
  medicine   616.129
    see also Cardiovascular
      diseases — humans
Heart pacers (Electronic)
  medicine   617.412 064 5
Heart stimulants
  pharmacokinetics   615.711
Heart surgery   617.412
Heart transplants   617.412 059 2
  see also Organ transplants
Heart valve diseases
  medicine   616.125
    see also Cardiovascular
      diseases — humans
Heartburn
  medicine   616.324
    see also Digestive system
      diseases — humans

Heat   536
  astrophysics   523.013
  biophysics   571.467
    humans   612.014 462
  crop damage   632.12
  effect on matter   536.4
  pathological effect   571.934 67
    medicine   616.989
  physics   536
Heat absorption   536.3
Heat capacity   536.6
Heat conduction   536.23
  engineering   621.402 23
Heat conduction in fluids   536.25
Heat conductivity
  materials science   620.112 96
Heat convection   536.25
  engineering   621.402 25
Heat distribution systems   621.402 8
Heat engineering   621.402
Heat engineers   621.402 092
Heat engines   621.402 5
Heat exchange
  engineering   621.402 2
  metallurgical furnaces   669.85
Heat exchangers   621.402 5
Heat exhaustion
  medicine   616.989
    see also Environmental
      diseases — humans
Heat loss
  electric circuits   621.319 21
Heat of fusion   536.42
Heat of vaporization   536.44
Heat perception   152.182 2
HEAT projectiles
  engineering   623.451 7
Heat pumps   621.402 5
  refrigeration engineering   621.563
Heat radiation   536.3
  engineering   621.402 27
Heat-resistant glass   666.155
Heat scattering   536.3
Heat storage   621.402 8
  solar engineering   621.471 2
Heat stress disorders   571.934 67
  humans
    medicine   616.989
    see also Environmental
      diseases — humans
Heat transfer   536.2
  chemical engineering   660.284 27
  engineering   621.402 2
  physics   536.2

Helena (Mont.)	T2—786 615
Helenopontus	T2—393 32
Helensburgh (Scotland)	T2—414 2
Helicobacter	579.323
Helicobacter infections	
medicine	616.330 14
see also Digestive system	
diseases — humans	
Heliconiaceae	584.88
Heliconias	584.88
botany	584.88
floriculture	635.934 88
Helicopter accidents	363.124 93
see also Air safety	
Helicopters	387.733 52
engineering	629.133 352
military engineering	623.746 047 2
piloting	629.132 525 2
transportation services	387.733 52
see also Aircraft	
Heliographs	
military engineering	623.731 2
nautical engineering	623.856 12
Heliotherapy	
medicine	615.831 4
Heliothis	595.78
agricultural pests	632.78
Heliotropes (Plants)	583.958
Heliports	387.736
engineering	629.136 16
military engineering	623.661 6
see also Airports	
Helium	553.971
chemistry	546.751
economic geology	553.971
gas technology	665.822
see also Chemicals	
Helium extraction	665.73
Hell	202.3
art representation	704.948 9
Christianity	704.948 2
arts	T3C—382 023
Christianity	236.25
Islam	297.23
literature	808.803 820 23
history and criticism	809.933 820 23
specific literatures	T3B—080 382 023
history and	
criticism	T3B—093 820 23
Hellbender (Salamander)	597.85
Hellebores	583.34
botany	583.34
floriculture	635.933 34

Hellenic languages		480
	T6—8	
Hellenic literatures		880
Hellenic sculpture		733.3
Hellenistic Greek language		487.4
	T6—87	
Hellenistic movement (Judaism)		296.81
Hellenistic period		
Egyptian history		932.021
Greek history		938.08
Mesopotamian history		935.06
Middle Eastern history		939.404
Palestinian history		933.03
Hellenistic World		938
	T2—38	
Hellespontus (Roman province)		939.21
	T2—392 1	
Helmets (Armor)		623.441 8
art metalwork		739.75
Helmets (Headwear)		391.43
see also Headwear		
Helminthologists		592.309 2
Helminthology		592.3
agriculture		632.623
medicine		616.962
plant crops		632.623
veterinary medicine		636.089 696 2
Heloderma		597.959 5
Helodermatidae		597.959 5
Helotiales		579.57
Help facilities (Computers)		005.3
development		005.15
Help-wanted advertising		659.193 311 24
Helping behavior		158.3
Helsinki (Finland)	T2—489 718	
Helvetia	T2—369 43	
Helvetic Republic		949.405
	T2—494	
Hemangiomas		
medicine		616.993 13
Hemapheresis		
pharmacology		615.39
Hematheia (Greece)	T2—495 65	
Hematite		
mineralogy		549.523
Hematologic agents		
pharmacokinetics		615.718
Hematologic diseases		
medicine		616.15
see also Cardiovascular		
diseases — humans		

Hematologic neoplasms
  incidence   614.599 941 8
  medicine   616.994 18
    see also Cancer — humans
Hematology   616.15
  diagnosis
    general disease   616.075 61
Hematopoiesis   573.155
  see also Hematopoietic system
Hematopoietic system   573.155
  animals   573.155
  diseases   573.155 39
    see also Hematopoietic
      system diseases
  human anatomy   611.41
  human physiology   612.41
  medicine   616.41
Hematopoietic system diseases   573.155 39
  animals   573.155 39
  humans   362.196 41
    cancer   362.196 994 41
      incidence   614.599 944 1
      medicine   616.994 41
      social services   362.196 994 41
      see also Cancer —
        humans
    geriatrics   618.976 41
    incidence   614.594 1
    medicine   616.41
    pediatrics   618.924 1
    pharmacokinetics   615.718
    social services   362.196 41
Hematuria
  medicine   616.63
  see also Urologic diseases —
    humans
Hemiascomycetes   579.562
Hemic disorders
  medicine   616.15
  see also Cardiovascular
    diseases — humans
Hemichordata   593.99
  paleozoology   563.99
Hemimetabola   595.73
Hemiprocnidae   598.762
Hemiptera   595.754
Hemispheres   T2—181
Hemlocks   585.2
  forestry   634.975 3
  lumber   674.144
  ornamental arboriculture   635.977 52
Hemoconia
  human physiology   612.117

Hemodialysis
  medicine   617.461 059
Hemoglobin
  human physiology   612.111 1
  medicine   616.151
Hemoglobin disorders
  medicine   616.151
  see also Cardiovascular
    diseases — humans
Hemolytic anemia
  medicine   616.152
  see also Cardiovascular
    diseases — humans
Hemolytic disease of the
  newborn
  pediatrics   618.921 5
  perinatal medicine   618.326 1
  see also Cardiovascular
    diseases — humans
Hemophilia
  medicine   616.157 2
  see also Cardiovascular
    diseases — humans
  pediatrics   618.921 572
Hemopoiesis   573.155
  see also Hematopoietic system
Hemopoietic system   573.155
  see also Hematopoietic system
Hemorheology
  humans   612.118 1
Hemorrhage
  medicine   616.157
  see also Cardiovascular
    diseases — humans
Hemorrhagic diseases
  medicine   616.157
  see also Cardiovascular
    diseases — humans
Hemorrhoids
  medicine   616.352
  see also Digestive system
    diseases — humans
Hemp (Apocynaceae)   583.956
Hemp (Cannabaceae)   583.45
  see also Hemp
Hemp (Fiber)   677.12
  botany   583.648
  crop   633.53
  textiles   677.12
    arts   746.041 2
  see also Textiles
Hemp (Musaceae)   584.88
Hemp pulp   676.14
Hemphill County (Tex.)   T2—764 817

Hempstead County (Ark.)	T2—767 54
Henan Sheng (China)	T2—511 8
Henbanes	583.959 3
Henderson County (Ill.)	T2—773 413
Henderson County (Ky.)	T2—769 87
Henderson County (N.C.)	T2—756 92
Henderson County (Tenn.)	T2—768 263
Henderson County (Tex.)	T2—764 227
Henderson Island (Pitcairn Island)	T2—961 8
Hendricks County (Ind.)	T2—772 53
Hendry County (Fla.)	T2—759 46
Hennenman (South Africa : District)	T2—685 3
Hennepin County (Minn.)	T2—776 57
Henophidia	597.967
Henrico County (Va.)	T2—755 453
Henry I, King of England	
English history	942.023
Henry I, King of France	
French history	944.021
Henry II, King of England	
English history	942.031
Henry II, King of France	
French history	944.028
Henry III, King of England	
English history	942.034
Henry III, King of France	
French history	944.029
Henry IV, King of England	
English history	942.041
Henry IV, King of France	
French history	944.031
Henry V, King of England	
English history	942.042
Henry VI, King of England	
English history	942.043
Henry VII, King of England	
English history	942.051
Henry VIII, King of England	
English history	942.052
Henry County (Ala.)	T2—761 31
Henry County (Ga.)	T2—758 435
Henry County (Ill.)	T2—773 38
Henry County (Ind.)	T2—772 64
Henry County (Iowa)	T2—777 95
Henry County (Ky.)	T2—769 385
Henry County (Mo.)	T2—778 462
Henry County (Ohio)	T2—771 15
Henry County (Tenn.)	T2—768 34
Henry County (Va.)	T2—755 692

Hepatic encephalopathy	
medicine	616.83
see also Nervous system diseases — humans	
Hepaticae	588.3
Hepatidae	588.3
Hepatitis	
medicine	616.362 3
see also Digestive system diseases — humans	
Hepatopsida	588.3
Heptarchy	942.015
Heptathlon	796.42
Heraclitean philosophy	182.4
Hērakleion (Greece : Regional unit)	T2—495 9
Heraldic design	744.62
decorative arts	744.62
insignia	929.6
Heraldry	929.6
design	744.62
Hérault (France)	T2—448 4
Herb gardens	635.7
Herb teas	641.357
agriculture	635.7
commercial processing	663.96
cooking with	641.657
food	641.357
home preparation	641.877
Herbaceous plants	582.12
landscape architecture	716
Herbaceous vines	582.189
Herbal medicine	615.321
Herbals	
pharmacognosy	615.321
see Manual at 615.1 vs. 615.2–.3	
Herbariums	580.74
Herbert (South Africa : District)	T2—687 13
Herbicides	632.954
agricultural use	632.954
chemical engineering	668.654
Herbivorous animals	591.54
Herbivorous Saurischia	567.913
Herbs	581.63
botany	581.63
commercial processing	664.805 7
cooking with	641.657
food	641.357
garden crop	635.7
pharmacognosy	615.321
see Manual at 615.1 vs. 615.2–.3	

Herpes labialis	
medicine	616.522
see also Skin diseases —	
humans	
Herpes simplex type 1	
medicine	616.522
see also Skin diseases —	
humans	
Herpes simplex type 2	
incidence	614.547
medicine	616.951 8
see also Communicable	
diseases — humans	
Herpes zoster	
medicine	616.522
see also Skin diseases —	
humans	
Herpesviridae	579.243 4
Herpesvirus diseases	
incidence	614.581 2
medicine	616.911 2
see also Communicable	
diseases — humans	
Herpetologists	597.909 2
Herpetology	597.9
Herrera (Panama : Province)	T2—728 724
Herring (Clupea harengus)	641.392
conservation technology	639.977 452
cooking	641.692
fishing	639.274 52
food	641.392
resource economics	333.956 452
zoology	597.452
Herring family	597.45
Herschel (South Africa :	
District)	T2—687 57
Hertford County (N.C.)	T2—756 155
Hertfordshire (England)	942.58
	T2—425 8
Hertsmere (England)	T2—425 895
Hertzog, James Barry Munnik	
South African history	968.054
Herzegovinians	T5—918 39
Hesperioidea	595.788
Hesperonesian languages	499.2
	T6—992
Hesperornithiformes	568.23
Hesse (Germany)	943.41
	T2—434 1
Hetero nitrogen compounds	547.593
chemical engineering	661.894
Hetero oxygen compounds	547.592
chemical engineering	661.8

Hetero sulfur compounds	547.594
chemical engineering	661.896
Heterobasidiomycetes	579.59
Heterocyclic compounds	547.59
chemical engineering	661.8
Heterogeneous grouping of	
students	371.252
Heterogenesis	571.884
Heteromyidae	599.359 8
Heterophony	781.283
Heteroptera	595.754
Heterosexuality	306.764
Heterosexuals	306.764
	T1—086 62
psychology	155.34
social welfare	362.896 2
Heterosomata	597.69
Hettinger County (N.D.)	T2—784 86
Heveas	583.69
botany	583.69
rubber crop	633.895 2
Heves Megye (Hungary)	T2—439 8
Hewu (South Africa :	
District)	T2—687 56
Hexacorallia	593.6
Hexactinellida	593.44
paleozoology	563.4
Hexadecimal system	513.5
Hexagonal chess	794.18
Hexapoda	595.7
see also Insects	
Hexateuch (Bible)	222.1
Hi-fi	
sound reproduction systems	621.389 332
Hiatal hernia	
regional medicine	617.559
Ḥibarī, al-Ḥusayn ibn al-Ḥakam	
Koran commentary	297.122 755
Hibernation	591.565
behavior	591.565
physiology	571.787
Hibiscuses	583.775
botany	583.775
floriculture	635.933 775
Hickman County (Ky.)	T2—769 98
Hickman County (Tenn.)	T2—768 434
Hickories	583.65
Hickory County (Mo.)	T2—778 496
Hidalgo (Mexico : State)	T2—724 6
Hidalgo County (N.M.)	T2—789 693
Hidalgo County (Tex.)	T2—764 492
Hidatsa Indians	978.400 497 527 4
	T5—975 274

High-temperature injury	571.934 67
humans	
medicine	617.11
High temperatures	536.57
biophysics	571.467
chemical engineering	660.296 87
chemistry	541.368 7
effect on materials	620.112 17
physics	536.57
High-tension electric	
transmission	621.319 13
High Veld (South Africa) T2—682	
High-velocity armor-piercing	
ammunition	623.451 8
High voice	783.3
High-voltage accelerators	539.732
High-volume data sets	005.7
High-yield bonds	332.632 34
Higher criticism	
Bible	220.66
Higher education	378
T1—071 1	
federal aid	379.121 4
law	344.074
public administrative support	353.88
public support	379.118
law	344.076 84
research	378.007 2
special education	371.904 74
Higher-order logic	511.3
Highland (Scotland) T2—411 5	
Highland cattle	636.223
Highland County (Ohio) T2—771 845	
Highland County (Va.) T2—755 89	
Highland Region (Scotland) T2—411 5	
Highland Rim T2—768 4	
Kentucky T2—769 6	
Tennessee T2—768 4	
Highlands (Papua New Guinea) 995.6	
T2—956	
Highlands (Scotland) 941.15	
T2—411 5	
Highlands County (Fla.) T2—759 55	
Highly volatile petroleum	
products	665.538 2
Highveld (South Africa) T2—682	
Highveld Ridge (South	
Africa : District) T2—682 78	
Highway accidents	363.125
see also Highway safety	
Highway engineers	625.709 2
Highway maps	912
Highway patrol	363.233 2

Highway post offices	383.42
see also Postal service	
Highway safety	363.125
engineering	625.702 89
law	343.094
public administration	353.98
social services	363.125
Highway transportation	388.31
see also Road transportation	
Highways	388.1
engineering	625.7
transportation services	388.1
see also Roads	
Hijacking	364.155 2
law	345.025 52
Hijrah	297.634
Hijras	306.768
Hikers	796.510 92
Hiking	796.51
Hilbert spaces	515.733
Hilbert transform	515.723
Hildburghausen (Germany :	
Landkreis) T2—432 26	
Hildebrand, Bruno	
economic school	330.154 2
Hildesheim (Germany) T2—435 95	
Hill climbing	796.522
Hill County (Mont.) T2—786 14	
Hill County (Tex.) T2—764 283	
Hillingdon (London,	
England) T2—421 83	
Hills	551.436
T2—143	
see also Mountains	
Hillsboro County (N.H.) T2—742 8	
Hillsborough County (Fla.) T2—759 65	
Hillsborough County (N.H.) T2—742 8	
Hillsdale County (Mich.) T2—774 29	
Himachal Pradesh (India) T2—545 2	
Himalaya Mountains T2—549 6	
Himalayan cat	636.83
Himalayish languages	495.4
T6—954	
Ḥimṣ (Syria : Province) T2—569 12	
Hinayana Buddhism	294.391
Hinchinbrook Island	
National Park (Qld.) T2—943 6	
Hinckley and Bosworth	
(England) T2—425 49	
Hindi language	491.43
T6—914 31	
Hindi literature	891.43
Hindi-speaking peoples T5—914 3	
Hindis T5—914 3	

402

Holguín (Cuba : Province)	T2—729 164	Hollow ware	
Holiday work	331.257 4	rubber	678.34
economics	331.257 4	Hollyhocks	635.933 775
personnel management	658.312 1	botany	583.775
Holidays	394.26	floriculture	635.933 775
arts	700.434	Holman (N.W.T.)	T2—719 3
	T3C—334	Holmes County (Fla.)	T2—759 965
cooking	641.568	Holmes County (Miss.)	T2—762 625
customs	394.26	Holmes County (Ohio)	T2—771 64
flower arrangements	745.926	Holmium	
folklore	398.236	chemistry	546.417
history and criticism	398.33	Holocaust, 1933–1945	940.531 8
handicrafts	745.594 16	arts	700.458 405 318
interior decoration	747.93		T3C—358 405 318
labor economics	331.257 6	biography	940.531 809 2
law	344.091	Christian theology	231.76
literature	808.803 34	European history	940.531 8
history and criticism	809.933 34	interreligious relations	261.26
specific literatures	T3B—080 334	Jewish theology	296.311 74
history and		literature	808.803 584 053 18
criticism	T3B—093 34	Holocaust denial	940.531 818
personnel management	658.312 2	Holocene epoch	551.793
religion	203.6	geology	551.793
Buddhism	294.343 6	paleontology	560.179 3
Christianity	263.9	Holocephali	597.38
devotional literature	242.3	paleozoology	567.38
sermons	252.6	Holographic images	774
Hinduism	294.536	Holography	774
Islam	297.36	arts	774
Judaism	296.43	engineering	621.367 5
liturgy	296.453	Holometabola	595.7
sociology	306.481 25	*see also* Insects	
Holiness	202.2	Holomorphic functions	515.98
Christian church attribute	262.72	Holostei	597.41
Christian doctrine	234.8	paleozoology	567.41
Holistic medicine	610	Holothurioidea	593.96
health	613	paleozoology	563.96
therapeutics	615.5	Holstein-Friesian cattle	636.234
Holistic psychology	150.193	Holt, Harold	
Holland	949.2	Australian history	994.061
	T2—492	Holt County (Mo.)	T2—778 115
ancient	936.92	Holt County (Neb.)	T2—782 745
	T2—369 2	Holu languages	496.393
Holland (England : County)	T2—425 39		T6—963 93
Holland (Kingdom)	949.205	Holy, The	211
	T2—492	Holy Communion	234.163
Hollies	635.977 398 2	public worship	264.36
botany	583.982	Anglican	264.030 36
ornamental arboriculture	635.977 398 2	texts	264.03
Hollow blocks	666.894	Roman Catholic	264.020 36
architectural construction	721.044 4	texts	264.023
building construction	693.4	theology	234.163
ceramic technology	666.894		

Home movies	791.433
Home nursing	
by professionals	610.734 3
health services	362.14
medicine	610.734 3
Home ownership	363.583
public administrative support	353.55
Home remedies	
therapeutics	615.88
Home repairs	690.802 88
home economics	643.7
see Manual at 690 vs. 643.7	
Home reserves (Armed forces)	355.37
Home rule	
law	342.042
local government	320.8
Home safety	363.13
see also Safety	
Home schooling	371.042
primary education	372.104 242
Home schools	371.042
Home selection	643.12
Home shopping	381.142
Home sites	
selection	643.12
Home video systems	777
engineering	621.388
videography	777
Home workshops	684.08
Homeland Bloc (Austrian	
political party)	324.243 602 4
Homelands (South Africa)	968.29
	T2—682 9
Cape of Good Hope	T2—687 5
Natal	T2—684
Orange Free State	T2—685 1
Homeless children	
social group	305.230 869 42
social welfare	362.775 692
Homeless families	362.592 3
Homeless people	305.569 2
	T1—086 942
social theology	201.762 5
Christianity	261.832 5
social welfare	362.592
Homeless shelters	362.592 83
Homeless women	
social group	305.484 42
social welfare	362.839 85
Homeless youth	
social welfare	362.775 692
Homel´ (Belarus : Voblasts)	T2—478 1
Homel´skaĩa voblasts´	
(Belarus)	T2—478 1

Homemakers	640.92
	T1—088 64
Homemaking	640
Homeomorphisms	514
Homeopathy	
therapeutic system	615.532
Homeostasis	
biology	571.75
see also Endocrine system	
human physiology	612.022
Homeowner's insurance	368.096
liability	368.56
see also Insurance	
Homes	640
home economics	640
social services	363.5
older people	362.61
see also Group homes	
see also Dwellings	
Homework	371.302 81
Homicidal behavior	
medicine	616.858 44
Homicide	364.152
ethics	179.7
law	345.025 2
social welfare	362.882
Homiletic illustrations	
Christianity	251.08
Homiletics	
Christianity	251
Homilies	204.3
Christianity	252
Homing	
manned space flight	629.453
space flight	629.41
unmanned space flight	629.433
Homing pigeons	
animal husbandry	636.596
Homing systems	
spacecraft	629.474 2
unmanned spacecraft	629.464 2
Hominidae	599.88
paleozoology	569.88
Hominoidea	599.88
paleozoology	569.88
Homo (Genus)	
paleozoology	569.9
Homo erectus	569.97
Homo neanderthalis	569.986
Homo sapiens	
paleontology	569.98
zoology	599.9
Homo sapiens neanderthalis	569.986
Homobasidiomycetes	579.59

Honsyū (Japan)	T2—521
Hood, Mount (Or.)	T2—795 61
Hood County (Tex.)	T2—764 522
Hood River County (Or.)	T2—795 61
Hooded seal	599.796
Hoodoo	133.4
religious practice	299.675
Hoofed mammals	599.6
see also Ungulates	
Hookahs	688.4
Hooked rugs	
arts	746.74
Hooker County (Neb.)	T2—782 777
Hooke's law	531.382
Hookworm infections	
medicine	616.965 4
see also Communicable	
diseases — humans	
Hoops (Gymnastic equipment)	796.443
Hoopstad (South Africa :	
District)	T2—685 3
Hoover, Herbert	
United States history	973.916
Hop, step, and jump	796.432
see also Track and field	
Hop tree	635.977 375
botany	583.75
ornamental arboriculture	635.977 375
Hopbushes	583.75
Hope	
Christianity	234.25
psychology	152.4
Hope (B.C.)	T2—711 37
Hope Island (B.C.)	T2—711 2
Hopefield (South Africa :	
District)	T2—687 32
Hopeh Province (China)	T2—511 52
Hopetown (South Africa :	
District)	T2—687 13
Hopewell (Va.)	T2—755 586
Hopf algebras	512.55
Hopi Indians	979.100 497 458
	T5—974 58
Hopi language	497.458
	T6—974 58
Hopi literature	897.458
Hopkins County (Ky.)	T2—769 823
Hopkins County (Tex.)	T2—764 274
Hoplocarida	595.379 6
Hoppers (Insects)	595.752
agricultural pests	632.752
Hoppers (Railroad cars)	385.34
engineering	625.24
see also Rolling stock	

Hops	641.23
agriculture	633.82
botany	583.648
brewing additive	641.23
Horary astrology	133.56
Horayot	296.123 4
Babylonian Talmud	296.125 4
Mishnah	296.123 4
Palestinian Talmud	296.124 4
Hordaland fylke (Norway)	T2—483 6
Hordeeae	584.926
Hordeum	584.926
Horehounds	583.96
Horgen (Switzerland :	
Bezirk)	T2—494 572 8
Horizontal bars (Gymnastic	
equipment)	796.442
Horizontal combinations	
(Enterprises)	338.804 2
see also Combinations	
(Enterprises)	
Horizontal property	
law	346.043 3
Hormic psychology	150.193
Hormones	571.74
animal physiology	573.44
biochemistry	571.74
humans	612.405
chemistry	547.7
human physiology	612.405
pharmacology	615.36
see also Endocrine system	
see Manual at 573.44 vs.	
571.74	
Hormozgān (Iran)	T2—557 5
Hormuz, Strait of	551.461 535
	T2—165 35
Horn carving	736.6
Horn concertos	784.289 418 6
Horn of Africa	963
	T2—63
Horn players	788.940 92
Hornbeams	583.65
Hornbills	598.78
Hornby Island (B.C.)	T2—711 2
Horned dinosaurs	567.915
Horned liverworts	588.3
Horney, Karen	
psychological system	150.195 7

Hospital insurance	368.382 7	Hostels	910.466
public administration	353.69	*see also* Lodging (Temporary	
see also Insurance		housing)	
Hospital libraries	027.662	Hostile environments	
administration	025.197 662	biology	578.758
collection development	025.218 766 2	ecology	577.58
Hospital ships	359.836 4	Hostile work environments	331.133
design	623.812 64	Hot air balloons	
military		engineering	629.133 22
engineering	623.826 4	sports	797.51
naval equipment	359.836 4	*see also* Air sports	
naval units	359.326 4	Hot-air heating	
Hospital ward management	362.173 068	buildings	697.3
Hospitalers of St. John of		Hot cake mixes	664.753
Jerusalem	255.791 2	Hot cakes	641.815 3
church history	271.791 2	Hot lines (Counseling services)	361.06
Hospitality		mental illness	362.204 251
ethics	177.1	suicide	362.288 1
etiquette	395.3	Hot-metal dipping	671.733
Hospitality industry	338.479 1	Hot peppers	641.338 4
accounting	657.837	agriculture	633.84
economics	338.479 1	food	641.338 4
household management	647.94	Hot rods	796.72
Hospitals	362.11	driving	629.284 86
accounting	657.832 2	engineering	629.228 6
American Revolution	973.376	repair	629.287 86
animal husbandry	636.083 21	sports	796.72
architecture	725.51	*see also* Automotive	
armed forces	355.72	vehicles — sports	
Civil War (United States)	973.776	Hot spices	641.338 4
construction	690.551	Hot Spring County (Ark.)	T2—767 42
energy economics	333.796 4	Hot springs	551.23
institutional housekeeping	647.965 1	Hot Springs County (Wyo.)	T2—787 43
landscape architecture	712.7	Hot Springs National Park	
law	344.032 11	(Ark.)	T2—767 41
liability law	346.031	Hot-water bottles	
meal service	642.56	rubber	678.34
pastoral theology	206.1	Hot-water heating	
Christianity	259.411	buildings	697.4
social theology	201.762 11	Hot-water pipes	
Christianity	261.832 11	buildings	696.6
social welfare	362.11	Hot-water supply	
World War I	940.476	buildings	696.6
World War II	940.547 6	household management	644.6
Host-parasite relationships	577.857	Hot weather	
Host-virus relationships		health	613.113
medical microbiology	616.910 1	Hot-weather cooking	641.591 3
Hostage taking		Hot-weather photography	778.75
criminology	364.154	Hot-working operations	
law	345.025 4	metals	671.3
Hostages	362.884	Hotbeds	631.583
Hostas	635.934 79	floriculture	635.982
botany	584.79	gardening	635.048 3
floriculture	635.934 79	manufacturing technology	681.763 1

Houses	643.1
architecture	728.37
construction	690.837
see also Dwellings	
Houses (Astrology)	133.530 42
Housewives	640.92
	T1—088 64
law	346.016 3
social group	305.436 4
Housing	363.5
animal husbandry	636.083 1
armed forces	355.12
economics	333.338
energy economics	333.796 3
home economics	643.1
law	344.063 635
psychological influence	155.945
public administration	353.55
sanitation services	363.729 8
social services	363.5
sociology	307.336
see Manual at 363.5, 363.6,	
363.8 vs. 338; *also at* 363.5	
vs. 307.336, 307.34; *also at*	
363.5 vs. 643.1	
Housing allowances	363.582
armed forces	355.12
see also Housing	
Housing conditions	363.51
see also Housing	
Housing cooperatives	334.1
Housing renewal	
area planning	711.59
community sociology	307.34
Housing succession	307.336
Houston (Tex.)	T2—764 141 1
Houston County (Ala.)	T2—761 295
Houston County (Ga.)	T2—758 515
Houston County (Minn.)	T2—776 11
Houston County (Tenn.)	T2—768 36
Houston County (Tex.)	T2—764 235
Hove (England)	T2—422 56
Hover flies	595.774
Hovercraft	
engineering	629.3
Howard, John	
Australian history	994.066
1996–1999	994.066
2000–2007	994.071
Howard County (Ark.)	T2—767 483
Howard County (Ind.)	T2—772 85
Howard County (Iowa)	T2—777 312
Howard County (Md.)	T2—752 81
Howard County (Mo.)	T2—778 285

Howard County (Neb.)	T2—782 43
Howard County (Tex.)	T2—764 858
Howden (England)	T2—428 39
Howe Sound (B.C.)	T2—711 31
Howell County (Mo.)	T2—778 85
Howitzers	355.822
engineering	623.427
military equipment	355.822
Howland Island	T2—969 9
Howler monkeys	599.855
Hrodzen (Belarus :	
Voblasts)	T2—478 8
Hrodzenskaĩa voblasts′	
(Belarus)	T2—478 8
Hsiang dialects	495.179 512 15
	T6—951 7
Hualapai Indians	T5—975 724
Hualapai language	497.572 4
	T6—975 724
Huambo (Angola :	
Province)	T2—673 4
Huancavelica (Peru :	
Region)	T2—852 8
Huang He (China)	T2—511
Huánuco (Peru : Region)	T2—852 2
Huasco (Chile : Province)	T2—831 48
Huastec Indians	T5—974 2
Huastec language	497.42
	T6—974 2
Huave Indians	T5—979
Huavean languages	497.9
	T6—979
Hubbard County (Minn.)	T2—776 85
Hubei Sheng (China)	T2—512 12
Huckaback fabrics	677.615
Huckleberries	641.347 32
botany	583.93
cooking	641.647 32
food	641.347 32
horticulture	634.732
Hudson Bay	551.461 327
	T2—163 27
Hudson Bay Region	T2—714 111
Hudson County (N.J.)	T2—749 26
Hudson River (N.Y. and	
N.J.)	T2—747 3
Hudspeth County (Tex.)	T2—764 95
Huehuetenango	
(Guatemala : Dept.)	T2—728 171
Huelva (Spain : Province)	T2—468 7
Huerfano County (Colo.)	T2—788 51
Huerta, Adolfo de la	
Mexican history	972.082 1
Huerteales	583.76

Huesca (Spain : Province) T2—465 55
Hugh Capet, King of France
  French history 944.021
Hughes, William Morris
  Australian history 994.041
Hughes County (Okla.) T2—766 72
Hughes County (S.D.) T2—783 29
Huguenots 284.5
  biography 284.509 2
  persecution of 272.4
Huichol Indians T5—974 544
Huichol language 497.454 4
  T6—974 544
Huichol literature 897.454 4
Huíla (Angola) T2—673 5
Huila (Colombia : Dept.) T2—861 39
Ḥukm 340.591 2
Huku language 496.394
  T6—963 94
Hull (England) T2—428 37
Hull, Clark Leonard
  psychological system 150.194 34
Ḥullin 296.123 5
  Babylonian Talmud 296.125 5
  Mishnah 296.123 5
Hulls (Ships)
  engineering 623.84
Humacao (P.R. : District) T2—729 59
Humala, Ollanta
  Peruvian history 985.064 6
Human-alien encounters 001.942
Human anatomy 611
  arts T3C—356 1
  literature 808.803 561
    history and criticism 809.933 561
  specific literatures T3B—080 356 1
    history and
     criticism T3B—093 561
  see Manual at 599.94 vs. 611;
    also at 612 vs. 611
Human behavior
  psychology 150
  social psychology 302
Human body
  arts T3C—356 1
  folklore 398.276 1
    history and criticism 398.353
  literature 808.803 561
    history and criticism 809.933 561
  specific literatures T3B—080 356 1
    history and
     criticism T3B—093 561
Human capital
  accounting 657.4

Human characteristics
  arts 700.453
    T3C—353
  literature 808.803 53
    history and criticism 809.933 53
  specific literatures T3B—080 353
    history and
     criticism T3B—093 53
Human chromosome
  abnormalities
    medicine 616.042
Human cloning
  ethics 176.22
  religion 205.662 2
    see also Reproduction —
     ethics — religion
    see also Reproduction —
     ethics
Human-computer interaction 004.019
  engineering 621.398 4
Human ecology 304.2
  biology 599.95
  social theology 201.77
    Christianity 261.88
    Judaism 296.38
  see Manual at 578 vs. 304.2,
    508, 910
Human embryo 612.646
  experimental research 616.027
    medical ethics 174.28
  physiology 612.646
  transplantation
    ethics 176.2
    see also Reproduction —
     ethics
  surgery 618.178 059 9
Human engineering 620.82
Human evolution 599.938
Human experimentation in
  medicine
  clinical trials 615.507 24
  ethics 174.28
    see also Medical ethics
  law 344.041 96
Human face recognition
  biometric identification
    computer science 006.248 399 5
Human factors engineering 620.82
  computers 621.39
Human figures
  art representation 704.942
  arts 700.456 1
    T3C—356 1
  drawing 743.4

Human figures (continued)
  literature 808.803 561
    history and criticism 809.933 561
    specific literatures T3B—080 356 1
      history and
        criticism T3B—093 561
  painting 757
Human genetics 599.935
Human geography 304.2
Human immunodeficiency
  viruses
  medical microbiology 616.979 201
Human information processing 153
Human life
  folklore 398.27
    history and criticism 398.35
    persons 398.22
  origin
    religion 202.2
      Christianity 233.11
      Islam 297.221
      Judaism 296.32
      philosophy of religion 213
    philosophy 128
  respect for
    ethics 179.7
    religion
      Jainism 294.456 97
Human microbiome 612.001 579
Human microbiota 612.001 579
Human milk diet 613.269
Human monkeypox 362.196 913
  incidence 614.521
  medicine 616.913
  see also Communicable
    diseases — humans
  social services 362.196 913
Human mpox 362.196 913
  incidence 614.521
  medicine 616.913
  social services 362.196 913
Human papillomavirus infections
  incidence 614.581
  medicine 616.911
  see also Communicable
    diseases — humans

Human physiology 612
  arts T3C—356 1
  literature 808.803 561
    history and criticism 809.933 561
    specific literatures T3B—080 356 1
      history and
        criticism T3B—093 561
  see Manual at 612 vs. 611;
    also at 612.1–.8; *also at*
    613 vs. 612, 615.8; *also at*
    616 vs. 612
Human pigmentation
  physical anthropology 599.95
Human qualities
  folklore 398.27
    history and criticism 398.353
Human races 305.8
  physical ethnology 599.97
  see also Ethnic groups
Human relations
  applied psychology 158.2
  business 650.13
  personnel management 658.314 5
    executives 658.407 145
    public administration 352.66
Human relations training
  personnel management 658.312 44
    executives 658.407 124 4
    public administration 352.669
Human reproduction 612.6
  see also Genital system
Human reproductive technology
  ethics 176.2
    see also Reproduction —
      ethics
  health 613.94
  infertility
    gynecology 618.178 06
    medicine 616.692 06
Human resource development 370.113
  see also Vocational education
Human resource management 658.3
             T1—068 3
  see also Personnel
    management
Human resources 331.11
  accounting 657.4
  armed forces 355.22
  economics 331.11
  utilization
    economics 331.125

Humidity control
air conditioning
buildings 697.932 3
spacecraft 629.477 5
Humility 179.9
moral theology 205.699
see also Virtues
Humiriaceae 583.69
Hummingbirds 598.764
conservation technology 639.978 764
resource economics 333.958 764
Humor 152.43
history and criticism 809.7
journalism 070.444
literary criticism
theory 808.7
literature 808.87
specific literatures T3B—7
psychology 152.43
rhetoric 808.7
sociology 306.481
specific subjects T1—020 7
see Manual at T1—0207 vs.
T3B—7, T3A—8 + 02,
T3B—802, T3B—8 + 02,
T3A—8 + 07, T3B—807,
T3B—8 + 07
Humorists 809.7
collected biography 809.7
specific literatures T3B—700 9
Humorous fiction 808.839 17
Humorous poetry 808.817
history and criticism 809.17
specific literatures T3B—107
specific literatures T3A—1
Humors (Psychology) 155.262
Humpback whale 599.525
Humpbacked flies 595.774
Humphreys County (Miss.) T2—762 48
Humphreys County (Tenn.) T2—768 37
Humus
soil science 631.417
Hunan Sheng (China) T2—512 15
Hundred Days, 1815 944.05
Hundred Years' War, 1337–1453 944.025
Hunedoara (Romania :
Judeţ) T2—498 4
Hưng Yên (Vietnam :
Province) T2—597 3
Hungana language 496.393
T6—963 93
Hungarian language 494.511
T6—945 11
Hungarian literature 894.511

Hungarian partridge 598.623 2
Hungarians T5—945 11
Hungary 943.9
T2—439
ancient 936.39
T2—363 9
Hunger
human physiology 612.391
psychology 152.188 6
social theology 201.763 8
Christianity 261.832 6
social welfare 363.8
Hunger strikes
social conflict 303.61
Hunt County (Tex.) T2—764 272
Hunter River (N.S.W.) T2—944 2
Hunterdon County (N.J.) T2—749 71
Hunters
commercial 639.109 2
sports 799.292
Hunting 799.2
arts T3C—357 9
commercial 639.1
economics 338.372 9
public administration 354.349
ethics 179.3
see also Animals —
treatment of — ethics
game laws 346.046 954 9
painting 758.3
products 338.372 9
commerce 381.432–.439
public administration 354.349
sports 799.2
arts 700.457 9
T3C—357 9
biography 799.292
child care 649.57
ethics 179.3
human physiology 612.044
journalism 070.449 799 2
law 344.099
literature
history and criticism 809.933 579
specific literatures T3B—080 357 9
history and
criticism T3B—093 579
motion pictures 791.436 579
physical fitness 613.711
public administrative support 353.78
safety 363.14
public administration 353.97
techniques 799.202 89

Hunting
  sports (continued)
    sociology 306.483
    television programs 791.456 579
Hunting and gathering societies 306.364
Hunting animals
  animal husbandry 636.088 8
Hunting dogs 636.75
  sports 799.234
Hunting lodges
  architecture 728.7
Huntingdon County (Pa.) T2—748 73
Huntingdonshire (England) T2—426 54
Huntington County (Ind.) T2—772 71
Huntington disease
  medicine 616.851
    see also Nervous system
      diseases — humans
Huntsville (Ala.) T2—761 97
Huon pine 585.3
  forestry 634.975 93
Hupa Indians T5—972
Hupa language 497.2
   T6—972
Hupeh Province (China) T2—512 12
Hurdlers 796.426 092
Hurdles (Race)
  horses 798.45
  humans 796.426
    biography 796.426 092
Hurdy-gurdies 787.69
  instrument 787.691 9
  music 787.69
  see also Stringed instruments
Huron (Ont. : County) T2—713 22
Huron, Lake (Mich. and
  Ont.) T2—774
  Michigan T2—774
  Ontario T2—713 2
Huron County (Mich.) T2—774 44
Huron County (Ohio) T2—771 25
Huron Indians 973.049 755 5
   T5—975 55
Huron language 497.555
   T6—975 55
Hurrian languages 499.9
   T6—999
Hurricanes 551.552
  meteorology 551.552
  social services 363.349 22
  weather forecasting 551.645 2
  weather modification 551.685 2
  see also Disasters

Hurunui District (N.Z.) T2—938 1
  Canterbury Region T2—938 1
  Nelson-Marlborough
    Region T2—937 9
Husband and wife 306.872
  law 346.016 3
Husbands 306.872 2
   T1—086 55
  social welfare 362.820 865 5
  see also Married men
Huskers
  manufacturing technology 681.763 1
Huskies 636.73
Husking 631.56
Hussain, Mamnoon
  Pakistani history 954.910 532
Hussein, King of Jordan
  Jordanian history 956.950 44
    1953–1967 956.950 43
    1967–1999 956.950 44
Hussein, Saddam
  Iraqi history 956.704 4
Hussein Onn, Datuk
  Malaysian history 959.505 3
Hussite Wars, 1419–1436 943.702 24
Hussites 284.3
Hutchinson County (S.D.) T2—783 384
Hutchinson County (Tex.) T2—764 821
Hutias 599.359
Hutterite Brethren 289.73
  biography 289.709 2
Hutu (African people) T5—963 946 1
HVAC (Building systems) 697
HVAP ammunition 623.451 8
Hwang Ho (China) T2—511
Hyacinths 635.934 79
  botany 584.79
  floriculture 635.934 79
Hyaenidae 599.743
Hyaline cartilage
  human histology 612.751 7
Hyalospongiae 593.44
  paleozoology 563.4
Hybrid computers 004.19
  architecture 004.259
  communications 004.619
    software 005.713 9
    software development 005.712 9
  engineering 621.391 9
  graphics software 006.689
  graphics software development 006.679
  interfacing 004.619
    software 005.713 9
    software development 005.712 9

Hypercholesterolemia
  medicine 616.399 7
    see also Digestive system
      diseases — humans
Hypercubes 516.158
Hyperfunctions 515.9
Hypergeometric polynomials 515.55
Hypericaceae 583.69
Hyperkinesia
  medicine 616.858 9
  pediatrics 618.928 589
Hyperlipidemia
  medicine 616.399 7
    see also Digestive system
      diseases — humans
Hypermarkets 381.149
  management 658.879
Hypermedia 006.7
Hyperons 539.721 64
Hyperopia
  optometry 617.755
    see also Eye diseases —
      humans
Hyperparathyroidism
  medicine 616.445
    see also Endocrine
      diseases — humans
Hyperpinealism
  medicine 616.48
    see also Endocrine
      diseases — humans
Hypersensitivity
  incidence 614.599 3
  medicine 616.97
Hypersonic flow 533.276
  air mechanics 533.62
  aeronautics 629.132 306
Hypertension
  medicine 616.132
    see also Cardiovascular
      diseases — humans
  pregnancy complications
  obstetrics 618.361 32
Hypertext 006.7
Hypertext databases
  computer science 005.759
Hyperthyroidism
  medicine 616.443
    see also Endocrine
      diseases — humans
Hypertrichosis
  medicine 616.546
    see also Skin diseases —
      humans

Hypertrophies
  skin
    medicine 616.544
    see also Skin diseases —
      humans
Hyperventilation
  medicine 616.208
    see also Respiratory tract
      diseases — humans
Hyphochytridiomycetes 579.53
Hyphomycetes 579.55
Hypnosis 154.7
Hypnotherapy
  medicine 615.851 2
Hypnotic phenomena 154.77
Hypnotic regression
  occultism 133.901 35
Hypnotics
  pharmacokinetics 615.782
Hypnotism 154.7
  parapsychology 133.89
Hypoadrenalism
  medicine 616.45
    see also Endocrine
      diseases — humans
Hypochondria
  medicine 616.852 5
    see also Mental disorders
Hypochondriasis
  medicine 616.852 5
    see also Mental disorders
Hypocreales 579.567 7
Hypoglycemia
  medicine 616.466
    see also Endocrine
      diseases — humans
Hypoparathyroidism
  medicine 616.445
    see also Endocrine
      diseases — humans
Hypopituitarism
  medicine 616.47
    see also Endocrine
      diseases — humans
Hypostatic union 232.8
Hypothalamus 573.459
  biology 573.459
  human anatomy 611.81
  human physiology 612.826 2
  medicine 616.8
  see also Nervous system

Ice cream	641.862
commercial processing	637.4
home preparation	641.862
Ice crossings	
railroad engineering	625.147
road engineering	625.792
Ice dancing	796.912
see also Winter sports	
Ice fishing	799.122
Ice formation	
aeronautics	629.132 4
Ice games	796.96
see also Winter sports	
Ice hockey	796.962
electronic games	794.869 62
see also Winter sports	
Ice hockey players	796.962 092
Ice milk	641.862
commercial processing	637.4
home preparation	641.862
Ice plants (Aizoaceae)	583.883
Ice roads	388.12
engineering	625.792
see also Roads	
Ice skaters	796.910 92
Ice skates	
manufacturing technology	688.769 1
Ice skating	796.91
biography	796.910 92
see also Winter sports	
Ice sports	796.9
equipment technology	688.769
see also Winter sports	
Ice storms	551.556
social services	363.349 26
Ice wine	641.222
commercial processing	663.22
Icebergs	551.342
Iceboating	796.97
see also Winter sports	
Icebreakers	387.28
design	623.812 8
engineering	623.828
see also Ships	
Icebreaking services	387.54
İçel İli (Turkey)	T2—564 6
ancient	T2—393 5
Iceland	949.12
	T2—491 2
Iceland pony	636.16
Icelanders	T5—396 1
Icelandic language	439.69
	T6—396 91
Icelandic literature	839.69
Icelandic people	T5—396 1
Ices	641.863
commercial processing	637.4
home preparation	641.863
Ichneumonoidea	595.79
Ichneumons	595.79
Ichnology	560.43
vertebrates	566
Ichthyologists	597.092
Ichthyology	597
Ichthyornithiformes	568.23
Ichthyosauria	567.937
Ichthyosis	
medicine	616.544
see also Skin diseases —	
humans	
Iconography	
design	744.2
drawing	743.9
fine arts	704.9
see Manual at 704.9 and	
753–758	
painting	753–758
see Manual at 704.9 and	
753–758	
use in advertising	659.104 5
Icons	
design	744.2
fine arts	704.948
Christianity	704.948 2
religious significance	203.7
Christianity	246.53
see also Symbolism —	
religious significance	
Ictaluridae	597.492
Ictalurus	597.492
Icteridae	598.874
Id (Psychology)	154.2
ʿĪd al-Aḍḥā	297.36
ʿĪd al-Fiṭr	297.36
Ida County (Iowa)	T2—777 422
Idaho	979.6
	T2—796
Idaho County (Idaho)	T2—796 82
Ideal states	321.07
see also Utopias	
Idealism	141
arts	T3C—13
education	370.12
literature	808.801 3
history and criticism	809.913
specific literatures	T3B—080 13
history and	
criticism	T3B—091 3

Île aux Grues (Quebec) — T2—714 735
Ile-de-France (France) — T2—443 6
Ile de la Tortue (Haiti) — T2—729 42
Île-d'Orléans (Quebec) — T2—714 476
Île-Dorval (Quebec) — T2—714 28
Île Verte (Quebec) — T2—714 764
Ileal diseases
  medicine — 616.34
    see also Digestive system
      diseases — humans
Ileitis
  medicine — 616.344 5
    see also Digestive system
      diseases — humans
iLembe District
  Municipality (South
  Africa) — T2—684 47
Ileostomy — 617.554 1
Îles-de-la-Madeleine
  (Quebec) — T2—714 797
Ileum — 573.378
  biology — 573.378
  human anatomy — 611.341
  medicine — 616.34
  surgery — 617.554 1
  see also Digestive system
Ilex — 583.982
Ilía (Greece) — T2—495 27
  ancient — T2—388
Ilium (Extinct City) — T2—392 1
Ill people — 305.908 7
   — T1—087 7
'Illah (Islamic law) — 340.591 2
Ille-et-Vilaine (France) — T2—441 5
Illecillewaet River (B.C.) — T2—711 68
Illegal immigration — 364.137
  law — 345.023 7
Illegitimacy — 306.874
  law — 346.017
Illegitimate children — 306.874
   — T1—086 945
    see also Children of unmarried
      parents
Illiciales — 584.24
Illicit distilling — 364.133 2
  law — 345.023 32
Illinois — 977.3
   — T2—773
Illinois Indians — T5—973 15
Illinois language — 497.315
   — T6—973 15
Illinois River (Ill.) — T2—773 5
Illiteracy — 302.224 4
  see also Literacy

Illiterate people — 305.56
   — T1—086 94
Illizi (Algeria : Province) — T2—657
Illness — 362.1
  medicine — 616
  see also Diseases — humans
Illocutionary acts — 401.452
  specific languages — T4—014 52
Illuminating engineering — 621.32
  see also Lighting
Illumination — 621.32
  see also Lighting
Illumination (Decorative arts) — 741.647
Illuminations (Performing arts) — 791.6
Illusions — 001.96
  psychology of perception — 153.74
  sensory perception — 152.1
Illustration
  arts — 741.6
    see Manual at 741.6 vs. 800;
      also at 744 vs. 741.6
  sociology — 302.226
Illustrations — T1—022
  notable books — 096.1
  see Manual at T1—0222 vs.
    T1—0223
Illustrators — 741.609 2
Illyria — 939.87
   — T2—398 7
Illyrian languages (Ancient
  Indo-European) — 491.993
   — T6—919 93
Illyricum — 939.87
   — T2—398 7
Ilm-Kreis (Germany :
  Landkreis) — T2—432 26
Ilmenite
  mineralogy — 549.523
ILO (Labor office) — 354.921 1
  law — 344.01
Ilocos Norte (Philippines) — T2—599 142
Ilocos Region (Philippines) — T2—599 14
Ilocos Sur (Philippines) — T2—599 144
Iloilo (Philippines :
  Province) — T2—599 535
Iloko language — 499.21
   — T6—992 1
Ilorin (Nigeria) — T2—669 57
Image manipulation
  computer science — 006.6
  digital photography — 771.44

Immunocomputing	006.382 5
Immunocytochemistry	571.964
medicine	616.079
Immunodiagnosis	
medicine	616.075 6
Immunogenetics	571.964 8
medicine	616.079 6
Immunoglobulins	571.967
humans	616.079 8
pharmacology	615.37
Immunologic diseases	
medicine	616.97
Immunologic drugs	
pharmacology	615.37
Immunology	571.96
humans	616.079
Immunotherapy	615.37
Imo State (Nigeria)	T2—669 46
Impact strength	
materials science	620.112 5
Impact studies (Environmental)	333.714
Impala	599.646
Impatiens	583.93
botany	583.93
Impeachment	342.068
chief executives	342.062
judges	347.014
Impeachment power (Legislative	
bodies)	328.345 3
Impediments to marriage	
law	346.016 2
Impendle (South Africa :	
District)	T2—684 7
Imperative programming	005.113
Imperia (Italy : Province)	T2—451 87
ancient	T2—371 4
Imperial County (Calif.)	T2—794 99
Imperial system (Measurement)	530.813
social aspects	389.15
Imperial Valley (Calif. and	
Mexico)	T2—794 99
Imperialism	325.32
international relations	327.1
Impersonation	792.028
illegal	364.163 3
law	345.026 33
motion pictures	791.430 28
radio	791.440 28
stage	792.028
television	791.450 28
Impetigo	
medicine	616.523
see also Skin diseases —	
humans	

Implant-supported dentures	
dentistry	617.693
Implication	
linguistics	401.454
specific languages	T4—014 54
Import quotas	382.52
see also Import trade	
Import tax	382.7
public finance	336.264
see also Customs (Tariff)	
Import trade	382.5
law	343.087 7
public administration	354.74
Impotence	
drug therapy	616.692 206 1
medicine	616.692 2
see also Male genital	
diseases — humans	
neurotic	
medicine	616.858 32
Impoverished people	305.569
	T1—086 942
see also Poor people	
Impressing equipment	621.984
Impression	
printing	686.23
Impressionism	
fine arts	709.034 4
literature	808.801 1
history and criticism	809.911
specific literatures	T3B—080 11
history and	
criticism	T3B—091 1
music	780.904
painting	759.054
Imprisonment	365
Impromptus	784.189 4
Improper integrals	515.43
Improvisation (Drama)	792.028
motion pictures	791.430 28
radio	791.440 28
stage	792.028
television	791.450 28
Improvisation (Music)	781.36
Improvisatory forms	784.189 4
Impulse control disorders	
medicine	616.858 4
see also Mental disorders	
Impulsive personality	
medicine	616.858 4
see also Mental disorders	
İmroz Island (Turkey)	T2—562 2
In-car entertainment	629.277 4

Individual income tax	336.242	Indonesian language	499.221
law	343.052 62		T6—992 21
public administration	352.44	Indonesian language (Bahasa	
public finance	336.242	Indonesia)	499.221
Individual land tenure		Indonesian languages	499.22
economics	333.323		T6—992 2
Individual proprietorships	338.72	Indonesian literature	899.221
see also Proprietorships		Indonesian literatures	899.22
Individual psychology	155.2	Indonesians	T5—992 2
children	155.418 2	Indoor air pollution	
late adulthood	155.671 82	health	613.5
Individual retirement accounts	332.024 014 5	Indoor air quality	
tax law	343.052 33	health	613.5
Individualism		Indoor amusements	793
economics	330.153	Indoor climbing	796.522 4
philosophy	141.4	*see also* Outdoor life	
political ideology	320.512	Indoor field hockey	796.355
social psychology	302.54	*see also* Ball games	
Individuality	155.2	Indoor games	793
children	155.418 2	Indoor gardening	
Individualized instruction	371.394	floriculture	635.965
Individualized reading instruction		Indoor music	781.534
primary education	372.417	Indoor photography	778.72
Indo-Aryan languages	491.1	Indoor recreation centers	790.068
	T6—911	architecture	725.84
Indo-Aryan literatures	891.1	Indoor temperatures	
Indo-Aryan period	934.02	health	613.5
Indo-Aryans	T5—914	Indre (France : Dept.)	T2—445 51
Indo-European languages	410	Indre-et-Loire (France)	T2—445 4
	T6—1	Indri	599.83
Indo-European literatures	800	Inductance meters	621.374 2
Indo-Europeans	T5—09	Induction (Logic)	
Indo-Germanic languages	410	philosophical logic	161
	T6—1	psychology	153.432
Indo-Hittite languages	410	Induction accelerators	539.734
	T6—1	Induction heating	621.402
Indo-Iranian languages	491.1	Induction of employees	
	T6—911	armed forces	355.223
Indo-Iranian literatures	891.1	personnel management	658.312 42
Indo-jazz	781.657 291 411	public administration	352.66
Indo-Pakistan Sign Language	419.54	Induction of hypnosis	154.76
	T6—999 854	Induction welding	671.521 5
Indo-Pakistan War, 1965	954.904 5	Inductive reasoning	161
Indo-Pakistan War, 1971	954.920 51	philosophical logic	161
Indochina (French		psychology	153.432
Indochina)	T2—597	Inductors	
Indochina (Southeast peninsula of		radio engineering	621.384 133
Asia)	959	Indulgences (Christian rite)	265.66
	T2—59	Indus River	T2—549 1
Indochinese War, 1946–1954	959.704 1	Indus script	494.899
Indochinese War, 1961–1975	959.704 3		T6—948 99
Indonesia	959.8		
	T2—598		

Inflammable materials	363.179 8
fire safety technology	628.922 2
public safety	363.179 8
technology	604.7
see also Hazardous materials	
Inflammation	
result of injury	
medicine	617.22
symptom	616.047 3
Inflammatory bowel diseases	
medicine	616.344
see also Digestive system	
diseases — humans	
Inflation (Economics)	332.41
accounting	657.48
personal finance	332.024
Inflection (Grammar)	415.95
specific languages	T4—595
Inflection (Phonology)	414.6
specific languages	T4—16
Inflection tables (Grammar)	
applied linguistics	418
specific languages	T4—82
Influence	
psychology	155.9
children	155.418 9
social psychology	302.13
Influence peddling	364.132 3
law	345.023 23
public administration	353.46
Influenza	
incidence	614.518
medicine	616.203
see also Respiratory tract	
diseases — humans	
Infographics	744.37
Informal logic	160
Informatics	
computer science	004
information science	020
Information	
civil rights issues	323.445
sociology	306.42
Information and referral services	025.52
Information architecture	006.7
design	744.35
Information centers	027
see also Libraries	
Information control	363.31
see also Censorship	
Information design	744.37
see Manual at 744 vs. 741.6	
Information display systems	
electronic engineering	621.381 542

Information exchange	
law	344.09
Information filtering systems	005.56
computer science	005.56
information science	025.04
Information fusion	005.74
Information gathering	
executive management	658.403 8
Information graphics	744.37
Information integration	005.74
Information literacy	
primary education	372.34
Information management	
executive management	658.403 8
military administration	355.688
office services	651
production management	658.503 6
public administration	352.38
Information policy	338.926
see Manual at 338.926 vs.	
352.745, 500	
Information processing in nature	570
Information retrieval	
information science	025.524
Information science	020
Information scientists	020.92
Information security	
management	658.472
Information services	025.52
public administration	352.74
Information sources	
use	028.7
Information storage and retrieval	
systems	025.04
computer science	005.74
law	343.099 9
management use	658.403 801 1
specific subjects	025.06
Information systems	004
Information technology	
computer science	004
social effects	303.483 3
Information theory	003.54
	T1—011 54
communications engineering	621.382 2
Informational programs	
management use	658.455
Informed consent	344.041 2
Informers	
criminal investigation	363.252
Informetrics	020.727
Infrared astronomy	522.683
Infrared cinematography	777.6

Injuries	
anesthesiology	617.967 1
biology	571.975
incidence	614.3
medicine	617.1
Injurious animals	591.65
Injurious microorganisms	579.165
Injurious organisms	578.65
Injurious plants	581.65
Ink drawing	741.26
Ink painting	751.425
Inka	T5—983 23
Inka period	985.019
Inks	667.4
Inland marine insurance	368.23
see also Insurance	
Inland revenue	336.2
law	343.04
Inland Sea (Japan)	551.461 455
	T2—164 55
Inland seas	551.482 9
	T2—168
biology	578.763 9
ecology	577.639
law of nations	341.444
Inland water transportation	386
engineering	629.048
waterways	627.1
law	343.096 4
public administration	354.78
transportation services	386
Inland water transportation	
workers	386.092
Inland waterway mail	383.143
Inland waterway security services	363.287 2
Inland waterways	386
engineering	627.1
hydrology	551.48
land economics	333.915
see also Inland water	
transportation	
Inlay trim	
furniture arts	749.5
wood handicrafts	745.512
Inlays	
dentistry	617.675
Inline hockey	796.356 62
Inline skater hockey	796.356 6
Inmates (Prisoners)	365.6
	T1—086 927
labor economics	331.51
legal status	344.035 6
Inn (Switzerland)	T2—494 732 7

Inn River	T2—436 42
Austria	T2—436 42
Switzerland	T2—494 732 7
Innate ideas	121.4
Innate reflexes	
psychology	152.322 3
Innate virtues (Christian doctrine)	234
Innatism	149.7
Inner cities	
community redevelopment	307.342
Inner-city residents	
government programs	353.533 3
Inner ears	573.89
human physiology	612.858
see also Ears	
Inner Hebrides (Scotland)	941.154
	T2—411 54
Inner Mongolia (China)	T2—517 7
Inner Mongolia	
Autonomous Region	
(China)	T2—517 7
Inner product spaces	515.733
Inner tubes	678.35
Innervation	573.85
human heart	612.178
human muscles	612.743
human physiology	612.81
human respiratory system	612.28
human skin	612.798
muscles	573.752 8
see also Nervous system	
Innisfail (Qld.)	T2—943 6
Innkeepers	647.940 92
Innlandet fylke (Norway)	T2—482 4
Innocent passage	341.4
Innomines	784.187 6
Innovation	
agent of social change	303.484
executive management	658.406 3
Inns	910.46
see also Hotels	
Innsbruck (Austria)	T2—436 424
Inoculation	
disease control	614.47
İnönü, İsmet	
Turkish history	956.102 5
Inorganic biochemistry	572.51
humans	612.015 24
Inorganic chemistry	546
applied	660
see Manual at 541 vs. 546;	
also at 549 vs. 546	
Inorganic drugs	
pharmacology	615.2

Instinctive movements	
psychology	152.324
Institutes (Adult education)	T1—071 5
Institutes (Roman law)	340.54
Institutional care	361.05
children	362.732
older people	362.61
Institutional cooking	641.57
Institutional economics	
(Economic school)	330.155 2
Institutional grounds	
landscape architecture	712.7
Institutional households	
household management	647.96
Institutional housekeeping	647
see Manual at 647 vs. 647.068,	
658.2, T1—0682	
Institutional investment	332.672 53
international	332.673 14
Institutional investors	332.672 53
international	332.673 14
Institutional nursing	610.733
Institutional publishers	070.594
Institutional repositories	027
Institutionalized children	
psychology	155.446
Institutions (Sociology)	306
see Manual at 302–307 vs. 320	
Instruction services	
museology	069.15
Instructional materials	371.33
primary education	372.133
reading	372.412
public control	379.156
see also Teaching materials	
Instructional materials centers	027.7
college libraries	027.7
school libraries	027.8
Instructional supervision	371.203
Instructional technology	371.33
Instructions to juries	347.075 8
criminal law	345.075
Instrument flying	629.132 521 4
Instrumental ensembles	784
Instrumental forms	784.18
Instrumentalism	144.5
Instrumentation	T1—028 4
aircraft	629.135
analytical chemistry	543.19
physics	530.7
weather reporting	551.635
Instruments	T1—028 4
Instruments (Music)	784.19
see also Musical instruments	

Insulating materials	
building materials	691.95
materials science	620.195
Insulation	
building construction	693.83
electrical circuits	621.319 37
heat engineering	621.402 4
steam engineering	621.185
Insulators	
electrical circuits	621.319 37
Insulin	572.565
biochemistry	572.565
human physiology	612.34
pharmacology	615.365
see also Digestive system;	
Endocrine system	
Insulin-dependent diabetes	362.196 462 2
medicine	616.462 2
pregnancy complications	
obstetrics	618.364 6
social services	362.196 462 2
see also Endocrine diseases —	
humans	
Insulin therapy	
psychiatry	616.891 2
Insurance	368
accounting	657.73
financial management	658.153
labor economics	331.255
law	346.086
malpractice	346.086 02
personnel management	658.325 4
public administration	354.85
Insurance agents	368.009 2
Insurance companies	368.006 5
accounting	657.836
credit functions	332.38
investment by	332.672 532
investment in	332.672 2
see also Insurance	
Insurance law	346.086
Insurance rates	368.011
Insured mail	383.182
see also Postal service	
Insurgency (Warfare)	355.021 8
Insurgent warfare	355.021 8
Intaglio printing	765
Intaglios	736.223
Intangible property	346.048
Intangible property risks	368.063
Integer programming	519.77
Integers	512.72
Integral calculus	515.43
Integral domains	512.4

Integral equations	515.45	Intellectual processes	153
numerical solutions	518.66	children	155.413
Integral geometry	516.362	Intellectual property	346.048
Integral inequalities	515.46	law	346.048
Integral operators	515.723	public administration	352.749
Integral transforms	515.723	Intellectual property infringement	346.048
Integrals	515.43	criminal law	345.026 6
Integrated circuits	621.381 5	criminology	364.166
computer engineering	621.395	law	346.048
Integrated development		Intellectualism	149.7
environments	005.1	Intellectuals	305.552
Integrated optics	621.369 3		T1—086 222
Integrated pest management	632.9	civil rights	323.322 22
Integrated programs	005.5	relations with government	323.322 22
Integrated services digital		Intelligence	153.9
networks	384	comparative psychology	156.39
engineering	621.382	educational psychology	370.152 9
Integration (Mathematics)	515.43	evolutionary psychology	155.7
Integration in education	379.263	human physiology	612.823 39
Integration theory	515.42	philosophy	128.3
Integro-differential equations	515.38	psychology	153.9
Integument	573.5	Intelligence (Animals)	591.513
animal physiology	573.5	Intelligence (Information)	327.12
descriptive zoology	591.47	armed forces	355.343 2
human anatomy	611.77	*see also* Unconventional	
human physiology	612.79	warfare	
medicine	616.5	executive management	658.472
Integument diseases		public administration	352.379
medicine	616.5	international relations	327.12
see also Skin diseases —		public administration	353.17
humans		military technology	623.71
Integumentary system		*see also* Espionage	
human physiology	612.79	Intelligence levels	153.9
Intellect	153.9	Intelligence tests	153.93
philosophy	128.3	Intelligent agents (Computer	
psychology	153.9	software)	006.302 854 36
Intellectual disabilities	362.3	Intelligent road transportation	
arts	T3C—356 1	systems	388.312
geriatrics	618.976 858 8	engineering	625.794
literature	808.803 561	Intelligent vehicle-highway	
history and criticism	809.933 561	system	388.312
specific literatures	T3B—080 356 1	engineering	625.794
history and		Intelligentsia	305.552
criticism	T3B—093 561		T1—086 222
medicine	616.858 8	Intensifying solutions	
nursing	616.858 802 31	photography	771.54
pediatrics	618.928 588	Intensity of light	535.22
social welfare	362.3	Intensive care	362.174
public administration	353.65	medicine	616.028
Intellectual freedom	323.44	nursing	616.028
library policies	025.213	social welfare	362.174
Intellectual history	001.09	*see also* Health services	
Intellectual life	001.1	Intention (Islamic law)	340.592 5
sociology	306.42		

Internal-combustion engines	621.43
automotive	629.25
electric generation	621.312 133
ships	623.872 3
Internal commerce	381
law	343.08
public administration	354.73
Internal ear diseases	
medicine	617.882
see also Ear diseases —	
humans	
Internal ears	573.89
human anatomy	611.85
human physiology	612.858
medicine	617.882
see also Ears	
Internal friction	
solid-state physics	530.416
Internal management auditing	658.401 3
public administration	352.43
Internal management audits	658.401 3
public administration	352.439
Internal medicine	616
Internal migration	304.809
community sociology	307.2
Internal organization	658.402
	T1—068 4
education	371.207
public administration	352.28
see Manual at 658.04 vs.	
658.114, 658.402	
Internal respiration	
human physiology	612.26
see also Respiratory system	
Internal revenue	336.2
law	343.04
Internal storage (Computers)	004.53
engineering	621.397 3
International administration	352.11
International agencies	
law	341.2
International arbitration	327.17
international politics	327.17
law of nations	341.522
International assistance	
economics	338.91
social welfare	361.26
governmental	361.6
International Association of	
Rebekah Assemblies	366.38
biography	366.380 92
International Bank for	
Reconstruction and	
Development	332.153 2
law	346.082 153 2
International banking	332.15
law	346.082 15
International banks	332.15
International borrowing	336.343 5
public administration	352.45
public finance	336.343 5
International business enterprises	338.88
International Church of the	
Foursquare Gospel	289.94
International Churches of Christ	286.635
International claims	
public administration	353.44
International commerce	382
see also Foreign trade	
International Committee of the	
Red Cross	361.772
International Communist	
Congress	324.175
International conflict	327.16
law	341.5
see also Wars	
International cooking	641.59
International cooperation	327.17
law	341.7
International Court of Justice	341.552
International courts	341.55
International crimes	364.135
law	345.023 5
International Criminal Police	
Organization	363.206 01
law	345.052
International debt	336.343 5
public administration	352.45
public finance	336.343 5
International development	
economics	338.91
International Development	
Association	332.153 2
International disputes	327.16
law	341.5
International economic assistance	338.91
International economic	
cooperation	337
International economic	
development	338.91
role of multinational	
enterprises	338.883
International economic law	343.07

444

Intestinal secretions	573.373 79
human physiology	612.33
see also Digestive system	
Intestine	573.37
biology	573.37
human anatomy	611.34
human physiology	612.33
medicine	616.34
surgery	617.554
see also Digestive system	
Intibucá (Honduras : Dept.)	T2—728 381
Intimacy	
applied psychology	158.2
Intimate partner abuse	362.829 2
criminology	364.155 53
law	345.025 553
medicine	616.858 22
social welfare	362.829 2
Intimate partner violence	362.829 2
criminology	
law	345.025 553
Intonation (Linguistics)	414.6
specific languages	T4—16
Intoxication	362.29
medicine	616.86
social welfare	362.29
see also Substance abuse	
Intractable pain	
medicine	616.047 2
Intrafamily relationships	306.87
Intragovernmental revenues	
public finance	336.18
Intramural college sports	796.043
Intramural sports	796.042
see also Sports	
Intranets	004.682
computer science	004.682
office use	651.792
Intraocular lenses	
ophthalmology	617.752 4
Intraoperative care	
surgery	617.919
Intraoperative complications	
surgery	617.919
Intrauterine contraceptives	
health	613.943 5
medicine	618.185 2
see also Birth control	
Intravenous anesthesia	
surgery	617.962
Intravenous feeding	
medicine	615.854 84
Intravenous medication	
administering	615.6

Intravenous therapy	
medicine	615.855
Intrinsic variables (Stars)	523.844 2
Introduced species	333.952 3
Introductory forms (Music)	784.189 2
Introit	264.36
music	782.323 5
Introversion	155.232
Intrusion detection	005.83
Intrusion prevention	005.83
Intrusions (Geology)	551.88
Intuition	153.44
epistemology	121.3
ethical systems	171.2
psychology	153.44
Intuitionism	143
Intuitionistic logic	
mathematical logic	511.36
Intuitionistic mathematics	511.36
Inuit	971.900 497 12
	T5—971 2
Inuit languages	497.12
	T6—971 2
Inuit literatures	897.12
Inuktitut	971.900 497 12
	T5—971 2
Inuktitut (Eastern Canada)	T5—971 24
Inuktitut language (Eastern	
Canada)	497.124
	T6—971 24
Inuktitut languages	497.12
	T6—971 2
Inuktitut literature (Eastern	
Canada)	897.124
Inuktitut literatures	897.12
Inupiat	T5—971 2
Inupiatun language	T6—971 2
Inupik language	497.12
	T6—971 2
Inuvik (N.W.T.)	T2—719 3
Inuvik (N.W.T. : Region)	T2—719 3
Invariant theory	512.74
algebra	512.944
Invariants	512.5
Invasion	
engineering defense	623.31
Invasion of privacy	323.448
criminology	364.156
law	345.025 6
criminal law	345.025 6
torts	346.033
political science	323.448
Invasive species	333.952 3
Inventions	600

Ion transport	
physiology	572.3
Ionia	T2—392 3
Ionia County (Mich.)	T2—774 54
Ionian Islands (Greece)	T2—495 5
Ionian Islands (Greece :	
Islands)	T2—495 5
ancient	T2—382
Ionian Sea	551.461 386
	T2—163 86
Ionic equilibriums	541.372 3
chemical engineering	660.297 23
Ionic philosophy	182.1
Ionioi Nēsoi (Greece)	T2—495 5
Ionioi Nēsoi (Greece :	
Islands)	T2—495 5
ancient	T2—382
Ionization	530.444
chemical engineering	660.297 22
chemistry	541.372 2
meteorology	551.561
plasma physics	530.444
Ionization chambers	
nuclear physics	539.772
Ionization of gases	530.444
electronic physics	537.532
Ionized gases	530.44
Ionizing radiation	539.722
biophysics	571.459
Ionosphere	538.767
	T2—161 4
meteorology	551.514 5
Ionospheric probes	
unmanned	629.435 2
Ions	
chemical engineering	660.297 2
electrochemistry	541.372
Iosco County (Mich.)	T2—774 74
Iowa	977.7
	T2—777
Iowa County (Iowa)	T2—777 653
Iowa County (Wis.)	T2—775 78
Iowa Indians	T5—975 2
Iowa language	497.52
	T6—975 2
Iowa River (Iowa)	T2—777 6
IPM (Pest management)	632.9
IPOs (Securities)	658.152 24
corporate law	346.066 2
financial management	658.152 24
investment economics	332.632 2
Ipswich (England)	T2—426 49
Ipswich (Qld.)	T2—943 2
IQ tests	153.93
Iqaluit (Nunavut)	T2—719 52
Iquique (Chile : Province)	T2—831 27
IRA (Retirement account)	332.024 014 5
tax law	343.052 33
Iran	955
	T2—55
ancient	935.7
	T2—357
Iran-Iraq War, 1980–1988	955.054 2
Irangi (African people)	T5—963 94
Irangi language	496.394
	T6—963 94
Iranian-Iraqi Conflict, 1980–1988	955.054 2
Iranian languages	491.5
	T6—915
Iranian literatures	891.5
Iranian Plateau	
ancient	935.7
	T2—357
Iranians (National group)	T5—915 5
Iraq	956.7
	T2—567
ancient	935
	T2—35
Iraq Civil War, 2014–2017	956.704 43
Iraq-Kuwait Crisis, 1990–1991	956.704 42
Iraq War, 2003–2011	956.704 43
Iraqi-Iranian Conflict, 1980–1988	955.054 2
Iraqis	T5—927 567
Irbid (Jordan : Province)	T2—569 542
Irbīl (Iraq : Province)	T2—567 2
IRBM (Missiles)	358.175 382
engineering	623.451 953
military equipment	358.175 382
Iredell County (N.C.)	T2—756 793
Ireland	941.7
	T2—417
ancient	936.17
	T2—361 7
see Manual at 941	
Ireland (Island)	941.5
	T2—415
ancient	936.15
	T2—361 5
Irian Barat	995.1
	T2—951
Irian Jaya (Indonesia)	995.1
	T2—951
Irian Jaya Barat (Indonesia)	T2—951 2
Iridaceae	584.75
Iridium	669.7
chemical engineering	661.064 3
chemistry	546.643
metallography	669.957

Ismailites	
Hadith	297.125 922
Koran commentary	297.122 754
religious law	297.140 182 2
Isobutylene rubber	678.72
Isoetales	587.9
paleobotany	561.79
Isolation	
disease control	614.45
social psychology	302.545
Isomerases	572.79
see also Enzymes	
Isomers	547.122 52
inorganic chemistry	541.225 2
organic chemistry	547.122 52
Isometric exercises	613.714 9
Isometric projection	
technical drawing	604.245
Isomorphism	511.326
crystallography	548.3
mathematics	511.326
Isonitriles	547.044
chemical engineering	661.894
Isopoda	595.372
Isoptera	595.736
Isotope structure	539.74
Isotopes	
chemical engineering	660.298 8
radiochemistry	541.388
Isoviha	948.970 134 9
Isparta İli (Turkey)	T2—564 3
ancient	T2—392 7
Isrā'	297.633
Israel	956.94
	T2—569 4
ancient	933.4
	T2—334
Biblical geography and history	220.9
Christian theology	231.76
Jewish theology	296.311 73
Israel-Arab War, 1948–1949	956.042
Israel-Arab War, 1967	956.046
Israel-Arab War, 1973	956.048
Israel-Lebanon-Syria Conflict,	
1982–1985	956.052
Israelis	T5—924
Israelites	T5—924
Issaquena County (Miss.)	T2—762 412
ISSN (Standard serial number)	025.343 2
Issoufou, Mahamadou	
Nigerien (Niger) history	966.260 54
Issuing houses	332.66
Istanbul (Turkey)	T2—496 18
ancient	T2—398 618

İstanbul İli (Turkey)	T2—496 18
Asia	T2—563 2
ancient	T2—393 13
Europe	T2—496 18
Isthmus of Corinth (Greece)	T2—495 22
Isthmus of Suez (Egypt)	T2—621 5
Istiḥsān (Islamic law)	
sources of fiqh	340.591 34
Istiophoridae	597.78
Istiṣḥāb (Islamic law)	
sources of fiqh	340.591 3
Istiṣlāḥ (Islamic law)	
sources of fiqh	340.591 36
Istiwā'īyah al-Wusṭá (South	
Sudan)	T2—629 5
Istria (Croatia)	T2—497 2
ancient	T2—373 9
Isuridae	597.33
Itä-Suomen lääni (Finland)	T2—489 75
Italian Communist Party	324.245 075 2
Italian Democratic Socialist Party	
(1952–1995)	324.245 072 2
Italian Democratic Socialist Party	
(2004–)	324.245 072
Italian drama	852
Italian fiction	853
Italian folk music	781.625 1
Italian folk songs	782.421 625 1
Italian greyhound	636.76
Italian language	450
	T6—51
Italian Liberal Party (1943–1994)	324.245 04
Italian Liberal Party (2004–)	324.245 04
Italian literature	850
Italian Peninsula	945
	T2—45
ancient	937
	T2—37
Italian poetry	851
Italian Popular Party	
(1919–1926)	324.245 028 2
Italian Popular Party	
(1994–2002)	324.245 082
Italian Republican Party	324.245 05
Italian Riviera (Italy)	T2—451 8
Italian Social Movement	
(Political party)	324.245 038
Italian Social Movement-Right	
National (Political party)	324.245 038
Italian Socialist Party	324.245 074 2
Italian Somaliland	T2—677 3
Italian Wars, 1494–1559	945.06
Italianate revivals	
architecture	724.52

Italians	T5—51	Ivan IV, Czar of Russia	
Italic languages	470	Russian history	947.043
	T6—7	Ivan VI, Emperor of Russia	
Italic literatures	870	Russian history	947.061
Italic peoples	T5—4	Ivano-Frankivs´k (Ukraine :	
Italo-Ethiopian War, 1935–1936	963.056	Oblast)	T2—477 9
Italy	945	Ivano-Frankivs´ka oblast´	
	T2—45	(Ukraine)	T2—477 9
ancient	937	Ivanovo (Russia : Oblast)	T2—473 3
	T2—37	Ivanovskaĩa oblast´ (Russia)	T2—473 3
see Manual at T2—45		Ivies	635.933 988
Italy (Kingdom)	945.082	botany	583.988
Italy, Central	945.6	floriculture	635.933 988
	T2—456	Ivoirians	T5—966 68
Italy, Northern	945.1	Ivorians	T5—966 68
	T2—451	Ivory	
Italy, Southern	945.7	manufacturing technology	679.43
	T2—457	Ivory carving	736.62
ancient	937.7	Ivory Coast	966.68
	T2—377		T2—666 8
Itapúa (Paraguay)	T2—892 126	*see also* Côte d'Ivoire	
Itasca County (Minn.)	T2—776 78	Ivory Coast people	T5—966 68
Itawamba County (Miss.)	T2—762 982	Ivrea (Margravate)	945.103
Iterative development		Iwate-ken (Japan)	T2—521 14
computer software		IWW (Labor)	331.886 097 3
development	005.111	Ixioliriaceae	584.7
Iterative methods	518.26	Ixonanthaceae	583.69
Ithaca (Greece : Regional		Ixopo (South Africa :	
unit)	T2—495 5	District)	T2—684 67
Ithaca (N.Y.)	T2—747 71	Izabal (Guatemala : Dept.)	T2—728 131
Ithaca Island (Greece)	T2—495 5	Izard County (Ark.)	T2—767 27
ancient	T2—383	İzmir İli (Turkey)	T2—562 5
Ithakē (Greece : Regional		ancient	T2—392 3
unit)	T2—495 5	İzmit (Turkey)	T2—563 3
Ithala Game Preserve (South			
Africa)	T2—684 2	**J**	
Ithna Asharites (Islamic sect)	297.821		
Hadith	297.125 921	J document (Biblical criticism)	222.106 6
Koran commentary	297.122 753	Jacamars	598.72
religious law	297.140 182 1	Jacanas	598.33
I'tikāf	297.576	Jacanidae	598.33
Itzá Indians	T5—974 27	Jack County (Tex.)	T2—764 544
Itzá language	497.427	Jack-in-the-pulpits	584.442
	T6—974 27	Jackals	599.772
IUD (Contraceptive)		Jackets (Clothing)	391.46
health	613.943 5	commercial technology	687.14
medicine	618.185 2	indoor garments	687.113
see also Birth control		outdoor garments	687.14
Iudaea	T2—334 9	customs	391.46
Ivan, the Terrible		indoor garments	391.473
Russian history	947.043	outdoor garments	391.46
Ivan III, Grand Duke of Russia			
Russian history	947.041		

Jackets (Clothing) (continued)
  home sewing 646.45
    indoor garments 646.433
    outdoor garments 646.45
  see also Clothing
Jackrabbits 599.328
Jacks (Fishes) 597.72
Jacks (Lifting mechanisms) 621.877
Jackson (Miss.) T2—762 51
Jackson, Andrew
  United States history 973.56
Jackson County (Ala.) T2—761 95
Jackson County (Ark.) T2—767 97
Jackson County (Colo.) T2—788 66
Jackson County (Fla.) T2—759 93
Jackson County (Ga.) T2—758 145
Jackson County (Ill.) T2—773 994
Jackson County (Ind.) T2—772 23
Jackson County (Iowa) T2—777 64
Jackson County (Kan.) T2—781 335
Jackson County (Ky.) T2—769 183
Jackson County (Mich.) T2—774 28
Jackson County (Minn.) T2—776 235
Jackson County (Miss.) T2—762 12
Jackson County (Mo.) T2—778 41
Jackson County (N.C.) T2—756 95
Jackson County (Ohio) T2—771 85
Jackson County (Okla.) T2—766 45
Jackson County (Or.) T2—795 27
Jackson County (S.D.) T2—783 572
Jackson County (Tenn.) T2—768 51
Jackson County (Tex.) T2—764 127
Jackson County (W. Va.) T2—754 31
Jackson County (Wis.) T2—775 51
Jackson Parish (La.) T2—763 92
Jacksonville (Fla.) T2—759 12
Jacob (Biblical patriarch) 222.110 92
Jacobi polynomials 515.55
Jacobite Church 281.63
  see also Eastern churches
Jacobite Patriarchate of Antioch 281.63
  see also Eastern churches
Jacob's ladders (Plants)
  botany 583.93
Jacobsdal (South Africa :
  District) T2—685 7
Jacquard-weave fabrics 677.616
  see also Textiles
Jacquard-weave rugs
  arts 746.72
Jacques-Cartier (Quebec) T2—714 474
Jacques-Cartier National
  Park (Quebec) T2—714 48

Jacques-Cartier River
  (Quebec) T2—714 474
Jade 553.876
  economic geology 553.876
  glyptics 736.24
  jewelry 739.27
  materials science 620.198
  mining 622.387 6
  occultism 133.255 387 6
    divination 133.322
  prospecting 622.188 76
Jadīda (Morocco : Province) T2—646 2
Jadite 553.876
  see also Jade
Jaegers 598.338
Jaén (Spain : Province) T2—468 3
Ja'far ibn Manşūr al-Yaman
  Koran commentary 297.122 754
Ja'farī school (Islamic law) 340.590 182 1
  religious law 297.140 182 1
Jagan, Cheddi
  Guyanese history 988.103 31
Jagan, Janet
  Guyanese history 988.103 32
Jagdeo, Bharrat
  Guyanese history 988.103 33
Jagellon dynasty 943.802 3
Jagersfontein (South
  Africa : District) T2—685 7
Jaguar 599.755
  big game hunting 799.277 55
  conservation technology 639.979 755
  resource economics 333.959 755
Jahangir, Emperor of Hindustan
  Indian history 954.025 6
Jahn-Teller effect (Physics) 530.416
Jai alai 796.364
  see also Ball games
Jail breaks 365.641
Jails 365.34
  see also Penal institutions
Jain architecture 720.954
Jain philosophy 181.044
Jain sculpture 730.954
Jain temples and shrines 294.435
  architecture 726.144
Jainism 294.4
  art representation 704.948 944
  arts 700.482 944
    T3C—382 944
Jains
  biography 294.409 2
Jaipuri dialect 491.479 7
    T6—914 79

Jaipuri literature	891.479	Jams	641.852
Jakarta (Indonesia)	959.822	commercial processing	664.152
	T2—598 22	home preparation	641.852
Jakun (Malaysian people)	T5—992 8	Jämtland landskap (Sweden)	T2—488 3
Jakun language	499.28	Jämtlands län (Sweden)	T2—488 3
	T6—992 8	Jan Mayen Island	T2—983
Jalapa (Guatemala : Dept.)	T2—728 142	Jansenism	273.7
Jalisco (Mexico)	T2—723 5	denominations	284.84
Jamaica	972.92	Jansenville (South Africa :	
	T2—729 2	District)	T2—687 53
Jamaica bayberry	583.732	Janūb Dārfūr (Sudan : State)	T2—627
Jamaican literature	810	Janūb Kurdufān (Sudan)	T2—628
Jamaicans	T5—969 729 2	Janūb Sīnā' (Egypt)	T2—531
Jambi (Indonesia)	T2—598 15	Japan	952
James (Biblical book)	227.91		T2—52
James, William		Japan, Sea of	551.461 454
personality theory	155.264		T2—164 54
James I, King of England		Japan Current	551.462 145
British history	941.061	Japanese	T5—956
English history	942.061	Japanese beetles	595.764 9
Scottish history	941.106 1	agricultural pests	632.764 9
James I, King of Scotland		Japanese calendar	529.329 56
Scottish history	941.104	Japanese cedar	585.5
James II, King of England		Japanese chess	794.18
British history	941.067	Japanese chin	636.76
English history	942.067	Japanese flower arrangements	745.922 52
Scottish history	941.106 7	Japanese flowering cherry	635.977 364 2
James II, King of Scotland		Japanese ink painting	751.425 2
Scottish history	941.104	Japanese language	495.6
James III, King of Scotland			T6—956
Scottish history	941.104	Japanese literature	895.6
James IV, King of Scotland		Japanese macaque	599.864 4
Scottish history	941.104	Japanese medlars	641.341 6
James V, King of Scotland		*see also* Loquats	
Scottish history	941.104	Japanese quail	598.627 2
James VI, King of Scotland		Japanese religions	299.56
Scottish history	941.106 1	Japanese river fever	
1567–1603	941.105	incidence	614.526 4
1603–1625	941.106 1	medicine	616.922 4
James Bay Region (Ont. and		*see also* Communicable	
Quebec)	T2—714 115	diseases — humans	
James River (N.D. and S.D.)	T2—783 3	Japanese spaniel	636.76
North Dakota	T2—784 5	Japanning	
South Dakota	T2—783 3	decorative arts	745.726
James River (Va.)	T2—755 4	technology	667.75
Jameson raid, 1895–1896	968.204 75	Jar cutting	
Jammeh, A. J. J.		decorative arts	748.202 86
Gambian history	966.510 32	Jarai	T5—992 2
Jammu and Kashmir (India :		Jarash (Jordan : Province)	T2—569 548
1954–2019)	T2—546	Jardins-de-Napierville	
Jammu and Kashmir (India :		(Quebec)	T2—714 35
2019-)	T2—546 3	Jargon	417.2
		specific languages	T4—7
		Jarḥ wa al-Taʻdīl (Hadith)	297.125 26

Jars	688.8	Jaws (continued)	
glass	666.192	regional medicine	617.522
decorative arts	748.82	surgery	617.522
technology	666.192	Jay County (Ind.)	T2—772 67
see also Containers		Jays	598.864
Jasmines	583.963	conservation technology	639.978 864
botany	583.963	resource economics	333.958 864
floriculture	635.933 963	Jaza'ir (Algeria : Province)	T2—653
perfume crop	633.81	Jazīrah (Sudan : State)	T2—626 4
see also Jessamines		Jazz	781.65
(Solanaceae)		songs	782.421 65
Jasper County (Ga.)	T2—758 583	Jazz bands	784.416 5
Jasper County (Ill.)	T2—773 74	Jazz dancing	793.3
Jasper County (Ind.)	T2—772 977	Jazz ensembles	785.065
Jasper County (Iowa)	T2—777 594	Jazz musicians	781.650 92
Jasper County (Miss.)	T2—762 575	singers	782.421 650 92
Jasper County (Mo.)	T2—778 72	Jazz pianists	786.216 509 2
Jasper County (S.C.)	T2—757 98	Jazz saxophonists	788.716 509 2
Jasper County (Tex.)	T2—764 159	Jazz singers	782.421 650 92
Jasper National Park (Alta.)	T2—712 332	Jazz trumpeters	788.921 650 92
Jász-Nagykun-Szolnok		Jazz vocals	782.421 65
Megye (Hungary)	T2—439 8	Jealousy	152.48
Jatakas	294.382 325	ethics	179.8
Jaundice		religion	205.698
medicine	616.362 5	psychology	152.48
see also Digestive system		*see also* Vices	
diseases — humans		Jean I, King of France	
Java (Indonesia)	T2—598 2	French history	944.024
Java man	569.97	Jean II, King of France	
Java Sea	551.461 474	French history	944.025
	T2—164 74	Jeep cavalry	357.54
Java War, 1825–1830	959.802 23	Jeeps	388.342
Javan pig	599.633 2	driving	629.283
Javanese	T5—992 22	engineering	629.222
Javanese language	499.222	military engineering	623.747 22
	T6—992 22	repair	629.287 2
Javanese literature	899.222	transportation services	388.342
Javelin hurling	796.435	*see also* Automobiles	
see also Track and field		Jeff Davis County (Ga.)	T2—758 827
Jawa (Indonesia)	T2—598 2	Jeff Davis County (Tex.)	T2—764 934
Jawa Barat (Indonesia)	T2—598 24	Jefferson, Thomas	
Jawa Tengah (Indonesia)	959.826	United States history	973.46
	T2—598 26	1801–1805	973.46
Jawa Timur (Indonesia)	T2—598 28	1805–1809	973.48
Jawāmi'		Jefferson City (Mo.)	T2—778 55
Hadith	297.125 4	Jefferson County (Ala.)	T2—761 78
Jawara, Dawda Kairaba		Jefferson County (Ark.)	T2—767 79
Gambian history	966.510 31	Jefferson County (Colo.)	T2—788 84
Jawless fishes	597.2	Jefferson County (Fla.)	T2—759 87
Jaws		Jefferson County (Ga.)	T2—758 663
fractures		Jefferson County (Idaho)	T2—796 58
medicine	617.156	Jefferson County (Ill.)	T2—773 793
human anatomy	611.92	Jefferson County (Ind.)	T2—772 13
human physiology	612.92	Jefferson County (Iowa)	T2—777 94

Jet attack bombers	358.428 3
engineering	623.746 34
military equipment	358.428 3
Jet bombers	358.428 3
engineering	623.746 34
military equipment	358.428 3
Jet close support aircraft	358.428 3
engineering	623.746 34
military equipment	358.428 3
Jet engines	621.435 2
aircraft	629.134 353
Jet fighter-bombers	358.428 3
engineering	623.746 34
military equipment	358.428 3
Jet fighters	358.438 3
engineering	623.746 44
military equipment	358.438 3
Jet fuel	665.538 25
Jet planes	387.733 49
engineering	629.133 349
military engineering	623.746 044
military equipment	358.418 3
transportation services	387.733 49
see also Aircraft	
Jet pumps	621.691
Jet skiing	797.37
Jet streams (Meteorology)	551.518 3
Jethou (Channel Islands)	T2—423 47
Jetties	
engineering	627.24
Jevons, William Stanley	
economic school	330.157
Jewelers	739.270 92
Jewell County (Kan.)	T2—781 22
Jewelry	391.7
customs	391.7
making	739.27
costume jewelry	688.2
handicrafts	745.594 2
fine jewelry	739.27
theft of	364.162 873 927
law	345.026 287 392 7
Jewelweeds	583.93
Jewish apocalypses	
pseudepigrapha	229.913
Jewish architecture	
ancient	722.33
Jewish Autonomous Region (Russia)	T2—577
Jewish Bible	221
see Manual at 221	
Jewish calendar	529.326
religion	296.43

Jewish-Christian dialogue	261.26
Christian theology	261.26
Jewish theology	296.396
Jewish Christians (Sects)	289.9
Jewish cooking	641.567 6
Jewish day schools	371.076
Jewish education	296.68
see Manual at 207.5, 268 vs. 200.71, 230.071, 292–299	
Jewish holidays	296.43
customs	394.267
liturgy	296.453
see also Holidays	
Jewish law	340.58
religion	296.18
Jewish philosophy	181.06
Jewish Publication Society Bible	221.520 8
Jewish religious schools	296.680 83
Jewish sacred music	781.76
public worship	782.36
music	782.36
religion	296.462
Jewish sculpture	732.3
Jews	T5—924
civilization	909.049 24
Holocaust, 1933–1945	940.531 8
social aspects	305.892 4
Jews (Religious group)	T1—088 296
biography	296.092
specific denominations	296.8
role of leaders	296.61
social aspects	305.696
see Manual at 296.092	
Jew's harps	786.887
see also Percussion instruments	
Jharkhand (India : State)	T2—541 27
Jiangsu Sheng (China)	T2—511 36
Jiangxi dialects	495.179 512 22
	T6—951 7
Jiangxi Sheng (China)	T2—512 22
Jicarilla Apache language	497.25
	T6—972 5
Jicarilla Indians	T5—972 5
Jig saws	621.934
wood handicrafts	745.513
Jigawa State (Nigeria)	T2—669 77
Jigs (Tools)	621.992
Jigsaw puzzles	793.73
Jihad	297.72
Jihlavský kraj (Czech Republic)	T2—437 22
Jihočeský kraj (Czech Republic)	T2—437 13

John, King of England
  English history 942.033
John, the Baptist, Saint 232.94
John I, King of France
  French history 944.024
John II, King of France
  French history 944.025
John III, King of Sweden
  Swedish history 948.503 23
John IV, Negus of Ethiopia
  Eritrean history 963.504 2
  Ethiopian history 963.042
John Brown's Raid, 1859
  Civil War (United States) cause 973.711 6
John Dories 597.64
Johnson, Andrew
  United States history 973.81
Johnson, Lyndon B. (Lyndon
  Baines)
  United States history 973.923
Johnson County (Ark.) T2—767 33
Johnson County (Ga.) T2—758 676
Johnson County (Ill.) T2—773 996
Johnson County (Ind.) T2—772 515
Johnson County (Iowa) T2—777 655
Johnson County (Kan.) T2—781 675
Johnson County (Ky.) T2—769 245
Johnson County (Mo.) T2—778 455
Johnson County (Neb.) T2—782 276
Johnson County (Tenn.) T2—768 99
Johnson County (Tex.) T2—764 524
Johnson County (Wyo.) T2—787 35
Johnson-Sirleaf, Ellen
  Liberian history 966.620 41
Johnston County (N.C.) T2—756 41
Johnston County (Okla.) T2—766 68
Johnston Island T2—969 9
Johor T2—595 1
Joinery 684.08
  construction 694.6
  ship hulls 623.844
  woodworking 684.08
Joining equipment 621.97
Joining metals 671.5
  decorative arts 739.14
  sculpture 731.41
Joint chiefs of staff 355.330 42
Joint committees
  legislative bodies 328.365 7
Joint custody 346.017 3

Joint diseases 573.783 9
  animals 573.783 9
  humans
    medicine 616.72
    see also Musculoskeletal
     diseases — humans
Joint operations (Armed forces) 355.46
Joint stock companies 338.7
  see also Business enterprises;
   Unincorporated business
   enterprises
Joint tenancy 346.042
Joint ventures 338.7
  law 346.068 2
  management of enterprises 658.044
   initiation 658.114 4
   see Manual at 658.04 vs.
    658.114, 658.402
  see also Business enterprises
Joints (Body parts) 573.78
  diseases 573.783 9
  extremities
   surgery 617.580 59
  human anatomy 611.72
  human physiology 612.752
  medicine 616.72
  surgery 617.472
  see also Musculoskeletal
   system
Joints (Geology) 551.84
Joinvilleaceae 584.9
Jokebooks 808.882
  see also Jokes
Jokes 808.882
  folk literature 398.7
  literature 808.882
   history and criticism 809.982
   specific literatures T3B—802
   individual authors T3A—8
  see Manual at T1—0207 vs.
   T3B—7, T3A—8 + 02,
   T3B—802, T3B—8 + 02,
   T3A—8 + 07, T3B—807,
   T3B—8 + 07; *also at*
   T3A—8 + 02, T3B—802,
   T3B—8 + 02 vs. 398.6,
   793.735
Joliette (Quebec : Regional
  County Municipality) T2—714 42
Jonah (Biblical book) 224.92
Jonathan, Goodluck Ebele
  Nigerian history 966.905 6
Jonathan, Leabua
  Lesotho history 968.850 31

Judges (Court officials)	347.014
biography	347.014 092
criminal courts	345.012 4
occupational ethics	174.3
Judges (Rulers)	
Palestinian history	933.02
Judging competitions	T1—079
Judging livestock	636.081 1
Judgment	
epistemology	121
psychology	153.46
Judgment Day	202.3
Christianity	236.9
Islam	297.23
Judgments (Law)	347.077
Judicial administration	347.013
criminal law	345.012 3
Judicial assistance	345.052
Judicial branch of government	347
Judicial cooperation	347.012
criminal law	345.012 2
Judicial discretion	347.012
criminal law	345.012 2
Judicial error	347.012
criminal law	345.012 2
Judicial-executive relations	320.404
law	342.044
Judicial institutions	
sociology	306.25
Judicial-legislative relations	320.404
law	342.044
Judicial power	347.012
chief executives	352.235
legislatures	328.345 3
Judicial process	347.05
Judicial review	347.012
criminal law	345.012 2
Judicial statistics	347.013
Judith (Deuterocanonical book)	229.24
Judith Basin County (Mont.)	T2—786 62
Judo	796.815 2
see also Combat sports	
Juggling	793.87
Juglandaceae	583.65
Juglandales	583.65
Jugnauth, Aneerood	
Mauritian history	969.820 42
Juices (Beverages)	641.34
commercial processing	663.63
home preparation	641.875
Jujitsu	796.815 2
see also Combat sports	

Jujubes	641.342
botany	583.646
cooking	641.642
food	641.342
orchard crop	634.2
Jujuy (Argentina : Province)	T2—824 1
Jukeboxes	621.389 33
Jula language	496.345
	T6—963 45
Julian calendar	529.42
Juliana, Queen of the Netherlands	
Dutch history	949.207 2
July Monarchy	944.063
Jum'ah	297.36
Jumble sales	381.195
Jump rope rhymes	398.8
Jumpers (Athletes)	796.432 092
Jumping	
field sports	796.432
biography	796.432 092
horses	798.25
skiing	796.933
Jumping mice	599.35
Juncaceae	584.95
Juncaginaceae	584.44
Juncos	598.883
Junction diodes	621.381 522
Junction transistors	621.381 528 2
Juncture (Linguistics)	414.6
specific languages	T4—16
June beetles	595.764 9
June bugs	595.764 9
Juneau (Alaska)	T2—798 2
Juneau County (Wis.)	T2—775 55
Juneberries	641.347 4
botany	583.642
cooking	641.647 4
food	641.347 4
horticulture	634.74
Junee (N.S.W.)	T2—944 8
Jungermanniales	588.3
Jungian psychology	150.195 4
personality theory	155.264 4
Jungle diseases	
medicine	616.988 3
see also Environmental	
diseases — humans	
Jungle fowl	598.625
Jungle tactics	355.423
Jungles	333.75
	T2—152
biology	578.734
ecology	577.34
see also Forest lands	

Juniata County (Pa.)	T2—748 47	Jury trial	347.052
Juniata River (Pa.)	T2—748 45	criminal law	345.056
Junín (Peru : Region)	T2—852 4	Just war theory	
Junior colleges (Two-year		ethics	172.42
colleges)	378.154 3	religion	205.624 2
Junior high schools	373.236	Christianity	241.624 2
see also Secondary education		Justice	
Junior schools (Primary schools)	372	arts	T3C—353
see also Primary education		ethics	172.2
Juniors (Girl Scouts)	369.463 4	religion	205.622
Junipers	585.4	Buddhism	294.356 22
Junk bonds	332.632 34	Christianity	241.622
Junqalī (South Sudan :		Hinduism	294.548 622
State)	T2—629 3	Islam	297.562 2
Jupiter (Planet)	523.45	Judaism	296.362 2
	T2—992 5	law	340.114
astrology	133.536	literature	808.803 53
unmanned flights to	629.435 45	history and criticism	809.933 53
Jura (France)	T2—444 7	specific literatures	T3B—080 353
Jura (Switzerland)	T2—494 36	history and	
Jura Mountains (France and		criticism	T3B—093 53
Switzerland)	T2—494 3	political science	320.011
France	T2—444 5	public administration	353.4
Switzerland	T2—494 3	social theology	201.76
Jura-Nord Vaudois		Christianity	261.8
(Switzerland)	T2—494 522 5	Islam	297.27
Jurassic period	551.766	Judaism	296.38
geology	551.766	Justice of God	214
paleontology	560.176 6	see also Theodicy	
Jurchen (Manchurian		Justices of the peace	347.016
people)	T5—941	occupational ethics	174.3
Jurchen language	494.1	Justification (Christian doctrine)	234.7
	T6—941	Jute	677.13
Juries	347.075 2	agricultural economics	338.173 54
criminal law	345.075	botany	583.775
Jurisdiction		fiber crop	633.54
courts	347.012	textiles	677.13
criminal law	345.012 2	arts	746.041 3
see Manual at 347		economics	338.476 771 3
government	342.041	see also Textiles	
law of nations	341.4	Jute pulp	676.14
persons (legal concept)	342.08	Jutiapa (Guatemala : Dept.)	T2—728 143
territory	342.041 3	Jutland (Denmark)	T2—489 5
Jurisprudence	340	Jutland peninsula	T2—489 5
Jurisprudential commentary		Denmark	T2—489 5
Koran	297.122 712 4	Germany	T2—435 12
Juristic acts	346.02	Juvenile correctional institutions	365.42
Juristic persons	346.013	see also Penal institutions	
Jurists (Judges)	347.014 092	Juvenile courts	345.081
Jurists (Lawyers)	340.092	Juvenile delinquency	364.36
Jury ethics	174.3	school problem	371.782
Jury instructions	347.075 8	Juvenile delinquents	364.36
Jury selection	347.075 2		T1—086 923
criminal law	345.075	home care	649.153

Juvenile delinquents (continued)
law   345.03
pastoral care
    Christianity   259.5
penal institutions   365.42
    see also Penal institutions
Juvenile justice   364.36
    criminology   364.36
    law   345.08
Juvenile literature   808.899 282
    history and criticism   809.892 82
    reviews   028.162
    rhetoric   808.068
    specific literatures   T3B—080 928 2
        history and criticism T3B—099 282
Juvenile procedure   345.08

K

K-mesons   539.721 62
K-theory   512.66
    algebra   512.66
    topology   514.23
Ka'bah (Mecca, Saudi Arabia)   297.352
Kabardian language   499.962 4
                                          T6—999 624
Kabardino-Balkaria (Russia) T2—475 2
Kabardino-Balkariĭa
    (Russia)   T2—475 2
Kabba language   496.566
                                          T6—965 66
Kabbah, Ahmad Tejan
    Sierra Leonean history   966.404 5
Kabbalah   296.16
    see also Cabala
Kabila, Joseph
    Congolese history   967.510 34
Kabila, Laurent-Désiré
    Congolese history   967.510 34
Kaboré, Roch Marc Christian
    Burkinan history   966.250 54
Kabuki theater   792.095 2
Kabwe man   569.98
Kabyle language   493.34
                                          T6—933 4
Kabyle literature   893.34
Kabyles   T5—933
Kacem (Morocco :
    Province)   T2—643 5
Kachin language   495.4
                                          T6—954
Kaczyński, Lech
    Polish history   943.805 73

Kadai languages   495.9
                                          T6—959
Kadai literatures   895.9
Kadai peoples   T5—959
Kadarites (Islamic sect)   297.835
Kaduna State (Nigeria)   T2—669 73
Kaffraria   T2—687 5
Kafiri languages   491.49
                                          T6—914 9
Kafiri literatures   891.49
Kafirs (Afghanistan people)   T5—914 9
Kafr al-Shaykh (Egypt)   T2—621
Kagawa-ken (Japan)   T2—523 5
Kagera Region (Tanzania)   T2—678 27
Kagoshima-ken (Japan)   T2—522 6
Kahoolawe (Hawaii)   T2—969 22
Kahramanmaraş İli (Turkey) T2—565 3
    ancient   T2—393 6
Kaikoura District (N.Z.)   T2—937 8
Kainah Indians   T5—973 52
Kainuu (Finland)   T2—489 763
Kaipara District (N.Z.)   T2—931 8
Kajiado County (Kenya)   T2—676 272
Kaka languages   496.396
                                          T6—963 96
Kakamega County (Kenya)   T2—676 284
Kakapo   598.71
    conservation technology 639.978 71
    resource economics   333.958 71
Kako languages   496.396
                                          T6—963 96
Kala-azar
    incidence   614.534
    medicine   616.936 4
    see also Communicable
        diseases — humans
Kalahari Desert   T2—688 3
    Botswana   T2—688 3
    South Africa   T2—687 16
Kalahari Gemsbok National
    Park (South Africa)   T2—687 16
Kalām (Islam)   297.2
Kalam District (Pakistan)   T2—549 122
Kalamazoo County (Mich.)   T2—774 17
Kalanga language (Tanzania and
    Congo)   496.394
                                          T6—963 94
Kalāt District (Pakistan)   T2—549 153
Kalâtdlisut language   497.12
                                          T6—971 2
Kalawao County (Hawaii)   T2—969 24
Kalbarri National Park
    (W.A.)   T2—941 2

Kangaroos	599.222
big game hunting	799.272 22
conservation technology	639.979 222
resource economics	333.959 222
Kangiqsliniq (Nunavut)	T2—719 58
KaNgwane (South Africa)	T2—682 73
Kankakee County (Ill.)	T2—773 63
Kankan (Guinea)	T2—665 2
Kannada language	494.814
	T6—948 14
Kannada literature	894.814
Kano State (Nigeria)	T2—669 78
Kansa Indians	T5—975 25
Kansas	978.1
	T2—781
Kansas City (Kan.)	T2—781 39
Kansas City (Mo.)	T2—778 411
Kansas City jazz	781.653
Kansas River (Kan.)	T2—781 3
Kansu Province (China)	T2—514 5
Kanta-Häme (Finland)	T2—489 716
Kantianism	142.3
Kantō Region (Japan)	T2—521 3
Kanuri (African people)	T5—965 37
Kanuri language	496.537
	T6—965 37
Kanuri languages	496.537
	T6—965 37
Kanuri literatures	896.537
Kaolack (Senegal : Region)	T2—663
Kaolin	553.61
economic geology	553.61
mining	622.361
Kaolinite	
mineralogy	549.67
Kaonde language	496.393
	T6—963 93
Kaons	539.721 62
Kapadokya (Turkey)	T2—564 1
Kapiti Coast District (N.Z.)	T2—936 1
Kapok	
botany	583.775
fiber crop	633.56
materials science	620.195
textiles	677.23
see also Textiles	
Kaposi's sarcoma	
incidence	614.599 947 7
medicine	616.994 77
see also Cancer — humans	
Kara-Kalpak language	494.34
	T6—943 4
Kara Sea	551.461 325
	T2—163 25

Karachaevo-Cherkesiia	
(Russia)	T2—475 2
Karachay-Balkar language	494.38
	T6—943 8
Karachay-Cherkessia	
(Russia)	T2—475 2
Karachi (Pakistan : District)	954.918 3
	T2—549 183
Karagwe (Kingdom)	967.610 1
	T2—676 1
Karaim language	494.38
	T6—943 8
Karaites	296.81
Karak (Jordan : Province)	956.956 3
	T2—569 563
Karakalpak (Uzbekistan)	T2—587
Karakalpak language	494.34
	T6—943 4
Karakoram Range	T2—546 7
Karaman İli (Turkey)	956.45
	T2—564 5
ancient	T2—392 7
Karanga (African people)	T5—963 975
Karanga kingdoms	968.910 1
Karanga language	496.397 5
	T6—963 975
Karate	796.815 3
physical fitness	613.714 815 3
see also Combat sports	
Karbalā' (Iraq : Province)	T2—567 5
Karbük İli (Turkey)	T2—563 7
Karditsa (Greece : Regional	
unit)	T2—495 4
Karelia (Region)	T2—471 5
Karelia (Russia)	T2—471 5
Karelian language	494.54
	T6—945 4
Karelian literature	894.54
Karelians	T5—945 4
Karen	T5—95
Karen languages	495
	T6—95
Kari languages (Bantu)	496.394
	T6—963 94
Karlovarský kraj (Czech	
Republic)	T2—437 15
Karlsruhe (Germany)	T2—434 643 6
Karlsruhe (Germany :	
Landkreis)	T2—434 643
Karlsruhe (Germany :	
Regierungsbezirk)	T2—434 64
Karma	202.2
Buddhism	294.342 2
Hinduism	294.522

Karma yoga	294.543 6	Kashubs	T5—918 5
Karnak (Egypt)	T2—323	Kassalā (Sudan : State)	T2—625
Karnali Pradesh (Nepal)	T2—549 66	Kassel (Germany)	T2—434 124
Karnataka (India)	T2—548 7	Kassel (Germany :	
Karnes County (Tex.)	T2—764 444	Regierungsbezirk)	T2—434 12
Kärnten (Austria)	T2—436 6	Kastamonu İli (Turkey)	T2—563 7
Karo, Joseph ben Ephraim		ancient	T2—393 17
Jewish legal codes	296.182	Kastoria (Greece : Regional	
Karoo (South Africa)	T2—687 39	unit)	T2—495 62
Karoo, Great (South Africa)	T2—687 39	Katanga (Congo)	T2—675 18
Karoo, Little (South Africa)	T2—687 37	Katanning (W.A.)	T2—941 2
Karoo, Northern (South		Katharevusa language (Modern	
Africa)	T2—687 13	Greek)	489.3
Karoo, Upper (South			T6—89
Africa)	T2—687 13	Katharevusa literature (Modern	
Karoo National Park (South		Greek)	889
Africa)	T2—687 39	Katherine (N.T.)	T2—942 95
Karpathos (Greece :		Katherine Gorge National	
Regional unit)	T2—495 87	Park (N.T.)	T2—942 95
Karpathos Island (Greece)	T2—495 87	Kativik Regional	
ancient	T2—391 7	Administration (Quebec)	T2—714 111
Kars İli (Turkey)	T2—566 26	Katmai National Park and	
ancient	T2—395 5	Preserve (Alaska)	T2—798 4
Karsts	551.447	Katoomba (N.S.W.)	T2—944 5
	T2—144	Katowice (Poland :	
see also Caves		Voivodeship)	T2—438 58
Karting	796.76	Katsina State (Nigeria)	T2—669 76
see also Automotive		Katsura tree	583.43
vehicles — sports		Katsura trees	583.44
Karts (Racing cars)	796.76	Kattang language	499.15
driving	629.284 8		T6—991 5
engineering	629.228 5	Kattegat (Denmark and Sweden)	551.461 336
repair	629.287 8		T2—163 36
sports	796.76	Katukinan languages	498.9
Kartvelian languages	499.968		T6—989
	T6—999 68	Katydids	595.726
Kasaï-Occidental (Congo)	T2—675 123	Kauai (Hawaii)	T2—969 41
Kasaï-Oriental (Congo)	T2—675 126	Kauai County (Hawaii)	T2—969 4
Kasem language	496.35	Kaufman County (Tex.)	T2—764 277
	T6—963 5	Kaunda, Kenneth D. (Kenneth	
Kasena language	496.35	David)	
	T6—963 5	Zambian history	968.940 41
Kashmir	T2—546	Kauris	585.3
India	T2—546	forestry	634.975 93
Pakistan	T2—549 13	Kavala (Greece : Regional	
Kashmiri language	491.499	unit)	T2—495 7
	T6—914 99	Kavieng (Papua New	
Kashmiri literature	891.499	Guinea)	T2—958 3
Kashmiris	T5—914 99	Kaw River (Kan.)	T2—781 3
Kashrut	296.73	Kawar	T5—914 92
Kashubian language	491.85	Kawartha Lakes (Ont.)	T2—713 64
	T6—918 5	Kawartha Lakes (Ont. :	
Kashubian literature	891.85	Lakes)	T2—713 67
Kashubians	T5—918 5	Kawau Island (N.Z. : Island)	T2—932 1

Kawerau (N.Z.)	T2—934 26	Kekchí Indians	T5—974 2
Kawerau District (N.Z.)	T2—934 26	Kekchí language	497.42
Kay County (Okla.)	T2—766 24		T6—974 2
Kayaking	797.122 4	Kekkonen, Urho	
see also Aquatic sports		Finnish history	948.970 33
Kayseri İli (Turkey)	T2—564 12	Kelaa des Srarhna	
ancient	T2—393 4	(Morocco : Province)	T2—646 4
Kazak language	494.345	Kelâat Es-Sraghna	
	T6—943 45	(Morocco : Province)	T2—646 4
Kazak literature	894.345	Kelantan	T2—595 1
Kazakh language	494.345	Kele languages (Democratic	
	T6—943 45	Republic of Congo)	496.396
Kazakh literature	894.345		T6—963 96
Kazakhs	T5—943 45	Kele languages (Gabon)	496.396
Kazakhstan	958.45		T6—963 96
	T2—584 5	Kelim	296.123 6
Kazakhstani	T5—943 45	Kelowna (B.C.)	T2—711 5
Kazaks	T5—943 45	Kelps	579.887
Kazoo	783.99	resource economics	333.953 8
Kea-Kythnos (Greece)	T2—495 85	Kemerovo (Russia : Oblast)	T2—573
Kearney County (Neb.)	T2—782 394	Kemerovskaĩa oblast′	
Kearny County (Kan.)	T2—781 425	(Russia)	T2—573
Kearsarge and Alabama, Battle		Kemper County (Miss.)	T2—762 683
of, 1864	973.754	Kempo	796.815 9
Keating, Paul		*see also* Combat sports	
Australian history	994.065	Kempsey (N.S.W.)	T2—944 3
Keats Island (B.C. : Island)	T2—711 31	Kempton Park (South	
Kebbi State (Nigeria)	T2—669 63	Africa : District)	T2—682 25
Kechika River (B.C.)	T2—711 85	Kenaf	
Kechua Indians	T5—983 23	botany	583.775
Kechua language	498.323	fiber crop	633.56
	T6—983 23	Kenai Fjords National Park	
Kechua literature	898.323	(Alaska)	T2—798 3
Kechuan Indians	T5—983 23	Kenai Peninsula (Alaska)	T2—798 3
Kechuan languages	498.323	Kenai Peninsula Borough	
	T6—983 23	(Alaska)	T2—798 3
Kedah	T2—595 1	Kendall County (Ill.)	T2—773 263
Keeling Islands	969.9	Kendall County (Tex.)	T2—764 886
	T2—699	Kendo	796.86
Keene's cement	666.92	Kenedy County (Tex.)	T2—764 473
Keeshond	636.72	Kenhardt District (South	
Keewatin (Nunavut)	T2—719 58	Africa)	T2—687 16
Keffa (Ethiopia)	T2—633	Kénitra (Morocco :	
Kefir	641.26	Province)	T2—643 5
home preparation	641.875	Kennebec County (Me.)	T2—741 6
Kegs		Kennebec River (Me.)	T2—741 22
wooden	674.82	Kennedy, John F. (John	
Keiskammahoek (South		Fitzgerald)	
Africa : District)	T2—687 54	United States history	973.922
Keïta, Ibrahim Boubacar		Kennelly-Heaviside layers	538.767 3
Malian history	966.230 54	Kennels (Dog housing)	636.708 31
Keith County (Neb.)	T2—782 89	Kenneth Kaunda District	
Kejimkujik National Park		Municipality (South	
(N.S.)	T2—716 33	Africa)	T2—682 43

Kettle-shaped drums   786.93
   see also Percussion instruments
Kettledrums   786.93
   see also Percussion instruments
Kettles (Geologic landforms)   551.315
Ketubbot   296.123 3
   Babylonian Talmud   296.125 3
   Mishnah   296.123 3
   Palestinian Talmud   296.124 3
Ketuvim   223
Keuka Lake (N.Y.)   T2—747 82
Kewa language   499.12
      T6—991 2
Kewaunee County (Wis.)   T2—775 62
Keweenaw County (Mich.)   T2—774 995
Keweenaw Peninsula
   (Mich.)   T2—774 99
Key accounts
   marketing management   658.804
   sales personnel
      organization   658.810 2
Key-value stores
   computer science   005.758
Key West (Fla.)   T2—759 41
Key word indexing   025.486
Keya Paha County (Neb.)   T2—782 725
Keyboard bands   784.6
Keyboard electrophones   786.59
   see also Keyboard instruments
Keyboard idiophones   786.83
   see also Percussion instruments
Keyboard instruments   786
   bands and orchestras   784
   chamber ensembles   785
      mixed   785.2
      single type   785.62–.65
   construction   786.192 3
      by hand   786.192 3
      by machine   681.86
   solo music   786
Keyboard stringed instruments   786
   see also Keyboard instruments
Keyboard wind instruments   786.5
   see also Keyboard instruments
Keyboarding   652.3
Keyboards (Computers)   004.76
   engineering   621.398 6
Keynesian economics   330.156
Keys   683.32
Keyword indexing   025.486
Kgalagadi District
   Municipality (South
   Africa)   T2—687 15

Kgalagadi Transfrontier
   Park (Botswana and
   South Africa)   T2—687 16
Khabarovsk (Russia : Kray)   T2—577
Khabarovskiĭ kraĭ (Russia)   T2—577
Khairpūr District (Pakistan)   T2—549 17
Khakassia (Russia)   T2—575
Khakasskaia respublika
   (Russia)   T2—575
Khalaf al-Qāri'
   Koran readings   297.122 404 52
Khalaj language (Turkic)   494.36
      T6—943 6
Khalji dynasty   954.023 4
Khalkha   T5—942 3
Khalkha Mongolian language   494.23
      T6—942 3
Khalkha Mongolian literature   894.23
Khama, Seretse
   Botswana history   968.830 31
Khama, Seretse Khama Ian
   Botswana history   968.830 34
Khamti   T5—959 19
Khánh Hòa (Vietnam :
   Province)   T2—597 5
Khantia-Mansia (Russia)   T2—573
Khanty   T5—945 1
Khanty language   494.51
      T6—945 1
Khanty literature   894.51
Khanty-Mansiĭskiĭ
   avtonomnyĭ okrug
   (Russia)   T2—573
Kharia language   495.95
      T6—959 5
Kharias   T5—959 5
Kharijites   297.83
Kharkiv (Ukraine : Oblast)   T2—477 5
Kharkivs′ka oblast′
   (Ukraine)   T2—477 5
Khartoum (Sudan : State)   T2—626 2
Khartūm (Sudan : State)   T2—626 2
Khasi   T5—959 3
Khasi language   495.93
      T6—959 3
Khaskovo (1987–1998)
   (Bulgaria : Oblast)   T2—499 6
Khaskovo (1999-)
   (Bulgaria : Oblast)   T2—499 65
Khaskovska oblast
   (1987–1998) (Bulgaria)   T2—499 6
Khaskovska oblast (1999-)
   (Bulgaria)   T2—499 65

Kidney failure
  medicine   616.614
    see also Urologic diseases —
      humans
Kidney stones
  medicine   616.622
    see also Urologic diseases —
      humans
Kidneys   573.496
  biology   573.496
  human anatomy   611.61
  human physiology   612.463
  medicine   616.61
  surgery   617.461
    see also Urinary system
Kiel (Germany)   T2—435 123
Kielce (Poland :
    Voivodeship)   T2—438 45
Kiên Giang (Vietnam)   T2—597 9
Kiesinger, Kurt Georg
  German history   943.087 6
Kiev (Ukraine : Oblast)   T2—477 7
Kievan Rus   947.7
  Belarussian history   947.8
  Russian history   947.02
  Ukrainian history   947.7
Kigali (Rwanda)   T2—675 71
Kigoma Region (Tanzania)   T2—678 28
Kikongo languages   496.393 1
                                 T6—963 931
Kikuyu (African people)   T5—963 954
Kikuyu-Kamba languages   496.395 3
                                 T6—963 953
Kikuyu language   496.395 4
                                 T6—963 954
Kikuyu literature   896.395 4
Kikwete, Jakaya Khalfan Mrisho
  Tanzanian history   967.804 4
Kilayim   296.123 1
  Mishnah   296.123 1
  Palestinian Talmud   296.124 1
Kildare (Ireland : County)   T2—418 5
Kildin Saami language   494.576
                                 T6—945 76
Kildin Sámi language   494.576
                                 T6—945 76
Kilifi County (Kenya)   T2—676 235
Kilimanjaro, Mount
    (Tanzania)   T2—678 26
Kilimanjaro National Park
    (Tanzania)   T2—678 26
Kilimanjaro Region
    (Tanzania)   T2—678 26

Kilis İli (Turkey)   T2—564 9
  ancient   T2—393 6
Kilkenny (Ireland : County)   T2—418 9
Kilkis (Greece : Regional
    unit)   T2—495 65
Killarney (Ireland)   T2—419 65
Killer cells   571.968
  human immunology   616.079 9
Killer whale   599.536
  conservation technology   639.979 536
  resource economics   333.959 536
Killifishes   597.665
Kilmarnock and Loudoun
    (Scotland)   T2—414 67
Kiln drying lumber   674.384
Kilns   666.436
  decorative arts   738.136
  sculpture   731.3
  technology   666.436
Kim, Chŏng-il
  North Korean history   951.930 51
Kim, Chŏng-ŭn
  North Korean history   951.930 52
Kim, Dae Jung
  South Korean history   951.950 5
Kim, Il-sŏng
  North Korean history   951.930 43
Kimbala languages   496.393
                                 T6—963 93
Kimball County (Neb.)   T2—782 973
Kimberley (B.C.)   T2—711 65
Kimberley (South Africa :
    District)   T2—687 14
Kimberley (W.A.)   T2—941 4
Kimble County (Tex.)   T2—764 878
Kimbundu language   496.393 2
                                 T6—963 932
Kimbundu literature   896.393 2
Kin recognition (Animals)   591.563
Kinbasket Lake (B.C.)   T2—711 68
Kincardine (Scotland)   T2—411 52
Kincardine and Deeside
    (Scotland)   T2—412 4
Kindergarten   372.218
    see also Elementary education;
      Primary education
Kindergarten teachers   372.11
Kindergarten teaching   372.110 2
Kindness
  ethics   177.7
    see also Love — ethics
Kinematics   531.112
  fluids   532.05
  gases   533.2

Kinyarwanda literature	896.394 61
Kiowa Apache Indians	T5—972 5
Kiowa Apache language	497.25
	T6—972 5
Kiowa County (Colo.)	T2—788 93
Kiowa County (Kan.)	T2—781 785
Kiowa County (Okla.)	T2—766 47
Kiowa Indians	978.004 974 92
	T5—974 92
Kiowa language	497.492
	T6—974 92
Kiowa literature	897.492
Kiowa-Tanoan Indians	T5—974 9
Kiowa-Tanoan languages	497.49
	T6—974 9
Kiranti languages	495.49
	T6—954 9
Kiranti literatures	895.49
Kirantish languages	495.49
	T6—954 9
Kirchner, Néstor	
Argentine history	982.072
Kirghiz	T5—943 47
Kirghiz language	494.347
	T6—943 47
Kirghiz literature	894.347
Kirghizia	T2—584 3
Kiribati	996.81
	T2—968 1
Kırıkkale İli (Turkey)	T2—563 8
ancient	T2—393 2
Kirin Province (China)	T2—518 8
Kirinyaga County (Kenya)	T2—676 265
Kiritimati (Kiribati)	T2—964
Kirkcaldy (Scotland :	
District)	T2—412 9
Kirkintilloch (Scotland)	T2—414 36
Kirkland (Quebec)	T2—714 28
Kırklareli İli (Turkey)	T2—496 15
Kirklees (England)	T2—428 13
Kirkuk (Iraq : Province)	T2—567 4
Kirkwood (South Africa :	
District)	T2—687 53
Kirlian photography	778.3
parapsychology	133.892
Kirov (Russia : Oblast)	T2—474 2
Kirovohrad (Ukraine :	
Oblast)	T2—477 6
Kirovohrads´ka oblast´	
(Ukraine)	T2—477 6
Kirovskaía oblast´ (Russia)	T2—474 2
Kırşehir İli (Turkey)	T2—564 1
ancient	T2—393 4

Kirstenbosch National	
Botanical Garden (South	
Africa)	T2—687 355
Kirundi language	496.394 65
	T6—963 946 5
Kirundi literature	896.394 65
Kisā'ī, 'Alī ibn Ḥamzah	
Koran readings	297.122 404 522
Kisangani (Congo)	T2—675 15
Kisii County (Kenya)	T2—676 298
Kiska, Andrej	
Slovak history	943.730 514
Kissi (African people)	T5—963 2
Kissi language	496.32
	T6—963 2
Kissimmee River (Fla.)	T2—759 53
Kissing	
customs	394
Kisumu County (Kenya)	T2—676 293
Kiswahili language	496.392
	T6—963 92
Kiswahili literature	896.392
Kit Carson County (Colo.)	T2—788 91
Kitchen utensils	643.3
manufacturing technology	683.82
Kitchener (Ont.)	T2—713 45
Kitchens	643.3
construction	690.44
home economics	643.3
plumbing	696.184
residential interior decoration	747.797
Kites (Aircraft)	629.133 32
recreation	796.158
Kites (Birds)	598.945
conservation technology	639.978 945
resource economics	333.958 945
Kitikmeot (Nunavut)	T2—719 55
Kitimat (B.C.)	T2—711 1
Kitimat-Stikine (B.C.)	T2—711 1
Kitsap County (Wash.)	T2—797 76
Kitsch	709.034 8
19th century	709.034 8
20th century	709.040 13
painting	759.058
Kittens	636.807
Kittitas County (Wash.)	T2—797 57
Kittson County (Minn.)	T2—776 99
Kituba language	496.393 1
	T6—963 931
Kitui County (Kenya)	T2—676 242
Kíustendilski oblast	
(Bulgaria)	T2—499 84
Kivallik (Nunavut)	T2—719 58

Kivu, Lake (Congo and	
Rwanda)	T2—675 17
Congo	T2—675 17
Rwanda	T2—675 71
Kiwi (Fruit)	641.344
botany	583.93
cooking	641.644
food	641.344
horticulture	634.4
Kiwis (Birds)	598.54
Kiyaka languages	496.393
	T6—963 93
Klamath County (Or.)	T2—795 91
Klamath Indians	979.400 497 412 2
	T5—974 122
Klamath-Modoc language	497.412 2
	T6—974 122
Klamath Mountains (Calif.	
and Or.)	T2—795 2
California	T2—794 21
Oregon	T2—795 2
Klaus, Václav	
Czech history	943.710 512
Kleberg County (Tex.)	T2—764 472
Kleptomania	362.27
medicine	616.858 42
social welfare	362.27
Klerk, F. W. de (Frederik	
Willem)	
South African history	968.064
Klerksdorp (South Africa :	
District)	T2—682 43
Klickitat County (Wash.)	T2—797 53
Klinefelter's syndrome	
medicine	616.680 42
see also Male genital	
diseases — humans	
Klingon (Artificial	
language)	T6—999 9
Klip River (South Africa :	
District)	T2—684 7
Kliprivier (South Africa :	
District)	T2—684 9
Klystrons	621.381 333
Knapp, Georg Friedrich	
economic school	330.154 2
Kneelers	
home sewing	646.21
household management	645.4
textile arts	746.95
Knees	612.98
physiology	612.98
regional medicine	617.582

Knees (continued)	
surgery	617.582 059
see also Lower extremities	
Knies, Karl	
economic school	330.154 2
Knife combat	
military training	355.548
Knife fighting	796.852
Knifefishes	597.48
Knighthood	
genealogy	929.7
Knighthood orders	929.71
Christian religious orders	255.791
church history	271.791
Knights (Chessmen)	794.144
Knights Hospitalers of St. John of	
Jerusalem	255.791 2
church history	271.791 2
Knights of Labor	331.883 309 73
Knights of Malta	255.791 2
church history	271.791 2
Maltese history	945.850 2
Knights of Pythias	366.2
biography	366.209 2
Knights Templars	255.791 3
church history	271.791 3
Knitted fabrics	677.661
see also Textiles	
Knitted laces	
arts	746.226
Knitted rugs	
arts	746.73
Knitting	677.028 245
arts	746.432
manufacturing technology	677.028 245
Knives	621.932
art metalwork	739.72
military engineering	623.441 2
Knob celery	641.351 28
see also Celeriac	
Knobs region (Ky.)	T2—769 5
Knockers	
artistic ironwork	739.48
Knossos (Extinct city)	939.18
	T2—391 8
Knots (Mathematics)	514.224 2
Knott County (Ky.)	T2—769 165
Knotted fabrics	677.66
see also Textiles	
Knotting (Seamanship)	623.888 2
Knotting textiles	677.028 2
arts	746.422
manufacturing technology	677.028 2
Know-Nothing Party (U.S.)	324.273 2

Knowability of God	212.6
see also Knowledge of God	
Knowledge	001
history	001.09
international organizations	
public administration	353.721 1
psychology	153.4
public administrative support	352.74
sociology	306.42
theory of	121
Knowledge acquisition	
computer science	006.331
Knowledge-based systems	006.33
Knowledge engineering	
computer science	006.332
Knowledge of God	212.6
Christianity	231.042
comparative religion	202.11
philosophy of religion	212.6
Knowledge organization	001.012
information science	025.4
Knowledge representation	
computer science	006.332
Knowsley (England)	T2—427 54
Knox County (Ill.)	T2—773 49
Knox County (Ind.)	T2—772 39
Knox County (Ky.)	T2—769 125
Knox County (Me.)	T2—741 53
Knox County (Mo.)	T2—778 315
Knox County (Neb.)	T2—782 59
Knox County (Ohio)	T2—771 52
Knox County (Tenn.)	T2—768 85
Knox County (Tex.)	T2—764 743
Knoxville (Tenn.)	T2—768 85
Knysna (South Africa : District)	T2—687 37
Knysna Lakes National Park (South Africa)	T2—687 37
Knysna National Lake Area (South Africa)	T2—687 37
Koala	599.25
Koasati Indians	T5—973 8
Koasati language	497.38
	T6—973 8
Kōbe-shi (Japan)	T2—521 874
København (Denmark)	T2—489 13
Københavns amt (Denmark)	T2—489 13
Koblenz (Germany)	T2—434 323
Koblenz (Germany : Regierungsbezirk)	T2—434 32
Kobuk Valley National Park (Alaska)	T2—798 6
Kocaeli İli (Turkey)	T2—563 3
ancient	T2—393 13

Kōchi-ken (Japan)	T2—523 3
Kodashim	296.123 5
Babylonian Talmud	296.125 5
Mishnah	296.123 5
Palestinian Talmud	296.124 5
Kodiak Island (Alaska)	T2—798 4
Kodiak Island Borough (Alaska)	T2—798 4
Koffiefontein (South Africa : District)	T2—685 7
Kogi State (Nigeria)	T2—669 56
Kohelet	223.8
Kohgiluyeh va Boyr Ahmad (Iran)	T2—556 8
Kohistani language	491.499
	T6—914 99
Kohistani literature	891.499
Kohistanis	T5—914 99
Kohl, Helmut	
German history	943.087 8
1982–1990	943.087 8
1990–1998	943.088 1
Kohlrabi	641.353 47
cooking	641.653 47
food	641.353 47
Koi	639.374 83
Koine (Greek language)	487.4
	T6—87
Koksilah River (B.C.)	T2—711 2
Kola nuts	583.775
Kola Peninsula (Russia)	T2—471 3
Kola trees	583.775
alkaloidal crop	633.76
botany	583.775
Kolda (Senegal : Region)	T2—663
Kolingba, André	
Central African history	967.410 52
Köln (Germany)	T2—435 514
Köln (Germany : Regierungsbezirk)	T2—435 51
Komandorski Islands (Russia)	T2—577
Komárom-Esztergom Megye (Hungary)	T2—439 7
Komati River	T2—679 1
Eswatini	T2—688 7
Mozambique	T2—679 1
South Africa	T2—682 73
Kombucha	641.26
Komga (South Africa : District)	T2—687 54
Komi	T5—945 3
Komi (Russia)	T2—474 3

Kosovo War, 1998–1999	949.710 315	Krill	595.389
Kosrae (Micronesia)	T2—966	Krio language	427.966 4
Kossuth County (Iowa)	T2—777 21		T6—217
Koster (South Africa :		Kristallnacht, 1938	940.531 842
District)	T2—682 41	Kristianstads län (Sweden)	T2—486 1
Kostroma (Russia : Oblast)	T2—473 3	Kronobergs län (Sweden)	T2—486 5
Kostromaia oblast′		Kroonstad (South Africa :	
(Russia)	T2—473 3	District)	T2—685 2
Kosygin, Aleksey Nikolayevich		Krosno (Poland :	
Russian history	947.085 3	Voivodeship)	T2—438 66
Koszalin (Poland :		Kru (African people)	T5—963 3
Voivodeship)	T2—438 16	Kru languages	496.33
Kota language (Dravidian)	494.81		T6—963 3
	T6—948 1	Kruger National Park (South	
Kota literature (Dravidian)	894.81	Africa)	T2—682 73
Kountché, Seyni		Krugersdorp (South Africa :	
Nigerien (Niger) history	966.260 52	District)	T2—682 22
Kováč, Michal		Krymskaia oblast′ (Ukraine)	T2—477 1
Slovak history	943.730 511	Krypton	
Koyukon Indians	T5—972	chemistry	546.754
Koyukon language	497.2	gas technology	665.822
	T6—972	Ku Klux Klan	322.420 973
Kozanē (Greece : Regional		Ku-ring-gai Chase National	
unit)	T2—495 62	Park (N.S.W.)	T2—944 1
Kpelle (African people)	T5—963 4	Kuala Lumpur (Malaysia)	T2—595 1
Kpelle language	496.34	Kuando Kubango Province	
	T6—963 4	(Angola)	T2—673 5
KPÖ (Austrian political party)	324.243 607 5	Kuba (Kingdom)	967.512 601
Kraft process	676.126		T2—675 126
Kraft wrapping paper	676.287	Kuba languages	496.396
Kraków (Poland :			T6—963 96
Voivodeship)	T2—438 62	Kubitschek, Juscelino	
Královéhradecký kraj		Brazilian history	981.062
(Czech Republic)	T2—437 18	Kublai Khan	
Krameriaceae	583.62	Asian history	950.22
Kranskop (South Africa :		Kuchean language	491.994
District)	T2—684 8		T6—919 94
Krasnodar (Russia : Kray)	T2—475 2	Kuczynski Godard, Pedro-Pablo	
Krasnodarskii krai (Russia)	T2—475 2	Peruvian history	985.064 7
Krasnoiarskii krai (Russia)	T2—575	Kudumane (South Africa :	
Krasnoyarsk (Russia : Kray)	T2—575	District)	T2—687 15
Krebs cycle	572.475	Kudus	599.642 3
Krefeld (Germany)	T2—435 535 7	Kudzu	583.63
Krētē (Greece)	T2—495 9	Kufuor, John Agyekum	
ancient	T2—391 8	Ghanaian history	966.705 3
Krētēs (Greece :		Kugluktuk (Nunavut)	T2—719 55
Decentralized		Kui (Dravidian people)	T5—948 24
administration)	T2—495 9	Kui language (Dravidian)	494.824
Kretschmer, Ernst			T6—948 24
personality theory	155.264	Kui literature (Dravidian)	894.824
Kreuzlingen (Switzerland :		Kuĭbyshev (Russia : Oblast)	T2—474 4
Bezirk)	T2—494 597	Kuĭbyshevskaia oblast′	
Kriel (South Africa :		(Russia)	T2—474 4
District)	T2—682 76		

Kwa languages	496.337
	T6—963 37
Kwa literatures	896.337
Kwa Zulu (South Africa)	T2—684
Kwajalein Atoll (Marshall Islands)	T2—968 3
Kwakiutl Indians	T5—979 53
Kwakiutl language	497.953
	T6—979 53
Kwale County (Kenya)	T2—676 237
Kwamhlanga (South Africa : District)	T2—682 76
KwaNdebele (South Africa)	T2—682 76
Kwangsi Chuang Autonomous Region (China)	T2—512 8
Kwangtung Province (China)	T2—512 7
Kwangwa languages	496.399
	T6—963 99
Kwanzaa	394.261 2
Kwara State (Nigeria)	T2—669 57
Kwashiorkor	
medicine	616.396
see also Digestive system diseases — humans	
Kwaśniewski, Aleksander	
Polish history	943.805 72
KwaZulu (South Africa)	T2—684
KwaZulu-Natal (South Africa)	968.4
	T2—684
Kweichow Province (China)	T2—513 4
Kwese language	496.393
	T6—963 93
KWIC indexing	025.486
KWOC indexing	025.486
Kwomtari-Baibai languages	T6—991 2
Kyabram (Vic.)	T2—945 4
Kyanite	
mineralogy	549.62
Kyffhäuserkreis (Germany : Landkreis)	T2—432 24
Kyïvs´ka oblast´ (Ukraine)	T2—477 7
Kyklades (Greece)	T2—495 85
Kyle and Carrick (Scotland)	T2—414 64
Kymen lääni (Finland)	T2—489 71
Kymenlaakso (Finland)	T2—489 713
Kymi (Finland : Lääni)	T2—489 71
Kyogle (N.S.W.)	T2—944 3
Kyoto (Japan)	T2—521 864
Kyoto (Japan : Prefecture)	T2—521 86
Kyrgyz	T5—943 47
Kyrgyz language	494.347
	T6—943 47

Kyrgyz literature	894.347
Kyrgyzstan	958.43
	T2—584 3
Kyrgyzstani	T5—943 47
Kyrie	264.36
music	782.323 2
Kythēra Island (Greece)	T2—495 2
Kyūshū Island (Japan)	T2—522
Kyūshū Region (Japan)	T2—522
Kyustendil (Bulgaria : Oblast)	T2—499 84
Kyusyu Island (Japan)	T2—522
Kyusyu Region (Japan)	T2—522

L

L-functions	512.73
La Altagracia (Dominican Republic : Province)	T2—729 385
La Bostonnais (Quebec)	T2—714 459
La Chaux-de-Fonds (Switzerland : District)	T2—494 381
La Coruña (Spain : Province)	T2—461 1
La Côte-de-Beaupré (Quebec)	T2—714 48
La Côte-de-Gaspé (Quebec)	T2—714 793
La Crosse County (Wis.)	T2—775 71
La Guajira (Colombia : Dept.)	T2—861 17
La Habana (Cuba)	T2—729 123
La Habana (Cuba : Province)	T2—729 124
La Haute-Côte-Nord (Quebec)	T2—714 172
La Haute-Gaspésie (Quebec)	T2—714 791
La Haute-Yamaska (Quebec)	T2—714 63
La Jacques-Cartier (Quebec)	T2—714 474
La Libertad (El Salvador : Dept.)	T2—728 422
La Libertad (Peru : Region)	T2—851 6
La Mancha (Spain)	T2—464
La Matanie (Quebec : Regional County Municipality)	T2—714 775
La Matapédia (Quebec : Regional County Municipality)	T2—714 778
La Mauricie National Park (Quebec)	T2—714 453
La Mitis (Quebec)	T2—714 773
La Moure County (N.D.)	T2—784 53

Labor force	331.11
Labor grievances	331.889 66
see also Grievances (Labor)	
Labor groups	
relations with government	322.2
Labor injunctions	
economics	331.893
law	344.018 93
Labor law	344.01
Labor leaders	331.880 92
biography	331.880 92
role and function	331.873 3
Labor-management bargaining	331.89
see also Collective bargaining	
Labor market	331.12
maladjustments	331.13
Labor mobility	331.127
Labor movements	331.8
economics	331.8
relations with government	322.2
Labor need	331.123
Labor parties	324.217
international organizations	324.17
Labor Party (Australia)	324.294 07
Labor productivity	331.118
economics	331.118
promotion of	
personnel management	658.314
Labor relations	331
economics	331
law	344.01
personnel management	658.315
	T1—068 3
military personnel	355.33
public administration	352.68
public administration	354.9
sociology	306.34
Labor requirements	331.123
Labor rights	331.011
law	344.010 1
Labor shortages	331.136
Labor supply	331.11
Labor surpluses	331.137
Labor systems	
economics	331.117
sociology	306.36
Labor theory of value	
Marxian theory	335.412
Labor turnover	331.126
economics	331.126
personnel management	658.314
Labor unions	331.88
accounting	657.861
benefits	331.873 5

Labor unions (continued)	
elections	331.874
law	344.018 8
membership	331.873 2
organization	331.87
personnel management	658.315 3
public administration	352.68
public administration	354.97
relations with government	322.2
social welfare	361.766
women workers	331.478
Labor use	
agricultural industries	338.16
Labor violence	
economics	331.893
labor economics	
law	344.018 93
Laboratories	001.4
architecture	727.5
chemistry	542.1
institutional housekeeping	647.995
interior decoration	747.875
school facilities	371.623
Laboratory animals	616.027
care and maintenance	636.088 5
medicine	616.027
Laboratory diagnosis	
medicine	616.075 6
Laboratory manuals	T1—078
research	T1—072 1
Laboratory method	371.382
Laboratory mice	616.027 333
animal husbandry	636.935 3
medicine	616.027 333
Laboratory rats	616.027 33
animal husbandry	636.935 2
medicine	616.027 33
Laborers	331.11
public administration	354.9
social class	305.562
	T1—086 24
Laboring class	305.562
	T1—086 23
see also Working class	
Laboulbeniales	579.567
Labour Party (Great Britain)	324.241 07
Labrador (N.L.)	971.82
	T2—718 2
Labrador Current	551.462 134
Labrador Sea	551.461 343
	T2—163 43
Labuan	T2—595 3

Labyrinth diseases
  medicine   617.882
    see also Ear diseases —
    humans
Labyrinth fishes   597.7
Labyrinthodontia   567.8
Labyrinths (Ears)
  human anatomy   611.85
  human physiology   612.858
  medicine   617.882
Lac (Switzerland)   T2—494 538
Lac-Édouard (Quebec)   T2—714 459
Lac la Biche (Alta.)   T2—712 33
Lac qui Parle County
  (Minn.)   T2—776 38
Lac-Saint-Jean-Est
  (Quebec : Regional
  County Municipality)   T2—714 148
Lac-Saint-Jean Region
  (Quebec)   T2—714 14
Lacalle Herrera, Luis Alberto
  Uruguayan history   989.506 72
Lacalle Pou, Luis
  Uruguayan history   989.506 78
Lacandón Indians   T5—974 27
Lacandón language   497.427
    T6—974 27
Laccadive, Minicoy, and
  Amindivi Islands (India) T2—548 1
Laccadive Sea   551.461 537
    T2—165 37
Laccoliths   551.88
Lacerations (Wounds)
  medicine   617.13
Lacertidae   597.958
Laces   677.653
  arts   746.22
  manufacturing technology   677.653
Lacewings   595.747
Lachlan River (N.S.W.)   T2—944 9
Lacings   677.76
Lackawanna County (Pa.)   T2—748 36
Laclede County (Mo.)   T2—778 815
Laconia (Greece)   T2—495 22
  ancient   T2—389
Lacquering   667.75
  decorative arts   745.726
  furniture arts   749.5
  woodwork
    buildings   698.34
Lacrimal apparatus
  human physiology   612.847
  ophthalmology   617.764

Lacrimal apparatus diseases
  ophthalmology   617.764
    see also Eye diseases —
    humans
Lacrosse
  biography   796.362 092
Lacrosse (Game)   796.362
    see also Ball games
Lacrosse players   796.362 092
Lactation   573.679
  biology   573.679
  human physiology   612.664
  obstetrics   618.71
Lactic acid bacteria   579.35
Lacto-ovo vegetarian diet   613.262
  cooking   641.563 6
  health   613.262
Lactobacillus   579.37
Lactococcus   579.355
Lactose   572.565
    see also Carbohydrates
Lactose-free cooking   641.563 97
Lactose-free diet
  health   613.268 7
Lactose-free foods   641.309 7
Lactose intolerance
  medicine   616.399 82
    see also Digestive system
    diseases — humans
Ladakh (India)   T2—546 7
Ladin language   459.94
    T6—599 4
Ladin literature   859.94
Ladino language   467.949 6
    T6—67
Ladino literature   860
Ladins   T5—599 4
Ladismith (South Africa :
  District)   T2—687 37
Ladoga Lake (Russia)   T2—471 5
Lady Frere (South Africa :
  District)   T2—687 56
Lady Grey (South Africa :
  District)   T2—687 57
Ladybrand (South Africa :
  District)   T2—685 1
Ladybugs   595.769
  culture   638.576 9
Lae (Papua New Guinea)   T2—957 1
Lafayette County (Ark.)   T2—767 57
Lafayette County (Fla.)   T2—759 816
Lafayette County (Miss.)   T2—762 83
Lafayette County (Mo.)   T2—778 453
Lafayette County (Wis.)   T2—775 79

Lafayette Parish (La.)	T2—763 47
Lafourche Parish (La.)	T2—763 39
Lag b'Omer	296.439
liturgy	296.453 9
Laghouat (Algeria :	
Province)	T2—657
Lagomorpha	599.32
paleozoology	569.32
Lagoons	551.461 8
	T2—168
biology	578.778
ecology	577.78
freshwater biology	578.763
freshwater ecology	577.63
freshwater hydrology	551.482
oceanography	551.461 8
Lagopus	598.633
Lagos (Chile : Region)	T2—835
Lagos Escobar, Ricardo	
Chilean history	983.066 3
Lagos State (Nigeria)	T2—669 1
LaGrange County (Ind.)	T2—772 79
Lagrange polynomials	515.55
Laguerre polynomials	515.55
Laguna (Philippines :	
Province)	T2—599 173
Laguna de Bay (Philippines)	T2—599 172
Lahn River (Germany)	T2—434 14
Lahnda language	491.419
	T6—914 19
Lahnda literature	891.419
Lahore District (Pakistan)	954.914 3
	T2—549 143
Lai Châu (Vietnam :	
Province)	T2—597 1
Laikipia County (Kenya)	T2—676 275 3
Laingsburg (South Africa :	
District)	T2—687 39
Laissez-faire economics	330.153
Laity (Church members)	262.15
	T1—088 28
biography	270.092
specific denominations	280
church government	262.15
pastoral theology	253
social group	305.6
Lajemmerais (Quebec)	T2—714 362
Lak-Dargwa languages	499.964
	T6—999 64
Lak language	499.964
	T6—999 64
Lake Abitibi (Ont. and	
Quebec)	T2—713 142

Lake and Peninsula	
Borough (Alaska)	T2—798 4
Lake Athabasca (Sask. and	
Alta.)	T2—712 41
Lake Barkley (Ky. and	
Tenn.)	T2—769 79
Lake Champlain	T2—747 54
New York	T2—747 54
Vermont	T2—743 1
Lake Champlain, Battle of, 1814	973.525 6
Lake Clark National Park	
and Preserve (Alaska)	T2—798 6
Lake Constance	T2—434 62
Germany	T2—434 62
Switzerland	T2—494 597
Lake County (Calif.)	T2—794 17
Lake County (Colo.)	T2—788 46
Lake County (Fla.)	T2—759 22
Lake County (Ill.)	T2—773 21
Lake County (Ind.)	T2—772 99
Lake County (Mich.)	T2—774 68
Lake County (Minn.)	T2—776 76
Lake County (Mont.)	T2—786 832
Lake County (Ohio)	T2—771 334
Lake County (Or.)	T2—795 93
Lake County (S.D.)	T2—783 35
Lake County (Tenn.)	T2—768 12
Lake Cumberland (Ky.)	T2—769 63
Lake Diefenbaker (Sask.)	T2—712 42
Lake District (England)	942.78
	T2—427 8
Lake Erie	T2—771 2
Ohio	T2—771 2
Ontario	T2—713 3
Lake Erie, Battle of, 1813	973.525 4
Lake Eyre (S. Aust.)	T2—942 38
Lake Francis Case (S.D.)	T2—783 38
Lake Gairdner (S. Aust.)	T2—942 38
Lake Garda (Italy)	T2—452 6
Lake Geneva (Switzerland	
and France)	T2—494 52
France	T2—445 84
Switzerland	T2—494 52
Lake George (N.Y.)	T2—747 51
Lake Hawea (N.Z.)	T2—939 5
Lake Huron (Mich. and	
Ont.)	T2—774
Michigan	T2—774
Ontario	T2—713 2
Lake ice	551.345
Lake Kivu (Congo and	
Rwanda)	T2—675 17
Congo	T2—675 17
Rwanda	T2—675 71

Lakes	551.482
	T2—169 2
biology	578.763
ecology	577.63
engineering	627.14
hydrology	551.482
influence on precipitation	551.577 5
interactions with atmosphere	551.524 8
landscape architecture	714
law	346.046 916 3
law of nations	341.444
recreational resources	333.784 4
recreational use	797
resource economics	333.916 3
law	346.046 916 3
water supply engineering	628.112
Lakes Entrance (Vic.)	T2—945 6
Lakes State (South Sudan)	T2—629 4
Lakōnia (Greece)	T2—495 22
ancient	T2—389
Lakota Indians	978.004 975 244
	T5—975 244
Lakota language	497.524 4
	T6—975 244
Lakshadweep (India)	T2—548 1
Lâm Đồng (Vietnam)	T2—597 6
Lama (Genus)	599.636 7
Lamaism	294.392 3
Lamar County (Ala.)	T2—761 86
Lamar County (Ga.)	T2—758 446
Lamar County (Miss.)	T2—762 19
Lamar County (Tex.)	T2—764 263
Lamarckism	576.827
Lamb (Meat)	641.363
commercial processing	664.92
cooking	641.663
food	641.363
Lamb County (Tex.)	T2—764 843
Lamba language	496.391
	T6—963 91
Lambayeque (Peru : Region)	T2—851 4
Lambda calculus	511.35
Lambeth (London, England)	T2—421 65
Lambton (Ont.)	T2—713 27
Lamé	677.616
Lamellibranchia	594.4
Lamellicornia	595.764 9
Lamentations (Bible)	224.3
Lamiales	583.96
L'Amiante (Quebec)	T2—714 712
Lamiids	583.95

Laminar flow	532.052 5
air mechanics	533.62
gas mechanics	533.215
liquid mechanics	532.515
Laminariales	579.887
Laminated fabrics	677.69
see also Textiles	
Laminated glass	666.154
Laminated plastic	668.492
Laminated wood	674.835
see also Wood	
Laminating plastics	668.414
Lamington National Park (Qld.)	T2—943 2
Lammermuir Hills (Scotland)	T2—413 6
Lamnidae	597.33
Lamniformes	597.3
Lamoille County (Vt.)	T2—743 35
Lamp shells	594.68
paleozoology	564.68
Lampasas County (Tex.)	T2—764 513
Lampblack	662.93
Lampedusa (Italy)	T2—458 22
Lampreys	597.2
Lampridiformes	597.64
Lamps	621.32
ceramic arts	738.8
furniture arts	749.63
manufacturing technology	683.83
mining	622.473
see also Lighting	
Lampshades	
handicrafts	745.593 2
Lampung	T5—992 248
Lampung (Indonesia)	T2—598 18
Lampung language	499.224 8
	T6—992 248
Lampung literature	899.224 8
Lampyridae	595.764 4
Lamu County (Kenya)	T2—676 232
Lamut	T5—941
Lamut language	494.1
	T6—941
LAN (Computer network)	004.68
see also Computer communications	
Lanai (Hawaii)	T2—969 23
Lanao del Norte (Philippines)	T2—599 776
Lanao del Sur (Philippines)	T2—599 757
Lanariaceae	584.7
Lanark (Ont. : County)	T2—713 82

Land reform	
economics	333.31
law	346.044
Land resettlement	
economics	333.31
Land resources	333.73
economics	333.73
public administration	354.34
see Manual at 333.73–.78 vs.	
333, 333.1–.5	
Land sailing	796.68
see also Sports	
Land sale	333.333
Land settlement	
economics	333.31
Land slugs	594.38
Land snails	594.38
see also Snails (Land)	
Land subdivision	333.3
law	346.043 77
public administration	354.34
Land surveys	333.08
economics	333.08
public land	333.18
technology	526.9
Land tenure	333.3
agricultural sociology	306.349
economics	333.3
law	346.043 2
sociology	306.32
see also Private property —	
land economics	
see Manual at 333.73–.78 vs.	
333, 333.1–.5	
Land titles	346.043 8
Land transfer	333.33
economics	333.33
law	346.043 6
Land transportation	388
engineering	629.049
military engineering	623.61
see also Ground transportation	
Land trusts	
law	346.068
Land use	333.731 3
agricultural surveys	631.47
community sociology	307.33
economics	333.731 3
law	346.045
see Manual at 333.73–.78 vs.	
333, 333.1–.5	
Land use planning	
arts	711
Land valuation	333.332

Land value taxation	336.225
Land vehicles	388.34
engineering	629.049
transportation services	388.34
see also Automotive vehicles	
Land vertebrates	596
Landbund (Austrian political	
party)	324.243 602 3
Landed gentry	305.523 2
	T1—086 21
genealogy	929.2
Lander County (Nev.)	T2—793 33
Landes (France : Dept.)	T2—447 15
Landesring der Unabhängigen	
(Swiss political party)	324.249 408
Landforms	551.41
	T2—14
geography	910.914
geomorphology	551.41
physical geography	910.021 4
Landfowl	598.6
sports hunting	799.246
Landing	
aeronautics	629.132 521 3
manned space flight	629.458 8
Landing (Military tactics)	355.422
Landing accidents	363.124 92
see also Air safety	
Landing craft	359.835 6
design	623.812 56
engineering	623.825 6
naval equipment	359.835 6
naval units	359.325 6
Landing fields	387.736
see also Airports	
Landing lights	629.135 1
Landing systems	
aircraft	629.134 381
spacecraft	629.474 2
unmanned spacecraft	629.464 2
Landkreise	320.83
see also Counties	
Landlord and tenant	333.54
law	346.043 4
Landlord-tenant relations	333.54
law	346.043 4
Landlords' liability insurance	368.56
see also Insurance	
Landowners	333.009 2
Landowning classes	305.523 2
	T1—086 21
Landquart (Switzerland :	
Region)	T2—494 732 1

Languedocien dialect
  (Occitan language)   T6—491
Lanier County (Ga.)   T2—758 817
Laniidae   598.862
Lanolin   665.13
Lansdowne, Henry Charles Keith
  Petty-FitzMaurice, Marquess
  of
    Indian history   954.035 4
Länsi-Suomen lääni
  (Finland)   T2—489 73
Lansing (Mich.)   T2—774 27
Lantern-eyed fishes   597.64
Lantern fishes   597.61
Lanthanide series
  chemistry   546.41
  economic geology   553.494
  metallurgy   669.291
Lanthanotidae   597.959 6
Lanthanum
  chemistry   546.411
Lanuvian language   479.4
   T6—794
Lao (Tai people)   T5—959 191
Lào Cai (Vietnam :
  Province)   T2—597 1
Lao language   495.919 1
   T6—959 191
Lao literature   895.919 1
Laoighis (Ireland)   T2—418 7
Laois (Ireland)   T2—418 7
Laos   959.4
   T2—594
Laotians   T5—959 191
Lap robes
  manufacturing technology   677.626
Laparoscopic surgery   617.550 597
Laparoscopy
  diagnosis   617.550 754 5
    gynecology   618.107 545
  surgery   617.550 597
Lapeer County (Mich.)   T2—774 42
Lapidary work   736.202 8
Lapin lääni (Finland)   T2—489 77
Laplace functions   515.53
Laplace transform   515.723
Lapland   T2—489 77
LaPorte County (Ind.)   T2—772 91
Lapp languages   494.57
   T6—945 7
Lapp literatures   894.57
Lappet embroidery   677.77
Lappi (Finland)   948.977
   T2—489 77

Lapping tools   621.922
Lappish languages   494.57
   T6—945 7
Lappish literatures   894.57
Lappland landskap
  (Sweden)   T2—488 8
Laprairie (Quebec : County)   T2—714 34
Lapse
  insurance   368.016
Laptev Sea (Russia)   551.461 325
   T2—163 25
Laptop computers   004.167
Lapwings   598.33
L'Aquila (Italy : Province)   T2—457 11
  ancient   T2—377 34
Lara (Venezuela)   T2—872 5
Larache (Morocco :
  Province)   T2—642
Laramie County (Wyo.)   T2—787 19
Laramie Mountains (Wyo.
  and Colo.)   T2—787 9
Larceny   364.162
  see also Theft
Larceny insurance   368.82
Larches   585.2
  forestry   634.975 7
  lumber   674.144
  ornamental arboriculture   635.977 52
  see also Tamaracks
Lard
  food technology   664.34
Large business   338.644
  economics   338.644
  management   658.023
  personnel management   658.303
Large format cameras   771.32
Large fruit flies   595.774
Large industry   338.644
Large intestine   573.379
  biology   573.379
  human anatomy   611.347
  human physiology   612.36
  medicine   616.34
  surgery   617.554 7
  see also Digestive system
Large-print publications
  bibliographies   011.63
  cataloging   025.349
  library treatment   025.179
Large-scale digital computers   004.12
  see also Mainframe computers
Large-scale systems   003.71

Large-type publications	
cataloging	025.349
library treatment	025.179
Largemouth bass	597.738 8
culture	639.377 388
sports fishing	799.177 388
Lari	598.338
Laridae	598.338
Larimer County (Colo.)	T2—788 68
Larisa (Greece : Regional	
unit)	T2—495 4
Larks	598.825
Larkspurs	635.933 34
botany	583.34
floriculture	635.933 34
Larne (Northern Ireland :	
Borough)	T2—416 13
Larue County (Ky.)	T2—769 713
Larvacea	596.2
Larvae	571.876
descriptive zoology	591.392
physiology	571.876
Laryngeal diseases	
medicine	616.22
see also Respiratory tract	
diseases — humans	
Laryngeal muscles	
human anatomy	611.22
Laryngitis	
medicine	616.22
see also Respiratory tract	
diseases — humans	
Laryngology	616.22
Larynx	573.925
biology	573.925
human anatomy	611.22
human physiology	612.233
speech	612.78
medicine	616.22
surgery	617.533
see also Respiratory system	
Las Animas County (Colo.)	T2—788 96
Las Palmas (Canary	
Islands : Province)	T2—649
Las Tunas (Cuba : Province)	T2—729 162
Las Vegas (Nev.)	T2—793 135
Laser coagulation	
surgery	617.058
Laser communications	
engineering	621.382 7
Laser microsurgery	617.058
Laser optical discs	384.558
see also Video recordings	
Laser printing	686.233
Laser surgery	617.058
Laser warfare	358.39
Laser weapons	
engineering	623.446
Laser welding	671.52
Lasers	621.366
Lashley, Karl Spencer	
psychological system	150.194 32
Lasithi (Greece)	T2—495 9
Lasqueti Island (B.C.)	T2—711 31
Lassen County (Calif.)	T2—794 26
Lassen Volcanic National	
Park (Calif.)	T2—794 24
L'Assomption (Quebec :	
Regional County	
Municipality)	T2—714 416
Lassos	
sports	799.202 82
Last Judgment	
Christianity	236.9
Last Supper	232.957
Latah County (Idaho)	T2—796 86
Latakia (Syria : Province)	T2—569 13
Latches	683.31
Late Middle Ages	940.19
Italy	945.04
Lombardian history	945.205
Piedmontese history	945.104
Sardinian history	945.903
Sicilian history	945.804
Tuscan history	945.504
Venetian history	945.304
Latent heat	536.4
chemical engineering	660.296 2
evaporation and condensation	536.44
fusion and solidification	536.42
thermochemistry	541.362
Latent structure analysis	519.535
Later Prophets (Biblical books)	224
Laterality	
psychology	152.335
Latex biscuits	678.522
Latex paints	667.63
Latexes	
chemistry	547.842 5
manufacturing technology	678.5
Lathers	541.345 14
chemical engineering	660.294 514
colloid chemistry	541.345 14
Lathes	621.942
Lathing	693.6
architectural construction	721.044 6
Latidae	597.72
Latimer County (Okla.)	T2—766 76

Latin America	980	Latvians	T5—919 3
	T2—8	Lauderdale County (Ala.)	T2—761 99
Latin American literature	860	Lauderdale County (Miss.)	T2—762 676
Latin American Spanish dialects	467.98	Lauderdale County (Tenn.)	T2—768 16
	T6—61	Lauds	264.15
Latin Americans	T5—68	music	782.324
Latin calligraphy	744.429 71	*see also* Liturgy of the hours	
Latin language	470	Laufen (Switzerland :	
	T6—71	Bezirk)	T2—494 331
Biblical texts	220.47	Laufenburg (Switzerland :	
see Manual at 471–475, 478		Bezirk)	T2—494 564 5
vs. 477		Laughter	
Latin literature	870	psychology	152.43
Latin peoples	T5—4	Launceston (Tas.)	T2—946 5
Latin squares	511.64	Launch complexes	
Latina (Italy : Province)	T2—456 23	guided missiles	623.451 9
ancient	T2—376 5	spacecraft	629.478
Latinian languages	479.4	Launch vehicles	
	T6—794	guided missiles	623.451 9
Latinos	T5—68	Launching	
Latinos (U.S.)	T5—680 73	manned space flight	629.452
Latitude	526.61	space flight	629.41
celestial navigation	527.1	unmanned space flight	629.432
Latium (Italy)		Laundering	667.13
ancient	T2—376	home economics	648.1
Latter Day Saint movement	289.3	Laundries	667.13
church government	262.093	construction	690.43
local church	254.093	plumbing	696.183
church law	262.989 3	sanitation services	363.729 9
doctrines	230.93	*see also* Sanitation	
catechisms and creeds	238.93	Laurales	584.288
general councils	262.593	Laurel County (Ky.)	T2—769 143
guides to Christian life	248.489 3	Laurel wax	665.12
missions	266.93	Laurels	584.288
moral theology	241.049 3	Laurels (Ericaceae)	583.93
priesthood	262.149 3	Laurels (Lauraceae)	584.288
public worship	264.093	Laurels (Saxifragales)	583.44
religious associations	267.189 3	Laurens County (Ga.)	T2—758 535
religious education	268.893	Laurens County (S.C.)	T2—757 31
temples	246.958 93	Laurentian Mountains	
theology	230.93	(Quebec)	T2—714 4
Latter Day Saints		Laurentians region	T2—714 24
biography	289.309 2	Laurentian Plateau	T2—714
Lattice dynamics		Ontario	T2—713 1
solid-state physics	530.411	Quebec	T2—714
Lattice plant	584.44	Laurentians (Quebec)	T2—714 24
Lattice point geometry	516.35	Laurentides (Quebec)	T2—714 242
Lattices (Crystals)	548.81	Laurentides (Quebec :	
Lattices (Mathematics)	511.33	Region)	T2—714 24
Latvia	947.96	Laurentides Provincial Park	
	T2—479 6	(Quebec)	T2—714 48
Latvian language	491.93	Laurentides Wildlife	
	T6—919 3	Reserve (Quebec)	T2—714 48
Latvian literature	891.93		

Lebanese adder	597.963 6	Lee County (Tex.)	T2—764 247
Lebanon	956.92	Lee County (Va.)	T2—755 735
	T2—569 2	Leeches	592.66
ancient	939.44	Leeds (England : City)	T2—428 19
	T2—394 4	Leeds and Grenville (Ont.)	T2—713 73
Lebanon Conflict, 1982–1985	956.052	Leeks	641.352 6
Lebanon County (Pa.)	T2—748 19	botany	584.78
Lebanon War, 2006	956.920 452	cooking	641.652 6
Lebel-sur-Quévillon		food	641.352 6
(Quebec)	T2—714 115	garden crop	635.26
Lebern (Switzerland)	T2—494 357 3	Leelanau County (Mich.)	T2—774 635
Lebesgue integral	515.43	Leer (Germany : Landkreis)	T2—435 917
Lebombo Mountains (South		Lee's invasion of Maryland, 1862	973.733 6
Africa)	T2—682 73	Leeton (N.S.W.)	T2—944 8
Lebowa (South Africa)	T2—682 55	Leeward Islands (West Indies)	972.97
Lecce (Italy : Province)	T2—457 53		T2—729 7
ancient	T2—377 65	Leeward Netherlands	
Lecco (Italy : Province)	T2—452 37	islands	T2—729 77
ancient	T2—372 265	Leflore County (Miss.)	T2—762 46
Lecterns		Left, The (German political	
church architecture	726.529 2	party)	324.243 074
Lectionaries (Public worship)	264.34	Left and right (Psychology)	152.335
Anglican	264.030 34	Left-hand techniques	
texts	264.032	music	784.193 66
preaching	251.6	Left-handedness	
Roman Catholic	264.020 34	psychology	152.335
texts	264.029	Left May languages	T6—991 2
Lecture method	371.396	Leftist parties	324.217
Christian religious education	268.632	international organizations	324.17
Lectures	080	Leftovers (Cooking)	641.552
museum services	069.15	Leg bones	
Lecturing		human anatomy	611.718
rhetoric	808.51	human physiology	612.751
Lecythidaceae	583.93	Leg exercises	613.718 88
LED (Diodes)	621.381 522	Leg muscles	
LED lighting	621.328	human anatomy	611.738
see also Lighting		Leg techniques	
Ledbury (England)	T2—424 2	music	784.193 8
Lee, Charles		Lega dei Ticinesi (Swiss political	
treason	973.383	party)	324.249 408 4
Lee, Hsien Loong		Lega-Kalanga languages	496.394
Singaporean history	959.570 53		T6—963 94
Lee, Kuan Yew		Lega nord (Italian political party)	324.245 084
Singaporean history	959.570 51	Legal accounting	657.834
Lee County (Ala.)	T2—761 55	Legal aid	362.586
Lee County (Ark.)	T2—767 89	law	347.017
Lee County (Fla.)	T2—759 48	criminal law	345.012 7
Lee County (Ga.)	T2—758 943	welfare law	344.032 58
Lee County (Ill.)	T2—773 36	social services	362.586
Lee County (Iowa)	T2—777 99	Legal codes	348.023
Lee County (Ky.)	T2—769 185	United States	348.732 3
Lee County (Miss.)	T2—762 935	Legal costs	
Lee County (N.C.)	T2—756 355	law	347.057
Lee County (S.C.)	T2—757 67		

Legislation (Enactment and repeal)	328.37	Legislative representation	328.334
law	342.057	Legislators	
Legislation (Laws and statutes)	348.02	biography	328.092
Legislative bodies	328	law	342.055
bibliographies of publications	011.532	personal privileges	328.347
law	342.05	role and function	328.33
see Manual at 909, 930–990 vs. 320		Legitimacy of government	320.011
		Legitimation	
Legislative branch	328	family law	346.017 5
law	342.05	Legnica (Poland : Voivodeship)	T2—438 52
Legislative budgets	352.48	Legs	591.479
see also Budgets (Public)		animal physiology	573.79
Legislative buildings		descriptive zoology	591.479
architecture	725.11	human anatomy	611.98
Legislative calendars	328.4–.9	human physiology	612.98
Legislative districts	328.334 5	regional medicine	617.58
Legislative drafting	328.373	surgery	617.580 59
Legislative duties	328.34	Legumes	583.63
law	342.052	botany	583.63
Legislative-executive relations	328.345 6	commercial processing	664.805 65
law	342.044	cooking	641.656 5
Legislative functions	328.34	edible fruits	641.344 6
law	342.052	cooking	641.644 6
Legislative hearings	328.345	food	641.344 6
law	348.01	orchard crop	634.46
United States	348.731	field crop	633.3
see Manual at 300–330, 355–390 vs. 342–347, 352–354		food	641.356 5
		garden crop	635.65
		see Manual at 633–635	
Legislative histories	348.01	Leguminales	583.63
United States	348.731	Lehigh County (Pa.)	T2—748 27
Legislative immunity	328.348	Lehurutshe (South Africa : District)	T2—682 47
Legislative institutions		Leicester (England)	T2—425 42
sociology	306.23	Leicestershire (England)	T2—425 4
Legislative investigation	328.345 2	Leiden (Netherlands)	T2—492 38
Legislative journals	328.4–.9	Leinster (Ireland)	T2—418
Legislative-judicial relations	320.404	Leiopelmatidae	597.86
law	342.044	Leipzig (Germany)	T2—432 122
Legislative lobbying	328.38	Leipzig (Germany : Direktionsbezirk)	T2—432 12
law	342.05		
Legislative organization	328.36	Leipzig (Germany : Regierungsbezirk)	T2—432 12
law	342.057		
Legislative oversight	328.345 6	Leiria (Portugal : District)	T2—469 41
Legislative powers	328.34	Leishmaniasis	
chief executives	352.235	incidence	614.534
law	342.052	medicine	616.936 4
Legislative privileges	328.347	*see also* Communicable diseases — humans	
Legislative procedures	328.1		
law	342.057	Leisure	790.1
Legislative process	328	educational objective	370.119
Legislative reference bureaus	027.65	ethics	175
Legislative reform	328.304	influence on crime	364.25
Legislative reporting	328.1		

Lepcha language	495.4
	T6—954
Lephalale (South Africa : District)	T2—682 53
Lepidodendrales	561.79
Lepidoptera	595.78
agricultural pests	632.78
Lepidosauria	597.94
paleozoology	567.94
Lepontine Alps (Italy and Switzerland)	T2—494 78
Leporidae	599.32
Lepospondyli	597.8
paleozoology	567.8
Leprosy	
incidence	614.546
medicine	616.998
see also Communicable diseases — humans	
Leptis Magna (Extinct city)	T2—397 4
Leptodactylidae	597.875
Leptolepis	567
Leptons	539.721 1
Leptostraca	595.379 2
Leptotyphlopidae	597.969
Leptureae	584.92
Lepus	599.328
L'Érable (Quebec)	T2—714 575
Lérida (Spain : Province)	T2—467 4
Lernaeopodoida	595.34
Les Appalaches (Quebec)	T2—714 712
Les Basques (Quebec)	T2—714 766
Les Chenaux (Quebec)	T2—714 455
Les Chutes-de-la-Chaudière (Quebec)	T2—714 59
Les Collines-de-l'Outaouais (Quebec)	T2—714 223
Les Etchemins (Quebec)	T2—714 72
Les Îles-de-la-Madeleine (Quebec)	T2—714 797
Les Jardins-de-Napierville (Quebec)	T2—714 35
Les Laurentides (Quebec)	T2—714 242
Les Maskoutains (Quebec)	T2—714 523
Les Moulins (Quebec)	T2—714 412
Les Pays-d'en-Haut (Quebec)	T2—714 244
Les Saintes Islands (Guadeloupe)	T2—729 76
Les Sources (Quebec)	T2—714 573
Lesbian, gay, bisexual, transgender identity	306.76
Lesbian, gay, bisexual, transgender people	306.76
	T1—086 6
Lesbianism	306.766 3
religion	200.866 43
Christianity	270.086 643
see also Homosexuality	
Lesbians	306.766 3
	T1—086 643
legal status	346.013 086 643
private law	346.013 086 643
psychology	155.344 3
religion	200.866 43
Christianity	270.086 643
pastoral theology	259.086 643
social welfare	362.839 66
victims of abuse	362.885 508 664 3
Lesbos (Greece : Regional unit)	T2—495 82
Lesbos Island (Greece)	T2—495 82
ancient	T2—391 2
Leslie County (Ky.)	T2—769 152
Lesotho	968.85
	T2—688 5
Lesotho people	T5—968 85
Lespedezas	633.364
botany	583.63
forage crop	633.364
Less developed countries	T2—172 4
Lesser Antilles	T2—729
Lesser celandine	583.34
Lesser panda	599.763
Lesser Slave Lake (Alta.)	T2—712 31
Lesser Sunda Islands (Indonesia)	T2—598 6
Lesson plans	371.302 8
Lesvos (Greece)	T2—495 82
Leszno (Poland : Voivodeship)	T2—438 49
Letaba (South Africa)	T2—682 59
Letcher County (Ky.)	T2—769 163
Lethal gases	
human toxicology	615.91
Lethbridge (Alta.)	T2—712 345
Lethrinidae	597.72
Letsie III, King of Lesotho	
Lesotho history	968.850 32
Letterform design	744.4
see Manual at 744.4 vs. 686.22	
Lettering	
architectural design	729.19
bookbinding	686.36
decorative arts	744.42
design	744.42

Lettering (continued)
  prints 769.5
  stone 736.5
  technical drawing 604.243
Letterpress
  mechanical printing technique 686.231 2
Letters (Correspondence) 383.122
  biography 920
      T1—092
  direct advertising 659.133
  etiquette 395.4
  office services 651.75
    rhetoric 808.066 651
  postal handling 383.122
  see also Postal service
Letters (Literature) 808.86
  criticism 809.6
    theory 808.6
  history and criticism 809.6
  rhetoric 808.6
  specific literatures T3B—6
    individual authors T3A—6
Letters of credit 332.77
  law 346.096
Letters rogatory 347.012
  criminal law 345.012 2
Lettish language 491.93
      T6—919 3
Lettish literature 891.93
Letts T5—919 3
Lettuce 641.355 2
  botany 583.983
  commercial processing 664.805 52
  cooking 641.655 2
  food 641.355 2
  garden crop 635.52
Lëtzebuergesch language T6—32
Lëtzeburgesch language 437.949 35
Leucite
  mineralogy 549.68
Leucocytes 571.96
  see also Leukocytes
Leuk (Switzerland : Bezirk) T2—494 794 8
Leukas (Greece : Regional
  unit) T2—495 5
Leukemia 362.196 994 19
  incidence 614.599 941 9
  medicine 616.994 19
  social services 362.196 994 19
  see also Cancer — humans
Leukocyte count
  human physiology 612.112 7

Leukocyte disorders
  cancer 362.196 994 19
    incidence 614.599 941 9
    medicine 616.994 19
    social services 362.196 994 19
    see also Cancer — humans
  medicine 616.154
    see also Cardiovascular
      diseases — humans
Leukocytes 571.96
  human biochemistry 612.112 1
  human histology 612.112
  human immunology 616.079
  human physiology 612.112
  medicine 616.154
  physiology 571.96
  see also Cardiovascular system
Leukocytosis
  medicine 616.154
    see also Cardiovascular
      diseases — humans
Leukopenia
  medicine 616.154
    see also Cardiovascular
      diseases — humans
Leukorrhea
  gynecology 618.15
    see also Female genital
      diseases — humans
Levant T2—56
Levees (Flood barriers) 627.42
Leveling (Surveying) 526.36
Levels of education 372–374
  see Manual at 371.01–.8 vs.
    372–374, 378; *also at*
    372.24 and 373.23
Leventina (Switzerland) T2—494 781
Lévis (Quebec) T2—714 59
Levitation (Spiritualism) 133.92
Leviticus 222.13
Levy County (Fla.) T2—759 77
Lewes (England : District) T2—422 57
Lewis and Clark County
  (Mont.) T2—786 615
Lewis County (Idaho) T2—796 84
Lewis County (Ky.) T2—769 295
Lewis County (Mo.) T2—778 345
Lewis County (N.Y.) T2—747 59
Lewis County (Tenn.) T2—768 432
Lewis County (W. Va.) T2—754 61
Lewis County (Wash.) T2—797 82
Lewisham (London,
  England) T2—421 63

Lewy body dementia
  medicine   616.833 6
    see also Nervous system
      diseases — humans
Lexical functional grammar   415.018 234
  specific languages   T4—501 823 4
Lexical semantics   401.43
Lexicographers   413.092
Lexicography   413.028
    T1—03
  specific languages   T4—302 8
Lexicology   401.4
  specific languages   T4—014
Lexington (Ky.)   T2—769 47
Lexington (Mass.)   T2—744 4
Lexington (Va.)   T2—755 853
Lexington, Battle of, 1775   973.331 1
Lexington County (S.C.)   T2—757 73
Leyte (Philippines)   T2—599 587
Leyte Island (Philippines)   T2—599 587
Lezghi language   499.964
    T6—999 64
Lezghian language   499.964
    T6—999 64
LGBT identity   306.76
LGBT people   306.76
    T1—086 6
LGBTQ identity   306.76
Lhasa apso   636.72
Lhomi language   495.4
    T6—954
Liability   346.022
  government   342.088
  schools   344.075
Liability for environmental
  damages   344.046
Liability insurance   368.5
  law   346.086 5
  see also Insurance
Liability of states
  law of nations   341.26
Liability risks   368.08
Liaoning Sheng (China)   T2—518 2
Liard River   T2—711 87
Libel   364.156
  law   345.025 6
    criminal law   345.025 6
    torts   346.034
Liberal Catholic Church   284.8
  see also Old Catholic churches
Liberal-Conservative Party
  (Canada)   324.271 04
Liberal Democrats (British
  political party)   324.241 06

Liberal education   370.112
Liberal Forum (Austrian political
  party)   324.243 606
Liberal parties   324.216
  international organizations   324.16
Liberal Party (Great Britain)   324.241 06
Liberal Party of Australia   324.294 05
Liberal Party of Canada   324.271 06
Liberal Party of New York State   324.274 708
Liberal theology   230.046
Liberale Partei der Schweiz   324.249 406
Liberale Parteien (Austrian
  political party)   324.243 602 6
Liberales Forum (Austrian
  political party)   324.243 606
Liberalism
  philosophy   148
  political ideology   320.51
Liberality
  ethics   177.7
Liberation theology   230.046 4
  political aspects   261.7
  Roman Catholic   230.2
  socioeconomic aspects   261.8
Liberecký kraj (Czech
  Republic)   T2—437 17
Liberia   966.62
    T2—666 2
Liberians   T5—966 62
Libertad (El Salvador :
  Dept.)   T2—728 422
Libertad (Peru : Region)   T2—851 6
Libertador General
  Bernardo O'Higgins
  (Chile)   T2—833 2
Libertarian parties   324.218
  international organizations   324.18
Libertarian Party (U.S.)   324.273 8
Libertarianism   320.512
Liberty (Personal freedom)   323.44
  philosophy   123.5
  see also Civil rights
Liberty (Political theory)   320.011
Liberty County (Fla.)   T2—759 923
Liberty County (Ga.)   T2—758 733
Liberty County (Mont.)   T2—786 13
Liberty County (Tex.)   T2—764 155
Libido   155.31
Libode (South Africa :
  District)   T2—687 58
Libra (Zodiac)   133.527 2
Librarians   020.92
  library operations
    role and function   023.2

Libraries	027
accounting	657.832
armed forces	355.346
law	344.092
operations	025
political aspects	021.8
public administrative support	352.744
publications for	
bibliographies	011.67
reviews	028.167
publishing	070.594
relationships	021
residential interior decoration	747.73
Libraries and museums	021.3
Library acquisitions	025.2
Library administration	025.1
Library aides	023.3
Library and state	021.8
Library assistants	023.3
Library boards	021.82
Library bookbinding	686.303 2
Library buildings	
architecture	727.8
area planning	711.57
institutional housekeeping	647.998
lighting	621.322 78
plant management	022.7
planning	022.3
Library catalogs	025.31
library science	025.31
maintenance	025.317
Library clerks	023.3
Library collections	
maintenance	025.8
Library commissions	021.82
Library-community relations	021.2
Library consortia	021.65
Library consultants	023.2
Library cooperation	021.64
Library directors	025.197 009 2
Library equipment	
management	022.9
Library extension	
public libraries	027.42
Library-government relations	021.8
Library information networks	021.65
Library materials	
preservation	025.84
selection policy	025.21
Library networks	021.65
Library of Congress	027.573
Library of Congress Classification	025.433
Library orientation	025.56

Library outreach programs	
public libraries	027.42
Library outreach services	
public libraries	027.42
Library paraprofessionals	023.3
Library policy (Government policy)	021.8
Library programs	025.5
Library regulations	025.56
Library science	020
arts	T3C—39
Library signs	025.56
Library systems	
cooperation	021.65
operations	025
Library systems analysts	023.2
Library technicians	023.3
Library trustees	021.82
Library use studies	025.58
Librettos	780
treatises	780.268
Libreville (Gabon)	T2—672 1
Libya	961.2
	T2—612
ancient	939.74
	T2—397 4
Libyan Desert	T2—612
Libyans	T5—927 612
Lice	595.756
disease carriers	571.986
medicine	614.432 4
Lice infestations	
medicine	616.572
see also Skin diseases — humans	
License agreements	343.07
License fees	
public revenues	336.16
License plates	929.9
Licensed designs	744.7
Licensing	352.84
economic law	343.07
enforcement	363.233
export trade	382.64
see also Export trade	
import trade	382.54
see also Import trade	
intangible property law	346.048
public administration	352.84
Lichees	641.346
see also Litchis	
Lichens	579.7
Lichfield (England : District)	T2—424 68

Lichtenburg (South Africa :
  District)   T2—682 47
Licking County (Ohio)   T2—771 54
Lie algebras   512.482
Lie detectors   363.254
  civil rights   323.448
  criminal investigation   363.254
  law of privacy   342.085 8
  law of self-incrimination   345.056
  personnel management   658.314
    selection procedures   658.311 2
Lie groups   512.482
Liechtenstein   943.648
      T2—436 48
  ancient   936.364 8
      T2—363 648
Lieder   782.421 68
Liège (Belgium : Province)   T2—493 46
Liens
  law   346.074
Liesegang rings   541.348 5
Liestal (Switzerland)   T2—494 335 4
Liestal (Switzerland :
  Bezirk)   T2—494 335
Lieutenant governors
  public administration   352.239
LiF (Austrian political party)   324.243 606
Life
  biological nature   570.1
  civil rights issues   323.43
  medical ethics   179.7
  origin   576.83
    see also Origin of life
  philosophy   113.8
  respect for
    ethics   179.1
    religion   205.691
      Buddhism   294.356 91
      Christianity   241.691
      Hinduism   294.548 691
      Islam   297.569 1
      Judaism   296.369 1
Life after death
  occultism   133.901 3
  philosophy   129
  religion   202.3
    Christianity   236.2
    Islam   297.23
    Judaism   296.33
    philosophy of religion   218
Life care communities   362.61
  see also Health care facilities

Life cycle   571.8
  animal behavior   591.56
  animal physiology   571.81
  animals   591.56
  arts   T3C—354
  customs   392
  developmental biology   571.8
  etiquette   395.2
  folklore   398.274
    history and criticism   398.354
  literature   808.803 54
    history and criticism   809.933 54
    specific literatures   T3B—080 354
      history and
        criticism   T3B—093 54
  microorganisms   571.842 9
  music   781.58
  physiology   571.8
  plants   571.82
Life estates   346.043 2
  land economics   333.323 4
Life expectancy   304.645
  human physiology   612.68
Life insurance   368.32
  law   346.086 32
    tax law   343.052 4
  see also Insurance
Life on other planets   576.839
Life rafts
  aircraft   629.134 43
Life sciences   570
Life sciences and religion   201.657
  Christianity   261.55
  Islam   297.265 7
  philosophy of religion   215.7
Life skills   646.7
  primary education   372.37
Life-support systems
  spacecraft   629.477
Lifeboats   387.29
  design   623.812 9
  engineering   623.829
  transportation services   387.29
  see also Ships
Lifelong education   374
      T1—071 5
  see also Adult education
Lifesaving equipment
  aircraft   629.134 43
  ships   623.865
Liffey, River (Ireland)   T2—418 3
Lift (Aeronautics)   629.132 33
Lift systems
  air-cushion vehicles   629.313

Lighting (continued)
museums	069.29
photography	778.7
plant management	658.24
public areas	628.95
religious significance	203.7
Christianity	246.6

see also Symbolism —
  religious significance

road transportation	388.312
videography	777.52
Lighting fixtures	621.32
ceramic arts	738.8
church architecture	726.529 8
furniture arts	749.63
household management	645.5
manufacturing technology	683.83

see also Lighting

Lightning	551.563 2
crop damage	632.15
Lightning arresters	621.317
Lightning protection	
buildings	693.898
Lightships	387.155
engineering	623.894 3
transportation services	387.155
Lignin	
recovery from pulp	676.5
Lignin-derived plastics	668.45
Lignite	553.22
economic geology	553.22
mining	622.332
properties	662.622 2
Lignum vitaes	583.62
Liguria (Italy)	945.18
	T2—451 8
ancient	T2—371
Ligurian language	491.993
	T6—919 93
Ligurian Republic	945.180 82
Ligurian Riviera (Italy)	T2—451 8
Ligurian Sea	551.461 382
	T2—163 82
Lihou (Channel Islands)	T2—423 49
Lihoumel (Channel Islands)	T2—423 49
Lij Yasu, Negus of Ethiopia	
Ethiopian history	963.053
Lilacs	635.933 963
botany	583.963
floriculture	635.933 963
L'Île-d'Orléans (Quebec)	T2—714 476
L'Île-Dorval (Quebec)	T2—714 28

Liliaceae	584.69
botany	584.69
floriculture	635.934 69
Liliales	584.6
Lilies	584.3
floriculture	635.934 69
Liliopsida	584

see Manual at 583–584

Lille (France)	T2—442 84
Lille Baelt (Denmark)	551.461 334
	T2—163 34
Lillooet (B.C.)	T2—711 31
Lillooet Lake (B.C.)	T2—711 31
Lillooet River (B.C.)	T2—711 3
Lilongwe (Malawi)	T2—689 7
Lily of the valley	635.934 79
botany	584.79
floriculture	635.934 79
Lima (Peru)	T2—852 55
Lima (Peru : Dept.)	T2—852 5
Lima (Peru : Province)	T2—852 55
Lima (Peru : Region)	T2—852 52
Lima beans	641.356 53
botany	583.63
commercial processing	664.805 653
cooking	641.656 53
field crop	633.37
food	641.356 53
garden crop	635.653
Limarí (Chile : Province)	T2—832 35
Limavady (Northern	
Ireland : District)	T2—416 14
Limbo	236.4
Limbu language	495.49
	T6—954 9
Limburg (Belgium :	
Province)	T2—493 24
Limburg (Netherlands)	T2—492 48
Limburger cheese	641.373 53
cooking	641.673 53
food	641.373 53
processing	637.353
Lime	553.68
economic geology	553.68
use as soil conditioner	631.821
Lime mortars	666.93
Lime trees (Malvaceae)	583.775
Limeaceae	583.88
Limerick (Ireland)	T2—419 45
Limerick (Ireland : County)	T2—419 4
Limericks	808.817 5
history and criticism	809.175
specific literatures	T3B—107 5
individual authors	T3A—1

Limes (Fruit)	641.343 37	Lincoln (Ont. : County)	T2—713 38
commercial processing	664.804 337	Lincoln, Abraham	
cooking	641.643 37	United States history	973.7
food	641.343 37	Lincoln County (Ark.)	T2—767 823
orchard crop	634.337	Lincoln County (Colo.)	T2—788 89
Limes (Lindens)		Lincoln County (Ga.)	T2—758 165
botany	583.68	Lincoln County (Idaho)	T2—796 34
forestry	634.972 77	Lincoln County (Kan.)	T2—781 532
Limes (Malvaceae)		Lincoln County (Ky.)	T2—769 625
botany	583.775	Lincoln County (Me.)	T2—741 57
forestry	634.972 77	Lincoln County (Minn.)	T2—776 365
Limestone	553.516	Lincoln County (Miss.)	T2—762 534
building material	691.2	Lincoln County (Mo.)	T2—778 37
economic geology	553.516	Lincoln County (Mont.)	T2—786 81
petrology	552.58	Lincoln County (N.C.)	T2—756 782
quarrying	622.351 6	Lincoln County (N.M.)	T2—789 64
Limestone County (Ala.)	T2—761 98	Lincoln County (Neb.)	T2—782 82
Limestone County (Tex.)	T2—764 285	Lincoln County (Nev.)	T2—793 14
Liming leather	675.22	Lincoln County (Okla.)	T2—766 35
Limit	515.222	Lincoln County (Or.)	T2—795 33
Limitation of actions	347.052	Lincoln County (S.D.)	T2—783 391
Limitation of rights	323.49	Lincoln County (Tenn.)	T2—768 624
Limited companies	338.74	Lincoln County (W. Va.)	T2—754 43
law	346.066 8	Lincoln County (Wash.)	T2—797 35
see also Corporations		Lincoln County (Wis.)	T2—775 27
Limited editions	094.4	Lincoln County (Wyo.)	T2—787 82
publishing	070.573	Lincoln Heath (England)	T2—425 3
Limited government	320.512	Lincoln National Park (S.	
Limited monarchies	321.87	Aust.)	T2—942 38
Limited war	355.021 5	Lincoln Parish (La.)	T2—763 91
Limnology	551.48	Lincoln Sea	551.461 327
biology	577.6		T2—163 27
Limoges (France)	T2—446 624	Lincoln Wolds (England)	T2—425 32
Limón (Costa Rica :		Lincolnshire (England)	T2—425 3
Province)	T2—728 61	Lindens	
Limousin (France)	T2—446 6	botany	583.775
Limousine services	388.321	forestry	634.972 7
urban	388.413 214	Lindi Region (Tanzania)	T2—678 24
Limousines	388.342 32	Lindley (South Africa :	
driving	629.283 32	District)	T2—685 1
engineering	629.222 32	Lindsey (England : County)	T2—425 31
repair	629.287 232	Line and staff organization	658.402
transportation services	388.342 32	armed forces	355.330 4
see also Automobiles		public administration	352.283
Limpets	594.32	Line cuts	
Limpopo (South Africa)	968.25	printing	686.232 7
	T2—682 5	Line dancing	793.36
Limpopo River	T2—679 2	Line engraving	765.2
Mozambique	T2—679 2	Line geometry	516.183
South Africa	T2—682 5	Line integrals	515.43
Linaceae	583.69	Line Islands	996.4
Linares (Chile : Province)	T2—833 7		T2—964
Lincoln (England)	T2—425 34	Line-outs	796.333 23
Lincoln (Neb.)	T2—782 293		

Line play	
American football	796.332 23
Linear A	492.6
	T6—926
see Manual at T6—926	
Linear accelerators	539.733
Linear algebra	512.5
Linear B	487.1
	T6—87
Linear closed-loop systems	
automation engineering	629.832
Linear differential equations	515.354
Linear equations	515.252
Linear logic	511.31
Linear operators	515.724 6
Linear programming	519.72
Linear systems	003.74
Linear topological spaces	515.73
Linen textiles	677.11
see also Textiles	
Lines (Electrical)	621.319 2
Lines (Mathematics)	516.152
Lineups (Criminal investigation)	363.258
Lingala language	496.396 86
	T6—963 968 6
Lingala literature	896.396 86
Lingayats	294.551 3
Lingerie	391.423 082
commercial technology	687.22
customs	391.423 082
home economics	646.34
home sewing	646.420 4
Lingga Islands (Indonesia)	T2—598 192
Lingua francas	401.3
Linguatula	592.76
Linguistic analysis	
philosophy	149.94
Linguistic change	417.7
specific languages	T4—7
Linguistic disorders	
medicine	616.855
see also Communication	
disorders	
special education	371.914
Linguistic groups	
sociology	305.7
Linguistic philosophies	149.94
Linguistics	410
computer applications	410.285
see Manual at 006.35 vs.	
410.285	
see Manual at 410	

Linguists	
language specialists	
specific languages	T4—092
linguistics specialists	410.92
specific languages	T4—092
philologists	409.2
specific languages	T4—092
Linhares, José Finol	
Brazilian history	981.061
Linin network	571.66
Linkage editors	005.43
Linked data	025.042 7
Linkers (Computer software)	005.43
Links (Mathematics)	514.224
Linlithgow, Victor Alexander	
John Hope, Marquess of	
Indian history	954.035 9
Linn County (Iowa)	T2—777 62
Linn County (Kan.)	T2—781 69
Linn County (Mo.)	T2—778 24
Linn County (Or.)	T2—795 35
Linoleum	645.1
building construction	698.9
household management	645.1
Linoleum-block printing	761.3
Linotype	
manufacturing technology	681.61
Linotype composition	
automatic	686.225 44
manual	686.225 42
Linsangs	599.742
Linseed oil	665.352
Linters	
plastic technology	668.411
Linz (Austria)	T2—436 24
Lion	599.757
big game hunting	799.277 57
conservation technology	639.979 757
resource economics	333.959 757
Lions, Gulf of (France)	551.461 382
	T2—163 82
Lions Bay (B.C.)	T2—711 33
Lions International	369.5
Lions River (South Africa :	
District)	T2—684 7
Lip diseases	
medicine	616.31
Lip-reed instruments	788.9
see also Brass instruments	
Lipari Islands (Italy)	T2—458 11
Lipases	572.757
see also Enzymes	
Lipectomy	617.952
Lipetsk (Russia : Oblast)	T2—473 5

Listening (continued)
child care	649.58
music training method	781.424
primary education	372.69
psychology	
communication	153.68
perception	153.733
recreation	790.138
social interaction	302.224 2
Listeria	579.37
Lists	T1—021 6
Litanies	264.13
music	782.292
Roman Catholic	264.027 4
Litchfield County (Conn.)	T2—746 1
Litchis	641.346
botany	583.75
cooking	641.646
food	641.346
orchard crop	634.6
Literacy	302.224 4
adult education	374.012 4
educational policy	379.24
linguistics	418.4
	T4—84
primary education	372.6
sociology	302.224 4
training	
personnel management	658.312 44
see also Illiteracy	
Literacy programs	379.24
adult education	374.012 4
Literary agents	
publishing	070.52
Literary criticism	809
sacred books	208.2
Bible	220.66
Talmud	296.120 66
specific literatures	T3B—09
see Manual at T3B—08 and T3B—09	
theory	801.95
see Manual at 800	
Literary forgeries	098.3
Literary forms	808.81–.88
criticism	809.1–.7
theory	808.1–.7
see Manual at 808.81–.88 and 809.1–.7	
history	809.1–.7
see Manual at 808.81–.88 and 809.1–.7	
rhetoric	808.1–.7
children's literature	808.068 1–.068 7

Literary forms (continued)
specific literatures	T3B—1–8
individual authors	T3A—1–8
translating	418.041–.048
specific languages	T4—804 1–804 8
see Manual at 800; *also at* 808.81–.88 and 809.1–.7	
Literary genres	808.81–.88
sacred books	208.2
Bible	220.66
Talmud	296.120 66
specific literatures	T3B—1–8
see Manual at T3B—102–107, T3B—205, T3B—308 vs. T3C—1, T3C—3	
see also Literary forms	
Literary hoaxes	098.3
Literary movements	808.801
history and criticism	809.91
specific literatures	T3B—080 1
history and criticism	T3B—091
Literary style	800
criticism	809
specific literatures	T3B—09
rhetoric	808
Literary themes	
arts	700.457
	T3C—357
folklore	398.277
history and criticism	398.357
literature	808.803 57
history and criticism	809.933 57
specific literatures	T3B—080 357
history and criticism	T3B—093 57
Literature	800
geographic treatment	T3C—93–99
see Manual at T3C—93–99; *also at* T3C—93–99, T3C—9174 vs. T3C—8	
history and criticism	809
specific literatures	T3B—09
influence on crime	364.254
primary education	372.64
translating	418.04
specific languages	T4—804
see also Arts	
see Manual at 741.6 vs. 800; *also at* 800; *also at* 800 vs. 398.2	

Literature (Black authors, African origin)	808.898 96
history and criticism	809.889 6
specific literatures	T3B—080 896
history and criticism	T3B—098 96
Literature and religion	201.68
Christianity	261.58
Islam	297.268
Judaism	296.378
Lithgow (N.S.W.)	T2—944 5
Lithium	669.725
chemical engineering	661.038 1
chemistry	546.381
economic geology	553.499
metallurgy	669.725
physical metallurgy	669.967 25
see also Chemicals	
Lithography	686.231 5
graphic arts	763
Lithology	552
Lithops	583.883
Lithosphere	551
Lithuania	947.93
	T2—479 3
Lithuanian language	491.92
	T6—919 2
Lithuanian literature	891.92
Lithuanians	T5—919 2
Litopterna	569.62
Little Barrier Island (N.Z.)	T2—932 4
Little Belt (Denmark)	551.461 334
	T2—163 34
Little Big Horn, Battle of the, 1876	973.82
Little brown bats	599.472
Little Church of France	284.8
Little Colorado River (N.M. and Ariz.)	T2—791 33
Little Kanawha River (W. Va.)	T2—754 2
Little Karoo (South Africa)	T2—687 37
Little league (Baseball)	796.357 62
Little River County (Ark.)	T2—767 55
Little Rock (Ark.)	T2—767 73
Little Sisters of the Poor	255.95
church history	271.95
Little theater	792.022 3
Liturgical dance	246.7
Liturgical drama	
music	782.298
choral and mixed voices	782.529 8
single voices	783.092 98

Liturgical music	782.29
instrumental forms	784.189 93
vocal forms	782.29
choral and mixed voices	782.529
single voices	783.092 9
Liturgical objects	203.7
Christianity	247
Judaism	296.461
Liturgical renewal	264.001
Liturgical year	263.9
devotional literature	242.3
sermons	252.6
Liturgy	203.8
Liturgy of the hours	264.15
Anglican	264.030 15
Roman Catholic	264.020 15
texts	264.024
Live-bearers	597.667
culture	639.376 67
Live-forevers (Plants)	583.44
Live Oak County (Tex.)	T2—764 447
Liver	573.38
biology	573.38
human anatomy	611.36
human physiology	612.352
medicine	616.362
surgery	617.556 2
see also Digestive system	
Liver diseases	
medicine	616.362
see also Digestive system diseases — humans	
Liverpool (England)	T2—427 53
Liverworts	588.3
Livestock	636
Livestock exhibition	636.081 1
Livestock feeding	636.084
Livestock feeds	636.085 5
see also Feeds	
Livestock judging	636.081 1
Livestock liability insurance	368.56
see also Insurance	
Livestock workers	636.009 2
Living Bible	220.520 83
Living chess	794.17
Living conditions	
armed forces	355.12
Living fossils	576.8
Living rooms	643.54
home economics	643.54
interior decoration	747.75
Living standard	
macroeconomics	339.47
Living stones	583.883

Living together	306.841
	T1—086 56
law	346.016 71
Livingston County (Ill.)	T2—773 61
Livingston County (Ky.)	T2—769 895
Livingston County (Mich.)	T2—774 36
Livingston County (Mo.)	T2—778 223
Livingston County (N.Y.)	T2—747 85
Livingston Parish (La.)	T2—763 14
Livonia	T2—479 8
Livonian language	494.54
	T6—945 4
Livonian literature	894.54
Livonian War, 1557–1582	947.043
Livonians	T5—945 4
Livorno (Italy : Province)	945.56
	T2—455 6
ancient	T2—375 62
Lizard fishes	597.61
Lizards	597.95
resource economics	333.957 94
Lizards as pets	639.395
Lizard's-tail (Plant)	584.284
Llama wool textiles	677.32
see also Textiles	
Llamas	636.296 6
Llandrindod Wells (Wales)	T2—429 51
Llanelli (Wales : Borough)	T2—429 65
Llangollen (Wales)	T2—429 37
Llano County (Tex.)	T2—764 62
Llano Estacado	T2—764 8
New Mexico	T2—789 3
Texas	T2—764 8
Llanquihue (Chile : Province)	T2—835 4
Llantrisant (Wales)	T2—429 78
Llanwrtyd Wells (Wales)	T2—429 56
Lliw Valley (Wales)	T2—429 82
Lloydminster (Sask. and Alta.)	T2—712 42
Lloyds of London	368.012 060 421 2
Loa (Chile)	T2—831 35
Loaches	597.48
Loaders (Computer software)	005.43
Loading equipment	
port engineering	627.34
ships	623.867
Loading operations	
materials management	658.788 5
ships	623.888 1
Loads	
bridge engineering	624.252
structural analysis	624.172
Loan brokers	332.3

Loan collections	
museology	069.56
Loan guarantees	
public administration	352.736
Loan services	
library science	025.6
museology	069.13
Loan words	412
specific languages	T4—24
Loans	332.7
capital management	658.152 24
economics	332.7
banking services	332.175 3
central banking	332.113
law	346.073
economic assistance	343.074 2
public administrative support	352.736
public revenues	336.15
administration	352.45
Loasaceae	583.92
Lobachevski geometry	516.9
Lobbying	324.4
law	342.05
legislative bodies	328.38
public relations	659.293 244
Lobi (African people)	T5—963 5
Lobi language	496.35
	T6—963 5
Lobo Sosa, Porfirio	
Honduran history	972.830 541
Lobster culture	639.64
Lobster fishing	639.54
Lobsters	641.395
commercial fishing	
economics	338.372 538 4
conservation technology	639.975 384
cooking	641.695
culture	639.64
fishing	639.54
food	641.395
commercial processing	664.94
resource economics	333.955 54
zoology	595.384
Local anesthesia	
surgery	617.966
Local-area networks	004.68
see also Computer communications	
Local bibliographies	015
Local Christian church	250
missions	266.022
specific denominations	280
see Manual at 260 vs. 250	

Locris (Greece)	T2—495 15
ancient	T2—383
Loculoascomycetes	579.564
Locusts (Animals)	595.726
agricultural pests	632.726
Locusts (Plants)	583.63
botany	583.63
forestry	634.973 63
Lodes	553.19
Lodges (Resort hotels)	910.462
see also Resorts	
Lodging (Temporary housing)	910.46
accounting	657.837
architecture	728
area planning	711.557
household management	647.94
landscape architecture	712.7
management	647.940 68
sanitation services	363.729 8
law	344.046 4
see also Sanitation	
travel	910.46
Lodi (Italy : Province)	T2—452 19
ancient	T2—372 28
Lodi dynasty	954.024 5
Łódź (Poland : Voivodeship)	T2—438 47
Łódź Ghetto	940.531 853 847
Lofoten (Norway)	T2—484 4
Lofoten Islands (Norway)	T2—484 4
Lofting	
ship hulls	623.842
Logan County (Ark.)	T2—767 37
Logan County (Colo.)	T2—788 75
Logan County (Ill.)	T2—773 57
Logan County (Kan.)	T2—781 135
Logan County (Ky.)	T2—769 76
Logan County (N.D.)	T2—784 56
Logan County (Neb.)	T2—782 795
Logan County (Ohio)	T2—771 463
Logan County (Okla.)	T2—766 33
Logan County (W. Va.)	T2—754 44
Loganberries	641.347 14
cooking	641.647 14
food	641.347 14
horticulture	634.714
Loganiaceae	583.956
Logarithms	512.922
algebra	512.922
arithmetic	513.22
Logbooks	
aeronautics	629.132 54
Loggers	634.980 92
Logging	634.98
Logic (Reasoning)	160
Logic circuits	621.395
Logic databases	
computer science	005.740 151 13
Logic design	
computer circuits	621.395
Logic operators	511.3
mathematical logic	511.3
philosophical logic	160
Logic programming	005.115
artificial intelligence	006.332
Logical atomism	146.5
Logical positivism	146.42
Logistics	
management	658.5
military operations	355.411
Logooli language	496.395
	T6—963 95
Logos (Christianity)	232.2
Logos (Design)	744.63
Logotypes	744.63
Logroño (Spain)	T2—463 54
Loir-et-Cher (France)	T2—445 3
Loire (France : Dept.)	T2—445 81
Loire-Atlantique (France)	T2—441 67
Loire River (France)	944.5
	T2—445
Loiret (France)	T2—445 2
Loja (Ecuador : Province)	T2—866 25
Lokāyata	181.46
Lolland (Denmark)	T2—489 3
Lollards	284.3
Lolo languages	495.4
	T6—954
Loloish languages	495.4
	T6—954
Lomandroideae	584.79
Lombardia (Italy)	945.2
	T2—452
ancient	T2—372 2
Lombards	
Italian history	945.01
Southern Italian history	945.701
Lombardy (Italy)	945.2
	T2—452
ancient	T2—372 2
Lombok (Indonesia)	T2—598 65
Lomé (Togo)	T2—668 1
Lomond, Loch (Scotland)	T2—414 2
Łomża (Poland : Voivodeship)	T2—438 36
London (England)	942.1
	T2—421
London (Ont.)	T2—713 26

Lories (Parrots)	598.71	Lotto	795.38
animal husbandry	636.686 5	Lotuses	635.933 38
Lorises	599.83	botany	583.38
Lorisidae	599.83	floriculture	635.933 38
Lorraine (France)	T2—443 8	Lotuxo-Teso languages	496.552 2
Lorraine, House of			T6—965 522
Tuscan history	945.507	Loudness	
1737–1801	945.507	acoustical engineering	620.21
1814–1860	945.508 3	Loudon County (Tenn.)	T2—768 863
Lorries	388.344	Loudoun County (Va.)	T2—755 28
engineering	629.224	Louga (Senegal : Region)	T2—663
see also Trucks		Lough Neagh (Northern	
Los Alamos County (N.M.)	978.958	Ireland)	T2—416
	T2—789 58	Louis VI, King of France	
Los Andes (Chile :		French history	944.022
Province)	T2—832 42	Louis VII, King of France	
Los Angeles (Calif.)	979.494	French history	944.022
	T2—794 94	Louis VIII, King of France	
Los Angeles County (Calif.)	979.493	French history	944.023
	T2—794 93	Louis IX, King of France	
Los Lagos (Chile : Region)	T2—835	French history	944.023
Los Picahos National Park		Louis X, King of France	
(Colombia)	T2—861 94	French history	944.024
Los Ríos (Ecuador)	T2—866 33	Louis XI, King of France	
Los Santos (Panama :		French history	944.027
Province)	T2—728 723	Louis XII, King of France	
Losengo language	496.396 86	French history	944.027
	T6—963 968 6	Louis XIII, King of France	
Losengo literature	896.396 86	French history	944.032
Loss (Financial management)	658.155	Louis XIV, King of France	
Loss (Psychology)	155.93	French history	944.033
Loss of citizenship	323.6	Louis XV, King of France	
penology	364.68	French history	944.034
Loss of territory	320.12	Louis XVI, King of France	
Loss of vote	324.62	French history	944.035
penology	364.68	1774–1789	944.035
Lost-wax casting		1789–1792	944.041
metals	671.255	Louis XVIII, King of France	
sculpture	731.456	French history	944.061
Lot (France)	T2—447 33	1814–1815	944.05
Lot-et-Garonne (France)	T2—447 18	1815–1824	944.061
Lotbinière (Quebec :		Louis Philippe, King of the	
Regional County		French	
Municipality)	T2—714 58	French history	944.063
Lothair II, Holy Roman Emperor		Louisa County (Iowa)	T2—777 926
German history	943.023	Louisa County (Va.)	T2—755 465
Lothian (Scotland)	T2—413 3	Louisbourg (N.S.)	T2—716 955
Lotteries	795.38	Louisiana	976.3
advertising	659.197 953 8		T2—763
occupational ethics	174.6	Louisiana French Creole	447.976 3
use in advertising	659.17		T6—417
Lottery income		Louisville (Ky.)	T2—769 44
public administration	352.44		
public finance	336.17		

Low-income people 305.569
                           T1—086 24
    see also Poor people
Low power television stations 384.55
Low-protein cooking 641.563 8
Low-protein diet
    health 613.282
Low-salt cooking 641.563 23
Low-salt diet
    health 613.285 223
Low-sodium cooking 641.563 23
Low-sodium diet
    health 613.285 223
Low-temperature biology
    humans 612.014 465
Low-temperature technology 621.56
Low temperatures 536.56
    biophysics 571.464
    chemical engineering 660.296 86
    chemistry 541.368 6
    effect on materials 620.112 16
    physics 536.56
Low veld (South Africa) T2—682 59
Low voice 783.5
Lowell (Mass.) T2—744 4
Lower Arrow Lake (B.C.) T2—711 62
Lower Austria (Austria) T2—436 12
Lower Avon River
    (England) T2—423 9
Lower Bavaria (Germany) T2—433 5
Lower California (Mexico) T2—722
Lower Canada 971.03
    Quebec 971.402
Lower chambers (Legislative
    bodies) 328.32
Lower classes 305.56
                         T1—086 24
    social welfare 362.892
Lower criticism
    Bible 220.404 6
Lower Egypt T2—621
    ancient T2—321
Lower extremities 612.98
    anatomy 611.98
    bones 612.751
        anatomy 611.718
        medicine 616.71
        physiology 612.751
        surgery 617.471
    fractures
        medicine 617.158
    joints
        medicine 616.72
        surgery 617.580 59

Lower extremities (continued)
    muscles
        anatomy 611.738
        physiology 612.98
        regional medicine 617.58
        surgery 617.580 59
Lower Franconia (Germany) T2—433 3
Lower Guinea 967.1
                         T2—671
Lower houses (Legislative
    bodies) 328.32
Lower Hutt City (N.Z.) T2—936 4
Lower legs
    regional medicine 617.584
    surgery 617.584
Lower Lusatia (Germany) T2—431 51
Lower Mamberamo languages 499.1
                         T6—991
Lower Mesopotamia T2—567 5
    ancient 935.5
                         T2—355
Lower middle class 305.55
                         T1—086 23
Lower Paleolithic Age 930.124
Lower Peninsula (Mich.) T2—774
Lower primary grades 372.241
    see also Primary education
Lower Saxony (Germany) T2—435 9
Lower Tugela (South
    Africa : District) T2—684 47
Lower Umfolozi (South
    Africa : District) T2—684 43
Lowland game birds 598.41
    conservation technology 639.978 41
    resource economics 333.958 41
    sports hunting 799.244
Lowlands (Scotland) T2—413
Lowndes County (Ala.) T2—761 465
Lowndes County (Ga.) T2—758 864
Lowndes County (Miss.) T2—762 973
Lowveld (South Africa) T2—682 59
Loxodonta 599.674
Loxton (S. Aust.) T2—942 33
Loyalty Islands (New
    Caledonia) T2—959 7
Loyalty oaths 323.65
    law 342.068 4
    obligation of citizens 323.65
    public personnel management 352.65
Loyalty of citizens 323.65
Lozère (France : Dept.) T2—448 1
Lozi (African people) T5—963 99
Lozi language 496.399
                         T6—963 99

Lullabies	781.582
folk literature	398.8
music	781.582
songs	782.421 582
Lumbee Indians	T5—973
Lumbee language	497.3
	T6—973
Lumber	674
economics	338.476 74
law	343.078 674
Lumber industry workers	674.092
Lumbering	634.98
Lumbermen	634.980 92
Lumberyards	674.32
Lumbini Pradesh (Nepal)	T2—549 65
Lumbriculida	592.64
Luminescence	535.35
materials science	620.112 95
mineralogy	549.125
Luminescence spectroscopy	543.56
Luminism	709.034 4
painting	759.054
Luminous paints	667.69
Luminous-tube lighting	621.327
see also Lighting	
Lumped-parameter systems	003.7
Lumpkin County (Ga.)	T2—758 273
Luna County (N.M.)	T2—789 68
Lunar flights	629.454
manned	629.454
unmanned	629.435 3
Lunch periods	
labor economics	331.257 6
personnel management	658.312 2
Lunchbox cooking	641.53
Luncheons	642
cooking	641.53
light meals	641.53
main meals	641.54
customs	394.125 3
light meals	394.125 3
main meals	394.125 4
Lunches	642
cooking	641.53
light meals	641.53
main meals	641.54
customs	394.125 3
light meals	394.125 3
main meals	394.125 4
Lunchrooms	647.95
see also Eating places	
Lunda (Kingdom)	967.340 1
	T2—673 4
Lunda languages	496.393
	T6—963 93
Lunda Norte (Angola)	T2—673 4
Lunda Sul (Angola)	T2—673 4
Lundu-Balong languages	496.396
	T6—963 96
Lüneburg (Germany : Regierungsbezirk)	T2—435 93
Lunenburg (N.S. : County)	971.623
	T2—716 23
Lunenburg County (Va.)	T2—755 643
Lung cancer	
incidence	614.599 942 4
medicine	616.994 24
see also Cancer — humans	
Lung diseases	
medicine	616.24
see also Respiratory tract diseases — humans	
Lungfishes	597.39
Lungless salamanders	597.859
Lungs	573.25
biology	573.25
human anatomy	611.24
human physiology	612.24
medicine	616.24
surgery	617.542
see also Respiratory system	
Lungu language	496.394
	T6—963 94
Luo (Kenyan and Tanzanian people)	T5—965 584 2
Luo language (Kenya and Tanzania)	496.558 42
	T6—965 584 2
Luo languages	496.558 4
	T6—965 584
Luo literature (Kenya and Tanzania)	896.558 42
Luorawetlin languages	494.6
	T6—946
Lupines	583.63
botany	583.63
field crop	633.367
floriculture	635.933 63
Lupus erythematosus	
medicine	616.772
see also Musculoskeletal diseases — humans	
Luristān (Iran)	T2—556 2
Lusaka (Zambia)	T2—689 4
Lusaka Province (Zambia)	T2—689 4
Lusatia (Germany)	T2—431 51

Lygeum	584.926
Lyginopteridaceae	561.595
Lying	
ethics	177.3
Lyman County (S.D.)	T2—783 58
Lyme disease	
incidence	614.574 6
medicine	616.924 6
see also Communicable	
diseases — humans	
Lymexyloidea	595.763
Lymph	573.16
biology	573.16
human histology	612.420 45
human physiology	612.42
Lymphatic diseases	573.163 9
animals	573.163 9
humans	362.196 42
cancer	362.196 994 42
glands	
incidence	614.599 944 6
medicine	616.994 46
incidence	614.599 944 2
medicine	616.994 42
social services	362.196 994 42
see also Cancer —	
humans	
geriatrics	618.976 42
incidence	614.594 2
medicine	616.42
pediatrics	618.924 2
pharmacokinetics	615.74
social services	362.196 42
surgery	617.44
Lymphatic glands	
human anatomy	611.46
human physiology	612.42
medicine	616.42
Lymphatic system	573.16
biology	573.16
diseases	573.163 9
see also Lymphatic diseases	
human anatomy	611.42
glands	611.46
human histology	612.420 45
human physiology	612.42
medicine	616.42
surgery	617.44
Lymphocytes	571.96
human cytology	612.420 46
human immunology	616.079

Lymphogranuloma venereum	
incidence	614.547
medicine	616.951 8
see also Communicable	
diseases — humans	
Lymphoid tissue	
human histology	612.420 45
Lymphokines	
human immunology	616.079
Lymphomas	
incidence	614.599 944 6
medicine	616.994 46
see also Cancer — humans	
Lynchburg (Va.)	T2—755 671
Lynching	364.134
law	345.023 4
Lynn County (Tex.)	T2—764 851
Lynx	599.753
conservation technology	639.979 753
resource economics	333.959 753
Lyon (France)	T2—445 823
Lyon County (Iowa)	T2—777 114
Lyon County (Kan.)	T2—781 62
Lyon County (Ky.)	T2—769 813
Lyon County (Minn.)	T2—776 363
Lyon County (Nev.)	T2—793 58
Lyonnais (France)	T2—445 82
Lyons, J. A. (Joseph Aloysius)	
Australian history	994.042
Lyrebirds	598.822
Lyres	787.78
instrument	787.781 9
music	787.78
see also Stringed instruments	
Lyric poetry	808.814
history and criticism	809.14
specific literatures	T3B—104
individual authors	T3A—1
Lyrics	780
treatises	780.268
Lysergic acid diethylamide abuse	362.294
medicine	616.863 4
personal health	613.83
social welfare	362.294
see also Substance abuse	
Lysosomes	571.655
Lyssavirus	579.256 6
Lythraceae	583.73
Lytton (B.C.)	T2—711 72
Lytton, Edward Robert Bulwer	
Lytton, Earl of	
Indian history	954.035 3
Lzhedmitriĭ I, Czar of Russia	
Russian history	947.045

Machine-readable catalog records			Mackinac, Straits of (Mich.)	T2—774 923
format	025.316		Mackinac County (Mich.)	T2—774 923
maintenance	025.317		Maclear (South Africa :	
retrospective conversion	025.317 3		District)	T2—687 57
Machine-Readable Cataloging			Macleay River (N.S.W.)	T2—944 3
format	025.316		Macomb County (Mich.)	T2—774 39
Machine-readable data			Macon (Ga.)	T2—758 552
representation	005.72		Macon County (Ala.)	T2—761 49
Machine-readable materials	302.231		Macon County (Ga.)	T2—758 513
see also Electronic resources			Macon County (Ill.)	T2—773 582
Machine sewing			Macon County (Mo.)	T2—778 27
home economics	646.204 4		Macon County (N.C.)	T2—756 982
Machine sheds			Macon County (Tenn.)	T2—768 484
agricultural use	631.25		Macoupin County (Ill.)	T2—773 83
Machine-shop practice	670.423		Macpherson, John, Sir	
agriculture	631.304		Indian history	954.031 1
Machine shorthand	653.3		Macquarie perch	597.73
Machine theory			Macramé	746.422 2
computer engineering	621.39		Macri, Mauricio	
computer science	004		Argentine history	982.074
mathematics	511.35		Macro-Gê languages	498.4
Machine tools	621.902			T6—984
Machine translating			Macro processors	005.45
linguistics	418.020 285 635		Macrobiotic diet	
specific languages	T4—802 028 563 5		health	613.264
Machinery	621.8		Macrocystis	579.887
Machinery insurance	368.7		Macroeconomic policy	339.5
see also Insurance			Macroeconomics	339
Machines in industry	338.06		*see Manual at* 332, 336 vs. 339	
Machining metals	671.35		Macrofungi	579.6
decorative arts	739.14		Macroinstructions	
sculpture	731.41		computer software	005.3
Machmeters	629.135 2		programming	005.13
Machynlleth (Wales)	T2—429 51		programs	005.3
Macías Nguema, Francisco			Macromolecules	572
Equatorial Guinean history	967.180 31		biochemistry	572
Mackay (Qld.)	T2—943 6		chemistry	547.7
Mackenzie (B.C.)	T2—711 82		Macrophages	571.968 5
Mackenzie (N.W.T. and			human immunology	616.079 95
Nunavut)	T2—719 3		Macropodidae	599.22
Mackenzie, Alexander			Macropus	599.222
Canadian history	971.052		Macroscelidea	599.337
MacKenzie District (N.Z.)	T2—938 8		paleozoology	569.337
Mackenzie King Island			Macrotonality	781.265
(N.W.T. and Nunavut)	T2—719 3		Macrouridae	597.63
Mackenzie Mountains			Macrura	595.384
(N.W.T. and Yukon)	T2—719 3		Macruronidae	597.632
Mackenzie River (N.W.T.)	T2—719 3		Ma'dabā (Jordan : Province)	T2—569 562
Mackerel	641.392		Madagascar	969.1
cooking	641.692			T2—691
fishing	639.277 82		Madang Province (Papua	
food	641.392		New Guinea)	T2—957 3
zoology	597.782		Madawaska (N.B. : County)	T2—715 54
Mackerel sharks	597.33		Madders	583.956

Made-for-television movies 791.43
  see Manual at 791.43 vs.
    791.45
Madeira Islands T2—469 8
Madeira vine 583.883
Madeleine, Îles-de-la-
  (Quebec) T2—714 797
Madera County (Calif.) T2—794 81
Madhvāchārya (Philosophy) 181.484 1
Madhya Pradesh (India) T2—543
Madhyamika Buddhism 294.392
Madikwe (South Africa :
  District) T2—682 41
Madison (Wis.) T2—775 83
Madison, James
  United States history 973.51
Madison County (Ala.) T2—761 97
Madison County (Ark.) T2—767 15
Madison County (Fla.) T2—759 85
Madison County (Ga.) T2—758 152
Madison County (Idaho) T2—796 55
Madison County (Ill.) T2—773 86
Madison County (Ind.) T2—772 57
Madison County (Iowa) T2—777 81
Madison County (Ky.) T2—769 53
Madison County (Miss.) T2—762 623
Madison County (Mo.) T2—778 91
Madison County (Mont.) T2—786 663
Madison County (N.C.) T2—756 875
Madison County (N.Y.) T2—747 64
Madison County (Neb.) T2—782 54
Madison County (Ohio) T2—771 55
Madison County (Tenn.) T2—768 27
Madison County (Tex.) T2—764 237
Madison County (Va.) T2—755 38
Madison Parish (La.) T2—763 81
Mádl, Ferenc
  Hungarian history 943.905 42
Madness 362.2
  individual interactions 302.542
Madonna and Child
  art representation 704.948 55
  arts T3C—382 329 2
Madras (India : State) T2—548 2
Madre de Dios (Peru :
  Region) T2—854 2
Madrid (Spain : Province) T2—464 1
Madrid Hurtado, Miguel de la
  Mexican history 972.083 4
Madrigals 782.43
  choral and mixed voices 782.543
  single voices 783.094 3
Madriz (Nicaragua) T2—728 523
Madtoms 597.492

Madura (Indonesia) T2—598 28
Madura language 499.223 4
  T6—992 234
Madura literature 899.223 4
Madurese T5—992 234
Madurese language 499.223 4
  T6—992 234
Madurese literature 899.223 4
Maduro, Nicolás
  Venezuelan history 987.064 3
Maduro, Ricardo
  Honduran history 972.830 537
Mafia 364.106
Mafraq (Jordan : Province) T2—569 597
  ancient T2—335 97
Magadan (Russia : Oblast) T2—577
Magadanskaĭa oblast'
  (Russia) T2—577
Magahi language 491.454 7
  T6—914 54
Magahi literature 891.454
Magallanes (Chile : Province) 983.644
  T2—836 44
Magallanes y Antártica
  Chilena (Chile) T2—836 4
Magari language 495.49
  T6—954 9
Magazine illustration 741.652
Magazines 050
  T1—05
  design 744.555
  see also Serials
Magdalen Islands (Quebec) T2—714 797
Magdalena (Colombia :
  Dept.) T2—861 16
Magdalena River
  (Colombia) T2—861
Magdeburg (Germany) T2—431 822
Magdeburg (Germany :
  Regierungsbezirk) T2—431 82
Magellan, Strait of (Chile and
  Argentina) 551.461 74
  T2—167 4
Maggiore, Lake (Italy and
  Switzerland) T2—451 65
  Italy T2—451 65
  Switzerland T2—494 788
Maggots 595.771 392
  agricultural pests 632.77
Magherafelt (Northern
  Ireland : District) T2—416 4
Maghreb T2—61
Magi (Christian doctrines) 232.923

Magic	133.43
arts	700.477
	T3C—377
folklore	398.2
history and criticism	398.4
literature	808.803 77
history and criticism	809.933 77
specific literatures	T3B—080 377
history and criticism	T3B—093 77
recreation	793.8
religious practice	203
sociology	306.4
Magic squares	511.64
Magicians (Occultists)	133.430 92
see also Legendary beings	
Magicians (Performers)	793.809 2
Magicians (Religious leaders)	200.92
biography	200.92
role and function	206.1
see Manual at 200.92 and	
201–209, 292–299	
Magicians' manuals	133.43
Magisterium	262.8
Magma	551.13
Magna Graecia	937.7
	T2—377
Magnēsia (Greece)	T2—495 4
Magnesia ad Maeandrum	
(Extinct city)	T2—392 3
Magnesia cement	666.95
Magnesite	
mineralogy	549.782
Magnesium	669.723
applied nutrition	613.285 2
biochemistry	572.523 92
humans	612.015 24
chemical engineering	661.039 2
chemistry	546.392
economic geology	553.492 9
materials science	620.187
metabolism	572.523 92
human physiology	612.392 4
metallography	669.957 23
metallurgy	669.723
metalworking	673.723
mining	622.349 29
organic chemistry	547.053 92
applied	661.895
physical metallurgy	669.967 23
see also Chemicals; Metals	
Magnesium soaps	668.125
Magnet schools	373.241

Magnetic bubble memory	004.563
engineering	621.397 63
Magnetic-core memory	004.53
engineering	621.397 3
Magnetic currents (Earth)	538.748
Magnetic diagnosis	
medicine	616.075 48
Magnetic disks (Computers)	004.563
engineering	621.397 63
Magnetic drums	004.563
engineering	621.397 63
Magnetic engineering	621.34
Magnetic engineers	621.340 92
Magnetic fields (Earth)	538.7
Magnetic induction	538.4
Magnetic ink character	
recognition	006.4
engineering	621.399 4
Magnetic levitation trains	388.42
see also Local rail transit	
systems	
Magnetic observations (Earth)	538.79
Magnetic phenomena	538.3
Magnetic properties	538.3
crystals	548.85
materials science	620.112 97
Magnetic prospecting	622.153
Magnetic relaxation	538.3
Magnetic resonance	538.36
Magnetic resonance imaging	
medicine	616.075 48
Magnetic resonance	
spectroscopes	
manufacturing technology	681.414 8
Magnetic resonance spectroscopy	
engineering	621.361
Magnetic separation	
ores	622.77
Magnetic storms (Earth)	538.744
Magnetic stripe encoding	
computer science	006.24
Magnetic substances	538.4
Magnetic surveys (Earth)	538.78
Magnetic tapes	
computer storage	004.563
engineering	621.397 63
music	786.75
see also Electrophones	
recordings	
engineering	621.382 34
Magnetic testing	
materials science	620.112 78
Magnetic variations	
(Geomagnetism)	538.74

Mail cars	385.33
engineering	625.23
see also Rolling stock	
Mail collection	383.145
Mail delivery	383.145
Mail fraud	364.136
law	345.023 6
Mail handling	383.1
office services	651.759
Mail-order catalogs	381.142 029
	T1—029
direct advertising	659.133
Mail-order houses	381.142
management	658.872
see also Commerce	
Mail service	383.1
see also Postal service	
Mailboxes	383.145
Mailing lists (Computer	
communications)	004.693
communications services	384.36
sociology	302.231 2
Maimonides, Moses	
Jewish legal writings	296.181
Main dishes (Cooking)	641.82
Main meals	642
cooking	641.54
customs	394.125 4
Main memory (Computers)	004.53
engineering	621.397 3
Main River (Germany)	T2—434
Main-sequence stars	523.88
Maine	974.1
	T2—741
Maine (France)	T2—441 6
Maine, Gulf of	551.461 345
	T2—163 45
Maine coon cat	636.83
Maine-et-Loire (France)	T2—441 8
Mainframe computers	004.12
architecture	004.252
communications	004.612
software	005.713 2
software development	005.712 2
engineering	621.391 2
graphics software	006.682
graphics software development	006.672
interfacing	004.612
software	005.713 2
software development	005.712 2
multimedia software	006.782
multimedia software	
development	006.772
multimedia-systems programs	006.782

Mainframe computers (continued)	
operating systems	005.442
performance evaluation	004.120 29
for design and improvement	004.252
software	005.32
systems analysis	004.252
systems design	004.252
see Manual at 004.11–.16	
Mainstream jazz	781.654
Mainstreaming	
education	371.904 6
gifted students	371.952
grouping of students	371.252
library services	027.663
Maintainability engineering	620.004 5
Maintenance	620.004 6
	T1—028 8
materials management	
public administration	352.554
plant management	658.202
	T1—068 2
public administration	352.564
public administration	352.54
Maintenance (Domestic relations)	346.016 63
Maintenance facilities	
spacecraft	629.478
Mainz	
(Rhineland-Palatinate,	
Germany)	T2—434 351
Maipuran languages	498.39
	T6—983 9
Maithili language	491.454 7
	T6—914 54
Maithili literature	891.454
Maitland (N.S.W.)	T2—944 2
Maize	641.331 5
Majolica	738.372
Major County (Okla.)	T2—766 29
Major medical insurance	368.382 8
law	346.086 382 8
see also Insurance	
Major Prophets (Biblical books)	224
Majorca (Spain)	T2—467 54
Majority (Age)	
customs	392.15
etiquette	395.24
law	346.013 083
music	781.584
Majoro, Moeketsi	
Lesotho history	968.850 32
Makaa-Njem languages	496.396
	T6—963 96
Makah Indians	T5—979 54

Makah language	497.954
	T6—979 54
Makasar	T5—992 264
Makasar language	499.226 4
	T6—992 264
Makasar literature	899.226 4
Makasar Strait	551.461 473
	T2—164 73
Make-ahead meals	
cooking	641.555
Makedonia (Greece :	
Periphereia)	T2—495 6
Makedonias-Thrakēs	
(Greece : Decentralized	
administration)	T2—495 7
Makeup	646.72
dramatic performances	792.027
motion pictures	791.430 27
stage	792.027
television	791.450 27
see also Cosmetics	
Makhshirin	296.123 6
Makira and Ulawa	
(Solomon Islands)	T2—959 38
Makkot	296.123 4
Babylonian Talmud	296.125 4
Mishnah	296.123 4
Palestinian Talmud	296.124 4
Mako sharks	597.33
Makonde (African people)	T5—963 97
Makonde language	496.397
	T6—963 97
Maku languages	498.9
	T6—989
Makua languages	496.397
	T6—963 97
Makueni County (Kenya)	T2—676 241
Makurdi (Nigeria)	T2—669 54
Makuria (Kingdom)	962.502 2
Malabar Independent Syrian	
Church	281.54
see also Eastern churches	
Malabo (Equatorial Guinea)	T2—671 86
Malabsorption syndromes	
medicine	616.399
see also Digestive system	
diseases — humans	
Malacca (State)	T2—595 1
Malacca, Strait of	551.461 565
	T2—165 65
Malachi (Biblical book)	224.99
Malachite	
mineralogy	549.785
Malaclemys	597.925 9

Malacology	594
Malacostraca	595.37
paleozoology	565.37
Maladjusted students	371.93
Maladjusted young people	
delinquent	364.36
	T1—086 923
home care	649.153
mentally ill	305.908 408 3
	T1—087 4
predelinquent	305.230 869 23
	T1—086 923
social welfare	362.74
Málaga (Spain : Province)	T2—468 5
Malagasy	T5—993
Malagasy language	499.3
	T6—993
Malagasy literature	899.3
Malagasy Republic	T2—691
Malaita (Solomon Islands)	T2—959 37
Malamulele (South Africa :	
District)	T2—682 57
Malan, D. F. (Daniel François)	
South African history	968.056
Malanje (Angola)	T2—673 4
Mälar, Lake (Sweden)	T2—487 2
Mälaren (Sweden)	T2—487 2
Malaria	
incidence	614.532
medicine	616.936 2
see also Communicable	
diseases — humans	
Malas Zénāwi	
Ethiopian history	963.072 1
Malaspina Peninsula (B.C.)	T2—711 31
Malatya İli (Turkey)	T2—565 4
ancient	T2—393 6
Malawi	968.97
	T2—689 7
Malawi (Kingdom)	968.970 1
	T2—689 7
Malawi, Lake	T2—689 7
Malawi people	T5—968 97
Malawians	T5—968 97
Malay Archipelago	T2—598
Malay Archipelago inner seas	551.461 473
	T2—164 73
Malay language	499.28
	T6—992 8
Malay languages	499.22
	T6—992 2
Malay literature	899.28
Malay Peninsula	T2—595 1

Malay-Polynesian languages	499.2
	T6—992
Malaya	T2—595 1
Malayalam language	494.812
	T6—948 12
Malayalam literature	894.812
Malayalis	T5—948 12
Malayan languages	499.22
	T6—992 2
Malayan literatures	899.2
Malayic languages	499.22
	T6—992 2
Malayo-Polynesian languages	499.2
	T6—992
Malayo-Polynesian languages of	
Sumatra	499.224
	T6—992 24
Malayo-Polynesians	T5—992
Malays (Asian people)	T5—992 8
Malaysia	959.5
	T2—595
Malaysia, East	T2—595 3
Malaysians	T5—992 8
Malcolm Island (B.C.)	T2—711 2
Maldive Islands	T2—549 5
Maldives	954.95
	T2—549 5
Maldivian language	491.489
	T6—914 89
Maldivian literature	891.489
Maldivians	T5—914 89
Maldon (England : District)	T2—426 756
Maldon (Vic.)	T2—945 3
Maldonado (Uruguay :	
Dept.)	T2—895 15
Male breast	
medicine	616.49
surgery	617.549
Male climacteric	
human physiology	612.665
Male genital diseases	
humans	362.196 65
anesthesiology	617.967 463
cancer	362.196 994 63
incidence	614.599 946 3
medicine	616.994 63
social services	362.196 994 63
see also Cancer —	
humans	
incidence	614.596 5
medicine	616.65
social services	362.196 65
surgery	617.463

Male genital system	573.65
anesthesiology	617.967 463
biology	573.65
human anatomy	611.63
human physiology	612.61
medicine	616.65
surgery	617.463
Male gods	202.113
Male infertility	
medicine	616.692 1
see also Male genital	
diseases — humans	
Male prostitution	306.743
Male reproductive system	573.65
animals	573.65
plants	575.65
see also Male genital system	
Male sex disorders	
medicine	616.69
see also Male genital	
diseases — humans	
Male sexual disorders	
medicine	616.69
see also Male genital	
diseases — humans	
Male-to-female transgender	
people	306.768
	T1—086 7
social services	362.897
Male-to-female transgender	
young people	
social services	362.785
Malecite-Passamaquoddy	
language	497.34
	T6—973 4
Malenkov, Georgi	
Russian history	947.085 2
Males (Human)	305.31
	T1—081 1
health	613.042 3
see also Men	
Malfeasance by employees	
labor economics	331.259 8
personnel management	658.314
Malfeasance in office	364.132
law	345.023 2
public administration	353.46
Malheur County (Or.)	T2—795 97
Mali	966.23
	T2—662 3
Mali Empire	966.201 7
	T2—662
Malians	T5—966 23

Malicious mischief insurance	368.12	Malta		945.85
see also Insurance			T2—458 5	
Malicious prosecution	346.033 4	ancient		937.85
Malignant neoplasms	571.978		T2—378 5	
see also Cancer		Maltases		572.756
Malignant tumors	571.978	see also Enzymes		
incidence	614.599 9	Malted alcoholic beverages		641.23
medicine	616.994	commercial processing		663.3
see also Cancer		home preparation		641.873
Mālik ibn Anas	297.125 58	Malted nonalcoholic beverages		641.26
Mālikī school (Islamic law)	340.590 181 3	commercial processing		663.6
religious law	297.140 181 3	home preparation		641.875
Malikites		Maltese	T5—927 9	
religious law	297.140 181 3	Maltese (Dog)		636.76
Mālikīyah		Maltese language		492.79
religious law	297.140 181 3		T6—927 9	
Malinke (African people)	T5—963 45	Maltese literature		892.79
Malinke language	496.345	Malthusian economic school		330.153
	T6—963 45	Malto language		494.83
Malis (Greece)	T2—383		T6—948 3	
Mallard	598.413 4	Malto literature		894.83
Malleability		Maltose		572.565
materials science	620.112 5	see also Carbohydrates		
Malleco (Chile)	T2—834 5	Maluku (Indonesia : islands)	T2—598 5	
Mallee (Vic. : District)	T2—945 9	Maluku (Indonesia :		
Mallet games	796.35	province)	T2—598 52	
Mallophaga	595.757	Maluku Utara (Indonesia)	T2—598 56	
Mallorca (Spain)	T2—467 54	Maluti (South Africa :		
Mallows	583.775	District)	T2—687 59	
Malls (Shopping centers)	381.11	Malvaceae		583.775
see also Shopping centers		Malvales		583.77
Malmesbury (South Africa :		Malvern (England)	T2—424 47	
District)	T2—687 32	Malvern Hills (England)	T2—424 47	
Malmöhus län (Sweden)	T2—486 1	Malvids		583.7
Malnutrition		Malvinas Islands		997.11
humans	362.196 39		T2—971 1	
incidence	614.593 9	see also Falkland Islands		
medicine	616.39	Malware		005.88
social services	362.196 39	Mam Indians	T5—974 2	
Malnutrition surveys	614.593 9	Mam language		497.42
Maloggia (Switzerland :			T6—974 2	
Distretto)	T2—494 732 8	Mambwe language		496.394
Maloja (Switzerland :			T6—963 94	
Region)	T2—494 732 8	Mamelukes		962.024
Małopolskie Voivodeship		Egyptian history		962.024
(Poland)	T2—438 62	Palestinian history		956.940 33
Malpighiaceae	583.69	Mammal nest beetles		595.764 2
Malpighiales	583.69	Mammalia		599
Malpractice	346.033	see also Mammals		
Malpractice insurance	368.564	Mammalogists		599.092
see also Insurance		Mammals		599
		agricultural pests		632.69
		animal husbandry		636
		art representation		704.943 29

Mammals (continued)	
arts	T3C—362 9
big game hunting	799.26
commercial hunting	639.11
conservation technology	639.9
control technology	628.969
agriculture	632.69
drawing	743.69
experimental animals	
medicine	616.027 3
paleozoology	569
resource economics	333.954
small game hunting	799.259
zoology	599
see Manual at 599	
Mammaplasty	618.190 592
Mammary glands	573.679
biology	573.679
gynecology	618.19
human anatomy	611.49
human cancer	
incidence	614.599 944 9
medicine	616.994 49
see also Cancer —	
humans	
human physiology	612.664
surgery	618.190 59
Mammee apple	583.69
Mammography	
medicine	618.190 757 2
Mammoplasty	618.190 592
Mammoth Cave National	
Park (Ky.)	T2—769 754
Man	301
see also Humans	
Man, Isle of	T2—427 9
Man-machine ratios	
production management	658.514
Man-machine systems	
ergonomics	620.82
computer science	004.019
engineering	621.398 4
Man-made environments	
biology	578.755
ecology	577.55
Man-made fibers	
paper	676.7
textiles	677.4
arts	746.044
see also Textiles	
Manabí (Ecuador)	T2—866 34
Managed care plans	362.104 258
insurance	368.382
see also Insurance	

Managed currency	332.46
Managed floating exchange rates	332.456 4
Management	658
	T1—068
armed forces	355.6
arts	700.455 3
	T3C—355 3
literature	808.803 553
history and criticism	809.933 553
personal aspects	658.409
public administration	351
sociology	302.35
see Manual at T1—068; *also*	
at T1—068 vs. 353–354;	
also at 330 vs. 650, 658	
Management accounting	658.151 1
public administration	352.43
Management auditing	658.401 3
public administration	352.43
Management audits	658.401 3
public administration	352.439
Management by objectives	658.401 2
public administration	352.36
Management consultants	658.46
public administration	352.373
Management environment	658.409 5
public administration	352.39
Management for legal	
compliance	658.12
Managerial accounting	658.151 1
public administration	352.43
Managerial finance	658.15
see also Financial management	
Managerial occupations	331.761 658
Managerial success	658.409
Managers	338.092
	T1—086 22
labor economics	331.761 658
social class	305.554
Managing change	658.406
military administration	355.686 7
public administration	352.367
Managing your boss	650.13
Managua (Nicaragua :	
Dept.)	T2—728 513
Manakins	598.822
Manapouri, Lake (N.Z.)	T2—939 6
Manāsik	297.352 4
Manassas (Va.)	T2—755 273 4
Manassas Park (Va.)	T2—755 273 6
Manatee County (Fla.)	T2—759 62
Manatees	599.55
conservation technology	639.979 55
resource economics	333.959 55

Manawatu District (N.Z.)	T2—935 6
Manawatu-Wanganui Region (N.Z.)	T2—935
Mancha	T2—464
Manche	551.461 336
	T2—163 36
Manche (France)	T2—442 12
Manchester (England)	T2—427 33
Manchester (N.H.)	T2—742 8
Manchester terrier (Standard dog)	636.755
Manchester terrier (Toy dog)	636.76
Manchineels	583.69
Manchu	T5—941
Manchu dynasty	951.03
Manchu languages	494.1
	T6—941
Manchu literatures	894.1
Manchuria	T2—518
Manda languages	496.391
	T6—963 91
Mandab, Strait of	551.461 532
	T2—165 32
Mandalas	203.7
Buddhism	294.343 7
Hinduism	294.537
Mandan Indians	T5—975 22
Mandan language	497.522
	T6—975 22
Mandarin Chinese language	495.1
	T6—951 1
Mandarin duck	598.412
Mandates	321.08
establishment	
World War I	940.314 26
World War II	940.531 426
see also Semisovereign states	
Mande (African people)	T5—963 45
Mande languages	496.34
	T6—963 4
Mande literatures	896.34
Mande-speaking peoples	T5—963 4
Mandeb, Bab el	551.461 532
	T2—165 32
Mandekan languages	496.345
	T6—963 45
Mandela, Nelson	
South African history	968.071
Mandera County (Kenya)	T2—676 223
Manding languages	496.345
	T6—963 45
Manding-Mokole languages	496.345
	T6—963 45
Mandingo (African people)	T5—963 45

Mandingo languages	496.345
	T6—963 45
Mandinka (African people)	T5—963 45
Mandinka languages	496.345
	T6—963 45
Mandolins	787.84
instrument	787.841 9
music	787.84
see also Stringed instruments	
Mandrakes	
botany	583.959 3
medicinal crop	633.883 959 3
Maneuvers (Military)	355.4
training	355.52
Manga	741.595 2
drawing	741.51
Manganese	669.732
chemical engineering	661.054 1
chemistry	546.541
economic geology	553.462 9
human toxicology	615.925 541
materials science	620.189 32
metallography	669.957 32
metallurgy	669.732
metalworking	673.732
mining	622.346 29
organic chemistry	547.055 41
applied	661.895
physical metallurgy	669.967 32
see also Chemicals; Metals	
Manganese group	
chemical engineering	661.054
chemistry	546.54
Mangaung Metropolitan Municipality (South Africa)	T2—685 4
Mangbetu (African people)	T5—965 6
Mangbetu language	496.56
	T6—965 6
Mange	
animals	
veterinary medicine	636.089 657 3
humans	
medicine	616.573
see also Skin diseases — humans	
Mangoes	641.344 4
botany	583.75
cooking	641.644 4
food	641.344 4
orchard crop	634.44
Mangosteens	641.346 55
agriculture	634.655
botany	583.69

Mangosteens (continued)
cooking — 641.646 55
food — 641.346 55
Mangrove swamp ecology — 583.176 98
Mangrove swamps — 577.698
  biology — 578.769 8
  ecology — 577.698
  see also Wetlands
Mangroves — 583.176 98
  Arecaceae — 584.5
  Verbenaceae — 583.96
Mangroves (Arecaceae) — 584.84
Mangroves (Myrtales) — 583.73
Mangroves (Verbenaceae) — 583.96
Mangue Indians — T5—976
Manhattan (New York,
  N.Y.) — T2—747 1
Manholes
  sewers — 628.25
Manhwa — 741.595 19
  drawing — 741.51
Manic-depressive illness
  medicine — 616.895
  see also Mental disorders
Manic psychoses
  medicine — 616.895
  see also Mental disorders
Manica (Mozambique :
  Province) — T2—679 4
Manicaland Province
  (Zimbabwe) — T2—689 1
Manicheism — 299.932
  Christian heresy — 273.2
Manicouagan (Quebec :
  Regional County
  Municipality) — T2—714 174
Manicure tools
  manufacturing technology — 688.5
Manicuring — 646.727
Maniema (Congo) — T2—675 17
Manifold topology — 514.34
Manifolds (Mathematics)
  geometry — 516.07
  topology — 514.34
Manihiki Atoll (Cook
  Islands) — T2—962 4
Manila (Philippines) — T2—599 16
Manila hemp
  botany — 584.88
  fiber crop — 633.571
Manila paper — 676.287

Manioc — 641.336 82
  botany — 583.69
  food — 641.336 82
  see also Cassava
Manipulators (Mechanism) — 629.893 3
Manipur (India) — T2—541 7
Manisa İli (Turkey) — T2—562 4
  ancient — T2—392 2
Manistee County (Mich.) — T2—774 62
Manitoba — 971.27
   — T2—712 7
Manitoba, Lake (Man.) — T2—712 72
Manitoulin (Ont.) — T2—713 135
Manitowoc County (Wis.) — T2—775 67
Manjimup (W.A.) — T2—941 2
Mankind — 301
  see also Humans
Mankwe (South Africa :
  District) — T2—682 41
Manned space flight
  engineering — 629.45
Manned spacecraft
  engineering — 629.47
Manners — 390
  child training — 649.6
  etiquette — 395
Mannheim (Germany) — T2—434 645 2
Manning Provincial Park
  (B.C.) — T2—711 5
Manor houses
  architecture — 728.8
Manpower
  armed forces — 355.22
  civilians — 355.23
  military law — 343.012
Manpower planning
  management — 658.301
Manpower shortages — 331.136
Mansel Island (Nunavut) — T2—719 52
Mansfield (England :
  District) — T2—425 23
Mansi — T5—945 1
Mansi language — 494.51
   — T6—945 1
Mansi literature — 894.51
Mansions
  architecture — 728.8
Manslaughter — 364.152 5
  law — 345.025 25
Mantels
  furniture arts — 749.62
Mantis shrimps — 595.379 6
Mantises — 595.727
  culture — 638.572 7

Mantle of earth	551.116	Manuscript editing	808.027
Mantodea	595.727	publishing	070.51
Mantova (Italy)	T2—452 81	Manuscript illumination	741.647
ancient	T2—373 181	Manuscript selection	
Mantova (Italy : Province)	T2—452 8	publishing	070.51
ancient	T2—373 18	Manuscripts	091
Mantras	203.7	bibliographies	011.31
Buddhism	294.343 7	cataloging	025.341 2
Hinduism	294.537	library treatment	025.171 2
Mantua (Italy)	T2—452 81	music	780
ancient	T2—373 181	treatises	780.262
Mantua (Italy : Province)	T2—452 8	Manx	T5—916 4
ancient	T2—373 18	Manx cat	636.822
Manual alphabet	419	Manx language	491.64
representing spoken language	418		T6—916 4
specific languages	T4—891	Manx literature	891.64
Manual arts		Manxmen	T5—916 4
primary education	372.5	Many-bodies problem	530.144
Manual of arms	355.547	astronomy	521
Manually coded English		Many-valued logic	511.312
American	428.917	Mao, Zedong	
British	428.914 1	Chinese history	951.05
Manually coded language	418	Maoism	335.434 5
specific languages	T4—891	economics	335.434 5
Manufactured gases	665.7	political ideology	320.532 309 51
Manufactured products	670	Maori	305.899 442
economics	338.476 7		T5—994 42
technology	670	Maori language	499.442
Manufacturers	338.476 709 2		T6—994 42
directories	338.767 025	Maori literature	899.442
Manufacturers' outlets	381.15	Maori Wars, 1843–1847	993.021
management	658.870 5	Maori Wars, 1860–1870	993.022
Manufacturing		Map coloring	511.56
ethics	174.4	Map drawing	526
production management	658.5	Map makers	526.092
taxes	336.207	Map making	526
technology	670	military engineering	623.71
see Manual at 671–679 vs.		military intelligence service	355.343 2
680		Map projections	526.8
Manufacturing industries	338.476 7	Map reading	912.014
accounting	657.867	Map thefts	364.162 891 2
public administration	354.66	law	345.026 289 12
Manufacturing wastes		Map turtles	597.925 9
water pollution engineering	628.168 37	Maple Ridge (B.C.)	T2—711 33
Manufacturing workers	670.92	Maple sugar	641.336 4
labor economics	331.767	agriculture	633.64
public administration	354.947	biochemistry	572.565
Manukau City (N.Z.)	T2—932 5	commercial processing	664.132
Manures	631.86	cooking	641.636 4
animal husbandry	636.083 8	food	641.336 4
Manus	T5—991 2	*see also* Carbohydrates	
Manus Province (Papua		Maple syrup	641.336 4
New Guinea)	T2—958 1	agriculture	633.64
		commercial processing	664.132

Maple syrup (continued)
  cooking   641.636 4
  food   641.336 4
  see also Carbohydrates
Maples   583.75
  botany   583.75
  forestry   634.972 2
  lumber   674.142
  ornamental arboriculture   635.977 375
Maplewood (N.J.)   T2—749 33
Mappings (Mathematics)   511.326
  topology   514
Maps   912
   T1—022 3
  aeronautics   629.132 54
  cartography   526
    military engineering   623.71
  cataloging   025.346
  design   744.37
  geography   912
  library treatment   025.176
  printing   686.283
  publishing   070.579 3
  theft of   364.162 891 2
    law   345.026 289 12
Maps (Functions)   511.326
Mapuche Indians   T5—987 2
Mapuche language   498.72
   T6—987 2
Mapuche literature   898.72
Mapudungu Indians   T5—987 2
Mapudungun language   498.72
   T6—987 2
Mapudungun literature   898.72
Mapulaneng (South Africa :
  District)   T2—682 73
Mapumulu (South Africa :
  District)   T2—684 47
Mapungubwe National Park
  (South Africa)   T2—682 57
Maputaland (South Africa)   T2—684 3
Maputo (Mozambique :
  Province)   T2—679 1
Maputo River   T2—684 2
  Mozambique   T2—679 1
  South Africa   T2—684 2
Maqāṣid al-sharī'ah (Islamic law)   340.591 1
Maqṭū'   297.125 21
Maqurrah (Kingdom)   962.502 2
   T2—625
Mar Thoma Church   281.54
  see also Eastern churches
Mar Thoma Syrian Church   281.54
  see also Eastern churches

Mara Region (Tanzania)   T2—678 27
Maracaibo, Gulf of (Colombia
  and Venezuela)   551.461 365
   T2—163 65
Maracaibo Lake
  (Venezuela)   T2—872 3
Maracas   786.885
  see also Percussion instruments
Marakele National Park
  (South Africa)   T2—682 53
Marakwet (African people)   T5—965 56
Marakwet language   496.556
   T6—965 56
Maramureş (Romania :
  Judeţ)   T2—498 4
Maranhão (Brazil)   T2—812 1
Marantaceae   584.88
Maraş İli (Turkey)   T2—565 3
Maratha   T5—914 61
Marathi language   491.46
   T6—914 61
Marathi literature   891.46
Marathon (Ancient site)   T2—385
Marathon County (Wis.)   T2—775 29
Marathon races   796.425 2
  see also Track and field
Marattiales   587.33
  paleobotany   561.73
Marble   553.512
  building material   691.2
  economic geology   553.512
  petrology   552.4
  quarrying   622.351 2
Marbled polecat   599.766
Marbles (Game)   796.2
  see also Sports
Marbling (Paper)
  bookbinding   686.36
Marbling (Woodwork)
  buildings   698.32
MARC format   025.316
Marcgraviaceae   583.93
March (Switzerland)   T2—494 752 1
March flies   595.772
March flies (Bibionidae)   595.772
March flies (Tabanidae)   595.773
Marchantiales   588.3
Marche (France : Province)   T2—446 8
Marche (Italy)   T2—456 7
  ancient   T2—374 5
Marches   784.189 7
Marches (Italy)   T2—456 7
  ancient   T2—374 5
Marching bands   784.83

Marine cooking	641.575 3	Marion County (Ga.)	T2—758 482
Marine ecology	577.7	Marion County (Ill.)	T2—773 794
Marine engineering	623.87	Marion County (Ind.)	T2—772 52
Marine fishes	597.177	Marion County (Iowa)	T2—777 83
culture	639.32	Marion County (Kan.)	T2—781 57
see also Fishes		Marion County (Ky.)	T2—769 51
Marine forces (Military service)	359.96	Marion County (Miss.)	T2—762 21
Marine geology	551.468	Marion County (Mo.)	T2—778 353
Marine hatchetfishes	597.5	Marion County (Ohio)	T2—771 514
Marine insurance	368.2	Marion County (Or.)	T2—795 37
see also Insurance		Marion County (S.C.)	T2—757 86
Marine invertebrates	592.177	Marion County (Tenn.)	T2—768 79
resource economics	333.955	Marion County (Tex.)	T2—764 193
Marine lizards (Mosasauridae)	567.95	Marion County (W. Va.)	T2—754 54
Marine mammals	599.5	Marionettes	791.53
paleozoology	569.5	making	
resource economics	333.959 5	handicrafts	745.592 24
Marine microorganisms	579.177	*see also* Puppets	
Marine navigation	623.89	Mariopteris	561.597
Marine organisms	578.77	Mariotype process	773.1
Marine pollution	363.739 4	Mariposa County (Calif.)	T2—794 46
see also Water pollution		Marital property	346.042
Marine reptiles (Paleontological		divorce law	346.016 64
grouping)	567.937	Marital psychotherapy	
Marine resources	333.916 4	psychiatry	616.891 562
public administration	354.369	Marital rights	346.016 3
Marine safety technology	623.888	Marital status	306.81
Marine scenes		Maritime (Russia: Kray)	T2—577
art representation	704.943 7	Maritime law	343.096
painting	758.2	*see Manual at* 341.45 vs.	
Marine science	551.46	343.0962	
see also Oceans		Maritime Provinces	971.5
Marine snakes	597.965		T2—715
Marine transportation	387.5	Marjoram	641.357
see also Ocean transportation		botany	583.96
Marine transportation facilities	387.15	*see also* Herbs	
see also Port facilities		Mark (Gospel)	226.3
Marine transportation safety	363.123	Markazī (Iran)	T2—552 7
see also Water		Marker drawing	741.26
transportation — safety		Markerwaard (Netherlands)	T2—492 2
Marine transportation workers	387.509 2	Market analysis procedure	
Marine waters	551.46	management	658.83
see also Oceans			T1—068 8
Marine zebra fishes	597.68	Market analysis reports	381
Marine zoology	591.77	Market economy	330.122
Mariner project	629.435 4	Market research procedure	
Marines (Armed forces)	359.96	management	658.83
Marinette County (Wis.)	T2—775 33		T1—068 8
Maring (Papua New Guinea		Market research reports	381
people)	T5—991 2	Market segmentation	
Mariology (Christian doctrines)	232.91	management	658.802
Marion County (Ala.)	T2—761 89	Market study procedure	
Marion County (Ark.)	T2—767 193	management	658.83
Marion County (Fla.)	T2—759 75		T1—068 8

Marriage (continued)	
religion	204.41
Buddhism	294.344 41
Christianity	248.4
Hinduism	294.544 1
Islam	297.577
Judaism	296.74
religious doctrine	202.2
Christianity	234.165
religious law	208.4
Christianity	262.9
Judaism	296.444
rites	203.85
Christianity	265.5
Judaism	296.444
liturgy	296.454 4
see also Public worship	
social theology	201.7
Christianity	261.835 81
Marriage contracts	346.016 2
Marriage counseling	
pastoral theology	206.1
Christianity	259.14
Judaism	296.61
psychotherapy	616.891 562
social welfare	362.828 6
Married men	306.872 2
	T1—086 55
family relationships	306.872 2
home economics	646.782
guides to Christian life	248.842 5
psychology	155.645 2
social welfare	362.820 865 5
Married people	306.872
	T1—086 55
Christian devotional literature	242.644
family relationships	
home economics	646.782
guides to religious life	204.41
Buddhism	294.344 41
Christianity	248.844
Hinduism	294.544 1
Islam	297.577
Judaism	296.74
see also Marriage —	
personal religion	
law	346.016 3
psychology	155.645
social group	306.872
social welfare	362.820 865 5
Married women	306.872 3
	T1—086 55
Christian devotional literature	242.643 5

Married women (continued)	
family relationships	306.872 3
home economics	646.782
guides to Christian life	248.843 5
labor economics	331.43
psychology	155.645 3
social welfare	362.839 52
Marrucinian language	479.7
	T6—797
Mars (Planet)	523.43
	T2—992 3
astrology	133.535
manned flights to	629.455 3
unmanned flights to	629.435 43
Marsá Maṭrūḥ (Egypt)	T2—621
Marsabit County (Kenya)	T2—676 244
Marseille (France)	T2—449 12
Marseilles	T2—449 12
Marsh flies	595.774
Marsh rabbit	599.324
Marshall County (Ala.)	T2—761 94
Marshall County (Ill.)	T2—773 515
Marshall County (Ind.)	T2—772 88
Marshall County (Iowa)	T2—777 55
Marshall County (Kan.)	T2—781 31
Marshall County (Ky.)	T2—769 91
Marshall County (Minn.)	T2—776 97
Marshall County (Miss.)	T2—762 88
Marshall County (Okla.)	T2—766 61
Marshall County (S.D.)	T2—783 13
Marshall County (Tenn.)	T2—768 585
Marshall County (W. Va.)	T2—754 16
Marshall Islands	996.83
	T2—968 3
Marshallese language	499.52
	T6—995 2
Marshals (Law)	347.016
criminal law	345.012 6
Marshals (Police)	363.282
Marshes	551.417
biology	578.768
ecology	577.68
see also Wetlands	
Marsian language	479.7
	T6—797
Marsiliales	587.3
Marsupial cats	599.27
Marsupial mice	599.27
Marsupial moles	599.27
Marsupial rats	599.27
Marsupialia	599.2
see also Marsupials	

Marsupials	599.2	Marxism	335.4
conservation technology	639.979 2	economics	335.4
paleozoology	569.2	political ideology	320.531 5
resource economics	333.959 2	Marxism-Leninism	335.43
Marsupicarnivora	599.27	economics	335.43
Martaban, Gulf of (Burma)	551.461 565	political ideology	320.532 2
	T2—165 65	Marxist-Christian dialogue	
Martens	599.766 5	Christian theology	261.21
Martes	599.766 5	Marxist-Leninists	335.430 92
Martha's Vineyard (Mass.)	T2—744 94	Marxist parties	324.217
Martial artists	796.809 2	Marxists	335.409 2
Martial arts	796.8	Mary, Blessed Virgin, Saint	232.91
biography	796.809 2	art representation	704.948 55
physical fitness	613.714 8	arts	T3C—351
see also Combat sports		private prayers to	242.74
Martial law	342.062 8	*see Manual at* 230–280	
Martigny (Switzerland :		Mary, Queen of Scots	
District)	T2—494 796 7	Scottish history	941.105
Martin, Lake (Ala.)	T2—761 53	Mary I, Queen of England	
Martin, Paul		English history	942.054
Canadian history	971.072	Mary II, Queen of England	
Martin County (Fla.)	T2—759 31	British history	941.068
Martin County (Ind.)	T2—772 382	English history	942.068
Martin County (Ky.)	T2—769 243	Scottish history	941.106 8
Martin County (Minn.)	T2—776 232	Mary Tudor, Queen of England	
Martin County (N.C.)	T2—756 45	English history	942.054
Martin County (Tex.)	T2—764 857	Maryborough (Qld.)	T2—943 2
Martinelli Berrocal, Ricardo		Maryborough (Vic.)	T2—945 3
Alberto		Maryland	975.2
Panamanian history	972.870 543		T2—752
Martingales	519.236	Masaba-Luyia languages	496.395
Martinicans	T5—969 729 82		T6—963 95
Martiniquais	T5—969 729 82	Masai (African people)	T5—965 522 6
Martinique	972.982	folk literature	398.208 996 552 26
	T2—729 82	Masai language	496.552 26
Martins	598.826		T6—965 522 6
Martinsville (Va.)	T2—755 693	Masai literature	896.552 26
Martyniaceae	583.96	Maṣāliḥ al-mursalah (Islamic	
Martyrs	200.92	law)	
biography	200.92	sources of fiqh	340.591 36
Christian	272.092	Masānīd	297.125 61
see Manual at 230–280		Masaya (Nicaragua : Dept.)	T2—728 514
role and function	206.1	Masbate (Philippines :	
see Manual at 200.92 and		Province)	T2—599 57
201–209, 292–299		Masbate Island (Philippines)	T2—599 57
Marwari language	491.479 7	Mascara (Algeria :	
	T6—914 79	Province)	T2—651
Marwari literature	891.479	Mascarene Islands	T2—698
Marxian parties		Mascoian languages	498.9
international organizations	324.17		T6—989
Marxian socialism	335.4	Mascots (Occultism)	133.44
economics	335.4	Masculinity	155.332
political ideology	320.531 5	Masers	621.381 336
		Maseru (Lesotho)	T2—688 5

Mashhūr (Hadith)	297.125 24
Mashona (African people)	T5—963 975
Mashonaland Central	
Province (Zimbabwe)	T2—689 1
Mashonaland East Province	
(Zimbabwe)	T2—689 1
Mashonaland West Province	
(Zimbabwe)	T2—689 1
Masire, Ketumile, Sir	
Botswana history	968.830 32
Masisi, Mokgweetsi Eric	
Keabetswe	
Botswana history	968.830 35
Masjid al-Ḥarām	297.352
Maskinongé (Quebec :	
Regional County	
Municipality)	T2—714 44
Maskoutains (Quebec)	T2—714 523
Masks	391.434
commercial technology	687.4
customs	391.434
home construction	646.478
see also Clothing	
Masks (Sculpture)	731.75
Masochism	
medicine	616.858 35
see also Mental disorders	
sociology	306.776
Mason County (Ill.)	T2—773 553
Mason County (Ky.)	T2—769 323
Mason County (Mich.)	T2—774 61
Mason County (Tex.)	T2—764 66
Mason County (W. Va.)	T2—754 33
Mason County (Wash.)	T2—797 97
Masonry	693.1
Masonry (Secret order)	366.1
Masonry adhesives	666.9
building materials	691.5
materials science	620.135
Masonry arch bridges	
construction	624.225
Masonry dams	627.82
Masonry materials	
architectural construction	721.044 1
materials science	620.13
structural engineering	624.183
Masons	693.109 2
Masons (Secret order)	366.1
Masques	782.15
literature	808.825
history and criticism	809.25
specific literatures	T3B—205
individual authors	T3A—2
music	782.15

Masques (continued)	
stage presentation	792.6
see also Theater	
Mass (Christian rite)	264.36
Anglican	264.030 36
texts	264.03
music	782.323
choral and mixed voices	782.532 3
single voices	783.093 23
Roman Catholic	264.020 36
texts	264.023
Mass (Substance)	531.14
air mechanics	533.6
gas mechanics	533.15
liquid mechanics	532.4
solid mechanics	531.5
Mass communication	302.2
communications services	384
law	343.099
social aspects	302.2
Mass culture	306
Mass deacidification	
bibliographic materials	025.84
Mass-energy equivalence	530.11
Mass hysteria	302.17
Mass media	302.23
accounting	657.84
election campaigns	324.73
influence on crime	364.254
instructional use	371.358
adult level	374.26
higher education	378.175 8
law	343.099
performances	
collectibles	791.407 5
religion	201.7
Christianity	261.52
evangelism	269.26
use by local Christian	
church	253.78
administration	254.3
Judaism	296.37
sociology	302.23
Mass media music	781.54
Mass movement (Geology)	551.307
Mass murder	364.152 34
Fairfield County (Conn.)	364.152 340 974 69
law	345.025 234
social welfare	362.882 93
Mass murderers	364.152 34
biography	364.152 340 92
Mass spectrometry	543.65
analytical chemistry	543.65
physics	539.602 87

Mass spectroscopy	543.65
analytical chemistry	543.65
physics	539.602 87
Mass transfer	530.475
chemical engineering	660.284 23
gaseous-state physics	530.435
liquid-state physics	530.425
physics	530.475
semiconductors	537.622 5
solid-state physics	530.415
Mass transit	388.4
see also Urban transportation	
Mass transport (Physics)	530.475
see also Mass transfer	
Mass transportation	388.042
law	343.093 3
transportation services	388.042
urban	388.4
see also Urban transportation	
see also Passenger services	
Mass wasting (Geology)	551.307
Massa-Carrara (Italy :	
Province)	T2—455 4
ancient	T2—375 4
Massa e Carrara (Italy :	
Province)	T2—455 4
ancient	T2—375 4
Massac County (Ill.)	T2—773 997
Massachusett Indians	T5—973 48
Massachusett language	497.348
	T6—973 48
Massachusetts	974.4
	T2—744
Massachusetts Bay (Mass.)	551.461 345
	T2—163 45
Massacre of innocents	232.92
Massage	615.822
physical fitness	613.72
therapeutics	615.822
Massif Central (France)	T2—445 9
Massively parallel	
supercomputers	004.35
Mast cell disease	
medicine	616.77
see also Musculoskeletal	
diseases — humans	
Mast cells	
human cytology	611.018 26
Mastectomy	616.994 490 59
Master and servant	
law	346.024
Master's degree	378.2
Masters Golf Tournament	796.352 66
Masterton District (N.Z.)	T2—936 8

Mastication	
human physiology	612.311
rubber	678.22
Mastiffs	636.73
Mastigomycotina	579.53
Mastocytosis	
medicine	616.77
see also Musculoskeletal	
diseases — humans	
Mastoid process diseases	
medicine	617.87
see also Ear diseases —	
humans	
Mastoid processes	
human anatomy	611.85
human physiology	612.854
medicine	617.87
Masts	623.862
Masturbation	
sociology	306.772
Masvingo Province	
(Zimbabwe)	T2—689 1
Mặt trận dân tộc giải phóng miền	
nam Việt Nam	959.704 332 2
Matabeleland North	
Province (Zimbabwe)	T2—689 1
Matabeleland South	
Province (Zimbabwe)	T2—689 1
Mataco-Guaicuru languages	498.7
	T6—987
Matagalpa (Nicaragua :	
Dept.)	T2—728 525
Matagalpan Indians	T5—978
Matagami (Quebec)	T2—714 115
Matagorda County (Tex.)	T2—764 132
Matamata Piako District	
(N.Z.)	T2—933 53
Matane (Quebec : Regional	
County Municipality)	T2—714 775
Matanie (Quebec : Regional	
County Municipality)	T2—714 775
Matanuska-Susitna Borough	
(Alaska)	T2—798 3
Matanzas (Cuba : Province)	T2—729 13
Matapédia (Quebec :	
Regional County	
Municipality)	T2—714 778
Matawinie (Quebec)	T2—714 418
Match-cover advertising	659.131
design	744.66
Match covers	741.694
Matches	662.5
Matching numbers contests	790.134
Matching theory	511.66

Maté	641.337 7	Maternally acquired antibodies	571.963 8
agriculture	633.77	Maternity garments	392
beverage	641.337 7	commercial technology	687.16
botany	583.982	customs	392
commercial processing	663.96	home economics	646.34
cooking with	641.637 7	home sewing	646.47
home preparation	641.877	*see also* Clothing	
Mate selection		Maternity insurance	368.424
customs	392.4	law	344.022 4
life skills	646.77	*see also* Insurance	
sociology	306.82	Maternity leave	331.257 630 852
Matekane, Sam		economics	331.257 630 852
Lesotho history	968.850 32	government-sponsored	
Matera (Italy : Province)	T2—457 72	insurance	368.454 008 52
ancient	T2—377 73	personnel management	658.312 2
Materia medica	615.1	Maternity services	362.198 2
see also Drugs		*see also* Health services	
(Pharmaceuticals)		Mathematical analysis	515
Material culture	306.46	Mathematical crystallography	548.7
Material remains	930.1	Mathematical economics	330.015 1
Materialism	146.3	economic school	330.154 3
Christian polemics	239.7	Mathematical games	793.74
Indian philosophy	181.46	Mathematical geography	526
Islamic polemics	297.298	Mathematical linguistics	410.151
Materialization (Spiritualism)	133.92	Mathematical logic	511.3
Materials	T1—028 4	computer programming	
architectural construction	721.04	languages	005.131
building construction	691	Mathematical models	511.8
engineering	620.11		T1—015 118
foundation engineering	624.153	systems	003
manufacturing technology	670		T1—011
nuclear reactors	621.483 3	Mathematical optimization	519.6
standards and specifications		*see also* Optimization	
production management	658.562	Mathematical physics	530.15
structural engineering	624.18	Mathematical programming	519.7
Materials costs		management decision making	658.403 3
financial management	658.155 3	Mathematical recreations	793.74
Materials engineers	620.110 92	Mathematical school	
Materials estimates	T1—029	(Economics)	330.154 3
building construction	692.5	Mathematical shortcuts	513.9
Materials handling		Mathematical statistics	519.5
materials management	658.781	Mathematicians	510.92
Materials-handling equipment	621.86	Mathematics	510
ships	623.867		T1—015 1
Materials management	658.7	arts	T3C—36
	T1—068 7	equipment	510.284
public administration	352.55	primary education	372.7
schools	371.67	*see Manual at* 510; *also at*	
Materials science	620.11	510, T1—0151 vs. 003,	
Matériel (Armed forces)	355.8	T1—011; *also at* 510,	
Maternal behavior (Animals)	591.563	T1—0151 vs. 004–006,	
Maternal deaths		T1—0285	
incidence	614.599 279	Mathews County (Va.)	T2—755 31
obstetrics	618.79	Mathieu functions	515.54

546

Maximum-security prisons	365.33	Māzandarān (Iran)	T2—552 3
see also Penal institutions		ancient	939.6
Maxwell's equations (Physics)	530.141		T2—396
Maxwell's thermodynamic		Mazatec Indians	T5—976
formulas	536.71	Mazdaism	295
May Day	394.262 7	Maze puzzles	793.738
Maya calendar	529.329 784 27	Mazowieckie Voivodeship	
Maya Indians	972.81	(Poland)	943.841
	T5—974 2		T2—438 41
Guatemala	972.81	Mazurkas	793.319 438
Mexico	972.6	music	784.188 4
Maya Indians (Yucatecan		Mbabane (Eswatini)	T2—688 7
Maya)	T5—974 27	Mbai language (Moissala)	496.566
Maya language	497.427		T6—965 66
	T6—974 27	Mbala (Congolese people,	
Maya literature	897.427	Bandundu region)	T5—963 93
Mayabeque (Cuba :		Mbam languages	T6—963 96
Province)	T2—729 126	Mbasogo, Teodoro Obiang	
Mayacaceae	584.95	Nguema	
Mayaguana Island		Equatorial Guinean history	967.180 32
(Bahamas)	T2—729 6	Mbay language	496.566
Mayagüez (P.R. : District)	T2—729 56		T6—965 66
Mayan calendar	529.329 784 27	Mbeki, Thabo	
Mayan languages	497.42	South African history	968.072
	T6—974 2	Mbere languages	496.396
Mayan period	972.810 16		T6—963 96
Mayans	972.81	Mbete languages	496.396
	T5—974 2		T6—963 96
Mayans (Yucatecan Maya)	T5—974 27	Mbeya Region (Tanzania)	T2—678 28
Mayapple	583.34	Mbibana (South Africa :	
Mayas	972.81	District)	T2—682 76
	T5—974 2	MBO (Management by	
Mayas (Yucatecan Maya)	T5—974 27	objectives)	658.401 2
Maydeae	584.924	public administration	352.36
Mayenne (France : Dept.)	T2—441 62	Mbole-Ena languages	496.394
Mayes County (Okla.)	T2—766 93		T6—963 94
Mayflies	595.734	Mboshi languages	496.396
Mayflower	583.34		T6—963 96
Mayflower (Berberidaceae)	583.34	Mbosi language	496.396
Mayo (Ireland : County)	T2—417 3		T6—963 96
Mayo, Richard Southwell		Mbukushu language	496.399
Bourke, Earl of			T6—963 99
Indian history	954.035 2	Mbum language	496.361
Mayonnaise	641.814		T6—963 61
food technology	664.37	Mbundu (Angolan people,	
home preparation	641.814	Benguela Province)	T5—963 99
Mayor-council government	320.854	Mbundu (Angolan people,	
Mayors	320.854	Luanda Province)	T5—963 932
public administration	352.232 16	Mbundu language (Benguela	
Mayotte	969.45	Province, Angola)	496.399
	T2—694 5		T6—963 99
Maypop	583.69	Mbundu language (Luanda	
Maysān (Iraq)	T2—567 5	Province, Angola)	496.393 2
			T6—963 932

Mbundu literature (Luanda
  Province, Angola)   896.393 2
McBride (B.C.)   T2—711 82
McClain County (Okla.)   T2—766 55
McCone County (Mont.)   T2—786 26
McCook County (S.D.)   T2—783 372
McCormick County (S.C.)   T2—757 36
McCracken County (Ky.)   T2—769 95
McCreary County (Ky.)   T2—769 135
McCulloch County (Tex.)   T2—764 67
McCurtain County (Okla.)   T2—766 64
McDonald County (Mo.)   T2—778 736
McDonough County (Ill.)   T2—773 42
McDowell County (N.C.)   T2—756 89
McDowell County (W. Va.)   T2—754 49
McDuffie County (Ga.)   T2—758 632
McEwen, John, Sir
  Australian history   994.061
McGregor River (B.C.)   T2—711 82
McHenry County (Ill.)   T2—773 22
McHenry County (N.D.)   T2—784 62
McIntosh County (Ga.)   T2—758 737
McIntosh County (N.D.)   T2—784 55
McIntosh County (Okla.)   T2—766 74
McKean County (Pa.)   T2—748 63
McKenzie County (N.D.)   T2—784 81
McKinley, William
  United States history   973.88
McKinley County (N.M.)   T2—789 83
McLean County (Ill.)   T2—773 59
McLean County (Ky.)   T2—769 826
McLean County (N.D.)   T2—784 75
McLennan County (Tex.)   T2—764 284
McLeod County (Minn.)   T2—776 52
McMahon, William
  Australian history   994.061
McMinn County (Tenn.)   T2—768 865
McMullen County (Tex.)   T2—764 452
McNairy County (Tenn.)   T2—768 29
McNaughton Lake (B.C.)   T2—711 68
McPherson County (Kan.)   T2—781 55
McPherson County (Neb.)   T2—782 793
McPherson County (S.D.)   T2—783 16
Mdantsane (South Africa :
  District)   T2—687 55
Mdutjana (South Africa :
  District)   T2—682 76
Mead   641.23
  commercial processing   663.4
Mead, Lake (Ariz. and
  Nev.)   T2—793 12
Meade County (Kan.)   T2—781 75
Meade County (Ky.)   T2—769 852
Meade County (S.D.)   T2—783 44

Meadow beauties   583.73
Meadow mice   599.354
Meadowlarks   598.874
Meadows   333.74
      T2—153
  biology   578.746
  ecology   577.46
  see also Grasslands
Meagher County (Mont.)   T2—786 612
Meal (Milling products)
  commercial processing   664.720 7
    wheat   664.722 73
Meals   642
  customs   394.125
  transportation services   388.042
    see also Passenger services
Mealworms   595.769
Mean   519.533
Mean value theorems   515.33
Meaning
  epistemology   121.68
  linguistics   401.43
    specific languages   T4—014 3
    see Manual at 401.43 vs.
      306.44, 401.45, 401.9,
      412, 415
Meaning-text theory (Linguistics) 410.184 2
  specific languages   T4—018 42
Measles
  incidence   614.523
  medicine   616.915
    see also Communicable
      diseases — humans
  pediatrics   618.929 15
Measure theory   515.42
Measurement   530.8
      T1—028 7
  chemistry   542.3
Measurement systems   530.81
  physics   530.81
  social aspects   389.15
Measurement theory   530.801
Measures   530.81
  see also Weights and measures
Measuring instruments
  electric measurement   621.37
  electronics   621.381 548
  manufacturing technology   681.2
  physics   530.7

Meat	641.36
commercial preservation	
technology	664.902 8
commercial processing	
economics	338.476 649
technology	664.9
cooking	641.66
food	641.36
home preservation	641.49
product safety	363.192 9
see also Food — product	
safety	
Meat cutting	664.902 9
Meat loaf	641.824
commercial processing	664.92
home preparation	641.824
Meat pies	
commercial processing	664.92
home preparation	641.824
Meath (Ireland)	T2—418 22
Meatless high-protein foods	
technology	664.64
Meats	641.36
see also Meat	
Mecca (Saudi Arabia)	T2—538
Islam	297.352
Mechanical bands	784.6
Mechanical barriers	
military engineering	623.31
Mechanical chess players	794.17
Mechanical conveyer systems	
office services	651.79
Mechanical deformation	
materials science	620.112 3
Mechanical drawing	604.2
Mechanical engineering	621
military applications	623.045
Mechanical engineers	621.092
Mechanical forces	530
biophysics	571.43
humans	612.014 41
extraterrestrial biophysics	
humans	612.014 53
materials science	620.112 3
Mechanical musical instruments	786.6
bands and orchestras	784
chamber ensembles	785
single type	785.66
construction	786.619 23
by hand	786.619 23
by machine	681.866
solo music	786.6
Mechanical pencils	
manufacturing technology	681.6

Mechanical processes	
printing	686.231
pulp to paper	676.2
wood pulp	676.122
Mechanical properties	
materials science	620.112 92
Mechanical separation	
ores	622.75
Mechanical stokers	
steam engineering	621.183
Mechanical systems	
ships	623.850 1
Mechanical toys	790.133
manufacturing technology	688.728
recreation	790.133
see also Toys	
Mechanical working	
metals	671.3
Mechanics	530
atmosphere	551.515
classical physics	531
engineering	620.1
foundation soils	624.151 36
physics	530
quantum physics	530.12
structures	624.17
Mechanics' liens	346.024
Mechanics of materials	620.112 3
Mechanics of particles	
classical physics	531.16
Mechanics of points	531.1
Mechanism (Philosophy)	146.6
Mechanisms	
engineering	621.8
Mechanization	
agricultural economics	338.161
control engineering	629.8
economics	338.064
factory operations engineering	670.427
mineral industries	338.26
production management	658.514
secondary industries	338.45
social effects	303.483
Mechanized bells	786.64
see also Mechanical musical	
instruments	
Mechanized cavalry	357.5
Mechanotherapy	
medicine	615.82
Mechitarists	255.17
church history	271.17
Méchouar de Casablanca	
(Morocco)	T2—643 8

Mecklenburg (Germany :
  State)   T2—431 7
Mecklenburg County (N.C.) T2—756 76
Mecklenburg County (Va.) T2—755 645
Mecklenburg-Strelitz
  (Germany : Landkreis) T2—431 72
Mecklenburg-Vorpommern
  (Germany)   T2—431 7
Mecoptera   595.744
Mecosta County (Mich.)   T2—774 52
Medal of Honor Legion (U.S.) 369.11
Medallions
  numismatics   737.22
Medals   T1—079
  armed forces   355.134 2
  numismatics   737.22
  religious significance   203.7
    see also Symbolism —
      religious significance
  research incentive   001.44
Médéa (Algeria : Province) T2—653
Medelpad landskap
  (Sweden)   T2—488 5
Media   302.23
  see also Mass media
Media (Ancient area)   935.75
    T2—357 5
Media centers   027
  see also Libraries
Media ethics   175
Media kits
  cataloging   025.349 6
  library treatment   025.179 6
Media production
  primary education   372.672
Median   519.533
Median Empire   935.750 4
    T2—357 5
Mediastinal diseases
  medicine   616.27
    see also Respiratory tract
      diseases — humans
Mediastinum
  human anatomy   611.27
  human physiology   612.25
  medicine   616.27
  surgery   617.545
Mediation
  labor economics   331.891 42
    public administration   354.97
  law   347.09
  law of nations   341.52

Mediation (continued)
  personnel management   658.315 4
    public administration   352.68
  social conflict   303.69
Medicaid   368.420 097 3
  law   344.730 22
  public administration   353.690 973
Medicaid fraud   364.163
  law   345.730 263
Medical accounting   657.834
Medical anthropology   306.461
Medical assistants   610.737 092
  role and function   610.737 069
  services   610.737
Medical astrology   133.586 1
Medical bacteriology   616.920 1
Medical care   362.1
  see also Health services
Medical care facilities
  area planning   711.555
Medical chemistry   615.19
Medical climatology   616.988
Medical emergencies   362.18
  medicine   616.025
  social services   362.18
Medical entomology   616.968
Medical ethics   174.2
  religion   205.642
    Buddhism   294.356 42
    Christianity   241.642
    Hinduism   294.548 642
    Islam   297.564 2
    Judaism   296.364 2
Medical examinations   616.075
Medical examiners   614.109 2
  law   347.016
    criminal law   345.012 6
Medical genetics   616.042
  law   344.041 96
Medical geography   614.42
Medical gymnastics
  therapeutics   615.82
Medical helminthology   616.962
Medical history taking   616.075 1
Medical installations (Armed
  forces)   355.72
Medical instruments   610.284
  manufacturing technology   681.761
  product safety   363.19
    public administration   353.99
    see also Product safety
Medical insurance   368.382 2
  public administration   353.69
  see also Insurance

Medicine shows	791.1
Medicines	615.1
see also Drugs	
(Pharmaceuticals)	
Medieval architecture	723
Medieval art	709.02
Medieval church modes	781.263
Medieval law	340.55
Medieval metrical romances	808.813 3
history and criticism	809.133
specific literatures	T3B—103 3
individual authors	T3A—1
Medieval music	780.902
Medieval painting	759.02
Medieval period	909.07
	T1—090 2
Austrian history	943.602
church history	270.3
Danish history	948.901
English history	942.03
European history	940.1
French history	944.02
German history	943.02
Italian history	945.01
Japanese history	952.02
Lombardian history	945.201
Norwegian history	948.101
Sardinian history	945.902
Scandinavian history	948.02
Sicilian history	945.801
Southern Italian history	945.701
specific centuries	909.1–.4
Swedish history	948.501
Tuscan history	945.501
Venetian history	945.301
see Manual at T1—0940902	
vs. T1—0902	
Medieval philosophy	
eastern	181
western	189
Medieval remedies	
therapeutics	615.880 902
Medieval sculpture	734
Medigap	368.382
see also Insurance	
Medina (England)	T2—422 8
Medina (Saudi Arabia)	T2—538
Islam	297.355 38
Medina Angarita, Isaías	
Venezuelan history	987.063 15
Medina County (Ohio)	T2—771 35
Medina County (Tex.)	T2—764 42

Medio Campidano (Italy :	
Province)	T2—459 8
ancient	T2—379 8
Mediolanum (Italy)	T2—372 271
Meditation	158.12
religion	204.35
Buddhism	294.344 35
Christianity	248.34
Hinduism	294.543 5
Islam	297.382
Sufi	297.438 2
Judaism	296.72
Meditations	158.128
religion	204.32
Buddhism	294.344 32
Christianity	242
Hinduism	294.543 2
Islam	297.382 4
Sufi	297.438 24
Judaism	296.72
Meditations (Music)	784.189 6
Mediterranean climate	551.691 28
Mediterranean region	909.098 22
	T2—182 2
ancient	937
	T2—37
climate	551.691 822
Mediterranean Sea	551.461 38
	T2—163 8
Mediterranean-type ecosystems	577.38
biology	578.738
Mediterranean-type plants	581.738
Mediterranean vegetation	581.738
Medium-security prisons	365.33
see also Penal institutions	
Mediums of exchange	332.4
Mediumship (Spiritualism)	133.91
Medlars	641.341 5
botany	583.642
cooking	641.641 5
food	641.341 5
orchard crop	634.15
Medulla oblongata	
human anatomy	611.81
human physiology	612.828
medicine	616.8
Medullosaceae	561.595
Medusae (Jellyfishes)	593.53
Medvedev, Dmitry	
Russian history	947.086 3
Medway (England)	T2—422 32
Meeker County (Minn.)	T2—776 49
Meerkat	599.742

Meetings	060	Melanesian languages	499.5
management use	658.456		T6—995
Megachiroptera	599.49	Melanesian literatures	899.5
paleozoology	569.4	Melanesians	T5—995
Megaloptera	595.747	Melanoma	
Megalopteris	561.597	incidence	614.599 947 7
Megapodiidae	598.64	medicine	616.994 77
Megaptera	599.525	*see also* Cancer — humans	
Megaric philosophy	183.6	Melanommatales	579.564
Megaris (Greece)	T2—384	Melanthiaceae	584.6
Megasporangia	575.665	Melastomataceae	583.73
Megaspores	571.845 2	Melatonin	
Meghalaya (India)	T2—541 64	human physiology	612.492
Megillah (Tractate)	296.123 2	Melayu Asli languages	499.28
Babylonian Talmud	296.125 2		T6—992 8
Mishnah	296.123 2	Melbourne (Vic.)	T2—945 1
Palestinian Talmud	296.124 2	Meleagrididae	598.645
Megillot (Bible)	221.044	Meleagris gallopavo	598.645
Mehedinți (Romania)	T2—498 4	Meles	599.767 2
Meighen, Arthur		Meliaceae	583.75
Canadian history	971.061 3	Melianthaceae	583.72
1920–1921	971.061 3	Melilla (Spain)	T2—641
1926	971.062 2	ancient	T2—397 12
Meigs County (Ohio)	T2—771 99	Melilotus	633.366
Meigs County (Tenn.)	T2—768 836	botany	583.63
Meiji period	952.031	forage crop	633.366
Me'ilah	296.123 5	Melinae	599.767
Babylonian Talmud	296.125 5	Meliorism	
Mishnah	296.123 5	philosophy	149.5
Meilen (Switzerland :		Mellette County (S.D.)	T2—783 63
Bezirk)	T2—494 572 9	Mellivorinae	599.767
Meiosis	571.845	Melmoth (South Africa)	T2—684 43
Meirionnydd (Wales)	T2—429 25	Melodeons	788.863
Meitnerium		instrument	788.863 19
chemistry	546.62	music	788.863
Mékinac (Quebec)	T2—714 457	*see also* Woodwind	
Meknès-El Menzeh		instruments	
(Morocco)	T2—645	Melodic reading	
Meknès-Tafilalt (Morocco)	T2—645	Koran	297.122 404 59
Mekong River	T2—59	Melodrama	792.27
Mekong River Delta		literature	808.825 27
(Vietnam and Cambodia)	T2—597 8	history and criticism	809.252 7
Melaka (State)	T2—595 1	specific literatures	T3B—205 27
Melamines	668.422 4	individual authors	T3A—2
Melancholy		stage presentation	792.27
arts	T3C—353	*see also* Theater	
literature	808.803 53	Melody	781.24
history and criticism	809.933 53	Meloidea	595.769
specific literatures	T3B—080 353	Melons	641.356 1
history and		botany	583.66
criticism	T3B—093 53	commercial processing	664.805 61
Melanconiales	579.55	cooking	641.656 1
Melanesia	995	food	641.356 1
	T2—95	garden crop	635.61

Melos (Greece)	T2—495 85
Melos Island (Greece)	T2—495 85
Melting	536.42
chemical engineering	660.284 296
metals	671.24
Melton (England : Borough)	T2—425 46
Melville (Sask.)	T2—712 44
Melville Peninsula	
(Nunavut)	T2—719 52
Membership lists	T1—06
directories	T1—025
Membrane lipids	572.577
Membrane processes	
chemical engineering	660.284 24
desalinization	628.167 4
water supply treatment	628.164
Membrane proteins	572.696
Membranes	
cytology	571.64
Membranophones	786.9
see also Percussion instruments	
Memoirs	920
	T1—092
Memorabilia	T1—075
Memorandums	
office use	651.755
Memorial buildings	725.94
Memorials	394.4
Holocaust, 1933–1945	940.531 864
see also Military	
commemorations	
Memorizing	
music training method	781.426
Memory	153.12
educational psychology	370.152 2
human physiology	612.823 312
philosophy	128.3
Memory (Computers)	004.5
engineering	621.397
Memory cards	004.568
engineering	621.397 68
Memory disorders	
medicine	616.83
see also Nervous system	
diseases — humans	
Memory management	005.435
Memphis (Extinct city)	T2—322
Memphis (Tenn.)	T2—768 19
Memphrémagog (Quebec)	T2—714 64
Memphrémagog Lake	
(Quebec)	T2—714 64
Men	305.31
	T1—081 1
art representation	704.942 3

Men (continued)	
arts	700.452 11
	T3C—352 11
biography	920.71
civil and human rights	323.331
criminal offenders	364.373
drawing	743.43
education	371.821 1
etiquette	395.142
fine arts	704.041
grooming	646.704 4
health	613.042 34
journalism for	070.483 46
labor economics	331.561
literature	808.803 521 1
history and criticism	809.933 521 1
specific literatures	T3B—080 352 11
history and	
criticism	T3B—093 521 1
painting	757.3
physical fitness	613.704 49
psychology	155.332
recreation	790.194
indoor	793.019 4
outdoor	796.081 1
relations with government	323.331
religion	200.811
Christianity	270.081 1
devotional literature	242.642
guides to Christian life	248.842
guides to life	204.408 11
sex hygiene	613.952
social aspects	305.31
see Manual at T1—081 *and*	
T1—08351, T1—08352,	
T1—08421, T1—08422	
Menabe (Kingdom)	969.101
	T2—691
Ménage à trois	
law	346.016 723
Menaḥot	296.123 5
Babylonian Talmud	296.125 5
Mishnah	296.123 5
Menarche	
human physiology	612.662
Menard County (Ill.)	T2—773 555
Menard County (Tex.)	T2—764 877
Mende (African people)	T5—963 48
Mende-Bandi languages	496.348
	T6—963 48
Mende language	496.348
	T6—963 48
Mende literature	896.348
Mendelevium	546.449

Mendel's laws	576.52
Mendicant religious orders	255.06
church history	271.06
Mending books	025.84
Mending textiles	
home economics	646.2
clothes	646.6
Mendip (England)	T2—423 83
Mendip Hills (England)	T2—423 83
Mendocino County (Calif.)	T2—794 15
Mendoza (Argentina : Province)	T2—826 4
Mendrisio (Switzerland : Distretto)	T2—494 786
Menelik II, Negus of Ethiopia	
Ethiopian history	963.043
Menger, Carl	
economic school	330.157
Mengistu Haile-Mariam	
Ethiopian history	963.071
Menhadens	597.45
fishing	639.274 5
Meniere's disease	
medicine	617.882
see also Ear diseases — humans	
Menifee County (Ky.)	T2—769 583
Menindee Lake (N.S.W.)	T2—944 9
Meningeal diseases	
medicine	616.82
see also Nervous system diseases — humans	
Meninges	573.862 5
human anatomy	611.81
human histology	612.820 45
human physiology	612.82
medicine	616.82
see also Nervous system	
Meningitis	
medicine	616.82
see also Nervous system diseases — humans	
Meningoencephalitis	
medicine	616.832
see also Nervous system diseases — humans	
Menispermaceae	583.34
Mennonite Church	289.7
church government	262.097
local church	254.097
church law	262.989 7
doctrines	230.97
catechisms and creeds	238.97
general councils	262.597
Mennonite Church (continued)	
guides to Christian life	248.489 7
missions	266.97
moral theology	241.049 7
public worship	264.097
religious associations	267.189 7
religious education	268.897
seminaries	230.073 97
theology	230.97
Mennonite cooking	641.566
Mennonites	
biography	289.709 2
Menominee County (Mich.)	T2—774 953
Menominee County (Wis.)	T2—775 356
Menominee Indians	977.400 497 313
	T5—973 13
Menomini Indians	T5—973 13
Menomini language	497.313
	T6—973 13
Menopause	
disorders	
gynecology	618.175
see also Female genital diseases — humans	
human physiology	612.665
social aspects	305.244 2
Menorca (Spain)	T2—467 52
Menorrhagia	
gynecology	618.172
see also Female genital diseases — humans	
Men's clothing	391.1
commercial technology	687.081 1
customs	391.1
home economics	646.32
home sewing	646.402
see also Clothing	
Men's liberation movement	305.32
Men's movements	305.32
Men's prisons	365.44
see also Penal institutions	
Men's rights	323.331
political science	323.331
Men's voices	782.8
choral and mixed voices	782.8
single voices	783.8
Menstruation	
human physiology	612.662
Menstruation disturbances	
gynecology	618.172
Mensuration	530.8
	T1—028 7
forestry	634.928 5
geometry	516.15

Menyanthaceae	583.983
Menzies, Robert, Sir	
Australian history	994.05
1939–1941	994.042
1949–1966	994.05
Mephitinae	599.768
Meprobamate	
pharmacokinetics	615.788 2
Merbein (Vic.)	T2—945 9
Mercantile credit	332.742
marketing management	658.882
Mercantilism (Economic school)	330.151 3
Mercantour National Park	
(France)	T2—449 4
Mercator projection	526.82
Merced County (Calif.)	T2—794 58
Mercedarians	255.45
church history	271.45
Mercenary troops	355.354
American Revolution	973.342
Mercer County (Ill.)	T2—773 395
Mercer County (Ky.)	T2—769 485
Mercer County (Mo.)	T2—778 213
Mercer County (N.D.)	T2—784 83
Mercer County (N.J.)	T2—749 65
Mercer County (Ohio)	T2—771 415
Mercer County (Pa.)	T2—748 95
Mercer County (W. Va.)	T2—754 74
Mercerizing textiles	677.028 25
Merchandisers	381.092
Merchandising	381
management	658.8
Merchant marine	387.5
see also Ocean transportation	
Merchant mariners	387.509 2
technologists	623.880 92
Merchant ships	387.2
design	623.812
engineering	623.82
freight services	387.544
power-driven	387.24
design	623.812 4
engineering	623.824
transportation services	387.24
transportation services	387.2
wind-driven	387.224
design	623.812 24
engineering	623.822 4
handling	623.882 24
transportation services	387.224
see also Ships	
Merchants	381.092
Mercia supremacy	942.015 7
Mercuries (Plants)	583.69
Mercury (Element)	669.71
chemical engineering	661.066 3
chemistry	546.663
economic geology	553.454
human toxicology	615.925 663
metallurgy	669.71
mining	622.345 4
organic chemistry	547.056 63
applied	661.895
physical metallurgy	669.967 1
toxicology	571.954 663
see also Chemicals; Metals	
Mercury (Planet)	523.41
	T2—992 1
astrology	133.533
unmanned flights to	629.435 41
Mercury fulminate	662.27
Mercury project	629.454
Mercury-vapor lighting	621.327 4
see also Lighting	
Mergansers	598.415
Merge sort (Computer science)	005.741
Mergers	338.83
accounting	657.96
banks	332.16
economics	338.83
law	346.066 26
management	658.162
Merging data	005.741
Mergini	598.415
Mérida (Spain)	T2—462 7
Mérida (Venezuela : State)	T2—871 3
Meridian (Miss.)	T2—762 677
Meridional instruments	522.2
Merina (Kingdom)	969.101
	T2—691
Merino, Manuel	
Peruvian history	985.064 8
Merino sheep	636.36
Meristem	575.48
Merit (Christian doctrine)	234
Merit awards	
personnel management	658.322 5
Merit pay	331.216 4
labor economics	331.216 4
personnel management	658.322 5
Merit system (Civil service)	352.63
Merits of Koran	297.122 32
Meriwether County (Ga.)	T2—758 455
Merkaz (Israel : District)	T2—569 47
Merkel, Angela	
German history	943.088 3
Merlucciid hakes	597.632
Merlucciidae	597.632

Mermaids	398.21
see also Legendary beings	
Mermen	398.21
see also Legendary beings	
Meroitic language	T6—96
Meromorphic functions	515.982
Meropidae	598.78
Merostomata	595.49
Merovingian dynasty	944.013
French history	944.013
German history	943.013
Merreden (W.A.)	T2—941 2
Merrick County (Neb.)	T2—782 423
Merrimac, Battle of Monitor and,	
1862	973.752
Merrimack County (N.H.)	T2—742 72
Merrimack River (N.H. and	
Mass.)	T2—742 72
Merritt (B.C.)	T2—711 72
Mersey, River (England)	T2—427 5
Merseyside (England)	T2—427 5
Mersin İli (Turkey)	T2—564 6
ancient	T2—393 5
Merthyr Tydfil (Wales :	
County Borough)	T2—429 75
Merton (London, England)	T2—421 93
Meru County (Kenya)	T2—676 246
Mesa County (Colo.)	T2—788 17
Mesa Verde National Park	
(Colo.)	T2—788 27
Mesabi Range (Minn.)	T2—776 77
Mescal	641.25
commercial processing	663.5
Mescalero-Chiricahua Apache	
language	497.256
	T6—972 56
Mescalero Indians	T5—972 56
Mescaline abuse	362.294
medicine	616.863 4
personal health	613.83
social welfare	362.294
see also Substance abuse	
Mesencephalon	
human anatomy	611.81
human physiology	612.826 4
medicine	616.8
Mesentery	
human anatomy	611.38
human physiology	612.33
medicine	616.38
surgery	617.558
Mesilinka River (B.C.)	T2—711 87
Mesmerism	154.7

Meso-American native languages	497
	T6—97
Meso-American native literatures	897
Meso-American native	
peoples	T5—970 72
Mesocricetus	599.356
Mesogastropoda	594.32
Mesolithic Age	930.13
Mesons	539.721 62
Mesopotamia	956.7
	T2—567
ancient	935
	T2—35
Mesopotamian architecture	722.51
Mesopotamian sculpture	732.5
Mesosauria	567.937
Mesosphere	551.514
Mesozoic era	551.76
geology	551.76
paleontology	560.176
Mesquakie language	497.314
	T6—973 14
Mesquite	583.633
Mess services (Armed forces)	355.341
Message passing	005.71
Messana (Italy)	T2—378 111
Messapian language	491.993
	T6—919 93
Messenger services	
internal office communication	651.79
office services	651.374 3
Messēnia (Greece)	T2—495 22
ancient	T2—389
Messiahs	
Christianity	232.1
Judaism	296.336
role and function	206.1
Messianic Judaism	289.9
Messianic prophecies	
Christianity	232.12
Judaism	296.336
Messianism	202.3
Judaism	296.336
Messina (Italy)	T2—458 111
ancient	T2—378 111
Messina (Italy : Città	
metropolitana)	T2—458 11
Messina (South Africa :	
District)	T2—682 57
Messina, Strait of (Italy)	551.461 386
	T2—163 86
Meta (Colombia)	T2—861 94

Metabolic diseases	571.944	Metallic salt processes	
humans	362.196 39	photography	772
incidence	614.593 9	Metallic soaps	668.125
medicine	616.39	Metallic solids	530.413
social services	362.196 39	Metallic wood-boring beetles	595.763
see also Digestive system		Metallizing	671.734
diseases — humans		Metallography	669.95
Metabolism	572.4	Metallurgical furnaces	669.8
animals	572.41	Metallurgists	669.092
bone diseases		Metallurgy	669
medicine	616.716	equipment manufacturing	
see also Musculoskeletal		technology	681.766 9
diseases — humans		Metals	669
human physiology	612.39	applied nutrition	613.285 1
inborn errors		architectural construction	721.044 7
medicine	616.390 42	architectural decoration	729.6
medicine	616.39	biochemistry	572.51
pharmacokinetics	615.739	humans	612.015 24
plants	572.42	building construction	693.7
see also Digestive system		building materials	691.8
Metacarpals		chemistry	546.3
human anatomy	611.717	decorative arts	739
Metadata		dowsing	133.323 3
information science	025.3	economic geology	553.4
format	025.316	foundation materials	624.153 6
Metaethics	170.42	handicrafts	745.56
Metagenesis	571.884	human toxicology	615.925 3
Metal engraving	765	materials science	620.16
Metal forming	671.3	metabolism	572.514
Metal furniture	645.4	human physiology	612.392 4
manufacturing technology	684.105	metallography	669.95
see also Furniture		military resources	355.242
Metal intaglio engraving	765	mineralogy	549.23
Metal manufacturing equipment		mining	622.34
manufacturing technology	681.767 1	organic chemistry	547.05
Metal-oxide-semiconductor		aliphatic	547.45
memory	004.53	applied	661.895
engineering	621.397 32	prospecting	622.184
Metal products	671.8	sculpture material	731.2
Metal relief engraving	761.8	ship design	623.818 2
Metal spraying	671.734	shipbuilding	623.820 7
Metal-work	671	structural engineering	624.182
see also Metalworking		textiles	677.53
Metalanguage	410.1	*see also* Textiles	
	T4—01	toxicology	571.954 3
Metalinguistics	410.1	*see also* Chemicals	
	T4—01	Metalworkers	669.092
Metallic compounds	546.3	metallurgy	669.092
chemical engineering	661.03	metalworking	671.092
Metallic fillings		Metalworking	671
dentistry	617.675	economics	338.476 71
Metallic glass	669.94	home workshops	684.09
Metallic inlays		ship hulls	623.843
dentistry	617.675	technology	671

Metamathematics	510.1	Methodist Church (continued)	
Metamorphic rocks	552.4	religious education	268.87
Metamorphosis (Biology)	571.876	seminaries	230.073 7
Metaphor	401.43	theology	230.7
linguistics	401.43	Methodist Church (U.S.)	287.631
literature	808.801 5	see also Methodist Church	
history and criticism	809.915	Methodist Church of Great	
rhetoric	808.032	Britain	287.536
Metaphysics	110	Methodist Episcopal Church	287.632
Metaponto (Italy)	T2—457 72	see also Methodist Church	
ancient	T2—377 73	Methodist Episcopal Church,	
Metatarsals		South	287.633
human anatomy	611.718	see also Methodist Church	
Metatheria	599.2	Methodist New Connexion	287.53
paleozoology	569.2	see also Methodist Church	
Metcalfe, Charles Theophilus		Methodist Protestant Church	287.7
Metcalfe, Baron		see also Methodist Church	
Indian history	954.031 4	Methodist sacred music	781.717
Metcalfe County (Ky.)	T2—769 693	public worship	782.322 7
Metchosin (B.C.)	T2—711 28	music	782.322 7
Meteor showers	523.53	religion	264.070 2
Meteorite craters	551.397	Methodists	
Meteorites	523.51	biography	287.092
mineralogy	549.112	Methodology (Principles)	T1—01
petrology	549.112	Metonymy	401.43
Meteoroids	523.51	linguistics	401.43
	T2—993	rhetoric	808.032
effect on space flight	629.416	Metric differential geometries	516.37
Meteorologists	551.509 2	Metric geometry	516.1
Meteorology	551.5	Euclidean	516.2
	T1—015 515	Metric spaces	514.325
aeronautics	629.132 4	Metric system	530.812
agriculture	630.251 5	law	343.075
law	344.095 5	social aspects	389.15
see Manual at 551.5 vs. 551.6		Metric topology	514.3
Meteors	523.51	Metrical romances	808.813 3
Meter (Music)	781.226	history and criticism	809.133
Meter (Prosody)	808.1	specific literatures	T3B—103 3
Methamphetamine abuse	362.299 5	individual authors	T3A—1
Methane		Metrication	389.16
biogas technology	665.776	Metro Manila (Philippines)	T2—599 16
Methane producing bacteria	579.321	Metro Vancouver (B.C.)	T2—711 33
Methanogenic bacteria	579.321	Metrology	
Methodist Church	287	commerce	389.1
church government	262.07	Metronomes	
local church	254.07	technology	681.118
church law	262.987	Metropolitan-area networks	004.67
doctrines	230.7	Metropolitan areas	307.764
catechisms and creeds	238.7	area planning	711.43
guides to Christian life	248.487	government	320.85
missions	266.7	public administration	352.167
moral theology	241.047	Metropolitana (Chile)	T2—833 1
public worship	264.07	Metteniusaceae	583.953
religious associations	267.187	Metz (France)	T2—443 853

Meurthe-et-Moselle
(France)   T2—443 82
Meuse (France)   T2—443 81
Meuse River   T2—492 4
   Belgium   T2—493 46
   Netherlands   T2—492 4
Mevleviyeh   297.482
Mexican-American Border
Region   T2—721
Mexican Americans   305.868 720 73
   T5—687 207 3
Mexican Hairless   636.76
Mexican literature   860
Mexican Revolution, 1910–1917   972.081 6
Mexican War, 1845–1848   973.62
Mexicans   T5—687 2
Mexico   972
   T2—72
Mexico, Gulf of   551.461 364
   T2—163 64
Mexico, Valley of (Mexico)   T2—725
Mexico City (Mexico)   T2—725 3
Mezereum   583.77
Mezuzot   296.461
Mezzo-soprano voices   782.67
   children's   782.77
     choral and mixed voices   782.77
     single voices   783.77
   general works   782.67
     choral and mixed voices   782.67
     single voices   783.67
   women's   782.67
     choral and mixed voices   782.67
     single voices   783.67
Mezzotinting   766.2
Mfecane   968.041
Mgeni River (South Africa)   T2—684 55
Mhala (South Africa :
District)   T2—682 73
Mhlatuze River (South
Africa)   T2—684 43
Miami (Fla.)   T2—759 381
Miami Beach (Fla.)   T2—759 381
Miami County (Ind.)   T2—772 84
Miami County (Kan.)   T2—781 68
Miami County (Ohio)   T2—771 48
Miami-Dade County (Fla.)   T2—759 38
Miami Indians   T5—973 15
Miami language (Algic)   497.315
   T6—973 15
Miami River (Ohio)   T2—771 7
Miao   T5—959 72
Miao language   495.972
   T6—959 72

Miao literature   895.972
Miao-Yao languages   495.97
   T6—959 7
MIAs   355.113
   see also Missing in action
Mica   553.674
   economic geology   553.674
   mineralogy   549.67
   mining   622.367 4
   synthetic   666.86
   technology   666.72
Micah (Biblical book)   224.93
Mice (Computers)   004.76
   engineering   621.398 6
Mice (Muridae)   599.35
   see also Rodents
Mice (Mus)   599.353
   agricultural pests   632.693 53
   animal husbandry   636.935 3
   experimental animals
     medicine   616.027 333
   household sanitation   648.7
Michael, Czar of Russia
   Russian history   947.047
Michael the Brave (Wallachia)
   Romanian history   949.801 5
Michelias   635.977 428 6
   botany   584.286
   ornamental arboriculture   635.977 428 6
Michif language   497.323
   T6—973 23
Michigan   977.4
   T2—774
Michigan, Lake   T2—774
Michoacán (Mexico : State)   T2—723 7
Michoacán de Ocampo
(Mexico)   T2—723 7
Micmac Indians   971.500 497 343
   T5—973 43
Micmac language   497.343
   T6—973 43
MICR (Computer science)   006.4
   engineering   621.399 4
Microanalysis (Chemistry)   543.22
Microascales   579.565
Microassembly languages   005.18
Microbes   579
   see also Microorganisms
Microbial diseases   571.98
   see also Communicable
   diseases
Microbiologists   579.092

Microbiology	579	Micrometeorology	551.66
applied	660.62	ecology	577.22
food	641.300 157 9	Micronesia	T2—965
commercial technology	664.001 579	Micronesia (Federated	
health	613.201 579	States)	T2—966
human physiology	612.001 579	Micronesian languages	499.52
intestine	612.330 157 9		T6—995 2
stomach	612.320 157 9	Micronesians	T5—995 2
medicine	616.904 1	Micronutrients	572.515
see Manual at 579.165		*see also* Trace elements	
vs. 616.9041; *also at*		Microorganisms	579
616.1–.9 vs. 616.1–.9		air pollution control	628.536
personal health		cell biology	571.629
environmental health	613.101 579	*see Manual at* 571.629 vs.	
Microbiotheriidae	599.27	571.29	
Microcephaly		cell culture	571.638 29
medicine	616.858 844	food technology	664.024
Microchemical analysis	543.22	human physiology	612.001 579
Microchemistry	543.22	medical microbiology	616.904 1
Microchiroptera	599.4	paleontology	561.9
paleozoology	569.4	physiology	571.29
Microcircuits	621.381 5	*see Manual at* 571.629 vs.	
Microclimatology	551.66	571.29	
ecology	577.22	resource economics	333.953
Microcode	005.18	respiration	572.472 9
Microcomputer workstations	004.16	Micropaleontology	560.47
see also Personal computers		Micropedology	631.433
Microcomputers	004.16	Microphones	621.382 84
see Manual at 004.11–.16		radio engineering	621.384 133
Microcontrollers	006.22	Microphotography	
Microcoryphia	595.723	technology	686.43
Microeconomics	338.5	Microprocessors	004.16
Microelectronic circuits	621.381 5	*see also* Personal computers	
Microelectronics	621.381	Microprogramming	005.18
social effects	303.483 4		T1—028 551 8
Microfiche	302.23	Microprograms	005.18
see also Microforms			T1—028 551 8
Microfilaments	571.654	Micropterus	597.738 8
Microfilms	302.23	Microreproductions	302.23
bibliographies	011.36	bibliographies	011.36
see also Microforms		*see also* Microforms	
Microform catalogs	025.313	Microscopes	502.82
Microforms	302.23	biology	570.282
bibliographies	011.36	manufacturing technology	681.413
cataloging	025.349 4	Microscopic analysis	
library treatment	025.179 4	chemistry	543.22
production		Microscopic metallography	669.950 282
office records	651.58	Microscopic objects	
technology	686.43	photography	778.31
publishing	070.579 5	Microscopic petrology	552.8
Microfossils	560.47	Microscopy	502.82
Microhylidae	597.89	biology	570.282
Microlithography		medical diagnosis	616.075 8
electronics	621.381 531	natural sciences	502.82

Microsporangia	575.65
Microsporida	579.48
Microstructure	
materials science	620.112 99
Microsurgery	617.05
Microtechnique	502.82
biology	570.282 7
Microtomy	502.82
biology	570.282 7
Microtonality	781.269
Microtubules	571.654
Microtus	599.354
Microwave aids	
marine navigation	623.893 3
Microwave cooking	641.588 2
Microwave dinners	
home serving	642.1
Microwave electronics	
engineering	621.381 3
physics	537.534 4
Microwave spectroscopes	
manufacturing technology	681.414 8
Microwave spectroscopy	543.6
analytical chemistry	543.6
engineering	621.361
physics	537.534 4
Microwaves	537.534 4
biophysics	571.453
humans	612.014 481
Micrurus	597.964 4
Mid & East Antrim	
(Northern Ireland)	T2—416 13
Mid Bedfordshire (England)	T2—425 63
Mid Devon (England)	T2—423 54
Mid Glamorgan (Wales)	T2—429 7
Mid Suffolk (England)	T2—426 45
Mid Sussex (England)	T2—422 65
Mid Ulster (Northern	
Ireland)	T2—416 4
Mid Wales	T2—429 5
Mid-Western State (Nigeria)	T2—669 3
Midair collisions	363.124 92
see also Air safety	
Midbrain	
human anatomy	611.81
human physiology	612.826 4
medicine	616.8
Middelburg (Eastern Cape,	
South Africa : District)	T2—687 56
Middelburg (Mpumalanga,	
South Africa : District)	T2—682 76
Middle age	305.244
Middle-aged men	305.244 1

Middle-aged people	305.244
	T1—084 4
civil rights	323.353
guides to Christian life	248.84
guides to religious life	
Judaism	296.708 44
health	613.043 4
labor economics	331.394
psychology	155.66
relations with government	323.353
religion	200.844
Christianity	270.084 4
social aspects	305.244
Middle-aged women	305.244 2
Middle-aged workers	331.394
Middle Ages	909.07
	T1—090 2
literature	
history and criticism	809.933 582 07
see also Medieval period	
Middle America	972
	T2—72
Middle American native	
languages	497
	T6—97
Middle American native	
literatures	897
Middle American native	
peoples	T5—970 72
Middle Atlantic States	974
	T2—74
Middle class	305.55
	T1—086 22
customs	390.1
dress	391.01
social welfare	362.892
Middle Congo	967.240 3
	T2—672 4
Middle-distance races	796.423
see also Track and field	
Middle ear diseases	
medicine	617.84
see also Ear diseases —	
humans	
Middle ears	
human anatomy	611.85
human physiology	612.854
medicine	617.84
Middle East	956
	T2—56
ancient	939.4
	T2—394
Middle East theater (World War	
II)	940.542 4

Midwifery	
law	344.041 5
medicine	618.2
Midwives	
law	344.041 5
role and function	618.202 33
Mie-ken (Japan)	T2—521 81
Mifepristone	
medicine	618.29
pharmacokinetics	615.766
Mifflin County (Pa.)	T2—748 46
Mignonettes	635.933 78
botany	583.78
floriculture	635.933 78
Migori County (Kenya)	T2—676 296
Migraine	
medicine	616.849 12
see also Nervous system	
diseases — humans	
Migrant agricultural workers	
economics	331.544
social class	305.563
Migrant workers	331.544
	T1—086 24
economics	331.544
social class	305.562
social welfare	362.85
Migration	304.8
political science	325
social theology	
Christianity	261.838
Migration (Animals)	591.568
birds	598.156 8
Migratory animals	591.568
Migratory birds	598.156 8
Mihai II, Viteazul, Voivode of	
Wallachia	
Romanian history	949.801 5
Mikasuki Indians	T5—973 8
Mikasuki language	497.38
	T6—973 8
Mikkeli (Finland : Province)	T2—489 75
Mikkelin lääni (Finland)	T2—489 75
Mikva'ot (Tractate)	296.123 6
Mikveh	296.75
Mila (Algeria : Province)	T2—655
Milam County (Tex.)	T2—764 288
Milan (Italy)	T2—452 11
ancient	T2—372 271
Milan (Italy : Metropolitan	
city)	T2—452 1
ancient	T2—372 27
Milano (Italy)	T2—452 11
ancient	T2—372 271

Milano (Italy : Città	
metropolitana)	T2—452 1
ancient	T2—372 27
Mildew	579.53
agricultural disease	632.43
materials science	620.112 23
Mildura (Vic.)	T2—945 9
Miletus	T2—392 3
Milieu therapy	
psychiatry	616.891 44
Militarism	355.021 3
ethics	172.42
see also War — ethics	
social theology	201.727 3
see also War — social	
theology	
sociology	303.66
Military accounting	657.835
Military administration	355.6
Military air transportation service	358.44
Military aircraft	358.418 3
armed forces equipment	358.418 3
engineering	623.746
Military alliances	355.031
armed forces	355.356
Military arts	355
Military assistance	355.032
law	342.041 2
Military attachés	355.032
Military bands	784.84
Military bases	355.7
law	343.015 7
Military buildings	
architecture	725.18
Military camps	355.7
Military capability	355.033 2
Military commemorations	355.16
Algerian Revolution	965.046 6
American Revolution	973.36
Chaco War	989.207 166
Civil War (England)	942.062 6
Civil War (Spain)	946.081 6
Civil War (United States)	973.76
Crimean War	947.073 86
Falkland Islands War	997.110 246
Franco-German War	943.082 6
Hundred Years' War	944.025 6
Indo-Pakistan War, 1971	954.920 516
Indochinese War	959.704 16
Iraq War, 2003–2011	956.704 436
Iraqi-Iranian Conflict	955.054 26
Korean War	951.904 26
Mexican War	973.626
Napoleonic Wars	940.276

Military missions	355.032
law	342.041 2
Military models	355.48
handicrafts	745.592 82
war games	355.48
Military music	781.599
songs	782.421 599
Military occupation	355.028
law of war	341.66
operations	355.49
Military offenses (Law)	343.014 3
Military operations	355.4
World War I	940.41
World War II	940.541
Military Order of Foreign Wars of the United States	369.11
Military pacts	355.031
Military penology	365.48
law	343.014 6
Military pensions	331.252 913 55
law	343.011 2
Military personnel	355.009 2
law	343.01
civil rights	342.085
law of war	341.67
role and function	355.33
Military personnel missing in action	355.113
see also Missing in action	
Military police	355.133 23
Military policy	355.033 5
Military prisons	365.48
law	344.035 48
penology	365.48
see also Penal institutions	
Military procurement	355.621 2
Military records management	355.688 7
Military relations	355.031
Military religious orders	255.791
church history	271.791
Military resources	355.2
law	343.013
Military schools (Higher education)	378.4–.9
see Manual at 378.4–.9 vs. 355.00711	
Military schools (Secondary education)	373.243
see also Secondary education	
Military schools (Service academies)	355.007 11
see Manual at 378.4–.9 vs. 355.00711	

Military science	355
arts	700.458 1
	T3C—358 1
literature	808.803 581
history and criticism	809.933 581
Military sealift commands	359.985
Military service (Conditions of work)	355.1
Military service (Manpower procurement)	355.223
ethics	172.42
see also War — ethics	
law	343.012
Military services	355
see also Armed services	
Military situation	355.03
Military societies	369.2
biography	369.209 2
United States	369.1
Military sociology	306.27
Military songs	782.421 599
Military supplies	355.8
Military supply ships	359.985 83
design	623.812 65
engineering	623.826 5
naval equipment	359.985 83
naval units	359.985 3
Military surgery	617.99
Military training	355.5
Military transportation	358.25
air forces	358.44
engineering	623.6
land forces	358.25
naval forces	359.985
Military transports (Ships)	359.985 83
see also Transports (Ships)	
Military units	355.31
American Revolution	973.34
Civil War (United States)	973.74
Confederate States of America	973.742
France	
American Revolution	973.347
Great Britain	
American Revolution	973.341
War of 1812	973.524 1
Poland	
American Revolution	973.346
Spain	
American Revolution	973.346
Spanish-American War	973.894
states of United States	
Civil War (United States)	973.744–.749
Sweden	
American Revolution	973.346

Military units (continued)
  United States
    Civil War (United States)   973.741
      War of 1812   973.524 3
    War of 1812   973.524
    World War I   940.41
    World War II   940.541
    see Manual at 930–990
Militia   355.37
Milk   641.371
  animal husbandry   636.088 42
    cow's milk   636.214 2
    see Manual at 636.1–.8 vs.
      636.088
  cooking   641.671
  food   641.371
  physiology   573.679
  processing   637.1
Milk-free cooking   641.563 971
Milk-free diet
  health   613.268 71
Milk-free foods   641.309 71
Milk River (Mont. and
  Alta.)   T2—786 1
Milk substitutes
  commercial processing   663.64
Milkfish   641.392
  cooking   641.692
  culture   639.375
  food   641.392
  zoology   597.5
Milking   637.124
Milkweeds   583.956
Milkworts   583.63
Milky Way   523.113
Mill, John Stuart
  economic school   330.153
Millard County (Utah)   T2—792 45
Mille Lacs County (Minn.)   T2—776 68
Milled soaps   668.124
Millennium
  Christianity   236.9
Milleporina   593.55
Miller County (Ark.)   T2—767 56
Miller County (Ga.)   T2—758 964
Miller County (Mo.)   T2—778 56
Millets   641.331 71
  botany   584.924
  commercial processing   664.72
  cooking   641.631 71
  food   641.331 71
  food crop   633.171
  forage crop   633.257 1
Milliammeters   621.374 4

Milliners   646.504 092
Millinery   646.504
  commercial technology   687.42
  home construction   646.504
Milling grains   664.72
Milling metals   671.35
Milling plants
  ore dressing   622.79
Milling tools   621.91
Millipedes   595.66
Millmerran (Qld.)   T2—943 3
Mills
  architecture   725.4
  construction   690.54
Mills County (Iowa)   T2—777 74
Mills County (Tex.)   T2—764 512
Milne Bay Province (Papua
  New Guinea)   T2—954 1
Milos
  botany   584.924
Milos (Greece)   T2—495 85
Milton Keynes (England)   T2—425 91
Milwaukee (Wis.)   T2—775 95
Milwaukee County (Wis.)   T2—775 94
Mimamsa (Philosophy)   181.42
Mimaropa (Philippines)   T2—599 3
Mime   792.3
  see also Theater
Mimicry (Biology)   578.47
  animals   591.473
  plants   581.47
Mimidae   598.844
Mimosaceae   583.633
Mimosas   583.633
  botany   583.633
  ornamental arboriculture   635.977 363 3
Mimosoideae   583.633
Mina (African people)   T5—963 37
Minangkabau   T5—992 244
Minangkabau language   499.224 4
    T6—992 244
Minangkabau literature   899.224 4
Minarets   297.351
  architecture   726.2
Minas Gerais (Brazil)   T2—815 1
Mind   128.2
  philosophy   128.2
  psychology   150
Mind reading   133.82
Mindanao Island
  (Philippines)   T2—599 7
Mindfulness   158.13
Mindfulness meditation   158.12
Mindoro (Philippines)   T2—599 3

Mindoro Occidental	
(Philippines)	T2—599 38
Mindoro Oriental	
(Philippines)	T2—599 36
Mine clearing	355.4
civilian operations	363.349 88
military engineering	623.26
operations	355.4
Mine drainage	622.5
water pollution engineering	628.168 32
Mine health	363.119 622
social services	363.119 622
technology	622.8
Mine laying (Military)	623.26
Mine railroads	622.66
Mine roof control	622.28
Mine safety	363.119 622
social services	363.119 622
technology	622.8
see also Safety	
Mine shafts	622.25
Mine surveys	622.14
Mine timbering	622.28
Mined lands	333.765
economics	333.765
law	346.046 765
reclamation technology	631.64
Minelayers	359.836 2
design	623.812 62
engineering	623.826 2
naval equipment	359.836 2
naval units	359.326 2
Miner County (S.D.)	T2—783 34
Mineral commodities	338.27
investment economics	332.644 2
Mineral County (Colo.)	T2—788 38
Mineral County (Mont.)	T2—786 84
Mineral County (Nev.)	T2—793 51
Mineral County (W. Va.)	T2—754 94
Mineral drugs	
pharmacology	615.2
Mineral fertilizers	631.8
economic geology	553.64
see also Fertilizers	
Mineral industries	338.2
enterprises	338.762 2
law	343.077
products	338.27
commerce	381.42
public administration	354.39
Mineral oils	
processing	665.4
Mineral pigments	553.662
Mineral resources	333.85
land economics	333.85
law	346.046 85
law	346.046 85
military science	355.242
public administration	354.39
Mineral rights	
law	346.043
private ownership	346.043
public control	346.046 85
public revenue	336.12
sale and rental	333.339
Mineral springs	
health resorts	613.122
therapeutics	615.853
Mineral surveys	
prospecting	622.13
Mineral waters	553.73
commercial processing	663.61
economic geology	553.73
health	613.287
therapeutics	615.853
Mineral waxes	
processing	665.4
Mineralized beverages	641.26
commercial processing	663.62
Mineralogists	549.092
Mineralogy	549
see Manual at 549 vs. 546; also at 549 vs. 548	
Minerals	553
applied nutrition	613.285
animal husbandry	636.085 27
biochemistry	572.51
humans	612.015 24
economic geology	553
economics	338.2
resources	333.85
law	346.046 85
folklore	398.26
history and criticism	398.365
legendary	398.465
real	398.365
metabolism	572.514
human physiology	612.392
mineralogy	549
public administration	354.39
resource economics	333.85
law	346.046 85
synthetic	666.86
Miners	622.092
labor economics	331.762 2
public administration	354.942 2

Minks (continued)	
trapping	639.117 662 7
zoology	599.766 27
Minna (Nigeria)	T2—669 65
Minneapolis (Minn.)	T2—776 579
Minneapolis Metropolitan	
Area (Minn.)	T2—776 579
Minnedosa (Man.)	T2—712 73
Minnehaha County (S.D.)	T2—783 371
Minnesang (Poetry)	808.814
history and criticism	809.14
specific literatures	T3B—104
individual authors	T3A—1
Minnesota	977.6
	T2—776
Minnesota River (S.D. and	
Minn.)	T2—776 3
Minnows	597.482
Minoan architecture	722.61
Minoan Linear A	492.6
	T6—926
see Manual at T6—926	
Minoan Linear B	487.1
	T6—87
Minoans	939.18
Minor arts	745
Minor Clerks Regular	255.56
church history	271.56
Minor Prophets (Bible)	224.9
Minor surgery	617.024
obstetrics	618.85
Minor tractates (Talmud)	296.123 7
Minorca (Spain)	T2—467 52
Minorities	305
	T1—08
bibliographies of works by	011.8
civil rights	323.1
education	371.82
government programs	353.53
legal status	346.013 08
constitutional law	342.087
private law	346.013 08
libraries for	027.63
personnel management	658.300 8
government employees	352.608
relations with government	323.1
social welfare	362
public administration	353.53
see Manual at T1—08; *also at*	
T1—08 and 306.2–.6	
Minorities (Ethnic and national)	305.8
	T1—089
psychology	155.8
social welfare	362.84

Minorities in education	370.8
Minority enterprises	338.642 2
economics	338.642 2
financial management	658.159 208
management	658.022 08
Minority groups (Ethnic and	
national)	305.8
	T1—089
psychology	155.8
social welfare	362.84
Minors	305.23
see also Young people	
Minors (Legal concept)	
legal status	346.013 083
private law	346.013 083
Minquiers (Channel Islands)	T2—423 48
Minsk (Belarus : Oblast)	T2—478 6
Minskaĩa voblastsʹ	
(Belarus)	T2—478 6
Minstrel shows	791.12
Mint (Herb)	641.338 2
botany	583.96
see also Flavorings	
Minting policies	332.46
Minto, Gilbert Elliot, Earl of	
Indian history	954.031 3
Minto, Gilbert John Murray	
Kynynmond Elliot, Earl of	
Indian history	954.035 6
Minuets	793.3
music	784.188 35
Minūfīyah (Egypt)	T2—621
Minutes	
office records	651.77
Minyā (Egypt : Province)	T2—622
Miocene epoch	551.787
geology	551.787
paleontology	560.178 7
Mirabel (Quebec)	T2—714 254
Miracle plays	
literature	808.825 16
history and criticism	809.251 6
specific literatures	T3B—205 16
individual authors	T3A—2
stage presentation	792.16
see also Theater	
Miracles	202.117
Christianity	231.73
of Jesus Christ	232.955
Gospels	226.7
of Mary	232.917
spiritual gift	234.13
Judaism	296.311 6
philosophy of religion	212

Mississippi County (Ark.)	T2—767 95
Mississippi County (Mo.)	T2—778 983
Mississippi River	T2—77
Arkansas	T2—767 8
Tennessee	T2—768 1
Mississippi River Delta	
(La.)	T2—763 3
Mississippian period	551.751
geology	551.751
paleontology	560.175 1
Missoula County (Mont.)	T2—786 85
Missouri	977.8
	T2—778
Missouri Compromise, 1820	973.54
Civil War (United States) cause	973.711 3
Missouri River	T2—78
Missouri	T2—778
Montana	T2—786
Nebraska	T2—782 2
North Dakota	T2—784 7
South Dakota	T2—783 3
Missouri Valley Siouan	
languages	497.527
	T6—975 27
Mist	541.345 15
colloid chemistry	541.345 15
applied	660.294 515
meteorology	551.575
Mistletoes	583.85
Mistresses (Extramarital	
relationships)	306.736
Misty Fjords National	
Monument (Alaska)	T2—798 2
Misumalpan languages	497.88
	T6—978 8
Mitanni (Ancient kingdom)	935.402
	T2—354
Mitchell (Qld.)	T2—943 4
Mitchell County (Ga.)	T2—758 973
Mitchell County (Iowa)	T2—777 234
Mitchell County (Kan.)	T2—781 23
Mitchell County (N.C.)	T2—756 865
Mitchell County (Tex.)	T2—764 729
Mitchell's Plain (South	
Africa : District)	T2—687 35
Mite infestations	
humans	
medicine	616.573
see also Skin diseases —	
humans	
Mites	595.42
agricultural pests	632.654 2
disease carriers	
medicine	614.433

Mithraism	299.15
Mitis (Quebec)	T2—714 773
Mitochondria	571.657
Mitochondrial DNA	572.869
Mitosis	571.844
Mitral valve diseases	
medicine	616.125
see also Cardiovascular	
diseases — humans	
Mitral valves	
human anatomy	611.12
human physiology	612.17
medicine	616.125
Mittelfranken (Germany)	T2—433 2
Mittelland (Switzerland)	T2—494 5
Mitten makers	685.409 2
Mittens	391.412
commercial technology	685.4
customs	391.412
home economics	646.3
home sewing	646.48
see also Clothing	
Mittimatalik (Nunavut)	T2—719 52
Mittlerer Oberrhein	
(Germany : Region)	T2—434 643
Mitzvot	
Jewish ethics	296.36
Jewish law	296.18
Miwok Indians	T5—974 133
Miwok language	497.413 3
	T6—974 133
Mixe Indians	T5—974 3
Mixe-Zoque languages	497.43
	T6—974 3
Mixed ability grouping in	
education	371.252
Mixed-bloods (People)	T5—05
Mixed descent	T5—05
Mixed drinks	641.874
commercial processing	663.1
Mixed economies	330.126
Mixed equations	515.38
Mixed languages	417.22
specific languages	T4—7
Mixed-level classrooms	371.25
Mixed marriage	306.84
law	346.016 76
Mixed martial arts	796.81
Mixed-media arts	
techniques	702.81
two-dimensional	740
Mixed reality	006.8
Mixed voices	782.5
Mixes (Pastry)	664.753

Model airplanes	629.133 134
military engineering	623.746 022 8
recreation	796.154
see Manual at 796.15 vs.	
629.0460228	
Model automobiles	629.221 2
recreation	796.156
see Manual at 796.15 vs.	
629.0460228	
Model boats	623.820 1
recreation	796.152
see Manual at 796.15 vs.	
629.0460228	
Model cars	629.221 2
recreation	796.156
see Manual at 796.15 vs.	
629.0460228	
Model land vehicles	629.221
military engineering	623.747 022 8
recreation	796.156
see Manual at 796.15 vs.	
629.0460228	
Model makers	688.109 2
Model ships	623.820 1
recreation	796.152
see Manual at 796.15 vs.	
629.0460228	
Model theory	511.34
Model trains	625.19
recreation	790.133
see Manual at 796.15 vs.	
629.0460228	
Model vehicles	629.046 022 8
recreation	796.15
see Manual at 796.15 vs.	
629.0460228	
Modeling	
plastic arts	730.28
pottery	666.442
arts	738.142
technology	666.442
primary education	372.53
sculpture	731.42
use in child care	649.51
Modeling (Fashion design)	746.92
Modeling (Simulation)	003
	T1—011
Models (Fashion)	746.920 92
Models (Molds)	
sculpture	731.43
Models (Representations)	688.1
	T1—022 8
arts	702.8
cataloging	025.349 6

Models (Representations) (continued)	
educational use	T1—078
handicrafts	745.592 8
see Manual at 745.5928	
library treatment	025.179 6
manufacturing technology	688.1
Models (Simulations)	003
	T1—011
management decision making	658.403 52
Modems	004.64
engineering	621.398 14
Modena (Italy)	T2—454 21
ancient	T2—372 621
Modena (Italy : Province)	T2—454 2
ancient	T2—372 62
Moderators	
nuclear engineering	621.483 37
Modern algebra	512
Modern architecture	724
Modern art	709.04
religious significance	203.7
Christianity	246.4
Modern dance	792.8
see also Theater	
Modern dance performers	792.802 809 2
Modern decoration	744.090 4
Modern differential geometry	516.362
Modern geometry	516.04
Modern Greek language	489.3
	T6—89
Modern Greek literature	889
Modern history	909.08
	T1—090 3
arts	T3C—358 208
specific centuries	909.5–.8
Modern Indic languages	491.4
	T6—914
Modern Indic literatures	891.4
Modern Indo-Aryan languages	491.4
	T6—914
Modern Indo-Aryan literatures	891.4
Modern jazz	781.655
Modern languages	410
Modern Latin peoples	T5—4
Modern literature	808.800 3
history and criticism	809.03
Modern music	780.903
Modern Paganism	299.94
Christian polemics	239.94
Modern painting	759.06
Modern pentathlon	796

Mohave language	497.572 2	Moldova	947.6
	T6—975 722		T2—476
Mohawk Indians	974.700 497 554 2	ancient	939.88
	T5—975 542		T2—398 8
Mohawk language	497.554 2	Molds (Fungi)	579.53
	T6—975 542	agricultural diseases	632.43
Mohawk River (N.Y.)	T2—747 6	Molds (Tools)	621.984
Mohegan Indians	974.600 497 344	Mole rats	599.35
	T5—973 44	Mole salamanders	597.858
Mohegan-Montauk-Narragansett		Mole Valley (England)	T2—422 165
language	497.344	Molecular biology	572.8
	T6—973 44	humans	611.018 16
Mohism (Chinese philosophy)	181.115	Molecular botany	572.82
Moi, Daniel Arap		Molecular computing	006.384 2
Kenyan history	967.620 42	Molecular electronics	621.381
Moism (Chinese philosophy)	181.115	Molecular evolution	572.838
Moisture		Molecular genetics	572.8
meteorology	551.57	humans	611.018 16
soil physics	631.432	Molecular physics	539.6
Moistureproof construction		astronomy	523.019 6
buildings	693.893	Molecular properties	
Mojave Desert (Calif.)	T2—794 95	materials science	620.112 99
Mokala National Park		Molecular spectra	539.6
(South Africa)	T2—687 14	Molecular spectroscopy	543.54
Mokerong (South Africa :		Molecular structure	541.22
District)	T2—682 53	biochemistry	572.33
Mokole languages	496.345	chemistry	541.22
	T6—963 45	physics	539.12
Mokopane (South Africa :		Molecular weights	541.222
District)	T2—682 53	Molecules	
Molasses	641.336	chemistry	541.22
commercial processing	664.118	physics	539.6
cooking with	641.636	Moles (Animals)	599.335
food	641.336	agricultural pests	632.693 35
Moldavia	T2—498 1	Moles (Disorder)	
Moldova	T2—476	medicine	616.55
Romania	T2—498 1	*see also* Skin diseases —	
Moldavia (Principality)	949.801 4	humans	
	T2—498 1	Molinism	273.7
Moldavian language	459	persecution of	272.5
	T6—591	Molise (Italy : Region)	T2—457 19
Moldavians	T5—591	ancient	T2—377 33
Molded pulp	676.182	Mollicutes	579.328
Molded rubber	678.34	Mollies	597.667
Molding		Molluginaceae	583.883
arts	730.28	Mollusca	594
ceramic arts	738.142	*see also* Mollusks	
sculpture	731.43	Molluscoidea	594.6
Molding glass	666.125	paleozoology	564.6
Molding latex	678.527	Molluscum contagiosum	
Molding plastics	668.412	medicine	616.522
Molding rubber	678.27	*see also* Skin diseases —	
Moldmaking		humans	
metal casting	671.23		

Monetary policy (continued)
  law   343.032 6
  macroeconomics   339.53
Monetary reform
  international   332.456 6
Monetary stabilization   332.415
  international banking   332.152
  law   346.082 152
Monetary standards   332.42
Monetary theory   332.401
Money   332.4
  arts   737.4
  economics   332.4
  law   343.032
  public administration   354.84
Money market funds   332.632 7
Money orders   332.76
  law   346.096
Money-saving cooking   641.552
Money-saving interior decorating   747.1
Money supply   332.4
  effect on value of money   332.414
Mong language   495.972
   T6—959 72
Mong literature   895.972
Mongkut, King of Siam
  Thai history   959.303 4
Mongo (African people)   T5—963 96
Mongo languages   496.396
   T6—963 96
Mongol dynasty   951.025
Mongol Empire   950.2
   T2—5
Mongolia   951.73
   T2—517 3
Mongolia (Region)   951.7
   T2—517
Mongolian language   494.23
   T6—942 3
Mongolian languages   494.2
   T6—942
Mongolian literature   894.23
Mongolian literatures   894.2
Mongolian People's Republic   951.73
   T2—517 3
Mongolians   T5—942 3
Mongoloid race   T5—95
Mongols   T5—942
Mongooses   599.742
Monifieth (Scotland)   T2—412 6
Moniliales   579.55
Moniligastrida   592.64
Monimiaceae   584.288

Monism
  philosophy   147.3
Moniteau County (Mo.)   T2—778 52
Monito del monte   599.27
Monitor and Merrimac, Battle of,
  1862   973.752
Monitor lizards   597.959 6
Monitorial system of education   371.39
Monitoring (Social control)   361.25
  see also Environmental
    monitoring
Monitors (Computers)
  control programs
    firmware   005.18
    control software   005.43
  video display screens   004.77
    engineering   621.398 7
Monitors (Disciplinarians)
  student discipline   371.59
Monk seals   599.795
Monkeypox
  humans   362.196 913
    incidence   614.521
    medicine   616.913
    see also Communicable
      diseases — humans
  social services   362.196 913
Monkeys   599.8
  animal husbandry   636.98
  experimental animals
    medicine   616.027 38
  see also Primates
Monkeys (New World)   599.85
Monkeys (Old World)   599.86
Monklands (Scotland)   T2—414 52
Monks   206.57
  Buddhist   294.365 7
  Christian   255
    biography   271.009 2
    see Manual at 230–280
    guides to Christian life   248.894 2
Monkshoods   583.34
Monmouth (Wales :
  District)   T2—429 98
Monmouth County (N.J.)   T2—749 46
Monmouthshire (Wales)   T2—429 9
Monmouthshire (Wales :
  County)   T2—429 98
Mono County (Calif.)   T2—794 48
Mono Indians   T5—974 57
Mono language   497.457
   T6—974 57
Monochromatic photography   778.62

Monseñor Nouel
(Dominican Republic :
Province)   T2—729 369 3
Monsoons   551.518 4
Monsteras   584.442
Monsters
  arts   700.47
    T3C—37
  literature   808.803 7
   history and criticism   809.933 7
   specific literatures   T3B—080 37
    history and
     criticism   T3B—093 7
  unexplained phenomena   001.944
Monstrilloida   595.34
Mont-Royal (Quebec)   T2—714 28
Mont-Tremblant National
  Park (Quebec)   T2—714 418
Montage   702.813
Montagnais Indians   971.400 497 32
    T5—973 2
Montagnais language   497.32
    T6—973 2
Montagnards (Vietnamese
  people)   T5—959 3
Montagu (South Africa :
  District)   T2—687 33
Montague County (Tex.)   T2—764 541
Montana   978.6
    T2—786
Montana (1987–1998)
  (Bulgaria : Oblast)   T2—499 1
Montana (1999-) (Bulgaria :
  Oblast)   T2—499 15
Montauk language   497.344
    T6—973 44
Montcalm (Quebec :
  Regional County
  Municipality)   T2—714 415
Montcalm County (Mich.)   T2—774 53
Monte-Carlo (Monaco)   T2—449 49
Monte Carlo method   518.282
Monte Cristi (Dominican
  Republic : Province)   T2—729 352
Monte Plata (Dominican
  Republic : Province)   T2—729 377
Monteiro, António Mascarenhas
  Cape Verdean history   966.580 32
Montenegrin language   491.829
    T6—918 29
Montenegrin literature   891.829
Montenegrins   T5—918 29

Montenegro   949.745
    T2—497 45
  ancient   939.874 5
    T2—398 745
Montérégie (Quebec)   T2—714 3
Monterey Bay (Calif.)   551.461 432
    T2—164 32
Monterey County (Calif.)   T2—794 76
Montessori method   371.392
  primary education   372.139 2
Montevideo (Uruguay :
  Dept.)   T2—895 13
Montezuma County (Colo.)   978.827
    T2—788 27
Montgomery (Wales :
  District)   T2—429 51
Montgomery County (Ala.)   T2—761 47
Montgomery County (Ark.)   T2—767 43
Montgomery County (Ga.)   T2—758 832
Montgomery County (Ill.)   T2—773 82
Montgomery County (Ind.)   T2—772 48
Montgomery County (Iowa)   T2—777 75
Montgomery County (Kan.)   T2—781 93
Montgomery County (Ky.)   T2—769 553
Montgomery County (Md.)   T2—752 84
Montgomery County (Miss.)   T2—762 642
Montgomery County (Mo.)   T2—778 382
Montgomery County (N.C.)   T2—756 74
Montgomery County (N.Y.)   T2—747 46
Montgomery County (Ohio)   T2—771 72
Montgomery County (Pa.)   T2—748 12
Montgomery County
  (Tenn.)   T2—768 45
Montgomery County (Tex.)   T2—764 153
Montgomery County (Va.)   T2—755 785
Monthey (Switzerland :
  District)   T2—494 796 9
Months   529.2
Montmagny (Quebec :
  Regional County
  Municipality)   T2—714 735
Montmorency County
  (Mich.)   T2—774 83
Monto (Qld. : Shire)   T2—943 5
Montour County (Pa.)   T2—748 39
Montpelier (Vt.)   T2—743 4
Montpellier (France)   T2—448 42
Montréal (Quebec)   T2—714 28
Montréal (Quebec : Urban
  agglomeration)   T2—714 28
Montréal-Est (Quebec)   T2—714 28
Montréal Island (Quebec)   T2—714 28
Montréal Metropolitan
  Community (Quebec)   T2—714 27

Moral offenses
  criminology 364.17
  law 345.027
Moral philosophers 170.92
  see Manual at 170.92 vs. 171
Moral philosophy 170
Moral realism 170.42
Moral Rearmament 267.16
Moral renewal (Christianity) 248.25
Moral sense
  ethical systems 171.2
Moral theology 205
  Buddhism 294.35
  Christianity 241
    see Manual at 241 vs. 261.8
  Hinduism 294.548
  Islam 297.5
    Sufi 297.45
  Judaism 296.36
Moral training
  home child care 649.7
Morale
  armed forces 355.123
  personnel management 658.314
  public administration 352.66
Morales, Jimmy
  Guatemalan history 972.810 536
Morales Ayma, Evo
  Bolivian history 984.054 2
Morality 170
  public control
    criminology 364.17
    law 345.027
    public administration 353.37
  religion 205
Morality plays
  literature 808.825 16
    history and criticism 809.251 6
    specific literatures T3B—205 16
      individual authors T3A—2
  stage presentation 792.16
  see also Theater
Morat, Lake of
  (Switzerland) T2—494 538
Moravia (Czech Republic) 943.72
   T2—437 2
Moravian Church 284.6
  see also Christian
    denominations
Moravian dialects 491.867
   T6—918 6
Moravian literature 891.86
Moravians (Ethnic group) T5—918 6

Moravians (Religious group)
  biography 284.609 2
Moravskoslezský kraj
  (Czech Republic) T2—437 28
Moray (Scotland) T2—412 2
Morays 597.43
Morazán (El Salvador) T2—728 433
Morbid obesity
  medicine 616.398
    see also Digestive system
      diseases — humans
  surgery 617.43
Morbihan (France) T2—441 3
Mordell conjecture 516.352
Mordellidae 595.769
Mordoviĩa (Russia) T2—474 6
Mordvin T5—945 6
Mordvin language 494.56
   T6—945 6
Mordvin literature 894.56
Mordvinia (Russia) T2—474 6
Moré (African people) T5—963 5
Moré language 496.35
   T6—963 5
Møre og Romsdal fylke
  (Norway) T2—483 9
Morehouse Parish (La.) T2—763 84
Morelos (Mexico) T2—724 9
Morels 579.578
Mores 306
  customs 390
  sociology 306
Moretele I (South Africa :
  District) T2—682 41
Moretele II (South Africa :
  District) T2—682 76
Morgan County (Ala.) T2—761 93
Morgan County (Colo.) T2—788 74
Morgan County (Ga.) T2—758 595
Morgan County (Ill.) T2—773 463
Morgan County (Ind.) T2—772 513
Morgan County (Ky.) T2—769 253
Morgan County (Mo.) T2—778 53
Morgan County (Ohio) T2—771 94
Morgan County (Tenn.) T2—768 74
Morgan County (Utah) T2—792 26
Morgan County (W. Va.) T2—754 96
Morgan horse 636.177
Morges (Switzerland :
  District) T2—494 522 3
Morgues 363.75
  architecture 725.597
Morice Lake (B.C.) T2—711 82
Morice River (B.C.) T2—711 82

Moridae	597.63	Morphophonology	414
Moringaceae	583.78	specific languages	T4—15
Mormon Church	289.332	Morphosyntax	415
see also Church of Jesus Christ		specific languages	T4—5
of Latter-day Saints		Morrill County (Neb.)	T2—782 95
Mormon tea	585.8	Morris County (Kan.)	T2—781 58
Mormons		Morris County (N.J.)	T2—749 74
biography	289.332 092	Morris County (Tex.)	T2—764 217
Mormyriformes	597.47	Morrison, Scott	
Morning after pills		Australian history	994.072
health	613.943 2	Morrison County (Minn.)	T2—776 69
medicine	618.182 5	Morrison plan	371.39
see also Birth control		Morrow County (Ohio)	T2—771 516
Morning-blooming plants		Morrow County (Or.)	T2—795 67
floriculture	635.953	Morse code telegraphy	384.14
Morning glories	635.933 959	wireless	384.524
botany	583.959	*see also* Telegraphy	
floriculture	635.933 959	Morsi, Mohamed	
Morning prayer	264.15	Egyptian history	962.056
Anglican	264.030 15	Mortal sin	241.31
texts	264.033	Mortality	
music	782.325	demography	304.64
choral and mixed voices	782.532 5	Mortar (Material)	666.9
single voices	783.093 25	building material	691.5
Mornington (Vic.)	T2—945 2	materials science	620.135
Morobe Province (Papua		Mortars (Weapons)	355.822
New Guinea)	T2—957 1	engineering	623.425
Moroccans	T5—927 64	military equipment	355.822
Morocco	964	Mortgage banks	332.32
	T2—64	law	346.082 32
ancient	939.712	public administration	354.86
	T2—397 12	Mortgage bonds	332.632 3
Morocco (Spanish zone)	T2—642	Mortgage certificates	332.632 3
Morogoro Region		Mortgage defaults	332.72
(Tanzania)	T2—678 25	Mortgage delinquencies	332.72
Morona-Santiago (Ecuador)	T2—866 43	Mortgage insurance	368.852
Morone	597.732	law	346.086 852
Moroni (Comoros)	T2—694 1	economic assistance	343.074 2
Moronidae	597.732	Mortgages	332.72
Morphine abuse	362.293	accounting	657.75
medicine	616.863 2	credit economics	332.72
personal health	613.83	investment economics	332.632 44
social welfare	362.293	law	346.043 64
see also Substance abuse		public administration	354.86
Morphing		Morton County (Kan.)	T2—781 715
computer graphics	006.696	Morton County (N.D.)	T2—784 85
Morphisms (Mathematics)	512.62	Morton National Park	
Morphogenesis	571.833	(N.S.W.)	T2—944 6
Morphology (Biology)	571.3	Mortuary chapels	
Morphology (Grammar)	415.9	architecture	726.8
specific languages	T4—59	Mortuary practice	363.75
Morphophonemics	414	*see also* Undertaking	
specific languages	T4—15	(Mortuary)	
		Moruya (N.S.W.)	T2—944 7

Morwell (Vic.)	T2—945 6	Mosses	588.2
MOS memory	004.53	paleobotany	561.8
engineering	621.397 32	*see also* Plants	
Mosaic diseases		Mossi (African people)	T5—963 5
agriculture	632.8	Mossi (Kingdom)	966.250 1
Mosaic glass			T2—662 5
arts	748.5	Mossi languages	496.35
Mosaic law (Bible)	222.1		T6—963 5
Mosaics	738.5		
architectural decoration	729.7	Mostaganem (Algeria :	
Mosasauridae	567.95	Province)	T2—651
Moscoso, Mireya		Mosul (Iraq)	T2—567 4
Panamanian history	972.870 541	Motacillidae	598.854
Moscovium	546.71	Motazilites	297.834
Moscow (Russia : Oblast)	T2—473 1	Koran commentary	297.122 74
Moscow Patriarchate	281.947	Motelkeepers	647.940 92
Moselle (France)	T2—443 85	Motels	910.46
Moselle River	T2—434 3	*see also* Hotels	
Moses		Motets	782.26
Biblical leader	222.109 2	choral and mixed voices	782.526
Islam	297.246	single voices	783.092 6
Mosetenan languages	498.9	Moth flies	595.772
	T6—989	Mother and child	306.874 3
Moshavim	307.776	Mother of God	
Moshoeshoe II, King of Lesotho		Christian doctrine	232.91
Lesotho history	968.850 31	Motherhood	306.874 3
1966–1990	968.850 31	Mothering Sunday	394.262 8
1995–1996	968.850 32	Mothers	306.874 3
Mosisili, Pakalitha Bethuel			T1—085 2
Lesotho history	968.850 32	Christian devotional literature	242.643 1
Moskovskaia oblast´		family relationships	306.874 3
(Russia)	T2—473 1	guides to Christian life	248.843 1
Mosques	297.351	psychology	155.646 3
architecture	726.2	social welfare	362.839 53
organization	297.65	Mother's Day	394.262 8
Mosquito control	363.78	Motherwell (Scotland :	
social welfare	363.78	District)	T2—414 52
technology	628.965 7	Moths	595.78
see also Pest control		agricultural pests	632.78
Mosquito Indians	972.850 049 788 2	culture	638.578
	T5—978 82	Motility	
Mosquito language	497.882	cytology	571.67
	T6—978 82	microorganisms	571.672 9
Mosquitoes	595.772	Motion	
disease carriers	571.986	celestial bodies	521
medicine	614.432 3	design	744.82
Moss animals	594.67	philosophy	116
Mössbauer spectroscopy		physics	531.11
physics	537.535 2	stars	523.83
Mossel Bay (South Africa :		Motion design	744.82
District)	T2—687 37	Motion picture advertising	659.14
Mosselbaai (South Africa :		Motion picture directors	791.430 233 092
District)	T2—687 37	Motion picture music	781.542
		Motion picture photography	777

Motion picture plays	791.437
see also Screenplays	
Motion picture projection	777.57
Motion picture scripts	791.437
rhetoric	808.066 791
Motion picture theaters	
architecture	725.823
Motion pictures	791.43
accounting	657.84
cataloging	025.347 3
communications services	384.8
ethics	175
influence on crime	364.254
instructional use	371.335 23
adult level	374.265 23
journalism	070.18
library treatment	025.177 3
performing arts	791.43
see Manual at 791.43,	
791.45 vs. 777	
public administration	354.75
sociology	302.234 3
use in advertising	659.152
see Manual at 384.54, 384.55,	
384.8 vs. 791.4	
Motion sickness	
medicine	616.989 2
see also Environmental	
diseases — humans	
Motion studies	
production management	658.542 3
psychology	152.3
Motions (Law)	347.052
Motivation	153.8
armed forces	355.123
education	
gifted students	371.956
educational psychology	370.154
learning psychology	153.153 4
personnel management	658.314
executives	658.407 14
public administration	352.66
primary education	
reading	372.42
Motivation research	
marketing management	658.834 2
Motlanthe, Kgalema	
South African history	968.073
Motley County (Tex.)	T2—764 752
Motocross	796.756
Motor bicycles	388.347 5
engineering	629.227 5
see also Motorcycles	
Motor functions	
human physiology	612.7
localization in brain	612.825 2
psychology	152.3
Motor homes	388.346
architecture	728.79
camper cooking	641.575
driving	629.284 6
engineering	629.226
repair	629.287 6
transportation services	388.346
travel	910
see also Automotive vehicles	
see Manual at 643.29, 690.879,	
728.79 vs. 629.226	
Motor horns	
music	786.99
see also Percussion	
instruments	
Motor land vehicles	388.34
engineering	629.2
transportation services	388.34
see also Automotive vehicles	
Motor learning	
psychology	152.334
Motor nerves	
human physiology	612.811
Motor organs	573.7
see also Musculoskeletal	
system	
Motor scooter racing	796.75
Motor skills	
educational psychology	370.155
Motor system	573.7
see also Musculoskeletal	
system	
Motor vehicle engineers	629.209 2
Motor vehicle insurance	368.092
inland marine	368.232
law	346.086 092
liability	368.572
see also Insurance	
Motor vehicle racing	796.7
see also Automotive	
vehicles — sports	
Motor vehicle registration plates	929.9
Motor vehicle transportation	
facilities	
architecture	725.38
area planning	711.73
Motor vehicles	388.34
engineering	629.2
transportation services	388.34
see also Automotive vehicles	

Motor yachting	797.125 6
Motor yachts	387.231 4
engineering	623.823 14
transportation services	387.231 4
see also Ships	
Motorboat racing	797.14
Motorboating	
sports	797.125
Motorboats	387.231
design	623.812 31
engineering	623.823 1
handling	623.882 31
transportation services	387.231
see also Ships	
Motorcycle accidents	363.125 9
see also Highway safety	
Motorcycle racers	796.750 92
Motorcycle racing	796.75
biography	796.750 92
see also Automotive	
vehicles — sports	
Motorcycle theft	364.162 862 922 75
law	345.026 286 292 275
Motorcycle transportation	
facilities	
area planning	711.73
Motorcycle troops (Armed	
forces)	357.53
Motorcycles	388.347 5
engineering	629.227 5
repair	629.287 75
riding	629.284 75
sports	796.75
theft of	364.162 862 922 75
law	345.026 286 292 275
transportation services	388.347 5
see also Automotive vehicles	
see Manual at 629.046 vs. 388	
Motorized homes	388.346
see also Motor homes	
Motorized infantry	356.16
Motors	621.4
Motorscooters	388.347 5
engineering	629.227 5
repair	629.287 75
see also Motorcycles	
Motorways	388.122
see also Roads	
Moulins (Quebec)	T2—714 412
Moultrie County (Ill.)	T2—773 675
Mound builders (Birds)	598.64
Mount Aspiring National	
Park (N.Z.)	T2—937 1
Mount Athos (Greece)	T2—495 65

Mount Ayliff (South	
Africa : District)	T2—687 59
Mount Buffalo National	
Park (Vic.)	T2—945 5
Mount Cook National Park	
(N.Z.)	T2—938 8
Mount Currie (South	
Africa : District)	T2—684 67
Mount Desert Island (Me.)	T2—741 45
Mount Elliott National Park	
(Qld.)	T2—943 6
Mount Etna (Italy)	T2—458 13
Mount Everest (China and	
Nepal)	T2—549 61
Mount Field National Park	
(Tas.)	T2—946 2
Mount Fletcher (South	
Africa : District)	T2—687 59
Mount Frere (South Africa :	
District)	T2—687 59
Mount Fuji (Japan)	T2—521 66
Mount Gambier (S. Aust.)	T2—942 34
Mount Hood (Or.)	T2—795 61
Mount Isa (Qld.)	T2—943 7
Mount Kaputar National	
Park (N.S.W.)	T2—944 4
Mount Kilimanjaro	
(Tanzania)	T2—678 26
Mount Lofty Ranges (S.	
Aust.)	T2—942 32
Mount McKinley National	
Park (Alaska)	T2—798 3
Mount Rainier National	
Park (Wash.)	T2—797 782
Mount Revelstoke National	
Park (B.C.)	T2—711 68
Mount Robson Provincial	
Park (B.C.)	T2—711 82
Mount Spec National Park	
(Qld.)	T2—943 6
Mount Waddington (B.C.)	T2—711 2
Mount Whitney (Calif.)	T2—794 86
Mountain ashes	583.73
Mountain ashes (Rosaceae)	583.642
Mountain biking	796.63
see also Cycling — sports	
Mountain building	551.82
Mountain climbing	796.522
equipment technology	688.765 22
see also Outdoor life	
Mountain goat	599.647 5
conservation technology	639.979 647 5
resource economics	333.959 647 5
Mountain laurel	583.93

Movement disorders
 medicine | 616.83
  see also Nervous system
   diseases — humans
Movement education
 primary education | 372.868
Movement perception
 human physiology | 612.88
  visual perception | 612.84
 psychology | 153.754
  visual perception | 152.142 5
Movies | 791.43
 see also Motion pictures
Movimento sociale italiano
 (Political party) | 324.245 038
Movimento sociale
 italiano-Destra nazionale
 (Political party) | 324.245 038
Moving and storage industry | 388.044
 law | 343.093 2
Moving household goods | 648.9
 freight services | 388.044
 personnel management | 658.383
Moving sidewalks | 388.41
Moving targets
 gun sports | 799.313
 physics | 531.112
Mower County (Minn.) | T2—776 17
Mowing | 631.55
Moxibustion
 therapeutics | 615.892
Moxico (Angola : Province) | T2—673 4
Moyle (Northern Ireland) | T2—416 14
Mozambicans | T5—967 9
Mozambique | 967.9
 | T2—679
Mozambique Channel | 551.461 525
 | T2—165 25
MP (Military Police) | 355.133 23
Mpendle (South Africa :
 District) | T2—684 7
Mpofu (South Africa :
 District) | T2—687 54
Mpongwe language | 496.396
 | T6—963 96
Mpox
 humans | 362.196 913
  incidence | 614.521
  medicine | 616.913
  social services | 362.196 913
Mpumalanga (South Africa) | 968.27
 | T2—682 7
Mqanduli (South Africa :
 District) | T2—687 58

MRI (Imaging)
 medicine | 616.075 48
MSG (Food additive)
 food technology | 664.4
M'Sila (Algeria : Province) | T2—655
Msinga (South Africa :
 District) | T2—684 8
Mswati III, King of Eswatini
 Swazi history | 968.870 3
Mthatha (South Africa :
 District) | T2—687 58
Mthethwa (Kingdom) | 968.403 8
 | T2—684
Mtonjaneni (South Africa :
 District) | T2—684 43
Mtunzini (South Africa :
 District) | T2—684 43
Mtwara Region (Tanzania) | T2—678 24
Mu-mesons | 539.721 14
Mu'allaq (Hadith) | 297.125 22
Mubārak, Muḥammad Ḥusnī
 Egyptian history | 962.055
Mucilage | 668.33
Muck (Scotland) | T2—411 54
Mucocutaneous leishmaniasis
 incidence | 614.534
 medicine | 616.936 4
  see also Communicable
   diseases — humans
Mucous membranes
 human histology | 611.018 7
Mud flows | 551.307
Mud fuels | 662.82
Mud puppies | 597.85
Mud turtles | 597.923
Mu'ḍal (Hadith) | 297.125 22
Mudéjar architecture | 720.946 090 2
Mudgee (N.S.W.) | T2—944 5
Mudīrīyat al-Sharqīyah
 (Egypt) | T2—621
Mudminnows | 597.5
Muffin mixes | 664.753
Muffins | 641.815 7
Mufflers (Automobile part) | 629.252
Muffs | 391.44
 commercial technology | 687.19
 fur | 685.24
 customs | 391.44
 see also Accessories (Clothing)
Mugabe, Robert Gabriel
 Zimbabwean history | 968.910 51
Mugilidae | 597.7
Muğla İli (Turkey) | T2—562 7
 ancient | T2—392 4

Multiple access systems
  computer communications   004.6
    see also Computer
      communications
  processing modes   004.3
    see also Processing
      modes — computer
      science
Multiple art   709.040 7
  sculpture   735.230 47
Multiple birth
  obstetrics   618.25
Multiple column tariffs   382.753
  see also Customs (Tariff)
Multiple cropping   631.58
Multiple deficiency states
  medicine   616.399
    see also Digestive system
      diseases — humans
Multiple dwellings
  architecture   728.31
Multiple flutes   788.37
  see also Woodwind
    instruments
Multiple intelligences   153.9
  educational psychology   370.152 9
  psychology   153.9
Multiple-line insurance coverage   368.09
Multiple-loop systems
  automation engineering   629.833
Multiple myeloma
  incidence   614.599 941 8
  medicine   616.994 18
    see also Cancer — humans
Multiple organ failure
  medicine   616.047 5
Multiple personality disorder
  medicine   616.852 36
    see also Mental disorders
Multiple pregnancy
  obstetrics   618.25
Multiple-purpose buildings   720.49
Multiple sclerosis   362.196 834
  medicine   616.834
  social services   362.196 834
  see also Nervous system
    diseases — humans
Multiple stars   523.841
Multiple-valued logic   511.312
Multiplexers
  communications engineering   621.382 16
  computer communications   004.66
    engineering   621.398 1

Multiplexing
  communications engineering   621.382 16
  computer communications   004.66
    engineering   621.398 1
Multiplication   512.92
  algebra   512.92
  arithmetic   513.213
Multiplicative properties   512.73
Multiplier (Economics)   339.43
Multiprocessing   004.35
  communications   004.618 5
    computer software   005.713 75
    computer software
      development   005.712 75
  computer software   005.375
  computer software
    development   005.275
  graphics software   006.687 5
  graphics software development   006.677 5
  interfacing
    computer software   005.713 75
    computer software
      development   005.712 75
  multimedia software   006.787 5
  multimedia software
    development   006.777 5
Multiprocessors   004.35
  engineering   621.391
Multiprogramming   005.434
  computer hardware   004.3
  systems software   005.434
  see also Processing modes —
    computer science
Multisensor data fusion   005.74
Multistage programming   519.703
Multistory buildings   720.483
  see also Tall buildings
Multistory houses
  architecture   728.372
Multitasking (Computer science)   005.434
  computer hardware   004.3
  see also Processing modes —
    computer science
Multitrophic interactions
  (Ecology)   577.16
Multiuser processing (Computer
  science)   004.3
Multivariate analysis   519.535
Multnomah County (Or.)   T2—795 49
Muluzi, Bakili
  Malawian history   968.970 42
Mumbai (India)   T2—547 92
Mummies
  customs   393.3

Mumps
  incidence   614.544
  medicine   616.313
    see also Digestive system
      diseases — humans
  pediatrics   618.923 13
Munchausen syndrome
  medicine   616.858 6
    see also Mental disorders
Munchausen syndrome by proxy
  medicine   616.858 223
    see also Child abuse
München (Germany)   T2—433 64
Münchwilen (Switzerland :
  Bezirk)   T2—494 593
Muncie (Ind.)   T2—772 65
Munda   T5—959 5
Munda languages   495.95
     T6—959 5
Munda literatures   895.95
Mundane astrology   133.5
Mundari language   495.95
     T6—959 5
Mundari literature   895.95
Munich (Germany)   943.364
     T2—433 64
Municipal annexation   320.859
  law   342.041 3
Municipal bankruptcy   336.368
Municipal bonds   332.632 33
  law   346.092 2
Municipal charters   342.02
Municipal colleges   378.052
    see also Higher education
Municipal contracts   352.532 14
Municipal corporations   320.85
  law   342.09
Municipal courts   347.02
Municipal engineering   628
Municipal engineers   628.092
Municipal finance   336.014
  law   343.03
  public administration   352.421 4
  public finance   336.014
Municipal franchises
  public revenue   336.16
Municipal government
  law   342.09
Municipal incorporation   320.85
Municipal theater   792.022
Municipal universities   378.052
    see also Higher education
Municipal wastes   363.728
    see also Waste control

Municipal water supply   363.61
  engineering   628.1
Municipalities   320.85
  law   342.09
    see Manual at T2—713 and
      T2—714
Munqatiʻ (Hadith)   297.125 22
Munsee Indians   T5—973 45
Munsee language   497.345
     T6—973 45
Münster (Germany :
  Regierungsbezirk)   T2—435 61
Munster (Ireland)   T2—419
Münster (Westphalia,
  Germany)   T2—435 614
Münsterland (Germany)   T2—435 61
Muntjacs   599.65
Muntz metal   669.3
  materials science   620.182
  metallography   669.953
  metallurgy   669.3
  metalworking   673.3
  physical metallurgy   669.963
Muong   T5—959 2
Muong language   495.92
     T6—959 2
Muons   539.721 14
Mura languages   498.9
     T6—989
Mural paintings   751.73
Murangʻa County (Kenya)   T2—676 264
Murcia (Spain : Region)   T2—467 7
Murder   364.152 3
  law   345.025 23
  social welfare   362.882 93
Murderers   364.152 3
  biography   364.152 309 2
Mureş (Romania)   T2—498 4
Muri (Switzerland : Bezirk)   T2—494 566 7
Muriatic acid
  chemical engineering   661.23
Muridae   599.35
Murine typhus
  incidence   614.526 2
  medicine   616.922 2
    see also Communicable
      diseases — humans
Müritz (Germany :
  Landkreis)   T2—431 72
Murjiites (Islamic sect)   297.837
Murmansk (Russia : Oblast)   T2—471 3
Murmanskaia oblastʻ
  (Russia)   T2—471 3
Muromachi period   952.023

Murray Bridge (S. Aust.)	T2—942 32	Muscular dystrophy	362.196 748
Murray County (Ga.)	T2—758 31	medicine	616.748
Murray County (Minn.)	T2—776 27	pediatrics	618.927 48
Murray County (Okla.)	T2—766 57	social services	362.196 748
Murray River (B.C.)	T2—711 87	*see also* Musculoskeletal	
Murray River (N.S.W.-S.		diseases — humans	
Aust.)	T2—944	Muscular rheumatism	
Murraysburg (South Africa :		medicine	616.742
District)	T2—687 39	*see also* Musculoskeletal	
Murres	598.33	diseases — humans	
conservation technology	639.978 33	Muscular tissue	
resource economics	333.958 33	human histology	612.740 45
Murrumbidgee River		Musculoskeletal diseases	573.739
(N.S.W.)	T2—944 8	animals	573.739
Mursal (Hadith)	297.125 222	veterinary medicine	636.089 67
Mursī, Muḥammad		humans	362.196 7
Egyptian history	962.056	anesthesiology	617.967 47
Murua Island (Papua New		cancer	362.196 994 7
Guinea)	T2—954 1	incidence	614.599 947
Murui language	498.9	medicine	616.994 7
	T6—989	social services	362.196 994 7
Murwillumbah (N.S.W.)	T2—944 3	*see also* Cancer —	
Mus	599.353	humans	
Muş İli (Turkey)	T2—566 72	geriatrics	618.976 7
ancient	T2—394 2	incidence	614.597
Mūsá		medicine	616.7
Islam	297.246	pediatrics	618.927
Musaceae	584.88	pharmacokinetics	615.77
Muṣannafat	297.125 56	social services	362.196 7
Muscat and Oman	T2—535 3	surgery	617.47
Muscatine County (Iowa)	T2—777 68	Musculoskeletal system	573.7
Musci	588.2	anesthesiology	617.967 47
Muscicapidae	598.848	animals	573.7
Muscidae	595.774	diseases	573.739
Muscle fatigue		*see also* Musculoskeletal	
human biochemistry	612.744	diseases	
Muscles	573.75	dislocations	
biology	573.75	medicine	617.16
drawing		fractures	
animals	743.6	medicine	617.15
humans	743.47	human anatomy	611.7
human anatomy	611.73	human histology	612.704 5
human biochemistry	612.744	human physiology	612.7
human biophysics	612.741	injuries	617.470 44
human physiology	612.74	medicine	616.7
injuries	617.473 044	sprains	
medicine	616.74	medicine	617.17
pharmacokinetics	615.773	surgery	617.47
surgery	617.473	Museologists	069.092
Muscogee County (Ga.)	T2—758 473	Museology	069
Muscular diseases			T1—075
medicine	616.74	arts	T3C—39
see also Musculoskeletal		Museum activities	069
diseases — humans			T1—075

594

Relative Index

		Music (continued)	
Museum catalogs	069.52	primary education	372.87
	T1—074	printing	686.284
Museum collections	069.5	public administrative support	353.77
	T1—074	publishing	070.579 4
Museum documentation	069.52	religion	203.7
	T1—075	attitude toward secular music	201.678
Museum equipment	069.3	Buddhism	294.343 7
Museum furnishings		Christianity	246.75
plant management	069.3	attitude toward secular	
Museum furniture		music	261.578
museology	069.33	Hinduism	294.537
Museum guidebooks	T1—074	Islam	
Museum labels	069.53	attitude toward secular	
Museum libraries	027.68	music	297.267 8
Museum objects		Jainism	294.437
circulation	069.132	Judaism	296.462
selection	069.51	public worship	203.8
Museum policy (Government		Christianity	264.2
policy)	069	Judaism	296.462
Museum registration methods	069.52	*see also* Sacred music —	
	T1—075	religious significance	
Museum science	069	research	780.72
Museum services	069.1	sociology	306.484 2
	T1—075	use in child care	649.51
Museums	069	*see Manual at* 780	
	T1—074	Music appreciation	781.17
architecture	727.6	primary education	372.872
area planning	711.57	Music boxes	786.65
fine arts	708	*see also* Mechanical musical	
see Manual at 704.9 and		instruments	
753–758		Music dictionaries	780.3
institutional housekeeping	647.996	Music editing	780.149
law	344.093	Music education	780.7
public administrative support	352.76	Music fusions	781.6
publishing	070.594	*see Manual at* 781.6	
Museveni, Yoweri		Music hall presentations	792.7
Ugandan history	967.610 44	*see also* Theater	
Musharraf, Pervez		Music halls	
Pakistani history	954.910 531	architecture	725.81
Mushrooms	579.6	Music instruction	780.7
agriculture	635.8	Music libraries	026.78
commercial processing	664.805 8	Music theory	781
cooking	641.658	Music therapy	
food	641.358	medicine	615.851 54
human toxicology	615.952 96	Musical aptitude tests	153.947 8
Music	780	Musical bows	787.92
aptitude tests	153.947 8	instrument	787.921 9
arts	T3C—357 8	music	787.92
ethics	175	*see also* Stringed instruments	
religion		Musical chairs (Recreation)	793.4
Christianity	241.65	Musical elements	781.2
see also Recreation — ethics			
folklore	398.277 8		
history and criticism	398.357 8		

595

Myers-Briggs personality	
inventory	155.283
applied psychology	158.15
Myers-Briggs typology	
personality theory	155.264 4
Mykolaïvs´ka oblast´	
(Ukraine)	T2—477 3
Mykolayiv (Ukraine :	
Oblast)	T2—477 3
Mykonos (Greece :	
Regional unit)	T2—495 85
Mykonos Island (Greece)	T2—495 85
Mynas	598.863
animal husbandry	636.68
Myocardial depressants	
pharmacokinetics	615.716
Myocardial diseases	
medicine	616.124
see also Cardiovascular	
diseases — humans	
Myocardial infarction	
medicine	616.123 7
see also Cardiovascular	
diseases — humans	
Myocardial ischemia	
medicine	616.123
see also Cardiovascular	
diseases — humans	
Myocarditis	
medicine	616.124
see also Cardiovascular	
diseases — humans	
Myocardium	
human anatomy	611.12
human physiology	612.17
medicine	616.124
Myodocopa	595.33
paleozoology	565.33
Myomorpha	599.35
Myopia	
optometry	617.755
see also Eye diseases —	
humans	
Myositis	
medicine	616.743
see also Musculoskeletal	
diseases — humans	
Myotis	599.472
Myoxidae	599.359 6
Myriangiales	579.564
Myriapoda	595.6
paleozoology	565.6
Myricaceae	583.65
Myricales	583.65
Myristicaceae	584.286
Myrmecophagidae	599.314
Myrothamnaceae	583.42
Myrtaceae	583.732
botany	583.732
edible fruits	641.344 2
cooking	641.644 2
food	641.344 2
orchard crop	634.42
Myrtales	583.73
Myrtle wax	665.12
Myrtles (Lauraceae)	584.288
Myrtles (Myricaceae)	583.65
Myrtles (Myrtaceae)	635.933 732
botany	583.732
floriculture	635.933 732
Myrtles (Oregon myrtle)	583.23
Myrtles (Wax myrtles)	583.43
Mysia (Turkey)	939.21
	T2—392 1
Mysidacea	595.375
Mysore (India : State)	T2—548 7
Mystacocarida	595.36
Mysteries	
occultism	135
unexplained phenomena	001.94
Mystery films	791.436 556
Mystery games	793.93
Mystery plays (Religious)	
literature	808.825 16
history and criticism	809.251 6
specific literatures	T3B—205 16
individual authors	T3A—2
stage presentation	792.16
see also Theater	
Mystery plays (Suspense)	792.27
literature	808.825 27
history and criticism	809.252 7
specific literatures	T3B—205 27
individual authors	T3A—2
stage presentation	792.27
Mystery programs	791.446 556
radio	791.446 556
television	791.456 556
Mystery stories	808.838 72
history and criticism	809.387 2
specific literatures	T3B—308 72
individual authors	T3A—3
Mystical body of Christ	262.77
Mystical Judaism	296.833
Mysticeti	599.5
paleozoology	569.5

N

Naiads (Plants)	584.445
Nail-care tools	
manufacturing technology	688.5
Nail diseases	
humans	
geriatrics	618.976 547
incidence	614.595 47
medicine	616.547
see also Skin diseases —	
humans	
pediatrics	618.925 47
pharmacokinetics	615.779
surgery	617.477
Nails (Body parts)	599.814 7
animal physiology	573.59
descriptive zoology	599.814 7
human anatomy	611.78
human physiology	612.799
medicine	616.547
personal care	646.727
surgery	617.477
see also Skin	
Nails (Fasteners)	621.884
arts	739.48
Nairn (Scotland : District)	T2—411 58
Nairobi (Kenya)	T2—676 25
Nais	788.37
see also Woodwind	
instruments	
Naja	597.964 2
Najadales	584.74
Najaf (Iraq : Province)	T2—567 5
Najas	584.445
Najd (Saudi Arabia)	T2—538
Najib Tun Razak, Datuk	
Malaysian history	959.506 2
Nakers	786.93
see also Percussion instruments	
Nakh languages	499.964 1
	T6—999 641
Nakhichevan (Azerbaijan)	T2—475 4
Nakho-Daghestan languages	499.964
	T6—999 64
Nakuru County (Kenya)	T2—676 271
Nam Định (Vietnam :	
Province)	T2—597 3
Nama language	496.1
	T6—961
Namakgale (South Africa :	
District)	T2—682 59
Namakwa District	
Municipality (South	
Africa)	T2—687 17
Namaqua National Park	
(South Africa)	T2—687 17
Namaqualand (South	
Africa)	T2—687 17
Nambiquaran languages	498.4
	T6—984
Namboku period	952.022
Name cards	
prints	769.5
Names	929.97
cataloging	025.322
customs	392.12
divination	133.33
etymology	412
specific languages	T4—2
geographic	910.014
gazetters	910.3
personal	929.4
law	346.012
Names of God	
Islam	297.211 2
Judaism	296.311 2
Namibe Province (Angola)	T2—673 5
Namibia	968.81
	T2—688 1
Namibians	T5—968 81
Naming ceremonies	
Judaism	296.443
Nampula (Mozambique)	T2—679 7
Namur (Belgium : Province)	T2—493 44
Nanai (Asian people)	T5—941
Nanai language	494.1
	T6—941
Nanaimo (B.C. : Regional	
District)	T2—711 2
Nance County (Neb.)	T2—782 425
Nancy (France)	T2—443 823
Nande (Zairian people)	T5—963 94
Nande languages	496.394
	T6—963 94
Nandi (East African people)	T5—965 56
Nandi (Zairian people)	T5—963 94
Nandi County (Kenya)	T2—676 279 7
Nandi language (Bantu)	496.394
	T6—963 94
Nandi languages (Nilotic)	496.556
	T6—965 56
Nanggroe Aceh Darussalam	
(Indonesia)	959.811
	T2—598 11
Nangklao, King of Siam	
Thai history	959.303 3
Nanjing (Jiangsu Sheng,	
China)	T2—511 36

Narrative poetry (continued)
  specific literatures   T3B—103
    individual authors   T3A—1
Narrogin (W.A. : Shire)   T2—941 2
Narrow-gage railroads   385.52
  see also Railroads
Nartheciaceae   584.52
Narwhal   599.543
Nasafī, 'Abd Allāh ibn Aḥmad
  Koran commentary   297.122 73
Nasā'ī, Aḥmad ibn Shu'ayb
  Hadith   297.125 53
Nasal sinus diseases
  medicine   616.212
    see also Respiratory tract
      diseases — humans
Nasal sinuses   573.26
  biology   573.26
  human anatomy   611.21
  human physiology   612.232
  medicine   616.212
  see also Respiratory system
Nash County (N.C.)   T2—756 47
Nashim   296.123 3
  Babylonian Talmud   296.125 3
  Mishnah   296.123 3
  Palestinian Talmud   296.124 3
Nashville (Tenn.)   T2—768 55
Nāsikh wa-al-mansūkh
  Hadith   297.125 163
  Koran   297.122 612
Naskapi Indians   T5—973 2
Naskapi language   497.32
    T6—973 2
Nasopharynx
  human anatomy   611.32
  human physiology   612.31
  medicine   616.21
Nasopharynx diseases
  medicine   616.21
    see also Respiratory tract
      diseases — humans
Nass River (B.C.)   T2—711 85
Nassarawa State (Nigeria)   T2—669 53
Nassau (Bahamas)   T2—729 6
Nassau County (Fla.)   T2—759 11
Nassau County (N.Y.)   T2—747 245
Nasser, Gamal Abdel
  Egyptian history   962.053
Nasser, Lake (Egypt and
  Sudan)   T2—623
Nasturtiums (Brassicaceae)   583.78

Nasturtiums (Tropaeolaceae)   635.933 78
  botany   583.78
  floriculture   635.933 78
Natal (South Africa)   968.405
    T2—684
Natal Drakensberg Park
  (South Africa)   T2—684 9
Natalia   968.404 2
    T2—684
Natantia   595.388
Natchez (Miss.)   T2—762 26
Natchez Indians   T5—979
Natchitoches Parish (La.)   T2—763 65
Nathalia (Vic.)   T2—945 4
Nation of Islam   297.87
Nation River (B.C.)   T2—711 82
Nation-states   321.05
National Action for People and
  Homeland (Swiss political
  party)   324.249 403
National advertising   659.131 2
National Alliance (Italian
  political party)   324.245 04
National Alliance of
  Independents (Swiss political
  party)   324.249 408
National anthems   782.421 599
National bankruptcy   336.368
National banks   332.122 3
National Baptist Convention of
  America   286.134
    see also Baptists
National Baptist Convention of
  the United States of America   286.133
    see also Baptists
National bibliographies   015
National borrowing   336.343 3
    see also National debt
National Botanic Gardens of
  South Africa   T2—687 355
National Capital (Papua New
  Guinea)   995.45
    T2—954 5
National Capital Region
  (Ont. and Quebec)   T2—713 84
  Ontario   T2—713 84
  Quebec   T2—714 221
National Capital Region
  (Philippines)   T2—599 16
National cemeteries   363.75
  landscape architecture   718.8
National characteristics   305.8
  psychology   155.89
National conferences of bishops   262.12

National wealth	339.3
conservation	339.49
Nationaldemokratische Partei	
(Austrian)	324.243 603 8
Nationaldemokratische Partei	
Deutschlands	324.243 03
Nationale Aktion für Volk und	
Heimat (Swiss political party)	324.249 403
Nationalism	320.54
arts	700.458 1
	T3C—358 1
folklore	398.278 1
history and criticism	398.358 1
literature	808.803 581
history and criticism	809.933 581
specific literatures	T3B—080 358 1
history and	
criticism	T3B—093 581
music	780.903 4
social theology	201.72
Christianity	261.7
West Bank	320.540 956 942
Nationalist China	T2—512 49
Nationalist parties	324.218 3
international organizations	324.183
Nationality (Citizenship)	323.6
see also Citizenship	
Nationality clubs	369.2
Nationalization of foreign	
property	
law	343.025 2
Nationalization of industry	338.924
law	343.07
Nationalization of property	333.14
land economics	333.14
law	343.025 2
Nationals, The (Australian	
political party)	324.294 04
Nationalsozialistische	
Arbeiterpartei (Austria)	324.243 602 38
Nationalsozialistische Deutsche	
Arbeiter-Partei (Austria)	324.243 602 38
Nationalsozialistische Deutsche	
Arbeiter-Partei (Germany)	324.243 023 8
Native American languages	497
	T6—97
South America	498
	T6—98
Native American literatures	897
South America	898
Native American peoples	T5—97
South America	T5—98
see also American native	
peoples	
Native American religions	299.7
North America	299.7
South America	299.8
Native elements	549.2
see also Chemicals	
Native metals	549.23
see also Metals	
Native peoples	305.8
see also Indigenous peoples	
Native plants	
floriculture	635.951
resource economics	333.953 3
Nativism	149.7
Nativity of Jesus Christ	232.92
NATO (Alliance)	355.031 091 821
law	341.72
Natrona County (Wyo.)	T2—787 93
Natuna Islands (Indonesia)	T2—598 192
Natural areas	333.951 6
biological resources	
conservation	333.951 6
land conservation	333.731 6
wildlife conservation	333.954 16
see also Wildlife reserves	
Natural childbirth	
obstetrics	618.45
Natural communities	577.82
Natural computing	006.38
Natural dyes	
technology	667.26
Natural environments	
health	613.1
Natural family planning	
health	613.943 4
medicine	618.184
see also Birth control	
Natural foods	641.302
Natural gas	553.285
economic geology	553.285
extraction	622.338 5
extractive economics	338.272 85
law	343.077 2
pipeline transportation	388.56
engineering	665.744
law	343.093 96
prospecting	622.182 85
public administration	354.46
public utilities	363.63
law	343.092 6
resource economics	333.823 3
law	346.046 823 3
technology	665.7
economics	338.476 657
see also Petroleum	

Neck (continued)
regional medicine 617.53
surgery 617.530 59
Neck muscles
human anatomy 611.733
Neckar-Odenwald-Kreis
(Germany : Landkreis) T2—434 645
Neckar River (Germany) T2—434 645
Necklaces 391.7
customs 391.7
making 739.278
costume jewelry 688.2
handicrafts 745.594 2
fine jewelry 739.278
Necks (Geology) 551.88
Neckwear 391.41
see also Accessories (Clothing)
Necrologies 920
Necromancy 133.9
Necropneumonia
medicine 616.245
see also Respiratory tract
diseases — humans
Necrotizing fasciitis
incidence 614.579 8
medicine 616.929 8
see also Communicable
diseases — humans
Necrotizing ulcerative gingivitis
medicine 616.312
see also Digestive system
diseases — humans
Nectarines 641.342 57
cooking 641.642 57
food 641.342 57
orchard crop 634.257
Nectria 579.567 7
Nedarim 296.123 3
Babylonian Talmud 296.125 3
Mishnah 296.123 3
Palestinian Talmud 296.124 3
Nederlandsche Oost-Indische
Compagnie
Indonesian history 959.802 1
Needlefishes 597.66
Needlepoint 746.442
Needlepoint laces 677.653
arts 746.224
manufacturing technology 677.653
Needles
home sewing 646.19
Needlestick injuries
medicine 617.143

Needlework
primary education 372.54
textile arts 746.4
Ñeembucú (Paraguay :
Dept.) T2—892 124
Nefertiti, Queen of Egypt
Egyptian history 932.014
Nega'im 296.123 6
Negation
philosophical logic 160
Negative income tax 362.582
law 344.032 582
Negatives (Photography) 771.43
distribution 771.48
manipulation 771.43
organization 771.48
preparation 771.43
preservation 771.45
storage 771.45
Negeri Sembilan T2—595 1
Negev (Israel) T2—569 49
Neglected children
social welfare 362.76
see also Child abuse
Negligence (Law) 346.032
Negotiable instruments 332.76
law 346.096
Negotiable order of withdrawal
accounts 332.175 22
Negotiation 302.3
collective bargaining 331.891 2
executive management 658.405 2
psychology 158.5
social psychology 302.3
Negro Methodist churches 287.8
see also Methodist Church
Negros Island (Philippines) T2—599 538
Negros Occidental
(Philippines) T2—599 538
Negros Oriental
(Philippines) T2—599 552
Nehemiah (Biblical book) 222.8
Nehru, Jawaharlal
Indian history 954.042
Nei Monggol Zizhiqu
(China) T2—517 7
Neighborhood centers
recreation centers 790.068
Neighborhoods 307.336 2
Neighbors
applied psychology 158.25
psychological influence 155.925
Neisseria 579.33
Nejd (Saudi Arabia) T2—538

Neoplasticism	709.040 52
painting	759.065 2
sculpture	735.230 452
Neoplatonism	186.4
ancient	186.4
Christian polemics	239.4
modern	141.2
Neopsychoanalytic systems	150.195 7
Neorealism	
philosophy	149.2
Neornithes	598
paleozoology	568
Neosho County (Kan.)	T2—781 95
Neotoma	599.357 3
Neotropical fruit bats	599.45
Nepal	954.96
	T2—549 6
Nepalese	T5—914 95
Nepali	T5—914 95
Nepali language	491.495
	T6—914 95
Nepali literature	891.495
Nepean River (N.S.W.)	T2—944 6
Nepenthaceae	583.887
Nepenthales	583.887
Nephews	306.87
	T1—085
Nephrite	553.876
see also Jade	
Nephritis	
medicine	616.612
see also Urologic diseases —	
humans	
Nephrology	616.61
Neptune (Planet)	523.48
	T2—992 8
astrology	133.539 1
Neptunium	546.432
see also Chemicals	
Nerve compression syndromes	
medicine	616.856
see also Nervous system	
diseases — humans	
Nerve fibers	573.85
human physiology	612.81
Nerve tissues	573.85
human histology	612.810 45
see also Nervous system	
Nerves	573.85
biology	573.85
human anatomy	611.83
human biochemistry	612.814
human biophysics	612.813
human physiology	612.81

Nerves (continued)	
medicine	616.856
surgery	617.483
see also Nervous system	
Nervous system	573.8
anesthesiology	617.967 48
biology	573.8
diseases	573.839
see also Nervous system	
diseases	
human anatomy	611.8
human biophysics	612.804 3
human histology	612.8
human physiology	612.8
medicine	616.8
pediatrics	618.928
perinatal medicine	618.326 8
pharmacokinetics	615.78
pregnancy complications	
obstetrics	618.368
surgery	617.48
see also Innervation	
Nervous system diseases	573.839
animals	573.839
veterinary medicine	636.089 68
veterinary pharmacokinetics	636.089 578
humans	362.196 8
anesthesiology	617.967 48
cancer	362.196 994 8
incidence	614.599 948
medicine	616.994 8
social services	362.196 994 8
see also Cancer —	
humans	
geriatrics	618.976 8
incidence	614.598
medicine	616.8
social services	362.196 8
surgery	617.481
symptoms	616.84
Neshoba County (Miss.)	T2—762 685
Nēsoi (Greece : Regional	
unit)	T2—495 12
Nesosilicates	
mineralogy	549.62
Ness, Loch (Scotland)	T2—411 56
Ness County (Kan.)	T2—781 46
Nesting	591.564
Nestorian churches	281.8
see also Eastern churches	
Nests	591.564
Net national product	339.32
Net-winged beetles	595.764 4

Neurobiology	573.8
humans	612.8
Neuroblastoma	
pediatrics	618.929 948
Neurochemistry	573.84
human physiology	612.804 2
Neurofibromatosis	
incidence	614.599 9
medicine	616.993 83
Neuroglia	
human cytology	612.810 46
Neurolinguistics	
disorders	
medicine	616.855
human physiology	612.823 36
Neurological diseases	573.839
see also Nervous system	
diseases	
Neurological language disorders	
medicine	616.855 2
see also Communication	
disorders	
Neurological nursing	616.804 231
Neurology	
medicine	616.8
Neuromuscular diseases	
medicine	616.744
see also Musculoskeletal	
diseases — humans	
Neuronal ceroid-lipofuscinosis	
medicine	616.83
see also Nervous system	
diseases — humans	
Neurons	573.853 6
human cytology	612.810 46
see also Nervous system	
Neuropharmacology	615.78
Neurophysics	
human physiology	612.804 3
Neurophysiology	573.8
humans	612.8
Neuropsychiatry	616.8
Neuropsychological tests	616.804 75
Neuropsychology	612.8
Neuropsychopharmacology	615.78
Neuroptera	595.747
Neuropteris	561.597
Neuroses	362.25
medicine	616.852
social welfare	362.25
see also Mental illness	
Neurosurgery	617.48

Neurosyphilis	
medicine	616.83
see also Nervous system	
diseases — humans	
Neurotic disorders	
medicine	616.852
see also Mental disorders	
Neuse River (N.C.)	T2—756 19
Neuston	592.176
Neutral countries	T2—171 83
law of war	341.64
World War I	940.335
diplomatic history	940.325
World War II	940.533 5
diplomatic history	940.532 5
Neutralist blocs	T2—171 6
Neutrality	
law of war	341.64
Neutrinos	539.721 5
Neutron radiation	
biophysics	571.459
humans	612.014 486
Neutron stars	523.887 4
Neutrons	539.721 3
Neutrophils	
human immunology	616.079
Nevada	979.3
	T2—793
Nevada County (Ark.)	T2—767 52
Nevada County (Calif.)	T2—794 37
Nevado del Huila National	
Park (Colombia)	T2—861 39
Neves, José Maria	
Cape Verdean history	966.580 35
Nevi	
medicine	616.55
see also Skin diseases —	
humans	
Nevi'im	224
Nevi'im aharonim	224
Nevi'im rishonim	222
Nevis	T2—729 73
Nevşehir İli (Turkey)	T2—564 14
ancient	T2—393 4
New Academy (Philosophy)	186.2
New Age movement	299.93
Christian polemics	239.93
occultism	130
Christian viewpoint	261.513
parapsychology	130
religion	299.93
see Manual at 299.93	
New Age religions	299.93
see Manual at 299.93	

New Testament Greek language 487.4
                            T6—87
New Testament pseudepigrapha 229.92
New Testament theology 230.041 5
New Thought 299.93
    Christian 289.98
New towns 307.768
    area planning 711.45
New Westminster (B.C.) T2—711 33
New World blackbirds 598.874
New World chameleons 597.954 8
New World flycatchers 598.823
New World fruit bats 599.45
New World monkeys 599.85
New World pitcher plants 583.93
New World polecats 599.768
New World porcupines 599.359 74
New World runners (Lizards) 597.958 2
New World seedeaters 598.883
New World vultures 598.92
New World warblers 598.872
New Year 394.261 4
    customs 394.261 4
       Jewish 394.267
    Jewish 296.431 5
       liturgy 296.453 15
New York (N.Y.) 974.71
                T2—747 1
New York (State) 974.7
                T2—747
New York Bay (N.Y.) 551.461 346
                T2—163 46
New York County (N.Y.) T2—747 1
New York jazz 781.653
New York Metropolitan
    Area T2—747 1
New Zealand 993
                T2—93
    see Manual at T2—93
New Zealand literature 820
New Zealand red pine 585.3
New Zealand Wars, 1843–1847 993.021
New Zealand Wars, 1860–1870 993.022
New Zealanders T5—23
Newar T5—954 9
Newari language 495.49
                T6—954 9
Newari literature 895.49
Newark (N.J.) T2—749 32
Newark and Sherwood
    (England) T2—425 24
Newaygo County (Mich.) T2—774 58
Newberry County (S.C.) T2—757 39

Newborn infants
    pediatrics 618.920 1
Newbury (England :
    District) T2—422 91
Newcastle (N.S.W.) T2—944 2
Newcastle (South Africa :
    District) T2—684 1
Newcastle-under-Lyme
    (England : Borough) T2—424 62
Newcastle upon Tyne
    (England) T2—428 76
Newfoundland 971.8
                T2—718
Newfoundland (Dog) 636.73
Newfoundland, Island of
    (N.L.) T2—718
Newfoundland and Labrador 971.8
                T2—718
Newham (London, England) T2—421 76
Newport (R.I.) T2—745 7
Newport (Wales : County
    Borough) T2—429 91
Newport County (R.I.) T2—745 6
Newport News (Va.) T2—755 416
Newry, Mourne & Down
    (Northern Ireland) T2—416 58
Newry and Mourne
    (Northern Ireland) T2—416 58
News agencies 070.435
News gathering 070.43
News media 070.1
News programs 070.43
News sources
    journalism 070.431
Newsgroups (Computer
    communications) 004.693
    communications services 384.36
    sociology 302.231 2
Newsletters 050
    design 744.55
    journalism 070.175
    see also Serials
Newspaper columns
    journalism 070.44
Newspaper illustration 741.65
Newspapers 070
                T1—05
    bibliographies 011.35
    design 744.55
    journalism 070.172
    postal handling 383.123
       see also Postal service
    publishing 070.572 2
    sociology 302.232 2

Nicholas II, Emperor of Russia	
Russian history	947.083
Nicholas County (Ky.)	T2—769 417
Nicholas County (W. Va.)	T2—754 69
Nickel	669.733 2
biochemistry	572.526 25
building construction	693.773 32
building material	691.873 32
chemical engineering	661.062 5
chemistry	546.625
decorative arts	739.56
economic geology	553.485
human toxicology	615.925 625
materials science	620.188
metallography	669.957 332
metallurgy	669.733 2
metalworking	673.733 2
mining	622.348 5
physical metallurgy	669.967 332
see also Chemicals; Metals	
Nickerie (Suriname :	
District)	T2—883 1
Nicola River (B.C.)	T2—711 72
Nicolet-Yamaska (Quebec)	T2—714 54
Nicollet County (Minn.)	T2—776 32
Nicomedia (Turkey)	T2—563 3
Nicotine	
human toxicology	615.952 395 93
Niddah (Tractate)	296.123 6
Babylonian Talmud	296.125 6
Mishnah	296.123 6
Palestinian Talmud	296.124 6
Niddah practice	296.742
Nidulariales	579.599
Nidwald (Switzerland)	T2—494 762
Nidwalden (Switzerland)	T2—494 762
Nieces	306.87
	T1—085
Niederbayern (Germany)	T2—433 5
Niederösterreich (Austria)	T2—436 12
Niedersachsen (Germany)	T2—435 9
Nielim language	496.361
	T6—963 61
Nielloing	
decorative arts	739.15
Nièvre (France)	T2—444 16
Niğde İli (Turkey)	T2—564 1
ancient	T2—393 4
Nigei Island (B.C.)	T2—711 2
Nigel (South Africa :	
District)	T2—682 23
Niger	966.26
	T2—662 6

Niger-Congo languages	496.3
	T6—963
Niger-Kordofanian languages	496.3
	T6—963
Niger people	T5—966 26
Niger River	T2—662
Niger State (Nigeria)	T2—669 65
Nigeria	966.9
	T2—669
Nigerians	T5—966 9
Nigeriens (People of Niger)	T5—966 26
Night-blooming plants	
floriculture	635.953
Night crawlers	592.64
culture	639.75
Night flying	629.132 521 4
Night journey of Muḥammad	297.633
Night lizards	597.959 8
Night photography	778.719
Night schools	
adult education	374.8
higher education	378.15
Night skies	
meteorology	551.566
Night tactics	355.423
Night work	331.257 4
personnel management	658.312 1
Nightclothes	391.426
see also Clothing	
Nightclub presentations	792.7
see also Theater	
Nighthawks	598.99
Nightingales	598.842
Nightjars	598.99
Nightmares	154.632
Nightshades	583.959 3
Nihali language	T6—948 9
Nihali-speaking people	T5—948 9
Nihilism	
arts	T3C—384
literature	808.803 84
history and criticism	809.933 84
specific literatures	T3B—080 384
history and	
criticism	T3B—093 84
philosophy	149.8
Nihonium	546.67
Niigata-ken (Japan)	T2—521 52
Niihau (Hawaii)	T2—969 42
Nijmegen (Netherlands)	T2—492 18
Nika language	496.395
	T6—963 95
Nīl (Sudan)	T2—625
Nīl al-Abyaḍ (Sudan)	T2—626 4

Nīl al Azraq (Sudan)	T2—626 4	Niobium	669.79
Nile River	T2—62	chemical engineering	661.052 4
Nile River Delta	T2—621	chemistry	546.524
Nilo-Saharan languages	496.5	economic geology	553.499
	T6—965	metallurgy	669.79
Nilo-Saharan literatures	896.5	physical metallurgy	669.967 9
Nilo-Saharan-speaking		*see also* Chemicals	
peoples	T5—965	Niobrara County (Wyo.)	T2—787 15
folk literature	398.208 996 5	Niobrara River (Wyo. and	
Nilotic languages	496.55	Neb.)	T2—782 7
	T6—965 5	Nipa palm	584.84
Nilotic peoples	T5—965 5	Nipissing (Ont. : District)	T2—713 147
Nimbarka (Philosophy)	181.484 3	Nipissing, Lake (Ont.)	T2—713 147
Nîmes (France)	T2—448 37	Nirvana	
Nīnawá (Iraq : Province)	T2—567 4	Buddhism	294.342 3
Ninepins	794.6	Hinduism	294.523
Nineteen eighties	909.828	Niska Indians	T5—974 12
	T1—090 48	Niter	553.64
Nineteen fifties	909.825	mineralogy	549.732
	T1—090 45	Nith, River (Scotland)	T2—414 7
Nineteen forties	909.824	Nithsdale (Scotland)	T2—414 7
	T1—090 44	Nitidulidae	595.769
Nineteen hundreds (Decade)	909.821	Nitrate fertilizers	631.842
	T1—090 41	chemical engineering	668.624 2
Nineteen nineties	909.829	Nitrates	553.64
	T1—090 49	chemical engineering	661.65
Nineteen seventies	909.827	economic geology	553.64
	T1—090 47	mineralogy	549.732
Nineteen sixties	909.826	mining	622.364
	T1—090 46	Nitration	547.27
Nineteen tens	909.821	chemical engineering	660.284 4
	T1—090 41	Nitriansky kraj (Slovakia)	T2—437 33
Nineteen thirties	909.823	Nitric acid	
	T1—090 43	chemical engineering	661.24
Nineteen twenties	909.822	Nitrides	
	T1—090 42	chemical engineering	661.65
Nineteenth century	909.81	Nitrification	572.545
	T1—090 34	Nitrifying bacteria	
Nineveh (Extinct city)	T2—354	agricultural use	631.847
Nineveh (Iraq : Province)	T2—567 4	Nitrifying crops	631.847
Ningsia Hui Autonomous		Nitriles	547.044
Region (China)	T2—517 5	chemical engineering	661.894
Ningxia Hui Zizhiqu		Nitrites	
(China)	T2—517 5	chemical engineering	661.65
Ningxia Huizu Zizhiqu		Nitro compounds	547.041
(China)	T2—517 5	chemical engineering	661.894
Ninh Bình (Vietnam :		Nitro dyes	667.252
Province)	T2—597 3	Nitrocellulose	662.26
Ninh Thuận (Vietnam :		textiles	677.461
Province)	T2—597 5	*see also* Textiles	
Ninth century	909.1	Nitrocellulose glue	668.33
	T1—090 21	Nitrogen	553.93
Ninth of Av	296.439	animal nutrition	572.544 1
		animal husbandry	636.085 21

Nitrogen (continued)
biochemistry — 572.54
chemical engineering — 661.071 1
chemistry — 546.711
economic geology — 553.93
gas technology — 665.824
organic chemistry — 547.04
  aliphatic — 547.44
  applied — 661.894
  aromatic — 547.64
see also Chemicals
Nitrogen compounds — 546.711 2
Nitrogen cycle
  (Biogeochemistry) — 577.145
Nitrogen fertilizers — 631.84
chemical engineering — 668.624
Nitrogen fixation — 572.545
Nitrogen removal
sewage treatment — 628.357
Nitrogen salts
chemical engineering — 661.65
chemistry — 546.711 24
Nitroglycerin
military engineering — 623.452 7
Nitrosation — 547.27
chemical engineering — 660.284 4
Nitroso compounds — 547.041
chemical engineering — 661.894
Nitroso dyes — 667.252
Nitrous oxide abuse — 362.299 3
medicine — 616.86
personal health — 613.8
social welfare — 362.299 3
see also Substance abuse
Niue — T2—962 6
Niue language — 499.484
  T6—994 84
Niue literature — 899.484
Niuean language — 499.484
  T6—994 84
Niuean literature — 899.484
Niueans — T5—994 84
Nivation — 551.38
Nivkh — T5—946
Nivkh language — 494.6
  T6—946
Nixon, Richard M. (Richard
  Milhous)
United States history — 973.924
Nīyah (Islamic law) — 340.592 5
Niyazov, Saparmurad
Turkmenistan history — 958.508 61
Nizhegorod (Russia :
  Oblast) — T2—474 1

Nizhegorodskaĩa oblast′
  (Russia) — T2—474 1
Nizhniy Novgorod (Russia :
  Oblast) — T2—474 1
Njabi languages — 496.396
  T6—963 96
Njebi languages — 496.396
  T6—963 96
Njem language — 496.396
  T6—963 96
Nkandla (South Africa :
  District) — T2—684 43
Nkangala District
  Municipality (South
  Africa) — T2—682 76
Nkomazi (South Africa :
  District) — T2—682 73
Nkoya languages — 496.393
  T6—963 93
Nkrumah, Kwame
  Ghanaian history — 966.705 1
Nkundo language — 496.396
  T6—963 96
Nkundu language — 496.396
  T6—963 96
NMR (Physics) — 538.362
NMR imaging
medicine — 616.075 48
NMSQT (Merit scholarship test) — 378.166 2
NNP (Macroeconomics) — 339.32
Nō
literature — 895.620 51
theater — 792.095 2
No-fault insurance — 368.5
law — 346.086 5
see also Insurance
No-fault motor vehicle insurance — 368.572 8
law — 346.086 572 8
see also Insurance
No-tillage — 631.581 4
Noah (Biblical person)
Bible stories — 222.110 950 5
Nobatia (Kingdom) — 962.502 2
  T2—625
Nobelium — 546.449
Nobility (Social class) — 305.522
  T1—086 21
customs — 390.23
dress — 391.023
genealogy — 929.7
Noble County (Ind.) — T2—772 76
Noble County (Ohio) — T2—771 95
Noble County (Okla.) — T2—766 27

Noncitizens (continued)
naturalization	323.623
political status	323.631
social group	305.906 91
social welfare	362.899 1
women	
social welfare	362.839 81
young people	
social welfare	362.779 1
Nonclassical logic	511.31
mathematical logic	511.31
philosophical logic	160.119 8
Noncombat services (Armed	
forces)	355.34
Noncombatants	
law of war	341.67
World War I	940.316 1
World War II	940.531 61
Noncommercial radio	384.54
Noncommercial television	384.554
Noncommissioned officers	355.009 2
role and function	355.338
Noncommissioned officers' clubs	355.346
Noncommunicable diseases	571.9
humans	
incidence	614.59
medicine	616.98
Noncommutative algebras	512.46
Noncommutative rings	512.46
Nonconformists (British	
churches)	280.4
see also Protestantism	
Nonconsequentialism	171.2
Noncrystalline solids	530.413
Nondairy coffee whiteners	
commercial processing	663.64
Nondestructive testing	
materials science	620.112 7
Nondifferentiable functions	515.8
Nondomesticated animals	
culture	639
Nondominant groups	305.56
	T1—086 93
see also Minorities	
Nondramatic vocal forms	782.2
choral and mixed voices	782.52
None (Divine office)	264.15
music	782.324
see also Liturgy of the hours	
Nonelectronic data processing	004.9
Nonets	
chamber music	785.19
vocal music	783.19

Nonexplosive ammunition	
military engineering	623.459
Nonferrous metals	669
architectural construction	721.044 7
building construction	693.72–.77
building materials	691.8
economic geology	553.4
materials science	620.18
metallography	669.95
metallurgy	669
metalworking	673
mining	622.34
physical metallurgy	669.96
ship design	623.818 2
shipbuilding	623.820 7
structural engineering	624.182 2–.182 9
see also Chemicals; Metals	
Nongoma (South Africa :	
District)	T2—684 2
Nongovernmental organizations	
(International agencies)	060
	T1—060 1
social welfare	361.77
Nongraded schools	371.255
Nonimpact printing	686.233
Nonlethal weapons	
manufacturing technology	683.4
military	355.82
military engineering	623.4
Nonlinear analysis	
functional analysis	515.724 8
Nonlinear closed-loop systems	
automation engineering	629.836
Nonlinear differential equations	515.355
Nonlinear equations	515.252
Nonlinear functional analysis	515.724 8
Nonlinear operators	515.724 8
Nonlinear optics	535.2
engineering	621.369 4
Nonlinear programming	519.76
Nonlinear systems	003.75
Nonlinguistic communication	302.222
	T1—014
Nonliterate people	305.56
	T1—086 94
Nonliterate societies	301.7
government	321.1
religion	201.4
Nonloom weaving	
arts	746.42
Nonmechanized data processing	004.9
Nonmetals	
biochemistry	572
chemistry	546.7

Nordic skiing	796.932
see also Winter sports	
Nordjyllands amt	
(Denmark)	T2—489 58
Nordland fylke (Norway)	T2—484 4
Nordrhein-Westfalen	
(Germany)	T2—435 5
Nordvorpommern	
(Germany : Landkreis)	T2—431 78
Nordwestmecklenburg	
(Germany : Landkreis)	T2—431 76
Nore River (Ireland)	T2—418 9
Norfolk (England)	942.61
	T2—426 1
Norfolk (Ont. : County)	T2—713 36
Norfolk (Va.)	T2—755 521
Norfolk Broads (England)	T2—426 17
Norfolk County (Mass.)	T2—744 7
Norfolk Island	T2—948 2
Noricum	936.36
	T2—363 6
Norite	552.3
Norman architecture	723.4
Norman County (Minn.)	T2—776 93
Normandie (France)	T2—442 1
Normandy (France)	T2—442 1
Normandy Invasion, 1944	940.542 142 1
Normans	T5—395
Southern Italian history	945.703
Normative ethics	170.44
Normed linear spaces	515.732
Nornalup National Park	
(W.A.)	T2—941 2
Norrbotten landskap	
(Sweden)	T2—488 8
Norrbottens län (Sweden)	T2—488 8
Norris Lake (Tenn.)	T2—768 935
Norrland (Sweden)	T2—488
Norse religion	293
Norseman (W.A.)	T2—941 7
Norte de Santander	
(Colombia)	T2—861 24
North Africa	961
	T2—61
ancient	939.7
	T2—397
North Africans	T5—927 61
North America	970
	T2—7
Chinese explorations	970.012
English explorations	970.017
French explorations	970.018
geography	917
Norse explorations	970.013

North America (continued)	
pre-Columbian claims	970.011
Spanish and Portuguese	
explorations	970.016
travel	917.04
Welsh explorations	970.014
see Manual at T2—73 vs.	
T2—71	
North American box turtles	597.925
North American catfishes	597.492
North American native languages	497
	T6—97
North American native literatures	897
North American native	
peoples	T5—97
sign languages	
for hearing people	419.108 997
North American red squirrels	599.363
North Americans	T5—1
North Athens (Greece)	T2—495 12
North Atlantic Ocean	551.461 31
	T2—163 1
North Atlantic Treaty	
Organization	355.031 091 821
law	341.72
North Ayrshire (Scotland)	T2—414 61
North Battleford (Sask.)	T2—712 42
North Borneo	T2—595 3
North Brabant (Netherlands)	T2—492 45
North Calotte	T2—48
North Canadian River	
(Okla.)	T2—766 1
North Carolina	975.6
	T2—756
North Cascades National	
Park (Wash.)	T2—797 73
North Caucasian languages	499.96
	T6—999 6
North central Caucasian	
languages	499.964 1
	T6—999 641
North Central State	
(Nigeria)	T2—669 73
North Central States	977
	T2—77
North Channel (Huron,	
Lake, Mich. and Ont.)	T2—713 132
North Channel (Ireland and	
Scotland)	551.461 337
	T2—163 37
North Coast (South Africa)	T2—684 47
North Dakota	978.4
	T2—784

North West Leicestershire (England) T2—425 48
North-Western Province (Zambia) T2—689 4
North-Western Region (China) T2—514
North Wiltshire (England) T2—423 12
North York (Toronto, Ont.) T2—713 541
North Yorkshire (England) T2—428 4
North Yorkshire Moors (England) T2—428 46
Northam (W.A.) T2—941 2
Northampton (England) T2—425 57
Northampton County (N.C.) T2—756 49
Northampton County (Pa.) T2—748 22
Northampton County (Va.) T2—755 15
Northampton Uplands (England) T2—425 56
Northamptonshire (England) T2—425 5
Northavon (England) T2—423 91
Northbrook, Thomas George Baring, Earl of
  Indian history 954.035 2
Northeast Caucasian languages 499.964
  T6—999 64
Northeast Turkic languages 494.33
  T6—943 3
Northeastern India 954.1
  T2—541
Northeastern States 974
  T2—74
Northern Aegean (Greece) T2—495 82
Northern Areas (Pakistan) T2—549 132
Northern Australia T2—942 9
Northern Bahr el Ghazal State (South Sudan) T2—629 4
Northern Bantu languages 496.394
  T6—963 94
Northern Baptists 286.131
  see also Baptists
Northern Britain 941.1
  T2—411
  ancient 936.11
Northern Cape (South Africa) 968.71
  T2—687 1
Northern coastal region (Papua New Guinea) 995.7
  T2—957
  see also Momase region (Papua New Guinea)
Northern Darfur (Sudan : State) T2—627
Northern dynasties
  Chinese history 951.015

Northern England 942.7
  T2—427
Northern Europe 948
  T2—48
  ancient 936.8
  T2—368
Northern France T2—442 7
Northern Free State District Municipality (South Africa) T2—685 2
Northern fur seal 599.797 3
Northern Hemisphere T2—181 3
Northern Ireland 941.6
  T2—416
  ancient 936.16
  T2—361 6
  see Manual at T2—41 and T2—42
Northern Italy 945.1
  T2—451
Northern Karoo (South Africa) T2—687 13
Northern Kordofan (Sudan) T2—628
Northern League (Italian political party) 324.245 084
Northern lights 538.768
Northern Mariana Islands T2—967
Northern Min dialects 495.179 512 45
  T6—951 7
Northern Mindanao (Philippines) T2—599 77
Northern Neck (Va.) T2—755 2
Northern Norway T2—484 3
Northern Ontario T2—713 1
Northern Paiute Indians T5—974 577
Northern Paiute language 497.457 7
  T6—974 577
Northern Panhandle (W. Va.) T2—754 1
Northern Province (Papua New Guinea) T2—954 2
Northern Province (Zambia) T2—689 4
Northern Region (China) T2—511
Northern Rhodesia 968.940 2
  T2—689 4
Northern Rockies (B.C.) T2—711 87
Northern Samar (Philippines) T2—599 582
Northern Sotho language 496.397 71
  T6—963 977 1
Northern Sotho literature 896.397 71
Northern Sporades (Greece) T2—495 4
  ancient T2—391 1
Northern State (Sudan) T2—625

Nothingness	111.5	Novels	808.83
Nothosauria	567.937	history and criticism	809.3
Notio Aigaio (Greece)	T2—495 85	specific literatures	T3B—3
Notions	646.19	individual authors	T3A—3
commercial technology	687.8	Novelties	
home sewing	646.19	manufacturing technology	688.726
Notios Tomeas Athēnōn		Novenas	264.7
(Greece)	T2—495 12	Novgorod (Russia : Oblast)	T2—472 2
Notodelphyoida	595.34	Novitiate (Monastic life)	248.894 25
Notostraca	595.32	women	248.894 35
Notoungulata	569.62	Novogrodskaia oblast′	
Notre-Dame-des-Anges		(Russia)	T2—472 2
(Quebec)	T2—714 471	Novosibirsk (Russia :	
Notre-Dame Mountains		Oblast)	T2—573
(Quebec)	T2—714 7	Novosibirskaia oblast′	
Nottingham (England)	T2—425 27	(Russia)	T2—573
Nottingham Island		NOW accounts	332.175 22
(Nunavut)	T2—719 52	Nowata County (Okla.)	T2—766 97
Nottinghamshire (England)	T2—425 2	Nowra (N.S.W.)	T2—944 7
Nottoway County (Va.)	T2—755 637	Nowy Sącz (Poland :	
Noturus	597.492	Voivodeship)	T2—438 62
Nouakchott (Mauritania)	T2—661	Noxubee County (Miss.)	T2—762 955
Noun phrases	415.5	Noyon, Treaty of, 1516	945.306
specific languages	T4—55	NP-complete problems	511.352
Nouns	415.54	Nqamakwe (South Africa :	
specific languages	T4—554	District)	T2—687 54
Noupoort (South Africa :		NQR (Physics)	538.362
District)	T2—687 13	Nqutu District of KwaZulu	
Nouveau-Québec (Quebec)	T2—714 11	(South Africa)	T2—684 8
Nouvelle-Aquitaine		NSAP (Austrian political party)	324.243 602 38
(France)	T2—446	NSDAP (Austrian political party)	324.243 602 38
Nouvelle-Beauce (Quebec)	T2—714 718	Nsikazi (South Africa :	
Nova Scotia	971.6	District)	T2—682 73
	T2—716	Ntabethemba (South	
Novaia Zemlia (Russia)	T2—986	Africa : District)	T2—687 56
Novák, Katalin		Ntcham language	496.35
Hungarian history	943.905 46		T6—963 5
Novara (Italy : Province)	T2—451 6	Ntomba language	496.396 8
ancient	T2—372 24		T6—963 968
Novas	523.844 6	Nubia	939.78
Novaya Zemlya (Russia)	T2—986		T2—397 8
Novelettes	808.83	Nubian languages	496.542
history and criticism	809.3		T6—965 42
specific literatures	T3B—3	Nubian literatures	896.542
individual authors	T3A—3	Nubians	T5—965 42
Novelists	809.3	Ñuble (Chile)	T2—833 8
collected biography	809.3	Nuckolls County (Neb.)	T2—782 372
specific literatures	T3B—300 9	Nuclear accidents	363.179 9
individual biography	T3A—3	public safety	363.179 9
Novellas	808.83	technology	621.483 5
history and criticism	809.3	*see also* Hazardous materials	
specific literatures	T3B—3	Nuclear activation analysis	543.63
individual authors	T3A—3		

Nuclear activities	539.75
see Manual at 530.416 vs. 539.75	
Nuclear chemistry	541.38
applied	660.298
Nuclear disarmament	327.174 7
law of nations	341.734
Nuclear energy	333.792 4
economics	333.792 4
law	343.092 5
physics	539.7
public administration	354.47
Nuclear energy industry	333.792 4
Nuclear energy insurance	368.7
see also Insurance	
Nuclear engineering	621.48
military applications	623.044
Nuclear engineers	621.480 92
Nuclear envelope	571.66
Nuclear family	306.855
Nuclear fission	539.762
Nuclear forces	355.021 7
Nuclear fuels	
economic geology	553.493
engineering	621.483 35
public administration	354.47
resource economics	333.854 93
Nuclear fusion	539.764
Nuclear hazards insurance	368.7
see also Insurance	
Nuclear heating	
buildings	697.79
Nuclear interactions	539.75
see Manual at 530.416 vs. 539.75	
Nuclear liability insurance	368.7
see also Insurance	
Nuclear magnetic resonance	538.362
imaging	
medicine	616.075 48
Nuclear magnetic resonance	
spectroscopy	543.66
Nuclear medicine	616.075 75
Nuclear membrane	571.66
Nuclear missile forces	358.17
Nuclear missiles	358.171 82
engineering	623.451 9
military equipment	358.171 82
Nuclear models	539.74
Nuclear nonproliferation	327.174 7
law of nations	341.734
Nuclear physicists	539.709 2
Nuclear physics	539.7
astronomy	523.019 7

Nuclear power plants	621.483
law	343.092 5
Nuclear power systems	
auxiliary systems	
spacecraft	629.474 43
propulsion	621.485
see also Nuclear propulsion	
Nuclear-powered automobiles	
engineering	629.229 6
Nuclear-powered submarines	359.938 34
design	623.812 574
engineering	623.825 74
naval equipment	359.938 34
Nuclear-powered vehicles	388.349 6
transportation services	388.349 6
Nuclear propulsion	621.485
aircraft	629.134 355
automotive	629.250 9
ships	623.872 8
spacecraft	629.475 3
Nuclear quadrupole resonance	538.362
Nuclear reactions	539.76
Nuclear reactors	621.483
Nuclear safety	363.179 9
public administration	353.999
public safety	363.179 9
technology	621.483 5
see also Hazardous materials	
Nuclear spectroscopy	543.6
Nuclear structure	539.74
Nuclear terrorism	363.325 5
see also Terrorism	
Nuclear warfare	355.021 7
civil defense	363.35
ethics	172.422
religion	205.624 22
Christianity	241.624 22
see also War — ethics	
operations	355.43
social theology	201.727 5
Christianity	261.873 2
Judaism	296.382 7
see also Disasters	
Nuclear weapons	355.825 119
control	327.174 7
law of nations	341.734
engineering	623.451 19
military equipment	355.825 119
see also Nuclear warfare	
Nuclei as particles	539.723 2
Nucleic-acid hybridization	572.84
Nucleic acid-protein interactions	572.84

Nutrition (continued)
  social welfare — 363.8
  law — 344.033
  see also Digestive system
  see Manual at 363.8 vs. 613.2,
    641.3
Nutrition disorders
  humans — 362.196 39
    incidence — 614.593 9
    medicine — 616.39
    pediatrics — 618.923 9
    social services — 362.196 39
    see also Digestive system
      diseases — humans;
      Nutritional diseases —
      humans
Nutrition support
  medicine — 615.854 8
Nutrition surveys — 363.82
Nutrition therapy
  medicine — 615.854
Nutritional diseases
  humans — 362.196 39
  see also Nutrition
    disorders — humans
Nutritional requirements — 572.39
Nutritional services
  health services — 362.176
  public administration — 353.56
  schools — 371.716
Nutritionists — 363.809 2
Nutritive organs — 573.3
  see also Digestive system
Nuts — 581.464
  commercial processing — 664.804 5
  cooking — 641.645
  descriptive botany — 581.464
  food — 641.345
  forest products — 634.987
  orchard crop — 634.5
  physiology — 575.67
Nuts (Fasteners) — 621.882
Nuweveld Range (South
  Africa) — T2—687 17
Nyakyusa-Ngonde language — 496.391
  T6—963 91
Nyalas — 599.642 3
Nyamira County (Kenya) — T2—676 299
Nyamwezi (African people) — T5—963 94
Nyamwezi language — 496.394
  T6—963 94
Nyandarua County (Kenya) — T2—676 268
Nyanga language — 496.394
  T6—963 94

Nyanja (African people) — T5—963 918
Nyanja language — 496.391 8
  T6—963 918
Nyanja literature — 896.391 8
Nyankore language — 496.395 6
  T6—963 956
Nyanza Province (Kenya) — T2—676 29
Nyasa, Lake — T2—689 7
Nyasaland — 968.970 2
  T2—689 7
Nyaya (Philosophy) — 181.43
Nyctaginaceae — 583.883
Nyctibiidae — 598.99
Nye County (Nev.) — T2—793 34
Nyerere, Julius K. (Julius
  Kambarage)
  Tanzanian history — 967.804 1
Nyeri County (Kenya) — T2—676 266
Nyika (Nika) language — 496.395
  T6—963 95
Nyika-Safwa languages — 496.391
  T6—963 91
Nyika-Taita languages — 496.395
  T6—963 95
Nyilamba-Langi languages — 496.394
  T6—963 94
Nylons (Plastics) — 668.423 5
  textiles — 677.473
  see also Textiles
Nymphaeaceae — 584.23
Nymphaeales — 584.23
Nymphomania
  medicine — 616.858 33
Nyngan (N.S.W.) — T2—944 9
Nynorsk language — 439.82
  T6—398 2
Nynorsk literature — 839.82
Nyon (Switzerland :
  District) — T2—494 522 1
Nyoro-Ganda languages — 496.395 6
  T6—963 956
Nytrils
  textiles — 677.474 4
  see also Textiles
Nyunga — T5—991 5
Nyungar dialects — 499.15
  T6—991 5
Nyusi, Filipe Jacinto
  Mozambican history — 967.905 4
Nzima (African people) — T5—963 38
Nzima language — 496.338
  T6—963 38

O

Obscenity (continued)
   postal handling   383.120 5
   social problem   364.174
Obscenity in speech   179.5
Observation
   descriptive research   001.433
               T1—072 3
Observatories
   architecture   727.5
   astronomy   522.1
Obsessive-compulsive disorder
   medicine   616.852 27
   see also Mental disorders
Obsidian   552.22
   glyptics   736.28
Obstacle courses (Military
   training)   355.544
Obstetrical disorders
   incidence   614.599 22
   medicine   618.2
Obstetrical nursing   618.202 31
Obstetrical surgery   618.8
Obstetricians   618.200 92
   law   344.041 2
   malpractice   344.041 21
   role and function   618.202 32
Obstetrics   618.2
   anesthesiology   617.968 2
   veterinary medicine   636.089 82
Obstructions
   intestine
      medicine   616.342
      see also Digestive system
         diseases — humans
      surgery   617.554
Obstructive pulmonary disease
   medicine   616.24
   see also Respiratory tract
     diseases — humans
Obwalden (Switzerland)   T2—494 764
Ocarinas   788.38
   see also Woodwind
     instruments
Occasional sermons
   Christianity   252.6
Occasionalism   147
Occasions of revelation of Koran   297.122 12
Occident   909.098 21
               T2—182 1
Occidental Mindoro
   (Philippines)   T2—599 38
Occidental region
   (Paraguay)   T2—892 2

Occitan language   449
               T6—491
Occitan literature   849
Occitanie (France)   T2—447 3
Occitans   T5—4
Occlusion disorders
   dentistry   617.643
   incidence   614.599 6
Occult sciences   130
Occultations   523.99
Occultism   130
   arts   T3C—37
   literature   808.803 7
     history and criticism   809.933 7
     specific literatures   T3B—080 37
       history and
         criticism   T3B—093 7
   religious practice   203
   see Manual at 001.9 *and* 130;
     also at 200 vs. 130
Occultism and religion   201.613
   Christianity   261.513
   Islam   297.261 3
   Judaism   296.371
Occultists   130.92
Occupational aptitude tests   153.94
Occupational diseases
   health   613.62
   medicine   616.980 3
   law   344.043 698 03
   see also Environmental
     diseases — humans
   workers' compensation law   344.021 8
Occupational ethics   174
   religion   205.64
     Christianity   241.64
Occupational groups   305.9
               T1—088
   customs   390.4
   dress   391.04
   journalism for   070.486
   religion
     Christianity
      guides to life   248.88
   see Manual at 305.9 vs. 305.5
Occupational guidance   331.702
   see also Vocational guidance
Occupational health   613.62
Occupational health nursing   610.734 6
Occupational health services
   personnel management   658.382
     public administration   352.67

Oceans (continued)	
influence on precipitation	551.577 5
interactions with atmosphere	551.524 6
law of nations	341.45
see Manual at 341.45 vs. 343.0962	
physical geology	551.46
public administration	354.369
United States	
public expenditures	354.369 246 097 3
resource economics	333.916 4
see Manual at T2—162	
Ocelot	599.752
animal husbandry	636.89
Ochil Hills (Scotland)	T2—412 8
Ochiltree County (Tex.)	T2—764 815
Ochnaceae	583.69
Ochotona	599.329
Ochotonidae	599.329
Oconee County (Ga.)	T2—758 193
Oconee County (S.C.)	T2—757 21
Oconee River (Ga.)	T2—758 6
Oconto County (Wis.)	T2—775 37
Ocotepeque (Honduras : Dept.)	T2—728 383
Ocotillo	583.93
OCR (Computer science)	006.424
Octal system (Numeration)	513.5
Octets	
chamber music	785.18
vocal music	783.18
Octopoda	594.56
paleozoology	564.56
Octopuses	594.56
cooking	641.694
food	641.394
commercial processing	664.94
Ocular motility disorders	
ophthalmology	617.762
see also Eye diseases — humans	
Ocular neuromuscular mechanism	
human physiology	612.846
ophthalmology	617.762
Odd Fellows	366.3
biography	366.309 2
Odd-toed ungulates	599.66
Odendaalsrus (South Africa : District)	T2—685 3
Oder-Spree (Germany : Landkreis)	T2—431 53
Oderland-Spree (Germany : Raumordnungsregion)	T2—431 53
Odes	808.814 3
history and criticism	809.143
specific literatures	T3B—104 3
individual authors	T3A—1
Odes of Solomon	229.912
Odessa (Ukraine : Oblast)	T2—477 2
Odes'ka oblast' (Ukraine)	T2—477 2
Odi (South Africa : District)	T2—682 41
Odia	T5—914 56
Odia language	491.456
	T6—914 56
Odia literature	891.456
Odisha (India)	T2—541 33
ODL (Open and distance learning)	371.35
adult education	374.4
higher education	378.175
Odobenidae	599.799
Odocoileus	599.652
Odocoileus hemionus	599.653
Odonata	595.733
Odontoceti	599.5
paleozoology	569.5
Odontopteris	561.597
Oea (Libya)	T2—397 4
Oestridae	595.774
Off-road biking	796.63
see also Cycling — sports	
Off-road vehicles	388.348 8
driving	629.283 042
engineering	629.228 8
military engineering	623.747
repair	629.287 042
transportation services	388.348 8
see also Automotive vehicles	
Offaly (Ireland)	T2—418 6
Offenbach am Main (Germany)	T2—434 163
Offenders	364.3
	T1—086 927
criminology	364.3
law	345.03
pastoral care	
Christianity	259.5
punishment	364.6
welfare services	364.6
Offenders with disabilities	364.308 7
Offenses against military discipline	355.133 4
Offenses against property	364.16
Holocaust, 1933–1945	940.531 813 2
restitution	940.531 814 4
law	345.026
social welfare	362.889 6

Ogun State (Nigeria)	T2—669 23
Ogwr (Wales)	T2—429 71
Ohau, Lake (N.Z.)	T2—938 97
Ohio	977.1
	T2—771
Ohio County (Ind.)	T2—772 123
Ohio County (Ky.)	T2—769 835
Ohio County (W. Va.)	T2—754 14
Ohio River	T2—77
Kentucky	T2—769
West Virginia	T2—754 1
Ohmmeters	621.374 2
Oholot	296.123 6
Oil (Petroleum)	553.282
economic geology	553.282
extraction	622.338 2
extractive economics	338.272 82
law	343.077 2
pipeline technology	665.544
processing	665.5
economics	338.476 655
enterprises	338.766 55
prospecting	622.182 82
public administration	354.45
public utilities	363.6
law	343.092 6
resource economics	333.823 2
law	346.046 823 2
see also Petroleum	
Oil beetles	595.769
Oil depletion allowance	336.243 16
tax law	343.052 34
Oil gas	665.773
Oil heating	
buildings	697.044
Oil lamps	621.323
see also Lighting	
Oil painting	751.45
Oil palms	633.851
agriculture	633.851
botany	584.84
Oil pollution	363.738 2
law	344.046 332
water supply engineering	628.168 33
see also Pollution	
Oil processes	
photographic printing	773.8
Oil-producing plants	
agriculture	633.85
Oil sands	553.283
see also Tar sands	

Oil shale	553.283
economic geology	553.283
mining	622.338 3
law	343.077 2
processing	665.4
Oil-soluble paint	667.62
Oil spills	363.738 2
law	344.046 332
water pollution engineering	628.168 33
Oil well flooding	622.338 2
Oil wells	622.338 2
Oilbird	598.99
Oiling	
woodwork	
buildings	698.33
Oils	
applied nutrition	613.284
food technology	664.3
hydraulic-power technology	621.204 24
industrial	665
materials science	620.198
metabolism	
human physiology	612.397
paint technology	667.622
Oilseed plants	
agriculture	633.85
Ointments	
pharmaceutical chemistry	615.19
Oirat	T5—942
Oirat-Kalmyk language	494.2
	T6—942
Oise (France)	T2—442 64
Ōita-ken (Japan)	T2—522 8
Ojibwa Indians	977.004 973 33
	T5—973 33
Ojibwa language	497.333
	T6—973 33
Ojibwa languages	497.33
	T6—973 3
Ojibwa literature	897.333
Ojibway Indians	T5—973 33
Okaloosa County (Fla.)	T2—759 982
Okanagan Lake (B.C.)	T2—711 5
Okanagan-Similkameen (B.C.)	T2—711 5
Okanogan County (Wash.)	T2—797 28
Okapi	599.638
Okayama-ken (Japan)	T2—521 94
Okeechobee, Lake (Fla.)	T2—759 39
Okeechobee County (Fla.)	T2—759 53
Okefenokee Swamp (Ga. and Fla.)	T2—758 752
Okfuskee County (Okla.)	T2—766 73

Okhotsk, Sea of	551.461 453	Old Catholic churches (continued)	
	T2—164 53	religious education	268.848
Okinawa Island (Japan)	T2—522 94	theology	230.48
Okinawa-ken (Japan)	T2—522 9	Old Catholics	
Oklahoma	976.6	biography	284.8
	T2—766	Old Church Slavic language	491.817 01
Oklahoma City (Okla.)	T2—766 38		T6—918 17
Oklahoma County (Okla.)	T2—766 38	Old Danish language	439.817 01
Oklahoma Panhandle		Old English language	429
(Okla.)	T2—766 13		T6—29
Oklahoma Territory	T2—766 1	Old English literature	829
Okmulgee County (Okla.)	T2—766 83	Old French language	447.01
Oko languages	496.33		T6—41
	T6—963 3	Old Frisian language	439.2
Okpe language	496.33		T6—392
	T6—963 3	Old Frisian literature	839.2
Okra	641.356 48	Old-growth forests	333.75
botany	583.775	*see also* Forest lands	
commercial processing	664.805 648	Old High German language	437.01
cooking	641.656 48		T6—31
food	641.356 48	Old Icelandic language	439.6
garden crop	635.648		T6—396 1
Oktibbeha County (Miss.)	T2—762 953	Old Icelandic literature	839.6
Oktoberfest	394.264 4	Old Indic language	491.29
Olacaceae	583.85		T6—912 9
Olancho (Honduras)	T2—728 33	Old Indic literature	891.29
Öland (Sweden)	T2—486 3	Old Italian language	457.01
Öland (Sweden : Island)	T2—486 3		T6—51
Olbia-Tempio (Italy :		Old Kingdom (Egypt)	932.012
Province)	T2—459 3	Old Latin language	477
ancient	T2—379 3		T6—71
Old age	305.26	Old Low Franconian language	439.31
Old-age and survivors' insurance	368.3		T6—393 1
government-sponsored	368.43	Old Low Franconian literature	839.31
law	344.023	Old Low German language	439.4
see also Insurance			T6—394
Old age homes	362.61	Old Low German literature	839.4
Old age pensions	331.252	Old Low Germanic languages	439
see also Pensions			T6—39
Old Bulgarian language	491.817 01	Old Low Germanic literatures	839
	T6—918 17	Old Norse language	439.6
Old Bulgarian literature	891.81		T6—396 1
Old Castile (Spain)	T2—463 5	Old Norse literature	839.6
Old Catholic churches	284.8	Old Northwest	977
church government	262.048		T2—77
local church	254.048	*see also* North Central States	
church law	262.984 8	Old people	305.26
doctrines	230.48		T1—084 6
catechisms and creeds	238.48	*see also* Older people	
guides to Christian life	248.484 8	Old Persian language	491.51
missions	266.48		T6—915 1
moral theology	241.044 8	Old Persian literature	891.51
public worship	264.048	Old Portuguese language	469.701
			T6—69

On-the-job training	331.259 2
	T1—071 55
personnel management	T1—068 3
executives	658.407 124
public administration	352.669
Ona Indians	T5—987
Onagraceae	583.73
Onchocerciasis	
incidence	614.555 2
medicine	616.965 2
see also Communicable	
diseases — humans	
Oncogenes	
medicine	616.994 042
Oncogenic viruses	579.256 9
Oncology	616.994
Oncopods	592.7
paleozoology	562.7
Oncorhynchus	597.56
Oncoviruses	579.256 9
Ondatra	599.357 9
Ondes martenot	786.73
see also Electrophones	
Ondo State (Nigeria)	T2—669 28
One-act plays	
literature	808.824 1
history and criticism	809.241
specific literatures	T3B—204 1
individual authors	T3A—2
One-dish cooking	641.82
One old cat	796.357 8
One-person corporations	338.74
management	658.045
see also Corporations	
One-person enterprises	
management	658.041
initiation	658.114 1
One-room schools	372.125
Onega Lake (Russia)	T2—471 5
Oneida County (Idaho)	T2—796 41
Oneida County (N.Y.)	T2—747 62
Oneida County (Wis.)	T2—775 25
Oneida Indians	974.700 497 554 3
	T5—975 543
Oneida Lake (N.Y.)	T2—747 62
Oneida language	497.554 3
	T6—975 543
Onions	641.352 5
botany	584.78
commercial processing	664.805 25
cooking	641.652 5
food	641.352 5
garden crop	635.25
Onionskin paper	676.282 3

Online advertising	659.144
Online auctions	381.177
management	658.877 7
Online catalogs	025.313 2
Online chat groups	004.693
communications services	384.36
sociology	302.231 2
Online etiquette	395.5
Online help facilities	005.3
development	005.15
Online information systems	004
Online marketing	381.142
management	658.872
Online processing	004
Online shopping	381.142
law	343.081 142
Online social networks	302.302 85
communications services	384.38
computer science	006.754
instructional use	371.334 675 4
sociology	302.302 85
Only children	306.874
	T1—085 4
family relationships	306.874
home care	649.142
psychology	155.442
Onomastics	929.97
etymology	412
specific languages	T4—2
geographic names	910.014
gazetters	910.3
personal names	929.4
Onondaga County (N.Y.)	T2—747 65
Onondaga Indians	T5—975 54
Onondaga language	497.554
	T6—975 54
Onslow County (N.C.)	T2—756 23
Ontario	971.3
	T2—713
see Manual at T2—713 and	
T2—714	
Ontario, Lake (N.Y. and	
Ont.)	T2—747 9
New York	T2—747 9
Ontario	T2—713 5
Ontario, Northern	T2—713 1
Ontario County (N.Y.)	T2—747 86
Ontologies	006.332
Ontology	111
Ontonagon County (Mich.)	T2—774 985
Onychophora	592.74
Onygenales	579.565
Onyx	553.87
see also Semiprecious stones	

Ophioglossales	587.33	Optical character recognition	006.424
paleobotany	561.73	computer engineering	621.399 4
Ophiurida	593.94	Optical communications	
Ophiuroidea	593.94	engineering	621.382 7
paleozoology	563.94	Optical components	
Ophthalmic nursing	617.702 31	cameras	771.35
Ophthalmologists	617.709 2	Optical computers	
role and function	617.702 32	engineering	621.391
Ophthalmology	617.7	*see Manual at* 006.37	
anesthesiology	617.967 7	vs. 006.42, 621.367,	
geriatrics	618.977 7	621.391, 621.399	
nursing	617.702 31	Optical crystallography	548.9
pediatrics	618.920 977	Optical data processing	621.367
Opiliaceae	583.85	computer science	006.42
Opilioacariformes	595.42	engineering	621.399 6
Opiliones	595.43	*see Manual at* 006.37 vs.	
Opisthobranchia	594.34	006.42, 621.367, 621.391,	
Opisthocomidae	598.74	621.399	
Opium		Optical detectors	
pharmacokinetics	615.782 2	manufacturing technology	681.25
pharmacology	615.323 35	Optical diagnosis	
Opium abuse	362.293	medicine	616.075 45
medicine	616.863 2	Optical digital discs	004.565
personal health	613.83	engineering	621.397 67
social welfare	362.293	Optical disc technology	621.382 7
see also Substance abuse		Optical engineering	621.36
Opium War, 1840–1842	951.033	military engineering	623.042
Opole (Poland :		Optical-fiber cable	
Voivodeship)	T2—438 55	computer science	004.64
Opolskie Voivodeship		engineering	621.398 1
(Poland)	T2—438 55	Optical-fiber communication	621.382 75
Opossum shrimps	595.375	Optical glass	666.156
Opossums	599.276	Optical illusions	152.148
Opossums (America)	599.276	Optical instruments	
Opossums (Australasia)	599.23	manufacturing technology	681.4
Opotiki District (N.Z.)	T2—934 28	Optical interconnects	621.369 3
Oppland fylke (Norway)	T2—482 5	Optical metallography	669.950 282
Opposition parties (Legislatures)	328.369	Optical pattern recognition	
Optic nerve diseases		computer science	006.42
incidence	614.599 7	engineering	621.399 4
ophthalmology	617.732	*see Manual at* 006.37	
see also Eye diseases —		vs. 006.42, 621.367,	
humans		621.391, 621.399	
Optic nerves	573.882 8	Optical properties	
animal physiology	573.882 8	materials science	620.112 95
human anatomy	611.84	Optical rotation	
human physiology	612.843	chemistry	541.7
ophthalmology	617.732	Optical scanning	
see also Eyes		computer science	006.42
Optical art	709.040 72	engineering	621.399 4
painting	759.067 2	Optical spectroscopes	
sculpture	735.230 472	manufacturing technology	681.414
Optical binaries	523.841		

Oranges (continued)
food	641.343 1
orchard crop	634.31
Orangutan	599.883
Oraon	T5—948 3
Oraon language	494.83
	T6—948 3
Oraon literature	894.83

Oratories (Chapels)
architecture	726.595
Oratorios	782.23
choral and mixed voices	782.523
Orators	809.5
collected biography	809.5
specific literatures	T3B—500 9
individual biography	T3A—5
Oratory	808.51

Orbital diseases
ophthalmology	617.78

see also Eye diseases —
humans

Orbital flights
manned	629.454
Orbitals (Quantum chemistry)	541.28
Orbits (Astromechanics)	521.3
astronautics	629.411 3
astronomy	521.3
comets	523.63
earth	525.3
moon	523.33

Orbits (Eye sockets)
human anatomy	611.84
ophthalmology	617.78
Orbits (Nuclear particles)	539.725
Orcaella	599.538
Orchard grass	633.22
botany	584.926
Orchards	634
Orchestra conductors	784.209 2
Orchestral harps	787.95

see also Stringed instruments
Orchestral music	784.2
Orchestras	784.2
Orchestras with solo instruments	784.23
Orchestras with toy instruments	784.46
Orchestras with vocal parts	784.22
Orchestration	781.374
Orchidaceae	584.72
Orchidales	584.72
Orchids	584.72
botany	584.72
floriculture	635.934 72
Orcinus	599.536
Ord River (W.A. : River)	T2—941 4

Order
philosophy	117
Order of DeMolay for Boys	366.108 351
Order of the Eastern Star	366.18
biography	366.180 92
Order statistics	519.5
Ordered algebraic structures	511.33
Ordered solids	530.413
Ordered topological spaces	514.32

Ordering
library acquisitions	025.23
materials management	658.72
Orders (Awards)	929.81
armed forces	355.134 2
numismatics	737.223
Orders (Societies)	369
Orders of knighthood	929.71
Ordinances	348.02
Ordinary differential equations	515.352
numerical solutions	518.63
Ordinary differentiation	515.33
Ordinary language philosophy	149.94
Ordinary of the mass	264.36
music	782.323 2
Ordination of clergy	206.1
Christianity	262.14
ecclesiology	262.14
sacrament	234.164
public worship	265.4
theology	234.164
Judaism	296.61
Ordination of women	206.108 2
Christianity	262.140 82
Judaism	296.610 82
Ordnance	355.8
engineering	623.4
air ordnance	623.746 1
naval ordnance	623.825 1
military equipment	355.8
air ordnance	358.418
naval ordnance	359.8

see Manual at 355–359 *vs.* 623

Ordos
Roman Catholic liturgy	264.021
Ordovician period	551.731
geology	551.731
paleontology	560.173 1
Ordu İli (Turkey)	T2—565 6
ancient	T2—393 37
Orduña (Spain)	T2—466 9
Ore dressing	622.7

see Manual at 622.22, 622.7
vs. 662.6, 669

Ore processing	622.7

Oreamnos	599.647 5
Örebro län (Sweden)	T2—487 6
Oregano	641.357
see also Herbs	
Oregon	979.5
	T2—795
Oregon County (Mo.)	T2—778 875
Oregon myrtle	584.288
Orel (Russia : Oblast)	T2—473 5
Orellana (Ecuador)	T2—866 414
Orenburg (Russia : Oblast)	T2—474 3
Orenburgskaia oblast'	
(Russia)	T2—474 3
Orense (Spain : Province)	T2—461 5
Ores	553
Oresund (Denmark and Sweden)	551.461 334
	T2—163 34
Organ banks	362.178 3
Organ builders	786.519 092
Organ cases	
church architecture	726.529 7
Organ concertos	784.265 186
Organ culture	571.538
humans	612.028
Organ donation	362.178 3
law	344.041 94
Organ transplants	362.197 954
law	344.041 94
medical ethics	174.297 954
see also Medical ethics	
social services	362.197 954
surgery	617.954
Organelles	571.65
Organic chemicals	
chemical engineering	661.8
Organic chemistry	547
analytical chemistry	543.17
applied	661.8
Organic compounds	547
biochemistry	572
humans	612.015 7
human toxicology	615.95
pollution	
ecology	577.278
toxicology	571.957
Organic drugs	
pharmacology	615.3
Organic evolution	576.8
Organic farming	631.584
Organic fertilizers	631.86
chemical engineering	668.63
Organic gardening	635.048 4
floriculture	635.987
Organic geochemistry	553.2

Organic materials	
materials science	620.117
Organic poisons	363.179 1
human toxicology	615.95
public safety	363.179 1
see also Hazardous materials	
Organic solids	530.413
Organically grown foods	641.302
agriculture	631.584
home economics	641.302
Organismic psychology	150.193
Organists	786.509 2
Organization (Management)	658.1
	T1—068 1
executive	658.402
production	658.51
public administration	352.2
see Manual at 658.04 vs.	
658.114, 658.402	
Organization of African Unity	341.249
public administration	352.116
Organization of American States	341.245
public administration	352.117
Organization of production	338.6
economics	338.6
management	658.51
	T1—068 5
Organizational behavior	302.35
management	658
Organizational change	
executive management	658.406
public administration	352.367
Organizations	060
	T1—06
business enterprises	338.7
law	346.06
organizational behavior	302.35
religious	206.5
see also Religious	
organizations	
social	369
see Manual at T1—025	
vs. T1—0601–0609;	
also at T1—0601–0609;	
also at T1—072 vs.	
T1—0601–0609	
Organized crime	364.106
law	345.02
Organohalogen compounds	547.02
alicyclic chemistry	547.52
aliphatic chemistry	547.42
biochemistry	572.556
human toxicology	615.951 2

Organometallic compounds	547.05	Orientale (Congo :	
aliphatic chemistry	547.45	Province)	T2—675 15
biochemistry	572.51	Orientation (Geography)	912.014
chemical engineering	661.895	Orientation of employees	
human toxicology	615.951 5	personnel management	658.312 42
Organonitrogen compounds	547.04	public administration	352.66
aliphatic chemistry	547.44	Orientational perception	
aromatic chemistry	547.64	psychology	152.188 2
Organophosphorus compounds	547.07	Oriente (Ecuador)	T2—866 4
aliphatic chemistry	547.47	Orienteering	796.582
Organosilicon compounds	547.08	*see also* Outdoor life	
aliphatic chemistry	547.48	Origami	736.982
Organosulfur compounds	547.06	Origin of legislation	328.372
aliphatic chemistry	547.46	Origin of life	576.83
aromatic chemistry	547.66	philosophy	113.8
Organotherapy		religion	202.4
pharmacology	615.36	Christianity	231.765
Organs (Musical instruments)	786.5	philosophy of religion	213
instrument	786.519	Origin of races	
music	786.5	physical ethnology	599.972
see also Keyboard instruments		Origin of the state	320.11
Oribi Gorge Nature Reserve		Origin of universe	523.12
(South Africa)	T2—684 63	philosophy	113
Orient	950	religion	202.4
	T2—5	Christianity	231.765
Oriental (Morocco)	T2—643 3	philosophy of religion	213
Oriental architecture	720.95	Original sin	233.14
ancient	722.1	Orinoco River (Venezuela)	T2—87
Oriental arts	709.5	Orinoquia Region	
Oriental churches	281.6	(Colombia)	T2—861 9
see also Eastern churches		Orioles	598.874
Oriental horses	636.11	Orissa (India)	T2—541 33
Oriental languages	490	Oristano (Italy : Province)	T2—459 4
	T6—9	ancient	T2—379 4
Oriental Mindoro		Oriya	T5—914 56
(Philippines)	T2—599 36	Oriya language	491.456
Oriental Orthodox churches	281.6		T6—914 56
doctrines	230.16	Oriya literature	891.456
catechisms and creeds	238.16	Orkney (Scotland)	T2—411 32
theology	230.16	Orkney Islands (Scotland)	941.132
see also Eastern churches			T2—411 32
Oriental philosophy	181	Orlah	296.123 1
Oriental region (Paraguay)	T2—892 1	Mishnah	296.123 1
Oriental rugs		Palestinian Talmud	296.124 1
arts	746.750 95	Orléanais (France)	T2—445 1
Oriental sculpture	730.95	Orléans (France)	T2—445 27
ancient	732.7	Orléans, Île-de (Quebec)	T2—714 476
Oriental shorthair cats	636.82	Orléans, Isle of (Quebec)	T2—714 476
Oriental sores		Orleans County (N.Y.)	T2—747 91
incidence	614.534	Orleans County (Vt.)	T2—743 23
medicine	616.936 4	Orleans Parish (La.)	T2—763 35
see also Communicable		Orléansville (Algeria :	
diseases — humans		Province)	T2—653
		Orlicz spaces	515.73

Orthography	411
applied linguistics	418
specific languages	T4—813
specific subjects	T1—014
linguistics	411
specific languages	T4—152
primary education	372.632
Orthomorphic projections	526.82
Orthopedic appliances	
manufacturing technology	681.761
Orthopedic equipment	617.9
Orthopedic nursing	616.702 31
Orthopedic shoes	
manufacturing technology	685.38
Orthopedic surgery	617.47
Orthopedics	616.7
Orthoptera	595.726
Orthopters	
engineering	629.133 36
Orthoptics	617.762
Orthorrhapha	595.773
Ortiz Rubio, Pascual	
Mexican history	972.082 43
Oruro (Bolivia : Dept.)	T2—841 3
Orvieto (Italy)	
ancient	T2—375 76
Oryctolagus	599.322
Oryx	599.645
conservation technology	639.979 645
resource economics	333.959 645
Oryzeae	584.92
Osage County (Kan.)	T2—781 643
Osage County (Mo.)	T2—778 58
Osage County (Okla.)	976.625
	T2—766 25
Osage Indians	978.004 975 254
	T5—975 254
Osage language	497.525 4
	T6—975 254
Osage orange	583.648
Osaka (Japan)	T2—521 834
Osaka (Japan : Prefecture)	T2—521 83
Osborne County (Kan.)	T2—781 215
Oscan language	479.9
	T6—799
Oscans	T5—79
Oscar I, King of Sweden and	
Norway	
Swedish history	948.504 1
Oscar II, King of Sweden	
Swedish history	948.504 2
Osceola County (Fla.)	T2—759 25
Osceola County (Iowa)	T2—777 116
Osceola County (Mich.)	T2—774 69

Oscillations	
solid-state physics	530.416
solids	531.32
Oscillatoriales	579.39
Oscillators	
electronic circuits	621.381 533
radio engineering	621.384 12
Oscillographs	621.374 7
electronic engineering	621.381 548 3
Oscilloscopes	621.381 548 3
Oscines	598.8
see Manual at 598.824–.88	
Osco-Umbrian languages	479.9
	T6—799
Osco-Umbrian literatures	879.9
Osco-Umbrians	T5—79
Oscoda County (Mich.)	T2—774 78
Osee (Biblical book)	224.6
Osetin language	491.59
	T6—915 9
Osetin literature	891.59
Oshkosh (Wis.)	T2—775 64
OSI (Computer communication)	004.62
Osilinka River (B.C.)	T2—711 85
Oslo fylke (Norway)	T2—482 1
Osmaniye İli (Turkey)	T2—564 7
ancient	T2—393 5
Osmanli language	494.35
	T6—943 5
Osmanli literature	894.35
Osmium	669.7
chemical engineering	661.064 1
chemistry	546.641
metallography	669.957
metallurgy	669.7
physical metallurgy	669.967
see also Chemicals	
Osmosis	530.425
physics	530.425
water supply treatment	628.164
Osmotic pressure	541.341 5
Osnabrück (Germany)	T2—435 911
Osorno (Chile : Province)	T2—835 3
Osoyoos (B.C.)	T2—711 5
Osprey	598.93
Osroene	T2—394 2
Osseous tissues	
human histology	612.751 045
Ossete language	491.59
	T6—915 9
Ossete literature	891.59
Ossetic language	491.59
	T6—915 9
Ossetic literature	891.59

Ossets	T5—915 9	Ostracoda	595.33
Ossicle diseases		paleozoology	565.33
medicine	617.842	Ostravský kraj (Czech	
see also Ear diseases —		Republic)	T2—437 28
humans		Ostriches	598.524
Ossicles		animal husbandry	636.694
human anatomy	611.85	Ostrobothnia (Finland)	T2—489 734
human physiology	612.854	Ostrogoths	T5—39
medicine	617.842	Italian history	945.01
Ostariophysi	597.48	Sicilian history	945.801
Osteichthyes	597	Ostrołęka (Poland :	
see also Fishes		Voivodeship)	T2—438 41
Osteitis		Ostropales	579.57
medicine	616.712	Ostvorpommern (Germany :	
see also Musculoskeletal		Landkreis)	T2—431 78
diseases — humans		Ostyak language	494.51
Osteitis deformans			T6—945 1
medicine	616.712	Ostyak literature	894.51
see also Musculoskeletal		Ostyak Samoyed language	494.4
diseases — humans			T6—944
Osteoarthritis		Ostyaks	T5—945 1
medicine	616.722 3	Osun State (Nigeria)	T2—669 26
see also Musculoskeletal		Oswego County (N.Y.)	T2—747 67
diseases — humans		Otago Region (N.Z.)	T2—939 1
Osteochondritis		Otariidae	599.797
medicine	616.712	Otariinae	599.797 5
see also Musculoskeletal		OTC market	332.643
diseases — humans		Otero County (Colo.)	T2—788 95
Osteoglossomorpha	597.47	Otero County (N.M.)	T2—789 65
paleozoology	567.47	Other minds	
Osteomyelitis		epistemology	121.2
medicine	616.715	Otididae	598.32
see also Musculoskeletal		Oto Indians	T5—975 2
diseases — humans		Oto language (Siouan)	497.52
Osteopathic physicians	610.92		T6—975 2
Osteopathy	610	Oto-Manguean languages	497.6
therapeutic system	615.533		T6—976
Osteoporosis		Otoe County (Neb.)	T2—782 273
medicine	616.716	Otolaryngology	617.51
see also Musculoskeletal		Otologists	617.809 2
diseases — humans		role and function	617.802 32
Östergötland landskap		Otology	617.8
(Sweden)	T2—486 8	anesthesiology	617.967 8
Östergötlands län (Sweden)	T2—486 8	geriatrics	618.977 8
Österreichische Volkspartei	324.243 604	pediatrics	618.920 978
Østfold fylke (Norway)	T2—482 3	surgery	617.805 9
Ostia (Italy)	T2—456 3	Otomí Indians	T5—976
ancient	T2—376 3	Otomí language	497.6
Ostinato	781.827		T6—976
instrumental	784.182 7	Otorohanga District (N.Z.)	T2—933 7
Østlandet (Norway)	T2—482	Otsego County (Mich.)	T2—774 84
Östlich Raron (Switzerland)	T2—494 794 2	Otsego County (N.Y.)	T2—747 74
Ostprignitz-Ruppin		Ottawa (Ont.)	T2—713 84
(Germany : Landkreis)	T2—431 54	Ottawa-Carleton (Ont.)	T2—713 84

Ottawa County (Kan.)	T2—781 26	Ouagadougou (Burkina	
Ottawa County (Mich.)	T2—774 15	Faso)	T2—662 5
Ottawa County (Ohio)	T2—771 212	Ouargla (Algeria : Province)	T2—657
Ottawa County (Okla.)	T2—766 99	Ouarzazate (Morocco :	
Ottawa Indians	T5—973 36	Province)	T2—646 6
Ottawa language	497.336	Ouattara, Alassane D.	
	T6—973 36	Ivorian history	966.680 54
Ottawa River (Quebec and		Ouds	787.82
Ont.)	T2—713 8	*see also* Stringed instruments	
Ontario	T2—713 8	Oudtshoorn (South Africa :	
Quebec	T2—714 2	District)	T2—687 37
Otter shrews	599.33	Oued (Algeria : Province)	T2—657
Otter Tail County (Minn.)	T2—776 89	Oued Eddahab-Lagouira	
Otterhound	636.753 6	(Morocco)	T2—648
Otters	599.769	Ouest (Haiti : Dept.)	T2—729 452
animal husbandry	636.976 9	Ouest lausannois	
conservation technology	639.979 769	(Switzerland)	T2—494 522 9
resource economics	333.959 769	Ouija board	133.932 5
small game hunting	799.259 769	Oujda-Angad (Morocco)	T2—643 3
Otters (River otters)	599.769 2	Ould Daddah, Mokhtar	
animal husbandry	636.976 92	Mauritanian history	966.105 1
conservation technology	639.979 769 2	Oulu (Finland : Province)	T2—489 76
resource economics	333.959 769 2	Oulun lääni (Finland)	T2—489 76
small game hunting	799.259 769 2	Oum el Bouaghi (Algeria :	
Otters (Sea otter)		Province)	T2—655
conservation technology	639.979 769 5	Ounce (Snow leopard)	599.755 5
resource economics	333.959 769 5	Ouray County (Colo.)	T2—788 22
Ottoman Empire	956.015	Ouse, River (Yorkshire,	
	T2—56	England)	T2—428 4
Algerian history	965.024	Out-of-body experience	133.95
Arabian history	953.03	Outagamie County (Wis.)	T2—775 39
Balkan Peninsula	949.603	Outaouais (Quebec :	
Egyptian history	962.03	Administrative region)	T2—714 22
Iraqi history	956.703	Outaouais Region (Quebec)	T2—714 22
Jordanian history	956.950 3	Outaouais Regional	
Lebanese history	956.920 34	Community (Quebec)	T2—714 221
Libyan history	961.202 4	Outboard motorboats	387.231 3
North African history	961.023	design	623.812 313
Palestinian history	956.940 34	engineering	623.823 13
Syrian history	956.910 3	transportation services	387.231 3
Tunisian history	961.103	*see also* Ships	
Turkish history	956.101 5	Outboard motors	623.872 34
Yemeni history	953.303	Outcrops (Geology)	551.85
Ottoman Turkish language	494.35	Outdoor advertising	659.134 2
	T6—943 5	Outdoor cooking	641.578
Ottoman Turkish literature	894.35	Outdoor education	371.384
Ouachita County (Ark.)	T2—767 66	Outdoor furniture	645.8
Ouachita Mountains (Okla.		cleaning	648.5
and Ark.)	T2—766 6	customs	392.36
Arkansas	T2—767 4	decorative arts	749.8
Oklahoma	T2—766 6	household management	645.8
Ouachita Parish (La.)	T2—763 87	manufacturing technology	684.18
Ouachita River (Ark. and		Outdoor games	796
La.)	T2—763 7	*see also* Sports	

Overindulgence	
ethics	178
Overland air-cushion vehicles	
engineering	629.322
military engineering	623.748 2
Overland mail	383.143
see also Postal service	
Overpopulation	363.91
Overseas information libraries	027.5
Overseas service	384.64
see also Telephone	
Oversewing	
bookbinding	686.35
Overshoes	678.33
Oversight	658.401 3
legislative function	328.345 6
management	658.401 3
military administration	355.685
public administration	352.35
independent agencies	352.88
Overtime pay	331.216 2
personnel management	658.322 2
Overtime work	331.257 2
personnel management	658.312 1
Overton County (Tenn.)	T2—768 684
Overtures	784.189 26
musical form	784.189 26
orchestral music	784.218 926
Overuse injuries	
medicine	617.172
Overwater air-cushion vehicles	387.2
engineering	629.324
military engineering	623.748 4
transportation services	387.2
inland water	386.22
ocean	387.2
Overweight people	
cooking for	641.563 5
reducing diet	613.25
Ovibos	599.647 8
Oviducts	
gynecology	618.12
Oviedo (Spain)	T2—461 9
Ovimbundu (African people)	T5—963 99
Oviraptor	567.912
Ovis	599.649
Ovis canadensis	599.649 7
Ovo-lacto vegetarian diet	613.262
cooking	641.563 6
health	613.262
ÖVP (Austrian political party)	324.243 604

Ovulation detection method	
health	613.943 4
medicine	618.184
see also Birth control	
Owen County (Ind.)	T2—772 43
Owen County (Ky.)	T2—769 393
Owenism	335.12
Owensboro (Ky.)	T2—769 864
Owl Creek Mountains (Wyo.)	T2—787 43
Owls	598.97
conservation technology	639.978 97
resource economics	333.958 97
Owners' liability insurance	368.56
see also Insurance	
Ownership	
communications industry	384.041
land economics	333.3
real property law	346.043 2
transportation services	388.049
Ownership equity	
accounting	657.76
Ownership flags	929.92
Ownership marks	929.9
	T1—027 7
animal husbandry	636.081 2
Ownership of land	333.3
Owsley County (Ky.)	T2—769 176
Owyhee County (Idaho)	T2—796 21
Oxalidaceae	583.68
Oxalidales	583.68
Oxazines	547.595
Oxazoles	547.592
chemical engineering	661.8
Oxdiazines	547.595
Oxdiazoles	547.595
Oxen	599.642 2
animal husbandry	636.216
Oxford (England)	942.574
	T2—425 74
Oxford (Ont. : County)	T2—713 46
Oxford County (Me.)	T2—741 75
Oxfordshire (England)	942.57
	T2—425 7
Oxidases	572.791
see also Enzymes	
Oxidation	541.393
Oxidation ditches	628.351
Oxidation ponds	628.351
Oxidation-reduction reaction	541.393
biochemistry	572.53
chemical engineering	660.284 43
organic chemistry	547.23

Pacific Ocean islands	990
	T2—9
geography	919
travel	919.04
Pacific Ocean theater (World	
War II)	940.542 6
Pacific region	T2—182 3
Pacific Rim National Park	
(B.C.)	T2—711 2
Pacific settlement of disputes	303.69
international relations	327.17
law of nations	341.52
sociology	303.69
Pacific Slope (U.S.)	T2—79
Pacifism	303.66
ethics	172.42
see also Peace — ethics	
international politics	327.172
social theology	201.727 3
see also Peace — social	
theology	
sociology	303.66
Pacifists	303.66
international politics	
biography	327.172 092
World War I	940.316 2
World War II	940.531 62
Pack animals (Beasts of burden)	636.088 2
Packaging	658.564
design	744.68
drugs (pharmaceuticals)	
preservation	615.18
electronics	621.381 046
engineering	688.8
law	343.075
production management	658.564
sales promotion	658.823
Packers (Agricultural tools)	
manufacturing technology	681.763 1
Packet switching (Data	
transmission)	
communications engineering	621.382 16
computer communications	004.662
computer engineering	621.398 1
Packing clothes	
home economics	646.6
Packing crops	631.56
Packing for shipment	
materials management	658.788 4
PACs (Action committees)	324.4
law	342.078

Padded toys	
making	688.724
handicrafts	745.592 4
technology	688.724
Paddle tennis	796.34
see also Sports	
Paddlefishes	597.42
Paddy rice	641.331 8
see also Rice	
Padova (Italy)	T2—453 21
ancient	T2—373 41
Padova (Italy : Province)	T2—453 2
ancient	T2—373 4
Padre Island (Tex.)	T2—764 47
Padua (Italy)	T2—453 21
ancient	T2—373 41
Padua (Italy : Province)	T2—453 2
ancient	T2—373 4
Paelignian language	479.7
	T6—797
Paeoniaceae	583.44
Paeoniales	583.44
Paestum (Extinct city)	T2—377 773
Paez language	498.2
	T6—982
Pagalu (Equatorial Guinea)	T2—671 86
Paganism	292
Christian polemics	239.3
Page, Earle, Sir	
Australian history	994.042
Page County (Iowa)	T2—777 78
Page County (Va.)	T2—755 94
Page design	
design	744.5
sociology	302.226
Pageantry	
performing arts	791.6
Pageants	394.5
customs	394.5
performing arts	791.62
Paget disease of bone	
medicine	616.712
see also Musculoskeletal	
diseases — humans	
Paging systems	
engineering	621.389 2
Pahang	T2—595 1
Pahari	T5—914 96
Pahari languages	491.496
	T6—914 96
Pahari literatures	891.496
Pahlavi language	491.53
	T6—915 3
Pahlavi literature	891.53

Paleogene period	551.782	Palladium	669.7
geology	551.782	chemical engineering	661.063 6
paleontology	560.178 2	chemistry	546.636
Paleogeography	551.7	metallography	669.957
Paleography	417.7	metallurgy	669.7
	T4—7	organic chemistry	547.056 362
handwriting	411.7	physical metallurgy	669.967
specific languages	T4—11	*see also* Chemicals	
Paleolithic Age	930.12	Pallets	
fine arts	709.011 2	wooden	674.82
painting	759.011 2	Palliative care	
sculpture	732.22	medicine	616.029
Paleomagnetism	538.727	Palm Beach County (Fla.)	T2—759 32
Paleontologists	560.92	Palm oil	641.338 51
Paleontology	560	cooking	641.638 51
see Manual at 551.7 vs. 560;		food	641.338 51
also at 576.8 vs. 560		food technology	664.36
Paleopalynology	561.13	Palm reading	133.6
Paleosiberian languages	494.6	Palm Sunday	263.925
	T6—946	devotional literature	242.35
Paleosiberian literatures	894.6	music	781.726
Paleosiberian peoples	T5—946	sermons	252.625
Paleovolcanism	551.210 901	Palm Valley National Park	
Paleozoic era	551.72	(N.T.)	T2—942 91
geology	551.72	Palma (Majorca)	T2—467 542
paleontology	560.172	Palma de Mallorca	
Paleozoology	560	(Majorca)	T2—467 542
Palermo (Italy)	T2—458 231	Palmae	584.84
Palermo (Italy : Città		*see also* Palms	
metropolitana)	T2—458 23	Palmales	584.84
ancient	T2—378 23	*see also* Palms	
Palestine	956.94	Palmerston North (N.Z.)	T2—935 8
	T2—569 4	Palmerston North City	
ancient	933	(N.Z.)	T2—935 8
	T2—33	Palmettos	584.84
Biblical geography and history	220.9	*see also* Palms	
Palestine Liberation Organization		Palmistry	133.6
history	956.940 5	Palmists	133.609 2
Palestinian Arab women	305.488 927 4	Palms	584.84
Palestinian Arabs	T5—927 4	botany	584.84
Palestinian architecture		forestry	634.974
ancient	722.33	ornamental arboriculture	635.977 484
Palestinian National Authority	351.569 42	ornamental gardening	635.934 84
Palestinian sculpture	732.3	paleobotany	561.45
Palestinian Talmud	296.124	Palmyra (Extinct city)	T2—394 32
Palestinians (Ethnic group)	T5—927 4	Palmyra Atoll (Line Islands)	T2—969 9
Palestinians (Palestinian		Palo Alto County (Iowa)	T2—777 155
National Authority)	T5—927 569 42	Palo Pinto County (Tex.)	T2—764 552
Palestrina (Italy)		Palomino horse	636.13
ancient	T2—376 3	Palouse River (Idaho and	
Pali language	491.37	Wash.)	T2—797 39
	T6—913 7	Palpigradi	595.452
Pali literature	891.37		
Palindromes	793.734		

Panicoideae	584.924
botany	584.924
forage crops	633.27
Panics (Economics)	338.542
Panicum	584.924
botany	584.924
food crop	633.171
Panjabi language	491.42
	T6—914 2
Panjabi literature	891.42
Panjabis	T5—914 21
Pannirtuuq (Nunavut)	T2—719 52
Pannonia	936.39
	T2—363 9
Panoan languages	498.4
	T6—984
Panoan peoples	T5—984
Panola County (Miss.)	T2—762 84
Panola County (Tex.)	T2—764 187
Panoramas	745.8
decorative arts	745.8
paintings	751.74
Panoramic cinematography	777.6
Panoramic photography	778.36
Panoramic videography	777.6
Panpipes	788.37
instrument	788.371 9
music	788.37
see also Woodwind	
instruments	
Panpsychism	141
Pans	
kitchen utensils	643.3
manufacturing technology	683.82
Pansies	635.933 69
botany	583.69
floriculture	635.933 69
Pantelleria Island (Italy)	T2—458 24
Pantheism	211.2
philosophy	147
Pantheistic religions	201.4
Panther (Puma)	599.752 4
conservation technology	639.979 752 4
resource economics	333.959 752 4
Panthera	599.755
Panto	792.38
see also Theater	
Pantodonta	569.62
Pantomime	792.3
Pantomime (Christmas	
entertainment)	792.38
see also Theater	
Pantomime (Silent entertainment)	792.3
see also Theater	

Pantomime (United Kingdom)	792.38
Pants (Trousers)	391.476
commercial technology	687.116
customs	391.476
home economics	646.3
home sewing	646.436
see also Clothing	
Pants (Undergarments)	391.423
see also Undergarments	
Papa Doc	
Haitian history	972.940 72
Papacy	262.13
Papago Indians	T5—974 552
Papakura District (N.Z.)	T2—932 6
Papal administration	262.136
Papal bulls and decrees	262.91
Papal infallibility	262.131
Papal schism, 1378–1417	282.090 23
Papal States	945.6
	T2—456
Papal systems (Ecclesiology)	262.3
Paparoa National Park	
(N.Z.)	T2—937 3
Papaveraceae	583.35
Papaverales	583.35
Papaws (Annonaceae)	641.344 1
botany	584.286
cooking	641.644 1
food	641.344 1
orchard crop	634.41
Papaws (Caricaceae)	583.78
Papaws (Caricaceae, Papayas)	641.346 51
see also Papayas	
Papayas	641.346 51
agriculture	634.651
botany	583.78
commercial processing	664.804 651
cooking	641.646 51
food	641.346 51
Paper	676
handicrafts	745.54
manufacturing technology	676
materials science	620.197
photographic materials	771.532 3
sculpture material	731.2
Paper airplanes	745.592
Paper bags	676.33
Paper boxes	676.32
handicrafts	745.54
Paper chromatography	543.84
Paper covers	
bookbinding	686.344
Paper cups	676.34
Paper cutting	736.98

Paradise	202.3
Christianity	236.24
Islam	297.23
Paradoxes	
logic	165
Paraffin (Kerosene)	665.538 3
Paraffin (Wax)	547.77
natural	665.4
petroleum product	665.538 5
Paraffins (Alkanes)	547.411
chemical engineering	661.814
Paragraphs	
rhetoric	808
Paraguarí (Paraguay)	T2—892 123
Paraguay	989.2
	T2—892
Paraguay River	T2—892
Paraguay tea	641.337 7
see also Maté	
Paraguayan literature	860
Paraguayan War, 1865–1870	989.205
Paraguayans	T5—688 92
Parah	296.123 6
Paraíba (Brazil : State)	T2—813 3
Paraíso (Honduras : Dept.)	T2—728 34
Parakeets	598.71
animal husbandry	636.686 5
Parakeets (Lovebirds)	636.686 4
animal husbandry	636.686 4
zoology	598.71
Paralegals	340.092
malpractice	347.050 41
practice	347.050 4
Paralipomena (Biblical books)	222.6
Parallax	
stars	523.81
Parallax corrections	522.9
Parallel bars (Gymnastic equipment)	796.442
see also Gymnastics	
Parallel giant slalom racing	796.939
see also Winter sports	
Parallel processing	004.35
Parallel processors	004.35
engineering	621.391
Parallel programming	005.275
Parallel slalom racing	796.939
see also Winter sports	
Parallelism	147
Paralympics	796.045 6
Paralysis	
medicine	616.842
see also Nervous system diseases — humans	
Paralysis agitans	
medicine	616.833
see also Nervous system diseases — humans	
Paralytic shellfish poisoning	
human toxicology	615.945
Paramagnetism	538.43
Paramaribo (Suriname : District)	T2—883 52
Paramecium	579.495
Parametric inference	519.54
Parametric statistical methods	519.5
Paramillo National Park (Colombia)	T2—861 26
Paramo	
ecology	577.538
Paramotoring	797.55
Paramours	306.736
Paramyxoviridae	579.256
Paraná (Brazil : State)	T2—816 2
Paraná River (Brazil-Argentina)	T2—822
Argentina	T2—822
Brazil	T2—816
Paranasal sinus diseases	
medicine	616.212
see also Respiratory tract diseases — humans	
Paranasal sinuses	
human anatomy	611.21
human physiology	612.232
medicine	616.212
Paranoid disorders	
medicine	616.897
see also Mental disorders	
Paranoid personality disorder	
medicine	616.858 1
see also Mental disorders	
Paranormal phenomena	130
Paranthropus	569.93
Paraphrase	
musical element	781.377
musical forms	781.826
instrumental	784.182 6
Paraplegia	
medicine	617.58
neurology	616.842
see also Nervous system diseases — humans	
Parapsychologists	130.92
Parapsychology	130
see Manual at 001.9 and 130	

Parental behavior (Animals)	591.563
Parental kidnapping	362.829 7
law	344.032 829 7
social welfare	362.829 7
see also Families — social	
welfare	
Parental leave	331.257 63
fathers	331.257 630 851
government-sponsored	
insurance	368.454 008 51
gay parents	331.257 630 866 4
government-sponsored	
insurance	368.454 008 664
government-sponsored	
insurance	368.454
labor economics	331.257 63
mothers	331.257 630 852
government-sponsored	
insurance	368.454 008 52
personnel management	658.312 2
Parental rights	346.017
Parenteral infusions	
administering	615.6
Parenteral nutrition	
medicine	615.854 84
Parenteral therapy	
medicine	615.855
Parenthood	306.874
child rearing	649.1
customs	392.3
sociology	306.874
Parenting	649.1
home economics	649.1
personal religion	204.41
Buddhism	294.344 41
Christianity	248.845
Hinduism	294.544 1
Islam	297.577
Judaism	296.74
sociology	306.874
Parents	306.874
	T1—085
Christian devotional literature	242.645
family relationships	306.874
guides to religious life	204.41
Buddhism	294.344 41
Christianity	248.845
Hinduism	294.544 1
Islam	297.577
Judaism	296.74
psychology	155.646
social welfare	362.82
law	344.032 82
public administration	353.533 1

Pareto, Vilfredo	
economic school	330.154 3
Pari-mutuel betting	798.401
Paria, Gulf of (Venezuela and	
Trinidad and Tobago)	551.461 366
	T2—163 66
Parianeae	584.922
Paridae	598.824
Paris (France)	T2—443 61
Paris, Treaty of, 1783	
United States history	973.317
Paris Commune, 1871	944.081 21
Paris metropolitan area	
(France)	T2—443 6
Parish houses	
architecture	726.4
Parish libraries	027.67
Parish missions	266.022
Parish welfare work	361.75
Parishes	250
administration	254
Park, Chung Hee	
South Korean history	951.950 43
Park buildings	
architecture	725.7
Park County (Colo.)	T2—788 59
Park County (Mont.)	T2—786 661
Park County (Wyo.)	T2—787 42
Park lodges	910.462
see also Resorts	
Park police	363.28
Park Range (Colo. and	
Wyo.)	T2—788 66
Parke County (Ind.)	T2—772 465
Parker County (Tex.)	T2—764 553
Parking	388.474
see also Parking facilities	
Parking aprons	625.889
Parking facilities	388.474
architecture	725.38
area planning	711.73
construction	690.538
law	343.098 2
public administration	354.765
urban transportation services	388.474
Parking turnouts	625.77
Parkinson disease	
drug therapy	616.833 061
medicine	616.833
see also Nervous system	
diseases — humans	
therapy	616.833 06

Parsi language (Pahlavi)	491.53
	T6—915 3
Parsi literature (Pahlavi)	891.53
Parsing (Computers)	
natural languages	415.028 563 5
specific languages	T4—502 856 35
Parsley	641.357
botany	583.988 2
see also Herbs	
Parsnip River (B.C.)	T2—711 82
Parsnips	641.351 4
botany	583.988 2
commercial processing	664.805 14
cooking	641.651 4
food	641.351 4
garden crop	635.14
Parsonages	
architecture	726.9
Part-of-speech tagging	415.028 563 5
specific languages	T4—502 856 35
Part songs	783.1
Part-time employment	331.257 27
personnel management	658.312 1
Part-time enterprises	
management	658.041
Part-time work	331.257 27
Part-whole relationships	111.82
Part-word method (Reading)	
primary education	372.465
Partei der Arbeit der Schweiz	324.249 407 4
Partei des Demokratischen	
Sozialismus (Germany)	324.243 074
Parthenogenesis	571.887
Parthenopaean Republic	945.707
Parthia	T2—396
Parthian Empire	935.064
Parti communiste français	324.244 075
Parti québécois	324.271 409 84
Partial differential equations	515.353
numerical solutions	518.64
Partial differential operators	515.724 2
Partial differentiation	515.33
Partial hearing loss	
medicine	617.8
see also Ear diseases —	
humans	
Partially ordered sets	511.332
Participatory democracy	323.042
Participatory management	331.011 2
personnel management	658.315 2
public administration	352.68
Participles	415.6
specific languages	T4—56
Particle acceleration	539.73

Particle beams	539.73
Particle board	674.836
Particle colliders	539.73
Particle mechanics	530.12
classical physics	531.16
quantum mechanics	530.12
see Manual at 530.475 vs.	
530.12, 531.16	
Particle physics	539.72
Particle radiation	539.72
biophysics	571.459
humans	612.014 486
nuclear physics	539.72
Particle swarm optimization	006.382 4
Particles (Grammar)	415.7
specific languages	T4—57
Particles (Matter)	
classical mechanics	531.16
meteorology	551.511 3
nuclear physics	539.72
technology	620.43
Partido Revolucionario	
Institucional (Mexico)	324.272 05
Parties (Entertainments)	793.2
see also Entertainments	
(Parties)	
see Manual at 392, 393, 394	
vs. 793.2	
Parties (Politics)	324.2
see also Political parties	
Partisan troops	356.15
Partitas	784.185 4
Partitions (Building element)	721.2
architecture	721.2
construction	690.12
interior decoration	747.3
Partitions (Mathematics)	
number theory	512.73
Partitions, 1772–1795 (Poland)	943.802 5
Partito comunista italiano	324.245 075 2
Partito d'azione (Italy :	
1853–1867)	324.245 026
Partito d'azione (Italy :	
1942–1947)	324.245 06
Partito dei lavoratori italiani	324.245 027
Partito della rifondazione	
comunista (Italy)	324.245 075
Partito democratico (Italy)	324.245 06
Partito democratico della sinistra	
(Italy)	324.245 07
Partito fascista repubblicano	
(Italy)	324.245 023 8
Partito liberale italiano	
(1943–1994)	324.245 04

Passenger automobiles (continued)
  transportation services   388.342
  see also Automobiles
Passenger services   388.042
  air   387.742
    airport services   387.736 4
    law   343.097 8
  automobile   388.321
    urban   388.413 21
  bus   388.322
    law   343.094 82
    terminal services   388.33
    urban   388.413 22
      terminal services   388.473
  canal   386.404 22
  ferries   386.6
  ground   388.042
    law   343.093 3
  inland waterway   386.242
    law   343.096 8
    port services   386.862
  lake   386.542
  law   343.093 3
  marine   387.542
    law   343.096 8
    port services   387.162
  ports   387.162
  public administration   354.763
  railroad   385.22
    law   343.095 8
    public administration   354.767 3
    special purpose   385.5
    terminal services   385.262
    urban   388.42
      terminal services   388.472
  river   386.352
Passenger ships
  power-driven   387.243
    design   623.812 43
    engineering   623.824 3
Passenger terminals
  architecture   725.3
  area planning   711.7
  construction   690.53
  inland waterway   386.852
  ports   387.152
  railroad   385.314
Passenger-train cars   385.33
  engineering   625.23
  see also Rolling stock
Passenger transportation   388.042
  see also Passenger services
Passer sparrows   598.887

Passeres   598.8
  see Manual at 598.824–.88
Passeriformes   598.8
  paleozoology   568.8
Passerines   598.8
Passifloraceae   583.69
  botany   583.69
  edible fruits   641.344 2
    cooking   641.644 2
    food   641.344 2
    orchard crop   634.42
Passiflorales   583.69
Passing
  American football   796.332 25
Passing off (Offense)   364.166 8
  law   345.026 68
Passion fruit   641.344 25
  cooking   641.644 25
  food   641.344 25
  orchard crop   634.425
Passion of Jesus Christ   232.96
  music   782.23
Passion plays
  literature   808.825 16
    history and criticism   809.251 6
    specific literatures   T3B—205 16
      individual authors   T3A—2
  religious significance   246.723
  stage presentation   792.16
  see also Theater
Passionflowers   583.69
  botany   583.69
  floriculture   635.933 69
Passionists   255.62
  church history   271.62
Passiontide   263.92
  devotional literature   242.34
  music   781.725 5
  sermons   252.62
Passive-aggressive personality
  disorder
  medicine   616.858 1
  see also Mental disorders
Passive resistance
  political action   322.4
  social conflict   303.61
Passive smoking
  human toxicology   615.952 395 93
  respiratory diseases   616.200 471
  see also Respiratory tract
    diseases — humans
Passover   296.437
  customs   394.267
  liturgy   296.453 7

Pathological biochemistry	571.94
human metabolic diseases	616.39
see also Digestive system	
diseases — humans	
Pathological gambling	
medicine	616.858 41
see also Mental disorders	
Pathological physiology	571.9
see also Pathology	
Pathological processes	
medicine	616.047
Pathological psychology	616.89
Pathology	571.9
cytology	571.936
humans	611.018 15
humans	616.07
injuries	
medicine	617.107
surgery	617.07
see Manual at 571–575 vs. 630	
Pathophysiology	571.9
see also Pathology	
Patience	179.9
moral theology	205.699
see also Virtues	
Patience (Game)	795.43
Patient compliance	
medicine	615.5
Patient education	
medicine	615.507 1
Patient isolation	
disease control	614.45
Patients' libraries	027.662
Patinating	
decorative arts	739.15
Patio furniture	645.8
see also Outdoor furniture	
Patio gardening	635.967 1
Patio lighting	621.322 9
see also Lighting	
Patios	721.84
architecture	721.84
construction	690.184
domestic	643.55
architecture	728.93
construction	690.893
home economics	643.55
Patmos Island (Greece)	T2—495 87
Patois	417.2
specific languages	T4—7
Patriarchal family	306.858
Patriarchate	262.13

Patriarchs	200.92
Biblical	222.110 922
biography	200.92
Christian	270.092
biography	270.092
specific denominations	280
see Manual at 230–280	
ecclesiology	262.13
see also Clergy — Christian	
Patriarchy (System of	
government)	321.1
Patricia Portion (Ont.)	T2—713 1
Patrick County (Va.)	T2—755 695
Patrilineal kinship	306.83
Patriotic holidays	394.26
law	344.091
see also Holidays	
Patriotic music	781.599
songs	782.421 599
Patriotic pageants	394.5
customs	394.5
performing arts	791.624
Patriotic societies	369.2
biography	369.209 2
United States	369.1
Patristic philosophy	189.2
Patristics (Christianity)	270
Patrol	
military operation	355.413
police services	363.232
Patrol boats (Military)	359.835 8
design	623.812 58
engineering	623.825 8
naval equipment	359.835 8
naval units	359.325 8
Patrol boats (Police)	363.286
design	623.812 63
engineering	623.826 3
police services	363.286
Patron and client	306.2
Patronage	306.2
political science	324.204
Patronage of individuals	T1—079
Pattern lumber	674.43
Pattern perception	
visual	
psychology	152.142 3
Pattern poetry	808.814
history and criticism	809.14
specific literatures	T3B—104
Pattern recognition	
computer science	006.4
	T1—028 564
engineering	621.399 4

Peace	
social theology (continued)	
Hinduism	294.517 273
Judaism	296.382 7
World War I	940.312
World War II	940.531 2
see also Social history	
Peace conferences	341.73
Peace Corps (U.S.)	361.6
Peace movements	327.172
sociology	303.66
Peace pipe	399
Peace River (Alta.)	T2—712 31
Peace River (B.C. :	
Regional district)	T2—711 87
Peace River (B.C. and Alta.)	T2—712 31
Alberta	T2—712 31
British Columbia	T2—711 87
Peace River (Fla.)	T2—759 57
Peace River-Liard (B.C.)	T2—711 87
Peace treaties	341.66
Peaceful occupation	
law of nations	341.722
Peaceful settlement of disputes	303.69
international relations	327.17
law of nations	341.52
sociology	303.69
Peacekeeping forces	355.357
law of nations	341.584
Peacekeeping operations	355.4
Peach County (Ga.)	T2—758 556
Peaches	641.342 5
botany	583.642
commercial processing	664.804 25
cooking	641.642 5
food	641.342 5
orchard crop	634.25
Peafowl	598.625 8
animal husbandry	636.595
Pe'ah	296.123 1
Mishnah	296.123 1
Palestinian Talmud	296.124 1
Peak District (England)	T2—425 11
Peanut flour	664.726
Peanut meal	664.726
Peanut worms	592.35
Peanuts	641.356 596
agricultural economics	338.173 368
botany	583.63
commercial processing	664.805 659 6
economics	338.476 647 26
technology	664.726
cooking	641.656 596
field crop	633.368

Peanuts (continued)	
food	641.356 596
garden crop	635.659 6
Pearl Harbor, Attack on, 1941	940.542 669 3
Pearl of Great Price (Latter Day	
Saint movement sacred book)	289.324
Pearl oysters	
culture	639.412
Pearl River (Miss. and La.)	T2—762 5
Pearl River County (Miss.)	T2—762 15
Pearlfishes	597.63
Pears	641.341 3
botany	583.642
commercial processing	664.804 13
cooking	641.641 3
food	641.341 3
orchard crop	634.13
Pearson, Lester B.	
Canadian history	971.064 3
Pearston (South Africa :	
District)	T2—687 53
Peas	641.356 5
botany	583.63
commercial processing	664.805 65
cooking	641.656 5
field crop	633.3
food	641.356 5
garden crop	635.65
Peas (Pisum sativum)	641.356 56
botany	583.63
commercial processing	664.805 656
cooking	641.656 56
field crop	633.37
food	641.356 56
garden crop	635.656
Peasants	305.563 3
	T1—088 63
Peasants' War, 1524–1525	943.031
Peat	553.21
economic geology	553.21
mining	622.331
properties	662.622 1
use as soil conditioner	631.826
Peat bogs	
biology	578.768 7
ecology	577.687
Peat coal	553.21
see also Peat	
Peat mosses	588.29
Peatlands	
biology	578.768 7
ecology	577.687
Peba-Yaguan languages	498.9
	T6—989

Pecans	641.345 2	Pediatric services	362.198 92
agriculture	634.52	*see also* Health services	
botany	583.65	Pediatric surgery	617.98
cooking	641.645 2	Pediatric therapeutics	615.542
food	641.345 2	Pediatric toxicology	615.900 83
Peccaries	599.634	Pediatricians	618.920 009 2
Pecopteris	561.597	role and function	618.920 023 2
Pecos County (Tex.)	T2—764 923	Pediatrics	618.92
Pecos River (N.M. and		*see Manual at* 616 vs. 618.92;	
Tex.)	T2—764 9	*also at* 618.92097 vs. 617	
New Mexico	T2—789 4	Pediculosis	
Texas	T2—764 9	medicine	616.572
Pectins	572.566	*see also* Skin diseases —	
biochemistry	572.566	humans	
food technology	664.25	Pedicuring	646.727
see also Carbohydrates		Pedigrees	
Pedagogy	370	animal husbandry	636.082 2
Pedal cars		Pediments	721.5
engineering	629.227 4	architecture	721.5
Pedaliaceae	583.96	construction	690.15
Pedaling		Pee Dee River (N.C. and	
music	784.193 8	S.C.)	T2—757 8
Peddie (South Africa :		Peel (Ont. : Regional	
District)	T2—687 54	municipality)	T2—713 535
Pedernales (Dominican		Peer counseling of students	371.404 7
Republic : Province)	T2—729 323	Peer group	
Pedestals	721.3	influence on crime	364.253
architecture	721.3	socialization	303.327
construction	690.13	Peer pressure	303.327
Pedestrian facilities	388.41	Peer review	
area planning	711.74	health services	362.106 8
landscape architecture	717	Peer-to-peer architecture	
use	388.41	computer science	004.652
Pedestrian malls	388.411	Peerage	
area planning	711.74	genealogy	929.7
landscape architecture	717	Pegasiformes	597.64
Pedestrian paths	388.12	Pegmatite dikes	553.16
area planning	711.74	determinative mineralogy	549.116
use	388.12	Peiraieus (Greece : Regional	
local	388.411	unit)	T2—495 12
Pedestrian traffic	388.41	Peking (China)	T2—511 56
law	343.098 1	Peking man	569.97
Pedi (African people)	T5—963 977 1	Pekingese (Dog)	636.76
Pedi language	496.397 71	Pelagian Islands	T2—458 22
	T6—963 977 1	Pelagianism	273.5
Pediatric cardiology	618.921 2	Pelargoniums	635.933 72
Pediatric dentistry	617.645	botany	583.72
Pediatric disorders		floriculture	635.933 72
incidence	614.599 292	Pelecaniformes	598.43
medicine	618.92	paleozoology	568.4
Pediatric gynecology	618.920 98	Pelecanoididae	598.42
Pediatric nursing	618.920 023 1	Pelgrimsrus 1 (South	
Pediatric pharmacology	615.108 3	Africa : District)	T2—682 73
Pediatric preventive measures	613.043 2		

Pelgrimsrus 2 (South Africa : District)	T2—682 73
Pelicans	598.43
Pella (Greece : Regional unit)	T2—495 65
Pellagra	
medicine	616.393
see also Digestive system diseases — humans	
Pelly Bay (Nunavut)	T2—719 55
Pelobatoidea	597.86
Pelomedusidae	597.929
Peloncillo Mountains (Ariz. and N.M.)	T2—789 693
Peloponnesian War, 431–404 B.C.	938.05
Peloponnēsos (Greece)	T2—495 22
Peloponnēsos (Greece : Peninsula)	T2—495 2
Peloponnēsou, Dytikē Hellada kai Ioniou (Greece : Decentralized administration)	T2—495 2
Peloponnesus (Greece)	T2—495 22
Peloponnesus (Greece : Peninsula)	T2—495 2
ancient	T2—386
Peloponnesus, Western Greece and the Ionian Islands (Greece : Decentralized administration)	T2—495 2
Pelvic bones	
human anatomy	611.71
medicine	616.71
Pelvic muscles	
human anatomy	611.736
Pelvic region	
human anatomy	611.96
human physiology	612.96
regional medicine	617.55
surgery	617.55
Pelycosauria	567.93
Pemba (Tanzania)	967.81
	T2—678 1
Pemba North (Tanzania)	T2—678 1
Pemba South (Tanzania)	T2—678 1
Pemberton (B.C.)	T2—711 31
Pembina County (N.D.)	T2—784 19
Pembrokeshire (Wales)	T2—429 62
Pemiscot County (Mo.)	T2—778 996
Pemón language	498.42
	T6—984 2
Pen-and-ink drawing	741.26

P'en ching	635.977 2
Peña Nieto, Enrique	
Mexican history	972.084 3
Penal colonies	365.34
see also Penal institutions	
Penal institutions	365
accounting	657.832
area planning	711.556
buildings	365.5
architecture	725.6
energy economics	333.796 4
institutional housekeeping	647.966
law	344.035
psychological influence	155.962
reform	365.7
Penal reform	364.6
Penalties	
personnel management	658.314 4
Penance	203.4
Christianity	234.166
public worship	265.6
theology	234.166
Penarth (Wales)	T2—429 89
Penas	787.6
see also Stringed instruments	
Pencil drawing	741.24
Pencil fishes	597.48
Pencils	
mechanical	681.6
wood-cased	674.88
Pend d'Oreille language	497.943 5
	T6—979 435
Pend d'Oreille literature	897.943 5
Pend Oreille County (Wash.)	T2—797 21
Pende (African people)	T5—963 93
Pende languages	496.393
	T6—963 93
Pender County (N.C.)	T2—756 25
Pendle (England)	T2—427 645
Pendleton County (Ky.)	T2—769 33
Pendleton County (W. Va.)	T2—754 91
Pendulum motion	531.324
Pendulums	531.324
clockworks	681.112
dowsing	133.323
fortune-telling	133.3
Penetrating wounds	
medicine	617.14
Penetration	
materials science	620.112 6
Penguins	598.47
Penicillin	
pharmacology	615.329 565 4

Peonies	635.933 44
botany	583.44
floriculture	635.933 44
Peons	305.56
	T1—086 25
People	T1—08
groups	T1—08
government programs	353.53
see Manual at T1—08	
individuals	T1—092
collected biography	T1—092 2
literature	
specific literatures	T3B—080 351
see also Persons	
(Individuals)	
see Manual at T1—08; *also at*	
T1—08 and 306.2–.6	
People movers	
engineering	621.868
People of God (Church)	262.7
People with developmental	
disabilities	305.908 5
	T1—087 5
education	371.92
social group	305.908 5
social services	362.196 8
intellectual disabilities	362.3
physical illness	362.196 8
People with disabilities	305.908
	T1—087
architecture for	720.87
arts	T3C—352 7
civil and human rights	323.37
United States	323.370 973
clothing	
home sewing	646.401
collected biography	T1—092 7
education	371.9
law	344.079 11
footwear for	
manufacturing technology	685.38
government programs	353.539
Holocaust, 1933–1945	940.531 808 7
home care	649.8
legal status	346.013 087
private law	346.013 087
United States	346.730 130 87
libraries for	027.663
administration	025.197 663
collection development	025.218 766 3
museum services	069.17
pastoral care	
Christianity	259.44

People with disabilities (continued)	
publications for	
reviews	028.163
recreation	790.196
indoor	793.019 6
outdoor	796.087
relations with government	323.37
social group	305.908
social welfare	362.4
biography	362.409 2
sports	796.087
see Manual at 796.08 vs.	
796.04	
see Manual at 362.1–.4 vs. 610	
People with handicaps	305.908
	T1—087
see also People with	
disabilities	
People with hearing impairments	305.908 2
	T1—087 2
education	371.912
legal status	
United States	346.730 130 872
library services	027.663
social group	305.908 2
social welfare	362.42
People with intellectual	
disabilities	305.908 4
	T1—087 4
criminal offenders	364.38
education	371.928
law	344.079 128
social welfare	362.3
People with learning	
disabilities	T1—087
education	371.9
social group	305.908 4
People with mental disabilities	
civil and human rights	323.374
criminal offenders	364.38
education	371.92
law	344.079 12
	344.079 14
guides to Christian life	248.862
Holocaust, 1933–1945	940.531 808 74
legal status	346.013 087 4
private law	346.013 087 4
social welfare	362.2
law	344.044
People with mental illness	305.908 4
	T1—087 4
criminal offenders	364.38
correctional institutions	365.46
see also Penal institutions	

674

Percichthyidae	597.73
Percidae	597.75
Perciformes	597.7
paleozoology	567.7
Percoidea	597.72
Percoidei	597.7
Percolation (Statistical physics)	530.13
Percolation theory	530.13
Percopsiformes	597.62
Percussed idiophones	786.84
set	786.84
single	786.884
see also Percussion instruments	
Percussion bands	784.68
Percussion caps	662.4
military engineering	623.454 2
Percussion ensembles	785.68
Percussion instruments	786.8
bands and orchestras	784
chamber ensembles	785
mixed	785.2–.5
single type	785.68
construction	786.819 23
by hand	786.819 23
by machine	681.868
solo music	786.8
Perdix perdix	598.623 2
Pereira, Aristides	
Cape Verdean history	966.580 31
Perennials (Plants)	582.16
floriculture	635.932
Pérez Molina, Otto	
Guatemalan history	972.810 535
Perfect binding	
bookbinding	686.35
Perfectionism	
ethical systems	171.3
personality trait	155.232
Perforating tools	621.95
Performance (Law)	346.022
Performance art	700
fine arts	709.040 755
20th century	709.040 755
21st century	709.050 155
techniques	702.81
Performance auditing	658.401 3
public administration	352.43
Performance audits	658.401 3
public administration	352.439
Performance awards	331.216 4
labor economics	331.216 4
personnel management	658.322 5

Performance contracting	
students	371.393
teachers	371.15
Performance evaluation	
computer science	004.029
engineering	621.390 29
for design and improvement	004.24
engineering	621.392
see Manual at 004.1 vs. 004.24	
executive management	658.401 3
military services	355.685
public administration	352.35
Performance evaluation of	
employees	658.312 5
public administration	352.66
Performance rating	
personnel management	658.312 5
executives	658.407 125
Performance scores	780
treatises	780.264
Performance standards	
commerce	389.63
personnel management	658.312 5
production management	658.562
Performance techniques	
music	781.43
singing	783.043
Performance tests	
automotive vehicles	629.282 4
Performances	790.2
ethics	175
music	780.78
Performers (Entertainers)	791.092
see Manual at 780.92 and 791.092	
Performing arts	790.2
public administrative support	353.77
sociology	306.484
see Manual at 780.079 vs. 790.2	
Performing arts centers	
architecture	725.83
area planning	711.558
Performing arts in music	780.079
Perfume-producing plants	
agriculture	633.81
economic botany	581.636
Perfumes	668.54
customs	391.63
Pergamum (Turkey)	T2—562 5
ancient	T2—392 3
Periapical abscesses	
dentistry	617.632

Pericardium	573.172 5		Periosteum	573.762 5
biology	573.172 5		human histology	612.751 045
human anatomy	611.11		*see also* Musculoskeletal	
human physiology	612.17		system	
medicine	616.11		Periostitis	
see also Cardiovascular system			medicine	616.712
Pericardium diseases			*see also* Musculoskeletal	
medicine	616.11		diseases — humans	
see also Cardiovascular			Peripheral control units	004.64
diseases — humans			engineering	621.398 1
Peridiscaceae	583.44		Peripheral nerves	573.85
Peridotite	552.3		human physiology	612.81
Peridural anesthesia			medicine	616.856
surgery	617.964		*see also* Nervous system	
Périgord (France)	T2—447 2		Peripheral nervous system	
Perimenopause			diseases	
disorders			medicine	616.856
gynecology	618.175		*see also* Nervous system	
see also Female genital			diseases — humans	
diseases — humans			Peripheral vascular diseases	
human physiology	612.665		medicine	616.131
Perimetrium	573.667 25		*see also* Cardiovascular	
human physiology	612.627		diseases — humans	
see also Female genital system			Peripherals (Computers)	004.7
Perinatal death				T1—028 547
medicine	618.392		engineering	621.398 4
Perinatal medicine	618.32		Perischoechinoidea	593.95
Perinatology	618.32		Periscopes	623.46
Perineum			Perissodactyla	599.66
human anatomy	611.96		paleozoology	569.66
human physiology	612.96		Peritoneal dialysis	
surgery	617.555		medicine	617.461 059
Period costumes			Peritoneal diseases	
home sewing	646.478		medicine	616.38
Period furniture	749.090 1–.090 5		*see also* Digestive system	
Period novels	808.838 1		diseases — humans	
history and criticism	809.381		Peritoneum	573.325
specific literatures	T3B—308 1		human anatomy	611.38
individual authors	T3A—3		human physiology	612.33
Periodic law	546.8		medicine	616.38
Periodic table	546.8		surgery	617.558
Periodicals	050		*see also* Digestive system	
	T1—05		Periwinkles (Plants)	
design	744.55		botany	583.956
see also Serials			Perjury	364.134
Periodicity (Biology)	571.77		law	345.023 4
Periodicity (Chemistry)	546.8		Perkins County (Neb.)	T2—782 88
Periodontal diseases			Perkins County (S.D.)	T2—783 45
dentistry	617.632		Perlis	T2—595 1
Periodontics	617.632		Permaculture	631.58
Periodontitis			Permafrost	551.384
dentistry	617.632		biology	578.758 6
			ecology	577.586
			engineering geology	624.151 36

Permanent Court of Arbitration	341.522 2	Perry County (Ark.)	T2—767 39
Permanent Court of International		Perry County (Ill.)	T2—773 93
Justice	341.552	Perry County (Ind.)	T2—772 29
Permanent deformation	531.385	Perry County (Ky.)	T2—769 173
materials science	620.112 33	Perry County (Miss.)	T2—762 175
see also Plasticity		Perry County (Mo.)	T2—778 694
Permanent education	374	Perry County (Ohio)	T2—771 59
	T1—071 5	Perry County (Pa.)	T2—748 45
see also Adult education		Perry County (Tenn.)	T2—768 38
Permanent magnetic fields		Persecutions (Christian church	
(Earth)	538.72	history)	272
Permanent-mold casting		Persepolis (Iran)	T2—357 72
metals	671.253	Pershing County (Nev.)	T2—793 53
Permanent waving	646.724	Persia	T2—55
Permanent way (Railroad)	385.312	ancient	935.7
engineering	625.1		T2—357
transportation services	385.312	Persian cat	636.832
Permeability		Persian Empire	935.05
foundation soils	624.151 36		T2—35
Permiaks	T5—945 3	Egyptian history	932.016
Permian languages	494.53	Mesopotamian history	935.05
	T6—945 3	Middle Eastern history	939.403
Permian literatures	894.53	Palestinian history	933.03
Permian period	551.756	Persian Gulf	551.461 535
geology	551.756		T2—165 35
paleontology	560.175 6	Persian Gulf Crisis, 1990–1991	956.704 42
Permians	T5—945 3	Persian Gulf Region	953
Permic languages	494.53		T2—53
	T6—945 3	ancient	939.49
Permic literatures	894.53		T2—394 9
Permskaia oblast′ (Russia)	T2—474 3	Persian Gulf States	953.6
Permutation groups	512.21		T2—536
Permutations (Mathematics)	511.64	ancient	939.49
Perm′ (Russia : Oblast)	T2—474 3		T2—394 9
Pernambuco (Brazil)	T2—813 4	Persian Gulf syndrome	
Pernik (Bulgaria : Oblast)	T2—499 86	medicine	616.98
Pernishka oblast (Bulgaria)	T2—499 86	Persian Gulf War, 1980–1988	955.054 2
Peromyscus	599.355	Persian Gulf War, 1991	956.704 42
Perón, Isabel		Persian language	491.55
Argentine history	982.064		T6—915 5
Perón, Juan Domingo		Persian literature	891.55
Argentine history	982.062	Persian rugs	
1946–1955	982.062	arts	746.755
1973–1974	982.064	Persian Wars, 500–479 B.C.	938.03
Perón, María Estela		Persians	T5—915 5
Argentine history	982.064	Persimmons	641.344 5
Peronosporales	579.546	botany	583.93
Perouse Strait	551.461 453	cooking	641.644 5
	T2—164 53	food	641.344 5
Peroxidation		orchard crop	634.45
chemical engineering	660.284 43	Persis	T2—357 72
Peroxisomes	571.655	Persistence	
Perquimans County (N.C.)	T2—756 144	insurance	368.016
Perry County (Ala.)	T2—761 44		

Personal narratives (continued)
Iraqi-Iranian Conflict	955.054 209 2
Korean War	951.904 209 2
Mexican War	973.620 92
South African War	968.048 092
Spanish-American War	973.890 92
Thirty Years' War	940.240 92
Vietnamese War	959.704 309 2
War of the Pacific	983.061 609 2
World War I	940.481
World War II	940.548 1

see Manual at 930–990
Personal property
law	346.047
private ownership	346.047
public ownership	343.023

Personal property tax 336.23
law	343.054
public administration	352.44
public finance	336.23

Personal religion 204
Buddhism	294.344
Christianity	240
Hinduism	294.54
Islam	297.57
Sufi	297.4
Judaism	296.7

Personal risks	368.07
Personal safety	613.6
	T1—028 9
primary education	372.37

Personal security
civil rights issues	323.43

Personal selling	381.1
management	658.85
	T1—068 8
Personal shorthand	653.18

Personal space
sociology	304.23

Personal survival
occultism	133.901 3

Personal wealth
taxes	336.24

Personalism
philosophy	141.5

Personality	155.2
applied psychology	158.1
children	155.418 2
educational psychology	370.153 2
folklore	398.273
history and criticism	398.353
philosophy	126
Personality (Law)	346.012

Personality assessment	155.28
applied psychology	158.15
Personality development	155.25

Personality disorders
medicine	616.858 1

see also Mental disorders
Personality inventories	155.283
applied psychology	158.15
Personality questionnaires	155.283
applied psychology	158.15
Personality tests	155.28
applied psychology	158.15
Personality types	155.26

Personalized reading instruction
primary education	372.417
Personifications (Religion)	202.14

Personnel
libraries	023
museums	069.63
office services	651.3

Personnel information
management	658.301
Personnel management	658.3
	T1—068 3
armed forces	355.61
executives	658.407
libraries	023
museums	069.63
public administration	352.6
schools	371.201
higher education	378.11
Personnel planning	658.301
Personnel policy	658.301

Personnel selection
management	658.311 2

Personnel transports
military engineering	623.746 5

Personnel utilization
management	658.312 8
public administration	352.66
Persons (Individuals)	T1—092
	T2—2
arts	700.451
	T3C—351
biography	920
	T1—092
collected biography	T1—092 2
folklore	398.22
history and criticism	398.352
groups	T1—08

see also People
see Manual at T1—08

Pesticides (continued)
  agricultural use   632.95
    see Manual at 632.95 vs.
      632.2–.8
  chemical engineering   668.65
  human toxicology   615.902
  pest control technology   628.96
  pollution   363.738 498
    ecology   577.279
    environmental engineering   628.529
    law   344.046 334
    see also Pollution
  public safety   363.179 2
    see also Hazardous materials
  toxicology   571.959
  water pollution engineering   628.168 42
Pests   591.65
  agriculture   632.6
  see also Pest control
PET (Tomography)
  medicine   616.075 75
Pet food   636.088 7
  animal husbandry   636.088 7
  manufacturing technology   664.66
Pet names   929.97
Petals   575.69
Pétanque   796.31
Petauridae   599.23
Petenaeaceae   583.76
Peter (Biblical books)   227.92
Peter I, Emperor of Russia
  Russian history   947.05
Peter II, Emperor of Russia
  Russian history   947.061
Peter III, Emperor of Russia
  Russian history   947.062
Peter Lougheed Provincial
  Park (Alta.)   T2—712 332
Peterborough (England :
  City)   T2—426 51
Peterborough (Ont. :
  County)   T2—713 67
Petermanniaceae   584.6
Petersburg (Va.)   T2—755 581
Petit basset griffon vendén   636.753 6
Petition
  civil right   323.48
PETN (Explosives)   662.27
Petorca (Chile : Province)   T2—832 48
Petra (Extinct city)   939.48
    T2—394 8
Petrels   598.42
Petri nets   511.35

Petrified Forest National
  Park (Ariz.)   T2—791 37
Petrified wood   561.16
Petro, Gustavo
  Colombian history   986.106 357
Petrochemicals   665.538
  chemical engineering   661.804
  human toxicology   615.951
  petroleum product   665.538
Petrogenesis   552.03
Petroglyphs   709.011 3
Petrography   552
Petrol   665.538 27
Petrolatum   665.538 5
Petroleum   553.28
  chemistry   547.83
  dowsing   133.323 7
  economic geology   553.28
  extraction   622.338
    equipment manufacturing
      technology   681.766 5
  extractive economics   338.272 8
    law   343.077 2
  pipeline transportation   388.55
    law   343.093 95
  processing   665.5
    economics   338.476 655
    enterprises   338.766 55
  prospecting   622.182 8
  public administration   354.45
  resource economics   333.823
    law   346.046 823
Petroleum chemicals   665.538
  chemical engineering   661.804
  petroleum product   665.538
Petroleum coke   665.538 8
Petroleum County (Mont.)   T2—786 28
Petroleum engineers   665.509 2
Petroleum gas   665.773
Petroleum geology   553.28
Petroleum industry   338.272 8
  law   343.077 2
Petrologists   552.009 2
Petrology   552
Petrosaviaceae   584.48
Petrosaviales   584.48
Petrusburg (South Africa :
  District)   T2—685 7
Pets   636.088 7
  art representation   704.943 2
  arts   T3C—362
  therapeutic use   615.851 58
  see Manual at 800, T3C—362
    vs. 398.245, 590, 636

Pettis County (Mo.)	T2—778 48
Petty officers	359.009 2
role and function	359.338
Petunias	635.933 959 3
botany	583.959 3
floriculture	635.933 959 3
Pews	247.1
architecture	726.529 3
Pewter	
decorative arts	739.533
Pezizales	579.578
Pfäffikon (Switzerland :	
Bezirk)	T2—494 574 5
Pfiesteriaceae	579.87
pH	541.372 8
chemical engineering	660.297 28
Phacidiales	579.57
Phaeophyceae	579.88
Phaeophyta	579.88
Phaethontidae	598.43
Phages	579.26
Phagocytes	571.968
human immunology	616.079 9
Phalaborwa (South Africa :	
District)	T2—682 59
Phalacrocoracidae	598.43
Phalaenopsis	584.72
botany	584.72
floriculture	635.934 72
Phalanger	599.232
Phalangeridae	599.232
Phalangeroidea	599.23
Phalanges	
human anatomy	611.718
hands	611.717
Phalangida	595.43
Phalansterianism (Socialist	
school)	
economics	335.23
Phalanxes (Military units)	355.31
Phalaris	584.926
Phalaropes	598.33
Phalaropodidae	598.33
Phallales	579.599
Phanarists	
Romanian history	949.801 5
Phanerite	552.3
Phanerozoic eon	551.7
Phanerozonia	593.93
paleozoology	563.93
Phantasms	133.14
Pharaoh hound	636.753 6
Phareae	584.922
Pharisees	296.812

Pharmaceutical arithmetic	615.140 151 3
Pharmaceutical chemistry	615.19
Pharmaceutical drugs	615.1
see also Drugs	
(Pharmaceuticals)	
Pharmaceutical services	
insurance	368.382 4
see also Insurance	
social welfare	362.178 2
Pharmaceutical technology	615.19
Pharmacists	615.109 2
law	344.041 6
Pharmacodynamics	615.7
see Manual at 615.1 vs. 615.7;	
also at 615.7 vs. 615.9	
Pharmacognosy	615.321
Pharmacokinetics	615.7
see Manual at 615.1 vs. 615.7;	
also at 615.2–.3 vs. 615.7;	
also at 615.7 vs. 615.9	
Pharmacologists	615.109 2
Pharmacology	615.1
adolescent medicine	615.108 35
pediatrics	615.108 3
veterinary medicine	636.089 51
see Manual at 615.1 vs. 615.7	
Pharmacopoeias	615.11
Pharmacy	615.1
law	344.041 6
Pharyngeal diseases	
medicine	616.32
see also Digestive system	
diseases — humans	
surgery	617.532
Pharynx	
human anatomy	611.32
human physiology	612.31
medicine	616.32
surgery	617.532
Phascolarctidae	599.25
Phase changes	530.474
see also Phase transformations	
Phase diagrams	530.474
metallurgy	669.94
see also Phase transformations	
Phase equilibria	530.474
see also Phase transformations	
Phase-locked loops	
electronic circuits	621.381 536 4
Phase modulators	
electronic circuits	621.381 536 4
Phase stability	530.474
see also Phase transformations	

Phase transformations	530.474	Philip II, King of France	
chemical engineering	660.296 3	French history	944.023
fluid-state physics	530.424	Philip II, King of Spain	
physics	530.474	Spanish history	946.043
solid-state physics	530.414	Philip III, King of France	
thermochemistry	541.363	French history	944.024
Phase transitions	530.474	Philip III, King of Spain	
see also Phase transformations		Spanish history	946.051
Phasemeters	621.374 9	Philip IV, King of France	
Phases		French history	944.024
moon	523.32	Philip IV, King of Spain	
Phasianidae	598.62	Spanish history	946.052
Phasianus colchicus	598.625 2	Philip V, King of France	
Phasmatodea	595.729	French history	944.024
Phasmida	595.729	Philip V, King of Spain	
Pheasants	598.625	Spanish history	946.055
animal husbandry	636.594	Philip VI, King of France	
conservation technology	639.978 625	French history	944.025
resource economics	333.958 625	Philippe, King of the Belgians	
sports hunting	799.246 25	Belgian history	949.304 5
Phelps County (Mo.)	T2—778 594	Philippians (Biblical book)	227.6
Phelps County (Neb.)	T2—782 392	Philippine-American War,	
Phencyclidine abuse	362.294	1898–1901	959.903 1
medicine	616.863 4	Philippine campaign, 1898	973.893 7
personal health	613.83	Philippine Independent Church	284.8
social welfare	362.294	*see also* Old Catholic churches	
see also Substance abuse		Philippine languages	499.21
Phenolics	668.422 2		T6—992 1
Phenology	578.42	Philippine literatures	899.21
Phenols	547.632	Philippine people	T5—992 1
chemical engineering	661.82	Philippine Sea	551.461 458
Phenomenalism	142.7		T2—164 58
Phenomenological psychology	150.192	Philippines	959.9
Phenomenology	142.7		T2—599
Phenotypes	576.53	Philippolis (South Africa :	
Phenylketonuria		District)	T2—685 7
medicine	616.399 5	Philipstown (South Africa :	
see also Digestive system		District)	T2—687 13
diseases — humans		Philistia	933.3
Phigalia (Extinct city)	T2—388		T2—333
Philadelphia (Pa.)	T2—748 11	Phillip Island (Vic.)	T2—945 2
Philadelphia County (Pa.)	T2—748 11	Phillips County (Ark.)	T2—767 88
Philanthropists	361.740 92	Phillips County (Colo.)	T2—788 77
Philanthropy		Phillips County (Kan.)	T2—781 17
ethics	177.7	Phillips County (Mont.)	T2—786 16
social welfare	361.74	Philodendrons	635.934 442
Philately	744.72	botany	584.442
Philemon (Biblical book)	227.86	floriculture	635.934 442
Philesiaceae	584.6	Philologists	409.2
Philibert II, Duke of Savoy		linguistics specialists	410.92
Piedmontese history	945.105	Philology	400
Philinoglossacea	594.34	linguistics	410
Philip I, King of France			
French history	944.022		

Philosophers	180–190
ancient	180
eastern	181
medieval western	189
modern	190
see Manual at 180–190	
Philosopher's stone	540.112
folklore	398.26
history and criticism	398.465
Philosophical anthropology	128
Philosophical commentary	
Koran	297.122 712 6
Philosophical counseling	128.4
Philosophical logic	160
Philosophy	100
	T1—01
arts	T3C—384
literature	808.803 84
history and criticism	809.933 84
specific literatures	T3B—080 384
history and	
criticism	T3B—093 84
primary education	372.8
see Manual at T1—01; *also at*	
200 vs. 100	
Philosophy and religion	201.61
Christianity	261.51
Islam	297.261
Judaism	296.371
Philosophy of language	121.68
linguistics	401
Philosophy of nature	113
Philosophy of religion	210
Philosophy of science	501
Philydraceae	584.86
Phiomorpha	599.359
Phishing	364.163 2
law	345.026 32
Phlebitis	
medicine	616.142
see also Cardiovascular	
diseases — humans	
Phlebotomy	
diagnosis	
general disease	616.075 61
Phloem	575.452
Phlorina (Greece : Regional	
unit)	T2—495 62
Phloxes	635.933 93
botany	583.93
floriculture	635.933 93
Phobias	
medicine	616.852 25
see also Mental disorders	

Phobic disorders	
medicine	616.852 25
see also Mental disorders	
Phoca	599.792
Phocidae	599.79
Phocis (Greece)	T2—495 15
ancient	T2—383
Phocoena	599.539
Phocoenidae	599.539
Phoenicia	939.44
	T2—394 4
Phoenician architecture	722.31
Phoenician language	492.6
	T6—926
Phoenician literature	892.6
Phoenician sculpture	732.944
Phoenicians	T5—926
Phoenicopteriformes	598.35
paleozoology	568.3
Phoenix	398.245 4
see also Legendary animals	
Phoenix (Ariz.)	T2—791 73
Phoka (African people)	T5—963 91
Phōkis (Greece)	T2—495 15
Pholidota	599.31
paleozoology	569.31
Phonemics	414
specific languages	T4—15
Phonetic method (Reading)	
primary education	372.465
Phonetic shorthand systems	
English language	653.42
Phonetics	414.8
primary education	372.465
specific languages	T4—158
Phonics	
primary education	372.465
Phonocardiography	
medicine	616.120 754 4
Phonodiscs	384
see also Sound recordings	
Phonograph records	384
see also Sound recordings	
Phonographs	621.389 33
Phonology	414
specific languages	T4—15
Phonons	
solid-state physics	530.416
Phonorecords	384
see also Sound recordings	
Phoridae	595.774
Phoronida	592.3
paleozoology	562.3

Phosphatases	572.755 3
see also Enzymes	
Phosphates	553.64
chemical engineering	661.43
economic geology	553.64
mineralogy	549.72
mining	622.364
Phosphatocopida	565.3
Phosphenes	
chemical engineering	661.87
Phosphinic acids	
chemical engineering	661.87
Phosphoacids	
chemical engineering	661.87
Phosphoalcohols	
chemical engineering	661.87
Phosphoaldehydes	
chemical engineering	661.87
Phosphoketones	
chemical engineering	661.87
Phospholipids	572.57
see also Lipids	
Phosphonic acids	
chemical engineering	661.87
Phosphonium compounds	
chemical engineering	661.87
Phosphoproteins	572.68
see also Proteins	
Phosphorescence	535.353
Phosphoric acid	
chemical engineering	661.25
Phosphorus	
applied nutrition	613.285
biochemistry	572.553
humans	612.015 24
chemical engineering	661.071 2
chemistry	546.712
metabolism	
human physiology	612.392 4
organic chemistry	547.07
aliphatic	547.47
applied	661.87
Phosphorus fertilizers	631.85
chemical engineering	668.625
Phosphorus salts	
chemical engineering	661.43
Photo-offset printing	686.232 5
Photo-optics	621.367
Photobacterium	579.34
Photobiochemistry	572.435
Photoceramic processes	773.6
Photochemistry	541.35
atmosphere	551.511
chemical engineering	660.295
Photocomposition	686.225 44
Photoconductive cells	621.381 542
Photoconductivity	537.54
Photocopying	686.4
equipment	686.402 84
manufacturing technology	681.65
library services	025.12
office use	652.4
technology	686.4
Photoduplication	686.4
see also Photocopying	
Photoelasticity	
materials science	620.112 95
Photoelectric components	621.381 542
Photoelectric photometry	
astronomy	522.623
Photoelectricity	537.54
Photoelectronic components	621.381 542
Photoemission	537.54
Photoemissive cells	621.381 542
Photoenamel processes	773.6
Photoengraving	686.232 7
Photogrammetry	526.982
military engineering	623.72
Photograph files	
police records	363.24
Photographers	770.92
see Manual at 779 vs. 770.92	
Photographic chemicals	771.5
chemical engineering	661.808
Photographic digital images	779
processing	771.4
Photographic equipment	771
manufacturing technology	681.418
Photographic images	779
arts	779
distribution	771.48
manipulation	771.44
organization	771.48
preparation	771.44
preservation	771.45
processing	771.4
storage	771.45
see Manual at 779 vs. 770.92	
Photographic photometry	
astronomy	522.622
Photographic prints	
processing	771.4
Photographic projection	771.48
motion pictures	777.57
transparencies (photographs)	771.48
Photographic surveying	526.982

Photographs 779
    T1—022 2
  arts 779
  criminal investigation 363.258
  processing 771.4
  see Manual at 779 vs. 770.92
Photography 770
  arts 770
  astronomy 522.63
  engineering 621.367
  green technology 771.402 86
  military engineering 623.72
  nuclear physics 539.778
  technique 771
  waste technology 771.402 86
Photogravure 686.232 7
Photointaglio 686.232 7
Photoionization of gases 530.444
Photojournalism 070.49
  education 371.897
Photolithography 686.232 5
Photoluminescence 535.355
Photomacrography 778.324
  cinematography 777.6
  videography 777.6
Photomechanical printing 686.232
Photometers
  manufacturing technology 681.415
Photometry 535.220 287
  astronomy 522.62
  engineering 621.321 1
Photomicrography 778.31
  biology 570.282
  cinematography 777.6
  science 502.82
  videography 777.6
Photomontage 778.8
Photomultipliers 621.381 542
Photon propulsion 629.475 4
Photonics 621.365
Photonovels 741.5
  see also Fotonovelas
Photons 539.721 7
Photonuclear reactions 539.756
Photopsychography 778.3
Photosensitive surfaces
  chemical engineering 661.808
  photography 771.53
Photosensitivity
  animals 573.88
    see also Eyes

Photosensitivity disorders
  medicine 616.515
    see also Skin diseases —
    humans
Photosphere
  sun 523.74
Photostating
  technology 686.45
Photostats
  technical drawing 604.25
Photosynthesis 572.46
Photosynthetic bacteria 579.38
Phototherapy
  medicine 615.831
Phototransistors 621.381 528
Phototubes 621.381 542
Photovoltaic cells 621.381 542
Photovoltaic effect 537.54
Photovoltaic generation 621.312 44
Phrase books 418
  specific languages T4—83
Phrase structure grammars 415.018 23
  specific languages T4—501 823
Phrases (Grammar) 415
  specific languages T4—5
Phrenology 139
Phrygia T2—392 6
Phrygia Pacatiana T2—392 6
Phrygia Salutaris T2—392 6
Phrygian language 491.993
  T6—919 93
Phrynophiurida 593.94
Phthiōtis (Greece) T2—495 15
  ancient T2—383
Phthiraptera 595.756
Phú Thọ (Vietnam :
  Province) T2—597 2
Phú Yên (Vietnam :
  Province) T2—597 5
Phutthayǫtfā Čhulālōk, King of
  Siam
  Thai history 959.303 1
Phycid hakes 597.632
Phycologists 579.809 2
Phycology 579.8
Phycomycetes 579.53
Phylacteries 296.461 2
Phyllocarida 595.379 2
Phyllodocida 592.62
Phyllosilicates
  mineralogy 549.67
Phyllostomatidae 599.45
Phyllostomidae 599.45

Phylogeny	576.88
animals	591.38
microorganisms	579.138
plants	581.38
Physarales	579.52
Physeter	599.547
Physeteridae	599.547
Physical anthropologists	599.909 2
Physical anthropology	599.9
Physical biochemistry	572.43
humans	612.015 83
Physical chemistry	541
applied	660.29
see Manual at 541 vs. 546	
Physical conditions of work	331.256
see also Work environment	
Physical constants	530.81
Physical crystallography	548.8
Physical diagnosis	
medicine	616.075 4
Physical distribution of goods	
management	658.788
	T1—068 8
Physical education	613.7
health	613.7
primary education	372.86
sports	796.07
Physical environment	
influence on crime	364.22
psychological influence	155.91
Physical ethnologists	599.970 92
Physical ethnology	599.97
Physical evidence	
criminal investigation	363.256 2
criminal law	345.064
law	347.064
Physical fitness	613.7
health	613.7
public administration	353.627 4
sociology	306.461 3
Physical geography	910.02
see Manual at 550 vs. 910;	
also at 909, 930–990 vs.	
910	
Physical geology	551
Physical gerontology	612.67
Physical illness	362.1
medicine	616
see also Diseases — humans	
Physical instruments	
manufacturing technology	681.753
Physical metallurgy	669.9
Physical mineralogy	549.12
Physical oceanography	551.46

Physical operations	
chemical engineering	660.284 2
Physical optics	535.2
Physical organic chemistry	547.13
Physical sciences	500.2
Physical therapy	
medicine	615.82
psychiatry	616.891 3
Physical training	
health	613.7
Physical typology	
influence on crime	364.24
Physical units	530.81
Physical yoga	
health	613.704 6
see Manual at 613.7046	
vs. 615.824, 615.851,	
615.852, 616–618	
therapeutics	615.824
see Manual at 613.7046	
vs. 615.824, 615.851,	
615.852, 616–618	
Physically disabled children	
home care	649.151
Physically disabled people	305.908
	T1—087
education	371.91
social group	305.908
social welfare	362.4
see also Physically	
handicapped people	
Physically handicapped people	305.908
	T1—087
see also Physically disabled	
people	
Physician and patient	610.696
Physician assistants	610.737 209 2
role and function	610.737 206 9
services	610.737 2
Physicians	610.92
health services	362.172
see also Health services	
law	344.041 2
malpractice	344.041 21
role and function	610.695
Physicians' liability insurance	368.564 2
see also Insurance	
Physicists	530.092
Physics	530
ecology	577.13
engineering	621
law	344.095 3

Pickles	
commercial preservation	664.028 6
cooking with	641.616 2
home preservation	641.462
Pickling foods	664.028 6
commercial preservation	664.028 6
home preservation	641.462
Pickup trucks	388.343 2
driving	629.284 32
engineering	629.223 2
repair	629.287 32
transportation services	388.343 2
see also Trucks	
Picnic areas	
road engineering	625.77
Picnic cooking	641.578
Picnics	642.3
Picornaviridae	579.257 2
Picramniaceae	583.745
Picramniales	583.745
Pictograms	
design	744.2
Pictorial arts	740
Pictorial journalism	070.49
Pictorial works	T1—022 2
Pictou (N.S. : County)	T2—716 13
Picture dictionaries	413.17
specific languages	T4—317
specific subjects	T1—03
Picture frames	684
furniture arts	749.7
wooden	674.88
Picture framing	749.7
Pictures	T1—022 2
bibliographies	011.376
cataloging	025.347 1
fine arts	740
instructional use	371.335 2
library treatment	025.177 1
textile arts	746.3
Pidgin English	427.9
	T6—217
Pidgins	417.22
specific languages	T4—7
see Manual at T4—7	
Pidyon haben	296.442 3
liturgy	296.454 23
Pie mixes	664.753
Piecework	331.216 4
labor economics	331.216 4
personnel management	658.322 5
Piedmont (Italy : Region)	945.1
	T2—451
ancient	T2—372 22

Piedmont (U.S. : Region)	T2—75
Alabama	T2—761 5
Georgia	T2—758 4
Maryland	T2—752 7
North Carolina	T2—756 5
South Carolina	T2—757 3
Virginia	T2—755 6
Piegan Indians	T5—973 52
Piemonte (Italy)	945.1
	T2—451
ancient	T2—372 22
see also Piedmont (Italy : Region)	
Pier foundations	624.158
Pierce, Franklin	
United States history	973.66
Pierce County (Ga.)	T2—758 792
Pierce County (N.D.)	T2—784 591
Pierce County (Neb.)	T2—782 56
Pierce County (Wash.)	T2—797 78
Pierce County (Wis.)	T2—775 42
Pieria (Greece)	T2—495 65
Pierre (S.D.)	T2—783 29
Pierre-De Saurel (Quebec)	T2—714 39
Piers (Columns)	721.3
architecture	721.3
construction	690.13
structural engineering	624.16
Piers (Port facilities)	387.15
engineering	627.31
see also Port facilities	
Pies	641.865 2
commercial processing	664.752 5
home preparation	641.865 2
Piet Retief (South Africa : District)	T2—682 78
Pietermaritzburg (South Africa)	T2—684 75
Pietermaritzburg (South Africa : District)	T2—684 7
Pietersburg (South Africa : District)	T2—682 56
Pietism	273.7
Piezoelectricity	537.244 6
Piezomagnetism	538.3
Pig iron	669.141 3
Pigeon English	427.9
	T6—217
Pigeons	598.65
agricultural pests	632.686 5
animal husbandry	636.596
sports hunting	799.246 5
Piggyback transportation	385.72
public administration	354.764

Plant location

management 658.21

    libraries 022.1

    museums 069.21

    schools 371.61

Plant maintenance

management 658.202

Plant management 658.2

T1—068 2

  libraries 022

  museums 069.2

  public administration 352.56

  schools 371.6

    special education 371.904 5

see also Facility management;

  Plants (Buildings and

  equipment) — management

see Manual at 647 vs. 647.068,

  658.2, T1—0682

Plant pathology 571.92

  agriculture 632

Plant pest control

  environmental engineering 628.97

Plant physiology 571.2

Plant propagation 631.53

  agriculture 631.53

  forestry 634.956 5

Plant protection 632.9

Plant quarantine 632.93

Plant regulators

  agriculture 631.89

  biology 571.72

Plant resources 333.953

  public administration 354.349

Plant respiration 572.472

Plant sanitation 363.729 5

  engineering 628.51

Plant selection 631.52

Plant shutdowns 338.604 2

Plant spacing (Agriculture) 631.53

Plant supports 631.546

  manufacturing technology 681.763 1

Plant training 631.546

Plant varieties

  agriculture 631.57

  resource economics 333.953 4

Plant viruses 579.28

  agriculture 632.8

Plantagenet, House of 942.03

  English history 942.03

  genealogy 929.72

  Irish history 941.503

Plantaginaceae 583.96

Plantagos 583.96

Plantain lilies 635.934 79

  botany 584.79

  floriculture 635.934 79

Plantains (Fruits) 641.347 73

  botany 584.88

  commercial processing 664.804 773

  cooking 641.647 73

  food 641.347 73

  horticulture 634.773

Plantains (Plantaginaceae) 583.96

Plantation crops 633

  see Manual at 633–635

Plantation houses

  architecture 728.8

Plantations

  community sociology 307.72

  system of production

    sociology 306.349

Planting 631.53

  equipment manufacturing

    technology 681.763 1

Plants 580

  agricultural pests 632.5

  agriculture 630

  anatomy 571.32

  art representation 704.943 4

  arts 700.464

T3C—364

  bacterial diseases 571.993 12

  Bible 220.858

  biography T1—092 9

  botany 580

  coevolution with insects 576.875

  communicable diseases 571.982

  comparative psychology 156.9

  conservation technology 639.99

  drawing 743.7

  endoparasitic diseases 571.999 2

  folklore 398.242

    history and criticism 398.368

     legendary 398.468

     real 398.368

  food source 641.303

    see Manual at 583–585 vs.

     600

  influence on precipitation 551.577 5

  landscape architecture 715

  literature 808.803 64

    history and criticism 809.933 64

    specific literatures T3B—080 364

     history and

      criticism T3B—093 64

  metabolism 572.42

  mycoses 571.995 12

Dewey Decimal Classification

Platelets	573.159
histology	573.159
human histology	612.117
human physiology	612.117
medicine	616.157
physiology	573.159
see also Cardiovascular system	
Plates (Musical instruments)	786.82
see also Bars (Musical instruments)	
Plates (Photosensitive surfaces)	661.808
chemical engineering	661.808
photography	771.532 2
Plates (Printing surfaces)	
flat surfaces	686.231 5
raised surfaces	686.231 4
Plates (Structural elements)	624.177 65
naval architecture	623.817 765
Plates (Tableware)	642.7
paper	676.34
Platform diving	797.24
see also Aquatic sports	
Platform foundations	624.156
Platform speeches	
literature	808.851
history and criticism	809.51
specific literatures	T3B—501
individual authors	T3A—5
rhetoric	808.51
Platforms (Party programs)	324.23
Platinotype processes	772.3
Platinum	669.24
chemical engineering	661.064 5
chemistry	546.645
economic geology	553.422
materials science	620.189 24
metallography	669.952 4
metallurgy	669.24
metalworking	673.24
mining	622.342 4
physical metallurgy	669.962 4
see also Chemicals; Metals	
Platinum metals	669.7
chemical engineering	661.063
chemistry	546.63
economic geology	553.495
metallography	669.957
metallurgy	669.7
physical metallurgy	669.967
Platinum printing-out process	772.3
Platinumwork	
decorative arts	739.24

Platonism	184
ancient	184
modern	141.2
Platoons (Military units)	355.31
Platt National Park (Okla.)	T2—766 57
Plattdeutsch	439.4
	T6—394
Plattdeutsch literature	839.4
Platte County (Mo.)	T2—778 135
Platte County (Neb.)	T2—782 52
Platte County (Wyo.)	T2—787 17
Platte River (Neb.)	T2—782
Platy	597.667
Platycopa	595.33
paleozoology	565.33
Platyhelminthes	592.4
paleozoology	562.4
Platypus	599.29
Platyrrhini	599.85
paleozoology	569.85
Platysternidae	597.926
Plaun (Switzerland)	T2—494 735 6
Play	790
child care	649.5
psychology	155
children	155.418
recreation	790
sociology	306.481
see also Recreation	
Play (Animals)	591.563
Play groups	
preschool education	372.21
Play schools	
primary education	372.21
Play therapy	
medicine	615.851 53
psychiatry	616.891 653
pediatrics	618.928 916 53
Player pianos	786.66
see also Mechanical musical instruments	
Playground equipment	
manufacturing technology	688.76
Playgrounds	796.068
Playing cards	795.4
manufacturing technology	688.754
Playing time	
musical technique	781.432
Plays	
literature	808.82
see also Drama (Literature)	
musical	782.14
music	782.14
stage presentation	792.6

Plucked idiophones	786.85
set	786.85
single	786.887
see also Percussion instruments	
Plucked instruments	787.7
see also Stringed instruments	
Plumas County (Calif.)	T2—794 29
Plumb-yews	585.3
Plumbaginaceae	583.88
Plumbaginales	583.88
Plumbago (Graphite)	553.26
see also Graphite	
Plumbers	696.109 2
Plumbing	696.1
household management	644.6
Plumbing fixtures	644.6
building construction	696.1
household management	644.6
Plumeria	583.956
botany	583.956
floriculture	635.933 956
Plums	641.342 2
botany	583.642
cooking	641.642 2
food	641.342 2
orchard crop	634.22
Plundering	364.16
law	345.026
Pluralism (Philosophy)	147.4
Pluralism (Religion)	201.5
Buddhism	294.335
Christianity	261.2
Hinduism	294.515
Islam	297.28
Judaism	296.39
Pluralism (Social sciences)	305.8
education	370.117
political science	323.1
sociology	305.8
Pluriarcs	787.93
instrument	787.931 9
music	787.93
see also Stringed instruments	
Plush	677.617
Plush-capped finch	598.88
Pluto (Planet)	523.492 2
	T2—992 9
astrology	133.539 2
Plutocracy	321.5
Plutonic rocks	552.3
Plutonium	669.293 4
chemical engineering	661.043 4
chemistry	546.434
human toxicology	615.925 434

Plutonium (continued)	
metallography	669.952 934
metallurgy	669.293 4
physical metallurgy	669.962 934
see also Chemicals	
Plymouth (England)	T2—423 58
Plymouth Brethren	289.9
Plymouth County (Iowa)	T2—777 16
Plymouth County (Mass.)	T2—744 82
Plymouth Rock chicken	636.582
Plywood	674.834
Plzeňský kraj (Czech Republic)	T2—437 14
PMS (Syndrome)	
gynecology	618.172
see also Female genital diseases — humans	
Pneumatic clocks	
technology	681.115
Pneumatic construction	693.98
architecture	721.044 98
Pneumatic control	629.804 5
Pneumatic conveyor systems	
office use	651.79
Pneumatic engineering	621.51
Pneumatic engineers	621.510 92
Pneumatic pumps	621.69
Pneumatic tools	621.904
Pneumatics	533
engineering	621.51
physics	533
Pneumoconiosis	
medicine	616.244
see also Respiratory tract diseases — humans	
Pneumocystis carinii pneumonia	
medicine	616.241 6
Pneumocystis pneumonia	
medicine	616.241 6
Pneumonia	
medicine	616.241
Po River (Italy)	T2—452
Poaceae	584.92
Poaching	364.162 859
birds	364.162 859 8
law	345.026 285 98
fish	364.162 859 7
law	345.026 285 97
law	345.026 285 9
mammals	364.162 859 9
law	345.026 285 99
Poales	584.9
paleobotany	561.49
Pocahontas County (Iowa)	T2—777 19

Pocahontas County (W. Va.)	T2—754 87
Pocket billiards	794.73
Pocket calculators	681.145
mathematics	510.284
Pocket gophers	599.359 9
Pocket mice	599.359 8
Pocket scores	780
treatises	780.265
Pocono Mountains (Pa.)	T2—748 2
Podargidae	598.99
Podcasting	791.46
instructional use	371.333 2
publishing	070.579 738
sociology	302.234
software	006.787 6
Podiatry	617.585
Podicipediformes	598.443
paleozoology	568.4
Podkarpackie Voivodeship (Poland)	T2—438 66
Podlaskie Voivodeship (Poland)	T2—438 36
Podocarpaceae	585.3
paleobotany	561.53
Podocarpuses	585.3
Podocopa	595.33
paleozoology	565.33
Podostemaceae	583.69
Podostemales	583.69
Poeciliidae	597.667
Poems	808.81
music	780
treatises	780.268
see also Poetry	
Poetic books (Old Testament)	223
pseudepigrapha	229.912
Poetic drama	
literature	808.82
history and criticism	809.2
specific literatures	T3B—2
individual authors	T3A—2
Poetics	808.1
Poetry	808.81
criticism	809.1
theory	808.1
history and criticism	809.1
rhetoric	808.1
specific literatures	T3B—1
individual authors	T3A—1
see Manual at T3B—1	
Poetry slams	808.545
Poets	809.1
collected biography	809.1
specific literatures	T3B—100 9
individual biography	T3A—1
Pogolo (African people)	T5—963 91
Pogolo languages	496.391
	T6—963 91
Pogonophora	592.3
paleozoology	562.3
Pogoro (African people)	T5—963 91
Pogoro languages	496.391
	T6—963 91
Pohamba, Hifikepunye Lucas	
Namibian history	968.810 42
Pohjanmaa (Finland)	T2—489 734
Pohjois-Karjala (Finland)	T2—489 758
Pohjois-Karjalan lääni (Finland)	T2—489 758
Pohjois-Pohjanmaa (Finland)	T2—489 767
Pohjois-Savo (Finland)	T2—489 752
Poikilothermy	571.76
Poinsett County (Ark.)	T2—767 96
Poinsettias	635.933 69
botany	583.69
floriculture	635.933 69
Point-of-sale advertising	659.157
Point processes	519.23
Point set topology	514.322
Point sets	511.33
Point-to-point communications	004.692
communications services	384.34
sociology	302.231 1
Pointe-Claire (Quebec)	T2—714 28
Pointe Coupee Parish (La.)	T2—763 454
Pointers (Dogs)	636.752 5
Pointillism	709.034 5
painting	759.055
Poison arrow frogs	597.877
Poison gas	
ethics	172.42
military engineering	623.459 2
Poison gas projectiles	623.451 6
Poison hemlocks	583.988 2
Poison ivies	583.75
Poison oaks	583.75
Poisoning	
human toxicology	615.9
incidence	615.904
Poisonous animals	591.65
human toxicology	615.94
Poisonous fishes	597.165
human toxicology	615.945

Poisonous food animals	
human toxicology	615.945
Poisonous microorganisms	579.165
Poisonous organisms	578.65
Poisonous plants	581.659
human toxicology	615.952
Poisons	363.179 1
human toxicology	615.9
personal safety	615.905
public safety	363.179 1
toxicology	571.95
see also Hazardous materials	
Poisson distribution	519.24
Poisson integral	515.43
Poisson-Stieltjes integral	515.43
Poisson's ratio	531.381
Poitiers (France)	T2—446 34
Poitou (France)	T2—446
Poitou-Charentes (France)	T2—446
Poker (Game)	795.412
Pokeweed	583.883
Polabian language	491.89
	T6—918 9
Polabian literature	891.89
Poland	943.8
	T2—438
Poland China swine	636.482
Polar bear	599.786
conservation technology	639.979 786
resource economics	333.959 786
Polar regions	T2—11
see also Frigid zones	
Polarimeters	
manufacturing technology	681.25
Polarimetry	
astronomy	522.65
Polaris missiles	359.981 782
engineering	623.451 97
military equipment	359.981 782
Polariscopic analysis	543.59
Polarization of light	535.52
Polarography	543.4
Polders	
engineering	627.549
Pole vaulting	796.434
see also Track and field	
Polecats (New World)	599.768
Polecats (Old World)	599.766 2
Polela (South Africa : District)	T2—684 67
Polemics	
Christianity	239
comparative religion	202

Polemics (continued)	
Islam	297.29
Judaism	296.35
Polemoniaceae	583.93
Polemoniales	583.93
Poles (People)	T5—918 5
Polesine (Italy)	T2—453 3
Police	363.2
law	344.052
public administration	353.36
sociology	306.28
Police boats	363.286
design	623.812 63
engineering	623.826 3
police services	363.286
Police buildings	
architecture	725.18
Police corruption	364.132 3
law	345.023 23
public administration	353.46
Police dogs	
animal husbandry	636.708 86
police services	363.2
Police functions	363.23
Police misconduct	364.132
Police officers	363.209 2
role and function	363.22
Police patrols	363.232
Police powers (Constitutional law)	342.041 8
Police questioning	363.254
Police records	363.24
Police services	363.2
see also Police	
Police surveillance	363.232
Policy making	320.6
executive management	658.401 2
military administration	355.684
political science	320.6
public administration	352.34
social processes	303.3
see Manual at 300, 320.6 vs. 352–354	
Policy studies	320.6
Poliomyelitis	
incidence	614.549
medicine	616.835
see also Nervous system diseases — humans	
pediatrics	618.928 35
Poliovirus	579.257 2
Polish language	491.85
	T6—918 51
Polish literature	891.85

Politicians
  biography 324.209 2
  characteristics 324.22
  ethics 172.2
Politics 320
  arts 700.458 1
    T3C—358 1
  folklore 398.278 1
    history and criticism 398.358 1
  journalism 070.449 32
  literature 808.803 581
    history and criticism 809.933 581
    specific literatures T3B—080 358 1
      history and
        criticism T3B—093 581
  sociology 306.2
  see Manual at 324 vs. 320
Politics and religion 322.1
  political science 322.1
  social theology 201.72
    Buddhism 294.337 2
    Christianity 261.7
    Hinduism 294.517 2
    Islam 297.272
      see Manual at 297.26–.27
    Judaism 296.382
  see Manual at 322.1 vs.
    201.72, 261.7, 292–299
Politics as a profession 324.22
Polk, James K. (James Knox)
  United States history 973.61
Polk County (Ark.) T2—767 45
Polk County (Fla.) T2—759 67
Polk County (Ga.) T2—758 375
Polk County (Iowa) T2—777 58
Polk County (Minn.) T2—776 95
Polk County (Mo.) T2—778 77
Polk County (N.C.) T2—756 915
Polk County (Neb.) T2—782 352
Polk County (Or.) T2—795 38
Polk County (Tenn.) T2—768 875
Polk County (Tex.) T2—764 165
Polk County (Wis.) T2—775 17
Polkas 793.33
  music 784.188 44
Poll tax 336.25
  law 343.062
  public administration 352.44
  public finance 336.25
  qualification for voting 324.62
Polled Shorthorn cattle 636.226
Pollen 571.845 2
  paleobotany 561.13

Pollen control
  air conditioning
    buildings 697.932 4
Pollination 571.864 2
  coevolution 576.875
Polling 324.65
Pollocks 641.392
  cooking 641.692
  food 641.392
  zoology 597.632
Pollutants 363.738
  law 344.046 33
  see also Pollution
Pollution 363.73
  criminology 364.145
    law 345.024 5
  crop damage 632.19
  ecology 577.27
  human toxicology 615.902
  law 344.046 32
  public administration 354.335
    cleanup 353.93
  social effects 304.28
  social theology 201.77
    Christianity 261.88
  social welfare 363.73
  toxicology 571.95
  see Manual at 333.7–.9 vs.
    363.1, 363.73, 577; *also at*
    363.73 vs. 571.95, 577.27
Pollution control equipment
  manufacturing technology 681.76
Pollution control technology 628.5
    T1—028 6
  aircraft 629.134 35
  architecture 720.47
  automotive 629.25
  construction 690.028 6
  glassmaking 666.14
  paper manufacturing 676.042
  petroleum 665.538 9
  plastic technology 668.419 2
  rubber manufacturing 678.29
  water 628.168
  wood products 674.84
Pollution liability insurance 368.563
  see also Insurance
Polo 796.353
  biography 796.353 092
  see also Ball games
Polo players 796.353 092
Polokwane (South Africa :
  District) T2—682 56

Polypodiopsida	587.3
paleobotany	561.73
Polyporales	579.597
Polypropylene	668.423 4
textiles	677.474 5
see also Textiles	
Polypteriformes	597.42
paleozoology	567.42
Polyradiculoneuritis	
medicine	616.856
see also Nervous system	
diseases — humans	
Polysaccharides	572.566
see also Carbohydrates	
Polystyrenes	668.423 3
Polytheism	211.32
comparative religion	202.11
philosophy of religion	211.32
Polytheistic religions	201.4
Polytopes	516.158
Polyurethane rubber	678.72
Polyurethanes	668.423 9
polyesters	668.422 5
thermoplastic	668.423 9
Polyvinyls	668.423 6
textiles	677.474 4
see also Textiles	
Polyzoa	594.67
Pomacanthidae	597.72
Pomacentridae	597.72
Pomaceous fruits	641.341
botany	583.642
cooking	641.641
food	641.341
orchard crops	634.1
Pombaline reforms	946.903 3
Pomegranates	641.346 4
agriculture	634.64
botany	583.73
cooking	641.646 4
food	641.346 4
Pomerania (Poland and	
Germany)	T2—438 16
Germany	T2—431 78
Poland	T2—438 16
Pomeranian (Dog)	636.76
Pomerelia (Poland)	T2—438 22
Pomeroon-Supenaam	
Region (Guyana)	T2—881 2
Pommel horse	796.442
Pomo Indians	979.400 497 574
	T5—975 74
Pomo languages	497.574
	T6—975 74

Pomorskie Voivodeship (Poland)	943.822
	T2—438 22
Pompeii (Extinct city)	937.725 68
	T2—377 256 8
Ponape (Micronesia)	T2—966
Ponape language	499.52
	T6—995 2
Ponca Indians	T5—975 253 9
Ponca language	497.525 39
	T6—975 253 9
Ponce (P.R. : District)	T2—729 57
Pond Inlet (Nunavut)	T2—719 52
Pondera County (Mont.)	T2—786 53
Pondicherry (India : Union	
Territory)	T2—548 6
Pondoland (South Africa)	T2—687 58
Ponds	551.482
	T2—169 2
biology	578.763 6
ecology	577.636
fish culture	639.31
hydrology	551.482
landscape architecture	714
resource economics	333.916 3
Pondweeds	584.742
Pondweeds (Potamogetonaceae)	584.447
Pongidae	599.88
paleozoology	569.88
Pongo	599.883
Pongola River	T2—684 2
Mozambique	T2—679 1
South Africa	T2—684 2
Ponies	636.16
Pons Variolii	
human anatomy	611.81
human physiology	612.826 7
medicine	616.8
Pontarddulais (Wales)	T2—429 82
Pontchartrain, Lake (La.)	T2—763 34
Pontederiaceae	584.86
Pontevedra (Spain :	
Province)	T2—461 7
Pontiac (Quebec : Regional	
County Municipality)	T2—714 21
Pontiac's Conspiracy, 1763–1764	973.27
Pontificale Romanum	264.025
Pontine Islands (Italy)	T2—456 23
Pontine Marshes (Italy)	T2—456 23
Pontoporiidae	599.538
Pontotoc County (Miss.)	T2—762 932
Pontotoc County (Okla.)	T2—766 69
Pontus (Roman diocese)	T2—393
Pontus (Roman province)	T2—393 3
Pontus Polemoniacus	T2—393 37

Population ecology	577.88
animals	591.788
microorganisms	579.178 8
plants	581.788
Population exchanges	325
Population genetics	576.58
Population geography	304.6
Population movement	304.8
Civil War (United States)	973.714
public administration	353.59
social theology	
Christianity	261.838
World War II	940.531 45
Population transfers	325
World War II	940.531 45
Populism	
political ideology	320.566 2
Populist Party (U.S.)	324.273 27
Populus	583.69
Poquoson (Va.)	T2—755 422
Porcelain	666.5
arts	738.2
materials science	620.146
technology	666.5
Porch furniture	645.8
see also Outdoor furniture	
Porches	721.84
architecture	721.84
construction	690.184
home economics	643.55
Porcupine fishes	597.64
Porcupines	599.359 7
Porcupines (New World)	599.359 74
Porcupines (Old World)	599.359 7
Pordenone (Italy : Ente di	
decentramento regionale)	T2—453 94
ancient	T2—373 94
Pore fungi	579.597
Porgies	597.72
sports fishing	799.177 2
Porifera	593.4
paleozoology	563.4
Porirua City (N.Z.)	T2—936 2
Pork	641.364
commercial processing	664.92
cooking	641.664
food	641.364
Pornography	
arts	700.453 8
	T3C—353 8
criminology	364.174
law	345.027 4
see also Crime	

Pornography (continued)	
ethics	176.7
religion	205.667
Christianity	241.667
fine arts	704.942 8
law	344.054 7
literature	808.803 538
history and criticism	809.933 538
specific literatures	T3B—080 353 8
history and	
criticism	T3B—093 538
painting	757.8
social problem	364.174
public administrative control	353.37
sociology	306.771
Porous materials	
materials science	620.116
Porous solids	530.413
Porphyria	
medicine	616.399
see also Digestive system	
diseases — humans	
Porphyrins	547.593
chemical engineering	661.894
Porphyry	552.3
Porpoises	599.539
Porrentruy (Switzerland :	
District)	T2—494 366
Port Arthur (Tas.)	T2—946 4
Port-au-Prince (Haiti)	T2—729 452
Port Augusta (S. Aust.)	T2—942 38
Port buildings	387.15
see also Port facilities	
Port Coquitlam (B.C.)	T2—711 33
Port Cros National Park	
(France)	T2—449 3
Port Cygnet (Tas.)	T2—946 2
Port Elizabeth (South	
Africa : District)	T2—687 52
Port	
Elizabeth-Uitenhage-Despatch	
industrial area	T2—687 52
Port facilities	387.15
architecture	725.34
area planning	711.76
engineering	627.3
military engineering	623.64
transportation services	387.15
inland waterway	386.85
see also Ports	
Port Fairy (Vic.)	T2—945 7
Port Harcourt (Nigeria)	T2—669 42
Port Hedland (W.A.)	T2—941 3

Portuguese-speaking countries	T2—175 69
Portuguese Timor	959.87
	T2—598 7
Portuguese water dog	636.73
Portulacaceae	583.883
Portulacas	583.883
Posey County (Ind.)	T2—772 34
Posidoniaceae	584.44
Position classification	658.306
Position-finding devices	
marine navigation	623.893
radio engineering	621.384 191
Positional astronomy	522
mathematical geography	526.6
Positive psychology	150.198 8
Positives (Photography)	771.44
distribution	771.48
manipulation	771.44
organization	771.48
preparation	771.44
preservation	771.46
storage	771.46
Positivism	146.4
ethics	171.2
Positron emission tomography	
medicine	616.075 75
Positrons	539.721 4
Posology	
pharmacology	615.14
Possible worlds	511.314
Possums	599.23
Possums (America)	599.276
Possums (Australasia)	599.23
Post-apartheid period	968.07
Post exchanges	355.341
Post-Keynesian economics	330.156
Post-mortem examination	
medicine	616.075 9
Post offices	383.42
architecture	725.16
see also Postal service	
Post-production	
videography	777.55
Post-traumatic stress disorders	
medicine	616.852 1
see also Mental disorders	
pediatrics	618.928 521
Postage stamps	383.23
design	744.72
investment economics	332.63
philately	744.72

Postage stamps (continued)	
postal service	383.23
see also Postal service	
printing	686.288
Postal cards	383.122
see also Postal service	
Postal clerks	383.492
Postal codes	383.145 5
see also Postal service	
Postal communication	383
see also Postal service	
Postal inspection	383.46
Postal insurance	368.2
see also Insurance	
Postal law	343.099 2
Postal offenses	364.136
law	345.023 6
Postal organization	383.4
law	343.099 25
Postal rates	383.23
law	343.099 23
Postal routes	383.143
law	343.099 25
Postal savings banks	332.22
Postal service	383
armed services	355.693
law	343.099 2
public administration	354.759
Postal service workers	383.492
Postal stationery	
philately	744.72
Postal zones	383.145
see also Postal service	
Postcard illustration	741.683
Postcards	383.122
philately	744.72
see also Postal service	
Postclassical Greek language	487.3
	T6—87
Postclassical Latin language	477
	T6—71
Postcoital contraceptives	
health	613.943 2
medicine	618.182 5
see also Birth control	
Postcoordinate indexing	025.47
Postdoctoral programs	378.155
Postencephalitic Parkinson disease	
medicine	616.833
see also Nervous system diseases — humans	

Postencephalitic Parkinson's
  disease
  medicine   616.833
    see also Nervous system
      diseases — humans
Posters
  arts   744.78
    illustration   741.674
    prints   769.5
  design   744.78
Postglacial epoch   551.793
  geology   551.793
  paleontology   560.179 3
Posthypnotic phenomena   154.774
Postimpressionism   709.034 6
  painting   759.056
Postludes   784.189 3
Postmarks
  philately   744.72
Postmasburg (South Africa :
  District)   T2—687 16
Postmenopause
  disorders
    gynecology   618.175
    see also Female genital
      diseases — humans
  human physiology   612.665
Postmodernism   149.97
  arts   700.411 3
            T3C—113
  literature   808.801 13
    history and criticism 809.911 3
    specific literatures T3B—080 113
      history and
        criticism   T3B—091 13
  philosophy   149.97
Postnatal care
  obstetrics   618.6
  social theology   201.762 198 6
Postnatal development
  humans   612.6
Postoperative care
  medicine   617.919 5
Postoperative complications
  medicine   617.919 5
Postpartum depression
  medicine   618.76
Postpartum hemorrhage
  obstetrics   618.7
Postpoliomyelitis syndrome
  incidence   614.549
  medicine   616.835
    see also Nervous system
      diseases — humans

Posts (Columns)   721.3
  architecture   721.3
  construction   690.13
Posts (Military installations) 355.7
  law   343.015 7
Poststructuralism
  philosophy   149.97
Posture   613.78
Postwar period (World War II) 909.825
            T1—090 45
Pot abuse   362.295
  medicine   616.863 5
  personal health   613.835
  social welfare   362.295
    see also Substance abuse
Pot gardening   635.986
Potable water   363.61
    see also Drinking water;
      Municipal water supply
Potamogetonaceae   584.447
Potamogetonales   584.44
Potaro-Siparuni Region
  (Guyana)   T2—881 87
Potash   546.383 22
  chemical engineering 661.334
Potash salts   553.636
  economic geology 553.636
  mining   622.363 6
Potassium   669.725
  chemical engineering 661.038 3
  chemistry   546.383
  metallurgy   669.725
  mining   622.363 6
  organic chemistry 547.053 83
    applied   661.895
  physical metallurgy 669.967 25
    see also Chemicals
Potassium alkalis   546.383 22
  chemical engineering 661.33
Potassium bicarbonate 546.383 22
  chemical engineering 661.333
Potassium carbonate 546.383 22
  chemical engineering 661.334
Potassium compounds 546.383 22
Potassium fertilizers   631.83
  chemical engineering 668.623
Potassium hydroxide 546.383 22
  chemical engineering 661.332
Potassium minerals
  economic geology 553.636
Potato printing   761
Potato starch
  food technology   664.22

Potato whiskey	641.25	Potter's wheels	666.43
commercial processing	663.5	decorative arts	738.13
Potatoes	641.352 1	sculpture	731.3
agriculture	635.21	technology	666.43
botany	583.959 3	Pottery	666.3
commercial processing	664.805 21	arts	738
cooking	641.652 1	technology	666.3
food	641.352 1	Poultry (Animals)	636.5
Potawatomi Indians	977.004 973 16	agricultural economics	338.176 5
	T5—973 16	zoology	598.6
Potawatomi language	497.316	Poultry (Meat)	641.365
	T6—973 16	commercial processing	664.93
Potchefstroom (South		economics	338.476 649 3
Africa : District)	T2—682 43	cooking	641.665
Potential energy	531.6	food	641.365
Potential offenders		home preservation	641.493
identification	364.41	Poured concrete	624.183 4
Potential theory	515.96	building construction	693.5
Potentiometers	621.374 3	with reinforcement	693.541
Potenza (Italy : Province)	T2—457 71	without reinforcement	693.521
ancient	T2—377 75	structural engineering	624.183 4
Potgietersrus (South Africa :		Poverty	362.5
District)	T2—682 53	arts	700.455 6
Potichomania			T3C—355 6
handicrafts	745.546	influence on crime	364.2
Potomac River	T2—752	law	344.032 5
Maryland	T2—752	literature	808.803 556
Virginia	T2—755 2	history and criticism	809.933 556
West Virginia	T2—754 9	specific literatures	T3B—080 355 6
Potoos	598.99	history and	
Potosí (Bolivia : Dept.)	T2—841 4	criticism	T3B—093 556
Potpourris (Dried plants)	668.542	macroeconomics	339.46
Pots		religious practice	204.47
kitchen utensils	643.3	Buddhism	294.344 47
manufacturing technology	683.82	Christianity	248.47
Potsdam (Germany)	T2—431 546	Hinduism	294.544 7
Potsdam (Germany : Bezirk)	T2—431 54	social theology	201.762 5
Potsdam-Mittelmark		Buddhism	294.337 625
(Germany : Landkreis)	T2—431 54	Christianity	261.832 5
Pottawatomie County (Kan.)	T2—781 32	Hinduism	294.517 625
Pottawatomie County		Judaism	296.38
(Okla.)	T2—766 36	social welfare	362.5
Pottawattamie County		public administration	353.533 2
(Iowa)	T2—777 71	social welfare facilities	362.583
Potted plants	635.986	architecture	725.55
houseplants	635.965	Poverty-stricken people	305.569
Potted trees	635.977		T1—086 942
houseplants	635.965	*see also* Poor people	
Potter County (Pa.)	T2—748 55	Powder metal products	671.87
Potter County (S.D.)	T2—783 19	Powder metallurgy	671.37
Potter County (Tex.)	T2—764 825	Powder post beetles	595.763
Potters	738.092	Powder processes	
		photographic printing	773.2

Pregnancy	573.67
biology	573.67
cooking for	641.563 19
human physiology	612.63
obstetrics	618.2
psychology	155.646 3
social services	362.198 2
veterinary medicine	636.089 82
Pregnancy complications	
obstetrics	618.3
Pregnancy programs in schools	371.714
Pregnancy toxemias	
obstetrics	618.361 32
Pregnant workers	331.44
economics	331.44
Prehistoric animals	560
Prehistoric archaeology	930.1
Prehistoric humans	569.9
Prehistoric periods	930.1
	T1—090 12
Prehistoric religions	201.42
Prejudice	303.385
ethics	177.5
see also Discrimination —	
ethics	
religion	200.8
Christianity	270.08
Judaism	296.08
sociology	303.385
Preliminary hearings	345.072
Preliminary Scholastic	
Assessment Test	378.166 2
Preludes	784.189 28
Premarital counseling	
Christian pastoral counseling	259.13
social welfare	362.828 6
see also Families — social	
welfare	
Premarital sexual relations	306.733
ethics	176.4
see also Sexual relations	
Premature birth	
obstetrics	618.397
Premature infants	
pediatrics	618.920 11
Premature labor	
obstetrics	618.397
Premenopause	
human physiology	612.665
Premenstrual syndrome	
gynecology	618.172
see also Female genital	
diseases — humans	

Premiers	352.23
cabinet governments	321.804 3
public administration	352.23
Premium television	384.555 4
see also Television	
Premonstratensians	255.19
church history	271.19
Přemyslid dynasty	943.702 23
Prenatal care	
obstetrics	618.24
Prentiss County (Miss.)	T2—762 985
Prenuptial contracts	346.016 62
Preoperative care	
surgery	617.919 2
Prep schools	373.222
see also Secondary education	
Prepaid dental insurance	368.382 3
see also Insurance	
Prepaid health insurance	368.382
see also Insurance	
Preparation of food (Cooking)	641.5
Preparatory schools	373.222
see also Secondary education	
Prepared doughs	664.753
Prepared ores	669.042
Prepared pianos	786.28
instrument	786.281 9
music	786.28
see also Keyboard instruments	
Prepositional phrases	415.7
specific languages	T4—57
Prepositions	415.7
specific languages	T4—57
Prerelease guidance centers	365.34
see also Penal institutions	
Prerelease programs	365.663
Presbyopia	
optometry	617.755
see also Eye diseases —	
humans	
Presbyterian Church	285
church government	262.05
local church	254.05
church law	262.985
doctrines	230.5
catechism and creeds	238.5
general councils	262.55
guides to Christian life	248.485
missions	266.5
moral theology	241.045
public worship	264.05
religious associations	267.185
religious education	268.85

Pressing clothes		Preventive detention	345.052 7
home economics	648.1	Preventive medicine	613
Pressing equipment	621.98	personal	613
Pressing glass	666.123	public	614.44
Pressing metals	671.33	animal husbandry	636.089 444
Pressing textiles	677.028 25	public administration	353.628
Pressure		*see Manual at* 362.1–.4 and	
biophysics	571.437	614.4–.5	
humans	612.014 415	Preveza (Greece : Regional	
extraterrestrial biophysics		unit)	T2—495 3
humans	612.014 535	Priapulida	592.3
mechanics	531.1	paleozoology	562.3
Pressure cooking	641.587	Price control (Government)	338.526
Pressure distribution		economics	338.526
aeronautics	629.132 35	law	343.083
Pressure groups	322.43	public administration	352.85
political process	324.4	Price County (Wis.)	T2—775 24
relations with government	322.43	Price-demand relationship	338.521 2
Pressure perception		Price determination	338.52
psychology	152.182 3	economics	338.52
Pressure regulators		marketing management	658.816
steam engineering	621.185	Price discrimination	
Pressure surge		criminology	364.168
engineering	620.106 4	trade law	343.072 5
Pressure vessels	681.760 41	Price-earnings ratio	332.632 21
Pressure welding	671.529	Price fixing	338.523
Pressurization		criminology	364.168
aircraft	629.134 42	law	345.026 8
manned spacecraft	629.477 5	economics	338.523
spacecraft	629.477 5	trade law	343.072 5
Pressurizing oils and gases	665.028 2	Price indexes	338.528
Presswork		Price leadership	338.523
printing	686.23	Price levels	338.528
Prestatyn (Wales)	T2—429 37	Price lists	T1—029
Preston (England : Borough)	T2—427 665	Price policy	338.52
Preston County (W. Va.)	T2—754 82	Price statistics	338.528
Prestressed concrete	624.183 412	Price-supply relationship	338.521 3
building construction	693.542	Price supports	
manufacturing technology	666.893	agricultural economics	338.18
materials science	620.137	law	343.076 1
structural engineering	624.183 412	public administration	354.528 5
Presumptions (Law)	347.064	economics	338.52
Presupposition		law	343.074 2
linguistics	401.454	public administration	352.85
specific languages	T4—014 54	Price trends	T1—029
Preteens	305.234	collectibles	T1—075
see also School children		Prices	338.52
Pretoria (South Africa)	T2—682 275	agricultural industries	338.13
Pretoria (South Africa :		economics	338.52
District)	T2—682 27	land economics	333.332 3
Pretrial procedure	347.072	macroeconomics	339.42
criminal law	345.072	mineral industries	338.23
Pretrial release	345.072		
Preventive dentistry	617.601		

Primers (Detonators)	662.4
military engineering	623.454 2
Primers (Readers)	418
specific languages	T4—86
for nonnative speakers	T4—864
Primitive art	700
nonliterate peoples	709.011
Primitive Baptists	286.4
see also Baptists	
Primitive Methodist Church	287.4
see also Methodist Church	
Primitive religions	201.42
Primitive societies	301.7
Primitive weapons	
art metalwork	739.744 1
Primitivism	
arts	700.414 5
	T3C—145
literature	808.801 45
history and criticism	809.914 5
specific literatures	T3B—080 145
history and criticism	T3B—091 45
Primorskiĭ kraĭ (Russia)	T2—577
Primor´ye (Russia : Kray)	T2—577
Primroses	583.93
botany	583.93
floriculture	635.933 93
Primulaceae	583.93
Primulales	583.93
Primulas	583.93
botany	583.93
floriculture	635.933 93
Prince (P.E.I.)	T2—717 1
Prince Albert (Sask.)	T2—712 42
Prince Albert (South Africa : District)	T2—687 39
Prince Albert's yew	585.3
Prince Edward (Ont.)	T2—713 587
Prince Edward County (Va.)	T2—755 632
Prince Edward Island	971.7
	T2—717
Prince Edward Islands	969.9
	T2—699
Prince George (B.C.)	T2—711 82
Prince George County (Va.)	T2—755 585
Prince George's County (Md.)	T2—752 51
Prince of Wales Island (Nunavut)	T2—719 55
Prince Rupert (B.C.)	T2—711 1
Prince William County (Va.)	T2—755 273 2

Princes	305.522
see also Royalty	
Princesses	305.522
see also Royalty	
Princeton (B.C.)	T2—711 5
Principal components analysis	519.535 4
Principals (Criminal law)	345.03
Principals (School)	
biography	371.200 92
public control	379.157
role and function	371.201 2
Print media	
journalism	070.17
sociology	302.232
Print specimens	686.22
Printed advertising	659.132
Printed books	094
Printed circuits	621.381 531
Printed ephemera	744.7
cataloging	025.342
Printed music	780
treatises	780.263
Printers	686.209 2
Printers (Equipment)	
computer science	004.77
engineering	621.398 7
manufacturing technology	681.62
Printing	686.2
photography	771.44
textile arts	746.62
textiles	667.38
Printing apparatus	
photography	771.44
Printing ink	667.5
Printing presses	
manufacturing technology	681.62
Printing solutions	
photography	771.54
Printing telegraphy	384.14
wireless	384.524
see also Telegraphy	
Printmakers	769.92
see Manual at 769.9	
Printmaking	
graphic arts	760
Prints	
arts	769
cataloging	025.347 1
library treatment	025.177 1
Prion diseases	
medicine	616.83
see also Nervous system diseases — humans	
Prions (Subviral organisms)	579.29

721

Private airplanes	
engineering	629.133 340 422
piloting	629.132 521 7
Private banks	332.123
Private bills	
enactment	328.378
Private carriers	388.041
truck	388.324 3
see also Freight services;	
Passenger services	
Private colleges	378.04
see also Higher education	
Private companies	338.7
law	346.066 8
see also Business enterprises	
Private detective services	363.289
Private duty nursing	610.732
Private education	371.02
law	344.072
see also Private schools	
Private enterprise	338.61
Private international law	340.9
see Manual at 340.9	
Private investment	332.6
economics	332.6
international	332.673
Private investors	332.6
economics	332.6
international	332.673
Private land	333.3
landscape architecture	712.6
see also Land	
Private law	346
Islamic law	346.167
Private libraries	027.1
catalogs	017.2
Private military companies	355.34
security services	363.289 8
Private parks	
landscape architecture	712.6
Private police services	363.289
Private presses	
bibliographies of publications	011.55
Private property	
land economics	333.3
see also Land tenure	
Private publishers	070.593
Private schools	371.02
adult education	374
public support	379.326
finance	371.206
law	344.076
higher education	378.04
public support	379.324

Private schools (continued)	
law	344.072
preschool education	
public support	379.322 2
primary education	372.104 22
public support	379.322
public policy	379.3
public support	379.32
secondary education	373.222
public support	379.323
special education	371.9
public support	379.328
see Manual at 371 vs. 353.8,	
371.2, 379	
Private television	384.550 65
Private universities	378.04
see also Higher education	
Private welfare services	361.7
see also Welfare services	
Privateering	
naval operations	359.4
see also Naval operations	
Privatization	338.925
Privets	635.933 963
botany	583.963
floriculture	635.933 963
Privilege escalation	
computer science	005.87
Privileges (Military awards)	355.134
Privileges of chief executives	
public administration	352.235
Privileges of diplomats	327.2
Privileges of legislators	328.347
Prize contests	
advertising	659.197 901 34
sales promotion	658.82
use in advertising	659.17
Prize law	343.096
law of nations	341.63
Prizes	T1—079
research	001.44
Pro-choice movement	362.198 88
law	342.087 8
United States	362.198 880 097 3
Pro-life movement	362.198 88
law	342.085
United States	362.198 880 097 3
	362.198 880 973
Probabilistic logic	511.318
mathematical logic	511.318
philosophical logic	160.119 88
Probabilistic methods	518.28
Probabilistic number theory	512.76

Probabilities	519.2	Procellariiformes	598.42
epistemology	121.63	paleozoology	568.4
gambling	795.015 192	Process	
insurance	368.01	philosophy of nature	116
management decision making	658.403 4	Process analysis	
primary education	372.79	production management	658.5
see Manual at 795.015192 vs.		Process control	003.5
519.27			T1—011 5
Probability calculus	519.2	chemical engineering	660.281 5
Probability distribution	519.24	production management	658.5
Probability theory	519.2	Process design	
Probate law	346.052	chemical engineering	660.281 2
Probation	364.63	Process management	
law	345.077	systems software	005.434
penology	364.63	Process metallurgy	669
public administration	353.39	Process philosophy	146.7
Probation after death	236.4	Process research	
Probation of teachers	371.144	production management	658.577
Probiotic foods	641.300 157 9	Process serving	347.072
cooking	641.563	Process theology	230.046
health	613.201 579	Processed cheese	641.373 58
Probiotics	615.329	cooking	641.673 58
food	641.300 157 9	food	641.373 58
health	613.201 579	manufacturing	637.358
pharmacology	615.329	Processing (Archives)	025.341 4
Problem employees		Processing (Libraries)	025.02
personnel management	658.304 5	Processing centers	
Problem of few bodies	530.14	library operations	025.02
Problem of <?ddc		Processing modes	
fotag="fo:inline" font-		computer science	004.3
style="italic"?>n<?ddc			T1—028 543
fotag="/fo:inline"?> bodies	530.144	communications	004.618
astronomy	521	software	005.713 7
Problem of three bodies	530.14	software development	005.712 7
astronomy	521	graphics software	006.687
Problem soils		graphics software	
floriculture	635.955	development	006.677
Problem solving	153.43	interfacing	
artificial intelligence	006.333	software	005.713 7
educational psychology	370.152 4	software development	005.712 7
executive management	658.403	multimedia software	006.787
psychology	153.43	multimedia software	
Problem students	371.93	development	006.777
Problems		operating systems	005.447
study and teaching	T1—076	software	005.37
Proboscidea	599.67	software development	005.27
paleozoology	569.67	*see Manual at* 004.1 vs.	
Proboscis worms	592.32	004.3	
Procaryotes	579.3	Processions	394.5
Procedural rights	347.05	customs	394.5
military	343.014 3	performing arts	791.6
public administration	352.88	religious rites	203.8
Procedure (Law)	347.05	Christianity	265.9

Processors	
computer hardware	004
engineering	621.39
see Manual at 004.1; *also at*	
004.1 vs. 004.3	
programming-language	
translators	005.45
Prochlorales	579.39
Proconsular Africa	T2—397 3
Procrastination	179.8
religion	205.698
Proctology	616.35
Procurators fiscal	345.411 01
Procurement	658.72
	T1—068 7
air forces	358.416 212
armed forces	355.621 2
naval forces	359.621 2
public administration	352.53
Procurement of capital	658.152 2
	T1—068 1
Procyon	599.763 2
Procyonidae	599.763
Produce (Agricultural products)	338.17
see also Agricultural products	
Produce trade	381.41
Producer brands	
sales promotion	658.827
Producer gas	665.772
Producers' cooperatives	334.6
management	658.87
Product accounts	
(Macroeconomics)	339.31
Product catalogs	338.020 29
	T1—029
secondary industries	
economics	338.402 9
see Manual at T1—025 vs.	
T1—029	
Product comparisons	T1—029
Product control	363.19
production management	658.56
see also Product safety	
Product counterfeiting	364.166 8
law	345.026 68
Product design	744.7
management	658.575 2
Product development	
management	658.575

Product directories	338.020 29
	T1—029
secondary industries	
economics	338.402 9
see Manual at T1—025 vs.	
T1—029	
Product displays	
design	744.68
Product evaluation	381.33
Product evaluations	T1—029
Product liability	346.038
production management	658.56
Product liability insurance	368.562
see also Insurance	
Product life cycle	
management	658.5
Product listings	T1—029
Product management	658.5
marketing	658.8
production	658.5
Product planning	658.503 8
Product recall	363.19
law	344.042
product safety	363.19
production management	658.56
Product returns	
marketing management	658.812
Product safety	363.19
criminology	364.142
criminal law	345.024 2
law	344.042
production management	658.56
social services	363.19
public administration	353.99
Product servicing	
marketing management	658.812
Product specifications	
production management	658.562
Product standards	
production management	658.562
Production (Performing arts)	792.023 2
ballet	792.84
motion pictures	791.430 232
musical plays	792.64
opera	792.54
radio	791.440 232
stage	792.023 2
television	791.450 232
Production capacity	
secondary industries	338.45
Production control	
management	658.5

Professionals	331.71
	T1—086 22
see also Professional workers	
Professions	331.71
	T1—023
Professors	378.12
Profit and loss statements	
financial management	658.151 2
Profit sharing	331.216 47
labor economics	331.216 47
personnel management	658.322 5
Profits	338.516
accounting	657.7
agricultural industries	338.13
financial management	658.155
income distribution	339.21
increasing	
financial management	658.155 4
mineral industries	338.23
production economics	338.516
secondary industries	338.43
taxes	336.243
law	343.052 44
public administration	352.44
Progeny	306.874
	T1—085 4
Prognosis	
medicine	616.075
Progoneata	595.6
paleozoology	565.6
Program auditing	658.401 3
public administration	352.43
Program audits	658.401 3
public administration	352.439
Program design	005.12
Program documentation	
preparation	005.15
text	005.3
Program evaluation techniques	
(Network analysis)	658.403 2
Program maintenance	005.16
Program music	781.56
Program notes (Music)	780.15
Program reliability	005.132 2
Program verification	005.14
Programmable calculators	510.285 41
see Manual at 004.1	
Programmable controllers	
control engineering	629.895
Programmed instruction	371.394 4
	T1—07
electronic	371.334
adult education	374.264

Programming	
dramatic performances	792.023 6
motion pictures	791.430 236
radio	791.440 236
stage	792.023 6
television	791.450 236
Programming (Mathematics)	519.7
Programming computers	005.13
see also Computer	
programming	
Programming language	
translators	005.45
Programming languages	005.13
computer graphics	006.663
Programs (Broadcasting)	384.544 3
communications	384.544 3
radiobroadcasting	384.544 3
communications	384.544 3
performing arts	791.44
television broadcasting	384.553 2
communications	384.553 2
performing arts	791.45
Programs (Computers)	005.3
	T1—028 553
see also Computer programs	
Programs (Party platforms)	324.23
Programs (Social action)	361.25
public administration	351
Progreso (Guatemala :	
Dept.)	T2—728 153
Progress	303.44
Progressions	515.24
Progressive Conservative Party of	
Canada	324.271 04
Progressive jazz	781.655
Progressive National Baptist	
Convention	286.135
see also Baptists	
Progressive Party (U.S. : 1912)	324.273 27
Progressive Party (U.S. : 1924)	324.273 27
Progressive Party (U.S. : 1948)	324.273 7
Progressive rock	781.66
Progressive taxation	336.293
Prohibited books	098.1
Prohibition Party (U.S.)	324.273 8
Prohibitive tariffs	382.73
see also Customs (Tariff)	
Project Apollo	629.454
Project Gemini	629.454
Project management	658.404
public administration	352.365
Project Mariner	629.435 4
Project Mercury	629.454
Project method of teaching	371.36

Propellers	
aircraft	629.134 36
ships	623.873
Proper integrals	515.43
Proper of the mass	264.36
music	782.323 5
choral and mixed voices	782.532 35
single voices	783.093 235
Property	
economic theory	330.17
Holocaust, 1933–1945	940.531 813 2
law	346.04
sociology	306.32
Property damage insurance	368.1
see also Insurance	
Property insurance	368.1
commercial	368.12
see also Insurance	
Property law	346.04
Property loss insurance	368.1
see also Insurance	
Property management	
public administration	352.5
Property offenses	364.16
law	345.026
social welfare	362.889 6
Property rights	323.46
law	346.042
Property risks	368.06
Property tax	336.22
law	343.054
public administration	352.44
Prophecies	133.3
occultism	133.3
religion	203.2
Biblical	220.15
eschatological	202.3
Christianity	236
Judaism	296.33
messianic	
Christianity	232.12
Judaism	296.336
Prophecy (Concept)	202.117
Christianity	231.745
spiritual gift	234.13
in Bible	220.15
Islam	297.211 5
Judaism	296.311 55
Prophetic books (Old Testament)	224
Prophetic books	
(Pseudepigrapha)	229.913
Prophetic message	
Bible	220.15
Prophetic office of Jesus Christ	232.8

Prophets	200.92
biography	200.92
Islam	297.246
role and function	206.1
see Manual at 200.92 and	
201–209, 292–299	
Prophets (Biblical books)	224
Prophylaxis	
public health	614.44
Propjet engines	
aircraft	629.134 353 2
Proportion (Architecture)	
horizontal plane	729.23
vertical plane	729.13
Proportion (Mathematics)	512.924
algebra	512.924
arithmetic	513.24
Proportional counters	
nuclear physics	539.773
Proportional representation	328.334 7
law	342.053
Proportional taxation	336.293
Propositional calculus	511.3
mathematical logic	511.3
philosophical logic	160
Propositions	
philosophical logic	160
Proprietary libraries	027.2
Proprietor's income	
macroeconomics	339.21
Proprietorships	338.72
accounting	657.91
economics	338.72
income tax	336.242 3
law	343.052 68
law	346.065
management	658.041
initiation	658.114 1
see Manual at 658.04 vs.	
658.114, 658.402	
taxes	336.207
law	343.068
Proprioceptive organs	
human anatomy	611.8
human physiology	612.88
Proprioceptive perception	
psychology	152.188 2
Propulsion systems	621.4
air-cushion vehicles	629.314
spacecraft	629.475
unmanned spacecraft	629.465

Proteins (continued)
  biochemistry   572.6
    humans   612.015 75
  chemistry   547.7
  metabolic disorders   571.946
    medicine   616.399 5
    see also Digestive system
      diseases — humans
  metabolism
    human physiology   612.398
Proteinuria
  medicine   616.63
    see also Urologic diseases —
      humans
Proteolytic enzymes   572.76
  see also Enzymes
Proterozoic era   551.715
  geology   551.715
  paleontology   560.171 5
Protest   303.6
  social action   361.23
Protest groups   322.4
Protest music   781.592
Protest stoppages   331.892
  see also Strikes (Work
    stoppages)
Protestant art
  religious significance   246.4
Protestant churches   280.4
  see also Protestantism
Protestant men
  religious associations   267.240 4
Protestant Methodists   287.53
  see also Methodist Church
Protestant People's Party of
  Switzerland   324.249 408 2
Protestant regions   T2—176 14
Protestant women
  religious associations   267.440 4
Protestant young adults
  religious associations   267.620 4
Protestantism   280.4
  church law   262.980 4
  conversion to   248.241
    from Roman Catholicism   248.244
    from specific denominations   248.241
  doctrines   230.044
  guides to Christian life   248.480 4
  missions   266
  moral theology   241.040 4
  public worship   264
  religious associations   267.180 4
  religious education   268.804

Protestantism (continued)
  seminaries   230.071 1
  theology   230.044
Protestants
  biography   280.409 2
Protista   579
  see also Microorganisms
Proto-Malay languages   499.28
    T6—992 8
Proto-Nordic language   439.5
    T6—395
Proto-Scandinavian language   439.5
    T6—395
Protobranchia   594.4
Protoceratops   567.915
Protocol (Diplomacy)   327.2
Protocols (Standards)
  communications engineering   621.382 12
  computer communications   004.62
  interfacing   004.62
Protocols (Treaties)
  law of nations   341.37
    texts   341.026
Protolepidodendrales   561.79
Protomycetales   579.562
Proton spin tomography   616.075 48
Protons   539.721 23
Protophytes   579
Protoplasm   571.6
Prototheria   599.29
  paleozoology   569.29
Protozoa   579.4
  medical microbiology   616.936 01
  paleontology   561.99
Protozoan diseases   571.994
  see also Protozoan infections
Protozoan infections   571.994
  agriculture   632.3
  animals   571.994 11
    veterinary medicine   636.089 693 6
  biology   571.994
  humans   362.196 936
    incidence   614.53
    medicine   616.936
    social services   362.196 936
  plants   571.994 12
    agriculture   632.3
  see also Communicable
    diseases
Protozoologists   579.409 2
Protozoology   579.4
  medicine   616.936 01
  paleontology   561.99
Protura   595.722

Pseudo-Demetrius I
  Russian history   947.045
Pseudo-Demetrius II
  Russian history   947.045
Pseudo gospels   229.8
Pseudoanalytic functions   515.98
Pseudoborniales   561.72
Pseudomonas   579.332
Pseudomonas infections
  incidence   614.57
  medicine   616.92
    see also Communicable
      diseases — humans
Pseudomorphism
  crystallography   548.3
Pseudonymous works
  bibliographies   014
Pseudopoda   571.67
Pseudoscorpiones   595.47
Psi phenomena   133.8
Psilophytales   561.74
Psilopsida   587.4
  paleobotany   561.74
Psilotales   587.4
  paleobotany   561.74
Psittaciformes   598.71
  paleozoology   568.7
Psittacosis
  animals
    veterinary medicine   636.686 539
  humans
    incidence   614.566
    medicine   616.958
      see also Communicable
       diseases — humans
Pskov (Russia : Oblast)   T2—472 3
Pskovskaĩa oblast′ (Russia)   T2—472 3
Psocoptera   595.732
Psophiidae   598.32
Psoriasis
  medicine   616.526
Psychedelic drugs
  pharmacokinetics   615.788 3
Psychedelics abuse   362.294
  medicine   616.863 4
  personal health   613.83
  social welfare   362.294
  see also Substance abuse
Psychiatric clinics   362.22
  see also Mental health services
Psychiatric disorders   362.2
  medicine   616.89
    see also Mental disorders

Psychiatric hospitals   362.21
  architecture   725.52
    see also Mental health services
Psychiatric insurance   368.382 5
  see also Insurance
Psychiatric nursing   616.890 231
Psychiatric social work   362.204 25
Psychiatrists
  law   344.041 2
  malpractice   344.041 21
Psychiatry   616.89
  geriatrics   618.976 89
  pediatrics   618.928 9
  see Manual at 616.89 vs.
    150.195
Psychic communication   133.8
Psychic gifts   133.8
Psychic healing
  medicine   615.852 8
Psychic messages   133.93
Psychic phenomena   133.8
Psychic surgery
  medicine   615.852 8
Psychic talents   133.8
Psychic therapy
  medicine   615.852 8
Psychoanalysis   150.195
  psychiatry   616.891 7
  psychology   150.195
  see Manual at 616.89 vs.
    150.195
Psychobiology   573.8
  humans   612.8
Psychodidae   595.772
Psychodrama
  psychiatry   616.891 523
Psychokinesis   133.88
Psycholinguistics   401.9
  specific languages   T4—019
Psychological causes of war   355.027 5
  World War I   940.311 4
  World War II   940.531 14
Psychological characteristics
  influence on crime   364.24
Psychological fiction   808.838 3
  history and criticism   809.383
  specific literatures   T3B—308 3
    individual authors   T3A—3
Psychological principles   T1—019
Psychological systems   150.19
  see Manual at 152–158 vs.
    150.19

Psychological themes		PT boats	359.835 8
arts	T3C—353	design	623.812 58
literature	808.803 53	engineering	623.825 8
history and criticism	809.933 53	naval equipment	359.835 8
specific literatures	T3B—080 353	naval units	359.325 8
history and		Ptarmigans	598.633
criticism	T3B—093 53	Pteranodon	567.918
Psychological therapies		Pteridophyllaceae	583.35
medicine	615.851	Pteridophyta	587
Psychological warfare	355.343 4	paleobotany	561.7
see also Unconventional		Pteridospermales	561.595
warfare		Pterobranchia	593.99
Psychologists	150.92	paleozoology	563.99
Psychology	150	Pteroclididae	598.65
	T1—019	Pterodactylus	567.918
information systems	025.061 5	Pteromedusae	593.55
statistics	150.151 95	Pterophyllum	597.74
see Manual at 302–307 vs.		Pteropoda	594.37
150, T1—019		Pteropodidae	599.49
Psychology (Animals)	591.5	Pterosauria	567.918
Psychology and religion	201.615	Pterygota	595.7
Christianity	261.515	paleozoology	565.7
Islam	297.261 5	Ptilogonatidae	598.853
Judaism	296.371	Ptolemaic dynasty	932.021
Psychology of religion	200.19	Puberty	612.661
Psychometrics	150.151 95	customs	392.14
tests	150.287	etiquette	395.24
Psychopathic personality		human physiology	612.661
medicine	616.858 2	music	781.583
see also Mental disorders		Public accounting	657.61
Psychopathology	616.89	law	346.063
Psychopharmacology	615.78	Public address systems	
Psychophysiology		engineering	621.389 2
humans	612.8	office use	651.79
Psychoses	362.26	Public administration	351
medicine	616.89	armed forces	355.6
see also Mental disorders		ethics	172.2
puerperal diseases		*see also* Political ethics	
medicine	618.76	subordinate jurisdictions	352.14
social welfare	362.26	support and control	353.33
Psychosexual disorders		*see Manual at* 351.3–.9	
medicine	616.858 3	vs. 352.13–.19; *also at*	
Psychosomatic medicine	616.08	352.13 vs. 352.15	
Psychosurgery	617.481	United States	
Psychotherapy		serial publications	351.730 5
psychiatry	616.891 4	West Bank	351.569 42
Psychotic disorders		*see Manual at* T1—068 vs.	
medicine	616.89	353–354; *also at* 320.9,	
see also Mental disorders		320.4 vs. 351; *also at* 363	
Psychotropic drugs		vs. 344.02–.05, 353–354	
pharmacokinetics	615.788	Public administrators	352.3
Psychrometrics		biography	351.092
air conditioning		executive management	352.3
buildings	697.931 5		

Punched card readers	004.76
computer engineering	621.398 6
Punched cards	004.56
electronic data processing	004.56
nonelectronic data processing	004.9
Punching tools	621.96
Punctuated equilibrium	576.82
Punctuation	411
specific languages	T4—11
Puncture wounds	
medicine	617.143
Punic language	492.6
	T6—926
Punic Wars, 264–146 B.C.	937.04
Punishment	
armed forces	355.133 25
law	345.077
penology	364.6
prisons	365.644
social control	303.36
social theology	201.764
Christianity	261.833 6
student discipline	371.54
Punjab (India)	954.552
	T2—545 52
Punjab (India : Province)	T2—545
Punjab (India : State)	T2—545 5
Punjab (Pakistan)	T2—549 14
Punjabi language	491.42
	T6—914 2
Punjabi literature	891.42
Punjabis	T5—914 21
Punk rock	781.66
Puno (Peru : Region)	T2—853 6
Puntarenas (Costa Rica :	
Province)	T2—728 67
Punting (Boating)	797.123
Punting (Kicking)	
American football	796.332 27
Punu language	496.396
	T6—963 96
Puppet films	791.433 4
Puppet masters	791.530 92
Puppet television programs	791.453 4
Puppeteers	791.530 92
Puppetry	791.53
Christian religious use	246.725
religious education	268.67
primary education	372.674
production scripts	791.538
Puppets	791.53
making	688.722 4
handicrafts	745.592 24
technology	688.722 4

Puppets (continued)	
performing arts	791.53
see also Toys	
Puracé National Park	
(Colombia)	T2—861 53
Puranas	294.592 5
Purari River (Gulf Province,	
Papua New Guinea)	T2—954 7
Purbeck (England)	T2—423 36
Purcell Mountains (B.C. and	
Mont.)	T2—711 65
Purchase contracts	
accounting	657.75
materials management	658.723
Purchase of real property	333.33
economics	333.33
private ownership	333.33
public ownership	333.13
law	346.043 62
private ownership	346.043 62
public ownership	343.025 2
Purchasing	658.72
	T1—068 7
see also Procurement	
Purchasing manuals	381.33
Purchasing power	339.42
cost of living	339.42
value of money	332.41
Purchasing power parity	332.456
Pure food control	363.192
see also Food — product safety	
Pure Land Buddhism	294.392 6
Pure mathematics	510
Pure sciences	500
see also Science	
Purépecha language	497.96
	T6—979 6
Purgatives	
pharmacokinetics	615.732
Purgatory	
Christianity	236.5
Purification	
oils and gases	665.028 3
petroleum distillates	665.534
Purified pulp	676.4
Purim	296.436
liturgy	296.453 6
Purines	547.596
chemical engineering	661.894
Puritanism	285.9
doctrines	230.59
moral theology	241.045 9
persecution of others	272.8

Pyramids (Buildings) (continued)
  Mayan   972.810 16
    Guatemala   972.810 16
    Mexico   972.650 16
  Mexican   972.01
  Toltec   972.017
Pyramids (Geometry)   516.156
Pyramids (Marketing)   381.1
  management   658.872
Pyrans   547.592
  chemical engineering   661.8
Pyrazoles   547.593
  chemical engineering   661.894
Pyrenees (France and Spain)   946.5
                             T2—465
  France   T2—447 3
  Spain   946.5
                             T2—465
Pyrénées-Atlantiques
  (France)   T2—447 16
Pyrenees National Park   T2—447 8
Pyrénées-Orientales
  (France)   T2—448 9
Pyrenomycetes   579.567
Pyridines   547.593
  chemical engineering   661.894
Pyrite
  mineralogy   549.32
Pyroclastic rocks   552.23
Pyrography   745.514
Pyromagnetism   538.3
Pyromania
  medicine   616.858 43
  see also Mental disorders
Pyrometallurgy   669.028 2
Pyrometers
  manufacturing technology   681.2
Pyrometry   536.52
Pyrophyllite
  mineralogy   549.67
Pyrotechnical devices
  military communications
    engineering   623.731 3
Pyrotechnics   662.1
Pyrotheria   569.62
Pyroxenes
  mineralogy   549.66
Pyrrhonic philosophy   186.1
Pyrroles   547.593
  chemical engineering   661.894
Pyrrophyta   579.87
Pythagorean philosophy   182.2
Pythagorean theorem   516.22
Pythoninae   597.967 8

Pythons   597.967 8

Q

Q fever
  incidence   614.526 5
  medicine   616.922 5
    see also Communicable
      diseases — humans
Q hypothesis (Gospels)   226.066
Qacentina (Algeria :
  Province)   T2—655
Qaḍārif (Sudan : State)   T2—625
Qādarīyah (Islamic sect)   297.835
Qaddafi, Muammar
  Libyan history   961.204 2
Qādirīyah (Sufi order)   297.48
Qādisīyah (Iraq)   T2—567 5
Qāhirah (Egypt : Province)   T2—621 6
Qalyūbīyah (Egypt)   T2—621
Qamani'tuaq (Nunavut)   T2—719 58
Qāri', Ḥamzah ibn Ḥabīb
  Koran readings   297.122 404 522
Qāri', Nāfi' ibn 'Abd al-Raḥmān
  Koran readings   297.122 404 522
Qatar   953.63
                             T2—536 3
  ancient   939.49
                             T2—394 9
Qataris   T5—927 536 3
Qattara Depression (Egypt)   T2—622
Qausuittuq (Nunavut)   T2—719 52
Qazvīn (Iran: Province)   T2—551 8
Qi gong   613.714 89
Qiblah   297.382
Qigong   613.714 89
Qikiqtaaluk (Nunavut)   T2—719 52
Qin dynasty   931.04
Qinā (Egypt : Province)   T2—623
Qing dynasty   951.03
Qinghai Sheng (China)   T2—514 7
Qirā'āt   297.122 404 5
Qirā'āt al-'ashr   297.122 404 52
Qirā'āt al-sab'   297.122 404 522
Qiyās (Islamic law)
  sources of fiqh   340.591 34
Qohelet   223.8
Qom (Iran : Province)   T2—552 6
Qoran   297.122
Quackery
  medicine   615.856
Quad roller hockey   796.356 64
Quadra Island (B.C.)   T2—711 2

Quasi contract	346.029	Queen Maud Land	T2—989
Quasi-judicial agencies	352.8	Queens (Chessmen)	794.146
Quaternary period	551.79	Queens (N.B.)	T2—715 42
geology	551.79	Queens (N.S. : Regional	
paleontology	560.179	municipality)	T2—716 24
Quaternions	512.5	Queens (New York, N.Y.)	T2—747 243
Quay County (N.M.)	T2—789 26	Queens (P.E.I.)	T2—717 4
Quays	387.15	Queens (Rulers)	352.23
engineering	627.31	*see also* Monarchs; Royalty	
see also Port facilities		Queenscliff (Vic.)	T2—945 2
Queanbeyan (N.S.W.)	T2—944 7	Queensland	T2—943
Quebec (Province)	971.4	Queenstown (South Africa :	
	T2—714	District)	T2—687 56
1867–1897	971.403 1	Queenstown (Tas.)	T2—946 6
1897–1936	971.403 2	Queenstown-Lakes District	
1936–1945	971.403 3	(N.Z.)	T2—939 5
1945–1960	971.404 1	Queer identity	306.76
1960–1976	971.404 2	Queer people	306.76
1976–1985	971.404 3		T1—086 6
1985–1994	971.404 4	Queleas	598.887
1994–1999	971.404 5	agricultural pests	632.688 87
see Manual at T2—713 and		Quenas	788.35
T2—714		*see also* Woodwind	
Québec (Quebec)	T2—714 471	instruments	
Québec (Quebec : Urban		Quenching metals	671.36
agglomeration)	T2—714 471	Quercoideae	583.65
Quebec Act, 1774	971.022	Querétaro (Mexico : State)	T2—724 5
Quebec Conference, 1864	971.049	Query languages	025.04
Québec Metropolitan		computer science	005.74
Community (Quebec)	T2—714 47	information science	025.04
Quebec Sign Language	419.714	Quesnay, François	
	T6—999 871 4	economic school	330.152
Quechan language	497.572	Quesnel (B.C.)	T2—711 75
	T6—975 72	Quesnel Lake (B.C.)	T2—711 75
Quechua Indians	T5—983 23	Quesnel River (B.C.)	T2—711 75
Quechua language	498.323	Question	
	T6—983 23	philosophical logic	160.119
Quechua literature	898.323	Question-answering systems	025.524 028 563 5
Quechuan Indians	T5—983 23	Questione meridionale	945.709
Quechuan languages	498.323	Questionnaires	
	T6—983 23	descriptive research	001.433
Queen Anne's County (Md.)	T2—752 34		T1—072 3
Queen Anne's lace	583.849	Questions and answers	
Queen Anne's lace (Apiaceae)	583.988 2	study and teaching	T1—076
Queen Anne's War, 1701–1714	940.252 6	Quetta District (Pakistan)	T2—549 152
North American history	973.25	Quetzals	598.73
Queen bees		Queuing processes	519.82
apiculture	638.145	Queuing theory	519.82
Queen Charlotte Islands		management decision making	658.403 4
(B.C.)	T2—711 12	Quezaltenango (Guatemala :	
Queen Charlotte Sound (B.C.)	551.461 433	Dept.)	T2—728 182
	T2—164 33	Quezon (Philippines :	
Queen Charlotte Strait (B.C.)	551.461 433	Province)	T2—599 179
	T2—164 33		

Rabbis (continued)
  training   296.071 1
  see Manual at 296.092
Rabbit hair textiles   677.35
  see also Textiles
Rabbits   599.32
  agricultural pests   632.693 2
  animal husbandry   636.932 2
  conservation technology   639.979 32
  experimental animals
    medicine   616.027 3
  resource economics   333.959 32
  small game hunting   799.259 32
  zoology   599.32
Rabies
  animals
    incidence   636.089 456 3
    veterinary medicine   636.089 695 3
  humans
    incidence   614.563
    medicine   616.953
    see also Communicable
      diseases — humans
Rabies virus   579.256 6
Rabun County (Ga.)   T2—758 123
Raccoons   599.763 2
  trapping   639.117 632
Race discrimination   305.8
  law   342.087 3
Race discrimination in
  employment   331.6
  law   344.016
Race relations   305.8
  arts   T3C—352 9
  religion   200.89
    Christianity   270.089
  sociology   305.8
Race walking   796.429
  see also Track and field
Racehorses   636.12
  sports   798.4
Racerunners (Lizards)   597.958 25
Races (Ethnology)   305.8
  physical ethnology   599.97
Races (Sports)   796
  see also Racing
Racetracks
  architecture   725.89
  automobiles   796.720 68
  horses   798.400 68
  humans   796.420 68
Rachidia (Morocco :
  Province)   T2—645

Racial characteristics
  physical ethnology   599.972
Racial conflict   305.8
  influence on crime   364.256
Racial discrimination   305.8
Racial groups   305.8
                           T1—089
  arts   T3C—352 9
Racial minorities   305.8
  see also Ethnic groups
Racially mixed people   T5—05
Racine County (Wis.)   T2—775 96
Racing   796
  aircraft   797.52
  animals   798
    dogs   798.8
    horses   798.4
  automobiles   796.72
  bicycles   796.62
  BMX bicycles   796.622
  boats   797.14
  cyclo-cross bicycles   796.624
  humans   796.42
  midget cars   796.76
  motor scooters   796.75
  motor vehicles   796.7
  motorcycles   796.75
  mountain bicycles   796.63
  road bicycles   796.626
  soapboxes   796.6
  track bicycles   796.628
  see also Sports
Racing animals
  animal husbandry   636.088 8
Racing cars   796.72
  driving   629.284 8
  engineering   629.228 5
  repair   629.287 8
  sports   796.72
  see also Automotive
    vehicles — sports
Racism   305.8
                           T1—089
  arts   T3C—352 9
  ethics   177.5
  see also Discrimination —
    ethics
  political ideology   320.569
  religion   200.89
    Christianity   270.089
Racism in textbooks
  public control   379.156

Rack railroads	385.6
engineering	625.33
transportation services	385.6
see also Railroads	
Racket games	796.34
equipment technology	688.763 4
Racketeering	364.106 7
law	345.02
Rackets	
biography	796.343 092
Rackets (Game)	796.343
see also Ball games	
Rackets players	796.343 092
Racketts	788.5
see also Woodwind	
instruments	
Racon	621.384 8
marine navigation	623.893 3
Radar	621.384 8
airport engineering	629.136 6
electronic engineering	621.384 8
marine navigation	623.893 3
military engineering	623.734 8
military gunnery	623.557
nautical engineering	623.856 48
weather reporting	551.635 3
Rade language	499.22
	T6—992 2
Radford (Va.)	T2—755 786
Radha Soami Satsang	294
Radial street patterns	
area planning	711.41
Radiant energy	539.2
Radiant panel heating	
buildings	697.72
Radiant points	
astronomy	523.53
Radiation	539.2
biophysics	571.45
humans	612.014 48
effect on materials	620.112 28
effect on space flight	629.416
meteorology	551.527
physics	539.2
solid-state physics	530.416
Radiation (Biological evolution)	576.84
Radiation biology	571.45
humans	612.014 48
Radiation chemistry	541.382
applied	660.298 2
Radiation dosimetry	
human biophysics	612.014 480 287
radiotherapy	615.842
Radiation injuries	571.934 5
agriculture	632.3
animals	571.934 51
veterinary medicine	636.089 698 97
humans	362.196 989 7
medicine	616.989 7
social services	362.196 989 7
see also Environmental	
diseases — humans	
plants	571.934 52
Radiation measurement	539.77
Radiation safety	363.179 9
public administration	353.999
see also Hazardous materials	
Radiation sickness	571.934 5
see also Radiation injuries	
Radiation therapy	
medicine	615.842
Radiation warfare	358.39
Radiation weapons	358.398 2
engineering	623.446
military equipment	358.398 2
Radiative heating	
buildings	697.1
Radiators	
heating buildings	697.07
steam	697.507
Radical Democratic Party (Swiss	
political party)	324.249 406
Radical Party (Italy)	324.245 06
Radical theory	512.4
Radicalism	
agent of social change	303.484
political ideology	320.53
Radicals (Chemicals)	541.224
Radiesthesia	133.323
Radii (Bones)	
human anatomy	611.717
Radio	384.5
accounting	657.84
communications services	384.5
engineering	621.384
influence on crime	364.254
instructional use	371.333 1
adult level	374.263 1
	T1—071 5
journalism	070.194
law	343.099 45
marine navigation	623.893 2
military engineering	623.734
nautical engineering	623.856 4
performing arts	791.44
public administration	354.75

Radio (continued)
  religion 201.7
    Christianity 261.52
      evangelism 269.26
      preaching 251.07
    use by local Christian
      church 253.78
        administration 254.3
  sociology 302.234 4
  see Manual at 384.54, 384.55,
    384.8 vs. 791.4
Radio adaptations 791.446
Radio advertising 659.142
Radio astronomy 522.682
Radio beacons
  engineering 621.384 191
Radio comment
  journalism 070.442
Radio communication 384.5
Radio compasses
  aircraft engineering 629.135 1
  engineering 621.384 191
  marine navigation 623.893 2
Radio control
  airport engineering 629.136 6
  engineering 621.384 196
Radio direction finders
  aircraft engineering 629.135 1
Radio drama 791.447
  see also Radio plays
Radio engineers 621.384 092
Radio evangelism 269.26
Radio frequency allocation 384.545 24
Radio frequency identification 006.245
  computer science 006.245
  engineering 621.384 192
Radio-frequency spectroscopes
  manufacturing technology 681.414 8
Radio genres 791.446
Radio music 781.544
Radio networks 384.540 65
  enterprises 384.540 65
  facilities 384.545 5
  performing arts 791.44
Radio news 070.43
Radio plays 791.447
  literature 808.822 2
    history and criticism 809.222
    specific literatures T3B—202 2
      individual authors T3A—2
  radio programs 791.447

Radio plays (continued)
  rhetoric 808.222
  see Manual at 791.437 and
    791.447, 791.457, 792.9;
    also at 808.82 vs. 791.437,
    791.447, 791.457, 792.9
Radio programs 384.544 3
  broadcasting 384.544 3
  performing arts 791.44
Radio public speaking 808.51
Radio relay
  telephone engineering 621.387 82
Radio scripts 791.447
  rhetoric 808.066 791
  see also Radio plays
Radio stations 384.545 3
  architecture 725.23
  engineering 621.384
  enterprises 384.540 65
  facilities 384.545 3
  performing arts 791.44
Radio telescopes 522.682
Radio towers
  architecture 725.23
Radio waves 537.534
  biophysics 571.453
    humans 612.014 481
  physics 537.534
  propagation and transmission 621.384 11
Radioactivation analysis 543.63
Radioactive fallout 363.738
  physics 539.753
  social problem 363.738
  see also Pollution
Radioactive materials
  public administration 353.999
  public safety 363.179 9
Radioactive pollution 363.738
  effect on natural ecology 577.277
  see also Pollution
Radioactive substances 539.752
Radioactive tracers
  analytical chemistry 543.63
Radioactive wastes 363.728 9
  environmental engineering 628.5
    air pollution 628.535
    water pollution 628.168 5
  law 344.046 22
  public administration 353.999
  social services 363.728 9
  technology 621.483 8
Radioactivity 539.752
Radioactivity prospecting 622.159

Rafflesiaceae	583.69
Rafflesiales	583.69
Raft zithers	787.73
see also Stringed instruments	
Rafting (Sports)	797.121
Rafts	386.229
design	623.812 9
engineering	623.829
transportation services	386.229
Rag pulp	676.13
Rāgas	781.264
Ragtime	781.645
Ragusa (Italy : Libero	
consorzio comunale)	T2—458 15
ancient	T2—378 15
Ragweeds	583.983
Ragworts	583.983
Rail fastenings	
railroad engineering	625.15
Rail transit services	388.42
see also Local rail transit	
systems	
Railings	
church architecture	726.529 6
Railroad accidents	363.122
see also Railroad safety	
Railroad atlases	385.022 3
specific areas	385.09
Railroad bridges	385.312
see also Bridges	
Railroad buildings	385.314
architecture	725.33
see also Railroad terminals	
Railroad cars	385.32–.34
see also Rolling stock	
Railroad construction workers	625.100 92
Railroad crossings	385.312
engineering	625.163
transportation services	385.312
Railroad engineers	625.100 92
Railroad freight stations	385.314
architecture	725.32
see also Railroad terminals	
Railroad insurance	
inland marine	368.233
see also Insurance	
Railroad mail	383.143
see also Postal service	
Railroad passenger stations	385.314
architecture	725.31
see also Railroad terminals	
Railroad police	363.287 4
Railroad post offices	383.42
see also Postal service	

Railroad safety	363.122
engineering	625.100 289
law	343.095
public administration	353.98
social services	363.122
Railroad stations	385.314
see also Railroad terminals	
Railroad terminals	385.314
architecture	725.31
area planning	711.75
engineering	625.18
special purpose	625.3–.6
institutional housekeeping	647.963 1
law	343.095 2
transportation services	385.314
special purpose	385.5
urban	388.472
Railroad ties	625.143
Railroad tracks	385.312
engineering	625.14
interurban railroads	625.65
local railroads	625.65
law	343.095 2
military engineering	623.631
transportation services	385.312
Railroad transportation	385
engineering	625.1
law	343.095
local transit	388.42
see also Local rail transit	
systems	
public administration	354.767
transportation services	385
see also Railroads	
Railroad transportation workers	385.092
Railroad workers	385.092
construction	625.100 92
Railroad yards	385.314
engineering	625.18
law	343.095 2
transportation services	385.314
Railroads	385
electrification	
technology	621.33
engineering	625.1
investment in	332.672 2
landscape architecture	713
military engineering	623.63
mining	622.66
transportation services	385
see also Railroad transportation	
Rails (Birds)	598.32
Rails (Railroads)	625.15

Railway carriages   385.32–.34
   see also Rolling stock
Railways   385
   see also Railroads
Rain   551.577
   crop damage   632.16
   meteorology   551.577
   weather forecasting   551.647 7
   weather modification   551.687 7
Rain forests   333.75
   T2—152
   biology   578.734
   ecology   577.34
   see also Forest lands
Rainbows   551.567
Rainbows (Girl Guides)   369.463 4
Raincoats   391.46
   customs   391.46
   home sewing   646.45
   see also Clothing
Rainfall   551.577
Rains County (Tex.)   T2—764 275
Rainy Lake (Minn. and
   Ont.)   T2—776 79
Rainy River (Minn. and
   Ont.)   T2—776 79
Rainy River (Ont. : District)   T2—713 117
Raised-character publications
   cataloging   025.349 2
   library treatment   025.179 2
   publishing   070.579 2
Raised characters
   printing   686.282
Raisi, Ebrahim
   Iranian history   955.063
Raja yoga   181.45
   Hinduism   294.543 6
   philosophy   181.45
Rajaonarimampianina, Hery
   Malagasy history   969.105 7
Rajasthan (India)   T2—544
Rajasthani language   491.479
   T6—914 79
Rajasthani literature   891.479
Rajasthani-speaking people   T5—914 79
Rajiformes   597.35
   paleozoology   567.35
Rajoelina, Andry
   Malagasy history   969.105 6
     2009–2014   969.105 6
     2019–   969.105 8
Rājshāhi (Bangladesh :
   Division)   T2—549 24

Rakotovao, Rivo
   Malagasy history   969.105 7
Raleigh (N.C.)   T2—756 55
Raleigh County (W. Va.)   T2—754 73
Rallidae   598.32
Rallies (Automobile sport)   796.73
   see also Automotive
     vehicles — sports
Ralls County (Mo.)   T2—778 355
RAM (Computer memory)   004.53
   engineering   621.397 3
Rama I, King of Siam
   Thai history   959.303 1
Rama II, King of Siam
   Thai history   959.303 2
Rama III, King of Siam
   Thai history   959.303 3
Rama IV, King of Siam
   Thai history   959.303 4
Rama V, King of Siam
   Thai history   959.303 5
Rama VI, King of Siam
   Thai history   959.304 1
Rama VII, King of Siam
   Thai history   959.304 2
Rama VIII, King of Thailand
   Thai history   959.304 3
Rama IX, King of Thailand
   Thai history   959.304 4
Rama X, King of Thailand
   Thai history   959.304 5
Ramadan   297.362
Ramakrishna movement   294.555
Raman effect   535.846
Raman spectroscopes
   manufacturing technology   681.414 6
Raman spectroscopy   543.57
   analytical chemistry   543.57
   engineering   621.361
   physics   535.846
Rāmānujāchārya (Philosophy)   181.483
Ramaphosa, Cyril
   South African history   968.075
Ramayana   294.592 2
Rameses II, King of Egypt
   Egyptian history   932.014
Ramie
   botany   583.648
   fiber crop   633.55
   textiles   677.15
   see also Textiles
Ramjet engines
   aircraft   629.134 353 5

Ramos, Fidel V.	
Philippine history	959.904 8
Ramos, Nereu	
Brazilian history	981.062
Ramotar, Donald	
Guyanese history	988.103 34
Ramphastidae	598.72
Ramps	721.83
architecture	721.83
canal engineering	627.135 3
construction	690.183
Ramses II, King of Egypt	
Egyptian history	932.014
Ramsey County (Minn.)	T2—776 58
Ramsey County (N.D.)	T2—784 36
Ramu languages	499.12
	T6—991 2
Rana	597.892
Ranales	583.34
Ranch-style houses	
architecture	728.373
Ranchers	636.010 92
Ranches	636.01
Ranchowner insurance	368.096
see also Insurance	
Randall County (Tex.)	T2—764 834
Randburg (South Africa :	
District)	T2—682 21
Randfontein (South Africa :	
District)	T2—682 22
Randolph County (Ala.)	T2—761 57
Randolph County (Ark.)	T2—767 24
Randolph County (Ga.)	T2—758 932
Randolph County (Ill.)	T2—773 92
Randolph County (Ind.)	T2—772 66
Randolph County (Mo.)	T2—778 283
Randolph County (N.C.)	T2—756 61
Randolph County (W. Va.)	T2—754 85
Random-access memory	004.53
engineering	621.397 3
Random fields	519.23
Random processes	519.23
Random walks	519.282
Ranganathan's Colon	
Classification	025.435
Range finders	
military engineering	623.46
photography	771.37
Range management	636.084 5
animal husbandry	636.084 5
forage agriculture	633.202

Rangelands	333.74
	T2—153
ecology	577.4
see also Grasslands	
Rangeley Lakes (Me. and	
N.H.)	T2—741 7
Ranger project	629.435 3
Rangers (Armed forces)	356.167
Rangers (Girl Guides)	369.463 5
Ranges (Stoves)	
manufacturing technology	683.88
Rangifer	599.658
animal husbandry	636.294 8
Rangitikei District (N.Z.)	T2—935 5
Hawke's Bay Region	T2—934 64
Manawatu-Wanganui	
Region	T2—935 5
Ranidae	597.89
Rank (Heraldry)	929.7
Rankin County (Miss.)	T2—762 59
Rankin Inlet (Nunavut)	T2—719 58
Ranks (Military grades)	355.33
Ranoidea	597.89
Ransom County (N.D.)	T2—784 315
Ransom insurance	368.82
Ranunculaceae	583.34
Ranunculales	583.34
Rao, P. V. Narasimha	
Indian history	954.052
Rap (Music)	781.649
songs	782.421 649
Rapanui language	499.4
	T6—994
Rapateaceae	584.9
Rape (Crime)	364.153 2
law	345.025 32
social welfare	362.883 92
Rape prevention	
self-defense	613.663
Rape victims	362.883 92
see also Victims of crime	
Rapes (Plants)	583.78
botany	583.78
oil crop	633.853
Rapeseed	
oil crop	633.853
Raphidiodea	595.747
Rapid calculations	513.9
Rapid reading	418.4
specific languages	T4—843 2
Rapid transit	388.4
see also Urban transportation	

Rapid transit facilities
  architecture 725.33
  area planning 711.75
Rapid transit railroads 388.42
  engineering 625.4
  see also Local rail transit
    systems
Rapides Parish (La.) T2—763 69
Rappahannock County (Va.) T2—755 395
Rappahannock River (Va.) T2—755 2
Rapping (Spiritualism) 133.92
Raptors (Birds) 598.9
  conservation technology 639.978 9
  resource economics 333.958 9
Rapture (Christian doctrine) 236.9
Raqqah (Syria : Province) T2—569 12
Rare animals 333.954 2
  biology 591.68
  resource economics 333.954 2
Rare birds 333.958 22
  biology 598.168
  resource economics 333.958 22
Rare book libraries 026.09
Rare books 090
  bibliographies 011.44
  cataloging 025.341 6
  library treatment 025.171 6
Rare dugong
  biology 599.559 168
Rare earths 669.291
  chemical engineering 661.041
  chemistry 546.41
  economic geology 553.494
  materials science 620.189 291
  metallography 669.952 91
  metallurgy 669.291
  physical metallurgy 669.962 91
  see also Chemicals
Rare fishes 333.956 8
  biology 597.168
  resource economics 333.956 8
Rare gases
  chemistry 546.75
  economic geology 553.97
  technology 665.822
Rare mammals 333.954 2
  biology 599.168
  resource economics 333.954 2
Rare plants 333.953 2
  biology 581.68
  resource economics 333.953 2
Rare reptiles 333.957 2
  biology 597.916 8
  resource economics 333.957 2

Rare species 333.952 2
  biology 578.68
  resource economics 333.952 2
Rare zebras
  biology 599.665 716 8
Rarefied-gas electronics 537.53
Raritan River (N.J.) T2—749 44
Rarotongan language 499.44
  T6—994 4
Ras al Khaimah (United
    Arab Emirates : Emirate) T2—535 7
Ra's al Khaymah (United
    Arab Emirates : Emirate) T2—535 7
Ras Tafari
  Ethiopian history 963.055
    as emperor 963.055
    as regent and king 963.054
Ras Tafari movement 299.676
Rashidun Caliphate 297.090 212
Raspberries 641.347 11
  botany 583.642
  commercial processing 664.804 711
  cooking 641.647 11
  food 641.347 11
  horticulture 634.711
Rasps 621.924
Rastafari, Jah
  Ethiopian history 963.055
    as emperor 963.055
    as regent and king 963.054
Rastafarians
  biography 299.676 092
Rastatt (Germany :
    Landkreis) T2—434 643
Rat control 363.78
  social welfare 363.78
  technology 628.969 3
  agriculture 632.693 52
  see also Pest control
Rat kangaroos 599.22
Ratchets 621.83
  music 786.886
  see also Percussion
    instruments
Rates (Prices)
  communications industry 384.041
  insurance 368.011
  transportation services 388.049
Rates (Real property taxes) 336.22
  law 343.054
  public finance 336.22
Rätikon Mountains T2—494 732 5

Ratio 512.924
  algebra 512.924
  arithmetic 513.24
Rational functions 512.96
Rational numbers 512.782
Rational psychology 150.192
Rationalism 149.7
  Christian polemics 239.7
  philosophy 149.7
  philosophy of religion 211.4
  political ideology 320.512
Rationality 128.33
Rationing 333.717
  law 343.07
  public administration 352.86
  social welfare 361.6
  see Manual at 333.7–.9 vs.
    363.6
Ratites 598.5
  animal husbandry 636.69
  paleozoology 568.5
Rats (Muridae) 599.35
  see also Rodents
Rats (Rattus) 599.352
  agricultural pests 632.693 52
  animal husbandry 636.935 2
  experimental animals
    medicine 616.027 33
  household sanitation 648.7
  pest control 363.78
    social welfare 363.78
    technology 628.969 3
      agriculture 632.693 52
    see also Pest control
  small game hunting 799.259 352
  zoology 599.352
Ratsiraka, Didier
  Malagasy history 969.105 2
    1975–1993 969.105 2
    1997–2002 969.105 4
Rattan
  basketwork crop 633.58
Rattan furniture 645.4
  manufacturing technology 684.106
  see also Furniture
Rattan textiles 677.54
  see also Textiles
Rattans 584.84
Ratting
  sports hunting 799.259 352
Rattle drums 786.96
  see also Percussion instruments
Rattled idiophones 786.885
  see also Percussion instruments

Rattles
  musical instruments 786.885
  see also Percussion
    instruments
Rattlesnake ferns 587.33
Rattlesnakes 597.963 8
Rattus 599.352
Rauwolfias 583.956
  botany 583.956
Ravalli County (Mont.) T2—786 89
Ravalomanana, Marc
  Malagasy history 969.105 5
Ravenna (Italy) T2—454 71
  ancient T2—372 671
Ravenna (Italy : Province) T2—454 7
  ancient T2—372 67
Ravens 598.864
Ravines 551.442
  T2—144
  geography 910.914 4
  geomorphology 551.442
  physical geography 910.021 44
Raw food diet
  health 613.265
Raw materials 333.7
  economics 333.7
  military resources 355.24
Rāwalpindi (Pakistan :
  District) T2—549 142
Rawlings, Jerry J.
  Ghanaian history 966.705 2
Rawlins County (Kan.) T2—781 125
Ray County (Mo.) T2—778 19
Ray-finned fishes 597
  see also Fishes
Ray tracing
  computer graphics 006.693
Rayon
  textiles 677.46
  arts 746.044 6
  see also Textiles
Rays (Fishes) 597.35
  cooking 641.692
  food 641.392
Rays (Nuclear physics) 539.722
Razavi Khorāsān (Iran) T2—559 2
Razgrad (Bulgaria : Oblast) T2—499 36
Rāzī, Muḥammad ibn Abī Bakr
  Koran commentary 297.122 73
Razing buildings 690.26
Razors
  manufacturing technology 688.5

Real functions	515.8
Real numbers	512.786
Real property	333.3
Real property insurance	368.096
see also Insurance	
Real property market	333.332 2
Real property tax	336.22
law	343.054
public administration	352.44
Real-time locating systems	910.285
	T1—028 5
engineering	621.384 192
Real-time processing	004.33
communications	004.618 3
computer software	005.713 73
computer software development	005.712 73
computer software	005.373
graphics software	006.687 3
graphics software development	006.677 3
interfacing	
computer software	005.713 73
computer software development	005.712 73
multimedia software	006.787 3
multimedia software development	006.777 3
software development	005.273
see also Processing modes — computer science	
Real-time programming	005.273
Real-valued functions	515.7
Real variable functions	515.8
Realia	
cataloging	025.349
library treatment	025.179
Realism	
education	370.12
fine arts	709.034 3
literature	808.801 2
history and criticism	809.912
specific literatures	T3B—080 12
history and criticism	T3B—091 2
painting	759.053
philosophy	149.2
sculpture	735.22
Realistic fiction	808.838 3
history and criticism	809.383
specific literatures	T3B—308 3
individual authors	T3A—3
Reality	
philosophy	111
Reamers	621.954

Reaping	631.55
Reapportionment (Legislatures)	328.334 5
Rear axles	
automotive engineering	629.245
Reason	128.33
epistemology	121.3
ethical systems	171.2
philosophical anthropology	128.33
theology	
Christianity	231.042
Reasoning	153.43
artificial intelligence	006.333
educational psychology	370.152 4
philosophical logic	160
psychology	153.43
Rebates	
law	343.072
Rebekah (Biblical matriarch)	222.110 92
Rebellion (Political offense)	364.131
law	345.023 1
Rebuses	793.73
Recall (Elections)	324.68
Recall (Information science)	025.04
Recall (Memory)	153.123
Recataloging	
library operations	025.39
Receivership	332.75
see also Bankruptcy	
Receiving operations	
materials management	658.728
Receiving sets	
radio	621.384 18
Recent epoch	551.793
geology	551.793
paleontology	560.179 3
Recently extinct species	333.952 2
see also entries beginning Rare	
Receptionists	
office services	651.374 3
Receptions	
meal service	642.4
Receptive processes (Psychology)	152.1
Recession (Economics)	338.542
Recidivists	364.3
	T1—086 927
Recipes	T1—021 2
cooking	641.5
Reciprocal equations	515.253
Reciprocal trade	382.9
law	343.087
Reciprocating engines	
aircraft	629.134 352

Reducing exercises
  physical fitness — 613.712
Reducing solutions
  photography — 771.54
Reduction (Chemical reaction) — 541.393
  organic chemistry — 547.23
Reduction in force
  economics — 331.259 6
    employment security — 331.259 6
    unemployment — 331.137
  law — 344.012 596
  personnel management — 658.313 4
    public administration — 352.69
Reductionism (Psychology) — 150.194
Reductive algebras — 512.55
Redwood (Sequoia) — 585.5
  forestry — 634.975 8
  lumber — 674.144
Redwood County (Minn.) — T2—776 35
Redwood National Park
  (Calif.) — T2—794 12
Reed instruments — 788.4
  see also Woodwind
    instruments
Reed organs — 786.55
  instrument — 786.551 9
  music — 786.55
  see also Keyboard instruments
Reedbucks — 599.645
Reedfishes — 597.42
Reeds — 584.92
  botany — 584.92
Reefs — 551.424
   — T2—142
  biology — 578.778 9
  ecology — 577.789
  geography — 910.914 2
  geomorphology — 551.424
  physical geography — 910.021 42
Reel-to-reel tapes (Computers) — 004.563
  engineering — 621.397 63
Reelfoot Lake (Tenn.) — T2—768 12
Reeling textiles — 677.028 22
  arts — 746.12
  manufacturing technology — 677.028 22
Reels (Dances) — 793.34
Reengineering
  executive management — 658.406 3
Reentry problems
  space flight — 629.415
Reeves County (Tex.) — T2—764 924
Refectories
  architecture — 726.79

Refereeing (Recreation) — 790.1
  American football — 796.332 3
  basketball — 796.323 3
  Canadian football — 796.335 3
  golf — 796.352 4
  ice hockey — 796.962 3
  rugby — 796.333 3
  soccer — 796.334 3
  tennis — 796.342 3
  volleyball — 796.325 3
  see also Sports
Reference — 401.456
  linguistics — 401.456
    specific languages — T4—014 56
  philosophy of language — 121.68
Reference books — 028.7
  bibliographies — 011.02
  reviews — 028.12
  use — 028.7
Reference groups
  social psychology — 302.5
Reference services — 025.52
Reference works — 028.7
  bibliographies — 011.02
  reviews — 028.12
  use — 028.7
Referendum (Legislation) — 328.23
Referral services
  physicians — 362.172
Refined grain
  commercial processing — 664.720 7
Reflection of light
  physics — 535.323
Reflection of sound
  engineering — 620.21
  physics — 534.204
Reflexes
  psychology — 152.322
Reflexology
  psychology — 150.194 4
Reflexology (Therapy) — 615.822 4
Reforestation — 333.751 53
  law — 346.046 751 53
  resource economics — 333.751 53
  silviculture — 634.956
Reform Judaism — 296.834 1
  liturgy — 296.450 46
Reform movements — 303.484
  agent of social change — 303.484
  relations with government — 322.44
  religion — 209
  social action — 361.24
Reform Party of Canada — 324.271 04

Reform schools	365.42	Reformed natural gas	665.773
see also Penal institutions		Reformed Presbyterian churches	285.136
Reformation	270.6	see also Presbyterian Church	
European history	940.23	Reformed refinery gas	665.773
German history	943.03	Refraction errors	
Reformation of offenders	364.601	incidence	614.599 7
Reformatories	365.34	optometry	617.755
juvenile offenders	365.42	see also Eye diseases —	
see also Penal institutions		humans	
Reformed Christians	284.2	Refraction of light	535.324
American	285.7	astronomical corrections	522.9
biography	285.709 2	Refraction of sound	
biography	284.209 2	acoustical engineering	620.21
European	284.2	Refractivity	
biography	284.209 2	materials science	620.112 95
Reformed Church	284.2	Refractometry	543.59
church government	262.042	Refractory materials	553.67
local church	254.042	economic geology	553.67
church law	262.984 2	materials science	620.143
doctrines	230.42	metallurgical furnaces	669.82
catechisms and creeds	238.42	technology	666.72
guides to Christian life	248.484 2	Refrigerants	
missions	266.42	refrigeration engineering	621.564
moral theology	241.044 2	Refrigerating foods	664.028 52
public worship	264.042	commercial preservation	664.028 52
religious associations	267.184 2	home preservation	641.452
religious education	268.842	Refrigeration	621.56
seminaries	230.073 42	alcoholic beverages	663.15
theology	230.42	nautical engineering	623.853 5
Reformed Church (American		Refrigeration engineers	621.560 92
Reformed)	285.7	Refrigerator cars	385.34
church government	262.057	engineering	625.24
local church	254.057	see also Rolling stock	
church law	262.985 7	Refrigerators	621.57
doctrines	230.57	kitchen appliances	641.452 028 4
catechisms and creeds	238.57	low-temperature engineering	621.57
guides to Christian life	248.485 7	Refugees	305.906 914
missions	266.57		T1—086 914
moral theology	241.045 7	asylum	323.631
public worship	264.057	citizenship law	342.083
religious associations	267.185 7	immigration law	342.082
religious education	268.857	Iraq War, 2003–2011	956.704 431
seminaries	230.073 57	law of nations	341.486
theology	230.57	political science	325.21
Reformed Church in America	285.732	political status	323.631
see also Reformed Church		social group	305.906 914
(American Reformed)		social theology	201.762 87
Reformed Church in the United		Christianity	261.832 8
States	285.733	social welfare	362.87
see also Reformed Church		public administration	353.533 8
(American Reformed)		women	
Reformed Episcopal Church	283.3	social welfare	362.839 814
see also Anglican Communion		young people	305.230 869 14
Reformed Hinduism	294.556	social welfare	362.779 14

Refugio County (Tex.)	T2—764 119		Region Zealand (Denmark)	T2—489 12
Refuse	363.728		Regional anatomy	
military sanitation	623.754		animals	573.993 3
waste technology	628.44		humans	611.9
rural	628.440 917 34		Regional anesthesia	
see also Waste control			surgery	617.964
Regalia	391		Regional associations	341.24
Regals (Music)	786.55		Regional bibliographies	015
instrument	786.551 9		Regional cytology	
music	786.55		humans	612.9
see also Keyboard instruments			Regional development	338.9
Regattas	797.14		law	343.074 6
Regeneration (Christian doctrine)	234.4		Regional field offices	
Regeneration (Developmental			public administration	352.288
biology)	571.889		Regional groups	305.8
Regensburg (Germany)	T2—433 47			T1—089
Reggae	781.646		Regional histology	571.59
songs	782.421 646		animals	573.99
Regge poles	539.721		humans	612.9
Reggio Calabria (Italy)	T2—457 831		plants	575.435 9
ancient	T2—377 831		Regional medicine	617.5
Reggio Calabria (Italy :			anesthesiology	617.967 5
Città metropolitana)	T2—457 83		geriatrics	618.977 5
ancient	T2—377 83		pediatrics	618.920 975
Reggio Emilia (Italy :			surgery	617.5
Province)	T2—454 3		*see Manual at* 617.5	
ancient	T2—372 63		Regional nationalism	320.54
Reggio nell'Emilia (Italy :			Regional organizations	341.24
Province)	T2—454 3		Regional physiology	571.59
ancient	T2—372 63		animals	573.99
Regiments (Military units)	355.31		humans	612.9
Regina (Sask.)	T2—712 445		plants	575.4
Región Autónoma del			Regional planning	307.12
Atlántico Norte			civic art	711.3
(Nicaragua)	T2—728 537		community sociology	307.12
Región Autónoma			economics	338.9
del Atlántico Sur			law	346.045
(Nicaragua)	T2—728 532		Regional surgery	617.5
Région de			anesthesiology	617.967 5
Bruxelles-Capitale			*see Manual at* 617.5	
(Belgium)	T2—493 32		Regional treatment	T1—09
Region Hovedstaden			Regionalist parties	324.218 4
(Denmark)	T2—489 13		Regions	T2—1
Region Midtjylland			Regions (Local government	
(Denmark)	T2—489 55		units)	320.83
Region Nordjylland			*see also* Counties	
(Denmark)	T2—489 58		Regions (State-level units)	321.023
Region of Southern			*see also* States (Members of	
Denmark (Denmark)	T2—489 52		federations)	
Région-Sherbrookoise			Registered mail	383.182
(Quebec)	T2—714 66		*see also* Postal service	
Region Sjælland (Denmark)	T2—489 12		Registered nursing assistants	610.730 92
Region Syddanmark			role and function	610.730 693
(Denmark)	T2—489 52			

Registered partners	306.841
	T1—086 56
Registered partnerships	306.841
	T1—086 56
law	346.016 71
Registration	352.84
see also Licensing	
Registration for military service	355.223 6
Registration of voters	324.64
Registration plates	929.9
Regression analysis	519.536
Regressive taxation	336.293
Regular Baptists	286.1
see also Baptists	
Regulation (Public	
administration)	352.8
Regulation of conduct	
armed forces	355.133
Regulations (Laws)	348.025
United States	348.732 5
Regulatory agencies	352.8
decisions	348.045
United States	348.734 5
law	342.066 4
rulings	348.045
United States	348.734 5
Rehabilitation	
geriatrics	618.977 03
health services	362.178 6
medicine	617.03
housing services	363.583
injuries	
medicine	617.103
natural resources	333.715 3
prisoner services	365.661
social services	362.042 5
Rehabilitation (Restoration of	
rights)	345.077
Rehabilitation training	362.042 5
labor economics	331.259 2
personnel management	658.312 44
public administration	352.669
Rehabilitative therapy	617.06
injuries	
medicine	617.106
Rehearsal	
musical technique	781.44
Reid, G. H. (George Houstoun)	
Australian history	994.041
Reigate and Banstead	
(England)	T2—422 17
Reign of Terror, 1793–1794	944.044
Reiki (Therapy)	
medicine	615.852

Reimbursement health insurance		368.382
see also Insurance		
Reims (France)	T2—443 22	
Reina, Carlos Roberto		
Honduran history		972.830 535
Reincarnation		
occultism		133.901 35
philosophy		129
religion		202.37
Buddhism		294.342 37
Hinduism		294.523 7
Reindeer		599.658
animal husbandry		636.294 8
conservation technology		639.979 658
resource economics		333.959 658
Reindexing		
library operations		025.39
Reinforced concrete		624.183 41
architectural construction		721.044 54
building construction		693.54
foundation materials		624.153 37
materials science		620.137
ship design		623.818 341
ship hulls		623.845 41
shipbuilding		623.820 7
structural engineering		624.183 41
Reinforced plastics		668.494
Reinforcement (Psychology)		153.85
Reinforcing plastics		668.416
Reinstatement (Military		
personnel)		355.114
Reinsurance		368.012 2
law		346.086 012 2
Reinventing government		352.3
REIT		332.632 47
Reitz (South Africa :		
District)	T2—685 1	
Reiwa period		952.052
Relapsing fevers		
incidence		614.574 4
medicine		616.924 4
see also Communicable		
diseases — humans		
Relation (Philosophy)		111
Relational databases		
computer science		005.756
Relational grammar		415.018 25
specific languages	T4—501 825	
Relations (Mathematics)		511.326
Relative indexing		025.47
Relatives (People)		306.87
	T1—085	
arts	T3C—352 5	

Religious studies	200.71
see Manual at 207.5, 268 vs.	
200.71, 230.071, 292–299	
Religious symbolism	203.7
art representation	704.948
painting	755
see also Symbolism —	
religious significance	
Religious therapy	
medicine	615.852
Reliquaries	
Christianity	247
Relishes	641.812
Relizane (Algeria :	
Province)	T2—651
Remarriage	306.81
ethics	173
Judaism	296.444
law	346.016
social theology	201.7
Christianity	261.835 84
Remedial education	
adult level	374.012
Remedial reading	418.4
primary education	372.43
specific languages	T4—842
Remedies (Legal actions)	347.077
Remembrance days	
Holocaust, 1933–1945	940.531 862
Reminiscences	920
	T1—092
biography	920
literature	808.883
history and criticism	809.983
specific literatures	T3B—803
individual authors	T3A—8
see Manual at T3A—8 + 03	
and T3B—803, T3B—8	
+ 03	
Remodeling of buildings	690.24
architecture	720.286
home economics	643.7
see Manual at 690 vs. 643.7	
Remodeling of clothes	646.4
Remonstrant churches	284.9
Remonstrants	
biography	284.9
Remote control	620.46
radio engineering	621.384 196
Remote-control models	796.15
see Manual at 796.15 vs.	
629.0460228	

Remote-control vehicles	
engineering	629.046
recreation	796.15
Remote procedure calls	005.71
Remote sensing technology	621.367 8
Remount services	357.2
Removal from office	
recall elections	324.68
Renaissance architecture	724.12
Renaissance art	709.024
religious significance	246.4
Renaissance decoration	744.090 24
Renaissance music	780.903 1
Renaissance painting	759.03
Renaissance period	
European history	940.21
Italian history	945.05
Renaissance revival architecture	724.52
Renaissance sculpture	735.21
Renal dialysis	
medicine	617.461 059
Renal disease	
medicine	616.61
see also Urologic diseases —	
humans	
Renal failure	
medicine	616.614
see also Urologic diseases —	
humans	
Renal hypertension	
medicine	616.132
see also Cardiovascular	
diseases — humans	
Rendering oils and gases	665.028 2
Rendezvous	
manned space flight	629.458 3
Renegotiation of government	
contracts	352.53
Renewable energy resources	333.794
economics	333.794
engineering	621.042
Renewal theory	519.287
Renfrew (Ont. : County)	T2—713 81
Renfrew (Scotland)	T2—414 37
Renfrew (Scotland :	
District)	T2—414 37
Renfrewshire (Scotland)	T2—414 37
Renmark (S. Aust.)	T2—942 33
Rennellese language	499.46
	T6—994 6
Rennes (France)	T2—441 54
Reno (Nev.)	T2—793 55
Reno County (Kan.)	T2—781 83

Renovation	690.24	Repentance	202.2
home economics	643.7	Christianity	234.5
see Manual at 690 vs. 643.7		Islam	297.22
Rensselaer County (N.Y.)	T2—747 41	Judaism	296.32
Rent		Repetition learning	
income distribution	339.21	psychology	153.152 2
land economics	333.5	Report writing (Study technique)	371.302 81
law	346.043 44	Reporters	070.430 92
public revenue	336.12	Reporting	
Rent (Economic theory)	333.012	executive management	658.45
Rent control	363.583	military administration	355.688
law	346.043 44	public administration	352.38
Rent subsidies	363.582	financial management	658.151 2
Rental collections		journalism	070.43
museology	069.56	Reports	
Rental housing	363.5	audits	657.452
household management		authorship techniques	808.066
apartments	647.92	financial management	658.151 2
Rental libraries	027.3	office records	651.78
Rental services		Repossession	347.077
museology	069.13	installment sales	346.074
Renting		Repoussé	
land economics	333.5	decorative arts	739.14
Renville County (Minn.)	T2—776 34	sculpture	731.41
Renville County (N.D)	T2—784 64	Representation	324.63
Reorganization		electoral politics	324.63
management	658.16	legislative districts	328.334 5
internal organization	658.402	political right	323.5
public administration	352.28	Representation theory	
public administration	352.2	operational calculus	515.722 3
Reorganized Church of Jesus		Representations	
Christ of Latter Day Saints	289.333	fine arts	704.9
see also Mormon Church		museology	069.134
Reoviridae	579.254	Representations of groups	512.22
Repairs	620.004 6	Repression	323.044
	T1—028 8	Reprieve	364.63
buildings	690.24	Reprimands	
see Manual at 690 vs. 643.7		personnel management	658.314 4
home economics	643.7	Reprints	
library materials	025.84	bibliographies	011.47
Reparation (Criminal justice)		Reprisals	
social welfare	362.881 87	international relations	327.117
Reparations		law	341.582
law of war	341.66	Reproducers	
revenue source	336.182	sound engineering	621.389 33
war		Reproduction	571.8
social services	363.349 887	animals	573.6
World War I	940.314 22	biology	571.8
World War II	940.531 422	ethics	176
Reparative surgery	617.952	religion	205.66
Repatriation	323.64	Buddhism	294.356 6
Repayment (Public debt)		Christianity	241.66
public finance	336.363	Hinduism	294.548 66
Repeal of legislation	328.37	Islam	297.566

Reproduction
  ethics
    religion (continued)
      Judaism   296.366
  human physiology
    primary education   372.372
  microorganisms   571.842 9
  plants   575.6
  see Manual at 571.8 vs. 573.6,
    575.6
Reproduction (Memory)   153.123
Reproductions
  arts   702.872
  paintings   751.5
Reproductive adaptation   578.46
  animals   591.46
  plants   581.46
Reproductive behavior (Animals)   591.56
Reproductive hormones   571.837 4
  see also Sex hormones
Reproductive organs   573.6
  see also Genital system
Reproductive system   573.6
  animals   573.6
    descriptive zoology   591.46
    physiology   573.6
    see also Genital system
  biology   573.6
  plants   575.6
    descriptive botany   581.46
    physiology   575.6
Reproductive technology
  ethics
    religion
      Christianity   241.662
    humans
      ethics   176.2
      see also Reproduction —
        ethics
  health   613.94
  infertility
    gynecology   618.178 06
    medicine   616.692 06
Reproductive toxicology
  medicine   616.650 71
Reprography   686
  equipment manufacturing
    technology   681.6
  library services   025.12
  office use   652.4
Reptantia   595.38
Reptiles   597.9
  agriculture   639.39
  art representation   704.943 279

Reptiles (continued)
  arts   T3C—362 79
  big game hunting   799.279
  commercial hunting   639.14
  conservation technology   639.977 9
  drawing   743.679
  food   641.396
    cooking   641.696
  paleozoology   567.9
  resource economics   333.957
  zoology   597.9
Reptiles as pets   639.39
Republic County (Kan.)   T2—781 24
Republic of Korea   951.95
         T2—519 5
Republic of South Africa   968
         T2—68
Republic of Texas   976.404
Republic of the Congo
  (Brazzaville)   967.24
         T2—672 4
Republican Party (U.S. :
  1792–1828)   324.273 26
Republican Party (U.S. : 1854–)   324.273 4
Republican Party of Germany   324.243 03
Republican River (Neb. and
  Kan.)   T2—781 2
  Kansas   T2—781 2
  Nebraska   T2—782 37
Republics   321.86
Republikaner (German political
  party)   324.243 03
Repudiation of debt
  public finance   336.368
Repulse Bay (Nunavut)   T2—719 58
Requiem mass   264.36
  music   782.323 8
    choral and mixed voices   782.532 38
    single voices   783.093 238
Required courses   375.002
  higher education   378.24
Requirements analysis
  computer science
    software   005.12
Requisition
  military resources   355.28
Reredoses   247.1
  architecture   726.529 6
Res judicata   347.077
Resampling methods   519.54
Rescission (Law)   346.022
Rescue aircraft
  military engineering   623.746 6

Rescue dogs
  animal husbandry — 636.708 86
  disaster relief — 363.348 1
Rescue operations — 363.348 1
  disaster relief — 363.348 1
  engineering — 628.92
  fire safety — 363.378 1
    technology — 628.922
  Holocaust, 1933–1945 — 940.531 835
  mining technology — 622.89
  seamanship — 623.888 7
Research — 001.4
          T1—072
  public administrative support — 352.74
  see Manual at T1—072 vs.
    T1—0601–0609
Research and development
  air force supplies — 358.407
  military science — 355.07
  naval forces — 359.07
  production management — 658.57
  public administration — 354.27
    noneconomic fields — 352.7
  public contract law — 346.023
Research buildings — 001.4
  see also Laboratories
Research ethics — 174
Research libraries — 027
Research methods — 001.42
          T1—072 1
  see Manual at
    T1—07201–07209 vs.
    T1—0721
Research reports
  biology — 570
  see Manual at 571–573 vs.
    610
  medicine — 610
  rhetoric — 808.02
Researchers — 001.409 2
Resedaceae — 583.78
Reservation systems
  transportation — 388.042
  air service — 387.742 2
  see also Passenger services
Reservations (Military
  installations) — 355.7
Reserve collections in libraries — 025.6
Reserve Officer Training Corps — 355.223 207 1173
Reserve requirements
  central banking — 332.113
Reserve status (Armed forces) — 355.113
Reserve training (Armed forces) — 355.223 2

Reserves (Armed forces) — 355.37
  air forces — 358.413 7
Reserves (Capital management) — 658.152 26
Reserves (Natural resources) — 333.711
Reservoir engineering
  oil extraction — 622.338 2
Reservoirs — 627.86
  biology — 578.763
  ecology — 577.63
  flood control — 627.44
  landscape architecture — 719.33
  recreational resources — 333.784 6
  recreational use — 797
  water supply engineering — 628.132
Resettlement
  community sociology — 307.2
  housing services — 363.583
    see also Housing
  public administration — 353.59
Residency (Training) — T1—071 55
Residential buildings — 643.1
  see also Dwellings
Residential cities
  area planning — 711.45
Residential finance — 332.722
Residential homes — 362.61
Residential land — 333.77
  area planning — 711.58
  community sociology — 307.336
  resource economics — 333.77
  taxation — 336.225
Residential water supply — 363.61
  economics — 333.912 2
Residents (Students)
  training — T1—071 55
Residues
  petroleum — 665.538 8
  wood — 674.84
Residues (Mathematics) — 512.72
Resignation of employees
  armed forces — 355.114
  personnel management — 658.313
    public administration — 352.69
Resin-derived plastics — 668.45
Resin-producing plants
  agriculture — 633.895
  economic botany — 581.636
Resins
  chemistry — 547.843 4
  commercial processing — 668.37
  fossil — 553.29
  materials science — 620.192 4
  recovery from pulp — 676.5

Respiratory tract diseases (continued)	
humans	362.196 2
cancer	362.196 994 2
incidence	614.599 942
medicine	616.994 2
social services	362.196 994 2
see also Cancer —	
humans	
geriatrics	618.976 2
incidence	614.592
medicine	616.2
nursing	616.200 423 1
pediatrics	618.922
pharmacokinetics	615.72
social services	362.196 2
surgery	617.54
Respiratory tract infections	
medicine	616.2
see also Respiratory tract	
diseases — humans	
Responsa (Jewish law)	296.185
Responses	
music	782.292
Responsibility	
executive management	658.402
law	346.022
military administration	355.685
public administration	352.35
Responsive readings	
public worship	203.8
Christianity	264.4
Judaism	296.45
Rest	
animal physiology	573.79
human physiology	612.76
physical fitness	613.79
Rest areas	
road engineering	625.77
Rest homes	362.61
see also Health care facilities	
Rest periods	
labor economics	331.257 6
personnel management	658.312 2
Restaurant cooking	641.572
Restaurant meal service	642.5
Restaurants	647.95
arts	T3C—356 4
economics	338.476 479 5
literature	808.803 564
history and criticism	809.933 564
see also Eating places	
Restaurateurs	647.950 92
Restigouche (N.B.)	T2—715 11

Restigouche River (N.B.	
and Quebec)	T2—715 11
Restionaceae	584.9
Restionales	584.9
Restitution (Criminal justice)	
social welfare	362.881 87
Restitution (Law of war)	341.66
Holocaust, 1933–1945	940.531 814 4
social services	363.349 887
Restitution coefficient	531.382
Restoration	T1—028 8
arts	702.88
cinematography	777.58
engineering	620.004 6
library materials	025.84
museology	069.53
videography	777.58
wooden furniture	684.104 42
Restoration (France), 1815–1848	944.06
Restoration (Great Britain),	
1660–1688	941.066
English history	942.066
Scottish history	941.106 6
Restoration (Spain), 1814–1833	946.072
Restoration (Spain), 1871–1873	946.073
Restoration movement (Christian	
movement)	286.6
biography	286.609 2
church government	262.066
local church	254.066
church law	262.986 6
doctrines	230.66
catechisms and creeds	238.66
guides to Christian life	248.486 6
missions	266.66
moral theology	241.046 6
public worship	264.066
religious associations	267.186 6
religious education	268.866
seminaries	230.073 66
theology	230.66
Restoration of natural resources	333.715 3
Restorative surgery	617.952
Restoring torques	
aeronautics	629.132 364
Restraint	
social control	303.36
Restraint of trade (Competition)	338.604 8
criminology	364.168
law	345.026 8
economics	338.604 8
law	343.072 3
Restrictive environments	
psychology	155.96

Retirement benefits	331.252
law	344.012 52
public employees	342.068 6
Retirement counseling	
personnel management	658.385
Retirement guides	
life skills	646.79
Retirement income	332.024 014
pensions	331.252
see also Pensions	
personal finance	332.024 014
tax economics	336.242 8
tax law	343.052 4
Retirement investment plans	332.024 014 5
Retirement planning	332.024 014
Retracts	514.24
Retraining	
labor economics	331.259 24
law	344.012 592 4
public employees	342.068 6
personnel management	658.312 43
social welfare	362.042 5
vocational education	370.113
Retreats (Military tactics)	355.422
Retreats (Religion)	
Christianity	269.6
Retribution	
penology	364.601
Retrieval of information	
information science	025.524
Retrievers	636.752 7
Retrospective conversion	
library operations	025.317 3
Retroviridae	579.256 9
medical microbiology	616.918 801
Retroviridae infections	
incidence	614.588
medicine	616.918 8
see also Communicable	
diseases — humans	
Retroviruses	579.256 9
Rett syndrome	
medicine	616.858 84
pediatrics	618.928 588 4
Return to Orthodox Judaism	296.715
Returned merchandise	
marketing management	658.812
Retziaceae	583.96
Reunification of Germany	943.087 8
Réunion	969.81
	T2—698 1
Reusability	
computer software	005.132 6
Reuss River (Switzerland)	T2—494 566

Revegetation	631.64
Revelation (Biblical book)	228
Revelation of God	212.6
Bible	220.13
Christianity	231.74
comparative religion	202.117
Islam	297.211 5
Judaism	296.311 5
philosophy of religion	212.6
Revelation of Koran	297.122 12
Revelstoke (B.C.)	T2—711 68
Revenue	336.02
financial management	658.155 4
law	343.036
public administration	352.44
public finance	336.02
Revenue budgets (Public)	352.48
see also Budgets (Public)	
Revenue cutters	363.286
design	623.812 63
engineering	623.826 3
police services	363.286
Revenue offenses	364.133
law	345.023 3
Revenue sharing	336.185
law	343.034
public administration	352.73
public finance	336.185
Revenue stamps	336.272
public finance	336.272
Revenue tariffs	382.72
see also Customs (Tariff)	
Reveries	154.3
Reverse dictionaries	413.1
specific languages	T4—31
Reverse osmosis	
desalinization	628.167 44
Review	
study and teaching	T1—076
Reviews	
ballet	792.845
books	028.1
films	791.437 5
musical plays	792.645
opera	792.545
radio programs	791.447 5
television programs	791.457 5
Revised English Bible	220.520 6
Revised Standard version Bible	220.520 42
Revised versions of Bible	220.520 4
Revival meetings	269.24
Revolution	303.64
ethics	172.1
political science	321.094

Revolution (continued)
  social change | 303.4
  social conflict | 303.64
  social theology | 201.72
    Buddhism | 294.337 2
    Christianity | 261.7
    Hinduism | 294.517 2
    Islam | 297.272 109 4
    Judaism | 296.382
  see Manual at 909, 930–990
    vs. 320.4, 321, 321.09
Revolution of 1891 (Chilean
    history) | 983.062
Revolution of 1911–1912
    (Chinese history) | 951.036
Revolution of 1918 (German
    history) | 943.085 1
Revolution of 1958 (Venezuelan
    history) | 987.063 3
Revolution of April 1870
    (Venezuelan history) | 987.062
Revolution of October 1945
    (Venezuelan history) | 987.063 2
Revolutionäre Marxistische Liga
    (Swiss political party) | 324.249 407 5
Revolutionary activities | 322.42
Revolutionary groups | 322.42
Revolutionary Marxist League
    (Swiss political party) | 324.249 407 5
Revolutionary unions
    labor economics | 331.886
Revolutionary warfare | 355.021 8
Revolutions of 1848 | 940.284
  German history | 943.074
Revolvers | 683.436
  art metalwork | 739.744 36
  manufacturing technology | 683.436
  military engineering | 623.443 6
Revues | 782.14
  music | 782.14
  stage presentation | 792.6
  see also Theater
Rewards
  armed forces | 355.134
  social control | 303.35
  student discipline | 371.53
Reweaving | 646.25
  clothing care | 646.6
  home sewing | 646.25
Rex cat | 636.822

Reye syndrome
  medicine | 616.83
  see also Nervous system
    diseases — humans
  pediatrics | 618.928 3
Reynolds County (Mo.) | T2—778 885
Reza Shah Pahlavi, Shah of Iran
  Iranian history | 955.052
RFD (Mail delivery) | 383.145
  see also Postal service
RFID (Radio frequency
    identification) | 006.245
  computer science | 006.245
  engineering | 621.384 192
Rh factor
  human physiology | 612.118 25
  incompatibility
    pediatrics | 618.921 5
    perinatal medicine | 618.326 1
  see also Cardiovascular
    diseases — humans
Rhabdocoela | 592.42
Rhabdofario | 597.57
Rhabdoviridae | 579.256 6
Rhade (Vietnamese people) | T5—992 2
Rhaetia | T2—369 47
  Austria | T2—363 64
  Switzerland | T2—369 47
Rhaetian Alps | T2—494 732
Rhaetian languages | 459.9
  | T6—599
Rhaetian literatures | 859.9
Rhaetians | T5—599
Rhaeto-Romanic languages | 459.9
  | T6—599
Rhaeto-Romanic literatures | 859.9
Rhagionidae | 595.773
Rhamnaceae | 583.646
Rhamnales | 583.646
Rhapsodies (Music) | 784.189 45
Rhea County (Tenn.) | T2—768 834
Rheas | 598.522
Rhegium (Italy) | T2—377 831
Rheiformes | 598.522
  paleozoology | 568.5
Rheims-Douay Bible | 220.520 2
Rhein-Neckar (Germany :
    Metropolregion) | T2—434 645
Rhein-Neckar-Kreis
    (Germany : Landkreis) | T2—434 645
Rhein-Pfalz-Kreis
    (Germany : Landkreis) | T2—434 353
Rheinfelden (Switzerland :
    Bezirk) | T2—494 564 3

Rheinhessen-Pfalz
  (Germany :
    Regierungsbezirk)   T2—434 35
Rheinland-Pfalz (Germany)   T2—434 3
Rheintal (Switzerland)   T2—494 721
Rhenish Prussia (Germany)   T2—434 3
Rhenium   669.7
  chemical engineering   661.054 5
  chemistry   546.545
  metallurgy   669.7
  physical metallurgy   669.967
  see also Chemicals
Rheology   531.113 4
Rheostats   621.317
Rhesus monkey   599.864 3
Rheto-Romance languages   459.9
           T6—599
Rheto-Romance literatures   859.9
Rhetoric   808
Rheumatic diseases
  medicine   616.723
  see also Musculoskeletal
    diseases — humans
Rheumatic fever
  incidence   614.597 23
  medicine   616.991
  see also Communicable
    diseases — humans
  pediatrics   618.929 91
Rheumatic heart disease
  medicine   616.127
  see also Cardiovascular
    diseases — humans
Rheumatism
  medicine   616.723
  see also Musculoskeletal
    diseases — humans
Rheumatoid arthritis
  medicine   616.722 7
  see also Musculoskeletal
    diseases — humans
Rheumatology   616.723
Rhinbund   943.06
Rhine, Confederation of the   943.06
Rhine Province (Germany)   T2—434 3
Rhine River   T2—434
  Germany   T2—434
  Switzerland   T2—494
Rhineland-Palatinate
  (Germany)   T2—434 3
Rhinencephalon
  human physiology   612.825
  medicine   616.8

Rhinoceroses   599.668
  conservation technology   639.979 668
  resource economics   333.959 668
Rhinocerotidae   599.668
Rhinology   616.21
Rhipiceroidea   595.763
Rhiptoglossidea   597.956
Rhizobium   579.334
Rhizocephala   595.35
Rhizomes   581.46
  descriptive botany   581.46
  physiology   575.497
Rhizomyidae   599.35
Rhizophoraceae   583.69
Rhizopodea   579.43
Rhizopus   579.53
Rhizosphere   577.57
Rhizostomeae   593.53
Rhode Island   974.5
           T2—745
Rhode Island Red chicken   636.584
Rhode Island Sound (Mass. and
  R.I.)   551.461 346
           T2—163 46
Rhodes (Greece : Island)   T2—495 87
  ancient   T2—391 6
Rhodes (Greece : Regional
  unit)   T2—495 87
Rhodesia (1964–1980)   968.910 4
           T2—689 1
Rhodesia and Nyasaland   968.903
           T2—689
Rhodesian man   569.98
Rhodesian ridgeback   636.753 6
Rhodesians   T5—968 91
Rhodium   669.7
  chemical engineering   661.063 4
  chemistry   546.634
  metallography   669.957
  metallurgy   669.7
  physical metallurgy   669.967
  see also Chemicals
Rhodobacter   579.385
Rhododendrons   583.93
  botany   583.93
  floriculture   635.933 93
Rhodope (Greece)   T2—495 7
Rhodope Mountains   T2—499 7
Rhodophyceae   579.89
Rhodophyta   579.89
Rhodopseudomonas   579.385
Rhoeadales   583.34
Rhön (Germany)   T2—433 3
Rhondda (Wales)   T2—429 78

Richards Bay (South Africa) T2—684 43
Richardson County (Neb.) T2—782 282
Richelieu River (Quebec) T2—714 3
Richland County (Ill.) T2—773 77
Richland County (Mont.) T2—786 23
Richland County (N.D.) T2—784 12
Richland County (Ohio) T2—771 28
Richland County (S.C.) T2—757 71
Richland County (Wis.) T2—775 75
Richland Parish (La.) T2—763 86
Richmond (B.C.) T2—711 33
Richmond (N.S. : County) T2—716 98
Richmond (Natal, South
    Africa : District) T2—684 7
Richmond (Northern Cape,
    South Africa : District) T2—687 13
Richmond (Va.) T2—755 451
Richmond County (Ga.) T2—758 64
Richmond County (N.C.) T2—756 34
Richmond County (N.Y.) T2—747 26
Richmond County (Va.) T2—755 23
Richmond River (N.S.W.) T2—944 3
Richmond upon Thames
    (London, England) T2—421 95
Richmondshire (England) T2—428 48
Richtersveld National Park
    (South Africa) T2—687 17
Ricinulei 595.455
Rickets
  medicine 616.395
  see also Digestive system
    diseases — humans
Rickettsiae
  medical microbiology 616.922 01
Rickettsial diseases 571.993 27
  agriculture 632.32
  animals 571.993 271 1
    veterinary medicine 636.089 692 2
  biology 571.993 27
  humans 362.196 922
    incidence 614.526
    medicine 616.922
    see also Communicable
      diseases — humans
    social services 362.196 922
  plants 571.993 271 2
    agriculture 632.32
Rickettsias 579.327
Rickshaws 388.341
  manufacturing technology 688.6

Riddles 808.882
  folk literature 398.6
  jokes
    literature 808.882
      history and criticism 809.982
      specific literatures T3B—802
      individual
        authors T3A—8
  literature 808.882
    history and criticism 809.982
    specific literatures T3B—802
      individual authors T3A—8
  recreation 793.735
  see Manual at T3A—8 + 02,
    T3B—802, T3B—8 + 02
    vs. 398.6, 793.735
Ridesharing 388.413 212
Riding-club buildings
  architecture 725.88
Riding horses (Breeds) 636.13
Riding horses (Recreation) 798.23
Ridley turtles 597.928
Riel's Rebellion, 1869–1870 971.051
Riel's Rebellion, 1885 971.054
Riemann hypothesis 512.73
Riemann integral 515.43
Riemann surfaces 515.93
Riemannian geometry 516.373
Riemannian manifolds 516.362
Riesz spaces 515.73
Rieti (Italy : Province) T2—456 24
  ancient T2—377 35
RIF (Layoff)
  economics 331.259 6
    employment security 331.259 6
    unemployment 331.137
  law 344.012 596
  personnel management 658.313 4
  public administration 352.69
Rif language 493.3
   T6—933
Rif Mountains (Morocco) T2—643 2
Riffle beetles 595.764 5
Rifle grenades 623.451 14
Rifles 683.422
  art metalwork 739.744 25
  manufacturing technology 683.422
  military engineering 623.442 5
  military equipment 355.824 25
  sports 799.202 832
Rift Valley fever
  incidence 614.588
  medicine 616.918

Rings (Jewelry)	391.72
customs	391.72
making	739.278 2
costume jewelry	688.2
handicrafts	745.594 2
fine jewelry	739.278 2
Rings (Mathematics)	512.4
number theory	512.74
Rings (Planets)	523.98
Ringworm	
medicine	616.579
see also Skin diseases —	
humans	
Rink bandy	796.963
Rink hockey	796.356 64
Rinks	
architecture	725.86
Rinzai	294.392 7
Rio Arriba County (N.M.)	T2—789 52
Rio Blanco County (Colo.)	T2—788 15
Rio Branco (Brazil :	
Territory)	T2—811 4
Rio de Janeiro (Brazil :	
State)	T2—815 3
Rio de la Plata (Argentina and	
Uruguay)	551.461 368
	T2—163 68
Río de la Plata (Viceroyalty)	982.024
	T2—82
Rio de Oro	T2—648
Rio Grande	T2—764 4
Colorado	T2—788 3
Mexico	T2—721
New Mexico	T2—789 6
Texas	T2—764 4
Rio Grande County (Colo.)	T2—788 37
Rio Grande do Norte	
(Brazil)	T2—813 2
Rio Grande do Sul (Brazil)	T2—816 5
Rio Grande Valley	T2—764 4
Rio Maputo	T2—684 2
Mozambique	T2—679 1
South Africa	T2—684 2
Río Muni	T2—671 83
Río Negro (Argentina)	T2—827 3
Río Negro (Uruguay)	T2—895 28
Río San Juan (Nicaragua)	T2—728 531
Rioja (Argentina : Province)	T2—824 6
Rioja (Spain)	T2—463 54
Ríos (Ecuador)	T2—866 33
Riot and civil commotion	
insurance	368.125
see also Insurance	
Riot control	363.323

Riot insurance	368.125
see also Insurance	
Rioting	364.143
law	345.024 3
Riots	303.623
political action	322.4
prisons	365.641
public safety	363.323
social conflict	303.623
social services	363.323
see also Disasters	
Riparian biology	578.768
Riparian ecology	577.68
Riparian rights	
law	346.043 2
Ripened cheeses	641.373 53
cooking	641.673 53
food	641.373 53
processing	637.353
Ripley County (Ind.)	T2—772 14
Ripley County (Mo.)	T2—778 894
Ripon, George Frederick Samuel	
Robinson, Marquess of	
Indian history	954.035 3
Risaralda (Colombia :	
Dept.)	T2—861 32
RISC (Computer science)	004.3
see also Processing modes —	
computer science	
Rishonim	296.180 92
Risk	
economics	338.5
insurance	368
Risk assessment	
natural resources	333.714
see Manual at 333.7–.9 vs.	
363.1, 363.73, 577	
public safety	363.102
social services	361.1
Risk capital	332.041 54
Risk factors	
medicine	616.071
Risk management	368
financial management	658.155
insurance	368
Risk of consequential loss	368.08
Risk perception	
social psychology	302.12
Risorgimento	945.083
Lombardian history	945.208 3
Piedmontese history	945.108 3
Venetian history	945.308 3
Ritavi (South Africa :	
District)	T2—682 59

Ritchie County (W. Va.)	T2—754 24
Rites	394
customs	394
magic	133.43
religion	203.8
African religions	299.613 8
Buddhism	294.343 8
Christianity	264
comparative religion	203.8
Hinduism	294.538
Islam	297.38
Judaism	296.45
music	782.3
witchcraft	133.43
see Manual at 392, 393, 394	
vs. 793.2	
Ritual bath	
Judaism	296.75
Ritual purity	
Islam	297.38
Judaism	
family purity	296.742
Ritual slaughter (Dietary laws)	204.46
Islam	297.576
Judaism	296.73
Rituale Romanum	264.025
Rituals	203.8
Rivas (Nicaragua : Dept.)	T2—728 517
River basins	
land economics	333.73
River beds	551.442
	T2—144
geography	910.914 4
geomorphology	551.442
physical geography	910.021 44
River boats	386.224 36
design	623.812 436
engineering	623.824 36
freight services	386.244
passenger services	386.242
transportation services	386.224 36
see also Ships	
River dogfishes	597.41
River dolphins	599.538
River ice	551.345
River mouths	
engineering	627.124
River Nile (Sudan)	T2—625
River otters	599.769 2
see also Otters (River otters)	
River police	363.287 2
River steamers	386.224 36
see also River boats	

River transportation	386.3
see also Inland water	
transportation	
Rivera (Uruguay : Dept.)	T2—895 34
Rivers	551.483
	T2—169 3
biology	578.764
ecology	577.64
geography	910.916 93
hydraulic engineering	627.12
hydrology	551.483
interactions with atmosphere	551.524 8
landscape architecture	714
law	346.046 916 2
law of nations	341.442
recreational resources	333.784 5
law	346.046 784 5
recreational use	797
resource economics	333.916 2
law	346.046 916 2
travel	910.916 93
water supply engineering	628.112
Rivers State (Nigeria)	T2—669 42
Riversdale (South Africa :	
District)	T2—687 37
Riverside County (Calif.)	979.497
	T2—794 97
Riverweeds	583.69
Riveting	671.59
decorative arts	739.14
sculpture	731.41
ship hulls	623.843 2
Riveting equipment	621.978
Rivets	621.884
Riviera	T2—449 4
France	T2—449 4
Italy	T2—451 8
Riviera (Switzerland)	T2—494 783
Riviera-Pays-d'Enhaut	
(Switzerland)	T2—494 524 7
Rivière-du-Loup (Quebec :	
Regional County	
Municipality)	T2—714 764
Rivière-du-Nord (Quebec)	T2—714 246
Rivne (Ukraine : Oblast)	T2—477 9
Rivnens′ka oblast′	
(Ukraine)	T2—477 9
Riwayah	297.125 16
Rizal (Philippines :	
Province)	T2—599 172
Rize İli (Turkey)	T2—566 22
ancient	T2—393 37
RML (Swiss political party)	324.249 407 5
RNA (Genetics)	572.88

RNA virus infections
animals
    veterinary medicine   636.089 691 8
humans
    incidence   614.588
    medicine   616.918
RNA viruses   579.25
Roach (Fish)   597.482
  sports fishing   799.174 82
Roaches   595.728
Road accidents   363.125
  see also Highway safety
Road camps (Correctional
  programs)   365.34
  see also Penal institutions
Road cycling   796.626
Road engineers   625.709 2
Road maintenance   625.761
Road maps   912
Road oils   665.538 8
Road rage   363.125 1
Road repair   625.761
Road running   796.425
  see also Track and field
Road safety   363.125
  see also Highway safety
Road tests
  automotive vehicles   629.282 4
Road transportation   388.31
  law   343.094
  public administration   354.77
  urban   388.413 1
Roadability tests
  automotive vehicles   629.282 5
Roadbeds
  railroad engineering   625.123
    interurban railroads   625.65
    local railroads   625.65
  road engineering   625.733
Roadrunners   598.74
Roads   388.1
  agricultural use   631.28
  area planning   711.7
  effect on natural ecology   577.272
  engineering   625.7
  forestry   634.93
  land economics   333.77
    acquisition and disposal   333.11
    urban land use   333.77
  landscape architecture   713
  law   343.094 2
  military engineering   623.62
  public administration   354.77
  transportation services   388.1

Roads (continued)
  urban   388.411
  use   388.314
    urban   388.413 14
Roadside areas   625.77
  road transportation   388.312
Roadside barriers   625.795
Roadside biology   578.755
Roadside ecology   577.55
Roadside shrines
  architecture   726.9
Roadside signs
  outdoor advertising   659.134 2
Roadsteads   387.1
  hydraulic engineering   627.22
  see also Ports
Roan antelope   599.645
Roane County (Tenn.)   T2—768 84
Roane County (W. Va.)   T2—754 36
Roanoke (Va.)   T2—755 791
Roanoke County (Va.)   T2—755 792
Roanoke Island (N.C.)   T2—756 175
Roanoke River (Va. and
  N.C.)   T2—756 16
  North Carolina   T2—756 16
  Virginia   T2—755 6
Roarers (Musical instruments)   783.99
Roasting
  home cooking   641.71
Robalos   597.72
Robben Island (South
  Africa)   T2—687 35
Robber flies   595.773
Robbery   364.155 2
  law   345.025 52
  social welfare   362.885
Robbery insurance   368.82
Robbery victims   362.885
Robert II, King of France
  French history   944.021
Robert-Cliche (Quebec)   T2—714 716
Roberts County (S.D.)   T2—783 12
Roberts County (Tex.)   T2—764 818
Robertson (South Africa :
  District)   T2—687 33
Robertson County (Ky.)   T2—769 415
Robertson County (Tenn.)   T2—768 464
Robertson County (Tex.)   T2—764 239
Robeson County (N.C.)   T2—756 332
Robins   598.842
Robinson Gorge National
  Park (Qld.)   T2—943 5
Robot hands   629.893 3
Robotics   629.892

Rocky Mountain spotted fever
incidence — 614.526 3
medicine — 616.922 3
see also Communicable
diseases — humans
Rocky Mountain Trench
(B.C. and Mont.) — T2—711
Rocky Mountains — T2—78
Alberta — T2—712 33
British Columbia — T2—711
Canada — T2—711
Colorado — T2—788
Montana — T2—786 5
New Mexico — T2—789 5
United States — T2—78
Utah — T2—792 2
Wyoming — T2—787 2
Rococo architecture — 724.19
Rococo art — 709.033 2
Rococo decoration — 744.090 33
Rococo music — 780.903 3
Rococo painting — 759.047
Rodent control — 363.78
see also Rodents — pest
control
Rodent-resistant construction — 693.844
Rodentia — 599.35
see also Rodents
Rodenticides — 632.951
agricultural use — 632.951
chemical engineering — 668.651
Rodents — 599.35
animal husbandry — 636.935
disease carriers — 571.986
medicine — 614.438
experimental animals
medicine — 616.027 33
paleozoology — 569.35
pest control — 363.78
social welfare — 363.78
technology — 628.969 3
agriculture — 632.693 5
home economics — 648.7
see also Rodent control
zoology — 599.35
Rodeos — 791.84
Rodney District (N.Z.) — T2—932 1
Rodopē (Greece) — T2—495 7
Rodopi Mountains — T2—499 7
Rodos (Greece : Regional
unit) — T2—495 87
Rodrigues Island
(Mauritius) — T2—698 2

Rodríguez, Abelardo L.
(Abelardo Luján)
Mexican history — 972.082 44
Rodríguez, Andrés
Paraguayan history — 989.207 41
Rodríguez, Miguel Angel
Costa Rican history — 972.860 524
Rods (Musical instruments) — 786.82
concussed — 786.872
friction — 786.862
set — 786.862
single — 786.888
percussed — 786.842
set — 786.842
single — 786.884 2
plucked — 786.85
set — 786.85
single — 786.887
see also Percussion instruments
Rods (Structural elements) — 624.177 4
Roe deer — 599.659
Roentgenium
chemistry — 546.65
Roentgenology
medicine — 616.075 72
Rogaland fylke (Norway) — T2—483 4
Roger Mills County (Okla.) — T2—766 16
Rogers County (Okla.) — T2—766 94
Roggeveld Range (South
Africa) — T2—687 17
Rogue River (Or.) — T2—795 21
Role and reference grammar — 415.018 34
specific languages — T4—501 834
Role conflict — 302.15
Role playing
psychiatry — 616.891 523
Role-playing games — 793.93
computerized games — 793.93
Role theory — 302.15
Rolette County (N.D.) — T2—784 592
Rolfing
therapeutics — 615.822
Roll (Aeronautics) — 629.132 364
Roll on/roll off shipping — 387.544 2
Roller bearings — 621.822
Roller hockey — 796.356 6
Roller painting — 751.49
Roller skates
manufacturing technology — 688.762 1
Roller skating — 796.21
see also Sports
Rollerblading — 796.21
Rollers (Agricultural tools)
manufacturing technology — 681.763 1

Roman Empire (continued)
  Spanish history   936.603
  Swiss history   936.940 2
  Tunisian history   939.730 3
  Welsh history   936.290 4
Roman Kingdom   937.01
     T2—37
Roman law   340.54
  medieval period   340.55
Roman philosophy   180.937
Roman question   945.084
Roman religion   292.07
Roman Republic   937.02
     T2—37
Roman revival architecture   724.22
Roman sculpture   733.5
Romana (Dominican
     Republic : Province)   T2—729 383
Romance language literatures   840
Romance languages   440
     T6—4
Romances (Music)   784.189 68
Romances (Prose)   808.83
  history and criticism   809.3
  medieval   808.83
    history and criticism   809.3
    specific literatures   T3B—3
      individual authors   T3A—3
  modern   808.838 5
    history and criticism   809.385
    specific literatures   T3B—308 5
      individual authors   T3A—3
Romances (Verse)   808.813 3
  history and criticism   809.133
  specific literatures   T3B—103 3
    individual authors   T3A—1
Romanesque architecture   723.4
Romanesque art   709.021 6
  religious significance   246.2
Romanesque decoration   744.090 21
Romanesque painting   759.021 6
Romanesque revival architecture   724.52
Romanesque sculpture   734.24
Romani language   491.497
     T6—914 97
Romani literature   891.497
Romania   949.8
     T2—498
  ancient   939.88
     T2—398 8
Romanian language   459
     T6—591
Romanian literature   859
Romanian Orthodox Church   281.949 8

Romanians   T5—591
Romanies   305.891 497
     T5—914 97
  Holocaust, 1933–1945   940.531 808 991 497
Romanov, House of   947.046
  genealogy   929.77
Romans (Ancient people)   T5—71
Romans (Biblical book)   227.1
Romansch   T5—599 6
Romansch language   459.96
     T6—599 6
Romansch literature   859.96
Romansh   T5—599 6
Romansh language   459.96
     T6—599 6
Romansh literature   859.96
Romantic fiction   808.838 5
  history and criticism   809.385
  specific literatures   T3B—308 5
    individual authors   T3A—3
Romanticism
  arts   700.414 5
     T3C—145
  decoration   744.090 34
  fine arts   709.034 2
  literature   808.801 45
    history and criticism   809.914 5
    specific literatures   T3B—080 145
      history and
        criticism   T3B—091 45
  music   780.903 4
  painting   759.052
  philosophy   141.6
  sculpture   735.22
Romany language   491.497
     T6—914 97
Romany law   340.520 899 149 7
Romany literature   891.497
Romany people   305.891 497
     T5—914 97
  Holocaust, 1933–1945   940.531 808 991 497
  religion
    Christianity
      pastoral theology   259.089 914 97
  social aspects   305.891 497
Romblon (Philippines :
  Province)   T2—599 52
Rome (Italy)   T2—456 32
  ancient   T2—37
     T2—376 3

Rome Capital (Italy :	
Metropolitan city)	T2—456 3
ancient	T2—376 3
Etruria	T2—375 9
Latium	T2—376 3
Rommelpots	786.98
see also Percussion instruments	
Ronde bosse	
ceramic arts	738.4
Rondônia (Brazil : State)	T2—811 1
Rondos	781.824
instrumental	784.182 4
Ronga language	496.397 8
	T6—963 978
Rood screens	247.1
architecture	726.529 6
Roodepoort (South Africa :	
District)	T2—682 21
Roof failure (Mining)	622.28
Roof furniture	645.8
see also Outdoor furniture	
Roof gardening	635.967 1
Roofers	695.092
Roofing	695
Roofing paper	676.289
Roofing tiles	666.732
Roofs	721.5
architecture	721.5
construction	690.15
Rooks (Birds)	598.864
Rooks (Chessmen)	794.143
Rooks County (Kan.)	T2—781 18
Rooming houses	910.464
see also Lodging (Temporary	
housing)	
Roosevelt, Franklin D. (Franklin	
Delano)	
United States history	973.917
Roosevelt, Theodore	
United States history	973.911
Roosevelt County (Mont.)	T2—786 22
Roosevelt County (N.M.)	T2—789 32
Root canal surgery	617.634 205 9
Root celery	641.351 28
see also Celeriac	
Root crops	635.1
agriculture	635.1
cooking	641.651
food	641.351
Root extraction (Mathematics)	512.923
arithmetic	513.23
Rootkits	005.88
Roots (Mathematics)	
number theory	512.72
Roots (Plants)	581.498
descriptive botany	581.498
physiology	575.54
Rope climbing	796.46
Roper River (N.T.)	T2—942 95
Ropes	677.71
knotting and splicing	623.888 2
materials science	620.197
power transmission	621.853
sculpture material	731.2
ship gear	623.862
structural engineering	624.189 7
Ropes (Gymnastic equipment)	796.443
Roraima (Brazil)	T2—811 4
Rorquals	599.524
Rorschach (Switzerland :	
Wahlkreis)	T2—494 722
Rorschach personality theory	155.264
Rorschach tests	155.284 2
Rosa (Plant)	583.644
Rosales	583.64
Rosary	242.74
Roscher, Wilhelm	
economic school	330.154 2
Roscommon (Ireland :	
County)	T2—417 5
Roscommon County (Mich.)	T2—774 76
Rose apples	583.732
Rose of Sharon (Malvaceae)	635.933 775
botany	583.775
floriculture	635.933 775
Rosé wine	641.222 32
commercial processing	663.223 2
Roseau County (Minn.)	T2—776 98
Rosebud County (Mont.)	T2—786 32
Rosefinches	598.885
Rosellas (Birds)	598.71
Rosemaling	745.723
Rosemary	641.357
botany	583.96
see also Herbs	
Roses	635.933 644
botany	583.644
floriculture	635.933 644
Roses, Wars of the, 1455–1485	942.04
Rosetta stone	493.1
Rosh Hashanah (Holy day)	296.431 5
customs	394.267
liturgy	296.453 15
Rosh Hashanah (Tractate)	296.123 2
Babylonian Talmud	296.125 2
Mishnah	296.123 2
Palestinian Talmud	296.124 2
Rosicrucianism	135.43

Rosicrucians	135.430 92
Rosidae	583.6
Rosids	583.6
Roskilde amt (Denmark)	T2—489 12
Ross and Cromarty (Scotland)	T2—411 56
Ross County (Ohio)	T2—771 82
Ross-on-Wye (England)	T2—424 2
Ross Sea (Antarctic regions)	551.461 74
	T2—167 4
Ross seal	599.796
Rossendale (England)	T2—427 63
Rossland (B.C.)	T2—711 62
Rostock (Germany)	T2—431 745
Rostock (Germany : Bezirk)	T2—431 74
Rostov (Russia : Oblast)	T2—474 9
Rostovskaĩa oblast′ (Russia)	T2—474 9
Rostral furniture	
church architecture	726.529 2
Rot	
agriculture	632.4
materials science	620.112 23
Rotary blowers	621.62
Rotary fans	621.62
Rotary files (Records management)	651.54
Rotary International	369.52
biography	369.520 92
Rotary pumps	621.66
hydraulic	621.252
Rotation	
celestial bodies	521
earth	525.35
sun	523.73
Rotation groups	512.2
Rotation of crops	
cultivation technique	631.582
economics	338.162
soil conservation	631.452
Rotational motion	531.113
classical mechanics	531.113
fluid mechanics	532.059 5
gas mechanics	533.295
liquid mechanics	532.595
solid bodies	531.34
ROTC (Reserve training)	355.223 207 1173
Rote learning	
education	371.39
psychology	153.152 2
Rother (England)	T2—422 52
Rotherham (England : Metropolitan Borough)	T2—428 23
Rotifera	592.52
Rotifers	592.52

Rotis	641.84
Rotisserie sports	794.9
Rotor ships	387.22
engineering	623.822
transportation services	387.22
see also Ships	
Rotorcraft	387.733 52
engineering	629.133 352
military engineering	623.746 047 2
transportation services	387.733 52
Rotors	
aircraft	629.134 36
machine engineering	621.82
Rotorua District (N.Z.)	T2—934 23
Bay of Plenty Region	T2—934 23
Waikato Region	T2—933 67
Rotterdam (Netherlands)	T2—492 385
Rottweiler	636.73
Rouen (France)	T2—442 52
Rouergue (France)	T2—447 4
Rough carpentry	694.2
Rough lumber	674.28
Roughness	
materials science	620.112 92
Roughy (Trachichthyidae)	597.64
Rouhani, Hassan	
Iranian history	955.062
Roulette	795.23
Roumania	949.8
	T2—498
ancient	939.88
	T2—398 8
Round-backed lutes	787.82
see also Stringed instruments	
Round dances	793.33
Roundabouts (Traffic circles)	388.13
area planning	711.7
engineering	625.7
transportation services	388.13
urban	388.411
Roundhouses	385.314
architecture	725.33
Roundworm-caused diseases	
humans	
incidence	614.555
medicine	616.965
see also Communicable diseases — humans	
Roundworms	592.57
Rousseff, Dilma	
Brazilian history	981.066
Roussillon (France : Province)	T2—448 9
Roussillon (Quebec)	T2—714 34

Routers (Computer networks)	004.645	Royal office of Jesus Christ	232.8
Routers (Woodworking tools)		Royal tennis	796.34
use in home woodworking	684.083 12	Royalty	305.522
Routes			T1—086 21
air	387.72	customs	390.22
bus	388.322 1	dress	391.022
urban	388.413 22	folklore	398.22
maritime	387.52	history and criticism	398.352
truck	388.324 2	genealogy	929.7
urban	388.413 24	social group	305.522
Routing		RSFSR (Russia)	947
production management	658.53		T2—47
transportation	388.041	RSS feeds	006.787 6
see also Scheduling —		RTLS (Real-time locating	
transportation		systems)	910.285
Routing (Computer networks)	004.665		T1—028 5
	621.382 16	engineering	621.384 192
communications engineering	621.382 16	RU486 (Drug)	
Routt County (Colo.)	T2—788 14	medicine	618.29
Rouville (Quebec)	T2—714 53	pharmacokinetics	615.766
Rouville (Quebec : Regional		Rúa, Fernando de la	
County Municipality)	T2—714 53	Argentine history	982.071
Rouxville (South Africa :		Ruanda language	496.394 61
District)	T2—685 7		T6—963 946 1
Rouyn-Noranda (Quebec)	T2—714 136	Ruanda literature	896.394 61
Rove beetles	595.764 2	Ruanda-Rundi languages	496.394 6
Rover Scouts	369.435		T6—963 946
Rovigo (Italy : Province)	T2—453 3	Ruanda-Urundi	967.570 3
ancient	T2—373 3		T2—675 7
Row houses		Ruapehu District (N.Z.)	T2—935 2
architecture	728.312	Rub'al-Khali	T2—538
Rowan County (Ky.)	T2—769 57	Rubato	781.46
Rowan County (N.C.)	T2—756 71	Rubber	678.2
Rowan trees	583.642	chemistry	547.842 6
Rowboat racing	797.14	handicrafts	745.57
Rowboats	386.229	materials science	620.194
design	623.812 9	shipbuilding	623.820 7
engineering	623.829	structural engineering	624.189 4
transportation services	386.229	Rubber bands	678.35
Rowing		Rubber hydrochloride	678.68
sports	797.123	Rubber industry workers	678.209 2
see also Aquatic sports		Rubber plant (Ficus)	635.933 648
Roxas, Manuel		botany	583.648
Philippine history	959.904 1	floriculture	635.933 648
Roxburgh (Scotland :		rubber crop	633.895
District)	T2—413 7	*see also* Ficus elastica; India	
Royal commissions	352.743	rubber tree	
Royal fern	587.3	Rubber products	678.3
Royal houses		Rubber-stamp printing	761
genealogy	929.7	Rubber stamps	
Royal Natal National Park		manufacturing technology	681.6
(South Africa)	T2—684 9	Rubber tree (Hevea)	633.895 2
Royal National Park		botany	583.69
(N.S.W.)	T2—944 6	rubber crop	633.895 2

Rubbings
  graphic arts 740
  research technique 739.522
Rubella
  incidence 614.524
  medicine 616.916
    see also Communicable
      diseases — humans
  pediatrics 618.929 16
Rubeola
  incidence 614.523
  medicine 616.915
    see also Communicable
      diseases — humans
  pediatrics 618.929 15
Rubiaceae 583.956
Rubidium 669.725
  chemical engineering 661.038 4
  chemistry 546.384
  metallurgy 669.725
    see also Chemicals
Rubies 553.84
  economic geology 553.84
  jewelry 739.27
  mining 622.384
  synthetic 666.88
Rubus 583.642
Rubus berries 641.347 1
  botany 583.642
    see also Cane fruits
Rudd, Kevin
  Australian history 994.072
Rudders 623.862
  aircraft 629.134 33
Rudolf, Lake (Kenya and
  Ethiopia) T2—676 276
Rudolf II, Holy Roman Emperor
  German history 943.034
Rues (Plants) 583.75
Ruffed grouse 598.635
  sports hunting 799.246 35
Rugby 796.333
  biography 796.333 092
    see also Ball games
Rugby (England : Borough) T2—424 85
Rugby League 796.333 8
Rugby players 796.333 092
Rugby Union 796.333
Rügen (Germany :
  Landkreis) T2—431 78
Rugs 645.12
  arts 746.7
  building construction 698.9
  household management 645.12

Rugs (continued)
  interior decoration 747.5
  manufacturing technology 677.643
    nonwoven felts 677.632
Ruhr River (Germany) T2—435 5
Ruiz Cortines, Adolfo
  Mexican history 972.082 8
Rukwa Region (Tanzania) T2—678 28
Rule-based programming 005.115
Rule of law 340.11
Rule of the road at sea
  law 343.096 6
  seamanship 623.888 4
Ruled surfaces 516.362
Rules committees (Legislatures) 328.365 8
Rules of order 060.42
  legislatures 328.1
    committees 328.365 3
Rum 641.259
  commercial processing 663.59
Rum, Isle of (Scotland) T2—411 54
Rumania 949.8
  T2—498
  ancient 939.88
    T2—398 8
Rumanians T5—591
Rumbas 793.33
  music 784.188 8
Ruminants 599.63
  animal husbandry 636.2
  paleozoology 569.63
Rummage sales 381.195
Rummy 795.418
Rumor
  social psychology 302.24
Runaway children 305.230 869 23
  T1—086 923
  social group 305.230 869 23
  social welfare 362.74
Rundi (African people) T5—963 946 5
Rundi language 496.394 65
  T6—963 946 5
Rundi literature 896.394 65
Runes 430
  divination 133.33
  Proto-Scandinavian language 439.5
Runge-Kutta method 518.63
Runnels County (Tex.) T2—764 724
Runners (Athletes) 796.420 92
Runners (Stolons) 581.46
  agricultural propagation 631.533
  descriptive botany 581.46
  physiology 575.499

Russian Orthodox Church
  Outside Russia   281.947
Russian Revolution, 1905   947.083
Russian Revolution, 1917   947.084 1
Russian Soviet Federated
  Socialist Republic   947
                     T2—47
Russian turnip   641.351 26
  see also Rutabagas
Russians   T5—917 1
Russo-Finnish War, 1939–1940   948.970 32
Russo-Japanese War, 1904–1905   952.031
Russo-Turkish War, 1877–1878   949.603 87
Rust
  materials science   620.112 23
Rust diseases
  agriculture   632.492
Rust flies   595.774
Rust fungi   579.592
Rust-resistant paints   667.69
Rustenburg (South Africa :
  District)   T2—682 41
Rustling   364.162 863 62
  law   345.026 286 362
Rusts (Fungi)   579.592
  agricultural diseases   632.492
Rutabagas   641.351 26
  botany   583.78
  commercial processing   664.805 126
  cooking   641.651 26
  food   641.351 26
  garden crop   635.126
  see also Russian turnip;
    Swedes (Plants); Swedish
    turnip
Ruth (Biblical book)   222.35
Ruth Segomotsi Mompati
  District Municipality
  (South Africa)   T2—682 46
Ruthenians (Ethnic group)   T5—917 91
Ruthenium   669.7
  chemical engineering   661.063 2
  chemistry   546.632
  metallography   669.957
  metallurgy   669.7
  physical metallurgy   669.967
  see also Chemicals
Rutherford County (N.C.)   T2—756 913
Rutherford County (Tenn.)   T2—768 57
Rutherfordium
  chemistry   546.51
Rutherglen (Scotland)   T2—414 57
Rutherglen (Vic.)   T2—945 5

Rutile
  mineralogy   549.524
Rutland (England)   T2—425 45
Rutland County (Vt.)   T2—743 7
Ruto, William
  Kenyan history   967.620 45
Ruvuma Region (Tanzania)   T2—678 25
RV (Vehicle)   388.346
  engineering   629.226
  see also Motor homes
RV camps   910.468
  household management   647.942
  see also Lodging (Temporary
    housing)
Rwanda   967.571
                T2—675 71
Rwanda language   496.394 61
                T6—963 946 1
Rwanda literature   896.394 61
Rwanda-Rundi languages   496.394 6
                T6—963 946
Rwandans   T5—967 571
Ryazan (Russia : Oblast)   T2—473 3
Rye   641.331 4
  botany   584.926
  commercial processing   664.72
  cooking   641.631 4
  food   641.331 4
  food crop   633.14
  forage crop   633.254
Rye-free cooking   641.563 931 4
Rye-free diet
  health   613.268 314
Rye-free foods   641.309 314
Ryedale (England)   T2—428 46
Rynchopidae   598.338
Ryukyu Islands   T2—522 9
Ryukyuans   T5—956
Rzeszów (Poland :
  Voivodeship)   T2—438 66

S

's-Gravenhage
  (Netherlands)   T2—492 382
Saale-Holzlandkreis
  (Germany : Landkreis)   T2—432 22
Saale-Orla-Kreis
  (Germany : Landkreis)   T2—432 22
Saale River (Germany)   T2—431 84
Saalfeld-Rudolstadt
  (Germany : Landkreis)   T2—432 22
Saam languages   494.57
                T6—945 7

Saami (European people)	T5—945 7	Sac language	497.314 9
Saami languages	494.57		T6—973 149
	T6—945 7	Saca, Elías Antonio	
Saami literatures	894.57	Salvadoran history	972.840 543
Saane (Switzerland)	T2—494 535	Sacatepéquez (Guatemala)	T2—728 162
Saanich (B.C.)	T2—711 28	Saccharides	572.56
Saanich Peninsula (B.C.)	T2—711 28	*see also* Carbohydrates	
Saar River (France and		Saccharolytic enzymes	572.756
Germany)	T2—434 2	*see also* Enzymes	
Saarbrücken (Germany)	T2—434 21	Saccharomyces	579.563
Saarbrücken (Germany :		Saccharomycetaceae	579.562
Regionalverband)	T2—434 21	Saccopharyngidae	597.43
Saarbrücken (Germany :		Saccorhiza	579.887
Stadtverband)	T2—434 21	Sachs Harbour (N.W.T.)	T2—719 3
Saarland (Germany)	T2—434 2	Sachsen (Germany)	T2—432 1
Saba (Netherlands Antilles)	T2—729 77	Sachsen-Anhalt (Germany)	T2—431 8
Sabab (Islamic law)	340.591 2	Sackville (N.B.)	T2—715 23
Sabah	T2—595 3	Sacoglossa	594.35
Sabbath	296.41	Sacramental furniture	247.1
Christianity	263.1	architecture	726.529 1
Judaism	296.41	Sacramentals	264.9
Sabbatianism	296.82	Sacramentaries	
Sabbatical leave	331.257 6	Roman Catholic	264.020 36
education	371.104	texts	264.023
higher education	378.121	Sacramento (Calif.)	T2—794 54
personnel management	658.312 2	Sacramento County (Calif.)	T2—794 53
Sabbatical Year (Judaism)	296.439 1	Sacramento Mountains	
Sabellian languages	479.7	(N.M.)	T2—789 65
	T6—797	Sacramento River (Calif.)	T2—794 5
Sabellian literatures	879.7	Sacraments	234.16
Sabellianism	273.3	public worship	265
Sabers	623.441 3	Anglican	264.030 8
art metalwork	739.722	texts	264.035
Sabiaceae	583.37	Roman Catholic	264.020 8
Sabie River (South Africa)	T2—682 73	texts	264.025
Sabina (Italy : Region)	T2—456 24	theology	234.16
ancient	T2—377 35	Sacred books	208.2
Sabine County (Tex.)	T2—764 177	Buddhism	294.382
Sabine Lake (La. and Tex.)	T2—763 52	Christianity	220
Sabine language	479.7	Latter Day Saint movement	289.32
	T6—797	Hinduism	294.592
Sabine Parish (La.)	T2—763 62	Islam	297.122
Sabine River (Tex. and La.)	T2—764 14	Jainism	294.482
Sable (Carnivorous mammal)	599.766 5	Judaism	296.1
Sable antelope	599.645	Bible	221
Sable Island (N.S.)	T2—716 99	*see Manual at* 221	
Sabotage	364.164	*see Manual at* 200 vs. 130	
armed forces	355.343 7	Sacred Heart religious orders	255.93
see also Unconventional		church history	271.93
warfare		Sacred music	781.7
labor economics	331.893	public worship	203.8
law	345.026 4	religious significance	203.7
Sabrata (Extinct city)	T2—397 4	*see also* Music — religion	
Sac County (Iowa)	T2—777 424		

Sacred music (continued)	
vocal forms	782.22
choral and mixed voices	782.522
instrumental forms	784.189 92
single voices	783.092 2
Sacred places	203.5
Buddhist	294.343 5
Christianity	263.042
Jerusalem	263.042 569 442
Hindu	294.535
Islam	297.35
Jerusalem	297.355 694 42
Mecca (Saudi Arabia)	297.352
Medina (Saudi Arabia)	297.355 38
Jain	294.435
Judaism	296.48
Jerusalem	296.482
public worship	203.8
Sikh	294.635
Sacred songs	782.25
choral and mixed voices	782.525
single voices	783.092 5
Sacred vocal music	782.22
Sacrifice of Jesus Christ	232.4
Sacrifices (Religion)	203.4
Judaism	296.492
Sacrilege	
criminology	364.188
law	345.028 8
Sacristies	
architecture	726.596
Ṣadaqah	297.54
Sadat, Anwar	
Egyptian history	962.054
Saddle block anesthesia	
surgery	617.964
Saddle fungi	579.578
Saddle horses	636.13
Saddlers	685.109 2
Saddlery	636.108 37
animal husbandry	636.083 7
horse rearing	636.108 37
manufacturing technology	685.1
Sadducees	296.813
Sadism	
medicine	616.858 35
see also Mental disorders	
sociology	306.775
Sadness	152.4
Sadomasochism	
medicine	616.858 35
see also Mental disorders	
sociology	306.775

Safari lodges	910.462
see also Resorts	
Safe-deposit services	332.178
Safes	683.34
Safety	363.1
law	344.047
management	658.408
	T1—068 4
personal safety	613.6
	T1—028 9
personnel management	658.382
public administration	352.67
public administration	353.9
social services	363.1
see Manual at 363 vs.	
302–307, 333.7, 570–590,	
600; *also at* 363.1	
Safety engineering	620.86
	T1—028 9
automotive	629.204 2
design	629.231
construction	690.22
military	623.75
roads	625.702 89
transportation	629.040 289
Safety equipment	
aircraft	629.134 43
automobile	629.276
plant management	658.28
ships	623.865
tool engineering	621.992
Safety management	658.408
	T1—068 4
Safety regulations	363.1
public administration	353.9
see Manual at 363.1; *also at*	
363.1 vs. 600	
Safety training	
personnel management	658.312 44
public administration	352.669
Safety valves	
steam engineering	621.185
Safflower	583.983
Saffron (Spice)	641.338 3
agriculture	633.83
botany	584.75
food	641.338 3
Safi (Morocco : Province)	T2—646 2
Safwa language	496.391
	T6—963 91
Saga-ken (Japan)	T2—522 3
Sagadahoc County (Me.)	T2—741 85
Sagarmāthā National Park (Nepal)	T2—549 61

Saint Gall (Switzerland : Canton)	T2—494 72
Saint Gall (Switzerland : Wahlkreis)	T2—494 723
Saint George's Channel (Ireland and Wales)	551.461 337
	T2—163 37
Saint Helena	997.3
	T2—973
Saint Helena Parish (La.)	T2—763 15
Saint James Parish (La.)	T2—763 31
Saint-Jean (Quebec : County)	T2—714 38
Saint John (N.B. : County)	T2—715 32
Saint John (V.I.)	T2—729 722
Saint John River (Me. and N.B.)	T2—715 5
Saint John the Baptist Parish (La.)	T2—763 32
Saint Johns River (Fla.)	T2—759 1
Saint Joseph County (Ind.)	T2—772 89
Saint Joseph County (Mich.)	T2—774 19
Saint Joseph religious orders	255.976
church history	271.976
Saint Kitts	T2—729 73
Saint Kitts-Nevis	972.973
	T2—729 73
Saint Kitts-Nevis-Anguilla	T2—729 73
Saint-Lambert (Quebec)	T2—714 37
Saint Landry Parish (La.)	T2—763 46
Saint-Laurent, Louis Stephen Canadian history	971.063 3
Saint-Laurent du Maroni (French Guiana)	T2—882
Saint Lawrence, Gulf of	551.461 344
	T2—163 44
Saint Lawrence County (N.Y.)	T2—747 56
Saint Lawrence River	T2—714
New York	T2—747 56
Ontario	T2—713 7
Quebec	T2—714
Saint Lawrence Seaway	386.509 714
	T2—714
Ontario	T2—713 7
Quebec	T2—714
Saint Louis (Mo.)	T2—778 66
Saint-Louis (Senegal : Region)	T2—663
Saint Louis County (Minn.)	T2—776 77
Saint Louis County (Mo.)	T2—778 65
Saint Lucia	972.984 3
	T2—729 843
Saint Lucie County (Fla.)	T2—759 29

Saint Martin	972.978
	T2—729 78
French West Indies	T2—729 78
Netherlands Antilles	T2—729 77
Saint Martin (Collectivity)	T2—729 78
Saint Martin Parish (La.)	T2—763 48
Saint Mary Parish (La.)	T2—763 42
Saint Marys, Lake (Ohio)	T2—771 415
Saint Mary's County (Md.)	T2—752 41
Saint Marys River (Ga. and Fla.)	T2—759 11
Saint Marys River (Mich. and Ont.)	T2—774 91
Saint-Maurice (Switzerland : District)	T2—494 796 8
Saint-Maurice River (Quebec)	T2—714 45
Saint Paul (Minn.)	T2—776 581
Saint Paul Island	969.9
	T2—699
Saint Petersburg (Russia)	T2—472 1
Saint Pierre and Miquelon	971.88
	T2—718 8
Saint-Simonism (Socialist school)	335.22
Saint Tammany Parish (La.)	T2—763 12
Saint Thomas (V.I.)	T2—729 722
Saint Thomas Christian churches	281.54
doctrines	230.154
catechisms and creeds	238.154
theology	230.154
see also Eastern churches	
Saint Thomas Evangelical Church of India	281.54
see also Eastern churches	
Saint Vincent	T2—729 844
Saint Vincent and the Grenadines	972.984 4
	T2—729 844
Sainte-Anne-de-Bellevue (Quebec)	T2—714 28
Sainte Genevieve County (Mo.)	T2—778 692
Saintes Islands (Guadeloupe)	T2—729 76
Saintonge (France)	T2—446 4
Saints	200.92
art representation	704.948 63
arts	T3C—382
biography	200.92
Christian	270.092
biography	270.092
specific denominations	280
see Manual at 230–280	
doctrines	235.2

Salesmen	381.092	Salmo salar	597.56
personnel management	658.304 4	Salmon	641.392
training	658.312 45	commercial fishing	639.275 6
Salford (England : City)	T2—427 32	conservation technology	639.977 56
Salian emperors		cooking	641.692
German history	943.023	culture	639.375 6
Salicaceae	583.69	economics	338.371 375 6
Salicales	583.69	food	641.392
Salientia	597.8	resource economics	333.956 56
Salinas de Gortari, Carlos		sports fishing	799.175 6
Mexican history	972.083 5	zoology	597.56
Salinas River (Calif.)	T2—794 76	Salmon Arm (B.C.)	T2—711 68
Saline County (Ark.)	T2—767 72	Salmon River (Idaho)	T2—796 82
Saline County (Ill.)	T2—773 992	Salmon River Mountains	
Saline County (Kan.)	T2—781 545	(Idaho)	T2—796 7
Saline County (Mo.)	T2—778 47	Salmonella	579.344
Saline County (Neb.)	T2—782 327	Salmonella diseases	571.993 44
Saline water	553.72	*see also* Salmonella infections	
Saline water conversion		Salmonella infections	571.993 44
water supply engineering	628.167	animals	571.993 44
Salinity		veterinary medicine	636.089 692 7
sea water	551.466 4	humans	362.196 927
soil science	631.416	incidence	614.511
Salisbury (S. Aust.)	T2—942 32	medicine	616.927
Salisbury Island (Nunavut)	T2—719 52	social services	362.196 927
Salisbury Plain (England)	T2—423 1	*see also* Communicable	
Salish Indians	978.600 497 943 5	diseases	
	T5—979 435	Salmonidae	597.55
Salish language	497.943 5	conservation technology	639.977 55
	T6—979 435	culture	639.375 5
Salishan Indians	979.700 497 94	resource economics	333.956 55
	T5—979 4	sports fishing	799.175 5
Salishan languages	497.94	Salmoniformes	597.5
	T6—979 4	paleozoology	567.5
Saliva	573.353 79	Salon orchestras	784.4
human physiology	612.313	Salop (England)	T2—424 5
see also Digestive system		Salpingitis	
Salivan languages	498.9	gynecology	618.12
	T6—989	*see also* Female genital	
Salivary gland diseases		diseases — humans	
medicine	616.316	Salsify	641.351 6
see also Digestive system		botany	583.983
diseases — humans		cooking	641.651 6
Salivary glands	573.353 79	food	641.351 6
biology	573.353 79	garden crop	635.16
human anatomy	611.316	Salt (Sodium chloride)	553.632
human physiology	612.313	applied nutrition	613.285 22
medicine	616.316	biochemistry	572.523 822 4
see also Digestive system		humans	612.015 24
Salix	583.69	chemistry	546.382 24
Sall, Macky		cooking with	641.6
Senegalese history	966.305 3	economic geology	553.632
Salliq (Nunavut)	T2—719 58	food technology	664.4
Salmo	597.57		

Salt (Sodium chloride) (continued)
- metabolism — 572.523 822 4
  - human physiology — 612.392 6
- mineralogy — 549.4
- mining — 622.363 2
- Salt-free cooking — 641.563 23
- Salt-free diet
  - health — 613.285 223
- Salt Lake City (Utah) — T2—792 258
- Salt Lake County (Utah) — T2—792 25
- Salt lakes — 551.482 9
  - biology — 578.763 9
  - ecology — 577.639
  - resource economics — 333.916 4
- Salt marshes
  - biology — 578.769
  - ecology — 577.69
- Salta (Argentina : Province) — T2—824 2
- Saltarellos — 793.319 45
  - music — 784.188 2
- Salto (Uruguay : Dept.) — T2—895 35
- Salton Sea (Calif.) — T2—794 99
- Saltpeter — 553.64
  - economic geology — 553.64
  - mineralogy — 549.732
- Salts — 546.34
  - biochemistry — 572.51
  - chemical engineering — 661.4
  - chemistry — 546.34
  - economic geology — 553.63
  - metabolism — 572.51
    - human physiology — 612.392 6
  - see also Chemicals; Salt (Sodium chloride)
- Saltwater biology — 578.77
- Saltwater desalinization — 628.167
- Saltwater ecology — 577.7
- Saltwater fishes — 597.177
  - culture — 639.32
  - see also Fishes
- Saltwater fishing — 639.22
  - commercial — 639.22
  - sports — 799.16
- Saltwater intrusion — 363.738
  - engineering — 628.114
  - social problem — 363.738
  - see also Pollution
- Saltwater lagoons — 551.461 8 / T2—168
  - biology — 578.778
  - ecology — 577.78
- Saltwater wetlands
  - biology — 578.769
  - ecology — 577.69

Saluda County (S.C.) — T2—757 38
Saluki — 636.753 2
Salvador, El — 972.84 / T2—728 4
- see also El Salvador
Salvadoran literature — 860
Salvadorans — T5—687 284
Salvage operations
- disaster relief — 363.348 1
- maritime law — 343.096 8
- maritime transportation — 387.55
- underwater engineering — 627.703
Salvation — 202.2
- Christianity — 234
- Islam — 297.22
- Judaism — 296.32
Salvation Army — 287.96
- see also Christian denominations
Salvator Rosa National Park (Qld.) — T2—943 5
Salvelinus — 597.554
Salviniales — 587.3
Salzburg (Austria) — T2—436 32
Salzburg (Austria : Land) — T2—436 3
Samaná (Dominican Republic : Province) — T2—729 365
Samar (Philippines) — T2—599 584
Samar Island (Philippines) — T2—599 584
Samara (Russia : Oblast) — T2—474 4
Samaria — T2—332
Samaritan Aramaic language — 492.29 / T6—922 9
Samaritan language — 492.29 / T6—922 9
- Biblical texts — 220.45
Samaritan literature — 892.29
Samaritans (Judaism) — 296.817
Samarium
- chemistry — 546.415
Samarskaĭa oblast' (Russia) — T2—474 4
Samaveda — 294.592 13
Samba (Game) — 795.418
Sambalic languages — 499.21 / T6—992 1
Sambar — 599.654
Sambas — 793.33
- music — 784.188 8
Samburu County (Kenya) — T2—676 275 7
Samburu language — 496.552 2 / T6—965 522
Same languages — 494.57 / T6—945 7
Same literatures — 894.57

Same-sex marriage	306.848	San Antonio (Tex.)	976.435 1
law	346.016 8		T2—764 351
Same-sex unions	306.848	San Antonio River (Tex.)	T2—764 12
law	346.016 8	San Augustine County	
Samhitas	294.592 1	(Tex.)	T2—764 175
Sámi (European people)	948.004 945 7	San Benito County (Calif.)	T2—794 75
	T5—945 7	San Bernardino County (Calif.)	979.495
Sámi languages	494.57		T2—794 95
	T6—945 7	San Bernardino Mountains	
Sámi literatures	894.57	(Calif.)	T2—794 95
Samnium	T2—377 3	San Blas Cuna Indians	T5—978 3
Samoa	996.14	San Blas Cuna language	497.83
	T2—961 4		T6—978 3
Samoan Islands	T2—961 3	San Blas Cuna literature	897.83
Samoan language	499.462	San Blas Kuna Indians	T5—978 3
	T6—994 62	San Blas Kuna language	497.83
Samoan literature	899.462		T6—978 3
Samoans	T5—994 62	San Blas Kuna literature	897.83
Samoic Outlier languages	499.46	San Cristóbal (Dominican	
	T6—994 6	Republic : Province)	T2—729 374
Samos (Greece : Regional		San Diego (Calif.)	T2—794 985
unit)	T2—495 82	San Diego County (Calif.)	T2—794 98
Samos Island (Greece)	T2—495 82	San Felipe (Chile :	
ancient	T2—391 4	Province)	T2—832 45
Samothrace Island (Greece)	T2—495 7	San Francisco (Calif.)	T2—794 61
ancient	T2—391 1	San Francisco Bay (Calif.)	551.461 432
Samoyed	T5—944		T2—164 32
Samoyed (Dog)	636.73	San Francisco Bay Area	
Samoyedic languages	494.4	(Calif.)	T2—794 6
	T6—944	San Francisco County (Calif.)	979.461
Samoyedic literatures	894.4		T2—794 61
Samper Pizano, Ernesto		San Francisco earthquake, 1906	979.461 051
Colombian history	986.106 352	San Gabriel Mountains	
Sample preparation		(Calif.)	T2—794 93
analytical chemistry	543.19	San hsiens	787.85
Samples		*see also* Stringed instruments	
sales promotion	658.82	San Jacinto County (Tex.)	T2—764 167
Sampling techniques	001.433	San Joaquin County (Calif.)	T2—794 55
	T1—072 3	San Joaquin River (Calif.)	T2—794 8
Sampling theory	519.52	San Jorge River (Colombia)	T2—861 12
Sampson County (N.C.)	T2—756 375	San Jose (Calif.)	T2—794 74
Samsun İli (Turkey)	T2—563 8	San José (Costa Rica :	
ancient	T2—393 32	Province)	T2—728 63
Samuel (Biblical books)	222.4	San José (Uruguay : Dept.)	T2—895 12
Samuel 1 (Biblical book)		San Juan (Argentina :	
Bible stories	222.430 950 5	Province)	T2—826 3
San (African people)	T5—961	San Juan (Dominican	
San Andres Mountains		Republic : Province)	T2—729 342
(N.M.)	T2—789 67	San Juan (P.R. : District)	T2—729 51
San Andrés y Providencia		San Juan County (Colo.)	T2—788 25
(Colombia)	T2—861 11	San Juan County (Utah)	T2—792 59
San Antonio (Chile :		San Juan County (Wash.)	979.774
Province)	T2—832 58		T2—797 74

Sandwell (England)	T2—424 94	Sanitation (continued)	
Sandwich construction	624.177 9	spacecraft	629.477 4
naval architecture	623.817 79	World War I	940.475 2
Sandwich panels		World War II	940.547 52
architectural construction	721.044 92	*see also* Waste control	
construction materials	693.92	Sanitation equipment	
wood	674.835	plant management	658.28
see also Wood		Sanitation facilities	
Sandwiches	641.84	area planning	711.8
Sandy soils		Sanitation services	363.72
floriculture	635.955	*see also* Sanitation	
Sangamon County (Ill.)	T2—773 56	Sanitoriums	362.16
Sangamon River (Ill.)	T2—773 55	mental illness	362.23
Sango language	496.361 6	physical illness	362.16
	T6—963 616	*see also* Health care facilities	
Sango literature	896.361 6	Sankara, Thomas	
Sangre de Cristo Mountains		Burkinan history	966.250 52
(Colo. and N.M.)	T2—788 49	Śaṅkarācārya (Philosophy)	181.482
Sanguinetti, Julio María		Sankhya (Philosophy)	181.41
Uruguayan history	989.506 71	Sankt Gallen (Switzerland)	T2—494 723 4
1985–1990	989.506 71	Sankt Gallen (Switzerland :	
1995–2000	989.506 73	Canton)	T2—494 72
Sanhedrin	296.67	Sankt Gallen (Switzerland :	
Sanhedrin (Tractate)	296.123 4	Wahlkreis)	T2—494 723
Babylonian Talmud	296.125 4	Şanlıurfa İli (Turkey)	T2—565 1
Mishnah	296.123 4	Sanpete County (Utah)	T2—792 563
Palestinian Talmud	296.124 4	Sanquianga National Park	
Sanikiluaq (Nunavut)	T2—719 52	(Colombia)	T2—861 58
Sanilac County (Mich.)	T2—774 43	Sansevierias	584.79
Sanirajak (Nunavut)	T2—719 52	Sanskrit language	491.2
Sanitariums	362.16		T6—912
mental illness	362.23	Vedas	294.592 104 1
physical illness	362.16	Sanskrit literature	891.2
see also Health care facilities		Santa Ana (El Salvador :	
Sanitary engineering	628	Dept.)	T2—728 412
military engineering	623.75	Santa Ana Mountains	
Sanitary engineers	628.092	(Calif.)	T2—794 96
Sanitary landfills	363.728	Santa Bárbara (Honduras)	T2—728 385
technology	628.445 64	Santa Barbara Islands	
sewage sludge	628.364	(Calif.)	T2—794 91
water pollution engineering	628.168 25	Santa Catarina (Brazil :	
see also Waste control		State)	T2—816 4
Sanitary napkins	677.8	Santa Clara County (Calif.)	T2—794 73
Sanitation	363.72	Santa Cruz (Argentina :	
armed forces	355.345	Province)	T2—827 5
customs	392.36	Santa Cruz (Bolivia : Dept.)	T2—843
home economics	648	Santa Cruz, Andrés	
law	344.046 4	Bolivian history	984.044
enforcement	363.233	Santa Cruz County (Ariz.)	T2—791 79
mining	622.49	Santa Cruz County (Calif.)	T2—794 71
public administration	353.93	Santa Cruz de Tenerife	
public facilities	353.94	(Canary Islands :	
ships	623.854 6	Province)	T2—649
social services	363.72		

800

Sarans
  textiles — 677.474 4
  see also Textiles
Sarasota County (Fla.) — T2—759 61
Saratoga County (N.Y.) — T2—747 48
Saratov (Russia : Oblast) — T2—474 6
Saratovskaĩa oblast′
  (Russia) — T2—474 6
Saravastivada Buddhism — 294.391
Sarawak — T2—595 4
Sarcodina — 579.43
Sarcoidosis — 362.196 429
  medicine — 616.429
  social services — 362.196 429
Sarcoma
  incidence — 614.599 9
  medicine — 616.994
  see also Cancer — humans
Sarcomastigophora — 579.4
Sarcophagidae — 595.774
Sarcopterygii — 597.39
  paleozoology — 567.39
Sardegna (Italy) — 945.9
   T2—459
  ancient — 937.9
   T2—379
Sardines — 641.392
  conservation technology — 639.977 45
  cooking — 641.692
  food — 641.392
  resource economics — 333.956 45
  zoology — 597.45
Sardines (Young herring) — 641.392
  fishing — 639.274 52
  zoology — 597.452
  see also Sardines
Sardinia (Italy) — 945.9
   T2—459
  ancient — 937.9
   T2—379
Sardinia (Kingdom) — 945.107
  Piedmontese history — 945.107
  Sardinian history — 945.907
Sardinian language — 459.982
   T6—599 82
Sardinian literature — 859.982
Sardinians — T5—599 82
Sardis (Extinct city) — T2—392 2
Saren (Switzerland) — T2—494 764 4
Sarganserland (Switzerland) — T2—494 729
Sargasso Sea — 551.461 362
   T2—163 62
  biology — 578.776 362
  ecology — 577.763 62

Sargassum — 579.888
Sargent County (N.D.) — T2—784 314
Sargodha District (Pakistan) — T2—549 14
Sarine (Switzerland) — T2—494 535
Sark (Channel Islands) — T2—423 45
Sarmatia — 939.52
   T2—395 2
Sarney, José
  Brazilian history — 981.064
Sarpy County (Neb.) — T2—782 256
Sarraceniaceae — 583.93
Sarraceniales — 583.93
Sarsaparillas — 584.6
Sarthe (France) — T2—441 7
Sasakian geometry — 516.373
Sashes (Clothing) — 391.44
  see also Accessories (Clothing)
Saskatchewan — 971.24
   T2—712 4
Saskatchewan River (Sask.
  and Man.) — T2—712 42
Saskatoon (Sask.) — T2—712 425
Sasolburg (South Africa :
  District) — T2—685 2
Sasquatch — 001.944
Sassafras
  botany — 584.288
  food — 641.338 2
Sassafras tea — 641.338 2
  commercial processing — 663.96
  cooking with — 641.638 2
  home preparation — 641.877
Sassanian Empire — 935.07
   T2—35
Sassari (Italy : Province) — T2—459 3
  ancient — T2—379 3
Sassou Nguesso, Denis
  Congolese history — 967.240 52
   1979–1992 — 967.240 52
   1997– — 967.240 54
SAT (Assessment test) — 378.166 2
Satakunnan maakunta
  (Finland) — T2—489 733
Satakunta (Finland) — T2—489 733
Satan
  Christianity — 235.47
  Islam — 297.216
  Judaism — 296.316
  occultism — 133.422
Satanism — 133.422
  religion — 299
Satellite cells
  human cytology — 612.810 46

Savings departments	332.175 2
Savoie (France)	T2—445 85
Savona (Italy : Province)	T2—451 84
ancient	T2—371 3
Savories	641.812
Savoy (Duchy)	T2—445 85
Savoy (France and Italy)	T2—445 85
Savoy, House of	
Italian history	945.084
Piedmontese history	945.105
Savu Sea	551.461 474
	T2—164 74
Sawdust	674.84
fuel	662.65
Sawfishes	597.35
Sawflies	595.79
agricultural pests	632.79
Ṣawm	297.53
Ṣawm Ramaḍān	297.362
Sawmill operations	674.2
Saws	621.934
music	786.888
see also Percussion instruments	
Sawtooth Mountains (Idaho)	T2—796 72
Sawtooth Range (Idaho)	T2—796 29
Sawyer County (Wis.)	T2—775 16
Saxhorns	788.97
instrument	788.971 9
music	788.97
see also Brass instruments	
Saxifragaceae	583.44
Saxifragales	583.44
Saxifrages	583.44
botany	583.44
floriculture	635.933 44
Saxons	
English history	942.017
Saxony (Germany)	T2—432 1
Saxony (Prussia)	T2—431 8
Saxony, House of	943.022
Saxony-Anhalt (Germany)	T2—431 8
Saxophones	788.7
instrument	788.719
music	788.7
see also Woodwind instruments	
Saxophonists	788.709 2
Say, Jean Baptiste	
economic school	330.153
Sayan Mountains (Russia)	T2—575
Sayyid dynasty	954.024 2

Scabies	
humans	
medicine	616.573
see also Skin diseases — humans	
Scalar field theory	515.63
Scalds	
medicine	617.11
Scale insects	595.752
agricultural pests	632.752
Scale mosses	588.3
Scales (Integument)	591.477
descriptive zoology	591.477
physiology	573.595
Scales (Maps)	912.014 8
Scales (Music)	781.246
Scalic formations (Music)	781.246
Scaliger, House of	
Venetian history	945.304
Scallops	641.394
conservation technology	639.974 4
cooking	641.694
fishing and culture	639.46
food	641.394
commercial processing	664.94
resource economics	333.955 46
zoology	594.4
Scalp diseases	
medicine	616.546
see also Skin diseases — humans	
Scaly anteaters	599.31
Scaly reptiles	597.94
Scaly-tailed possums	599.232
Scandentia	599.338
paleozoology	569.338
Scandinavia	948
	T2—48
ancient	936.8
	T2—368
Scandinavian languages	439.5
	T6—395
Scandinavian literatures	839.5
Scandinavian religion	293
Scandinavians	T5—395
Scandium	669.290 1
chemical engineering	661.040 1
chemistry	546.401
economic geology	553.494 2
metallurgy	669.290 1
see also Chemicals; Metals	
Scanners	
computer graphics	006.62

Scaphopoda	594.29
paleozoology	564.29
Scapolite	
mineralogy	549.68
Scapulas	
human anatomy	611.717
Scarabaeidae	595.764 9
Scarabaeoidea	595.764 9
Scarabs	
glyptics	736.209 32
Scarborough (England :	
Borough)	T2—428 47
Scarborough (Toronto, Ont.)	T2—713 541
Scarification	
customs	391.65
Scarlatina	
incidence	614.522
medicine	616.929 87
see also Communicable	
diseases — humans	
Scarlet fever	
incidence	614.522
medicine	616.929 87
see also Communicable	
diseases — humans	
Scarves	391.41
home sewing	646.48
see also Accessories (Clothing)	
Scarves (Table linens)	
arts	746.96
Scatophagidae	595.774
Scattered disk objects	523.494
Scattering (Physics)	539.758
solid-state physics	530.416
Scattering of light	535.43
meteorology	551.566
Scavenger cells	571.968
human immunology	616.079 9
Scenarios	
music	780
treatises	782.002 69
Scene paintings	751.75
Scene understanding	
artificial intelligence	006.37
Scenery	
dramatic performances	792.025
motion pictures	791.430 25
stage	792.025
television	791.450 25
Scenic rivers	333.784 5
law	346.046 784 5
natural resources	333.784 5
Scent hounds	636.753 6

Scent recognition	
biometric identification	
computer science	006.248 353 79
Schaffhausen (Switzerland)	T2—494 586
Schaffhausen (Switzerland :	
Canton)	T2—494 58
Scheduled castes	305.568 8
see also Dalits	
Scheduling	
broadcasting services	384.544 2
radio	384.544 2
television	384.553 1
education	371.242
production management	658.53
transportation	388.041
air	387.740 42
automobile	388.321
bus	388.322 042
urban	388.413 22
canal	386.404 204 2
ferries	386.6
inland waterway	386.240 42
lake	386.540 42
marine	387.540 42
railroad	385.204 2
urban	388.42
river	386.350 42
truck	388.324 042
urban	388.413 24
Scheelite	
mineralogy	549.74
Schefferville (Quebec)	T2—714 117
Schenectady County (N.Y.)	T2—747 44
Scheuchzeriaceae	584.44
Schiffli embroidery	677.77
Schipperke	636.72
Schisandraceae	584.24
Schism between Eastern and	
Western Church	270.38
Schisms	
Christianity	262.8
church history	273
Judaism	296.67
Schist	552.4
Schistosomiasis	
incidence	614.553
medicine	616.963
see also Communicable	
diseases — humans	
Schizanthuses	635.933 959 3
botany	583.959 3
floriculture	635.933 959 3

Schizoid personality disorder
  medicine 616.858 1
  see also Mental disorders
Schizomida 595.45
Schizomycetes 579.3
Schizophrenia 362.26
  medicine 616.898
  social welfare 362.26
  see also Mental disorders
Schizophyta 579.3
Schleicher County (Tex.) T2—764 876
Schleswig-Holstein
  (Germany) T2—435 12
Schleswig-Holstein War, 1864 943.076
Schley County (Ga.) T2—758 495
Schmalkalden-Meiningen
  (Germany : Landkreis) T2—432 26
Schmalkaldic War, 1546–1547 943.031
Schmidt, Helmut
  German history 943.087 7
Schmitt, Pál
  Hungarian history 943.905 44
Schmoller, Gustav von
  economic school 330.154 2
Schnauzers 636.73
Schoharie County (N.Y.) T2—747 45
Scholarship 001.2
Scholarships 371.223
                   T1—079
  higher education 378.34
  law 344.079 5
  research 001.44
Scholastic Assessment Test 378.166 2
Scholastic philosophy 189.4
  modern 149.91
Scholz, Olaf
  German history 943.088 4
School adjustment 370.158
School administration 371.2
  see Manual at 371 vs. 353.8,
    371.2, 379
School administrators
  biography 371.200 92
  public control 379.157
  role and function 371.201 1
School and society 306.432
School assemblies 371.895
School attendance 371.294
  compulsory education 379.23
  law 344.079 2
School attendance districts 379.153 5
School boards 353.822 5
  local public education 379.153 1
  public education 353.822 5

School bonds 379.13
School boys T1—083 41
School buildings 371.6
  see also Educational buildings
School cafeterias 371.716
School calendar 371.23
School camps 796.542 2
School children 305.234
                   T1—083 4
  development
    human physiology 612.654
  home care 649.124
  psychology 155.424
  reading
    library science 028.534
  social aspects 305.234
  transportation 371.872
School choice 379.111
School closings 379.153 5
School cooking 641.571
School credits 371.218
School custodians 371.68
School day 371.244
  law 344.079 2
School desegregation 379.263
  law 344.079 8
School discipline 371.5
School districts 379.153 5
  liability 344.075
School dropouts 371.291 3
School enrollment 371.219
  secondary education 373.121 9
School environment
  psychological influence 370.158
School equipment 371.67
  higher education 378.196 7
  special education 371.904 5
School etiquette 395.5
School excursions 371.384
School facilities 371.6
  see also Educational buildings
School failure 371.285
School furniture 371.63
School girls T1—083 42
School grounds 371.61
  landscape architecture 712.7
School hygiene 371.71
School improvement programs 371.207
School integration 379.263
School journalism 371.897
School leavers 371.291 3
  secondary education 373.129 13
School-leaving age 379.23

Schweizerischer		Science fiction	
Nationalpark		arts (continued)	
(Switzerland)	T2—494 732 7	history and criticism	809.387 62
Schwerin (Germany)	T2—431 76	motion pictures	791.436 15
Schwerin (Germany :		radio programs	791.446 15
Bezirk)	T2—431 76	specific literatures	T3B—308 762
Schwyz (Switzerland)	T2—494 752 64	individual authors	T3A—3
Schwyz (Switzerland :		television programs	791.456 15
Bezirk)	T2—494 752 6	Science laboratories	507.2
Schwyz (Switzerland :		architecture	727.55
Canton)	T2—494 752	Science museums	507.4
Sciaenidae	597.725	architecture	727.65
Sciaenops	597.725	Science policy	338.926
Sciaridae	595.772	*see Manual at* 338.926 vs.	
Sciatica		352.745, 500	
medicine	616.856	Science projects in schools	507.8
see also Nervous system		Sciences (Knowledge)	001
diseases — humans		*see also* Knowledge	
Science	500	Sciences (Natural sciences)	500
	T1—015	*see also* Science	
arts	700.46	Scientific exemptions	
	T3C—36	customs duties	382.78
folklore	398.26	Scientific instruments	
history and criticism	398.36	manufacturing technology	681.75
information systems	025.065	Scientific method	001.42
law	344.095		T1—072 1
libraries	026.5	Scientific principles	500
literature	808.803 6		T1—015
history and criticism	809.933 6	*see Manual at* T1—015 vs.	
specific literatures	T3B—080 36	T1—0245–0246	
history and		Scientific recreations	793.8
criticism	T3B—093 6	Scientific socialism	335.423
painting	758.95	Scientific surveys	508
primary education	372.35	Scientific techniques	T1—072 1
public administrative support	352.745	Scientific toys	790.133
social effects	303.483	manufacturing technology	688.725
see Manual at 303.483 vs.		recreation	790.133
306.45, 306.46		*see also* Toys	
sociology	306.45	Scientific travels	508
see Manual at 303.483 vs.		Scientific writing	808.066 5
306.45, 306.46		Scientists	509.2
use in agricultural industries	338.16	Islamic polemics	297.298
see Manual at 500 vs. 001		works for	T1—024 5
Science and religion	201.65	*see Manual at* T1—015 vs.	
Buddhism	294.336 5	T1—0245–0246	
Christianity	261.55	Scientology	299.936
Hinduism	294.516 5	biography	299.936 092
Islam	297.265	Scilly, Isles of (England)	T2—423 79
Judaism	296.375	Scilly Isles (England)	T2—423 79
philosophy of religion	215	Scincidae	597.957
Science fair projects	507.8	Scincomorphoidea	597.957
Science fiction	808.838 762	Scintillation	
arts	700.415	atmospheric optics	551.565
	T3C—15		

Scintillation counters
nuclear physics 539.775
Sciomyzidae 595.774
Scioto County (Ohio) T2—771 87
Scioto River (Ohio) T2—771 5
Scissors 621.93
home sewing 646.19
Sciuridae 599.36
paleozoology 569.36
Sciurus 599.362
Scleral diseases
ophthalmology 617.719
see also Eye diseases —
humans
Scleras
human anatomy 611.84
human physiology 612.841
ophthalmology 617.719
Sclerenchyma 571.585
Scleroderma
medicine 616.544
see also Skin diseases —
humans
Scleroproteins 572.67
see also Proteins
Scolecophidia 597.969
Scolioidea 595.79
Scoliosis
medicine 616.73
see also Musculoskeletal
diseases — humans
Scolopacidae 598.33
Scolytidae 595.768
Scombridae 597.782
Scombroidei 597.78
Sconces
furniture arts 749.63
Scones 641.815 7
Scooters 388.347 5
engineering 629.227 5
see also Motorcycles
Scopelomorpha 597.61
paleozoology 567.61
Score reading 781.423
primary education 372.873
Scores (Music) 780
cataloging 025.348 8
library treatment 025.178 8
treatises 780.26
see Manual at 780.26; *also at*
782
Scoring systems
contract bridge 795.415 4

Scorpaeniformes 597.68
paleozoology 567.68
Scorpio (Zodiac) 133.527 3
Scorpion fishes 597.68
Scorpion flies 595.744
Scorpion venom
human toxicology 615.942
Scorpions 595.46
Scotch broom 583.63
Scotia Sea 551.461 73
T2—167 3
Scotland 941.1
T2—411
ancient 936.11
T2—361 1
see Manual at T2—41 and
T2—42; *also at* 941
Scotland. Children's Hearings 345.411 08
Scotland. Court of Appeal 345.411 016 3
Scotland. Court of First Instance 345.411 016 2
Scotland. Court of Session 347.411 023
Scotland. Court of Session. Inner
House 347.411 035
Scotland. Court of Session. Outer
House 347.411 024
Scotland. Court of the Lord Lyon 347.411 04
Scotland. Crown Counsel 345.411 01
Scotland. District Court 345.411 012
Scotland. High Court of
Justiciary 345.411 016
Scotland. House of Lords (Court
of last resort) 347.411 039
Scotland. Licensing Appeals
Court 347.411 04
Scotland. Licensing Courts 347.411 04
Scotland. Lord Advocate 345.411 01
Scotland. Sheriff Court 347.411 021
criminal law 345.411 014
Scotland. Sheriff-Principal 347.411 032
Scotland. Solicitor-General 345.411 01
Scotland County (Mo.) T2—778 312
Scotland County (N.C.) T2—756 335
Scots T5—916 3
Scots language (English dialect) 427.941 1
T6—21
Scott County (Ark.) T2—767 44
Scott County (Ill.) T2—773 455
Scott County (Ind.) T2—772 183
Scott County (Iowa) T2—777 69
Scott County (Kan.) T2—781 43
Scott County (Ky.) T2—769 425
Scott County (Minn.) T2—776 54
Scott County (Miss.) T2—762 655
Scott County (Mo.) T2—778 97

Scott County (Tenn.)   T2—768 71
Scott County (Va.)   T2—755 732
Scottburgh (South Africa)   T2—684 63
Scottish Borders (Scotland)   T2—413 7
Scottish deerhound   636.753 2
Scottish English dialect   427.941 1
   T6—21
Scottish Gaelic language   491.63
   T6—916 3
Scottish Gaelic literature   891.63
Scottish Gaels   T5—916 3
Scottish Highlands
   (Scotland)   T2—411 5
Scottish literature
   English   820
   Gaelic   891.63
Scotts Bluff County (Neb.)   T2—782 98
Scottsdale (Tas.)   T2—946 4
Scouring compounds   668.127
Scouting movement   369.43
Scouting organizations   369.43
Scows   387.29
   design   623.812 9
   engineering   623.829
   transportation services   387.29
   see also Ships
Scranton (Pa.)   T2—748 37
Scrap metal   363.728 8
   metallurgy   669.042
   social services   363.728 8
   see also Waste control
Scrapbooking   745.593 8
Scrapbooks
   handicrafts   745.593 8
Scraped idiophones   786.886
   see also Percussion instruments
Scratch pad paper   676.286
Scratchboard drawing   741.29
Screamers (Birds)   598.41
Screen process printing   686.231 6
Screening
   chemical engineering   660.284 22
   ores   622.74
   sewage treatment   628.34
   water supply treatment   628.162 2
Screenplays   791.437
   literature   808.823
    history and criticism   809.23
    specific literatures   T3B—203
    individual authors   T3A—2
   motion pictures   791.437
   music   780
    treatises   780.268

Screenplays (continued)
   rhetoric   808.23
   see Manual at 791.437 and
    791.447, 791.457, 792.9;
    also at 808.82 vs. 791.437,
    791.447, 791.457, 792.9
Screens   645.4
   church architecture   726.529 6
   church furniture   247.1
   decorative arts   749.3
   see also Furniture
Screenwriting   808.23
Screven County (Ga.)   T2—758 695
Screw-cutting tools   621.944
Screw pines   584.55
Screwdrivers   621.972
Screws   621.882
Scribes
   Judaism   296.461 5
    biography   296.461 509 2
Scrimshaws   736.69
Script shorthand systems   653.428
Scripts
   motion pictures   791.437
    see also Screenplays
   puppetry   791.538
   radio   791.447
   stage productions   792.9
   television   791.457
Scripture readings
   public worship
    Christianity   264.34
Scriptures (Religion)   208.2
   see also Sacred books
Scroll saws   621.934
   wood handicrafts   745.513
Scrollwork
   furniture arts   749.5
   wood handicrafts   745.513
Scrophulariaceae   583.96
Scrophulariales   583.96
Scrotum   573.655 25
   biology   573.655 25
   human anatomy   611.63
   human physiology   612.614
   medicine   616.67
   see also Male genital system
Scrotum diseases
   medicine   616.67
    see also Male genital
    diseases — humans

Sea turtles	597.928
conservation technology	639.977 928
resource economics	333.957 928
Sea urchins	593.95
harvest and culture	639.7
Sea walnuts	593.8
Sea warfare	359
Seabed	551.468
law of nations	341.455
see also Ocean floor	
Seabed mining	622.295
Seabees (Naval forces)	359.982
Seaborgium	546.53
Seadromes	
engineering	629.136 1
Seafaring life	910.45
music about	781.595
Seafood	641.392
commercial processing	664.94
cooking	641.692
home preservation	641.494
Seahorses	597.679 8
Sealants	668.38
building materials	691.99
materials science	620.199
structural engineering	624.189 9
Sealers (Hunters)	639.290 92
Sealing (Hunting)	639.29
economics	338.372 979
law	343.076 929
Sealing devices	621.885
Seals (Animals)	599.79
conservation technology	639.979 79
hunting	639.29
resource economics	333.959 79
Seals (Devices)	929.9
insignia	929.9
numismatics	737.6
SEALs (Military units)	359.984
Seam welding	671.521 3
Seamanship	623.88
Seamen	387.509 2
navy enlisted personnel	359.009 2
role and function	359.338
see also Sailors	
Seamoths	597.64
Seamstresses	646.209 2
Seaplanes	387.733 47
engineering	629.133 347
transportation services	387.733 47
see also Aircraft	
Seaports	387.1
see also Ports	
Search algorithms	005.741

Search and seizure	
criminal investigation	363.252
law	345.052 2
Search dogs	
animal husbandry	636.708 86
disaster relief	363.348 1
Search engines	025.042 52
Search for moving target	531.112
Search strategy	
information science	025.524
Search trees (Computer science)	005.741
Searching data	005.741
Searcy County (Ark.)	T2—767 195
Seas	551.46
	T2—162
see also Oceans	
Seascapes	
art representation	704.943 7
drawing	743.837
painting	758.2
Seashells	594.147 7
Seashore animals	591.769 9
Seashores	551.457
	T2—146
biology	578.769 9
ecology	577.699
health	613.12
see also Coasts	
Seasickness	
medicine	616.989 2
see also Environmental diseases — humans	
Seasonal adaptation	578.43
animals	591.43
plants	581.43
Seasonal affective disorder	
medicine	616.852 7
see also Mental disorders	
Seasonal changes	
health	613.11
Seasonal cooking	641.564
Seasonal holidays	394.26
see also Holidays	
Seasonal houses	
architecture	728.7
Seasonal music	781.524
Seasonal parties	793.22
Seasonal unemployment	331.137 044
Seasoning lumber	674.38
Seasonings	641.338 2
cooking with	641.638 2
Seasons	508.2
arts	T3C—33
astronomy	525.5

Seasons (continued)

biological adaptation	578.43
effect on natural ecology	577.23
folklore	398.236
history and criticism	398.33
influence on crime	364.22
literature	808.803 3
history and criticism	809.933 3
specific literatures	T3B—080 33
history and criticism	T3B—093 3
music	781.524
natural history	508.2

Seat belts

aircraft	629.134 43
automobiles	363.125 7
engineering	629.276
highway safety	363.125 7
law	343.094 4

Seat ejectors

aircraft	629.134 386

Seats

automobile	629.26
Seattle (Wash.)	T2—797 772
Seatwork	371.3
Seawalls	627.58
flood control	627.42
port engineering	627.24
shore protection	627.58
Seawater	551.46
desalinization	628.167
oceanography	551.46
water supply evaluation	628.116

see also Oceanography

Seawater intrusion	363.738
engineering	628.114
social problem	363.738

see also Pollution

Seawater supply

ship sanitation	623.854 3
Seaweeds	579.88
cooking	641.698
culture	639.89
food	641.398
resource economics	333.953 8

Sebaceous gland diseases

medicine	616.53

see also Skin diseases — humans

Sebaceous glands	573.537 9
biology	573.537 9
human anatomy	611.77
human physiology	612.793

Sebaceous glands (continued)

medicine	616.53

see also Skin

Sebastian County (Ark.)	T2—767 36

Seborrhea

medicine	616.53

see also Skin diseases — humans

Secernentea	592.57

Secession

United States history	973.713
Second-class mail	383.123

see also Postal service

Second Coming of Christ	236.9
Second Crusade, 1147–1149	956.014
Second Empire (France)	944.07
Second International	324.174
Second language acquisition	401.93
applied linguistics	418
education	418.007 1
specific languages	T4—8
audio-lingual approach	T4—834
education	T4—800 71
formal approach	T4—824
specific languages	T4—019

see Manual at 407.1, T1—071 vs. 401.93, T4—019, 410.71, 418.0071, T4—80071

Second languages

primary education	372.65
Second Republic (Austria)	943.605 3
Second Republic (France)	944.07
Second Republic (Spain)	946.081
Secondary batteries	621.312 424
Secondary education	373
	T1—071 2
federal aid	379.121 3
law	344.074
public administrative support	353.8
public support	379.113
law	344.076 83
special education	371.904 73

see Manual at 372.24 and 373.23

Secondary industries

	338.4
enterprises	338.7
law	343.078

see Manual at 343.078 vs. 343.08

mergers	338.83

Secondary industries (continued)

multinational enterprises	338.88
see also International enterprises	
products	338.4
commerce	381.45
foreign	382.45
public administration	354.73
public administration	354.6
restrictive practices	338.82

Secondary recovery

oil extraction	622.338 2

Secondary roads	388.12
see also Roads	

Secondary school buildings

architecture	727.2

Secondary school graduates

choice of vocation	331.702 33
labor force	331.114 43
unemployment	331.137 804
Secondary school libraries	027.822 3
Secondary school teaching	373.110 2
Secondary schools	373
	T1—071 2
see also Secondary education	
Secondary sexual characteristics	591.46
physical anthropology	599.936
Secondary storage (Computers)	004.56
engineering	621.397 6
Secondhand stores	381.19
management	658.87
see also Commerce	

Secret agents

criminal investigation	363.252

Secret codes

computer science	005.824
Secret police	363.283
Secret societies	366
Secretarial accounting	657.2
Secretarial bookkeeping	657.2
Secretariat (United Nations)	352.113
Secretaries	651.374 109 2
office services	651.374 1
Secretaries of state	352.293
see Manual at 352–354	
Secretary bird	598.9
Secretion	571.79
biology	571.79
human physiology	612.4
medicine	616.4
see also Endocrine system	
Secretory organs	571.79
biology	571.79
human anatomy	611.4

Secretory organs (continued)

human physiology	612.4
see also Endocrine system	
Sections (Architectural design)	729.1
Sects (Religion)	209
Buddhism	294.39
sources	294.385
Christianity	280
Hinduism	294.55
sources	294.595
Islam	297.8
Jainism	294.49
Judaism	296.8
sources	296.15
sources	208.5
see Manual at 201–209 and 292–299	
Secular cantatas	782.48
choral and mixed voices	782.548
single voices	783.094 8
Secular holidays	394.26
see also Holidays	
Secular humanism	211.6
Christian polemics	239.7

Secular institutes

Christianity	255.095
church history	271.095
women	255.909 5
church history	271.909 5
Secular trends (Economics)	338.54
Secular vocal music	782.4
choral and mixed voices	782.54
single voices	783.094
Secularism	211.6
religious freedom	
law	342.085 22

Secured transactions

law	346.074
Securities	332.632
corporate law	346.066 6
income tax	336.242 6
law	343.052 46
investment economics	332.632
law	346.092 2
printing	686.288
public administration	354.88
theft of	364.162 833 263 2
law	345.026 283 326 32
Securities brokers	332.62
law	346.092 6
public administration	354.88
Securities exchange	332.642
international	332.65

Seeds (continued)
  physiology 575.68
  sowing 631.531
    forestry 634.956 5
    ornamental plants 635.915 31
Seeland (Switzerland) T2—494 545 3
Seeland (Switzerland :
    Verwaltungsregion) T2—494 545
Sees
    Christian ecclesiology 262.3
Sefrou (Morocco : Province) T2—643 4
Sefton (England) T2—427 59
Segesta (Extinct city) T2—378 24
Segmented worms 592.6
Segovia (Spain : Province) T2—463 57
Segregation in education 379.263
    law 344.079 8
Sei whale 599.524
Seibo (Dominican
    Republic : Province) T2—729 384
Seiches 551.463
  lakes 551.482
  oceanography 551.463
Seine-et-Marne (France) T2—443 7
Seine-Maritime (France) T2—442 5
Seine River (France) T2—443 6
Seine-Saint-Denis (France) T2—443 62
Seining
  sports 799.13
Seismic prospecting 622.159 2
Seismic sea waves 551.463 7
Seismic waves 551.22
Seismography 551.220 287
Seismology 551.22
Seismosaurus 567.913
Sekgosese (South Africa :
    District) T2—682 57
Sekhukhune District
    Municipality (South
    Africa) T2—682 55
Sekhukhuneberg Range
    (South Africa) T2—682 55
Sekhukhuneland (South
    Africa : District) T2—682 55
Selachii 597.3
  paleozoology 567.3
Selaginellales 587.9
Selangor T2—595 1
Selby (England : District) T2—428 45
Select committees
  legislative bodies 328.365 7
Selected laws 348.024
  United States federal laws 348.732 4
Selection of animals 636.081

Selection procedures
  personnel management 658.311 2
    public administration 352.65
Selective dissemination of
    information 025.525
Selective service 355.223 63
  law 343.012 2
Selenides
  mineralogy 549.32
Selenium
  biochemistry 572.555
  chemical engineering 661.072 4
  chemistry 546.724
  metallurgy 669.79
  organic chemistry 547.057 24
    applied 661.895
Selenography 919.91
Seletar (Malaysian people) T5—992 8
Seleucid Empire 935.062
  T2—35
Self
  literature 808.803 84
    history and criticism 809.933 84
    specific literatures T3B—080 384
    history and
      criticism T3B—093 84
  philosophy 126
    arts T3C—384
  psychology 155.2
    arts T3C—353
Self-acceptance 155.2
  applied psychology 158.1
Self-actualization 155.2
  applied psychology 158.1
Self-adjoint operator algebras 512.556
Self-confidence 155.2
  applied psychology 158.1
Self-contained communities 307.77
Self-control 179.9
  moral theology 205.699
  psychology 153.8
    development 155.25
  see also Virtues
Self-defense 613.66
  children 613.660 83
  military training 355.548
  personal safety 613.66
  women 613.660 82
  young people 613.660 83
Self-defense (Law) 345.04
Self-destructive behavior
  medicine 616.858 2
Self-determination of states 320.15
  law of nations 341.26

Self-development reading	
library science	028.8
Self-driving cars	629.222
engineering	629.222
Self-employed people	
income tax	
law	343.052 6
Self-employment enterprises	
management	658.041
initiation	658.114 1
Self-esteem	155.2
applied psychology	158.1
Self-financing	332.041 52
Self-help devices	
injured people	617.103
Self-help groups	361.43
Self-hypnosis	
therapeutic use	615.851 22
Self-improvement	
applied psychology	158.1
Self-incrimination	345.056
Self-instruction	371.394 3
Self-organizing systems	003.7
Self-publishing	070.593
Self-realization	155.2
applied psychology	158.1
ethical systems	171.3
Self-reliance	179.9
child training	649.63
see also Virtues	
Self-respect	155.2
applied psychology	158.1
Selinus (Extinct city)	T2—378 24
Seljuk dynasty	956.014
Middle Eastern history	956.014
Turkish history	956.101 4
Selkirk (Man.)	T2—712 74
Selkirk Mountains	T2—711 68
Selkup language	494.4
	T6—944
Selling	381
commerce	381
management	658.81
	T1—068 8
techniques for individuals	658.85
Selwyn District (N.Z.)	T2—938 5
Semaeostomeae	593.53
Semang	T5—959 3
Semang languages	495.93
	T6—959 3
Semantic computing	006
Semantic web	025.042 7

Semantics		
linguistics		401.43
specific languages	T4—014 3	
see Manual at 401.43 vs.		
306.44, 401.45, 401.9,		
412, 415		
philosophical system		149.94
philosophy of language		121.68
Semaphores		
military engineering		623.731 2
nautical engineering		623.856 12
Semara (Morocco :		
Province)	T2—648	
Semi-detached houses		
architecture		728.312
Semi-enclosed spaces		
architecture		721.84
Semi-industrial unions		331.883 3
see also Labor unions		
Semiarid lands		551.415
	T2—154	
see also Arid lands		
Semibituminous coal		553.24
properties		662.622 4
see also Coal		
Semicircular canal diseases		
medicine		617.882
see also Ear diseases —		
humans		
Semicircular canals		
human physiology		612.858
medicine		617.882
Semiconductivity		537.622
materials science		620.112 972
Semiconductor circuits		621.381 5
Semiconductor memory		004.53
engineering		621.397 32
Semiconductor storage		004.568
engineering		621.397 68
Semiconductors		621.381 52
chemical engineering		660.297 7
electrochemistry		541.377
physics		537.622
radio engineering		621.384 134
television engineering		621.388 32
Semidetached houses		
architecture		728.312
Semidiesel engines		621.436
ships		623.872 36
Semidiesel locomotives		385.366
engineering		625.266
transportation services		385.366
see also Rolling stock		
Semigroups		512.27

Semimetals	
chemistry	546.71
economic geology	553.499
mineralogy	549.25
Seminaries	200.711
Christianity	230.071 1
Judaism	296.071 1
Seminars	371.37
higher education	378.177
Seminole County (Fla.)	T2—759 23
Seminole County (Ga.)	T2—758 996
Seminole County (Okla.)	T2—766 71
Seminole Indians	975.900 497 385 9
	T5—973 859
Seminole language	497.385 9
	T6—973 859
Seminole War, 1818	973.54
Seminole War, 1835–1842	973.57
Semionotiformes	597.41
Semiotics	302.2
linguistics	401.4
specific languages	T4—014
specific subjects	T1—014
philosophy	121.68
social aspects	302.2
Semiprecious stones	553.87
carving	736.2
economic geology	553.87
jewelry	739.27
materials science	620.198
mining	622.387
occultism	133.255 387
divination	133.322
prospecting	622.188 7
synthetic	666.88
Semiregular variable stars	523.844 26
Semirigid airships	387.732 6
engineering	629.133 26
military engineering	623.743 6
transportation services	387.732 6
see also Aircraft	
Semisecret societies	366
Semiskilled workers	331.794
labor economics	331.794
labor force	331.114 2
personnel management	658.304 4
unemployment	331.137 804
Semisovereign states	321.08
law of nations	341.27
public administration	353.15
specific states	351.3–.9
Semites	T5—92
religion	299.2

Semitic languages	492
	T6—92
Biblical texts	220.4
Semitic literatures	892
Semitic peoples	T5—92
religion	299.2
Semitrailers (Freight)	388.344
engineering	629.224
see also Trucks	
Semnān (Iran)	T2—552 4
Sena language	496.391
	T6—963 91
Senari language	496.35
	T6—963 5
Seneca County (N.Y.)	974.769
	T2—747 69
Seneca County (Ohio)	T2—771 24
Seneca Indians	974.700 497 554 6
	T5—975 546
Seneca language	497.554 6
	T6—975 546
Senegal	966.3
	T2—663
Senegal languages	496.321
	T6—963 21
Senegalese	T5—966 3
Senegambia	966.305 1
	T2—663
Senegambian languages	496.321
	T6—963 21
Senekal (South Africa : District)	T2—685 1
Senescence	571.878
see also Aging	
Senga-Sena languages	496.391
	T6—963 91
Senile dementia	
geriatrics	618.976 831
medicine	616.831
see also Nervous system diseases — humans	
Senior citizens	305.26
	T1—084 6
see also Older people	
Senior high schools	373.238
see also Secondary education	
Seniority	
labor economics	331.259 6
personnel management	658.312
Seniors (Girl Scouts)	369.463 5
Sennas	583.634
Senneville (Quebec)	T2—714 28
Senoic languages	495.93
	T6—959 3

Sensation	152.1	Sentences (Grammar)	415
biology	573.87	specific languages	T4—5
epistemology	121.35	Sentences (Legal decisions)	345.077
see also Sense organs		penology	364.6
Sensationalism (Philosophical		Sentencing	345.077 2
school)	145	Sentential calculus	511.3
Sensations (Art styles)	709.040 7	mathematical logic	511.3
20th century	709.040 7	philosophical logic	160
21st century	709.050 1	Sentiments	152.4
Sense knowledge	121.35	Senufo (African people)	T5—963 5
Sense organs	573.87	Senufo language	496.35
animal physiology	573.87		T6—963 5
descriptive zoology	591.4	Sepals	575.69
human anatomy	611.8	Separate maintenance	346.016 68
human histology	612.8	Separate property	346.042
human physiology	612.8	divorce law	346.016 64
see also Nervous system		Separated men	306.892
Senses	573.87	Separated people	306.89
psychology	152.1		T1—086 53
see also Sense organs		family relationships	306.89
Sensitive plants	583.633	guides to religious life	
Sensitivity in plants	575.98	Christianity	248.846
Sensitivity training		law	346.016 68
applied psychology	158.2	social group	306.89
social psychology	302.14	social welfare	362.829 4
Sensitometry	661.808	Separated women	306.893
Sensor fusion	005.74	social welfare	362.839 59
Sensor networks	006.25	Separation (Domestic relations)	306.89
Sensorineural hearing loss		ethics	173
medicine	617.886	Judaism	296.444 4
see also Ear diseases —		law	346.016 68
humans		social theology	201.7
Sensors		Christianity	261.835 89
manufacturing technology	681.2	Separation from parents	
Sensory evaluation		child psychology	155.44
food	664.072	Separation from service	
Sensory functions	573.87	personnel management	658.313
human physiology	612.8	public administration	352.69
localization in brain		Separation of powers	320.404
human physiology	612.825 5	law	342.044
see also Nervous system		Separation processes	
see Manual at 612.8 vs. 152		chemical engineering	660.284 2
Sensory influences		Separatist parties	324.218 4
psychology	155.911	Sephardic liturgy	296.450 42
Sensory nerves	573.872 8	Sepik-Ramu languages	499.12
human physiology	612.811		T6—991 2
see also Nervous system		Sepik River (New Guinea)	T2—957 5
Sensory perception	152.1	Sepioidea	594.58
comparative psychology	156.21	Sepoy Mutiny, 1857–1858	954.031 7
educational psychology	370.155	Sept-Rivières (Quebec)	T2—714 176
epistemology	121.35	Septets	
psychological influence	155.911	chamber music	785.17
see Manual at 153.7 vs. 152.1;		vocal music	783.17
also at 612.8 vs. 152			

Septic tanks		Serfs	306.365
technology	628.368	T1—086 25	
Septicemia		customs	390.25
incidence	614.577	dress	391.025
medicine	616.944	Serging	646.204 4
see also Communicable		Sergipe (Brazil)	T2—814 1
diseases — humans		Seri Indians	T5—975 7
puerperal diseases		Serial murderers	364.152 32
incidence	614.545	biography	364.152 320 92
obstetrics	618.74	Serial murders	364.152 32
Septoria	579.55	law	345.025 232
Septuagint	221.48	social welfare	362.882 93
Sepulchral slabs	736.5	Serial publications	050
Sequatchie County (Tenn.)	T2—768 77	T1—05	
Sequatchie River (Tenn.)	T2—768 77		
Sequence	264.36	*see also* Serials	
music	782.323 5	Serialism	
Sequences (Mathematics)	515.24	music	781.33
Sequences of integers	512.72	Serials	050
Sequencing		T1—05	
production management	658.53	bibliographies	011.34
Sequential analysis	519.54	cataloging	025.343 2
Sequential machines	511.35	design	744.55
Sequoia National Park		indexes	050
(Calif.)	T2—794 86	journalism	070.175
Sequoias	585.5	library treatment	025.173 2
forestry	634.975 8	postal handling	383.123
Sequoyah County (Okla.)	T2—766 81	*see also* Postal service	
Serbia	949.71	publishing	070.572
	T2—497 1	sociology	302.232 4
ancient	939.871	Sericulture	638.2
	T2—398 71	Series (Mathematics)	515.243
Serbia and Montenegro	949.710 31	Series (Publications)	
	T2—497 1	bibliographies	011.48
Serbian language	491.82	Serigraphy	764.8
	T6—918 2	Sermon on the Mount	226.9
Serbian literature	891.82	Christian moral theology	241.53
Serbian Orthodox Church	281.949 71	Sermon outlines	251.02
Serbians	T5—918 2	Sermon preparation	206.1
Serbo-Croatian language	491.82	Christianity	251.01
	T6—918 2	*see also* Preaching	
Serbo-Croatian literature	891.82	Sermons	204.3
Serbs	T5—918 2	Christianity	252
Serenades	784.185 6	Islam	297.37
Serengeti National Park		Jewish	296.47
(Tanzania)	T2—678 27	Serology	
Serer (African people)	T5—963 21	medicine	616.079 5
Serer language	496.321	diagnosis	616.075 6
	T6—963 21	Serous membranes	
Serer-Sine language	496.321	human histology	611.018 7
	T6—963 21	Serows	599.647
Serfdom	306.365	Serpentine	553.55
		building material	691.2
		economic geology	553.55
		mineralogy	549.67

Sétif (Algeria : Province)   T2—655
Seto-naikai (Japan)   551.461 455
   T2—164 55
Sets   511.32
Settat (Morocco : Province)   T2—643 9
Setters (Dogs)   636.752 6
Setting (Literature)   808.802 2
   history and criticism   809.922
   specific literatures   T3B—080 22
    history and criticism   T3B—092 2
Setting (Performances)   792.025
   motion pictures   791.430 25
   stage   792.025
   television   791.450 25
Settlement (Insurance)   368.014
Settlement (Population)   307.14
   land reform   333.31
   public administration   353.59
Settlement (Real estate)   346.043 73
Settling
   water supply treatment   628.162 2
Setúbal (Portugal : District)   T2—469 44
Seven last words on cross   232.963 5
Seven Readings (Koran)   297.122 404 522
Seven Weeks' War, 1866   943.076
Seven Years' War, 1756–1763   940.253 4
   North American history   973.26
Seveners (Islamic sect)   297.822
   Hadith   297.125 922
   Koran commentary   297.122 754
   religious law   297.140 182 2
Sevenoaks (England :
   District)   T2—422 36
Seventeenth century   909.6
   T1—090 32
Seventh century   909.1
   T1—090 21
Seventh-Day Adventist Church   286.732
   see also Adventists
Seventh-Day Baptists   286.3
   see also Baptists
Severance pay   331.216 6
   personnel management   658.322 2
Severance tax   336.271 6
   law   343.055
Severn, River (Wales and
   England)   T2—424
   England   T2—424
   Wales   T2—429 51
Severnaĩa Osetiĩa (Russia)   T2—475 2
Severnaĩa Zemlĩa (Russia)   T2—987
Severnaya Zemlya (Russia)   T2—987
Severočeský kraj (Czech
   Republic)   T2—437 16

Severomoravský kraj
   (Czech Republic)   T2—437 28
Sevier County (Ark.)   T2—767 47
Sevier County (Tenn.)   T2—768 893
Sevier County (Utah)   T2—792 55
Seville (Spain : Province)   T2—468 6
Sewage disposal   363.728 493
   social services   363.728 493
   technology   628.36
   see also Sewage treatment
Sewage effluent   363.728 493
   disposal technology   628.362
   social services   363.728 493
   water pollution engineering   628.168 2
   see also Sewage treatment
Sewage irrigation   628.362 3
Sewage lagoons
   sanitary engineering   628.351
Sewage sludge   363.728 493
   sanitary engineering   628.364
   social services   363.728 493
   use as fertilizer   631.869
   see also Sewage treatment
Sewage treatment   363.728 493
   law   344.046 22
   military engineering   623.753
   social services   363.728 493
   technology   628.3
   see also Waste control
Seward County (Kan.)   T2—781 735
Seward County (Neb.)   T2—782 324
Seward Peninsula (Alaska)   T2—798 6
Sewerage   628.2
Sewers   628.2
Sewing   646.2
   home economics   646.2
   primary education   372.54
Sewing equipment   646.19
   home sewing   646.19
   manufacturing technology   681.767 7
Sewing machines
   home economics   646.204 4
   manufacturing technology   681.767 7
Sewing materials   646.1
   commercial technology   687.8
   home economics   646.1
Sex   306.7
   arts   700.453 8
   T3C—353 8
   customs   392.6
   ethics   176.4
   evolution   576.855
   folklore   398.273 8
    history and criticism   398.353 8

Sex (continued)		Sex hormones	571.837 4
human physiology	612.6	biology	571.837 4
literature	808.803 538	animal reproduction	573.637 4
history and criticism	809.933 538	human physiology	612.6
specific literatures	T3B—080 353 8	pharmacology	615.366
history and		*see also* Genital system	
criticism	T3B—093 538	Sex hygiene	613.95
psychology	155.3	school programs	371.714
adolescents	155.53	Sex instruction	613.907 1
children	155.43	home child care	649.65
religious worship	202.12	primary education	372.372
sociology	306.7	Sex manuals	613.96
theological anthropology	202.2	Sex offenses	364.153
Christianity	233.5	law	345.025 3
Sex addiction		social welfare	362.883
medicine	616.858 33	Sex role	305.3
Sex cells	571.845		T1—081
Sex characteristics		arts	700.452 1
animals	591.46		T3C—352 1
physical anthropology	599.936	literature	
Sex crimes	364.153	specific literatures	T3B—080 352 1
law	345.025 3	history and	
school problem	371.786	criticism	T3B—093 521
social welfare	362.883	psychology	155.33
Sex differences	578.46	Sexadecimal system	513.5
animals	591.46	Sexes	
physical anthropology	599.936	evolution	576.855
psychology	155.33	psychology	155.33
adolescents	155.53	social aspects	305.3
children	155.43	Sexism	305.3
sociology	305.3	Sexism in textbooks	
Sex differentiation	571.882	public control	379.156
Sex differentiation disorders		Sext	264.15
medicine	616.694	music	782.324
Sex discrimination against men	305.32	*see also* Liturgy of the hours	
Sex discrimination against		Sextants	
women	305.42	astronomy	527.028 4
labor economics	331.413 3	Sextets	
law	344.014 133	chamber music	785.16
law	342.087 8	vocal music	783.16
Sex discrimination in education	370.81	Sexual abstinence	
law	344.079 8	health	613.9
Sex disorders		birth control	613.94
gynecology	618.17	Sexual abuse of adolescents	
see also Female genital		medicine	616.858 36
diseases — humans		Sexual abuse of children	362.76
medicine	616.69	medicine	616.858 36
see also Genital diseases —		school problem	371.786
humans		*see also* Child abuse	
Sex education	613.907 1	Sexual abuse victims	362.883
home child care	649.65	counseling	362.883 86
primary level	372.372	legal aid	362.883 86
		social welfare	
		law	344.032 883

Sexual behavior (Animals)	591.562
Sexual desire disorders	
psychiatry	616.858 3
Sexual deviation	
criminology	364.153 6
law	345.025 36
medicine	616.858 3
Sexual disorders	
gynecology	618.17
see also Female genital	
diseases — humans	
medicine	616.69
see also Genital diseases —	
humans	
psychiatry	616.858 3
Sexual division of labor	306.361 5
Sexual ethics	176.4
religion	205.664
see also Sexual relations —	
ethics — religion	
see also Sexual relations —	
ethics	
Sexual excitement	
psychology	155.31
Sexual factors in evolution	576.855
Sexual harassment	
prevention	
personnel management	658.314 5
Sexual harassment of women	
labor economics	331.413 3
sociology	305.42
Sexual intercourse	
psychology	155.35
sociology	306.77
Sexual love	306.7
psychology	155.3
Sexual minorities	306.76
see also LGBT people	
Sexual orientation	306.76
arts	700.453
	T3C—353
literature	808.803 53
history and criticism	809.933 53
specific literatures	T3B—080 353
history and	
criticism	T3B—093 53
psychology	155.34
religion	200.866
social groups	T1—086 6
sociology	306.76
Sexual orientation and gender	
identity (SOGI)	306.76

Sexual practices	306.77
psychology	155.35
public control	
public administration	353.37
sociology	306.77
Sexual relations	306.7
customs	392.6
ethics	176.4
religion	205.664
Buddhism	294.356 64
Christianity	241.664
Hinduism	294.548 664
Islam	297.566 4
Judaism	296.366 4
laws of family purity	296.742
social theology	201.7
Christianity	261.835 7
sociology	306.7
technique	613.96
Sexual reproduction	571.8
animals	573.6
microorganisms	571.845 29
plants	575.6
see also Genital system	
Sexual selection (Animals)	591.562
Sexuality	
arts	700.453 8
	T3C—353 8
literature	808.803 538
history and criticism	809.933 538
specific literatures	T3B—080 353 8
history and	
criticism	T3B—093 538
psychology	155.3
Sexually abused children	
pediatrics	618.928 583 6
social theology	201.762 76
Christianity	261.832 72
social welfare	362.76
Sexually transmitted diseases	
incidence	614.547
medicine	616.951
law	344.043 695 1
see also Communicable	
diseases — humans	
Seychelles	969.6
	T2—696
Seychellois	T5—969 696
Seymour River	
(Columbia-Shuswap,	
B.C.)	T2—711 68
Sforza, House of	
Lombardian history	945.206

Shape
  animals 591.41
  biological organisms 578.41
  plants 581.41
Shape theory (Topology) 514.24
Shaped charges
  military engineering 623.454 5
Shapers (Tools) 621.912
Shaping metals
  decorative arts 739.14
  sculpture 731.41
Shar-Pei 636.72
Share renting
  agricultural land economics 333.335 563
  land economics 333.563
Sharecroppers 306.365
                 T1—088 63
Sharecropping 306.365
  economics 333.335 563
Shared custody 306.89
Shared memory 005.71
Shareholders' meetings
  law 346.066 6
Shares (Corporate equity
  securities) 332.632 2
Sharia 340.59
  religious law 297.14
  secular law 340.59
Shāriqah (United Arab
  Emirates : Emirate) T2—535 7
Shārjah (United Arab
  Emirates : Emirate) T2—535 7
Sharkey County (Miss.) T2—762 414
Sharks 597.3
  commercial fishing 639.273
  cooking 641.692
  food 641.392
  paleozoology 567.3
  sports fishing 799.173
  zoology 597.3
Sharkskin fabrics 677.615
  see also Textiles
Sharp County (Ark.) T2—767 23
Sharp-tailed grouse 598.637 8
Sharpeville Massacre, 1960 968.058
Sharpshooters 356.162
Sharq al-Istiwā'īyah (South
  Sudan) T2—629 5
Sharqīyah (Egypt) T2—621
Shasta County (Calif.) T2—794 24
Shastri, Lal Bahadur
  Indian history 954.043
Shavers
  manufacturing technology 688.5

Shaving 646.724
  customs 391.5
  personal care 646.724
Shavings
  wood 674.84
Shavuot 296.438
  liturgy 296.453 8
Shawano County (Wis.) T2—775 36
Shawinigan (Quebec) T2—714 453
Shawkānī, Muḥammad ibn ʿAlī
  Koran commentary 297.122 755
Shawls 391.44
  see also Accessories (Clothing)
Shawnee County (Kan.) T2—781 63
Shawnee Indians 974.004 973 17
                  T5—973 17
Shawnee language 497.317
                  T6—973 17
Shawnigan Lake (B.C.) T2—711 2
Shawns 788.52
  see also Woodwind
    instruments
Shearing animals 636.083 3
Shearing sheds
  architecture 725.37
Shearing stress
  effect on materials 620.112 45
Shearing textiles 677.028 25
Shears 621.93
  home sewing 646.19
Shearwaters 598.42
Sheaths (Nerve tissue) 573.852 5
  human histology 612.810 45
  see also Nervous system
Sheaths (Tendon) 573.753 56
  see also Tendon sheaths
Sheaves (Mathematics) 514.224
Sheboygan County (Wis.) T2—775 69
Sheds
  architecture 725.372
  construction 690.537 2
  domestic
    architecture 728.922
    construction 690.892 2
Sheehan's syndrome
  obstetrics 618.7
Sheep 636.3
  animal husbandry 636.3
  big game hunting 799.276 49
  zoology 599.649
Sheep dogs 636.737

Sheep's milk	641.371 7
cooking	641.671 7
food	641.371 7
processing	637.17
Sheep's wool textiles	677.31
arts	746.043 1
see also Textiles	
Sheet metal	671.823
Sheet music illustration	741.66
Sheeting	
rubber	678.36
Sheets	645.4
arts	746.97
home sewing	646.21
household equipment	645.4
Sheffield (England : City)	T2—428 21
Shehitah	296.73
Shekalim	296.123 2
Mishnah	296.123 2
Palestinian Talmud	296.124 2
Shekhar, Chandra	
Indian history	954.052
Shelburne (N.S. : County)	T2—716 25
Shelby County (Ala.)	T2—761 79
Shelby County (Ill.)	T2—773 798
Shelby County (Ind.)	T2—772 59
Shelby County (Iowa)	T2—777 484
Shelby County (Ky.)	T2—769 435
Shelby County (Mo.)	T2—778 323
Shelby County (Ohio)	T2—771 45
Shelby County (Tenn.)	T2—768 19
Shelby County (Tex.)	T2—764 179
Sheldon, William Herbert	
personality theory	155.264
Shelf fungi	579.597
Shelf ice	551.342
Shelflisting	
library science	025.428
Shelikof Strait (Alaska)	551.461 434
	T2—164 34
Shell carving	736.6
Shell model (Nuclear physics)	539.743
Shell parakeets	636.686 4
Shellac	667.79
Shellfish	594
commercial fishing	
economics	338.372 4
conservation technology	639.974
cooking	641.694
culture	639.4
economics	338.371 4
fishing	639.4
food	641.394
commercial processing	664.94

Shellfish (continued)	
resource economics	333.955
sports fishing	799.254
zoology	594
Shellfishing	
economics	338.372 4
sports	799.254
Shelling crops	631.56
Shells (Ammunition)	
artillery	623.451 3
small arms	
military engineering	623.455
Shells (Animals)	591.477
carving	736.6
descriptive zoology	591.477
mollusks	594.147 7
handicrafts	745.55
physiology	573.77
Shells (Structural elements)	624.177 62
naval architecture	623.817 762
structural engineering	624.177 62
concrete	624.183 462
Shelter	
social welfare	361.05
Sheltered employment	362.404 848
see also Employment	
services — social services	
Sheltered housing	362.61
Shelving	
household management	645.4
library collections maintenance	025.81
library plant management	022.4
manufacturing technology	684.162
Shemittah	296.439 1
Shenandoah County (Va.)	T2—755 95
Shenandoah National Park	
(Va.)	T2—755 9
Shenandoah River Valley (Va.	
and W. Va.)	975.59
	T2—755 9
Shengs	788.82
see also Woodwind	
instruments	
Shensi Province (China)	T2—514 3
Shepherd's purse	583.78
Shepparton (Vic.)	T2—945 4
Shepway (England)	T2—422 395
Sherbet	641.863
commercial processing	637.4
home preparation	641.863
Sherbrooke (Quebec)	T2—714 66
Sherbrooke (Quebec :	
Regional County	
Municipality)	T2—714 66

Sherburne County (Minn.)	T2—776 66	Shigella	579.34
Sheridan County (Kan.)	T2—781 145	Shigellosis	
Sheridan County (Mont.)	T2—786 218	incidence	614.516
Sheridan County (N.D.)	T2—784 76	medicine	616.935 5
Sheridan County (Neb.)	T2—782 92	*see also* Communicable	
Sheridan County (Wyo.)	T2—787 32	diseases — humans	
Sheriffs		Shih Tzu (Dog)	636.76
law	347.016	Shiites	297.82
police services	363.282	*see also* Shia Islam	
Sherman County (Kan.)	T2—781 115	Shikoku Island (Japan)	T2—523
Sherman County (Neb.)	T2—782 44	Shikoku Region (Japan)	T2—523
Sherman County (Or.)	T2—795 64	Shilha language	493.3
Sherman County (Tex.)	T2—764 813		T6—933
Sherman's March to the Sea,		Shilluk (African people)	T5—965 584
1864	973.737 8	Shilluk language	496.558 4
Sherry	641.222 609 468 8		T6—965 584
commercial processing	663.226 094 688	Shimane-ken (Japan)	T2—521 96
Sherwood Forest (England)	T2—425 24	Shin (Sect)	294.392 6
Shetland (Scotland)	T2—411 35	Shina language	491.499
Shetland Islands (Scotland)	T2—411 35		T6—914 99
Shetland pony	636.16	Shina literature	891.499
Shevi'it	296.123 1	Shinano River (Japan)	T2—521 52
Mishnah	296.123 1	Shiners	597.482
Palestinian Talmud	296.124 1	Shingles (Disease)	
Shevu'ot	296.123 4	medicine	616.522
Babylonian Talmud	296.125 4	*see also* Skin diseases —	
Mishnah	296.123 4	humans	
Palestinian Talmud	296.124 4	Shingles (Roofing)	695
Shewa (Ethiopia)	T2—633	Shinto	299.561
Sheyenne River (N.D.)	T2—784 3	art representation	704.948 995 61
Shi language	496.394	Shinto philosophy	181.095 61
	T6—963 94	Shinto temples and shrines	299.561 35
Shia Islam	297.82	architecture	726.195 61
doctrines	297.204 2	Shintoism	299.561
Hadith	297.125 92	Shintoists	
Koran commentary	297.122 75	biography	299.561 092
relations with Sunni Islam	297.804 2	Shinyanga Region	
schools of law	340.590 182	(Tanzania)	T2—678 28
religion	297.140 182	Ship accidents	363.123
worship	297.302	*see also* Water	
Shiatsu		transportation — safety	
therapeutics	615.822 2	Ship canals	386.4
Shiawassee County (Mich.)	T2—774 25	engineering	627.137
Shielding		transportation services	386.4
nuclear reactors	621.483 23	interoceanic	386.42
Shields (Armor)	623.441 8	noninteroceanic canals	386.47
art metalwork	739.752	*see also* Canals	
Shieldtail snakes	597.967	Ship canneries	
Shift systems	331.257 25	engineering	623.824 8
Shift work	331.257 25	Ship fitting	623.843 3
personnel management	658.312 1	Ship flags	929.92
Shifting cultivation		Ship gear	623.862
agricultural technology	631.581 8	Ship handling	623.881
Shiga-ken (Japan)	T2—521 85		

Shoe buckles	391.7
customs	391.7
making	739.278
costume jewelry	688.2
handicrafts	745.594 2
fine jewelry	739.278
Shoe repairers	685.310 092
Shoemakers	685.310 092
Shoes	391.413
commercial technology	685.31
customs	391.413
see also Clothing	
Shoghi, Effendi	
works by	297.938 6
Shogi	794.18
Shona (African people)	T5—963 975
Shona language	496.397 5
	T6—963 975
Shona literature	896.397 5
Shooting game	
sports	799.21
see also Hunting — sports	
Shooting stars (Plants)	583.93
Shoots (Plants)	581.495
descriptive botany	581.495
physiology	575.4
Shop stewards	331.873 3
Shop technology	670.42
Shoplifting	364.162 32
law	345.026 232
Shoppers' clubs	381.149
management	658.879
Shopping	381.1
etiquette	395.53
see also Commerce	
Shopping bags	
design	744.68
Shopping centers	381.11
architecture	725.21
area planning	711.552 2
management	658.87
see also Commerce	
Shopping malls	381.11
see also Commerce; Shopping	
centers	
Shops (Retail trade)	381.1
architecture	725.21
management	658.87
see also Commerce	
Shoran	621.384 8
marine navigation	623.893 3
Shore, John, Baron Teignmouth	
Indian history	954.031 1
Shore biology	578.769 9
Shore birds	598.33
sports hunting	799.243 3
Shore ecology	577.699
Shore flies	595.774
Shore protection	333.917 16
engineering	627.58
land economics	333.917 16
Shore reclamation	333.917 153
engineering	627.58
land economics	333.917 153
Shorebirds	598.33
sports hunting	799.243 3
Shorelands	551.457
	T2—146
see also Coasts	
Shorelines	551.458
	T2—146
geography	910.914 6
geomorphology	551.458
physical geography	910.021 46
Shoring	
structural engineering	624.152
Short-haired cats	636.82
Short-necked lutes	787.8
see also Stringed instruments	
Short-order cooking	641.57
Short-range ballistic missiles	358.175 282
engineering	623.451 952
military equipment	358.175 282
Short-range weather forecasting	551.636 2
Short stories	808.831
history and criticism	809.31
specific literatures	T3B—301
individual authors	T3A—3
Short takeoff and landing	
airplanes	
engineering	629.133 340 426
Short-term capital	
financial management	658.152 44
Short-term government securities	336.31
Short-term loans receivable	
financial management	658.152 44
Short track speed skating	796.914
Shortages	
agricultural industries	338.17
natural resources	333.711
production	338.02
secondary industries	338.47
Shorthair cats	636.82
Shorthand	653
Shorthorn cattle	636.222
Shorts (Clothing)	391.476
see also Pants (Trousers)	

Shut-in people (continued)	
recreation	790.196
indoor	793.019 6
outdoor	796.087 7
Shutters (Cameras)	771.36
Shuttle cars	
mining	622.66
Shyness	155.232
SI (Metric system)	530.812
social aspects	389.15
Sialidae	595.747
Siam	T2—593
Siam, Gulf of	551.461 472
	T2—164 72
Siamang	599.882
Siamese	T5—959 11
Siamese cat	636.825
Siamese fighting fish	597.7
Siamese language	495.91
	T6—959 11
Siamese literature	895.91
Siassi Islands (Papua New	
Guinea)	T2—957 1
Siaya County (Kenya)	T2—676 292
Sibasa (South Africa :	
District)	T2—682 57
Siberia (Russia)	957
	T2—57
Siberia, Eastern (Russia)	T2—575
Siberia, Western (Russia)	957.3
	T2—573
Siberian husky	636.73
Siberian Yupik	T5—971 4
Siberian Yupik languages	T6—971 4
Sibiu (Romania : Judeţ)	T2—498 4
Sibley County (Minn.)	T2—776 33
Siblings	306.875
	T1—085 5
child care handbooks	649.102 45
family relationships	306.875
home care	649.143
psychological influence	155.924
psychology	155.443
adulthood	155.646
Sibyls	
parapsychology	133.324 8
religion	206.1
Sichuan Sheng (China)	T2—513 8
Sicilian dialect	T6—51
Sicilianas	793.3
music	784.188 3

Sicily (Italy)	945.8
	T2—458
ancient	937.8
	T2—378
Sicily (Kingdom)	945.8
Sicily, Strait of	551.461 381
	T2—163 81
Sick leave	331.257 62
economics	331.257 62
government-sponsored	
insurance	368.452
personnel management	658.312 2
Sick people	305.908 7
	T1—087 7
architecture for	720.877
clothing	
home sewing	646.401
collected biography	T1—092 7
cooking for	641.563 1
devotional literature	
Christianity	242.4
government programs	
(nonhealth)	353.539
guides to religious life	204.42
Christianity	248.861
health services	362.1
public administration	353.6
home care	649.8
pastoral care	206.1
Christianity	259.41
recreation	790.196
indoor	793.019 6
outdoor	796.087 7
religious rites	203.8
Christianity	265.82
social group	305.908 7
social theology	201.762 1
Christianity	261.832 1
social welfare	362.1
see Manual at 362.1–.4 vs.	
610	
Sickle cell anemia	
medicine	616.152 7
see also Cardiovascular	
diseases — humans	
Sickness	362.1
medicine	616
see also Diseases — humans	
Sickness insurance	368.382
see also Insurance	
Sidama (African people)	T5—935
Sidamo (African people)	T5—935
Sidamo languages	493.5
	T6—935

Siddha medicine
  therapeutic system   615.538 4
Siddurim   296.45
Side arms
  art metalwork   739.72
  military engineering   623.44
Side-blown flutes   788.32
  see also Woodwind
    instruments
Side chapels
  architecture   726.595
Side dishes   641.81
Side drums   786.94
  see also Percussion instruments
Side effects of drugs
  pharmacokinetics   615.704 2
Side-necked turtles   597.929
Side-sewing
  bookbinding   686.35
Sideline markets   381.1
  see also Commerce
Sideline stores   381.1
  see also Commerce
Sidereal clocks
  astronomy   522.5
Sidereal day   529.1
Sidereal month   523.33
Siderite
  mineralogy   549.782
Siders (Switzerland :
  Bezirk)   T2—494 796 1
Sideshows   791.35
Sidewalks   388.411
  road engineering   625.88
  transportation services   388.411
Sidi Bel Abbès (Algeria :
  Province)   T2—651
Sidi Bernoussi-Zenata
  (Morocco)   T2—643 8
Sidi Kacem (Morocco :
  Province)   T2—643 5
Sidi-Youssef-Ben-Ali
  (Morocco)   T2—646 4
Sidings (Railroads)   625.163
Sidings (Walls)
  buildings   698
  wood   674.43
Sidney (B.C.)   T2—711 28
Sidon (Lebanon)   T2—569 2
  ancient   T2—394 4
Sidonian architecture   722.31
SIDS (Syndrome)
  pediatrics   618.920 26

Siedlce (Poland :
  Voivodeship)   T2—438 41
Siege of Vicksburg, 1863   973.734 4
Siege warfare   355.44
Siemens process   669.142 2
Siena (Italy)   T2—455 81
  ancient   T2—375 66
Siena (Italy : Province)   T2—455 8
  ancient   T2—375 66
Sieradz (Poland :
  Voivodeship)   T2—438 47
Sierra (Ecuador)   T2—866 1
Sierra County (Calif.)   T2—794 36
Sierra County (N.M.)   T2—789 67
Sierra Leone   966.4
      T2—664
Sierra Leoneans   T5—966 4
Sierra Madre del Sul
  (Mexico)   T2—727 3
Sierra Madre Occidental
  (Mexico)   T2—723
Sierra Madre Oriental
  (Mexico)   T2—724
Sierra Nevada de Santa
  Marta National Park
  (Colombia)   T2—861 16
Sierra Nevada Mountains
  (Calif. and Nev.)   T2—794 4
Sierra Region (Ecuador)   T2—866 1
Sierre (Switzerland :
  District)   T2—494 796 1
Sieves (Mathematics)   512.73
Sifakas   599.83
Siftings
  cereal grains
    commercial processing   664.720 8
    wheat   664.722 8
Sight   573.88
  see also Vision
Sight method (Reading)
  primary education   372.462
Sight-reading (Music)   781.423
  primary education   372.873
Sighthounds   636.753 2
Sighting apparatus
  military engineering   623.46
Sigillography   929.9
  insignia   929.9
  numismatics   737.6
Sigismund III, King of Poland
  and Sweden
  Swedish history   948.503 24
Sigmodon   599.357 2

Sigmoid colon	
human anatomy	611.347
human physiology	612.36
medicine	616.34
surgery	617.554 7
Sigmoid flexure	
human anatomy	611.347
human physiology	612.36
medicine	616.34
surgery	617.554 7
Sign language literatures	899.98
Sign languages	419
	T6—999 8
for deaf people	419
specific languages	419.4–.9
for hearing people	419.1
primary education	372.6
special education	371.912 46
Sign painting	667.6
Signage	
design	744.87
Signal corps	358.24
Signal generators	
electronics	621.381 548
Signal processing	621.382 2
Signal propagation	
communications engineering	621.382 4
satellite communication	621.382 54
Signal theory	003.54
communications engineering	621.382 23
systems	003.54
Signals	302.23
communications engineering	621.382 2
railroad transportation	385.316
engineering	625.165
law	343.095 2
transportation services	385.316
road transportation	388.312 2
engineering	625.794
law	343.094 6
transportation services	388.312 2
social psychology	302.23
street transportation	388.413 122
engineering	625.794
law	343.098 2
transportation services	388.413 122
transportation	388.041
engineering	629.040 289
law	343.093
transportation services	388.041
Signatures (Design)	744.63
Signboards	
social psychology	302.23

Signed English	
American	428.917
British	428.914 1
Signets	
numismatics	737.6
Signs	302.23
advertising	659.134
design	744.87
law	346.045
social psychology	302.23
transportation	388.041
engineering	629.040 289
transportation services	388.041
wooden	674.88
see also Signals	
Ṣiḥāḥ	
Hadith	297.125 4
Siirt İli (Turkey)	T2—566 78
ancient	T2—394 2
Sikh gurus	294.609 2
biography	294.609 2
role and function	294.663
Sikh philosophy	181.046
Sikh temples and shrines	294.635
architecture	726.146
Sikhism	294.6
art representation	704.948 946
Islamic polemics	297.294
Sikhism and Islam	294.615
Islamic view	297.284 6
Sikh view	294.615
Sikhs	
biography	294.609 2
Sikkim (India)	T2—541 67
Sikkimese	T5—914 17
1975–	T5—914 11
Sikoku Island (Japan)	T2—523
Sikoku Region (Japan)	T2—523
Siksika Indians	978.004 973 52
	T5—973 52
Siksika language	497.352
	T6—973 52
Silage	636.086 2
forage crop	633.2
Silence	
musical element	781.236
Silencers (Automobile part)	629.252
Silencers (Firearms)	
manufacturing technology	683.4
Silesia	T2—438 5
Czech Republic	T2—437 28
Poland	T2—438 5
Silesian War, 1740–1742	943.054
Silesian War, 1744–1745	943.054

Silesian War, 1756–1763	940.253 4
Silhouettes	741.7
animals	591.41
cutting	736.984
drawing	741.7
plants	581.41
Silicates	
mineralogy	549.6
Silicon	553.6
chemical engineering	661.068 3
chemistry	546.683
economic geology	553.6
materials science	620.193
organic chemistry	547.08
aliphatic	547.48
applied	661.88
see also Chemicals	
Silicon salts	
chemical engineering	661.43
Silicones	668.422 7
Silicosis	
medicine	616.244
see also Respiratory tract	
diseases — humans	
Silistra (Bulgaria : Oblast)	T2—499 38
Silk books	096.2
Silk cotton tree	583.775
Silk ribbon embroidery	746.447
Silk-screen printing	686.231 6
graphic arts	764.8
textile arts	746.62
Silk textiles	677.39
arts	746.043 9
see also Textiles	
Silk tree	583.633
Silkworms	638.2
culture	638.2
zoology	595.78
Silky flycatchers	598.853
Silky terrier	636.76
Sillimanite	
mineralogy	549.62
Sills (Geology)	551.88
Silo machinery	
manufacturing technology	681.763 1
Silos	633.208 68
Silphidae	595.764 2
Silt	
petrology	552.5
reservoir engineering	627.86
river engineering	627.122
Silurian period	551.732
geology	551.732
paleontology	560.173 2
Siluriformes	597.49
paleozoology	567.49
Silver	669.23
chemical engineering	661.065 4
chemistry	546.654
economic geology	553.421
extractive economics	338.274 21
materials science	620.189 23
metallography	669.952 3
metallurgy	669.23
metalworking	673.23
mining	622.342 3
physical metallurgy	669.962 3
see also Chemicals; Metals	
Silver Bow County (Mont.)	T2—786 68
Silver coins	332.404 2
investment economics	332.63
monetary economics	332.404 2
numismatics	737.4
Silver processes	
photography	772.4
Silver question	332.423 097 3
Silver standard	332.422 3
Silverfish (Insects)	595.723
Silverpoint drawing	741.25
Silversides	597.66
Silversmithing	739.23
Silversmiths	739.230 92
Silverware	
arts	739.238 3
table setting	642.7
Silviculture	634.95
Simaroubaceae	583.75
Simbu Province (Papua New Guinea)	T2—956 7
Simcoe (Ont. : County)	T2—713 17
Simdlangentsha (South Africa : District)	T2—684 2
Simḥat Torah	296.433 9
liturgy	296.453 39
Similarity (Mathematics)	516.2
Simile	808.032
Simmering	
home cooking	641.73
Simmonds' disease	
medicine	616.47
see also Endocrine	
diseases — humans	
Simonstown (South Africa : District)	T2—687 35
Simple microscopes	
biology	570.282 3
Simple proteins	572.66
see also Proteins	

Simples
  pharmacognosy 615.321
Simplexes 514.223
Simpson County (Ky.) T2—769 735
Simpson County (Miss.) T2—762 585
Simpson Desert National
  Park (Qld.) T2—943 7
Simpson Peninsula
  (Nunavut) T2—719 55
Simulation 003
  T1—011
  engineering 620.004 4
  instructional use 371.397
  management decision making 658.403 52
  mathematics 511.8
Simuliidae 595.772
Simultaneous play (Chess) 794.17
Sin 202.2
  Buddhism 294.342 2
  Christianity 241.3
    original sin 233.14
  Hinduism 294.522
  Islam 297.22
  Judaism 296.32
  moral theology 205
    Buddhism 294.35
    Christianity 241.3
    Hinduism 294.548
    Islam 297.5
    Judaism 296.36
Sinai (Egypt) 953.1
  T2—531
Sinai Campaign, 1956 956.044
Sinai Peninsula (Egypt) T2—531
  ancient 939.48
  T2—394 8
Sinaloa (Mexico : State) T2—723 2
Sindh (Pakistan) T2—549 18
Sindhi T5—914 25
Sindhi language 491.41
  T6—914 11
Sindhi literature 891.41
Sine-Saloum (Senegal) T2—663
Sinfonia concertantes 784.184 5
Sinfoniettas 784.184
  musical form 784.184
  orchestral music 784.218 4
Singapore 959.57
  T2—595 7
Singapore Strait 551.461 472
  T2—164 72
Singeing textiles 677.028 25
Singers 782.009 2

Singh, Charan
  Indian history 954.052
Singh, Manmohan
  Indian history 954.053 2
Singh, Vishwanath Pratap
  Indian history 954.052
Singida Region (Tanzania) T2—678 26
Singine (Switzerland) T2—494 539
Singing 783.043
Singing games 796.13
Single column tariffs 382.752
  see also Customs (Tariff)
Single fatherhood 306.874 22
Single idiophones 786.88
  see also Percussion instruments
Single-lens reflex cameras 771.32
Single-line outlets (Marketing) 381.14
  see also Commerce
Single men 306.815 2
  T1—086 52
  psychology 155.642 2
  social group 306.815 2
Single motherhood 306.874 32
  social welfare 362.839 532
Single mothers 306.874 32
  social welfare 362.839 532
Single-parent family 306.856
  social theology 201.7
    Christianity 261.835 856
  social welfare 362.829 4
    see also Families — social
      welfare
Single parents 306.856
  child care handbooks 649.102 43
  religion 204.41
Single people 306.815
  T1—086 52
  psychology 155.642
  social group 306.815
Single-photon
  emission-computed
  tomography 616.075 75
Single-piece processes
  production management 658.533
Single-reed bagpipes 788.49
  see also Woodwind
    instruments
Single-reed instruments 788.6
  see also Woodwind
    instruments
Single-shot pistols 683.432
  see also Pistols
Single-sideband radio systems 621.384 153
Single-stage programming 519.702

836

Siros (Greece : Regional unit)	T2—495 85
Sisal	
botany	584.79
fiber crop	633.577
Sīsī, ʿAbd al-Fattāḥ	
Egyptian history	962.056
Siskins	598.885
Siskiyou County (Calif.)	T2—794 21
Sisonke District Municipality (South Africa)	T2—684 67
Sissach (Switzerland : Bezirk)	T2—494 339
Sissi, Abdel-Fatah el- Egyptian history	962.056
Sīstān va Balūchestān (Iran)	T2—558 3
Sister-brother relationship	306.875 3
Sister-sister relationship	306.875 4
Sisters	306.875
	T1—085 5
see also Siblings	
Sisters (Nurses)	610.730 92
role and function	610.730 69
Sisters (Women religious)	255.9
biography	271.900 2
see Manual at 230–280	
guides to Christian life	248.894 3
Sisters and brothers	306.875 3
psychology	155.443
Sisters of Bon Secours	255.94
church history	271.94
Sisters of Charity	255.91
church history	271.91
Sisters of Mercy	255.92
church history	271.92
Sistrums	786.885
see also Percussion instruments	
Sistrurus	597.963 8
SiSwati language	496.398 7
	T6—963 987
SiSwati literature	896.398 7
Sit-ins	
social conflict	303.61
Sitars	787.82
see also Stringed instruments	
Site planning	
architecture	720.28
Site selection	
home economics	643.12
nuclear engineering	621.483 2
Sitka (Alaska)	T2—798 2
Sitten (Switzerland)	T2—494 796 44

Sitten (Switzerland : District)	T2—494 796 4
Sittidae	598.82
Situation ethics	171.7
Situational influences psychology	155.93
Sivas İli (Turkey)	T2—565 5
ancient	T2—395 5
Siwa language	493.3
	T6—933
Siwi language	493.3
	T6—933
Six Days' War, 1967	956.046
Six-man football	796.332 8
Sixteenth century	909.5
	T1—090 31
Sixth century	909.1
	T1—090 21
Sixth-form colleges	373.238
Siyabuswa (South Africa)	T2—682 76
Siyanda District Municipality (South Africa)	T2—687 16
Size	530.81
animals	591.41
biological organisms	578.41
plants	581.41
Size of enterprise	338.64
economics	338.64
microeconomics	338.514 4
Size of farm	
economics	338.16
Size perception	
psychology	153.752
Size standards	
commerce	389.62
production management	658.562
Sizing coal	662.623
Sizing ores	622.74
Sizing paper	676.234
Sizuoka-ken (Japan)	T2—521 65
Sjælland (Denmark)	T2—489 1
Sjogren's syndrome	
medicine	616.775
see also Musculoskeletal diseases — humans	
Ska (Music)	781.646
Skagerrak (Denmark and Norway)	551.461 336
	T2—163 36
Skagit County (Wash.)	T2—797 72
Skamania County (Wash.)	T2—797 84
Skåne län (Sweden)	T2—486 1
Skåne landskap (Sweden)	T2—486 1

Skin diseases
  humans
    cancer (continued)
      social services — 362.196 994 77
      see also Cancer —
        humans
    geriatrics — 618.976 5
    incidence — 614.595
    medicine — 616.5
    pediatrics — 618.925
    pharmacokinetics — 615.778
    social services — 362.196 5
    surgery — 617.477
Skin diving — 797.232
Skin glands
  human physiology — 612.793
Skinks — 597.957
Skinner, B. F. (Burrhus Frederic)
  psychological system — 150.194 34
Skipjack (Tuna) — 597.783
Skipper flies — 595.774
Skippers — 595.788
Skips (Containers) — 622.68
Skirmishing (Tactics) — 355.422
Skirts — 391.477
  commercial technology — 687.117
  customs — 391.477
  home economics — 646.34
  home sewing — 646.437
  see also Clothing
Skis — 796.93
  manufacturing technology — 688.769 3
Skitswish Indians — T5—979 43
Skitswish language — 497.943
                   T6—979 43
Skittles — 794.6
Skolt Saami language — 494.576
                   T6—945 76
Skolt Sámi language — 494.576
                   T6—945 76
Skuas — 598.338
Skull
  anthropometry — 599.948
  fractures
    medicine — 617.155
  human anatomy — 611.715
  human physiology — 612.751
  medicine — 616.71
  surgery — 617.514
Skull base
  surgery — 617.514
Skunk cabbages — 584.442
Skunks — 599.768

Sky
  atmospheric optics — 551.565
  meteorology — 551.5
  religious worship — 202.12
Sky color — 551.566
Sky marshals — 363.287 6
Skydivers — 797.560 92
Skydiving — 797.56
  biography — 797.560 92
  see also Air sports
Skye, Island of (Scotland) — 941.154
                   T2—411 54
Skye and Lochalsh
  (Scotland) — T2—411 54
Skylights — 721.5
  architecture — 721.5
  construction — 690.15
Skyros Island (Greece) — T2—495 15
  ancient — T2—391 1
Skyscrapers — 720.483
  see also Tall buildings
Skysurfing — 797.56
  see also Air sports
Slabs
  structural engineering — 624.177 2
    concrete — 624.183 42
Slacks — 391.476
  see also Pants (Trousers)
Slag (Metallurgy) — 669.84
Slalom skiing — 796.935
Slander — 364.156
  ethics — 177.3
  law — 345.025 6
    criminal law — 345.025 6
    torts — 346.034
Slang — 417.2
  specific languages — T4—7
  see Manual at T4—7
Slang dictionaries — T1—03
Slash-and-burn agriculture
  technology — 631.581 8
Śląskie Voivodeship
  (Poland) — T2—438 58
Slate — 553.54
  building material — 691.2
  economic geology — 553.54
  petrology — 552.4
  quarrying — 622.354
Slaughterhouse residues
  use as fertilizer — 631.843
Slaughterhouses
  meat processing — 664.902 9
Slave kings
  Indian history — 954.023 2

Small fruits	581.464
horticulture	634.7
see also Berries	
Small game hunting	
sports	799.25
Small-group reading	
primary education	372.416 2
Small groups	302.34
pastoral work	
Christianity	253.7
Small industry	338.642
Small intestine	573.378
biology	573.378
human anatomy	611.341
human physiology	612.33
medicine	616.34
surgery	617.554 1
see also Digestive system	
Small-scale systems	003.7
Small states	321.06
international role	327.101
Small towns	307.762
Smallmouth bass	597.738 8
Smallpox	
incidence	614.521
medicine	616.912
see also Communicable	
diseases — humans	
Smara (Morocco : Province) T2—648	
Smart cards	006.246
banking services	332.178
computer science	006.246
credit economics	332.76
Smartphone cameras	771.32
Smartphones	004.167
Smartwatches	004.167
Smell	573.877
animal physiology	573.877
human physiology	612.86
Smell disorders	
medicine	616.856
see also Nervous system	
diseases — humans	
Smell perception	
psychology	152.166
Smelting	669.028 2
Smelts	641.392
cooking	641.692
food	641.392
zoology	597.5
Smilacaceae	584.6
Smilaxes (Asparagaceae)	
botany	584.79
Smilaxes (Smilacaceae)	584.6

Smith, Adam	
economic school	330.153
Smith, Ian Douglas	
Zimbabwean history	968.910 4
Smith County (Kan.)	T2—781 213
Smith County (Miss.)	T2—762 582
Smith County (Tenn.)	T2—768 52
Smith County (Tex.)	T2—764 225
Smithers (B.C.)	T2—711 82
Smithfield (South Africa : District)	T2—685 7
Smithton (Tas.)	T2—946 5
Smocking	
arts	746.44
Smog	363.739 2
air pollution	363.739 2
pollution technology	628.532
see also Pollution	
Smoke	541.345 15
colloid chemistry	541.345 15
applied	660.294 515
pollution technology	628.532
Smoke bomb launchers	623.445
Smoke bombs	623.451 6
Smoke damage insurance	368.12
see also Insurance	
Smoke pollution	363.738 7
see also Pollution	
Smoke signals	
design	744.26
social psychology	302.222
Smoke trees (Anacardiaceae)	583.75
Smoke trees (Fabaceae)	583.63
Smoked foods	
cooking	641.616 5
Smokeless powder	
military engineering	623.452 6
Smokers' supplies	688.4
Smoking	394.14
addiction	362.296
medicine	616.865
personal health	613.85
social welfare	362.296
see also Substance abuse	
customs	394.14
Smoking cessation	
medicine	616.865 06
Smoking foods	664.028 6
commercial preservation	664.028 6
home preservation	641.465
Smolensk (Russia : Oblast)	T2—472 7
Smolenskaia oblast' (Russia)	T2—472 7
Smolian (Bulgaria : Oblast)	T2—499 72

Smolyan (Bulgaria : Oblast)	T2—499 72
Smooth muscle tissues	
human histology	612.740 45
SMP (Insurance)	368.094
see also Insurance	
Smuggling	364.133 6
law	345.023 36
Smut fungi	579.593
agricultural diseases	632.493
Smuts	579.593
agricultural diseases	632.493
Smuts, Jan Christiaan	
South African history	968.053
1919–1924	968.053
1939–1948	968.055
Smyrna (Turkey)	T2—562 5
ancient	T2—392 3
Smyth County (Va.)	T2—755 723
Snacks	642
commercial processing	664.6
cooking	641.53
customs	394.125 3
Snail farming	639.483 8
Snails	594.3
Snails (Land)	594.38
agricultural pests	632.643 8
control technology	628.964
culture	639.483 8
food	641.394
commercial processing	664.95
cooking	641.694
zoology	594.38
Snake eels	597.43
Snake flies	595.747
Snake-necked turtles	597.929
Snake plants	584.79
Snake River (Wyo.-Wash.)	T2—796 1
Idaho	T2—796 1
Oregon	T2—795 7
Washington	T2—797 4
Wyoming	T2—787 55
Snake venom	
human toxicology	615.942
Snakeflies	595.747
Snakeheads (Fishes)	597.64
Snakes	597.96
resource economics	333.957 96
small game hunting	799.257 96
Snakes as pets	639.396
Snap beans	641.356 52
botany	583.63
cooking	641.656 52
food	641.356 52
Snapdragons	635.933 96
botany	583.96
floriculture	635.933 96
Snappers (Fishes)	597.72
cooking	641.692
food	641.392
sports fishing	799.177 2
Snapping beetles	595.765
Snapping turtles	597.922
Snare drums	786.94
see also Percussion instruments	
Snares Islands (N.Z.)	T2—939 9
Sneeuberg (South Africa)	T2—687 56
Snipe flies	595.773
Snipers	356.162
Snipes (Birds)	598.33
Snobbishness	
arts	T3C—353
literature	808.803 53
history and criticism	809.933 53
specific literatures	T3B—080 353
history and	
criticism	T3B—093 53
Snohomish County (Wash.)	T2—797 71
Snooker	794.735
Snooks	597.72
sports fishing	799.177 2
Snoring	
medicine	616.209
Snorkeling	797.232
Snout beetles	595.768
Snow	551.578 4
building construction	693.91
meteorology	551.578 4
weather forecasting	551.647 84
weather modification	551.687 84
Snow camping	796.54
Snow carving	736.94
Snow-compacted roads	388.12
engineering	625.792
see also Roads	
Snow control	
airport engineering	629.136 37
road engineering	625.763
Snow cover	551.578 46
biology	578.758 6
ecology	577.586
see also Snow	
Snow drifts	551.578 47
Snow fences	
railroad engineering	625.13
road engineering	625.763
Snow goose	598.417 5

Snow leopard	599.755 5	Soaps	668.12
conservation technology	639.979 755 5	Soapstone	553.55
resource economics	333.959 755 5	building material	691.2
Snow monkey	599.864 4	economic geology	553.55
Snow-on-the-mountain (Plant)	583.69	quarrying	622.355
Snow removal		Soaring	
airport engineering	629.136 37	aeronautics	629.132 31
road engineering	625.763	sports	797.55
road transportation	388.312	*see also* Air sports	
Snow sports	796.9	Sobhuza II, King of Swaziland	
equipment technology	688.769	Swazi history	968.870 3
see also Winter sports		Sobolev spaces	515.782
Snow surveys	551.579	Sóc Trăng (Vietnam :	
Snowballs (Plants)	635.933 987	Province)	T2—597 9
botany	583.987	Soccer	796.334
floriculture	635.933 987	electronic games	794.863 34
Snowboard cross	796.939	rules	796.334 020 22
see also Winter sports		*see also* Ball games	
Snowboarding	796.939	Soccer players	796.334 092
see also Winter sports		Soccer shoes	
Snowdonia (Wales)	T2—429 25	manufacturing technology	688.763 34
Snowfall	551.578 4	Soccsksargen (Philippines)	T2—599 74
see also Snow		Social acceptance	302.14
Snowmobiles	388.348 8	Social action	361.2
driving	629.283 042	Social adjustment	302.14
engineering	629.228 8	Social anthropologists	306.092
repair	629.287 042	Social anthropology	306
sports	796.94	Social attitudes	303.38
transportation services	388.348 8	Social behavior	302
see also Off-road vehicles		*see Manual at* 302–307 vs. 156	
Snowplowing		Social behavior (Animals)	591.56
railroad engineering	625.100 288	Social breakdown	361.1
road engineering	625.763	Social casework	361.32
Snowplows		Social causes of war	355.027 4
railroad engineering	625.22	World War I	940.311 4
Snowsheds	625.13	World War II	940.531 14
Snowshoeing	796.92	Social change	303.4
see also Winter sports		Social choice	302.13
Snowshoes		Social classes	305.5
manufacturing technology	688.769 2		T1—086 2
Snowstorms	551.555	civil rights	323.322
social services	363.349 25	customs	390.2
see also Disasters		dress	391.02
Snowy Mountains (N.S.W.)	T2—944 7	relations with government	323.322
Snuffboxes		religion	200.862
handicrafts	745.593 4	Christianity	270.086 2
Snyder County (Pa.)	T2—748 49	social welfare	362.892
Soap carving	736.95	*see Manual at* 305.9 vs. 305.5	
Soap operas	791.446	Social classification	025.487
radio programs	791.446	Social classification systems	025.487
television programs	791.456	Social clubs	367
Soapberries	583.75	Social conflict	303.6
Soapbox racing	796.6	influence on crime	364.256
see also Sports		public safety	363.32

Social conservatism	
political ideology	320.52
Social contract	320.11
Social control	303.33
Social credit money	332.56
Social Credit Party of Canada	324.271 05
Social customs	390
armed forces	355.1
Social dancing	793.3
Social decay	303.45
Social democracy	335.5
economic system	335.5
political ideology	320.531 5
Social democratic parties	324.217 2
international organizations	324.172
Social Democratic Party of	
Austria	324.243 607 2
Social Democratic Party of	
Germany	324.243 072
Social Democratic Party of	
Switzerland	324.249 407 2
Social Democratic Worker Party	
(Austria)	324.243 602 7
Social deterioration	303.45
Social determinants	
individual psychology	155.234
Social dysfunction	
collective behavior	302.17
individual interactions	302.542
individual reactions	302.54
Social education	370.115
Social engineering (Computer	
security)	364.163
Social environment	
psychological influence	155.92
Social equality	305
religion	200.8
Christianity	270.08
Judaism	296.08
Social ethics	170
sociology	303.372
Social evolution	303.4
Social forecasts	303.49
Social gerontology	362.6
Social groups	305
T1—08	
influence on crime	364.253
religion	200.8
Christianity	270.08
Judaism	296.08
see Manual at T1—08; *also at*	
306 vs. 305, 909, 930–990	

Social history	306.09
Algerian Revolution	965.046 1
American Revolution	973.31
Chaco War	989.207 161
Civil War (England)	942.062 1
Civil War (Spain)	946.081 1
Civil War (United States)	973.71
Crimean War	947.073 81
Falkland Islands War	997.110 241
Franco-German War	943.082 1
Hundred Years' War	944.025 1
Indo-Pakistan War, 1971	954.920 511
Indochinese War	959.704 11
Iraq War, 2003–2011	956.704 431
Iraqi-Iranian Conflict	955.054 21
Korean War	951.904 21
Mexican War	973.621
Napoleonic Wars	940.271
Persian Gulf War, 1991	956.704 421
South African War	968.048 1
Spanish-American War	973.891
Thirty Years' War	940.241
Vietnamese War	959.704 31
War of 1812	973.521
War of the Pacific	983.061 61
World War I	940.31
World War II	940.531
Social identity	305
Social indexing	025.487
Social inequality	305
Social influence	302.13
psychology	155.92
Social innovation	303.484
Social insects	595.79
physiology of caste	571.882 157 9
Social institutions	306
see Manual at 302–307 vs. 320	
Social insurance	368.4
law	344.02
public administration	353.54
see also	
Government-sponsored	
insurance; Insurance	
Social interaction	302
Social justice	303.372
law	340.115
Social law	344.01
Social learning	303.32
Social legislation	344.01
Social market economy	330.126

Social themes
  arts (continued)
    folklore — 398.275
      history and criticism — 398.355
    literature — 808.803 55
      history and criticism — 809.933 55
      specific literatures — T3B—080 355
        history and
          criticism — T3B—093 55
Social theology — 201.7
  Buddhism — 294.337
  Christianity — 261
    see Manual at 241 vs. 261.8;
      also at 260 vs. 250
  Hinduism — 294.517
  Islam — 297.27
  Judaism — 296.38
Social understanding — 302.12
Social values — 303.372
Social welfare — 361
  see also Welfare services
Social welfare reformers — 361.240 92
Social work — 361.3
Social workers — 361.309 2
Socialism — 335
  economics — 335
  political ideology — 320.531
  sociology — 306.345
  see Manual at 335 vs. 306.345,
    320.53
Socialist communities — 307.77
Socialist ethics — 171.7
Socialist International — 324.174
Socialist Labor Party (U.S.) — 324.273 7
Socialist parties — 324.217 4
  international organizations — 324.174
Socialist Party (U.S.) — 324.273 7
Socialist Party of Italian Workers
  (1893–1895) — 324.245 027
Socialist Party of Italian Workers
  (1925–1927) — 324.245 027
Socialist Party of Italian Workers
  (1947–1951) — 324.245 072 2
Socialist Party of Proletarian
  Unity (Italy : 1943–1947) — 324.245 074 2
Socialist Party of Proletarian
  Unity (Italy : 1947–1951) — 324.245 074
Socialist Unity Party of Germany — 324.243 075
Socialist Worker Party
  (Switzerland) — 324.249 407 5
Socialist Workers Party (U.S.) — 324.273 7
Socialists — 335.009 2
Socialization — 303.32

Socially disadvantaged children — 305.230 869 4
  home care — 649.156 7
  psychology — 155.456 7
  social group — 305.230 869 4
Socially disadvantaged people — 305.56
               T1—086 94
  government programs — 353.53
  libraries for — 027.6
  religion — 200.869 4
    Hinduism — 294.508 694
  social group — 305.56
  social welfare — 362
    public administration — 353.53
Socially responsible investments — 332.604 2
Societies — 060
  fraternal organizations — 369
  see also Nonprofit
    organizations
Society — 301
Society Islands — T2—962 1
Society of Christian Israelites — 289.9
Society of Friends — 289.6
  biography — 289.609 2
  church government — 262.096
    local church — 254.096
  church law — 262.989 6
  doctrines — 230.96
    catechisms and creeds — 238.96
  general councils — 262.596
  guides to Christian life — 248.489 6
  missions — 266.96
  moral theology — 241.049 6
  persecution of — 272.8
  public worship — 264.096
  religious associations — 267.189 6
  religious education — 268.896
  seminaries — 230.073 96
  theology — 230.96
Society of Jesus — 255.53
  church history — 271.53
Society of the Cincinnati — 369.13
Socinianism — 289.1
Sociobiology — 304.5
  animal behavior — 591.56
  biological ecology — 577.8
  ethical systems — 171.7
  human behavior — 304.5
  see Manual at 302–307 vs. 156
Socioeconomic classes — 305.5
               T1—086 2
  see also Social classes

Sofia (Bulgaria)	T2—499 9
Soft drinks	641.26
see also Nonalcoholic beverages	
Soft-fiber crops	633.5
Soft rock	781.66
Soft-shelled turtles	597.926
Soft toys	
making	688.724
handicrafts	745.592 4
technology	688.724
Soft-winged flower beetles	595.763
Softball	796.357 8
see also Ball games	
Softening (Water treatment)	628.166 6
Software	005.3
	T1—028 553
cataloging	025.344
coding	005.13
see Manual at 005.1 vs. 005.13	
graphics	006.68
library treatment	025.174
multimedia systems	006.78
see Manual at T1—0285; *also at* 004 vs. 005; *also at* 005.1 vs. 005.3; *also at* 005.3	
Software compatibility	005.132 4
Software design	005.12
Software development	005.1
	T1—028 551
graphics	006.66
multimedia systems	006.76
see Manual at 005.1 vs. 005.13; *also at* 005.1 vs. 005.3; *also at* 005.268 vs. 005.265, 005.269	
Software development methods	005.111
Software documentation	
preparation	005.15
text	005.3
Software engineering	005.1
Software frameworks	005.1
Software maintenance	005.16
Software measurement	005.146
Software metrics	005.146
Software packages	005.3
Software patterns	005.132 67
Software piracy	346.048 2
criminal law	345.026 62
criminology	364.166 2
law	346.048 2
Software portability	005.132 4
Software reengineering	005.166

Software reliability	005.132 2
management	005.132 206 8
Software security	005.8
Software testing	005.14
Software verification	005.14
Softwoods	
forestry	634.975
lumber	674.144
Sof͞ia Alekseevna, Regent of Russia	
Russian history	947.049
Sogdian language	491.53
	T6—915 3
Sogdian literature	891.53
Sogdiana	T2—396
SOGI (Sexual orientation and gender identity)	306.76
Soglo, Nicéphore Dieudonné	
Beninese history	966.830 52
Sogn og Fjordane fylke (Norway)	T2—483 8
Soil	631.4
see also Soils	
Soil acidity	631.42
Soil alkalinity	631.42
Soil biochemistry	
soil science	631.417
Soil biology	578.757
agriculture	631.46
Soil chemistry	631.41
Soil classification	631.44
Soil compaction	624.151 363
Soil conditioners	631.82
chemical engineering	668.64
Soil conservation	333.731 6
agriculture	631.45
land economics	333.731 6
law	346.046 731 6
public administration	354.343 4
Soil consolidation	624.151 362
Soil ecology	577.57
Soil erosion	551.302
agriculture	631.45
engineering	627.5
geology	551.302
see also Erosion	
Soil factors	
floriculture	635.955
Soil fertility	631.422
Soil formation	551.305
frost action	551.38
Soil mechanics	624.151 36
agriculture	631.433
engineering geology	624.151 36

Soil mechanics (continued)	
railroad engineering	625.122
road engineering	625.732
Soil moisture	631.432
Soil physics	
soil science	631.43
Soil pollution	363.739 6
law	344.046 34
public administration	354.343 5
social welfare	363.739 6
technology	628.55
see also Pollution	
Soil science	631.4
Soil stabilization	624.151 363
Soil surveys	631.47
agriculture	631.47
engineering	624.151 7
Soil temperature	631.436
Soil texture	
agriculture	631.433
conditioners	631.826
Soil working	631.51
equipment manufacturing	
technology	681.763 1
Soilless culture	631.585
Soils	631.4
	T2—148
agriculture	631.4
biology	578.757
ecology	577.57
engineering geology	624.151
materials science	620.191
petrology	552.5
railroad engineering	625.122
road engineering	625.732
Sojas	583.63
Sōka Gakkai	294.392 8
Sokoto State (Nigeria)	T2—669 62
Sokotrans	T5—929
Sokotri language	492.9
	T6—929
Sokotri literature	892.9
Sokotri people	T5—929
Solanaceae	583.959 3
Solanales	583.959
Solano County (Calif.)	T2—794 52
Solar batteries	621.312 44
Solar cells	621.312 44
Solar collectors	621.472
Solar day	529.1
Solar desalinization	628.167 25
Solar energy	333.792 3
architectural consideration	720.472 4
astronomy	523.72
Solar energy (continued)	
economics	333.792 3
engineering	621.47
law	343.092 8
public administration	354.48
Solar energy-powered	
automobiles	
engineering	629.229 5
Solar energy-powered vehicles	388.349 5
engineering	629.229 5
transportation services	388.349 5
Solar engineers	621.470 92
Solar engines	621.473
automotive	629.250 8
ships	623.872 7
Solar flares	523.75
Solar furnaces	621.477
Solar granulation	523.74
Solar heating	621.47
buildings	697.78
Solar houses	643.2
architecture	728.370 472 4
home economics	643.2
see also Dwellings	
Solar interior	523.76
Solar prominences	523.75
Solar radiation	523.72
meteorology	551.527 1
Solar system	523.2
	T2—99
Solar wind	523.58
Soldering	671.56
decorative arts	739.14
sculpture	731.41
Soldering equipment	621.977
Soldier beetles	595.764 4
Soldier flies	595.773
Soldierfishes	597.64
Soldierly qualities	355.13
Soldiers	355.009 2
law	343.01
civil rights	342.085
law of war	341.67
Soldiers of fortune	355.354
Sole bargaining rights	331.889 6
Sole proprietorships	338.72
see also Proprietorships	
Sole traders	
law	346.068
Solenodons	599.33
Solenogastres	594.2
Soles (Fishes)	597.69
cooking	641.692
food	641.392

Soleure (Switzerland :
  Canton)   T2—494 35
Solicitors (Lawyers)   340.092
Solid dynamics   531.3
Solid foams   541.345 13
  chemical engineering   660.294 513
Solid-gas interfaces   530.417
Solid geometry   516.23
  analytic   516.33
  Euclidean   516.23
Solid-liquid interfaces   530.417
Solid mechanics
  engineering   620.105
Solid particles   530.413
  classical mechanics   531.16
  solid-state physics   530.413
Solid propellants   662.26
  aircraft   629.134 351
  military engineering   623.452 6
  spacecraft   629.475 24
Solid solutions
  metallurgy   669.94
Solid-state chemistry   541.042 1
Solid-state lasers   621.366 1
Solid-state physics   530.41
  see Manual at 548 vs. 530.41
Solid-state storage   004.568
  engineering   621.397 68
Solid wastes   363.728 5
  law   344.046 22
  social services   363.728 5
  technology   628.44
  see also Waste control
Solidification   536.42
  metallurgy   669.94
Solids
  chemical engineering   660.041
  expansion and contraction   536.414
  geometry   516.156
  heat transfer   536.23
  sound transmission   534.22
  specific heat   536.63
  state of matter   530.41
Solifugae   595.48
Solihull (England :
  Metropolitan Borough)   T2—424 97
Solipsism
  epistemology   121.2
Solís Rivera, Luis Guillermo
  Costa Rican history   972.860 531
Solitaire   795.43
Solitary confinement   365.644

Solitude
  psychology   155.92
  religious practice   204.47
    Christianity   248.47
Solo instruments   786–788
  bands and orchestras   784
  chamber ensembles   785
Solo voices   783.2
Sologne (France)   T2—445 3
Sololá (Guatemala : Dept.)   T2—728 164
Solomon, King of Israel
  Biblical leader   222.530 92
  Palestinian history   933.02
Solomon Islands   995.93
      T2—959 3
Solomon River (Kan.)   T2—781 2
Solomon Sea   551.461 476
      T2—164 76
Solothurn (Switzerland)   T2—494 357 7
Solothurn (Switzerland :
  Canton)   T2—494 35
Solothurn-Lebern
  (Switzerland)   T2—494 357
Solpugida   595.48
Solubility   541.342
  chemical engineering   660.294 2
Soluble soaps   668.124
Solutes   541.348 3
  chemical engineering   660.294 83
Solution chemistry   541.34
  applied   660.294
Solution mining   622.22
Solutions (Pharmaceuticals)
  pharmaceutical chemistry   615.19
Solutrean culture   930.128
Solvent abuse   362.299 3
Solvent extraction
  chemical engineering   660.284 248
Solvents   541.348 2
  chemical engineering   660.294 82
  organic   661.807
Solway Firth (England and
  Scotland)   551.461 337
      T2—163 37
Sólyom, László
  Hungarian history   943.905 43
Somali   T5—935 4
Somali Democratic Republic   967.73
      T2—677 3
  people   T5—935 4
Somali-Ethiopian Conflict,
  1978–1991   963.071
Somali kelel (Ethiopia)   T2—632

Sooke (B.C.)	T2—711 28	Sorgo	633.62
Sooke Lake (B.C.)	T2—711 28	forage crop	633.257 4
Sophia, Regent of Russia		syrup crop	633.62
Russian history	947.049	Soria (Spain : Province)	T2—463 55
Sophistic philosophy	183.1	Soriano (Uruguay : Dept.)	T2—895 27
Sophonias (Biblical book)	224.96	Soricidae	599.336
Sopranino recorders	788.363	Sørlandet (Norway)	T2—483 1
see also Woodwind		Sororities	369.082
instruments		education	371.856
Soprano recorders	788.364	Sorosilicates	
see also Woodwind		mineralogy	549.63
instruments		Sorrel (Polygonaceae)	641.355 6
Soprano saxophones	788.72	botany	583.888
see also Woodwind		cooking	641.655 6
instruments		food	641.355 6
Soprano voices	782.66	garden crop	635.56
children's	782.76	Sorrento (Vic.)	T2—945 2
choral and mixed voices	782.76	Sorrow	152.4
single voices	783.76	Sorsogon (Philippines :	
general works	782.66	Province)	T2—599 185
choral and mixed voices	782.66	Sort algorithms	005.741
single voices	783.66	Sorting data	005.741
women's	782.66	Sorting machines	
choral and mixed voices	782.66	manufacturing technology	681.14
single voices	783.66	Soshanguve (South Africa :	
Sør-Trøndelag fylke		District)	T2—682 27
(Norway)	T2—484 1	Sotah	296.123 3
Sorbet	641.863	Babylonian Talmud	296.125 3
commercial processing	637.4	Mishnah	296.123 3
home preparation	641.863	Palestinian Talmud	296.124 3
Sorbian language	491.88	Sotalia	599.538
	T6—918 8	Soteriology	202.2
Sorbian literature	891.88	Christianity	234
Sorbs	T5—918 8	Islam	297.22
Sorcerers (Religious leaders)	200.92	Judaism	296.32
biography	200.92	Sotho (African people)	T5—963 977
role and function	206.1	Sotho languages	496.397 7
see Manual at 200.92 *and*			T6—963 977
201–209, 292–299		Sotho-Tswana languages	496.397 7
Sordariales	579.567		T6—963 977
Sorex	599.336 2	Soto	294.392 7
Sorghum sugars	641.336 2	Soufflés	641.82
commercial processing	664.133	Souk Ahras (Algeria :	
food	641.336 2	Province)	T2—655
see also Sugar		Soul	128.1
Sorghum syrup	641.336 2	philosophy	128.1
commercial processing	664.133	religion	202.2
food	641.336 2	Christianity	233.5
see also Sugar		Islam	297.225
Sorghums	584.924	Judaism	296.32
botany	584.924	Soul food cooking	641.592 960 73
forage crop	633.257 4	Soul music	781.644
grain crop	633.174	songs	782.421 644
syrup crop	633.62		

South Asian languages	T6—911
South Asian theater (World War II)	940.542 5
South Asians	T5—914
South Athens (Greece)	T2—495 12
South Atlantic Ocean	551.461 35
	T2—163 5
South Atlantic States	975
	T2—75
see also Southeastern States	
South Australia	T2—942 3
South Ayrshire (Scotland)	T2—414 64
South Bedfordshire (England)	T2—425 63
South Bend (Ind.)	T2—772 89
South Bucks (England)	T2—425 98
South Cambridgeshire (England)	T2—426 57
South Carolina	975.7
	T2—757
South Caucasian languages	499.968
	T6—999 68
South Central States	976
	T2—76
South China Sea	551.461 472
	T2—164 72
South Coast (South Africa)	T2—684 5
South Cotabato (Philippines)	T2—599 744
South Dakota	978.3
	T2—783
South Derbyshire (England)	T2—425 19
South Dobruja	T2—499 42
South Downs (England)	T2—422 6
South Dravidian languages	494.81
	T6—948 1
South Dravidian literatures	894.81
South Dravidians	T5—948 1
South-East Sulawesi (Indonesia)	T2—598 48
South frigid zone	T2—116
South Georgia and South Sandwich Islands	T2—971 2
South Georgia Island	T2—971 2
South Glamorgan (Wales)	T2—429 87
South Gloucestershire (England)	T2—423 91
South Halmahera-West New Guinea languages	499.5
	T6—995
South Hams (England)	T2—423 592
South Herefordshire (England)	T2—424 2
South Holland (England)	T2—425 39
South Holland (Netherlands)	T2—492 38
South Island (N.Z.)	T2—937
South Kalimantan (Indonesia)	T2—598 36
South Karelia (Finland)	T2—489 711
South Kesteven (England)	T2—425 38
South Khorāsān (Iran)	T2—559 2
South Korea	951.95
	T2—519 5
South Koreans	T5—957 051 95
South Lakeland (England)	T2—427 83
South Lanarkshire (Scotland)	T2—414 57
South Mbundu languages	496.399
	T6—963 99
South Norfolk (England)	T2—426 19
South Northamptonshire (England)	T2—425 59
South Orange (N.J.)	T2—749 33
South Orkney Islands	T2—989
South Osset (Georgia)	T2—475 8
South Ostrobothnia (Finland)	T2—489 736
South Oxfordshire (England)	T2—425 79
South Pacific Ocean	551.461 48
	T2—164 8
South Pembrokeshire (Wales)	T2—429 62
South Platte River (Colo. and Neb.)	T2—788 7
South Pole	T2—989
South Ribble (England)	T2—427 67
South Saami language	494.572 2
	T6—945 722
South Saami literature	894.572 2
South Sámi language	494.572 2
	T6—945 722
South Sámi literature	894.572 2
South Sandwich Islands	T2—971 2
South Sardinia (Italy)	T2—459 8
ancient	T2—379 8
South Saskatchewan River (Alta. and Sask.)	T2—712 42
South Savo (Finland)	T2—489 755
South Semitic languages	492.8
	T6—928
South Semitic literatures	892.8
South Shetland Islands	T2—989
South Slavic languages	491.81
	T6—918 1
South Slavic literatures	891.81
South Slavic peoples	T5—918 1

Southern Nations, Nationalities, and Peoples Federal State (Ethiopia)   T2—633
Southern Paiute Indians   T5—974 576 9
Southern Paiute language   497.457 69
  T6—974 576 9
Southern Province (Zambia)   T2—689 4
Southern question (Italy)   945.709
Southern Rhodesia   968.910 2
  T2—689 1
Southern Sotho language   496.397 72
  T6—963 977 2
Southern Sotho literature   896.397 72
Southern Sporades (Greece)   T2—495 87
  ancient   T2—391 6
Southern States   975
  T2—75
  War of 1812   973.523 8
Southern Tiwa Indians   T5—974 97
Southern Tiwa language   497.497
  T6—974 97
Southern Turkic languages   494.36
  T6—943 6
Southern Uplands (Scotland)   T2—413 7
Southern Vietnam   T2—597 7
Southern Yemen   953.35
  T2—533 5
Southern Yemenis   T5—927 533 5
Southland District (N.Z.)   T2—939 6
Southland Region (N.Z.)   T2—939 6
Southport (Qld.)   T2—943 2
Southwark (London, England)   T2—421 64
Southwest, New   979
  T2—79
Southwest, Old   976
  T2—76
Southwest jazz   781.653
Southwest Pacific Ocean   551.461 47
  T2—164 7
Southwest Turkic languages   494.36
  T6—943 6
Southwestern Ontario   T2—713 2
Southwestern States   T2—79
Soutpansberg (South Africa : District)   T2—682 57
Soutpansberg (South Africa : Mountains)   T2—682 57
Sovereigntist parties   324.218 4
Sovereignty   320.15
  law of nations   341.26

Sovereignty of God   212.7
  Christianity   231.7
  comparative religion   202.112
  Judaism   296.311 2
  philosophy of religion   212.7
Soviet Central Asia   958.4
  T2—584
Soviet communism   335.43
  economics   335.43
  political ideology   320.532 2
Soviet people   T5—917
Soviet Union   947.084
  T2—47
  Asia   957
  T2—57
Soviets (People)   T5—917
Sow bugs   595.372
Soweto (South Africa)   T2—682 21
Soweto Uprising, 1976   968.062 7
Sowing   631.531
Soy oil   641.356 55
  cooking   641.656 55
  food   641.356 55
  food technology   664.368
Soy sauce   641.356 55
  food   641.356 55
Soyas   583.63
Soybean flour   664.726
Soybean glue   668.33
Soybean meal   664.726
Soybean milk
  commercial processing   663.64
Soybeans   583.74
  agricultural economics   338.173 34
  botany   583.63
  commercial processing   664.805 655
  economics   338.476 647 26
  technology   664.726
  cooking   641.656 55
  field crop   633.34
  food   641.356 55
  garden crop   635.655
Soyfoods
  commercial processing technology   664.726
Sozialdemokratische Arbeiterpartei (Austria)   324.243 602 7
Sozialdemokratische Partei der Schweiz   324.249 407 2
Sozialdemokratische Partei Deutschlands   324.243 072
Sozialdemokratische Partei Österreichs   324.243 607 2

Spacecraft gunnery	623.556
Spacecraft rendezvous	
manned space flight	629.458 3
Spaces (Mathematics)	516
combinatorial topology	514.224
geometry	516
Spadefoots	597.86
Spaghetti	641.822
commercial processing	664.755
home preparation	641.822
Spain	946
	T2—46
ancient	936.6
	T2—366
Spalacidae	599.35
Spalding County (Ga.)	T2—758 443
Spaniards	T5—61
Spaniels	636.752 4
Spanish	T5—61
Spanish America	980
	T2—8
Spanish-American literature	860
Spanish-American War, 1898	973.89
societies	369.181
Spanish Americans	T5—68
Spanish Armada, 1588	942.055
Spanish drama	862
Spanish fiction	863
Spanish folk music	781.626 1
Spanish folk songs	782.421 626 1
Spanish Guinea	T2—671 8
Spanish language	460
	T6—61
foreign language instruction	
primary education	372.656 1
Spanish literature	860
Spanish Merino sheep	636.366
Spanish-Moroccan War,	
1859–1860	964.03
Spanish Morocco	T2—642
Spanish moss	584.98
Spanish plums	641.344 4
botany	583.75
cooking	641.644 4
food	641.344 4
Spanish poetry	861
Spanish Sahara	T2—648
Spanish satire	867
Spanish Succession, War of the,	
1701–1714	940.252 6
North American history	973.25
Spanish West Africa	T2—648
Spanners	621.972
Spar varnishes	667.79

Sparganium	584.99
Sparidae	597.72
Spark control devices	
automotive	629.258
Spark-ignition engines	621.434
automotive	629.250 4
ships	623.872 34
Sparkling wine	641.222 4
commercial processing	663.224
Sparrows	598.883
Sparrows (Fringillidae)	598.883
Sparrows (Passer)	598.887
Spars	623.862
Sparta (Greece)	T2—495 22
ancient	T2—389
Spartan supremacy	938.06
Spartanburg County (S.C.)	T2—757 29
Spas	
health	613.122
therapeutics	615.853
Spatial behavior	
human ecology	304.23
Spatial databases	
computer science	005.753
Spatial perception	
psychology	153.752
Spatial planning	
arts	711
Spatsizi River (B.C.)	T2—711 85
SPD (German political party)	324.243 072
Speaker recognition	
biometric identification	
computer science	006.248 392
computer science	006.248 392
engineering	621.399 4
Speakers (Communications	
devices)	621.382 84
Speaking	
applied linguistics	418
specific languages	T4—83
rhetoric	808.5
Speaking in tongues	234.132
Speaking voices	782.96
choral and mixed voices	782.96
single voices	783.96
Spearfishes	597.78
Spearfishing	799.14
Spears	623.441 5
art metalwork	739.72
sports	799.202 82
Special assessments	336.2
law	343.042
public administration	352.44

Speech errors	401.9	Spellers	418
specific languages	T4—019	specific languages	T4—813
Speech-impaired people	T1—087	Spelling	411
special education	371.914 2	applied linguistics	418
Speech output devices	006.54	specific languages	T4—813
engineering	621.399	specific subjects	T1—014
Speech perception	401.95	linguistics	411
specific languages	T4—019	specific languages	T4—152
Speech processing		primary education	372.632
computer science	006.454	standard language	410
Speech recognition		Spelling checkers (Computer	
computer science	006.454	software)	005.52
engineering	621.399 4	Spelling reform	418
Speech synthesis		specific languages	T4—813
computer science	006.54	Spells	203.32
engineering	621.399	Spells (Occultism)	133.44
Speech therapy		Spelthorne (England)	T2—422 12
medicine	616.855 06	Spelunkers	796.525 092
special education	371.914 2	Spelunking	796.525
Speeches	080	biography	796.525 092
literary criticism		*see also* Outdoor life	
theory	808.5	Spence Bay (Nunavut)	T2—719 55
literature	808.85	Spencer County (Ind.)	T2—772 31
history and criticism	809.5	Spencer County (Ky.)	T2—769 455
specific literatures	T3B—5	Spending	339.47
individual authors	T3A—5	Sperm	571.845 1
rhetoric	808.5	Sperm banks	362.178 3
Speechreading		Sperm whale	599.547
applied linguistics		Spermaceti	
specific languages	T4—895 4	chemical engineering	665.13
Speechwriting	808.5	Spermatocidal agents	
Speed control devices	621.812	health	613.943 2
Speed drills and tests		medicine	618.182
keyboarding	652.307	pharmacokinetics	615.766
shorthand	653.15	Spermatophyta	580
Speed letters		*see also* Plants	
office use	651.75	Spermophilus	599.365
Speed limits	388.314 4	Sperrin Mountains	
law	343.094 6	(Northern Ireland)	T2—416 2
urban	388.413 144	Spey, River (Scotland)	T2—411 58
Speed reading	418.4	Spezia (Province)	T2—451 83
specific languages	T4—843 2	Sphaeropsidales	579.55
Speed skating	796.914	Sphaerosepalaceae	583.77
Speedboats	387.231	Sphagnales	588.29
design	623.812 31	Sphalerite	
engineering	623.823 1	mineralogy	549.32
handling	623.882 31	Sphecoidea	595.798
transportation services	387.231	Sphenisciformes	598.47
see also Ships		paleozoology	568.4
Speedways		Sphenocleaceae	583.959
automobile racing	796.720 68	Sphenodontidae	597.945
Speller-dividers	413.1	Sphenophyllales	561.72
specific languages	T4—31	Sphenopsida	587.2
		paleobotany	561.72

Spinets	786.4
instrument	786.419
music	786.4
see also Keyboard instruments	
Spink County (S.D.)	T2—783 217
Spinner dolphins	599.534
Spinning (Fishing)	799.126
Spinning machines	
textile technology	677.028 52
Spinning textiles	677.028 22
arts	746.12
manufacturing technology	677.028 22
Spinor algebras	512.57
Spinor analysis	515.63
Spinosaurus	567.912
Spinulosa	593.93
Spiny anteaters	599.29
Spiny eels	597.7
Spiny-headed worms	592.33
Spiny rats	599.359
Spiny-rayed fishes	597.64
Spiral gears	621.833 3
Spirals	516.152
Spireas	635.933 642
botany	583.642
floriculture	635.933 642
Spires	721.5
architecture	721.5
construction	690.15
Spirit leveling	526.36
Spirit photography	133.92
Spirit varnishes	667.79
Spirit writings	133.93
Spirits (Discarnate beings)	133.9
apparitions	133.1
Spiritual beings	202.1
Christianity	235
Spiritual direction	206.1
Christianity	253.53
Spiritual exercises	204.3
Christianity	248.3
Spiritual gifts	
Christian doctrines	234.13
Spiritual healing	
medicine	615.852
religion	203.1
African religions	299.613 1
Christianity	234.131
miracles	231.73
miracles	202.117
Native American religions	299.713 1
Spiritual life	204.4
Buddhism	294.344 4
Christianity	248.4

Spiritual life (continued)	
Hinduism	294.544
Islam	297.57
Judaism	296.7
Spiritual renewal	203
Christianity	269
Islam	297.3
Spiritual therapies	
medicine	615.852
Spiritual warfare	235.4
Spiritual world	
occultism	133.901 3
Spiritualism	133.9
comparative religion	202.1
literature	808.803 7
history and criticism	809.933 7
specific literatures	T3B—080 37
history and criticism	T3B—093 7
philosophy	141
therapy	
medicine	615.852 8
Spiritualists	133.909 2
Spirituality	204
Buddhism	294.344
Christianity	248
Hinduism	294.54
Islam	297.57
Judaism	296.7
Spirituals	782.253
choral and mixed voices	782.525 3
single voices	783.092 53
Spirochetes	579.32
Spitsbergen Island (Norway)	T2—981
Spleen	573.155 5
biology	573.155 5
human anatomy	611.41
human physiology	612.415
medicine	616.41
surgery	617.551
see also Hematopoietic system	
Spleenworts	587.3
Splenic diseases	
medicine	616.41
see also Hematopoietic system diseases — humans	
Splicing	
ropes and cables	623.888 2
Splines	511.422 3
Split-level houses	
architecture	728.373
Split T formation	796.332 22

Sportswear (Activewear)   796
   see also Activewear
Sportswear (Casual wear)   391
   see also Casual wear
Sporulation   571.847
Spot removal
   household sanitation   648.1
Spot tests (Chemicals)   543.22
Spot welding   671.521 3
Spotsylvania County (Va.)   T2—755 365
Spotted dolphins   599.534
Spotted seal   599.792
Spotted turtle   597.925 7
Spouse abuse   362.829 2
   criminology   364.155 53
   law   345.025 553
   family relationships   306.872
   medicine   616.858 22
   social welfare   362.829 2
   see also Family violence
Spouses   306.872
   T1—086 55
   law   346.016 3
   see also Married people
Spouses of alcoholics
   medicine   616.861 9
   social welfare   362.292 3
Spouses of clergy
   Christianity   253.22
    biography   270.092
     specific denominations   280
     see Manual at 230–280
    pastoral theology   253.22
Spouses of substance abusers
   medicine   616.869
   social welfare   362.291 3
Sprains
   medicine   617.17
Sprang
   arts   746.422 4
Sprat   641.392
   cooking   641.692
   food   641.392
   zoology   597.452
Spratly Islands   T2—59
Spray painting   667.6
Sprayed latex   678.538
Spraying
   agricultural pest control   632.94
   painting   667.6
Spraying plants
   manufacturing technology   681.763 1
Spread formation
   American football   796.332 22

Spread latex   678.538
Spread rubber   678.36
Spreading latex   678.527
Spreadsheets (Computer
   software)   005.54
Sprechgesang   782.97
   choral and mixed voices   782.97
   single voices   783.97
Spree-Neisse (Germany :
   Landkreis)   T2—431 51
Spring   508.2
   music   781.524 2
   see also Seasons
Spring-flowering plants   581.43
   floriculture   635.953
Spring guns
   art metalwork   739.73
Springboard diving   797.24
   biography   797.240 92
   see also Aquatic sports
Springbok   599.646
Springfield (Ill.)   T2—773 56
Springfield (Mass.)   T2—744 26
Springhaas   599.359
Springs (Mechanisms)   621.824
   automotive engineering   629.243
   railroad engineering   625.21
Springs (South Africa :
   District)   T2—682 25
Springs (Water)   551.498
   water supply engineering   628.112
Springtails   595.725
Sprinkler systems
   fire technology   628.925 2
Sprinters   796.422 092
Sprints   796.422
   biography   796.422 092
Spruce budworm
   forest pest   634.975 267 8
Spruces   585.2
   forestry   634.975 2
   lumber   674.144
SPS (Swiss political party)   324.249 407 2
Spur gears   621.833 1
Spurge laurel   583.77
Spurges (Euphorbiaceae)   583.69
Spurious knowledge   001.9
Sputtering (Physics)
   solid-state physics   530.416
Spy stories   808.838 72
   history and criticism   809.387 2
   specific literatures   T3B—308 72
    individual authors   T3A—3

Staff trees	583.67	Stammering	
Staffing patterns	658.312 8	medicine	616.855 4
Stafford (England :		*see also* Communication	
Borough)	T2—424 64	disorders	
Stafford County (Kan.)	T2—781 813	pediatrics	618.928 554
Stafford County (Va.)	T2—755 26	Stamp Act, 1765–1766	
Staffordshire (England)	942.46	United States history	973.311 1
	T2—424 6	Stamp tax	336.272
Staffordshire Moorlands		law	343.057
(England)	T2—424 61	public administration	352.44
Stag beetles	595.764 9	public finance	336.272
Stage fright	792.028 019	Stamping metals	671.334
motion pictures	791.430 280 19	decorative arts	739.14
radio	791.440 280 19	sculpture	731.41
stage	792.028 019	Stamping tools	621.984
television	791.450 280 19	Stamps (Postage)	383.23
Stage presentations	792	*see also* Postage stamps	
see also Theater		Stamps (Seals)	
Stagecoach transportation	388.322 8	design	744.7
Stagecoaches	388.341	numismatics	737.6
manufacturing technology	688.6	Stand-up comedians	792.760 280 92
transportation services	388.341	Stand-up comedy	792.76
Stagflation	332.41	Standard deviation	519.534
Staghorn ferns	587.3	Standard-gage railroads	385
Stags	599.65	*see also* Railroads	
big game hunting	799.276 5	Standard industrial classifications	338.020 12
Stained glass		Standard language	
arts	748.5	applied linguistics	418
Staining (Microscopy)	502.82	education	418.007 1
biology	570.282 7	specific languages	T4—800 71
Staining (Woodwork)		description and analysis	411–415
buildings	698.32	specific languages	
Stainless steel	669.142	applied linguistics	T4—8
decorative arts	739.4	description and analysis	T4—1–5
see also Steel		Standard Malay language	499.28
Stains			T6—992 8
manufacturing technology	667.2	Standard Malay literature	899.28
Stairs	721.832	Standard of living	
architecture	721.832	macroeconomics	339.47
construction	690.183 2	Standard time	389.17
Stalin, Joseph		Standardbred horse	636.175
Russian history	947.084 2	Standardization	389.6
Stalingrad, Battle of, 1942–1943	940.542 174 7		T1—021 8
Stalk-eyed flies	595.774	commerce	389.6
Stalkers		law	343.075
biography	364.158 092	production management	658.562
Stalking	364.158	public administration	352.83
law	345.025 8	Standardized tests	371.262
social welfare	362.888	primary education	372.126 2
Stalking victims	362.888	reading	372.482
see also Victims of crime		*see Manual at* 371.262 vs.	
Stamens	575.65	371.264	
Stamford (Conn.)	T2—746 9		

Stegosauria	567.915
Stegosaurus	567.915 3
Steiermark (Austria)	T2—436 5
Stein algebras	512.55
Steiner-Waldorf method	371.391
Stellar evolution	523.88
Stellar magnitudes	523.822
Stellar radiation	523.82
Stellenbosch (South Africa : District)	T2—687 33
Stelleroidea	593.93
paleozoology	563.93
Steller's sea cow	599.559 168
Stem cells	
experimental research medicine	616.027 74
Stem vegetables	
garden crops	635.3
Stemonaceae	584.55
Stemonitales	579.52
Stems (Plants)	581.495
descriptive botany	581.495
physiology	575.4
reproductive adaptation	581.46
Stenciling	
decorative arts	745.73
Stencils	
mechanical printing technique	686.231 6
office use	652.4
Stenella	599.534
Stenographers	651.374 109 2
office services	651.374 1
Stenographic machines	
manufacturing technology	681.61
Stenography	653.14
Stenolaemata	594.67
Stepbrothers	306.875
	T1—085 5
see also Siblings	
Stepchildren	306.874 7
	T1—085 4
Stepfamilies	306.874 7
Stephanotises	583.956
Stephen, King of England	
English history	942.024
Stephens County (Ga.)	T2—758 132
Stephens County (Okla.)	T2—766 53
Stephens County (Tex.)	T2—764 546
Stephenson County (Ill.)	T2—773 33
Stepmothers	
social welfare	362.839 57
Stepparents	306.874 7
	T1—085
Steppes	333.74
	T2—153
biology	578.744
ecology	577.44
see also Grasslands	
Stepps (Scotland)	T2—414 52
Steps	
landscape architecture	717
Stepsisters	306.875
	T1—085 5
see also Siblings	
Stercorariidae	598.338
Sterculia	583.775
Sterculiaceae	583.775
Sterea Hellada (Greece)	T2—495 15
Stereo systems	
automobile	629.277 4
Stereochemistry	547.122 3
inorganic chemistry	541.223
organic chemistry	547.122 3
Stereology	502.82
biology	570.282
Stereophonic sound systems	
engineering	621.389 334
Stereoscopic cinematography	777.65
Stereoscopic photography	778.4
Stereoscopic projection	778.4
Stereoscopic videography	777.65
Stereotypes	
sociology	303.385
Sterility	
gynecology	618.178
see also Female genital diseases — humans	
medicine	616.692
see also Genital diseases — humans	
Sterilization (Birth control)	363.97
health	613.942
social services	363.97
surgery	
tubal ligation	618.120 59
vasectomy	617.463
see also Birth control	
Sterilization (Microorganism elimination)	
public health	614.48
spacecraft	629.477 4
surgery	617.910 1
Sterkspruit (South Africa : District)	T2—687 57
Sterkstroom (South Africa : District)	T2—687 56
Sterling County (Tex.)	T2—764 871

Stock purchase plans	331.216 49
Stock rights	332.632 2
Stock speculation	332.632 28
Stock tickers	384.14
wireless	384.524
see also Telegraphy	
Stock warrants	332.632 2
Stockbridge Indians	T5—973 449
Stockholders' meetings	
law	346.066 6
Stockholm (Sweden)	T2—487 3
Stockholms län (Sweden)	T2—487 3
Stockings	391.423
see also Hosiery	
Stockmen	636.009 2
Stockpiles	
secondary industries	338.47
Stockport (England :	
Metropolitan Borough)	T2—427 34
Stocks	332.632 2
accounting	657.76
corporate law	346.066 6
income tax	336.242 6
law	343.052 46
law	346.092 2
see Manual at 332.6322 vs.	
332.6323	
Stocks (Matthiola)	583.78
Stockton-on-Tees	
(England : Borough)	T2—428 51
Stockton Plateau (Tex.)	T2—764 92
Stockyards	
animal husbandry	636.083 1
Stoddard County (Mo.)	T2—778 95
Stoic ethics	171.2
Stoic philosophy	188
Stoichiometry	541.26
applied chemistry	660.7
Stoke-on-Trent (England)	942.463
	T2—424 63
Stokes County (N.C.)	T2—756 64
Stokes' integral	515.43
STOL airplanes	
engineering	629.133 340 426
Stoles	391.46
commercial technology	687.14
fur	685.24
see also Outerwear	
Stolons	581.46
agricultural propagation	631.533
descriptive botany	581.46
physiology	575.499

Stomach	573.36
biology	573.36
human anatomy	611.33
human physiology	612.32
medicine	616.33
surgery	617.553
see also Digestive system	
Stomach cancer	
incidence	614.599 943 3
medicine	616.994 33
see also Cancer — humans	
Stomach diseases	
medicine	616.33
see also Digestive system	
diseases — humans	
Stomach ulcers	
medicine	616.334
see also Digestive system	
diseases — humans	
Stomatopoda	595.379 6
Stomiatiformes	597.5
Stomiatoidei	597.5
Stomiiformes	597.5
Stone	553.5
architectural construction	721.044 1
architectural decoration	729.6
building construction	693.1
building materials	691.2
economic geology	553.5
materials science	620.132
sculpture material	731.2
structural engineering	624.183 2
Stone Age	930.12
	T1—090 12
Stone carving	736.5
Stone County (Ark.)	T2—767 283
Stone County (Miss.)	T2—762 162
Stone County (Mo.)	T2—778 794
Stone flies	595.735
Stone fruits	
botany	583.642
orchard crops	634.2
Stone lithography	763.22
Stone pavements	625.82
Stone plants	583.883
Stone sculpturing	731.463
Stonecrops	583.44
Stonewall County (Tex.)	T2—764 737
Stoneware	666.6
arts	738.3
technology	666.6
Stoneworts	579.839
Stop motion (Animation)	777.7

Stopwatches	
technology	681.118
Storage	
cinematography	777.58
coal technology	662.624
gas technology	665.742
home economics	648.8
museology	069.53
	T1—075
negatives	771.45
petroleum technology	665.542
positives (photographs)	771.46
videography	777.58
warehouse management	658.785
water supply engineering	628.13
Storage (Computers)	004.5
	T1—028 545
engineering	621.397
Storage (Mathematics)	519.83
Storage area networks (Computer	
networks)	004.687
Storage areas	
home economics	643.5
Storage batteries	621.312 424
Storage buildings	
architecture	725.35
Storage centers	
library role	021
Storage containers	
warehouse management	658.785
Storage elevators	
architecture	725.36
Storage of office records	651.53
Storage services	388.044
see also Freight services	
Storaxes	583.674
Storaxes (Styracaceae)	583.93
Store Bælt (Denmark)	551.461 334
	T2—163 34
Store detectives	363.289
Stores (Retail trade)	381.1
architecture	725.21
institutional housekeeping	647.962 1
management	658.87
see also Commerce	
Storey County (Nev.)	979.356
	T2—793 56
Storing clothes	
home economics	646.6
Storing crops	631.568
Storing electric power	621.312 6
Storing food	
home economics	641.48
Storing food (Animal behavior)	591.53

Storing household goods	648.8
Storks	598.34
Storm insurance	368.122
see also Insurance	
Storm petrels	598.42
Storm sewers	628.212
Storm surges	
oceanography	551.463
Stormberg Range (South	
Africa)	T2—687 56
Stormont, Dundas and	
Glengarry (Ont.)	T2—713 75
Storms	551.55
meteorology	551.55
social services	363.349 2
weather forecasting	551.645
weather modification	551.685
see also Disasters	
Storstrøms amt (Denmark)	T2—489 12
Story County (Iowa)	T2—777 546
Storytelling	808.543
child care	649.58
library services	027.625 1
primary education	372.677
rhetoric	808.543
Stour, River	
(Wiltshire-Dorset,	
England)	T2—423 3
Stoves	
ceramic arts	738.8
heating buildings	697.22
household appliances	644.1
kitchen appliances	643.3
manufacturing technology	683.88
Strabane (Northern Ireland :	
District)	T2—416 2
Strabismus	
ophthalmology	617.762
see also Eye diseases —	
humans	
Strafford County (N.H.)	T2—742 5
Straightening tools	621.98
Strain gauges	
materials science	620.112 302 87
Strains	531.381
bridge engineering	624.252
materials science	620.112 3
naval architecture	623.817 6
physics	531.381
structural analysis	624.176
Strains (Injuries)	
medicine	617.17
Strait of Dover	551.461 336
	T2—163 36

Strait of Georgia (B.C.)	551.461 433
	T2—164 33
Strait of Gibraltar	551.461 381
	T2—163 81
Strait of Hormuz	551.461 535
	T2—165 35
Strait of Juan de Fuca (B.C. and	
Washington)	551.461 432
	T2—164 32
Strait of Magellan (Chile and	
Argentina)	551.461 74
	T2—167 4
Strait of Malacca	551.461 565
	T2—165 65
Strait of Mandab	551.461 532
	T2—165 32
Strait of Messina (Italy)	551.461 386
	T2—163 86
Strait of Sicily	551.461 381
	T2—163 81
Straits	
law of nations	341.446
Straits of Florida	551.461 363
	T2—163 63
Straits of Mackinac (Mich.)	T2—774 923
Stralsund (Germany)	T2—431 78
Strand (South Africa :	
District)	T2—687 35
Strange particles	539.721 6
Strangeness (Nuclear physics)	539.721 6
Strangers	
applied psychology	158.27
psychological influence	155.927
Strangford Lough (Northern	
Ireland)	T2—416 54
Strasbourg (France)	T2—443 954
Strasburgeriaceae	583.742
Strasser, Valentine E. M.	
Sierra Leonean history	966.404 4
Strategic arms limitation	327.174 7
Strategic Defense Initiative	358.174
Strategic geography	355.47
Strategic management	658.401 2
military administration	355.684
public administration	352.34
Strategic materials	355.24
land economics	333.8
law	343.01
military science	355.24
Strategic missile forces	358.17
land	358.175 4
navy	359.981 7

Strategic missiles	358.171 82
engineering	623.451 9
law of nations	341.738
military equipment	358.171 82
Strategic planning (Management)	658.401 2
military administration	355.684
public administration	352.34
Strategic weapons	358.171 82
engineering	623.451 9
law of nations	341.738
military equipment	358.171 82
Strategy	355.02
Civil War (United States)	973.730 1
military operations	355.4
overall military objectives	355.02
World War I	940.401
World War II	940.540 1
see also Military history	
Stratford Avon River	
(England)	T2—424 4
Stratford District (N.Z.)	T2—934 85
Manawatu-Wanganui	
Region	T2—935 3
Taranaki Region	T2—934 85
Stratford-on-Avon	
(England : District)	T2—424 89
Strathclyde (Scotland)	T2—414
Strathkelvin (Scotland)	T2—414 36
Strathmore (Scotland)	T2—412 6
Stratifications (Rock formations)	551.81
economic geology	553.14
specific areas	554–559
Stratigraphic paleobotany	561.11
Stratigraphic paleontology	560.17
Stratigraphic paleozoology	560.17
Stratigraphy	551.7
Stratiomyidae	595.773
Stratosphere	551.514 2
	T2—161 3
Straw pulp	676.14
Strawberries	641.347 5
botany	583.642
commercial processing	664.804 75
cooking	641.647 5
food	641.347 5
horticulture	634.75
Stream of consciousness	
literature	808.802 5
history and criticism	809.925
specific literatures	T3B—080 25
history and	
criticism	T3B—092 5
Streaming (Education)	371.254

String beans	641.356 52
see also Snap beans	
String ensembles	785.7
String games	793.96
String orchestras	784.7
String quartets	785.719 4
String theory	539.725 8
String trios	785.719 3
Stringed instruments	787
bands and orchestras	784
chamber ensembles	785
mixed	785.2–.5
single type	785.7
construction	787.192 3
by hand	787.192 3
by machine	681.87
solo music	787
Strings	677.71
Strip cartoons	741.56
see also Comic strips	
Strip cropping (Soil conservation)	631.456
Strip-mined lands	333.765
economics	333.765
law	346.046 765
reclamation technology	631.64
Strip mining	622.292
law	343.077
Striped bass	641.392
cooking	641.692
culture	639.377 32
food	641.392
sports fishing	799.177 32
zoology	597.732
Striped dolphins	599.534
Striped polecat	599.766
Striped weasels	599.766 3
Striper (Striped bass)	641.392
see also Striped bass	
Stroboscopic photography	621.367
Stroessner, Alfredo	
Paraguayan history	989.207 3
Stroke (Disorder)	
medicine	616.81
see also Nervous system	
diseases — humans	
Stromatoporoidea	563.58
Stromboli (Italy)	T2—458 11
Stromiatiformes	597.5
Stromiiformes	597.5
Strong interaction (Nuclear	
particles)	539.754 8
Strongboxes	683.34

Strontium	669.725
chemical engineering	661.039 4
chemistry	546.394
metallurgy	669.725
physical metallurgy	669.967 25
see also Chemicals	
Strophic form	781.823
instrumental	784.182 3
Stroud (England : District)	T2—424 19
Struck board zithers	787.74
see also Stringed instruments	
Struck drums	786.92
see also Percussion instruments	
Struck stringed instruments	787.7
see also Stringed instruments	
Structural analysis	624.17
bridges	624.25
construction	690.21
naval architecture	623.817 1
Structural chemistry	541.2
Structural clay products	666.73
materials science	620.142
Structural control (Engineering)	624.171
Structural crystallography	548.81
Structural decoration	729
see Manual at 729	
Structural design	624.177 1
naval architecture	623.817 71
Structural dynamics	624.171
Structural elements	721
architecture	721
area planning	711.6
construction	690.1
engineering	624.17
Structural engineering	624.1
see Manual at 624 vs. 624.1	
Structural engineers	624.109 2
Structural failure	624.171
Structural foam products	668.493
Structural geology	551.8
Structural linguistics	410.181
grammar	415.018 1
specific languages	T4—501 81
specific languages	T4—018 1
Structural materials	
construction	691
nuclear reactors	621.483 32
Structural optimization	624.177 13
Structural polysaccharides	572.566 8
Structural proteins	572.67
Structural stability	624.171
Structural stone	553.5
see also Stone	
Structural theory	624.17

Students (continued)
  relations with government — 323.383 718
  role in counseling — 371.404 7
Studies (Rooms) — 643.58
  home economics — 643.58
  residential interior decoration — 747.73
Studies (Subject-oriented
  programs) — T1—07
Studios
  broadcast engineering — 621.384
  communications engineering — 621.382 3
  photography — 771.1
Study abroad — 370.116
Study and teaching — T1—07
Study clubs — 367
Study collections
  museology — 069.55
Study facilities — 371.621
Study groups
  adult education — 374.22
Study methods — 371.302 81
Study scores — 780
  treatises — 780.265
Study skills — 371.302 81
Stuffed toys
  making — 688.724
   handicrafts — 745.592 4
   technology — 688.724
Stunt animals
  animal husbandry — 636.088 8
Stunt flyers — 797.540 92
Stunt flying — 797.54
  biography — 797.540 92
  see also Air sports
Stuntmen — 791.430 280 92
Stunts
  motion pictures — 791.430 28
  television — 791.450 28
Sturgeons — 597.42
Sturnidae — 598.863
Stutsman County (N.D.) — T2—784 52
Stutterers — T1—087
Stutterheim (South Africa :
  District) — T2—687 54
Stuttering
  medicine — 616.855 4
  see also Communication
   disorders
  pediatrics — 618.928 554
  special education — 371.914 2
Stuttgart (Germany) — T2—434 715
Stuttgart (Germany :
  Regierungsbezirk) — T2—434 71

Stuttgart (Germany :
  Region) — T2—434 71
Stylasterina — 593.55
Style
  fine arts — 701.8
   drawing — 741.018
  literary criticism — 809
   specific literatures — T3B—09
  painting — 750.18
  rhetoric — 808
Style checkers (Computer
  software) — 005.52
Style manuals — 808.027
  typing — 652.3
Style sheet languages — 006.74
Styles (Fine arts) — 709
  see Manual at 704.9
   and 753–758; also at
   709.012–.015, 709.02–.05
   vs. 709.3–.9
Stylidiaceae — 583.983
Stylobasium — 583.63
Stylommatophora — 594.38
Styracaceae — 583.93
Styrenes — 668.423 3
Styria (Austria) — T2—436 5
Suazo Córdova, Roberto
  Honduran history — 972.830 532
Sub-Saharan Africa — 967
  — T2—67
Subantarctic Islands (N.Z.) — T2—939 9
Subatomic particles — 539.72
Subconscious — 154.2
  comparative psychology — 156.4
  educational psychology — 370.15
  philosophy — 127
Subcontracting — 346.022
  armed forces — 355.621 2
  management — 658.405 8
Subcontracting fees
  labor economics — 331.216 6
Subcultures — 306.1
Subdivision of land — 333.3
  law — 346.043 77
  public administration — 354.34
Subgroups — 512.2
Subia languages — 496.399
  — T6—963 99
Subject analysis
  information science — 025.4
Subject and predicate (Grammar) — 415
  specific languages — T4—5
Subject authority files — 025.47

Substance abuse (continued)
  health insurance   368.382 5
    see also Insurance
  law   344.044 6
    criminal law   345.027 7
    social welfare law   344.044 6
  literature   808.803 561
    history and criticism   809.933 561
    specific literatures   T3B—080 356 1
      history and
        criticism   T3B—093 561
  medicine   616.86
  pastoral theology   206.1
    Christianity   259.429
  personal health   613.8
  personnel management   658.382 2
    public administration   352.67
  pregnancy complications
    obstetrics   618.368 6
  primary education   372.378
  prisoner services   365.667 29
  religious guidance   204.42
    Christianity   248.862 9
  school problem   371.784
  social theology   201.762 29
    Christianity   261.832 29
  social welfare   362.29
    public administration   353.64
  transportation safety   363.120 1
    traffic accidents   363.125 14
  see Manual at 616.86 vs.
    158.1, 204.42, 248.8629,
    292–299, 362.29
Substance abusers   362.290 92
                T1—087 4
Substance-related disorders
  medicine   616.86
  perinatal medicine   618.326 86
  pregnancy complications
    obstetrics   618.368 6
Substitute teaching   371.141 22
Substitution (Chemical reaction)   541.39
  organic chemistry   547.2
Substructural logic   511.31
Subsurface mining   622.2
Subsurface resources
  land economics   333.8
  public administration   354.39
Subsurface water   553.79
  see also Groundwater
Subterranean land vehicles
  engineering   629.292
Subtiaba-Tlapanec languages   497.9
                T6—979

Subtraction   512.92
  algebra   512.92
  arithmetic   513.212
Subtractive processes
  color photography   778.66
Subtropical climate   551.691 28
Subtropical ecology   577.091 28
Subtropical fruits
  cooking   641.646
  food   641.346
  orchard crops   634.6
Subtropics   T2—128
Subud   299.933
Suburban administration   352.169
Suburban areas   307.74
                T2—173 3
  literature
    history and criticism   809.933 582 097 33
    see also Suburbs
Suburban biology   578.756
Suburban ecology   577.56
Suburban sociology   307.74
Suburban transportation   388.4
  railroad
    engineering   625.4
Suburbs   307.74
                T2—173 3
  psychological influence   155.943
  public administration   352.169
    control by higher
      jurisdictions   353.336 9
Subversion (Political)   327.12
  see also Subversive activities
Subversive activities   327.12
  armed forces   355.343 7
    see also Unconventional
      warfare
  criminology   364.131
    criminal law   345.023 1
  international politics   327.12
  political groups   322.42
  public administration   353.17
Subversive groups   322.42
Subversive material
  postal handling   383.120 5
Subviral organisms   579.29
Subway stations   388.472
  architecture   725.31
  construction   690.531
  transportation services   388.472
Subway transportation   388.42
  see also Subways (Rail)
Subways (Pedestrian)   388.411

Sugar crops	633.6
Sugar-free cooking	641.563 837
Sugar-free diet	
health	613.283 32
Sugar-free foods	641.309 36
Sugar maple	633.64
botany	583.75
syrup crop	633.64
Sugar substitutes	
food technology	664.5
Sugarcane	633.61
agricultural economics	338.173 61
agriculture	633.61
botany	584.924
Sugars	572.565
see also Carbohydrates	
Sūhāj (Egypt : Province)	T2—623
Suharto	
Indonesian history	959.803 7
Suhl (Germany)	T2—432 26
Suhl (Germany : Bezirk)	T2—432 26
Sui dynasty	951.016
Suicidal behavior	362.28
medicine	616.858 445
see also Suicide	
Suicide	362.28
criminology	364.152 2
law	345.025 22
customs	394.88
ethics	179.7
religion	205.697
Buddhism	294.356 97
Christianity	241.697
Hinduism	294.548 697
Judaism	296.369 7
medicine	616.858 445
pastoral care	206.1
Christianity	259.428
social theology	201.762 28
Christianity	261.832 28
social welfare	362.28
see also Mental illness	
Suidae	599.633
Suiformes	599.633
Suir River (Ireland)	T2—419 1
Suitcases	
manufacturing technology	685.51
Suites	784.185 8
Suits (Clothing)	391.473
commercial technology	687.113
customs	391.473
home economics	646.3
home sewing	646.433
see also Clothing	
Suits (Law)	347.053
procedure	347.050 4
Sukarno	
Indonesian history	959.803 5
Sukhothai (Kingdom)	959.302 2
Sukkah	296.123 2
Babylonian Talmud	296.125 2
Mishnah	296.123 2
Palestinian Talmud	296.124 2
Sukkot	296.433
liturgy	296.453 3
Suku (African people)	T5—963 93
Suku language	496.393
	T6—963 93
Sukuma (African people)	T5—963 94
Sukuma-Nyamwezi languages	496.394
	T6—963 94
Sukunka River (B.C.)	T2—711 87
Sulawesi (Indonesia)	T2—598 4
Sulawesi Barat (Indonesia)	T2—598 46
Sulawesi languages	499.226
	T6—992 26
Sulawesi Selatan (Indonesia)	T2—598 47
Sulawesi Tengah (Indonesia)	T2—598 44
Sulawesi Tenggara (Indonesia)	T2—598 48
Sulawesi Utara (Indonesia)	T2—598 42
Sulaymānīyah (Iraq : Province)	T2—567 2
Sulfate process	
wood pulp	676.126
Sulfated hydrocarbons	668.14
Sulfated oils	668.14
Sulfates	546.723 24
chemical engineering	661.63
mineralogy	549.75
Sulfides	546.723 2
chemical engineering	661.63
mineralogy	549.32
organic chemistry	547.061
Sulfinic acids	547.066
chemical engineering	661.896
Sulfite process	
wood pulp	676.125
Sulfites	546.723 24
chemical engineering	661.63
Sulfonation	547.27
chemical engineering	660.284 4
Sulfones	547.065
chemical engineering	661.896
Sulfonic acids	547.067
chemical engineering	661.896

Sun-dried blocks
  architectural construction   721.044 22
  building construction   693.22
Sun spiders   595.48
Sun tables
  earth astronomy   525.38
Sunan (Hadith)   297.125 5
Sunbeam snakes   597.967
Sunburn
  medicine   616.515
  see also Skin diseases —
    humans
Sunbury (N.B.)   T2—715 43
Sunbury (Vic.)   T2—945 2
Sunda Islands   T2—598
Sunda Islands, Lesser
  (Indonesia)   T2—598 6
Sunda language   499.223 2
    T6—992 232
Sunda literature   899.223 2
Sundanese   T5—992 232
Sundanese language   499.223 2
    T6—992 232
Sundanese literature   899.223 2
Sunday
  Christian observance   263.3
  music   781.522 2
Sunday school   268
  Jewish   296.680 83
Sunday school buildings
  administration   268.2
  architecture   726.4
Sunday work   331.257 4
  economics   331.257 4
  personnel management   658.312 1
Sunderland (England :
  Metropolitan Borough)   T2—428 71
Sundews   583.887
Sundials
  technology   681.111 2
Sunfishes   597.738
Sunflower County (Miss.)   T2—762 47
Sunflowers   583.983
  botany   583.983
  floriculture   635.933 983
Sung dynasty   951.024
Sunlight-favoring plants
  floriculture   635.954
Sunni Islam   297.81
  doctrines   297.204 1
  Koran commentary   297.122 73
  relations with Shia Islam   297.804 2

Sunni Islam (continued)
  schools of law   340.590 181
    religion   297.140 181
  worship   297.301
Sunnites   297.81
  see also Sunni Islam
Sunshine Coast (B.C.)   T2—711 31
Sunshine law   342.066 2
Sunspiders   595.48
Sunspots   523.74
  geomagnetic effects   538.746
Sunwar language   495.49
    T6—954 9
Suomi language   494.541
    T6—945 41
Suomi literature   894.541
Super Bowl (Football)   796.332 648
Superannuation (Pension)   331.252
Supercolliders   539.736
Supercomputers   004.11
  architecture   004.251
  communications   004.611
    software   005.713 1
    software development   005.712 1
  engineering   621.391 1
  graphics software   006.681
  graphics software development 006.671
  interfacing   004.611
    software   005.713 1
    software development   005.712 1
  multimedia software   006.781
  multimedia software
    development   006.771
  operating systems   005.441
  performance evaluation   004.110 29
    for design and improvement 004.251
  software   005.31
  software development   005.21
  systems analysis   004.251
  systems design   004.251
  see Manual at 004.11–.16
Superconducting supercolliders   539.736
Superconductivity   537.623
  engineering   621.35
  materials science   620.112 973
Superconductor circuits   621.381 5
Superconductors   537.623
  engineering   621.35
Supercritical fluid
  chromatography   543.86
Supercritical gas chromatography 543.86
Supercross   796.756
Superego
  subconscious   154.2

Superfluidity	530.42
Supergiant slalom skiing	796.935
see also Winter sports	
Supergravity	530.142 3
Superheaters	
nuclear reactors	621.483 4
steam engineering	621.197
Superintendents of schools	
biography	371.200 92
public control	379.157
role and function	371.201 1
Superior (Wis.)	T2—775 11
Superior, Lake	T2—774 9
Michigan	T2—774 9
Ontario	T2—713 12
Superior courts	347.02
Superior intelligence	153.98
Supermarkets	381.149
discount stores	381.149
management	658.879
food stores	381.456 413
management	658.879
Supernatural	
arts	700.47
	T3C—37
literature	808.803 7
specific literatures	T3B—080 37
history and	
criticism	T3B—093 7
occultism	130
Supernatural beings	
religious	202.11
see also Gods and goddesses	
secular	398.21
see also Legendary beings	
Supernovas	523.844 65
Supersonic flow	533.275
air mechanics	533.62
aeronautics	629.132 305
Superstitions	001.96
folklore	398.41
Superstores	381.149
management	658.879
Superstring theory	539.725 8
Superstrings	539.725 8
Supersymmetry	539.725
Supertanker berthing areas	387.1
engineering	627.22
see also Ports	
Supervised activities	
child care	649.5

Supervision of dramatic	
performances	792.023
motion pictures	791.430 23
radio	791.440 23
stage	792.023
television	791.450 23
Supervision of employees	658.302
executive personnel	658.407
library personnel	023.9
military personnel	355.330 41
public administration	352.66
Supervisors	
labor economics	331.794
role and function	658.302
Suppers	642
cooking	641.53
light meals	641.53
main meals	641.54
customs	394.125 3
light meals	394.125 3
main meals	394.125 4
Supplemental budgets (Public)	352.48
see also Budgets (Public)	
Supplies	
armed forces	355.8
management	658.7
armed forces	355.621
public administration	352.55
office services	651.29
Supply (Quantity)	
communications industry	384.041
forecasts	338.02
agricultural industries	338.17
production economics	338.02
secondary industries	338.47
microeconomics	338.521 3
natural resources	333.711
transportation services	388.049
Supply and demand	338.521
monetary economics	332.401
production economics	338.521
Supply depots (Armed forces)	355.75
Supply management	658.7
armed forces	355.621
public administration	352.55
Supply services (Armed forces)	355.621
issuing units	355.341
Supply ships (Military)	359.985 83
see also Military supply ships	
Supply-side economics	330.155 4
Support (Domestic relations)	346.016 63
Support groups	361.43

Supporting garments	391.423
commercial technology	687.2
customs	391.423
home sewing	646.42
see also Clothing	
Suppressed books	098.1
Suppuration	571.937 9
Supramolecular chemistry	547.122 6
inorganic chemistry	541.226
Supranational states	321.04
Suprasegmental phonology	414.6
specific languages	T4—16
Supreme courts	347.035
criminal law	345.014 44
Suras (Koran)	
Arabic text	297.122 42
commentary	297.122 72
Surety bonds	
insurance	368.84
Suretyship	346.074
Surf riding	797.32
see also Aquatic sports	
Surface-active agents	668.1
Surface chemistry	541.33
applied	660.293
Surface engineering	620.44
Surface finishing	
home woodworking	684.084
wooden furniture	684.104 3
Surface integrals	515.43
Surface-mined lands	333.765
economics	333.765
reclamation technology	631.64
Surface mining	622.292
Surface-painted enamels	
ceramic arts	738.46
Surface physics	530.417
liquids	530.427
solids	530.417
Surface processes (Geology)	551.3
see Manual at 551.302–.307	
vs. 551.35	
Surface prospecting	622.12
Surface rail transit systems	388.42
engineering	625.6
public administration	354.769
transportation services	388.42
Surface refinishing	
wooden furniture	684.104 43
Surface tension	530.427
chemical engineering	660.293
Surface tillage	631.581

Surface-to-air guided missiles	358.174 82
engineering	623.451 94
military equipment	358.174 82
Surface-to-air missile forces	358.174
Surface-to-surface guided	
missiles	358.171 82
engineering	623.451 95
military equipment	358.171 82
Surface-to-underwater guided	
missiles	358.176 82
engineering	623.451 96
military equipment	358.176 82
Surface transportation	388
mining	622.69
see also Ground transportation	
Surface treatment	
metals	671.7
Surface water	553.78
	T2—169
economic geology	553.78
hydrology	551.48
resource economics	333.91
Surfaced lumber	674.42
Surfaces	
geometry	
algebraic	516.352
configurations	516.154
differential	516.36
integral	516.362
Surfacing roads	625.8
dirt roads	625.75
paved roads	625.8
Surfactants	668.1
Surfers	797.320 92
Surfers Paradise (Qld.)	T2—943 2
Surfing	797.32
biography	797.320 92
see also Aquatic sports	
Surgeons	617.092
law	344.041 2
malpractice	344.041 21
role and function	617.023 2
Surgery	617
gynecology	618.105 9
obstetrics	618.8
veterinary medicine	636.089 7
see Manual at 616 vs. 617.4;	
also at 617	
Surgery (Topology)	514.72
Surgical abortion	362.198 88
medicine	618.88
see also Abortion	
Surgical assistants	
role and function	617.023 3

Surgical complications		Surrey Heath (England)	T2—422 13
anesthesiology	617.960 41	Surrogate motherhood	306.874 3
medicine	617.919	ethics	176.2
Surgical dressings		*see also* Reproduction —	
use	617.93	ethics	
Surgical equipment	617.9	law	346.017
Surgical gauzes	677.8	Surry County (N.C.)	T2—756 65
manufacturing technology	677.8	Surry County (Va.)	T2—755 562
use	617.93	Sursee (Switzerland : Amt)	T2—494 555
Surgical infections		Surselva (Switzerland)	T2—494 735 8
medicine	617.919 5	Surveillance	
Surgical insurance	368.382 2	civil rights issue	323.448 2
see also Insurance		engineering	621.389 28
Surgical nurses		law	345.052
role and function	617.023 1	law enforcement	363.232
Surgical nursing	617.023 1	Survey methodology	001.433
Surgical physician assistants			T1—072 3
role and function	617.023 32	Surveying	526.9
Surgical shock		canal engineering	627.131
medicine	617.21	dam engineering	627.81
Surgical technicians		railroad engineering	625.11
role and function	617.023 3	road engineering	625.723
Surianaceae	583.63	Surveying equipment	
Surigao del Norte		manufacturing technology	681.76
(Philippines)	T2—599 723	Surveyors	526.909 2
Surigao del Sur		Surveys	
(Philippines)	T2—599 724	descriptive research	001.433
Surinam toad	597.865		T1—072 3
Suriname	988.3	marketing management	658.83
	T2—883	marketing reports	381
Surinamers	T5—914 1	public administration	352.75
Surmic languages	496.54	Survival	613.69
	T6—965 4	Survival analysis	519.546
Surnames	929.42	Survival housekeeping	613.69
Surpluses		Survival skills	613.69
agricultural industries	338.17	Survival training (Military	
military supplies	355.621 37	training)	355.54
natural resources	333.711	Survivors' insurance	368.3
production	338.02	government-sponsored	368.43
secondary industries	338.47	law	344.023
Surrealism		*see also* Insurance	
arts	700.411 63	Sus	599.633 2
	T3C—116 3	Susa (Extinct city)	T2—357 64
fine arts	709.040 63	Susanna (Deuterocanonical book)	229.6
literature	808.801 163	Sushi	641.82
history and criticism	809.911 63	Susliks	599.365
specific literatures	T3B—080 116 3	Suspended ceilings	
history and		buildings	698
criticism	T3B—091 163	Suspended sentence	364.63
painting	759.066 3	Suspense drama	792.27
sculpture	735.230 463	literature	808.825 27
Surrey (B.C.)	T2—711 33	history and criticism	809.252 7
Surrey (England)	942.21	specific literatures	T3B—205 27
	T2—422 1	individual authors	T3A—2

Suspense drama (continued)
stage presentation 792.27
see also Theater
Suspense stories 808.838 72
history and criticism 809.387 2
specific literatures T3B—308 72
individual authors T3A—3
Suspension bridges
construction 624.23
Suspension of rights 323.49
Suspension systems
automotive engineering 629.243
Suspensions (Chemistry) 541.34
chemical engineering 660.294
Susquehanna County (Pa.) T2—748 34
Susquehanna River T2—748
Maryland T2—752 74
Pennsylvania T2—748
Susquehanna River, West
Branch (Pa.) T2—748 5
Sussex (England) T2—422 5
Sussex cattle 636.222
Sussex County (Del.) T2—751 7
Sussex County (N.J.) T2—749 76
Sussex County (Va.) T2—755 565
Sustainability 304.2
human ecology 304.2
technology 628
T1—028 6
Sustainable architecture 720.47
Sustainable development 338.927
Sustainable engineering 628
T1—028 6
Sustainable horticulture 635.028 6
Sustainable living
household management 640.286
Sustainable technology 628
T1—028 6
Sustut River (B.C.) T2—711 85
Susu language 496.34
T6—963 4
Sutherland (Scotland) T2—411 52
Sutherland (South Africa :
District) T2—687 17
Sūtrapiṭaka 294.382 3
Suttapiṭaka 294.382 3
Suttee 393.930 954
customs 393.930 954
Hindu practice 294.538 8
Sutter County (Calif.) T2—794 34
Sutton (London, England) T2—421 92
Sutton County (Tex.) T2—764 879
Sutures
surgical use 617.917 8

Suwałki (Poland :
Voivodeship) T2—438 32
Suwannee County (Fla.) T2—759 82
Suwannee River (Ga. and
Fla.) T2—759 8
Suwaydā' (Syria : Province) T2—569 14
Suways (Egypt : Province) T2—621 5
SV40 (Virus) 579.244 5
Svalbard (Norway) T2—981
Svan language 499.968
T6—999 68
Svealand (Sweden) T2—487
Sverdlovsk (Russia : Oblast) T2—474 3
Sverdlovskaĩa oblast'
(Russia) T2—474 3
Svetambara (Jainism) 294.492
SVP (Swiss political party) 324.249 403
Swabia (Germany) T2—434 6
Bavaria T2—433 7
Swabian Alps (Germany) T2—434 73
Swabian dialect 437.943 37
T6—33
Swabian Jura (Germany) T2—434 73
Swabians
Sicilian history 945.804
Southern Italian history 945.704
Swahili language 496.392
T6—963 92
Swahili literature 896.392
Swahili-speaking peoples T5—963 92
Swain County (N.C.) T2—756 96
Swale (England) T2—422 33
Swale, River (England) T2—428 48
Swallow-tanager 598.875
Swallowers (Chiasmodontidae) 597.7
Swallowers (Saccopharyngidae) 597.43
Swallows 598.826
Swamp eels 597.64
Swamp rats 599.35
Swamps 551.417
biology 578.768
ecology 577.68
see also Wetlands
Swan Hill (Vic.) T2—945 9
Swan River (W.A.) T2—941 2
Swans 598.418
animal husbandry 636.681
Swansea (Wales) 942.982
T2—429 82
Swanskin fabrics 677.624
see also Textiles
Swaps (Finance) 332.645 7
Swarm intelligence
computer science 006.382 4

Swarming of bees	595.799 156
apiculture	638.146
Swartruggens (South	
Africa : District)	T2—682 41
Swat (Pakistan)	T2—549 122
Swati language	496.398 7
	T6—963 987
Swazi (Ethnic group)	T5—963 987
Swazi (National group)	T5—968 87
Swazi language	496.398 7
	T6—963 987
Swazi literature	896.398 7
Swaziland	968.87
	T2—688 7
see also Eswatini	
Swearing	
customs	394
ethics	179.5
Sweat gland diseases	
medicine	616.56
see also Skin diseases —	
humans	
Sweat glands	573.537 9
biology	573.537 9
human anatomy	611.77
human physiology	612.793
medicine	616.56
see also Skin	
Sweaters	391.46
commercial technology	687.14
home sewing	646.45
see also Outerwear	
Sweden	948.5
	T2—485
ancient	936.85
	T2—368 5
Swedenborgianism	289.4
Swedenborgians	
biography	289.409 2
Swedes	T5—397
Swedes (Plants)	641.351 26
see also Rutabagas	
Swedish Empire	948.503 4
Finnish history	948.970 134
Swedish history	948.503 4
Swedish language	439.7
	T6—397
Swedish literature	839.7
Swedish people	T5—397
Swedish turnip	641.351 26
see also Rutabagas	
Sweep generators	
electronics	621.381 548

Sweeping	
housecleaning	648.5
Sweet bay	641.357
botany	584.288
see also Herbs	
Sweet cider	641.341 1
commercial processing	663.63
cooking with	641.641 1
food	641.341 1
Sweet clovers	633.366
botany	583.63
forage crop	633.366
Sweet corn	641.356 72
commercial processing	664.805 672
cooking	641.656 72
food	641.356 72
garden crop	635.672
Sweet gale	583.65
Sweet Grass County (Mont.)	T2—786 64
Sweet gums	583.44
botany	583.44
forestry	634.973 44
ornamental arboriculture	635.977 344
Sweet herbs	641.357
see also Herbs	
Sweet peas (Flowers)	635.933 63
botany	583.63
floriculture	635.933 63
Sweet peppers	641.356 43
botany	583.959 3
commercial processing	664.805 643
cooking	641.656 43
food	641.356 43
garden crop	635.643
Sweet potatoes	641.352 2
agriculture	635.22
botany	583.959
commercial processing	664.805 22
cooking	641.652 2
food	641.352 2
Sweet sorghums	633.62
Sweetened condensed milk	641.371 424
cooking	641.671 424
food	641.371 424
processing	637.142 4
Sweeteners	
commercial processing	664.1
Sweetleaf	583.674
Sweetleaf (Symplocaceae)	583.93
Sweets (Candy)	641.853
commercial processing	664.153
home preparation	641.853
Sweets (Desserts and	
confections)	641.86

Sweetwater County (Wyo.)	T2—787 85
Swellendam (South Africa : District)	T2—687 36
Swells (Wind effects)	551.463
lakes	551.482
Świętokrzyskie Voivodeship (Poland)	T2—438 45
Swift County (Minn.)	T2—776 41
Swift Current (Sask.)	T2—712 43
Swifts	598.762
Swimmers	797.210 92
Swimming	797.21
animal behavior	591.57
biography	797.210 92
physical fitness	613.716
see also Aquatic sports	
Swimming pools	797.2
architecture	725.74
domestic	643.556
architecture	728.962
construction	690.896 2
home economics	643.556
public	797.2
architecture	725.74
construction	690.574
sanitation services	363.729 2
see also Sanitation	
Swindon (England : Borough)	T2—423 13
Swine	636.4
Swing (Golf)	796.352 3
Swing (Music)	781.654
Swisher County (Tex.)	T2—764 838
Swiss	T5—35
Swiss cheese	641.373 54
cooking	641.673 54
food	641.373 54
processing	637.354
Swiss Democrats (Political party)	324.249 403
Swiss-German dialect	437.949 4
	T6—35
Swiss Germans	T5—35
Swiss Labour Party	324.249 407 4
Swiss Liberal Party	324.249 406
Swiss literature	
French	840
German	830
Italian	850
Swiss National Park	T2—494 732 7
Swiss People's Party	324.249 403
Switchboard operators	
office services	651.374 3
Switchboards	
communications services	384.65
telephony	621.387
Switches	
electrical engineering	621.317
interior wiring	621.319 24
railroad engineering	625.163
Switching	
communications engineering	621.382 16
computer communications	004.66
engineering	621.398 1
computer engineering	621.395
telephone engineering	621.385 7
Switching circuits	
electronics	621.381 537
Switching equipment	
electrical engineering	621.317
Switching theory	
electronics	621.381 537 2
Switzerland	949.4
	T2—494
ancient	936.94
	T2—369 4
Switzerland County (Ind.)	T2—772 125
Swivel embroidery	677.77
Sword dances	793.35
Sword fighting	796.86
Sword lilies	635.934 75
botany	584.75
floriculture	635.934 75
Swordfish	597.78
Swordplay	796.86
Swords	623.441 3
art metalwork	739.722
Swordtail (Fish)	597.667
Sycamores	583.44
forestry	634.973 44
ornamental arboriculture	635.977 344
Sycamores (Platanaceae)	583.38
botany	583.38
forestry	634.973 38
ornamental arboriculture	635.977 338
Sydney (N.S.W.)	994.41
	T2—944 1
Syenite	553.52
economic geology	553.52
petrology	552.3
quarrying	622.352
Sylhet (Bangladesh : Division)	T2—549 27
Syllabaries	411
specific languages	T4—11
Syllabi (Outlines)	T1—020 2
Syllogisms	166

Synchro-cyclotrons	539.735
Synchronic linguistics	410
see Manual at 410	
Synchronized skating	796.912
see also Winter sports	
Synchronized swimming	797.217
see also Aquatic sports	
Synchronized trampoline	796.474
Synchronous accelerators	539.735
Synchronous converters	621.313 5
Synchronous generators	621.313 4
Synchronous machinery	621.313 3
Synchronous transfer modes	
communications engineering	621.382 16
computer communications	004.66
engineering	621.398 1
Synchroscopes	621.374 9
Synchrotrons	539.735
Synclines	551.86
Syncretism	
philosophy	148
Syndetic structure	025.322 2
authority files	025.322 2
subject authority files	025.47
Syndicalism	335.82
economics	335.82
political ideology	320.53
sociology	306.34
Syndicated crime	364.106 8
Syndicates	
banking	332.16
real estate investment	332.632 47
unincorporated business	
enterprises	338.7
see also Business	
enterprises;	
Unincorporated business	
enterprises	
Synecology	577.8
animals	591.78
microorganisms	579.178
plants	581.78
Synesthesia	
psychology	152.189
Syngnathidae	597.679
Synod of Bishops	262.136
Synod of Evangelical Lutheran	
Churches	284.132 3
see also Lutheran church	
Synodontidae	597.61
Synods	
Christian ecclesiology	262.4
presbyterian polity	262.42

Synonym dictionaries	413.1
specific languages	T4—312
specific subjects	T1—03
Synopses	T1—020 2
music	780
treatises	780.269
vocal music	
treatises	782.002 69
Synoptic Gospels	226
Synoptic problem (Gospels)	226.066
Syntax	415
specific languages	T4—5
Synthesis	
chemical engineering	660.284 4
chemistry	541.39
organic chemistry	547.2
Synthesizers	786.74
instrument	786.741 9
music	786.74
see also Electrophones	
Synthetic building materials	666.89
Synthetic chemicals	
organic	661.805
Synthetic drugs	
pharmacology	615.31
Synthetic drugs of abuse	362.299
personal health	613.8
social welfare	362.299
see also Substance abuse	
Synthetic dyes	667.25
Synthetic fuels	662.66
Synthetic gems	666.88
Synthetic glue	668.31
Synthetic meat	664.64
Synthetic minerals	666.86
Synthetic perfumes	668.544
Synthetic petroleum	662.662
Synthetic textile fibers	677.4
Synthetism	709.034 7
painting	759.057
Syphilis	
incidence	614.547 2
medicine	616.951 3
see also Communicable	
diseases — humans	
Syracusae (Italy)	T2—378 141
Syracuse (Italy)	T2—458 141
ancient	T2—378 141
Syracuse (Italy : Free	
municipal association)	T2—458 14
ancient	T2—378 14
Syracuse (N.Y.)	T2—747 66

Tabanidae	595.773
Tabankulu (South Africa : District)	T2—687 59
Ṭabaqāt al-Ruwāh	297.125 261
Ṭabarānī, Sulaymān ibn Aḥmad	
Hadith	297.125 63
Ṭabarī	
Koran commentary	297.122 73
Ṭabarsī, al-Faḍl ibn al-Ḥasan	
Koran commentary	297.122 753
Tabasaran language	499.964
	T6—999 64
Tabasco (Mexico : State)	T2—726 3
Tabby	
building construction	693.22
Tabernacles	
Christian church furniture	247.1
architecture	726.529 1
Judaism	296.49
Tabes dorsalis	
medicine	616.83
see also Nervous system	
diseases — humans	
Tablas	786.93
see also Percussion instruments	
Tablature	780.148
Table decorations	642.8
Table furnishings	642.7
Table linens	642.7
arts	746.96
home sewing	646.21
table setting	642.7
Table manners	395.54
Table Mountain (Western Cape, South Africa)	T2—687 356
Table Mountain National Park (South Africa)	T2—687 356
Table salt	553.632
see also Salt (Sodium chloride)	
Table service	642.6
Table setting	642.6
Table tennis	796.346
biography	796.346 092
see also Ball games	
Table tennis players	796.346 092
Table tipping (Spiritualism)	133.92
Tableaux	793.24
Tablecloths	642.7
arts	746.96
home sewing	646.21
table setting	642.7

Tables (Furniture)	645.4
decorative arts	749.3
outdoor	645.8
see also Outdoor furniture	
see also Furniture	
Tables (Lists)	T1—021
Tabletop fountains	745.594 6
Tabletop photography	778.8
Tablets (Pharmaceuticals)	
pharmaceutical chemistry	615.19
Tableware	642.7
earthenware	666.68
arts	738.38
technology	666.68
glass	
arts	748.2
gold	
arts	739.228 3
handicrafts	745.593
ironwork	
arts	739.48
porcelain	666.58
arts	738.28
technology	666.58
pottery	666.3
arts	738
technology	666.3
silver	
arts	739.238 3
table setting	642.7
wood	
arts	736.4
Taboos	390
Tabora Region (Tanzania)	T2—678 28
Tabulated materials	T1—021
Tacanan languages	498.9
	T6—989
Tachinid flies	595.774
Tachinidae	595.774
Táchira (Venezuela)	T2—871 2
Tachometers	
technology	681.118
Tachyglossidae	599.29
Tackles (Mechanisms)	621.863
Tackling	
American football	796.332 26
Tacna (Peru : Region)	T2—853 5
Tacoma (Wash.)	T2—797 788
Tacos	641.84
Tactical exercises (Military training)	355.54
Tactical geography	355.47
Tactical missile forces	358.175 2

Tajikistan	958.6
	T2—586
ancient	939.6
	T2—396
Tajikistani	T5—915 7
Tajwīd	297.122 404 59
Tāk Sin, King of Siam	
Thai history	959.302 4
Takapuna (N.Z.)	T2—932 2
Take-overs	338.83
see also Mergers	
Takeoff	
aeronautics	629.132 521 2
manned space flight	629.452
space flight	629.41
unmanned space flight	629.432
Takeoff accidents	363.124 92
see also Air safety	
Takhrījāt	297.125 7
Takla Lake (B.C.)	T2—711 82
Talbot County (Ga.)	T2—758 483
Talbot County (Md.)	T2—752 32
Talc	553.676
economic geology	553.676
mineralogy	549.67
mining	622.367 6
technology	666.72
Talca (Chile : Province)	T2—833 5
Talented people	305.908 9
	T1—087 9
Taliaferro County (Ga.)	T2—758 616
Talismans	133.44
Islamic popular practices	297.39
numismatics	737.23
religious significance	203.7
see also Symbolism —	
religious significance	
Talk shows	791.446
radio programs	791.446
television programs	791.456
Talking books	
bibliographies	011.384
Tall buildings	720.483
architecture	720.483
construction	690.383
fire hazards	363.379
see also Fire safety	
Tall oil	
recovery from pulp	676.5
Talladega County (Ala.)	T2—761 61
Tallahassee (Fla.)	T2—759 88
Tallahatchie County (Miss.)	T2—762 455
Tallapoosa County (Ala.)	T2—761 53

Tallapoosa River (Ga. and Ala.)	T2—761 5
Tallit	296.461
Tallow	665.2
Tallow tree	583.69
Talmud	296.12
Talmud Bavli	296.125
Talmud Yerushalmi	296.124
Talmudic literature	296.12
Talmudic period	956.940 2
Talon, Patrice	
Beninese history	966.830 55
Talpidae	599.335
Talurqjuak (Nunavut)	T2—719 55
Tama County (Iowa)	T2—777 56
Tama National Park (Colombia)	T2—861 24
Tamahaq language	493.38
	T6—933 8
Tamahaq literature	893.38
Tamang language	495.4
	T6—954
Tamanrasset (Algeria : Province)	T2—657
Tamar, River (England)	T2—423 5
Tamar River (Tas.)	T2—946 5
Tamaracks	585.2
see also Larches	
Tamaricaceae	583.88
Tamaricales	583.88
Tamarind	641.344 6
botany	583.63
cooking	641.644 6
food	641.344 6
orchard crop	634.46
Tamarins	599.84
conservation technology	639.979 84
resource economics	333.959 84
Tamarisk	583.88
Tamashek language	493.38
	T6—933 8
Tamashek literature	893.38
Tamasheq language	493.38
	T6—933 8
Tamasheq literature	893.38
Tamaulipas (Mexico)	T2—721 2
Tamazight language	493.33
	T6—933 3
Tamazight literature	893.33
Tambacounda (Senegal : Region)	T2—663
Tambourines	786.95
see also Percussion instruments	
Tambov (Russia : Oblast)	T2—473 5

Taos Indians	978.900 497 496
	T5—974 96
Taos language	497.496
	T6—974 96
Taounate (Morocco : Province)	T2—643 2
Taourirt (Morocco : Province)	T2—643 3
Tap dancing	792.78
see also Theater	
Tapas	641.812
Tape drives (Computers)	
computer science	004.563
engineering	621.397 63
Tape players	
automobile	629.277 4
sound reproduction	621.389 324
Tape recorders	
automobile	629.277 4
sound reproduction	621.389 324
Tape recordings	
sound reproduction	621.389 324
Tapes (Adhesives)	668.38
Tapes (Computers)	
computer science	004.563
engineering	621.397 63
Tapes (Recording devices)	621.382 34
Tapes (Sound)	384
bibliographies	011.38
see also Sound recordings	
Tapes (Textiles)	677.76
Tapestries	677.64
manufacturing technology	677.64
textile arts	746.3
Tapestry makers	746.392
Tapestry-woven rugs	
arts	746.72
Tapestry yard goods	677.642
Tapeworm-caused diseases	
incidence	614.554
medicine	616.964
see also Communicable diseases — humans	
Tapeworms	592.46
Taphonomy	560.41
Taphrinales	579.562
Tapia	
building construction	693.22
Tapioca	641.336 82
cooking	641.636 82
food	641.336 82
Tapiridae	599.66
Tapirs	599.66
Tapisciaceae	583.76

Tapping tools	621.955
Taps (Valves)	621.84
Taqlīd (Islamic law)	
sources of fiqh	340.591 38
Tar	
materials science	620.196
Tar pavements	625.85
Tar sands	553.283
economic geology	553.283
mining	622.338 3
law	343.077 2
processing	665.4
Taraba State (Nigeria)	T2—669 89
Tarahumara Indians	972.160 049 745 46
	T5—974 546
Tarahumara language	497.454 6
	T6—974 546
Tarahumaran languages	497.454 6
	T6—974 546
Taranaki Region (N.Z.)	T2—934 8
Taranto (Italy)	
ancient	T2—377 67
Taranto (Italy : Province)	T2—457 55
ancient	T2—377 67
Taranto, Gulf of (Italy)	551.461 386
	T2—163 86
Tarapacá (Chile : Region)	T2—831 2
Tararua District (N.Z.)	T2—935 7
Manawatu-Wanganui Region	T2—935 7
Wellington Region	T2—936 9
Tarascan languages	497.96
	T6—979 6
Tarasco Indians	972.370 049 796
	T5—979 6
Tarasco language	497.96
	T6—979 6
Tardigrada	592.72
Tardive dyskinesia	
medicine	616.83
see also Nervous system diseases — humans	
Taree (N.S.W.)	T2—944 2
Tarentum (Italy)	T2—377 67
Tarf (Algeria : Province)	T2—655
Target selection	
military gunnery	623.557
Target shooting	799.3
arts	700.457 9
	T3C—357 9
child care	649.57
ethics	175
human physiology	612.044
journalism	070.449 799 3

Tatar suzerainty	
Russian history	947.03
Tatars	T5—943 87
Crimean	T5—943 88
Tatarstan (Russia)	T2—474 5
Tate County (Miss.)	T2—762 85
Tatted fabrics	677.663
see also Textiles	
Tatting	
arts	746.436
Tattnall County (Ga.)	T2—758 775
Tattooing	
customs	391.65
Taung (South Africa :	
District)	T2—682 46
Taunton Deane (England)	T2—423 85
Taunus (Germany)	T2—434 16
Taupo, Lake (N.Z.)	T2—933 9
Taupo District (N.Z.)	T2—933 9
Bay of Plenty Region	T2—934 24
Hawke's Bay Region	T2—934 63
Manawatu-Wanganui	
Region	T2—935 13
Waikato Region	T2—933 9
Tauranga District (N.Z.)	T2—934 21
Taurus (Zodiac)	133.526 3
Taurus Mountains (Turkey)	T2—564
Tautomerism	547.122 52
inorganic chemistry	541.225 2
organic chemistry	547.122 52
Tavastia Proper (Finland)	T2—489 716
Tawhid	297.211 3
Tawi-Tawi (Philippines)	T2—599 98
Tawitawi (Philippines)	T2—599 98
Tax accounting	657.46
law	343.042
income tax	343.052 044
Tax administration	352.44
law	343.04
see Manual at 343.04–.06 vs.	
336.2, 352.44	
Tax appeals	
law	343.042
Tax assessment	336.2
income tax	336.241
law	343.052 042
law	343.042
property tax	336.222
law	343.054 2
public administration	352.44
Tax auditing	
law	343.04

Tax avoidance	336.206
income tax	336.241 6
corporate	336.243 16
law	343.052 3
personal	336.242 16
law	343.04
property tax	336.22
law	343.054 3
public finance	336.206
Tax collection	352.44
law	343.042
Tax credits	336.206
income tax law	343.052 37
see also Tax avoidance	
Tax deductions	336.206
see also Tax avoidance	
Tax evasion	364.133 8
law	345.023 38
Tax-exempt organizations	
law	343.066
Tax-exempt securities	
law	346.092 2
Tax exemptions	336.206
see also Tax avoidance	
Tax expenditures	336.206
Tax incentives	336.206
income tax law	343.052 304
see also Tax avoidance	
Tax incidence	336.294
Tax law	343.04
see Manual at 343.04–.06 vs.	
336.2, 352.44	
Tax limitations	
law	343.034
Tax lists	
genealogy	929.3
Tax loopholes	336.206
see also Tax avoidance	
Tax planning	
law	343.04
income tax	343.052
Tax rates	336.2
import tax	336.265
Tax rebates	336.206
see also Tax avoidance	
Tax reduction	336.206
see also Tax avoidance	
Tax reform	336.205
income tax	336.241 5
corporate	336.243 15
personal	336.242 15
Tax returns	
income tax law	343.052 044

Tax shelters	336.206	Taylor County (Ky.)	T2—769 673
income tax law	343.052 38	Taylor County (Tex.)	T2—764 727
investment economics	332.604 22	Taylor County (W. Va.)	T2—754 55
see also Tax avoidance		Taylor County (Wis.)	T2—775 26
Taxales	585.6	Tayside (Scotland)	T2—412 8
paleobotany	561.56	Taza (Morocco : Province)	T2—643 2
Taxation	336.2	Taza-Al Hoceïma-Taounate	
American Revolution cause	973.311 4	(Morocco)	T2—643 2
see also Taxes		Tazewell County (Ill.)	T2—773 54
Taxation power (Legislative		Tazewell County (Va.)	T2—755 763
bodies)	328.341 2	TCA cycle	572.475
Taxes	336.2	Te Anau, Lake (N.Z.)	T2—939 6
accounting	657.46	Tea	641.337 2
financial management	658.153	agricultural economics	338.173 72
law	343.04	agriculture	633.72
macroeconomic policy	339.525	botany	583.93
public administration	352.44	commercial processing	
litigation	353.43	economics	338.476 639 4
Taxicab drivers	388.413 214 092	technology	663.94
Taxicab service	388.413 214	cooking with	641.637 2
law	343.098 2	customs	394.15
public administration	354.765 3	food	641.337 2
transportation services	388.413 214	home preparation	641.877
Taxicabs	388.342 32	Tea Act, 1773	
driving	629.283 32	United States history	973.311 5
engineering	629.222 32	Tea leaves	
repair	629.287 232	divination	133.324 4
transportation services	388.342 32	Teacher-administrator relations	371.106
see also Automobiles		Teacher aides	371.141 24
Taxidermy	590.752	Teacher burnout	371.100 19
Taxodiaceae	585.5	Teacher certification	371.12
paleobotany	561.55	Teacher-community relations	306.432
Taxonomic biology	578	education	371.19
plants	580	sociology	306.432
Taxonomic nomenclature	578.014	Teacher education	370.711
see Manual at 579–590		Teacher evaluation	371.144
Taxonomy (Biology)	578.012	Teacher exchanges	370.116 3
Tay, River (Scotland)	T2—412 8	law	344.08
Tây Ninh (Vietnam :		Teacher morale	371.100 19
Province)	T2—597 7	Teacher-parent conferences	371.103
Tay-Sachs disease		Teacher-parent relations	371.192
medicine	616.858 845	Teacher participation in	
pediatrics	618.928 588 45	administration	371.106
Taya, Maawiya Ould Sid'Ahmed		Teacher qualifications	371.12
Mauritanian history	966.105 3	higher education	378.124
Tayammum	297.38	Teacher-staff relations	371.106
Tayassuidae	599.634	Teacher-student relations	371.102 3
Taylor, Charles Ghankay		Teacher training	370.711
Liberian history	966.620 33		T1—071 1
Taylor, Zachary		Teacher turnover	371.14
United States history	973.63	Teacher workload	371.141 2
Taylor County (Fla.)	T2—759 86	Teachers	371.1
Taylor County (Ga.)	T2—758 493	biography	371.100 92
Taylor County (Iowa)	T2—777 79	higher education	378.12

Teachers (continued)
  law   344.078
  public control   379.157
  religious educators   207.509 2
    Christian   268
      biography   268.092
        see Manual at 230–280
      role and function   268.3
    Jewish   296.68
      biography   296.680 92
      role and function   296.68
  role in guidance   371.404 6
  workload   371.141 2
    higher education   378.122 12
Teachers' assistants   371.141 24
Teachers' colleges   370.711
Teaching   371.102
                              T1—071
  educational psychology   370.15
  higher education   378.125
  law   344.078
  professional education   370.711
  special education   371.904 3
Teaching (Spiritual gift)   234.13
Teaching aids   371.33
                              T1—078
Teaching load   371.141 2
  higher education   378.122 12
Teaching machines
  adult education   374.264
Teaching materials   371.33
  see also Instructional materials
Teaching methods   371.3
                              T1—071
  personnel training   658.312 404
  primary education   372.13
  religious education   207.5
    Christianity   268.6
  special education   371.904 3
Teaching office of the church   262.8
Teaching orders (Christianity)   255.03
  church history   271.03
  women   255.903
    church history   271.903
Teachings of Jesus Christ   232.954
Teak
  botany   583.96
  forestry   634.973 96
  lumber   674.144
Team handball   796.327
Team management   658.402 2
  see also Work teams
Team teaching   371.148
Teamsters   388.324 092

Tear ducts
  human physiology   612.847
Tear gas
  manufacturing technology   683.45
  military engineering   623.459 2
Tear-gas canister launchers   623.445
Teas (Meals)   642
  cooking   641.53
    light meals   641.53
    main meals   641.54
  customs   394.125 3
    light meals   394.125 3
    main meals   394.125 4
Teasels   583.987
Teasing   302.3
Tebboune, Abdelmadjid
  Algerian history   965.055
Tébessa (Algeria : Province) T2—655
Technetium
  chemical engineering   661.054 3
  chemistry   546.543
Technical assistance
  economics   338.91
  public finance   336.185
Technical chemistry   660
Technical drawing   604.2
Technical education   T1—071
Technical high schools   373.246
  see also Secondary education
Technical libraries   026.6
Technical processes (Libraries)   025.02
Technical reports
  cataloging   025.343 6
  library treatment   025.173 6
Technical services (Libraries)   025.02
Technical training   607
  armed forces   355.56
Technical writing   808.066
Techno music   781.648
Technological archaeology   609.009
Technological innovations
  agricultural industries   338.16
  cause of social change   303.483
    see Manual at 303.483 vs.
      306.45, 306.46
  economics   338.064
  executive management   658.406 2
  mineral industries   338.26
  production management   658.514
Technological instruments
  manufacturing technology   681.76
Technological unemployment   331.137 042

Technologists	609.2
works for	T1—024 6
see Manual at T1—015 vs.	
T1—0245–0246	
Technology	600
art representation	704.949 6
arts	700.456
	T3C—356
folklore	398.276
history and criticism	398.356
law	344.095
literature	808.803 56
history and criticism	809.933 56
specific literatures	T3B—080 356
history and	
criticism	T3B—093 56
painting	758.96
primary education	372.358
production management	658.514
public administrative support	352.745
social effects	303.483
see Manual at 303.483 vs.	
306.45, 306.46	
sociology	306.46
see Manual at 303.483 vs.	
306.45, 306.46	
see Manual at 300 vs. 600	
Technology and religion	201.66
Christianity	261.56
Islam	297.266
Judaism	296.376
philosophy of religion	215
Technology assessment	303.483
economic development	338.9
public administration	354.27
health services potential	362.104 2
natural resources impact	333.714
safety risk	363.1
social change potential	303.483
Technology transfer	338.926
economics	338.926
law	343.074
Tecophilaeaceae	584.7
Tectibranchia	594.37
Tectonics	551.8
Tectosilicates	
mineralogy	549.68
Teddy bears	
making	688.724 3
handicrafts	745.592 43
technology	688.724 3

Teenage boys	305.235 1
	T1—083 51
see also Young men — under	
twenty-one	
Teenage fathers	306.874 2
social welfare	362.787 42
Teenage girls	305.235 2
	T1—083 52
see also Young women —	
under twenty-one	
Teenage mothers	306.874 3
social welfare	362.787 43
Teenage pregnancy	
obstetrics	618.200 835
social welfare	362.787 43
Teenagers	305.235
	T1—083 5
see also Adolescents	
Tees, River (England)	T2—428 5
Teeth	591.44
animal physiology	573.356
anthropometry	599.943
dentistry	617.6
descriptive zoology	591.44
diseases	573.356 39
see also Tooth diseases	
human anatomy	611.314
human physiology	612.311
Teeth diseases	573.356 39
see also Tooth diseases	
Tefillin	296.461 2
Tegucigalpa (Honduras)	T2—728 371
Tehama County (Calif.)	T2—794 27
Tehran (Iran)	T2—552 5
Tehran (Iran : Province)	T2—552 5
Tehuantepec, Gulf of (Mexico)	551.461 41
	T2—164 1
Tehuantepec Canal	386.447
Teichmüller spaces	515.94
Teignbridge (England)	942.355
	T2—423 55
Teignmouth, John Shore, Baron	
Indian history	954.031 1
Teiidae	597.958 2
Tejan Kabbah, Ahmad	
Sierra Leonean history	966.404 5
Teke languages	496.396
	T6—963 96
Tekirdağ İli (Turkey)	T2—496 16
Tekrur (Kingdom)	966.301
	T2—663
Tel Aviv (Israel : District)	T2—569 48
Telangana (India)	T2—548 4

Telangiectasis		Telephone (continued)	
medicine	616.148	public administration	354.75
see also Cardiovascular		sociology	302.235
diseases — humans		wireless	384.53
Telangitis		communications services	384.53
medicine	616.148	Telephone answering machines	
see also Cardiovascular		engineering	621.386 7
diseases — humans		office services	651.73
Telecommunication	384	Telephone books	910.25
accounting	657.84	*see Manual at* T1—025 vs.	
communications services	384	T1—029	
engineering	621.382	Telephone calls	384.64
law	343.099 4	wireless	384.534
public administration	354.75	*see also* Telephone	
Telecommunication workers	384.092	Telephone counseling	361.06
Telecommuting	331.256 8	Telephone engineers	621.385 092
labor economics	331.256 8	Telephone etiquette	395.59
personnel management	658.312 3	Telephone lines	
Teleconferencing		communications services	384.65
instructional use	371.358	Telephone-order houses	381.142
Telecontrol		management	658.872
engineering	620.46	*see also* Commerce	
radio engineering	621.384 196	Telephone selling	381.142
Telefacsimile	384.14	management	658.872
see also Facsimile transmission		techniques for individuals	658.85
Telefax	384.14	Telephone services	384.64
see also Facsimile transmission		wire	384.64
Telegraphy	384.1	wireless	384.534
communications services	384.1	Telephone shopping	381.142
engineering	621.383	Telephone stations	
law	343.099 4	communications services	384.65
military engineering	623.732	wireless	384.535
nautical engineering	623.856 2	Telephone switching systems	621.387
public administration	354.75	Telephones	621.386
sociology	302.235	automobile	629.277
wireless	384.52	office services	651.73
Telegraphy stations		Telephony	384.6
communications industry	384.15	*see also* Telephone	
Telemark fylke (Norway)	T2—482 8	Telephotography	778.322
Telemarketing	381.142	Telepresence	384.556
management	658.872	sociology	302.234 5
Teleology	124	Telescopes	522.2
philosophy	124	astronomy	522.2
philosophy of religion	210	manufacturing technology	681.412 3
Teleorman (Romania)	T2—498 2	Teleshopping	381.142
Teleostei	597	law	343.081 142 8
see also Fishes		*see also* Commerce	
Telepathists	133.820 92	Teletext	004.69
Telepathy	133.82	communications services	384.33
Telephone	384.6	*see also* Computer	
communications services	384.6	communications	
engineering	621.385	Teletype	384.14
law	343.099 43	wireless	384.524
military engineering	623.733	*see also* Telegraphy	

Telford and Wrekin (England)	T2—424 56
Telford pavements	625.86
Teller County (Colo.)	T2—788 58
Tellurides	
mineralogy	549.32
Tellurium	
chemical engineering	661.072 6
chemistry	546.726
economic geology	553.499
metallurgy	669.79
Telopea	583.38
Telpherage	621.868
Teltow-Fläming (Germany : Landkreis)	T2—431 54
Telugu	T5—948 27
Telugu language	494.827
	T6—948 27
Telugu literature	894.827
Tem (African people)	T5—963 5
Tem language	496.35
	T6—963 5
Temer, Michel	
Brazilian history	981.066
Témiscamingue (Quebec : Regional County Municipality)	T2—714 137
Témiscouata (Quebec : Regional County Municipality)	T2—714 762
Temne (African people)	T5—963 2
Temne language	496.32
	T6—963 2
Temotu (Solomon Islands)	T2—959 39
Temouchent (Algeria : Province)	T2—651
Tempeh	641.356 55
Tempera painting	751.43
Temperament (Musical instruments)	784.192 8
Temperament (Psychology)	155.262
Temperance	178
see also Virtues	
Temperate basses	597.73
Temperate Zones	T2—12
Temperate zones	
diseases	
medicine	616.988 2
see also Environmental diseases — humans	
Temperature	536.5
biophysics	571.46
humans	612.014 46
health	613.1

Temperature (continued)	
meteorology	551.525
physics	536.5
seawater	551.465 3
meteorological effect	551.524 6
weather forecasting	551.642 5
Temperature adaptation	578.42
animals	591.42
plants	581.42
Temperature changes	
effect on materials	620.112 15
geologic work	551.39
meteorology	551.525 3
Temperature control	
buildings	697.932 2
mining	622.43
ships	623.853
spacecraft	629.477 5
Temperature-salinity relationships	551.466 43
Tempering glass	666.129
Tempering metals	671.36
Templars	255.791 3
church history	271.791 3
Temple of Jerusalem	296.491
Temples	203.5
architecture	726.1
Buddhist	294.343 5
Hindu	294.535
Jain	294.435
Jewish	296.65
see also Synagogues	
Jewish temple in Jerusalem	296.491
Latter Day Saint movement	246.958 93
Shinto	299.561 35
Sikh	294.635
Tempo (Music)	781.22
Temporal constructions (Grammar)	415
specific languages	T4—5
Temporal databases	
computer science	005.753
Temporal logic	511.314
Temporal power of pope	262.132
Temporary buildings	720.444
architecture	720.444
construction	690.344
Temporary deformation	531.382
materials science	620.112 32
see also Elasticity	
Temporary employees	331.257 29
Temporary employment	331.257 29
Temporary help	331.257 29
Temporary help services	331.128

Temporary housing	
social welfare	361.05
Temporary marriage	306.847
law	346.016 77
Temporary unions	306.847
law	346.016 77
Temporomandibular joint	
dysfunction	
regional medicine	617.522
Temptation	
moral theology	205
Christianity	241.3
Temptation of Jesus Christ	232.95
Temuan (Malaysian people)	T5—992 8
Temuan language	T6—992 8
Temurah	296.123 5
Babylonian Talmud	296.125 5
Mishnah	296.123 5
Ten Commandments	222.16
moral theology	
Christianity	241.52
Judaism	296.36
Ten kingdoms (China)	951.018
Ten Readings (Koran)	297.122 404 52
Ten Sikh gurus	294.609 2
biography	294.609 2
role and function	294.663
Ten Thousand Islands (Fla.)	T2—759 44
Tenancy	
land economics	333.53
law	346.043 4
Tenant-landlord relations	333.54
law	346.043 4
Tenants' liability insurance	368.56
see also Insurance	
Tenbury Wells (England)	T2—424 47
Tench	597.482
sports fishing	799.174 82
Tenda (African people)	T5—963 2
Tenda language	496.32
	T6—963 2
Tende-Yanzi languages	496.396
	T6—963 96
Tender offers (Securities)	332.632 2
financial economics	332.632 2
law	346.066 2
management	658.16
production economics	338.83
Tenderizers	
food technology	664.4
Tendinitis	
medicine	616.75
see also Musculoskeletal	
diseases — humans	

Tendon diseases	
medicine	616.75
see also Musculoskeletal	
diseases — humans	
Tendon sheath diseases	
medicine	616.76
see also Musculoskeletal	
diseases — humans	
Tendon sheaths	573.753 56
human anatomy	611.75
human physiology	612.75
medicine	616.76
see also Musculoskeletal	
system	
Tendons	573.753 56
biology	573.753 56
human anatomy	611.74
human physiology	612.75
medicine	616.75
surgery	617.474
see also Musculoskeletal	
system	
Tendrils	581.48
Tendring (England)	T2—426 725
Tène period	936.02
Tenebrionidae	595.769
Tenedos Island (Turkey)	T2—562 2
ancient	T2—391 1
Tenements	647.92
architecture	728.314
construction	690.831 4
household management	647.92
see also Dwellings	
Tenericutes	579.328
Tennant Creek (N.T.)	T2—942 95
Tennessee	976.8
	T2—768
Tennessee River	T2—768
Alabama	T2—761 9
Tennessee	T2—768
Tennessee Walking Horse	636.13
Tennessine	546.73
Tennis	796.342
electronic games	794.863 42
equipment technology	688.763 42
see also Ball games	
Tennis courts	796.342 068
Tennis players	796.342 092
Tenor horns	788.974
see also Brass instruments	
Tenor recorders	788.366
see also Woodwind	
instruments	

Tenor saxophones	788.74
see also Woodwind instruments	
Tenor viols	787.64
see also Stringed instruments	
Tenor voices	782.87
choral and mixed voices	782.87
single voices	783.87
Tenos Island (Greece)	T2—495 85
Tenpins	794.6
Tenrecs	599.33
Tensas Parish (La.)	T2—763 79
Tension (Mechanical stress)	
effect on materials	620.112 41
Tension headache	
medicine	616.849 14
see also Nervous system diseases — humans	
Tensor algebra	512.57
Tensor analysis	515.63
Tensor calculus	515.63
Tent shows	792.022
Tentaculata	593.8
Tenterfield (N.S.W.)	T2—944 4
Tentering textiles	677.028 25
Tenth century	909.1
	T1—090 21
Tenth of Muḥarram	297.36
Tents	796.540 284
manufacturing technology	685.53
Tenure	331.259 6
labor economics	331.259 6
law	
public employees	342.068 6
personnel management	658.312
teachers	371.104
higher education	378.121 4
public administration	354.98
Tepiman languages	497.455
	T6—974 55
Tepo language	496.33
	T6—963 3
Tequila (Distilled liquor)	641.25
commercial processing	663.5
Tequila (Plant)	584.79
Ter Saami language	494.576
	T6—945 76
Ter Sámi language	494.576
	T6—945 76
Teramo (Italy : Province)	T2—457 15
ancient	T2—374 9
Teratogenic agents	
medicine	616.043

Teratology	
biology	571.976
medicine	616.043
Terbium	
chemistry	546.416
Terce	264.15
music	782.324
see also Liturgy of the hours	
Terengganu	T2—595 1
Tergeste (Italy)	T2—373 91
Term life insurance	368.323
see also Insurance	
Term limitation	
chief executives	352.23
legislators	328.33
Term logic	160
Terminal ballistics	
military engineering	623.516
Terminal care	362.175
children	
social welfare	362.198 920 05
ethics	179.7
law	344.041 97
medicine	616.029
nursing	616.029
pastoral theology	206.1
Christianity	259.417 5
social theology	201.762 175
Christianity	261.832 175
social welfare	362.175
Terminals (Computers)	004.75
engineering	621.398 5
graphics	006.62
engineering	621.399 6
Terminals (Transportation)	388.04
see also Transportation facilities	
Termination	
insurance	368.016
Terminology	401.4
	T1—014
dictionaries	413
specific languages	T4—014
dictionaries	T4—3
usage (Applied linguistics)	T4—81
see Manual at T4—3 vs. T4—81	
usage (Applied linguistics)	418
Termite damage prevention	691.14
Termite-resistant construction	693.842
Termites	595.736
control technology	628.965 7

Ternary form	781.822 3
instrumental	784.182 2
Ternary system (Numeration)	513.5
Terni (Italy : Province)	T2—456 52
ancient	T2—374 4
Etruria	T2—375 76
Umbria	T2—374 4
Ternopil′ (Ukraine : Oblast)	T2—477 9
Ternopil′s′ka oblast′ (Ukraine)	T2—477 9
Terns	598.338
Terpenes	
chemistry	547.71
Terra-cotta	
architectural construction	721.044 3
building construction	693.3
building materials	691.4
materials science	620.142
Terrace (B.C.)	T2—711 85
Terrace houses	
architecture	728.312
Terraces	
landscape architecture	717
Terracing (Soil conservation)	631.455
Terrapins	597.925
Terrariums	578.073
animals	590.73
floriculture	635.982 4
plants	580.73
Terrebonne Parish (La.)	T2—763 41
Terrell County (Ga.)	T2—758 935
Terrell County (Tex.)	T2—764 922
Terrestrial ecology	577
Terrestrial photogrammetry	526.982 5
Terrestrial radiation	
meteorology	551.527 2
Terrestrial turtles	597.924
Terriers	636.755
Terriers (Toy dogs)	636.76
Territorial property	320.12
law of nations	341.42
Territorial waters	
law	342.041 3
law of nations	341.448
Territoriality	
animal behavior	591.566
human ecology	304.23
Territories (Local government units)	320.83
see also Counties	
Territories (State-level units)	321.023
see also States (Members of federations)	

Territories under international	
control	321
law	341.29
public administration	353.159
Territory of states	320.12
law	342.041 3
law of nations	341.42
Terrorism	363.325
criminology	364.131 7
law	345.023 17
ethics	172.1
international relations	327.117
prevention	
management	658.473
social conflict	303.625
social welfare	362.889 317
Terry cloth	677.617
Terry County (Tex.)	T2—764 859
Tersinidae	598.875
Tertiary education	378
	T1—071 1
see also Higher education	
Tertiary period	551.78
geology	551.78
paleontology	560.178
Tertiary recovery	
oil extraction	622.338 2
Teruel (Spain : Province)	T2—465 51
Terumot	296.123 1
Mishnah	296.123 1
Palestinian Talmud	296.124 1
Teso (African people)	T5—965 522
Teso language	496.552 2
	T6—965 522
Teso-Turkana languages	496.552 2
	T6—965 522
Tessellations (Mathematics)	516.132
Euclidean geometry	516.213 2
Tessin (Switzerland)	T2—494 78
Test, River (England)	T2—422 732
Test anxiety	371.260 19
Test bias	
education	371.260 13
psychology	150.287
Test construction	
education	371.261
	T1—076
teacher-prepared tests	371.271
Test reliability	
education	371.260 13
Test-taking skills	
education	371.26

Test-tube babies
  ethics   176.2
    see also Reproduction —
      ethics
  medicine   618.178 059 9
Test tubes   542.2
Test validity
  education   371.260 13
Test Valley (England)   T2—422 732
Testaments
  pseudepigrapha   229.914
Testes   573.655
  biology   573.655
  human anatomy   611.63
  human physiology   612.614
  medicine   616.68
  see also Male genital system;
    Testicles
Testicles   573.655
  see also Testes
Testicular cancer
  incidence   614.599 946 3
  medicine   616.994 63
  see also Cancer — humans
Testicular diseases
  medicine   616.68
    see also Male genital
      diseases — humans
Testing   T1—028 7
  chemistry   542.3
  education   371.26
     T1—076
    teacher-prepared tests   371.271
  physics   530.8
Testing devices
  electronics   621.381 548
  manufacturing technology   681.2
  radio engineering   621.384 133
Tests   T1—028 7
  education   371.26
     T1—076
    teacher-prepared tests   371.271
    see Manual at 371.262 vs.
      371.264
  personnel selection   658.311 25
  public administration   352.65
Testudines   597.92
  paleozoology   567.92
Testudinidae   597.924
Testudinoidea   597.92

Tetanus
  incidence   614.512 8
  medicine   616.931 8
    see also Communicable
      diseases — humans
Tete (Mozambique :
  Province)   T2—679 5
Tetela languages   496.396
     T6—963 96
Teton County (Idaho)   T2—796 54
Teton County (Mont.)   T2—786 55
Teton County (Wyo.)   T2—787 55
Teton Indians   978.004 975 244
     T5—975 244
Teton language   497.524 4
     T6—975 244
Teton Range (Wyo. and
  Idaho)   T2—787 55
Tétouan (Morocco :
  Province)   T2—642
Tetrahedrite
  mineralogy   549.35
Tetrameristaceae   583.93
Tetrao   598.634
Tetraodontiformes   597.64
Tetraonidae   598.63
Tetrapoda   596
Tetras   597.48
Teuso languages   496.57
     T6—965 7
Teuthoidea   594.58
Teutoburg Forest
  (Germany)   T2—435 65
Teutonic Knights   255.791 4
  church history   271.791 4
Tevul Yom   296.123 6
Tewa Indians   978.900 497 494
     T5—974 94
Tewa language   497.494
     T6—974 94
Tewa literature   897.494
Tewkesbury (England :
  Borough)   T2—424 12
Texada Island (B.C.)   T2—711 31
Texas   976.4
     T2—764
Texas, East   T2—764 14
Texas County (Mo.)   T2—778 84
Texas County (Okla.)   T2—766 135
Texas Panhandle (Tex.)   T2—764 8
Texas Republic   976.404
Texoma, Lake (Okla. and
  Tex.)   T2—766 61

Text editors (Computer programs)
  programming aids   005.13
Text editors (Computer software) 005.52
  programming aids   005.13
Text encoding   005.72
Text messaging   384.534
  communications services   384.534
  sociology   302.234 45
Text processing   005.52
Textbook bias   371.32
  public control   379.156
Textbooks   371.32
  bibliographies   011.7
  law   344.077
  public control   379.156
  teaching use   371.32
Textile arts   746
Textile chemicals   677.028 35
Textile handicrafters   746.092
Textile handicrafts   746
Textile plants (Living organisms) 677
  see Manual at 583–585 vs. 600
Textile printing   667.38
Textile workers   677.009 2
Textiles   677
  equipment manufacturing
    technology   681.767 7
  field crops   633.5
  handicrafts   746
  home sewing   646.11
  manufacturing technology   677
    economics   338.476 77
    law   343.078 677
  materials science   620.197
  product safety   363.19
    see also Product safety
  sculpture material   731.2
  ship design   623.818 97
  shipbuilding   623.820 7
Texts (Music)   780
  treatises   780.268
Textual criticism
  literature   809
    specific literatures   T3B—09
    theory   801.959
  sacred books   208.2
    Bible   220.404 6
    Talmud   296.120 4
Texture
  materials science   620.112 92
Texture (Music)   781.28
Thaba Nchu (South Africa : District)   T2—685 4

Thabamoopo (South Africa : District)   T2—682 56
Thabane, Thomas Motsoahae
  Lesotho history   968.850 32
Thabazimbi (South Africa : District)   T2—682 53
Thabo Mofutsanyana
  District Municipality
  (South Africa)   T2—685 1
Thai   T5—959 11
Thái Bình (Vietnam : Province)   T2—597 3
Thai language   495.91
    T6—959 11
Thai literature   895.91
Thái Nguyên (Vietnam : Province)   T2—597 1
Thailand   959.3
    T2—593
Thailand, Gulf of   551.461 472
    T2—164 72
Thal (Switzerland : Bezirk)   T2—494 353 7
Thal-Gäu (Switzerland)   T2—494 353
Thalamus
  human anatomy   611.81
  human physiology   612.826 2
  medicine   616.8
Thalassemia
  medicine   616.152
    see also Cardiovascular
    diseases — humans
Thaliacea   596.2
Thallium   669.79
  chemical engineering   661.067 8
  chemistry   546.678
  metallurgy   669.79
  physical metallurgy   669.967 9
  see also Chemicals
Thallobionta   579
Thallophyta   579
Thames, River (England)   T2—422
Thames Coromandel
  District (N.Z.)   T2—933 23
Thamesdown (England)   T2—423 13
Thanet (England)   T2—422 357
Thanh Hóa (Vietnam : Province)   T2—597 4
Thanksgiving   394.264 9
  cooking   641.568
  handicrafts   745.594 164 9
Thao (Taiwan people)   T5—992 5
Thar Desert (India and Pakistan)   T2—544

Tharaka Nithi County
  (Kenya)   T2—676 247
Thasos (Greece : Regional
  unit)   T2—495 7
Thasos Island (Greece)   T2—495 7
  ancient   T2—391 1
Thatch grasses   584.924
Thayer County (Neb.)   T2—782 335
The Pas (Man.)   T2—712 72
The Weald (England)   T2—422 5
Theaceae   583.93
Theales   583.93
Theater   792
  accounting   657.84
  influence on crime   364.254
  instructional use   371.399
  Japan   792.095 2
  performing arts   792
  primary education   372.66
  religious significance   203.7
    Christianity   246.72
      religious education   268.67
    see also Arts — religious
      significance
  sociology   306.484 8
Theater etiquette   395.53
Theater-in-the-round   792.022 8
Theater television   384.556
  see also Television
Theaters (Buildings)
  architecture   725.822
  area planning   711.558
  institutional housekeeping   647.968 22
  music   781.538
Theatines   255.51
  church history   271.51
Theatrical costumes   792.026
  dramatic performances   792.026
  home sewing   646.478
  see also Costumes
Theatrical dancing   792.78
Theatrical performers   792.028 092
Theban supremacy   938.06
Thebes (Egypt : Extinct
  city)   T2—323
Thebes (Greece)   T2—384
Thecodontia   567.91
Thecosomata   594.34
Theft   364.162
  law   345.026 2
  prevention
    household security   643.16
    management   658.473

Theft
  prevention (continued)
    museology   069.54
         T1—075
Theft insurance   368.82
Theism   211.3
  Christianity   231
  comparative religion   202.11
  Islam   297.211
  Judaism   296.311
  philosophy of religion   211.3
Theistic religions   201.4
Theists   211.309 2
Thelephoraceae   579.6
Theligonum   583.956
Thelon Game Sanctuary
  (N.W.T. and Nunavut)   T2—719 3
Thelon River (N.W.T. and
  Nunavut)   T2—719 58
Thematic apperception tests   155.284 4
Thematic catalogs   780.216
Theme and variations   781.825
  instrumental   784.182 5
Theme parks   791.068
  see also Amusement parks
Themes
  arts   700.42–.49
         T3C—3
    see Manual at T3C—3
  literature   808.803
    history and criticism   809.933
    specific literatures   T3B—080 3
    history and
      criticism   T3B—093
    see Manual at
      T3B—102–107,
      T3B—205, T3B—308 vs.
      T3C—1, T3C—3
  musical element   781.248
Theocracy   321.5
  political ideology   320.55
  political system   321.5
  religion   201.721
    Christianity   261.73
Theodicy   202.118
  Christianity   231.8
  comparative religion   202.118
  Islam   297.211 8
  Judaism   296.311 8
  philosophy of religion   214
Theodore I, Czar of Russia
  Russian history   947.044

Theodore II, Negus of Ethiopia
  Eritrean history   963.504 1
  Ethiopian history   963.041
Theodore III, Czar of Russia
  Russian history   947.049
Theologians   202.092
  Christian   230.092
    Protestant   230.044 092
         230.044 092
    see Manual at 230–280
Theological anthropology   202.2
Theological seminaries
  Christianity   230.071 1
Theology   202
  Buddhism   294.342
  Christianity   230
  Hinduism   294.52
  Islam   297.2
    Sufi   297.41
  Judaism   296.3
Theophanies
  Christianity   231.74
Theoretical biochemistry   572.33
  humans   612.015 82
Theoretical chemistry   541.2
  see Manual at 541 vs. 546
Theoretical organic chemistry   547.12
Theory   T1—01
  see Manual at T1—01
Theosis
  Christian doctrine   234.8
Theosophists
  biography   299.934 092
Theosophy   299.934
Theotokos   232.91
Thera (Greece : Regional
  unit)   T2—495 85
Thera Island (Greece)   T2—495 85
  ancient   T2—391 5
Therapeutic charms   203.326
  occultism   133.446
Therapeutic manipulations
  medicine   615.82
Therapeutic services   362.178
  see also Health services
Therapeutic spells   203.326
  occultism   133.446
Therapeutic systems   615.53
  see Manual at 615.53
Therapeutic touch
  medicine   615.852
Therapeutics   615.5
  adolescent medicine   615.508 35
  pediatrics   615.542

Therapeutics (continued)
  veterinary medicine   636.089 55
  see Manual at 613 vs. 612,
    615.8; *also at* 615.8
Therapists   615.509 2
Therapsida   567.93
Therapy   615.5
  see Manual at 617
Theravada Buddhism   294.391
Theremins   786.73
  see also Electrophones
Thérèse-De Blainville
  (Quebec)   T2—714 248
Therevidae   595.773
Thermal analysis   543.26
Thermal capacity   536.6
Thermal conductivity   536.201 2
Thermal convective storms   551.554
Thermal cracking
  petroleum   665.533
Thermal diffusivity   536.201 4
Thermal dissociation   541.364
  chemical engineering   660.296 4
Thermal effects of electricity   537.624
Thermal engineering   621.402
Thermal expansion   536.41
Thermal forces
  materials science   620.112 1
Thermal insulation   693.832
Thermal ocean power conversion   333.914
Thermal perception   152.182 2
Thermal pollution   363.739 4
  effect on natural ecology   577.627 26
  social welfare   363.739 4
  water supply engineering   628.168 31
  see also Pollution
Thermal properties
  materials science   620.112 96
Thermal waters   333.88
  economics   333.88
  geophysics   551.23
Thermal weapons   623.446
Thermionic converters   621.312 43
Thermistors   621.381 548
Thermit welding   671.529
Thermobiology   572.436
  biochemistry   572.436
  body temperature   571.76
  humans   612.014 46
Thermobiophysics   571.46
  humans   612.014 46
Thermochemistry   541.36
  biochemistry   572.436
  chemical engineering   660.296

Thermocouples	536.52
Thermodynamics	536.7
biochemistry	572.436
chemical engineering	660.296 9
chemistry	541.369
engineering	621.402 1
meteorology	551.522
physics	536.7
Thermoelectric generation	621.312 43
Thermoelectricity	537.65
Thermography	
medicine	616.075 4
Thermogravimetry	543.26
Thermoluminescence	535.356
Thermometry	536.502 87
Thermonuclear reaction	539.764
Thermonuclear reactors	621.484
Thermopenetration	
therapeutics	615.832 3
Thermoplastic elastomers	678
Thermoplastic plastics	668.423
Thermosbaenacea	595.373
Thermosetting plastics	668.422
Thermostats	
air conditioning buildings	697.932 2
heating buildings	697.07
Thermotherapy	
medicine	615.832
Theropoda	567.912
Thesauri (Controlled	
vocabularies)	025.47
Thesauri (Synonym dictionaries)	413.1
specific languages	T4—312
specific subjects	T1—03
Theses (Academic)	378.242
bibliographies	011.75
rhetoric	808.066 378
specific places	015
Thesprōtia (Greece)	T2—495 3
Thessalia (Greece)	T2—495 4
Thessalias-Stereas Helladas	
(Greece : Decentralized	
administration)	T2—495 15
Thessalonians (Biblical books)	227.81
Thessalonikē (Greece :	
Regional unit)	T2—495 65
Thessaly (Greece)	949.54
	T2—495 4
ancient	T2—382
Thessaly and Central Greece	
(Greece : Decentralized	
administration)	T2—495 15
Theta function	515.984

Theunissen (South Africa :	
District)	T2—685 3
Thiazoles	547.594
Thierstein (Switzerland)	T2—494 355 3
Thiès (Senegal : Region)	T2—663
Thigh muscles	
human anatomy	611.738
Thighs	612.98
physiology	612.98
regional medicine	617.582
surgery	617.582
see also Lower extremities	
Thimbles	
home sewing	646.19
Thin-film circuits	621.381 5
Thin-film memory	004.53
engineering	621.397 32
Thin-film technology	621.381 52
Thin films	530.427 5
liquid-state physics	530.427 5
solid-state physics	530.417 5
Thin-layer chromatography	543.84
Things (Law)	346.04
Things (Philosophy)	111
Thinking	153.42
human physiology	612.823 342
psychology	153.42
Thinners	
paint technology	667.624
Thio acids	547.064
chemical engineering	661.896
Thioalcohols	
chemical engineering	661.896
Thioaldehydes	547.065
chemical engineering	661.896
Thioethers	547.061
chemical engineering	661.896
Thioketones	547.065
chemical engineering	661.896
Thiophenes	547.594
Thiqāt (Hadith)	297.125 262
Thira (Greece : Regional	
unit)	T2—495 85
Third-class mail	383.124
see also Postal service	
Third Crusade, 1189–1192	956.014
Third International	324.175
Third Order Regular of St.	
Francis	255.38
church history	271.38
women	255.973
church history	271.973

Third orders	
religious orders	255.094
church history	271.094
women	255.909 4
church history	271.909 4
Third parties (Law)	346.022
Third Reich	943.086
Third Republic (France)	944.081
Third stream jazz	781.681 75
Third World (Developing regions)	T2—172 4
Third World (Unaligned blocs)	T2—171 6
Thirst	
human physiology	612.391
psychology	152.188 6
Thirteen Articles of Faith (Judaism)	296.3
Thirteenth century	909.2
	T1—090 22
Thirty Years' War, 1618–1648	940.24
Thistles	583.983
Thlaping Tlaro (South Africa : District)	T2—687 15
Thohoyandou (South Africa : District)	T2—682 57
Thomas County (Ga.)	T2—758 984
Thomas County (Kan.)	T2—781 132
Thomas County (Neb.)	T2—782 774
Thomist philosophy	189.4
modern	149.91
Thompson (Man.)	T2—712 71
Thompson, John S. D. (John Sparrow David), Sir	
Canadian history	971.055
Thompson-Nicola (B.C.)	T2—711 72
Thompson River (B.C.)	T2—711 72
Thonga (African people)	T5—963 97
Thonga language	496.397
	T6—963 97
Thoracic surgery	617.540 59
Thoracica	595.35
Thorax	573.996
biology	573.996
human anatomy	611.94
human physiology	612.94
regional medicine	617.54
surgery	617.540 59
Thorium	669.292 2
chemistry	546.422
economic geology	553.493
metallurgy	669.292 2
see also Chemicals; Metals	

Thorndike, Edward L. (Edward Lee)	
psychological system	150.194 4
Thorns	581.47
descriptive botany	581.47
physiology	575.457
Thorough bass	781.47
Thoroughbred horse	636.132
Thothmes III, King of Egypt	
Egyptian history	932.014
Thought	153.42
philosophy	128.3
psychology	153.42
Thousand Islands (N.Y. and Ont.)	T2—747 58
New York	T2—747 58
Ontario	T2—713 7
Thrace	T2—495 7
ancient	939.861
	T2—398 61
Bulgaria	T2—499 5
Greece	T2—495 7
Thrace, Eastern (Turkey)	949.61
	T2—496 1
ancient	939.861
	T2—398 61
Thracian language	491.993
	T6—919 93
Thraco-Phrygian languages	491.993
	T6—919 93
Thrashers (Birds)	598.844
Thraupidae	598.875
Thread	677.028 62
home sewing	646.19
manufacturing technology	677.028 62
Threatened species	333.952 2
see also entries beginning with Rare	
Threats	
international relations	327.117
social control	303.36
Three-day event (Horsemanship)	798.242
Three-dimensional chess	794.18
Three-dimensional graphics	
computer graphics	006.693
Three-dimensional printing	621.988
Three-quarter play	
rugby	796.333 25
Three Rivers (England)	T2—425 88
Three-wheel automobiles	
engineering	629.222
Three-wheel motorcycles	
engineering	629.227 5

Three-wheeled automobiles	
engineering	629.222
Three-wheeled motor vehicles	
engineering	629.222
Three-wheeled motorcycles	
engineering	629.227 5
Three wise men (Christian	
doctrines)	232.923
Thresholds (Psychology)	152.1
quantitative studies	152.82
Threskiornithidae	598.34
Thrift industry	332.32
law	346.082 32
public administration	354.86
Thrift institutions	332.32
law	346.082 32
public administration	354.86
Thrift shops	381.19
Thrifts (Plants)	635.933 88
botany	583.88
floriculture	635.933 88
Thrips	595.758
Throat	
human anatomy	611.32
human physiology	612.31
medicine	616.31
regional medicine	617.531
surgery	617.531 059
Throat diseases	
medicine	616.31
see also Digestive system	
diseases — humans	
Throckmorton County	
(Tex.)	T2—764 735
Thrombin	
human physiology	612.115
Thrombocytes	573.159
human histology	612.117
see also Cardiovascular system	
Thromboembolisms	
arteries	
medicine	616.135
see also Cardiovascular	
diseases — humans	
veins	
medicine	616.145
see also Cardiovascular	
diseases — humans	
Thrombophlebitis	
medicine	616.142
see also Cardiovascular	
diseases — humans	

Thromboses	
arteries	
medicine	616.135
see also Cardiovascular	
diseases — humans	
lungs	
medicine	616.249
see also Respiratory tract	
diseases — humans	
medicine	616.135
see also Cardiovascular	
diseases — humans	
veins	
medicine	616.145
see also Cardiovascular	
diseases — humans	
Throttles	
automotive	629.258
Throughways	388.122
see also Roads	
Thrushes	598.842
Thrust (Aeronautics)	629.132 33
Thừa Thiên-Huế (Vietnam)	T2—597 4
Thulium	
chemistry	546.418
Thumb pianos	786.85
see also Percussion instruments	
Thun (Switzerland :	
District)	T2—494 541 6
Thun, Lake of (Switzerland)	T2—494 541 6
Thunder Bay (Ont. :	
District)	T2—713 12
Thunderstorms	551.554
social services	363.349 24
Thuner See (Switzerland)	T2—494 541 6
Thunnus	597.783
Thur River (Switzerland)	T2—494 59
Thurgau (Switzerland)	T2—494 59
Thüringen (Germany)	T2—432 2
Thuringia (Germany)	T2—432 2
Thuringian Forest	T2—432 26
Thurniaceae	584.95
Thurrock (England)	T2—426 78
Thurston County (Neb.)	T2—782 227
Thurston County (Wash.)	T2—797 79
Thutmose III, King of Egypt	
Egyptian history	932.014
Thylacine	599.27
Thymallus	597.559
Thyme	641.357
botany	583.96
see also Herbs	
Thymelaeaceae	583.77
Thymelaeales	583.77

Ties (Neckwear) 391.41
see also Accessories (Clothing)
Ties (Railroad) 625.143
Tift County (Ga.) T2—758 882
Tiger 599.756
  big game hunting 799.277 56
  conservation technology 639.979 756
  resource economics 333.959 756
Tiger beetles 595.762
Tiger fishes (Characidae) 597.48
Tiger shark 597.34
Tigerfishes (Characidae) 597.48
Tigerflowers
  botany 584.75
Tightrope walking
  circuses 791.34
  sports 796.46
Tigray kelel (Ethiopia) T2—634
Tigre (African people) T5—928
Tigré language 492.82
    T6—928 2
Tigré literature 892.82
Tigrigna language T6—928 3
Tigrigna literature 892.83
Tigrinya (African people) T5—928
Tigrinya language 492.83
    T6—928 3
Tigrinya literature 892.83
Tigris River T2—567 4
Tigua Indians T5—974 96
Tigua language 497.496
    T6—974 96
Tijānīyah 297.48
Tikar (African people) T5—963 6
Tikar language 496.36
    T6—963 6
Tilapias 641.392
  cooking 641.692
  culture 639.377 4
  food 641.392
  zoology 597.74
Tile drains 666.733
Tile furniture 645.4
  manufacturing technology 684.106
  see also Furniture
Tile piping 666.733
Tiles
  architectural construction 721.044 3
  building construction 693.3
  building materials 691.4
  ceramic arts 738.6
  floor coverings
    building construction 698.9
  materials science 620.142

Tiles (continued)
  rubber 678.34
  structural engineering 624.183 6
Tilia 583.775
Tiliaceae 583.775
Tilings (Mathematics) 516.132
  Euclidean geometry 516.213 2
Till (Geologic landforms) 551.315
Till (Geologic material) 551.314
Tillage 631.51
Tillamook County (Or.) T2—795 44
Tillman County (Okla.) T2—766 46
Tillodontia 569.31
Timaliidae 598.834
Timaru District (N.Z.) T2—938 7
Timber 338.174 98
  agricultural economics 338.174 98
  building material 691.1
  resource economics 333.751 1
  see Manual at 583–585 vs. 600
Timber resources 333.751 1
  see also Forest lands
Timber truss bridges
  construction 624.218
Timber wolf 599.773
Timbre (Sound)
  musical element 781.234
Timbre perception
  psychology 152.157
Time
  arts 701.8
    T3C—384
    drawing 741.018
  chronology 529
  literature 808.803 84
    history and criticism 809.933 84
    specific literatures T3B—080 384
     history and
      criticism T3B—093 84
  philosophy 115
  sociology 304.237
Time (Music) 781.22
Time and date recorders
  technology 681.118
Time clocks
  technology 681.118
Time deposits 332.175 2
Time estimates
  building construction 692.5
  commercial T1—029
Time-invariant systems 003.8
Time-lapse cinematography 777.6
Time-lapse videography 777.6

Time management	650.11
business	650.11
executives	658.409 3
home economics	640.43
Time of day	
influence on crime	364.22
Time of Troubles, 1605–1613	947.045
Time payments (Wages)	331.216 2
personnel management	658.322 2
Time perception	153.753
Time series	519.232
Time-series analysis	519.55
Time-sharing (Computers)	005.434
computer hardware	004.3
systems software	005.434
Time-sharing (Real estate)	333.323 4
economics	333.323 4
law	346.043 3
Time studies	
production management	658.542 1
Time systems	389.17
Time-varying systems	003.8
Time wage rate	331.216 2
personnel management	658.322 2
Time zones	389.17
Timepieces	
technology	681.11
Times	
arts	T3C—33
folklore	398.236
history and criticism	398.33
literature	808.803 3
history and criticism	809.933 3
specific literatures	T3B—080 33
history and criticism	T3B—093 3
music	781.52
religious observance	203.6
Christianity	263
Islam	297.36
Judaism	296.43
Timesaving cooking	641.555
Timework	331.216 2
personnel management	658.322 2
Timiş (Romania)	T2—498 4
Timiskaming (Ont.)	T2—713 144
Timor Island (Indonesia)	T2—598 68
Timor Sea	551.461 574
	T2—165 74
Timor Tengah (Indonesia)	T2—598 68
Timor Timur	959.87
	T2—598 7
Timothy (Biblical books)	227.83

Timothy (Grass)	633.24
botany	584.926
forage crop	633.24
Timpani	786.93
Timur	
Asian history	950.24
Tin	669.6
architectural construction	721.044 76
building construction	693.76
building material	691.86
chemical engineering	661.068 6
chemistry	546.686
decorative arts	739.532
economic geology	553.453
materials science	620.185
metallography	669.956
metallurgy	669.6
metalworking	673.6
mining	622.345 3
physical metallurgy	669.966
see also Chemicals; Metals	
Tin soldiers	
handicrafts	745.592 82
Tinamiformes	598.55
paleozoology	568.5
Tinamous	598.55
Tindouf (Algeria : Province)	T2—657
Tinea	
medicine	616.579
see also Skin diseases —	
humans	
Tineoidea	595.78
Tinian (Northern Mariana	
Islands)	T2—967
Tinne Indians	T5—972
Tinned foods	
cooking	641.612
product safety	363.192 9
see also Food — product	
safety	
Tinos (Greece : Regional	
unit)	T2—495 85
Tinos Island (Greece)	T2—495 85
Tinsel	
textiles	677.76
see also Textiles	
Tintype process	772.14
Tioga County (N.Y.)	T2—747 77
Tioga County (Pa.)	T2—748 56
Tipaza (Algeria : Province)	T2—653
Tipiṭaka	294.382
Tippah County (Miss.)	T2—762 923
Tippecanoe County (Ind.)	T2—772 95

Tipperary (Ireland : County)	941.92
	T2—419 2
Tipping	
economics	331.216 6
etiquette	395.5
Tipton County (Ind.)	T2—772 555
Tipton County (Tenn.)	T2—768 17
Tipulidae	595.772
Tires	678.32
automotive engineering	629.248 2
Tirmidhī, Muḥammad ibn 'Īsá	
Hadith	297.125 43
Tirol (Austria)	943.642
	T2—436 42
Tiryns (Extinct city)	T2—388
Tishah b'Av	296.439
liturgy	296.453 9
Tishomingo County (Miss.)	T2—762 995
Tissemsilt (Algeria :	
Province)	T2—651
Tissue anatomy	571.533
humans	611.018
Tissue banks	362.178 3
Tissue biology	571.5
humans	611.018
Tissue culture	571.538
experimental research	
medicine	616.027
humans	612.028
Tissue degeneration	571.935
Tissue differentiation	571.835
Tissue grafting	
surgery	617.954
Tissue morphology	571.533
humans	611.018
Tissue paper	676.284 2
handicrafts	745.54
Tissue regeneration	571.889 35
humans	611.018
Tissue respiration	572.47
human physiology	612.26
see also Respiratory system	
Tissues	571.5
humans	611.018
Titanium	669.732 2
chemical engineering	661.051 2
chemistry	546.512
economic geology	553.462 3
materials science	620.189 322
metallography	669.957 322
metallurgy	669.732 2
metalworking	673.732 2
physical metallurgy	669.967 322
see also Chemicals; Metals	

Titanium group	
chemical engineering	661.051
chemistry	546.51
Tithes	
Christian practice	248.6
local church fund raising	254.8
Titicaca Lake (Peru and	
Bolivia)	T2—841 2
Bolivia	T2—841 2
Peru	T2—853 6
Title (Property)	346.043 8
law	346.043 8
public administration	354.34
Title examinations	346.043 8
Title insurance	368.88
law	346.086 88
Title manipulation	
subject cataloging	025.486
Title searching	346.043 8
Titles of honor	
genealogy	929.7
Titling	
cinematography	777.55
technical drawing	604.243
videography	777.55
Titmice	598.824
Tito, Josip Broz	
Yugoslavian history	949.702 3
Titoism	335.434 4
economics	335.434 4
political ideology	320.532 309 497
Titration	543.24
Titus (Biblical book)	227.85
Titus County (Tex.)	T2—764 215
Tiumenskaia oblast'	
(Russia)	T2—573
Tiv (African people)	T5—963 6
Tiv language	496.36
	T6—963 6
Tivi (African people)	T5—963 6
Tivi language	496.36
	T6—963 6
Tiwa Indians	T5—974 96
Tiwa language	497.496
	T6—974 96
Tiwi language (Melville Island)	499.15
	T6—991 5
Tizi Ouzou (Algeria :	
Province)	T2—653
Tiznit (Morocco : Province)	T2—646 6
Tlaxcala (Mexico : State)	T2—724 7
Tlemcen (Algeria :	
Province)	T2—651

922

Tlingit Indians 979.800 497 27
    T5—972 7
Tlingit language 497.27
    T6—972 7
TMJ dysfunction
  regional medicine 617.522
TNT (Explosive) 662.27
  military engineering 623.452 7
Toadfishes 597.62
Toads 597.87
Toadstools 579.6
Toamasina (Madagascar :
  Province) T2—691
Toasting 394.12
  see also Toasts
Toasts 394.12
  customs 394.12
  literature 808.851
    history and criticism 809.51
    specific literatures T3B—501
     individual authors T3A—5
  rhetoric 808.512
Toba Batak T5—992 246 2
Toba Batak language 499.224 62
    T6—992 246 2
Toba Batak literature 899.224 62
Tobacco
  agricultural economics 338.173 71
    law 343.076 371
  agriculture 633.71
  botany 583.959 3
  customs 394.14
  ethics 178.7
  human toxicology 615.952 395 93
  manufacturing technology 679.7
    economics 338.476 797
  smuggling 364.133 6
    law 345.023 36
Tobacco abuse 362.296
  effect on fetus
    perinatal medicine 618.326 86
  medicine 616.865
  personal health 613.85
  pregnancy complications
    obstetrics 618.368 6
  social welfare 362.296
  see also Substance abuse
Tobacco industry workers 679.709 2
Tobacco smuggling 364.133 6
  law 345.023 36
Tobacco substitutes 688.4
Tobago 972.983
    T2—729 83
Tobias (Deuterocanonical book) 229.22

Tobit (Deuterocanonical book) 229.22
Tobogganing 796.95
Tobote language 496.35
    T6—963 5
Tocantins (Brazil) T2—811 7
Toccatas 784.189 47
Tocharian language 491.994
    T6—919 94
Tocharish language 491.994
    T6—919 94
Tochigi-ken (Japan) T2—521 32
Tocopilla (Chile : Province) T2—831 32
Toda (Dravidians) T5—948 1
Toda language 494.81
    T6—948 1
Toda literature 894.81
Today's English Bible 220.520 82
Todd County (Ky.) T2—769 77
Todd County (Minn.) T2—776 88
Todd County (S.D.) T2—783 62
Tofieldiaceae 584.44
Tofu 641.356 55
  commercial processing 664.805 655
  cooking 641.656 55
  food 641.356 55
Togaviridae 579.256 2
Toggenburg (Switzerland) T2—494 726
Togo 966.81
    T2—668 1
Togoland 966.810 2
    T2—668 1
  Ghana T2—667
  Togo T2—668 1
Togolese T5—966 81
Tōhoku Region (Japan) T2—521 1
Tohono O'Odham Indians 979.100 497 455 2
    T5—974 552
Tohono O'Odham language 497.455 2
    T6—974 552
Tohono O'Odham literature 897.455 2
Tohorot (Order or tractate) 296.123 6
  Babylonian Talmud 296.125 6
  Mishnah 296.123 6
  Palestinian Talmud 296.124 6
Toilet paper 676.284 2
Toilet training 649.62
Toilets
  construction 690.42
Tojiki language 491.57
    T6—915 7
Tok Pisin 427.995 3
    T6—217
Toka (African people) T5—963 91

Toka language	496.391
	T6—963 91
Tokamaks	621.484
Tokat İli (Turkey)	T2—565 6
ancient	T2—393 37
Tokelau Islands	996.15
	T2—961 5
Tokelau language	499.46
	T6—994 6
Tokelauan dialect	499.46
	T6—994 6
Tokelauans (New Zealand	
people)	T5—994 6
Token coins	332.404 3
Tokens	
numismatics	737.3
Tokharian language	491.994
	T6—919 94
Tokugawa period	952.025
Tokushima-ken (Japan)	T2—523 4
Tokyo (Japan)	T2—521 35
Tolecraft	745.723
Toledo (Ohio)	T2—771 13
Toledo (Spain : Province)	T2—464 3
Toledo Bend Reservoir (La.	
and Tex.)	T2—763 62
Toledo District (Belize)	T2—728 24
Toledo Manrique, Alejandro	
Peruvian history	985.064 4
Toleration	179.9
moral theology	205.699
social theology	201.723
Christianity	261.72
see also Virtues	
Toliara (Madagascar :	
Province)	T2—691
Tolima (Colombia : Dept.)	T2—861 36
Tolland County (Conn.)	T2—746 43
Tolls	
roads	388.114
transportation services	388.049
Tollways	388.122
see also Roads	
Tolman, Edward Chace	
psychological system	150.194 34
Tolna Megye (Hungary)	T2—439 7
Toltec empire	972.017
	T2—72
Tom Green County (Tex.)	T2—764 721
Tomahawks	623.441 4
Tomatoes	641.356 42
botany	583.959 3
commercial processing	664.805 642
cooking	641.656 42

Tomatoes (continued)	
food	641.356 42
garden crop	635.642
Tombigbee River (Miss. and	
Ala.)	T2—761 2
Tombs	
architecture	726.8
Tomography	
medicine	616.075 7
Tompkins County (N.Y.)	T2—747 71
Tomsk (Russia : Oblast)	T2—573
Tomskaia oblast' (Russia)	T2—573
Tonal systems (Music)	781.26
Tonality	781.258
Tonbridge and Malling (England)	942.237 2
	T2—422 372
Tønder amt (Denmark)	T2—489 52
Tone color	
musical element	781.234
perception	
psychology	152.157
Tone River (Japan)	T2—521 3
Tonga	996.12
	T2—961 2
Tonga (Mozambique and	
South African people)	T5—963 97
Tonga (Zambian people)	T5—963 91
Tonga language (Inhambane)	496.397
	T6—963 97
Tonga language (Nyasa)	496.391
	T6—963 91
Tonga language (Tonga Islands)	499.482
	T6—994 82
Tonga language (Zambesi)	496.391
	T6—963 91
Tonga literature (Tonga Islands)	899.482
Tongaat (South Africa)	T2—684 5
Tongaland (South Africa)	T2—684 3
Tongan language	499.482
	T6—994 82
Tongan literature	899.482
Tongans	T5—994 82
Tongariro National Park	
(N.Z.)	T2—935 2
Tongic languages	499.48
	T6—994 8
Tongue	573.357
biology	573.357
human anatomy	611.313
human physiology	612.312
tasting	612.87
medicine	616.31
surgery	617.522
see also Digestive system	

Tops (Clothing) (continued)
  home economics — 646.3
  home sewing — 646.435
  see also Clothing
Tops (Coverings)
  automobile — 629.26
Toradja languages — 499.226
  T6—992 26
Toradjas — T5—992 26
Torah (Bible) — 222.1
Torah scrolls — 296.461 5
Toraja (Indonesian people) — T5—992 26
Toraja languages — 499.226
  T6—992 26
Toraja Sa'dan language — 499.226
  T6—992 26
Torbay (England) — T2—423 595
Torches — 621.323
  see also Lighting
Torfaen (Wales) — T2—429 97
Tories
  Canadian history — 971.024
  United States history — 973.314
Torino (Italy) — T2—451 21
  ancient — T2—372 221
Torino (Italy : Città
  metropolitana) — T2—451 2
  ancient — T2—372 22
Tornadoes — 551.553
  meteorology — 551.553
  social services — 363.349 23
  weather forecasting — 551.645 3
  weather modification — 551.685 3
  see also Disasters
Torne River (Sweden and
  Finland) — T2—488 8
Tornedalen Finnish — 494.54
  T6—945 4
Tornedalen Finnish literature — 894.54
Toronto (Ont.) — T2—713 541
Toros Dağları (Turkey) — T2—564
Torpedo boats — 359.835 8
  design — 623.812 58
  engineering — 623.825 8
  naval equipment — 359.835 8
  naval units — 359.325 8
Torpedoes (Ammunition) — 359.825 17
  engineering — 623.451 7
  naval equipment — 359.825 17
Torpedoes (Fishes) — 597.35
Torquay (Vic.) — T2—945 2
Torque — 531.34
Torrance County (N.M.) — T2—789 63

Torres Strait (Qld. and Papua
  New Guinea) — 551.461 476
  T2—164 76
Torres Strait Islanders — T5—991 2
Torres Strait Islands (Qld.) — T2—943 8
Torricelli languages — T6—991 2
Torricelliaceae — 583.988
Torrid zone — T2—13
  see also Tropics
Torridge (England) — T2—423 51
Torrijos Espino, Martín
  Panamanian history — 972.870 542
Torsion (Mathematics) — 516.36
Torsion (Mechanics)
  effect on materials — 620.112 43
Tort liability — 346.03
Tortillas — 641.815
Tortoises — 597.924
  conservation technology — 639.977 924
  resource economics — 333.957 924
Tortola (V.I.) — T2—729 725
Tortricoidea — 595.78
Torts — 346.03
  see Manual at 345.02 vs.
  346.03
Tortuga Island (Haiti) — T2—729 42
Torture — 364.675
  criminal investigation — 363.254
  ethics — 179.75
  military intelligence service — 355.343 2
  penology — 364.675
  war customs — 399
Toruń (Poland :
  Voivodeship) — T2—438 26
Tory Party (Great Britain) — 324.241 02
Toscana (Italy) — 945.5
  T2—455
  ancient — 937.5
  T2—375
Tosefta — 296.126 2
Total derivatives — 515.33
Total differentiation — 515.33
Total productive maintenance — 658.202
Total quality management — 658.401 3
  production management — 658.562
Total war — 355.02
Totalitarian government — 321.9
Totalitarianism — 320.53
Totem poles
  religious significance — 299.713 7
  sculpture — 731.77
Totemic kinship — 306.83
Totemism — 202.11
Totonac Indians — T5—979

Totonacan languages	497.9
	T6—979
Totonicapán (Guatemala :	
Dept.)	T2—728 181
Tottori-ken (Japan)	T2—521 93
Touadéra, Faustin-Archange	
Central African history	967.410 55
Touareg	T5—933
Toucans	598.72
animal husbandry	636.68
Touch	573.875
animal physiology	573.875
human physiology	612.88
psychology	152.182
see also Nervous system	
Touch football	
American	796.332 8
Canadian	796.335 8
Touch-me-nots	583.79
Touch-me-nots (Balsaminaceae)	583.93
Touch techniques	
music	784.193 68
Touchtone devices	
computer science	004.76
engineering	621.398 6
Toulouse (France)	T2—447 367
Toumani Touré, Amadou	
Malian history	966.230 53
Touracos	598.74
Touraine (France)	T2—445 4
Touré, Ahmadou	
Malian history	966.230 53
Touré, Ahmed Sékou	
Guinean history	966.520 51
Touré, Amadou Toumani	
Malian history	966.230 53
Tourette syndrome	
medicine	616.83
see also Nervous system	
diseases — humans	
Tourism	910
economics	338.479 1
recreation	790.18
sociology	306.481 9
travel	910
see also Travel	
Tourist exemptions	
customs duties	382.78
see also Customs (Tariff)	
Tourist industry	338.479 1
air service	387.742
boat service	387.542
bus service	388.322 2
urban	388.413 22

Tourist industry (continued)	
economics	338.479 1
law	343.078 91
transportation law	343.093 3
public administration	354.73
railroad service	385.22
sociology	306.481 9
transportation services	388.042
Tourmaline	553.87
mineralogy	549.64
see also Semiprecious stones	
Tournaments (Contests)	
customs	394.7
Tournaments (Graphs)	511.54
Tours (France)	T2—445 45
Towada Lake (Japan)	T2—521 12
Towboats	387.232
design	623.812 32
engineering	623.823 2
see also Ships	
Towed boats	387.29
design	623.812 9
engineering	623.829
transportation services	387.29
see also Ships	
Toweling	
arts	746.98
Towels	643.52
arts	746.98
home economics	643.52
home sewing	646.21
Tower Hamlets (London,	
England)	942.15
	T2—421 5
Towers (Structural elements)	721.5
architecture	721.5
Christian church architecture	726.597
construction	690.15
Towers (Structures)	
architecture	725.97
Towhees	598.883
Town halls	
architecture	725.13
Town planning	307.121 6
see also City planning	
Towner County (N.D.)	T2—784 38
Townhouses	643.1
architecture	728.312
see also Dwellings	
Towns	307.76
see also Cities	
Towns County (Ga.)	T2—758 282
Townshend Acts, 1767	
United States history	973.311 2

Townsville (Qld.)	T2—943 6
Toxic chemicals	363.179 1
hazardous materials technology	604.7
chemical engineering	660.280 4
pollution	363.738 4
see also Pollution	
public safety	363.179 1
see also Hazardous materials	
Toxic drug reactions	
pharmacokinetics	615.704
Toxic materials	363.179
see also Hazardous materials	
Toxic shock syndrome	
incidence	614.579 7
medicine	616.929 7
see also Communicable	
diseases — humans	
Toxic spills	363.728 7
see also Waste control	
Toxic torts	346.038
Toxic wastes	363.728 7
technology	628.42
see also Waste control	
Toxicity testing	615.907
Toxicologists	615.900 92
Toxicology	571.95
adolescent medicine	615.900 835
medicine	615.9
see Manual at 615.7 vs.	
615.9	
pediatrics	615.900 83
veterinary medicine	636.089 59
Toxins	
human toxicology	615.95
toxicology	571.957
Toxoids	
pharmacology	615.372
Toy dogs	636.76
Toy instrument orchestras	784.46
Toy makers	688.720 92
Toy Manchester terrier	636.76
Toy soldiers	
handicrafts	745.592 82
Toy theaters	791.5
Toyama-ken (Japan)	T2—521 53
Toys	790.133
cataloging	025.349 6
customs	394.3
library treatment	025.179 6
making	688.72
handicrafts	745.592
technology	688.72

Toys (continued)	
product safety	363.19
law	344.042 35
see also Product safety	
recreation	790.133
use in child care	649.55
Toys (Dogs)	636.76
TPM (Maintenance management)	658.202
TQM (Management)	658.401 3
production management	658.562
Trà Vinh (Vietnam)	T2—597 8
Trabzon İli (Turkey)	T2—565 8
Trace elements	572.515
applied nutrition	613.285
animal husbandry	636.085 27
biochemistry	572.515
humans	612.015 24
metabolism	
human physiology	612.392 4
Trace fossils	560.43
Tracer testing	
materials science	620.112 73
Trachea	573.26
biology	573.26
human anatomy	611.23
human physiology	612.234
medicine	616.23
surgery	617.533
see also Respiratory system	
Tracheal diseases	
medicine	616.23
see also Respiratory tract	
diseases — humans	
Tracheitis	
medicine	616.23
see also Respiratory tract	
diseases — humans	
Trachemys	597.925 9
Tracheophytes	580
see also Plants	
Trachichthyidae	597.64
Trachoma	
incidence	614.599 7
ophthalmology	617.772
see also Eye diseases —	
humans	
Trachylina	593.55
Track (Sports)	796.42
see also Track and field	
Track and field	796.42
arts	700.457 9
	T3C—357 9
biography	796.420 92
child care	649.57

Traffic control	388.041
air transportation	387.740 426
see also Air traffic control	
canal transportation	386.404 204 2
inland waterway	386.240 42
lake transportation	386.540 42
railroad transportation	385.204 2
engineering	625.165
river transportation	386.350 42
road transportation	388.312
engineering	625.794
law	343.094 6
police services	363.233 2
public administration	354.772 8
urban	388.413 12
law	343.098 2
Traffic control failures	363.120 1
air transportation	363.124 18
railroad transportation	363.122 1
see also Transportation safety	
Traffic engineering (Urban)	388.413 12
law	343.098
public administration	354.772 8
Traffic flow (Road)	388.31
urban	388.413 1
Traffic noise	363.741
see also Noise	
Traffic patterns	
highways	388.314 3
streets	388.413 143
Traffic regulations	343.094 6
urban transportation	343.098
Traffic safety	363.125
see also Highway safety;	
Transportation safety	
Traffic signals	388.312 2
see also Traffic signs	
Traffic signs	388.312 2
engineering	625.794
law	343.094 6
transportation services	388.312 2
urban	388.413 122
law	343.098 2
Traffic surveys	
roads	388.314
urban	388.413 14
Traffic violations	364.147
law	345.024 7
Traffic volume	
highways	388.314 2
streets	388.413 142
Trafficways	
engineering	629.047
landscape architecture	713

Trafford (England)	T2—427 31
Tragedies (Drama)	792.12
literature	808.825 12
history and criticism	809.251 2
specific literatures	T3B—205 12
individual authors	T3A—2
stage presentation	792.12
see also Theater	
Tragedy	
arts	T3C—162
literature	808.801 62
history and criticism	809.916 2
specific literatures	T3B—080 162
history and	
criticism	T3B—091 62
Tragelaphus	599.642 3
Tragicomedies (Drama)	
literature	808.825 23
history and criticism	809.252 3
specific literatures	T3B—205 23
individual authors	T3A—2
Tragulidae	599.63
Trail (B.C.)	T2—711 62
Trailer camps	910.468
household management	647.942
see also Lodging (Temporary	
housing)	
Trailer parks	647.92
area planning	711.58
household management	647.92
Trailers (Freight)	388.344
engineering	629.224
see also Trucks	
Trailers (Passenger)	388.346
architecture	728.79
engineering	629.226
pulling	629.284 6
repair	629.287 6
travel	910
see also Motor homes	
Traill County (N.D.)	T2—784 14
Train accidents	363.122
see also Railroad safety	
Trainers (Aircraft)	
military engineering	623.746 2
Training	
armed forces	355.5
child care	649.6
employee education	370.113
see also Vocational	
education	
Training plants	631.546

Training programs	
personnel management	658.312 404
public administration	352.669
public administration	354.968
Training schools (Correctional	
institutions)	365.42
see also Penal institutions	
Training teachers	T1—071 1
Trains	385.37
engineering	625.2
sanitation services	363.729 3
see also Sanitation	
transportation services	385.37
see also Rolling stock	
Traits	
individual psychology	155.232
Trajectories	
military engineering	623.514
Tramp routes	387.523
Trampoline	796.474
Trampolining	796.474
biography	796.474 092
see also Gymnastics	
Tramps	305.569
	T1—086 942
Trams	
engineering	625.66
Tramways	388.46
engineering	625.6
public transportation	354.769
transportation services	388.46
Trance music	781.648
Trance phenomena (Hypnotism)	154.772
Tranquilizer abuse	362.299
medicine	616.86
personal health	613.8
social welfare	362.299
see also Substance abuse	
Tranquilizers	
pharmacokinetics	615.788 2
Trans-Neptunian objects	523.49
	T2—992 9
Trans-New Guinea languages	499.12
	T6—991 2
Trans Nzoia County	
(Kenya)	T2—676 278 3
Trans-Uranian planets	523.48
Transaction processing systems	005.745
Transaction tax	336.27
law	343.055
public administration	352.44
public finance	336.27

Transactional analysis	
applied psychology	158.2
system	158.9
psychiatry	616.891 45
Transborder data flow	384.3
computer communications	
services	384.3
law	344.09
Transcarpathia (Ukraine :	
Oblast)	T2—477 9
Transcaucasus	947.5
	T2—475
Transcendence of God	212.7
see also Attributes of God	
Transcendental functions	515.22
Transcendental meditation	158.125
system	158.9
Transcendental numbers	512.73
Transcendentalism	
arts	T3C—384
literature	808.803 84
history and criticism	809.933 84
specific literatures	T3B—080 384
history and	
criticism	T3B—093 84
philosophy	141.3
Transcription (Genetics)	572.884 5
Transcription (Language)	
linguistics	411
specific languages	T4—11
shorthand notes	653.14
Transcription (Music)	781.37
Transduction (Genetics)	571.964 8
Transepts	
Christian church architecture	726.592
Transfection	571.964 8
Transfer (Law)	346.043 6
Transfer of employees	
personnel management	658.312 8
public administration	352.66
Transfer of learning	
psychology	153.154
Transfer painting	
pottery	666.45
arts	738.15
technology	666.45
Transfer payments	
macroeconomic policy	339.522
Transfer RNA	572.886
Transfer students	371.291 4
higher education	378.169 14
Transfer tax (Inheritance)	336.276
law	343.053

Transfer tax (Transactions)	336.27
law	343.055
public finance	336.27
Transferases	572.792
see also Enzymes	
Transfiguration of Jesus Christ	232.956
Transfinite numbers	511.322
Transformation (Genetics)	571.964 8
Transformation of energy	531.68
Transformational grammar	415.018 22
specific languages	T4—501 822
Transformations (Mathematics)	511.326
geometry	516.1
mathematical logic	511.326
Transformer substations	621.312 6
Transformers (Electrical equipment)	621.314
Transforms	515.723
Transgender adolescents	
social services	362.785
Transgender children	
home care	649.156 4
Transgender identity	306.768
Transgender people	306.768
	T1—086 7
labor economics	331.5
psychology	155.33
social welfare	362.897
Transgender young people	
home care	649.156 4
social services	362.785
Transgenic mammals	
experimental animals	
medicine	616.027 3
Transient magnetism (Geomagnetism)	538.74
Transients (Electricity)	621.319 21
Transistors	621.381 528
television engineering	621.388 32
Transit insurance	368.2
see also Insurance	
Transit police	363.287
Transit tax	382.7
public finance	336.263
see also Customs (Tariff)	
Transition metals	
chemical engineering	661.06
chemistry	546.6
Transitional flow	532.052 6
gas mechanics	533.216
liquid mechanics	532.516
Transits	523.99
Mercury	523.91
Venus	523.92

Transkei (South Africa)	T2—687 58
Translating	
linguistics	418.02
specific languages	T4—802
specific subjects	418.03
specific languages	T4—803
Translation (Genetics)	572.645
Translation (Linguistics)	418.02
specific languages	T4—802
specific subjects	418.03
specific languages	T4—803
Translations	
bibliographies	011.7
Translator stations	384.554
see also Television	
Translators (Computer science)	
microprogramming languages	005.18
programming languages	005.45
Translators (Interpreters)	
specific languages	T4—802 092
Transliteration	411
specific languages	T4—11
Translocation (Genetics)	572.877
Transmigration	
occultism	133.901 35
philosophy	129
Transmission devices	
automotive engineering	629.244
Transmission facilities	
communications engineering	621.382 3
Transmission media	
computer communications	004.64
engineering	621.398 1
Transmission modes	
communications engineering	621.382 16
computer communications	004.66
engineering	621.398 1
Transmission of light	535.3
Transmission of sound	534.2
see also Sound	
Transmitters	
radio engineering	621.384 131
television engineering	621.388 31
Transmitting electricity	621.319
Transmitting heat	
engineering	621.402 2
Transmitting steam	621.185
Transnational Radical Party (Italy)	324.245 06
Transoceanic flights	
engineering	629.130 916 2
Transonic flow	533.274
air mechanics	533.62
aeronautics	629.132 304

Transylvania Colony	976.902
	T2—769
Transylvania County (N.C.)	T2—756 93
Traoré, Moussa	
Malian history	966.230 51
Trapani (Italy : Libero	
consorzio comunale)	T2—458 24
ancient	T2—378 24
Trapeze work	
circuses	791.34
sports	796.46
Trappers	639.109 2
Trapping	639.1
commercial	639.1
sports	799.2
Trappists	255.125
church history	271.125
Traps	
military engineering	623.31
Traps Islands (N.Z.)	T2—939 9
Trapshooters	799.313 209 2
Trapshooting	799.313 2
biography	799.313 209 2
see also Target shooting	
Traralgon (Vic.)	T2—945 6
Trás-os-Montes (Portugal)	T2—469 2
Trás-os-Montes e Alto	
Douro (Portugal)	T2—469 2
Trash (Art style)	709.034 8
19th century	709.034 8
20th century	709.040 13
Trauma centers	362.18
Traumatic neuroses	
medicine	616.852 1
see also Mental disorders	
Traumatic shock	
medicine	617.21
Traumatology	
medicine	617.1
Travel	910
arts	700.42
	T3C—32
economics	338.479 1
literature	808.803 2
history and criticism	809.933 2
specific literatures	T3B—080 32
history and criticism	T3B—093 2
meal service	642.3
natural history	508
recreation	790.18

Travel (continued)	
sociology	306.481 9
see Manual at 550 vs. 910;	
also at 900; also at 909,	
930–990 vs. 910; also at	
913–919	
Travel by bicycle	910
Travel cooking	641.575
Travel diseases	
medicine	616.980 2
see also Environmental	
diseases — humans	
Travel facilities	910.46
see also Lodging (Temporary	
housing)	
Travel guides	910.202
Travel health	613.68
Travelers	910.92
Traveling displays	
transportation advertising	659.134 4
Traveling shows	791.1
Traveling-wave tubes	621.381 335
Traverse County (Minn.)	T2—776 435
Traversing (Surveying)	526.33
Travertine	553.516
Travis County (Tex.)	T2—764 31
Trawlers	387.28
design	623.812 8
engineering	623.828 2
see also Ships	
Treason	364.131
American Revolution	973.381
law	345.023 1
Treasure County (Mont.)	T2—786 313
Treasure hunting	622.19
Treasury bills	332.632 32
see also Government securities	
Treasury certificates	332.632 32
see also Government securities	
Treasury departments (Public	
administration)	352.4
Treasury notes	332.632 32
see also Government securities	
Treaties	341.37
sources of law of nations	341.1
texts	341.026
Treaty Establishing a	
Constitution for Europe, 2004	341.242 202 65
Treaty Establishing the European	
Community, 1957	341.242 202 65
Treaty of Campo Formio, 1797	945.307
Treaty of Nice, 2001	341.242 202 65
Treaty of Noyon, 1516	945.306

Treaty of Paris, 1783
  United States history   973.317
Treaty of Verdun, 843   943.021
Treaty of Versailles, 1783
  United States history   973.317
Treaty of Versailles, 1919
  European history   940.314 1
Treaty on European Union, 1992   341.242 202 65
Treaty powers (Legislative
  bodies)   328.346
Trebizond İli (Turkey)   T2—565 8
Treble recorders   788.365
  see also Woodwind
    instruments
Treble viols   787.63
  see also Stringed instruments
Treble voices
  men's   782.86
    choral and mixed voices   782.86
    single voices   783.86
  women's   782.66
  see also Soprano voices
Trebuchets   355.822
  engineering   623.422
  military equipment   355.822
Tredegar (Wales)   T2—429 95
Tree-adjoining grammar   415.018 26
  specific languages   T4—501 826
Tree crops   634
Tree frogs   597.878
Tree kangaroos   599.22
Tree lily   584.55
Tree of heaven   635.977 375
  botany   583.75
  ornamental arboriculture   635.977 375
Tree planting   634.956 5
  ornamental arboriculture   635.977
Tree shrews   599.338
Tree squirrels   599.362
Tree swifts   598.762
Treenware   674.88
Trees   582.16
  art representation   704.943 4
  arts   T3C—364 216
  drawing   743.76
  forestry   634.9
  landscape architecture   715.2
  literature   808.803 642 16
    history and criticism   809.933 642 16
    specific literatures   T3B—080 364 216
      history and
        criticism   T3B—093 642 16
  ornamental agriculture   635.977
  paleobotany   561.16

Trees (continued)
  religious worship   202.12
  see Manual at 633–635; *also at*
    635.9 vs. 582.1
Trees (Mathematics)   511.52
Trefoils   633.32
  botany   583.63
  forage crop   633.32
Trego County (Kan.)   T2—781 165
Treinta y Tres (Uruguay :
  Dept.)   T2—895 22
Trellises
  plant training   631.546
Trematoda   592.48
Trematode infections
  incidence   614.553
  medicine   616.963
    see also Communicable
      diseases — humans
Tremellales   579.59
Trempealeau County (Wis.)   T2—775 49
Trench mouth
  medicine   616.312
    see also Digestive system
      diseases — humans
Trench warfare   355.44
Trenčiansky kraj (Slovakia)   T2—437 38
Trent, River (England)   T2—425
Trentino-Alto Adige (Italy)   945.38
                        T2—453 8
  ancient   T2—373 7
Trento (Italy : Province)   T2—453 85
  ancient   T2—373 75
Trenton (N.J.)   T2—749 66
Trespass (Law)   346.036
Treutlen County (Ga.)   T2—758 682
Treviño (Spain)   T2—466 7
Treviso (Italy)   T2—453 61
  ancient   T2—373 65
Treviso (Italy : Province)   T2—453 6
  ancient   T2—373 65
Triakidae   597.36
Trial-and-error learning
  psychology   153.152 4
Trial courts   347.02
  criminal law   345.014 2
Trial of Jesus Christ   232.962
Trial practice   347.075
  criminal law   345.075
Trial procedure   347.075
Trials (Law)   347.07
  criminal law   345.07
Triangles (Geometry)   516.154

Triangles (Music)   786.884 2
  see also Percussion instruments
Triangulation   526.33
Triassic period   551.762
  geology   551.762
  paleontology   560.176 2
Triathlon   796.425 7
  see also Track and field
Tribal communities   307.772
  government   321.1
Tribal fighting (Military tactics)   355.425
Tribal groups   305.8
Tribal land
  economics   333.2
Triboelectricity   537.21
Tribology   621.89
Tribulation (Christian doctrine)   236.9
Tribunals
  papal administration   262.136
Tricarboxylic acid cycle   572.475
Triceratops   567.915 8
Trichechidae   599.55
Trichechus   599.55
Trichiales   579.52
Trichinosis
  incidence   614.562
  medicine   616.965 4
    see also Communicable
      diseases — humans
Trichiuridae   597.78
Trichoderma   579.567 7
Trichomycetes   579.53
Trichoptera   595.745
Trick cinematography   777.9
Trick games   793.5
Trick photography   778.8
Trick videography   777.9
Tricks   793.8
  manufacturing technology   688.726
Tricuspid valve
  human anatomy   611.12
  human physiology   612.17
  medicine   616.125
Tricuspid valve diseases
  medicine   616.125
    see also Cardiovascular
      diseases — humans
Tricycles
  engineering   629.227 3
  repair   629.287 73
  riding   629.284 73
Trier (Germany)   T2—434 313
Trier (Germany :
  Regierungsbezirk)   T2—434 31

Trieste (Italy)   T2—453 931
  ancient   T2—373 91
Trieste (Italy : Ente di
  decentramento regionale)   T2—453 93
  ancient   T2—373 9
Trifolium   633.32
  botany   583.63
  forage crop   633.32
Trigg County (Ky.)   T2—769 79
Trigger circuits
  electronics   621.381 537
Triggerfishes   597.64
Trigonometric leveling   526.38
Trigonometry   516.24
Trihydroxy aromatics   547.633
Trikala (Greece : Regional
  unit)   T2—495 4
Trilateration   526.33
Trilliums   584.6
  botany   584.6
  floriculture   635.934 6
Trills   781.247
Trilobita   565.39
Trimble County (Ky.)   T2—769 375
Trimeniaceae   584.24
Trimmers   621.93
Trimmings
  textiles   677.7
Trinidad   972.983
                              T2—729 83
Trinidad and Tobago   972.983
                              T2—729 83
Trinidadians   T5—969 729 83
Trinitarians (Religious order)   255.42
  church history   271.42
Trinity   231.044
  art representation   704.948 52
  arts   T3C—382 310 44
Trinity County (Calif.)   T2—794 14
Trinity County (Tex.)   T2—764 172
Trinity River (Tex.)   T2—764 14
Trinity Sunday   263.94
  devotional literature   242.38
  music   781.729 4
  sermons   252.64
Trionychidae   597.926
Trios
  chamber music   785.13
  vocal music   783.13
Triphenylmethane dyes   667.254
Tripiṭaka   294.382
Triple Alliance, War of the,
  1865–1870   989.205

Tropical plants	581.709 13
floriculture	635.952 3
Tropical rain forests	
biology	578.734
ecology	577.34
Tropics	T2—13
biology	578.091 3
ecology	577.091 3
Troposphere	551.513
	T2—161 2
Trotskyism	335.433
economics	335.433
political ideology	320.532 3
Trotskyist International	324.175
Trotters (Horses)	636.175
Troubadour poetry	808.814
history and criticism	809.14
specific literatures	T3B—104
individual authors	T3A—1
Troubled young people	
home care	649.153
social welfare	362.74
Trough zithers	787.72
see also Stringed instruments	
Troughs	
music	786.82
concussed	786.874
friction	786.864
set	786.864
single	786.888
percussed	786.844
set	786.844
single	786.884 4
see also Percussion	
instruments	
Troup County (Ga.)	T2—758 463
Trousdale County (Tenn.)	T2—768 482
Trousers	391.476
see also Pants (Trousers)	
Trout	641.392
commercial fishing	639.275 7
conservation technology	639.977 57
cooking	641.692
culture	639.375 7
economics	338.371 375 7
food	641.392
resource economics	333.956 57
sports fishing	799.175 7
zoology	597.57
Trout-perches	597.62
Trover and conversion	346.036
Trovoada, Miguel	
Sao Tomean history	967.150 22

Troy (Extinct city)	939.21
	T2—392 1
Truancy	371.295
law	344.079 2
Truant officers	371.295
Trucial States	T2—535 7
Truck accidents	363.125 9
see also Highway safety	
Truck cavalry	357.54
Truck farming	635
Truck terminals	388.33
transportation services	388.33
urban	388.473
Truck transportation	388.324
law	343.094 83
public administration	354.765 4
transportation services	388.324
urban	388.413 24
law	343.098 2
Truckers	388.324 092
Trucks	388.344
agricultural use	631.373
driving	629.284 4
engineering	629.224
military engineering	623.747 4
operation	388.324 044
urban	388.413 24
repair	629.287 4
transportation services	388.344
see also Articulated lorries;	
Automotive vehicles;	
Lorries; Semitrailers	
(Freight); Trailers (Freight)	
Trudeau, Justin	
Canadian history	971.074
Trudeau, Pierre Elliott	
Canadian history	971.064 4
1968–1979	971.064 4
1980–1984	971.064 6
True bugs	595.754
True cedars	585.2
True fungi	579.5
True lice	595.756
True seals	599.79
True swifts	598.762
True wasps	595.798
True water beetles	595.762
Truffles	641.358
agriculture	635.8
biology	579.57
commercial processing	664.805 8
cooking	641.658
food	641.358
Trujillo (Venezuela : State)	T2—871 4

Tswa-Ronga languages	496.397 8	Tubes	
	T6—963 978	music (continued)	
Tswana (African people)	T5—963 977 5	percussed	786.845
Tswana language	496.397 75	set	786.845
	T6—963 977 5	single	786.884 5
Tswana literature	896.397 75	*see also* Percussion	
Tu language	T6—942	instruments	
Tuamotu Islands	T2—963 2	Tübingen (Germany :	
Tuareg	T5—933	Regierungsbezirk)	T2—434 73
Tuareg language	493.38	Tubuai Islands	T2—962 2
	T6—933 8	Tubular bridges	
Tuareg literature	893.38	construction	624.21
Tuatara	597.945	Tubular drums	786.94
Tubal pregnancy		*see also* Percussion instruments	
obstetrics	618.31	Tubulidentata	599.31
Tubal sterilization		paleozoology	569.31
health	613.942	Tucano Indians	T5—983 5
see also Birth control		Tucano language	498.35
surgery	618.120 59		T6—983 5
Tubas	788.98	Tucanoan languages	498.35
instrument	788.981 9		T6—983 5
music	788.98	Tucker County (W. Va.)	T2—754 83
see also Brass instruments		Tucson (Ariz.)	T2—791 776
Tube feeding		Tucumán (Argentina)	T2—824 3
medicine	615.854 82	Tudor, House of	942.05
Tube zithers	787.72	English history	942.05
see also Stringed instruments		genealogy	929.72
Tuberales	579.57	Irish history	941.505
Tuberculosis	362.196 995	Tufa	552.5
incidence	614.542	Tuff	552.23
medicine	616.995	Tug Fork	T2—754 4
law	344.043 699 5	Kentucky	T2—769 2
social services	362.196 995	West Virginia	T2—754 4
see also Communicable		Tug services	387.166
diseases — humans		inland ports	386.866
Tubers	581.46	law	343.096 7
cooking	641.652	Tugboats	387.232
descriptive botany	581.46	design	623.812 32
food	641.352	engineering	623.823 2
food crops	635.2	*see also* Ships	
nursery production	631.526	Tugela (South Africa)	T2—684 47
ornamental plants	635.915 26	Tugela River (South Africa)	T2—684
physiology	575.498	Tughluk dynasty	954.023 6
planting	631.532	Tuition	371.206
ornamental plants	635.915 32	higher education	378.106
Tubes		Tuktoyaktuk (N.W.T.)	T2—719 3
music	786.82	Tuktut Nogait National Park	
concussed	786.875	(N.W.T.)	T2—719 3
friction	786.865	Tula (Russia : Oblast)	T2—473 4
set	786.865	Tulameen River (B.C.)	T2—711 5
single	786.888	Tulare County (Calif.)	T2—794 86

Tularemia		Tundras (continued)	
incidence	614.573 9	ecology	577.586
medicine	616.923 9	geography	910.915 3
see also Communicable		geomorphology	551.453
diseases — humans		physical geography	910.021 53
Tularosa Valley (N.M.)	T2—789 65	Tung oil	665.333
Tulbagh (South Africa :		Tung tree	583.69
District)	T2—687 33	Tungstates	
Tulcea (Romania : Judeţ)	T2—498 3	mineralogy	549.74
Tulip tree	584.286	Tungsten	669.734
botany	584.286	chemical engineering	661.053 6
forestry	634.974	chemistry	546.536
Tulips	635.934 69	economic geology	553.464 9
botany	584.69	materials science	620.189 34
floriculture	635.934 69	metallography	669.957 34
Tulita (N.W.T.)	T2—719 3	metallurgy	669.734
Tulles	677.654	metalworking	673.734
see also Textiles		mining	622.346 49
Tulsa County (Okla.)	T2—766 86	physical metallurgy	669.967 34
Tulums	788.49	*see also* Chemicals; Metals	
see also Woodwind		Tungurahua (Ecuador)	986.615
instruments			T2—866 15
Tul'skaîa oblast' (Russia)	T2—473 4	Tungus	T5—941
Tumbes (Peru : Region)	T2—851 2	Tungus languages	494.1
Tumble bugs	595.764 9		T6—941
Tumbler Ridge (B.C.)	T2—711 87	Tungus-Manchu languages	494.1
Tumbling	796.472		T6—941
see also Gymnastics		Tungusic languages	494.1
Tumbling flower beetles	595.769		T6—941
Tumboa plant	585.8	Tungusic literatures	894.1
Tumbuka (African people)	T5—963 91	Tungusic peoples	T5—941
Tumbuka language	496.391	Tunica County (Miss.)	T2—762 86
	T6—963 91	Tunicata	596.2
Tumors	571.978	paleozoology	566
humans		Tuning	784.192 8
incidence	614.599 9	Tunis (Tunisia)	T2—611
medicine	616.994	Tunisia	961.1
see also Cancer			T2—611
Tunas	641.392	ancient	939.73
commercial fishing	639.277 83		T2—397 3
conservation technology	639.977 783	Tunisians	T5—927 611
cooking	641.692	Tunnel diodes	621.381 522
food	641.392	Tunnel engineers	624.193 092
resource economics	333.956 783	Tunnel vaults	721.45
zoology	597.783	architecture	721.45
Tunas (Cuba : Province)	T2—729 162	construction	690.145
Tunbridge Wells (England :		Tunneling (Construction)	624.193
Borough)	942.238	mining	622.26
	T2—422 38	Tunneling (Physics)	530.416
Tunceli İli (Turkey)	T2—566 75	semiconductors	537.622 6
ancient	T2—394 2	Tunnels	388.13
Tundras	551.453	architecture	725.98
	T2—153	construction	624.193
biology	578.758 6	military engineering	623.68

Tunnels (continued)	
mining	622.26
psychological influence	155.964
public administration	354.76
transportation services	388.13
railroads	385.312
roads	388.13
Tununirusiq (Nunavut)	T2—719 52
Tuolumne County (Calif.)	T2—794 45
Tupaiidae	599.338
paleozoology	569.338
Tuparro National Park	
(Colombia)	T2—861 92
Tupelos	583.92
Tupí Indians	T5—983 832
Tupí language	498.383 2
	T6—983 832
Tupí languages	498.38
	T6—983 8
Tupí literature	898.383 2
Tupinambá Indians	T5—983 83
Tupinambá language	498.383
	T6—983 83
Tupper, Charles, Sir	
Canadian history	971.055
Tuque (Quebec)	T2—714 459
Turacos	598.74
Turbellaria	592.42
Turbines	621.406
hydraulic power	621.24
steam engineering	621.165
Turbojet engines	621.435 2
aircraft	629.134 353 3
Turbojet fuel	665.538 25
Turbomachines	621.406
Turboprop airplanes	387.733 43
engineering	629.133 343
transportation services	387.733 43
see also Aircraft	
Turboprop engines	
aircraft	629.134 353 2
Turboramjet engines	
aircraft	629.134 353 4
Turbots	597.69
Turbulence	
oceanography	551.462
Turbulent flow	532.052 7
aeronautics	629.132 32
air mechanics	533.62
gas mechanics	533.217
liquid mechanics	532.517
Turco-Tataric languages	494.3
	T6—943
Turcomans	T5—943 64

Turdidae	598.842
Turf	
floriculture	635.964 2
Turfanish language	491.994
	T6—919 94
Tŭrgovishte (Bulgaria :	
Oblast)	T2—499 34
Turin (Italy)	T2—451 21
ancient	T2—372 221
Turin (Italy : Metropolitan	
city)	T2—451 2
ancient	T2—372 22
Turing machines	511.35
Turkana (African people)	T5—965 522
Turkana, Lake (Kenya and	
Ethiopia)	T2—676 276
Turkana County (Kenya)	T2—676 276
Turkana language	496.552 2
	T6—965 522
Turkestan	958.4
	T2—584
Turkey	956.1
	T2—561
ancient	939.2
	T2—392
Turkey (Meat)	641.365 92
commercial processing	664.93
cooking	641.665 92
food	641.365 92
Turkey in Europe	949.61
	T2—496 1
ancient	939.861
	T2—398 61
Turkey vulture	598.92
Turkeys	636.592
animal husbandry	636.592
conservation technology	639.978 645
resource economics	333.958 645
sports hunting	799.246 45
zoology	598.645
Turkic languages	494.3
	T6—943
Turkic literatures	894.3
Turkic peoples	T5—943
Turkish baths	613.41
Turkish language	494.35
	T6—943 5
Turkish literature	894.35
Turkish rugs	
arts	746.756 1
Turkish Thrace	949.61
	T2—496 1
ancient	939.861
	T2—398 61

Tutankhamen, King of Egypt
  Egyptian history   932.014
Tutoring   371.394
Tutsi (African people)   T5—963 946 1
Tuva (Russia)   T2—575
Tuva-Altai languages   494.33
                                 T6—943 3
Tuvalu   996.82
                                 T2—968 2
Tuvalu language   499.46
                                 T6—994 6
Tuvaluans   T5—994 6
Tuvinian language   494.33
                                 T6—943 3
Tuyên Quang (Vietnam :
  Province)   T2—597 1
TV   384.55
  see also Television
TV dinners
  commercial processing   664.65
  home serving   642.1
Tverskaĩa oblast′ (Russia)   T2—472 8
Tver′ (Russia : Oblast)   T2—472 8
Tweed, River (Scotland and
  England)   T2—413 7
Tweeddale (Scotland)   T2—413 7
Tweedsmuir Provincial Park
  (B.C.)   T2—711 82
Tweezers
  manufacturing technology   688.5
Twelfth century   909.1
                                 T1—090 21
Twelve patriarchs
  pseudepigrapha   229.914
Twelve prophets (Bible)   224.9
Twelve step programs
  devotional literature   204.32
    Christianity   242.4
  pastoral theology   206.1
    Christianity   259.429
  religious guidance   204.42
    Christianity   248.862 9
  social theology   201.762 29
    Christianity   261.832 29
  substance abuse
    rehabilitation   616.860 3
    therapy   616.860 6
Twelve-tone system   781.268
Twelve Tribes   933.02
Twelvers (Islamic sect)   297.821
  Hadith   297.125 921
  Koran commentary   297.122 753
  religious law   297.140 182 1

Twentieth century   909.82
                                 T1—090 4
Twenty-first century   909.83
                                 T1—090 5
Twenty-one (Game)   795.423
Twi (Ghanaian people)   T5—963 385
Twi language (Ghana)   496.338 5
                                 T6—963 385
Twi literature (Ghana)   896.338 5
Twiggs County (Ga.)   T2—758 545
Twilight   525.7
  meteorology   551.566
Twill-woven rugs
  arts   746.72
Twin Cities Metropolitan
  Area (Minn.)   T2—776 579
Twin Falls County (Idaho)   T2—796 37
Twines   677.71
Twining
  arts   746.42
Twins   306.875
  obstetrics   618.25
  psychology   155.444
  see also Siblings
Twisters (Tornadoes)   551.553
  see also Tornadoes
Twisting textiles   677.028 22
  arts   746.12
  manufacturing technology   677.028 22
Two-Spirit people   306.760 899 7
Two-way radios
  automobile   629.277
Two-wheel motor vehicles
  engineering   629.227 5
Two-wheeled motor vehicles
  engineering   629.227 5
Tyler, John
  United States history   973.58
Tyler County (Tex.)   T2—764 163
Tyler County (W. Va.)   T2—754 19
Tympanic membrane diseases
  medicine   617.85
    see also Ear diseases —
      humans
Tympanic membranes
  human anatomy   611.85
  human physiology   612.854
  medicine   617.85
Tympanuchus   598.637
Tyndale Bible   220.520 1
Tyne, River (England)   T2—428 7
Tyne and Wear (England)   T2—428 7

Type 1 diabetes	362.196 462 2	Typographic masterpieces	
medicine	616.462 2	books	094.4
pregnancy complications		Typographical designs	
obstetrics	618.364 6	graphic arts	744.4
social services	362.196 462 2	sociology	302.226
see also Endocrine diseases —		Typography	744.47
humans		design	744.47
Type 2 diabetes	362.196 462 4	sociology	302.226
medicine	616.462 4	*see Manual at* 744.4 vs. 686.22	
pregnancy complications		Typology (Linguistics)	410.1
obstetrics	618.364 6	grammar	415.01
social services	362.196 462 4	specific languages	T4—501
see also Endocrine diseases —		Typology (Psychology)	155.26
humans		Typology (Theology)	
Type ornaments	686.22	Biblical interpretation	220.64
Type theory	511.3	Christian doctrines	232.1
Typecasting	686.221	Talmudic interpretation	296.120 64
printing technology	686.22	Tyrannidae	598.823
Typeface design	744.45	Tyrannosaurus	567.912 9
Typefaces	744.452	Tyranny	321.9
printing technology	686.22	Tyrant flycatchers	598.823
Typefounding		Tyre (Lebanon)	T2—569 2
printing technology	686.22	ancient	T2—394 4
Typesetters	744.472 092	Tyrian architecture	722.31
Typesetting	744.472	Tyrol (Austria)	943.642
printing technology	686.225		T2—436 42
Typewriter art	740	Tyrolean zithers	787.75
Typewriters	652.3	*see also* Stringed instruments	
manufacturing technology	681.61	Tyrone (Northern Ireland)	T2—416 4
office practice	652.3	Tyrrell County (N.C.)	T2—756 172
Typewriting	652.3	Tyrrhenian Sea	551.461 383
Typewriting analysis			T2—163 83
criminal investigation	363.256 5	Tytonidae	598.97
Typha	584.99	Tyumen (Russia : Oblast)	T2—573
Typhaceae	584.99	Tzeltal Indians	T5—974 28
Typhales	584.99	Tzeltal language	497.428
Typhlopidae	597.969		T6—974 28
Typhlopoidea	597.969	Tzotzil Indians	T5—974 287
Typhoid fever		Tzotzil language	497.428 7
incidence	614.511 2		T6—974 287
medicine	616.927 2	Tzotzil literature	897.428 7
see also Communicable		Tzutujil Indians	T5—974 2
diseases — humans		Tzutujil language	497.42
Typhoons	551.552		T6—974 2
see also Hurricanes			
Typhus		**U**	
incidence	614.526 2		
medicine	616.922 2	Uasin Gishu County	
see also Communicable		(Kenya)	T2—676 279 3
diseases — humans		Ubangi-Shari	967.410 3
Typing	652.3		T2—674 1
Typists	651.374 109 2	Ubangian languages	496.361
office services	651.374 1		T6—963 61

Ubombo (South Africa : District) T2—684 3
Ubykh language 499.962
T6—999 62
Ucayali (Peru : Region) T2—854 3
Uckermark (Germany : Landkreis) T2—431 53
Uckermark-Barnim (Germany : Raumordnungsregion) T2—431 53
Udine (Italy : Ente di decentramento regionale) T2—453 91
ancient T2—373 81
Udmurt language 494.53
T6—945 3
Udmurt literature 894.53
Udmurtia (Russia) T2—474 6
Udmurtiîa (Russia) T2—474 6
Udmurts T5—945 3
Uecker-Randow (Germany : Landkreis) T2—431 78
UFOs (Objects) 001.942
Uganda 967.61
T2—676 1
Ugandans T5—967 61
Ugarit (Extinct city) T2—394 33
Ugaritic language 492.67
T6—926 7
Ugaritic literature 892.67
Ugliness
personal
arts T3C—353
literature 808.803 53
history and criticism 809.933 53
specific literatures T3B—080 353
history and criticism T3B—093 53
Ugrians T5—945 1
Ugric languages 494.51
T6—945 1
Ugric literatures 894.51
Ugric peoples T5—945 1
Ugu District Municipality (South Africa) T2—684 63
UHF radio systems 621.384 151
Uíge (Angola : Province) T2—673 2
Uighur T5—943 23
Uighur language 494.323
T6—943 23
Uighur literature 894.323
Uillean pipes 788.49
see also Woodwind instruments

Uilleann pipes 788.49
see also Woodwind instruments
Uinta County (Wyo.) T2—787 84
Uinta Mountains (Utah and Wyo.) T2—792 14
Uintah County (Utah) T2—792 21
Uitenhage (South Africa : District) T2—687 53
Ukaan language 496.33
T6—963 3
Ukhahlamba District Municipality (South Africa) T2—687 57
uKhahlamba Drakensberg Park (South Africa) T2—684 9
Ukraine 947.7
T2—477
ancient 939.52
T2—395 2
Ukrainian Autocephalous Orthodox Church 281.947 7
Ukrainian language 491.79
T6—917 91
Ukrainian literature 891.79
Ukrainian Orthodox Church (Kyivan Patriarchate) 281.947 7
Ukrainian Orthodox Church (Moscow Patriarchate) 281.947 7
Ukrainians T5—917 91
Ukuleles 787.89
instrument 787.891 9
music 787.89
see also Stringed instruments
Ukẓin 296.123 6
Ulama
role and function 297.61
Ulawa (Solomon Islands) T2—959 38
Ulbricht, Walter
German history 943.108 75
Ulcerations
skin
medicine 616.545
see also Skin diseases — humans
Ulcerative colitis
medicine 616.344 73
Ulcers
digestive system
medicine 616.343
see also Digestive system diseases — humans
Ulema
role and function 297.61

uMgungundlovu District Municipality (South Africa) — T2—684 7
Umhlanga (South Africa) — T2—684 5
Umingmaktok (Nunavut) — T2—719 55
uMkhanyakude District Municipality (South Africa) — T2—684 3
Umlazi (South Africa : District) — T2—684 5
Umm al-Qaiwain (United Arab Emirates : Emirate) — T2—535 7
Umm al-Qaywayn (United Arab Emirates : Emirate) — T2—535 7
Umpiring (Recreation) — 790.1
  American football — 796.332 3
  baseball — 796.357 3
  Canadian football — 796.335 3
  cricket — 796.358 3
  rugby — 796.333 3
  soccer — 796.334 3
  volleyball — 796.325 3
  see also Sports
Umpqua River (Or.) — T2—795 29
Umrah — 297.352 5
UMT (Military training) — 355.225
Umtata (South Africa : District) — T2—687 58
Umvoti (South Africa : District) — T2—684 8
Umzimkulu (South Africa : District) — T2—684 67
Umzinto (South Africa : District) — T2—684 63
uMzinyathi District Municipality (South Africa) — T2—684 8
UN (United Nations) — 341.23
Unaligned blocs — T2—171 6
Unami language — 497.345
  T6—973 45
Unani medicine
  therapeutic system — 615.53
Unarmed combat — 796.81
  military training — 355.548
  sports — 796.81
Unborn children
  law — 346.017 1
Unclaimed estates — 346.057
Uncles — 306.87
  T1—085
Unconscious
  philosophy — 127
  psychology — 154.2

Unconventional warfare — 355.343
  Algerian Revolution — 965.046 8
  American Revolution — 973.385
  Chaco War — 989.207 168
  Civil War (England) — 942.062 8
  Civil War (Spain) — 946.081 8
  Civil War (United States) — 973.785
  Crimean War — 947.073 88
  Falkland Islands War — 997.110 248
  Franco-German War — 943.082 8
  Hundred Years' War — 944.025 8
  Indo-Pakistan War, 1971 — 954.920 518
  Indochinese War — 959.704 18
  Iraq War, 2003–2011 — 956.704 438
  Iraqi-Iranian Conflict — 955.054 28
  Korean War — 951.904 28
  Mexican War — 973.628
  Napoleonic Wars — 940.278
  Persian Gulf War, 1991 — 956.704 428
  South African War — 968.048 8
  Spanish-American War — 973.898
  Thirty Years' War — 940.248
  Vietnamese War — 959.704 38
  War of the Pacific — 983.061 68
  World War I — 940.485
  World War II — 940.548 5
Uncovered spaces
  architecture — 721.84
Undaria — 579.887
Underachievers (Students) — 371.28
  special education — 371.9
Underberg District (South Africa) — T2—684 67
Undercover police work — 363.232
Underdeveloped areas — T2—172 4
Underemployed people — 331.13
Underemployment — 331.13
Undergarments — 391.423
  commercial technology — 687.2
  customs — 391.423
  home sewing — 646.42
  see also Clothing
Underglaze painting — 666.45
  arts — 738.15
  technology — 666.45
Underground architecture — 720.473
Underground areas
  environmental psychology — 155.964
Underground construction — 624.19
Underground disposal — 363.728
  sewage sludge disposal — 628.366
  solid waste technology — 628.445 66
  see also Waste control
Underground electrical lines — 621.319 23

Unicameral legislatures	328.39	Union County (Fla.)	T2—759 14
UNICEF (Children's Fund)	362.7	Union County (Ga.)	T2—758 285
public administration	353.536 211	Union County (Ill.)	T2—773 995
Unicoi County (Tenn.)	T2—768 982	Union County (Ind.)	T2—772 625
Unicorn fishes	597.64	Union County (Iowa)	T2—777 853
Unicorn plants	635.933 96	Union County (Ky.)	T2—769 885
botany	583.96	Union County (Miss.)	T2—762 925
floriculture	635.933 96	Union County (N.C.)	T2—756 755
Unicorns	398.245 4	Union County (N.J.)	T2—749 36
see also Legendary animals		Union County (N.M.)	T2—789 23
Unicycles		Union County (Ohio)	T2—771 532
engineering	629.227 1	Union County (Or.)	T2—795 71
Unidentified flying objects	001.942	Union County (Pa.)	T2—748 48
Unification Church	289.96	Union County (S.C.)	T2—757 41
biography	289.960 92	Union County (S.D.)	T2—783 392
see also Christian		Union County (Tenn.)	T2—768 935
denominations		Union dues checkoff	331.889 6
Unified field theory	530.142	Union federations	331.872
Unified operations (Armed		*see also* Labor unions	
forces)	355.46	Union Islands	996.15
Uniflagellate molds	579.53		T2—961 5
Uniform algebras	512.55	Union leaders	331.880 92
Uniform functions	515.22	biography	331.880 92
Uniform spaces	516	role and function	331.873 3
geometry	516	Union of Christian and Center	
topology	514.32	Democrats (Italian political	
Uniform titles		party)	324.245 082
cataloging	025.322	Union of Kalmar	948.03
Uniforms	391.48	*see also* Kalmar Union	
armed forces	355.14	Union of Soviet Socialist	
issue and use	355.81	Republics	947.084
see Manual at 355.1409			T2—47
commercial technology	687.15	Union of the Comoros	969.41
customs	391.48		T2—694 1
see also Clothing		Union organizing	331.891 2
Unincorporated business		Union Parish (La.)	T2—763 89
enterprises	338.7	Union pipes	788.49
law	346.068	*see also* Woodwind	
management	658.044	instruments	
initiation	658.114 4	Union racketeering	364.106 7
see Manual at 658.04 vs.		Union recognition	331.891 2
658.114, 658.402		Union republics (Soviet Union)	321.023
production economics	338.7	*see also* States (Members of	
see also Business enterprises		federations)	
Unincorporated societies	060	Union security	331.889
see also Nonprofit		Union shop	331.889 2
organizations		Union sympathizers	
Unión (El Salvador : Dept.)	T2—728 434	Civil War (United States)	973.717
Union (Philippines)	T2—599 146	Union Valdôtaine (Italian	
Union catalogs	025.31	political party)	324.245 084
bibliography	017	Uniondale (South Africa :	
library cooperation	021.642	District)	T2—687 37
library science	025.31		
Union County (Ark.)	T2—767 61		

United Nations International
   Children's Emergency Fund
   public administration   353.536 211
United Nations treaties series   341.026 2
United Pentecostal Church   289.94
United Presbyterian Church in
   the U.S.A.   285.131
   see also Presbyterian Church
United Presbyterian Church of
   North America   285.134
   see also Presbyterian Church
United Provinces of Central
   America   972.804
       T2—728
   Costa Rican history   972.860 42
   Guatemalan history   972.810 42
   Honduran history   972.830 4
   Nicaraguan history   972.850 42
   Salvadoran history   972.840 42
United Provinces of the
   Netherlands   949.204
       T2—492
United Reformed Church in the
   United Kingdom   285.232
   see also Presbyterian Church
United Socialist Party (Italy :
   1922–1930)   324.245 027
United Socialist Party (Italy :
   1969–1971)   324.245 072 2
United Society of Believers in
   Christ's Second Appearing   289.8
   see also Christian
     denominations
United States   973
       T2—73
   Dutch explorations   973.19
   English explorations   973.17
   French explorations   973.18
   geography   917.3
   Norse explorations   973.13
   Spanish and Portuguese
     explorations   973.16
   travel   917.304
   see Manual at T2—73 vs.
     T2—71
United States. Central
   Intelligence Agency   327.127 3
United States. Continental
   Congress
   United States history   973.312
United States. Court of Customs
   and Patent Appeals   347.732 8
United States. Navy. SEALs   359.984

United States. Supreme Court   347.732 6
   reports   348.734 13
United States Code   348.732 3
United States customary
   measurements   530.813
United States federal law reporter
   system for the Atlantic region   348.734 22
United States federal reporter
   system for the Northeast
   region   348.734 23
United States federal reporter
   system for the Northwest
   region   348.734 24
United States federal reporter
   system for the Pacific region   348.734 28
United States federal reporter
   system for the South region   348.734 27
United States federal reporter
   system for the Southeast
   region   348.734 25
United States federal reporter
   system for the Southwest
   region   348.734 26
United States national reporter
   system   348.734 2
United States of Colombia   986.106 1
       T2—861
   Colombian history   986.106 1
   Panamanian history   972.870 3
United States Pacific seawaters   551.461 432
       T2—164 32
United States people
   (National group)   T5—13
United States Sanitary
   Commission
   Civil War (United States)   973.777
Uniting Church in Australia   287.93
   see also Christian
     denominations
Unitized cargo services   385.72
   public administration   354.764
Units   530.81
Unity   111.82
   Christian church   262.72
Unity School of Christianity   289.97
   see also Christian
     denominations
Unity State (South Sudan)   T2—629 3
Universal algebra   512
Universal bibliographies   011.1
Universal Decimal Classification   025.432
Universal history   909
Universal House of Justice
   works by   297.938 7

Upland game birds	598.6
conservation technology	639.978 6
resource economics	333.958 6
sports hunting	799.246
Upland rice	
food crop	633.179
Upper Arrow Lake (B.C.)	T2—711 62
Upper atmosphere	551.514
winds	551.518 7
Upper Austria (Austria)	T2—436 2
Upper Avon River	
(England)	T2—424 4
Upper Bavaria (Germany)	T2—433 6
Upper Canada	971.03
	T2—71
Ontario	971.302
	T2—713
Upper chambers (Legislative	
bodies)	328.31
Upper class	305.52
	T1—086 21
Upper Demerara-Berbice	
Region (Guyana)	T2—881 4
Upper Egypt	T2—623
ancient	932.3
	T2—323
Upper extremities	612.97
anatomy	611.97
bones	612.751
anatomy	611.717
medicine	616.71
physiology	612.751
surgery	617.471
fractures	
medicine	617.157
joints	
medicine	616.72
surgery	617.57
muscles	
anatomy	611.737
physiology	612.97
regional medicine	617.57
surgery	617.570 59
Upper Franconia (Germany)	T2—433 1
Upper Guinea	T2—665
Upper houses (Legislative	
bodies)	328.31
Upper Hutt City (N.Z.)	T2—936 5
Upper Karoo (South Africa)	T2—687 13
Upper Mesopotamia	T2—567 4
ancient	935.4
	T2—354
Upper Nile State (South	
Sudan)	T2—629 3

Upper Palatinate (Germany)	T2—433 4
Upper Paleolithic Age	930.128
Upper Peninsula (Mich.)	T2—774 9
Upper Takutu-Upper	
Essequibo Region	
(Guyana)	T2—881 84
Upper Volta	966.250 3
	T2—662 5
see also Burkina Faso	
Upper Volta people	T5—966 25
Uppland landskap (Sweden)	T2—487 4
Uppsala län (Sweden)	T2—487 4
Upshur County (Tex.)	T2—764 222
Upshur County (W. Va.)	T2—754 62
Upson County (Ga.)	T2—758 486
Upton County (Tex.)	T2—764 863
Upton upon Severn	
(England)	T2—424 47
Upwelling	
oceanography	551.462
Ur (Extinct city)	935.501
	T2—355
Urabá, Gulf of (Colombia)	551.461 365
	T2—163 65
Ural-Altaic languages	494
	T6—94
Ural-Altaic literatures	894
Ural Mountains (Russia)	947.43
	T2—474 3
Uralic languages	494.5
	T6—945
Uralic literatures	894.5
Uraninite	
mineralogy	549.528
Uranium	669.293 1
chemical engineering	661.043 1
chemistry	546.431
economic geology	553.493 2
extractive economics	338.274 932
human toxicology	615.925 431
materials science	620.189 293 1
metallography	669.952 931
metallurgy	669.293 1
mining	622.349 32
physical metallurgy	669.962 931
prospecting	622.184 932
see also Chemicals; Metals	
Urantia	299.93
Uranus (Planet)	523.47
	T2—992 7
astrology	133.538
Urban administration	352.16

Urinary calculi
  medicine — 616.622
    see also Urologic diseases —
      humans
Urinary diseases — 573.493 9
  see also Urologic diseases
Urinary incontinence
  medicine — 616.62
    see also Urologic diseases —
      humans
Urinary system — 573.49
  anesthesiology — 617.967 461
  biology — 573.49
  diseases — 573.493 9
    see also Urologic diseases
  human anatomy — 611.61
  human histology — 612.460 45
  human physiology — 612.46
  medicine — 616.6
  surgery — 617.461
Urination disorders
  medicine — 616.62
    see also Urologic diseases —
      humans
Urine
  human physiology — 612.461
Urochordata — 596.2
  paleozoology — 566
Urodela — 597.85
  paleozoology — 567.8
Urogenital diseases — 573.639
  animals — 573.639
    veterinary medicine — 636.089 66
  humans
    cancer
      incidence — 614.599 946
      medicine — 616.994 6
    medicine — 616.6
    pharmacokinetics — 615.76
    surgery — 617.46
Urogenital organs — 573.6
  see also Urogenital system
Urogenital system — 573.6
  diseases — 573.639
    see also Urogenital diseases
  human anatomy — 611.6
  human physiology — 612.46
  medicine — 616.6
  surgery — 617.46
  see also Genital system;
    Urinary system
Urologic diseases — 573.493 9
  animals — 573.493 9
    veterinary medicine — 636.089 66

Urologic diseases (continued)
  humans — 362.196 6
    anesthesiology — 617.967 461
    cancer — 362.196 994 61
      incidence — 614.599 946 1
      medicine — 616.994 61
      social services — 362.196 994 61
      see also Cancer —
        humans
    geriatrics — 618.976 6
    incidence — 614.596
    medicine — 616.6
    pediatrics — 618.926
    pharmacokinetics — 615.761
    social services — 362.196 6
    surgery — 617.461
  see also Urogenital diseases
Urology — 616.6
Uropeltidae — 597.967
Uropygi — 595.453 2
Ursidae — 599.78
  paleozoology — 569.78
Ursulines — 255.974
  church history — 271.974
Ursus — 599.78
Ursus americanus — 599.785
Ursus arctos — 599.784
Ursus maritimus — 599.786
Urticaceae — 583.648
Urticales — 583.648
Urticaria
  medicine — 616.517
    see also Skin diseases —
      humans
Uru-Chipaya languages — 498.9
  — T6—989
Uruguay — 989.5
  — T2—895
Uruguay River — T2—822
  Argentina — T2—822
  Uruguay — T2—895
Uruguayan literature — 860
Uruguayans — T5—688 95
Usability
  computer software — 005.019
  computers — 004.019
Usage (Applied linguistics) — 418
  specific languages — T4—8
Uşak İli (Turkey) — T2—562 8
  ancient — T2—392 6
Use tax — 336.271
  law — 343.055
  public administration — 352.44
  public finance — 336.271

Uto-Aztecan Indians	978.004 974 5
	T5—974 5
Uto-Aztecan languages	497.45
	T6—974 5
Utopian socialism	335.02
English system	335.12
Utopias	321.07
arts	T3C—372
literature	808.803 72
history and criticism	809.933 72
specific literatures	T3B—080 372
history and	
criticism	T3B—093 72
political system	321.07
socialism	335.02
Utrecht (Netherlands :	
Province)	T2—492 32
Utrecht (South Africa :	
District)	T2—684 1
Uttar Pradesh (India)	954.2
	T2—542
Uttarakhand (India)	T2—545 1
Uttaranchal (India)	T2—545 1
Uttlesford (England)	T2—426 712
Uudenmaan lääni (Finland)	T2—489 718
Uudenmaan maakunta	
(Finland)	T2—489 718
Uusimaa (Finland)	T2—489 718
Uvalde County (Tex.)	T2—764 432
Uveal diseases	
incidence	614.599 7
ophthalmology	617.72
see also Eye diseases —	
humans	
Uveas	
human anatomy	611.84
human physiology	612.842
ophthalmology	617.72
Uyghur	T5—943 23
Uyghur language	494.323
	T6—943 23
Uyghur literature	894.323
Uzbek	305.894 325
	T5—943 25
Uzbek language	494.325
	T6—943 25
Uzbek literature	894.325
Uzbekistan	958.7
	T2—587
ancient	939.6
	T2—396
Uzbekistani	T5—943 25

V

Vaal River (South Africa)	T2—682
Vaal Triangle (South	
Africa)	T2—682 23
Vaalbos National Park	
(South Africa)	T2—687 14
Vaasa (Finland : Lääni)	T2—489 73
Vaasan Lääni (Finland)	T2—489 73
Vacation homes	643.25
architecture	728.72
construction	690.872
home economics	643.25
see also Dwellings	
Vacation schools	
adult education	374.8
Vacations	
labor economics	331.257 6
personnel management	658.312 2
recreation	790.1
sociology	306.481 25
Vaccination	
disease control	614.47
law	344.043
Vaccines	
pharmacology	615.372
Vaccinia	
incidence	614.521
medicine	616.913
see also Communicable	
diseases — humans	
Vacuoles	571.655
Vacuum deposition	
metal finishing	671.735
Vacuum electronics	537.53
Vacuum metallizing	671.735
Vacuum metallurgy	669.028 4
Vacuum pumps	621.55
Vacuum technology	621.55
Vacuum tubes	
electronics	621.381 512
radio engineering	621.384 132
Vacuum ultraviolet spectroscopes	
manufacturing technology	681.414 5
Vacuum ultraviolet spectroscopy	
physics	535.845
Vacuums	533.5
engineering	621.55
Vagala language	496.35
	T6—963 5
Vagina	
gynecology	618.15
human anatomy	611.67
human physiology	612.628

958

Vaginal diaphragms	
health	613.943 5
medicine	618.185
see also Birth control	
Vaginal diseases	
gynecology	618.15
see also Female genital diseases — humans	
Vaginiperineotomy	
obstetrical surgery	618.85
Vagrancy	364.148
law	345.024 8
Vagrants	305.569
	T1—086 942
Vai (African people)	T5—963 4
Vai language	496.34
	T6—963 4
Vaiśeṣika (Philosophy)	181.44
Vaisheshika (Philosophy)	181.44
Vaishnavism	294.551 2
Vaisnavism	294.551 2
Vajiralongkorn, King of Thailand	
Thai history	959.304 5
Vajiravudh, King of Siam	
Thai history	959.304 1
Val-de-Marne (France)	T2—443 63
Val-de-Ruz (Switzerland : District)	T2—494 383
Val-de-Travers (Switzerland)	T2—494 389
Val-d'Oise (France)	T2—443 67
Val-Saint-François (Quebec)	T2—714 65
Val Verde County (Tex.)	T2—764 881
Valais (Switzerland)	T2—494 79
Valdivia (Chile : Province)	T2—835 2
Valdotanian Union (Italian political party)	324.245 084
Vale of Glamorgan (Wales)	T2—429 89
Vale of White Horse (England)	T2—425 76
Vale Royal (England)	T2—427 14
Valemount (B.C.)	T2—711 82
Valence (Chemistry)	541.224
Valencia (Spain : Province)	T2—467 63
Valencia (Spain : Region)	T2—467 6
Valencia County (N.M.)	T2—789 92
Valentine's Day	394.261 8
handicrafts	745.594 161 8
Valerians	583.987

Validation	
computer software	
development	005.14
data	005.72
file processing	005.74
Valises	
manufacturing technology	685.51
Vallabhācārya (Philosophy)	181.484 4
Valladolid (Spain : Province)	T2—462 3
Valle (Honduras : Dept.)	T2—728 352
Valle d'Aosta (Italy)	945.11
	T2—451 1
ancient	T2—372 21
Valle del Cauca (Colombia)	T2—861 52
Vallée-de-la-Gatineau (Quebec)	T2—714 224
Vallée de l'Or (Quebec)	T2—714 139
Vallée-du-Richelieu (Quebec)	T2—714 365
Vallemaggia (Switzerland)	T2—494 789
Valley County (Idaho)	T2—796 76
Valley County (Mont.)	T2—786 17
Valley County (Neb.)	T2—782 48
Valley Forge	
United States history	973.334 1
Valley of Mexico (Mexico)	T2—725
Valley winds	551.518 5
Valleys	551.442
	T2—144
geography	910.914 4
geomorphology	551.442
physical geography	910.021 44
Valois, House of	944.025
genealogy	929.74
Valparaíso (Chile : Province)	T2—832 55
Valparaíso (Chile : Region)	T2—832 4
Valréas (France)	T2—445 88
Valuation	
businesses	
financial management	658.15
law	346.065
investment economics	332.632 21
real property	333.332
law	346.043 7
Valuation of assets	
accounting	657.73
Valuation theory	515.78
Value	T1—01
labor theory	
Marxian economics	335.412
microeconomics	338.521

Value-added networks 004.69
  computer communications
    services 384.33
  see also Computer
    communications
Value-added tax 336.271 4
  law 343.055
  public administration 352.44
  public finance 336.271 4
Value analysis (Cost control) 658.155 2
Value cognition
  psychology 153.45
Values
  epistemology 121.8
  social control 303.372
Valvatida 593.93
Valverde (Dominican
  Republic : Province) T2—729 357
Valves 621.84
  internal-combustion engines 621.437
Valvular activity
  heart
    human physiology 612.171
Valvular heart diseases
  medicine 616.125
  see also Cardiovascular
    diseases — humans
Vampire bats 599.45
Vampires 398.21
  see also Legendary beings
Vampyromorpha 594.55
Van Allen radiation belts 538.766
Van Buren, Martin
  United States history 973.57
Van Buren County (Ark.) T2—767 29
Van Buren County (Iowa) T2—777 98
Van Buren County (Mich.) T2—774 13
Van Buren County (Tenn.) T2—768 657
Van İli (Turkey) T2—566 28
  ancient T2—395 5
Van pools 388.413 212
Van Wert County (Ohio) T2—771 413
Van Zandt County (Tex.) T2—764 276
Vanadates
  mineralogy 549.72
Vanadium 669.732
  chemical engineering 661.052 2
  chemistry 546.522
  economic geology 553.462 6
  materials science 620.189 32
  metallography 669.957 32
  metallurgy 669.732
  metalworking 673.732

Vanadium (continued)
  organic chemistry
    applied 661.895
  physical metallurgy 669.967 32
  see also Chemicals; Metals
Vanadium group
  chemical engineering 661.052
  chemistry 546.52
Vance County (N.C.) T2—756 532
Vancouver (B.C.) T2—711 33
Vancouver Island (B.C.) 971.12
                    T2—711 2
Vandal language 439.9
                    T6—399
Vandal period
  Libyan history 939.740 4
  Moroccan history 939.712 05
  North Africa 939.704
  Tunisian history 939.730 4
Vandalic language 439.9
                    T6—399
Vandalism 364.164 4
  law 345.026 44
  schools 371.782
Vandalism insurance 368.12
  see also Insurance
Vandals (Germanic people) T5—39
  Sardinian history 945.901
Vanderbijlpark (South
  Africa : District) T2—682 23
Vanderburgh County (Ind.) T2—772 33
Vanderhoof (B.C.) T2—711 82
Vanderkloof Dam (South
  Africa) T2—687 13
Vänern (Sweden) T2—486 7
Vanga shrikes 598.8
Vanillas 641.338 2
  botany 584.72
  see also Flavorings
Vanishing species 333.952 2
  see also entries beginning with
    Rare
Vanoise, Parc national de la
  (France) T2—445 85
Vanrhynsdorp (South
  Africa : District) T2—687 32
Vans 388.343 4
  driving 629.284 34
  engineering 629.223 4
  repair 629.287 34
  transportation services 388.343 4
  see also Trucks
Vanuatu 995.95
                    T2—959 5

Vapor lighting 621.327
  see also Lighting
Vapor-phase deposition
  metal finishing 671.735
Vapor plating
  metal finishing 671.735
Vaporization 536.44
Var (France) T2—449 3
Varactors 621.381 522
Varanidae 597.959 6
Varanus 597.959 6
Varanus komodoensis 597.959 68
Vardar Macedonia T2—497 6
Vardar River T2—497 6
Varela Rodríguez, Juan Carlos
  Panamanian history 972.870 544
Varese (Italy : Province) T2—452 2
  ancient T2—372 25
Vargas, Getúlio
  Brazilian history 981.061
Variable annuities
  insurance 368.375
  see also Insurance
Variable costs 338.514 2
  financial management 658.155 3
Variable life insurance 368.325
  see also Insurance
Variable rate securities 332.632 044
Variable stars 523.844
Variables 511.326
Variation (Biology) 576.54
  humans 599.94
Variations (Mathematics) 515.64
Variations (Musical forms) 781.825
  instrumental 784.182 5
Varicella
  incidence 614.525
  medicine 616.914
    see also Communicable
      diseases — humans
Varicose veins
  medicine 616.143
    see also Cardiovascular
      diseases — humans
Varietal wines 641.22
  commercial processing 663.2
Varieties
  agriculture 631.57
Variety drama
  literature 808.825 7
    history and criticism 809.257
    specific literatures T3B—205 7
      individual authors T3A—2

Variety shows 792.7
  see also Theater
Variety stores 381.14
  see also Commerce
Variola major
  incidence 614.521
  medicine 616.912
    see also Communicable
      diseases — humans
Variola minor
  incidence 614.521
  medicine 616.912
Varix
  medicine 616.143
    see also Cardiovascular
      diseases — humans
Varmints
  small game hunting 799.25
Värmland landskap
  (Sweden) T2—487 7
Värmlands län (Sweden) T2—487 7
Varna (1987–1998)
  (Bulgaria : Oblast) T2—499 4
Varna (1999-) (Bulgaria :
  Oblast) T2—499 45
Varnenska oblast
  (1987–1998) (Bulgaria) T2—499 4
Varnenska oblast (1999-)
  (Bulgaria) T2—499 45
Varnish trees 583.77
Varnish trees (Sapindaceae) 583.75
Varnishes 667.79
Varnishing 667.79
  technology 667.79
  woodwork
    buildings 698.34
Varsinais-Suomi (Finland) T2—489 731
Vas Megye (Hungary) T2—439 7
Vasa, House of 948.503 2
  Finnish history 948.970 132
  Swedish history 948.503 2
Vascongadas (Spain) T2—466
Vascular circulation 573.18
  human physiology 612.13
    see also Cardiovascular system
Vascular cryptogams 587
Vascular dementia
  medicine 616.812
    see also Nervous system
      diseases — humans
Vascular diseases
  medicine 616.13
    see also Cardiovascular
      diseases — humans

Vascular diseases (continued)
  pregnancy complications
    obstetrics   618.361 3
Vascular headaches
  medicine   616.849 1
  see also Nervous system
    diseases — humans
Vascular plants   580
  see also Plants
Vascular seedless plants   587
Vascular surgery   617.413
Vasectomy (Birth control)
  health   613.942
  see also Birth control
  surgery   617.463
Vases
  sculpture   731.72
Vaslui (Romania : Judeţ)   T2—498 1
Vasoconstrictors (Drugs)
  pharmacokinetics   615.71
Vasoconstrictors (Nerves)
  human physiology   612.18
Vasodilators (Drugs)
  pharmacokinetics   615.71
Vasodilators (Nerves)
  human physiology   612.18
Vasomotors
  human physiology   612.18
Vasopressin
  human physiology   612.492
  pharmacology   615.363
Västerbotten landskap
  (Sweden)   T2—488 7
Västerbottens län (Sweden)   T2—488 7
Västergötland landskap
  (Sweden)   T2—486 7
Västernorrlands län
  (Sweden)   T2—488 5
Västmanland landskap
  (Sweden)   T2—487 5
Västmanlands län (Sweden)   T2—487 5
Västra Götalands län
  (Sweden)   T2—486 7
VAT (Tax)   336.271 4
  law   343.055
  public administration   352.44
  public finance   336.271 4
Vaterländische Front (Austrian
  political party)   324.243 602 43
Vatican City   945.634
     T2—456 34
  ancient   T2—376 3
Vättern (Sweden)   T2—486 4
Vaucluse (France : Dept.)   T2—449 2

Vaud (Switzerland)   T2—494 52
Vaudeville   792.7
  see also Theater
Vaudreuil-Soulanges
  (Quebec)   T2—714 26
Vault (Gymnastic equipment)   796.442
  see also Gymnastics
Vaults   721.43
  architecture   721.43
  construction   690.143
Vaupés (Colombia)   T2—861 65
Vázquez, Tabaré
  Uruguayan history   989.506 75
    2005–2010   989.506 75
    2015–2020   989.506 77
VdU (Austrian political party)   324.243 603
Veal   641.362
  commercial processing   664.92
  cooking   641.662
  food   641.362
Vector algebra   512.5
Vector analysis   515.63
Vector bundles   514.224
Vector calculus   515.63
Vector geometry   516.182
Vector processing   004.35
Vector processors   004.35
  engineering   621.391
Vector quantities
  mechanics   531.112
Vector spaces   512.52
Vector-valued functions   515.7
Vectorcardiography
  medicine   616.120 754 7
Vectors (Disease carriers)   571.986
  biology   571.986
  medicine   614.43
Vedanta (Philosophy)   181.48
Vedas   294.592 1
  Sanskrit texts   294.592 104 1
Vedda   T5—914 8
Vedic language   491.29
     T6—912 9
Vedic literature   891.29
Vedic period   934.02
Vedic religion   294.509 013
Vega (Dominican Republic :
  Province)   T2—729 369 7
Vegan cooking   641.563 62
Vegan diet   613.262 2
  cooking   641.563 62
  health   613.262 2

Velocity of flow	
air mechanics	533.62
fluid mechanics	532.053 2
gas mechanics	533.27
liquid mechanics	532.57
Velocity of light	535.24
Velocity of sound	534.202
Velocity of stars	523.83
Velocity theory	
monetary economics	332.401
Velour	677.617
see also Textiles	
Velvet	677.617
see also Textiles	
Velveteen	677.617
see also Textiles	
Venango County (Pa.)	T2—748 96
Venda (African people)	T5—963 976
Venda (South Africa)	T2—682 57
Venda language	496.397 6
	T6—963 976
Venda literature	896.397 6
Vendean War, 1793–1800	944.042
Vendée (France)	T2—441 69
Vendettas	
influence on crime	364.256
Vending machines	629.82
Vendor selection	
library acquisitions	025.233
materials management	658.722
Vendors and purchasers	346.043 63
Veneers	674.833
architectural decoration	729.6
Venereal diseases	
incidence	614.547
medicine	616.951
law	344.043 695 1
see also Communicable	
diseases — humans	
Venetia	T2—373
Venetia (Italy : Region)	945.3
	T2—453
Venetiaan, Runaldo Ronald	
Surinamese history	988.303 22
1991–1996	988.303 22
2000–2010	988.303 24
Venetian Republic	945.308 3
Venetic language	479.4
	T6—794
Veneto (Italy)	945.3
	T2—453
ancient	T2—373
Venezia (Italy)	T2—453 11

Venezia (Italy : Città	
metropolitana)	T2—453 1
ancient	T2—373 5
Venezuela	987
	T2—87
Venezuela, Gulf of (Colombia	
and Venezuela)	551.461 365
	T2—163 65
Venezuelan literature	860
Venezuelans	T5—688 7
Venial sin	241.31
Venice (Italy)	T2—453 11
ancient	T2—373 5
Venice (Italy : Metropolitan	
city)	T2—453 1
ancient	T2—373 5
Venice (Republic)	945.3
Venice, Gulf of (Italy)	551.461 385
	T2—163 85
Venison	641.391
commercial processing	664.92
cooking	641.691
food	641.391
Venomous snakes	597.961 65
Venoms	
human toxicology	615.942
Venous diseases	
medicine	616.14
see also Cardiovascular	
diseases — humans	
Venous embolisms	
medicine	616.145
see also Cardiovascular	
diseases — humans	
Venous thromboses	
medicine	616.145
see also Cardiovascular	
diseases — humans	
Ventersburg (South Africa :	
District)	T2—685 3
Ventersdorp (South Africa :	
District)	T2—682 43
Venterstad (South Africa :	
District)	T2—687 57
Ventilation	
aircraft	629.134 42
automobile	629.277 2
buildings	697.92
household management	644.5
library buildings	697.978
plant management	022.8
mining	622.42
museums	069.29
plant management	658.25

Ventilation (continued)	
sewers	628.23
underground construction	624.19
vehicles	629.040 289
Ventilation engineers	697.920 92
Ventricle diseases (Heart)	
medicine	616.12
see also Cardiovascular	
diseases — humans	
Ventricles (Heart)	
human anatomy	611.12
human physiology	612.17
medicine	616.12
Ventricular fibrillation	
medicine	616.128
see also Cardiovascular	
diseases — humans	
Ventriloquism	793.89
Ventura County (Calif.)	T2—794 92
Venture capital	332.041 54
Venture Scouts	369.435
Venus (Planet)	523.42
	T2—992 2
astrology	133.534
unmanned flights to	629.435 42
Venus's flytrap	583.887
Veps	T5—945 4
Veps language	494.54
	T6—945 4
Veps literature	894.54
Veracruz (Mexico : State)	T2—726 2
Veraguas (Panama :	
Province)	T2—728 722
Verandas	721.84
Verb phrases	415.6
specific languages	T4—56
Verb tables	
applied linguistics	418
specific languages	T4—82
Verbal communication	302.224
psychology	153.6
Verband der Unabhängigen	
(Austrian political party)	324.243 603
Verbania (Italy : Province)	T2—451 65
ancient	T2—372 245
Verbano-Cusio-Ossola	
(Italy)	T2—451 65
ancient	T2—372 245
Verbenaceae	583.96
Verbenas	635.933 96
botany	583.96
floriculture	635.933 96
Verbs	415.6
specific languages	T4—56

Vercelli (Italy : Province)	T2—451 7
ancient	T2—372 23
Verd antique marble	553.55
economic geology	553.55
quarrying	622.355
Verdicts	347.075
criminal law	345.075
Verdun, Treaty of, 843	943.021
Vereeniging (South Africa :	
District)	T2—682 23
Vérendrye Wildlife Reserve	
(Quebec)	T2—714 224
Verification	
computer software	
development	005.14
musical instruments	784.192 7
Vermicides	632.951
agricultural use	632.951
chemical engineering	668.651
Vermiculite	553.678
economic geology	553.678
mining	622.367 8
Vermiform appendix	
human anatomy	611.345
human physiology	612.33
medicine	616.34
surgery	617.554 5
Vermiform appendix diseases	
medicine	616.34
see also Digestive system	
diseases — humans	
Vermilion County (Ill.)	T2—773 65
Vermilion Parish (La.)	T2—763 51
Vermillion County (Ind.)	T2—772 462
Vermont	974.3
	T2—743
Vernon (B.C.)	T2—711 5
Vernon County (Mo.)	T2—778 44
Vernon County (Wis.)	T2—775 73
Vernon Parish (La.)	T2—763 61
Verona (Italy)	T2—453 41
ancient	T2—373 21
Verona (Italy : Province)	T2—453 4
ancient	T2—373 2
Verrucae	
medicine	616.544
see also Skin diseases —	
humans	
Versailles (France)	T2—443 663
Versailles, Treaty of, 1783	
United States history	973.317
Versailles, Treaty of, 1919	
European history	940.314 1

Verse drama
literature 808.82
history and criticism 809.2
specific literatures T3B—2
individual authors T3A—2
Versification 808.1
Version
obstetrical surgery 618.82
Version control
computer software 005.3
Verte, Île (Quebec) T2—714 764
Vertebrate viruses 579.2
Vertebrates 596
agricultural pests 632.66
conservation technology 639.9
paleozoology 566
resource economics 333.954
zoology 596
Vertical combinations
(Enterprises) 338.804 2
see also Combinations
(Enterprises)
Vertical lift rotors
aircraft 629.134 36
Vertical-speed indicators 629.135 2
Vertical takeoff and landing
aircraft 387.733 5
engineering 629.133 35
military engineering 623.746 047
transportation services 387.733 5
Vertigo
medicine 616.841
see also Nervous system
diseases — humans
Vervains 635.933 96
botany 583.96
floriculture 635.933 96
Verwoerd, Hendrik Frensch
South African history 968.058
Very-high-frequency radio
systems 621.384 151
Very large scale integration 621.395
Very-low-frequency radio
systems 621.384 153
Vesicles 571.655
Vespers 264.15
Anglican 264.030 15
texts 264.034
music 782.324
see also Liturgy of the hours
Vespertilionidae 599.47
Vespoidea 595.798

Vessel flutes 788.38
see also Woodwind
instruments
Vessels
music 786.82
concussed 786.876
friction 786.866
set 786.866
single 786.888
percussed 786.846
set 786.846
single 786.884 6
see also Percussion
instruments
Vessels (Nautical) 387.2
see also Ships
Vest-Agder fylke (Norway) T2—483 2
Vested rights (Pensions) 331.252 2
see also Pensions
Vesterålen (Norway) T2—484 4
Vestfold fylke (Norway) T2—482 7
Vestfold og Telemark fylke
(Norway) T2—482 7
Vestibular diseases
medicine 617.882
see also Ear diseases —
humans
Vestibular perception 152.188 2
Vestibules (Ears)
human anatomy 611.85
human physiology 612.858
medicine 617.882
Vestibulocochlear nerve diseases
medicine 617.886
see also Ear diseases —
humans
Vestinian language 479.7
T6—797
Vestland fylke (Norway) T2—483 6
Vestlandet (Norway) T2—483 3
Vestments 391.48
commercial technology 687.15
customs 391.48
see also Clothing
Vests (Undergarments) 391.423
see also Undergarments
Vests (Waistcoats) 391.473
commercial technology 687.113
customs 391.473
home sewing 646.433
see also Clothing
Vestsjælland (Denmark) T2—489 12
Veszprém Megye (Hungary) T2—439 7

Vicksburg, Siege of, 1863	973.734 4
Victimology	362.88
Victims of abuse	362.885 5
social welfare	362.885 5
Victims of crime	362.88
	T1—086 949
artists	704.086 949
church work	259.086 949
criminal law	345.050 46
insurance	368.82
law	344.028
school programs	371.782
social welfare	362.88
law	344.032 88
public administration	353.533 7
Victims of identity theft	362.889 639 3
Victims of oppression	
social welfare	362.87
public administration	353.533 8
Victims of political crimes	362.889 31
Victims of property offenses	362.889 6
Victims of terrorism	362.889 317
Victims of war	305.906 95
	T1—086 948
Victims of war crimes	362.889 38
Victor Amadeus II, King of Sardinia	
Piedmontese history	945.107
Sardinian history	945.907
Victor Amadeus III, Duke of Savoy	
Piedmontese history	945.107
Sardinian history	945.907
Victor Emmanuel I, King of Sardinia	
Piedmontese history	945.108 2
1796–1815	945.108 2
1815–1861	945.108 3
Victor Emmanuel II, King of Italy	
Italian history	945.084
Lombardian history	945.208 4
Piedmontese history	945.108 4
Sardinian history	945.908 4
Sicilian history	945.808 4
Southern Italian history	945.708 4
Tuscan history	945.508 4
Venetian history	945.308 4
Victor Emmanuel III, King of Italy	
Italian history	945.091
Lombardian history	945.209 1
Piedmontese history	945.109 1
Sardinian history	945.909 1

Victor Emmanuel III, King of Italy (continued)	
Sicilian history	945.809 1
Southern Italian history	945.709 1
Tuscan history	945.509 1
Venetian history	945.309 1
Victor Harbour (S. Aust.)	T2—942 32
Victoria	994.5
	T2—945
Victoria (B.C.)	T2—711 28
Victoria (N.B. : County)	T2—715 53
Victoria (N.S. : County)	T2—716 93
Victoria (Ont. : County)	T2—713 64
Victoria (Seychelles)	T2—696
Victoria, Lake	T2—678 27
Victoria, Queen of Great Britain	
British history	941.081
English history	942.081
Scottish history	941.108 1
Victoria County (Tex.)	T2—764 125
Victoria East (South Africa : District)	T2—687 54
Victoria Falls	T2—689 1
Victoria Island (Nunavut and N.W.T.)	T2—719 55
Victoria swine	636.484
Victoria West (South Africa : District)	T2—687 13
Victorian architecture	724.5
Victualing	
aircraft	387.736 4
boats	387.168
buses	388.33
ships	387.168
trains	385.26
transportation services	388.041
Vicuña	599.636 7
animal husbandry	636.296
Vicuña wool textiles	677.32
see also Textiles	
Video animation	777.7
Video art	777
computer art	776.6
Video cassettes	384.558
see also Video recordings	
Video discs	
computer storage	004.565
engineering	621.397 67
recordings	384.558
see also Video recordings	
Video display components	621.381 542 2
Video display screens	
computer science	004.77
engineering	621.398 7

Video games	794.8	Videotex	004.69
music	781.54	communications services	384.33
Video mini-series	791.45	*see also* Computer	
see Manual at 791.43 vs.		communications	
791.45		Vidin (Bulgaria : Oblast)	T2—499 12
Video photography	777	Vieira, João Bernardo	
Video production	384.558	Guinean (Guinea-Bissau)	
communications services	384.558	history	966.570 32
videography	777	1980–1999	966.570 32
Video recorders	384.558	2005–2009	966.570 34
communications services	384.558	Vielles	787.69
engineering	621.388 33	instrument	787.691 9
videography	777.36	music	787.69
Video recording	777	*see also* Stringed instruments	
Video recordings	384.558	Vienna (Austria)	943.613
bibliographies	011.373		T2—436 13
cataloging	025.347 3	Vienne (France : Dept.)	T2—446 3
communications services	384.558	Vieques Island (P.R.)	T2—729 59
engineering	621.388 332	Vierwaldstätter See	
instructional use	371.335 23	(Switzerland)	T2—494 557
adult level	374.265 23	Việt-Cộng (Vietnamese history)	959.704 332 2
library treatment	025.177 3	Viet-Muong languages	495.92
music	780		T6—959 2
treatises	780.267	Viet-Muong literatures	895.92
see Manual at 780.26		Viet-Muong peoples	T5—959 2
performing arts	791.43	Vietcong (Vietnamese history)	959.704 332 2
videography	777.38	Vietnam	959.7
Video records	384.558		T2—597
see also Video recordings		Vietnamese	T5—959 22
Video tapes	384.558	Vietnamese communism	335.434 6
see also Video recordings		Vietnamese language	495.922
Videocassettes	384.558		T6—959 22
see also Video recordings		Vietnamese literature	895.922
Videoconferencing	384.556	Vietnamese War, 1961–1975	959.704 3
instructional use	371.335 8	North Vietnam	959.704 331
sociology	302.234 5	societies	369.2
Videodiscs		United States	369.186
computer storage	004.565	South Vietnam	959.704 332
engineering	621.397 67	Viewdata	004.69
recordings	384.558	*see also* Computer	
see also Video recordings		communications	
Videography	777	Viewer access	
see Manual at 791.43, 791.45		communications services	384.555 3
vs. 777		Viewfinders	771.37
Videorecordings	384.558	Vige language	496.35
see also Video recordings			T6—963 5
Videorecords	384.558	Vigesimal system (Numeration)	513.5
see also Video recordings		Vigo County (Ind.)	T2—772 45
Videotapes	384.558	Vihiga County (Kenya)	T2—676 282
see also Video recordings		Vihuelas	787.86
Videotelephony	384.556	instrument	787.861 9
sociology	302.234 5	music	787.86
		see also Stringed instruments	
		Vijnana Buddhism	294.392

Viken fylke (Norway)	T2—482 2
Viking Mars Program	629.435 43
Viking period	948.022
Danish history	948.901 4
Norwegian history	948.101 4
Swedish history	948.501 4
Vikings	T5—395
Vila Nova, Carlos	
Sao Tomean history	967.150 26
Vila Real (Portugal :	
District)	T2—469 23
Vilas County (Wis.)	T2—775 23
Vîlcea (Romania)	T2—498 2
Viljoenskroon (South	
Africa : District)	T2—685 2
Villa Clara (Cuba :	
Province)	T2—729 142
Villages	307.762
	T2—173 2
area planning	711.43
government	320.8
cities	320.85
see Manual at T2—4–9	
Villancicos	782.43
carols	782.281 723
Villas	
architecture	728.8
Vinayapiṭaka	294.382 2
Vincentians	255.77
church history	271.77
Vindelicia	T2—363 3
Vinegar	
commercial processing	664.55
cooking with	641.62
Vinegar flies	595.774
Vines	582.18
floriculture	635.974
landscape architecture	715.4
see Manual at 635.9 vs. 582.1	
Vĩnh Long (Vietnam :	
Province)	T2—597 8
Vĩnh Phúc (Vietnam :	
Province)	T2—597 2
Vinnytsa (Ukraine : Oblast)	T2—477 8
Vinnyt͡s′ka oblast′	
(Ukraine)	T2—477 8
Vinton County (Ohio)	T2—771 837
Vinylidene chlorides	668.423 7
Vinyls	668.423 6
textiles	677.474 4
see also Textiles	
Vinyons	
textiles	677.474 4
see also Textiles	
Viola concertos	784.273 186
Viola da gambas	787.65
instrument	787.651 9
music	787.65
see also Stringed instruments	
Viola d'amores	787.66
instrument	787.661 9
music	787.66
see also Stringed instruments	
Violaceae	583.69
Violales	583.69
Violas	787.3
instrument	787.319
music	787.3
see also Stringed instruments	
Violence	303.6
arts	700.455 2
	T3C—355 2
ethics	179.7
religion	205.697
Buddhism	294.356 97
Christianity	241.697
Hinduism	294.548 697
Islam	297.569 7
Judaism	296.369 7
literature	808.803 552
history and criticism	809.933 552
specific literatures	T3B—080 355 2
history and	
criticism	T3B—093 552
public safety	363.32
social conflict	303.6
Violence in schools	371.782
Violence in the workplace	
prevention	
management	658.473
Violent behavior	
medicine	616.858 2
Violent crimes	364.15
prevention	364.4
self-defense	613.66
social welfare	362.88
see also Crime	
Violets	583.69
botany	583.69
floriculture	635.933 69
Violin concertos	784.272 186
Violin family	787.2
see also Stringed instruments	
Violin makers	787.219 092
Violinists	787.209 2

Violins	787.2	Virginia Beach (Va.)	T2—755 51
instrument	787.219	Virginia City (Nev.)	T2—793 56
music	787.2	Virginia cowslip	635.933 958
see also Stringed instruments		botany	583.958
Violoncellists	787.409 2	floriculture	635.933 958
Violoncellos	787.4	Virginia creeper	583.79
instrument	787.419	Virginia deer	599.652
music	787.4	conservation technology	639.979 652
see also Stringed instruments		resource economics	333.959 652
Viols	787.6	Virginia reels	793.34
instrument	787.619	Virginia willow	583.44
music	787.6	Virginity of Mary	232.913
see also Stringed instruments		Virgo (Zodiac)	133.526 7
Vipera	597.963 6	Viroids	579.29
Viperfishes	597.5	Virologists	579.209 2
Viperidae	597.963	Virology	579.2
Vipers	597.963	medicine	616.910 1
Viral diseases	571.992	Virtual memory	005.435
see also Virus diseases		computer hardware	004.5
Viral hepatitis		computer software	005.435
medicine	616.362 3	Virtual museums	069
see also Digestive system		Virtual private networks	004.678 4
diseases — humans		Virtual reality	006.8
Viral pneumonia		computer art	776
medicine	616.241 4	Virtual reference services	
Viral skin diseases		(Libraries)	025.52
incidence	614.595 22	Virtue	179.9
medicine	616.522	*see also* Virtues	
see also Skin diseases —		Virtues	179.9
humans		arts	700.453
Vireolaniidae	598.878		T3C—353
Vireonidae	598.878	literature	808.803 53
Vireos	598.878	history and criticism	809.933 53
conservation technology	639.978 878	specific literatures	T3B—080 353
resource economics	333.958 878	history and	
Virgin birth of Jesus Christ	232.921	criticism	T3B—093 53
Virgin Gorda (V.I.)	T2—729 725	religion	205.699
Virgin Islanders	T5—969 729 72	Buddhism	294.356 99
Virgin Islands	972.972	Christianity	241.4
	T2—729 72	Hinduism	294.548
Virgin Islands, British	T2—729 725		294.548 699
Virgin Islands National Park		Islam	297.5
(Saint John, V.I.)	T2—729 722	Judaism	296.369 9
Virgin Islands of the United		Virus diseases	571.992
States	972.972 2	agriculture	632.8
	T2—729 722	animals	571.992 11
Virginals	786.4	veterinary medicine	636.089 691
instrument	786.419	biology	571.992
music	786.4	humans	362.196 91
see also Keyboard instruments		incidence	614.58
Virginia	975.5	medicine	616.91
	T2—755	social services	362.196 91
Virginia (South Africa :			
District)	T2—685 3		

Virus diseases (continued)
plants 571.992 8
agriculture 632.8
see also Communicable
diseases
Viruses (Computer security) 005.88
Viruses (Microorganisms) 579.2
medical microbiology 616.910 1
see Manual at 579.24–.25
Visas 323.67
law 342.082
political science 323.67
public administration 353.13
Visayan Islands
(Philippines) T2—599 5
Visceral leishmaniasis
incidence 614.534
medicine 616.936 4
see also Communicable
diseases — humans
Visceral perception
psychology 152.188 6
Visconti, House of
Lombardian history 945.205
Viscose rayon 677.463
see also Textiles
Viscosity 531.113 4
fluid mechanics 532.053 3
gas mechanics 533.28
liquid mechanics 532.58
solid mechanics 531.4
Viscous flow 532.053 3
gas mechanics 533.28
liquid mechanics 532.58
Vises 621.992
Viseu (Portugal : District) T2—469 31
Vishnuism 294.551 2
Visibility
aeronautics 629.132 4
meteorology 551.568
Visible light 535
see also Light
Visible light spectroscopes
manufacturing technology 681.414 3
Visigothic domination
Spanish history 946.01
Visigoths T5—39
Vision 573.88
artificial intelligence 006.37
arts 701.8
epistemology 121.35
human physiology 612.84
painting 750.18

Vision (continued)
psychology 152.14
see also Eyes
Visions
religious experience 204.2
Christianity 248.29
Viśiṣṭādvaita (Philosophy) 181.483
Visitation rights (Domestic law) 346.017 3
Visitation Sisters 255.975
church history 271.975
Visiting housekeepers
social welfare 362.828 3
Visiting nurses 610.734 3
medicine 610.734 3
social welfare 362.14
Visp (Switzerland : Bezirk) T2—494 794 6
Vistula River T2—438
Visual arts 700
Visual-auditory memory 153.134
Visual binaries 523.841
Visual communication 302.226
design 744
sociology 302.226
Visual communication systems 744.26
Visual design 744
see Manual at 744 vs. 741.6
Visual display units
computer science 004.77
engineering 621.398 7
Visual effects
dramatic performances 792.024
see also Special effects —
dramatic performances
Visual hierarchy 744.35
Visual language 744.26
Visual logic 744.32
Visual memory 153.132
Visual novels 741.5
Visual perception
psychology 152.14
Visual programming 005.118
Visual signaling
communications services 384
design 744.26
military engineering 623.731
nautical engineering 623.856 1
Visualization (Psychology) 153.32
Visually impaired children
home care 649.151 1
Visually-impaired people 305.908 1
T1—087 1
education 371.911
library services 027.663
social welfare 362.41

Vitaceae	583.79
Vitales	583.79
Vitalism	147
Vitamin D treatment	
milk processing	637.141
Vitamin therapy	615.328
Vitamins	572.58
applied nutrition	613.286
animal husbandry	636.085 28
biochemistry	572.58
humans	612.399
chemistry	547.7
metabolism	
human physiology	612.399
pharmacology	615.328
Vitebsk (Belarus : Voblasts)	T2—478 4
Vitebskaîa voblasts'	
(Belarus)	T2—478 4
Viterbo (Italy)	T2—456 251
ancient	T2—375 8
Viterbo (Italy : Province)	T2—456 25
ancient	T2—375 8
Viticulture	634.8
Vitiligo	
medicine	616.55
see also Skin diseases —	
humans	
Vitoria (Spain)	T2—466 5
Vitreous bodies	
human anatomy	611.84
human physiology	612.844
ophthalmology	617.746
Vitreous body diseases	
ophthalmology	617.746
see also Eye diseases —	
humans	
Viverridae	599.742
Vivisection	
ethics	179.4
see also Animals —	
treatment of — ethics	
Vizcarra, Martín	
Peruvian history	985.064 8
Vizcaya (Spain)	T2—466 3
Vizsla	636.752
Vlaams-Brabant (Belgium)	T2—493 31
Vladimir (Russia : Oblast)	T2—473 3
Vladimirskaîa oblast'	
(Russia)	T2—473 3
VLF radio systems	621.384 153
VLSI (Computer circuits)	621.395
VMM insurance	368.12
see also Insurance	
Vocabulary	401.4
dictionaries	413
specific languages	T4—014
dictionaries	T4—3
usage (Applied	
linguistics)	T4—81
see Manual at T4—3 vs.	
T4—81	
usage (Applied linguistics)	418
Vocabulary development	
primary education	372.44
Vocal communication	
animals	596.159 4
physiology	573.92
Vocal cord diseases	
medicine	616.22
see also Respiratory tract	
diseases — humans	
Vocal cords	573.925
biology	573.925
medicine	616.22
surgery	617.533
see also Respiratory system	
Vocal duets	783.12
Vocal expression	
psychology	152.384 2
Vocal forms	782
Vocal music	782
biography	782.009 2
diction	783.043
see Manual at 782	
Vocal quartets	783.14
Vocal trios	783.13
Vocalises	782.4
Vocalists	782.009 2
Vocalization	
animals	596.159 4
physiology	573.92
Vocation (Career)	331.7
see also Occupations;	
Vocational guidance	
Vocation (Religious calling)	253.2
ecclesiology	262.1
guides to life	248.892
monastic and religious orders	255
men	255
guides to life	248.894 22
women	255.9
guides to life	248.894 32
Vocational counseling	331.702
see also Vocational guidance	
Vocational education	370.113
	T1—071
adult level	374.013

Vocational education (continued)	
on the job	331.259 2
personnel management	658.312 4
	T1—068 3
secondary level	373.246
Vocational guidance	331.702
	T1—023
economics	331.702
education	371.425
personnel management	658.385
psychology	158.6
Vocational interest tests	153.94
Vocational interests	
applied psychology	158.6
Vocational qualifications	331.114
see also Qualifications of	
employees	
Vocational rehabilitation	362.042 5
see also Employment	
services — social services	
Vocational schools	370.113
see also Vocational education	
Vocational training	370.113
	T1—071 5
Vochysiaceae	583.73
Vodka	641.25
commercial processing	663.5
Vodou	299.675
Vodouism	299.675
Vogul	T5—945 1
Vogul language	494.51
	T6—945 1
Vogul literature	894.51
Voice	
human physiology	612.78
music	783
see Manual at 782	
preaching	251.03
rhetoric of speech	808.5
Voice (Grammar)	415.6
specific languages	T4—56
Voice culture	783.043
Voice disguisers (Musical	
instruments)	783.99
Voice disorders	
medicine	616.855 6
see also Communication	
disorders	
Voice input devices	006.454
computer engineering	621.399 4
Voice instruments	783.99
Voice mail systems	
office services	651.73

Voice output devices	006.54
computer engineering	621.399
Voice prints	
criminal investigation	363.258
Voice recognition	
biometric identification	
computer science	006.248 392
criminal investigation	363.258
Voice synthesis	006.54
computer engineering	621.399
Voiōtia (Greece)	T2—495 15
Voivodina (Serbia)	T2—497 1
Volatiles (Volcanic gases)	551.23
Volcanic ash	552.23
Volcanic gases	551.23
Volcanic rocks	552.2
Volcanoes	551.21
ancient period	551.210 901
disaster services	363.349 5
see also Disasters	
Voles	599.354
Volga languages, Middle	494.56
	T6—945 6
Volga literatures, Middle	894.56
Volga River (Russia)	T2—474
Volgograd (Russia : Oblast)	T2—474 7
Volgogradskaîa oblast'	
(Russia)	T2—474 7
Volition	153.8
Volksrust (South Africa :	
District)	T2—682 78
Volleyball	796.325
biography	796.325 092
see also Ball games	
Volleyball cards	796.325 075
Volleyball courts	796.325 068
Volleyball players	796.325 092
Vologda (Russia : Oblast)	T2—471 9
Vologodskaîa oblast'	
(Russia)	T2—471 9
Volscian language	479.7
	T6—797
Volsinii (Terni, Italy)	T2—375 76
Volsinii (Viterbo, Italy :	
Extinct city)	T2—375 83
Volsinii Novi (Extinct city)	T2—375 83
Volsinii Veteres (Italy)	T2—375 76
Volt-ammeters	621.374 6
Volta-Comoe languages	496.338
	T6—963 38
Volta River (Ghana)	T2—667
Voltage detectors	621.374 3
Voltaic languages	496.35
	T6—963 5

Vredendal (South Africa :	
District)	T2—687 32
Vryburg (South Africa :	
District)	T2—682 46
Vryheid (South Africa :	
District)	T2—684 2
VTOL aircraft	387.733 5
engineering	629.133 35
military engineering	623.746 047
transportation services	387.733 5
Vulcanization	678.24
latex	678.524
rubber	678.24
Vulcanized papers	676.284 5
Vulcanized rubber	678.34
Vulci (Extinct city)	T2—375 82
Vulgar Latin language	477
	T6—71
Vulgate Bible	220.47
Vulpes	599.775
Vultures	598.92
Vultures (New World)	598.92
Vultures (Old World)	598.94
Vulva	
gynecology	618.16
human anatomy	611.67
human physiology	612.628
Vulvar diseases	
gynecology	618.16
see also Female genital	
diseases — humans	
Vuwani (South Africa :	
District)	T2—682 57
Východočeský kraj (Czech	
Republic)	T2—437 18
Východoslovenský kraj	
(Slovakia)	T2—437 35
Vysočina kraj (Czech	
Republic)	T2—437 22

W

W*-algebras	512.556
Waadt (Switzerland)	T2—494 52
Waadtländer Nordjura	
(Switzerland)	T2—494 522 5
Wabash County (Ill.)	T2—773 78
Wabash County (Ind.)	T2—772 83
Wabash River (Ind.)	T2—772 4
Wabasha County (Minn.)	T2—776 13
Wabaunsee County (Kan.)	T2—781 61
Wachirālongkǭn, King of	
Thailand	
Thai history	959.304 5

Wade, Abdoulaye	
Senegalese history	966.305 2
Wadena County (Minn.)	T2—776 87
Wādī al-Jadīd (Egypt)	T2—622
Wading birds	598.3
sports hunting	799.243
Wafers (Electronics)	621.381 52
Waffle mixes	664.753
Waffles	641.815 3
Wage differentials	331.22
Wage discrimination	331.215 3
Wage payment systems	331.216
Wage policy	331.21
Wage-price policy	339.5
inflation control	332.415
Wage scales	331.216
personnel management	658.322 2
Wages	331.21
accounting	657.742
economics	331.21
law	344.012 1
public employees	342.068 6
personnel management	658.32
	T1—068 3
armed forces	355.64
executives	658.407 2
public administration	352.67
public administration	354.98
taxation	336.242 2
law	343.052 42
public administration	352.44
public finance	336.242 2
Wages fund theory	331.210 1
Wagga Wagga (N.S.W.)	T2—944 8
Wagner tubas	788.98
see also Brass instruments	
Wagoner County (Okla.)	T2—766 87
Wagons	388.341
agricultural use	631.373
manufacturing technology	688.6
Wagtails	598.854
Waḥdah (South Sudan)	T2—629 3
Wahhābīyah (Islamic sect)	297.814
Wahid, Abdurrahman	
Indonesian history	959.804 1
Wahkiakum County (Wash.)	T2—797 91
Waiheke Island (N.Z.)	T2—932 4
Waikato District (N.Z.)	T2—933 3
Waikato Region (N.Z.)	T2—933
Waimakariri District (N.Z.)	T2—938 2
Waimate District (N.Z.)	T2—938 93
Waipa District (N.Z.)	T2—933 57
Wairarapa (N.Z.)	T2—936 6
Wairoa District (N.Z.)	T2—934 62

Wallowa Mountains (Or.)	T2—795 73
Wallpaper	676.284 8
handicrafts	745.54
household management	645.2
interior decoration	747.3
Walls (Building element)	721.2
architecture	721.2
construction	690.12
interior decoration	747.3
Walls (Structures)	
agricultural use	631.27
architecture	725.96
Walnuts	641.345 1
botany	583.65
cooking	641.645 1
food	641.345 1
forestry	634.973 65
nut crops	634.51
Walpiri	T5—991 5
Walpiri language	499.15
	T6—991 5
Walras, Léon	
economic school	330.157
Walrus	599.799
Walsall (England :	
Metropolitan Borough)	T2—424 92
Walsh County (N.D.)	T2—784 18
Walthall County (Miss.)	T2—762 22
Waltham Forest (London,	
England)	T2—421 72
Walton County (Fla.)	T2—759 97
Walton County (Ga.)	T2—758 212
Waltzes	793.33
music	784.188 46
Walvis Bay (Namibia)	T2—688 1
Walworth County (S.D.)	T2—783 18
Walworth County (Wis.)	T2—775 89
Wampanoag Indians	974.400 497 348
	T5—973 48
Wampanoag language	497.348
	T6—973 48
Wanaka, Lake (N.Z.)	T2—939 5
Wandering Jews	584.86
Wandering Jews (Plants)	584.86
Wandsworth (London,	
England)	T2—421 66
Wanganui District (N.Z.)	T2—935 4
Wangaratta (Vic.)	T2—945 5
Wanica (Suriname :	
District)	T2—883 57
Wannsee-Konferenz (1942 :	
Berlin, Germany)	940.531 844
Wansdyke (England)	T2—423 98
Wapello County (Iowa)	T2—777 93

Wapiti	599.654 2
animal husbandry	636.294 42
big game hunting	799.276 542
conservation technology	639.979 654 2
Waqf	
law	346.064 2
Islamic law	346.167 064 2
War	355.02
arts	700.458 1
	T3C—358 1
effect on natural ecology	577.274
ethics	172.42
religion	205.624 2
Buddhism	294.356 242
Christianity	241.624 2
Hinduism	294.548 624 2
Islam	297.562 42
Judaism	296.362 42
folklore	398.278 2
history and criticism	398.358 1
law	341.6
literature	808.803 581
history and criticism	809.933 581
specific literatures	T3B—080 358 1
history and	
criticism	T3B—093 581
military science	355.02
social effects	303.485 8
social theology	201.727 3
Buddhism	294.337 273
Christianity	261.873
Hinduism	294.517 273
Islam	297.27
Judaism	296.382 7
sociology	303.66
see also Wars	
War and emergency legislation	343.01
War and emergency powers	
administrative law	342.062
constitutional law	342.041 2
War crime trials	341.690 268
War crimes	364.138
criminal investigation	363.259 38
criminal law	345.023 8
law of nations	341.69
social welfare	362.889 38
War customs	399
War dances	399
War games	
military science	355.48
recreation	793.92
computerized games	793.92
War loan interest	336.182
War memorials	725.94

War neuroses
  medicine 616.852 12
    see also Mental disorders
War news
  journalism 070.433 3
War of 1812 973.52
War of nerves 327.14
War powers (Legislative bodies) 328.346
War relief 363.349 88
War risk insurance 368.14
  see also Insurance
War risk life insurance 368.364
  see also Insurance
War victims 305.906 95
               T1—086 948
  artists 704.086 948
  arts T3C—352 694 8
  law of war 341.67
  literature 808.803 526 948
    history and criticism 809.933 526 948
  motion pictures 791.436 526 948
  social group 305.906 95
  social services 363.349 8
  theater 792.086 948
  young people 305.230 869 48
War victims as artists 704.086 948
War with Algiers, 1815 973.53
Warao Indians T5—989
Warao language 498.9
               T6—989
Warao literature 898.9
Waratahs 583.38
Warble flies 595.774
Warblers (Old World) 598.843
Ward (Law) 346.018
Ward County (N.D.) T2—784 63
Ward County (Tex.) T2—764 914
Ward management 362.173 068
  medicine 610.733
Wards (Election districts) 328.334 5
Ware County (Ga.) T2—758 794
Warehouse clubs 381.149
  management 658.879
Warehouse management 658.785
  military supplies 355.621 3
Warehouse receipts
  law 346.096
Warehouses
  architecture 725.35
Warehousing 388.044
  commerce 381
  transportation services 388.044
  see also Freight services

Warfare 355.02
  see also War
Warlocks (Occultists) 133.430 92
  see also Legendary beings
Warm-blooded animals 599
  paleozoology 569
Warmbad (South Africa :
  District) T2—682 53
Warmbaths (South Africa :
  District) T2—682 53
Warmińsko-Mazurskie
  Voivodeship (Poland) T2—438 32
Warning systems 363.35
  civil defense 363.35
  law 344.053 5
  military engineering 623.737
  public administration 353.95
Warrab State (South Sudan) T2—629 4
Warragul (Vic.) T2—945 6
Warrant officers 355.009 2
  role and function 355.332
Warrants (Law) 345.052
Warranty 343.08
Warren (N.S.W.) T2—944 9
Warren County (Ga.) T2—758 625
Warren County (Ill.) T2—773 415
Warren County (Ind.) T2—772 96
Warren County (Iowa) T2—777 82
Warren County (Ky.) T2—769 74
Warren County (Mo.) T2—778 386
Warren County (N.C.) T2—756 52
Warren County (N.J.) T2—749 78
Warren County (N.Y.) T2—747 51
Warren County (Ohio) T2—771 763
Warren County (Pa.) T2—748 67
Warren County (Tenn.) T2—768 653
Warren County (Va.) T2—755 97
Warrenton (South Africa :
  District) T2—687 14
Warrick County (Ind.) T2—772 32
Warrington (England :
  Borough) T2—427 19
Warrnambool (Vic.) T2—945 7
Wars 355.02
  history 900
  military analysis 355.48
  military science 355.02
  social services 363.349 8
  see also Disasters; War
  see Manual at 900; *also at*
    930–990

Wars between France and Holy Roman Empire, 1521–1599	
French history	944.028
Italian history	945.06
Wars of the Roses, 1455–1485	942.04
Warsaw (Poland : Voivodeship)	T2—438 41
Warsaw Ghetto	940.531 853 841
Warsaw Pact	355.031 094 7
Warsaw Treaty Organization	355.031 094 7
Warships	359.83
ancient and medieval	359.832
design	623.812 1
engineering	623.821
handling	623.882 1
naval equipment	359.83
naval units	359.32
power-driven	359.83
design	623.812 5
engineering	623.825
naval equipment	359.83
wind-driven	359.832
design	623.812 25
engineering	623.822 5
Wart snakes	597.967
Wartburgkreis (Germany : Landkreis)	T2—432 26
Warthog	599.633
Warts	
medicine	616.544
see also Skin diseases — humans	
Warwick (England : District)	T2—424 87
Warwickshire (England)	942.48
	T2—424 8
Warwickshire Avon River (England)	T2—424 4
Wasatch County (Utah)	T2—792 23
Wasatch Range (Utah and Idaho)	T2—792 2
Idaho	T2—796 44
Utah	T2—792 2
Wasco County (Or.)	T2—795 62
Waseca County (Minn.)	T2—776 195
Wash, The (England)	T2—425 3
Washabaugh County (S.D.)	T2—783 64
Washakie County (Wyo.)	T2—787 34
Washboards	
music	786.886
see also Percussion instruments	
Washburn County (Wis.)	T2—775 15

Washing clothes	
home economics	648.1
Washing coal	662.623
Washing fabrics	
home economics	648.1
Washing machines	
manufacturing technology	683.88
Washington	979.7
	T2—797
Washington (D.C.)	975.3
	T2—753
see also District of Columbia	
Washington (District)	976.803
	T2—768
Washington, George	
United States history	973.41
1789–1793	973.41
1793–1797	973.43
Washington County (Ala.)	T2—761 243
Washington County (Ark.)	T2—767 14
Washington County (Colo.)	T2—788 79
Washington County (Fla.)	T2—759 963
Washington County (Ga.)	T2—758 672
Washington County (Idaho)	T2—796 25
Washington County (Ill.)	T2—773 88
Washington County (Ind.)	T2—772 22
Washington County (Iowa)	T2—777 923
Washington County (Kan.)	T2—781 273
Washington County (Ky.)	T2—769 493
Washington County (Md.)	T2—752 91
Washington County (Me.)	T2—741 42
Washington County (Minn.)	T2—776 59
Washington County (Miss.)	T2—762 42
Washington County (Mo.)	T2—778 64
Washington County (N.C.)	T2—756 165
Washington County (N.Y.)	T2—747 49
Washington County (Neb.)	T2—782 245
Washington County (Ohio)	T2—771 98
Washington County (Okla.)	T2—766 96
Washington County (Or.)	T2—795 43
Washington County (Pa.)	T2—748 82
Washington County (R.I.)	T2—745 9
Washington County (Tenn.)	T2—768 97
Washington County (Tex.)	T2—764 245
Washington County (Utah)	T2—792 48
Washington County (Va.)	T2—755 725
Washington County (Vt.)	T2—743 4
Washington County (Wis.)	T2—775 91
Washington Parish (La.)	T2—763 11
Washita County (Okla.)	T2—766 42
Washita River (Tex. and Okla.)	T2—766 5
Washo Indians	T5—975 76

Washo language	497.576
	T6—975 76
Washoe County (Nev.)	T2—793 55
Washtenaw County (Mich.)	T2—774 35
Wāsiṭ (Iraq)	T2—567 5
Wasmosy, Juan Carlos	
Paraguayan history	989.207 42
Wasps	595.79
agricultural pests	632.79
Wasseramt (Switzerland)	T2—494 359 3
Wasseramt-Bucheggberg	
(Switzerland)	T2—494 359
Waste control	363.728
law	344.046 2
production management	658.567
public administration	353.93
social services	363.728
spacecraft	629.477 4
technology	628.4
see also Waste technology;	
Wastes	
Waste disposal	363.728
see also Waste control; Waste	
technology	
Waste heat	333.793
Waste lands	333.731 37
Waste management	363.728
see also Waste control	
Waste technology	628.4
	T1—028 6
architecture	720.475
construction	690.028 6
glassmaking	666.14
nuclear engineering	621.483 8
paper manufacturing	676.042
petroleum	665.538 9
plastics	668.419 2
rubber manufacturing	678.29
rural	628.409 173 4
wood products	674.84
see also Waste control	
Waste utilization	
production management	658.567
Wastelands	
public administration	354.34
Wastepaper pulp	676.142
Wastes	363.728
energy production	
economics	333.793 8
fuel technology	662.87
law	344.046 2
pollution technology	628.5
social services	363.728

Wastes (continued)	
utilization	
animal feed	636.085 56
production management	658.567
water pollution engineering	628.168
see also Waste control; Waste	
technology	
Wastewater	363.728 4
see also Waste control	
Watauga County (N.C.)	T2—756 843
Watchdog agencies	352.88
Watchdogs	636.73
Watches	681.114
art metalwork	739.3
technology	681.114
Watchmakers	681.114 092
Watchworks	
technology	681.112
Water	553.7
biochemistry	572.539
humans	612.015 22
chemical engineering	661.08
chemistry	546.22
disease transmission	614.43
dowsing	133.323 2
economic geology	553.7
folklore	398.26
history and criticism	398.364
geologic agent	551.35
see Manual at 551.302–.307	
vs. 551.35	
health	613.287
hydraulic engineering	627
hydraulic-power technology	621.204 22
law	346.046 91
materials science	620.198
metabolism	
human physiology	612.392 3
meteorology	551.57
plant management	658.26
prospecting	628.114
public administration	354.36
public works	
public administration	354.362 77
religious worship	202.12
resource economics	333.91
law	346.046 91
sanitary engineering	628.1
supply services	363.61
treatment engineering	628.162
Water absorption	
plants	575.76
Water-atmosphere interactions	551.524
microclimatology	551.66

Water balance	551.48
Water bears	592.72
Water beetles	595.762
Water birds	598.176
conservation technology	639.978 176
paleozoology	568.4
resource economics	333.958 28
Water bodies	551.46
	T2—16
influence on precipitation	551.577 5
physical geology	551.46
public administration	354.36
Water buffalo	636.293
animal husbandry	636.293
zoology	599.642
Water chestnuts	583.765
Water chestnuts (Lythraceae)	583.732
Water clocks	
technology	681.111
Water clovers	587.3
Water collection systems	
engineering	628.142
Water conservation	333.911 6
agriculture	631.7
engineering	628.13
law	346.046 911 6
public administration	354.363 4
resource economics	333.911 6
Water detention ponds	627.44
Water distribution systems	363.61
engineering	628.144
Water diversion	
engineering	627.123
flood control	627.45
Water drainage	
buildings	696.13
Water-electrolyte balance	
biochemistry	571.75
humans	612.015 22
Water-electrolyte imbalances	571.937 5
medicine	616.399 2
see also Digestive system	
diseases — humans	
Water features	
landscape architecture	714
Water fixtures	
buildings	696.1
Water fleas	595.32
Water games	797.25
Water gardens	635.967 4
Water gas	665.772
Water hammer	
engineering	620.106 4
Water heaters	
buildings	696.6
manufacturing technology	683.88
Water hyacinths	584.86
Water ices (Desserts)	641.863
commercial processing	637.4
home preparation	641.863
Water impoundment	
flood control	627.44
Water-lifting devices	621.69
Water lilies (Nymphaeaceae)	635.934 23
botany	584.23
floriculture	635.934 23
Water mains	628.15
Water mills	621.21
Water ouzels	598.832
Water pageantry	797.203
Water plantains	584.44
Water pollution	363.739 4
effect on natural ecology	577.627
law	344.046 343
public administration	354.363 5
sanitary engineering	628.168
social welfare	363.739 4
toxicology	571.95
see also Pollution	
Water polo	797.252
see also Aquatic sports	
Water poppy	584.44
Water power	333.914
economics	333.914
electrical engineering	621.312 134
law	343.092 4
public administration	354.362 7
Water purification	628.162
Water-repellent fabrics	677.682
see also Textiles	
Water resources	333.91
engineering	627
law	346.046 91
public administration	354.36
Water reuse	363.728 4
see also Waste control	
Water rights	
law	346.043 2
public control	346.046 91
sale and rental	333.339
Water safety	363.123
public administration	353.987
sports	797.200 289
see also Safety	
Water scavenger beetles	595.763
Water skiers	797.350 92

Water skiing	797.35	Waterclovers	587.3
biography	797.350 92	Watercolor painting	751.422
see also Aquatic sports		Watercresses	641.355 6
Water softeners		botany	583.78
buildings	696.12	cooking	641.655 6
hot-water supply	696.6	food	641.355 6
Water-soluble mediums		garden crop	635.56
painting	751.42	Waterfalls	T2—169 4
Water-soluble paints	667.63	hydrology	551.484
Water solutions	541.342 2	Waterford (Ireland)	T2—419 15
chemical engineering	660.294 22	Waterford (Ireland :	
Water spangles	587.3	County)	T2—419 1
Water sports	797	Waterfowl	598.41
see also Aquatic sports		conservation technology	639.978 41
Water storage (Plant physiology)	575.78	food	641.391
Water striders	595.754	cooking	641.691
Water supply	363.61	resource economics	333.958 41
economic geology	553.7	sports hunting	799.244
engineering	628.1	zoology	598.41
household management	644.6	Waterfowling	799.244
law	343.092 4	Waterleafs	583.958
military engineering	623.751	Waterloo (Ont.)	T2—713 45
plumbing	696.12	Waterloo (Ont. : Regional	
public administration	354.366	municipality)	T2—713 44
ships	623.854	Waterloo, Battle of, 1815	940.274 2
social services	363.61	Watermarks	676.280 27
spacecraft	629.477 3	Watermeals	584.442
see Manual at 363.61		Watermelons	641.356 15
Water table	551.492	botany	583.66
Water temperatures		commercial processing	664.805 615
meteorology	551.524	cooking	641.656 15
oceanography	551.465 3	food	641.356 15
Water towers	628.13	garden crop	635.615
Water transportation	387	Waterpower	333.914
engineering	629.048	Waterproof construction	
law	343.096	buildings	693.892
military engineering	623.8	Waterproof fabrics	677.682
public administration	354.78	*see also* Textiles	
safety	363.123	Watersheds	
law	343.096	land economics	333.73
public administration	353.987	Waterspouts (Tornadoes)	551.553
see also Marine		*see also* Tornadoes	
transportation safety		Waterton-Glacier	
transportation services	387	International Peace Park	
Water treatment	628.162	(Mont. and Alta.)	T2—786 52
Water turbines	621.24	Alberta	T2—712 34
Water voles	599.354	Montana	T2—786 52
Water witching	133.323 2	Waterton Lakes National	
Waterberg (South Africa :		Park (Alta.)	T2—712 34
District)	T2—682 53	Waterval-Boven (South	
Waterberg District		Africa : District)	T2—682 76
Municipality (South		Waterways (Inland	
Africa)	T2—682 53	transportation)	386
Waterbuck	599.645	*see also* Inland waterways	

Waterwheels	621.21
Waterworks	363.61
see also Water supply	
Watford (England)	T2—425 892
Watling Island (Bahamas)	T2—729 6
Watonwan County (Minn.)	T2—776 29
Watson, John Christian	
Australian history	994.041
Watsonian behaviorism	150.194 32
Watt-hour meters	621.374 5
Wattled crows	598.8
Wattles (Fabaceae)	583.633
botany	583.633
forestry	634.973 633
ornamental arboriculture	635.977 363 3
Wattmeters	621.374 6
Waukesha County (Wis.)	T2—775 93
Waupaca County (Wis.)	T2—775 38
Waushara County (Wis.)	T2—775 57
Wave action	551.36
Wave functions	530.124
Wave guides	
microwave electronics	621.381 331
Wave mechanics	530.124
Wave-particle duality	530.124
Wave propagation	
microwave electronics	621.381 31
radio engineering	621.384 11
Wave theories	530.14
electricity	537.12
light	535.13
modern physics	530.14
Wave transmission	
microwave electronics	621.381 31
radio engineering	621.384 11
Wavelets (Mathematics)	515.243 3
Wavell, Archibald Percival	
Wavell, Earl of	
Indian history	954.035 9
Waveney (England)	T2—426 41
Waveney, River (England)	T2—426 19
Waverley (England)	T2—422 19
Waves	
air mechanics	533.62
fluid mechanics	532.059 3
gas mechanics	533.293
liquid mechanics	532.593
mechanics	531.113 3
oceanography	551.463
quantum theory	530.124
solid mechanics	531.33
Wax beans	641.356 52
see also Snap beans	
Wax carving	736.93

Wax myrtles	583.65
Wax painting	751.46
Waxbills	598.886
Waxes	665.1
biochemistry	572.57
chemistry	547.77
sculpture material	731.2
Waxing	
woodwork	
buildings	698.33
Waxwings	598.852
Way of the Cross	232.96
Roman Catholic liturgy	264.027 4
Wayfinding	
design	744.87
Wayne County (Ga.)	T2—758 756
Wayne County (Ill.)	T2—773 792
Wayne County (Ind.)	T2—772 63
Wayne County (Iowa)	T2—777 88
Wayne County (Ky.)	T2—769 64
Wayne County (Mich.)	T2—774 33
Wayne County (Miss.)	T2—762 573
Wayne County (Mo.)	T2—778 92
Wayne County (N.C.)	T2—756 395
Wayne County (N.Y.)	T2—747 87
Wayne County (Neb.)	T2—782 57
Wayne County (Ohio)	T2—771 61
Wayne County (Pa.)	T2—748 23
Wayne County (Tenn.)	T2—768 39
Wayne County (Utah)	T2—792 54
Wayne County (W. Va.)	T2—754 47
Waynesboro (Va.)	T2—755 912
Weah, George	
Liberian history	966.620 42
Weak interaction (Nuclear	
particles)	539.754 4
Weakfish	597.725
Weakley County (Tenn.)	T2—768 24
Weald, The (England)	T2—422 5
Wealden (England)	T2—422 51
Wealth	330.16
distribution	339.2
economic theory	330.16
ethics	178
religion	205.68
Buddhism	294.356 8
Christianity	241.68
Hinduism	294.548 68
macroeconomics	339.3
Wealth tax	336.22
law	343.054

Web sites
  bibliographies   025.042 2
    specific subjects   025.06
    see Manual at 011.39 vs.
       005.3029, 016.0053,
       025.04; *also at* 011.39
       vs. 005.3029, 016.0053,
       025.0422
  cataloging   025.344
  computer science   006.7
  design   744.85
  development   006.7
  information systems   025.042 2
Web software development   006.76
Webb County (Tex.)   T2—764 462
Webcasting   006.787 6
  instructional use   371.334 678 76
  publishing   070.579 738
  sociology   302.234
Weber County (Utah)   T2—792 28
Webster County (Ga.)   T2—758 916
Webster County (Iowa)   T2—777 51
Webster County (Ky.)   T2—769 883
Webster County (Miss.) T2—762 697
Webster County (Mo.)   T2—778 823
Webster County (Neb.)   T2—782 374
Webster County (W. Va.) T2—754 65
Webster Parish (La.)   T2—763 96
Weddell Sea (Antarctic regions) 551.461 73
                      T2—167 3
Weddell seal   599.796
Wedding clothes   392.54
  commercial technology   687.16
  customs   392.54
  home sewing   646.476
  see also Clothing
Wedding music   781.587
Wedding planning   392.52
Wedding receptions   392.5
  customs   392.5
  parties   793.23
  see Manual at 392, 393, 394
    vs. 793.2
Wedding-related parties   793.23
Weddings   392.5
  customs   392.5
    dress   392.54
    see also Clothing
  etiquette   395.22
  flower arrangements   745.926
  handicrafts   745.594 1
  interior decoration   747.93
  rites   203.85

Weed killers   632.5
  agriculture   632.5
  chemical engineering   668.654
  environmental engineering 628.97
Weeding (Library collections) 025.216
Weeds   632.5
  control   363.78
    agriculture   632.5
    environmental engineering 628.97
    social services   363.78
  economic botany   581.652
Weeks   529.2
Weenen (South Africa :
  District)   T2—684 9
Weevils   595.768
  agricultural pests   632.768
Weight
  biological organisms   578.41
  plants   581.41
Weight-gaining diet
  health   613.24
Weight lifters   796.410 92
Weight lifting   613.713
  biography   796.410 92
  physical fitness   613.713
  sports   796.41
  see also Sports
Weight-losing diet
  health   613.25
Weight-losing programs
  dietetics   613.25
  exercises   613.712
  health   613.712
Weighting (Compensation)
  labor economics   331.216 6
  personnel management 658.322 2
Weightlessness
  space flight   629.418
Weights and measures   530.81
  law   343.075
  physics   530.81
  public administration   352.83
  social use   389.1
  standardization   389.62
  see also Measures
Weimar (Germany)   T2—432 241
Weimar Republic   943.085
Weimaraner (Dog)   636.752
Weimarer Land (Germany :
  Landkreis)   T2—432 24
Weinfelden (Switzerland :
  Bezirk)   T2—494 595
Weirs   627.883
Weld County (Colo.)   T2—788 72

Welsh	T5—916 6
Welsh Borders (England and Wales)	T2—424
Welsh Calvinistic Methodist Church	285.235
see also Presbyterian Church	
Welsh corgis	636.737
Welsh language	491.66
	T6—916 6
Welsh literature	891.66
English	820
Welsh Marches (England and Wales)	T2—424
Welsh pony	636.16
Welshpool (Wales)	T2—429 51
Welwitschiales	585.8
Welwyn Hatfield (England)	T2—425 86
Wendish language	491.88
	T6—918 8
Wendish literature	891.88
Wendish people	T5—918 8
Wends	T5—918 8
Wens (Disorder)	
medicine	616.53
see also Skin diseases — humans	
Wentworth (Ont.)	T2—713 52
Wepener (South Africa : District)	T2—685 7
Werdenberg (Switzerland : Wahlkreis)	T2—494 728
Werewolves	398.245 4
see also Legendary animals	
Werribee (Vic.)	T2—945 2
Weser-Ems (Germany : Regierungsbezirk)	T2—435 91
Weser River (Germany)	T2—435 9
Wesleyan Conference	287.53
see also Methodist Church	
Wesleyan Methodist Church	287.1
see also Methodist Church	
Wesleyan Reform Union	287.534
see also Methodist Church	
Wesleyan Reformers	287.53
see also Methodist Church	
Wesselsbron (South Africa : District)	T2—685 3
Wessex supremacy	942.016
West (U.S.)	978
	T2—78
art representation	704.949 978
arts	700.458 78
	T3C—358 78

West (U.S.) (continued)	
drama	808.829 358 78
history and criticism	809.293 587 8
literature	808.803 587 8
history and criticism	809.933 587 8
specific literatures	T3B—080 358 78
history and criticism	T3B—093 587 8
see also Westerns — fiction	
West (Western world)	909.098 21
	T2—182 1
West Africa	966
	T2—66
West Africans	T5—966
West Aramaic people	T5—922
West Athens (Greece)	T2—495 12
West Atlantic languages (Africa)	496.32
	T6—963 2
West Attica (Greece)	T2—495 12
West Azerbaijan (Iran)	T2—554
West Bank	956.942
	T2—569 42
ancient	933.2
	T2—332
West Baton Rouge Parish (La.)	T2—763 452
West Bengal (India)	T2—541 4
West Berkshire (England : District)	T2—422 91
West Berlin (Germany)	T2—431 554
West Branch Susquehanna River (Pa.)	T2—748 5
West Carroll Parish (La.)	T2—763 83
West Coast District Municipality (South Africa)	T2—687 32
West Coast National Park (South Africa)	T2—687 32
West Coast Region (N.Z.)	T2—937 1
West Devon (England)	T2—423 53
West Dorset (England)	T2—423 31
West Dunbartonshire (Scotland)	T2—414 32
West Feliciana Parish (La.)	T2—763 17
West Flanders (Belgium)	T2—493 12
West Frisian Islands (Netherlands)	T2—492 13
West Germanic languages	439
	T6—39
West Germanic literatures	839
West Germany (1949–1990)	943.087
	T2—43
West Glamorgan (Wales)	T2—429 82
West Indian boxwood	583.45

Western Europe	940
	T2—4
ancient	936
	T2—36
Western Finland (Finland)	T2—489 73
Western flower arrangements	745.922 4
Western folk music modes	781.263
Western France	T2—446
Western front	
World War I	940.414 4
Western Greece (Greece)	T2—495 27
Western Hemisphere	T2—181 2
Western Hemisphere	
intergovernmental	
organizations	341.245
Western Highlands (Papua New	
Guinea)	995.65
	T2—956 5
Western Hindi languages	491.43
	T6—914 3
Western Hindi literatures	891.43
Western Isles (Scotland)	T2—411 4
Western Kordofan (Sudan)	T2—628
Western Macedonia	
(Greece)	T2—495 62
Western Mediterranean	
region	T2—182 21
ancient	936
	T2—36
Western Mediterranean Sea	551.461 381
	T2—163 81
Western New Guinea (Indonesia)	995.1
	T2—951
Western Nilotic languages	496.558
	T6—965 58
Western Oregon	T2—795 1
Western Panjabi language	491.419
	T6—914 19
Western philosophy	190
Western popular music	781.64
country music	
songs	782.421 642
songs	782.421 64
Western Province (Kenya)	T2—676 28
Western Province (Papua	
New Guinea)	T2—954 9
Western Province (Solomon	
Islands)	T2—959 31
Western Province (Zambia)	T2—689 4
Western Saami languages	494.572
	T6—945 72
Western Sahara	964.8
	T2—648

Western Samar	
(Philippines)	T2—599 584
Western Sámi languages	494.572
	T6—945 72
Western Samoa	996.14
	T2—961 4
Western Samoans	T5—994 62
Western Siberia (Russia)	T2—573
Western States (U.S.)	978
	T2—78
Western stories	808.838 74
history and criticism	809.387 4
specific literatures	T3B—308 74
individual authors	T3A—3
Western Turkic languages	494.38
	T6—943 8
Western Visayas	
(Philippines)	T2—599 53
Western Washington	T2—797 6
Western world	909.098 21
	T2—182 1
Westerns	
fiction	808.838 74
history and criticism	809.387 4
specific literatures	T3B—308 74
individual authors	T3A—3
motion pictures	791.436 587 8
radio programs	791.446 587 8
television programs	791.456 587 8
Westland District (N.Z.)	T2—937 1
Westland National Park	
(N.Z.)	T2—937 1
Westlich Raron	
(Switzerland)	T2—494 794 5
Westmeath (Ireland)	T2—418 15
Westminster (London, England)	942.132
	T2—421 32
Westmoreland County (Pa.)	T2—748 81
Westmoreland County (Va.)	T2—755 24
Westmorland (N.B. :	
County)	T2—715 23
Westmount (Quebec)	T2—714 28
Weston County (Wyo.)	T2—787 14
Westonaria (South Africa :	
District)	T2—682 22
Westösterreich (Austria)	T2—436 4
Westphalia (Germany)	T2—435 6
Wet-collodion process	772.14
Wet-weather photography	778.75
Wetar Island (Indonesia)	T2—598 52
Wetland animals	591.768

White collar crime	364.168
law	345.026 8
White collar workers	331.792
	T1—086 22
labor economics	331.792
labor force	331.119 042
labor market	331.129 042
labor unions	331.883 6
personnel management	658.304 4
social class	305.55
White corpuscles	571.96
human histology	612.112
human immunology	616.079
human physiology	612.112
see also Cardiovascular system	
White County (Ark.)	T2—767 76
White County (Ga.)	T2—758 277
White County (Ill.)	T2—773 96
White County (Ind.)	T2—772 93
White County (Tenn.)	T2—768 66
White dwarfs	523.887
White elephant sales	381.195
White-footed mice	599.355
White-fronted goose	598.417 3
White mangrove	583.763
White mangrove (Combretaceae)	583.73
White Mountains (N.H. and Me.)	T2—742 2
White Nile (Sudan : State)	T2—626 4
White Nile River	T2—629 3
White perch	597.732
White Pine County (Nev.)	T2—793 15
White race	305.809
	T5—09
White River (Ark. and Mo.)	T2—767 2
White River (Ind.)	T2—772 3
White River (South Africa : District)	T2—682 73
White Rock (B.C.)	T2—711 33
White Sands National Monument (N.M.)	T2—789 65
White Sea (Russia)	551.461 324
	T2—163 24
White shark	597.33
White slave traffic	364.153 4
law	345.025 34
White supremacy political ideology	320.569 09
White-tailed deer	599.652
big game hunting	799.276 52
conservation technology	639.979 652
resource economics	333.959 652
White whale	599.542

White wine	641.222 2
commercial processing	663.222
fortified	641.222 6
sparkling	641.222 4
commercial processing	663.224
Whitefish Bay (Mich. and Ont.)	T2—774 91
Whitefishes	597.55
Whiteflies	595.752
Whitehorse (Yukon)	T2—719 1
Whites	305.809
	T5—09
race identity	305.809
Whiteshell Provincial Park (Man.)	T2—712 74
Whiteside County (Ill.)	T2—773 35
Whitetip shark	597.34
Whitewash	667.63
Whitewashing buildings	698.2
Whitfield County (Ga.)	T2—758 324
Whiting (Kingfish)	597.725
Whitings (Cods)	597.633
Whitings (Whitefishes)	597.55
Whitlam, Gough Australian history	994.062
Whitley County (Ind.)	T2—772 75
Whitley County (Ky.)	T2—769 132
Whitman County (Wash.)	T2—797 39
Whitney, Mount (Calif.)	T2—794 86
Whitsunday	263.94
devotional literature	242.38
music	781.729 3
sermons	252.64
Whitsunday Group (Qld.)	T2—943 6
Whitsunday Island National Park (Qld.)	T2—943 6
Whittling	736.4
Whole-class reading primary education	372.416 4
Whole-language approach primary education	372.62
language arts	372.62
reading	372.475
Whole life insurance	368.326
see also Insurance	
Whole tonality	781.266
Whole-word method (Reading) primary education	372.462
Wholesale clubs	381.149
management	658.879
Wholesale marketing	381.2
management	658.86
see also Commerce	

Willingdon, Freedman
  Freedman-Thomas, Marquess
  of
    Indian history   954.035 8
Willisau (Switzerland :
  Amt)   T2—494 553
Williston (South Africa :
  District)   T2—687 17
Williston Lake (B.C.)   T2—711 87
Willmore Wilderness
  Provincial Park (Alta.)   T2—712 332
Willowmore (South Africa :
  District)   T2—687 53
Willows   583.69
  botany   583.69
  ornamental arboriculture   635.977 369
Willowvale (South Africa :
  District)   T2—687 54
Wills   346.054
  genealogy   929.3
Willy-willies (Hurricanes)   551.552
  see also Hurricanes
Wilmington (Del.)   T2—751 2
Wilmington (N.C.)   T2—756 27
Wilmot Proviso, 1847   973.61
  Civil War (United States) cause 973.711 3
Wilson, Woodrow
  United States history   973.913
Wilson cloud chambers
  nuclear physics   539.777
Wilson County (Kan.)   T2—781 925
Wilson County (N.C.)   T2—756 43
Wilson County (Tenn.)   T2—768 54
Wilson County (Tex.)   T2—764 445
Wilsons Promontory
  National Park (Vic.)   T2—945 6
Wiltshire (England)   T2—423 1
Wimmera (Vic. : District)   T2—945 8
Wimmera River (Vic.)   T2—945 9
Winburg (South Africa :
  District)   T2—685 3
Winches   621.864
Winchester (England : City) T2—422 735
Winchester (Va.)   T2—755 991
Wind   551.518
  crop damage   632.16
  geologic agent   551.37
Wind bands   784.8
Wind Cave National Park
  (S.D.)   T2—783 95
Wind chimes   786.872
  see also Percussion instruments

Wind-driven ships   387.204 3
  design   623.812 043
  engineering   623.820 3
  modern   387.22
    design   623.812 2
    engineering   623.822
    handling   623.882 2
    transportation services   387.22
  transportation services   387.204 3
  see also Ships
Wind energy   333.92
Wind engines   621.45
Wind ensembles   785.43
Wind erosion   551.372
Wind instruments   788
  bands and orchestras   784
  chamber ensembles   785
  construction   788.192 3
    by hand   788.192 3
    by machine   681.88
  solo music   788
Wind loads   624.175
Wind-powered electric
  generation   621.312 136
Wind propulsion   621.45
Wind River Range (Wyo.) T2—787 6
Wind scorpions   595.48
Wind tunnels
  aircraft   629.134 52
Wind waves
  oceanography   551.463
Windham County (Conn.) T2—746 45
Windham County (Vt.)   T2—743 9
Windhoek (Namibia)   T2—688 1
Windlasses   621.864
Windmills   621.453
Window-box gardens   635.967 8
Window displays
  advertising   659.157
Window furnishings   645.3
  home sewing   646.21
  household management   645.3
  manufacturing technology   684
Window gardening   635.967 8
Window glass   666.152
Window insurance   368.6
  see also Insurance
Window managers (Systems
  software)   005.437
Windowing software   005.437

Windows	
automobile	629.266
buildings	721.823
architecture	721.823
construction	690.182 3
interior decoration	747.3
Windscreen wipers	678.35
automobile	629.276
Windscreens	
automobile	629.266
Windshield wipers	678.35
automobile	629.276
Windshields	
automobile	629.266
Windsor (N.S.)	T2—716 35
Windsor (Ont.)	T2—713 32
Windsor, Edward, Duke of	
British history	941.084
English history	942.084
Scottish history	941.108 4
Windsor, House of	941.08
British history	941.08
English history	942.08
genealogy	929.72
Scottish history	941.108
Windsor and Maidenhead	
(England)	942.296
	T2—422 96
Windsor County (Vt.)	T2—743 65
Windsor Tableland National	
Park (Qld.)	T2—943 6
Windstorm insurance	368.122
see also Insurance	
Windsurfing	797.33
Windward Islands	972.984
	T2—729 84
Wine	641.22
commercial processing	663.2
cooking with	641.622
home economics	641.22
home preparation	641.872
Wings (Air force units)	358.413 1
Wings (Airplanes)	
engineering	629.134 32
Wings (Animals)	591.479
descriptive zoology	591.479
birds	598.147 9
insects	595.714 79
physiology	573.798
Wings (Naval air units)	359.943 4
Winkler County (Tex.)	T2—764 913
Winn Parish (La.)	T2—763 66
Winnebago, Lake	T2—775 64
Winnebago County (Ill.)	T2—773 31

Winnebago County (Iowa)	T2—777 22
Winnebago County (Wis.)	T2—775 64
Winnebago Indians	T5—975 26
Winnebago language	497.526
	T6—975 26
Winneshiek County (Iowa)	T2—777 32
Winnipeg (Man.)	T2—712 743
Winnipeg, Lake (Man.)	T2—712 72
Winnipegosis, Lake (Man.)	T2—712 72
Winnipesaukee, Lake (N.H.)	T2—742 4
Winona County (Minn.)	T2—776 12
Winooski River (Vt.)	T2—743 17
Winston County (Ala.)	T2—761 74
Winston County (Miss.)	T2—762 692
Winter	508.2
music	781.524 8
see also Seasons	
Winter air conditioning	
building systems	697.933 2
Winter flounder	597.694
Winter-flowering plants	581.43
floriculture	635.953
Winter Olympic Games	796.98
see also Sports	
Winter sports	796.9
arts	700.457 9
	T3C—357 9
child care	649.57
ethics	175
human physiology	612.044
journalism	070.449 796 9
law	344.099
literature	
history and criticism	809.933 579
specific literatures	T3B—080 357 9
history and	
criticism	T3B—093 579
motion pictures	791.436 579
physical fitness	613.711
public administrative support	353.78
safety	363.14
public administration	353.97
techniques	796.902 89
sociology	306.483
television programs	791.456 579
see also Sports	
Winteraceae	584.282
Wintergreens	583.93
flavorings	641.338 2
see also Flavorings	
Winter's bark	584.282
Winterthur (Switzerland :	
Bezirk)	T2—494 574 7

Wire communication systems	384.6	Wit and humor	152.43
see also Telephone		Witbank (South Africa :	
Wire services		District)	T2—682 76
journalism	070.435	Witch hazels (Plants)	583.44
Wire-stitching		Witchcraft	203.3
bookbinding	686.35	arts	700.477
Wire walking			T3C—377
sports	796.46	literature	808.803 77
Wired communications	004.6	history and criticism	809.933 77
Wirehaired pointing griffon	636.752	specific literatures	T3B—080 377
Wireless communication	384.5	history and	
communications services	384.5	criticism	T3B—093 77
engineering	621.384	occultism	133.43
law	343.099 45	religious practice	203.3
public administration	354.75	African religions	299.613 3
Wireless communications	004.6	modern revivals	299.94
Wires		arts	T3C—382 999 4
electrical circuits	621.319 33	Native American religions	299.713 3
metal	671.842	sociology	306.4
power transmission	621.854	Witches (Occultists)	133.430 92
sculpture material	731.2	persecution by Church	272.8
structural engineering	624.177 4	*see also* Legendary beings	
Wiretapping		Witches (Religious leaders)	200.92
criminal investigation	363.252	biography	200.92
electronic engineering	621.389 28	modern revivals of old	
law	345.052	religions	299.94
Wireworms	595.765	role and function	206.1
agricultural pests	632.765	*see Manual at* 200.92 and	
Wirral (England)	T2—427 51	201–209, 292–299	
Wirt County (W. Va.)	T2—754 26	Witham, River (England)	T2—425 3
Wisconsin	977.5	Withholding tax	336.242 2
	T2—775	law	343.052 424
Wisconsin Evangelical Lutheran		Withlacoochee River (Fla.)	T2—759 7
Synod	284.134	Witness bearing	248.5
see also Lutheran church		Witnesses	347.066
Wisconsin River (Wis.)	T2—775	police interrogation	363.254
Wisdom literature (Bible)	223	trial procedure	347.075
Apocrypha	229.3	Witotoan languages	498.9
Old Testament	223		T6—989
pseudepigrapha	229.912	Witrivier (South Africa :	
Wisdom of God	212.7	District)	T2—682 73
Christianity	231.6	Witsieshoek (South Africa :	
comparative religion	202.112	District)	T2—685 1
Judaism	296.311 2	Wittmund (Germany :	
philosophy of religion	212.7	Landkreis)	T2—435 917
Wisdom of Solomon (Bible)	229.3	Witwatersrand (South	
Wise County (Tex.)	T2—764 532	Africa)	T2—682 2
Wise County (Va.)	T2—755 743	Wives	306.872 3
Wise men (Christian doctrines)	232.923		T1—086 55
Wisent	599.643	social welfare	362.839 52
Wismar (Germany)	T2—431 76	*see also* Married women	
Wisterias	635.933 63	Wives of alcoholics	
botany	583.63	social welfare	362.292 3
floriculture	635.933 63		

Wives of clergymen
  Christianity 253.22
  see also Spouses of
    clergy — Christianity
Wives of substance abusers
  social welfare 362.291 3
Wizardry 133.43
  occultism 133.43
  religious practice 203.3
    modern revivals 299.94
Wizards (Occultists) 133.430 92
  see also Legendary beings
Wizards (Religious leaders) 200.92
  biography 200.92
  role and function 206.1
  see Manual at 200.92 and
    201–209, 292–299
Włocławek (Poland :
  Voivodeship) T2—438 26
Wobblies 331.886 097 3
Wodehouse (South Africa :
  District) T2—687 57
Wodonga (Vic.) T2—945 5
Województwo Dolnośląskie
  (Poland) T2—438 52
Województwo
  Kujawsko-Pomorskie
  (Poland) T2—438 26
Województwo Łódzkie
  (Poland) T2—438 47
Województwo Lubelskie
  (Poland) T2—438 43
Województwo Lubuskie
  (Poland) T2—438 12
Województwo Małopolskie
  (Poland) T2—438 62
Województwo Mazowieckie
  (Poland) T2—438 41
Województwo Opolskie
  (Poland) T2—438 55
Województwo Podkarpackie
  (Poland) T2—438 66
Województwo Podlaskie
  (Poland) T2—438 36
Województwo Pomorskie
  (Poland) T2—438 22
Województwo Śląskie
  (Poland) T2—438 58
Województwo
  Świętokrzyskie (Poland) T2—438 45
Województwo
  Warmińsko-Mazurskie
  (Poland) T2—438 32

Województwo
  Wielkopolskie (Poland) T2—438 49
Województwo
  Zachodniopomorskie
  (Poland) T2—438 16
Wok cooking 641.774
Woking (England) T2—422 142
Wokingham (England :
  District) T2—422 94
Wolds, The (England) T2—428 3
Wolf children 155.456 7
Wolf-Rayet stars 523.88
Wolfe County (Ky.) T2—769 213
Wolfhounds 636.753 5
Wolfram 669.734
  see also Tungsten
Wolframite
  mineralogy 549.74
Wolfsbanes 583.34
Wolfville (N.S.) T2—716 34
Wollastonite
  mineralogy 549.66
Wollongong (N.S.W.) T2—944 6
Wolmaransstad (South
  Africa : District) T2—682 43
Wolof (African people) T5—963 214
Wolof language 496.321 4
     T6—963 214
Wolof literature 896.321 4
Wolverhampton (England) T2—424 91
Wolverine 599.766
Wolves 599.773
  animal husbandry 636.977 3
  conservation technology 639.979 773
  predator control technology 636.083 9
    conservation technology 639.966
  resource economics 333.959 773
  zoology 599.773
Wombats 599.24
Women 305.4
     T1—082
  advertising images and themes 659.104 552 2
  art representation 704.942 4
  arts 700.452 2
     T3C—352 2
  Bible 220.830 54
  biography 920.72
  civil and human rights 323.34
    see also Women's rights
  criminal offenders 364.374
  drawing 743.44
  education 371.822
  etiquette 395.144
  fine arts 704.042

Women (continued)			
government programs	353.535	
grooming	646.704 2	
health	613.042 44	
journalism for	070.483 47	
labor economics	331.4	
legal status	346.013 082	
constitutional law	342.087 8	
private law	346.013 082	
United States	346.730 130 82	
literature	808.803 522	
history and criticism	809.933 522	
specific literatures	T3B—080 352 2	
history and		
criticism	T3B—093 522	
painting	757.4	
physical fitness	613.704 5	
political organizations	324.3	
psychology	155.333	
recreation	790.194	
indoor	793.019 4	
outdoor	796.082	
relations with government	323.34	
religion	200.82	
Christianity	270.082	
devotional literature	242.643	
guides to Christian life	248.843	
guides to life	204.408 2	
Islam	297.082	
guides to life	297.570 82	
Judaism	296.082	
guides to life	296.708 2	
see also Women and religion		
roller skating	796.210 82	
sex hygiene	613.954	
social aspects	305.4	
social welfare	362.83	
public administration	353.535	
suffrage	324.623	
see Manual at T1—081 and		
T1—08351, T1—08352,		
T1—08421, T1—08422		
Women and religion	200.82	
see also Women — religion		
Women authors (Literature)	808.899 287	
specific literatures	T3B—099 287	
Women clergy	200.92	
biography	200.92	
Christian	270.092	
biography	270.092	
specific denominations	280	
see Manual at 230–280		
ordination	262.140 82	

Women clergy		
Christian (continued)	
pastoral theology	253.082
see also Clergy — Christian	
Judaism	296.092
see also Women rabbis	
ordination	206.108 2
role and function	206.108 2
see Manual at 200.92 and	
201–209, 292–299	
Women in arts	700.82
Women in combat	355.408 2
Women in education	370.82
Women in secondary education	373.082
Women of the Bible	220.920 82
Women rabbis	296.092
biography	296.092
specific denominations	296.8
ordination	296.610 82
role and function	296.610 82
Women workers	331.4
economics	331.4
public administration	354.908 2
sociology	305.43
Women's baseball	796.357 8
Women's basketball	796.323 8
Women's clothing	391.2
commercial technology	687.082
customs	391.2
home economics	646.34
home sewing	646.404
see also Clothing	
Women's football	796.332 8
Women's movements	305.42
Women's political organizations	324.3
Women's prisons	365.43
see also Penal institutions	
Women's rights	323.34
law	342.087 8
law of nations	341.485 8
political science	323.34
sociology	305.42
Women's shelters	362.838 3
Women's suffrage	324.623
Women's units (Armed forces)	355.348
Women's voices	782.6
choral and mixed voices	782.6
single voices	783.6
Wonderboom (South	
Africa : District)	T2—682 27
Wood	575.46
architectural construction	721.044 8
architectural decoration	729.6
biology	575.46

Wood (continued)	
building material	691.1
fuel	333.953 97
chemical technology	662.65
resource economics	333.953 97
handicrafts	745.51
lumber technology	674
materials science	620.12
sculpture material	731.2
ship design	623.818 4
shipbuilding	623.820 7
structural engineering	624.184
Wood boring beetles	595.764 8
Wood briquettes	662.65
Wood Buffalo National Park	
(Alta.)	T2—712 32
Wood carving	736.4
Wood construction	694
Wood County (Ohio)	T2—771 16
Wood County (Tex.)	T2—764 223
Wood County (W. Va.)	T2—754 22
Wood County (Wis.)	T2—775 52
Wood duck	598.412 3
conservation technology	639.978 412 3
resource economics	333.958 412 3
Wood engraving	761.2
Wood flour	674.84
Wood laminates	674.835
see also Wood	
Wood lice	595.372
Wood mice (Apodemus)	599.358 5
Wood mice (Peromyscus)	599.355
Wood oil	665.33
Wood pavements	625.83
Wood products	674.8
Wood products workers	674.809 2
Wood pulp	676.12
Wood rats	599.357 3
Wood sculpturing	731.462
Wood shavings	674.84
Wood shrews	599.332
Wood shrikes	598.8
Wood snakes	597.967
Wood sorrels	583.68
Wood-stove cooking	641.58
Wood swallows	598.8
Wood technology	
equipment manufacturing	
technology	681.767 6
Wood turtle	597.925 7
Wood-using technologies	674.8
Wood warblers	598.872
Woodburning	745.514
Woodbury County (Iowa)	T2—777 41
Woodchuck	599.366
small game hunting	799.259 366
Woodcocks	598.33
sports hunting	799.243 3
Woodcraft	
camp activity	796.545
Woodcreepers	598.822
Wooden furniture	645.4
manufacturing technology	684.104
see also Furniture	
Wooden ships	
construction	623.820 7
Wooden shoes	391.413
commercial technology	685.32
customs	391.413
see also Clothing	
Woodend (Vic.)	T2—945 3
Woodenware	674.88
Woodford County (Ill.)	T2—773 53
Woodford County (Ky.)	T2—769 465
Woodland Indians	T5—97
Woodlands	333.75
	T2—152
see also Forest lands	
Woodlark Island (Papua	
New Guinea)	T2—954 1
Woodlots	
agroforestry	634.99
Woodpeckers	598.72
Woodruff County (Ark.)	T2—767 92
Woods (Golf equipment)	796.352 32
Woods, Lake of the	T2—776 81
Canada	T2—713 11
Minnesota	T2—776 81
Woods County (Okla.)	T2—766 21
Woodson County (Kan.)	T2—781 923
Woodspring (England)	T2—423 96
Woodward County (Okla.)	T2—766 19
Woodwind bands	784.89
Woodwind instruments	788.2
bands and orchestras	784
chamber ensembles	785
mixed	785.2–.5
single type	785.8
construction	788.219 23
by hand	788.219 23
by machine	681.882
solo music	788.2
Woodwork	
interior decoration	747.3
Woodworking	684.08
carpentry	694
home workshops	684.08
lumber technology	674

Woody plants	582.16	Words (continued)	
landscape architecture	715	specific languages	T4—014
Woody vines	582.18	dictionaries	T4—3
Wool		usage (Applied	
animal husbandry	636.088 45	linguistics)	T4—81
Wool growing	636.314 5	*see Manual at* T4—3 vs.	
Wool textiles	677.31	T4—81	
arts	746.043 1	usage (Applied linguistics)	418
see also Textiles		Work	331
Wool wax	665.13	social theology	
Woolly monkeys	599.858	Christianity	261.85
Worcester (England)	T2—424 48	*see also* Labor	
Worcester (South Africa :		Work (Mechanics)	531.6
District)	T2—687 33	Work (Physiological exertion)	573.79
Worcester County (Mass.)	T2—744 3	human physiology	612.042
Worcester County (Md.)	T2—752 21	Work animals	636.088 6
Worcestershire (England)	942.44	Work areas	
	T2—424 4	home economics	643.58
Word-attack skills (Reading)		Work associates	
primary education	372.46	applied psychology	158.26
Word classes	415	psychological influence	155.926
specific languages	T4—5	Work at home	
Word dividers (Dictionaries)	413.1	labor economics	331.256 7
specific languages	T4—31	Work camps (Correctional	
Word formation	415.92	programs)	365.34
specific languages	T4—592	*see also* Penal institutions	
Word games	793.734	Work cars	385.32
computerized games	793.734	engineering	625.22
Word grammar	415.018 4	transportation services	385.32
specific languages	T4—501 84	*see also* Rolling stock	
Word of God		Work environment	331.256
Bible	220.13	economics	331.256
Jesus Christ	232.2	engineering	620.8
Word order	415	personnel management	658.38
specific languages	T4—5	public administration	352.67
Word origins	412	public administration	354.98
specific languages	T4—2	safety	363.11
Word processing	005.52	public administration	353.96
Word-recognition method		*see also* Industrial safety	
primary education	372.462	sanitation	363.729 5
Word sense disambiguation		public administration	353.94
natural language processing	401.430 285 635	Work ethic	306.361 3
specific languages	T4—014 302 856 35	Work force	331.11
Word study		Work-force diversity	331.133
primary education	372.61	personnel management	658.300 8
Word usage		Work furloughs	
rhetoric	808	penology	365.65
Words	401.4	Work groups	658.402 2
	T1—014	*see also* Work teams	
dictionaries	413	Work load	
music	780	production management	658.54
treatises	780.268	Work music	781.593

Work periods	331.257	Worker rights	331.011
economics	331.257	law	344.010 1
personnel management	658.312 1	Worker security	331.259 6
public administration	352.67	law	344.012 596
public administration	354.98	public employees	342.068 6
Work places	331.256	public administration	354.98
see also Work environment		Worker self-management	338.69
Work pressures		personnel management	658.315 2
executive management	658.409 5	theory of union role	331.880 1
Work productivity		Workers	331.11
personnel management		economics	331.11
public administration	352.66	public administration	354.9
promotion of		social class	305.562
personnel management	658.314	Workers' compensation	
Work release		insurance	368.41
penology	365.65	employers' liability	368.56
Work satisfaction	331.012	government-sponsored	368.41
see also Job satisfaction		law	344.021
Work sharing	331.257 2	personnel management	658.325 4
Work shifts	331.257 25	public administration	353.69
Work songs	782.421 593	*see also* Insurance	
Work stress		Workers with developmental	
labor economics	331.256	disabilities	331.595
Work studies		Workers with disabilities	331.59
production management	658.54	economics	331.59
Work-study plan	371.227	government programs	354.908 7
higher education	378.37	law	344.015 9
secondary education	373.28	personnel management	658.300 87
Work-study programs	371.225	Workers with hearing	
higher education	378.365	impairments	331.592
Work teams	658.402 2	Workers with visual impairments	331.591
group decision making	658.403 6	Workflow	
internal organization	658.402 2	production management	658.53
personnel utilization		Workhouses (Correctional	
public administration	352.66	institutions)	365.34
production management	658.533	*see also* Penal institutions	
quality control	658.562	Working capital	332.041 2
Work training	370.113	financial management	658.152 44
see also Vocational education		Working class	305.562
Work vehicles			T1—086 23
automotive engineering	629.225	civil rights	323.322 3
driving	629.284 5	customs	390.1
repair	629.287 5	dress	391.01
Workaholism		lower class	T1—086 24
personality trait	155.232	middle class	T1—086 23
Workbooks	T1—076	relations with government	323.322 3
Workday	331.257 23	social welfare	362.85
economics	331.257 23	public administration	354.9
personnel management	658.312 1	Working-class parties	324.217
Worker control of industry	338.69	international organizations	324.17
production economics	338.69	Working conditions (Physical)	331.256
theory of union role	331.880 1	*see also* Work environment	
Worker parties	324.217		
international organizations	324.17		

Working dogs (Breeds of dogs)	636.73
see Manual at 636.70886, 636.70888 vs. 636.73, 636.752	
Working dogs (Dogs as working animals)	636.708 86
see Manual at 636.70886, 636.70888 vs. 636.73, 636.752	
Working environment	331.256
see also Work environment	
Working mothers	
economics	331.44
Working ships	387.2
engineering	623.82
power-driven	387.248
engineering	623.824
transportation services	387.248
small craft	387.204 26
engineering	623.820 26
transportation services	387.204 26
transportation services	387.2
wind-driven	387.226
engineering	623.822 6
transportation services	387.226
see also Ships	
Workmen's compensation insurance	368.41
see also Workers' compensation insurance	
Workplace diversity	331.133
personnel management	658.300 8
Workplace environment	331.256
see also Work environment	
Workplace violence	
prevention	
management	658.473
Workplaces	331.256
see also Work environment	
Workshops (Seminars)	T1—071 5
Workshops (Workrooms)	
agriculture	631.304
Workstations (Microcomputers)	004.16
see also Personal computers	
Workweek	331.257
economics	331.257
personnel management	658.312 1
World Bank	332.153 2
law	346.082 153 2
World-circling travel	910.41
World community	
law of nations	341.2
World Community of al-Islam in the West	297.87

World Court	341.552
World Cup competition	
soccer	796.334 668
World fairs	907.4
see also Exhibitions	
World government	321.04
law	341.21
World history	909
arts	700.458 2
	T3C—358 2
literature	808.803 582
history and criticism	809.933 582
specific literatures	T3B—080 358 2
history and criticism	T3B—093 582
World music	780
see Manual at 781.6 vs. 780, 780.9	
World Party of Socialist Revolution	324.175
World politics and religion	
social theology	201.727
Christianity	261.7
Judaism	296.382 7
see also Politics and religion — social theology	
World series (Baseball)	796.357 646
World Trade Organization	382.92
World views	140
World War I, 1914–1918	940.3
	T1—090 41
societies	369.2
United States	369.186
World War II, 1939–1945	940.53
	T1—090 44
Netherlands	940.534 92
societies	369.2
United States	369.186
World Wide Web	025.042
computer science	004.678
hypertext	006.7
information management	
public administration	352.380 285 467 8
information systems	025.042
publishing	070.579 73
sociology	302.231
see Manual at 004.678 vs. 006.7, 025.042, 384.33	
Worm-caused diseases	571.999
agriculture	632.623
animals	571.999 1
veterinary medicine	636.089 696 2

Worm-caused diseases (continued)
  humans
    incidence   614.552
    medicine   616.962
    see also Communicable
      diseases — humans
  plants   571.999 2
    agriculture   632.623
Worm culture   639.75
WORM discs   004.565
  engineering   621.397 67
Worm farming   639.75
Worm gears   621.833 3
Worm lizards   597.948
Worm snakes   597.969
Worms   592.3
  agricultural pests   632.623
  culture   639.75
  paleozoology   562.3
  plant crop pests   632.623
Worms (Computer security)   005.88
Worms (Germany)   T2—434 352
Wormwood   641.338 2
  botany   583.983
  see also Flavorings; Herbs
Wororan languages   499.15
      T6—991 5
Worry   152.46
Worship   204.3
  Buddhism   294.344 3
  Christianity   248.3
  Hinduism   294.543
  Islam   297.3
    Sufi   297.43
  Judaism   296.45
Worth
  epistemology   121.8
Worth County (Ga.)   T2—758 945
Worth County (Iowa)   T2—777 232
Worth County (Mo.)   T2—778 143
Worthing (England)   T2—422 68
Wounds
  biology   571.975
  incidence   614.3
  medicine   617.1
Woven felt   677.62
  see also Textiles
Wrangel Island (Russia)   T2—577
Wrangell-Saint Elias
  National Park and
  Preserve (Alaska)   T2—798 3
Wrapping paper   676.287

Wraps (Clothing)   391.46
  commercial technology   687.19
  home sewing   646.45
  see also Outerwear
Wraps (Stuffed foods)   641.84
Wrasses   597.7
Wreaths   745.926
Wreckage studies
  aeronautics   629.132 55
  automotive   629.282 6
  naval architecture   623.817 6
  seamanship   623.888 5
  structural analysis   624.176
Wrecking bars   621.93
Wrecking buildings   690.26
Wrekin, The (England :
  District)   T2—424 56
Wren-tit   598.834
Wrenches   621.972
Wrens   598.833
Wrestlers   796.812 092
Wrestling   796.812
  biography   796.812 092
  see also Combat sports
Wrexham (Wales: County
  Borough)   T2—429 39
Wrexham Maelor (Wales)   T2—429 39
Wright County (Iowa)   T2—777 274
Wright County (Minn.)   T2—776 51
Wright County (Mo.)   T2—778 825
Wrigley (N.W.T.)   T2—719 3
Wrinkle-resistant fabrics   677.681
  see also Textiles
Wrist techniques
  music   784.193 64
Wrists   612.97
  physiology   612.97
  regional medicine   617.574
  surgery   617.574
  see also Upper extremities
Write once read many discs   004.565
  engineering   621.397 67
Write once read many drives   004.565
  engineering   621.397 67
Writing
  personal improvement
    applied psychology   158.16
  therapeutic use
    medicine   615.851 63
    psychiatry   616.891 663
Writing (Manual skill)   652.1
Writing instruments
  manufacturing technology   681.6

X

Xenosauridae	597.959
Xenungulata	569.62
Xeroderma	
medicine	616.544
see also Skin diseases — humans	
Xerography	686.442
equipment manufacturing technology	681.65
office use	652.4
technology	686.442
Xeronemataceae	584.7
Xhariep District Municipality (South Africa)	T2—685 7
Xhosa (African people)	T5—963 985
Xhosa language	496.398 5
	T6—963 985
Xhosa literature	896.398 5
Xiang dialects	495.179 512 15
	T6—951 7
Xinca language	497.9
	T6—979
Xinjiang Uygur Zizhiqu (China)	T2—516
Xinjiang Weiwuer Zizhiqu (China)	T2—516
Xiphiidae	597.78
Xiphosura	595.492
paleozoology	565.492
Xizang Zizhiqu (China)	T2—515
Xoloitzcuintli	636.76
Xosa language	496.398 5
	T6—963 985
Xosa literature	896.398 5
Xylariales	579.567
Xylem	575.46
Xylophones	786.843
see also Percussion instruments	
Xyridaceae	584.9

Y

Yacht basins	
engineering	627.38
Yacht racing	797.14
see also Aquatic sports	
Yachting	797.124 6
see also Aquatic sports	
Yachts	387.204 23
engineering	623.820 23
handling	623.881 23

Yachts (continued)	
power-driven	387.231 4
engineering	623.823 14
transportation services	387.231 4
transportation services	387.204 23
wind-driven	387.223
design	623.812 23
engineering	623.822 3
transportation services	387.223
see also Ships	
Yad ha-ḥazaḳah	296.181 2
YaDabub behér béhérasbočenā hezboč kelel (Ethiopia)	T2—633
Yadayim	296.123 6
Yadkin County (N.C.)	T2—756 66
Yadkin River (N.C.)	T2—756 68
Yagua language	498.9
	T6—989
Yahya Khan, Aga Muhammad Pakistani history	954.904 6
Yajurveda	294.592 14
Yak	599.642 2
Yaka (African people)	T5—963 93
Yakama Indians	979.700 497 412 7
	T5—974 127
Yakama language	497.412 7
	T6—974 127
Yakima County (Wash.)	T2—797 55
Yakima River (Wash.)	T2—797 55
Yakut	T5—943 32
Yakut language	494.332
	T6—943 32
Yakut literature	894.332
Yakutat (Alaska)	T2—798 2
Yakutia (Russia)	T2—575
Yalobusha County (Miss.)	T2—762 82
Yalova İli (Turkey)	T2—563 3
ancient	T2—393 13
Yamagata-ken (Japan)	T2—521 16
Yamaguchi-ken (Japan)	T2—521 97
Yamal-Nenets (Russia)	T2—573
Yamal-Nenetskiĭ avtonomnyĭ okrug (Russia)	T2—573
Yamanashi-ken (Japan)	T2—521 64
Yambasa languages	496.396
	T6—963 96
Yambol (Bulgaria : Oblast)	T2—499 55
Yamhill County (Or.)	T2—795 39
Yami (Taiwan people)	T5—992 5
Yamoussoukro (Ivory Coast)	T2—666 8

Yams (Convolvulaceae)		Yarn	677.028 62
botany	583.959	home sewing	646.19
Yams (Dioscorea)	641.352 3	manufacturing technology	677.028 62
agriculture	635.23	Yaroslavl′ (Russia : Oblast)	T2—473 2
botany	584.52	Yarra River (Vic.)	T2—945 2
commercial processing	664.805 23	Yaruro language	498.9
cooking	641.652 3		T6—989
food	641.352 3	Yass (N.S.W.)	T2—944 7
Yams (Sweet potatoes)	641.352 2	Yates County (N.Y.)	T2—747 82
see also Sweet potatoes		Yaunde-Fang languages	496.396
Yancey County (N.C.)	T2—756 873		T6—963 96
Yang ch'ins	787.74	Yavapai County (Ariz.)	T2—791 57
see also Stringed instruments		Yavapai Indians	T5—975 724
Yangtze River (China)	T2—512	Yavapai language	497.572 4
Yankton County (S.D.)	T2—783 394		T6—975 724
Yanomam languages	498.92	Yaw (Aeronautics)	629.132 364
	T6—989 2	Yawning	
Yanomamo Indians	305.898 92	human physiology	612.21
	T5—989 2	Yaws	
Yanomamo language	498.92	medicine	616.523
	T6—989 2	*see also* Skin diseases —	
Yanzi language	496.396	humans	
	T6—963 96	Yayi, Boni	
Yao (African people)	T5—963 97	Beninese history	966.830 54
Yao (Southeast Asian		Yazd (Iran : Province)	T2—559 4
people)	T5—959 78	Yazoo County (Miss.)	T2—762 49
Yao language (Southeastern		Yazoo Mississippi Delta	
Asia)	495.978	(Miss. : Region)	T2—762 4
	T6—959 78	Yazoo River (Miss.)	T2—762 4
Yao languages (Africa)	496.397	Year-round school	371.236
	T6—963 97	Year-round systems	
Yao literature (Southeastern		air conditioning	697.933 4
Asia)	895.978	Yearbooks	050
Yaoundé (Cameroon)	T2—671 1		T1—05
Yap (Micronesia)	T2—966	encyclopedia	030
Yapese language	499.52	publishing	070.572
	T6—995 2	Yearly Conference of People	
Ya'qūb al-Ḥaḍramī		Called Methodists	287.53
Koran readings	297.122 404 52	*see also* Methodist Church	
Yaqui Indians	T5—974 542	Years	529.2
Yaqui language	497.454 2	Yeast breads	641.815
	T6—974 542	Yeasts	579.562
Yaqui literature	897.454 2	Yeasts (Basidiomycetes)	579.59
Yaracuy (Venezuela)	T2—872 6	Yeasts (Common yeasts)	579.563
Yar'adua, Umaru Musa		leaven	664.68
Nigerian history	966.905 5	Yeasts (Saccharomycetaceae)	579.562
Yard goods	677.632	Yell County (Ark.)	T2—767 38
Yard sales	381.195	Yellow-dog contracts	331.894
management	658.87	Yellow-eyed grass	584.9
see also Commerce		Yellow fever	
Yards		incidence	614.541
landscape architecture	712.6	medicine	616.918 54
Yare, River (England)	T2—426 1	*see also* Communicable	
Yarmouth (N.S. : County)	T2—716 31	diseases — humans	

Yellow-green algae	579.82
Yellow Medicine County	
(Minn.)	T2—776 37
Yellow pages (Directories)	T1—029
see Manual at T1—025 vs.	
T1—029	
Yellow poplar	584.286
forestry	634.974
Yellow River (China)	T2—511
Yellow Sea	551.461 456
	T2—164 56
Yellowknife (N.W.T.)	T2—719 3
Yellowstone County	
(Mont.)	T2—786 39
Yellowstone National Park	T2—787 52
Montana	T2—786 661
Yellowstone River	T2—786 3
Yellowwoods	585.3
Yeltsin, Boris Nikolayevich	
Russian history	947.086 1
Yemen	953.3
	T2—533
ancient	939.49
	T2—394 9
Yemen (People's Democratic	
Republic)	953.350 52
	953.350 52
	T2—533 5
	T2—533 5
Yemen (Republic of Yemen)	953.305 3
	T2—533
Yemen (Yemen Arab Republic)	953.320 52
	T2—533 2
Yemen Arab Republic	953.320 52
	T2—533 2
Yemenis	T5—927 533
Northern Yemen	T5—927 533 2
Southern Yemen	T5—927 533 5
Yên Bái (Vietnam :	
Province)	T2—597 1
Yenisei Ostyak	T5—946
Yenisei-Ostyak language	494.6
	T6—946
Yenisei Samoyed language	494.4
	T6—944
Yeppoon (Qld.)	T2—943 5
Yersinia	579.34
Yersinia infections	
incidence	614.573
medicine	616.923
see also Communicable	
diseases — humans	
Yeshivot	296.071 1

Yevamot	296.123 3
Babylonian Talmud	296.125 3
Mishnah	296.123 3
Palestinian Talmud	296.124 3
Yevrey Autonomous Region	
(Russia)	T2—577
Yews	585.6
Yeye language	496.399
	T6—963 99
Yezidis	
religion	299.159
Yi dynasty	951.902
Yiddish language	439.1
	T6—391
Yiddish literature	839.1
Yield point (Mechanics)	531.381
Yields	
crop production	631.558
Yin dynasty	931.02
Yindjibarndi language	499.15
	T6—991 5
YMCA (Association)	267.3
Ynys Môn (Wales)	T2—429 21
Yo-Yos	796.2
Yoakum County (Tex.)	T2—764 849
Yobe State (Nigeria)	T2—669 87
Yodo River (Japan)	T2—521 83
Yoga	181.45
Buddhism	294.344 36
comparative religion	204.36
health	613.704 6
see Manual at 613.7046	
vs. 615.824, 615.851,	
615.852, 616–618	
Hinduism	294.543 6
philosophy	181.45
psychological therapies	
medicine	615.851
see Manual at 613.7046	
vs. 615.824, 615.851,	
615.852, 616–618	
spiritual therapies	
medicine	615.852
see Manual at 613.7046	
vs. 615.824, 615.851,	
615.852, 616–618	
therapeutics	615.824
see Manual at 613.7046	
vs. 615.824, 615.851,	
615.852, 616–618	
Yogacara Buddhism	294.392

Young men
under twenty-one (continued)
   journalism for   070.483 36
   psychology   155.532
   publications for
    bibliographies   011.624 1
   sex hygiene   613.953
   social aspects   305.235 1
   social welfare   362.708 3
   see also Adolescent boys
   see Manual at T1—081 and
    T1—08351, T1—08352,
    T1—08421, T1—08422
Young Men's Christian
  Association camps   796.542 2
Young Men's Christian
  Associations   267.3
Young parents
  social welfare   362.787 4
Young people   305.23
           T1—083
  arts   700.452 3
           T3C—352 3
  civil and human rights   323.352
   law   342.087 72
  education   371.82
  government programs   353.536
  grooming   646.704 6
  guides to religious life   204.408 3
   Christianity   248.82
   Judaism   296.708 3
  journalism for   070.483 2
  legal aid   362.716
  legal status   346.013 083
   constitutional law   342.087 72
   private law   346.013 083
  libraries for   027.625
  literature   808.803 523
   history and criticism   809.933 523
   specific literatures   T3B—080 352 3
    history and
     criticism   T3B—093 523
  material assistance   362.71
  publications for
   bibliographies   011.62
   reviews   028.162
  reading
   library science   028.5
  reading interests   028.55
  relations with government   323.352

Young people (continued)
  religion   200.83
   Christianity   270.083
    devotional literature   242.62
    pastoral care   259.2
    religious education   268.432
   Judaism   296.083
    religious education   296.680 83
  sex hygiene   613.951
  social aspects   305.23
  social welfare   362.7
   public administration   353.536
Young people's books
  bibliographies   011.62
Young people's societies   369.4
  biography   369.409 2
Young women   305.242 2
           T1—084 22
  etiquette   395.124 2
  journalism for   070.483 47
  psychology   155.65
  social aspects   305.242 2
  social welfare   362
  under twenty-one   305.235 2
           T1—083 52
   etiquette   395.123 3
   health   613.042 43
   journalism for   070.483 37
   psychology   155.533
   publications for
    bibliographies   011.624 2
   sex hygiene   613.955
   social welfare   362.708 3
  victims of crimes   362.880 842 2
  see Manual at T1—081 and
    T1—08351, T1—08352,
    T1—08421, T1—08422
Young Women's Christian
  Associations   267.5
Young workers   331.34
Youngstown (Ohio)   T2—771 39
Youth   305.235
           T1—083 5
  over twenty   305.242
           T1—084 2
  see also Young adults
  see also Adolescents
Youth hostels   910.466
  see also Lodging (Temporary
    housing)
Yozgat İli (Turkey)   T2—563 8
  ancient   T2—393 32
Ytterbium
  chemistry   546.419

Zamakhsharī, Maḥmūd ibn 'Umar
   Koran commentary   297.122 74
Zambales (Philippines)   T2—599 152
Zambezi River   T2—679
Zambézia (Mozambique)   T2—679 6
Zambia   968.94
    T2—689 4
Zambians   T5—968 94
Zamboanga del Norte
    (Philippines : Province)   T2—599 783
Zamboanga del Sur
    (Philippines)   T2—599 785
Zamboanga Peninsula
    (Philippines : Region)   T2—599 78
Zamboanga Sibugay
    (Philippines)   T2—599 787
Zamfara State (Nigeria)   T2—669 61
Zamora (Spain : Province)   T2—462 4
Zamora-Chinchipe
    (Ecuador)   T2—866 44
Zamość (Poland :
    Voivodeship)   T2—438 43
Zamucoan languages   498.9
    T6—989
Zande (African people)   T5—963 61
Zande language   496.361
    T6—963 61
Zander   597.758
Zanichelliaceae   584.74
Zanjān (Iran : Province)   T2—551 6
Zante (Greece)   T2—495 5
Zanzibar   967.81
    T2—678 1
Zanzibar Central/South
    (Tanzania)   T2—678 1
Zanzibar North (Tanzania)   T2—678 1
Zanzibar Urban/West
    (Tanzania)   T2—678 1
Západočeský kraj (Czech
    Republic)   T2—437 14
Západoslovenský kraj
    (Slovakia)   T2—437 33
Zaparoan languages   498.9
    T6—989
Zapata County (Tex.)   T2—764 483
Zaporizhzhya (Ukraine :
    Oblast)   T2—477 3
Zaporiz´ka oblast´ (Ukraine)   T2—477 3
Zapotec Indians   T5—976 8
Zapotec language   497.68
    T6—976 8
Zapotec literature   897.68
Zapotecan languages   497.68
    T6—976 8

Zaragoza (Spain : Province)   T2—465 53
Zaramo language   496.391
    T6—963 91
Zardārī, Āṣif 'Alī
    Pakistani history   954.910 532
Zarma (African people)   T5—965 8
Zarma language   496.58
    T6—965 8
Zarqā' (Jordan : Province)   T2—569 593
    ancient   T2—335 93
Zarwāl, al-Yamīn
    Algerian history   965.054
Zarzuelas   782.12
    music   782.12
    stage presentation   792.5
Zastron (South Africa :
    District)   T2—685 7
Zavala County (Tex.)   T2—764 437
Zavim   296.123 6
Zawā'id   297.125 64
Zaydī school (Islamic law)
    religious law   297.140 182 4
Zaydī school (Islamic law)   340.590 182 4
Zaydites (Islamic sect)   297.824
    Hadith   297.125 924
    Koran commentary   297.122 755
    religious law   297.140 182 4
Zealand (Denmark)   T2—489 1
Zealots (Judaism)   296.81
Zebra fishes (Freshwater)   597.482
    culture   639.374 82
Zebra fishes (Marine)   597.68
Zebra plant (Marantaceae)   635.934 88
    botany   584.88
    floriculture   635.934 88
Zebras   599.665 7
    animal husbandry   636.18
Zebus   636.291
Zechariah (Biblical book)   224.98
Zedillo Ponce de León, Ernesto
    Mexican history   972.083 6
Zeeland (Netherlands :
    Province)   T2—492 42
Zeewolde (Netherlands)   T2—492 2
Zeiformes   597.64
Zelaya, Manuel
    Honduran history   972.830 538
Zeman, Miloš
    Czech history   943.710 513
Zen Buddhism   294.392 7
    biography   294.392 709 2
Zener diodes   621.381 522
Zeolite
    mineralogy   549.68

Zombiism
  African religions — 299.675
Zonal regions — T2—1
Zone time — 389.17
Zones of latitude
  astronomical geography — 525.5
Zonguldak İli (Turkey) — T2—563 7
  ancient — T2—393 17
Zoning — 333.731 7
  area planning — 711
    urban — 711.4
  land use — 333.731 7
    urban — 333.771 7
  law — 346.045
  public administration — 354.333
    urban — 354.353
Zoo animals — 590.73
  animal husbandry — 636.088 9
Zooflagellates — 579.42
Zoological gardens — 590.73
  see also Zoos
Zoological paleoecology — 560.45
Zoological specimens
  preservation — 590.752
Zoologists — 590.92
Zoology — 590
Zoomastigophorea — 579.42
  paleontology — 561.992
Zoonoses — 571.98
  animals
    veterinary medicine — 636.089 695 9
  humans — 362.196 959
    incidence — 614.56
    medicine — 616.959
    social services — 362.196 959
  see also Communicable
  diseases
Zooplankton — 592.177 6
  freshwater — 592.176
Zoos — 590.73
  animal care — 636.088 9
  architecture — 727.659
  landscape architecture — 712.5
Zoque Indians — T5—974 3
Zoque language — 497.43
   — T6—974 3
Zoraptera — 595.738
Zorilla — 599.766
Zoroastrian philosophy — 181.05
Zoroastrianism — 295
Zoroastrians
  biography — 295.092
Zosteraceae — 584.44

Zouagha-Moulay Yacoub
  (Morocco) — T2—643 4
Zoug (Switzerland : Canton) — T2—494 756
Zoysieae — 584.92
Zucchini — 641.356 2
  see also Squashes
Zug (Switzerland) — T2—494 756 4
Zug (Switzerland : Canton) — T2—494 756
Zug, Lake (Switzerland) — T2—494 756
Zuger See (Switzerland) — T2—494 756
Zuid-Holland (Netherlands) — T2—492 38
Zuidelijke IJsselmeerpolders
  (Netherlands) — T2—492 2
Zuider Zee (Netherlands) — T2—492 2
Zulia (Venezuela) — T2—872 3
Zulu (African people) — 305.896 398 6
   — T5—963 986
Zulu language — 496.398 6
   — T6—963 986
Zulu literature — 896.398 6
Zulu War, 1879 — 968.404 5
Zululand (South Africa) — 968.404
   — T2—684
Zululand District
  Municipality (South
  Africa) — T2—684 2
Zuma, Jacob
  South African history — 968.074
Zuni Indians — 978.900 497 994
   — T5—979 94
Zuni language — 497.994
   — T6—979 94
Zuni literature — 897.994
Zurich (Switzerland) — T2—494 572 6
Zurich (Switzerland :
  Canton) — T2—494 57
Zurich, Lake of
  (Switzerland) — T2—494 572
Zurzach (Switzerland :
  Bezirk) — T2—494 564 7
Zuzus — 787.92
  see also Stringed instruments
Zwelitsha (South Africa :
  District) — T2—687 55
Zygnematales — 579.837
Zygomycetes — 579.53
Zygophyllaceae — 583.62
Zygophyllales — 583.62
Zygote intrafallopian transfer
  surgery — 618.178 059 9
Zygotes — 571.864
Zymases — 572.791
  see also Enzymes
Zyrian — T5—945 3